# Encyclopedia of Political Economy

edited by Phillip Anthony O'Hara

Volume 2: L–Z

London and New York

First published 1999
by Routledge
11 New Fetter Lane, London, EC4P 4EE
29 West 35th Street, New York, NY 10001
© 1999 Routledge

Typeset in Times by Routledge
Printed and bound in Great Britain by T.J. International Ltd, Padstow, Cornwall

*British Library Cataloguing in Publication Data*
A catalogue record for this book is available from the British Library

*Library of Congress Cataloging-in-Publication Data*
Encyclopedia of political economy / edited by Phillip Anthony O'Hara.
p.    cm.
Includes bibliographical references and index.
(set: alk. paper). (v. 1 alk. paper). (v. 2 alk. paper).
1. Economics–Encyclopedias I. O'Hara, Phillip Anthony.
HB61.E554 1998                                97–48471
330′.03–DC21                                   CIP

ISBN 0-415-15426-X (set)
ISBN 0-415-18717-6 (v. 1)
ISBN 0-415-18718-4 (v. 2)

# Contents

# L

## labor force

The labor force is defined as the sum of those persons who are employed and those who are unemployed. Before defining these terms, we should note that the definitions have been developed in conformity with the nature of CAPITALISM and would not have meaning in pre-capitalist economies. For example, it is important to define and measure unemployment because unemployment is a serious problem in capitalist economies but not in prior modes of production (see RESERVE ARMY OF LABOR). In addition, the labor force is confined to those who either work for wages or are seeking such work. Therefore, work outside of the labor market is ignored, despite the fact that it may be socially useful labor (see HOUSEHOLD LABOR; HOUSEHOLD PRODUCTION AND NATIONAL INCOME).

### Definitions

To determine the size of the labor force, surveys of households are taken periodically by national governments to determine how many persons are in each category. Therefore, when using labor force data, care must be taken to insure that they have been put on a common footing. The focus on households excludes some persons from the data by definition. In the United States, for example, persons living in institutions such as prisons and nursing homes are excluded from the surveys, but those in the armed forces are included. In Canada, on the other hand, members of the armed forces are excluded as are indigenous peoples living on native "reserves."

Given the various exclusions and inclusions, the focus of the surveys is upon labor market activity in some period prior to that in which the survey is conducted. The goal is to determine how many persons are "employed" and how many are "unemployed." Once again, however, the definitions of "employed" and "unemployed" vary between countries, and have changed periodically as well. In the United States, for example, the "employed" are those 16 and older who worked at least one hour for pay in the previous week, plus those who worked without pay for at least 15 hours in a family business, plus those who have jobs but did not work in the previous week due to illness, leave, vacation, strikes and so forth.

The "unemployed" are those who are not employed but who have actively sought work in the last four weeks, plus those who have not sought work due to temporary layoff or the start of a new job (Sorrentino 1993). All other persons, that is, those neither employed nor unemployed, are placed in the category "not in the labor force." Notice that, in the United States, persons under 16 years old are placed in this last category by definition. In Canada the age is 15. In many nations such age minima would be much too high, due to the widespread use of child labor; even in the advanced capitalist nations, they exclude millions of young workers from the labor force count.

### Useful statistics

Given the definitions of labor force, employed and unemployed, it is possible to calculate a number of useful statistical "rates." The unemployment rate is equal to the number of people unemployed divided by the number of people in the labor force. The employment rate is equal to the number of people employed divided by the population over 16 years old.

The labor force participation rate is equal to the number of people in the labor force divided by the population over 16. These rates can be measured for any group within the population, provided that the sample size is large enough. For example, unemployment rates are frequently calculated by race, sex, age, education, industry and occupation. In addition, other statistics are easily measured, such as the long-term (over a certain period, e.g. fifty-two weeks) unemployment rate.

## Flaws in the definitions

From the perspective of those who are critical of capitalism, the definitions of the labor force and its component parts are seriously flawed (see Yates 1994). First, the category "labor force" includes only those either engaged in or seeking wage labor. Those who are not, are placed in the category "not in the labor force," whether or not they are engaged in work. Full-time homemakers are not counted as workers, despite their arduous and critical labors. The definition of "labor force" clearly stigmatizes homemakers, who are overwhelmingly women, since it reflects a basic capitalist value, namely, that those who do not work for pay are inferior to those who do (see also DOMESTIC LABOR DEBATE; FAMILY WAGE; GENDER DIVISION OF LABOR). Similarly, those who barter their labor directly for goods and services and those who engage in production for immediate home consumption are excluded from the labor force.

Second, the definition of "unemployed" greatly underestimates the amount of surplus labor. Two significant groups are excluded from the unemployed. The first group are those who work part-time (defined in the United States as less than 35 hours per week) but want full-time work and who are not counted as partially unemployed (or under-employed). This group includes those whose hours of work have been cut against their will, and those seeking full-time employment but only able to find part-time work (Tilly 1995). Counting "involuntary part-time" workers as fractionally unemployed adds between one-half and three and one-half percentage points to the

unemployment rates in most advanced capitalist economies.

The second group that is excluded are those who give up looking for work because they believe that no work is available; they are counted as "not in the labor force" and not as unemployed. These "discouraged workers" typically suffer the same range of difficulties as those who are officially unemployed, so a strong argument can be made for including them as unemployed. Japan's fabled low unemployment rate would grow by more than four percentage points if discouraged workers were counted as unemployed. The curious thing about both types of "underemployment" is that governments do keep track of them; they simply do not publicize them (see Sorrentino 1993).

## Important trends

Despite the weaknesses of official labor market definitions, the data collected do allow us to discern some important trends. First, in capitalist economies the labor force comes to encompass nearly all of labor. The labor force participation rate grows as peasants are driven from their land, and as homemakers are driven into the market (see INDUSTRIALIZATION). At the same time, an ever smaller proportion of the labor force is engaged in agriculture. In the most advanced capitalist economies, less than five percent of the labor force is employed in farming (Hobsbawm 1994).

Second, most capitalist economies exhibit marked increases in the labor force participation of women. This occurs for a variety of reasons, not least of which is the demand by women themselves for equal access to paid labor. However, it is still the case that women tend to be concentrated in certain occupations, such as clerical work, elementary school teaching and nursing, which are relatively poorly paid and which often recreate in the paid labor force stereotypical female roles in the home.

Third, the trend in employment is toward work in service-producing industries and away from those which produce goods (see LABOR

PROCESS; DIVISION OF LABOR). This has been the consequence of rapid labor-saving technological change in goods production, increased demand for services consequent upon economic growth, and enormous need for managerial, clerical and financial labor required by modern management control techniques (Braverman 1974). However, service production has not been immune to the replacement of people by machines, corporate downsizing and the like, so the rapid growth in service employment may be reaching its limit (Greenbaum 1995).

Fourth, while capitalist economies have always generated considerable unemployment, they no longer appear to be able to create jobs for staggeringly large numbers of persons (see UNEMPLOYMENT AND UNDEREMPLOYMENT). Unemployment, broadly defined to include involuntary part-time and discouraged workers, has been growing since the 1970s and shows no signs of long-term moderation. Worldwide there are now roughly 800 million underemployed workers, representing a ticking time bomb of social and political turmoil (Yates 1994). Unemployment is typically especially severe among ethnic and racial minorities. In the United States, for example, the labor force participation rate of African-American men is relatively low and declining, indicating that they are becoming increasingly discouraged about their employment prospects. A similar trend is found among both young and old men in Great Britain (Beechey and Perkins 1987).

## Conclusion

This growth of unemployment has greatly enhanced the insecurity of the employed and allowed employers to restructure their workforces so that a rapidly growing proportion of all employees have become "contingent workers." That is, they no longer enjoy or have hope of gaining employment with meaningful job security. Again in the United States, at least one-tenth of all employment is contingent, that is, involuntary part-time, temporary, leased,

done in the home or independently contracted (Henson 1995).

## See also:

cost of job loss; unemployment: policies to reduce; wage determination

## Selected references

Beechey, Veronica and Perkins, Teresa (1987) *A Matter of Hours: Women, Part-Time Work and the Labour Market*, Cambridge: Polity Press.

Braverman, Harry (1974) *Labor and Monopoly Capital: The Degradation of Work in the Twentieth Century*, New York: Monthly Review Press.

Greenbaum, Joan (1995) *Windows on the Workplace: Computers, Jobs, and the Organization of Office Work in the Late Twentieth Century*, New York: Monthly Review Press.

Henson, Kevin D. (1995) *Just a Temp*, Philadelphia: Temple University Press.

Hobsbawm, Eric (1994) *The Age of Extremes: A History of the World, 1914–1991*, New York: Pantheon.

Sorrentino, Constance (1993) "International Comparisons of Unemployment Indicators." *Monthly Labor Review* 116(3): 3–24.

Tilly, Chris (1995) *Half a Job: Bad and Good Part-Time Jobs in a Changing Labor Market*, Philadelphia: Temple University Press.

Yates, Michael D. (1994) *Longer Hours, Fewer Jobs: Employment and Unemployment in the United States*, New York: Monthly Review Press.

MICHAEL D. YATES

# labor and labor power

## Significance of the distinction

The terms "labor" and "labor power" are two of the most important concepts in Marx's political economy of CAPITALISM. Generally speaking, under capitalism, labor is the social practice of workers producing commodities and value in the sphere of production, under the direction of capitalists or their functionaries for a certain period of labor time (e.g. eight hours per work day). Labor power, on the other hand, is the capacity of workers to labor; their human potential, knowledge and experience, which is (in a generalized sense) exchanged in the market for wages (see Gintis and Bowles 1981). Capitalists must pay workers enough in the form of wages to enable the reproduction of labor power. When this capacity is activated in the labor process, under conditions of general commodity exchange, labor contributes to the production of value and (usually) surplus value.

The value created by labor in a normal working day (total labor time, e.g. eight hours) must be greater than the equivalent value of labor power (necessary labor time, e.g. four hours) for surplus labour time and exploitation to exist (e.g. four hours). In other words, the value of commodities (newly created) is determined by the amount of socially necessary labor materialized in commodities. This includes the value of labor power and surplus value. The value of labor power, on average, equals the value incorporated in wage goods. Exploitation or surplus value is precisely the difference between the value created by *living labor* and the value of labor power. Thus, labor power is a very special commodity since its use value, becoming actualized as labor and hence value, is greater than its exchange value (which is equal to wage goods on average). For this surplus value to be produced under capitalism, labor power must be of at least a certain minimum level of skill, speed and efficiency for the industry or sphere in question. (See EXPLOITATION AND SURPLUS VALUE.)

Total value of the commodity thus equals surplus value ($SV$) plus variable capital ($V$; wages) created by living labor; plus depreciated constant capital and materials ($C$, or dead labor): usually shown as $C + V + SV$.

## Marx on labor in general

MARX wrote on the general nature of labor and the specific social relations underlying labor in capitalism. On the general relations, in Chapter 7 of Volume I of *Das Kapital* Marx (1867: 283) writes: "Labor is, first of all a process between man and nature, a process by which man, through his own actions, mediates, regulates and controls the metabolism between himself and nature." To this, Marx adds that, apart "from the exertion of the working organs, a purposeful will is required for the entire duration of work" (Marx 1867: 284).

A literal interpretation of these sentences implies that, for Marx, "labor" is itself a process between nature and a specific, purposeful activity of mankind. The simple elements of the labor process include work, the object on which that work is performed, and instruments of work (Marx 1867: 284). The result of "labor," whether narrowly or broadly defined, is a "product" or "a use-value, a piece of natural material adopted to human needs by means of a change in its form" (Marx 1867: 287).

## Labor power

Besides being a process or a purposeful productive activity, Marx also conceives of "labor" as "an expenditure" (or activation) "of human labor-power" (Marx 1867: 137). "Labor power," in turn, is defined as "labor capacity, the aggregate of those mental and physical capabilities existing in the physical form, the living personality, of a human being" (Marx 1867: 270).

In capitalism, according to Marx, labor power itself becomes a commodity. The "value of labor power" is said to be "determined, as in the case of every other commodity, by the labor-time necessary for the production, and consequently also the reproduction, of this specific article." This "necessary labor time" is equivalent to the "value of means of subsistence necessary for the maintenance of its owner" (Marx 1867: 274). The "number and extent" of these means of subsistence, in turn, depend on such things as the "physical peculiarities," "history," "habits and expectations" and the "level of civilization" of the country in which the worker lives. They also depend on the cost of the "worker's replacements, i.e. his children, in order that this race of peculiar commodity-owners may perpetuate its presence on the market" (Marx 1867: 275).

## Concrete and abstract labor

We now turn to labor when the object of production is a commodity, with a use-value and a value. Now, according to Marx, labor acquires a twofold character: "concrete" or "useful labor"; and "abstract labor." Useful labor relates to "productive activity of a definite kind, carried on with a definite aim" (Marx 1867: 133), such as mining gold, growing wheat, and knitting wool (Marx 1859: 29). "Abstract labor" is seen by Marx to be "labor in which abstraction is made from all the concrete forms and useful properties of actual work"; and as "the reduction of all kinds of actual labor to their common character of being human labor in general, of being the expenditure of human labor-power" (Marx 1867: 159–60).

Marx believes that this abstraction emanates from real or historical processes of capitalism, and not from a mental generalization. This stems from the reduction of different kinds of labor to the "labor realized" in the universal equivalent; everything is reduced to money (see COMMODITY FETISHISM). For Marx, if useful labor becomes "objectified" as a use-value, then abstract labor becomes "materialized" as "value" in the production of commodities. In other words, "value" is the same thing as "materialized" abstract labor (see Likitkijsomboon 1995; Krause 1982).

## Further research

Much controversy has emerged in the contemporary literature concerning the concepts of labor and labor power. Some scholars have argued that an emphasis should be placed on the institutional conditions underlying the reproduction of labor power, since labor power is not a commodity in the usual sense of the term. The role played by the family and the state are critical for the formation of creative human capacities inherent in labor power (see Gintis and Bowles 1981; Delphy and Leonard 1992: ch. 3). Here, the labor theory of value becomes less a theory of relative prices and more an analysis of those cultural, political and social practices underlying both the reproduction of labor power, and the extraction of surplus labor in the production process (Gintis and Bowles 1981). For an "analytical Marxian" critique of the theory underlying this labor–labor power distinction see Skillman (1996–7).

## See also:

circuit of social capital; class; class processes; classes of capitalism; domestic labor debate; economic surplus; household labor; labor theory of value; Marxist political economy: contemporary varieties; productive and unproductive labor; reserve army of labor

## Selected references

Delphy, Christine and Leonard, Diana (1992) *Familiar Exploitation: A New Analysis of Marriage in Contemporary Western Societies*, Cambridge: Polity Press.

Fayazmanesh, Sasan (1994) "Marx's Semantics and the Logic of the Derivation of Value," *Research in the History of Economic Thought and Methodology* 12: 65–91.

Gintis, Herbert and Bowles, Samuel (1981) "Structure and Practice in the Labor Theory of Value," *Review of Radical Political Economics* 12(4): 1–26.

Krause, Ulrich (1982) *Money and Abstract Labor*, London: New Left Books.

Likitkijsomboon, Pichit (1995) "Marxian Theories of Value-Form," *Review of Radical Political Economics* 27(2): 73–105.

Marx, Karl (1859) *A Contribution to the Critique of Political Economy*, New York: International Publishers, 1976.

—— (1867) *Das Kapital*, vol. 1, published as *Capital, Volume 1*, New York: Vintage Books, 1977.

—— (1976) *Value: Studies by Karl Marx*, trans.

Albert Dragstedt, London: New Park Publications.

Skillman, Gilbert L. (1996–97) "Marxian Value Theory and the Labor–Labor Power Distinction," *Science and Society* 60(4): 427–51.

SASAN FAYAZMANESH
PHILLIP ANTHONY O'HARA

# labor-managed enterprises

The theory of the enterprise managed by workers is today largely based on the WARD–VANEK MODEL OF SELF-MANAGEMENT, first developed by Benjamin Ward (1958). The cooperative principles which underlie it include the diffusion of the entrepreneurial role amongst all partners in the firm, and the rule of "one worker, one vote."

In Volume 3 of *Das Kapital*, MARX wrote that the worker-managed enterprise "provide[s] the proof that the capitalist has become superfluous." Many times he expressed a favorable view of the cooperative movement. In 1867, for instance, he wrote:

> We acknowledge the co-operative movement as one of the transforming forces of society based ... on class antagonism. Its great merit is to show that the present paupering, and despotic system of the subordination of labor to capital can be superseded by the republican and beneficent system of the association of free and equal producers.
>
> (Marx 1969: 81)

One finds favorable opinions of cooperatives also among other great economists of the past, such as, for example, John Stuart Mill and Alfred Marshall. It may appear strange, therefore, that a return of theoretical interest in labor-managed firms arose only after Ward's article was published in 1958.

## Merit of self-management

The principal merit of the self-managed firm lies above all in the greater democracy of these firms, where all those participating in the productive activity are responsible, including financially, for the outcomes achieved. Furthermore, firms run by workers eliminate the domination of capital over labor which, as Marx has argued, is the domination of things over human beings. (See COMMODITY FETISHISM.) In eliminating the domination of capital over labor, firms run by workers eliminate capitalist EXPLOITATION and reduce ALIENATION.

One of the merits of labor-managed enterprises is a reduction of wage inflation, due to a reduction in conflicting claims between capital and labor (see INFLATION: CONFLICTING CLAIMS APPROACH). Also worth mentioning is the reduction in unemployment since, during recessions, workers would prefer to reduce working hours than risk losing their jobs.

## Types of self-managed firms

There are various types of firms managed by workers. The most important distinction is, perhaps, between the "labor-managed firm" (LMF), which is financed exclusively by borrowed capital; and the "worker-managed firm" (WMF), which employs reinvested profits. Another important distinction is between firms which allow the sale of the position of partner, and those in which workers who leave the firm lose all property rights in the firm. In this context, a less important distinction is between publicly and privately owned corporations.

When the firm is self-financed, the problem arises as to whether the income distributed to the individual worker should take account of the number of years of service to the firm or not. If one does not take account of the years of service (as is usually proposed), the earnings on savings that the longer standing partners have reinvested in the firm contribute equally to the earnings of old and new partners alike. The irrationality of this rule produces the double problem of (a) hindering the acquisition of new partners as existing workers have less incentive to share the fruits of their savings with the new arrivals, and hence (b) reducing investment in the firm. On the latter, the income accruing to partners who help finance an investment will be lower since, in the future, they will have to divide the fruits of their investment also among newer partners who did not contribute. On the other hand, if in establishing the income to be attributed to each partner one takes account of the years of service, one needs to calculate for each year the value of partners' investments in that year. This would make the calculation of the correct distribution of income among partners very complicated.

## Labor-managed firm

The LMF is examined in some detail because it is the "pure" form of the self-managed firm, which overturns the capital–labor relationship. The LMF is a firm in which labor "hires" capital, paying it a fixed income, making all the choices regarding productive activity and appropriating the surplus. Similar to the LMF is the self-financing, self-managed firm which, in order to distinguish between labor and capital income, attributes a share of the funds put aside for investment in the firm to each partner and undertakes to pay interest on the sum thus raised.

If the owners of capital have no role in the running of the firm, it is of little interest to know who owns the capital employed in the productive activity. Those in favor of public ownership note that what is usually lent is financial rather than physical capital (above all because of difficulties in monitoring the maintenance of physical capital goods) and there is no reason, therefore, to attribute property rights over the firm to its capitalist backers. On the other hand, even if the workers of the firm buy the capital goods, they cannot become owners of the firm's capital goods without becoming capitalists themselves. Therefore, since it is not appropriate for ownership of capital goods to be in the hands of either capitalists or workers (and because they have to be owned by someone), ownership must presumably be attributed to the state.

As to the possibility of selling the position of partner on the market, analyzed theoretically by Sertel (1982) among others, this would solve the problem of underinvestment. The sale of positions eliminates the tendency toward underinvestment because all partners have an incentive to maximize the net value of the firm. However, this would possibly allow the entry into the firm of new partners who were not desired or approved by the existing partners.

## Demerits

As to criticisms, one needs to begin with Pantaleoni who, in 1898, observed that "the professed co-operative principles, if implemented logically and universally, would lead to the same price formation" as under capitalism. This is contradicted by the Ward and Vanek model, which makes it clear that the self-managed firm tends to maximize the average income of the worker-partners, not the profits on capital invested. This leads to significant differences between capitalist and self-managed firms.

As to more specific criticisms, the principal one concerns difficulties in raising finance. A firm which seeks exclusively external financing may face difficulties in raising funds because risk is not shared by workers (borrowers are not investing their own capital in the firm). However, the self-managed firm which does not reinvest its own capital may raise funds from partners through voluntary loans, or perhaps also through compulsory loans by partners decided by majority vote.

An important criticism was put forward by Alchian and Demsetz (1972), who suggested that in the self-managed firm monitoring activities are undertaken by all and are, therefore, less effective than monitoring in the capitalist firm undertaken by a specific person or persons. However, nothing prevents the self-managed firm from appointing a specific person or persons to monitor the activities of workers, although it may be unnecessary. In the MONDRAGÓN experiment, costs of supervision are minimal due to low worker alienation and subtle peer pressure.

## See also:

anarchism; community; market socialism; participatory democracy and self-management; social ownership and property; socialism and communism

## Selected references

Alchian, Armen A. and Demsetz, Harold (1972) "Production, Information Costs and Economic Organization," *American Economic Review* 62.

Marx, Karl and Engels, Friedrich (1969) *Selected Works*, vol. 2, Moscow: Progress Publishers.

Pantaleoni, Maffio (1898) "An Attempt to Analyse the Concepts of 'Strong' and 'Weak' in their Economic Connection," *Economic Journal* 8 (June).

Sertel, Murat R. (1982) *Workers and Incentives*, Amsterdam: North Holland.

Vanek, Jaroslav (1970) *The General Theory of Labor-Managed Market Economies*, Ithaca, NY: Cornell University Press.

Ward, Benjamin (1958) "The Firm in Illyria: Market Syndicalism," *American Economic Review* 48(4).

BRUNO JOSSA

# labor market discrimination

Labor market discrimination is the unequal treatment of persons in the LABOR FORCE in such areas as hiring, pay, promotion, training opportunities, and mentoring, based solely on their membership in particular identifiable demographic groups. Groups which are often discriminated against include females, blacks and Latinos, the elderly and the disabled. In short, labor market discrimination occurs when two persons, otherwise identically qualified, receive disparate treatment based solely on group membership.

## Types of discrimination

Janice Madden (1973) defined three types of labor market discrimination; plus there are two ancillary forms of discrimination:

- wage discrimination, which occurs when wage differentials are not based on productivity differences;
- occupational discrimination, which occurs when the proportion of members of a group (such as females or blacks) in an occupation is based on factors other than PRODUCTIVITY differences; and
- cumulative discrimination, which occurs when a person has low productivity due to past discrimination (such as deficient on-the-job training or mentoring);
- pre-labor market discrimination, similar to cumulative discrimination, which occurs when a person has low productivity because of inferior educational opportunities due to discrimination;
- societal discrimination, a precursor to both labor market and occupational discrimination, which is based on the belief that some jobs are more "appropriate" for certain groups, such as nurses "should be" females and doctors "should be" males.

Occupational discrimination, which is also called occupational segregation, occurs when members of different groups (such as males or females) are concentrated in different occupations (see GENDER DIVISION OF LABOR). By this definition, since women comprise about 46 percent of the entire US labor force, occupational segregation would be suspected if the proportion of women in a particular occupation differed greatly from 46 percent, *ceteris paribus*. As an example, assume that equally qualified males and females apply for jobs at a bank, but the women are hired as tellers and the men are hired as management trainees. Even if male and female tellers get identical wages and male and female management trainees get identical salaries, occupational discrimination is present because females and males are "steered" to different job classifications. Social "norms" and personal preferences may explain some cases of occupational segregation.

## Nature of discrimination

The existence of labor market discrimination is shown by the fact that in the USA women earned only 75 cents (on average) for every dollar men earned in 1995, based on a comparison of full-time year-round workers (see WOMEN'S WAGES: SOCIAL CONSTRUCTION OF). While part of this gap is due to wage discrimination and occupational segregation, women also earn less than men due to wage differentials that are based on productivity differences. Such differences are generally caused by women having less work experience and less seniority than men, because most women have to spend time out of the labor force at child care and housekeeping.

## Laws and treaties

Pay discrimination by gender is illegal in the USA as a result of the Equal Pay Act of 1963, which requires that men and women must be paid at the same rate when doing substantially the same work (even with different job titles) for the same employer, at the same location. A typical violation of the Equal Pay Act would be for hospitals to hire men as orderlies and women as nurses' aides, and pay orderlies more than nurses' aides, even though both groups do substantially the same work. Note that it is not discrimination to base pay rates on factors that genuinely affect productivity, such as education, on-the-job training or seniority.

A problem with the Equal Pay Act was that it did not provide for equal treatment of the sexes in the areas of hiring and promotion. This situation was partially remedied *de jure* by Title VII of the Civil Rights Act of 1964, which outlaws labor market discrimination by "race, color, religion, sex, or national origin" in all aspects of employment, such as hiring, firing, promotion and compensation. The Office of Equal Employment Opportunity (later renamed the Equal Employment Opportunity Commission (EEOC)) was established to enforce compliance with Title VII.

Article 119 of the Treaty of Rome (which established the European Economic Community) guarantees equal pay for equal work by gender. Joyce Jacobsen (1994) found that equal pay laws were in effect in fifteen of the largest capitalist industrialized societies, from Canada (1951) to Japan (1987). Women earned less than men in every country for which reliable data are available.

## Neoclassical theory of discrimination

Gary Becker (1957) is generally credited with developing the neoclassical theory of labor market discrimination. He differentiated between prejudice, which is the irrational dislike of members of a group, and discrimination, which is a behavior (the unequal treatment of persons based solely on their membership in a particular identifiable demographic group) resulting from prejudice. He treated discrimination as if it were a commodity for which people have a preference; people with a "taste for discrimination" will act in various ways to avoid dealing with the group they are prejudiced against, even if such discrimination causes them to forego income or face higher costs.

According to Becker's theory, an employer who discriminates acts as if members of the disfavored group have undesirable characteristics which cause them to be more expensive to employ (by a percentage called the discrimination coefficient). Therefore, the employer either refuses to hire members of the disfavored group(s), or hires them only if they are willing to work at a lower wage. Note that employers may discriminate because of their own personal prejudices; because they believe that their employees are prejudiced, so that hiring members of the disfavored group(s) will cause strife within their workforce (and therefore reduce productivity); and/or that their customers are prejudiced, so that hiring members of the disfavored group(s) will drive customers away.

## Statistical discrimination

Kenneth Arrow (1973) is one of the developers of the theory of statistical discrimination. He defined statistical discrimination as acting on the basis of stereotypes, treating every member of a group as if she or he had the typical values of that group's real or imagined characteristics. An employer will preferentially hire from the groups believed to be more productive, and avoid hiring from groups considered to be less productive. A common example would be avoiding hiring women because women are more likely to take time off from work than men, due to pregnancy or responsibility for child care.

## Political economy perspectives

The Marxist–feminist view of gender discrimination, as posited by Heidi Hartmann (1976), has two major components. The first is attributed to a tradition of patriarchal societies, in which the father or husband has all the power in the family; accordingly, husbands oppress their wives by making them bear the brunt of household work and child raising. The second, which came with the advent of capitalism, has capitalists and male workers maintaining the hierarchical GENDER DIVISION OF LABOR by keeping women in subordinate occupations. According to this theory, women earn less than men which encourages women to enter marriage, where husbands force wives to take on the responsibility for domestic work, thus maintaining the cycle of female oppression. As a corollary, women therefore have less time to devote to the labor market, thus reducing their chance of advancing in the job hierarchy. Marxist-feminists see the traditions of patriarchy and capitalism as interlocking to keep women at a lower status.

Barbara Bergmann's (1971) crowding theory posits that women/blacks are discouraged (by "social custom" or outright discrimination) from entering male/white dominated occupations, and thus are forced into female/black dominated occupations. By the action of market forces, the decreased supply of workers results in higher pay for males/whites, while the increased supply ("crowding") of workers results in lower pay for females/blacks. Such occupational segregation is believed to be a major cause of pay inequalities by gender and race.

The model of discrimination associated with Lester Thurow (1969) and Michael Reich (1981) is particularly applicable to discrimination by race. This theory posits that employers practice racial discrimination because they can benefit from the resulting racial segregation of their work force. This segregation enables the employers to use a "divide and conquer" strategy that reduces the bargaining power of both white and black workers. Reich, along with David Gordon and other associates, contributed much to the development of labor market segmentation theory (see SEGMENTED AND DUAL LABOR MARKETS).

According to the dual labor market model of Peter Doeringer and Michael Piore (1971), the labor market has two classes of jobs: primary market jobs which pay well, with fringe benefits, have opportunity for advancement and provide steady employment; and secondary market jobs which pay poorly, lack fringe benefits, have little opportunity for advancement and do not provide steady employment. By means of discrimination by employers and/or unions, the primary labor market jobs are reserved for members of the favored groups, while members of the disfavored groups are relegated to the secondary labor market jobs.

Darity and Williams (1985) discuss four types of competition: classical, Marxist, neoclassical and Austrian. By definition, classical and Marxist competition contain rigidities which impede market forces, and therefore allow the long-run existence of employer-implemented discrimination. Darity and Williams also criticize the view that cultural differences in attitudes and work habits among racial and ethnic groups explains wage differentials among these groups. Market competition should bring about the transfer of cultural traits to low achievers. Instead of cultural differences, they point to social class as the explanation of discrimination.

Wage discrimination between two groups

can be estimated statistically by using the residual method (see Oaxaca and Ransom 1994).

The current method of allowing market forces to determine pay rates seems perfectly proper to many free market economists, who consider interference with the market to be an economic sin. However, feminist economists and many other political economists believe that the market is distorted by discrimination in some of the ways described above, thereby forcing members of disfavored groups to accept lower wages than employers pay to members of favored groups. Both AFFIRMATIVE ACTION and COMPARABLE WORTH have been proposed as ways to combat such discrimination in the labor market.

## See also:

culture of poverty; discrimination in the housing and mortgage market; race, ethnicity, gender and class

## Selected references

Arrow, Kenneth J. (1973) "The Theory of Discrimination," in Orley Ashenfelter and Albert Rees (eds), *Discrimination in Labor Markets*, Princeton, NJ: Princeton University Press.

Becker, Gary (1957) *The Economics of Discrimination*, 2nd edn, Chicago: University of Chicago Press, 1971.

Bergmann, Barbara (1971) "The Effect on White Incomes of Discrimination in Employment," *Journal of Political Economy* 79: 294–313.

Darity, William A., Jr. and Williams, Rhonda M. (1985) "Peddlers Forever?: Culture, Competition, and Discrimination," *American Economic Review Papers and Proceedings* 75(2): 256–61.

Doeringer, Peter B. and Piore, Michael J. (1971) *Internal Labor Markets and Manpower Analysis*, Lexington, MA: D.C. Heath & Co.

Hartmann, Heidi (1976) "Capitalism, Patriarchy, and Job Segregation by Sex," in Martha Blaxall and Barbara Reagan (eds), *Women and the Workplace: The Implications of Occupational Segregation*, Chicago: University of Chicago Press.

Jacobsen, Joyce P. (1994) *The Economics of Gender*, Cambridge, MA: Blackwell.

Madden, Janice F. (1973) *The Economics of Sex Discrimination*, Lexington, MA: Lexington Books.

Oaxaca, Ronald L. and Ransom, Michael R. (1994) "On Discrimination and the Decomposition of Wage Differentials," *Journal of Econometrics* 61: 5–21.

Reich, Michael (1981) *Racial Inequality: A Political Economy Analysis*, Princeton, NJ: Princeton University Press.

Thurow, Lester (1969) *Poverty and Discrimination*, Washington DC: The Brookings Institute.

Wolff, Edward (1997) *Economics of Poverty, Inequality, and Discrimination*, Cincinnati, OH: South-Western College Publishing.

EMILY P. HOFFMAN

# labor markets and market power

To what extent do market conditions determine the ability of workers to affect their conditions of work, inclusive of all pecuniary and non-pecuniary benefits? A host of economic theorists from Marxian to neoclassical perspectives have argued that the conditions of work, inclusive of wages, are largely determined by the forces of supply and demand, at least in the long run. The existence of worker power implies that conditions of work can be influenced by employees, independently of market forces; the equilibrium conditions of work would be different in the absence of worker or union power.

The power of workers is often associated with the unionization of labor, but can also refer to legislation which strengthens the bargaining power of labor. Nonetheless, it is also related to institutional interventions in the economy such as proactive union legislation, minimum wage legislation, unemployment insurance, social welfare, public health care and the like which serve to improve the bargaining power of workers. In the event that the power of labor is increased, conventional economic wisdom argues that this will increase unit costs and reduce profits, thereby endangering the individual firm's competitive position, as well as reducing output, employment and the growth potential in the larger economy.

## Classical economists

The contemporary view on labor markets and market power is rooted in the assumptions which underlie the works of the great eighteenth and nineteenth-century economists. For example, to the question of how successful labor's efforts against capital might prove to be, Karl Marx (1865: 71–2) wrote that the market price of labor "will, in the long run, adapt itself to its *value*; that, therefore, despite all the ups and downs, and do what he may, the working man will, on an average, only receive the value of his labor [power]...which is determined by the necessities required for its maintenance and reproduction...."

Compare Marx's pessimism on what can be achieved in a market economy to Adam Smith's perspective detailed in the *Wealth of Nations* (1776: 68–81). He argues that that it is important for workers to organize, so as to establish a countervailing power against the master (the owners of capital); otherwise the masters will always achieve a bargaining advantage against labor. However, in the long run, try as they may, workers can only earn a subsistence wage, unless they find themselves in a rapidly growing, prosperous economy, wherein the demand for labor exceeds supply. In other words, market power ultimately determines effective worker power. Smith favors the high-wage, tight labor market scenario, however, in that he maintains that higher wages encourage higher productivity: "Where wages are high, accordingly, we shall always find the workmen more active, diligent, and expeditious, than where they are low..." (Smith 1776: 81).

This particular thread in Smith's theoretical cloth distinguishes him from much of the contemporary thinking on the subject.

## Orthodox treatment

The modern conventional economic view on labor markets and market power was clearly articulated by George Stigler (1946) in his discussion of minimum wage legislation. Here, government imposes a minimum wage which is above what the market would generate in the absence of such legislation. The specific case Stigler makes against minimum wage legislation is easily generalized to the potential economic impact which other efforts to affect the free workings of the labor market might have. Stigler argues that minimum wage legislation can be expected to reduce aggregate output and result in an increase in unemployment; marginally benefiting those workers who previously earned just below the minimum and drastically reducing the earnings of those workers who were far below the minimum. The net effect of minimum wage legislation is clearly negative, from the perspective of the theoretical prism used by George Stigler and of the conventional wisdom then and now.

This type of modeling has been extended to an analysis of trade UNIONS by Albert Rees (1963). Stigler admits that these negative effects can be partially or even completely avoided if workers and management are shocked into increasing their productivity by minimum wage legislation. This possibility is assumed to be a theoretical special case in a world where competitive conditions drive economic agents into operating at maximum efficiency along the production possibility frontier.

## Stylized facts and recent work

A fundamental problem with this dominant analytical perspective is its inconsistency with the stylized facts. The bulk of the empirical evidence suggests that minimum wage legislation and trade unions do not have the negative effects predicted by contemporary economic theory (Card and Krueger 1995; Mishel and

Voos 1992). This suggests that, over the long run, conditions of work can be improved by increasing the power of labor for any given state of market forces, without negatively impacting upon the firm and the overall economy. However, for this to be true the underlying assumptions of the conventional economic wisdom must be flawed, for given these assumptions its logic is impeccable.

The recent work on efficiency wage and X-efficiency theories shows that wage rates and overall conditions of work clearly impact upon labor productivity. This is because the quantity and quality of effort is a discretionary variable: economic agents are not typically operating along the production possibility frontier and are, therefore, typically X-inefficient (Altman 1992, 1996; Leibenstein 1987). A more detailed and sophisticated throwback to the observations of Adam Smith, this contemporary, heterodox approach to labor market analysis, especially its X-efficiency variants (Altman 1992, 1996; see also Gordon 1996), argues that what is the exception to the rule in conventional analysis, is the rule in the actual economy. Hence workers can improve their working conditions without negatively affecting the firm or economy in terms of cost, price or profit. This is not to say that labor market conditions do not affect the capacity of workers to improve their economic standing.

However, in a world where working conditions and labor productivity are positively and causally related, tight labor markets need not negatively affect the economy. Nor need one expect that institutional arrangements, such as trade unions and minimum wage legislation (which tend to improve labor's bargaining position irrespective of the state of the market), will impact negatively on the economy. In fact, the heterodox modeling of the labor market would suggest the opposite, with significant implications for public policy.

## See also:

economic power; efficiency wages; health and safety in the workplace; industrial relations

## Selected references

Altman, Morris (1992) "The Economics of Exogenous Increases in Wage Rates in a Behavioral/X-Efficiency Model of the Firm," *Review of Social Economy* 50: 163–92.
—— (1996) *Human Agency and Material Welfare: Revisions in Microeconomics and their Implications for Public Policy*, Boston: Kluwer Academic Publishers.
Card, David and Krueger, Alan B. (1995) *Myth and Measurement: The New Economics of the Minimum Wage*, Princeton, NJ: Princeton University Press.
Gordon, David M. (1996) *Fat and Mean: The Corporate Squeeze of Working Americans and the Myth of Managerial "Downsizing"*, New York: Free Press.
Leibenstein, Harvey (1987) *Inside the Firm: The Inefficiencies of Hierarchy*, Cambridge, MA: Harvard University Press.
Marx, Karl (1865) *Wages, Price and Profit*, Peking: Foreign Language Press, 1965.
Mishel, Lawrence and Voos, Paula B. (eds) (1992) *Unions and Economic Competitiveness*, Armonk, NY: M.E. Sharpe.
Rees, Albert (1963) "The Effects of Unions on Resource Allocation," *Journal of Law and Economics* 6: 69–78.
Smith, Adam (1776) *An Inquiry into the Nature and Causes of the Wealth of Nations*, New York: Modern Library, 1937.
Stigler, George J. (1946). "The Economics of Minimum Wage Legislation," *American Economic Review* 36: 358–65.

MORRIS ALTMAN

# labor process

In *Das Kapital*, Karl MARX developed his famous letter scheme, M-C...P...C'-M', to analyze capitalist ACCUMULATION. A capitalist enterprise takes money capital (M) and purchases constant and variable capital (C) in competitive markets. This commodity capital is converted, inside of the workplace or the sphere of production (...P...), into another set of commodities (C′) which the firm then returns to the market for sale (C′-M′). Then the process repeats itself, on a larger scale if possible. As Marx said: "Accumulate, accumulate, that is Moses and the prophets" (see CIRCUIT OF SOCIAL CAPITAL).

Marx argued that the key to the firm's ability to accumulate was its power to extract unpaid or surplus labor from its workers. That is, profits originate inside of the workplace, in the movement from C to C′. To insure maximum surplus labor, therefore, it is necessary for the employer to exercise as much control as possible over the combination of the constant and variable capital. This combination is called the "labor process." Since the constant capital is inert (dead labor, as Marx so aptly called it), controlling the labor process amounts to controlling the laborer. The workers sell only their ability to work, their labor power, and it is the aim of capital to convert this into maximum labor (see LABOR AND LABOR POWER). However, given the circumstances of capitalist production, workers can and do resist (see EXPLOITATION AND SURPLUS VALUE).

There is considerable debate among radical economists concerning the development of the labor process in CAPITALISM. One approach, pioneered by Harry Braverman, argues for a more or less progressive development by capital of what might be called "control mechanisms," each of which successively increases the power of employers to extract surplus labor from their workers. At the dawn of capitalist production, capitalists had to rely upon the workers available to them, namely the skilled male workers who dominated the trades of the feudal guilds. At first, merchant-capitalists "put out" raw materials to craftsmen who worked them up into final products in their homes. While this system helped to drive weavers and other craftsmen into destitution, it was also subject to theft of materials and irregular delivery. These weaknesses led to its replacement by the factory system, in which workers would be herded into a central workplace and work under the employer's direct supervision.

The centralization of production was the precondition for the rapid development of more sophisticated control mechanisms. First, the managers observed that skilled workers often divided their tasks into subtasks or details to work more efficiently when they had a large number of items to produce. This led them to begin to substitute unskilled "detail" workers, often women and children, for skilled workmen. This greatly enhanced management's control of the labor process (and cheapened it as well) because troublesome workers could now be easily replaced. In addition, detail workers would not have the knowledge necessary to organize the production of commodities. The conceptualization of work could be monopolized by the employer. The detailed DIVISION OF LABOR gave tremendous impetus to the use of machinery, and machines enhanced managerial control by allowing management to increase its control over the pace of work.

According to Braverman, management's initial attempts to control the labor process were unsystematic until the advent of "scientific management," pioneered by Frederick Taylor (see TAYLORISM). Taylor argued that the key to managerial control over the labor process was for the employer to gain a monopoly over the conceptualization of work. This could be done through detailed study and analysis of work (his famous time and motion studies), the establishment of rigid standards for the performance of work and the systematic hiring of workers who would work according to these standards. Taylor's vision of the workplace was that of a smoothly working machine, with the workers laboring as human machines.

Taylor's ideal was implemented by capitalists such as Henry Ford, but Ford's assembly line was so inhospitable to workers that they quit in droves. Ford then introduced various nontechnical control devices such as the five-dollar day and his famous sociology department which introduced a variety of paternalistic initiatives such as language lessons and home visits to promote good moral behavior. Since Ford's somewhat primitive methods, employers have introduced personnel departments to accomplish the job of habituating workers to Tayloristic management.

Modern managerial control of the labor process has reached its apogee in the system developed by the Japanese automobile companies. Just as Ford's system has been called "Fordism," the Japanese model may be called "Toyotism" since its basic features were engineered by the Toyota Corporation. In this model production is rigidly Taylorized before production actually begins. Each step of every job is preplanned down to the smallest detail with almost no variation allowed. Workers are systematically recruited through a lengthy process of interviews and tests, including role-playing exercises to determine which workers will be able to function efficiently in this environment. The team concept of work is utilized, with work done by teams, each of whose members has mastered a variety of unskilled tasks. No relief workers are allowed so as to discourage absenteeism, and pressure is constantly exerted upon workers (through just-in-time inventory, for example) to force them to work faster (see FORDISM AND THE FLEXIBLE SYSTEM OF PRODUCTION).

Braverman's analysis has been challenged on a number of grounds. These include a romanticization of craft work, an incomplete definition of the concept of skill, an overestimation of the importance of Taylorism, a neglect of the larger set of social relationships outside of the labor process, and, most critically, the failure to consider the struggle of working people against managerial control and the effects which this struggle has had upon the control mechanisms themselves. Perhaps it is true that Braverman exaggerated the creative aspects of craft work in early capitalism. He did fail to see that our notion of skill may be socially constructed, so that, for example, certain activities done by men are considered skilled while others of equal difficulty but done by women are not.

However, much of the critique of Braverman is based upon a misunderstanding of his method of analysis. He analyzed at the same level of abstraction as did Marx in Volume 1 of *Das Kapital*, concentrating upon the exploitative capital–labor relationship and abstracting

from everything else. This was especially useful given that this allowed him to focus upon what is central to capitalism – and what is all but universally ignored by mainstream social science – namely the extraction of surplus value from the working class. Of course, not all skills have been eliminated from work and new skills may be created as others are destroyed; but the tendency in all capitalist workplaces is to de-skill labor, and none of Braverman's critics have convincingly shown otherwise. Likewise, not all workplaces have yet been Taylorized and perhaps some cannot be. This does not mean that the centralization of the conceptualization of work in management is not a basic tendency of capitalism. Certainly the arguments put forward that team-based production is a radical departure from Taylorism must seem naive to those who work under this "management by stress" system.

It is fair to say that Braverman's examination of the labor process is incomplete. Management's attempts to control it generate responses from workers, and these in turn compel employers to make adjustments or develop new control mechanisms. For example, the centralization of workers in factories makes it easier for them to organize collectively, and the detailed division of labor shows workers concretely that they are all alike. Yet knowing these things, while it deepens our understanding of capitalism, takes nothing away from Braverman's analysis of capitalism's underlying tendencies. Likewise, it is true that the labor process is embedded within a society which has multiple dimensions, all of which (the state, the system of education, IDEOLOGY and so on) must be studied and any of which might, at any given time, be more important than the labor process for a clear understanding of capitalism. However, the capital–labor relationship is the central feature of capitalism and therefore must be central in all theories concerning its nature.

## See also:

gender division of labor; segmented and dual labor markets; social structure of accumulation:

capital–labor accord; work, labor and production: major contemporary themes

## Selected references

Aronowitz, Stanley and DiFazio, William (1994) *The Jobless Future: Sci-Tech and the Dogma of Work*, Minneapolis, MN: University of Minnesota Press.

Berggren, Christian (1992) *Alternatives to Lean Production: Work Organization in the Swedish Auto Industry*, Ithaca, NY: ILR Press.

Braverman, Harry (1974) *Labor and Monopoly Capital: The Degradation of Work in the Twentieth Century*, New York: Monthly Review Press.

Foster, John Bellamy (1994) "*Labor and Monopoly Capital* Twenty Years After: An Introduction," *Monthly Review* 46(6).

Marx, Karl (1867) *Das Kapital*, published as *Capital, Volume I*, New York: International Publishers, 1967.

Parker, Mike and Slaughter, Jane (1994) *Working Smart: A Union Guide to Participation Programs and Reengineering*, Detroit: Labor Notes.

Thompson, E.P. (1963) *The Making of the English Working Class*, New York: Vintage Books.

Thompson, Paul (1983) *The Nature of Work: An Introduction to Debates on the Labor Process*, London: Macmillan.

MICHAEL D. YATES

# labor theory of value

## Introduction

Few concepts in the history of economics have been so very differently and contentiously understood, interpreted, criticized, debated and applied as the labor theory of value. It is imbued with a shifting but always intense aura of contestation. It is important for the author of this brief discussion to make his partisan position explicit.

There are multiple labor theories of value in the history (including the present) of economics. As with other theories of value (focused, for example, on utility or market power), the labor theories of value shed light on some aspects of economic processes while they also obscure other aspects. That labor theory of value which I find most persuasive is Marx's (although it too has had different and contesting interpretations). The basic issues posed for political economy by these various labor theories of value will hopefully become clearer in what follows.

To begin with some sharp demarcations, while Marx is usually associated and often credited with the inauguration of a labor theory of value, there are good reasons to question the association and to reject the credit outright (Rubin 1972; Meek 1973; Dobb 1973; Itoh 1980: 47ff). Adam Smith and David Ricardo, before Marx, were the great proponents and popularizers of a theory (which had some earlier formulations as well) that the values of commodities depended in some fundamental way upon and so reflected the amount of toil and trouble humans had to commit to their production, that is, to their cost. In more formal terms, the hypothesis holds that the relative prices of commodities established in market exchanges depend upon and are therefore proportional to their labor-determined values. Marx explicitly acknowledges at various points in his work that he was indebted to – although he also critically transformed – the labor theories of value propounded by Smith and Ricardo.

Indeed, for much of the nineteenth century most economists were comfortable with one or another CLASSICAL POLITICAL ECONOMY version (i.e. Smithian, Ricardian or Marxian) of a labor theory of value. True, some did not want to accord to productive labor the role of sole determinant of commodity values. Those who followed Smithian economics were likely to add other factors such as entrepreneurs' profit goals, land and buyers' desires, along with labor as playing at least some secondary roles in shaping commodity values. However, it was only with the neoclassical revolution begun in the 1870s that overt, determined hostility to a labor theory of value yielded an alternative theory.

## Implications of labor theories

Clearly one motive for neoclassical economics was distress over certain implications drawn from the labor theory of value. Ricardian socialism and Marxism were movements then widely understood to advocate that if labor caused all value, the laborers were entitled to all the value. In this theoretical light, persons other than laborers – share-owners, landlords, merchants *et al.* – had far lesser or no rightful claims to portions of that value. The huge portions they did obtain were thefts from the working class which could and should revolt against this state of affairs.

The neoclassical critique attacked the claim that the labor needed to produce commodities alone caused and explained their values. It propounded a multiple-causation approach to values, such that labor, capital, land and still other factors all contributed to commodity values. On the basis of this critique, NEOCLASSICAL ECONOMICS offered an alternative that sharply demoted the role of labor: commodity values depended conjointly on three different factors: (1) individuals' ranked preferences among commodities, (2) the technology available to convert nature into commodities, and (3) the initial endowments of wealth (land, labor and capital) that each individual contributed to production. By banishing any labor theory of value altogether from economics, the neoclassical tradition facilitated its own rapid rise to become the hegemonic paradigm within economics for most of the twentieth century.

## Forms of the labor theory

Nonetheless, forms of the labor theory of value did survive and develop in this century. All of them reacted, in one way or another, to the neoclassical critique and alternative. While neoclassical economists warrant the "neo" in their name by tracing their lineage to Adam Smith, contemporary labor theories of value connect themselves rather to Marx or Ricardo.

In most cases, this has meant throwing down the gauntlet to neoclassical theory's reduction of commodity values chiefly to the subjective notions of utility and of individual preferences among utilities. That is, modern labor theories of value often reduce commodity values not to subjective utility, but rather to the objective phenomenon of labor. The debate, then, has been utility theory of value versus labor theory of value.

This has been and continues to be mostly a very determinist debate (see DETERMINISM AND OVERDETERMINATION). Debaters argue over which theory "better" explains what essential factor(s) determine commodity values and, therefore, which theory better explains how entire economies work. The widest development and use of modern labor theories of value has occurred among Marxist economists. Partly this occurred because the authorities in socialist countries where Marxist theory was officially endorsed (for example, the USSR, China, Eastern Europe and elsewhere), utilized labor theories of value in calculating administered valuations of output and making economic planning and investment decisions.

By contrast, in countries with predominantly private capitalist economic systems, Marxists have given sharply varying amounts of prominence to labor theories of value in constructing their critical analyses of those systems and advocating socialist transformations. Some Marxists state flatly that Marx's (or indeed any) labor theory of value "is false" as an explanation of relative price formation in a capitalist economy (Roemer 1988: 47). Others have absorbed Piero Sraffa's work (see SRAFFA) into varying revisions of a Marxian labor theory of value (see survey in Howard and King 1992: 227–310). Still other Marxists have continued to use rather traditional views of Marx's labor theory of value to ground a basic understanding of capitalist economies, with an emphasis on relative price formation (by labor) within them. This has meant focusing social analysis primarily on production as the "economic base" that determines how a society's "superstructure of politics and culture" functions and evolves. That is, the labor theory of value orients those who use it in their work (theoretical, academic and practical) toward production and how its structures (ownership of productive property, technology and so on) determine relative prices, income distribution, economic and social injustice, economic crisis and long-term tendencies of economic and social change.

## Transformation problem

To sustain their applications and developments of Marx's labor theory of value, Marxists have had to defend it against many attacks. This has produced a vast literature of debate on the TRANSFORMATION PROBLEM. Begun a century ago by an Austrian founder of the neoclassical tradition, Eugen von Bohm-Bawerk, the critique held that Marx's logic precluded making labor inputs into production consistent essential determinants of commodity prices. Marxists countered with mathematical demonstrations of how labor values did determine (or were "transformed" into) relative prices that were proportional to labor values. Successive waves of debaters proposed solutions, criticized them, proposed alternative solutions and sustained new criticisms. All debaters shared a focus on the problem as one of showing how the relative prices of commodities had the labor inputs into their production as their ultimate determinants (Howard and King 1992: 227–310). No closure of this debate was ever achieved, and none is now in sight.

## Purpose of the labor theory?

Such a remarkably unresolved debate has recently suggested to many Marxists that the debaters may have posed the problem in an unresolvable way. Perhaps Marx's theory of value is not about explaining market prices as being proportional to labor values as the crucial alternative to the neoclassical economists' essentialist focus on utility. Marx's theoretical and political interests did not lead him to focus on analyzing prices. For Marx, the notion that political economy must have as its necessary foundation an essential determinat-ion of market prices entails an unwarranted capitulation to neoclassical economics and its contemporary HEGEMONY. The foundational focus on prices is their central issue; it need not and should not be the focus of Marxist theory (see Hilferding's arguments in Sweezy 1975).

What, then, is the purpose of a labor theory of value if not to explain market prices (setting aside whether or how well it performs that task)? The answer begins with the idea that what mattered most for Marx was not commodity exchange values, but rather the internal constitution of each commodity's value. Marx defines value as that aspect of every commodity that reflects the labor (he called it "abstract" labor) needed to produce it. The value of each commodity produced in the capitalist system comprises the sum of both a necessary value and a surplus value. Both of these values have to do with the labor involved in producing that commodity. The laborer who performs the labor that conveys value to a commodity receives back a portion of that value, a wage, as compensation for labor performed. Marx defined this wage, this returned portion of the value produced, as what was "necessary" for the laborer to reproduce and reapply his or her labor in producing more of the commodity.

The remaining portion of the laborer's labor, which Marx called "surplus" labor, produced a value that was not returned to the laborer as a wage. Such "surplus value" accrued not to the laborer who produced it but to others socially positioned (by custom, law and so on) to take it into their hands instead (see LABOR AND LABOR POWER). For Marx, what other theorists and activists had missed or only dimly glimpsed – the production and social distribution of such surplus values – was the central core of what his work contributed to social consciousness.

Marx's major work, Das Kapital, opens with a brief "labor theory of value" section, mainly to take his readers from what they thought economics was about (markets and prices) to what he wanted them to think about instead (uncompensated surplus labor). He then used the theoretical apparatus of the necessary-surplus differentiation to define classes in terms of producers over and against appropriators of surplus labor. The production, appropriation, and distribution of surplus labor as it exists in CAPITALISM – in the form of surplus value – then form the central objects of the vast bulk of *Das Kapital*'s three volumes.

To conclude, Marx's labor theory of value aims to focus those who encounter it primarily on production as the site where necessary and surplus labor occur and confront each other (in the relationship he called exploitation). On that basis, Marx's work then traces out the complex social forms and consequences of exploitation. Marx barely began that tracing. It was left to his followers afterwards, as they developed and changed his initial insights and as they contended with a capitalism which, as Marx insisted, is always changing (Resnick and Wolff 1987: ch. 3).

## Labor inputs and prices

This discussion perhaps leaves a lingering question: how do labor inputs influence the prices that actually obtain in commodity markets? The probable answer is this: what Marx's theory does is to define commodity values as equivalent to their abstract labor inputs. In contrast, commodity prices occurring in actual markets are overdetermined by an infinity of contributing factors (climate, politics, CULTURE, TECHNOLOGY, and so on). Among these are labor inputs, that is, values and the class differences plus class conflicts they reflect and reveal. The point and purpose of Marx's labor theory of value was to teach us about the existence of class, class conflict and all their social consequences including, among many others, their participation in the complex overdetermination of commodities' market prices. From this standpoint, it makes little sense to theorize the relative price of commodities as being reducible to merely their values or labor inputs. To proceed as though Marx's labor theory of value aims to "explain" market prices is to view Marx through the lens of neoclassical theory, a confusion of not only different but also fundamentally opposed paradigms. Trying to squeeze and distort Marx's theory into the framework and goals of neoclassical theory entails what philosophers call a "category mistake."

## See also:

commodity fetishism; economic surplus; Marxist political economy: contemporary varieties; productive and unproductive labor; turnover time of capital; use value and exchange value; value foundation of price

## Selected references

Dobb, Maurice (1973) *Theories of Value and Distribution Since Adam Smith*, Cambridge: Cambridge University Press.

Howard, M.C. and King, J.E. (1992) *A History of Marxian Economics*, vol. 2; *1929–1990*, Princeton, NJ: Princeton University Press.

Itoh, Makoto (1980) *Value and Crisis*, New York: Monthly Review Press.

Meek, Ronald L. (1973) *Studies in the Labour Theory of Value*, 2nd edn, London: Lawrence & Wishart.

Resnick, Stephen and Wolff, Richard (1987) *Knowledge and Class: A Marxian Critique of Political Economy*, Chicago: University of Chicago Press.

Roemer, John E. (1988) *Free to Lose: An Introduction to Marxist Economic Philosophy*, Cambridge, MA: Harvard University Press.

Rubin, Isaak Illich (1972) *Essays on Marx's Theory of Value*, 3rd edn, Detroit: Black & Red.

Sweezy, Paul (ed.) (1975) *Karl Marx and the Close of His System and Bohm-Bawerk's Criticism of Marx*, London: The Merlin Press.

Wolff, Richard and Resnick, Stephen (1987) *Economics: Marxian Versus Neoclassical*, Baltimore, MD: The Johns Hopkins University Press.

RICHARD D. WOLFF

# land reform

Land reform directly or indirectly redistributes and/or redefines PROPERTY rights to agricultural lands. Put more simply, land reform changes who owns land, or how land is owned. It has classically been understood as a redistributive policy relevant to reforming highly inegalitarian economies, where a relatively few individuals own most of the land. This entry focuses on classical redistributive reforms and land reforms which accompany agricultural decollectivization (see also INDIGENOUS TENURE SYSTEMS).

## Redistributive reforms

At its simplest level, redistributive land reform can be understood as a response to a syndrome of social, economic and political inequality built around an unequal distribution of land ownership. In some instances, land reform has been a rallying cry for revolutionary movements which often intend more sweeping economic reforms. Mexico in the early twentieth century, Bolivia and China at mid-century, Cuba in the 1960s and Nicaragua in the 1970s are all examples. In other instances, land reform has been part of a preemptive strike, meant to quell local unrest while preserving the dominant organization of an economy. US-supported land reforms efforts of various intensities throughout Latin America in the 1960s, following the Cuban revolution, exemplify this land reform impulse, as does the Salvadoran land reform of the 1980s. The more autonomous land reform undertaken by Peru in the 1960s and 1970s, and land reforms initiated by various states in post-colonial India, also seem to fit this mode. Indeed, land reform programs implemented under US tutelage after the Second World War in Japan, Korea and Taiwan are frequently cited as the most successful cases of land reform.

Given these various circumstances under which redistributive land reform has appeared, it is not surprising that land reform has been subjected to radically distinctive interpretations. Alain de Janvry (1981), for example,

suggests that for the most part Latin American land reforms had little to do with improving the lot of poor rural people, and were intended to stabilize and spur the growth of agrarian capitalism.

In Asian and other economies where land was typically operated by small-scale tenant farmers, even if it was owned by a class of wealthy landlords, so-called "land to the tiller" land reforms were fairly straightforward. They required a transfer of ownership rights to tenants, but no major reorganization of production at the farm level. The pre-reform operation of the land rental or tenancy markets in these economies in fact seemed to confirm the economic superiority of small-scale farming.

Such was not the case in Latin America, parts of southern Africa and elsewhere, where large-scale holdings were typically operated as single large-scale units utilizing hired labor. Architects of redistributive reform in these countries often had difficulty accepting the efficiency of small-scale farming, and opted for land reform programs that preserved large-scale production by granting former estate workers ownership shares in a cooperative farm. Reforms in Chile, Cuba, the Dominican Republic, Honduras, Nicaragua, Peru and El Salvador, among others, relied heavily upon producer cooperatives (see Carter and Mesbah 1994). In some other countries, (notably the Soviet Union and China), land previously cultivated on a small-scale was collectivized, partly in pursuit of imagined technological superiority of larger scale farming.

## Economic case for land reform

Questions of political (and redistributive) intent and impact aside, land reform has also been economically controversial. The so-called "economic case for land reform" has often been part and parcel of the call for redistributive reform, both in the heyday of Latin American reforms (see Dorner 1992) and in contemporary South Africa (see Binswanger and Deininger 1993). Two propositions support this case. First, small-scale holdings are more productive per-unit land area, and are economically more efficient because they can rely exclusively on self-supervising and productive family labor. Second, the redistribution of income generated by land reform creates a larger domestic market for consumer goods, spurring the growth of the local industrial and service sectors. If correct, this economic case for land reform would seem to imply that land reform entails no economic tradeoffs. It also implies that even the politics of redistributive reform should be relatively simple, since it should be possible to forge a political alliance between peasants and industrial capitalists to carry it out.

Is small-scale farming economically advantageous? Answers to this question have been many, including the notion that large-scale farmers have been economically irrational, or that governments have systematically subsidized large-scale farming, artificially repressing the advantages of small-scale agriculture.

Recently, largely theoretical work has explored a radical perspective in which competitive market economies fail to realize an "efficient distribution of land," thus making it possible to boost the performance of the economy by land redistribution. Central to these analyses are various sorts of intrinsically imperfect markets for labor, capital or risk which prevent the decentralized market economy from realizing an efficient outcome (for example, see Dasgupta and Ray 1986). These analyses lay the foundation for a novel type of neo-institutionalist (or perhaps neo-Marxian) perspective which, while rooted in the methodological individualism of neoclassical economics, indicates that the distribution of property rights over the means of production matters in fundamental ways.

Understanding the reasons why poor households have trouble accessing land through the market is of immediate practical relevance to debates about harnessing the land market as an instrument of redistributive land reform. Current interest in doing so is intense in a number of countries where state expropriation and redistribution of land is seen as politically or economically infeasible (notably South Africa, but also in a number of Latin American countries). The World Bank has, for instance, proposed a scheme of modest subsidies to poor individuals which, it argues, will suffice to let them buy their way into the land market now that economic liberalization has swept away various subsidies argued to have artificially propped up largescale farming (Binswanger and Deininger 1993). Other analysts argue that deeper reforms are needed to repair imperfect capital and other markets, which constrain the ability of poor individuals to access land via market transactions. In this argument, the state may be needed to break up large concentrations of power in order for market-assisted land reforms to be successful in the long term (see Carter and Barham 1996; Lipton 1993).

## Second-generation land reforms

The large-scale production cooperatives created by many agrarian reforms have, in nearly all instances, moved toward "second-generation" land reforms. These reforms are characterized by land and other cooperatively owned assets being subdivided and distributed as at least partially private property to co-operative members. There is debate over the degree to which this reform dynamic identifies the failure of the cooperative model of production. Putterman (1985) argues that the state often retained important rights of control in these cooperatives, damaging their functioning. Other analysts interpret this dynamic as reflecting an intrinsic COMMON PROPERTY RESOURCES problem. China offered the most striking example of this phenomenon in the early 1980s, when the "household responsibility system" was adopted. In this system, households were granted long-term leasehold contracts to land, encumbered with the responsibility for production quotas and other social obligations. It coincided with a period of rapid agricultural growth (Putterman 1995). In other countries, the impact of second generation reforms have been less striking (Carter and Mesbah 1994).

The powers that be in some of the transition economies of Eastern Europe and the former Soviet Union seem decidedly reluctant to subdivide and privatize existing large-scale, cooperative farms. The modest reconcentration of land following Chile's second-generation land reform sparked fresh debate about the competitiveness of small-scale agriculture. In China itself, agricultural growth has slowed since the mid-1980s, and there is ongoing debate about a third-generation reform which might either recollectivize land or completely privatize land rights, giving current lease-holders full and freely marketable rights to leasehold land. Not surprisingly, these debates about second and third-generation agrarian reform quickly confront the issue of the economic viability and stability of small-scale agriculture which is central to discussions about redistributive land reforms.

## See also:

land rights movements

## Selected references

Bardhan, Pranab (1994) "Economics of Development and the Development of Economics," *Journal of Economic Perspectives* 7(2): 129–42.

Binswanger, Hans and Deininger, Klaus (1993) "South African Land Policy: Historical Legacy and Current Policy Options," *World Development* 21(9): 1451–76.

Carter, Michael R. and Barham, Bradford (1996) "Level Playing Fields and Laissez Faire: Post-Liberalization Development Policy in Inegalitarian Agrarian Economies," *World Development* 24(7): 1133–50.

Carter, Michael R. and Mesbah, Dina (1994) "Land Reform and the Rural Poor in Latin America: The Future of State Mandated and Market Mediated Land Reform," in Jacques van der Gaag and Michael Lipton (eds), *Including the Poor*, Washington, DC: The World Bank.

Dasgupta, Partha and Ray, Debraj (1986) "Inequality as a Determinant of Malnutrition and Unemployment: Theory," *Economic Journal* 96(4): 1011–34.

Dorner, Peter (1992) *Latin American Land Reforms: A Retrospective Analysis*, Madison, WI: University of Wisconsin Press.

Janvry, Alain de (1981). *The Agrarian Question and Reformism in Latin America*, Baltimore, MD: Johns Hopkins University Press.

Lipton, Michael (1993). "Land Reform as Commenced Business: The Evidence Against Stopping," *World Development* 21(4): 641–57.

Putterman, Louis (1985) "Extrinsic versus Intrinsic Problems of Production Cooperatives," *Journal of Development Studies* 21.

—— (1995) *Continuity and Change in Rural China*, Cambridge: Cambridge University Press.

MICHAEL R. CARTER

# land rights movements

Indigenous peoples in territories subjected to European conquest dating from the late fifteenth century onward have managed to focus national and international attention on their subjugation and dispossession. These various movements, primarily concentrated in Australia, Canada, New Zealand, South America and the United States, began in different places at different times over the past several decades.

In New Zealand, there was a single treaty between the British Crown and the Maori peoples. The Treaty of Waitangi, signed by the ranking British officer in New Zealand and 500 different Maori chiefs during 1840, became the primary instrument of dispossession of Maori. The Australian immigrants from England saw no reason for treaties since the Aborigines were assumed not to have title to the lands taken from them. In North America, the governments of Canada and the United States negotiated a large number of separate treaties with the many distinct Indian tribes as the Europeans flooded in. Some of these treaties entailed the payment of nominal sums of money for land and other assets. As in New Zealand, the North American treaties were not based on the existence of native title but arose, instead, from the presumption of possession.

## Political movements and laws

Beginning in the late 1960s, a number of indigenous peoples began to organize political movements to re-establish their autonomy, and to reclaim lands taken from them. The Alaska Native Claims Settlement Act of 1971 provided Alaskan natives with over $900 million and with 44 million acres of federal lands. In Australia, the proposed Kakadu National Park provided the impetus for recreating Aboriginal land rights in the far north (Western *et al.* 1994). Legislation authorized governmental assistance to native peoples in the area of the park, but more importantly the new legal structure authorized joint management of park lands acknowledged to belong to aboriginal peoples. Kakadu National Park recognizes the cultural heritage of the aboriginal peoples and blends resource conservation principles into a regime of "co-management" of the Park. More recently, in the 1990s, the "Mabo" and "Wik" judgments of the Australian High Court have provided the foundation for unprecedented rights for Aborigines in relation to traditional sacred sites and lands.

When Arizona and California were engaged in serious legal battles over allocation of water from the lower Colorado River, their quest took second place to the water rights "reserved" by the US Supreme Court for Native Americans in Arizona. In the Great Lakes region of Michigan, Minnesota and Wisconsin, the Chippewa Indians have been engaged in legal battles with the three states to regain "treaty rights" over traditional hunting and fishing grounds. When lands were ceded to the United States by the Chippewa Indians in the late nineteenth century, the Chippewa retained the right to hunt, fish, trap and gather wild rice. Over the years, state governments have acted to eliminate all hunting and fishing by Indians off their reservations. In a series of decisions in Wisconsin in the late 1980s, those "off reservation" treaty rights were restored by federal judges. Now, Chippewa Indians in Wisconsin may exercise treaty rights to hunt and fish off their reservation as long as their activities do not threaten the viability of wildlife. The Great Lakes Indian Fish and Wildlife Commission collaborates with state-level conservation departments in the three states in yet another illustration of co-management.

## The case of South Africa

Although South Africa presents an entirely different dimension of land rights movements, the democratic transition underway there since 1990 can be thought of as the ultimate triumph of indigenous peoples over the historical process of European conquest. The early South African regimes were not materially different from those found elsewhere. However, following the Second World War, when "old-fashioned" colonialism went out of style, and when many nations embarked on a more congenial relationship with their native inhabitants, the government of South Africa took a decided turn away from liberalization. Forced removals, usually in the middle of the night, resulted in the relocation of approximately 75 percent of the total population into "homelands" comprising less than 14 percent of the land. These black homelands were then governed by puppet black rulers propped up with financial and military assistance from Johannesburg. The intense population pressure in the homelands, coupled with the withdrawal of male workers to the mines and factories, left the homelands bereft of their best workers and destitute. Poverty compounded the problems of natural resource degradation.

Unlike other land rights movements, the transition in South Africa is an instance of a clear majority finally overthrowing a distinct minority. Roughly 15 percent of the population of South Africa is of European origins, yet this minority had controlled all aspects of economic and political life in the country since 1652.

Today, following the adoption of a new constitution, South Africa faces a prodigious land-reform problem. Land claims courts will have a set period of time to receive filings by the dispossessed. While this process moves forward, there are efforts to facilitate the purchase of white-owned farms by blacks. While most land rights movements are concerned with restoring some level of autonomy and cultural identity to indigenous peoples, the revolution in South Africa will significantly overturn 300 years of dispossession and suppression by a white minority.

## Treaties and conventions

In most places, however, the land claims of indigenous groups are still confounded by national governments that have little interest in seeming to bend before the political pressure of small, often economically marginal, groups. The governments of China and India refuse to accept the concept of indigenous peoples because of the formidable task of establishing antecedence. Even where it is obvious which groups are, in fact, antecedent, the pertinent law is by no means clear. Of course indigenous peoples will claim, usually with good cause, that the law rarely helps them. On the other hand, nations with well-developed legal traditions adopt the canons of construction in which the language of treaties must be interpreted as the indigenous peoples would have understood it. Even then, these local treaties often are less than they would seem, and certainly less than the indigenous peoples would like for them to be. New Zealand is a case in point.

As above, here we see a clear – though brief – treaty between a colonizing power (Britain) and over 500 chieftains. Even so, it took legislative action by the government of New Zealand (in 1975) to acknowledge the pertinence of the Treaty of Waitangi. In the United States, the Eleventh Amendment to the Constitution prevents individuals and groups suing the federal government unless it agrees to be party to a suit. The various states and the national government are reluctant participants in the process of redress.

Therefore, indigenous peoples often find more legal traction in the form of international treaties and conventions. The Treaty of Waitangi is not the kind of external treaty obligation to which the government of New Zealand historically need pay much attention. On the other hand, New Zealand has become a party to several human rights instruments: the International Covenant on Civil and Political Rights, the International Covenant on Economic, Social and Cultural Rights, the Optional Protocol to the International Covenant on Civil and Political Rights, the International Convention on the Elimination of all Forms of Racial Discrimination, and the Convention on the Elimination of All Forms of Discrimination Against Women. In essence, these international obligations bind governments in ways that local treaties do not. Within this international legal environment, it is then possible to apply the principles of local treaties such as Waitangi. This has been the course of events in New Zealand (Brownlie 1992).

## Conclusion

The land rights movement among indigenous peoples is strengthened by a growing sense of awareness and power among widely scattered peoples. A few international conferences have provided a forum for sharing ideas and strategies. Full autonomy from national governance is a distant dream. But enhanced opportunities for self-determination, and a renewed commitment to their land-based legacy, seem within reach for most indigenous peoples.

## See also:

colonialism and imperialism: classic texts; cultural capital; culture; hunter–gatherer and subsistence societies; justice; land reform; race in political economy: major contemporary themes; racism; rights

## Selected references

Bromley, Daniel W. (1994) "The Enclosure Movement Revisited: The South African

Commons," *Journal of Economic Issues* 28: 357–65.

—— (1995) "South Africa: Where Land Reform Meets Land Restitution," *Land Use Policy* 12: 99–103.

Brownlie, Ian (1992) *Treaties and Indigenous Peoples*, Oxford: Clarendon Press.

Orange, Claudia (1987) *The Treaty of Waitangi*, Sydney: Allen & Unwin.

Western, David, Wright, Michael and Strum, Shirley (eds) (1994) *Natural Connections: Perspectives in Community-Based Conservation*, Washington, DC: Island Press.

Wilmsen, Edwin N. (ed.) (1989) *We Are Here: Politics of Aboriginal Land Tenure*, Berkeley, CA: University of California Press.

DANIEL W. BROMLEY

# language, signs and symbols

According to INSTRUMENTAL VALUE THEORY, value is that which provides for cultural continuity and noninvidious social reproduction. The key to this definition is the recognition that "culture matters," implying a paramount role for cultural symbols. Symbols, including language and signs, constitute representations which give tangibility to thoughts, ideas and concepts, which in themselves have no intrinsic form. The symbolic anthropologist Clifford Geertz defines clusters of symbols as "historically created systems of meaning in terms of which we give form, order, point, and direction to our lives" (Geertz 1973: 52). Symbols link individuals spatially and temporally by providing a common source of information and communication, contributing to the development of communal values and facilitating the development of social networks. Symbols and language are human creations, constituting "meaning," which is passed from age to age, a continuum of thought or social mores. These common values and resulting social relations guide behavior through the establishment of communal norms, learned and shared attributes or CULTURE.

Symbols provide the context wherein historical concepts are made tangible and accessible to current generations. Language, as the fundamental medium of communication, is a crucial system for transmitting historical progress, recreating the past and reapplying the existing symbols to new contexts. This results in problem solving based on continuous experiences and accumulated knowledge (Hoijer 1960: 196–209). That is, cultural and social evolution and progress are enabled by symbolic preservation of historical achievement. This is not to say that all symbols ensure "progress," but that, at a minimum, they embody accumulated knowledge and experience, making this knowledge accessible to current and future generations.

Symbols and common language are critical for successful adaptation to environmental changes. Groups of associated significant symbols, in that they are accessible in common, provide a guide for shared beliefs and value. Inasmuch as these symbols are interpreted through social discourse and experience, they render a historic, ordered system of relations. As Geertz writes:

> Culture is a system of symbols by which man confers significance upon his own experience. Symbol systems, human-created, shared, conventional, ordered, and indeed learned, provide human beings with a meaningful framework for orienting themselves to one another, to the world of social interaction... so the symbol system is the information source that, to some measurable extent, gives shape, direction, particularity, and point to an ongoing flow of activity.
> (Geertz 1973: 250)

Thorstein Veblen, John Dewey, Emile Durkheim, Karl Polanyi and Clifford Geertz, among others, have asserted that the fulfillment of human life is about the development of the individual, but always within a context of meaning and social interaction. Value is not merely a means to satisfy individual wants and needs, but also has an inseparable communal component. Socially constructive change, including the adoption of new technologies, should not destroy significant symbolic images which orient individuals and groups to their social and physical milieu. Some vestige of the past must be maintained to avoid uprooting society. It does not mean that the evolution of culture should be prohibited, but that change should allow for the society to reproduce itself, maintaining "the continuity of life meanings, experiences, and interpersonal relations" (Stanfield 1984: 22).

Substantiation of the value of symbols may best be established through the negative case. Although genetic elements can guide human behavior along a narrow path of basic survival, without a "cultural continuity" of development, meaningful existence is impaired and social reproduction crippled. Geertz warns that without social symbols, man's behavior would be virtually ungovernable, a mere chaos of pointless acts and exploding emotions, his experience virtually shapeless (Geertz 1973: 46).

Here, it is useful to borrow from sociologist Emile Durkheim his concept of anomie. Anomie means without tradition and custom and the associated norms, values, mores and goals which constrain behavior (Durkheim 1984: 339). Similar to Karl Polanyi's DISEMBEDDED ECONOMY, where social interaction is subordinated to other systems (namely economic), anomie defines social dysfunction, due to a lack of integration into *the historic and symbolic fabric of society*. The outcome of anomie includes the rise of social pathologies, including suicide, violence and other regressive behavior.

Preservation of symbol and language associations aids in social and cultural adaptation and is consistent with the principle of MINIMAL DISLOCATION of instrumental resources. Dislocation is minimized by maintaining the essence of identity and cultural orientation as it is evidenced in social symbols. When symbols are lost or cease to aid in the interpretation of the social and political environment, then social structures find no point of reference. This is the meaning of "social discontinuity," the severing of cultural norms and social structure. During periods of social discontinuity there is a loss of meaningful symbology. Inconsistencies arise between remaining symbols and actual social interaction. The inconsistencies lead to disorientation and eventually to discontinuity and the breakdown of institutional frameworks. The typical cause of social disintegration is rapid social and technological change, which affects the ability of symbol systems to facilitate interpretation of the social environment. As the social structure reacts to the rapid changes, it diverges from the existing symbology or culture, which changes at a slower rate. However, the reverse can also be true. The destruction of symbols by rapid growth and technological change can lead to social discontinuity.

The preservation of language, sign and symbol systems is not an argument against change, but an assertion that continuity of culture and symbolic integration is necessary to assimilate change and social evolution. Effective change will be embedded in the social fabric, thereby not contradicting solidarity or community relations but maintaining them. Preservation efforts provide for the physical manifestation of the continual sociocultural element, establishing the "primacy of society" and social solidarity. In that symbol systems constitute culture, their preservation ensures a vehicle for social reproduction.

The implication for economics is that as "culture matters," so too does history. Symbols are a necessary component of analysis as they aid in identification of the elements of continuity or PATH DEPENDENCY between past and present institutional arrangements. As the current social and economic context is only one of many possible outcomes, the impact of symbol systems and language imply that there are no universal "laws" of progress or economic development. The transmission of culture through symbols and via language leads to differentiated human systems, including kinship, communal, political and economic systems.

Neoclassical economics, however, has assumed away the importance of social symbols and culture by constructing the self-interested, atomistic agent. "Homo economicus" is assumed to maximize only its own well-being in a rationally consistent manner, without regard for social patterns of behavior or historical precedence. When individual behavior appears to reflect institutional influences – culture, habit or social values – the neoclassical school asserts that homo economicus is still deliberately and consciously pursuing his or her own hedonistic desires. Such assumptions discount cultural symbols and, hence, neglect an important determinant of behavior which may appear irrational in the context of "economic man" but very rational in terms of the "socio-cultural whole person."

Institutional, feminist, ecological, social and postmodern political economists acknowledge the importance of culture explicitly, and symbols implicitly. These schools acknowledge that value is a social construct, affected by the dominant symbolic influences, among other things. Moreover, it is recognized that too great an emphasis on self-interested pursuits devoid of social context (i.e. capitalism) may come at the detriment of coherent symbol systems and cultural stability. Acknowledgment of the significance of language, sign and symbol in valuation and social reproduction, then, implies an immutable association between economic and social systems.

## See also:

conventions; evolution and coevolution; holistic method; institutional change and adjustment; institutions and habits; modernism and postmodernism; time; value judgments and world views

## Selected references

Durkheim, E. (1984) *The Division of Labor in Society*, trans. by W.D. Halls, New York: Free Press.

Geertz, C. (1973) *The Interpretation of Cultures*, HarperCollins Publishers.

Herbert, E. (1991) *Culture and Anomie*, Chicago: University of Chicago Press.

Hoijer, H. (1960) "Language and Writing," in Harry L. Shapiro (ed.) *Man, Culture, and Society*, New York: Oxford University Press.

Stanfield, J.R. (1984) "Social Reform and Economic Policy," *Journal of Economic Issues* 18(1).

KARIN SABLE

# laws of political economy

Broadly speaking, there are two conceptions of laws: one focusing on empirical phenomena such as the events of experience, and the other focusing typically on non-empirical phenomena such as the entities that cause or facilitate these events.

## Positivist conception of laws

The first and most common conception of law in political economy stems from a positivist understanding of science. The version of positivism pertinent here is essentially a theory of the nature and limits of knowledge. Although positivism prioritizes epistemology (theories of knowledge), ontology (theories of existents) is not banished. Rather, an implicit ontology consisting of the objects of experience is concealed within this epistemology. What exists is reduced to what can be known through experience, and this in turn is reduced to unconnected, atomistic episodes or events. Now, if particular knowledge is of events, then the possibility of general (including scientific) knowledge must be of the regular patterns or constant conjunctions, if any, that these events reveal. The primary objects of science become events, and laws result from recording their constant conjunctions. A law is a statement about a constant conjunction of events, whether observed or conjectured, and may be styled as "whenever event $x$ then event $y$." Since this conception of law is encouraged by Hume's analysis of causality, it is referred to as Humean law. A Humean law just is the constant conjunction of events.

## Critical realist conception of laws

The alternative conception of law derives (in its modern form) from a critical realist conception of science, in particular from an analysis of the nature of experimental practices and results (Bhaskar 1978; Lawson 1997). The analysis starts with two observations. First, virtually all of the constant conjunctions of events that are of interest to science (including probabilistic ones) only occur in experimental situations, ignoring the possibility that they may occur accidentally and/or over some restricted spatio-temporal region, and/or be trivial. The point of experiment is to close the system by creating a particular set of conditions that will isolate the interesting causal mechanism from all those that are not of interest. The interesting causal mechanism is then allowed to operate unimpeded and the results, the constant conjunctions, are recorded. Hence, Humean law is more accurately styled as: "whenever event $x$, then event $y$, under conditions $z$." Second, the conclusions derived from experimental situations where conditions $z$ exist (i.e. in closed systems) are often successfully applied outside experimental situations when the conditions do not hold (i.e. in open systems).

## Critical issues relating to laws

If, however, a law is just a constant conjunction of events, and constant conjunctions are by definition not found outside closed systems, then one must conclude: (1) that outside closed systems there are no laws, and (2) that the question of what governs events in open systems is unaddressed. Moreover, it leaves the observation that the results obtained from closed systems are often successfully applied in open systems without any valid explanation.

If, therefore, events manifesting themselves as constant conjunctions are not found in open systems whence Humean law cannot govern or explain them, then something else must govern and explain them. The most likely candidates are the mechanisms that causally govern or facilitate the events that are experienced. The primary objects of science become causal mechanisms and the powers they possess in virtue of their intrinsic structures. To exemplify, the primary objects of zoology become the genetic mechanisms that predispose a kitten to

develop into a cat. A law is a statement about these causal mechanisms and their powers.

These causal mechanisms act transfactually; that is, once their powers are exercised, they continue to govern events causally. This is done irrespective of the conditions under which they operate, and/or the resultant form in which these events manifest themselves, that is, as constant or non-constant conjunctions. The resultant form of events depends upon the interaction of a network of causal mechanisms, some of which may act as countervailing mechanisms. The transfactual nature of causal mechanisms implies that, from the critical realism perspective, laws must be conceived of as tendencies. Laws as tendencies are claims about mechanisms and their causal powers; they are not claims about the conditions under which the mechanisms operate, or about the results of their operation.

It is not uncommon, however, to find adherents of the Humean conception of law attempting to interpret this law along the lines of a tendency. There are three commonly held (mis)interpretations of laws as tendencies (Lawson 1998). Humean law might be interpreted:

- as a trend (for example, wages tend to rise over time);
- as a high relative frequency of a given subset of a class of possible events (for example, as the supply of money increases, the general price level tends to increase soon after);
- as a counterfactual claim about what would come about under certain conditions (for example, if wages were to rise, employment would fall under certain conditions – where these conditions may be explicit as in the four Marshallian conditions of derived demand, or implicit as in a *ceteris paribus* clause).

In none of the three interpretations does attention focus on mechanisms and their causal powers. Instead, attention focuses on conditions, and/or results in the form of events and the constant conjunctions they are presumed to reveal. Since the conditions are effectively attempts to close the system, and the constant conjunctions are constitutive of the closed system, the three interpretations are exposed to the same critique as Humean law discussed above. While commonly held, the interpretation of Humean law as tendency is unfounded.

## Marx's analysis of laws

Whereas laws based on a Humean conception abound in political economy, for example, laws of demand and supply, Verdoorn's Law and so on, examples of laws as tendencies are rare. An example of the latter is, arguably, Marx's FALLING RATE OF PROFIT TENDENCY and the counteracting tendencies. Marx describes a tendency as "a law whose absolute action is checked, retarded, and weakened by counteracting circumstances" (*Das Kapital* 3: 235). Marx's focus is not on conditions and/or results, but on causes. His justification for the existence of the falling rate of profit tendency does not take the form of an attempt to discover constant conjunctions in the events, that is, between variables like the organic composition of capital and profit rates. Neither does he attempt to establish the conditions under which such a constant conjunction would occur; rather, he offers an analysis of mechanisms and their causal powers. Stated simply, Marx demonstrates how both tendency and counter-tendency are grounded in the same causal mechanism, namely, the drive to increase the productivity of labor when labor power appears in the commodity form. The tendency, once exercised, continues to act, irrespective of the conditions or the resultant form in which the ensuing events manifest themselves.

## See also:

critical realism; dialectical method

## Selected references

Bhaskar, R. (1978) A *Realist Theory of Science*, Brighton: Harvester Wheatsheaf.

Lawson, T. (1997) *Economics and Reality*, London and New York: Routledge.

—— (1998) "Tendencies," in J. Davis, W. Hands and U. Maki, *Handbook of Economic Methodology*, Aldershot: Elgar.

Marx, K. (1894) *Das Kapital*, vol. 3, published as *Capital Volume III*, Lawrence & Wishart, 1984.

STEVE FLEETWOOD

# Lewis's theory of economic growth and development

Born in the West Indies in 1915, W. Arthur Lewis took his PhD at the London School of Economics, where he taught for a short time before moving to Manchester. In 1959 he became vice-chancellor of the University of the West Indies. He left there in 1963 to take up the chair in political economy at Princeton, a post that he held until his death in 1991. His two most famous works, an article on economic development with unlimited supplies of labor (1954) and his book on *The Theory of Economic Growth* (1955), were both written during his time at Manchester.

His book sets out a comprehensive framework for studying economic development. In it he identifies three proximate causes of growth: efforts to economize, increases in knowledge and its application, and increases in capital and other resources per head. He also considers the various kinds of environments and institutions which are favorable to the emergence of growth. His 1954 article spawned a massive literature and is the main subject of this entry. While his name will long be associated with the study of economic development, he also wrote on tariffs, the economic history of the world economy and specific nations, cost–benefit analysis and planning. In 1979, Arthur Lewis was awarded the Nobel Prize for Economics (jointly with Theodore Schultz) for "pioneering research into economic development, with particular consideration of the problems of developing countries."

## Classical elements

Lewis's formal model(s) of economic development contain many elements of CLASSICAL POLITICAL ECONOMY (see Lewis 1958). These include the notion that the wage of unskilled labor is exogenous as far as buyers of labor in the modern sector are concerned. Another way of putting this is to say that the wage (in the short term at least) is not determined by the neoclassical forces of supply and demand for labor. Rather, it is fixed or pre-determined by economic and social circumstances in the traditional sector.

Another classical element important in the Lewis model is the connection between savings and the DISTRIBUTION OF INCOME. Together with Adam Smith and other classical economists, Lewis sees the basic problem as low savings. The key to development is to be found in mechanisms which dramatically increase the savings rate. Increased savings, in a capitalist economy, come mainly if not entirely from savings out of the profits of the capitalists:

> The reason why savings are low in an underdeveloped economy relatively to national income is not that the people are poor, but that capitalists' profits are low relative to national income. As the capitalist sector expands, profits grow relatively, and an increasing proportion of national income is reinvested.
>
> (Lewis 1954: 190)

## Lewis's basic model

Lewis's basic model may be set out as follows. First, let us assume two sectors in the economy. One, a capitalist or modern sector, uses physical capital owned by the capitalists and employs wage-labor for profit. Although it is common to equate this sector with manufacturing, there is no reason why the capitalist sector might not include capitalist elements such as plantations in the agriculture sector. The other sector is an overpopulated traditional or subsistence sector. Here the organization of production is small scale, with family activity being the norm. In this sector, output is assumed to be shared equally among the workers, and therefore their wage is related to the average product of labor in that sector and not the marginal product. At least some of the labor in the traditional sector may be characterized as "surplus labor," in the sense that it can be withdrawn from the sector without any noticeable loss of output. This is because, in this sector, productivity at the margin is very low and may even be zero or negative.

Lewis argues that, in the early phases of INDUSTRIALIZATION, the capitalist sector will be able to hire labor at the going wage in the subsistence sector plus a margin. Lewis suggests that the margin may be as high as 30–50 percent, to compensate for the higher cost of living and the real and psychological costs of moving. Since, by assumption, the average product of labor in the modern sector will be above the marginal product of labor of the last unit hired, the capitalist is able to obtain profits on the intra-marginal units of labor. These profits, again by assumption, are reinvested in the form of new physical capital goods. This process of capital ACCUMULATION increases the marginal (and average) product of labor in the modern sector, the amount of labor hired (at the constant wage), the capitalist's surplus, savings and investment, and so on. As productivity increases in the capitalist sector, so too does the profit share and with it the savings rate.

The key to the model is the notion that the supply of labor to the modern sector is infinitely elastic at the going wage rate. In other words, capitalists will not have to continually raise wages to attract increasing amounts of labor into the modern sector. One reason for this will be the existence of disguised unemployment in the traditional sector where the marginal product is "negligible, zero or even negative" (Lewis 1954: 141). In the extreme case of the Lewis model, where the marginal product of labor in producing the wage good is negative, it is possible to accumulate capital goods while not giving up the production of consumer goods. In this situation investment is undertaken with the aid of surplus labor. The transfer of such labor into the modern sector allows the marginal product of labor in the traditional sector (and thus the supply of food) to remain constant, or to rise at the same time as investment is rising.

## Criticisms of the model

The model has been subject to a number of criticisms, especially since some of its key assumptions do not appear to fit the reality of life in most contemporary Third World countries. First, the model assumes that employment transfer proceeds at the same rate as capital accumulates in the modern sector. However, there may be labor saving advances going on. Indeed, in most third world countries, the capacity of the industrial sector to absorb labor has turned out to be rather small. Also, many industrialized countries have seen marked labor shedding by their own manufacturing sectors in the past decade or two. Second, implicit in the model is the notion that there is surplus labor in rural areas and full employment in urban areas. Research indicates that the reverse is more likely to be true in many Third World countries. Third, nominal and real urban wages in the capitalist sector of many Third World countries appear to be able to rise rapidly, even when there is substantial unemployment. Fourth, the model presumes the existence of entrepreneurs who will act in the way specified. Some would argue that the major problem of economic development is to create the conditions under which an entrepreneurial class will come into being.

## Extensions by Fei and Ranis

Lewis's model of growth has occupied a central position in the literature of development economics since it was first published in 1954. His model was later extended by Fei and Ranis (1964), who saw the development process as occurring in three stages. The first stage was essentially that modelled by Lewis. In their second stage, the transfer of labor out of agriculture results in a shortage of agricultural output, a rise in the (relative) price of agricultural products, and a rise in wages in the modern sector. In their third stage, invest-

ment takes place in the agricultural sector and with it we see the commercialization of agriculture. As a result of this process, the real wage tends to equality with the marginal product of labor in both the traditional and modern sectors and so dualism comes to an end.

## See also:

capitalism; development political economy: major contemporary themes; newly industrialized Asian nations

## Selected references

Fei, J. and Ranis, G. (1964) *Development of the Labour Surplus Economy: Theory and Policy*, New York: Oxford University Press.

Gersovitz, M. (1982) *The Theory and Experience of Economic Development: Essays in Honour of Sir Arthur Lewis*, London: George Allen & Unwin.

Lewis, W.A. (1954) "Economic Development with Unlimited Supplies of Labour," *Manchester School* 22: 139–91.

—— (1955) *The Theory of Economic Growth*, London: George Allen & Unwin.

—— (1958) "Unlimited Labour: Further Notes," *Manchester School* 26: 1–32.

—— (1972) "Reflections on Unlimited Labour," in L. DiMarco (ed.) *International Economics and Development*, New York: Academic Press, 75–96.

—— (1983) *Selected Economic Writings of W. Arthur Lewis*, ed. M. Gersovitz, New York: New York University Press.

ROBERT DIXON

# liability management

Broadly speaking, liability management refers to the ability of banks to increase their lending activity by borrowing funds which appear on the liability side of their balance sheet, without having to dispose of their marketable assets (such as Treasury bills). In a more narrow sense, liability management is associated with wholesale financial markets and interbank arrangements, with banks competing for certificates of deposits (CDs) or other similar financial instruments. Because liability management has recently been associated with a spate of financial innovations, which have made monetary control even more difficult than it was before, it has attracted the interest of central bankers and academics. There are, however, two different interpretations of liability management among non-orthodox economists, which we shall call the traditional view and the radical view.

## Traditional view

The traditional perspective is that liability management is the latest stage in the historical development of banking systems (Chick 1986; Niggle 1991). According to this traditional view, mainstream monetary theory is based either on commodity money or on a stable base–reserve–multiplier process, with causality running from high-powered money to money and credit aggregates, which was vindicated in the early stages of banking. Before the advent of liability management, banks would passively wait for deposits, and only expand their lending activity if new depositors came forth. The attracted deposits were taken as a pool of funds, available for lending. Banks would mainly manage their asset side, making sure that sufficient secondary reserves were available; that is, making sure they had enough marketable assets to sell, in case of substantial deposit withdrawals or if more private loans needed to be made.

This passive behavior of banks, consistent with the causal story of orthodox monetary theory, would be overturned with the advent of liability management. According to the traditional view, liability management has transformed banks into active economic agents, who search aggressively for customers and adjust their liabilities later (Podolsky 1986: 159–60). Some authors even go so far as to claim that, as a result of liability management by the banks, the expansion of monetary and credit aggregates is supply-led (Chick 1986: 117, 122; Howells 1995). Commercial banks, rather than firms and households, would thus determine the rate of growth of credit money. In this extreme form, there is a similarity between liability management and the monetarist story: in both cases there can be an excessive creation of money and hence inflation. In the first case (the traditional non-orthodox view), it is the result of the greed of bankers, who lend beyond all reasonable limits; in the second case (MONETARISM), it is a consequence of the incompetence of the officials at the central bank.

## Radical view

There is, however, another view of liability management – the radical non-orthodox view. According to this new view, liability management is not an innovation that would have transformed the process of banking intermediation (Goodhart 1989: 30). Those who hold the radical view often believe that scriptural credit-money historically preceded commodity money, and that mainstream monetary theory was never historically relevant, even in the first stages of banking (see Heinsohn and Steiger 1983; and Courbis et al. 1991). Since money is endogenous and credit-driven, liability management is a permanent feature. Banks are perpetually engaged in passive liability management, as they must first consent to loans, and later search for funds to finance the deposits which are leaking out. If all banks are growing at approximately the same rate, leakages will be compensated for by deposits incoming from rival institutions. Liabilities will thus automatically adjust to the autonomous growth of assets. This is not necessarily the case, however. In Europe and the United States, some large banks (the business banks) have systematically been indebted toward smaller institutions (the deposit banks). As a consequence, business banks have been forced to enter into active liability management, borrowing funds from deposit banks to compensate for the differential in the rates of growth of their loans and of their deposits.

## Institutional analysis

Notwithstanding the active liability management at the level of the individual bank, active liability management at the systemic level has long been observed. According to a distinction made by John Hicks, we can contrast pure overdraft banking systems from market-financed banking systems (Renversez 1996). While the latter correspond to mainstream monetary theory, the former match banking systems that hold virtually no liquid assets. All overdraft systems are compelled to practice liability management as a logical necessity. Any adjustment is done on the liability side, simply because no adjustment from the asset side is possible. Banks as a whole, when they are in need of banknotes for their customers or in need of compulsory reserves, cannot get them by selling liquid assets to the central bank since they hold no Treasury bills. They obtain all of their high-powered money by borrowing it from the central bank.

When banks of these overdraft systems increase their loan portfolio, they are eventually required to augment their borrowings from the central bank. Most European banking systems, for instance the French system, have structurally been indebted to the central bank. The Japanese banking system is also of the overdraft type, as are most of the banking systems in the less developed countries. The argument to be found in the traditional view, that liability management would be a new phase in the development of financial systems, thus does not seem to be a correct assessment of the actual evolution of financial systems throughout the world.

In the case of financial systems of the American type, at least until recently, the dynamics were quite different, since commercial banks held large amounts of government bonds that central banks were disposed to repurchase. In some circumstances the central bank refused to do so, in which case the commercial banks were driven to the discount window, as in overdraft banking systems. Over the last two decades, as a result of the emphasis over anti-inflation policies, banks have been subjected to systematic refusals from the central bank to accommodate. Furthermore, the secondary reserves of Treasury bills and bonds, which were a vestige of the vast amounts of bonds accumulated during the Second World War, were depleted by the early 1960s, forcing banks to find other means to face unexpected deposit withdrawals without selling these precautionary assets or without calling back loans (Goodhart 1989: 32). Liability management has surged back. Indeed, as is recalled by Moore (1988: 27–8), active liability management was part of the American banking system in the 1920s, but it receded with the overabundance of primary and secondary asset reserves in the following two or three decades. Since the 1960s it has been back in favor.

## See also:

endogenous money and credit; financial innovations; financial instability hypothesis; monetary circuit; money, credit and finance: history; money, credit and finance: major contemporary themes

## Selected references

Chick, Victoria (1986) "The Evolution of the Banking System and the Theory of Saving, Investment and Interest," *Economies et Sociétés* 20(8–9): 111–26.

Courbis, Bernard, Fromier, Eric and Servet, Jean-Michel (1991) "Enrichir l'économie politique de la monnaie par l'histoire," *Revue Économique* 42(2): 315–38.

Goodhart, Charles (1989) "Has Moore become too horizontal?," *Journal of Post Keynesian Economics* 12(1): 29–34.

Heinsohn, Gunnar and Steiger, Otto (1983) "Private Property, Debts and Interest or the Origin of Money and the Rise and Fall of Monetary Economies," *Studi Economici* 21: 3–56.

Howells, Peter G.A. (1995) "The Demand for Endogenous Money," *Journal of Post Keynesian Economics* 18(1): 89–106.

Moore, Basil J. (1988) *Horizontalists and*

*Verticalists: The Macroeconomics of Credit Money*, Cambridge: Cambridge University Press.

Niggle, Christopher J. (1991) "The Endogenous Money Supply Theory: An Institutionalist Appraisal," *Journal of Economic Issues* 25(1): 137–51.

Podolsky, T.M. (1986) "Control of a Monetary Quantity: Constraint or Contumacy," *British Review of Economic Issues* 7(17): 1–37.

Renversez, Françoise (1996) "Monetary Circulation and Overdraft Economy," in Ghislain Deleplace and Edward J. Nell (eds), *Money in Motion: The Post Keynesian and Circulation Approaches*, London: Macmillan.

MARC LAVOIE

**LIBERALISM, GLOBAL:** *see* global liberalism

# liberation theology

Liberation theology is one of several theologies which have emerged in the second half of the twentieth century focusing on justice issues (others include feminist theology, environmental theology and black theology in South Africa and North America). Two common features unite these justice theologies. First, each represents theological reflection upon the experience of groups seeking transformation of specific elements of the postwar global order: the property relations of international capitalism, patriarchy, the environmental impact of global capitalism and institutionalized racism. Secondly, these theologies employ modes of social analysis which diverge from both the traditional framework of Christian social thought and the liberal framework of mainstream economics. Combining these, the distinguishing features of liberation theology can be said to be the experience of social revolution from which it emerges and the mode of analysis employed in interpreting that experience.

## History and basic tenets

Liberation theology first emerged from the experience of poverty and oppression among the propertyless classes of Central and South America during the 1960s and 1970s. Finding traditional Roman Catholic social thought inadequate for the task of interpreting their experience and spurred by the reforming spirit of Vatican II, Latin American faith communities involved in social transformation forged a new theology (some of the central texts are Gutierrez 1973, 1983; Míguez Bonino 1975; Sobrino 1978; Boff and Boff 1984). Central to that task were two things: first, the reading of sacred texts and interpretation of Catholic tradition from the perspective of the poor and oppressed of Central and South America; and second, interpreting the social position and options of the poor and oppressed in terms of radical social analysis. Over the past thirty years, liberation theology has played an important role in revolutionary movements across Central and South America (for example, a leading liberation theologian, Ernesto Cardenal, was minister of culture in the Sandinista government in Nicaragua during the 1980s). Latin American liberation theology has also played a significant role in the evolution of theology in Europe and North America, where traditional Christian social thought has had to come to terms with its militant compassion for the oppressed (Lernoux 1982).

## Injustice, poverty and abuse of power

The reading and interpretation of sacred texts within lay communities of resistance (sometimes called "base Christian communities") is an often overlooked core ingredient of liberation theology. It is a mistake to treat liberation theology on purely theoretical grounds. The theological treatises that have appeared are reflections upon, and are grounded in, lay communities reading and interpreting, within the context of their own experience of social resistance, the Old Testament stories of liberation from injustice, the prophetic voices raised against the abuse of power, and the New

Testament stories of Mary and the early church community. Out of the readings of those texts has emerged one basic theological premise which lay communities of resistance and theologians of liberation alike take as primary: God speaks and acts on behalf of the poor and the oppressed. Commonly identified as "the preferential option for the poor," this theological premise is now widely accepted, not only in the justice theologies from which it emerged, but also among those writing about social theory from more traditional Christian theological perspectives.

## Poverty, oppression and liberation

But what constitutes poverty, who is oppressed, and how would liberation appear? Traditional Christian theology focused attention on spiritual poverty, the oppression of living in a world characterized by the spiritual battle between the forces of good and evil, and the promise of ultimate victory beyond the boundaries of our life and world. Echoing Marx's challenge to the Hegelians (philosophers have been satisfied to describe the world; the point is to change it), liberation theology has challenged communities of faith in Latin American, Africa and Asia to resist social, economic and political oppression and seek liberation from the material forces of cultural production, which constitute the source of their poverty, through social transformation. This challenge has been the major source of dialogue and debate between liberation theologians, those who employ other approaches to Christian social theology and social theorists.

## Challenges to liberation theology

The Vatican and other Christian social theorists have challenged liberation theology on the grounds that it is inherently Marxist. While this is not necessarily true, it is the case that faith communities of resistance and theologians of liberation draw upon social theories which place power relations at the center of social and economic analysis. Dialectical social theories, such as dependency theory, have often

been employed in liberation theology for a number of reasons. First, they explicitly identify the social position within which the faith communities of resistance exist (standing in opposition to the dominant mode of cultural production). Second, they emphasize the conflict within society between the alternative interests of social groups, and suggest the possibility of social transformation. Radical social theorists find in liberation theology a significant ally, especially in popular education. For example, Freire's (1972) pedagogy of *conscientización* has been widely adopted as a model for bringing together radical social theory and the experience of ordinary people in oppressed situations.

The most recent development in liberation theology has been its migration to sub-Saharan Africa and Asia during the last two decades. In these new environs, liberation theology has been reshaped in keeping with the issues confronting communities of resistance on those two continents (Ferm 1986).

## See also:

community; ethics and morality; exploitation; human dignity; inequality; justice; rights

## Selected references

Boff, Leonardo and Boff, Clodovis (1984) *Salvation and Liberation: In Search of a Balance Between Faith and Politics*, Maryknoll, NY: Orbis Books.

Ferm, Deane William (ed.) (1986) *Third World Liberation Theologies: A Reader*, Maryknoll, NY: Orbis Books.

Freire, Paulo (1972) *Pedagogy of the Oppressed*, New York: Seabury Press.

Gutierrez, Gustavo (1973) *A Theology of Liberation: History, Politics and Salvation*, Maryknoll, NY: Orbis Books.

—— (1983) *The Power of the Poor in History*, Maryknoll, NY: Orbis Books.

Lernoux, Penny (1982) *Cry of the People: The Struggle for Human Rights in Latin America – The Catholic Church in Conflict with US Policy*, Harmondsworth: Penguin.

Míguez Bonino, José (1975) *Doing Theology in a Revolutionary Situation*, Philadelphia: Fortress Press.

Sobrino, Jon (1978) *Christology at the Crossroads: A Latin American Approach*, Maryknoll, NY: Orbis Books.

ROSS B. EMMETT

# limits to growth

Does the scarcity of energy and matter and the earth's finite capacity to supply environmental services, including the absorption of industrial wastes, place limits on global ECONOMIC GROWTH? This question is at the center of the "limits to growth" debate.

## Against limits

Those who argue against the "limits to growth" proposition suggest that resource and environmental scarcities can be overcome through the discovery of new reserves and technological advance. Energy scarcities can be avoided by finding new sources of supply, such as new reserves of oil or natural gas, or by inventing new technologies, such as more efficient photovoltaic cells that can take advantage of solar energy or nuclear fusion. Materials scarcities can be overcome not only by finding new sources of supply, but also through the invention of new materials that use relatively abundant minerals or renewable resources and improvements in recycling TECHNOLOGY.

As energy and materials become scarce, rising prices are said to stimulate the search for new reserves and new technologies. Market forces will thus solve the problem of resource scarcity. Damage to the natural environment may not be completely alleviated through voluntary bargaining. However, judicious public policies that use market forces, such as marketable emission permits, will resolve the problems of environmental deterioration.

## Limits argument

Those who believe that there are limits to growth suggest that conventional economic thought ignores the reality of the law of entropy and the limited ability of the global ecosystem to supply environmental services. Economic production and consumption is inherently entropic, converting high-quality low-entropy energy and matter into low-quality high-entropy waste that is potentially damaging to human health and ecological processes. Fossil fuel energy resources are finite, as is the flow per unit time of usable solar energy. Matter cannot be infinitely rearranged, and 100 percent recycling is an impossibility (see ENTROPY, NEGENTROPY AND THE LAWS OF THERMODYNAMICS).

Rising prices and technological advances cannot resolve what is, in the end, an ultimate scarcity of usable matter and energy. Moreover, the scale of the global ecosystem and its capacity to provide essential environmental resources and services is inherently limited. These limits relate to the capacity for waste absorption and nutrient recycling, the maintenance of climatic stability, plant pollination, clean air and water, fertile soil, harvestable plant and animal material, genetic resources and natural amenities.

Economic growth, by initiating damaging waste emissions and causing the human appropriation of natural ecosystems, reduces the capacity of the global ecosystem to supply these critical environmental resources and services. To its peril, NEOCLASSICAL ECONOMICS tends to treat the problem of environmental disruption as a relatively minor market failure problem, which is easily patched up by getting the prices right through voluntary deals between polluters and those hurt by POLLUTION, as well as through government regulation.

## History and controversy

The "limits to growth" debate was fostered by the publication of a book of that title in 1972 (Meadows *et al.* 1972). This book was a report on a global economic simulation study for the

Club of Rome's Project on the Predicament of Mankind. The book basically argued that current trends in economic growth would result in global production overshooting the earth's finite capacity to supply natural resources. Using a computer simulation of the global economy, the authors showed that overshooting global natural resource production capacity would result in a collapse of industrial output and food production and, with a lag, population decline. They also showed that a doubling of the natural resource base would fail to prevent collapse, because pollution becomes a limiting factor by reducing food production and increasing death rates.

The stabilization of population alone, in their simulation model, fails to prevent economic collapse. This is because continuing industrial growth depletes non-renewable resources. Finally, by undertaking a mix of policies, sustainable and stable global levels of food and industrial production can be achieved. These policies include reduced non-renewable resource consumption, a shift toward consumption of less resource-intensive services, reduced pollution emissions, increased soil conservation, a reduction in the size of the industrial capital stock and an increase in its durability. An appropriate policy mix that limits resource throughput and pollution emissions thus avoids the economic collapse that would come with a continuation of current trends.

## Critics of limits

The "limits to growth" simulation model was roundly criticized for its failure to incorporate market mechanisms. Conventional economists quickly pointed out that prices for non-renewable resources would rise in the face of increasing scarcity, decreasing resource use slowly over time and avoiding sudden collapse. Moreover, higher prices would encourage the substitution of more abundant for scarce resources, thus stimulating the search for new technologies that would use non-renewable resources more efficiently, increase recycling and intensify the search for new reserves. In an updated sequel, *Beyond the Limits* (Meadows *et al.* 1992), the authors address these criticisms and revise their simulation model, but still arrive at similar conclusions.

## Related research

The "limits to growth" debate is part of a larger controversy over the relationship between the global ecosystem and the global economy. The conventional view, represented by Barnett and Morse (1963), is that the economic system contains its own "antidotes to a general increase of resource scarcity." Scarcity will induce price increases that will in turn bring forth resource-saving technology. Since natural resource prices have remained largely stable, Barnett and Morse find no evidence of growing natural resource scarcity.

The dissenters, represented by Georgescu-Roegen (1971) and Daly (1991), suggest that the entropy law cannot be defeated by technological change, and that human society must quickly bring to a halt the squandering of the earth's limited resources. The conventional circular flow analysis that appears in all introductory texts misleads students by denying the role of natural and environmental resources in the economy. Rather than being circular, economic flows are linear, characterized by the input of high-quality low-entropy energy/matter. According to Daly, the optimum scale of the global economy has been exceeded and new policies are needed to reduce and stabilize resource throughput which is required to maintain the stock of human artifacts.

One strategy to help to accomplish this is marketable depletion permits for non-renewable resource inputs and marketable emission permits for damaging waste outputs. Quantitative growth requiring additional resource throughput would be limited as a result; but qualitative development would still be possible, through improvements in the quality of the stock of human artifacts.

The empirical question of resource and environmental limits to growth is currently being addressed by ecological economists. Ecological economics is an interdisciplinary framework of analysis, utilizing the work of Georgescu-Roegen and Daly, as well as more conventional neoclassical models. Among the many empirical findings of these economists is the discovery that the energy cost of extraction is increasing for a large class of minerals. This suggests that, once energy scarcity sets in, the real costs of minerals extraction will rise (Costanza 1991). The research of this group has also helped to verify the serious consequences of continuing environmental degradation associated with a global economic expansion that is heavily dependent on fossil fuels and other polluting and ecosystem damaging forms of technology.

## See also:

bioeconomics; ecological radicalism; environmental and ecological political economy: major contemporary themes; Green Party; quality of life; steady-state economy; sustainable development

## Selected references

Barnett, H.J. and Morse, Chandler (1963) *Scarcity and Growth: The Economics of Natural Resource Availability*, Washington, DC: Resources for the Future.

Costanza, R. (1991) *Ecological Economics: The Science and Management of Sustainability*, New York: Columbia University Press.

Daly, H.E. (1991) *Steady-State Economics*, 2nd edn, Washington, DC: Island Press.

Georgescu-Roegen, N. (1971) *The Entropy Law and the Economic Process*, Cambridge: Harvard University Press.

Meadows, D.H., Meadows, D.L., Randers, J. and Behrens, W.W. (1972) *Limits to Growth*, New York: Universe Books.

Meadows, D.H., Meadows, D.L. and Randers, J. (1992) *Beyond the Limits*, Post Mills, VT: Chelsea Green.

DOUGLAS E. BOOTH

# liquidity preference

Liquidity preference has traditionally been understood as the demand for a portfolio with a higher proportion of liquid assets, that is, assets which are readily marketable at minimal risk of capital loss. Money is the perfectly liquid asset. However, liquidity is an attribute which can be assigned in greater or lesser degree to a wide range of assets, real as well as financial. Recent usage of the concept refers also to the size of the portfolio itself, since a change in the liquidity preference of banks may be expressed by an expansion of bank lending; or a change in household liquidity preference could be expressed by a greater willingness to borrow, for example.

## Keynes's theory

The term is most closely associated with KEYNES (1936), who introduced liquidity preference as one of the three ultimate psychological factors in the determination of output and employment. Using the term interchangeably with the demand for money, Keynes outlined the importance of liquidity preference in determining the rate of interest. Since the rate of interest is "the reward for parting with liquidity for a specified period," rather than "a return to saving or waiting as such" (Keynes 1936: 167), it is a monetary phenomenon rather than a real phenomenon. Keynes thus emphasized the possibility of monetary variables having a lasting influence on real variables, that is, of money being non-neutral (see MONETARY THEORY OF PRODUCTION).

Keynes (1936: ch. 17) further broke down liquidity preference according to three motives: transactions demand, precautionary demand and speculative demand. He focused on speculative demand both as providing the vehicle for monetary policy to change the rate of interest (through interest rate sensitivity), and for instigating changes in the rate of interest irrespective of monetary policy. Speculative demand for money is demand induced by the expectation of capital loss from holding alternative assets. Since capital losses are associated with rising interest rates, the speculative demand for money is high when interest rates are low and expected to rise. In the extreme case, where there is a conviction that interest rates can only rise, the monetary authorities are powerless to drive market interest rates down further by open market purchases, because of the strength of the speculative demand for money; this is the liquidity trap case.

## Response to Keynes

In the immediate responses to Keynes's *General Theory*, the discussion of liquidity preference was broadened in two ways. First, there was the suggestion of a fourth motive, the finance motive, whereby there is a temporary demand for liquidity in anticipation of expenditure. The meaning and status of this motive has been a matter of some debate. Second, Townshend (1937) extended the notion of liquidity beyond money, to be considered as an attribute of a much wider range of assets, directly challenging orthodox value theory.

Within orthodox economics, the response was to incorporate liquidity preference into what became the neoclassical synthesis. By expressing the demand for money as a stable demand for real balances relative to income and the interest rate, it could be shown that a fall in prices would reduce the demand for nominal money balances (the real balance effect), counteracting the liquidity trap. The argument, then, was that the interest rate could always adjust to a level which would allow the labor market to clear, making money neutral, at least in the long run. The discussion of liquidity preference then became a discussion of the degree of interest sensitivity of the demand for money, which had only short-run significance.

In the meantime, in the UK, the *Report of the Radcliffe Committee* developed the liquidity preference concept along Townshend lines. Radcliffe (1959) argued that it was liquidity, rather than money as such, which influenced expenditure plans. However, liquidity is both unquantifiable and uncontrollable by direct means. Monetary policy should, therefore, be directed to interest rates rather than monetary aggregates, because interest rate changes can alter total liquidity. His analysis further focused on the process of liquidity creation within the financial system, and the importance of expectations of credit availability for perceptions of liquidity. Radcliffe thus broadened the scope of liquidity preference theory, combining it with an analysis of credit creation which presaged modern developments in post-Keynesian theory. Shackle's (1968) work on expectations, money and investment in turn encouraged parallel developments in neo-Austrian monetary economics.

## Critique of liquidity preference

One of those who gave evidence to the Radcliffe Committee, Nicholas Kaldor, took the analysis of credit creation further in developing the idea of the money supply as being endogenously generated by the private sector (Kaldor 1982) (see ENDOGENOUS MONEY AND CREDIT). Indeed, Kaldor argued that Keynes had encouraged the development of the neoclassical synthesis with his theory of liquidity preference, which had fitted well into the orthodox framework. If, as Kaldor argued, the banking system responds passively to credit demand, given the interest rate set by the central bank, then the central bank must passively stand by to supply any additional reserves required to back additional credit creation. This process is independent of the level of liquidity preference which, accordingly, loses its significance. This emphasis on credit creation, rather than the instabilities of liquidity preference, also characterizes institutionalist monetary theory.

## Recent work on liquidity preference

Davidson (1968) and Chick (1973) maintained the significance of liquidity preference, emphasizing the interconnectedness of time, UNCERTAINTY and money. Recent developments in post-Keynesian monetary theory have reasserted this significance, incorporating a broad interpretation of the concept of liquidity preference as applying to a wide range of assets, and extending it to the banks themselves. Keynes himself had set a precedent for the latter development (see Dow 1996), in passages which anticipate the endogenous money approach in emphasizing the private sector in determining credit creation. But Keynes emphasized the power of the banks, while the modern endogenous money theorists have emphasized the passivity of the banks in the face of credit demand. By considering the liquidity preference of banks, the supply of credit itself is seen to be a function of liquidity preference; a fall in bank liquidity preference leads to a rise in bank assets and liabilities, as well as a changing composition of assets. By considering the liquidity preference of borrowers in their investment decisions, as well as the disposition of their assets, the demand for credit is also seen to be a function of liquidity preference. Thus, households and firms may increase their borrowing and asset purchases, as well as changing the composition of their assets, in response to a fall in liquidity preference. The concept of liquidity preference thus now applies to the size of portfolios as well as their disposition.

A further recent, indeed ongoing, development in the liquidity preference concept stems from work on Keynes's philosophy, with its implications for our understanding of his theory of uncertainty and expectations. This work puts new emphasis on the precautionary demand for money. The speculative demand for money is a demand which is formulated when financial investors behave as if they know the probability distributions of asset prices, that is, they act as if they are certain (within stochastic variation). This was what had made the speculative demand for money so easy to incorporate in the neoclassical synthesis. Since it was grafted onto a theoretical framework which assumed stability of economic functions, there was no cause for shifts in speculative demand, and the other motives referred to the (stable) income level.

The precautionary demand has received some attention in orthodox circles as a buffer stock demand for money, emphasizing the need for money to cover stochastic variations in requirements. But the "Keynes philosophy approach" has emphasized the extent to which processes are not stochastic, and thus the limitations to modeling behavior as if based on the presumption of certainty. The precautionary motive thus refers to a recognition of uncertainty; the greater that recognition, the greater is the precautionary demand for money, and thus the higher are interest rates (Runde 1994). Thinking in this area is still progressing, with further analysis of the relationship between weight of evidence, the state of confidence and expectations, and their implications for the different elements of liquidity preference.

## See also:

monetary policy and central banking functions; money, credit and finance: major contemporary themes; post-Keynesian political economy: major contemporary themes; speculation

## Selected references

Chick, Victoria (1973) *The Theory of Monetary Policy*, London: Gray-Mills.

Davidson, Paul (1968) *Money and the Real World*, London: Macmillan.

Dow, Alexander C. and Dow, Sheila C. (1989) "Endogenous Money Creation and Idle Balances," in J. Pheby (ed.), *New Directions in Post-Keynesian Economics*, Aldershot: Edward Elgar.

Dow, Sheila C. (1996) "Endogenous Money," in G.C. Harcourt and P. Riach (eds), *A "Second Edition" of the General Theory*, London: Routledge.

Kaldor, Nicholas (1982) *The Scourge of Monetarism*, Oxford: Oxford University Press.

Keynes, John Maynard (1936) *The General Theory of Employment, Interest and Money*, London: Macmillan.

Radcliffe, Lord (1959) *Report of the Committee on the Workings of the Monetary System*, London: HMSO.

Runde, Jochen (1994) "Keynesian Uncertainty

and Liquidity Preference," *Cambridge Journal of Economics* 18(2): 129–44.

Shackle, George L.S. (1968) *Expectations, Investment and Income*, 2nd edn, Oxford: Oxford University Press.

Townshend, Hugh (1937) "Liquidity Premium and the Theory of Value," *Economic Journal* 47(March): 156–69.

SHEILA DOW

# long waves of economic growth and development

"Long waves" is the notion that there are long-term dynamic phases in the evolution of CAPITALISM, characterized by alternating periods of relatively booming economic conditions followed by more recessed and unstable economic conditions. They are also known as Kondratieff waves or cycles. During the first half of each wave, ECONOMIC GROWTH and ACCUMULATION are rapid, but eventually the rate of profit and accumulation decline on average for a considerable period. Usually each phase of capitalist evolution is of the order of 40–60 years in duration, with the high economic growth phase lasting 20–40 years, followed by less intense growth and more instability for 20–40 years.

The basic idea behind long waves is that the durable structures of the economy evolve over time in relatively complex patterns of development and demise. These durable structures include different forms of capital, depending on the theorist: fixed capital, social relations of capital, technological and knowledge capital, institutional capital and spatial capital. The main debates in long waves cover issues such as what form of capital is emphasized, which processes to concentrate on in the analysis, the nature of periodicity, plus UNEVEN DEVELOPMENT and CORE–PERIPHERY ANALYSIS.

## Phases of capitalism

Most long wave analysts believe that there have been four main waves (or phases) in the evolution of industrial capitalism: (1) the industrial revolution and competitive capitalism, 1780s–1840s; (2) large-scale industry, 1840s–1890s; (3) financial oligopoly capitalism, 1890s–1930s; and (4) postwar Fordist–Keynesian capitalism, late 1940s–1990s.

*Industrial revolution.* The first wave was during the period 1780s–1840s, the era of the industrial revolution. During this era (especially in Britain and the USA), the competitive forces of industry propelled the foundations for an industrial society based on wage labor, commodity production, and a class of industrial entrepreneurs in the manufacturing, agricultural and mining sectors. The TECHNOLOGY of the industrial revolution was based on cotton textiles, iron and steam power, new methods of crop rotation, steam blasting for smelting iron, the spinning mule, the reverberating furnace and the power loom (see Mager 1987: 75). The long-wave upswing made way for the downswing by 1820 as the rate of profit failed to sustain investment in capital and FINANCIAL CRISES became worse, culminating in the depression of the 1840s (depressions tend to occur near the end of the downswing of waves).

*Large-scale industry.* The second wave was during the 1840s–1890s, the era of large-scale industry. Especially important for the upswing were the machine-made steam engine, extensive railway developments, and gold discoveries in California and Australia. Europe and many of the settler colonies joined Britain and the USA in benefiting from the second Kondratieff upswing. However, the 1870s–1890s, popularly known as the "great contraction," saw the trend toward low profitability and hence lower accumulation and growth.

*Financial and oligopoly capitalism.* The third wave, during the 1890s–1930s, is known as the era of financial and oligopoly capitalism. Big financial and commercial capitalists began to dominate manufacturing and agricultural capital in most core nations. Electricity and chemicals were the leading sectors in core nations, and labor unions were an important part of the new industrial landscape. Industry became more concentrated. The period 1897–1912 was the most profitable period of the upswing. Downswing emerged especially in the mid–late 1920s. The GREAT DEPRESSION of 1929–39 (including the recessed period of the late 1930s) was the culmination of the third Kondratieff downswing.

*Fordist–Keynesian capitalism.* The fourth wave, during the 1940s–1990s, known as the postwar era of Fordism and Keynesian capitalism, was the age of the internal combustion engine, semi-automatic assembly line processes, segmentation of the labor market, the welfare state, a capital–labor accord, US hegemony and the stability of the patriarchal family. The Second World War provided the initial impetus to recovery, and the new institutions set the pattern for growth and accumulation during the 1950s and 1960s. However, a Kondratieff downswing emerged in the mid-1970s as the profit rate declined through greater wage, raw material, fiscal and financial pressures. Three major recessions emerged during the mid-1970s, the early 1980s and the early 1990s: a major depression has not yet emerged, perhaps because of "lender of last resort" facilities and big government (see FINANCIAL INSTABILITY HYPOTHESIS). Some call this downswing a "silent depression."

## History of long wave theory

Long wave theory and empirical analysis have advanced considerably since the early efforts of Hyde Clarke in 1847, Tugan-Baranowski in 1894, Parvus in 1901, van Gelderen in 1913, de Wolff and Kondratieff in the 1920s and Schumpeter in 1939. Long wave theories have consistently been committed to the development of a dynamic, evolutionary theory of modern economies. The debate up until the 1940s centered on questions of whether waves are propelled by the life of durable fixed capital (de Wolff and Kondratieff), or innovation (Schumpeter), or whether they are broad, less deterministic evolutionary forces of considerable variation and metamorphosis (Parvus, van Gelderen and Trotsky).

Nikolai Kondratieff's empirical analysis was one of the most advanced of the early generation of long wave scholars. He developed five main empirical hypotheses, including the role of bunching of inventions and innovations, expansion of the world market, agricultural prices and gold, plus wars and revolutions. These hypotheses have been a constant source of research even up to the present time (see Mager 1987).

Joseph SCHUMPETER'S THEORY OF INNOVATION, DEVELOPMENT AND CYCLES was influenced by Kondratieff. His brilliant *Theory of Economic Development*, published in 1911, was a general theory of innovation and cycles. It was not until *Business Cycles* emerged in 1939 that long waves were given a specific place in his analysis. He employed a method of successive approximations: start with steady state equilibrium, then introduce development through innovation, which creates surplus value and low amplitude cycles (recovery and recession). Then introduce credit, which increases the amplitude to four phases: boom, recession, depression and recovery (in that order). The length of the cycles depends on the durability of the capital and the lags involved.

Schumpeter made the simplifying assumption that there were three cycles: Kitchin cycle (3–5 years), Juglar cycle (7–11 years), and Kondratieff cycles (long waves; 35–60 years); and that there are three Kitchins to every Juglar and six Juglars to every Kondratieff. He recognized that capitalism is inherently unstable, and help may be needed from the state if the downswing involves entrenched negative expectations about the future.

Schumpeter was criticized on many counts: for having a lone entrepreneur rather than a modern transnational corporation (by Baran and Sweezy), for abstracting from Keynesian employment theory (by Oskar Lange), for not "proving" the notion of the "swarming of innovation" (Kuznets), for not specifying the nature of the reference cycle and so on (see Garvy 1946). But certainly, despite these criticisms, in the 1950s business cycles and waves were popular topics in the textbooks and the journals (Rostow, Hansen, Kuznets and so on). In the 1960s, traditional Keynesian employment theory and policy became more dominant, and long-term analyses of the evolution and cyclical nature of capitalism were less common. But from the late 1960s and early 1970s onwards, this changed as the capitalist system underwent major change and challenges, and a revival of political economy developed in the 1960s–1990s.

## Modern theories of long waves

Ernest Mandel in the 1964 *Socialist Register* was one of the first to see the forces of transformation and disarray emerging in the world economy during the fourth Kondratieff wave of the postwar era (1940s–1990s). In *Late Capitalism* in 1975 and *Long Waves of Capitalist Development* in 1980 he went on to develop his theory of the long wave, which was a fusion of the earlier work of Trotsky, Kondratieff and Schumpeter. His theory was based around changes in the rate of profit affecting investment and growth (and vice versa). He argued that the upswing is not inevitable but may result from a combination of forces influencing the rate of profit: power and struggle, competition, war and revolution, which become manifested as new sectors and technologies. The downswing of the wave is endogenously driven by a rise in the organic COMPOSITION OF CAPITAL as the capitalist process itself results in a FALLING RATE OF PROFIT TENDENCY.

Many other theories (re)surfaced in the 1960s and 1970s. For instance, drawing from one of Kondratieff's main hypotheses, W.W. Rostow continued to argue (as he did in the 1950s) that the relative price of agricultural and manufacturing goods is the critical phenomenon. In his many books and articles he included sectors and markets in the long wave process. His emphasis on real historical time is commendable. On the other hand, his theory has produced of late a peculiar periodicity: 1951–1972 is a downswing, 1972 onwards is an upswing.

Jay Forrester resurrected de Wolff and Kondratieff's theory of durable fixed capital during the 1970s in the Systems Dynamic National Model Project at the Massachusetts Institute of Technology. In this "capital investment" approach, long waves are generated by long-term capital overexpansion and decline associated with the capital goods sector. There are three sectors: consumer goods, capital goods which produce capital goods, and capital goods which produce consumer goods. An upswing is linked to greater consumer demand propelling complex long-lag expansions of the capital goods sector. With the "bootstraps mechanism" the capital goods sector "pulls itself up by its own bootstraps" (by producing more of itself) before it can satisfy consumer demand. Longer lags are introduced with price, credit, and innovation feedbacks.

Overproduction from the early 1970s, in industries such as shipbuilding, factories, warehouses and motor vehicles, was due to the optimistic expectations that arose during expansion, beyond what is justified on the basis of marginal productivity. The economy operates well below average capacity for twenty or thirty years as most of the lags become reversed. Many modern political economists would see this theory as being rather deterministic; however, they are likely to agree that fixed capital is an important part of a wider story of growth and transformation.

There are four main contemporary political economy approaches to long waves. They are based on historical TIME, institutions and/or technology, human and natural processes, CIRCULAR AND CUMULATIVE CAUSATION, and long-term EVOLUTION AND COEVOLUTION.

First, in Europe, Gerhard Mensch led the modern Schumpeterian trend in *Stalemate in Technology* (1979), which emphasized sectoral transformations. Christopher Freeman in his monographs and edited books has done much to refine and develop work on TECHNOLOGY plus INNOVATION, EVOLUTION AND CYCLES. Major themes include the weak correlation between downswings and innovation; the need for the state to facilitate profitability during long downswings through technology and other policies; and leading sectors analysis (see two special issues of the journal *Futures*, in August and October 1981).

Second, also in Europe, Carlotta Perez and Andrew Tylecote extended this Schumpeterian influence to issues taken seriously by the REGULATION APPROACH (originating in France), which studies the dialectic between technology and institutions. Long upswings develop when technology and institutions are in dynamic rapport with each other. For instance, Fordism only led to upswing in the 1940s and 1950s when the dominant semi-automatic assembly line processes in motor vehicle and consumer durables industries developed a suitable accord between capital and labor and an active mode of demand for final consumer goods. The technical requirements of innovation and production need to be dynamically balanced by distributive stability and markets. However, in the 1960s and early 1970s, Fordism had reached the end of its dynamic life (see FORDISM AND THE FLEXIBLE SYSTEM OF PRODUCTION) and a new mode of post-Fordism, or the flexible mode of accumulation, is only in its infancy in the 1990s.

Third, David Gordon (1980) developed a sophisticated analysis of institutional change in the SOCIAL STRUCTURES OF ACCUMULATION (SSA) explanation of waves. This approach was influenced by the regulation school and the resurgence of interest in political economy in the 1960s and 1970s. The SSA theory of long-term capitalist evolution posits that the building of a new set of institutions provides the certainty and stability necessary for sustained investment during long upswing. For example, in the postwar era (1940s–1990s), the institutions associated with US hegemony, the capital–labor accord, the welfare state, a new financial SSA and stable relations within the family propelled a suitable regime for rapid investment and growth during the 1950s and 1960s. However, many critical institutions gradually deteriorated as full employment and major obstacles to capital reduced the rate of profit and hence accumulation from the late 1960s onwards into the 1990s. A long wave upswing may emerge into the twenty-first century if the institutional innovations are suitable.

This SSA approach teaches us that institutions, which individual capitalists by themselves are usually powerless to influence, provide the solution to stability and economic growth, but also that solutions are only temporary. New technological relations and sociopolitical processes take time to rebuild and reshape, especially in a market-based system with its DISEMBEDDED ECONOMY. A considerable literature has developed in the SSA tradition.

Lastly, WORLD-SYSTEMS ANALYSIS has for years examined the unequal changes and transformations involved in core–periphery relations over long real time. Many different periodicities of long-term motion (50, 100 and 300-year waves) have been studied. Immanuel Wallerstein, Andre Gunder Frank, Giovanni Arrighi, Samir Amin and their colleagues have related long waves and longer movements to Third World debt, world hegemony, industrial relations, sectoral transformation, family relations and many other areas. Much of this work emanates from the Fernand Braudel Center at Binghamton in New York State (see the journal called *Review* published by this Center).

Long waves is a growing, interesting, popular and relevant field of inquiry to those scholars who value a holistic, interdisciplinary, historical and institutional analysis of the forces which condition long-term accumulation and growth. Policies tend to emphasize the need for protective responses to the market, the technological choices of the future, and the influence of institutions on economic behavior. Associated with this is a pragmatic analysis of long-term economic organization and change.

## Conclusion

Despite this optimism, there are many challenges to scholars who are studying long waves. For instance, critiques emerge from time to time. These critiques try to establish that there are problems in verifying long-wave periodicities, or that the long-wave theory does not have an endogenous explanation of the upswing, or that statistical techniques are inadequate. Many criticisms inadequately emphasize that modern-wave students are not proposing a deterministic approach, and are more interested in long historical trends and uneven developments than strict periodicities, amplitudes and regularities.

To surmount these challenges, scholars will need to emphasize the complexity of change, situate national trends in a global context, improve their statistical analysis of complex variables, and show how the durable structures of the economy evolve over time in more detail. Long wave analysis in the future, it is hoped, will become less a theory of regularized economic behavior and more an evolutionary approach to long-term transformations in the world, regional and national economies. Each of the political economy approaches to long waves is in the adolescent phase of maturity. Much work and interest lies ahead.

## See also:

business cycle theories; evolutionary economics: major contemporary themes; hegemony in the world economy; holistic method; knowledge, information, technology and change

## Selected references

Barr, Kenneth (1979) "Long Waves: A Selected Annotated Bibliography," *Review* 2(4).

Berry, Brian J.L. (1991) *Long-Wave Rhythms in Economic Development and Political Behaviour*, Baltimore: Johns Hopkins University Press.

Duijn, J.J. van (1983) *The Long Wave in Economic Life*, London: Allen & Unwin.

Freeman, C. (ed.) (1983) *Long Waves in the World Economy*, London: Butterworth.

Garvy, George (1946) "Kondratieff's theory of Long Cycles," *Review of Economic Statistics* 25(4).

Goldstein, Joshua (1988) *Long Cycles: Prosperity and War in the Modern Age*, New Haven: Yale University Press.

Gordon, David M. (1980) "Stages of Accumulation and Long Economic Cycles," in T.

Hopkins and I. Wallerstein (eds.) *Processes of the World-System*, London: Sage.

Kleinknecht, Alfred, Mandel, Ernest and Wallerstein, Immanuel (1992) *New Findings in Long-Wave Research*, London: Macmillan.

Mager, Nathan H. (1987) *The Kondratieff Waves*, New York: Praeger.

Marshall, Michael (1987) *Long Waves of Regional Development*, New York: St Martin's Press.

O'Hara, Phillip Anthony (1994) "An Institutionalist Review of Long Wave Theories: Schumpeterian Innovation, Modes of Regulation, and Social Structures of Accumulation," *Journal of Economic Issues* 28(2).

Tylecote, Andrew (1992) *Long Waves in the World Economy: The Current Crisis in Historical Perspective*, London and New York: Routledge.

PHILLIP ANTHONY O'HARA

# Lowe's instrumental method

Adolph Lowe (1893–1995) was a central figure in the "Kiel School" of political economy and the business cycle debates of the 1920s and 1930s. He held several important positions in the Weimar government, as well as a professorship at Frankfurt before his dismissal by the Nazis in 1933. He spent the remainder of the 1930s at the University of Manchester, before moving in 1941 to the Graduate Faculty of the New School for Social Research for the remainder of his lengthy career. Lowe's contributions range from analyses of growth, cycles, and technical change to methodology, the history of economic thought, political philosophy and public policy. All of these themes play a role in his political economics.

## Significance of industrial capitalism

Lowe studied the technological structure of industrial capitalism in the 1920s and early 1930s. This led him to the view that since the structural characteristics of the modern system were not adequately depicted by the data of traditional theory, economic "laws," such as "supply and demand," no longer applied with a high degree of reliability. Small-scale, labor-intensive production, carried out by independent producers with low fixed costs and operating at low levels of mechanization, makes for greater mobility. It therefore results in a high degree of adaptability to price and quantity variations. However, large-scale, modern industrial capitalism, with its huge fixed costs, capital-intensive methods and rapidly changing technologies, is characterized by great immobility, and thus an inability to make rapid adjustments. Nevertheless, in his elaborations of these views from the 1930s through to the 1950s, Lowe held steadfast to the view that the traditional method, if refined, could be used to analyze the modern system.

By the mid-1950s, however, Lowe began to develop the thesis that historical changes to the structure of capitalist society had altered the object of economic inquiry in such a way that the traditional method had to be abandoned. Analysis henceforth had to be conducted within an alternative, "instrumental" methodological framework (Lowe uses this term in his own sense; it has no connection with, for example, Friedman's use of the term). He believed that socioeconomic and technological conditions ironically rendered the traditional deductive method relatively appropriate for the period before modern industrial capitalism (see, for example, Lowe 1959: 163, 1965: 46, 68ff). But with the structural transformation of industrial capitalism and associated feedback effects resulting in environmental, institutional, behavioral, and socio-psychological changes, the traditional deductive method was no longer applicable (see, for example, Lowe 1959: 163–6, 1969a: 3, 11, 32, 1969b:169, 170–71, 180). Such transformations include the increasing concentration and centralization of capital, the rapid pace of technological change, the emerging middle classes in the industrialized nations, the increasing role of the state in the economy and the environmental impact of economic growth.

## The inclusive concept of order

From the end of the 1950s, Lowe explicitly rejected the argument that the historical transformation from early industrialization to modern industrial capitalism merely indicated a shift from one kind of stable system to another (see, for example, Lowe 1969b: 181). The traditional "deductive method [is] inapplicable...[because] neither the macro-movements of modern markets nor the underlying micro-patterns of behavior exhibit the degree of orderliness that is essential for scientific generalization" (Lowe 1969b: 180). The ability to make abstract generalizations that may serve as highest level hypotheses, from which deduction can proceed, requires that the research object exhibit some minimum degree of orderliness. Without such minimum order, the generalizations necessary for the employment of the traditional deductive method cannot be made.

Discussion of Lowe's methodological work has focused on his thesis that the regular behavioral and motivational patterns upon which scientific generalizations depend can no longer be trusted. In Lowe's "inclusive concept of order," however, the ability to identify reliable and stable phenomena is a necessary but not sufficient condition for the appropriate application of the traditional deductive method (1969a: 15). It is also required that the macro-outcomes of such behavioral and motivational patterns be consistent with society's macro goals (1969a: 6, 7). "Order" must thus be understood in the "double-sense" of underlying *regularity* of the research object and *socially satisfactory macro-outcomes*.

## Satisfactory macroeconomic outcomes

This position is certainly foreign to the traditional method, and contrary to the usual view that theorizing about an economic system is separable from whether or not that system produces an outcome that is consistent with society's goals. In such a view, if society does not approve of the outcomes, economic policy is undertaken. This, of course, is the traditional distinction between positive and normative economics. But Lowe emphatically rejects the approach that neglects a consideration of macro-outcomes at the ground level of theoretical analysis as "a radical positivism interested only in the explanation and prediction of movements, 'wherever they might lead'" (1969a: 7). Furthermore, he believes that "primary interventions" – traditional liberal utilitarian policies – are no longer adequate to address the inability of the market system to result in goal-adequate outcomes (1969b: 169, 188–9). The separation of positive and normative "can no longer be justified... recent developments demand the conscious integration of the analytical and normative aspects" (1967: 180).

Rather than taking only the initial conditions as known and addressing theory to predicting outcomes, Lowe proposed also taking as known a predetermined end-state: a vision of the desired outcomes. The task, then, becomes the derivation or the discovery of the unknown technical and social path(s) by which those outcomes might be achieved; the behavioral and motivational patterns capable of setting the system onto a suitable path; and the environmental context(s) capable of encouraging or inducing these patterns, and policies ("controls") shaping and creating the environmental context(s). For Lowe, a "suitable path" refers to an instrumentally-derived route to an independently determined end. Economic theory must not determine the ends (macro goals), but devise the means for their attainment.

## Structural and force analysis

The "instrumental method" begins from where we want to go and works backwards to our present state, or a state within our reach (Lowe 1965: 143–4). Analysis works backwards from the macro goals to the structural-technological conditions for their attainment. This is the realm of "structural analysis," which is analytically "prior" to "force analysis" (the consideration of suitable motivations and behaviors). In other words, the technical means capable of accomplishing some goal(s) may be

derived in advance of the suitable action directives. Because structural analysis precedes force analysis, investigations of the physical-technical consistency conditions relevant for goal attainment may be undertaken without any reference to assumptions concerning behavior or motivation. The procedure is, therefore, independent of any behavioral assumptions (1969a: 23–4; 1969b: 182).

Such independence from behavioral assumptions broadens the range of economic theory. Remember that Lowe believed the traditional deductive method to be relatively appropriate for the special case where motivational and behavioral patterns promoted a minimal degree of orderliness, such as that found during the early period of capitalism. Instrumentalism encompasses this special case, as well as other cases where actual motivational and behavioral patterns do not satisfy these conditions (1969a: 32). Political economics may be seen as a general theory of economic structure and behavior in the sense that it requires no initial assumptions concerning the nature of either.

## Instrumental-deductive method

Since the traditional deductive method is no longer possible, it might be thought that deduction itself is rendered obsolete. However, through the conscious recreation of the conditions appropriate for its application, the possibility for powerful economic reasoning of this type is recaptured. Lowe's analysis thus provides the foundation for "the restoration of deductive theory" (Lowe 1992: 326–7). Since the conditions are established by design and control, Lowe refers to the alternative replacing the traditional deductive method as the "instrumental-deductive method," which he considered to be "the core of Political Economics" (1969b: 179).

Far from endorsing "rational planning," Lowe explores the possibilities of instrumental inference as a policy discovery procedure. This involves investigating aspects of the policy formulation process that employ "tacit knowledge," "retroduction" and other heuristic problem-solving techniques. Lowe describes implicit search procedures and tactics of problem solving that are "taken for granted" in the scientific community, yet for the most part remain behind the scenes. Lowe's call is for making these conscious and recognizing their potential contribution to enhancing the power and success of the policy formulating process.

## See also:

capitalism; Heilbroner's worldly philosophy; normative and positive economics

## Selected references

Lowe, Adolph (1935) *Economics and Sociology: A Plea for Cooperation in the Social Sciences*, London: George Allen & Unwin.

—— (1959) "The Practical Uses of Theory: Comment," *Social Research* 26: 161–6.

—— (1965) *On Economic Knowledge: Toward a Science of Political Economics*, enlarged edition, Armonk, NY: M.E. Sharpe, 1977.

—— (1967) "The Normative Roots of Economic Value," in S. Hook (ed.) *Human Values and Economic Policy*, New York: New York University Press.

—— (1969a) "Toward a Science of Political Economics," in R.L. Heilbroner (ed.), *Economic Means and Social Ends: Essays in Political Economics*, Englewood Cliffs, NJ: Prentice Hall; repr. in A. Oakley (ed.) (1987), *Essays in Political Economics: Public Control in a Democratic Society*, Brighton: Wheatsheaf Press.

—— (1969b) "Economic Means and Social Ends: A Rejoinder," in R.L. Heilbroner (ed.), *Economic Means and Social Ends: Essays in Political Economics*, Englewood Cliffs, NJ: Prentice Hall; repr. in A. Oakley (ed.) (1987), *Essays in Political Economics: Public Control in a Democratic Society*, Brighton: Wheatsheaf Press.

—— (1976) *The Path of Economic Growth*, Cambridge: Cambridge University Press.

—— (1988) *Has Freedom a Future?*, New York: Praeger.

—— (1992) "Adolph Lowe (born 1893)," in P. Arestis and M. Sawyer (eds) *A Biographical Dictionary of Dissenting Economists*, Aldershot: Edward Elgar.

MATHEW FORSTATER

# M

## Maddison's analysis of growth and development

The rich interplay between technical and institutional analysis, with a strong dose of economic history, is central to Angus Maddison's analysis of ECONOMIC GROWTH and development. His studies, which are typically comparative and span generations, are rooted in a rich array of compatible time series and cross-section data sets he developed and integrated into a user-friendly format (Maddison 1987, 1991). Indeed, it is the data sets produced by Maddison which fostered a flood of pioneering empirical work in economics, often unrelated to his own, and which remain one of his critical scholarly contributions.

Maddison's analysis builds upon and extends the work and methodology of many scholars. He pays particular homage to Simon Kuznets and Colin Clark for developing national income accounting; to Martin Gilbert and Irving Kravis for devising a superior method of making national income estimates comparable across nations; to Wilfred Salter for developing the concept of embodied technical progress; to Theodore Schultz for developing the concept of HUMAN CAPITAL and for emphasizing the possible significance of education and knowledge to growth; and to Edward Denison for developing the growth accounting methodology.

### Growth and development: ultimate and proximate causes

The focus of Maddison's work remains an analysis of the advanced capitalist economies. However, Maddison often incorporates an analysis of less developed countries into his discussion for comparative purposes and, indeed, has published studies on less developed countries, past and present. Overall, he attempts to explain the process of growth and development and lack thereof from a historical perspective. In particular, he has endeavored to isolate those variables, be they institutional, social, political, cultural or purely economic, which have fostered or hindered the process of economic development. Maddison's analyses typically consist of two components. On the one hand he engages in establishing what he refers to as "ultimate causality," which considers the importance of institutional and other unmeasurable factors, such as politics, CULTURE and economic polities, in enabling nations to grow and develop. This is in the grand tradition of Max Weber and Karl Marx.

On the other hand, Maddison also attempts to determine proximate or technocratic causation where measurable variables such as output, labor, capital and land are technically considered in the causal schema. In the latter case, one can determine the statistical relationship between variables. But also, this correlation may be suggestive of causality and point to further research toward determining ultimate causality. Technical progress, although not quantifiable in any direct or exact manner, is approximated using a combination of proximate and ultimate analysis.

The clearest example of Maddison's approach to analyzing the question of growth and development are his most recent analytical works focusing on the developed world. What factors have facilitated the process of economic development and growth over historical TIME? In terms of ultimate causality, Maddison finds that central to the process of economic development has been the evolution of particular social, political and cultural forms that are conducive to economic growth. Central to these changes is the recognition that economic agents can transform the forces of nature to meet their own needs and that the course of economic development is not simply determined by circumstance and the whims of market forces. In a phrase, the "West" adopted the scientific-rational approach to life. In addition, private property rights were protected and nurtured and financial institutions were developed to meet the needs of a capitalist economy. The nation-state also helped to foster trade, commercial and intellectual links between regions. At another level, techniques of firm organization developed which were conducive to the growth process. Finally, the West's family structure and organization was more supportive of fertility control and, thus, to the ACCUMULATION of capital (see SOCIAL AND ORGANIZATIONAL CAPITAL).

In other words, the institutions and cultures of democratic capitalist nation-states, as distinguished from the other alternative institutional forms, hold one of the vital secrets to understanding the relative economic success of the "West." But this is not all. Within the developed world, more refined institutional intragroup differences exist which help explain differences in the pattern and path of economic development. On top of this, public policy plays a determining role in the overall process of growth and development.

## Stylized facts and convergence

Maddison's detailed technical analysis leads him to suggest certain "stylized facts." One of these highlights the strong statistical relationship between the growth and the level of the capital stock in the form of plant and equipment per capita, the growth and the level of human capital per capita, and the level and the rate of growth of gross domestic product per capita. He argues that the capital stock is very important to the growth process, since investing in plant and equipment facilitates the introduction of best practice TECHNOLOGY, embodied in the capital stock in the production

process. Maddison also underlines the importance of capital stock in the form of infrastructure. For this reason, a fast rate of economic growth requires a high rate of capital formation. Both the quantity and the quality of education is also of importance, since only an educated POPULATION can make it possible for an economy to engage seriously in technological progress through the development, refining, fostering and application of new technologies. Trade is another factor isolated by Maddison as being of considerable importance to the growth process.

Another stylized fact relates to convergence. Maddison recognizes that, although considerable convergence has taken place among the developed countries since the Second World War, there has been an absence of convergence on a global level, although some less developed economies in Asia and Latin America have experienced some catch-up. Since 1820, real per capita GDP has increased thirteenfold among the developed nations compared to only four times in Africa. Asia's per capita GDP increased eightfold and Latin America's per capita output increased sevenfold. Even in the absence of significant global convergence, the economies of the poorer nations tended to grow. However, convergence was not inevitable among the developed countries or between the developed and the less developed nations. In addition, it is not inevitable for leaders to become laggards; much depends upon institutional factors as well as public policy.

Maddison argues that the leaders in the growth process can also serve as a proxy for the technological leaders: they are at the technological frontier. If the laggards adopt appropriate institutional structures and engage in necessary policies, they should catch up with the leaders. This, Maddison argues, was the case with Holland when it displaced Flanders as the lead country in the beginning of the sixteenth century; with Britain when it displaced Holland as the lead country in the aftermath of the Napoleonic Wars; and with the United States when it displaced Britain as the lead country by the end of the nineteenth century. In the meantime, the British policy of favoring the financial sector contributed to Britain's laggard economic performance (see HEGEMONY IN THE WORLD ECONOMY). Maddison also argues that poor policy was, to a certain extent, responsible for the developed world falling behind the United States prior to the Second World War. In addition, colonialism and imperialism hindered the process of economic development in the less developed world.

In his analysis of India and Pakistan since the Moghuls, for example, he argues that the British conquered a relatively backward and inegalitarian society, one which was not at all conducive to growth and development. The British conquest of this region was, therefore, not the cause of its underdevelopment. However, Britain's prolonged stay in the region into the twentieth century, after introducing a variety of positive reforms, hindered the growth of what was to become India and Pakistan. Colonialism in itself was not necessarily the cause of underdevelopment here or elsewhere. In the cases of Holland, Britain and the United States, rapid capital accumulation joined with technological progress was the cornerstone of the growth process and of the transformation of laggards to leaders and vice versa, albeit the institutional and policy environment had to be just right.

## Postwar golden age and decline

Following the Second World War to 1973, the developed world, which soon incorporated Japan, experienced a "Golden Age" of growth. This was an era of convergence among this club of nations. In fact, convergence continued among the developed countries in the years following the "Golden Age." Once again, rapid capital accumulation and technical progress, with the laggards filling in their technology gap with the United States, was critical to the process of convergence. However, so was the policy context of this era which was characterized by the adoption of Keynesian-type macroeconomic policies, which stabilized demand, kept unemployment and real interest rates at low levels, and thereby created buoyant attitudes, which ultimately stimulated investment

(see KEYNESIAN REVOLUTION). Also of considerable importance was investment in knowledge in both the private and public sectors, and the opening up of trade.

The Golden Age came to an end in 1973 with the oil price shock and the collapse of the BRETTON WOODS SYSTEM. Inflation became significant and slaying the inflationary dragon became the name of the game, even after inflation rates returned to low levels by the 1980s. Governments throughout the West abandoned Keynesian policy and this had the effect of reducing the pace of growth and development in the West below its potential. This growth rate in per capita output was, nevertheless, almost double the average rate achieved in the 1870–1950 period. Only in Africa were growth rates in the post-1973 period disastrous, falling below zero. In fact, on average Asia's post-1973 growth rates bettered any achieved in previous eras (despite recent instability). Public policy played a critical role in determining these differential outcomes.

## Conclusion

Angus Maddison leaves us with a rigorous and open-ended analysis of growth and development which combines the detailed compilation of relevant national data sets, a technical analysis of these estimates, and an examination of the evolving historical, institutional, and policy constraints of the economies examined. Since, for Maddison, economic agents can affect their economic destiny by affecting their nation's institutions and policies, one must incorporate an understanding of the latter if the complex process of growth and development is to be understood. The technical analysis, necessarily important, will remain incomplete and even misleading if not combined with the unquantifiable institutional analysis.

## See also:

institutions and habits; productivity slowdown;

regulation approach; social structures of accumulation

## Selected references

Maddison, Angus (1971) *Class Structure and Economic Growth: India and Pakistan since the Moghuls*, London: Allen & Unwin.

—— (1985) *Two Crises: Latin America and Asia, 1929–38 and 1973–83*, Paris: OECD.

—— (1987) "Growth and Slowdown in Advanced Capitalist Economies: Techniques of Quantitative Assessment," *Journal of Economic Literature* 25: 649–98.

—— (1988) "Ultimate and Proximate Growth Causality: A Critique of Mancur Olson on the Rise and Decline of Nations," *Scandinavian Economic History Review* 36: 25–9.

—— (1991) *Dynamic Forces In Capitalist Development: A Long-Run Comparative View*, Oxford and New York: Oxford University Press.

—— (1994) "Explaining the Economic Performance of Nations, 1820–1989," in William J. Baumol, Richard R. Nelson and Edward N. Wolff (eds), *Convergence of Productivity: Cross-National Studies and Historical Evidence*, New York: Oxford University Press, 20–61.

—— (1995) *Monitoring the World Economy:1820–1992*, Paris: OECD.

MORRIS ALTMAN

# market socialism

## Introduction

Market socialism is the general designation for a number of models of economic systems. On the one hand, the market mechanism is utilized to distribute economic output, to organize production and to allocate factor inputs. On the other hand, the ECONOMIC SURPLUS accrues to society at large rather than to a CLASS of private (capitalist) owners, through some form of collective, public or social ownership of capital. The term has also been used to describe market-oriented reforms in some centrally planned economies since the Second World War, among the more notable being Yugoslavia, Poland, Hungary, China and Vietnam.

The role of the market in socialist economics received scant attention in the early post-Marx period, as the market mechanism was associated in Marx's writings with capitalist relations. It was not until after the Russian Revolution, and the problems of transition from independent commodity production and capitalist market forms to a system of command planning, that serious debate about the role of the market in a socialist economy developed. An important debate was developed by Enrico Barone, Ludwig von Mises, Oskar Lange, Fred Taylor, Friedrich Hayek and others, and became known as the SOCIALIST CALCULATION DEBATE.

Some other issues that relate to market-orientated reforms under socialism include the Yugoslav program of PARTICIPATORY DEMOCRACY AND SELF-MANAGEMENT, the Spanish MONDRAGÓN experiment, post-1970 reforms in the former Eastern bloc, and aspects of SOCIAL DEMOCRACY. This entry concentrates on some contemporary models plus reforms in China and Vietnam.

## Contemporary models

Differentiating market socialism from the MARKETS of CAPITALISM implies, at a minimum, some "socialization" of the ownership of capital. The *allocation* of goods and services would still be primarily laissez-faire, as under capitalism. Capital *ownership*, however, would be less fully private. In order of increasing decentralization (at least) three forms of socialized ownership can be distinguished: state-owned firms, employee- (or socially) owned firms, and citizen ownership of equity.

The first is the model of state ownership, in the Lange–Lerner model of a central planning board that owns all investment funds and auctions them to corporations that are managed by its own employees. These employees are required to maximize their firms' profits or share value.

The second is the model of employee ownership, in the WARD–VANEK MODEL OF SELF-MANAGEMENT of firms owned by their current and retired employees. These firms would still be dependent upon the state for credit. Alternative forms include the Horvat-Yugoslavian self-management model of social ownership, where the state would be the prime source of financial capital; and Mondragón-type worker cooperatives, where capital is generated internally from the membership and from cooperative and other financial institutions.

The third is the citizen ownership theory, in the Frydman–Rapaczynski or Bardhan–Roemer model of voucher equity shares to be distributed freely to the public, to be reinvested as the individual sees fit. Voucher shares would not be subject to individual bequest, but would revert to public redistribution upon the death of their holder (see Roemer in Roosevelt and Belkin 1994; Roemer 1994).

Each form faces theoretical and practical difficulties around information and incentives. State ownership must ensure that its employee-managers have incentives for maximizing the value of the capital entrusted to them, yet without making them the owners of that capital. In capitalist corporations this "principal–agent problem" is addressed by making managers substantial owners. However, this does not address the broader "stakeholder" interests.

Such arguments point toward a second form of socialized capital, that owned (or managed) by firm employees whose interests will coincide, at least in part, with the community in which they reside. The classic arguments against a system of employee-owned firms are the limitation on the mobility and diversification of capital; underinvestment due to the limited time horizon of workers; and the perverse demand–employment relationship implied in the Ward–Vanek model of self management. However, capital immobility, the horizon problem and the perverse employment implications can be addressed, as Saul Estrin and others have argued, through external financing (see Le Grand and Estrin 1990: 165–92).

This leads us to the third form of social ownership, through a more equal initial distribution of corporate equity. The importance of employee pension funds, which now control 20–30 percent of all common stock in most OECD countries, is widely recognized. Pension portfolios are typically not held in one's "own" enterprise or industry, but are highly diversified, similar to most privately held mutual funds. Rather than being controlled directly by their beneficiary employees, they are vested for them. In his *Unseen Revolution*, published in 1976, the well-known management theorist Peter Drucker claimed that pension funds were reconciling employees' need for financial security with capital's need to be mobile and diversified, a form of "pension fund socialism."

Contemporary campaigns focusing on this dynamic include the explicitly socialist Meidner program, and the advocacy of voucher privatization by Polish economists Roman Frydman and Andrzej Rapaczynski. However, in practice, a recent attempt at voucher privatization in Poland has been politically stalemated. In Russia, its redistributional effect has been minimal. Employee management groups have been able to buy up "their" firms at deep discounts, and Russian citizens saw the value of their vouchers destroyed by inflation. Only in the Czech republic has voucher PRIVATIZATION been carried out somewhat as planned, with many large companies privatized and with both Western and domestic mutual funds handling most of the citizen shares.

But if pension funds are a "natural" evolution of capitalism, how does one distinguish voucher-based socialization from voucher privatization as in the Czech republic? The difference may lie in the role that banks must play in allocating new sources of credit. Economists such as Roemer and Bardhan develop a comprehensive model for a citizen-equity socialism, one that relies upon a considerable spirit of public service from the managers of a banking system that would be highly centralized along German or Japanese lines (see Roemer 1994).

Another, more familiar theoretical issue that ties market socialism to market capitalism, however, is the efficiency of markets *per se*. That is, the justification for market socialism usually assumes that decentralized markets are far more statically and dynamically efficient than centralized planning. This leaves aside the persistent macroeconomic question of "involuntary unemployment," however weak one may find its micro-foundations. Such micro-foundations may ultimately be found to rest on the severe limits to human information processing, on chaotically unstable market equilibria, or both.

This criticism does not apply to most of the authors surveyed here, and especially not to Roemer. Roemer retains macroeconomic management in his version of market socialism. He argues that a more equal distribution of income would render such management more politically representative, and thus more concerned with the distributional effects of public goods and investment policy.

This raises the question of the function and type of planning required in a market socialist system. At one end of the spectrum are those who argue that without central planning, at least of capital accumulation, the system will not be socialist. At the other extreme are those who maintain that with anything more than just indicative (information) planning, the system would not be market. Most advocates of market socialism argue against microeconomic planning but stress the importance of macroeconomic planning. It would preferably be democratic and participatory macro-planning, as a form of information system and coordination instrument (see Le Grand and Estrin 1990: 100–38) .

## Market reforms in China and Vietnam

The market reforms of Eastern Europe and the former Soviet Union have been accompanied by severe economic collapse. The reforms have led to rates of GDP collapse in these countries far worse than during the GREAT DEPRESSION of the 1930s. This is a seeming indictment of the "shock therapy" of price liberalization and minimal government intervention in the transition to private capitalism. Yet as Poland, Hungary and the Czech Republic regained positive economic growth in the mid-1990s, the earlier shock therapy has been seen as ultimately justified.

The contrast between this doleful East European experience and the spectacular growth of China and Vietnam could not be more striking. Yet it was largely ignored by Western economists up until the mid-1990s, when it became too spectacular to ignore. Whereas the former Soviet-bloc economies were in absolute decline up until at least the mid to late 1990s, the People's Republic of China had maintained a real growth rate of over 9 percent for more than a decade, and Vietnam had similar growth since its reforms of 1989. What is the basis of this?

Both countries began their reform process through programs to return control of the land to village authorities and individual peasant families. In Vietnam, this was known as the *doi moi*, or "new road" reforms. The peasant family is obviously a much less complex form of social ownership than a corporation. To that extent, the transformation of property rights has been relatively easy in the largely peasant economies of China and Vietnam.

Another important difference stressed by some is the maintenance of a "strong state" in China and Vietnam. In the former Soviet bloc, by contrast, the end of one-party control was coincident with the weakening and even the wholesale dissolution of the state itself, and with this weakening, a general scramble to seize state property through any means.

The experience of economic reform in the former communist countries underscores the importance of building a social consensus on property rights, rather than accepting standard Western prescriptions. Thus, the end of state communism seems to corroborate the emphasis market socialists place on establishing new property rights, as opposed to changing other government programs. At the same time, this experience shows how difficult any fundamental reform of property rights will be.

## See also:

social ownership and property; socialism and communism

## Selected references

Le Grand, Julian and Estrin, Saul (eds) (1990) *Market Socialism*, Oxford: Clarendon Press.

Paul, Ellen Frankel, Miller, Fred D., Jr and Paul, Jeffrey (eds) (1989) *Socialism*, Oxford: Basil Blackwell.

Roemer, John E. (1994) *A Future for Socialism*, Cambridge, MA: Harvard University Press.

Roosevelt, Frank and Belkin, David (eds) (1994) *Why Market Socialism? Voices from "Dissent"*, Armonk, NY: M.E. Sharpe.

PAUL PHILLIPS
JAMES STODDER

# market structures

The structure of a market or an industry involves characteristics such as the number and size distribution of firms, the elasticity of demand and the conditions of entry and exit. In the structure–conduct–performance (SCP) paradigm, industrial structure is viewed as an important determinant of industrial performance. This includes price–cost margins, profitability, ADVERTISING AND THE SALES EFFORT and RESEARCH AND DEVELOPMENT. While this paradigm has lost much of its former dominance in orthodox industrial economics in the past decade or so, it still retains influence and is widely taught. We will follow the convention of using the terms "market" and "industry" interchangeably, though the term "industry structure" is suggestive of more concern with the production side, whereas "market structure" also suggests demand conditions. The SCP paradigm built on the notion that profitability would be higher under monopoly than under perfect (or monopolistic) competition,

and generalized this to postulate that a more concentrated industrial structure would lead to higher profitability than a less concentrated one (for a review of the evidence see Sawyer 1985: ch. 6).

## Perfect competition

A number of distinct industrial (or market) structures can be identified, in terms of the number of firms, conditions of entry and the nature of the product(s) (homogeneous or heterogeneous). Perfect competition is characterized by a large number of firms with free entry (at least in the long run), where firms produce a homogeneous product and are price takers. In the short run, a firm adjusts output so that marginal cost equals price and, in the long run, free entry ensures that firms operate where average costs are at a minimum. This has proved to be a powerful result, in the sense that competition appears to offer allocative and technical efficiency, even if doubts can be raised as to whether the competition of the real world has any correspondence to the competition of a static equilibrium perfect competition. Competition conveys some sense of a process of rivalry and seeking to outdo others: the static equilibrium of perfect competition can convey none of that. Further, departures from those structural characteristics can readily be labeled "imperfections," with the clear implication that those departures should be corrected.

A market in which there are no barriers to entry or to exit has been labeled a perfectly contestable one (Baumol *et al.* 1982). The ability of potential entrants to enter and leave an industry at will severely limits the actions of incumbent firms, and replicates many of the results of perfect competition.

## Monopoly

The polar extreme from perfect competition is monopoly: the single firm protected by substantial barriers to entry, involving price in excess of marginal cost and average variable costs above the minimum. Monopoly involves higher price and lower output (as compared with an equivalent perfectly competitive industry) and generates monopoly welfare loss (for a survey see Sawyer 1985: ch. 14). The situation of monopoly (and more generally of oligopoly) does not face the competitive pressures on costs, and hence monopoly may exhibit some degree of technical or X INEFFI-CIENCY. The potential supernormal profits may be captured by managers and workers in the form of higher wages and salaries.

The central notion of the structure–conduct–performance approach came from the idea that differences in industrial structure (between perfect competition and monopoly) lead to differences in performance (specifically the relationship between price and marginal cost). A related notion is that the position in structural terms of an industry, along the spectrum between perfect competition and monopoly, would influence (if not determine) the relative performance of the industry (as between perfect competition and monopoly).

## Monopolistic competition

Monopolistic competition (first formulated in Chamberlin 1933) focuses on the heterogeneity of the goods produced within an industry, the effect of which is that a firm faces a negatively-sloped demand curve for its product. The long-run equilibrium position, as illustrated in Figure 7, involves the tangency between the demand curve and the cost curve. This involves excess capacity and raises the question as to whether the costs involved in product differ-entiation (which means higher unit costs equal to ST ) are balanced by the benefits of choice and diversity.

There are many remaining theoretical diffi-culties with monopolistic competition. For example, can the boundaries of an industry be drawn in terms of a range of products, when there may be a long chain of substitutes? The use of monopolistic competition, rather than perfect competition, has become increasingly popular in orthodox circles, notably in macro-economics and in international trade theory. Many of the implications of the use of monopolistic competition rather than perfect competition flow from the excess capacity result of monopolistic competition, and the observa-tion that firms will be operating subject to diminishing costs. For macroeconomics, this means that as demand expands, costs and prices tend to fall, and real wages and employment rise (thus overturning the conventional negative relationship between real wages and employ-ment) (see, for example, Dixon and Rankin 1994). For international trade theory, mono-polistic competition suggests that trade brings benefits of lower costs and exploitation of INCREASING RETURNS TO SCALE. With product differentiation there can be intra-industry trade, whereas traditional trade theory focuses on the growth of inter-industry trade (see, for example, Krugman and Obstfeld 1997).

## Oligopoly

Oligopoly is the situation of a few firms dominating an industry, usually being pro-tected by barriers to entry. There can be little doubt that oligopoly is the dominant market structure in capitalist economies, with mature industries at the national and international level generally being controlled by a small number of firms. A key element has long been recognized as the interdependence between firms which the fewness of firms engenders. More specifically, the profits of one firm depend in a noticeable manner on the actions of its rivals, as well as the firm itself. The decisions of firm $A$ will affect the profits of other firms as well as its own profits, and other firms are likely to respond to firm $A$'s initial decision on price and output. Hence, firm $A$ may take into account the other firms' likely reactions when it makes it decisions. Further, joint profits would be higher if firms were to cooperate than if they take uncoordinated decisions. But cooperation and collusion faces problems of implementation and enforcement, although the takeover is an effective collusive device.

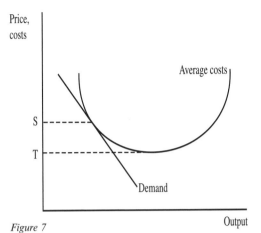

*Figure 7*

## Cournot and Cournot–Nash models

Numerous theories of oligopoly have been developed, starting from the work of Cournot. These theories vary in the manner in which the interdependence between firms is treated, the relationship between incumbent firms and potential entrants, and the degree of effective collusion. They also differ in the technique of analysis, which has moved away from the use of calculus to game theory. The theories of oligopoly vary in relation to what assumptions firm *A* makes as to how other firms will respond to *A*'s actions.

Under the Cournot assumption, each firm acts as though other firms will maintain their output. To illustrate this, consider an industry with *n* firms producing a homogeneous product, subject to constant variable costs and facing a linear demand curve. Then for firm *i* profit ($\Pi$) becomes:

$$\Pi_i = (a + bQ)q_i - dq_i \qquad (1)$$

where $p = a + bQ$ is the demand curve for the industry, $d$ the level of unit costs and $Q$ is industry output and hence equal to $q_i + Q_i$. The first-order condition for firm $i$ is then:

$$\frac{d\Pi_i}{dq_i} = (a + bQ) + q_i b \frac{\partial Q}{\partial q_i} - d = 0 \qquad (2)$$

The Cournot behavioral assumption is that $\partial Q / \partial q_i = 1$, since firm $i$ believes that the only variation in total output arises from the variation in its own output. With that simpli-

fication, summing over all of the *n* firms (assumed to face the same unit costs *d*) gives output and price as:

$$Q = n/(n+1) \cdot (d - a)/b \qquad (3)$$

$$p = a/(n+1) + dn/(n+1) \qquad (4)$$

Under perfect competition, price equals marginal cost as a condition of profit maximization, and price equals average cost as the zero (supernormal) profits condition. In this case, average and marginal costs are equal at *d*, so price would equal *d* and the competitive output would be $(d - a)/b$. With *n* firms, the level of output under the Cournot–Nash model in equilibrium is $n/(n+1)$ of the competitive equilibrium output. For monopoly $n = 1$, and the level of output is one half of the competitive level and price is $(a + d)/2$. For duopoly, $n = 2$, and there the output level is two-thirds of the competitive level. As the number of firms (*n*) increases, the value of the term $n/(n+1)$ tends to unity, and hence the equilibrium level of output tends toward the competitive level.

Many variants on the behavioral assumption (equivalent to making an assumption on $\partial Q / \partial q_i$) can be (and have been) used. Significant variants include those which allow a degree of dominance by one firm over the others, and those which focus on the possibilities for collusion, since total profits will generally be higher with some form of co-operation between the firms. Some of the variants retain the basic prediction that fewer firms and more collusion will generate higher profits, whereas others are not able to make any such predictions.

## Workable competition

Workable competition has been an influential variant of the SCP approach, and, while it is now little discussed in the academic literature, it retains an influence over industrial policy (see, for example, Sosnick 1958). The central idea of workable competition could be summarized as the rejection of perfect competition as a worthwhile attainable ideal. Perfect competition may remain an ideal, but there are costs associated with attaining it fully. But others would note the obstacles of pervasive uncertainty, lack of full information, and dynamic considerations (especially research and development), which are assumed to be absent in perfect competition, but which would prevent the attainment of perfect competition in practice. Yet others would not see perfect competition as an ideal to strive for. It may be that economies of scale require firms to be of a significant size relative to the market; or that the choice and variety of product differentiation would be lost under the homogeneity of perfect competition; or that research and development requires some departure from perfect competition.

## Important issues

In the theoretical discussions, it is generally assumed that the definition of the industry does not present any particular difficulties. In perfect competition (and, indeed, in monopoly and often in oligopoly), the industry is identified with the production of a particular product, and the industry at any particular time is composed of those firms which produce the product concerned (and the households who purchase that product). In empirical work, the definition of an industry cannot be so readily solved. In practice, two particular difficulties arise over the definition of an industry. One refers to the appropriate level of aggregation, and how finely or otherwise an industry should be defined. For example, is the appropriate level to include those firms producing a particular model of motor car (i.e. just one firm), all cars in a particular range of engine size, all medium-priced cars, all cars, all forms of personal transport? And so on. Similar questions can be raised in terms of geographical spread. The other difficulty relates to the boundaries of an industry. For example, is product $X$ a close enough substitute for product $Y$ for both of them to be included in the same market? The theory of monopolistic competition brought the problem of the definition and boundaries of an industry into the theoretical domain.

An important ingredient in the approaches discussed in this entry is that the structure of an industry conditions and constrains the behavior of the firms in the industry, thereby influencing the performance of the industry. The industry is the basic unit of analysis, whereas in other traditions (notably the Austrian and the Marxian) the firm is the basic unit of analysis. The orthodox theorizing on industrial structure has been with the standard profit maximizing, comparative static framework, and the firm treated largely as a "black box."

## Kalecki and monopoly capital

Kalecki's notion of the degree of monopoly draws a number of important implications from the SCP approach (see MONOPOLY, DEGREE OF). His work should be seen as indicating that the market power of firms influences the mark-up of price over costs (with average direct costs assumed to be constant with respect to output). Also, the market power of firms influences the share of profits in national income and the real wage (see PRICING).

Within the political economy tradition, the monopoly capital school (associated with authors such as Baran and Sweezy, KALECKI, Steindl and Cowling) draws on the SCP approach, and on the significance of market structure (for a survey see Sawyer 1988). The MONOPOLY CAPITALISM approach observes a rising trend of industrial concentration, and from that the implication that the profit share will tend to rise (as the price–cost margin rises). The effect of this shift away from wages toward profits on aggregate demand is significant: it would be expected to lower consumer expenditure, though it may raise investment. For a simple, closed, private sector economy, we have $s_w W + s_p \Pi = I$, where $W$ is wages and $\Pi$ profits, $I$ investment, and $s_w$ and $s_p$ the propensities to save out of wages and profits, respectively. Re-writing with $m$ as the profit share, we have $s_w(1 - m) + s_p m = I / Y$. As the degree of monopoly rises, the profit share rises. Further, it can be readily seen that as $m$ rises output $Y$ falls, unless there is a corresponding rise in investment.

**See also:**

competition and the average rate of profit; corporate hegemony; Kalecki's macro theory of profits; Kalecki's principle of increasing risk

### Selected references

Bain, J.S. (1956) *Barriers to New Competition*, Cambridge, MA: Harvard University Press.

Baran, P. and Sweezy, P. (1966) *Monopoly Capital*, New York: Monthly Review Press.

Baumol, W., Panzar, J. and Willig, R. (1982) *Contestable Markets and the Theory of Industrial Structure*, New York: Harcourt Brace Jovanovich.

Chamberlin, E. (1933) *The Theory of Monopolistic Competition*, Cambridge, MA: Harvard University Press.

Cowling, K. (1982) *Monopoly Capitalism*, London: Macmillan.

Dixon, H. and Rankin, N. (1994) "Imperfect Competition and Macroeconomics: A Survey," *Oxford Economic Papers* 46.

Krugman, P. and Obstfeld, Morris (1997) *International Economics: Theory and Policy*, 4th edn, Reading, MA: Addison-Wesley.

Sawyer, M. (1985) *Economics of Industries and Firms*, 2nd edn, London: Croom Helm.

—— (1988) "Theories of Monopoly Capitalism," *Journal of Economic Surveys* 2.

Sosnick, S.H. (1958) "A Critique of the Concepts of Workable Competition," *Quarterly Journal of Economics* 82.

MALCOLM SAWYER

# markets

Markets are socially constructed means to effect the exchange of present values for current and future benefit streams. They arise to mitigate the perceived imbalance of abundance and scarcity between individuals over time. Markets are allocative mechanisms whereby price signals indicate opportunities for exchange. They are coordinating structures whereby the revealed subjective values of market participants are thought to reflect the expression of free will.

### Ownership and mere possession

However, markets are more than mere signals of relative values. Markets are means by which we exchange ownership of expected value. The difference between the mere *exchange* of expected value, and the exchange of *ownership* of expected value is fundamental. This difference depends on some authority system willing to sanction the exchange of ownership. Put simply, market participants can exchange money and bread, but only the state (or some authority system, such as a village chief) can affirm an exchange of ownership of bread and money. In the absence of this, market participants exchange mere possession of expected value. One must never confuse possession with ownership; possession is a physical phenomenon, while ownership is a socially constructed circumstance. Only a state can confer the legal situation called "ownership." Otherwise, one has mere possession.

### Markets are social constructions

It is sometimes thought that markets are spontaneous and natural, and it is often claimed that markets have existed as long as there have been more than two individuals. While exchange may indeed be as old as the human race, mere exchange – while necessary – is not sufficient to establish a market. The distinction between possession and ownership relates to this difference. But there is a more fundamental issue at hand. To say that markets have existed "forever" is to leave the impression that markets are naturally free and autonomous institutional processes. On the contrary, markets must be socially constructed (Polanyi 1957). "Efficient" markets – perhaps sometimes epitomized by stock and commodity exchanges – require an elaborate and complex structure of rules and conventions. Indeed, it is this structure of institutions (working rules) that allows markets to function with relatively low TRANSACTION COSTS for the transactors. In the absence of institutional arrangements to facilitate markets across space and time, markets would shrink to small domains limited by the geographical reach of personal trust. Institutional arrangements, therefore, constitute a collective good that substitutes socially constructed assurance for personal trust across transactors. Markets arise from socially created and codified domains of exchange.

The powerful idea of Adam Smith's "invisible hand" must not obscure the fact that the conditions for markets must be carefully crafted and protected. Stock and commodities markets are to some degree efficient precisely because of the institutional structure within which they are embedded. Three examples of this institutional set up include the prohibition of insider trading, transparent and codified accounting procedures of those firms trading in such markets, and the presence of governmental or other entities to monitor these markets.

Markets are thought to provide a reasonable measure of "relative social value." It is true that market-clearing prices – under certain strict assumptions – offer some evidence of the exchange value to the transactors of the items whose ownership has changed hands. But the signals to emanate from markets are only relatively accurate (as opposed to precise) indicators of relative value if the circumstances of that exchange meet the conditions which justify the procedural affirmation that market prices indeed reflect true social value. In the absence of those preconditions, the exchange value from any particular transaction carries little normative significance. This explains our interest in "perfect" markets. A perfect market is one in which information is costless and widely available, no transactor is large enough to exert an influence over price, complete factor mobility obtains, and entry is relatively easy.

## Perfect and imperfect markets

Consider an example from labor markets.

There has long been a concern that women earn a lower wage (or salary) for the same job performed by men. Those who believe that market prices reflect true social value will insist that these differential wages are explained (justified) by real differences in productivity at the margin (where the exchange of labor for money occurs). Others will insist that market imperfections (discrimination, relatively pliant female workers) explain the wage differential. Do gender-based wage differentials reflect the "true" value of women and men in the same jobs? Unfortunately we have no way of knowing "true" values and so we must rely on a procedural definition. We say that if markets are reasonably "perfect," then the signals emanating therefrom (market wage rates) indeed reflect "true" values.

## Freedom and choice

Economists tend to like markets because they have been taught that markets assure individual freedom. Amartya Sen (1993) suggests that the idea of markets and freedom cannot be understood without recognizing three constituents of freedom: autonomy, opportunity and immunity. Autonomy concerns the freedom to choose. Opportunity concerns the freedom to achieve. Immunity concerns the freedom from encroachment by others. Those who believe that markets guarantee freedom stress autonomy (choice), and a limited version of immunity. The limited interest in immunity shows up in a deep aversion to encroachment by governments (say in the form of "regulation"), but ambivalence about market-sanctioned encroachment. We see this in the distaste of market advocates for regulations that redefine working conditions in private firms. While regulations are seen as an encroachment on owners of firms, the absence of those regulations is not seen as encroachment on workers. This selective perception owes its origins to the belief that markets are natural processes that must be left alone.

The third constituent of freedom, opportunity, is even more troublesome for those who claim that markets guarantee freedom. For instance, civil rights laws that prohibit firms denying service to members of certain groups are sometimes seen as an intervention into so-called "free markets." Thus an opportunity for the owner of the firm clashes with an opportunity for the individual who is turned away. Markets do not assure opportunity freedom.

## Coercion and command

In a related vein, the received wisdom in economics is that there is no coercion in markets. The history of centrally planned economies – and the evident abuses of the Soviet state – spawned a presumption about the civic wonders of so-called free markets. However, markets necessarily entail coercion. Market participants bring a range of capacities to the discipline of a market economy. Indeed, the "efficiency" of market economies arises from the threat of failure facing all participants. It is only the constant peril of extinction that keeps firms alert and agile; and, of course, it is the threat of dismissal that holds the attention of employees. In this important sense, firms and markets are domains of coercion exerting a relentless discipline on all (Bromley 1989).

A "market economy" is said to be one in which price signals play a significant role in resource allocation, output decisions, and – to some extent – the allocation of income among owners of the factors of production (land, labor, capital, and entrepreneurship). As against this, we have a "planned" economy. However, as with most dichotomies, this one conceals as much as it reveals. The failure arises not from the false distinction, but rather from the fact that "market" economies are in fact dominated by domains of command rather than domains of willful transacting guided by price. All firms are domains of command. As Herbert Simon (1991) reminds us, market economies are really vast networks of organizations. All of us belong to a number of organizations – families, firms, religions, private clubs, universities – in which price is largely irrelevant to allocational decisions (Ben-Porath 1980). When Ronald Coase (1937) inquired about the nature of the firm,

he was addressing one of the enduring fictions of economics. Coase wondered why, if markets are so efficient and costless, are there domains of command (firms)? The answer is that market processes entail non-trivial transaction costs that domains of command (firms) can avoid.

## Market failure and social problems

Finally, a word about "market failure." The current constellation of prices (and costs) is simply an artifact of the existing institutional setup: property rights, the distribution of endowments and incomes, and the nature and extent of other entitlements. If transaction costs (information costs, contracting costs and enforcement costs) are high enough, markets will not exist (Coase 1960). Markets tend to fail if there are considerable (negative) externalities, which cannot "naturally" be internalized into market prices (see Bromley 1990; Mishan 1980). In other words, there may be considerable pollution, injury, alienation, disease and inequality which are ingrained in the corporate market system. If the extent of these externalities is considerable, then it is said that there may be an argument for the state to intervene and impose taxes or other means to reduce these social costs; that is, so long as the cost of state intervention is not too high.

Some political economists argue that the existence of these negative results of production are endogenously ingrained in the workings of the private market system. A system dependent on private initiative and selfishness creates social problems. The market process does not incorporate in its valuation system directly the social costs of production. Therefore, such a system tends to destroy social and natural capital in the process of building private capital. This manifests in unstable growth, ALIENATION, POLLUTION, INEQUALITY of income and the destruction of public property. This double movement of CAPITALISM, private initiative and public squalor, is the central tendency of capitalism which has historically necessitated discretionary fiscal and monetary policy, health and safety legislation in the workplace and a social security network (see Polanyi 1957). This is the reality which is hidden from the market, yet it is the dominance of the market that creates it.

## See also:

business cycle theories; collective social wealth; disembedded economy; economic rationalism or liberalism; global liberalism; markets and exchange in pre-modern economies; neoclassical economics; regulation and deregulation: financial; social and organizational capital; welfare state

## Selected references

Ben-Porath, Yoram (1980) "The F-Connection: Families, Friends, and Firms and the Organization of Exchange," *Population and Development Review* 6: 1–30.

Bromley, Daniel W. (1989) *Economic Interests and Institutions: The Conceptual Foundations of Public Policy*, Oxford: Blackwell.

—— (1990) "The Ideology of Efficiency: Searching for a Theory of Policy Analysis," *Journal of Environmental Economics and Management* 19: 86–107.

Coase, Ronald N. (1937) "The Nature of the Firm," *Economica* 4: 386–405.

—— (1960) "The Problem of Social Cost," *Journal of Law and Economics* 3: 1–44.

Dahlman, Carl J. (1979) "The Problem of Externality," *Journal of Law and Economics* 22: 141–62.

Mishan, E.J. (1980) "How Valid Are Economic Evaluations of Allocative Changes?," *Journal of Economic Issues* 14: 143–61.

Polanyi, Karl (1957) *The Great Transformation*, Boston: Beacon Press.

Sen, Amartya (1993) "Markets and Freedoms: Achievements and Limitations of the Market Mechanism in Promoting Individual Freedoms," *Oxford Economic Papers* 45: 519–41.

Simon, Herbert A. (1991) "Organizations and Markets," *Journal of Economic Perspectives* 5: 25–44.

DANIEL W. BROMLEY

# markets and exchange in pre-modern economies

"Pre-modern" is an all-inclusive term for the economic systems that have preceded CAPITALISM. Capitalism's development since the sixteenth century has been gradual and frequently disruptive. Both before and during its evolution there have been a variety of economic systems throughout the world; these include hunter–gatherer, slave, feudal, mercantile and Asiatic systems, among others. There were, of course, quite diverse variants of these systems that coexisted and were regionally and culturally distinct. Within these variants there also existed a wide array of market and exchange relationships.

## Capitalism: the first and only market economy?

Yet even though economic anthropology suggests that MARKETS and exchange are antecedent to capitalism, European capitalism's appearance is unprecedented because it is considered the first and only "market economy." As Hungarian economist Karl Polanyi states: "A chain-reaction was started – what before was merely isolated markets was transformed into a self-regulating *system* of markets. And with the new economy, a new society sprang into being" (Polanyi 1968: 61). Thus, a common feature of pre-modern economies is that, although markets and exchange usually existed, they were not the dominant feature of the societies.

For example, ports of trade were a common feature of pre-modern societies. They existed in all parts of the world, from the Syrian coast as early as 2000 BC to the Upper Guinea coast of Africa, from the Aztec–Maya region of the Gulf of Mexico to Calcutta in India. These ports of trade were often "neutrality devices" between insecure regions and generally did not have "price-making markets." As Polanyi (1968: 239) argues, "governmental administration prevailed over the 'economic' procedure of competition." Ports of trade, as sophisticated as they were, did not form a "system" driven by market exchange and competition. In fact, just what a "market system" actually is continues to be a subject of intense debate.

The discussion of markets and exchange in pre-modern economies forms part of a wider historical debate, originating at least as early as Adam Smith's statement in *The Wealth of Nations* that people have an inherent "propensity to truck, barter and exchange." What Smith and many of today's neoclassical theorists argue is that capitalism's emergence was both organic and spontaneous (see Stanfield 1986). The argument revolves around the concept of "inherent propensity." If followed to its logical conclusion, it implies that capitalism may be qualitatively different than its precursors but represents the progressive culmination of behaviors that are natural to humankind.

There is little doubt that capitalism is the first system in which basic needs for food, clothing, and shelter are met through the process of exchange in markets. Even though markets, trade, and money existed in many pre-modern societies, they were not the primary institutions used for meeting basic material needs. Yet the conventional wisdom in neoclassical theory is that the emergence of generalized markets and exchange in capitalism does not represent a radical departure from its antecedents. A frequent interpretation of this is that pre-modern markets and exchange were like the dormant seeds of capitalism waiting for the proper conditions to sprout into a mature system. This again suggests to neoclassical theorists that capitalism's appearance in sixteenth-century Europe was organic and spontaneous and, therefore, progressive.

On the other hand, radical theorists including Polanyi view the development of capitalism as not only a qualitative departure from all pre-modern systems, but as a traumatic revolutionary event that was not at all organic nor spontaneous. As Polanyi states:

No society could, naturally, live for any length of time unless it possessed an economy of some sort; but previously to our time no economy has ever existed that, even in principle, was controlled by markets. In spite of the chorus of academic incantations so persistent in the nineteenth century, gain and profit made on exchange never before played an important part in human economy.

(Polanyi 1944: 43)

For Polanyi, the market system "handed over the fate of man and nature to the play of an automaton running in its own grooves and governed by its own laws. Nothing similar had ever been witnessed before" (Polanyi 1968: 62). What made the appearance of capitalism so revolutionary, in other words, was that humankind's fate was subordinated to the impersonal competition of supply and demand. For Polanyi and radical theorists, in capitalism "markets rule people," while in pre-modern societies "people rule markets"; although, in pre-modern economies, the "people" often took the form of ruling classes and cultural institutions.

## Exchange and markets in pre-modern societies

Still, there is a consensus in economics that markets and exchange had a narrower, more constricted role to play in pre-modern societies. Stanfield suggests that "in all but the most primitive societies, there is also division of labor with the concomitant necessity of integrative institutions to coordinate economic activities. These institutions have at least superficial similarities – market-places, trade, monetary objects, and accounting devices" (Stanfield 1990: 199). Using Polanyi's terminology, these economic activities were "embedded" in their respective social structures (see DISEMBEDDED ECONOMY). They were not part of a separate and autonomous economic sphere as in modern capitalism. Markets and exchange were subordinated to the laws, customs and traditions that defined the CULTURE of the society. For instance, Athens in the fifth century BC had the "agora" or marketplace, but it was subordinated to the Athenian polis: "It was (in modern terms) an artificial construct of limited access and dependent for supply, rates of currency, and price control upon the sanctions provided by the polity" (Polanyi 1968: 311).

To say that economic activity was subordinated and embedded in the various cultures implies that there was not as much individual economic freedom as in capitalism. Economic self-interest was not allowed the freer expression of the market system. The "economic motives" of profit and fear of unemployment were conspicuously absent. As Polanyi states:

> the motive of gain was specific to merchants, as was valour to the knight, piety to the priest, and pride to the craftsman. The notion of making the motive of gain universal never entered the heads of our ancestors. At no time prior to the second quarter of the nineteenth century were markets more than a subordinate feature in society.
>
> (Polanyi 1968: 67)

The fear-and-greed, carrot-and-stick motives prevalent today replaced the custom, obligation and moral norms that motived the individual in pre-modern economies.

Thus, markets and exchange were governed by each society's cultural norms. Many of these pre-modern societies were basically self-sufficient agricultural societies, where markets for specific goods existed but were controlled by customs and sanctions. For example, in Hellenic Greece and feudal Europe, an operative concept of the "just price" existed. Products might be bought and sold in markets but with the understanding that the price negotiated was one in which neither party's economic status was altered. A "just price" left both buyer and seller with the same standard of living – neither richer nor poorer. By contrast, in a modern market system the price is frequently the result of the impersonal and competitive forces of supply and demand. Justice is not an issue.

Additionally, what was traded and exchanged in pre-capitalist markets was frequently surplus output. The trade was often ritualistic as well. One village might trade some of its surplus grain to another tribe or village in exchange for surplus cloth. A social and political ritual might govern the actual process of exchange. If the surpluses were not traded then neither party would suffer extreme hardship, because each was essentially self-sufficient. The terms of trade may or may not involve a form of money. But if money was involved, it was, again, subject to the norms established by the groups. Unlike our contemporary market system, this was not a "market-driven" process. The motives were less "economic" than "social" or "political." Polanyi says that "if so-called economic motives were natural to man, we would have to judge all early and primitive societies as thoroughly unnatural" (Polanyi 1968: 66).

Were markets and exchange in pre-modern societies *necessarily* primitive and unsophisticated? The answer is no. From the time of Alexander the Great (300 BC) until the fall of the Roman Empire in the second century AD, economic activity in the Mediterranean region was very market-oriented and quite elaborate. There was intra-Mediterranean trade in slaves, grain and various luxuries (see Polanyi 1977). Yet this type of exchange and market was largely subordinated to political sanctions. Impersonal and competitive market forces did not rule Ptolemaic Egypt, Rome or Byzantium. In other parts of the world a similar type of governed trade occurred. Whether one examines Mayan civilization, Chinese dynasties, Trobriand Islanders, or other indigenous peoples the conclusion is the same: exchange and markets existed but were not the driving forces within their respective cultures. These were not "economic" societies in the contemporary sense.

## Problematical future of market economies

Is the study of markets and exchange in pre-modern societies important for our future? The answer to this depends in part on whether or not we are convinced that capitalism, including the "new global economy," is the "best of all possible worlds." For neoclassical defenders of capitalism, the downfall of the Soviet model in

Eastern Europe and the former Soviet Union, coupled with marketization reforms in China, suggests that market capitalism has triumphed. However, some radical critics take exception and look to the pre-modern role of markets and exchange for insights in envisioning a sustainable world of the twenty-first century.

There is evidence to suggest that a market system is closely correlated with the competitive and limitless struggle for profits. The market system, in other words, seems to be a "driven" system. Competition drives each and every economic player to search for more profits, more production, more markets, and more goods and services. Additionally, consumers are said to have insatiable appetites for more and better products. With infinite wants and the limitless quest for profits, production becomes only a means to ends that are always beyond our reach. Ultimately, more growth is seen as the answer.

There is both concern and evidence at this point that ecological and global biospheric limits may force us to accept LIMITS TO GROWTH. The dilemma for the twenty-first century may be that an insatiable market system cannot coexist within a finite biosphere. Perhaps such a dilemma will focus attention on how markets and exchange can be "re-embedded" in such a way that their allocative role can be retained yet subordinated to the global requirement of sustainability. If this is true, then the embedded character of markets and exchange in pre-modern economies may point the way toward a sustainable future. We may return, once again, to the condition that "people rule markets" rather than being ruled by them. Sahlins states that "there may be two possible courses to affluence. Wants may be 'easily satisfied' either by producing much or desiring little" (Sahlins 1972: 2). Our contemporary market system is one premised upon producing much. On the other hand, by subordinating markets and exchange to the requirements of sustainability, we not only share and learn from the pre-modern economies, but take the alternative path of desiring little; what Sahlins calls the "Zen road to affluence."

## See also:

Asiatic mode of production; economic anthropology: history; economic anthropology: major contemporary themes; feudalism; gifts; hegemony; hunter–gatherer and subsistence societies; mode of production and social formation; Polanyi's views on integration; slavery; socialism and communism; sustainable development

## Selected references

Polanyi, Karl (1944) *The Great Transformation*, New York: Octagon Books, 1975.
—— (1968) *Primitive, Archaic, and Modern Economies: Essays of Karl Polanyi*, ed. George Dalton, Boston: Beacon Press.
—— (1977) *The Livelihood of Man*, ed. Harry Pearson, New York: Academic Press.
Sahlins, Marshall (1972) *Stone Age Economics*, London: Tavistock, 1974.
Stanfield, J.R. (1986) *The Economic Thought of Karl Polanyi*, London: Macmillan.
—— (1990) "Karl Polanyi and Contemporary Economic Thought," in Kari Polanyi-Levitt (ed.), *The Life and Work of Karl Polanyi*, New York: Black Rose Books, 195–207.

DOUG M. BROWN

# marriage

Most economists deal with households without paying much attention to household composition and to the institutions which regulate households. The political economy of marriage provides an economic analysis of household formation and dissolution, and of production and distribution within marriage, while taking account of the political and legal constraints which influence the way individuals marry and function within marriages.

Marriage can be defined as a sexual and household union of two or more individuals with the anticipation that it will be durable. Theoretically, the union could involve any number of people and either or both sexes, but in Western society, this usually involves heterosexual marriage of one male and female, and the reproduction of children (see SEXUALITY). Most research dealing with the political economy of marriage has been inspired by three intellectual traditions: Marxist economics, neoclassical economics and game theory. Historically, for instance, many feminists have taken insights from these schools, and more recently in particular these insights have become rather eclectic (see the journal *Feminist Economics* for examples).

## Marxist tradition

Ever since Engels' *Origins of the Family, Private Property, and the State*, first published in 1884, Marxist economists have recognized that much production and reproduction occurs within families. Scholars trained in this tradition have emphasized women's economic role as producers in the household, their traditional role being the maintenance and reproduction of the work force (e.g. Himmelweit and Mohun 1977). Early Marxists such as Engels emphasized the impact of property structures on marriage and the family. Many contemporary economic analyses of marriage examining the impact of men's political power on women's relative well-being (see FEMINIST POLITICAL ECONOMY: MAJOR CONTEMPORARY THEMES) have been influenced by Marxist thought (see Folbre 1994).

One theme in this work examines the importance of non-market relations associated with married people within a family. While being unwaged, most housework impinges on economic performance through both production and the reproduction of caring relationships between people. Women tend to attend to these chores much more than men possibly due to the asymmetrical distribution of income, wealth and power in society in favor of men and the GENDER DIVISION OF LABOR. To the extent that this labor is rewarded less than its economic value, a form of EXPLOITATION occurs in the household. According to Marxist feminists, the marriage vow, PATRIARCHY, and the gender division of labor have contributed to

an inferior position of women. (see Heath and Ciscel 1988; Delphy and Leonard 1992; see CLASS STRUCTURES OF HOUSEHOLDS; DOMESTIC LABOR DEBATE; SOCIAL STRUCTURE OF ACCUMULATION: FAMILY).

## Becker and the spousal market

A second tradition is based on Gary Becker's neoclassical theory of marriage, first published in 1973 (see HOME ECONOMICS, NEW). While this research draws on the tools of individual utility maximization and marriage market analysis, it recognizes the influence of the legal and political systems. Marriage market analysis is very similar to labor market analysis (see Grossbard-Shechtman 1993). Consider some of the production occurring within marriage, such as cleaning, listening, or gardening, and define spousal labor as work performed for the benefit of a spouse. Given that many women can potentially substitute for each other's spousal labor, and the same can be said for men, there will be markets for spousal labor.

In a market for female spousal labor, women are on the supply side and men on the demand side. The market has an aggregate upward-sloping supply of spousal labor by women, and a downward-sloping demand by men. If a market equilibrium is obtained, the intersection of demand and supply determines how many people marry and how much time they spend working in marriage (the quantity and production dimension) and how much spousal workers get paid for their work (the price and distribution dimension). It follows from here that the value of an individual's time in marriage is a function of marriage market conditions. Similarly, one could have markets for men's spousal labor.

As is the case with any other market, marriage markets function within a political economy. Laws, customs and policies typically prevent these markets from clearing at the levels corresponding to a free market solution. Nevertheless, economists writing on marriage in the tradition of the new home economics consider that individual wives and husbands are influenced by the market value of time in marriage established in marriage markets. After marriage, an individual's actual value of time in marriage may differ from that market value due to the existence of one-to-one ties and divorce costs. Intra-marriage bargaining may occur.

## Game theory and marriage

A third tradition in the political economy of marriage deals with bargaining between husbands and wives. This tradition, started by Marilyn Manser, Murray Brown, Marjorie McElroy and Mary Jane Horney in the early 1980s, relies on (cooperative and non-cooperative) GAME THEORY. These theories typically take marriage as given and analyze the determinants of production in marriage and distribution between husband and wife. This perspective is useful in analyzing how husbands and wives make decisions regarding the allocation of joint resources (see Lundberg and Pollack 1996).

## Role of institutions

Political, legal and religious institutions affect men and women's value in marriage by influencing (1) the levels of demand or supply, and therefore the market value of time in marriage; (2) the prevalence of a market mechanism in the allocation of brides and grooms into marriages; or (3) bargaining rules and resources inside a marriage. Here are a few examples. Laws regulating marriage and divorce influence aggregate conditions in markets for spousal labor. No-fault divorce laws, which lower the value of divorce settlements traditional women can expect, are likely to lower the supply of women's spousal labor. Where divorce is prohibited, marriage markets are less free to facilitate reallocation of husbands and wives and market value in marriage is less likely to vary with duration of marriage. Laws which automatically allocate custody over children to husbands or to wives at divorce will also influence the relative marriage market values of men and women, as well as the bargaining power of individual husbands and wives in a particular marriage.

Other examples of laws and practices influencing marriage market values include regulations concerning the minimum age at marriage, exogamy and polygamy. Rules raising the minimum age at marriage are likely to increase the marriage market value of young women of marriageable age. Cultures often impose gender-asymmetric rules on exogamy, that is, who can marry outside a group. For instance, Islam does not impose restriction on Moslem men's marriages to non-Moslem women, but Moslem women are not supposed to marry outside their religion. This asymmetry will hurt women's market value in marriage. In contrast, asymmetric polygamy allowing men to have multiple wives but not vice versa is likely to benefit women's market value in marriage.

Furthermore, value in marriage and allocation into marriages depends on whether a market mechanism or a command mechanism regulates the allocation process. Where command mechanisms prevail, one expects more divergence from (free) market value of time in marriage. Command mechanisms have more influence where physical domestic violence, typically aimed at women, is tolerated more. At the extreme, if men feel free to kill their female relatives over issues of sexual behavior, women's freedom to make their own marriage choices will be limited, leading to women's inability to capture the market value of their time in marriage. Domestic violence against women may be more prevalent in cultures and in situations where the market value of women's time would otherwise be very high, such as polygamous societies. Whether people are free to chose their own mates or whether they are forced to follow their parents' choice is another dimension of the extent of allocation by command.

## Consumption and labor supply

The political economy of marriage helps to explain various aspects of marriage and divorce, such as the incidence of marriage and divorce, the type of marriage (formal or consensual union), and the number of wives in a polygamous society. It is also helpful in explaining topics closer to the core of economics, such as consumption and labor supply. Some applied work in this field explains why child-oriented and wife-oriented consumption is more likely to occur when wives have greater access to the family's income (Thomas 1990).

The political economy of marriage has also contributed to the study of labor supply. Studies have shown that marriage and divorce institutions, sex ratios and individual resources of value in marriage markets affect the labor force participation of married women (Peters 1986; Grossbard-Shechtman 1993). The political economy of marriage has helped explain political movements as well. According to Heer and Grossbard-Shechtman (1981), the rapid growth of feminism in the USA in the early 1970s was partially the result of entry into adulthood of large numbers of women born during the baby-boom period of the late 1940s and early 1950s. Given that, on average, men's age at marriage exceeds that of women, baby-boom women faced a small demand for their spousal labor, and the market value of their time in marriage was lower than that of preceding cohorts of US women. One of the reasons why feminist ideology appealed so strongly to young women at that time is that they needed help in adjusting to objectively lower market value of time in marriage, and therefore lower opportunities for traditional marriage.

## Conclusion

Being a new field, the political economy of marriage is in the process of integrating its various intellectual traditions. The various schools of thought tend to ignore each other. Many economists trained in the Marxist feminist tradition cast Becker and other neoclassical economists as villains, even though most Beckerian analyses of marriage are compatible with structural analysis and game theory. Most game theorists of marriage include minimal marriage market analyses, and most neoclassical economists ignore the research of economists taking a Marxist feminist perspective. Opportunities for political economists of marriage to interact with colleagues trained in a different tradition are rapidly increasing with the advance of computerized communication and with the internationalization of academia. (See Guttentag and Secord 1983.)

## See also:

family wage; gender; household labour; household production and national income

## Selected references

Delphy, Christine and Leonard, Diana (1992) *Familiar Exploitation: A New Analysis of Marriage in Contemporary Western Societies*, Cambridge: Polity Press.

Folbre, Nancy (1994) *Who Pays for the Kids? Gender and the Structures of Constraint*, London: Routledge.

Grossbard-Shechtman, Shoshana A. (1993) "Marriage Market Models," in Mario Tommasi and Kathryn Ierulli (eds), *The New Economics of Human Behavior*, Cambridge: Cambridge University Press.

Guttentag, Marcia and Secord, Paul (1983) *Too Many Women: The Sex Ratio Question*, London: Sage.

Heath, Julia A. and Ciscel, David H. (1988) "Patriarchy, Family Structure, and the Exploitation of Women's Labor," *Journal of Economic Issues* 22(September): 781–94.

Heer, David M. and Grossbard-Shechtman, Amyra (1981) "The Impact of the Female Marriage Squeeze and the Contraceptive Revolution on Sex Roles and the Women's Liberation Movement in the United States, 1960 to 1975," *Journal of Marriage and the Family* 43: 49–65.

Himmelweit, S. and Mohun, S. (1977) "Domestic Labor and Capital," *Cambridge Journal of Economics* 1: 15–31.

Lundberg, Shelly and Pollack, Robert A. (1996) "Bargaining and Distribution in Marriage," *Journal of Economic Perspectives* 10(4) 139–58.

MacElroy, Marjorie B. and Horney, Mary Jane

(1981) "Nash Bargained Household Decisions: Toward a Generalization of the Theory of Demand," *International Economic Review* 22: 333–49.

Manser, Marilyn and Brown, Murray (1980) "Marriage and Household Decision Making: a Bargaining Analysis," *International Economic Review* 21: 31–44.

Peters, Elizabeth H. (1986) "Marriage and Divorce: Informational Constraints and Private Contracting," *American Economic Review* 76: 437–54.

Thomas, Duncan (1990) "Intra-Household Resource Allocation: An Inferential Approach," *Journal of Human Resources* 25: 635–64.

SHOSHANA GROSSBARD-
SHECHTMAN

# Marx, Karl Heinrich

Karl Marx (1818–83) was born in Trier, Prussia (now Germany). His father was a liberal-minded lawyer, and his mother a dedicated homemaker. The Prussian government was autocratic, but Marx's family, his school and town were influenced by the Enlightenment and the 1830 revolution. He completed a PhD in philosophy at the University of Jena in 1841, but was unable to gain a university lectureship due to government repression of non-orthodox views and behavior.

Instead he turned to journalism, editing a liberal newspaper in Cologne, *Rheinische Zeitung*, which was banned within a year. In 1843 he moved to Paris, the center of radical thought and politics, and began editing a magazine, *Die Deutsch-Franzosische*, as well as writing the famous *Economic and Philosophical Manuscripts of 1844* and meeting his lifelong friend, Friedrich Engels. It was in Paris that Marx became a communist and first seriously studied political economy.

Due to pressure from Prussia, he was expelled from France in 1845 and settled in Belgium for three years. There he wrote a draft of *The German Ideology* (1845–6) with Engels, which set out the main postulates of the "materialistic conception of history," the idea that social existence determines consciousness. Marx's first published book emerged in 1847, the *Poverty of Philosophy* (in French), being a critique of Proudhon's idealistic socialism. Soon after, Marx and Engels were commissioned to write the *Communist Manifesto* by the Communist League, and it was published just prior to the 1848 revolutions in Europe (in which Marx and Engels were active).

Marx was expelled from Belgium in 1848, and moved back to (revolutionary) Prussia, where he edited a popular daily paper, *Die Neue Rheinische Zeitung*. The paper was banned and Marx was expelled from Prussia when counter-revolution took hold. Subsequently, he migrated to England in 1849 where he lived most of the rest of his life.

## Marx's main ideas in political economy

In London, Marx divided his time between study, politics, journalism and his family. He realized that to understand the potential for social and political change it is necessary to study political economy. This he did in further detail at the British Museum during the 1850s and, after the economic crisis of 1856–7, he wrote a prodigious 1,000 page manuscript which set out his main theory of radical political economy, now known as the *Grundrisse* manuscripts of 1857–8. This work, one of the many he wrote for "self-clarification" rather than publication, provided the foundations of his main published work, the magnum opus, *Das Kapital*, which emerged in three volumes, the first in 1867 in German (Volumes 2 and 3 were edited by Engels after his death).

Three main influences – neo-Hegelian philosophy, utopian socialism and CLASSICAL POLITICAL ECONOMY – became the main sources of criticism out of which emerged Marx's brilliantly original ideas about the "inner motion of capitalism" (political economy) and historical and dialectical materialism (see DIALECTICAL METHOD). In the *Communist Manifesto*, for instance, Marx and Engels argued that the inner workings of capitalism propel a central contradiction: the dual forces of incessant ACCUMULATION of capital and socioeconomic fragmentation and instability. This dual motion is endogenously ingrained in the system, and can change qualitatively only with a change in the mode of production. All of Marx's subsequent works sought to detail and develop this endogenous perspective of the unstable growth and development of capitalism.

Some scholars used to think that Marx's early analysis of ALIENATION in the *Economic and Philosophical Manuscripts of 1844* was dropped in his more mature works. The English publication of the *Grundrisse* (1857–8) in 1973 dispelled this myth. In the *1844 Manuscripts*, Marx examined the system of capitalist ownership of the means of production, and the dominance of commodity production, in which workers are alienated from their product, from themselves, from other workers, and from their species being (human beings are social animals). This theme is developed to a higher level in the *Grundrisse*, where he postulates that workers produce a surplus value which can return in a material form as machinery and control systems utilized in the capitalist process to reproduce their alienated and exploited existence. The greater the extent of alienation of value and product from workers, the greater is the surplus product. The same theme exists in *Das Kapital*, although here it is treated in a more pragmatic and realistic fashion, with the emphasis being placed on EXPLOITATION.

Also in the *Grundrisse*, Marx developed a framework for studying the economic system of capitalism as a mode of production. He explored the need for a "six-book plan," commencing with (1) capital, and dialectically linking this with (2) wage labor and (3) landed property, the three main classes of capitalism, followed by (4) the state and (5) foreign trade and finance, and culminating in a concrete analysis of (6) the world market and economic crises. He never completed this project, probably getting no further than "capital" (Oakley 1983) (see MARX'S METHODOLOGY OF POLITICAL ECONOMY).

The major categories and theories of Marx's political economy were developed or formalized in the *Grundrisse*. Some of the ideas developed in the *Grundrisse*, on commodity production and money, plus some notes on historical materialism, emerged in Marx's first published book on political economy, *A Contribution to a Critique of Political Economy*, which was virtually ignored when it first emerged in 1859. During the early and mid 1860s he worked on a massive three-volume work (part of an even larger manuscript) called *Theories of Surplus Value* (1862–3), which includes important ideas about surplus value, PRODUCTIVE AND UNPRODUCTIVE LABOR, and a critical analysis of Ricardo's theory of accumulation. Then in 1867 he finally published the first volume of his magnum opus, *Das Kapital*, in German. Volumes 2 (1885) and 3 (1894) of *Das Kapital* were published posthumously by Engels in German, based on manuscripts and fragments left by Marx.

*Das Kapital* corresponds broadly with at least the first of the six-book plan, (1) capital, which includes a critical analysis of the capitalist production process (*Das Kapital* Volume 1), the circulation process of capital (Volume 2), and the system of capitalist production as a whole (Volume 3). The production process examines the system of commodity production: use value and exchange value, LABOR AND LABOR POWER, the production of value, surplus value and exploitation in the LABOR PROCESS, the system of large-scale industry, and the RESERVE ARMY OF LABOR. Institutionalized conflict between capital and labor is a major theme in this work.

The circulation process of capital comprises the CIRCUIT OF SOCIAL CAPITAL, the TURNOVER TIME OF CAPITAL and REPRODUCTION: SIMPLE AND EXPANDED. Special emphasis is placed on the macroeconomic linkages between the purchasing of labor power and means of production, the production of surplus value, the realization of demand on the market, the further reinvestment of surplus value and so on in a circular process, as well as a two-sector model of growth and reproduction of capital.

Capitalist production as a whole includes the

system of competition, sectors with differing levels of productivity, the transformation of values into prices (see TRANSFORMATION PROBLEM), the FALLING RATE OF PROFIT TENDENCY and counter-tendencies, the system of credit and banking, and the relationship between production and distribution.

## Main contribution of Marx

The main theoretical contribution of Marx was in laying bare the exploitative and contradictory motion of capitalism. He recognized that while on the surface markets appear to be based on equal exchange, liberty and freedom, one needs to look deeper and more holistically into the fabric of capitalism to understand how workers are exploited, how business cycles arise and how the potential exists for liberating human beings from the impersonal and inhumane workings of the capitalist system. Behind the veil of markets is the exercise of ECONOMIC POWER, the production of surplus labor, the unequal distribution of income and wealth, the cyclical process of growth and unemployment and social fragility. As the principal theoretician of the working class, historically speaking, Marx changed the trend from "utopian" to "scientific" socialism.

## Marx's influence

His influence, directly or indirectly, has been enormous over the last hundred and fifty years. Two periods of influence stand out (after his death): 1890–1928 and 1965–85. During the first period, many political parties adopted Marxist principles and a generation of scholars were working along Marxist lines, especially in Germany and Russia. Rosa Luxemburg, Vladimir Lenin, Rudolf Hilferding, Nikolai Bukharin, Nicolai Kondratieff, I.I. Rubin and Henryk Grossman, in particular, made contributions to political economy during this period. However, while revisionism led to evolutionary socialism in Germany, through the works of Eduard Bernstein and others (see SOCIAL DEMOCRACY), in the USSR Joseph Stalin systematically rooted out every haven

of creative (Marxist) thought during 1928–54. Marx's socialism had little in common with the Soviet experience because the Soviet Union started as an undeveloped nation; the Stalinist dictatorship was worlds removed from Marx's vision of a society based on workers' control and participatory democracy to reduce exploitation; and the USSR lacked a system of human RIGHTS to protect people from abuses of power.

During the 1940s and 1950s, Marxist political economy was kept alive in the West through the creative efforts of Maurice Dobb, Paul Sweezy, Oskar Lange, Michal Kalecki and others. It was not until the mid-1960s that the second era of creative Marxist thought commenced, especially in the USA, the UK, Europe, Australia and, to a lesser extent, in South America, Africa and Asia. Marx's ideas were a central part of the revival of political economy which has continued to this day. Many of his manuscripts have been recently translated into English, and dozens of textbooks have emerged, including Ernest Mandel's *Marxist Economic Theory* in 1968, David Harvey's *Limits to Capital* in 1982, John King and Michael Howard's *Political Economy of Marx* in 1975, and the more mathematical *Marx's Economics* by Michio Morishima, in 1973.

Marx developed a theoretical framework which is still to this day being debated, utilized, applied, improved, modified and criticized. Marx's political economy, including his dialectical method, have been useful for understanding contemporary problems of CLASS, business cycles, cyclical crisis, UNEMPLOYMENT AND UNDEREMPLOYMENT, inflation, ECONOMIC POWER, competition, ACCUMULATION, domestic labor, the FALLING RATE OF PROFIT TENDENCY and FINANCIAL CRISES. Currently there are various groupings of Marxist political economists: postmodern Marxists, rational choice Marxists and fundamentalists, plus many radical economists who modify and extend his theories to important areas such as the labor market, the state, the family, the financial system and the world economy. Marx's influence lives on.

## See also:

Marxist political economy: history; Marxist political economy: major contemporary varieties

## Selected references

Bottomore, Tom (ed.) (1990) *A Dictionary of Marxist Thought*, 2nd edn, Oxford: Blackwell.

Bukharin, Nikolai Ivanovich (1919) *Economic Theory of the Leisure Class*, New York and London: Monthly Review Press, 1972.

Cutler, Anthony, Hindess, Barry, Hirst, Paul and Hussain, Athar (1977–8) *Marx's "Capital" and Capitalism Today*, 2 vols, London: Routledge & Kegan Paul.

Eatwell, John, Milgate, Murray and Newman, Peter (eds) (1990) *The New Palgrave: Marxian Economics*, London: Macmillan.

Luxemburg, Rosa (1913) *The Accumulation of Capital*, London: Routledge & Kegan Paul, 1951.

Mandel, Ernest (1971) *The Formation of the Economic Thought of Karl Marx*, London and New York: New Left Books and Monthly Review.

Nicolalevsky, Boris and Maenchen-Helfen, Otto (1933) *Karl Marx: Man and Fighter*, Harmondsworth: Penguin, 1973.

Oakley, Allen (1983) *A Bibliographical Analysis of Marx's Critical Theory*, London: Routledge.

Rader, Melvin (1979) *Marx's Interpretation of History*, New York: Oxford University Press.

Volkov, M.I. (1985) *A Dictionary of Political Economy*, Moscow: Progress Publishers.

PHILLIP ANTHONY O'HARA

# Marx's methodology of political economy

This entry concentrates on how Karl MARX inquired into and then presented his work on the political economy of CAPITALISM. We look at three main issues: the differences between the methods of presentation and inquiry; the relationship between capitalism as it appears and as it is scientifically understood; and Marx's six-book plan for his economic works.

## Methods of inquiry and presentation

In the "Postface" to the second edition of Volume 1 of *Das Kapital*, written in 1873, Marx differentiated between the method of inquiry and the method of presentation of his political economy of capitalism. Inquiry is the process of study, analysis and thinking, which "has to appropriate the material in detail, analyze its different forms of development and to track down their inner connection" (Marx 1873: 102). Only after this has been done can the method of presentation be activated, which is the anticipated published form of his work as seen by the public and scholars.

Some insight into this question is gained from Marx's *Grundrisse* manuscripts of 1857–8, especially the so-called "Introduction" to this work. Among the issues discussed is, first and foremost, how economic writings traditionally begin. In the first section of the "Introduction," for example, Marx notes that the point of departure of presentation for many eighteenth-century economic writings is production in general, that is, what all forms of production have in common. Linked to this is the trend for some certain political economists to "present production ... as distinct from distribution etc., as encased in eternal natural laws independent of history, at which opportunity *bourgeois* relations are then quietly smuggled in as the inevitable natural laws on which society in the abstract is founded" (Marx 1857–8: 87). Thus, rather than concentrating on those classes and tendencies specific to particular economic systems, they "extinguish all historic differences under *general human laws*" (Marx 1857–8: 87).

Marx argues that the general characteristics can be useful, but that a treatise on the capitalist economy must bring forth the specific features of this system, even if in an elemental (general or abstract) form at the start. As the method of presentation proceeds, the analysis should become more concrete. But, how should the specific forms of the economic system be developed? One method, in the seventeenth-century tradition, "always begin[s] with the living whole, with population, nation, state, several states, etc.; but they always conclude by discovering through analysis a small number of determinant, abstract, general relations such as division of labour, money, value, etc." (Marx 1857–8: 100). The second method is a later tradition, which begins from simple, abstract concepts and, through a process of continuous concretization, constructs a complex concept of the living whole. As Marx said, this second method involves ascending "from the simple relations, such as labor, division of labor, need, exchange value, to the level of the state, exchange between nations and the world market." The latter method, according to Marx, "is obviously the scientific method" (Marx 1857–8: 100–1).

However, for Marx, starting with the simplest relations, such as "labor," does not result in abstracting from specific economic systems. This is because, as he said, labor "achieves practical truth as an abstraction only as a category of the most modern society" (Marx 1857–8: 105), i.e. capitalism. In other words, under capitalism labor is reduced to socially comparable terms in the division of labor, subject to pressures which of necessity make it of a minimal degree of productivity and socially valid as value. Hence individual labor is reduced to simple social labor.

Thus the proper point of departure of political economy, according to Marx, is the result of the real, historical process of the development of capitalist society, and not a mental generalization. In his later writings, Marx often refers to such an abstraction as "real" or "historical abstraction" (Marx 1857–8: 449; see also Echeverria 1989; Carver 1980).

A considerable literature has emerged about why Marx started Volume 1 of *Das Kapital* with the "commodity" (see Fayazmanesh 1994; Murray 1990). The "commodity" is an abstraction, but a real historical abstraction. Marx thus starts *Das Kapital* with commodities in general, rather than specific markets such as shops, banks or the share market; and the

commodity is, according to Marx, "the simplest economic concretum"; the most elemental unit of bourgeois society (Marx 1879–80: 215). As Marx said:

> Beginnings are always difficult in all sciences. The understanding of the first chapter, especially the section that contains the analysis of commodities, will therefore present the greatest difficulty.... Moreover, in the analysis of the economic forms neither microscopes nor chemical agents are of assistance. The power of abstraction must replace both. But for bourgeois society, the commodity-form of the product of labor, or the value-form of the commodity, is the economic cell-form.
>
> (Marx 1873: 89–90)

Therefore, the commodity was chosen since it is the dominant general form in which labor and value are represented in capitalist society. The analysis is abstract, but commodity production is a central characteristic of capitalism. The commodity is immediately linked with value and labor, and gradually linked to the specific forms of production, surplus value and large-scale industry characteristic of capitalism as the volume develops.

## Science and sense perception

As Marx works on the production process of capitalism, he observes how highly theoretical concepts, such as value and surplus value, would appear on the surface of the capitalist society as the common sense concepts of price and profit. Indeed, to the extent that he works on the theory of competition in the *Grundrisse*, he comes to believe that, at the level of sense perception of the capitalist economy, a theoretical inversion takes place. For example, to the capitalist and like-minded economists, wages and profit, instead of being conditioned by value, would determine value (see COMMODITY FETISHISM).

Marx's subsequent work on the manuscripts which constitute the drafts of different volumes or sections of *Das Kapital*, would further strengthen the distinction between scientific understanding and sense perception of capitalism. In these notes, as well as in the first volume of *Das Kapital*, Marx often *compares* the object of political economy to that of the natural sciences, particularly astronomy (but, of course, in its totality political economy is different to the natural sciences). For example, he writes: "a scientific analysis of competition is possible only if we grasp the inner nature of capital, just as the apparent motion of heavenly bodies are intelligible only to someone who is acquainted with their real motion, which are not perceptible to the senses" (Marx 1873: 433). In the same vein, he writes elsewhere: "all science would be superfluous if the form of *appearance* of things directly coincided with their *essence*" (Marx 1894: 956; emphasis added).

The "road traveled by capital," to use an expression of Marx, involves not only a movement from less to more concrete concepts, but, at the same time, a movement from inner connections to the external necessity, where inversions and illusions are explained. The first three volumes of *Das Kapital*, for instance, well reflect the movement from essential relations (such as value and surplus value) to more outward appearances (such as price and profit).

## Marx's plan for his economic treatise

From the late 1850s to the early 1860s, Marx drafted various plans for presenting his economic treatise. Oakley (1983), who discusses these plans in detail, summarizes them as generally including the following successive and increasingly concrete books: (1) capital, (2) landed property, (3) wage labor, (4) the state, (5) foreign trade, and (6) world market and crises.

The totality of the "six-book plan" never materialized in Marx's lifetime. It has been suggested that *Das Kapital* – in so far as it includes a discussion of wage labor and landed property – presents a change in this general plan (Rosdolsky 1977). But there are indications, such as a reference in *Das Kapital* itself to a "special study of wage-labor" (never written), that Marx did not give up this grand plan, and that it should be left to other scholars to complete. If this is correct, then only book (1) ever materialized in Marx's work of

presentation, as the three volumes of *Das Kapital*: production (Volume 1), circulation (Volume 2), and the unity of production and circulation (Volume 3).

This six-book plan is critical for two reasons. First, Marx had in mind examining his major concepts in association with the conditions of existence of the dominant classes and institutions of capitalism, by a series of increasingly concrete and integrative models. And secondly, while Marx obviously abandoned the idea of completing this plan in his lifetime, he may still have considered a similar plan to be necessary for the development of a critical political economy of capitalism. This has important implications for scholars who concentrate on "capital," yet do not include models of the other conditions of existence of classes and spheres of capitalism (see O'Hara 1999). The work of Lebowitz (1992), for instance, examines in detail the need to integrate the wage labor book into an analysis of "capital."

## Conclusion

There are differences of opinion about Marx's analysis of value theory, the transformation problem, crisis theory, competition and so on. An important reason for this may be the lack of attention being paid to Marx's concept of science and the scientific method. It is not possible to understand Marx's theories without paying attention to questions of methodology.

## See also:

determinism and overdetermination; dialectical method; Marxist political economy: major contemporary varieties

## Selected references

Carver, Terell (1980) "Marx's 1857 Introduction," *Economy and Society* 9(2): 197–203.
Echeverria, Rafael (1989) "Critique of Marx's 1857 Introduction," in Ali Rattansi (ed.), *Ideology, Method and Marx: Essays from "Economy and Society"*, London and New York: Routledge.

Fayazmanesh, Sasan (1994) "Marx's Semantics and The Logic of the Derivation of Value," *Research in the History of Economic Thought and Methodology* 12: 65–91.

Lebowitz, Michael (1992) *Beyond Capital: Marx's Political Economy of the Working Class*, Basingstoke: Macmillan.

Marx, Karl (1857–8) *Grundrisse*, Harmondsworth: Penguin, 1973.

—— (1858) "Letter from Marx to Engels in Manchester, 2 April 1858," in Karl Marx and Friedrich Engels, *Selected Correspondence 1844–1895*, Moscow: Progress Publishers, 1976.

—— (1867) *Das Kapital*, vol. 1, published as *Capital, Volume 1*, Harmondsworth: Penguin, 1976.

—— (1873) "Postface to the Second Edition," in *Capital, Volume 1*, Harmondsworth: Penguin, 1976.

—— (1879–80) "Marginal Notes on Wagner," in Karl Marx, *Value Studies by Marx*, London: New Park Publications, 1976.

—— (1894) *Das Kapital*, vol. 3, published as *Capital, Volume 3*, Harmondsworth, Penguin, 1981.

Moseley, Fred and Campbell, Martha (1997) *New Investigations of Marx's Method*, Atlantic Highlands, NJ: Humanities Press.

Murray, Patrick (1990) *Marx's Theory of Scientific Knowledge*, Atlantic Highlands, NJ and London: Humanities Press International.

Oakley, Allen (1983) *The Making of Marx's Critical Theory: A Bibliographical Analysis*, London: Routledge & Kegan Paul.

O'Hara, Phillip Anthony (1999) *Marx, Veblen and Modern Institutional Economics: Principles and Dynamics of Capitalism*, Cheltenham: Edward Elgar.

Rosdolsky, Roman (1977) *The Making of Marx's Capital*, London: Pluto Press.

Sawyer, Malcolm (1983) *Marx's Method: Ideology, Science and Critique in "Capital"*, Brighton: Harvester Press, and Atlantic Highlands, NJ: Humanities Press.

SASAN FAYAZMANESH
PHILLIP ANTONY O'HARA

# Marxist political economy: history

MARX regarded himself both as a stern critic of classical (or scientific) political economy and, in an important sense, as its culmination. CLASSICAL POLITICAL ECONOMY, he believed, had begun in the late seventeenth century, with William Petty in England and Pierre Boisguillebert in France. It reached a climax with David Ricardo's *Principles of Political Economy and Taxation* in 1817, but then rapidly degenerated into crude apologies for capitalism. Thus Marx wrote voluminously, almost compulsively, on Adam Smith and Ricardo, but very little on John Stuart Mill and nothing at all on William Stanley Jevons and his marginalist contemporaries. Maurice Dobb (1973) is entirely faithful to Marx's own interpretation in describing two streams of economic theory which emanated from Smith: the "vulgar" economics which led directly to neoclassical analysis and eventually to modern orthodoxy, and the socialist political economy of Marx and his followers. In his critical dissection of classical theory, Marx drew heavily – as is well known – on German philosophy (above all G.W.F. Hegel) and on French socialism (Charles Fourier, the Comte de Saint-Simon and their disciples). Less widely acknowledged but equally important was the influence of early English critics of capitalism, especially the so-called "Ricardian socialists" John Francis Bray, Thomas Hodgskin and William Thompson, to whose writings he was introduced by Friedrich Engels in Manchester in the mid-1840s.

## Principal components of Marx's work

From these diverse sources Marx constructed a political economy which had two principal components: a general theory of economic systems, and a specific model of CAPITALISM. His general theory of the structure and evolution of modes of production emphasized the performance of surplus labor by the propertyless classes and the various methods by which its fruits were appropriated by the owning classes. Tension between the "forces of production" and these "social relations of production" was the driving force in all historical development (see Cohen 1978). By far the most advanced CLASS society was the capitalist mode of production, defined by the relationship between wage labor and capital. Marx believed capitalism to be uniquely dynamic and uncontrollably destructive of pre-capitalist societies. His analysis of labor and surplus labor in capitalist production, and of the concealment of their true nature under the fetishistic value-form, led him to more specific propositions concerning EXPLOITATION, economic crises and the inevitable replacement of capitalism by socialist relations of production which were, he believed, already evident in embryo within the existing social order (see SOCIALISM AND COMMUNISM).

Marx's conception of political economy was broad enough to preclude any sharp distinction between "economic" and "non-economic" writings, and the development of his ideas was sufficiently continuous to discredit the notion of a sharp epistemological break in his thinking. However, while themes central to Marxian political economy can be found in Marx's own *Economic and Philosophical Manuscripts* of 1844 and *Poverty of Philosophy* of 1847, in Engels' *Outlines of a Critique of Political Economy* of 1843, and of course in the 1848 *Communist Manifesto*, Marx's economic ideas crystallized in the late 1850s and early 1860s (Oakley 1983). The decade beginning in 1857 saw the writing of the "rough draft" eventually published as the *Grundrisse* (1857–8); the much shorter *A Contribution to a Critique of Political Economy* (1859); the huge manuscript on the history of classical economics which finally surfaced, in the early twentieth century, as *Theories of Surplus Value*; Volume 1 of *Das Kapital,* which appeared in 1867; and the untidy texts which Engels edited after Marx's death in 1883 and published as Volumes 2 and 3 of *Das Kapital.*

In his introduction to the second volume of *Das Kapital*, published in 1885, Engels announced the existence of a solution to the problem of transforming labor values into equilibrium prices of production and surplus values into profits, and challenged Marx's bourgeois critics to say what it was. The resulting "prize essay competition" attracted entries from both supporters and opponents of the LABOR THEORY OF VALUE, none of whom met with much success. Marx's own solution appeared late in 1894, in the long-delayed Volume 3, but disappointed many of his followers. It drew a biting critique from the prominent Austrian marginalist, Eugen von Böhm-Bawerk, who objected two years later that Marx had failed to resolve the glaring contradiction between his theory and capitalist reality. In 1904 the Austro-Marxist Rudolf Hilferding defended Marx's objectivist method against the subjectivist theory of value, which was further attacked by Nikolai Bukharin in his *Economic Theory of the Leisure Class*, completed in 1914. Technical aspects of the TRANSFORMATION PROBLEM were largely ignored until Ladislaus von Bortkiewicz, in two important articles published in 1906–7, provided a general mathematical solution to the problem and exposed the limitations of Marx's own analysis.

## Early post-Marx debate and developments

A more important challenge to Marxian political economy came from within the socialist movement, with Eduard Bernstein's "revision" of Marx's claims concerning capitalist development and the prospects for socialism (Howard and King 1989: chaps 4–6). Bernstein maintained that real wages were rising, not falling; the concentration and centralization of capital was proceeding only very slowly and crises were becoming less rather than more severe. In consequence the German proletariat showed no more taste for revolution than their fellow workers in Britain and America. Socialists, or social democrats, should aim for peaceful, piecemeal reforms in alliance with middle-class liberals, and abandon Marx's apocalyptic vision of revolutionary change. Bernstein's heresy provoked a series of polemical replies from Karl Kautsky and Rosa

Luxemburg, and a more temperate restatement and refinement of Marxian theory from Rudolf Hilferding.

Hilferding's *Finance Capital*, published in 1910, remains the most significant book in twentieth-century Marxian political economy. It provides a systematic treatment of questions which Marx had posed, without answering: those concerning the role of money, the increasingly close relationship between financial and industrial capital, the rise of the giant CORPORATION and the growth of state intervention. For Hilferding, "FINANCE CAPITAL", a term which encapsulates these developments, represented a new stage of capitalism, being illiberal, undemocratic, nationalistic and aggressive. In its economic policy, finance capital had forsaken the earlier cosmopolitan commitment to free trade and embraced imperialism, which Hilferding defined as a "struggle for economic territory" that threatened the onset of a world war.

In her 1913 *Accumulation of Capital*, Rosa Luxemburg reached the same conclusion by a different route. Strongly influenced by underconsumptionists like J.C.L Simonde de Sismondi and the Russian populists, Luxemburg claimed that Marx's Volume 2 of *Das Kapital* models of growth in a closed, two-sector capitalist economy were hopelessly flawed. The system could not generate sufficient markets by itself: demand from capitalists and workers was necessarily inadequate to "realize" all the surplus value produced. Thus, "external" sources of purchasing power were required, whether from "petty bourgeois" classes within the capitalist countries or from pre-capitalist modes of production outside. Continuous imperialist expansion was therefore a condition of survival for capitalism; but it was also profoundly contradictory, as the expansion of the system dissolved first the "natural economy" of backward societies and then the simple commodity production which arose in its place. Capitalism needed noncapitalist customers, but in seeking them out it simultaneously destroyed them. (See COLONIALISM AND IMPERIALISM: CLASSIC TEXTS.)

Few German Marxists were convinced by

Luxemburg's analysis, even though most regarded underconsumption as the principal cause of economic crises. In Russia, too, her revolutionary conclusions proved more attractive than her arguments. Orthodox Marxists like Plekhanov and Lenin had always been hostile to populist ideas, emphasizing not only the peculiarities of Russian capitalism but also the inevitability of its triumph over precapitalist forms. On this, at least, they agreed with the most distinguished of the Russian revisionists, Mikhail Tugan-Baranowski. Tugan, in fact, was well known for his vigorous defense of the proposition that there were in principle no limits to the expansion of aggregate demand within a closed capitalist system.

Bolshevik writers on imperialism, however, attacked not Luxemburg (who shared their internationalist opposition to the First World War) but Kautsky, who early in 1914 had denied the inevitability of the conflict. Kautsky identified a potentially new and more advanced stage of "ultra-imperialism" in which the rival capitalist powers would sink their differences and form a global cartel to facilitate the peaceful exploitation of non-capitalist territories. This was mercilessly criticized first by Bukharin, in his 1915 *Imperialism and World Economy*, and then in the following year by Lenin, who drew on Bukharin, Hilferding and the English liberal, J.A. Hobson, in his celebrated polemic, *Imperialism: the Highest Stage of Capitalism*. Kautsky's vision was utopian, they argued. The "law of uneven and combined development" (see UNEVEN DEVELOPMENT) rendered stable international cartels impossible even in individual industries, since new, more dynamic, low-cost producers could never resist the temptation to launch price wars against their older-established and therefore less progressive competitors. The same applied *a fortiori* to agreements between entire capitalist states.

After the October revolution of 1917 the gap between communist and social democratic versions of Marxian political economy became unbridgeable. The Bolsheviks maintained that capitalism had become "moribund," losing its former vigor and offering the world's workers and peasants nothing but intensified exploitation and the constant threat of war. German social democrats replied by adopting much of the old revisionist platform: in the new phase of "organized capitalism" (as Hilferding put it), rapid progress toward socialism was possible through bourgeois-democratic institutions, and there was no longer any reason to fear world war. Thus, while Lenin, Bukharin, Trotsky and other Russian Marxists debated the planned INDUSTRIALIZATION of the Soviet Union, Kautsky denounced the Bolshevik revolution as a dead end and dismissed an autonomous Russian socialism as a chimera.

## Later debates and developments

Significant advances in the economic theory of socialism were made in the 1920s by Russian economists like Preobrazhensky and Feldman. By 1929, with Stalin's assumption of supreme power and the beginning of forced industrialization under the first Five Year Plan, genuine intellectual inquiry had become impossible in the Soviet Union. Thereafter, creative work in Marxian political economy was confined to the West, where the onset of the GREAT DEPRESSION stimulated the development of more coherent crisis models (see Howard and King 1992: ch. 1). New variants of underconsumption theory were proposed by Otto Bauer in 1936 and by Paul Sweezy in 1942, both linking a slowdown in consumption expenditure to the growth of monopoly and the corresponding decline in the wage share in net output. Henryk Grossmann drew on Bauer's prewar critique of Luxemburg in his excavation of the analysis in Volume 3 of *Das Kapital* of the FALLING RATE OF PROFIT TENDENCY, which Grossmann regarded as an essential law of capitalist development and as the fundamental, underlying cause of all economic crises. Other writers suggested a synthesis of the two approaches, sometimes adding elements of a third: the possibility (emphasized by Maurice Dobb) that the profit rate might fall because the rate of exploitation declined at the peak of the boom as real wages rose.

While in the 1930s Marxian economics enjoyed a significant growth of interest among academic theorists, after 1945 it faced a series of profound intellectual challenges. The first was to account for the revival of the world capitalist economy, since the "long boom" which continued until the early 1970s took everyone by surprise. The most popular explanation centered on the unprecedented level of armament expenditures, which could be interpreted both as offsetting the falling rate of profit and – as Sweezy and his collaborator Paul Baran claimed in their 1964 *Monopoly Capital* – as an outlet for otherwise unusable surplus value. More openly Keynesian writers such as Joan Robinson preached the social democratic message that capitalism had changed: trade unions kept real wages rising in line with labor productivity, while increasing public consumption was guaranteed by the welfare state. Ernest Mandel and others stressed the truce in the class war produced by Nazism and world war, which had prevented a squeeze on profits as a result of working class militancy. When, from 1973 onwards, growth slowed down and mass unemployment reappeared, Marxian economists invoked these arguments in reverse. Underconsumption, falling rate of profit and "over-accumulation" (rising wage share) theories of crisis were all cited to account for the return of serious recession.

A second challenge was posed by academic critics of the labor theory of value. Using the techniques of modern linear economics, Paul Samuelson, Nobuo Okishio, Piero Sraffa and Ian Steedman demonstrated that labor values were derived, not primitive, magnitudes; that the entire transformation problem was nothing more than an unnecessary detour, since prices of production could be calculated directly from input–output data; and that, in models with alternative production processes and fixed capital, strange paradoxes could arise in the relationships between values, prices and profits. The same analysis showed that there was nothing inevitable or "essential" about the tendency, described in Volume 3 of *Das Kapital*, for the rate of profit to decline; indeed, technical progress would increase the profit rate unless real wages rose. To make sense of

"Marx after Sraffa," these critics argued, labor values must be given up and replaced by a SURPLUS APPROACH TO POLITICAL ECONOMY formulated in "price of production" terms. These conclusions were vehemently opposed by more orthodox Marxists, on the grounds that they fetishized the production of commodities and ignored the role of human labor as the central organizing principle of Marx's political economy (Steedman *et al*. 1981).

The third area of contention was imperialism (Brewer 1980). A variety of critics of the Hilferding–Lenin theory claimed that it had been both overtaken by events and captured by bourgeois nationalists. As to the first charge, the traditional Marxian analysis was deemed incapable of explaining the post-1945 decolonization, the suppression of imperialist rivalries and their replacement by United States "super-imperialism," or the rapid industrialization of many previously backward areas, especially in East Asia. The Leninist doctrine that capitalism was incapable of revolutionizing production in the Third World was developed further by Paul Baran, Andre Gunder Frank and Samir Amin. This doctrine was attacked (by, for instance, Bill Warren) as being inconsistent with Marx's vision of the capitalist mode of production as an irresistible universalizing force, and as a reactionary idea which only served the interests of peripheral capitalists. In the 1960s the Vietnam War briefly reinvigorated the conventional analysis, which appeared to receive further support from the secular decline in the poor countries' terms of trade and, in the 1980s, from the Latin American debt crisis. But imperialism is no longer a crucial concept in most versions of Marxian political economy (in its place we have the more eclectic WORLD-SYSTEMS ANALYSIS and INTERNATIONAL POLITICAL ECONOMY).

Fourth, Marxian economists had to confront the unpleasant realities of the Soviet system. Here they did rather well, producing a number of alternative models which were both consistent with historical materialism and less static than the specter of an apparently invincible and unchanging "totalitarianism" raised by bourgeois political scientists. The-

ories of bureaucratic collectivism, state capitalism, the Soviet Union as a new form of class society, as a "bureaucratically deformed workers' state," all allowed for internal conflict and social contradictions which threatened the survival of the ruling elite. The events of 1989–91 thus came as less of a surprise for Marxian political economists than their mainstream counterparts. This, it must be admitted, is true only at the level of criticism: positive proposals for an economics of socialism which might avoid the distortions and abuses of the Stalinist experience are still in their infancy (see SOCIALISM AND COMMUNISM; MARKET SOCIALISM; PARTICIPATORY DEMOCRACY AND SELF-MANAGEMENT).

## Selected references

Brewer, Anthony (1980) *Marxist Theories of Imperialism: A Critical Survey*, London: Routledge and Kegan Paul.

Cohen, G.A. (1978) *Karl Marx's Theory of History: A Defence*, Princeton, NJ: Princeton University Press.

Dobb, Maurice H. (1973) *Theories of Value and Distribution Since Adam Smith: Ideology and Economic Theory*, Cambridge: Cambridge University Press.

Howard, M.C. and King, J.E. (1989) *A History of Marxian Economics: Volume I, 1883–1929*, London: Macmillan and Princeton, NJ: Princeton University Press.

—— (1992) *A History of Marxian Economics: Volume II, 1929–1990*, London: Macmillan and Princeton, NJ: Princeton University Press.

Oakley, Allen (1983) *The Making of Marx's Critical Theory: A Bibliographical Analysis*, London: Routledge & Kegan Paul.

Steedman, Ian *et al*. (1981) *The Value Controversy*, London: Verso.

M.C. HOWARD
J.E. KING

# Marxist political economy: major contemporary varieties

Marxist political economy has always been a contested terrain of alternative interpretations. The rich, complex and sometimes contradictory writings of Marx would alone have assured that. In addition, since Marxist thinking, writing and political organizations have spread across the entire globe in the hundred years since his death, Marxism's interactions with many diverse cultures only increased the range of different conceptions of Marxist political economy. Here we can only sketch some of the major tendencies important today.

A few basic tenets are held in common by virtually all kinds of Marxist political economy. CAPITALISM is the chief object of criticism. However, Marxist political economy seeks much more than reforms or improvements of capitalism. The aim is for a transition to socialism or communism understood as alternative social structures. Lastly, most kinds of Marxist political economy envision socialism or communism as the contemporary culmination of historical tendencies toward democracy, equality, and collectivity that have challenged and plagued capitalist and other exploitative social systems and sometimes provoked revolutions against them. (See SOCIALISM AND COMMUNISM.)

Marxist political economists differ over their definitions of capitalism, socialism and communism. Because these differences are so basic, the arguments among differently persuaded Marxist political economists have sometimes been as intense as their oppositions to political economies that celebrate capitalism. Moreover, since Marxism is an internal critique of capitalism generated by capitalism itself, it has usually operated as the beleaguered minority position. Marxist political economists typically find themselves severely criticized, attacked, ostracized and/or ignored by the supporters of capitalism. This situation has also contributed to the differences among the alternative interpretations of Marxist political economy.

## Property-theoretic school

In disputing what capitalism is, one major tendency of Marxist political economy reasons in terms of (a) how productive property is owned and (b) how resources and products are distributed socially. Not only does this tendency include such major figures of twentieth-century Marxist political economy as Maurice Dobb, Paul Sweezy, Paul Baran and Ernest Mandel; it also remains alive and well among contemporary Marxist political economists such as John Roemer (1986), Anwar Shaikh (1990) and Andrew Glynn (1990). It also has been the tendency most often endorsed by governments and political parties that have called themselves Marxist (Howard and King 1992).

In this view, capitalism exists when (a) factories, land, money, buildings and so on are privately owned, and (b) individuals exchanging what they privately own in markets is the mode of distributing resources and products. Capitalism is seen here as a "class system" in the sense of a conflict between a propertied and a propertyless class mediated in and by markets. Socialism and communism are then conceived as social arrangements in which productive property is collectively (i.e. socially) owned by everyone (hence classes of propertied versus propertyless disappear), and in which resources and products are distributed by planned allocations rather than through markets. Within this tendency, "socialists" and "communists" debate how far to go and how fast in collectivizing property, in having a centralized state act as agent for the collectivity, in replacing markets with planning and, in Marx's dramatic phrase, replacing labor with need as the basis for distributing products.

This kind of Marxist political economy focuses on PROPERTY (who owns what) and ECONOMIC POWER (who decides the disposition of resources and products: individuals and enterprises in markets or state officials through planning and administration). These aspects of what Marx called a society's "relations of production" comprise this Marxist political economy's ENTRY POINT into analyzing society, and it also constructs its concrete analyses on that basis. Its proponents also seek to demonstrate that the injustices, inefficiencies and crises of capitalist systems flow ultimately from their private property and market systems. They likewise argue the superiority of socialism and/or communism to be essentially determined by their collective property and planning.

With property and economic power as its entry points, this kind of Marxist political economy uses a deterministic logic to reduce virtually every other aspect of society to effects of the economy understood as basically its particular arrangements of property and economic power. Such an economic determinism makes a society's politics and culture merely the effects of property and economic power (or, in a slightly weaker formulation, the economy is made "more" determinant of politics and culture than they are of it). When pushed to explain how and why particular regimes of property plus economic power over distribution arise, such Marxist political economists sometimes refer to developments in TECHNOLOGY (Marx's "forces of production") as ultimate cause.

Powerful political movements (for example, the Second, Third and Fourth Internationals) more or less "officially" endorsed variants of this version of Marxist political economy, in part because it captured the spirit and imagination of all sorts of anti-capitalist aspirations and movements. It became the prevalent, orthodox interpretation over the twentieth century. However, as those movements changed or disappeared, other versions of Marxist political economy – always present and active – challenged that orthodoxy. Marxist political economy is now a matter of increasingly equal and divergent schools.

## Power-theoretic school

One unorthodox variation of Marxist political economy makes power its "entry point" into social analysis, rather than property and distribution (market versus planning) systems. Its central concern is how power – political and cultural as well as economic – is distributed socially. Who rules and who is ruled – who gives and who takes orders – is far more important than who owns and how things get distributed. Classes are then differently defined, not in terms of property but rather in terms of who does and does not wield authority. Marxist political economists such as Charles Bettelheim (1976–8) and Michel Aglietta (1976) seem to hold these views.

This kind of Marxist political economy criticizes capitalism because its structure and operations are fundamentally based upon and reproduce unequal distributions of power (see ECONOMIC POWER). The power to control workers in production coincides with the power to control citizens in the polity, to set cultural priorities and practices, and much else. Hierarchies rather than democratic distributions of power everywhere characterize capitalisms. In contrast, democratic power distributions are made central to socialisms and communisms. Marxists endorsing this kind of Marxist political economy have often called themselves democratic socialists or social democrats to underscore their primary concern with power distributions (rather than distributions of resource and product ownerships).

This power-theoretic school of Marxist political economy does, however, share the orthodoxy's commitment to deterministic logic. Both schools seek to explain capitalism's injustices, inefficiencies and crises as ultimately reducible to their respective entry points. Thus, the power-theoretic Marxists believe that redistributing political power in democratic directions is *the* way fundamentally to undermine capitalism and construct socialism or communism. In contrast, the property-theoretic Marxists believe that redistributing property in the means of production – from private to social or collective ownership – and substituting planning for markets are the strategic priorities to the same ends.

The USSR, from 1917 to its demise in the 1980s, provoked confrontations between the property-theoretic and power-theoretic schools of Marxist political economy (Howard and King 1992). The former celebrated the USSR's achievement as socialism (because property had been collectivized and markets suppressed in favor of planning). The power theoretic Marxist political economy countered by denouncing the USSR as a deformed socialism, an undemocratic socialism, or no real socialism at all. For them, precisely because power remained unequally distributed inside the USSR (for example, monopolized by the Communist Party), its claim to have achieved socialism was bogus. In these debates, "communists" often came to mean mainly those Marxists whose entry points were property and modes of distribution, while "socialists" were those whose entry point was the distribution of power. Of course, communists were also concerned with power and socialists with property and distribution systems, but what distinguished them were the analytical and political primacy they accorded their different entry points.

## Hybrid formulations

Marxism's expansion across the twentieth century produced many hybrid formulations of Marxist political economy. These hybrids combined various aspects of the property and power theoretic alternatives, often under the heading of "relations of production" (see Resnick and Wolff 1987). Taken together, the property, power and hybrid formulations shared a commitment to determinism in their social theory. They tended to presume, as unproblematic, that analysis entailed (1) finding the ultimately determining factors, and (2) showing how they determine the ways in which economies and societies function and change. Their disagreement centered on what those factors were.

Moreover, they argued over which kind of Marxist political economy best grasped the actual workings – "laws of motion" – of economic systems. In these arguments, Marxist political economists participated in the kind of thinking called "modernism." For modernists, social analysis entails the search for a single truth of "the world out there." Science is this search for truth which human beings progressively approximate as they hypothesize, test and distinguish truth from falsity. Modernists likewise presume that the complexity of any society's structure and change can be "understood" by finding the simplicity lying beneath the surface and governing that complexity. In other words, modernists presume that some ultimately determining factors can be located and shown to give shape, direction and purpose to the initially daunting complexity of any society.

The Marxist political economies discussed above did not originate modernist modes of thinking. Others, rarely critics of capitalism, deserve the credit for modernism. But many Marxist political economists replicated modernist ways of thinking. Such Marxists rarely asked whether modernist ways of thinking might function, alongside other ways of thinking typical of capitalist societies, to support capitalism and oppose the rise of anti-capitalist ideas and social movements. Thus, much of the now century-old debate between pro-capitalist political economies and their Marxist adversaries has occurred on the shared terrain of modernism as if that terrain were the only and the necessary basis for all thought and action.

## Postmodern Marxist political economy

However, some Marxist political economists challenged modernism following up on suggestions in that direction by Lenin, Lukacs, Gramsci and Althusser (see Resnick and Wolff 1987: chaps 1–2; and many articles published in *Rethinking Marxism* since 1988). They argued, for example, that there is no one absolute truth about society; there are only alternative ways human beings have found to conceptualize social development. As there is no one "correct" way to dance, pray, eat, love and so on, there is no "correct" way to analyze society. Different ways of thinking – different entry points, different logics – yield different understandings of societies. Theorists either admit the contest of different theories – each with its idea/standard of "truth" – or they refuse and proceed on the absolute basis that one theory is correct and the others false. To admit the irreducible difference of alternative political economies invites questions. Why are some theories believed and others ignored? How do particular theories connect to attitudes toward and movements for change within particular societies? Theorists who reject modernism proceed on the basis that different theories emerge from a society's contradictions to reflect and to shape it in different ways. Proceeding in this non-modernist way, such theorists have acquired the label, "postmodernists" (see MODERNISM AND POSTMODERNISM). Marxists among them have developed a postmodern Marxist political economy.

Postmodern Marxist political economy does more than depart from its modernist precursor on the central presumption about what theories do and what truth(s) is (are). Where modernist Marxists presume and therefore "find" the key essential causes of economic and social events and show how those causes determine those events, postmodern Marxists presume and proceed otherwise. For them, every economic or social event is determined by everything else going on in its environment. Instead of being determined by essential causes, events are overdetermined.

Postmodern Marxist political economy's commitment to overdetermination – as against all determinisms – has significant analytical consequences (see DETERMINISM AND OVERDETERMINATION). No theory can take into account the infinity of factors combining to overdetermine any event chosen for scrutiny. All any theory can do – and all any theory ever did – is to fasten upon a very few overdeterminants of its object and formulate some of their connections to that object. Marxist political economy sees itself and other theories as so many alternative explanations; all are unavoidably partial, different ways of selecting particular factors to connect in particular ways to objects of explanation.

The current most-developed form of postmodern Marxist political economy makes its entry point a particular definition of Marx's concept of class (Callari *et al*. 1994). CLASS, for postmodern Marxist political economy, is that

economic process whereby the people who produce goods and services generate more (a "surplus") than they themselves obtain for their consumption. To inquire into any society's class structure is to uncover how this surplus is produced, who receives it first (who "appropriates" it) and, finally, how these receivers dispose of it. There are different ways (class structures) of producing, appropriating and disposing of such surpluses (feudal, capitalist, communist and so on). Most societies are presumed to include combinations of them in differing proportions and engaged in complex, contradictory interactions with one another. Postmodern Marxist political economy is concerned to analyze the influences that a society's particular class structures exert upon all its non-class dimensions.

Postmodern Marxist political economy's entry points are both causes and effects of its practitioners' concerns to displace certain class structures in favor of others. To be displaced are those defined as exploitative: where the producers of surplus pass it to other persons, not themselves producers, who then dispose of it. The feudal landlords, the industrial capitalists and the slave masters were all exploitative. Postmodern Marxist political economy seeks to contribute to the disappearance of exploitative class structures by identifying where, when and how they exist and interact with their social contexts. Postmodern Marxist political economy likewise seeks to support social transitions to non-exploitative class structures (socialism and communism) by specifying the conditions that can contribute to such transitions. Postmodern Marxist political economy defines communism as the collective production, appropriation, and disposition of the surplus by the producers themselves (Resnick and Wolff 1987).

## Linkages with feminists and environmentalists

The debates among and between modernist and postmodernist Marxist political economy depend not only on their differing concepts and arguments. They are overdetermined also by the non- and anti-Marxist political economies that contest with them and by all the non-theoretical aspects of social life. Recent trends in non-Marxist political economy deserve some explicit mention in this regard. Feminist and environmentalist political economies present yet other entry points into economic and social analysis, different from the various class entry points of both modernist and postmodernist Marxist political economy. Feminist entry points are GENDER and gender differentiations, while environmentalists make the transformations (usually destructive) of nature their entry points. Such political economies are complexly influenced by both Marxist and anti-Marxist political economies. Differences within feminist and environmentalist political economies emerge much as they did within all other political economies. However, nearly all Marxist political economies have recently sought bridges to and alliances with feminist, environmentalist and other trends of POLITICAL ECONOMY.

## Conclusion

Marxist political economies today find themselves in a remarkable situation. The range of differences and debates among them is now wider and more lively than it has been for years. Interactions among them and with non-Marxist political economies are yielding fruitful new insights and research programs and attracting a new generation. At the same time, the demise of the USSR and many of its allies facilitated a sharp decline in the adherents of orthodox Marxist political economy. As capitalisms everywhere shed their welfare state masks and return to the rapaciousness of the nineteenth century, their victims recommence the search for explanations of and alternatives to capitalism. In this environment, the prognoses for Marxist political economies are rather upbeat.

## See also:

environmental and ecological political economy: major contemporary themes; feminist political economy: major contemporary themes; Marxist political economy: history

## Selected references

Aglietta, Michel (1976) *A Theory of Capitalist Regulation*, London: New Left Books, 1979.
Bettelheim, Charles (1976–8) *Class Struggles in the USSR*, 2 vols, Brighton: Harvester.
Callari, Antonio, Cullenberg, Stephen and Biewener, Carole (eds) (1994) *Marxism in the Postmodern Age*, New York: Guilford Publications.
Fraad, Harriet, Resnick, Stephen and Wolff, Richard (1994) *Bringing It All Back Home: Class, Gender and Power in the Modern Household*, London: Pluto Press.
Glynn, Andrew (1990) "Contradictions of Capitalism," in John Eatwell, Murray Milgate and Peter Newman (eds), *The New Palgrave: Marxian Economics*, London: Macmillan.
Howard, M.C. and King, J.E. (1992) *A History of Marxian Economics: 1929–1990*, Princeton, NJ: Princeton University Press.
Resnick, Stephen and Wolff, Richard (1987) *Knowledge and Class: A Marxist Critique of Political Economy*, Chicago: University of Chicago Press.
Roemer, John (ed.) (1986) *Analytical Marxism*, New York: Cambridge University Press.
Shaikh, Anwar (1990) "Capital as a Social Relation," in John Eatwell, Murray Milgate and Peter Newman (eds), *The New Palgrave: Marxian Economics*, London: Macmillan.

RICHARD D. WOLFF

# Marxist political economy: relationship to other schools

## Commonalities

Marxist political economy shares many of the concerns and objectives of the other "post-classical" schools of POLITICAL ECONOMY, identified by Lavoie (1992) (among them the post-Keynesian, radical institutionalist, Kaleckian, feminist and radical). All post-classical schools attribute an important analytical role to CLASS and emphasize the production of wealth instead of the allocation of existing resources. They argue that CAPITALISM is crisis prone, generates UNEVEN DEVELOPMENT, reproduces INEQUALITY, and tends to create poverty and ALIENATION. They defend the rights of women, minorities and the poor, and wish to preserve some degree of state intervention in the economy as a potential platform for popular pressure against capital.

The alternatives to capitalism advocated by Marxist political economy and by the other schools of political economy also have much in common, at least in the short run. (For a theoretical critique of capitalism and an ingenious democratic political program for the left, see Sherman (1995).) In the long run, however, important differences exist because no other school of political economy shares Marxist political economy's uncompromising critique of capitalism, and its rejection of wage labor as the basis of economic exploitation.

## Differences

Methodologically, important differences exist between Marxist political economy and the other post-classical schools, in spite of broad agreement on the importance of realism, a HOLISTIC METHOD and procedural rationality. In their more abstract works, Marxist writers generally try to emulate Marx's systematic dialectic analysis in the first chapters of *Das Kapital*. Among other things, this rules out the intervention of individuals, except as representatives of broader economic categories. This systematic DIALECTICAL METHOD stands in sharp contrast to the approaches followed by neoclassical economics and the other post-classical schools.

In his work, Marx uses dialectics to identify the most important features of the subset of real relations being analyzed, and their internal CONTRADICTIONS, as the means to understanding the sources and limits of their dynamics. He does this through (a) the development of the contradictions within and between concepts, (b) the incorporation of historically specific material when this is warranted, and (c) the distinction between concepts belonging to different levels of abstraction, which should not be conflated. This method implies that theories are unable to capture reality immediately and should proceed in stages that correspond to the level of abstraction of the concepts employed. It also implies that the explanatory power of each concept depends on its level of abstraction. Relatively abstract concepts such as value capture essential aspects of capitalism, but may not be easily grasped empirically. In contrast, relatively concrete concepts such as profit are easier to grasp empirically, but lack explanatory power; they must be explained by recourse to more abstract concepts (see MARX'S METHODOLOGY OF POLITICAL ECONOMY).

## Problems with other schools

From this perspective, the neoclassical school tends to be criticized for being empiricist, and for its methodological individualism (see NEOCLASSICAL ECONOMICS: CRITIQUE). Marxist writers often extend criticisms to other schools of political economy. In particular, it has been argued they some of the latter are "middle-range theories" and that, like neoclassical economics, they often conflate the levels of abstraction involved in their analyses. Middle-range theories such as radical political economy and feminist political economy are located between grand theories (such as neoclassical economics, and Marxist political economy) and working hypotheses, and derive their concepts from immediate generalizations from reality. This makes radical political economy's work on, for example, SEGMENTED AND DUAL LABOR MARKETS, intuitively clear and appealing to writers of different persuasions. However, because of its imprecise connection with broader theories, radical political economy's findings often lack conceptual content and may border on the tautological (Sayer 1995).

Feminist political economy has made considerable advances, for instance, in the analysis of PATRIARCHY and the unveiling of male bias in economic theory and policy (Hartmann 1979). However, it has been criticized by Marxists for its eclecticism and emphasis on a structured narrative or description of female oppression, rather than on its explanation (Fine 1992). Similar arguments have been made against RADICAL INSTITUTIONALISM. In spite of their theoretical and political affinity with Marxism (see Dugger 1989; Stanfield 1995) and the fairness and clarity of Veblen's (1906) critique of Marx, radical institutionalist analyses have been criticized by Marxists for their lack of focus and of a distinctive theory of value.

Marxist political economy's critique of post-Keynesianism, Kaleckianism and Sraffianism is based on their alleged methodological insufficiencies. This can be seen in two different ways. It can be seen, first, in their lack of recognition of the primacy of production and, consequently, the use of concepts of circulation or distribution, such as in monopoly power or endogenous money and credit, as organizing principles. Second, it can be seen in the inconsistent use of social categories as being simultaneously representative of social relations and as aggregated individual relations.

For example, Sraffians construct economy-wide price equations from the aggregation of individual agents in competition. In contrast, in their analysis of distribution the wage and profit rates are formed through the clash between workers and capitalists as classes (Fine 1980). Post-Keynesian and Kaleckian analyses have similar shortcomings. They often consider the level of aggregate demand the primary object of analysis, and argue that it is determined by the level of social variables such as wages and profits. However, wages and profits are ultimately determined by aggregation over individual choices, which denies the operational meaning of CLASS. In contrast, Marxist political economy starts from the relationship between labor and capital at the point of production. This leads to the derivation of class conflict from the capitalist monopoly of the means of production and the institution of wage labor. Individuals enter

this picture primarily as personifications of class relations, and classes retain their principal role throughout the analysis.

## Critique of Marxist political economy

Marxist political economy has been criticized, especially by some Sraffians, for its reliance on the allegedly metaphysical and redundant concept of value, and for internal inconsistency as revealed by the transformation problem. In response, Marxist writers argue that the unwillingness of Sraffians (and others) to admit the validity of concepts such as value derive from their rejection of Marx's method. Other schools have criticized Marxist political economy heavily for its dogmatic defense of Marx's writings, and for the methodological inflexibility which can make it difficult to incorporate new material into the theory (for example, the oppression of women by men).

## Post-classical research program

In spite of these (sometimes acrimonious) disputes, there is much scope for the further development of the post-classical research program. In their work, each school of political economy has tended to prioritize a different aspect of the economy. For example, Marxists have written extensively about the social impact of changes in technologies and work practices. Post-Keynesians and institutionalists have done much work on the dynamic nature of capitalism and the role of social conventions and institutions. Sraffians highlight the logical shortcomings of neoclassical economics. Kaleckians emphasize the need for realism in economics. Radicals and feminists deplore the ahistorical and asocial character of mainstream analyses, quite apart from pursuing their own positive research agendas. This can obviously lead to much cross-fertilization, for instance, in the theories of money and credit, business cycles and financial crises, the exploitation of specific social groups such as workers or people of 'color' (see Lippitt 1996; Sherman 1991), and to the further development of a cogent challenge to neoclassical economics.

## Conclusion

In sum, differences between economic theories are often due to the distinct methodological and political perspectives of their proponents, and to the diverse causal structures employed, which are partly a reflection of the way in which individual and social categories are combined in each of them. The clashes between them indicate the extent to which such differences are allowed to dominate, and prevent constructive dialogue.

## See also:

feminist political economy: major contemporary themes; institutional political economy; Kalecki, Michal; political economy: schools; post-Keynesian political economy: major contemporary themes; Sraffian political economy

## Selected references

Dugger, W. (1989) *Radical Institutionalism: Contemporary Voices,* New York: Greenwood Press.

Fine, B. (1980) *Economic Theory and Ideology*, London: Edward Arnold.

—— (1992) *Women's Work and the Capitalist Family*, London: Routledge.

Hartmann, H. (1979) "The Unhappy Marriage of Marxism and Feminism: Towards a More Progressive Union," *Capital and Class*, Summer: 1–33.

Lavoie, Marc (1992) *Foundations of Post-Keynesian Economic Analysis*, Aldershot: Edward Elgar.

Lippit, V. (1996) *Radical Political Economy*, Armonk, NY: M.E. Sharpe.

O'Hara, Phillip Anthony (1997) "Veblen's Critique of Marx's Philosophical Preconceptions of Political Economy," *The European Journal of the History of Economic Thought* 4: 65–91.

Sayer, Andrew (1995) *Radical Political Economy: A Critique*, London: Blackwell.

Sherman, H. (1991) *The Business Cycle: Growth and Crisis under Capitalism*, Princeton, NJ: Princeton University Press.

—— (1995) *Reinventing Marxism*, Baltimore, MD: Johns Hopkins University Press.

Stanfield, J. R. (1995) *Economics, Power and Culture: Essays in the Development of Radical Institutionalism*, Basingstoke: Macmillan.

Veblen, T. (1906) "The Socialist Economics of Karl Marx and His Followers: 1. The Theories of Karl Marx" *Quarterly Journal of Economics* 20: 575–95.

ALFREDO SAAD FILHO

# medieval Arab-Islamic economic thought

In 1964, the late Joseph Spengler, writing on the economic thought of Ibn Khaldun 1332–1404, noted that "one is compelled to infer that [in Muslim scholarship]...knowledge of economic behavior was very great indeed" (Spengler 1964: 304). Unfortunately, however, the late Joseph SCHUMPETER created a blind spot by labeling the centuries between the Greeks and St Thomas Aquinas (AD 1225–74), broadly between the ninth and fourteenth centuries AD, as "blank," in that nothing of relevance to economics was supposedly written anywhere. However, during this period, numerous Arab-Islamic scholastics wrote voluminously on philosophical and theological issues, including economics, and their writings influenced various dimensions of Latin European scholarship. Some prominent names are al-Farabi (Alfarabus, 870–950, Ibn Sina (Avicenna, 980–1033), al-Ghazali (Algazal, 1058–1111), Ibn Rushd (Averroes, 1126–98), Ibn Taimiyah (1263–1328).

## Social welfare and wealth

An overriding theme throughout their works is the concept of *masalah*, or social welfare (the common good). Guided by the Scriptures, all human affairs, economic and others, are viewed in terms of *masalih* (utilities) and *mafasid* (disutilities). Pursuit of economic activities is not merely desirable, but imperative for salvation, tantamount to worship and "calling" (al-Ghazali 2: 60, 83). There is no distinction between the sacred and the secular: both spheres are essential for salvation. Socio-economic progress is to be pursued as divinely ordained, obligatory duties; if these duties are unfulfilled, worldly life would collapse and humanity would perish (al-Ghazali 2: 32). Further, these scholars recognize acquisitive, wealth accumulation tendencies as normal, though greed is condemned (al-Ghazali 3: 234). Wealth is viewed as the "greatest test" (al-Ghazali 3: 51). There is little sympathy for those who choose to be poor or attribute their misfortunes to the "will of God" (al-Ghazali 4: 265). The following themes are especially important in these writings.

## Voluntary exchange and the evolution of markets

Given the emphasis on individual economic pursuits and socioeconomic welfare, the evolution of MARKETS is viewed as being part of the "natural order," an expression of self-motivated desires to engage in voluntary exchange. Thus:

> farmers live where farming tools are not available. Blacksmiths and carpenters live where farmers are lacking. Naturally, they want to satisfy needs by giving up in exchange part of what they possess. Farmers bring produce to markets and anything unsold or unexchanged is sold at a lower price to traders who store the produce and sell at a profit. True for all kinds of goods. The motive is profit.
>
> (al-Ghazali 3: 227)

And, "to force people to sell something that is not obligatory to sell or to restrict them from selling permissible objects is unjust and unlawful" (Ibn Taimiyah 1976: 25). Moreover, "If desires for goods increase while supply decreases, price rises. But if supply increases and desire decreases, price declines" (Ibn Taimiyah 1968, 8: 583).

Clearly, free market demand–supply interactions are suggested, though not couched in modern terms. There are references to "prevailing prices, as determined by market practices," a concept named as "just price" by some Islamic and Latin scholastics, and even "equilibrium" price by others. However, excessive profits must not result from fraud; sellers must be guided by benevolence and "profit" in the Hereafter (al-Ghazali 2: 75–6, 79, 84). Indeed, these scholars, like St Thomas Aquinas a century later, discuss "ethics of market behavior."

## Production activities

These authors discuss production activities in terms of their social importance. The production of necessities is especially viewed as being socially obligatory (al-Ghazali 2: 83). Al-Ghazali particularly discusses a tripartite classification, similar to contemporary discussions, differentiating between (1) basic industries (food, clothing, shelter), (2) ancillary industries (adjuncts to others, such as iron, minerals, forests), and (3) complementary activities (bakers, millers and so on). While the first group is most important, all three must be promoted as socially obligatory duties. "If people abandon them, they could not survive... and God has blessed people with skills for different occupations" (al-Ghazali 2: 83). Al-Ghazali discusses stages of production, specialization and DIVISION OF LABOR, including vertically structured production from the farmer to the miller to the baker. Seven centuries before Adam Smith's example of the pin factory, al-Ghazali uses the example of a needle in discussing specialization and division of labor (al-Ghazali 4: 119).

## Money, counterfeit and interest

Among the numerous medieval Islamic scholastics, al-Ghazali and Ibn Taimiyah discuss the problems of barter and the evolution of money in some detail:

> Sometimes people need what they do not own and own what they do not need. For example, a person has saffron but needs a

camel and one who owns a camel wants saffron. However, there must be a measure of the two in exchange; the camel-owner cannot give whole camel for a quantity of saffron – there is no direct proportionality. Such barter transactions will be cumbersome. A medium is needed to determine their value in exchange. When their grades are ascertained, one can determine equality between the two. A camel may equal 100 dinars and a quantity of saffron worth 100 dinars, so the two quantities are equal to each other, and each equal to 100 dinars. But dirhams and dinars are not needed for themselves. They are created to change hands and establish rules for exchange with justice and for buying goods which have utility. Money as such has no particular form or feature of its own – like a mirror has no color but reflects all colors.

(al-Ghazali 4: 91–3)

Obviously, these scholars are aware of the "barter problems."

Counterfeiting and currency debasement are condemned by these scholastics. Such money "is worse than stealing a thousand dirhams" (al-Ghazali 2: 73). Ibn Taimiyah offers similar insights. Both anticipate the French scholar, Nicholas Oresme (1328–82), who is often credited with what later became known as "Gresham's Law," that "bad money drives out good money."

For medieval Islamic scholastics, as for Jewish and Christian scholastics, the prohibition of interest is absolute, as per the Scriptures. Charging interest on borrowing–lending transactions can lead to injustice and exploitation and deflects money from its key function, which, as with the Latin scholastics, consists in measuring the utility of objects in exchange. Money itself is "sterile," and "is not created to earn money, and doing so is a transgression" (al-Ghazali 4: 192).

## The role of the state

Islamic scholastics consider the state to be a necessary institution, for the proper function-

ing of society's economic affairs and for the fulfillment of divinely-ordained social obligations: "The state and religion are inseparable pillars of an orderly society. Religion is the foundation.... If either pillar is weak, society will crumble" (al-Ghazali 1: 17). The state evolves because "man's ability to fulfill his needs persuades him to live in a civilized society with cooperation; but human tendencies like jealousy, competition, and selfishness can create conflicts. Thus, collective arrangement becomes necessary to check those tendencies" (al-Ghazali 2: 13).

These writers generally discuss state functions along lines usually attributed to classical economists. In order to promote economic prosperity, the state must establish JUSTICE, peace, security and stability. "Where injustice and oppression are present, the people have no foothold;...the state falls into decay, the public revenues diminish...and prosperity fade[s] among the people" (Bagley 1964: 56, quoting al-Ghazali). Within the free market framework, an unbridled "invisible hand" is not advocated; circumstances such as market imperfections, emergencies and the promotion of social welfare may warrant state intervention (Ibn Taimiyah 1976: 256).

With respect to public finances, these authors discuss various revenue sources, such as taxes and public borrowing, including concern for equity, behavioral effects such as incentives/disincentives, and administration and compliance. Public expenditures should extend to functions such as the promotion of socioeconomic justice, the elimination of poverty and provision of socioeconomic infrastructure for economic development (al-Ghazali 2: 130).

An important public institution that is discussed by numerous early Islamic scholars is al-Hisbah, which is entrusted to a public official known as a *muhtasib* (the equivalent of a grand ombudsman). As an antecedent of contemporary anti-trust/regulatory institutions, al-Hisbah's function, comprehensively defined: "was to check harmful market practices, to promote what is good and forbid what is evil, particularly in those areas where the authority of other public officials could not reach" (Ibn Taimiyah 1976: 18).

## See also:

Islamic political economy

## Selected references

Bagley, F.R. (ed. and trans.) (1964) *Al-Ghazali's Nasihat al-Maluk* (Al-Ghazali's Book of Counsel for Rulers), New York: Oxford University Press.

al-Ghazali, Abu Hamid (n.d.) *Ihya Ulum al-Din* (Revival of the Religious Sciences), 4 vols, Beirut: Dar al-Nadwah.

Ghazanfar, S.M. (1991) "Scholastic Economics and Arab Scholars: The Great Gap Thesis Reconsidered," *Diogenes: International Review of Humane Sciences*, April–June.

Ghazanfar, S.M. and Islahi, A. Azim (1990) "Economic Thought of an Arab Scholastic: Abu Hamid Al-Ghazali (AD 1058–1111)," *History of Political Economy*, Fall.

—— (1992) "Explorations in Medieval Arab-Islamic Economic Thought: Some Aspects of Ibn Taimiyah's Economics," in S. Todd Lowry (ed.), *Perspectives on the History of Economic Thought*, Aldershot: Edward Elgar.

Ibn Taimiyah (1968) *Majmu' Fatawa*, 35 vols, Riyad: Matabi al-Riyad, AH 1381–7.

—— (1976) *Al-Hisbah fi'l Islam* (Public Duties in Islam), ed. Salah Azzam, Cairo: Dar al-Sha'ab.

Schumpeter, Joseph (1994) *History of Economic Analysis*, Oxford and New York: Oxford University Press.

Spengler, Joseph (1964) "Economic Thought of Islam: Ibn Khaldun," *Contemporary Studies in Society and History*.

S.M. GHAZANFAR

# mercantilism

The nature and merits of "mercantilism" have provoked one of the most significant debates in the history of economic thought. It is typically treated as a body of economic thought, but the label also encompasses a system of politico-economic practices. The relevant period is that of Western Europe, roughly between 1500 and 1800. The label itself is a belated product of nineteenth-century German interpreters.

## Nature of mercantilism

"Mercantilism" can be reasonably interpreted as the philosophy and practice of national economic power. It has been simply expressed as the symbiosis of "wealth" and "power," that is, wealth in the service of national power and vice versa. The era was one of contemporaneous nation building and expansion in commerce and industry. The two motifs are distinct but indissoluble. The common ground reflected the pragmatic alliance of monarch and commercial interests against their foreign counterparts, and against the old landed interest and urban guilds.

The culture of mercantilism is complex, as befits an age in transition. The age gives birth to the "rationalist" spirit, succoring secular and scientific thought. Mercantilist culture is also "corporatist," spawning attempts to reconstruct the socially unifying elements of feudalism and Catholicism in a secular and "individualist" age (Williams 1961).

Mercantilist practices reflect a long struggle for social coherence and stability, given dynastic conflict and economic transformation. Economic crises had a profound impact on the contemporary mind. Here was a premonition of the crisis-prone character of a system increasingly organized on capitalist principles. In England, the 1550s, the 1620s and the 1690s were crisis-prone periods evoking responses aimed at short-term stabilization and at longer term solutions.

In sixteenth-century France, a relatively advanced economy was set back by twenty-five years of civil and religious strife after 1570. Mercantilism took off in seventeenth-century France which, at first admiring of Spain, then looked to the commercial success of the Dutch and the English for models "to catch up." French mercantilism reached its zenith in the administration of Jean-Baptiste Colbert, financial controller under Louis XIV from 1661 to his death in 1683.

## Mercantilist regimes and practices

Mercantilist regimes are associated with a self-conscious support of an indigenous manufacturing capacity. The fostering of a woolen textile industry in England exemplifies this ambition. More broadly, mercantilist regimes emphasized a balanced economy – hence the importance of colonies, for commodities unattainable at home. A viable agriculture was seen as important, both for social stability and for military provisioning. Military provisioning also led to an emphasis on shipping (and materials like lumber) and fisheries.

Mercantilist practices underwent much evolution, especially in England. There was an early preoccupation with the retention of bullion, including legislation to impede its export. Bullion was deemed necessary for the commutation of feudal dues, and for lubricating the rapid rise in commerce. Moreover, England, being without mines, necessarily fed its needs from abroad. This was an age of monarchical ascendancy, and "bullionism" was functional to England's needs for enhanced power (Beer 1938). Ethics remained predominantly mediaeval, antagonistic to commercial imperatives. There was much regulation of domestic trade and of employment conditions.

The seventeenth century witnessed significant changes, with the gradual shift in the balance of power from the Crown to commercial interests, as well as rising conflict between the commercial interests themselves. These conflicts generated a language of "free trade" and "natural liberty," but this was the rhetoric of specific interests and did not reflect the values of a later age. The preoccupation with bullion declined, partly because of an improved institutional framework of credit and finance. Regulation gradually took on a more "modern" character (Lipson 1931). The granting of monopoly charters and guild regulations fell away, freeing up domestic trade. For revenue purposes, the Crown relied increasingly on customs duties. Behind these customs duties a formidable apparatus of protection was belatedly established (Davis 1966).

## Gradual decline of mercantilism

The protectionist components of British mercantilism were gradually dismantled during the nineteenth century. Argument from ascendant liberalist principles played a part. Centuries of war had generated an impasse, more from exhaustion than from enlightenment as to its futility. The loss of the American colonies forced a more flexible approach to the white settler colonies. More fundamentally, England was by then the dominant economic and military power; "mercantilist" aims could thus be achieved by more formally enlightened means, ushering in an era of "free trade imperialism."

Other countries did not generally follow Britain's example. France moved in a similar direction during the Second Empire (1852–70), afterwards renouncing that tendency. Elsewhere a second generation of industrializing powers – the USA, Germany and Japan – looked more to the practices prevalent in Britain's industrial ascent rather than those in its supremacy.

## Scholarly interpretations

Mercantilism remains an elusive subject, with succeeding generations of scholars interpreting the period in the light of their own conceptual frameworks and philosophical predispositions (Wilson 1957). Members of the nineteenth-century HISTORICAL SCHOOL, for instance, emphasized the systemic character of mercantilism, with an ideological sympathy for their subject.

Eli Heckscher (1931) and Jacob Viner (1937, 1968) are the touchstones of twentieth-century interpretation. Both approached mercantilism from a classical/neoclassical analytical perspective and from an ideological perspective centered on free trade. Adam Smith is their spiritual father. Mercantilist thought is judged as unethical, a system oriented toward the special interests of the mercantile class. It has also been judged as pre-scientific; arguments for a surplus on trade neglected the presumed equilibrating tendencies of trade, as later articulated in the "specie-flow mechanism."

Within the orthodox tradition, a crude interpretation has often reigned. Mercantilism is viewed as the association of national wealth with the accumulation of bullion. This view has always lacked credibility, as the mercantilist emphasis on bullion was instrumental toward more tangible ends.

A more plausible center of gravity for mercantilism is an emphasis on the balance of trade (more accurately, "overbalancing" exports). A trade surplus was consistently seen as a vehicle for domestic development. However, the explanation for this process changed over the seventeenth century, from an emphasis on the inflow of bullion to a "foreign-paid incomes" doctrine. Here, the "export of work" (especially through value-added goods) would ensure that foreigners essentially underwrote a country's economic development (Magnusson 1994). The underlying view of trade remained essentially a "beggar-thy-neighbor" phenomenon. It is this conflictual emphasis and strategic orientation that has led political scientists to coin the expression "neo-mercantilism" for what they interpret as the reproduction of mercantilist practices in recent history.

The condemnation of mercantilism within orthodox economics has led to academic neglect of the subject. This neglect is reflected in popular usage, in which mercantilism is crudely associated with protectionist policies, and thus with any divergence from a "free trade" ideal.

## A revival of interest?

Interest in mercantilism may be undergoing a revival (Magnusson 1994). Magnusson argues for an internal dynamic of mercantilist thought, not strictly driven by objective changes. He claims a broad range of mercantilist opinion, but argues for an overall coherence, based on a common acceptance of the wealth/power nexus. Magnusson claims that this robust discourse produced a technical vocabulary which gave birth to modern economics. He neglects mercantilist practice, but his work has restored legitimacy to the study of mercantilism.

## See also:

classical political economy; free trade and protection; trade policy

## Selected references

Beer, M. (1938) *Early British Economics*, London: Allen & Unwin.

Blaug, Mark (1991) *Pioneers in Economics*, vol. 4, *The Early Mercantilists*, and vol. 5, *The Later Mercantilists*, Aldershot: Edward Elgar.

Davis, Ralph (1966) "The Rise of Protection in England, 1689–1786," *Economic History Review* 19(2): 306–17; repr. in Blaug (1991).

Heckscher, Eli F. (1931) *Mercantilism*, 2 vols, London: Allen & Unwin, 1955.

Lipson, E. (1931) *The Economic History of England*, vols II– III, *The Age of Mercantilism*, London: Adam & Charles Black, 1956.

Magnusson, Lars (1994) *Mercantilism: The Shaping of an Economic Language*, London: Routledge.

Viner, Jacob (1937) *Studies in the Theory of International Trade*, London: Allen & Unwin.

—— (1968) "Mercantilist Thought," *International Encyclopedia of the Social Sciences*, New York: Macmillan and the Free Press.

Williams, W.A. (1961) *The Contours of American History*, Cleveland: World Publishing Co.

Wilson, Charles (1957) "Mercantilism: Some Vicissitudes of an Idea," *Economic History Review* 10(2): 181–8; repr. in Blaug (1991).

EVAN JONES

# methodological individualism and collectivism

## Methodological individualism

Methodological individualism is a doctrine that builds upon the intuition that the ultimate constituents of the social world are individuals, and that social events are brought about by particular people (Watkins 1973b). It has been advanced as an ontological thesis concerning the nature of social objects and properties, a semantic thesis concerning the meaning of social concepts, and an explanatory thesis concerning legitimate explanation in the social sciences. In one or more of these guises, it can been be traced through the ancient Greeks, Thomas Hobbes and, importantly, the later writings of Max Weber.

In its most coherent and important form, methodological individualism can be taken as the explanatory thesis that all explanations of the structure and change of the phenomena that form the object of social science investigation are to be conducted solely in terms of the intentions, beliefs, goals, and actions of various individuals (Elster 1986). The main controversies generated by advocates of methodological individualism have centered on the attacks on "collectivism," understood as the doctrine that there are supra-individual entities that are prior to the individual in the explanatory order.

This "collectivism" or "methodological holism" (Watkins 1973b) is closely associated with structural or functional forms of explanation. Advocates of methodological individualism argue against claims such as, for instance, that the state (a supra-individual entity) has the function of acting in the interests of the bourgeoisie, or that the structures of capitalism are such that individuals are determined to act in certain ways. To this end, Hayek (1955) and Popper (1957) argued against the "fallacy" of treating social predicates as referring to entities rather than treating them as components of models or theoretical constructs. It was argued that if social predicates such as "capitalism" were taken as "given objects" (Hayek), then social scientists would be tempted to discern the various "laws" governing these objects. Hayek and Popper both appear to be committed to the ontological version of methodological individualism, where only individuals are taken as real. In its extreme form, individuals are regarded atomistically, thus denying any genuine explanatory power to relations between individuals (e.g. "is more powerful than").

The relationship between methodological individualism and economics is somewhat complex. Although most Austrian economists have advocated methodological individualism, Hayek himself seems to reject it in his later work, arguing that societies are composed of rules which have certain functions (see Austrian school of political economy). Many proponents of methodological individualism regard it as a critique of Marxism, especially Marxist political economy, yet this has not prevented authors such as Elster and Roemer attempting to interpret Marx in terms of methodological individualism. However, opponents have objected that the individualistic basis of methodological individualism necessarily contradicts certain key Marxist ideas. It is worth noting that, although Elster and Roemer utilize rational choice theory, this is not necessarily implied by a commitment to methodological individualism.

At first sight, the apparent compatibility between methodological individualism and rational choice theory, coupled with recent attempts to provide a micro-foundation for macroeconomics, appear to suggest strong affinities between methodological individualism and neoclassical economics. However, as Kenneth Arrow has noted, although neoclassical economics does appear to agree that all explanations must refer to the actions of individuals, "every economic model one can think of includes irreducible social principles and concepts" (1994: 2). Arrow is not only referring to the frequent reference to households, firms, corporations and so on in economic models, but is arguing that a term such as "technical information" is irreducibly social.

This indicates the main difficulty facing methodological individualism. The majority of advocates favor a reductionist strategy, in which case all theories referring to social entities and events such as classes, nations, churches and so on must in principle be reducible to theories referring only to individuals. This entails that there is a strong connection between social properties and individual properties. Although identity would be the strongest form of connection, this is not necessary as reductionism only requires that instantiations of, say, social and individual properties can be linked by bridging laws, where such laws identify properties from the different theoretical discourses.

The most feasible form of reductionism for methodological individualism is type–type, where a type is a set of individual token objects or events that satisfy some description or share some property. For example, the type "firm" is the set of particular things having the property of being a firm. Consequently, for the reductionist intent of methodological individualism to be successful, instantiations of a certain type sharing some social property must be reducible to instantiations of a certain type sharing some individual property, coupled with suitable bridging laws.

Kincaid (1986) has shown that, according to methodological individualism, individuals exhaust the social world, in the sense that every entity in the social realm is either an individual or sum of individuals. Individuals are also said to determine the social world, in the sense that once all the relevant facts about individuals are set, then so too are all the facts about the social domain. Given this, the social can be said to supervene on the individual, where any two domains exactly alike in terms of the individuals and individual relations comprising them would share the same social properties. This entails that social predicates, taken as standing for properties, are coextensive with individual predicates. Consequently, type–type coextension obtains, and social types can in theory be reduced to individual types, via suitable laws.

## Methodological collectivism

However, the methodological individualism project faces a number of problems. First, there is the problem of multiple realization. This arises because it is logically possible that any social predicate, such as "firm" or "bureaucracy," can be realized by any number of different relations between individuals, in the same way that the predicate "fitness" does not necessarily correspond to any single configuration of physical facts about an organism. Social predicates appear to be multiply realizable, and thus the social does not supervene on the individual: there is no necessary coextension between social and individual predicates. Consequently, given multiple realizability, type–type reduction is not possible, and thus the reductionist strategy does not seem plausible. This is also the case with any token–token reduction: for example, any token bureaucracy persists through structural changes in the individual tokens realizing it.

However, just as each social event is not coextensive with any individual predicate, so individual acts do not uniquely determine their social description. Individual actions may have many social descriptions, depending upon context, which also appears to prevent the required law-like coextensionality of predicates. Individual behavior, even if described in individual terms, is not uniquely correlated with some social description.

For example, in explaining an individual action such as "firing a gun," it can be described in different ways, depending upon the context. Further, in explaining this action, it may be necessary to refer to social roles; for example, being a soldier. This introduces a third problem: even if reductionism were feasible, and coextension could be established, any workable individualistic social theory will, in all likelihood, presuppose social facts. In this context, Ruben (1985) points out that social explanations of the contents of beliefs may be more fundamental then individual beliefs. For example, if an explanation is offered as to why individuals rationally hold the true belief that some societies are matrilineal, it would seem that this must refer to the fact that some societies are matrilineal. In this case, and contra Elster, some "supra-individual entity" (matrilineal society) is explanatory prior to individual belief.

Given these problems, an advocate of methodological individualism may abandon the reductionist claim, arguing that the main concern is with providing explanations of individual, or token, objects or events. Explanation would thus be conducted on a "case by case" basis. However, this would appear to preclude any possibility of asking the forms of questions frequently raised in the social sciences, concerning explanations as to why certain kinds of events occur.

Tuomela (1984) has attempted to answer some of these objections by arguing that (a) other types of reduction are possible besides type–type bridging law reductions, and (b) it is possible for the methodological individualist to be ontologically committed to individuals, and yet be a conceptual holist, thus admitting that there are irreducible social properties. Tuomela thus only advocates a partial reduction of holistic social concepts to individual ones. However, at this stage it remains unclear whether alternative types of reduction are feasible.

## See also:

collective social wealth; community; critical realism; dialectical method; feminist philosophy of science; holistic method; human action and agency; knowledge, information, technology and change; paradigms; social and organizational capital; storytelling and pattern models; value judgments and world views

## Selected references

Arrow, Kenneth J. (1994) "Methodological Individualism and Social Knowledge," *American Economic Review* 84(2): 1–9.

Elster, John (1986) *Making Sense of Marx*, Cambridge: Cambridge University Press.

Hayek, Friedrich von (1955) *The Counter-revolution of Science*, New York: Glencoe Press.

Kincaid, H. (1986) "Reduction, Explanation, and Individualism," *Philosophy of Science* 53: 492–513.

O'Neill, John O. (ed.) (1973) *Modes of Individualism and Collectivism*, London: Heinemann.

Popper, Karl (1957) *The Poverty of Historicism*, London: Routledge & Kegan Paul.

Ruben, David Hillel (1985) *The Metaphysics of the Social World*, London: Routledge & Kegan Paul.

Tuomela, R. (1984) *A Theory of Social Action*, Dordrecht: Riedel.

Watkins, John W. (1973a) "Historical Explanation in the Social Sciences," in John O. O'Neill (ed.), *Modes of Individualism and Collectivism*, London: Heinemann.

—— (1973b) "Methodological Individualism: A Reply," in John O. O'Neill (ed.), *Modes of Individualism and Collectivism*, London: Heinemann.

STEPHEN D. PARSONS

# methodology in economics

## Increased interest in methodology

Recent years have witnessed an increased interest in economic methodology (see Hausman 1994: 1–4). Some argue that this is due to a combination of facts, such as that economies are not performing as well as they used to and the breakdown of the Keynesian–neoclassical synthesis in economics. In a situation in which the population doubts economists and economists doubt themselves, the question arises as to how long irony and cynicism can sustain the economics profession. The hope is that the disillusionment of today's graduate students, tomorrow's elite, may hold a promise for the future. Therefore, space has been created for methodology to point out flaws in current economic theory and directions for future contributions.

Others attribute the mushrooming literature

in economic methodology to theoretical reasons, for instance, the fact that other social sciences are increasingly using economics as a role model. At the same time, economists are starting to subject fundamental claims of modern mainstream economics to stringent psychological testing.

Finally, this growth may be due to new developments in the philosophy of science. In particular, philosophers of science have shown a growing interest in analyzing the actual practice of science and some have turned their attention to economics.

## Questions in methodology

Traditionally, (positivist) philosophers of science have been interested in finding answers to questions such as, what is the best way to go about the study of methodology? Is there a single approach, or a plurality? Is methodology essentially a prescriptive discipline, a descriptive one, or both? What should it be? What is the best response to the perennial problem of theory choice? (See Caldwell 1994: 6–7.) More recently, (growth of knowledge) philosophy of science has taken up questions such as, does (and should) scientific activity take place within a single theoretical framework, or many? Does science change incrementally, or by explosive, discontinuous revolutions? Do terms in different theories share meanings, or are different theories by nature either incommensurable or incomparable? (See Caldwell 1994: 91–3.)

In economic methodology, these issues have been translated into questions such as, what are the goals of economics? In what ways are economic claims established? What methods are employed? What is the conceptual structure of economic theories? How do concepts in economics relate to concepts in the natural sciences? Or, to what extent can economics be united to, or reduced to, physics? Is economics the same kind of science as are the natural sciences, or might the social sciences be a species of science different from that of the natural sciences? Can or ought the social sciences model themselves on the natural sciences? Is the structure of theories and explanations the same? Are the concepts of theories and explanations the same? Are the goals the same? Is it the case that, given human free will, human behavior is intrinsically unpredictable and thus not subject to economic laws? What is the role of social science in guiding conduct? Is this role unproblematic? (See Hausman 1994: 1–28.)

## Problems with the traditional view

According to the traditional philosophical view of science, the criteria by which knowledge claims are to be judged are universal and ahistorical, and the conclusions of science are determined by the natural world rather than by the social world. Recently, this view has come under attack for being beset by grave difficulties. In particular, it has been argued that the principle of the uniformity of nature is best seen, not as an assumption that analysts of science themselves have to make about the natural world, but as a part of scientists' resources for constructing their accounts of that world. The factual content of science should not be treated as a culturally unmediated reflection of a stable external world. Fact and theory, observation and presupposition are interrelated in a complex manner. The empirical conclusions of science must be seen as interpretative constructions, dependent for their meaning upon and limited by the cultural resources available to a particular social group at a particular point in time. Similarly, general criteria for assessing scientific knowledge claims cannot be applied universally, independently of social context, as traditional philosophy of science had previously assumed. These criteria are always open to varied interpretations and are given meaning in terms of particular scientists' specific intellectual commitments, presuppositions and objectives.

"Rational reconstruction" of the world according to some foolproof mechanical procedure is now widely seen as unattainable. It is not that rational argument and justification have been abandoned, but rather that a more modest appraisal is now made of what they can be expected to achieve. Furthermore, not only are philosophers of science context-bound, but the vast majority have limited themselves to discussion with other philosophers. Therefore, what we get is not philosophy of science, but the ideas that philosophers have about each other's ideas about science. Philosophy of science is thus twice-removed from science itself. As a result, the great majority of scientists are almost entirely isolated from trends in orthodox philosophy of science and, if they have any view at all, it is to dismiss it as irrelevant to the practice of science. In their attempt to understand the world, today's scientists hope that by some little understood process of communal reasonableness, their own interpretations of phenomena will converge with those of others.

## Recent developments in methodology

In response, three recent developments may be discerned in philosophy of science. First, there is a trend toward anti-foundationalism, stimulated by the realization that philosophy of science is incapable of providing an a priori "grounding" of scientific knowledge (see FOUNDATIONALISM AND ANTI-FOUNDATION-ALISM). Second, philosophers of science are moving toward naturalism in their attempt to look at actual science – biological, cognitive or social science – for guidance on epistemological and philosophical issues. Third, there is a tendency to think of science in social terms.

Given the lively research in the third area, it deserves further attention (see Pickering 1992). As the influence of the discredited a priori philosophies has faded, science studies scholars have sought to extend and modify their work in order to produce, for the first time, a genuine sociology of scientific knowledge. Starting from the idea that the social dimensions of science must be taken seriously because science is interestingly and constitutively social all the way into its technical core, sociologists of scientific knowledge study science as a complex form of social activity. They argue that there is nothing in the physical world that uniquely determines scientists' conclusions. Instead,

sociologists of scientific knowledge study the actual practice and culture of science, by looking closely at the ways in which scientists construct their accounts of the world and at the ways in which variations in social context influence the formation and acceptance of scientific assertions.

It is interesting to note that some science studies scholars have even turned to economics for insights into the practice and culture of science (see Hands 1997). This has resulted, for example, in analyse of science as a capitalist market economy in which agents are maximizing producers who competitively and greedily pursue their self-interest and discussions of credit and credibility, exchange and trade-off, and opportunism in science. Obviously attempts to develop an economic analysis of economics raise reflexive concerns.

## Current economic methodology

Current economic methodology mirrors these developments in philosophy of science through its move in two separate directions (see Backhouse 1994). First, economic methodologists engage in debates over traditional philosophy of science. This direction includes "postmodernist" arguments against the project of methodology in general, philosophically-based criticism of Popperian methodology, attempts to apply falsificationist methodology to the analysis of economics, attempts to "salvage" something from the Popperian tradition, and defenses of falsificationism. Second, economic methodologists attempt to "recover practice." This direction is followed by RHETORIC and discourse analysis, sociology of scientific knowledge, philosophical analysis of practice and attempts to reform practice.

One very lively field of research in this second area is feminist methodology (see Ferber and Nelson 1993). Issues raised in this field fall into one or more of five categories. First, feminist methodologists analyze the role of women economists. The drawback of this discussion is that it typically does not focus on the pressures constraining women economists. Second, the role of women in economic life has been examined in feminist methodology. The problem with this analysis is that it is frequently based on androcentric standards through its focus on women's contributions to the men's world. Third, some feminist methodologists see women as victims of male dominance in economic life. The pitfall of this discussion is that it creates the false impression that women have only been victims. Fourth, feminist methodologists have argued for a transformed logic of science in general and economics in particular. This critical approach analyzes masculinist ideologies in both the content and the methodologies of economic inquiry. There have been calls for a transformed logic of feminism in feminist methodology. This constructive approach seeks to transform science in general, and economics in particular, for feminist ends.

In addition, economic methodologists have taken up analyses of several special questions. First, what does prediction in economics mean? In particular, economists must circumvent the problem of self-defeating public predictions. Second, what does replication in economics mean? Do we replicate in economics? Based on different definitions of replication, economic methodologists have given several explanations for the lack of replication in economics.

Third, what is so special about econometrics? In particular, economic methodologists have focused on the lack of discussion of probability in econometrics, the problems it faces in justifying the error term, the fact that the hybrid of techniques used in econometrics has only been defended after the fact, the tenuous nature of exogeneity assumptions in solving identification problems, the false idol of objectivity, and the tensions between realism and instrumentalism on the one hand, and determinism and indeterminism on the other hand.

Fourth, can GAME THEORY and/or experimental economics provide an alternative empirical practice? As pointed out by economic methodologists, game theory is not well formulated, employs a babble of solution concepts, is faced with multiple equilibria, uses highly contingent models, encounters tensions between its conceptual foundation and application, and does not solve the arbitrariness problems confronted by general equilibrium theory. In addition, some economic methodologists argue that game theory and experimental economics can be seen as one of three reactions to the problems associated with algorithmic rationality pointed out by Gödel's theorem in mathematics. First, game theory and experimental economics are connected with von Neumann's mathematics. Whereas von Neumann sought to ground mathematics in actual practice, game theory and experimental economics attempted to ground rationality in actual practice. Second, Debreu's regular economics is linked to Bourbaki's mathematics. Whereas Bourbaki sought to axiomatize and formalize all good mathematics, Debreu attempted to clean up existence proofs in economics. Finally, Herbert Simon's bounded rationality is connected with Alan Turing's artificial intelligence. Whereas the Turing test illustrated the problems in telling the difference between machines and people, Simon sought to find rationality by building imitation people that confront complexity and computability.

Next, what is the definition, interpretation and status of rational choice? And how can it be tested? Some economic methodologists argue that the rationality postulate is inconsistent with philosophical foundations, that the common knowledge assumption is incoherent, insufficient and circular, that rational choice theory is self-defeating in cases of coordination and commitment, that there are non-choice sources of information on preferences and welfare, that choice may reflect a compromise among a variety of considerations, and that the connection between norms and self-interest is tenuous. (See RATIONALITY AND IRRATIONALITY.)

Sixth, how can existence, uniqueness and stability of general equilibrium be shown? Economic methodologists have illustrated that the heterogeneity of agents must be limited to prove existence, uniqueness and stability. In response to the Sonnenschein–Mantel–Debreu result, economists have even been led to resort to the representative agent model.

Finally, what is the proper domain of economics? Is it appropriate to use markets and market reasoning in certain areas? Can economics be studied in isolation from moral and cultural presuppositions?

## Conclusion

Methodology is relevant for economics because many economists anguish over whether their subject is a science, or started out in one of the sciences; or are overly eager to copy the sciences. Yet, there are several problems in imitating the sciences in economics. The world is constantly changing, images of science are constantly changing, and the problems in philosophy of science carry over to economics in its imitation. Hence, it is encouraging to witness the increased interest of economic methodologists in the actual practice and culture of economics.

## See also:

critical realism; determinism and over-determination; dialectical method; feminist philosophy of science; holistic method; methodological individualism and collectivism; modernism and postmodernism; pragmatism; storytelling and pattern models; value judgments and world views

## Selected references

Backhouse, Roger E. (ed.) (1994) *New Directions in Economic Methodology*, London: Routledge.

Caldwell, Bruce J. (1994) *Beyond Positivism: Economic Methodology in the Twentieth Century*, London: Routledge.

Ferber, Marianne A. and Nelson, Julie A. (eds) (1993) *Beyond Economic Man*, Chicago: University of Chicago Press.

Hands, D. Wade (1997) "Caveat Emptor: Economics and Contemporary Philosophy of Science," *Philosophy of Science* 64 (proceedings): 107–16.

Hausman, Daniel M. (ed.) (1994) *The Philosophy of Economics: An Anthology*, Cambridge: Cambridge University Press.

Klamer, Arjo and Colander, David (1990) *The Making of an Economist*, Boulder, CO: Westview Press.

Pickering, Andrew (ed.) (1992) *Science as Practice and Culture*, Chicago: University of Chicago Press.

ESTHER-MIRJAM SENT

# methodology of scientific research programs

In 1970, Imre Lakatos published an essay entitled "The Methodology of Scientific Research Programmes," as part of the proceedings to a conference structured as a debate between Thomas Kuhn and Karl Popper. The context in which Lakatos presented his theory is important, since it is best understood as an attempt to retain both the critical-rational elements of Popper's philosophy of science and the relativist elements of Kuhn's history and sociology of knowledge: "The 'dogmatism' of 'normal science' does not prevent growth as long as we combine it with the Popperian recognition that there is good, progressive normal science, and as long as we retain the determination to eliminate, under certain objectively defined conditions, some research programmes" (Lakatos 1970: 89–90).

## Naive and sophisticated falsification

For Lakatos, Popper's falsificationism presents a heroic and appealing image of scientific progress. According to Popper, although we cannot "know" truth we can "know" falsity, and science progresses by stating boldly and clearly the conditions under which a proposition will be rejected (falsified). However, for Lakatos, this is a *naive* falsificationism: it ignores the fact that scientific practice embodies a high degree of conventionalism, where propositions are not ruthlessly rejected when confronted with apparently contradictory evidence: "no experimental result can ever kill a theory: any theory can be saved from counterinstances either by some auxiliary hypothesis or by a suitable reinterpretation of its terms" (Lakatos 1970: 32).

Since any individual theory can be amended rather than falsified in light of "contradictory" experimental evidence, the *chain* of theories in which it is one link needs to be appraised. This is a *sophisticated* falsificationism because it appraises only this series of theories, rather than specific elements of it, and it is this series of theories that constitutes a research program:

> one of the crucial features of sophisticated falsificationism is that it replaces the concept of theory as the basic concept of the logic of discovery by the concept of series of theories. It is a succession of theories and not one given theory which is appraised as scientific or pseudo-scientific. But the members of such series of theories are usually connected by a remarkable continuity which welds them into research programmes.
>
> (Lakatos 1970: 47)

Lakatos argues that this continuity is akin to Kuhnian normal science, and the research program similar to the notion of PARADIGMS. Indeed, Lakatos interchanges Kuhn's terminology with his own at various points.

## Negative and positive heuristics

A research program is constituted by two sets of methodological rules. First, the "negative heuristic" specifies paths of research to avoid, and is designed to insulate from criticism a cluster of "hard core" propositions and beliefs. The negative heuristic effectively quarantines the hard core, which can then be taken as background knowledge during the course of research. Concrete research is guided by a second set of methodological rules, which form the "positive heuristic" of the program. The positive heuristic provides the guide for further research; the permissible range of inquiry: "The positive heuristic sets out a program which lists a chain of ever more complicated models simulating reality: the scientist's atten-

tion is riveted on building his [sic] models following instructions which are laid down in the positive part of the program. He ignores actual counterexamples, the available 'data'" (Lakatos 1970: 50). The articulation of the program through auxiliary hypotheses, adaptation of initial conditions, changes in observational techniques, etc., forms a protective belt around the hard core, and this protective belt "has to bear the brunt of tests and get adjusted and re-adjusted, or even completely replaced, to defend the thus-hardened core" (Lakatos 1970: 48).

## Appraisal of research programs

Lakatos uses the word "program" to emphasize that the line of research guided by the positive heuristic is usually laid down at the outset: an agenda for further research is specified on the basis of an initial, very simplistic model. Lakatos uses Bohr's elaboration of the atomic model as his example, whereby Bohr ignored criticisms of his initial simple models of atomic structure because he knew that these working models would be developed in subsequent "versions." It is not difficult to find similar examples in economics. Both neoclassical and Marxist economics begin with highly simplified models, essentially one-commodity worlds. However, these are only taken as departure points for the further elaboration of each research program. Often this elaboration proceeds at the purely theoretical level, involving conceptual innovations and mathematical sophistication (often ignoring empirical testing). The question is not the validity of these initial models, or any of the individual models which proceed on their bases, but rather the successive chain of elaborations, the whole program. It thus shifts emphasis from the individual theory to the process of theory change.

Lakatos argues that there is a rational means by which a research program can be appraised, thereby retaining the critical element of Popperian philosophy. Lakatos argues that a program is theoretically progressive if each new theory in the chain predicts some hitherto unexplained, novel fact. It is, in addition, empirically progressive "if some of this excess empirical content is also corroborated, that is if each new theory leads us to the actual discovery of some new fact.... We regard a theory in the series "falsified" when it is superseded by a theory with higher corroborated content" (Lakatos 1970: 33–4).

Lakatos went on to emphasize that a research program need only be intermittently progressive, rather than continuously progressive, in terms of predicting novel facts. A program may for a period appear to be degenerating, yet may eventually lead to a progressive problem shift through some innovation in its protective belt of propositions. The possibility of renewal provides a rational basis for the dogmatic adherence to a hard core that often epitomizes the history of science: if science followed Popper's strictures too closely – rejecting a program that appears to be falsified – its progress might be hobbled. A degree of dogmatism is healthy.

Lakatos also uses this notion of progressive and degenerative programs as a way of assessing rival programs, rather than just a means of evaluating the chain of theories that make up an individual program. He rejects Kuhn's belief that science is usually characterized by extended periods of peaceful normal science under the dominance of a single paradigm. Rather, he argues, both as a historical assessment and as a normative judgment, that science has progressed through the competition of rival research programs. An entire program is falsified when a rival can explain its previous success while anticipating in addition theoretically novel facts (1970: 69), thereby providing an objective reason for culling the range of rival research programs.

## Methodological pluralism

Nevertheless, despite this objective criterion for appraising rival programs, the methodology of scientific research programs provides a rational basis for methodological pluralism. If a research program need only occasionally be progressive, then a rejection of a program during a degenerative stage may be premature. Because the future often holds out the promise of progressive innovation, it is not clear at what point one can make a final judgment that a research program has lost all hope of redemption, and should be abandoned in favor of a rival. This plea for methodological pluralism situates Lakatos between the ruthless competition and elimination of "falsified" theories (advocated by Popper), and the universally dominant paradigm that is beyond judgment for an extended period (advocated by Kuhn).

## Appeal of the methodology of scientific research programs in economics

This combination of Kuhn's relativism and Popper's rationalism gives the methodology of scientific research programs a wide appeal within economics. The critical element of appraisal appeals to the orthodoxy (Weintraub 1985), while the arguments in favor of methodological pluralism appeal to heterodox theorists. There have been many attempts to apply the methodology of scientific research programs to the history of economics, most notably the collection of essays in Latsis (1976). These attempts, though, reveal some of the difficulties in actually operationalizing Lakatos's key concepts. For example, it is not clear at what level of theoretical aggregation the term "research program" applies. Some have taken this to apply at a broad level, so that there is a "neoclassical program" (Latsis and Coats, in Latsis 1976), while others have applied it to more narrowly conceived sets of ideas, such that the "monetarist" program differs in its hard-core beliefs from the "Keynesian" program (Leijonhufvud, in Latsis 1976). Similarly, whether Lakatos has in fact provided objective criteria for program appraisal is doubtful (Rosenberg 1986). The assessment as to when a research program is said to be progressing or degenerating, especially when compared to rival programs, will often be predetermined from the perspective from which the appraisal is being made (Leijonhufvud, in Latsis 1976: 78–9).

## See also:

methodology in economics; paradigm

## Selected references

Lakatos, I. (1970) "The Methodology of Scientific Research Programmes," in I. Lakatos and A. Musgrave (eds), *Criticism and the Growth of Knowledge*, Cambridge: Cambridge University Press; repr. in J. Worrall and G. Currie (eds), *The Methodology of Scientific Research Programmes. Philosophical Papers*, vol. 1, Cambridge: Cambridge University Press, 1978.

Latsis, S.J. (ed.) (1976) *Method and Appraisal in Economics*, Cambridge: Cambridge University Press.

Rosenberg, A. (1986) "Lakatosian Consolations for Economists," *Economics and Philosophy* 2: 127–39.

Weintraub, E. Roy (1985) *General Equilibrium Analysis: Studies in Appraisal*, Cambridge: Cambridge University Press.

GEORGE ARGYROUS

# military expenditure in developing countries

In 1990 military expenditure by developing countries was estimated to be around $100 billion. This represents approximately one-sixth of total world expenditure on defense (SIPRI 1992). From the end of the Second World War up until the mid-1980s, military expenditure by developing countries grew rapidly. Since 1984, when it peaked at close to $135 billion, military expenditure by developing countries has been declining by around 3–4 percent per year in real terms. In 1985 the defense burden for Asian developing countries was 4.4 per cent and by 1990 it had fallen to 3.5 percent. Similarly, the defense burden (the proportion of GDP spent on defense) for Middle Eastern and North African developing countries fell from 11.0 to 8.1 percent and from 5.8 to 3.9 percent respectively for the same

period. This downward trend is reflected in declines in the defense burden for most developing countries. Finally, the ratio of military expenditure to central government expenditure for developing countries fell from 17.0 percent in 1985 to 16.1 percent by 1990 (Hewitt 1993).

## Long-term decline in expenditures?

It is not clear at this stage whether this represents a sustained downward trend in military expenditure. There are a number of reasons why the post-1984 decline in military expenditures by developing countries may not be long lived. Conflicts in the Third World during the Cold War years were often part of a policy of surrogate containment by the USA and the USSR. Wars in the Third World were often proxy conflicts that were contained to specific locations and which did not spill over into direct conflict between the superpowers. The decline in military aid that went with the end of the Cold War had the effect of reducing military spending. However, as developing countries begin to take on more of their own defense responsibilities military expenditure may begin to rise again in the longer term. The 1990s have also seen a rise in the number of disputes over territory and resources and these have the potential to escalate into military conflict. The dispute between China, the Philippines, Vietnam and Brunei over the potentially resource rich Spratly Islands represents one such example.

## Military spending and economic growth

There has been a considerable amount of research conducted into the question of whether military expenditure by developing countries promotes or detracts from economic growth. The seminal research in this field was conducted by Benoit (1973, 1978). Benoit studied the relationship between the defense burden and the rate of ECONOMIC GROWTH for forty-four developing economies over the period 1950 to 1965. He concluded that countries with heavy defense burdens generally had the most rapid rate of growth and those with low defense burdens had the lowest growth rates. Benoit hypothesized that military spending led to economic growth by promoting capital formation and spin-offs, which in turn permitted resource mobilization in the private sector (1978). This has subsequently become known as the "Benoit effect."

Some researchers have been extremely critical of Benoit's methodology and maintain that there is little link between military expenditure and growth (see Biswas and Ram 1986). Other researchers accept the existence of a "Benoit effect," but maintain that the positive direct effect of military expenditure on economic growth is outweighed by negative effects. For example, Deger and Smith (1983) made use of a three-equation simultaneous system to test the relationship between the rate of economic growth, the savings ratio, and the defense burden for fifty developing economies. The estimated growth equation showed a positive correlation between the defense burden and the rate of economic growth, thereby supporting Benoit's conclusion that military expenditure has a positive direct effect on economic growth by resource mobilization. However, the results also indicated that military expenditure has a stronger negative indirect effect on economic growth by reducing saving. Overall, they estimated that an increase in military expenditure by 1 percent would lead to a fall in per capita GNP of 0.2 percent.

More recently, Chowdhury (1991) has used Granger causality tests to determine the presence and direction of causality between economic growth rates and military spending for fifty-five developing countries. His results indicate that for some developing countries there is no evidence of any causal link between the two variables, but for others there is. The causal link can go either way depending on the situation in each country.

Despite considerable research into the relationship between military expenditure and economic growth in developing economies little consensus has emerged. If anything can be concluded it is that it is not possible to make broad generalizations about the relationship

between military expenditure and economic growth across countries. Each country has to be considered on its own and with reference to its unique stage of development, the exact nature of the military spending being studied and the strategic environment in which each country exists.

By nature, most of the research into this area has been econometric. However, some of this research has been unsatisfactory because correlation has too often been confused with causality. Where researchers have discovered evidence of correlation between military expenditure and economic growth, the interpretation of their results has inappropriately led them to conclude causation. Benoit's original study is one such example.

Serious problems exist with respect to deficiencies in the data available to researchers. Data are published annually by the Stockholm International Peace Research Institute (SIPRI). Although the range of data on military expenditure has improved in recent years, a great number of developing countries remain secretive when it comes to releasing data. Quite often data on military expenditure represent the best educated guess by SIPRI. A further problem concerns gaps in the data. The most obvious gap with respect to developing countries is the lack of data for China. Additionally, there is the problem of researchers having to rely upon time series that are very small. The largest time series available for most developing countries are in the range of 35–40 years. This makes it extremely difficult for researchers to come up with meaningful results using econometric techniques.

## Social, cultural and political impact

There is also the issue of the social, cultural and political impact of military spending. Since the end of the Second World War, many millions of people have died in conflicts in the Third World. One can only guess at the personal and social costs associated with this tragic carnage. Furthermore, a great number of people have suffered at the hands of military dictatorships (many of which were financially and logistically supported by the superpowers during the Cold War), which ruthlessly suppressed personal freedom and popular democratic movements.

## See also:

budget deficit; effective demand and capacity utilization; fascism; fiscal policy; human development index; Keynesian revolution; state and government; technology

## Selected references

Benoit, E. (1973) *Defense and Economic Growth in Developing Countries*, Boston: D.C. Heath.
—— (1978) "Growth and Defense in Developing Countries," *Economic Development and Cultural Change* 26(2): 271–80.
Biswas, B. and Ram, R. (1986) "Military Expenditures and Economic Growth in Less Developed Countries: An Augmented Model and Further Evidence," *Economic Development and Cultural Change* 34: 361–73.
Chowdhury, A.R. (1991) "A Causal Analysis of Defense Spending and Economic Growth," *Journal of Conflict Resolution* 35(1): 80–97.
Deger, S. and Smith, R. (1983) "Military Expenditure and Growth in Less Developed Countries," *Journal of Conflict Resolution* 27(2): 335–53.
Hewitt, D.P. (1993) *Military Expenditures 1972–1990: The Reasons behind the Post-1985 Fall in Military Spending*, New York: IMF Working Paper WP/93/18.
Stockholm Institute of Peace Research (SIPRI) (1992) *World Armaments and Disarmaments: SIPRI Year Book*, Philadelphia: Taylor & Francis.

MALCOLM COOK

# minimal dislocation

The principle of minimal dislocation, first formally stated by J. Fagg Foster (1981), is a theoretical proposition that plays a critical role in the neoinstitutionalist theory of INSTITU-TIONAL CHANGE AND ADJUSTMENT. It identifies one of two major noninvidious (nonceremonial) constraints on the process of progressive institutional change. The other is explained by the principle of RECOGNIZED INTERDEPENDENCE.

The principle of minimal dislocation sheds light on the sustainable limits of institutional changes that occur in the wake of technological innovations in the arts and sciences. It sets forth the view that "progressive" institutional changes that make possible higher levels of instrumental efficiency in the problem-solving processes of the community, through the incorporation of technological innovations, may bring about dislocations of instrumentally warranted behavior in other parts of the institutional structure. The theory holds that, given the complexity of the institutional structure of society and the highly unpredictable nature of the impact of institutional changes on that structure, such dislocations are probably unavoidable even when institutional changes are carefully planned. Though they may be unavoidable, dislocations should be minimized if technological innovations in one part of the institutional structure are to result in net gains for the community as a whole.

## Fundamental tenets

The principle of minimal dislocation rests on three fundamental ideas. The first is that the institutional structure of society takes on the character of an "organic whole" (Veblen 1899: 201). Related to this is the recognition that changes in the behavioral patterns of one institution have the potential for bringing about changes in behavioral patterns throughout the entire institutional fabric of society. The second idea is the somewhat commonplace recognition that technological innovation usually involves displacement of older technologies. The third is a corollary of the principle of CEREMONIAL ENCAPSULATION. It is the notion that instrumentally (or technologically) warranted behaviors are often encapsulated by the ceremonially warranted status and power structure of society.

According to the theory, progressive institutional change involves the displacement of ceremonially warranted patterns of behavior by instrumentally (technologically) warranted patterns of behavior (Bush 1987: 1101–3). When this happens, there is a high probability that instrumentally warranted behavior that is ceremonially encapsulated will be displaced, along with the socially wasteful ceremonial practices that encapsulate it. The principle of minimal dislocation holds that technological innovations should be incorporated into the problem-solving processes of the community (through progressive institutional change) in such a way as to minimize the dislocation of older (but still potentially useful) technologies. They should also minimize the dislocation of technologies previously ceremonially encapsulated in the discarded ceremonially warranted patterns of behavior.

### Empirical and policy analysis

The principle of minimal dislocation serves to direct both empirical inquiries and policy formation. It helps to focus empirical inquiry on the consequences a technological innovation may have on the overall instrumental efficiency of a community. Imagine, for example, that the introduction of a new machine and/or chemical process proves to have a greater negative impact on the ecological system than older (or different) technologies. The introduction of this new machine (along with the appropriate institutional changes) may have the long-term effect of reducing the sustainability of the ecological system by causing a maximum dislocation of technologies that are more appropriate to the maintenance of the ecosystem.

In the area of policy formation, a careful assessment of the dislocative effects of alternative technologies becomes an indispensable component of democratic decision making. There is almost always more than one technological approach available for the solution of a given problem. One important way of sorting out the competing claims of vested interests promoting different technologies is to apply the criterion of minimal dislocation.

### See also:

collective social wealth; culture; disembedded economy; evolutionary economics: major contemporary themes; innovation, evolution and cycles; institutional political economy: major contemporary themes; knowledge, information, technology, and change; neo-institutionalism; social and organizational capital; technology; Veblen

### Selected references

Ayres, C.E. (1944) *The Theory of Economic Progress*, 3rd edn, Kalamazoo, MI: New Issues Press, Western Michigan University, 1978.

Bush, Paul D. (1987) "The Theory of Institutional Change," *Journal of Economic Issues* 21(3): 1075–1116.

Foster, J. Fagg (1981) "The Papers of J. Fagg Foster," *Journal of Economic Issues* 15(4): 857–1012.

Tool, Marc R. (1979) *The Discretionary Economy: A Normative Theory of Political Economy*, Santa Monica, CA: Goodyear Publishing Co.

Veblen, Thorstein B. (1899) *The Theory of the Leisure Class*, New York: Augustus M. Kelley, 1975.

PAUL D. BUSH

# Minsky's Wall Street paradigm

The Wall Street paradigm denotes Hyman Minsky's ideas about the financial dynamics of capitalist economies. Minsky originated the term in 1975 in his book, *John Maynard Keynes*, writing that:

> whereas classical economics and the neo-classical synthesis are based upon a barter paradigm ... Keynesian theory rests upon a speculative-financial paradigm – the image is

of a banker making his deals on a Wall Street.... [Hence,] the relevant paradigm is a City [of London] or a Wall Street where asset holdings as well as current transactions are financed by debts.

(Minsky 1975: 57–8, 73)

Minsky developed his ideas further in Minsky (1986) and in other writings (for an overview see Dymski and Pollin 1992).

For Minsky, financial dynamics of two kinds are crucial determinants of outcomes in advanced capitalist economies: financial fragility at the level of economic units, and financial instability at the level of the economy as a whole. The build-up of financial fragility, in his view, invariably accompanies capitalist ACCUMULATION processes. Recurrent financial instability has had consequences so devastating as to induce significant institutional changes that have, in turn, altered the dynamic of capitalist growth itself.

Minsky developed his ideas through a close reading and appreciation of Keynes's *General Theory*. In his view, Keynesian theory rests on three core elements: UNCERTAINTY, the volatility of investment and the cyclical character of capitalist ECONOMIC GROWTH. As Minsky puts it, "Keynesian economics is the economics of permanent disequilibrium" (1975: 68).

## Analysis of individual economic units

All economic units can be viewed as having balance sheets for which assets equal liabilities plus net worth. Firms and households must continually make decisions about whether to take on large-scale projects whose payoffs are far in the future, and thus are unpredictable in the sense of Keynesian uncertainty. Any assets committed to these projects must be financed internally or externally. Internal financing of assets – that is, the use of retained earnings and cash on hand to purchase assets – entails few difficulties. However, external financing of assets generates financial risk; it forces the firm to take on interest payment obligations, to promise dividends and/or to cede partial control to external parties. A firm issuing debt

or equity instruments must meet the financial commitments to which these instruments give rise, independently of the success or failure of the project they finance. Financing commitments are locked in when investment is undertaken, not after, and remain even if anticipated returns are not realized.

The financial fragility of economic units emerges from their balance-sheet positions. The financial commitments and returns entailed in liability and asset positions, respectively, create net positive or negative cash flows, or what Minsky terms a "financial structure." Financial structures fall into three categories: robust structures (hedge finance), in which a firm can meet its financing obligations with a considerable margin of safety (and thus has positive net cash flow), fragile structures (speculative finance), in which expected net cash flow is positive but realized net cash flow may be negative, and Ponzi finance, in which actual and expected net cash flows are negative (see HEDGE, SPECULATIVE AND PONZI FINANCE).

## Analysis of economic dynamics

What determines the proportions of hedge, speculative and Ponzi units, and how can Ponzi units arise? This is where the dynamic component of the Wall Street paradigm, which Minsky termed the FINANCIAL INSTABILITY HYPOTHESIS, emerges. In cyclical expansions, units move systematically from hedge to speculative financial structures. This shift is triggered by the higher than anticipated profits and share prices during expansions. Economic units seeking to exploit burgeoning market opportunities take on more debt as a means of increasing the pace of their investment spending.

As cyclical growth proceeds, more and more units increase their leverage (their ratios of debt to equity), and hence precommit more and more of their cashflow to interest payments. A mature economic expansion comes to resemble a bubble, as pessimistic news is discounted and optimistic news overemphasized. As debt loads build up, so systemic financial fragility increases, because ever smaller deviations from optimistic revenue projections will result in negative cashflow for an ever-growing share of economic units. In Minsky's view, a key pressure point in the build-up of financial fragility is the extent of misalignment between the price of producing real assets and the valuation of those real assets in centralized financial markets. Minsky pointed out that financial prices react quickly to every shift in financial market opinion, while cost prices depend on real market processes and move much more slowly. As an expansion proceeds, financial prices race ahead of cost prices – ironically encouraging still more investment and debt financing, since any new real asset will be valued at a premium in financial markets.

At some point, the bubble bursts and asset prices collapse. An adverse event anywhere in the economy quickly spreads across the economy, because fragile financial structures are widespread. What happens next depends on the role of government in the economy. In what Minsky termed the "small government era" before the Second World War, financial crises had devastating immediate consequences: the collapse of price levels, the failure of innumerable businesses and banks and widespread unemployment throughout the regularly employed workforce. However, Minsky argued that FINANCIAL CRISES have not led to depression since the Second World War because of the emergence of the "big government era." The key elements of this era are the central bank's willingness to serve as a lender of last resort and the presence of government spending as a large and stable source of aggregate demand. Financial crises in the big government era have resulted not in widespread bust, but instead in recurrent inflationary pressure and upward shifts in government debt levels. This shift is by no means permanent; eliminating the stabilizing role of central bank policy and government deficits would cause the re-emergence of volatile cyclical behavior.

In sum, the Wall Street paradigm views every state of the economy as being transitory. The responses of economic units to any given state soon undermine it and lead to new levels of financial fragility and economic growth.

## Money market capitalism

In his latter years, Minsky focused on an emerging "stage" of CAPITALISM, which he termed "money market capitalism" (Minsky 1996). In this new stage, financial forces would have ever greater scope due to the dominance of Wall Street funds, managed according to the single criterion of the highest short-run return. In effect, Wall Street itself will finally dictate the dynamics described in the Wall Street paradigm. Minsky warned that with the growth of non-bank lending, central banks were losing day-to-day contact with the markets in which positions were made. The consequence is that rapid swings in the price and availability of cash would become ever more pronounced, in spite of regulatory interventions aimed at stabilizing these prices and flows. Still new adaptations in government intervention would be required to prevent the re-emergence of recurrent episodes of unbridled speculative growth, followed by deep and socially costly recessions.

## See also:

endogenous money and credit; liability management; monetary policy and central banking functions; monetary theory of production; money, credit and finance: major contemporary themes; social structure of accumulation: financial; speculation; speculative bubbles and fundamental values

## Selected references

Dymski, Gary A. and Pollin, Robert (1992) "Hyman Minsky as Hedgehog: The Power of the Wall Street Paradigm," in Steven Fazzari and Dmitri Papadimitriou (eds), *Financial Conditions and Macroeconomic Performance*, Armonk, NY: M.E. Sharpe, 27–62.
Minsky, Hyman P. (1975) *John Maynard Keynes*, New York: Columbia University Press.

—— (1986) *Stabilizing An Unstable Economy*, New Haven, CT: Yale University Press.

—— (1996) "Uncertainty and the Institutional Structure of Capitalist Economies," *Journal of Economic Issues* 30(2): 357–68.

GARY A. DYMSKI

# Mitchell's analysis of business cycles

Wesley Clair Mitchell (1874–1948) was born in Rushville, Illinois. His academic life was spent mainly at Columbia University and the National Bureau of Economic Research (NBER) in New York City. His contribution to political economy was mainly in the area of business cycle analysis. His theory of business cycles is customarily called the "business-economy" theory. Arguably the best known explanation of instability in the pre-Keynes era, Mitchell's explanation of business cycles is "eclectic," because he refused to select a single or even a few factors to which he was willing to attribute the cycle. It is true that the widening and narrowing of the cost–price discrepancy, in effect the change in profit margins over the cycle, was for Mitchell a critical factor, but it impinged upon and was reflected in a diverse set of real, financial and psychological factors.

Mitchell regarded business cycles as "congeries of interrelated phenomena," which were based on "the main facts of economic history." Thus, his first task was to examine literally hundreds of time series with some care in an effort to tease from the record the recurring patterns of interrelations which might form the basis for a theory of instability.

## Definition of business cycle

This very empirical approach led to Mitchell's definition of cycles, arguably the most widely quoted definition of business cycles we have today:

> Business cycles are a type of fluctuation found in the aggregate economic activity of nations that organize their work mainly in business enterprise: a cycle consists of expansions occurring at about the same time in many economic activities, followed by similarly general recessions, contractions and revivals which merge into the expansion of the next cycle: this sequence of changes is recurrent but not periodic; in duration business cycles vary from more than one year to ten or twelve years; they are not divisible into shorter cycles of similar character with amplitude approximating their own.
>
> (Burns and Mitchell 1946: 3)

## Endogenous instability of investment

Embedded in this definition are a number of aspects of business cycles that Mitchell regarded as critical. The source of instability arises from within the character of an enterprise system and the fluctuating perceptions of profit possibilities. This is comparable to Keynes's emphasis on the instability of investment (shifts in the marginal efficiency of investment). Mitchell insisted that each phase of the cycle merges into the next phase because his view of instability was essentially dynamic; he did not distinguish growth from cycles but focused rather on the instability of growth rates. Cycles are recurring but not periodic (that is, the term "cycles" is in fact a misnomer) and what one calls a business cycle is different both from seasonal variation and from instability brought on by long-run phenomena (for example, construction cycles or long waves).

Mitchell's theory of cycles is based on a careful study of a number of "typical" interrelationships over the cycle. A key attribute is that these relationships produce a pattern of stresses and strains, which alternately facilitate and impede the investment process (mostly by altering the entrepreneur's view of profit possibilities). These stresses and strains tend to be cumulative in nature, rather than being offsetting as would be the case were the economy subject to a tendency for small disturbances to be "self-correcting" rather than cumulating into larger disturbances. Thus, in the final analysis, Mitchell's explanation of business cycles fits in with a number of others which stress the endogenous instability of investment (VEBLEN, KEYNES, SCHUMPETER and MARX, in particular).

The flavor of Mitchell's endogenously generated cumulative-stresses-and-strains theory may be illustrated by the following summary of what happens at the critical upper turning point:

> To sum up: The very conditions that make a business profitable gradually evolve conditions that threaten a reduction of profits. When the increase in business [activity]... taxes the productive capacity of the existing industrial equipment, the early decline of supplementary costs per unit of output comes gradually to a standstill. Meanwhile the expectation of making satisfactory profits induces active bidding among business enterprises for materials, labor, and loan funds, and sends up their prices. At the same time, the poorer parts of the industrial equipment are brought back into use, the efficiency of labor declines, and the incidental wastes of management rise. Thus the prime costs of doing business become heavier. After these processes have been running cumulatively for a while, it becomes difficult to advance selling prices fast enough to avoid a reduction of profits by the encroachment of costs.
>
> (Mitchell 1941: 61)

Thus we see that Mitchell's description of the critical activity preceding the upper turning point incorporates many of the factors he regards as pivotal in explaining business cycles: the change in profit margins, the lag of costs behind prices, the cumulative processes in real, financial, and psychological activity which increase the tensions preceding a business cycle peak, and the role of the quest for profits under conditions of uncertainty in keeping the entire process going.

## Phases in the cycle

A reading of Mitchell underscores the critical dynamic perspective which his view of business cycles encompasses. At bottom, his theory traces the path by which cyclical phases merge the one into the next. As Mitchell says:

> The theory of business cycles presented...is a descriptive analysis of the processes of cumulative change by which a revival of activity develops into intense prosperity, by which this prosperity engenders a crisis, by which crisis turns into depression, and by which depression, after growing more severe for a time, finally leads to such a revival of activity as that with which the cycle began.
>
> (Mitchell 1941: 149)

Readers will note that Mitchell referred to prosperity, crisis, depression and revival as the "phases which merge the one into the next." The terminology has changed: today we customarily refer to expansion, peak, recession and trough to cover the same four parts of the business cycle. Expansion is the cumulatively expanding part of the cycle in which ultimately stresses and strains both narrow profit margins and increasingly eradicate optimistic expectations. Peak is the preferred designation today for the point in time (determined *ex post* by a committee of experts coordinated through the National Bureau of Economic Research) when "the preponderance of evidence" suggest that, on balance, the economy has ceased expanding and has started to contract. The contraction, also a period of cumulative interaction, is the period during which liquidation increases in various parts of the economy: in firms' inventories, in firms' debts, in the outstanding loans of the financial sector and so on. All this gradually leads to renewed optimism and a more favorable view of investment opportunities. The trough is a point in time, chosen *ex post*, when the preponderance of evidence suggests that, on balance, the economy has ceased contracting and is once again expanding.

## Institutionalist tradition

Writers have consistently observed that Mitchell's theory of cycles was thus in the institutionalist tradition. Milton Friedman once commented:

> To Mitchell, economic theory was more than orthodox economic theory. It was a set of hypotheses explaining economic behavior in all its leading manifestations, and he was himself almost exclusively concerned with a part of economic theory that was largely outside the main stream of economic thought...the dynamic adjustment of the economic system as a whole.
>
> (Friedman 1952: 240)

Friedman goes on to note that it was no doubt Veblen, Mitchell's professor at the University of Chicago, who stimulated his interest in the process of economic change.

### Conclusion

If Mitchell was once regarded as the progenitor of "measurement without theory," today he is recognized as having had seminal insights into the fundamental interrelationships which characterize a dynamic enterprise-driven economy and as such his insights into how such economies generate instability have been acknowledged as well. The widespread interest in monitoring business cycle indicators is ongoing corroboration of the legacy he left to modern students of business cycles.

### See also:

business cycle theories; circular and cumulative causation; institutional political economy: history; long waves of economic growth and development

### Selected references

Burns, Arthur F. and Mitchell, Wesley C. (1946) *Measuring Business Cycles*, New York: National Bureau of Economic Research.
Friedman, Milton (1952) in Arthur Burns (ed.), *Wesley Clair Mitchell, The Economic Scientist*, New York: National Bureau of Economic Research.
Mitchell, Wesley Clair (1941) *Business Cycles and Their Causes*, Berkeley: CA University of California Press.

PHILIP A. KLEIN

# mode of production and social formation

Mode of production is the concept used by the Marxian tradition to describe the essential economic core of any society. Being comprised of both relations and forces of production, a mode is understood to govern not only other parts of the economic system, including its circulation of goods and credit, but also a society's politics and CULTURE as well. Because of this ultimately determining role, the mode has been portrayed as the base of society, upon which sits its determined economic system (the distribution of produced wealth and credit), the determined superstructure (the production and enforcement of laws and rules), and the production and dissemination of cultural meanings.

### Reproduction, contradiction and resolution

This ordering of society into an essential economic cause and its determined effects – sometimes referred to as economic determinism – endows enormous causal significance upon a mode of production. For example, one is supposedly able to figure out or literally deduce all kinds of non-modal social behavior from the economic behavior of a mode of production. This may include why and in what ways people in a society dress, speak, read and generally think the way they do, and the diverse ways they order each other's behavior, to the complex and varied ways they distribute their produced wealth. Put differently, explanations for their function and functioning in society rest, after all is said and done, with an analysis of the mode of production (see DETERMINISM AND OVERDETERMINATION).

Different forms of relations and forces of

production comprise different modes of production and, hence, produce different developments, including revolutionary conjunctures. Typically, Marxists have used the terms primitive communism, SLAVERY, the ASIATIC MODE OF PRODUCTION, FEUDALISM, CAPITALISM and socialism to describe these different modes of production. Each of these produces and governs a correspondingly different economic system and superstructure. For example, a capitalist mode of production comprising capitalist relations and forces of production determines its corresponding forms of distribution of goods, as well as politics and culture. A feudal mode produces its corresponding forms of distribution of wealth, as well as politics and culture, and so forth. Marxists also have understood that any given society (what they call a social formation) may consist of a number of coexisting modes of production, plus their corresponding economic systems and superstructures. Such a social formation would receive its societal adjective of capitalist, feudal and so on, depending upon which of these modes is dominant in that social formation.

The development of any social formation – its reproductive or revolutionary status – can be traced to the behavior of its dominant or governing mode of production. When the dominant mode's relations and forces of production are said to correspond to one another, the mode of production, and therefore the social formation in question, is understood to reproduce itself. When, however, those relations of production are in conflict (contradiction) with the forces of production, the continuation of that mode becomes untenable and a revolutionary transition is set in motion from existing to a new mode of production.

For example, in a capitalist social formation, the development of its dominant capitalist mode of production produces a dramatic change in the forces of production, namely the technical way production occurs. The latter is marked by socializing masses of workers into large corporate conglomerations. However, the still private capitalist relations of production, conceived as private possession of the means of production, become a fetter on the further development of the forces. Private possession of the means of production and its accompanying private profits, markets, and inevitable business cycles block the further development of the forces of production. The fundamental contradiction of the capitalist mode of production, and hence of the capitalist social formation, is its inability to achieve the full benefits of its own socialization of the forces of production. A revolutionary conjuncture is brought about by this contradictory noncorrespondence between the relations and forces of production. (See CONTRADICTIONS.)

A socialist or communist revolution eliminates this fetter on the forces of production. It resolves the fundamental contradiction between these two essential societal forces by socializing the relations of production (collectivizing ownership of the means of production), thereby bringing them into correspondence with the previously socialized forces of production. A newly dominant communist mode of production both releases the constraint on the forces of production, thereby ushering in an era of plenty, and generates a new political and cultural superstructure, thereby ending the former ALIENATION of one human being from another.

## Critical questions

Three critical questions have arisen within political economy in regard to mode of production analysis. One question concerns the meaning of a mode's two essential components, the forces and relations of production. Another questions the presumed causal relationship between the relations and forces of production, and between the mode of production, the economic system and the superstructure. A third question is directed at the causal relationship among different modes, particularly between capitalist and noncapitalist modes of production. One can think of political economy as being divided into contending schools, depending on answers provided and positions taken in regard to these questions.

Turning to the first of the above questions,

the mode of production takes on a variety of different meanings in the Marxian literature, because of different meanings attached to its constituent relations and forces of production. Relations have been conceived in terms of (a) possession of means of production (as in the above example); (b) surplus labor appropriation; (c) relations of effective power or control; and (d) combinations of these and still other components (for examples, see Balibar, in Althusser and Balibar 1975: part III, ch. l; Hindess and Hirst 1975: 9–12; Cohen 1978: chaps 2–3; Callinicos 1982: ch. 6). Forces also have been understood variously in this literature in terms of techniques of production, the labor process, labor power and still others. Because of this ambiguity, the boundary drawn between what is and what is not supposed to be located in the base (or in the economic system or superstructure) remains problematic.

In terms of the second question, the primacy awarded to a mode of production in any societal analysis emerged as a problem as soon as it was introduced by Marx and then further explained by Engels (Marx 1970: 20–1; Engels 1890). Reacting to criticisms directed against economic determinism, Engels (and others over the years) tried to formulate a middle way that would allow Marxism to hold onto the causal primacy of the mode while simultaneously enabling other components such as circulation and credit within the economic system, and politics and culture within the superstructure, to determine societal development. The result has been an approach that permits a mode of production to determine which of several societal forces will dominate a society.

For example, a capitalist mode determines that the economy dominates a capitalist society. Capitalist workers, forced by their economic status of being dispossessed from the means of production, sell the only thing they own, their labor power, to survive. These capitalist relations of production compel them to become sellers of labor power, thereby rendering surplus labor to the capitalist buyers who possess the means of production (see LABOR AND LABOR POWER). Unlike capitalist workers, feudal serfs possess the means of

production and, consequently, are not forced by their economic status to render surplus labor to lords. These contrasting feudal relations of production determine that religion intervenes to compel them to produce a surplus for lords. Whereas the economy dominates under capitalism, religion (or politics) dominates in non-capitalist systems. In the last instance, however, the relations of production determine whether it will be economics or noneconomics that dominates in any society.

While most theorists emphasize the determining role of the relations of production (Balibar in Althusser and Balibar 1975), others specify that role for the forces of production (Cohen 1978). In the latter approach, the march of production techniques determines the kind of production relations in society, and hence the kind of mode that appears there. Consequently that mode, ultimately structured by its forces of production, generates the rest of the economic system and the required superstructure.

Irrespective of whether it is the relations or forces of production that are conceived to be the last instant determinant, critics still see a one-way causation in which economics ultimately determines the effectivity of non-economics in any society. The middle way remains thoroughly economistic in its explanation of how change emerges in and travels through any society. Furthermore, it remains at best politically naive in looking only to changes in the base for the emergence of potentially revolutionary movements in and challenges to any existing society.

The third question involves the nature of a social formation comprising different modes of production (Wolpe 1980). Typically, the capitalist mode has been conceived to govern and determine the function and survival of these other modes of production. For example, the causal relationship between capitalist and non-capitalist modes of production is conceived to operate in only one direction. The capitalist mode of production becomes dominant, either by undermining and eventually destroying noncapitalist modes of production, or by molding these other modes to its changing requirements. Whether it be feudal destruction or survival, the capitalist mode remains nonetheless secure in its privileged role as the determining cause.

Some political economists have rejected mode of production analysis, not only for its continuing conceptual ambiguities but above all because of its relentless economic determinism (Hindess and Hirst 1977; Laclau and Mouffe 1985). Economic determinism conceives of the economic base as a self-reproducing entity within society, with the consequence of demoting the revolutionary potential of other parts of the economic system, as well as politics and culture. Others have criticized mode of production and social formation analyses for their essentialization of capitalism: the development of a social formation is reduced to the development of its capitalist mode of production, thereby rendering noncapitalist modes as derivative from and subordinate to capitalism (Wolpe 1980).

## Conclusion

What is needed is an analysis of the contradictory relationships between different modes of production, in which modes serve both to sustain and to undermine one another (McIntyre 1996). However, dialectical reasoning is generally absent from much of mode of production analysis, because of its longstanding attempt to ground social analysis in some ultimately determining but never determined relations or forces of production (see DIALECTICAL METHOD).

## See also:

class; class processes; disembedded economy; Marxist political economy: major contemporary varieties; socialism and communism

## Selected references

Althusser, Louis and Balibar, Etienne (1975) *Reading Capital*, London: New Left Books.
Callinicos, Alex (1982) *Is There A Future For Marxism?*, Atlantic Highlands, NJ: Humanities Press.
Cohen, G.A. (1978) *Karl Marx's Theory of History*, Princeton, NJ: Princeton University Press.
Engels, F. (1890) "Engels to Joseph Bloch, 21–2 September," in K. Marx and F. Engels, *Selected Correspondence*, 3rd revised edn, Moscow: Progress Publishers, 1975, 394–6.
Hindess, Barry and Hirst, Paul (1975) *Pre-Capitalist Modes of Production*, London and Boston: Routledge & Kegan Paul.
—— (1977) *Mode of Production and Social Formation*, London: Macmillan.
Laclau, Ernesto and Mouffe, Chantal (1985) *Hegemony and Socialist Strategy*, London and New York: Verso.
Marx, Karl (1970) *Critique of Political Economy*, New York: International Publishers.
McIntyre, Ric (1996) "Mode of Production, Social Formation, and Uneven Development, or Is There Capitalism In America?," in A Callari and D. Ruccio (eds), *Postmodern Materialism and the Future of Marxist Theory*, Hanover and London: Wesleyan University Press, 231–53.
Wolpe, Harold (1980) *The Articulation of Modes of Production*, London and Boston: Routledge & Kegan Paul.

RIC McINTYRE
STEPHEN RESNICK

# modernism and postmodernism

## Modernism

In social science, *modernity* refers to social conditions marked by a trend toward rationalization. The institutions of modernity typically include CAPITALISM, industrialism, urbanization, the nation state, bureaucracy and a professional military. *Modernism* refers to the cultural expression or celebration of modernity, which can take the form of a general style, outlook or habits or, in a specific aesthetic sense, an art movement. As an art movement, modernism is variously periodized from the 1890s to 1920, or 1960. Generally much more attention has been devoted to modernity and to modernization (the process of achieving modernity) than to modernism. Modernism used to refer mainly to art, but recently, probably because of postmodernism, it is also regarded as an outlook in social science. With postmodernism it is the other way round: most discussion is about postmodernism and relatively little about postmodernity.

## Modernism in political economy

In political economy, modernism refers to the affirmation of modernity. Marshall Berman (1988) portrays Karl MARX as a thinker who, while criticizing capitalism, affirms its modern character. Note Marx's dictum about the sixteenth century: "The conquest of the world market is the beginning of modern capitalism." In countless passages Marx celebrated the drive of the bourgeoisie and capitalism's "ever revolutionizing character" which makes for continuous transformation, does away with "rural idiocy," with backwardness and stagnation. Marx embraced science and industrial technology as progressive: witness the distinction between "utopian socialism" and "scientific socialism," and the scientific ethos of historical materialism. The commitment to science defines traditional Marxist epistemology as well as politics. This modernist commitment was one of the reasons Marx and Engels generally welcomed Western colonialism, as a process of "creative destruction."

In this sense, both capitalism and socialism have been modernist, committed to progress defined as a function of rationalization and applied science. Part of this concerns the infrastructure of industrialism. The "convergence thesis," which formed part of modernization theory during the postwar period, followed from this premise: in time capitalism and communism would overcome their ideological differences and gradually converge upon their structural similarities as industrial societies. Beyond the general commitment to applied science and rationalization, universalism and progress, modernism refers to specific forms of industrialism.

This includes TAYLORISM, or scientific time management in assembly-line production, which also served as a model for Soviet INDUSTRIALIZATION. Antonio Gramsci coined the term "Fordism" (along with "Americanism") to describe a form of mass production sustained by mass consumption. A further corollary of mass production has been "mass society." Charlie Chaplin's movie *Modern Times* evokes several of these elements. Modernism has been criticized for its nineteenth-century positivist epistemology, faith in science, narrow Cartesian cosmology and Western ethnocentrism. Conventional modernists view progress as being historically centered in and emanating from the West, through the familiar itinerary of the Renaissance, the scientific revolution, the Enlightenment, empire and colonialism, and global capitalism.

## Postmodernism

The core meaning of postmodernism is relativism and "disbelief in great narratives" such as those of emancipation, freedom, humanity. In architecture and art, where the term was first used, it refers to styles that depart from utilitarian functionalism. For Lyotard (1979), since Auschwitz, the Gulag and Hiroshima, the promises of the Enlightenment and modernity have been exhausted. In social theory, postmodernism refers to a wide spectrum of views, from nihilism à la Baudrillard to critical theory revisited, or from sckeptic to affirmative postmodernism, in the words of Pauline Rosenau (1992). The postmodern may refer to *postmodernity*, a condition, and to *postmodernism*, an outlook or mode of reflexivity (Bauman 1992), although this distinction is not always maintained.

## Postmodernism in political economy

In political economy, the first concern is with postmodernity as a condition. Postmodernity refers to general features of or trends in the organization of production, consumption and social life which may be distinct enough to be considered a break with modernity. An example is post-industrial society, which refers to a society where the majority of the work force is employed in services rather than manufacturing. Post-Fordism refers to combined changes in production, which becomes less standardized; in consumption, which becomes more volatile and fluid; and in political regulation, with the passing of the WELFARE STATE and Keynesian demand management (Amin 1994). Post-Fordist production methods, in contrast with Fordist mass production, are characterized as "flexible accumulation", "Toyotism", "just-in-time capitalism", or "lean production", terms which concern the organization and regulation of production and strategies of industrial location (Harvey 1989) (see FORDISM AND THE FLEXIBLE SYSTEM OF PRODUCTION).

General features of postmodern political economy are the growing importance of consumption relative to production, the large size of the cultural sector and the growth of the informational economy. Baudrillard (1981) refers to the political economy of the sign. The notion of "reflexive accumulation" takes this a step further, to the aestheticization or semioticization of economies, the growing design intensity of production, style and brand name consciousness in consumption, and the prominent role of marketing (Lash and Urry 1994). Further dimensions of a postmodern condition are globalization and the decentering of the West, in view of the emergence of newly industrialized economies, especially in Pacific Asia, along with the "Third Worldization" of metropolitan societies (Lee 1994).

Another familiar theme is the fragmented, de-centered or multi-centered character of social formations, as in the "postmodern city." All these elements are contested as to whether they occur or are significant, whether they should be so designated, or whether they add up to "postmodernity." In political economy, as generally, these features are not necessarily termed postmodern; alternative terms may be "late", "advanced", "high", "radical", "reflex-ive" or "neo-modernity", especially if one considers modernity as an incomplete project.

One can diagnose postmodern conditions without adopting postmodernism as a perspective; in other words, postmodernism can be treated as an object. Thus, according to Jameson (1991), postmodernism is merely the cultural expression of late capitalism. Alternatively, it can serve as a premise. This may take the form of adopting certain methodologies, in particular post-structuralism and discourse analysis; deconstruction and subverting binary and dichotomous thinking; anti-foundationalism; and anti-essentialism; avoiding homogenization; and acknowledging "difference."

These methodological premises may well be adopted in combination with Marxism and critical theory; arguably some of these methodologies are beginning to form part of a general social science tool kit. Thus, constructivism – which is increasingly becoming part of social science common sense – starts out from the constructed character of social phenomena, which goes together very well with discourse analysis as a tool to examine the process of construction. A further step is to adopt postmodernism as a perspective, which generally means the assumption of a definite break with modernity to highlight the contingent, fragmented and hybrid character of contemporary conditions, and the decentering of the subject. Like modernism, postmodernism has been criticized for its Western ethnocentric bias, although it has been applied outside the West as well. In modern political economy, postmodernism has influenced certain trends of neo-Marxism (see the journal *Rethinking Marxism*), Veblenian institutionalism (see the *Journal of Economic Issues*), feminism (*Feminist Economics*), and to some degree social political economy (*Review of Social Economy*).

### See also:

determinism and overdetermination; entry point; foundationalism and anti-foundationalism; Marxist political economy: major contemporary varieties

## Selected references

Amin, Ash (ed.) (1994) *Post-Fordism: A Reader*, Oxford: Blackwell.

Baudrillard, J. (1981) *For a Critique of the Political Economy of the Sign*, St Louis, MO: Telos Press.

Bauman, Z. (1992) *Intimations of Postmodernity*, London: Routledge.

Berman, Marshall (1988) *All that is Solid Melts Into Air: The Experience of Modernity*, New York: Penguin.

Harvey, D. (1989) *The Condition of Postmodernity*, Oxford: Blackwell.

Jameson, F. (1991) *Postmodernism, or the Cultural Logic of Late Capitalism*, London: Verso.

Lash, Scott and Urry, John (1994) *Economies of Signs and Space*, London: Sage.

Lee, Raymond L.M. (1994) "Modernization, Postmodernism and the Third World," *Current Sociology* 42(2).

Lyotard, Jean François (1979) *La Condition postmoderne*, Paris: Editions de Minuit.

Rosenau, Pauline (1992) *Postmodernism and the Social Sciences*, Princeton, NJ: Princeton University Press.

JAN NEDERVEEN PIETERSE

# Mondragón

One of the most successful examples of cooperative economic relations has occurred in and around the village of Mondragón, in the Basque region of Spain. The Mondragón group of cooperatives was founded in 1956 with a single enterprise employing 24 workers, and by 1994 had grown to more than one hundred cooperatives employing 24,875 workers. In addition to industrial cooperatives, a variety of supporting secondary cooperatives have been created, including a bank, a social security cooperative, a technical college, a research and development cooperative, education cooperatives, agricultural cooperatives, and service and consumer cooperatives. The products of the industrial cooperatives include refrigerators, ranges, washing machines, bicycles, capital goods, tools, engineering instruments, and electrical and electronic goods (the main brand name is Fagor).

## History

A central figure in the founding of the Mondragón cooperatives was Don José Maria Arizmendi, a parish priest appointed to Mondragón in 1941. He had studied Catholic social thought and was concerned with the economic problems facing Mondragón in the wake of the fall of the Basque region to Franco in the Spanish Civil War. He was instrumental in establishing a technical training school to provide local youth with industrial skills and instruction in cooperative values. In 1956, five graduates of the school started an enterprise, Ulgor, to produce space heaters and gas ranges. Once legal problems were worked out, Ulgor was converted to cooperative ownership, and over the years it has expanded its product line and increased its total employment considerably. The development of the cooperative system as a whole accelerated after the establishment of a cooperative bank in 1960, the Caja Laboral Popular (People's Savings Bank) under the tutelage of Don José Maria. The purpose of the bank was to provide financial, technical and social assistance to cooperatives agreeing to a formal contract of association with the bank.

## Significance of Mondragón

Radical and progressive social theorists have looked to cooperatives as an alternative to capitalist forms of economic organization since the early days of the industrial revolution. Cooperative principles were first established in England in the 1840s by the Rochdale Pioneers who established consumer and producer cooperatives. While consumer cooperatives persisted and were relatively successful in England, producer cooperatives were largely a failure. Those that succeeded initially were bought out by capitalists and converted to a conventional form of business organization.

Don José Maria was aware of the checkered history of producer cooperatives, and sought to establish a framework embodying the principles of cooperation but overcoming the limitations of cooperatives. The historical development of producer cooperatives as an alternative to capitalism had been inhibited by insufficient access to capital, limited incentives for initial organization, an absence of a drive for growth, and difficulties reconciling democratic control with the attainment of scale economies.

In the Mondragón system, the problems of insufficient capital and entrepreneurial resources are overcome through the activities of the cooperative bank. The bank not only has the mission of providing capital to cooperatives, but it also has a management services division that assists individuals who want to start new cooperatives, providing them with product ideas as well as startup capital and technical expertise. Through the contract of association, individual cooperatives are required to allocate their surplus earnings in specified proportions to reserves, partly going to individual workers in the form of long-term savings accounts, partly to investment and partly to social projects. Surplus earnings are distributed to individual savings accounts in proportion to labor incomes, and these accounts can only be withdrawn on retirement or departure from the cooperative. Surplus earnings have thus forced the bank to seek new loan outlets, and have provided a powerful incentive to foster growth of the cooperative system in order to generate lending opportunities. This incentive coincides with the basic mission of the cooperative system, to expand employment opportunities in the Basque area.

The problem of conflict between economic democracy and the attainment of scale economies is overcome by subdividing cooperatives into separate organizations when they get too large, and by creating groups of interconnected cooperatives that subdivide production processes and enter into income sharing agreements. Within each cooperative, managers are hired by member-elected management boards for fixed terms. To avoid internal tension over income distribution, historically, pay limits were set for the highest paid of 3–5 times the pay of the lowest paid worker. Mondragón cooperatives have also developed internal self-management schemes in an attempt to go beyond formal democracy and extend democratic control to the shop floor.

Mondragón proves that a system of producer cooperatives can be successful in the context of a market economy. Because the workers themselves receive title to surplus earnings and democratically control their own cooperatives, the problems of EXPLOITATION and ALIENATION, as discussed by MARX, are significantly reduced. By ensuring that members have continual employment (retraining and education are provided to workers within the cooperative system), Mondragón overcomes the problem of economic insecurity faced by those who work for conventional capitalist enterprises. Mondragón demonstrates that the mission of employment creation works just as well as profit maximization as a central economic motivation.

## Research on Mondragón

The development of Mondragón as a cooperative system has not occurred at the expense of economic performance. In the 1970s, labor PRODUCTIVITY, total factor productivity, worker earnings and growth were greater in the Mondragón cooperatives than in any comparable business in the Spanish economy (Thomas and Logan 1982). In the 1990s, Lutz (1997) puts Mondragón among the ten biggest firms in Spain in terms of assets. One possible explanation for this growth is higher levels of worker motivation and productivity associated with worker ownership and democratic participation (Booth 1987). Some researchers have suggested that this system of cooperative productive production could be developed further in other areas of the world in order to foster regional economic development and a less exploitative system of business organization (Booth 1987; Ellerman 1983; Lutz 1997). Ellerman (1983) argues that Mondragón institutional forms can be readily adapted to US circumstances.

While economic democracy, as manifested in Mondragón, has appealing qualities, it undoubtedly faces significant ideological and organizational barriers in the USA and many other nations. Socially motivated entrepreneurs, like Don José Maria, are needed initially to implement the needed institutional framework in sympathetic communities. The individualist attitudes at large in the US population constitute a major barrier to the creation of a cooperative economy. However, in some nations the cooperative is a common and relatively successful form of business organization.

### Recent changes at Mondragón

The cooperative was reorganized in 1991 into the Mondragón Cooperative Corporation (MCC), which now has about $9 billion in assets. Its sales and exports are booming, despite Spain's entry into the European Community. Economically it is now much more centralized, with every cooperative director reporting to a divisional manager of MCC. It has responded to the pressure of low-wage competition from abroad by setting up half a dozen plants abroad (for example, in Mexico and China), which are not yet run as cooperatives. It has also started to hire temporary workers who are not yet members of the cooperative, and hence do not share in decision-making and profits. Some managers are now paid ten to fifteen times the lowest wage, although the 1:6 pay ratio for lowest to highest generally applies to workers.

All of these measures are controversial, but they are still decided democratically by cooperative members who elect the Cooperative Congress, which in turn elects the MCC members who make the main decisions (see Lutz 1997). These changes to the Mondragón cooperative system have increased alienation, inequality and industrial tension significantly. But the basic structure of decision-making remains, and the investment provided by the company in education, research and cooperative association continues. The Mondragón

experiment is a successful model for the social organization of business, despite the recent challenges it has faced.

### See also:

economic surplus; labor process; labor-managed enterprises; participatory democracy and self-management; social and organizational capital

### Selected references

Booth, D.E. (1987) *Regional Long Waves, Uneven Growth, and the Cooperative Alternative*, New York, Praeger.
Ellerman, D.P. (1983) "A Model Structure for Cooperatives: Worker Co-ops and Housing Co-ops," *Review of Social Economy* 52–67.
Lutz, M.A. (1997) "The Mondragón Cooperative Complex: Community Enterprise in Action," *International Journal of Social Economics*: 24: 1404–21.
Thomas, H. and Logan, C. (1982) *Mondragón: An Economic Analysis*, London: George Allen & Unwin.
Whyte, W.F. and Whyte, K.K. (1988) *Making Mondragón: The Growth and Dynamics of the Worker Cooperative Complex*, Ithaca, NY: ILR Press.

DOUGLAS E. BOOTH

# monetarism

The doctrine of monetarism was pioneered by the Chicago-based economist Milton Friedman in the 1950s and 1960s (see for example Friedman 1956, 1968). It became an integral part of economic policy making in the 1970s and 1980s. This was especially so in the United Kingdom, which became a laboratory experiment for monetarism under the leadership of Margaret Thatcher, and also in the United States under President Ronald Reagan, and in many other nations (see REAGANOMICS AND THATCHERISM). The doctrine draws its inspiration from the classical quantity theory of money which goes back at least to David Hume's essay "Of Money" in 1752. The essence of the theory is that increases in the money supply will cause increases in the price level; or, to put it another way, there is an inverse relation between the quantity of money and its value. In the words of Friedman "inflation is always and everywhere a monetary phenomenon" (in a causal sense).

## Versions of the quantity theory

There are several different versions of the quantity theory of money, each using an identity or equilibrium condition. One is the Fisher equation of exchange:

$$MV = PT \tag{1}$$

where $M$ is the quantity of money, $V$ is the velocity of circulation of money, $T$ is the volume of all transactions (including intermediate goods and financial assets), and $P$ is the average price of those transactions. The equation is definitionally true because a given value of transactions ($PT$) must be matched by an equivalent value of purchasing power ($MV$). But for an increase in $M$ to lead to an equal increase in $P$, clearly $V$ and $T$ must be assumed constant (see below).

A second version of the quantity theory of money is the later income version in which $T$ in equation (1) is replaced by $Y$. $Y$ measures only those transactions that enter into the value of national income (i.e. transactions in final goods and services), so that $P$ is the average price of final goods and services (what is now called the GDP deflator). This is one of the price indexes used by countries for measuring the rate of inflation. $V$ is the income velocity of circulation of money, not the total velocity. Clearly, if increases in the money supply are to lead to equal increases in inflation, $V$ and $Y$ must be constant. Classical believers in the quantity theory of money assumed that $V$ was constant because they recognized only a transactions demand for money related to the purchase of goods. Unless the time interval between the receipt of income and expenditure changes, there is no reason why $V$ should be variable. $Y$

was assumed to be constant, because of the assumption in all of classical (pre-Keynesian) economic theory that economies tend naturally to long run full employment of resources through the workings of the price mechanism.

A third version of the quantity theory of money is the so-called Cambridge cash-balance equation:

$$M = k_d PY \tag{2}$$

where $k_d$ is defined as the demand to hold money per unit of money income. Thus, $k_d PY$ is the demand for money, $M$ is the supply of money, and in equilibrium the supply and demand for money must be equal. Comparing equations (1) and (2), $k_d$ is the reciprocal of the velocity of circulation of money. But in the Cambridge equation, which focuses on the demand for money, an asset demand for money is also recognized (as well as a transactions demand) which may vary with the rate of interest. Using the Cambridge equation, $M$ and $P$ will only be causally related if $k_d$ and $Y$ are constant (see VELOCITY AND THE MONEY MULTIPLIER).

## Keynes's critique of the quantity theory

Keynes (1936) in his *General Theory of Employment, Interest and Money* attacked the mechanistic quantity theory of money on the grounds that it could not be assumed that $k_d$ and $Y$ are constant. He treated the money supply as exogenously determined by the central bank, but argued that the demand to hold money may vary with supply, and that if there is less than full employment in an economy, $Y$ will not be constant either. Thus, how increases in the money supply affect prices depends on how money affects interest rates; how interest rates affect the demand for money and the components of aggregate demand, and the responsiveness of aggregate supply to changes in aggregate demand. Keynes also makes the point that inflation may occur through rising costs long before the full employment level of income is reached, which the quantity theory of money precludes.

## Friedman's monetarism

Friedman, in resurrecting the quantity theory of money as part of his attack on Keynes and Keynesianism, uses the Cambridge cash-balance equation, and most of his work is designed to show, that in the long run, $k_d$ is stable and disequilibrium between the supply and demand for money is rectified by rising prices. His theory of monetarism is therefore a theory about the demand for money, which he regards as a stable function of a limited number of independent variables. To argue that inflation is always and everywhere a monetary phenomenon in a causal sense, however, implies not only that the demand to hold money is a stable function of money income, but also that the money supply is exogenously determined, and not determined by the process of inflation itself. Moreover, finding that changes in the money supply precede changes in the price level (as Friedman does) is not necessarily proof that money is causal.

## Critique of monetarism

A major criticism of the Friedman doctrine, stressed by Kaldor (1982) and other post-Keynesian economists, is that the vast bulk of the money supply in modern economies is credit money which only comes into existence because it is demanded, to meet the needs of trade. It is more likely, therefore, that it is not changes in the money supply driving prices but price (and output) changes driving the money supply. If this is so, $k_d$ in equation (2) will be found to be stable, but this is evidence not that the money supply is causal in the inflation process, but the opposite; that the money supply is endogenous (see ENDOGENOUS MONEY AND CREDIT). Likewise, changes in money preceding changes in prices cannot be taken to mean that money is causal since agents will demand money in advance of production to finance the higher cost of intermediate inputs.

## Thatcher's monetarism

Margaret Thatcher's brand of monetarism was based on four basic beliefs. The first was the Friedman view that money is the villain of the piece in the inflation process. The second was that the major cause of increases in broad money (M3) is the size of the public sector borrowing requirement (PSBR). To control M3, it is necessary to control the PSBR, as if the PSBR is never funded by selling bonds to the public, and that private sector demand for money is irrelevant as a determinant of supply. Third was the article of faith that government spending crowds out private spending, either directly if resources are fully employed (resource crowding out), or indirectly through rising interest rates to finance an ever-growing PSBR (financial crowding out) (see BUDGET DEFICIT). Fourth, there was belief in the concept of a natural rate of unemployment, and if governments attempted to reduce unemployment below what was regarded as the natural rate, there would be ever-accelerating inflation. All unemployment is essentially voluntary.

## Critique of Thatcher's monetarism

The monetarist experiment implemented in the UK from 1979 turned out to be an economic nightmare. The target money supply variable was M3 money, and the instrument of control was to reduce the size of the PSBR progressively from over £10 billion to zero. This was designed to give signals to markets and economic agents that the rate of inflation would gradually fall, so that workers should moderate wage demands and price themselves back into work. As it turned out, it proved impossible to control the growth of M3 money to within the target ranges, but the size of the PSBR and the rate of inflation did come down – the opposite of what monetarism predicted. The fiscal deficit contracted and the rate of interest soared – again, the opposite relationship postulated by monetarism. The exchange rate appreciated which, together with tight monetary and fiscal policy, produced a deep slump. Wage and price inflation moderated, but at the cost of heavy unemployment.

Friedman blamed the UK's failure to meet M3 targets on the incompetence of the Bank of England. However, it was soon recognized that the only way to control the supply of money in a credit-based economy is to control the demand through raising its price, i.e. by higher interest rates. Wage inflation was also recognized as a source of price inflation, and an attempt was made to impose a wages policy in the public sector. After only three years, the monetarist experiment began to crumble, but the damage to the economy had already been done with negative growth, falling investment, the destruction of manufacturing industry, and unemployment rising to over 3 million.

## Conclusion

Friedman monetarism (monetarism Mark I) as an intellectual fashion has died a slow death, and its stronger version, the new classical macroeconomics (or monetarism Mark II), pioneered by Robert Lucas, has fared no better. The quantity theory of money and the doctrine of monetarism are too simple and mechanical to be able to accommodate the complex interaction between costs, prices and the money supply in a modern credit-driven economy, and to disentangle the various inflationary impulses that exist in the real world.

## See also:

liquidity preference; monetary circuit; monetary policy and central banking functions; money, credit and finance: major contemporary themes

## Selected references

Friedman, M. (1956) "The Quantity Theory of Money – A Restatement," in M. Friedman (ed.), *Studies in the Quantity Theory of Money*, Chicago: University of Chicago Press.

—— (1968) "The Role of Monetary Policy," *American Economic Review*, 58(1).

Kaldor, N. (1982) *The Scourge of Monetarism*, Oxford: Oxford University Press.

Keynes, J.M. (1936) *The General Theory of Employment Interest and Money*, London: Macmillan.

A.P. THIRLWALL

# monetary circuit

According to the monetary circuit approach, CAPITALISM can be best depicted as a sequence of concatenated phases set in a discrete time interval, rather than as timeless simultaneous exchanges emphasized by neoclassical theory. This sequential process of capitalist production is initiated by the creation of purchasing power by banks, which is assumed to go toward monetary payments of inputs made prior to the production and selling of output in the commodity market. Within this monetary view of the capitalist process as a whole, it is the differential access to money which shapes various asymmetries of power relations among social agents, and is the principal factor determining the real structure of the economy, namely the level and sectoral allocation of employment, size and composition of output, DISTRIBUTION OF INCOME and the rate of ACCUMULATION.

## History

This is an approach that has its antecedents in the writings of MARX on the circuit of money capital, and in the work of Wicksell with his development of the first macroeconomic scheme of money creation and circulation entirely in terms of "pure credit" (Bellofiore 1992). Further extended by Austro-German and British writers during the interwar period, in more recent times this approach has been revived by the FRENCH CIRCUIT SCHOOL (Alain Parguez, Frédéric Poulon and Bernard Schmitt, preceded by Jacques Le Bourva) and by Italian writers (Augusto Graziani and

Marcello Messori), who have developed fruit-ful exchanges with post-Keynesians (see Dele-place and Nell 1996).

## Endogenous money and debt

In opposition to the orthodox view which traces money to a commodity, "circuitists" claim that, in a true monetary economy, money is a symbol or token (see MONEY, CREDIT AND FINANCE: HISTORY). More pre-cisely, money is a credit instrument in a triangular transaction in which payments are settled by means of promises to pay from a third agent (a bank). Consequently, circuitists devote special attention to the creation and destruction of money, which they depict as a strictly endogenous variable (see ENDOGENOUS MONEY AND CREDIT). They reject the neoclas-sical interpretation of the money stock as a multiple of the monetary base, the latter being determined by government deficits financed via central bank borrowing, as well as the thesis of a precedence of deposits over loans. Instead, they argue that, even outside Wick-sell's pure credit economy, money remains nothing but a debt. In a mixed-money system, bank deposits and central bank liabilities (reserves and notes outstanding) are a con-sequence of private bank loans and/or central bank advances to commercial banks and governments. Thus, "loans make deposits" and the banking system as a whole faces no constraints on monetary creation, other than the limits set endogenously by the interaction of the various agents in the financial system.

## Simple circuit model

The simplest circuit model assumes a closed economy, without a government sector or central bank. The basic agents are (a) the commercial banking sector, (b) firms and (c) households (workers). Money enters the econ-omy when banks grant firms the initial finance needed to commence production. This com-mand over the flow of credit money provides entrepreneurs, together with banks, power to control the whole process of production and

distribution. The monetary circuit can be logically separated into three distinct phases. At the beginning of the period of the circuit, the banking system creates purchasing power *ex nihilo*, which enables firms to cover current costs of production (wages and intermediate goods). During this first phase, the bargaining between firms and trade unions in the labor market sets the level of money wages, within a range conditioned by negotiations between banks and firms in the money market. This money market determines the level of short-term interest rates, together with the amount of credit advances to firms.

According to the monetary circuit view, employment and the size and composition of output are affected mainly by the autonomous decisions of entrepreneurs about production, which are implemented during the period. Within the final phase, however, workers freely choose how to divide their money income between consumption and saving. Money demand for consumption goods in relation to supply made available to workers by firms settles the price of consumption goods and, hence, the level of real wages. Saving instead may be channeled through the financial mar-ket, in which securities issued by firms are purchased at a long-term rate of interest, or be kept as money balances (including bank deposits).

If the flow of savings goes entirely toward the acquisition of securities in the financial market, firms would get back from households all of the initial finance, whose effect would be to allow entrepreneurs to extinguish the principal of their loans. This would signify the complete closure of the circuit, since all credit initially advanced would be destroyed. In this framework, the role of the financial market is to allow firms to recover the leakages due to the existence of household saving. If, on the other hand, some of the flow of savings is retained as liquid balances (bank deposits), this net addition to the money stock would merely reflect firms' outstanding debt not yet reim-bursed at the end of the circuit. The perma-nence of a money stock, therefore, signals an equivalent credit of households to the banking sector.

## Initial and final finance

A distinction between initial finance and final finance is useful here. Banks provide the "initial" finance of credit money needed to begin the production process, regardless of whether it be production of consumption or investment goods. "Final" finance to repay firms' total initial financing of production comes both from sales in the consumption goods market and from new securities issues in the financial market. Purchases of capital goods can be undertaken by households in the financial market (where stocks are sold to savers), and/or among firms themselves (through the expenditures of their net revenues). If the fraction of total output devoted to investment goods production exceeds the rate of household saving, the flow of investment in excess of voluntary saving would be financed through what some authors would describe as "forced saving," namely through a rise in consumption goods prices (Graziani 1994: 80–5). Others prefer to argue that the gap is financed through a corporate levy, reflecting the ability of firms to capture net revenues by pricing their output so as to realize some target rate of return consistent with corporate final financing requirements (Parguez 1996: 167–71). This would allow firms to reimburse part of the initial credit advances via the mechanism of what, in Kaleckian PRICING literature, is dubbed "internal finance."

## Payment of interest

Within the monetary circuit, firms as a whole cannot obtain more money than was initially injected. From a macroeconomic point of view, the non-financial business sector may capture sufficient revenues to repay both principal and interest (net of what banks may pay on deposits), only because of the existence of net exports and/or government budget deficits that give rise to a net monetary creation. In a closed system without government, firms may pay interest only by surrendering a share of real output, with interest being a tax levied on net revenue.

## Economic surplus

The circuit approach is fundamentally opposed to neoclassical economics with regard to both the role of saving and distribution theory. Entrepreneurs decide the quota of real output that workers could acquire in the consumption goods market where the latter spend their money wage. The residual ECONOMIC SURPLUS is partly appropriated by the banking (and rentier) sector as the real return for finance, and partly by the industrial sector in the form of profit. Thus, as KEYNES and KALECKI recognized, firms earn what they spend, while workers spend what they earn, with the banking sector claiming a share of firms' revenues. Those who have a privileged "command" over money claim real resources, while those who own only labor power are entitled merely to a money income. Saving, being part of the income emerging after production and bank finance, cannot be a precondition for capital accumulation. Producer sovereignty, rather than individual intertemporal preferences for consumption, dominates the capitalist process.

## See also:

circuit of social capital; monetary theory of production; producer and consumer sovereignty

## Selected references

Bellofiore, R. (1992) "Monetary Macroeconomics before the *General Theory*, the Circuit Theory of Money in Wicksell, Schumpeter and Keynes," *Social Concept* 6(2): 47–89.

Deleplace, G. and Nell, E.J. (eds) (1996) *Money in Motion*, Basingstoke: Macmillan.

Graziani, A. (1989) "The Theory of the Monetary Circuit," *Thames Papers in Political Economy*, Spring.

—— (1994) *La teoria monetaria della produ-*

*zione*, Arezzo: Banca Popolare dell'Etruria e del Lazio.

Parguez, A. (1996) "Financial Markets, Unemployment and Inflation within a Circuitist Framework," *Économies et sociétés* 30(2–3): 163–92.

RICCARDO BELLOFIORE<br>MARIO SECCARECCIA

# monetary policy and central banking functions

## Central bank functions and tools

Central banks exist in all developed countries; and all developed countries entrust central banks with a number of important economic functions. According to the neoclassical view, the main objective of the central bank is to maintain the value of the domestic currency by keeping inflation under control.

Central banks are given other responsibilities as well. They are supposed to be lenders of the last resort for the economy, and they are supposed to regulate and supervise the financial sector of the economy. In this capacity, they monitor the compliance of financial institutions with various rules and regulations (like capital requirements, rules on consumer lending and regulations on the interest rates that banks can pay to depositors). They can close down financial institutions that repeatedly fail to adhere to the central bank rules and regulations. Central banks also set margin requirements on brokerage accounts, and can intervene in foreign exchange markets to influence the value of the domestic currency.

To achieve these objectives, the central bank is given certain powers to regulate banks, financial institutions and financial markets as well as powers that give it some control of the domestic money supply and domestic interest rates. The three most important tools of a central bank are: (1) its ability to lend money to banks and other financial institutions, and its ability to set interest rates for these loans, (2) its ability to set reserve requirements, or the fraction of a bank's liabilities to depositors it must keep on hand and not lend out, and (3) its ability to buy and sell government securities (usually referred to as "open market operations").

## Three schools of thought on monetary policy

According to the neoclassical view, monetary authorities are thought to control the monetary base (also called "high-powered money"), which consists of currency held by the public and bank reserves. This is what the central bank can directly control, because it is central banks that create high-powered money. Whenever they purchase government securities and whenever they make loans to banks, the monetary base increases by an amount equal to the loan or the open market operation. The goal of monetary policy, however, is to control the money supply and overall macroeconomic performance (primarily, the price level). Hence, the links between the monetary base and the money supply, and between the money supply and the price level, become important in employing monetary policy.

The traditional view of monetary policy centers on the close relationships between the monetary base and the money supply and between the money supply and the price level. The authorities manage to reach a desired value for the price level, which is the final target of monetary policy, by carefully controlling the monetary base (see Friedman 1991).

The traditional Keynesian approach does not think that there is a clear and simple relationship between money and prices in economies. According to Keynes and Keynesians, the quantity of money in circulation determines the rate of interest rather than the price level (which depends on production costs and especially on money wages) (see Weintraub 1978: 43–8). In the Keynesian view, monetary policy has to be conducted in order to affect the equilibrium level of income (and of employment) through the rate of interest. For example, in the neoclassical synthesis of Keynesian theory, unemployment is presented as a phenomenon that can be fought by an expansion of the money supply (Modigliani 1963).

The post-Keynesian approach agrees with this critique, but also criticizes the neoclassical view by emphasizing problems with the relationship between the monetary base and the money supply. In particular, many post-Keynesians hold that the central bank does not find it convenient (or does not have the capability) to control the money supply through controlling the monetary base (Kaldor 1958; Wray 1990; Musella and Panico 1995). The arguments supporting this critique are twofold.

First, the central bank does not control all the channels through which the monetary base is created. For example, national governments usually retain the right to print and circulate currency. Also, because it performs the role of lender of last resort, the central bank cannot refuse to provide loans to commercial banks when they ask for it. If, in this case, the central bank tries to control the monetary base, money and financial markets can become more unstable and FINANCIAL INNOVATIONS can increase. Either of these events would prevent the central bank from reaching its policy targets (Minsky 1957).

Second, commercial banks have the opportunity to expand the amount of loans (and thus the money supply) independently of any increase to the monetary base (Tobin 1963). Actually, commercial banks are price makers and quantity takers, inside given limits. They draw up agreements with their customers, giving them wide overdraft margins. Many companies, in developed financial systems, have prearranged lines of credit on overdraft facilities with their bankers (Moore 1988: 24). This phenomenon implies that the quantity of money (or credit) in circulation, inside given limits, tends to increase as the demand for money increases, and is independent of variations in the monetary base.

According to post-Keynesian political economists, the supply of money is determined by the demand for money, which is dependent on the price level, level of income and rate of interest. As prices increase, or as economic activity expands, firms must borrow more money and banks generally comply. Central banks or monetary authorities determine the rate of interest, while the level of income depends on real factors such as the marginal efficiency of capital, fiscal policy, income distribution and the rate of interest.

Finally, in the post-Keynesian approach, monetary policy is looked at more broadly than in the neoclassical model. Monetary and fiscal policy cannot have different goals, but are both coordinated in the pursuit of national economic stability. This implies that the central bank cannot concentrate on price stability, leaving to different authorities the pursuit of other objectives. Both fiscal and monetary authorities have to contribute to the fulfillment of their macroeconomic goals: a high and stable level of employment, reasonable stability of the internal purchasing power of money, steady economic growth and improvement of the standard of living (see Musella and Panico 1995: xviii–xx). Hence, according to the post-Keynesians, central banking is concerned with the stability of financial markets in order to achieve the stability of the economy.

## Simplified models of different schools

The neoclassical framework of money and prices can be summarized in a highly simplified fashion, by the following equations where $M$ is the money supply, $B$ is the monetary base and $P$ is the price level:

$$M = f(B) \tag{1}$$
$$P = g(M) \tag{2}$$

Hence, we can derive:

$$P = \phi(B) \quad \text{(where } \phi = fg) \tag{3}$$

It is easy to obtain from (3) the value of the monetary base that the central bank has to establish in order to reach the desired target of the price level:

$$B = \phi^{-1}(P) \tag{4}$$

The most recent version of the neoclassical theory of monetary policy has been expounded in the writings of Friedman (for example, Friedman 1991).

The traditional Keynesian approach criticizes the quantity theory of money and considers equation (2) to be an incorrect representation of the role of money in the economic process. According to Keynes and Keynesians, the quantity of money in circulation must be considered relevant for the determination of the rate of interest ($r$), not of the price level (that depends on production costs ($C$), and especially on money wages; see, for example, Weintraub (1978: 43–8). So, a Keynesian system of equations can be written in this way:

$$M = f(B) \tag{1}$$
$$r = g(M) \tag{2'}$$
$$P = h(C) \tag{3'}$$
$$C = C^* \tag{4'}$$

where $C^*$ is a given level of production costs. Hence, in the Keynesian view, monetary policy has to be conducted in order to affect the equilibrium level of income (and of employment) through the rate of interest.

In the post-Keynesian approach, the neoclassical thesis has been criticized in a more radical way. In fact, post-Keynesians agree with the Keynesian critique of equation (2), but they emphasize also the limits of the traditional interpretation of equation (1). Post-Keynesians in particular, as mentioned above, consider that the central bank does not find it convenient (or it does not have the capability) to control the money supply through the control of the monetary base.

A post-Keynesian model can be written as follows:

$$B = f(M) \tag{1''}$$
$$M^d = z(P, Y, r) = M^s \tag{2''}$$
$$P = h(C) \tag{3'}$$
$$C = C^* \tag{4'}$$
$$r = r^* \tag{5}$$
$$Y = Y(e, g, r, l) \tag{6}$$

Equation (2'') states that the supply of money is determined by the demand for money, which is dependent on the price level, level of income ($Y$) and rate of interest. Equation (5) states that in the post-Keynesian approach, the rate of interest is determined by the monetary authorities, while equation (6) states that the level of income depends on real factors, such as the marginal efficiency of capital ($e$), fiscal policy ($g$), income distribution ($l$), and the rate of interest ($r$). Hence, according to the post-Keynesians, central banking is concerned especially with the stability of financial markets in order to achieve the stability of the economy.

## See also:

endogenous money and credit; liability management; money, credit and finance: major contemporary themes; money, nature and role of

## Selected references

Friedman, M. (1991) *Monetarist Economics*, Oxford: Basil Blackwell.

Kaldor, N. (1958) "Monetary Policy, Economic Stability and Growth," Memorandum submitted to the Radcliffe Committee on the Working of the Monetary System, 23 June, *Principal Memoranda of Evidence*, Cmnd 827, London: HMSO, 1960, 146–53; repr. in N. Kaldor, *Essays on the Economic Policy I*, London: Duckworth, 128–53.

Minsky, H.P. (1957) "Central Banking and Money Market Changes," *Quarterly Journal of Economics* 71(2): 171–87.

Modigliani, F. (1963) "The Monetary Mechanism and its Interaction with Real Phenomena," *Review of Economic and Statistics* 45(February): 79–107.

Moore, B.J. (1988) *Horizontalists and Verticalists: The Macroeconomics of Credit Money*, Cambridge: Cambridge University Press.

Musella, M. and Panico, C. (eds) (1995) *Money Supply in the Economic Process*, Aldershot: Edward Elgar.

Tobin, J. (1963) "Commercial Banks as Creators of 'Money'," in D. Carson (ed.), *Banking and Monetary Studies*, Homewood, IL: Irwin, 408–19.

Weintraub, S. (1978) *Capitalism's Inflation and Unemployment*, Reading, MA: Addison-Wesley.

Wray, R. (1990) *Money and Credit in Capitalist Economies*, Aldershot: Edward Elgar.

MARCO MUSELLA

# monetary theory of production

## Nature and components

The monetary theory of production, as opposed to the theory of a real-exchange economy, is the theoretical core of many heterodox approaches to POLITICAL ECONOMY. This especially includes J.M. Keynes's *General Theory of Employment, Interest and Money*, post-Keynesian extensions and developments thereof, particular Marxian perspectives, and institutionalist thought.

Almost exclusively applied to the analysis of capitalist or "entrepreneurial" economies, the monetary theory of production encompasses these key components:

- the goal of capitalist production is to sell output for more money than was expended on buying the inputs used producing it, i.e. profit measured in monetary terms;
- commercial banks play a central role in endogenously creating both the wherewithal for firms to purchase the required inputs of production, and the system's ability to generate monetary profits;
- economic decisions are made within a context of fundamental uncertainty; and
- all economic agents, worker households, rentiers, and firms, need to make portfolio decisions within such a context.

Money is, consequently, not neutral in both the short-period and the long-period.

## Similarity in heterodoxy

The development of the monetary theory of production was a central and fundamental step in Keynes's break with classical/neoclassical economics and in the building of his general theory (Keynes 1971–83, vol. 13: 408–11). He recognized that this "distinction between a cooperative economy and an entrepreneur economy" is similar to Marx's observation that, in a capitalist economy, the goal of the capitalist is to part with money in order to obtain more money (1867: 248–57). Although KEYNES paid homage to MARX, he felt that Marx did not get very far with this observation (Keynes 1971–83, vol. 29: 81).

Marx and Keynes were not the only critics of the orthodoxy of their day, with a vision that the essential character of the capitalist economy lay in its monetary production nature. Others include Thorstein VEBLEN, Clarence Ayres and other institutionalists, Joseph SCHUMPETER, J.A. Hobson and Silvio Gesell. The monetary theory of production is a distinguishing characteristic of heterodox economists as compared with the classical, neoclassical or new classical orthodoxy. Consequently, modern adherence to the monetary theory of production can be found in a variety of specific and sometimes incomplete forms, ranging from post-Keynesian, Kaleckian, regulation, French Circuit, Marxian, institutional, Schumpeterian and social economics perspectives.

## Orthodox money neutrality

The monetary theory of production stands in contradistinction to the real-exchange theory of classical, neoclassical and new classical economics. Orthodoxy sees money as being neutral in the long run: the economy can be analyzed "as if" monetary considerations do not exist, money is imposed exogenously on the economy, and fundamental uncertainty is systematically assumed away. Consequently, "the most serious challenge that the existence of money poses to the theorist is this: the best developed [neoclassical] model of the economy cannot find room for it. The best developed model is, of course, the Arrow–Debreu version of a Walrasian general equilibrium" (Hahn 1981: 1). When production is also forced into the picture, "all hell is let loose (and) for what might look a little like actual economies, we have nothing to offer" (Hahn 1981: 32).

## Circuit of money capital

Most recognizably schematized by Marx's "circuit of money capital," $M \rightarrow C \ldots P \ldots C' \rightarrow M'$ (1899: 109–43), the search for monetary profit is mediated by a time-consuming production process, and involves the monetary (M) purchase of the commodity (C) inputs, $M \rightarrow C$, the activation of the inputs within the sphere of production ($\ldots P \ldots$), and the sale of the produced commodities (C') for a hopefully larger (M') amount of money, $C' \rightarrow M'$ (see MONETARY CIRCUIT; CIRCUIT OF SOCIAL CAPITAL). Short-term expectations of sales need to be formed in order to determine the quantities of output to be produced, and the inputs to be purchased in advance of sales occurring.

These expectations can, of course, be disappointed (Keynes 1971–83, vol. 7: 46–51). Time is also involved in selling the output after it has been produced, i.e. its circulation time (Marx 1889: 200–206). The explicit incorporation of fixed capital, of which Marx was an early proponent (1889: 268–305), brings to the fore the heterogeneous physical inputs that are repeatedly used over many periods. This involves long-lasting monetary commitments, and highlights the role of long-term EXPECTATIONS (Keynes 1971–83, vol. 7: 147–64).

Within the monetary theory of production it is explicitly recognized that the purchase of labor power and circulating and fixed capital inputs to production need financing. Banks are, directly or indirectly, the endogenous providers of this finance (Davidson 1978: 269–337; Wray 1990: 72–4) (see ENDOGENOUS MONEY AND CREDIT). Production is thus the key avenue by which money enters the economy and, contrary to real-exchange analyses, money "is not created like the manna from heaven of a Patinkinesque world, or dropped by helicopter as in Friedman's construction" (Davidson 1978: 147).

## Uncertainty and liquidity preference

The monetary theory of production is one set within a context of true uncertainty where there is no perfect foresight, no full set of contingent markets and no reducibility to a context of risk (Davidson 1978: 9–32). As a result, the social and institutional creation of short-term and long-term expectations becomes meaningful. This uncertainty is created and sustained within a persistent process of technical progress, dynamic change and institutional renovation (see Marx 1867: 762–876; Schumpeter 1942: 81–6; see SCHUMPETER'S THEORY OF INNOVATION, DEVELOPMENT AND CYCLES).

Within this uncertain context, money becomes logically a store of value (Keynes 1971–83, vol. 14: 115) and monetary liquidity and portfolio decisions become crucial (see LIQUIDITY PREFERENCE; SPECULATION). This is best reflected in Keynes's general theory of value, where the expected return of holding any durable asset is determined by $q - c + l + a$; where $q$ is the expected yield from holding the asset, $c$ is the carrying cost of the asset, $l$ is the partially-subjectively determined liquidity premium of the asset, and $a$ is the expected appreciation or depreciation of the value of the asset with respect to the domestic unit of account.

In equilibrium, when all expected own rates of return are equalized across all durable assets, the expected return on the most liquid asset ("money") establishes the standard return that all other durable assets must exceed in order to induce wealth holders to part with liquidity. These considerations determine, among other things, the amount of investment in fixed capital that is undertaken and the resulting major macroeconomic magnitudes like employment, income and profit.

Money's liquidity considerations are part of all decisions in the monetary theory of production. All production and related actions need to be financed in the monetary theory of production. As Keynes (1971–83, vol 23: 408–409) put it, the monetary theory of production describes "an economy in which money plays a part of its own and affects motives and decisions and ... the course of events cannot be predicted in the long period or in the short, without a knowledge of the behavior of money between the first state and the last."

## See also:

accumulation; animal spirits; financial instability hypothesis; Kalecki's macro theory of profits; money, credit and finance; major contemporary themes

## Selected references

Davidson, Paul (1978) *Money and the Real World*, 2nd edn, London: Macmillan.

Hahn, Frank (1981) *Money and Inflation*, Cambridge, MA: MIT Press.

Keynes, John Maynard (1971–83) *The Collected Writings of John Maynard Keynes*, London: Macmillan, and Cambridge: Cambridge University Press.

Marx, Karl (1867) *Das Kapital*, vol. 1, published as *Capital: A Critique of Political Economy, Vol. I*, New York: Vintage, 1977.

—— (1889) *Das Kapital*, vol. 2, published as *Capital: A Critique of Political Economy, Vol. II*, New York: Vintage, 1981.

Schumpeter, Joseph A. (1942) *Capitalism, Socialism and Democracy*, New York: Harper, 1975.

Wray, L. Randall (1990) *Money and Credit in Capitalist Economies*, Aldershot: Edward Elgar.

JOHAN DEPREZ
L. RANDALL WRAY

# money

Money is generally considered to be that universally accepted medium that enters into every exchange in a monetized economy. While there is no adequate, single definition for money, an acceptable, though vague, explanation might be "money is as money does" or, as Gertrude Stein put it an article in the *Saturday Evening Post*, "Whether you like it or whether you do not, money is money and that is all there is about it" ("Money," 13 July 1936: 88).

## Brief history

The history of money is so ancient as to be lost in the mists of time. There is evidence that precious metals may have been used as a commodity money (items functioning as money having value in their own right) as early as 20,000 BC. Currency, in the form of coins, is much more recent. Herodotus noted the use of coins in the ancient kingdom of Lydia in the seventh century BC, and many monetary historians believe that coins may have come into use a few hundred years earlier, in India. Fiat money (money that only functions as money because of the mutual acceptance by market participants), was first seen between AD 1500 and 1600 with the inception of warehouse banking. Fractionally backed fiat currency became quite common shortly thereafter as currency custodians realized that the entire store of money was rarely called for all at once. Most currencies today are pure fiat currency (fiat money not backed by the physical store of any commodity).

## Money and value

Money is unique due to its relationship with all other goods: money is used to denominate the "value" of other goods as the unit of account. As Simmel (1907) suggested, the money value of a good is the objectification of that good's intrinsic, subjective value. Further, Marx stated that: "Money degrades all the gods of mankind and turns them into commodities. Money is the universal and self-constituted value set upon all things. It has therefore robbed the whole world, of both nature and man, of its original value" (Marx 1844: 41).

Marx noted that money is merely a historical phenomenon that reflects economic and social development. Essentially all economies in the transition from primitive to modern society use money. The primary consequence of this nearly irresistible spread of money is "the inexorable homogenization and flattening of social ties" (Zelizer 1994: 2).

## Major functions of money

The primary function of money is to operate as a medium of exchange, or "circulation" in Marxian parlance. It also serves as a unit of account and as a store of value (a unit of money can be spent either today or in the future). A related function is that it operates as a standard of deferred payment (future prices are denominated in money terms). In order for money to exist, there must be defensible PROPERTY rights. Without the concept of property, there is no true trade. The classical concept of the origins of money suggests that money arose due to the inherent inconveniences of barter (the large number of required prices and the "double coincidence of want" necessary for a direct transaction).

Money may play a more crucial role, however, as Heinsohn and Steiger (1983) suggested. The original breakdown of community, or tribal, security that occurred with the creation of private property may have directly motivated the invention of money. Its primary purpose, then, is to act as a readily transferable stock of assets or wealth as a personal hedge against uncertainty, that can then be borrowed or lent as the need arises. In sum, money serves to control assets or, more succinctly put, money is power. The existence of money can, therefore, contribute to the dominance of an elite CLASS by allowing the intergenerational transfer of accumulated power, in the form of wealth (see CLASS PROCESSES).

## Monetized economies

Money, however, is more than a set of characteristics or functions. It is intrinsically linked to the economy. Economies can be classified either as "monetary" or "natural/barter." Contrary to popular supposition, Heinsohn and Steiger (1983) pointed out that money is not the sign of a monetized economy but the result of it. Specifically, Keynes (1930) suggested that it is possible to have a monetized economy without physical money (electronic transfers can serve the purpose, for example). It is the existence of private property and the creditor–debtor relationship that is the hallmark of a monetized economy. Creditor–debtor relationships require the ready transference of a security stock of assets (the primary purpose of money) on which a liquidity premium is paid. Heinsohn and Steiger (1983) went so far as to demonstrate that the etymology of the Latin word for "money" arises not from barter or trade but from debts and contracts.

In the modern capitalist society, money (or rather credit, since money is essentially endogenous in a credit-based society) and the hoarding of capital are the preconditions for economic crisis. Whenever monetary authorities do not accommodate the reserve needs of the financial markets, the banking system and, therefore, the economy at large will be destabilized (de Brunhoff 1973) (see MONETARY POLICY AND CENTRAL BANKING FUNCTIONS; FREE BANKING).

The post-Keynesian and institutionalist viewpoints recognize that money is inseparable from the economy. In fact, the direction of causality most frequently cited by orthodox economics, that of money affecting the economy (see VELOCITY AND THE MONEY MULTIPLIER), should be reversed. When left alone, the financial system will attempt to create the necessary liquidity required by the economy via financial innovation. Examples include the emergence of certificates of deposit (CDs), money market accounts, repurchase agreements and bank bills (bills of exchange). It is only when monetary authorities attempt to prevent bank reserves from growing at the pace required by the economy that the liquidity of the banking system will be endangered. In the short run, such restrictive actions may cause a financial crisis, a cyclical downturn and/or a rise in the level of interest rates (Arestis and Eichner 1988).

## See also:

endogenous money and credit; financial crises;

financial innovations; liability management; monetary theory of production

## Selected references

Arestis, Philip and Eichner, Alfred S. (1988) "The Post-Keynesian and Institutionalist Theory of Money and Credit," *Journal of Economic Issues* 22(4): 1003–21.

de Brunhoff, Suzanne (1973) *Marx on Money*, trans. Maurice J. Goldbloom, New York: Urizen.

Heinsohn, Gunnar and Steiger, Otto (1983) "Private Property, Debts and Interest or: the Origin of Money and the Rise and Fall of Monetary Economies," *Studi Economici* 21: 3–55.

Keynes, John Maynard (1930) *Treatise on Money*, London: Macmillan.

Marx, Karl (1844) *A World Without Jews*, New York: Philosophical Library, 1959.

—— (1867) *Das Kapital*, vol. 1, New York: International Publishers, 1970.

Simmel, Georg (1907) *The Philosophy of Money*, ed. David Frisby, trans. Tom Bottomore and David Frisby, London: Routledge, 1990.

Zelizer, Viviana (1994) *The Social Meaning of Money*, New York: Basic Books.

NANCY J. BURNETT

# money, credit and finance: history

The dominant orthodoxy in monetary theory is based on a tradition of "real" analysis and a "commodity" view of money which can be generically denoted as the quantity theory tradition. The quantity theory, to which the majority of mainstream economists directly or indirectly subscribe, is primarily the offspring of an intellectual movement originating in the Middle Ages. It developed in direct opposition to what was the then established view dominating European intellectual discourse for over a millennium.

## Cartalist view of money

The then alternative, known as the "nominalist" or "cartalist" theory, regarded money as a mere token established by convention. The traditional functions of money, as medium of exchange and unit of account, had to do with the legal status bestowed on it by the state authority and not with the intrinsic worth of the commodity chosen for legal tender. Money, being the ultimate liability of the state, is a creation of the legal system that sanctions and determines its nominal value as a monetary unit. This widely held view found its intellectual and legal justification in writings of the ancient philosophers, such as Plato and Aristotle, and in Roman jurisprudence. Owing its existence to the state, money appears as a necessary element of social integration and a critical mechanism for the distribution of economic benefits of the DIVISION OF LABOR.

Only when appropriated privately for other purposes, such as in the case of usury, does money take on a destabilizing role which ancient philosophers found morally unjustified. With the state's right of seignorage (through its legal authority over the mint), this widely-held view regarding the state administered value of money also provided a convenient theory, particularly for cash-starved medieval centralizing authorities who commonly practiced currency debasement as a way of overcoming their liquidity constraints and dealing with pressing problems of public finance.

## Metallist view of money

Opposed to the use made of this cartalist theory, there emerged a competing "commodity" or, more precisely, "metallist" view of money broadly associated with the works especially of such fourteenth-century scholastic writers as Nicholas Oresme. Representing the views of the nascent commercial classes, these writers were opposed to the widespread practice of currency alteration and some of them ultimately came to question the philosophical basis of the medieval authorities' right of seignorage. For these critics, the old cartalist conception was based on the erroneous belief that money's crucial legal property of fungibility (establishing the legal nominal equivalence of monetary units in circulation) could be conferred on commodities merely by government decree. Rejecting this view on the basis of a powerful theoretical construct that was later dubbed Gresham's Law, they opted for the principle that money ought not only be fungible in the legal sense but it should also be homogeneous with regard to the physical property of each monetary unit in circulation.

In a pure metal-based monetary system in which the state's privilege is largely taken away, and where money now appears as a scarce asset without seemingly being conceived as a state liability, the risks of alterations leading to problems of inflation and, finally, to a flight from money are reduced. As long as the metallic standard is adhered to, the existence of physical barriers to monetary expansion would be the ultimate guarantee against inflation and arbitrary taxation by the state. The rising bourgeoisie, who thrived on commercial expansion based on monetary exchanges, would thus be safe from the perceived instabilities connected with a perpetually altered currency system.

This commodity or metallist theory of money as an asset, without correspondingly being conceived as someone's liability, became established and served specific imperialist needs during the mercantilist era. Centralizing monarchs, in conjunction with the powerful commercial classes, became concerned with acquiring command over precious metals. This is not to imply that the cartalist theory had completely lost its appeal. In opposition to some of the leading metallists of the period such as Child, Petty, Locke, Cantillon and Hume, there emerged formidable cartalist opponents such as Barbon, Law and Steuart (Vickers 1959: 31). For instance, developing what later came to be described as the Real Bills doctrine, Law pointed to "good security" (such as land) rather than metal convertibility as the criterion for notes issuance (Green 1992: 118). Unfortunately, the failure of Law's system

in France put an end, temporarily, to the possible appeal of both the original cartalist approach and its more modern version, the credit theory of money (the latter being subsequently popularized over a century later by the Banking School) (see Rist 1940: 62).

## Bullionists and the currency principle

Of historical importance, however, the metallist theory was, above all, the critical step toward the nineteenth-century monetary orthodoxy as first developed by the bullionists over the issue of a convertible currency and then later enunciated in the currency principle in Britain. If, because of convenience and security, state-backed fiat money becomes indispensable, what ought to be the rules governing such a monetary system? The advocates of this principle, such as Ricardo, not only argued that currency should be convertible to bullion but that it "should vary precisely as would a purely specie circulation and that there should be permitted no discretionary departure from such manner of variation whatsoever" (Mints 1945: 75).

The monetary system would be self-regulating as long as money adheres to a metallic standard, whereby its supply is not at the discretion of the monetary authority but is, in a sense, exogenous to the authority itself. Accordingly, one must tie the hands of the state by imposing a transparent rule for issuing money on the basis of a clearly-defined standard. Any departure from such a rule by producing a state liability that, say, is excessive in relation to its commodity base would bring about inflationary consequences. Inflation, therefore, is merely a visible symptom of a process of monetary "debasement" of the state liability, analogous to what had been defended by earlier medieval writers.

## Modern quantity theory

As modern monetary systems slowly moved away from metallic standards (gold and bimetallism) and the theory itself witnessed its golden age during the post-1870 period, only the exogeneity aspect of the original analytical framework of the quantity theory remained intact, especially in its twentieth-century re-incarnations in the writings of Fisher, Pigou and Friedman (see Laidler 1991). Yet, despite this evolution, as numerous critics have emphasized (Rogers 1989: 171–6), this commodity conception of money, as a stock that individuals wish to hold still, forms the key underlying presupposition of dominant neo-Walrasian monetary theory (see MONETARISM).

## Alternative endogenous money views

During the last two centuries, opponents of orthodoxy developed competing views. As emphasized by numerous contemporary writers who have studied the intellectual history of endogenous money theory (see Wray 1990), the issue of endogeneity emerged as the first and principal line of attack against both the original commodity view and its modern offsprings. In a commodity-money world, the assumption of money exogeneity may be appropriate since money appears as an asset the supply of which is resource constrained, and does not appear as someone's liability. In a credit-money world of private bank money, such an assumption becomes meaningless. For the nineteenth-century advocates of the banking principle, money was a good *sui generis*, whose critical characteristics of liquidity and endogeneity prevented it from being tied to any one commodity or group of commodities.

What the currency theorists neglected to recognize was the essential role played by banks as creators of endogenous money. Bank credit is money and, unlike commodity money, what is an asset must necessarily be someone else's liability. Through the loans-deposits process, credit-money is created at the initiative of the borrower. Over-issue of banknotes could never arise since the money supply is essentially demand driven. Whether it be the eighteenth-century world of goldsmith banking or the ultimate Wicksellian analogy of a pure credit economy, the money supply now appears as an endogenous outcome of private decisions.

As a further outgrowth of the Banking principle, there came the discovery of a monetary circuit, arising from Tooke's articulation of the law of reflux. Following Tooke's flux/reflux principle, credit-money first emerges to finance productive activities in accordance, say, with the Real Bills doctrine. Once firms capture revenues from the sphere of circulation, this initial injection of credit is extinguished by means of its ultimate reflux to the banking and financial system. Emphasis is placed, therefore, on the flows of credit rather than on the stock of money and, perhaps more importantly, the emphasis is on the circular nature of credit flows. MARX later embraced a particular variant of this approach when he specified his famous circuit of money-capital $M \rightarrow C \rightarrow M'$, and highlighted the problem of the reflux of credit-money in Volume 3 of *Das Kapital*, as being critical to both the realization of surplus value and an understanding of financial crises (see CIRCUIT OF SOCIAL CAPITAL). By the late nineteenth century, an alternative view to the dominant quantity-theory orthodoxy had thus emerged to explain the genesis and persistence of the credit cycle. Much like Marx's analysis, for heterodox writers such as Veblen, crises took the form of recurrent periods of liquidation of previous build-up of credit brought about by the interaction of the financial system with activities of absentee owners or rentiers.

Throughout the twentieth century, the theory of money endogeneity has remained the principal line of criticism of orthodoxy. Admittedly, this competing theory has also been a characteristic feature of some nonconformist writings such as those of Hayek and the free banking theorists, on the one hand, and of the Swedish followers of Wicksell and SCHUMP-ETER, on the other. However, the concept of money-supply endogeneity describes, during the postwar period, primarily the work of post-Keynesian theorists who have built on the original views put forth by KEYNES in his *Treatise on Money* and in his later writings on the finance motive. In the 1950s, elements of this theory first resurfaced in the work of the Radcliffe Commission (Britain) and in the writings of Gurley and Shaw (USA) and Le Bourva (France). This was followed during the

1960s and 1970s by the work of numerous post-Keynesian writers, such as Kaldor, Davidson and Minsky.

However, within the ENDOGENOUS MONEY AND CREDIT camp, opinions diverged on the issue of the slope of the money supply curve, which has led to two opposing theories: the horizontalists (represented by Kaldor and Moore) who believe that interest rates are set exogenously with the supply of money being perfectly elastic at a given rate of interest, and the structuralists (or liquidity preference theorists) who support the view that interest rates are determined endogenously within the financial markets and are positively related to overall demand pressures in the economy (see MONEY, CREDIT AND FINANCE: MAJOR CONTEMPORARY THEMES). Despite such differences, all these critics of monetary orthodoxy subscribe to the fundamental post-Keynesian position that the supply of money is purely demand driven along the lines of nineteenth-century supporters of the Banking principle. At the same time, a revival of Tooke's famous flux/reflux principle has also occurred with the advent of the Franco-Italian school of the MONETARY CIRCUIT that conceptually integrates Keynes's theory of the finance motive, the Kaleckian theory of profit, Schumpeter's analysis of the credit circuit and some of the original work of the Banking School (see also the FRENCH CIRCUIT SCHOOL).

In addition to this principal line of attack with regards to money endogeneity, heterodox monetary theorists historically have also rejected the dominant commodity view of money for a number of less well-known reasons. Among the most famous of these critiques, there is the spillover from the physical sciences with the recognition and application of ENTROPY, NEGENTROPY AND LAWS OF THERMODYNAMICS to monetary theory. If, as classical and neoclassical theorists surmised, money should be treated *as if* it were a commodity, then should it not also suffer the same natural consequences afflicting the physical world? Unlike physical goods that depreciate over time, debt money grows with compound interest and, therefore, largely seems to escape the effects of entropy. To prevent the periodic realignment or financial crises that arise because of this asymmetry between money and physical goods, these late nineteenth- and early twentieth-century heterodox thinkers, such as Silvio Gesell and Frederick Soddy, inferred that this imbalance could be eliminated only by systematically taxing liquid holdings (see Seccareccia 1997). Though less celebrated, these heterodox ideas were recognized by Keynes in the *General Theory* as important undercurrents of thought in the diagnosis of capitalism.

## See also:

monetary theory of production

## Selected references

Green, Roy (1992) *Classical Theories of Money, Output and Inflation: A Study in Historical Economics*, London: Macmillan.

Laidler, David E.W. (1991) *The Golden Age of the Quantity Theory: The Development of Neoclassical Monetary Economics, 1870–1914*, Princeton, NJ: Princeton University Press.

Mints, Lloyd W. (1945) *History of Banking Theory in Great Britain and the United States*, Chicago: University of Chicago Press.

Rist, Charles (1940) *History of Monetary and Credit Theory*, New York: Macmillan.

Rogers, Colin (1989) *Money, Interest and Capital*, Cambridge: Cambridge University Press.

Seccareccia, Mario (1997) "Early Twentieth-Century Heterodox Monetary Thought," in Avi J. Cohen, Harald Hagemann and John Smithin (eds), *Money, Financial Institutions and Macroeconomics*, Boston: Kluwer-Nijhoff.

Vickers, Douglas (1959), *Studies in the Theory of Money, 1690–1776*, Philadelphia: Chilton.

Wray, L. Randall (1990) *Money and Credit in Capitalist Economies*, Aldershot: Edward Elgar.

MARIO SECCARECCIA

# money, credit and finance: major contemporary themes

## Introduction

KEYNES argued that money is the most liquid asset, used due to UNCERTAINTY, and that the division between money and non-money liquid assets is arbitrary. Money is generally defined by its primary functions – medium of exchange and means of payment – and those liquid assets that best serve these purposes are called money. Post-Keynesian political economy, however, has tended to define money as a "time machine" that transfers purchasing power from the present to the future (the store of value function). While any asset can do this, money is the only generally accepted means of payment in the present and the future (Davidson 1978).

Others have focused on SPECULATION and the speculative demand for money (Rousseas 1992). Some emphasize that modern money is just a debt issued by banks, the central bank, the treasury, and potentially by any firm that is believed to be credit worthy (Minsky 1986). No sharp line is drawn between "money" and "credit." Rather, any debt which is denominated in the unit of account, and which can be converted near par against central bank liabilities is "money." Others (the FRENCH CIRCUIT SCHOOL, in particular) define money as the particular invention of banks, created whenever banks provide loans.

An important approach is that of the Cartalists (and Keynes in the *Treatise on Money*), who believed that money is that which is accepted at public pay offices (for example, in payment of taxes and other obligations to the government). The government not only enforces "legal tender laws," it decides what shall be accepted as "legal tender." This means that when banks grant "credit" they also create "money," and this special status is conferred on them because the government accepts their liabilities. While other institutions can grant credit they cannot create money.

Finally, finance refers to purchasing power required for expenditure, and income flows may finance spending flows at the individual level. Where income is insufficient, if one can issue liabilities to "buy now, pay later," then spending is debt financed. Finance is usually distinguished from funding. Generally, finance refers to short-term indebtedness incurred, for example, during the construction phase of an investment project. Funding refers to the "take-out" long-term bonds (or equity) issued when the project is complete (see FINANCE CAPITAL).

## Endogenous money

A critical contribution of heterodoxy to macroeconomics is the development of an ENDOGENOUS MONEY AND CREDIT approach. This is now generally accepted by all heterodox economists, including institutionalists, post-Keynesians, Circuitistes and many Marxists (see Lavoie 1992; Deleplace and Nell 1996; Smithin 1994; Wray 1990). To be sure, endogenous money has not been developed out of whole cloth; rather, there is a direct lineage from the Banking School through Marx, to the Cartalists and Knapp, and finally to Keynes and some of his followers.

A modern "revival" began with early postwar debates concerning the velocity of money, beginning with Kaldor but with important extensions being made by Rousseas and Minsky. These early developments were partially a reaction to the truncated "money sector" of the neoclassical synthesis, and to policy discussions concerning the ability of central banks to control inflation through control over the money supply. Briefly, Kaldor argued that, as velocity could increase essentially without limit, central banks would be powerless in attempts to control the money supply.

Minsky's extension argued that attempts to constrain bank lending would induce FINANCIAL INNOVATIONS, which expand velocity and render central banks ineffective. Both Rousseas and Minsky emphasized the positive relationship between interest rates and velocity, so that tight money policy would cause a substitution of "near" money for "narrow" money, thus increasing velocity (see Wray 1990; Rousseas 1992). Even if the central bank controlled narrow money, this would have no necessary impact on broader money and spending.

In the "mainstream" approach, financial institutions are essentially ignored, the money supply is directly controlled by the central bank, and money demand is a function of current income and interest rates. The heterodox approach – especially that of the American post-Keynesians – evolved as an understanding of the operation of financial institutions and markets improved. According to Minsky (1986), banks (like all firms) take positions in assets by issuing liabilities. So long as expected income flows exceed expected debt service, with a sufficient margin for error and net income, banks "make loans" by "issuing deposits." Others, such as Dymski (in Deleplace and Nell 1996) and Moore (1988), have continued to develop the "banking firm" analysis. By treating banks like other firms, it became apparent that the simple "money multiplier" and "exogenous money supply" of orthodoxy could not be reconciled with profit-seeking behavior by either banks or their customers.

The recognition (by Davidson 1978, Minsky 1986 and others) that spending must be *financed*, eliminated the supposed independence between the "IS" and "LM" curves (or, the "real" and "money" sectors): the "money supply" would expand along with spending. This was a far more decisive break with orthodoxy than was the "variable velocity" argument.

However, if a country had adopted effective and legally required reserve ratios, how could banks expand lending and deposits if the central bank stood fast and refused to supply needed reserves? Two lines of defense were taken. Minsky, especially, relied on the observation that banks can economize on reserves, primarily by "operating on liabilities" – that is, by issuing liabilities with lower reserve requirements – but also by reducing excess reserves. On the other hand, first Kaldor and then Moore emphasized that, in practice, central banks do not refuse to supply legally required reserves, for this would pressure banks

to break the law (see Moore 1988; Wray 1990). This led to the conclusion that, no matter what the central bank announces as its target, in practice, on any given day all it can do is administer the rate at which reserves will be supplied.

## Circuitistes and horizontalists

Another tradition which has contributed to the understanding of money and credit, but with less emphasis on the "technical" details of financial institution practices, is the French-Italian "Circuitiste" approach. This can be traced from Schumpeter, Le Bourva and Schmitt (see Deleplace and Nell 1996). Here, the emphasis is on the logical necessity of providing finance before spending can be activated. Often a pure credit economy is assumed, with bank loans providing finance to firms to begin the production cycle (paying wages and other costs). Deposits then flow to households concomitantly with incomes, and then back to firms as households consume. The circuit is "closed" when receipts of firms are sufficient to retire the original loans.

Thus, Circuitistes reject the independence of "real" and "monetary" sectors even more forcefully than do post-Keynesians. Furthermore, Circuitistes tend to focus on money as a "flow" (that finances spending), while post-Keynesians have tended to focus on money as a "hoard," held to "lull disquietude" in the face of an uncertain future (see Wray, in Deleplace and Nell 1996).

In some respects, the Circuitiste approach is close to a particular variant of post--Keynesianism, horizontalism, the fullest development of which is Moore (1988; see also Smithin 1994). According to Moore, the central bank "administers" short-term interest rates (and not just the overnight rate) as the marginal supplier of reserves. Banks "mark up" over the overnight rate to obtain the short-term retail loan rate, and "mark down" to obtain the retail deposit rate.

"Wholesale" short-term rates are market determined, as each individual bank tries to rectify any mismatch of retail loans and deposits. Finally, long-term rates are determined by the market's expectation of the future short-term interest rate. According to Moore, a bank merely announces a retail loan rate of interest and then fully accommodates all demand for loans at that interest rate. The supply of loans is "horizontal" and supply conditions play no role. Because the central bank "administers" all short-term rates and long-term rates are determined by expectations of future short-term rates, Keynes's LIQUIDITY PREFERENCE theory of interest rates is rejected.

Similarly, as Kregel (1986) argued, much of the Circuitiste literature also ignores or rejects the liquidity preference approach. On the other hand, Dow, Chick and Wray have explicitly incorporated liquidity preference theory within an endogenous money approach. Also, Wray has argued that Keynes did have an endogenous money approach and that the Circuitiste analysis is consistent with Keynes's approach (see Wray 1990; Lavoie 1992; Wray, in Deleplace and Nell 1996).

## Structuralists

Another critique of horizontalism comes from the structuralists (Lavoie 1992; Pollin, in Deleplace and Nell 1996). They argue the mark-up is actually not stable, that it varies over the business cycle, and that its variations are consistent with a liquidity preference approach or with the FINANCIAL INSTABILITY HYPOTHESIS. Briefly, over the business cycle, especially during the upswing, balance sheets – including those of banks – become increasingly illiquid and risky. Interest rates begin to rise, and the mark-up rises as banks and other financial institutions become concerned with increasingly illiquid positions. Further, central banks begin to squeeze banks, primarily due to fears of inflation, by increasing actual and perceived pressure to limit loan expansion. Banks do not perceive reserves supplied at the discount window to be perfect substitutes for nonborrowed reserves; thus, central bank constraint changes bank behavior.

Banks never simply announce an interest rate and then meet all demand at that rate. The quantity and price of loans supplied is always negotiated, as banks take into account their own balance sheet positions, the positions of their customers, the expected ease with which reserves might be obtained and expected changes of central bank policy. Furthermore, central bank constraints hasten the transition to fragility as banks engage in liability management and innovation, stretching liquidity and increasing fragility.

## Conclusion

Whatever their stripe, heterodox economists generally prefer policy directed to keeping interest rates low, as did Keynes in his call for euthanasia of the rentier (see Wray 1990; Lavoie 1992; Smithin 1994; Lavoie, in Deleplace and Nell 1996). Some, including Moore (1988), believe that this will ensure a high level of aggregate demand. Others, however, following Keynes, are skeptical that low interest rates alone will stimulate demand. Nevertheless, low interest rates will reduce the share of income going to rentiers, and will lower the "stakes of the game," thereby reducing the incentive for speculative dominance at the expense of industry. Heterodoxy also generally prefers low unemployment over low inflation as a goal of policy, with many doubting the central bank's ability to control inflation, or preferring alternative policy (such as incomes policies and profit margin controls) to fight inflation (Davidson 1978) (see MONETARY POLICY AND CENTRAL BANKING FUNCTIONS).

Heterodoxy has also examined "micro credit" issues, arguing that traditional banks neglect large portions of society. Topics analyzed include DISCRIMINATION IN THE HOUSING AND MORTGAGE MARKET, credit rationing, issues related to credit, community development banking and "fringe" banking. Also important are policies to encourage banks to expand services to disadvantaged groups.

## See also:

financial crises; liability management; monetary circuit; money, nature and role of

## Selected references

Davidson, P. (1978) *Money and the Real World*, London: Macmillan.

Deleplace, G. and Nell, E.J. (eds) (1996) *Money in Motion: The Post Keynesian and Circulation Approaches*, New York: St Martin's Press.

Kregel, J.A. (1986) "Shylock and Hamlet, or Are There Bulls and Bears in the Circuit," *Economies et Sociétés, Monnaie et Production* 20(8–9):11–22.

Lavoie, M. (1992) *Foundations of Post Keynesian Analysis*, Aldershot: Edward Elgar.

Minsky, H.P. (1986) *Stabilizing an Unstable Economy*, New Haven, CT: Yale University Press.

Moore, B.J. (1988) *Horizontalists and Verticalists: The Macroeconomics of Credit Money*, Cambridge: Cambridge University Press.

Rousseas, S. (1992) *Post Keynesian Monetary Economics*, 2nd edn, Armonk, NY: M.E. Sharpe.

Smithin, J. (1994) *Controversies in Monetary Economics: Ideas, Issues, and Policy*, Aldershot: Edward Elgar.

Wray, L.R. (1990) *Money and Credit in Capitalist Economies: The Endogenous Money Approach*, Aldershot: Edward Elgar.

L. RANDALL WRAY

# monopoly capitalism

## Introduction

The roots of monopoly capital theory go back in the nineteenth century to Karl MARX, in the early twentieth century to V.I. Lenin and Rudolf Hilferding, in the middle part of the century to Michal KALECKI, Joseph Steindl, Paul Baran and Paul Sweezy, and more recently to Keith Cowling and his associates. A starting point for the theory of monopoly capitalism is the observation that rising centralization and concentration has been a general feature of CAPITALISM. It produces industries dominated by a few oligopolists who can raise prices, relative to costs, through implicit and explicit collusion as well as the erection and reinforcement of barriers to entry. There may still be considerable rivalry amongst firms but their collective market power rises, leading to increases in prices (relative to costs, including, notably, wages). Hence the share of profits in national income tends to rise at the expense of wages.

Since the propensity to save out of profits is considerably higher than the propensity out of wages, this shift in the DISTRIBUTION OF INCOME reduces consumer expenditure; although it may encourage investment as profitability may have risen. However, on the other hand, investment would be discouraged through the reduction in consumer demand (which may be reflected in reduced capacity utilization), and through the reduction in competition. The imperative to ACCUMULATION is lessened, as the survival pressures on firms decline. Oligopoly may be less conducive to investment and technical change than atomistic competition, and there is a tendency towards stagnation (see particularly Steindl 1952).

## Oligopolistic and monopolistic structures

Marx viewed the process of competition under capitalism as involving processes of centralization and concentration, and thereby oligopolistic and monopolistic structures emerge. Lenin saw that atomistic competition had evolved into oligopoly in the most developed capitalist countries of his time. The monopoly capitalism stage of capitalism involved monopolies playing a "decisive role in economic life." Linked with this is "the merging of bank capital with industrial capital, and the creation, on the basis of 'finance capital', of a financial oligarchy" (Lenin 1916; see also Hilferding 1910). The international monopolies share the world out amongst themselves, and the major capitalist countries continue the territorial division of the world.

Kalecki adopted the general view that economies were oligopolistic and monopolistic rather than competitive. He introduced the idea that the mark-up of price over direct costs would depend on the market power of the firms involved, summarized by the term "degree of monopoly." The degree of monopoly would depend on the degree of concentration, the extent of tacit collusion between firms, and on advertising and sales promotion. He later (Kalecki 1971) discussed the effects of trade union activity on the degree of monopoly. Kalecki developed from his PRICING equation the consequences of the degree of monopoly for the distribution of income as between wages and gross profits. He expected that concentration, and hence the degree of monopoly, would generally rise over time, leading to a rising share of profits in national income (see WAGE AND PROFIT SHARE and MONOPOLY, DEGREE OF).

Kalecki also indicated (see, for example, Kalecki 1954) that there would be a slowdown in the growth of capitalist economies in the later stages of development, arising from a decline in the intensity of innovation. This is linked in part to the declining importance of discoveries of new sources of raw materials, of new land to be developed, and so on, and from the rise of "assembly industries" which would not generate much technical advance.

## Generation and absorption of the surplus

The central theme of Baran and Sweezy (1966) was described as "the generation and absorption of the economic surplus under conditions of monopoly capitalism." The dominant firm is "a large-scale enterprise producing a significant share of the output of an industry, or several industries, and able to control its prices, the volume of its production, and the types and amounts of investments." The ECONOMIC SURPLUS is defined as "the difference between what a society produces and the costs of producing it."

In their analysis, the modern large corporation is controlled by the board of directors and the chief executive officer, but still operates in the interests of the owners. Large corporations thus strive for as much profit as possible. There is a considerable coincidence of interest between board of directors and shareholders, and outside interests (such as customers, suppliers and bankers) are often represented on the board of directors for interests to be harmonized. The management of a corporation is self-perpetuating, with one generation of managers often appointing or influencing the next generation. Each corporation seeks and usually achieves financial independence through the provision of internal finance for its investment program (see OWNERSHIP AND CONTROL OF THE CORPORATION).

In Baran and Sweezy's approach there is "the tendency of surplus to rise." The surplus at the firm level is the excess of revenue over costs, and includes profits and unnecessary costs (including advertising and sales promotion expenditure). The rise in profit margins is seen to arise as a side effect of falling real costs. Much of Baran and Sweezy (1966) is concerned with "the absorption of the surplus," which they explore in terms of capitalists' consumption and investment, ADVERTISING AND THE SALES EFFORT, civilian government, plus militarism and imperialism. In each case, the expenditure of the surplus, directly or indirectly, helps to support the maintenance of that surplus. The absorption of the surplus is a macroeconomic rather than a microeconomic problem. Indeed, the macroeconomic "solution" to the absorption of the surplus may operate to the short-run detriment of the individual firm.

## Cowling and transnational corporations

Cowling (1982) provides a formalization and development of the Kaleckian degree of monopoly, and also serves to link the monopoly capital approach with the structure–conduct–performance paradigm of orthodox industrial economics. He also seeks to integrate some of the managerialist literature, specifically insofar as managers are seen to have some power to capture profits for themselves. Managers have some degree of control over the disposal of the surplus and hence of its division between (reported) profits and fixed costs. Since the fixed costs include the manager's own remuneration and perks, the managers will have an incentive to inflate fixed costs at the expense of profits. The conflict between owners and managers is essentially a distributional conflict over sharing out the surplus, rather than involving questions of efficiency and the determination of price and output. The firm as an organization seeks to maximize the surplus which it gains, followed by a conflict over the distribution of the surplus between reported profits and managerial salaries.

There are a variety of linkages between domestic producers and foreign producers, through agreements and joint ventures. Often and more significantly they are parts of the same entity, that is, TRANSNATIONAL CORPORA-TIONS. The foreign producer may accept the domestic producer as price leader, so that the degree of monopoly may not be upset (although the domestic producer would lose market share). The transnational enterprise will make its decision on where to produce on grounds of cost minimization. Indeed, for a transnational production enterprise to move to a lower cost country may well increase the effective degree of monopoly through a reduction in costs.

The international dimension of the operations of large firms has often been featured in theorizing on monopoly capital. In the early stages of monopoly capitalism, the world was divided into the advanced industrialized countries undertaking the bulk of industrial production, and the non-industrialized countries supplying much of the raw materials and serving as export markets for the advanced industrialized countries. The rivalry between firms (and hence between countries) was for the control of raw materials and export rights. In the more recent stages of monopoly capitalism, the supply of raw materials has become of less significance and industrialization has spread to more countries. A transnational enterprise, by definition, owns and controls production facilities in more than one country. The spread of transnational production can involve production in both developed and developing countries, which involve, *inter alia*, quite different wage levels.

Cowling and Sugden (1987) argue that the transnational enterprise is able to weaken the power of workers and thereby lower wages and/or raise the intensity of labor. These arguments indicate that the rise of transnationals may lead to a rise in the degree of monopoly, rather than a decline as is often argued. The profit share of national income tends to rise as a consequence, exacerbating the stagnationist tendencies. The significance of transnational (as opposed to uninational) operations arises from the changing relationship between labor, capital and the state. The ability of trade unions to organize across countries to match the cross-country organization of transnationals is very limited. Governments are likely to be in competition with one another to attract footloose investment, and lack the ability (or willingness) to cooperate on an inter-governmental level to match the power of transnationals.

## See also:

centralized private sector planning; corporate hegemony; corporate objectives; effective demand and capacity utilization; interlocking directorships; Kalecki's macro theory of profits; labor markets and market power; market structures; Schumpeterian competition; transfer pricing

## Selected references

Baran, Paul and Sweezy, Paul M. (1966) *Monopoly Capital*, New York: Monthly Review Press.

Cowling, K. (1982) *Monopoly Capitalism*, London: Macmillan.

Cowling, K. and Sugden, R. (1987) *Transnational Monopoly Capitalism*, Brighton: Wheatsheaf.

Hilferding, R. (1910) *Finance Capital*, ed. T. Bottomore, trans. M. Watnick and S. Gordan, London: Routledge & Kegan Paul, 1981.

Kalecki, M. (1954) *Theory of Economic Dynamics*, London: George Allen & Unwin.

—— (1971) "The Class Struggle and the Distribution of National Income," *Kyklos* 24: 1–8.

Lenin, V.I. (1916) *Imperialism: The Highest*

*State of Capitalism*, in *Selected Works*, vol. 5, London: Lawrence & Wishart, 1936.

Sawyer, M. (1988) "Theories of Monopoly Capitalism," *Journal of Economic Surveys* 2.

Steindl, J. (1952) *Maturity and Stagnation in American Capitalism*, Oxford: Basil Blackwell, 1976.

MALCOLM SAWYER

# monopoly, degree of

Michal KALECKI's notion of the "degree of monopoly" is the connection between his influential characterization of PRICING (Kalecki 1940) in advanced industrial economies and his distribution theory (Kalecki 1938). As such, it is often considered an essential element in the post-Keynesian "microfoundations of macroeconomics," even if this identification is, for reasons that will become clear, more problematic than perhaps first appears.

## Standard presentation

The standard presentation – Feiwel (1975) is perhaps representative – starts with industries in which competition is, in one or more sense, imperfect. There are a small number of firms with constant unit prime costs $c$, the sum of productive labor $w$ and raw material costs per unit $m$, each operating below their "practical capacity constraints." It is then asserted that each firm "marks up" $c$ in order to cover the costs of overheads and to realize some positive net profit per unit, so that $p = (1+k)c$. The mark-up $k$ reflects, but is not equivalent to, the degree of monopoly. More controversial, perhaps, it is then often supposed that the value of $k$ is determined *ex ante* and is, under normal conditions, demand invariant.

Commodities are assumed to enter the sphere of circulation with a price. Within this framework, the "degree of monopoly" is a "catch all" of sorts, a representation, in the broadest possible terms, of both the form(s) and extent of competition. It therefore comprises "traditional" considerations: the number of firms, the structure of demand, the nature of strategic interaction, the regulatory environment and the influence of potential competition, to name some of the most obvious. It also comprises a number of "untraditional" considerations, as Kalecki (1971) himself underscored in later work: for instance, the balance of power between firms and workers, plus industrial norms and CONVENTIONS.

It follows that within such industries, sales proceeds $P$ are equal to $(1 + k)(W + M)$, where $W$ and $M$ are the wage and raw material bills, in which case labor's share in sectoral revenue $W/P$ is equal to $(1/1+k)(z/1 + k)$, where $z = W/M$. This is often understood to mean that $k$ and $z$ then "determine" labor's share, in which case $W/P$ or, for that matter, the real wage, $w/p$, is constant for each "degree of monopoly," unless $z$ is itself demand-sensitive. If the degree of monopoly increases, however, labor's share will fall, and vice versa.

Income distribution, in the aggregate, is then explained in terms of a weighted average of sectoral distributions: $W^*/P_* = (1/1+k^*)(z^*/1+z^*)$, where $W^*/P^*$ is labor's share in net national income, a function of the modified $k^*$ and $z^*$ and, to the extent that it determines the sectoral weights, the composition of aggregate demand, itself a function of the distribution of income. At this level, $k^*$ is often (also) understood in terms of a much broader class conflict over distributional shares, and therefore shares a number of important features with Marxian characterizations of the rate of surplus value.

## Mark-ups, prime costs and orthodoxy

From its roots in the 1930s, two concerns have dominated the relevant literature: (1) do firms in fact impose constant mark-ups over constant unit prime costs, and (2) to what extent is the Kaleckian model of the firm consistent with more orthodox characterizations of profit maximization under conditions of "imperfect" competition? The first has its modern roots in Richard Kahn's (1989) fellowship dissertation, and its most familiar expression in the empirical work of the Oxford Research Group, in particular Hall and Hitch (1939). If the first is still unsettled – some Kaleckians now believe that $k^*$ rises in booms and falls in busts, for example – it is the second that remains more controversial. In particular, Kalecki's eventual insistence that he had "not assume[d] that the firm attempt[ed] to maximize its profits in any precise sort of manner," (1965:12), which followed his much earlier endorsement of Lerner's (1934) more orthodox definition and measure of market power, failed to resolve matters.

From a neoclassical perspective, the connection between the Kaleckian and mainstream characterizations seems almost obvious, at least in the simple case of static monopolies. With constant marginal costs $c$, the conventional first order profit maximization condition $mr = mc$ can be written $p (1 - 1/e) = c$, where $e$ is the absolute value of the price elasticity of demand, in which case the *ex post* mark-up $k$ must equal $1/(e - 1)$, which some have (mis)-understood to mean that market power is first and foremost a positive function of consumer need. Even in this special case, however, $k$ will not be constant unless demand shifts assume a particular and (it is reasonable to suppose) contrived form.

Much more important, the Kaleckian $k$ was (and still is) intended to be much broader than this, inasmuch as the profit maximization problems of "real world monopolists" are neither static nor certain. Monopolists often confront uncertain sequences of connected demand functions and otherwise "imperfect" labor and credit markets in the face of potential competition and other constraints on price formation. To the extent that there are uncertainties such as these, the proposition that each behaves "as if" constant prime costs were "marked up" is not prima facie inconsistent with profit maximization. McDonald and Solow (1981), for example, articulate an otherwise static (and orthodox) model of LABOR MARKETS AND MARKET POWER in which the monopolist must confront a unionized work force, and find that constant shares are consistent with profit maximization in the face of fluctuations in demand.

The relationship between the Kaleckian and neoclassical treatments becomes still more obscure when there are a small number of firms, each of which exerts substantial market power. The "solution" of each firm's profit maximization problem is, in even the simplest model, a function of its expectations about its rivals' probable behavior(s), its expectations about its rivals' expectations about its own behavior, and so on. While recent advances in GAME THEORY have sometimes facilitated the formalization of strategic interaction, the modern literature is often indeterminate, a problem (if indeed it is this) that becomes even more pronounced in richer models. It is in this context that Kalecki's "as if" firm becomes an attractive and tractable construction, one rooted in observed *macroeconomic* behavior, however.

## Macroeconomics of microeconomics

In the end, the Kaleckian firm is perhaps best understood in terms of the search for the "macrofoundations of microeconomics." Marcuzzo (1996), for example, reminds us that Kalecki himself was an active participant in Sraffa's seminars in the 1930s and the director of the NIESR Cambridge Research Scheme. Both of these were concerned with explanations of the (more or less) constant distributive shares, a phenomenon that most understood was inconsistent with Keynes's own views on the operation of effective demand. Kalecki's "as if" firm is the simplest possible microstructure consistent with such behavior. To the extent that such constructs continue to find (more limited, perhaps) empirical support, and to the extent that it is much less obvious now than it once seemed that Kalecki's "rule of thumb" prices are inconsistent with profit maximization in complicated economic environments, the "degree of monopoly" will remain a prominent feature of the post--Keynesian and other heterodox literatures.

## See also:

Kalecki's macro theory of profits; Kalecki's principle of increasing risk; market structures

## Selected references

Feiwel, George R. (1975) *The Intellectual Capital of Michal Kalecki*, Knoxville, TN: University of Tennessee Press.

Hall, R.L. and Hitch, C.J. (1939) "Price Theory and Business Behavior," *Oxford Economic Papers* 2: 12–45.

Kahn, Richard F. (1989) *The Economics of the Short Period*, London: Macmillan.

Kalecki, Michal (1938) "The Determinants of Distribution of the National Income," *Econometrica* 6: 97–112.

—— (1940) "The Supply Curve of an Industry Under Imperfect Competition," *Review of Economic Studies* 7: 91–122.

—— (1965) *Theory of Economic Dynamics*, 2nd edn, London: Allen & Unwin.

—— (1971) *Selected Essays on the Dynamics of the Capitalist Economy (1933–1970)*, Cambridge: Cambridge University Press.

Lerner, Abba (1934) "The Concept of Monopoly and the Measurement of Monopoly Power," *Review of Economic Studies* 1(June): 157–75.

Marcuzzo, Maria Cristina (1996) "Alternative Microeconomic Foundations for Macroeconomics," *Review of Political Economy* 8(1): 7–22.

McDonald, Ian and Solow, Robert (1981) "Wage Bargaining and Employment," *American Economic Review* 71(December): 896–908.

PETER HANS MATTHEWS

MORALITY: *see* ethics and morality

# Myrdal's contribution to political economy

## Introduction

Gunnar Myrdal (1898–1987) was born in rural Sweden and studied law and economics at the University of Stockholm, where he received his doctorate in 1927. He was a student of several brilliant Swedish economists, such as Knut Wicksell, Eli F. Heckscher and Gustav Cassel. He made a number of important contributions to modern political economy. The most notable concerned his analysis of the difference between *ex ante* and *ex post* analysis, the problem of value premises in economic theorizing, the concept and practice of the WELFARE STATE, the study of social problems such as race, a study of underdeveloped regions, such as South Asia, and the further development of the principle of CIRCULAR AND CUMULATIVE CAUSATION. All this makes him a true political economist of almost classical dimensions, although he usually preferred to call himself an institutionalist (see Myrdal 1978; see INSTITUTIONAL POLITICAL ECONOMY: HISTORY).

## Early work

His earliest work was in pure theory and dealt with price formation and economic change, focusing on the role of EXPECTATIONS (not translated). Soon after his dissertation, Myrdal became involved in meta-theoretical reflection about the implicit values in the science of economics, which he found inherently conservative. He was lecturing on these controversial issues in the late 1920s, and collected his notes in a Swedish publication (1930), which much later was translated into English (by his close collaborator Paul Streeten) as *The Political Element in the Development of Economic Theory* (in 1953).

His first academic chair was in political economy and public finance (1933–9). This was a time when economics was in the midst of the Keynesian revolution and the language of economics was changing. The young Myrdal was very much part of this transformation, and became a member of what later became known as the "Stockholm School," which in some respects anticipated the new macroeconomic approach. Myrdal had the opportunity to serve as economic advisor to the much respected Swedish minister of finance, Ernst Wigforss, who at the time was more aware of the new economic thinking than were many economists.

## Policy questions

Myrdal wanted economics to serve a public purpose, which had to be made explicit in the research process. He was involved in modern POPULATION policy (along with Alva Myrdal), and served as a member of the Swedish parliament (1935–8), chairman of a Swedish Postwar Planning Commission (1943–5), and Minister of Commerce in the postwar social democratic government. This government was quite radical, in expecting a "socialist harvest," but the party had to face a decline in political support in the 1948 elections. Like many other economists at the time, Myrdal anticipated a postwar depression. For the purpose of economic stabilization he engineered a major trade agreement with the Soviet Union, an agreement that became intensely unpopular in Sweden. So began Myrdal's international career as a civil servant, working for ten years (1947–57) as the Executive Secretary of the United Nations Economic Commission for Europe (ECE). These practical experiences substantively influenced the direction of his research as well as the methods employed, towards a strong problem-oriented approach.

## Race and development

By then Myrdal was already internationally known academically for his work on the race question in the USA, carried out during the war, and resulting in the two-volume *An American Dilemma* (1944). This book is a most significant work, since it contains all the ingredients that formed his profile as a scientific worker: awareness of the value dimension, preparedness to make explicit the fundamental values which influenced the research process, dissatisfaction with the limitations of economics, the ambition to combine economic, social and political factors into a dynamic understanding of society, the idea of circular and cumulative causation, and the urge to achieve a real change in socioeconomic life. The "American creed" of justice and liberty, which had served as the value basis in *An American Dilemma,* remained also his own value orientation, together with European SOCIAL DEMOCRACY.

Whether dealing with one small country or the international system, he firmly believed in the power of political intervention and the moral soundness and economic usefulness of redistribution of resources as a condition for development. Development theory became an interest in the 1950s when he published his very influential *Economic Theory and Underdeveloped Regions* (1957). This contributed to the recognition of "backwardness" (later "underdevelopment") as a specific problem that needed a specialized discipline.

During 1957–67 Myrdal engaged in a monumental study of development in South Asia, which resulted in the three-volume *Asian Drama: An Inquiry into the Poverty of Nations* (1968). Here the modernization ideals, as expressed by the Indian political elite, took the place of the "American creed" as the basic value orientation. Myrdal soon realized that governments throughout the region were very different from the rational politician of the Swedish model. Thus a major theme of this work was the "softness" of the South Asian state: "softness" implying a gap between real and professed intentions.

*Asian Drama* was the culmination of an era in development studies. At that time the field became dominated by more leftist perspectives. Myrdal, the reformist, showed little sympathy for this radical trend in spite of the fact that he in a sense had anticipated the notion of "development of underdevelopment" in his earlier theory of the "backwash effects" of trade.

Myrdal belongs to the core group of pioneers in development studies, together with scholars such as Arthur Lewis, Raúl Prebisch, Hans Singer and Dudley Seers. Perhaps more than anyone else he epitomized the basic creed of the discipline. This creed included the view of underdevelopment as a complex of intertwined variables forming a vicious circle, and the usefulness of rational state intervention to create a change for the better. To him, development was the movement upwards of the whole social system (see DEVELOPMENT POLITICAL ECONOMY: HISTORY).

## Conclusion

In 1974 Myrdal received the Nobel Memorial Prize in Economic Science, which he somewhat ironically shared with Friedrich von Hayek, a conservative economist. Soon after came the general farewell to "Keynesianism" and the counter-revolution in development economics during the 1980s. Intervention was now seen as bad. Nevertheless, many of Myrdal's contributions were durable and are a critical part of modern POLITICAL ECONOMY. This is especially the case for the notion of CIRCULAR AND CUMULATIVE CAUSATION, examining issues within the framework of the linkages between economic, social and political factors, and emphasizing the importance of VALUE JUDGMENTS AND WORLD VIEWS in theories and perspectives of scholarly endeavor.

## See also:

culture of poverty; holistic method; political economy: major contemporary themes

## Selected references

Dostaler, G., Ethier, D. and Lepage, L. (eds) (1992) *Gunnar Myrdal and His Works*, London: Harvest House.

Myrdal, Gunnar (1930) *The Political Element in the Development of Economic Theory*, New York: Simon & Schuster, 1969.

—— (1939) *Monetary Equilibrium*, New York: Augustus M. Kelley, 1965.

—— (1944) *An American Dilemma: The Negro Problem and Modern Democracy*, 2 vols, New York: Pantheon Books.

—— (1957) *Economic Theory and Underdeveloped Regions*, New York: Harper.

—— (1960) *Beyond the Welfare State: Economic Planning and its International Implications*, New Haven, CT: Yale University Press.

—— (1968) *Asian Drama: An Inquiry into the Poverty of Nations*, 3 vols, New York: Twentieth Century Fund.

—— (1973) *Against the Stream: Critical Essays on Economics*, New York: Pantheon.

—— (1978) "Institutional Economics," *Journal of Economic Issues* 12(4): 771–83.

Streeten, P. (1990) "Gunnar Myrdal," *World Development* 18(7): 1031–7.

BJÖRN HETTNE

# N

## natural capital

There are two main categories of capital: natural and human created forms. The natural capital concept purports to express the direct linkages between the environment and development, based on the fact that the production of goods and services depends on renewable and non-renewable resources being extracted from the environment. Natural capital, therefore, refers to nature-based means of producing goods and services (Daly and Cobb 1989: 71–2). This includes the stock of environmentally provided assets such as soil, the atmosphere, the forests, wildlife and water. Assets which combine human-made and natural capital are called hybrid or cultivated capital; examples are food, wood and natural fibres. Natural capital has become increasingly important, due to fears of scarcity and the failure of the conventional System of National Accounts (SNA) to internalize environmental costs and benefits in the measurement of economic performance.

### Definition and types

Pearce *et al.* (1990: 1) define natural capital as, "the stock of all environmental and natural resource assets, from oil in the ground to the quality of soil and ground water, from the stock of fish in the oceans to the capacity of the globe to recycle and absorb carbon." According to Pearce *et al.* (1990: 4), SUSTAINABLE DEVELOPMENT entails "the non-depreciation of the natural capital stock"; a constant capital stock or non-negative change in the stock of natural resources and environmental quality.

It is important to distinguish between two types of natural capital stocks. First, there is the "existing stock," which is the stock that exists at a point in time. Second, there is the "optimal capital stock," which includes an assessment of the costs and benefits of changing the natural capital stocks. The sustainability of natural capital can be maintained by observing the optimal rather than the existing natural capital stocks. Resource conservation is often said to serve non-efficiency objectives, whereas optimality tends to be defined only in terms of efficiency. However, even in terms of efficiency, the existence of a valuation function which is linked to the existing endowment of natural resources adds emphasis to the conservation of existing stocks (Pearce *et al.* 1990). The latter is based on the fact that optimal natural capital stocks have both economic and non-market social values.

Based on sustainable development, conserving the stock of natural capital is said to be consistent with JUSTICE in respect of the socially disadvantaged, different generations and nature. Conservation of natural capital is related to our ignorance about the nature of the interactions between environment, economy and society. It is also related to an aversion to risk arising from the social and economic damage arising from external "shocks," such as drought and plagues, or "stress" such as soil erosion and agro-chemical residues.

### Significance for the national accounts

Natural capital transcends conventional definitions of capital, which ignore the environment in their calculation of the costs and benefits of production and consumption. The traditional System of National Accounts (SNA) is problematic since it neglects natural resource scarcities, environmental quality and social costs, and therefore reduces sustainable productivity and human health and welfare. The United Nations System of National Accounts has been modified to cater for these shortcomings, and a "System of Integrated Environment and Economic Accounting" (SEEA) has been devised (United Nations 1993). Many developing and developed countries have adopted some measures of environmental accounting (Norway, France, the Netherlands and Costa Rica are among the first countries to adopt SEEA). However, the full economic implications of incorporating natural capital in day-to-day economic transactions have not been appreciated by most economists.

## Sustainability

Natural capital entered the sustainable development fray through the work of many contemporary environmental and ecological economists. Although environmental and ecological economists agree on the importance of natural capital, they tend to disagree on how it can be sustained. Strong sustainability refers to the maintenance of each category of capital (including natural capital) or the maintenance of natural capital. Weak sustainability focuses on the maintenance of income or production, allowing for substitution and technological progress. The latter aims at the maintenance of the overall capital stock, rather than each of its components.

A number of measures have been devised to guide policy. For instance, according to Daly (1991), an earlier view (incorporating weak sustainability) was that if natural capital can be exchanged for an equal amount of technological or human capital, then the system is sustainable. This raises the question of how much economic growth results from the depreciation or destruction of natural resources. (See CAPITAL AND THE WEALTH OF NATIONS.)

Hanley et al. (1997) took the debate further by examining the idea of a non-declining natural capital stock (based on strong sustainability). It is important "to allow future generations to reach the same level of utility as the average held by this generation . . . .[Thus] holding constant ... the natural capital stock becomes the rule of sustainable development" (1997: 528). They then asked the question "How much of natural capital can be held constant?" and gave three possible answers:

(1) the existing level, (2) the level consistent with maintaining the critical element of natural capital, and (3) some amount in between these two. All three of these alternatives, however, assume that we can measure the value of natural capital at any point in time; in other words, that the different elements of natural capital be aggregated together in comparable units.

(Hanley et al. 1997: 528)

These three options themselves pose a problem of how to disaggregate natural capital stocks. (Hanley has compared this approach with the "safe minimal standards approach" (1997: 530).)

Costanza and Daly (1992) propose that (strong) sustainable development can be achieved only if the current level of depletion of natural capital is halted by taking a number of steps. One of these measures is by striving "to hold throughput or consumption of Total Natural Capital (TNC) constant at present levels by charging for TNC consumption, especially energy" (by way of an additional tax). This can then be linked to reduced income tax for the poor. Similar views have been expressed and elaborated in Costanza (1991), Jansson et al. (1994), and Prugh and Costanza (1995).

## See also:

cost–benefit analysis; cultural capital; entropy, negentropy and the laws of thermodynamics; environmental valuation; gross domestic product and net social welfare; human capital; limits to growth; quality of life; social and organizational capital; steady-state economy

## Selected references

Costanza, Robert and Daly, H.E. (1992)

"Natural Capital and Sustainable Development," *Conservation Biology* 6.

Costanza, Robert (ed.) (1991) *Ecological Economics: The Science and Management of Sustainability*, New York: Columbia University Press.

Daly, H.E. (1991) *Ecological Economics and Sustainable Development*, World Bank Environmental Department Paper No. 1991–24, Washington, DC: World Bank.

Daly, H.E. and Cobb, John B. (1989) *For the Common Good: Redirecting the Economy Toward Community, the Environment and a Sustainable Future*, Boston: Beacon Press.

Jansson, Ann-Mari, Hammer, Monica, Folke, C. and Costanza, Robert (eds) (1994) *Investing in Natural Capital: The Ecological Economics Approach to Sustainability*, New York: Island Press.

Hanley, Nick, Shogren, Jason F. and White, Ben (1997) *Environmental Economics in Theory and Practice*, Basingstoke: Macmillan.

Hartwick, J.M. (1977) "Intergenerational Equity and the Investing of Rents From Exhaustible Resources," *American Economic Review* 67(5).

Pearce, David, Barbier, Edward and Markandya, Anil (1990) *Sustainable Development: Economic and Environment in the Third World*, Aldershot: Edward Edgar.

Prugh, Thomas and Costanza, Robert (1995) *Natural Capital and Human Economic Survival*, International Society for Ecological Economics (ISEE) Press, Solomons, MD: Chelsea Green Publications.

United Nations (1993) *Integrated Environmental and Economic Accounting: Interim Version*, New York: United Nations.

M.A. MOHAMED SALIH

# natural rights

Throughout its history, political economy has been closely linked to the philosophy of natural law and natural rights. Political economy as a separate intellectual discipline grew out of the natural law/natural rights tradition of the eighteenth century (Schumpeter 1954), and thus owes its origins at least partly to this philosophical tradition. Of equal significance has been the influence of natural law concepts and ideas on the subsequent development of economics over the past two centuries, an influence which persists in current NEOCLASSICAL ECONOMICS. Natural law and natural rights philosophy continue to remain fundamental concepts in modern economic theory, especially neoclassical economic theory, because they are embedded in the preconceptions adopted and accepted, often unconsciously, by economists (Veblen 1919).

Natural law philosophy influences the form and content of economics, its method of analysis and its subject of analysis, what is included and what is excluded, but the most important lasting influence of the natural law tradition on economic theory can be seen in the VALUE JUDGMENTS AND WORLD VIEWS explicitly or implicitly made by economic theorists and in the legitimation and ideological role economic theory often plays. A critical understanding of modern economic theory, therefore, must first comprehend and expose the natural law preconceptions upon which much of economic orthodoxy rests.

## Natural law outlook

The natural law tradition is as old as philosophy, and as diverse. During the Renaissance period, the emphasis of this tradition started to shift away from the theological natural law theories of the scholastics, and toward a tradition which stressed natural rights. Although there were substantial changes in accepted dogmas, the essential natural law vision remained, and still remains, intact. Essential to this vision is the universality and sacrosanctness of the particular theory being espoused. We shall call this vision "the natural law outlook."

## Main elements

There are three essential elements in the

natural law outlook, an examination of which will help to illuminate the lasting importance of this vision to modern economic theory. The first is a belief in a social physics that the social universe, like the natural universe, is regulated by universal, invariant laws. Both the INDIVI-DUAL AND SOCIETY are subject to a set of universal laws which, once discovered, can be applied to any time and place. This fundamental belief is behind "economics imperialism," the often amusing and occasionally tragic idea that neoclassical economic theory can be used to explain all social behavior, regardless of time and place.

The second characteristic of the natural law outlook is naturalism, the belief that what exists can be explained – in fact must be explained – solely by natural causes. In economics, the accepted natural causes are human nature (rational economic "man") and "mother" nature (scarcity), which are the only legitimate final causes. These natural causes are to be juxtaposed with social or cultural causes, social and historical context. The last essential aspect of the natural law outlook is the derivation of a natural moral theory. In one of the greatest philosophical contradictions, the openly positivist tradition of modern economics culminates in the argument that its conclusions are not only based on nature (natural laws) but, it further argues, they are normative prescriptions. They compose what is and what ought to be (see NORMATIVE AND POSITIVE ECONOMICS).

The "social physics" aspect of the natural law outlook has had a profound effect on the development of political economy and economic theory. It is the belief in a "social physics" that is behind the use of models and metaphors from the natural sciences to construct economic theories and models. The influence of these models and metaphors is now widely known by historians of political economy, thanks especially to the work of Philip Mirowski (1988, 1989). A lasting effect of economists' "physics envy" is the rise of mathematical formalism and the rigid adherence to equilibrium as the central organizing idea. It is no exaggeration to say that modern

economic orthodoxy, and some schools of heterodoxy, simply cannot think outside of an equilibrium framework.

Yet the idea of equilibrium does not come from observing market activity, but is a displaced concept from the natural sciences and is the foundation upon which the use of natural metaphors in economics rests. The use of static equilibrium as the dominant heuristic tool for understanding CAPITALISM is certainly one of the most perplexing questions in the history of economic thought, for capitalist societies are anything but static equilibria. The benefit to economic theory of using static equilibrium as the central organizing concept has been the appearance of having a rigorous (scientific) theory. The cost has been reducing the extent to which is comprehends long-term dynamics (see EQUILIBRIUM, DISEQUILIBRIUM AND NON-EQUILIBRIUM).

The naturalism aspect of the natural law outlook has led to the separation of economics from political economy. Taking naturalism seriously eventually led to the elimination of historical and social context from the hard core of economic explanations. Although the exclusion of history and society was necessary for the development of mathematical formalism, the latter was needed to incorporate final "natural" causes.

## Justification of laissez-faire

The derivation of natural moral theory has provided the foundation for the use of economic theory to support specific ideological viewpoints. The main strength of the legitimating role of economic theory is that it allows one set of ideological viewpoints to posture as if their conclusions were unbiased scientific conclusions, while those opposing them were merely expressing their value laden opinions. At its apex, this tendency has justified laissez-faire economic policies as if they were based on natural laws. Always behind the legitimation activities of economists is the belief that markets are "natural" institutions and market outcomes are natural outcomes, and the institutions necessary for markets, such as private property rights, are "natural rights."

The absurdity and inhumanity of this perspective was clearly exposed during the Irish famine of the mid-nineteenth century. With millions starving, food was exported from Ireland to England, all defended by the argument that intervention would be contrary to the market, private property and natural law. A similarly absurd, and potentially equally tragic, commitment to laissez-faire is being played out in the former Soviet Union. Here the premise underlying the Western-supported reforms is the belief that stable and efficient markets are the result of natural forces, and all that is required is the removal of government interference and protection of private property rights. This view ignores externalities, the DISEMBEDDED ECONOMY, and the fact that instituting and protecting private property RIGHTS is an act of government laying down the basic rules.

## Conclusion

Neoclassical economics has been especially influenced by the natural law and natural rights philosophy in how it conceptualizes the economy, what it includes and excludes from its analysis, and what are legitimate and illegitimate conclusions to be reached by economic theory. We would be hard pressed to find a more important influence on economic theory.

## See also:

determinism and overdetermination; holistic method; human action and agency; laws of political economy; monetarism; political economy; time; value judgments and world views

## Selected references

Clark, Charles M.A. (1992) *Economic Theory and Natural Philosophy*, Aldershot: Edward Elgar.
Mirowski, Philip (1988) *Against Mechanism*, Totawa, NJ: Rowman & Littlefield.
—— (1989) *More Heat than Light*, Cambridge: Cambridge University Press.
Schumpeter, Joseph (1954) *History of Economic Analysis*, Oxford: Oxford University Press.
Veblen, Thorstein (1919) *The Place of Science in Modern Civilization and other Essays*, New Brunswick, NJ: Transactions Publishers, 1990.

CHARLES M.A. CLARK

# needs

## Needs and wants

To appreciate the issues posed by the existence of needs, consider the example of an individual consumer who lives in a world of two very distinct goods: one fulfills a need (food for her child), the other fulfills a want (diamonds). This person is thought to have a given "endowment," and faces a market-determined price ratio that establishes the relative price between the two goods. The neoclassical theory of consumer behavior indicates that, since all goods are gross substitutes, there must be a finite price ratio which will induce our maximizing individual to forgo an adequate supply of her child's food in order to purchase more diamonds.

Moreover, given the individual's preferences, economists typically describe such a choice as "rational behavior." While this example is consistent with the canons of instrumental reason, as embodied in the orthodox theory of consumer choice, most thinking people would find fault with the result. Clearly we have an instance of an unmet need and for this reason an irresponsible, or even criminal, consumer.

The problem is with the level of abstraction inherent in the theory. Goods, as specific items, satisfy different kinds of demands among and between different consumers. Sometimes these demands are needs rather than wants. For many people diamonds are desirable. On the other hand, feeding a child is almost always a necessity. Given their respective roles in a typical consumer's life, these goods are not commensurable. In such cases, the principle of gross substitutability breaks down.

Economic theory was not always blind to these issues. In juxtaposition to the neoclassical theory, the CLASSICAL POLITICAL ECONOMY approach to consumption was based on a crude but intelligible theory of needs. In place of wants, it proposed a notion of "subsistence." Subsistence meant a bundle of commodities that would enable a household to reproduce itself over a given period of time. Consumption in excess of this amount would consist of "luxuries."

## Marx on needs

The "early" Karl MARX, drawing upon the philosopher G.W.F. Hegel (1821: 122–34), considered the category of needs to be more complex than that depicted in classical economics. Marx proposed that needs took on a variety of attributes: his list included animal needs, artificial needs, human needs and social needs (Marx 1844: 147–64). The first category, that of animal needs, captured the basics of survival and not much more. Such needs could be easily satisfied, as was demonstrated by George Stigler (1945). Outside of a Third World context, a substantive theory of needs cannot be built around such a narrow definition. However, the theory of needs is not limited to biological existence. Human beings have various dimensions to their lives which suggests the existence of a more complex set of needs.

In a manner reminiscent of Rousseau, Marx thought that the second category, artificial needs, are introduced to modernity through the agency of the capitalist market. In order to increase sales, merchants must convince people that they are continually subject to unmet needs. This process was necessary to extend the size of the market and, for this reason, vital to the operation of an expanding capitalist economy. It follows that the process of production must be associated with some mechanism that will ensure the expansion of needs within the POPULATION. This critical

assessment of artificial needs is no longer unique to Marx; it represents part of the contemporary critique of consumer society (Galbraith 1958: chaps 10–11; Schor 1992: ch. 5).

## Human and social needs

The understanding of needs, as discussed in Hegel and the early Marx, contains the beginnings of a theory of both human needs and social needs. David Levine (1988: ch. 1) treats human needs as those needs that a person requires in order to develop and retain a "personality structure." The theory contends that people make consumption decisions as part of a pattern that expresses and supports a vision of who they are as individuals. This set of human needs can be distinguished from social needs. Social needs fulfill the specifically human desire to establish ourselves as particular persons who are simultaneously linked to, yet distinct from, the larger society of individuals. Social theorists have long known that all people, including the very poor, strive to fulfill their human and social needs. Unfortunately, economists, classical and neoclassical, have not made a sustained effort to understand the importance of these needs in the sphere of consumption.

## Hierarchy of needs

The role of needs in an analytical theory of consumption has been given its strongest presentation in a recent book by Marc Lavoie (1992: ch. 2). Building upon a framework proposed and developed by Mark Lutz and Kenneth Lux (1979: chaps 1–3), Lavoie posits the existence of a recognizable hierarchy of needs. Within any category we have a degree of choice as to how we may meet that set of needs. In the example of consumer choice presented earlier, the parent would first buy food for her child, but she might also "comparison shop" within the category "food" for, say, generic brands and other low-cost substitutes.

When this "basic" need for food is fulfilled, she would then turn to a less pressing need, such as entertainment. Then within this second category, she would again make comparisons between specific choices, along the lines depicted in the standard theory. In this way preferences between categories are lexicographic, but within each category standard indifference curves hold sway (Lavoie 1992: 78–85). Thus Lavoie's approach simultaneously maintains the core notion of substitution, even as it rejects the neoclassical principle of gross substitutability (see POST-KEYNESIAN THEORY OF CHOICE).

## Conclusion

Viewed from the perspective of economic theory, the category of needs has important implications for both the theory of exchange and the political economy of a market society. First, by reasserting the importance of income effects in consumption, the theory of needs undermines the uniqueness and stability of any given position of general economic equilibrium. This has important implications for the "law of demand." Second, if it is the case that people are, or can be shown to be, trading in order to fulfill needs, it follows that they may be subject to systemic EXPLOITATION in a free and fair market (Prasch 1995). When individuals have needs which are pressing, unmet and exacerbated by market forces, a just society may have an obligation to remove the provision of such commodities from an unregulated market system (Winfield 1988: chaps 10–11).

If we can sustain a needs/wants distinction in the realm of economic theory, policies such as subsidies for home heating oil, minimum wages, workplace safety regulations and so on have an economic logic to support them. Finally, a theory of needs has the potential to provide a more determinate and meaningful foundation for the theory of consumption. Specifically, it extricates consumer theory from its naive dependence on methodological individualism and instrumental reason.

## See also:

conspicuous consumption and emulation; dis-

embedded economy; humanistic economics; inequality; justice; markets; methodological individualism and collectivism; rights

## Selected references

Galbraith, John Kenneth (1958) *The Affluent Society*, Boston: Houghton Mifflin.

Hegel, G.W.F. (1821) *Philosophy of Right*, trans. T.M. Knox, New York: Oxford University Press, 1967.

Lavoie, Marc (1992) *Foundations of Post Keynesian Economic Analysis*, Brookfield, VT: Edward Elgar.

Levine, David P. (1988) *Needs, Rights, and the Market*, Boulder, CO: Lynne Rienner Publishers.

Lutz, Mark and Lux, Kenneth (1979) *The Challenge of Humanistic Economics*, Reading, MA: Benjamin Cummings.

Marx, Karl (1844) *The Economic and Philosophical Manuscripts of 1844*, ed. Dirk Struik, New York: International Publishers, 1964.

Prasch, Robert E. (1995) "Towards a General Theory of Market Exchange," *Journal of Economic Issues* 29(3): 807–28.

Schor, Juliet (1992) *The Overworked American: The Unexpected Decline of Leisure*, New York: Basic Books.

Stigler, George J. (1945) "The Cost of Subsistence," *Journal of Farm Economics* 27(2): 358–65.

Winfield, Richard Dien (1988) *The Just Economy*, New York: Routledge.

ROBERT E. PRASCH

# Nelson and Winter's analysis of the corporation

Joseph SCHUMPETER (1911, 1950) set forth a conception whereby episodic change is a natural and essential characteristic of a capitalist economy. Nelson and Winter (1982) build this approach into an evolutionary theory of economic change. The focus of their microeconomic analysis is on corporate behavior in an environment of technological and organizational innovation.

## Rules and techniques

At any given time, the behavior of the individual corporation is governed by its current decision rules and operating techniques. Both rules and techniques are simply thought of as routines whose presence in the firm is subject to historical and evolutionary explanation. These rules are not typically equivalent to deliberate optimization over some well defined set of alternatives.

## Innovation process

In the longer run, two classes of dynamic mechanisms are at work. Rule changes may occur through the process of RESEARCH AND DEVELOPMENT, and by imitation due to the observed success of other firms. The term "search" is used to denote rule-change processes at the firm level. The central feature is the trial-and-error (stochastic) character of the innovation process. That is, a successful innovation may not result from this (costly) research and development program. At the level of the market, aggregate outcomes change as a consequence of the economic selection mechanism. The selection mechanism, transient profits and losses associated with innovation, determines the exit of established firms and the entry of potential competitors.

Period-to-period analysis concerns the development and maintenance by the firm of the routines that constitute productive knowledge, that is, a persistent search for new rules by the firm. Firm search activities involve the manipulation and recombination of the actual technological and organizational ideas and skills associated with a particular economic context. The results of the search are recorded in the "space" of economic measures such as unit cost, PRODUCTIVITY or input coefficient magnitudes. Research and development expenditure by the firm gives it a chance to find a better technique for use in the next period.

Further, it is assumed that, when the search process provides a rule that is more profitable than the currently employed rule at prevailing prices, then it is adopted. This assumption asserts that innovative behavior is motivated by a calculation of the profit consequences from a contemplated course of action rather than from realized (maximal) results (Winter 1971: 247).

## Competition

At an industry level, the forces of search are complemented by an economic selection mechanism, whereby the fit replace the unfit. Profitable firms expand by adding new capacity, profitable new firms enter and unprofitable firms contract, altering the industry state (the weighting of the different decision rules in current use). The analysis requires a delineation of the set of actual firms and potential competitors whose behavior is to be studied. Further, the nature of the decision rules that determine entry or exit, expansion or contraction are specified below.

## Market prices

The current decision rules of the firms, through their input and output decisions, determine the prevailing market prices. Prices determine profitability and, in conjunction with the investment and capital market rules, the rates of expansion or contraction of individual firms. With the size of the firms altered, the firm decision rules imply different input and output decisions, hence different price and profitability signals, and so on. By this process, aggregate input and output prices for the sector undergo change, even if the search process does not modify the individual firm decision rules (Nelson and Winter 1974: 893).

When individual firm rules do change, the phenomena of search and selection are simultaneous, interacting aspects of the evolutionary process. The same prices that provide selective feedback also influence the directions of search. Through the joint action of search and selection the firms evolve over time, with the condition of the industry during a specific time period bearing the seeds of its condition on the following day (Nelson and Winter 1974: 893–4).

## Computer simulation models

The complex process of search and selection is analyzed by Nelson and Winter using computer simulation models. Prior to simulation, the selection environment must be characterized. This involves the specification of the conditions (functional form and elasticity) of supply and demand for current inputs and outputs, and the functioning of financial and capital markets (credit availability and lending requirements) facing the firms of the sector.

The experimental design sets, for example, two different levels for each of the experimental factors in a simulation. Factors considered of interest will vary with the focus of the study, and might include the pace of latent productivity growth, the variance of research draws around latent productivity, the difficulty of imitation and so on. For $n$ experimental factors, $2^n$ simulations are identified. The experimental design identifies the numerical context for comparison of simulation regimes, and is defined by specifying the values of the numerous parameters in the model. The objective in choosing these values need not be to represent any particular empirical situation, but rather to achieve general empirical plausibility together with theoretical simplicity and familiarity.

A run of the simulation model corresponds to picking an initial industry state and then letting the model generate, stochastically, the series of subsequent states. The open question is: what happens as the industry matures? Established firms may "pull away"; their technological performance is such as to leave them beyond the reach of any challenge from new entry. This case is registered in concentration-increasing stochastic growth, and eventually there will be a few large, old firms which generate most of the progress. In the polar opposite case, the early entrants find it difficult to move beyond their original achievements.

New possibilities emerge and are seized by new entrants, driving the older firms into decline and perhaps out of existence. The problem is to explain the relative role of entrants and established firms. What determines the strength of the challenge that established firms face from innovative entry? For a particular industry, the supply (or potential supply) of innovative entry in a particular time period is determined by the joint occurrence of innovation ideas relevant to the industry, with entrepreneurial traits and disposition, that will lead to a serious consideration of an entry attempt (Winter 1984: 296–7).

Simulations provide a specific quantitative illustration of an interpretation of SCHUMPE-TERIAN COMPETITION. Freedom from tractability constraints of available analytical techniques is the main advantage of simulation. This freedom can be exploited in a preliminary exploration of a variety of model formulations. Simulation also makes possible intuition relevant to a careful scrutiny of detailed quantitative examples. A study of a range of simulations may also lead to the perception of unanticipated regularities, and the development of new hypotheses about the behavior of the model (Nelson and Winter 1977: 272).

## See also:

conventions; innovation, evolution and cycles; Schumpeterian political economy; technology

## Selected references

Nelson, Richard and Winter, Sidney (1974) "Neoclassical vs. Evolutionary Theories of Economic Growth: Critique and Prospectus," *Economic Journal* 84: 886–905.

—— (1977) "Simulation of Schumpeterian Competition," *American Economic Review* 67: 271–6.

—— (1982) *An Evolutionary Theory of Economic Change*, Cambridge, MA: Harvard University Press.

Schumpeter, Joseph (1911) *The Theory of Economic Development*, Cambridge, MA: Harvard University Press, 1961.

—— (1950) *Capitalism, Socialism and Democracy*, 3rd edn, New York: Harper.

Winter, Sidney (1971) "Satisficing, Selection, and the Innovating Remnant," *Quarterly Journal of Economics* 85: 237–61.

—— (1984) "Schumpeterian Competition in Alternative Technical Regimes," *Journal of Economic Behaviour and Organisation* 5: 287–320.

HARRY BLOCH<br>GARY MADDEN

# neoclassical economics

## Introduction

The rise to dominance of neoclassical economics coincided with the rapid professionalization of economics at the end of the nineteenth century. Seventy years later, the numerically dominant group of professional economists in academia, business and government were not even distinguishing between neoclassical economics and economics. Neoclassical economics had achieved the status of the orthodox, the economics of the mainstream (see Hausman 1992). However, neoclassical economics was by no means a homogeneous and consistent entity, so that it faced challenges from within but also from heterodox developments "outside" (see NEOCLASSICAL ECONOMICS: CRITIQUE). Yet its impact and influence on those who "do economics" is so widespread that it has without doubt touched them all.

Thorstein VEBLEN has been identified (Aspromourgos 1986) as the first to attach the label "neoclassical" to the study of the economics of Alfred Marshall. This reflected an acceptance of Marshall's assertion that his predominantly microeconomic analysis preserved a continuity with CLASSICAL POLITICAL ECONOMY (Bharadwaj 1989). Later, neoclassical economics was increasingly identified with marginal analysis, whether narrowly or broadly defined, encompassing rationality, choice theoretic behavior and constrained maximization, usually in competitive markets. The publication of Samuelson's *Foundations of Economic Analysis* in 1948 reinforced a trend toward the mathematization of economics, and provided a further fillip for the increasingly technical approach to economics.

By the mid-1950s, Samuelson had coined the term "grand neoclassical synthesis" to describe the combination of neoclassical microeconomics and purportedly "Keynesian" macroeconomics (see Arestis 1992). Other schools of economics emerged, emphasizing the microeconomic underpinnings of a range of approaches to macroeconomics. There is considerable diversity within neoclassical economics, and as the new millennium approaches there is still controversy over its methodology and the nature of the problems it addresses. There is also an occasional challenge to its HEGEMONY.

## Origins and distinguishing characteristics

The precise timing of the emergence of neoclassical economics is still in dispute. It has usually been linked with the emergence of the utilitarian elements of the subjective theory of value. European economists were producing essentially "marginal" analysis as early as the 1830s–1850s. Examples include the work of J.H. von Thunen (1783–1850), Antoine Cournot (1801–77) and H.H. Gossen (1810–58). However, the early development of neoclassical economics is usually cited as occurring later. For instance, it is sometimes associated with Jevons, Menger and Walras and dated in the 1860s and 1870s; sometimes it is associated with Marshall and dated in the 1880s; and sometimes it is associated with the rise to dominance of the economics of utility maximization techniques as late as the 1960s (see Black *et al.* 1973).

Regardless of its timing, the distinguishing characteristics of neoclassical economics are now clear. In methodology, there is a strong tendency to abstraction and a reliance on deductive reasoning, which invariably involves the application of mathematical techniques. The emphasis is on the individual, who is seen as a rational utility maximizer, making choices at the margin, usually in competitive markets; which are characterized by market clearing and equilibrium outcomes. Firms too are seen as maximizers, subject to constraints imposed by production functions, which are characterized by diminishing marginal products. Substitution at the margin is the driving principle behind all economic decisions. Thus the optimal allocation of resources is of central concern and is achieved when all markets clear. When this occurs, general equilibrium prevails and issues of unemployment are irrelevant. Of course, none of this can be distilled from a reading of any one of the early theorists of the marginal foundations of neoclassical economics.

It is the writing of William Stanley Jevons in the Anglophone world and Carl Menger and Leon Walras in Europe which has most often been linked to significant developments in marginal analysis. The contribution of these three writers was similar but not identical. Menger provided only verbal illustrations of his marginal utility theory; Jevons used the calculus and Walras, who was the superior mathematician, provided a more insightful and complex analysis based on his general equilibrium theory. All three developed the marginal conditions for utility maximization but their value theory, especially that of Menger and Jevons, was defective and incomplete. However, the basis for the use of marginal analysis, mathematics and statistics in economics was laid, while Walras paved the way for sophisticated general equilibrium models stressing the interrelatedness of the various sectors of the economy.

Alfred Marshall has often been presented as the "father" of neoclassical economics. So much of modern microeconomic theory can be traced to him that the label may be regarded as having some validity. It was Marshall's objective to present economics in a form which was palatable to the average "business man" and to popularize economic study. Despite his competence as a mathematician, his only major work, the *Principles of Economics*, relegated the mathematics to the footnotes. Although he often stressed the interrelatedness of the economy, he developed partial equilibrium

analysis for product markets, reserving a somewhat inadequate form of general equilibrium analysis for factor markets.

Marshall's greatest impact on economics was through his popularization of an idea found earlier in A.J. Dupuit's writings, that of the "Marshallian cross" (supply and demand curves). Assuming that the marginal utility of money was constant, Marshall developed the conditions for utility maximization and the famous Marshallian demand curve. On the supply side, he developed the theory of production and cost under the three (functional not real) TIME periods. He also invented the much used and maligned elasticity concepts. In disequilibrium, supply price differed from demand price, which set off adjustments in quantities first and later in prices to establish equilibrium.

The concepts of consumer surplus and producer surplus were refined by Marshall and used to analyze the welfare consequences of various taxes. His conception of internal and external economies is one of the most durable of his discoveries, paving the way for further developments in welfare economics and in the economics of development. Apart from the important insights which can be gleaned from the concept of quasi-rent, his distribution theory, based on marginal productivity, has never been regarded as especially insightful or profound.

## Early twentieth-century neoclassical schools

By the turn of the century, the marginal analysis underlying neoclassical economics was well established. Distinct neoclassical schools had emerged, although some of their contributions have subsequently been absorbed into the dominant tradition. In the first three decades of the twentieth century, neoclassical economics was predominantly Marshallian economics, especially in the Anglophone countries. Marshall's successor as professor of economics at Cambridge, A.C. Pigou, made some significant advances in welfare economics, paving the way for a diversity of approaches in the "new welfare economics."

In Italy, Vilfredo Pareto (1848–1923) established the conditions for optimal consumption, based on preference orderings and without reference to the measurability of utility, which paved the way for the development of the famous "Pareto optimality" criterion. In the United States, John Bates Clark (1847–1938) and Irving Fisher (1867–1947) made important contributions to aspects of the theory of distribution. In Austria, the followers of Menger, led by Böhm-Bawerk (1851–1914), extended the theory of subjective value; while Lionel Robbins (1899–1984) and Friedrich von Hayek (1899–1992) extended and developed the work of the AUSTRIAN SCHOOL OF POLITICAL ECONOMY.

## Market structure

In 1926, the publication of a paper by Piero Sraffa on "The Laws of Returns Under Competitive Conditions" contributed to the earlier criticism of Marshallian cost analysis under competitive conditions by J.H. Clapham (also at Cambridge) and F.H. Knight (in the United States). The central issue was the character of a competitive market and the incompatibility of decreasing costs with competitive equilibrium. As a result, "market structure" became an issue of central concern, which led to important works by Joan Robinson in Britain and Edward Chamberlin in the United States.

Chamberlin's theory of monopolistic competition abandoned the price taking behavior of perfect competition in favor of price setting by firms. Product differentiation was an important element of his theory, which still maintained the assumption of atomistic behavior. Chamberlin's contribution to the theory of monopoly and his revival of the term "oligopoly" is now part of the standard undergraduate teaching program. Robinson's theory of imperfect competition, which she later disowned, used a similar analytical apparatus to Chamberlin, and led to substantially similar results and also had a large

impact on the subsequent teaching of neoclassical economics. Her work on the static analysis of the firm and comparative statics was analytically superior to Chamberlin's and she extended it in two important respects, to monopsonistic exploitation in labor markets and to monopolistic price discrimination.

## Post-Second World War developments

After 1945, the center of gravity in neoclassical economics shifted inexorably to the United States. The mathematization process, which had been presaged by Fisher fifty years earlier and resisted, proceeded apace with the publication of Samuelson's *Foundations* (1947) and the rapid growth of the numbers of technically competent economists. Much of the groundwork had been laid by J.R. Hicks, sometimes working jointly with R.G.D. Allan in the interwar period.

Hicks's best-known neoclassical work, *Value and Capital*, published in 1946, reproduced in a coherent form results discovered earlier, including the Hicks–Allan rediscovery of the Slutsky theorem and the establishment of the principle of marginal substitution as a centerpiece of demand theory. Hicks came to this through his neoclassical theory of wages, in which the elaboration of the elasticity of substitution was a major element. The most important consequence of Hicks's work was the gradual revival of general equilibrium theory. In this he demonstrated, first, the application of comparative statics to the problem, and second, the application of general equilibrium theory in a dynamic context, including expectations of the future, through the invention of a temporary equilibrium technique.

In the post-1945 period the agenda of neoclassical economics widened. The collaboration in the United States between the Hungarian-born mathematician John von Neumann and the German-born economist Oskar Morgenstern, who had links to the Austrian school, saw the publication of a pathbreaking book, *The Theory of Games and Economic Behaviour* in 1944. Economists could now analyze cooperative and non-cooperative small group interactions and a wide range of applications were made to oligopoly, bilateral monopoly, bargaining and various forms of coalition. Developments in utility theory were also stimulated by GAME THEORY, including the incorporation of uncertainty into the analysis through the concept of expected utility, or through K.J. Arrow's state preference theory. Fruitful extensions occurred through G.S. Becker's HUMAN CAPITAL theory, which treated time as a commodity and has stimulated endless empirical applications, to the labor market in particular.

In macroeconomics, Samuelson's "grand neoclassical synthesis" incorporated individual choice theoretic utility maximizing behavior and profit maximizing behavior by firms in a laissez-faire economic system. This IS–LM analysis, with the standard neoclassical production function tacked on, has dominated macroeconomic teaching. Competitive markets with flexibility of wages and prices ensured that Walrasian general equilibrium prevailed.

The emergence of STAGFLATION in the 1960s saw the rise to prominence of MONETARISM, also within the neoclassical tradition. Dissatisfaction with the adaptive expectations hypothesis, which predicted the possibility of short run trade-offs between inflation and unemployment, led to the rational expectations hypothesis of new classical macroeconomics. This theory predicted the absence of a trade off between inflation and unemployment in the short and long run and supported a "policy ineffectiveness proposition."

However, both theoretical and empirical weaknesses soon emerged, and some rational expectations proponents developed real business cycle models to predict economic fluctuations. Although still in the neoclassical mold, these models called for a high degree of substitutability between present and future consumption among suppliers of labor and lacked monetary underpinnings. There are some parallels between new classical economics and one wing of the New Keynesian school, which also subscribes to rational expectations in a general equilibrium framework. Their emphasis is on micro-foundations for macroeconomics, with unemployment being explained by institutional constraints leading to aggregate inefficiency.

Although Samuelson and von Neumann had written on the theory of economic growth, it was a famous paper by Robert Solow, "A Contribution to the Theory of Economic Growth" in 1956, which inspired numerous related pieces. Solow's model was labeled "neoclassical" because he employed a linear homogeneous production function, which allowed continuous substitution between capital and labor; and also because he adopted the marginal productivity theory of factor pricing.

The model generated a balanced growth rate which was independent of the savings rate and determined solely by the growth rate of the population and technology. The model was extended to more than one sector with technical progress and to include alternative production functions and variable savings rates. Empirical and policy analysis focused on the relative contributions of technical change and capital accumulation, the impact of taxation and choice of the optimal growth path.

Edmund S. Phelps, in 1961, was the first to demonstrate the "golden rule" of capital accumulation: "the steady growth state that gives the maximum path of consumption ... is the one along which national consumption equals the national wage bill and thus national saving equals 'profits'" (Phelps 1987: 536). Subsequent work became highly mathematical and analytically sterile, until another revival of interest in "new growth theories" occurred in the 1980s. These theories, which have been labeled endogenous growth theories, grapple with the apparent failure of the convergence prediction of neoclassical theory and with its perceived adherence to competitive markets. The proposed alternative shows how endogenous forces generate ECONOMIC GROWTH through a variety of externalities and increasing returns in imperfectly competitive markets.

## Modern mainstream economics

Most of the developments in neoclassical

economics have been absorbed into the dominant mainstream and now form the major fare in standard microeconomics textbooks. This material is predominantly concerned with optimization by agents operating under conditions of certainty. By contrast, contemporary developments which find their way into the journals and the graduate courses in economics are mainly concerned with economic behavior under uncertainty (not to be confused with post-Keynesian UNCERTAINTY).

The starting point for these contemporary developments is the von Neumann–Morgenstern expected utility analysis of economic agents maximizing under uncertainty. Information constraints and asymmetries generate uncertainty which is analyzed by generating subjective expected utility functions. Extensions and applications of this theory have been made to the analysis of insurance and labor markets focusing on issues of signaling, screening and adverse selection, as well as principal–agent problems such as moral hazard. Despite a plethora of developments and applications of expected utility theory, it has faced a major theoretical challenge associated with the failure of the so called "independence" axiom to hold. This version of the Allais paradox and more recently the related Machina paradox (see Cook and Levi 1990) have led to challenges to the conventional neoclassical assumption that economic agents always act rationally. Attempts to develop theory without the linearity of the independence axiom are still in their infancy.

The theory of games is another major development, but here the uncertainty faced by economic agents is affected by interdependence between agents, in contrast to expected utility theory where the uncertainty depends on the state of nature. Games are usually classified into cooperative and non-cooperative ones, but most of the recent emphasis has been on non-cooperative games. There have been some applications of cooperative games to the bilateral bargaining problem and Herbert Simon's concept of bounded rationality has been used to explain some of the apparently irrational predictions of bargaining theory.

Cooperative game theory has also had an important role in recent expositions of general equilibrium theory.

However, developments in non-cooperative games have been dominant. Maximization of utility or profits are still the motivating forces of economic agents. Most of the interesting applications have been made to duopoly or oligopoly markets, contributing to the illumination of the process of price competition. These theories have become increasingly complex, incorporating simultaneous and dynamic sequential move games. Experimental economics has tested various neoclassical theories, including expected utility theory. By artificially simulating some characteristics of markets, which conventional theory cannot deal with, additional light has been cast on economic processes.

## Conclusion

Despite a variety of challenges the hegemony of neoclassical economics remains intact. Its increasing heterogeneity now appears to be one of its strengths. Through this heterogeneity neoclassical economics has been able to rise to these challenges and to satisfy some of its critics. Mirowski's alternative interpretation argues that neoclassical economics "is best described as a sequence of distinct orthodoxies, surrounded by a penumbra of quasi-rivals; and that it is this, more than any deductive or inductive 'successes,' which accounts for its longevity" (1994: 68). For the foreseeable future, neoclassical economics will remain the dominant paradigm in economics.

## See also:

economic rationalism or liberalism; free banking; institutionalism: old and new; political economy; public choice theory; public goods, social costs and externalities; rationality and irrationality; Reaganomics and Thatcherism; rent-seeking and vested interests

## Selected references

Arestis, Philip (1992) *The Post-Keynesian Approach to Economics*, Aldershot: Edward Elgar.

Aspromourgos, A. (1986) "On the Origins of the Term 'Neoclassical'", *Cambridge Journal of Economics* 10: 265–270.

Bharadwaj, K. (1989) *Themes in Value and Distribution*, London: Unwin Hyman.

Black, R.D.C., Coats, W.A. and Goodwin, C.D.W. (eds) (1973) *The Marginal Revolution in Economics: Interpretation and Evaluation*, Durham, NC: Duke University Press.

Cook, Karen Schweers and Levi, Margaret (1990) *The Limits of Rationality*, Chicago: University of Chicago Press.

Hausman, D.M. (1992) *The Inexact and Separate Science of Economics*, Cambridge: Cambridge University Press.

Hicks, J.R. (1946) *Value and Capital*, Oxford: Clarendon Press.

Mas-Colell, A., Whinston, M.D. and Green, J.R. (1995) *Microeconomic Theory*, New York: Oxford University Press.

Mirowski, P. (1994) "What Are the Questions?," in R. Backhouse (ed.), *New Directions in Economic Methodology*, New York: Routledge.

Phelps, E.S. (1987) "Golden Rule," in John Eatwell, Murray Milgate and Peter Newman (eds), *The New Palgrave Dictionary of Economics*, London: Macmillan, vol 2.

Samuelson, P.A. (1947) *Foundations of Economic Analysis*, Cambridge, MA: Harvard University Press.

RAY PETRIDIS

# neoclassical economics: critique

The neoclassical paradigm has been contested in a variety of different ways. The criticisms are telling and the alternative models are robust and varied. Nonetheless, neoclassical economics has managed to retain its hegemonic status. For most orthodox economists, neoclassical economics *is* economics – the unmarked category – the norm to which all other heterodox schools are compared. The hallmark of neoclassical economics is that the theory of value and distribution is also a theory of output: prices, output and distribution are determined simultaneously (Eatwell and Milgate 1983). Economies are seen as comprising rational economic individuals, who maximize their utility subject to the constraints placed on them by prices, incomes and, in more complex models, logical (not real historical) TIME. Formal mathematical models are used to trace out the implications of consumers' and firms' behaviors, which are determined at the margin. Equilibrium prices and quantities for commodities and factors of production are determined simultaneously by the intersection of their respective demand and supply functions; any imbalance between demand and supply exerts pressure on prices to adjust quickly to a new market clearing level. If no market imperfections are present, then the price system will result in an economically efficient allocation of resources (see NEOCLASSICAL ECONOMICS).

## Institutions and culture

By the end of the nineteenth century, neoclassical economics was established as a science with a systematic theory and a well-defined set of research techniques. Classical physics provided the methodological paradigm. Nonetheless, its scientific efficacy was questioned from the start. Its critics asserted that using a theory based on static conditions with deterministic outcomes to describe the modern industrial economy was simply bad science. Thorstein VEBLEN (1909), founder of institutional political economy, argued that the most consequential facts observable in economic life are growth and change, but marginal analysis could shed no light on either phenomenon since all institutional and cultural phenomena were regarded as outside the domain of analysis. According to Veblen, limiting economic inquiry to deductive generalizations is the fatal weakness of marginal analysis. His critique of the construction of agency in the neoclassical model is similar. The hedonic calculus conceived all human conduct to be a rational response to the exigencies of a particular situation, and it underplays the influence of INSTITUTIONS AND HABITS, conventions and so forth. Veblen argued that this shuts off inquiry at precisely the point where scientific interest begins since the driving forces behind economic activity are imagination and creativity, forces that tend to remain outside neoclassical models (see INSTITUTIONALISM: OLD AND NEW).

Joan Robinson, one of the most influential post-Keynesian economists, offered criticisms in a similar vein (see ROBINSON'S CONTRIBUTION TO POLITICAL ECONOMY). Robinson (1980) argued that the propositions that structure neoclassical economics bear little resemblance to the structure and evolution of the actual economy. The study of the prices of commodities and the behavior of individuals and firms cannot be understood outside the context of the specific legal, political and economic systems in which they are set. However, the setting in which demand and supply are analyzed has no resemblance to modern CAPITALISM; it is a setting more characteristic of a rural fair where peasants and artisans barter their surplus products. Likewise, the emphasis on consumer choice in consumption theory renders invisible the inequalities of income distribution between families, and obscures the fact that income is the most important determinant of demand. She was also critical of the Marshallian concept of the representative firm, and its implication that there is an upper limit on the size of firms. The growth of large (transnational) corporations is still largely ignored in the basic theory of mainstream economics.

## Capital theory

Robinson (1953) may be credited with beginning the Cambridge controversies in capital theory, controversies that starkly exposed the logical deficiencies in the neoclassical treatment of value and distribution (see CAPITAL THEORY DEBATES). She criticized the ambig-uous nature of the capital variable in the neoclassical production function. In that account, capital is both an amount of savings and a stock of goods yielding profits to their owners. Robinson argued that it was incorrect to talk of these as though they were the same things because they do not coexist in time; when profits are being earned, capital has ceased to be money and has become plant and equipment. It was, in her opinion, impossible to find a measure of capital that is independent of distribution and the rate of interest (Harcourt 1972).

Sraffa (1960) had a profound influence on the direction of the controversies (see SRAF-FIAN POLITICAL ECONOMY). His analysis showed that the proposition that profits are determined by the marginal product of capital is meaningless because we would have to know the level of prices to know the value of capital, and we would have to know the rate of profit to know relative prices. Thus, the neoclassical treatment of distribution is tautologous. Sraffa is responsible for introducing the notions of RESWITCHING and CAPITAL REVERSING into the debates. Reswitching implies the possibility that the same technique may be the most profitable at a number of different interest rates even though other techniques are more profitable at rates in between. Capital reversing implies the possibility that the capital–labor ratio is positively related to the rate of profit. The assumption of a diminishing marginal rate of substitution between capital and labor is a fundamental pillar in neoclassical theory, a pillar that is effectively undermined by Sraffa's analysis.

## Money and uncertainty

The neutrality of money is another important pillar in the neoclassical edifice that has been subject to criticism from both institutionalists and post-Keynesians. Veblen considered it naive to treat money simply as an expedient of consumption. In practice people accumulate wealth and hold money for a wide variety of reasons such as status and privilege. Moreover, monetary institutions exert real effects on all facets of economic activity. In the neoclassical system, however, the whole money economy is absorbed by metaphor to reappear as a refined and sterilized system of barter. Since the distinguishing feature of a modern economy is its pecuniary nature, Veblen argued that neoclassical economics misses the main facts of economic life, including the nature of business cycles and unemployment.

Mirowski (1989), a contemporary institutionalist, sheds further light on this curious treatment of money in the neoclassical system. He argues that the late nineteenth-century marginalists hoped that the concept of utility would lead to a unified understanding of all economic phenomena in the same way that the law of conservation of energy unified physics at that time. However, they did not recognize the full implications of the conservation principle for their theoretical construct. The assumption of money neutrality is one result of the misunderstanding of the conservation principle. This principle implies that all goods may be transformed into utility, and hence into other goods through the intermediary act of trade. Money is unnecessary; it is an intermediate medium that goods must pass through before they are transformed into utility.

The notion of money neutrality is also subject to critique in post-Keynesian political economy (see POST-KEYNESIAN POLITICAL ECONOMY: MAJOR CONTEMPORARY THEMES). Davidson (1978), for instance, points out that in a world of perfect competition, with a Walrasian auctioneer assuring simultaneous equilibrium, it would be irrational to hold money as a store of value. In a post-Keynesian world of UNCERTAINTY – a world where future events cannot have probability ratios assigned to them – people hold money to guard against unforeseen changes in the future. Davidson argues that the problem of maintaining liquidity is a universal one and profoundly affects nearly every aspect of economic life, including economic instability and (involuntary) unemployment. Yet neoclassical analysis defines away the problem with the assumption of money neutrality. Other post-Keynesians (Eichner 1983) argue that neoclassical theory

violates well-established epistemological rules of science. Indifference curves, which underpin the theory of demand, and isoquants, which provide the foundation for production theory, are metaphysical constructs with no empirical counterparts. Eichner argues that neoclassical theory is little more than a set of deductions predicated on a set of nonscientific axioms.

## Capitalism and social relations

The Marxist critique begins from the notion that the starting point for political economy must be society rather than the individual. The laws of motion of capitalist society – production, distribution, ACCUMULATION and growth – are far more fundamental to economic inquiry than a theory of relative prices and resource allocation. Hilferding (1920) argued that the phenomenon of capitalist society cannot be understood if commodities or capital are considered in isolation. From a Marxist perspective, capitalism makes the existence of the individual person dependent upon the social relationships and CLASS in which he or she is placed; thus social relationships determine economic phenomena. Neoclassical economics, with its subjective theory of value, disregards this social nexus and thus effectively excludes real economics. Similarly, Dobb (1937) argued that treating the laws of exchange in abstraction from the more fundamental social relations of production is a source of problematical theorizing. Moreover, the subjective theory of value renders the concept of surplus meaningless and effectively obscures the real nature of capitalism (see MARXIST POLITICAL ECONOMY: MAJOR CONTEMPORARY VARIETIES).

## Gender, race and social groups

Exposing the importance of gender, race, class, and position is a central concern in feminist political economy (see FEMINIST POLITICAL ECONOMY: MAJOR CONTEMPORARY THEMES). Feminist critics argue that the assumption of rationality, central to neoclassical theory, is a profoundly gendered and incomplete account of human agency. Nelson (1996) points out that the neoclassical conception of agency excludes dependent children, the elderly and the infirm. This exclusion renders invisible a wide variety of economically significant relationships that do not fit into the rubric of rational maximization. Folbre (1995) argues that neoclassical economics cannot offer an adequate conceptualization of caring labor, i.e. labor that is undertaken out of affection or a sense of responsibility for other people. There are similar problems in the neoclassical treatment of the family. The new home economics renders invisible people who form groups that do not conform to the Victorian ideal of the family and naturalizes patriarchal gender relations. Williams (1993) reminds us that not only does *homo economicus* bear the imprint of his fathers' profoundly gendered lives, but that these fathers were the children of an imperialist world, a world in which racism appeared natural and colonialism was dictated by common sense. Thus, neoclassical theory embodies and naturalizes hierarchies of GENDER, nationality, SEXUALITY, class and race. Strassmann (1993) examines the relationship between RHETORIC and power in economics. She argues that the myth of the open marketplace of ideas hides the role of personal, social and political values in the neoclassical narrative, and this serves to maintain the power and disciplinary authority of its established practitioners.

Finally, the radical critique draws on a variety of the above-mentioned heterodox schools of thought. It is centered on ethical issues rather than primarily methodological ones. According to radical political economists, neoclassical theory is ideological in that it naturalizes inequality of income, wealth and power. It is deficient because it ignores the interactions of economics, politics and CULTURE. Since it is fundamentally centered in a western, First-World viewpoint, it ignores the harmful effects of market EXPLOITATION on Third World countries, indigenous peoples and other persons who live on the margins of contemporary economic society (see UNION FOR RADICAL POLITICAL ECONOMICS).

## See also:

Austrian school of political economy; collective social wealth; development economics: orthodox; disembedded economy; economic power; equilibrium, disequilibrium and non-equilibrium; ethics and morality; holistic method; instrumental value theory; methodological individualism and collectivism; monetarism; normative and positive economics; political economy; producer and consumer sovereignty; storytelling and pattern models

## Selected references

Davidson, Paul (1978) *Money and the Real World*, London: Macmillan.

Dobb, Maurice (1937) *Political Economy and Capitalism*, New York: International Publishers.

Eatwell, John and Milgate, Murray (1983) "Introduction," in John Eatwell and Murray Milgate (eds), *Keynes's Economics and the Theory of Value and Distribution*, New York: Oxford University Press.

Eichner, Alfred S. (1983) "Why Economics is Not Yet a Science," in Alfred Eichner (ed.), *Why Economics is Not Yet a Science*, Armonk, NY: M.E. Sharpe, 205–41.

Folbre, Nancy (1995) "Holding Hands at Midnight: The Paradox of Caring Labor," *Feminist Economics* 1(Spring): 73–92.

Harcourt, G.C. (1972) *Some Cambridge Controversies in the Theory of Capital*, Cambridge: Cambridge University Press.

Hilferding, Rudolf (1920), in Paul M. Sweezy (ed.), *Karl Marx and the Close of His System by Eugene von Böhm-Bawerk and Böhm-Bawerk's Criticism of Marx by Rudolf Hilferding*, New York: Augustus Kelley, 1949.

Mirowski, Philip (1989) *More Heat Than Light*, Cambridge: Cambridge University Press.

Nelson, Julie A. (1996) *Feminism, Objectivity and Economics*, London, Routledge.

Robinson, Joan (1953) "The Production Function and the Theory of Capital," *Review of Economic Studies* 22: 81–106.

—— (1980) "The Disintegration of Economics," in Joan Robinson, *What are the Questions? And Other Essays*, Armonk, NY: M.E. Sharpe, 60–67.

Sraffa, Piero (1960) *The Production of Commodities By Means of Commodities: A Prelude to the Critique of Economic Theory*, Cambridge: Cambridge University Press.

Strassmann, Diana (1993) "The Stories of Economics and the Power of the Storyteller," *History of Political Economy* 25: 146–65.

Veblen, Thorstein (1909) "The Limitations of Marginal Utility," *Journal of Political Economy* 17: 620–36.

Weeks, John (1989) *A Critique of Neoclassical Macroeconomics*, London: Macmillan.

Williams, Rhonda M. (1993) "Race, Deconstruction, and Emergent Agenda of Feminist Economic Theory," in Marianne A. Ferber and Julie A. Nelson (eds) *Beyond Economic Man*, Chicago: University of Chicago Press, 144–52.

DRUCILLA K. BARKER

# neoinstitutionalism

The term "neoinstitutional" economics was first employed by Marc R. Tool in his doctoral dissertation in 1953 (Tool 1953). It was picked up from Tool's dissertation by Louis J. Junker, who introduced it into the published literature (Junker 1968). Allan Gruchy also employed the term in his presidential address to the Association for Evolutionary Economics (AFEE) in 1969 (Gruchy 1969), but his use of the term is a bit more inclusive than Tool's (Bush 1995). Tool coined the term to identify a coherent institutionalist methodology that arises from Clarence E. Ayres's integration of Thorstein Veblen's social analysis with John Dewey's philosophy. Following Tool, American institutionalists practicing the "old institutional economics" have used the term to identify those contributions to the institutionalist literature that are either explicitly based on this Veblen–Dewey methodology or are fundamentally compatible with it.

Confusion in the use of the term has recently surfaced because "neoinstitutionalism" has been appropriated by some of the "new (neoclassical) institutionalists" (i.e. the "new institutional" economists) to refer to their own work (Eggertsson 1990). While it would be incompatible with the tenets of free inquiry to insist that a term such as "neo-institutionalism" be given only one possible usage, it is fair to say that it muddies the terminological waters for "new" institutionalists to appropriate this term, when it has been used for over forty years to identify a point of view fundamentally different from their own.

## Normative character of methodology

A diagnostic feature of neoinstitutional thought is the normative character of both its methodology and its substantive analysis. Sheehan and Tilman have observed that "instrumental valuation is the linchpin that today holds the neoinstitutional movement in economics together" (1992: 198). The meaning and significance of instrumental valuation in neoinstitutional economics is by no means settled in the American institutionalist literature. Some prominent American institutionalists have questioned the validity of the perspective set forth by Tool and others. Some leaders in the British/European movement of evolutionary-institutional economics may also find it philosophically unpalatable. Be that as it may, instrumental valuation, which is based on Dewey's pragmatic instrumentalist philosophy of inquiry and valuation (Dewey 1938, 1939, respectively), lies at the heart of the neoinstitutionalist paradigm (Tool 1986).

Methodologically, the theory of instrumental valuation holds that "objectivity" in science is not a matter of eliminating all normative propositions from inquiry. On the contrary, science is itself a system of values. Scientific inquiry inescapably and continuously involves the making of choices. These choices, in turn, affect the way in which behavior within the community of scientists is correlated in the conduct of inquiry. Consequently, "objectivity" in inquiry turns on the question as to what kind of values and modes of valuation facilitate scientific inquiry. Standards of scientific objectivity properly require that all absolutistic moral injunctions imposed on science from without are, indeed, to be excluded from scientific inquiry. Instrumental valuation, on the other hand, is itself generic to the scientific process. It generates value judgments that are "self-correcting," because they are tested by their consequences for the pursuit of inquiry. "The values of science," as Jacob Bronowski put it, "are the inescapable conditions of its practice" (Bronowski 1965: 60).

## Instrumental valuation

The concept of instrumental valuation plays a major role in the neoinstitutionalist approach to the theory of institutional change. In explaining institutional change, neoinstitutionalists focus on what they call the "institutional dichotomy," which hypothesizes that there are two fundamentally different kinds of modes of valuation that correlate behavior in all institutions: the ceremonial and the instrumental. Ceremonial values warrant patterns of status and power through use of distinctions (invidious distinctions) between individuals and groups of individuals with respect to their presumed inherent worth as human beings. They justify the encapsulation of science and technology for the purpose of preserving and extending differential advantages of one group over another. In consequence, ceremonial valuation inhibits institutional change and protects the status quo. Instrumental valuation, on the other hand, warrants patterns of behavior that the society depends upon in the problem-solving processes attendant to the provisioning of the community. Instrumental valuation is inherent in the dynamic process of "technological innovation" (very broadly defined), which gives rise to institutional change (see INSTRUMENTAL VALUE THEORY).

From the neoinstitutionalist perspective, "progress" is defined by Tool's "social value principle." This states that sustainable, progressive institutional changes "provide for the continuity of life and the noninvidious recrea-

tion of community through the instrumental use of knowledge" (Tool 1979: 293).

## See also:

Ayres's contribution to political economy; ceremonial encapsulation; institutional change and adjustment; institutional political economy: major contemporary themes; institutions and habits;; minimal dislocation; pragmatism; value judgments and world views; Veblen

## Selected references

Bronowski, Jacob (1965) *Science and Human Values*, New York: Harper & Row.

Bush, Paul D. (1995) "Marc Tool's Contributions to Institutional Economics," in Charles M.A. Clark (ed.), *Institutional Economics and the Theory of Social Value: Essays in Honor of Marc R. Tool*, Boston: Kluwer Academic Publishers, 1–28.

Dewey, John (1938) *Logic: The Theory of Inquiry*, in Jo Ann Boydston (ed.), *John Dewey: The Later Works, 1925–1953*, vol. 12, Carbondale, IL: Southern Illinois University Press, 1986.

—— (1939) "The Theory of Valuation," in Jo Ann Boydston (ed.), *John Dewey: The Later Works, 1925–1953*, vol. 13, Carbondale, IL: Southern Illinois University Press, 1988.

Eggertsson, Thráinn (1990) *Economic Behavior and Institutions*, Cambridge: Cambridge University Press.

Gruchy, Allan G. (1969) "Neoinstitutionalism and the Economics of Dissent," *Journal of Economic Issues* 3(1): 3–17.

Junker, Louis J. (1968) "Theoretical Foundations of Neo-Institutionalism," *American Journal of Economics and Sociology* 27(2): 197–213.

Sheehan, Michael F. and Tilman, Rick (1992) "A Clarification of the Concept of 'Instrumental Valuation' in Institutional Economics," *Journal of Economic Issues* 26(1): 197–208.

Tool, Marc R. (1953) "The Philosophy of Neo-Institutionalism: Veblen, Dewey, and Ayres,"

Ph.D. dissertation, Boulder, CO: University of Colorado.

— (1979) *The Discretionary Economy: A Normative Theory of Political Economy*, Santa Monica, CA: Goodyear Publishing Co.

— (1986) *Essays in Social Value Theory: A Neoinstitutionalist Contribution*, Armonk, NY: M.E. Sharpe.

PAUL D. BUSH

**NEW HOME ECONOMICS:** *see* home economics, new

**NEW INSTITUTIONALISM:** *see* institutionalism: relationship between old and new

# newly industrialized Asian nations

Over the thirty-five years from 1960 to 1995, East and South-East Asia has been by far the most rapidly growing region in the world. The four countries or regions showing the most dynamic economic growth started as less developed countries and joined the ranks of the industrialized countries during this period. Often referred to as the "four little tigers" or "Asian tigers," they include South Korea, Taiwan, Hong Kong and Singapore. A decade or so later, other countries in the region began to emulate their performance, with real gross domestic product (GDP) typically growing at rates in excess of 6 percent per year. The "new Asian tigers" include Malaysia, Thailand and

*Table 4* Economic performance indicators

| | Average annual growth rates (%) | | | | GDI (% of GNP) | | | |
|---|---|---|---|---|---|---|---|---|
| | 1960–70 | 1970–80 | 1980–90 | 1990–94 | 1960 | 1970 | 1980 | 1994 |
| Hong Kong | 10.0 | 9.2 | 6.9 | 5.7 | 18 | 21 | 35 | 31 |
| Singapore | 8.8 | 8.3 | 6.4 | 8.3 | 11 | 39 | 46 | 32 |
| South Korea | 8.6 | 9.6 | 9.4 | 6.6 | 11 | 25 | 32 | 38 |
| Taiwan | 9.6 | 9.7 | 7.9 | 6.8 | 20 | 26 | 34 | 25 |
| Malaysia | 6.5 | 7.9 | 5.2 | 8.4 | 14 | 22 | 30 | 39 |
| Indonesia | 3.9 | 7.2 | 6.1 | 7.6 | 8 | 16 | 24 | 29 |
| Thailand | 8.4 | 7.1 | 7.6 | 8.2 | 16 | 26 | 29 | 40 |

| | Average annual export growth (%) | | | | 1994 per capita GNP (US$) |
|---|---|---|---|---|---|
| | 1960–70 | 1970–80 | 1980–90 | 1990–94 | |
| Hong Kong | 12.7 | 9.7 | 14.4 | 14.3 | 21,650 |
| Singapore | 4.2 | 4.2 | 10.0 | 12.3 | 22,500 |
| South Korea | 34.7 | 23.5 | 12.0 | 10.6 | 8,260 |
| Taiwan | 22.4 | 17.2 | 10.4 | 7.7 | 11,597 |
| Malaysia | 6.1 | 4.8 | 10.9 | 12.9 | 3,480 |
| Indonesia | 3.5 | 7.2 | 2.9 | 10.8 | 880 |
| Thailand | 5.2 | 10.3 | 14.0 | 14.6 | 2,410 |

*Sources*: World Bank: *World Development Report* (*WDR*) 1996: 189, 208–9, 212–13; *WDR* 1994: 164–5, 178–9, 186–7; *WDR* 1984: 220–21, 224–7, 234–5, New York: Oxford University Press; Directorate General of Budget, Accounting and Statistics, Executive Yuan, Republic of China (Taiwan): *Statistical Yearbook of the Republic of China* (*SYRC*) 1995: 160–61, 166–9; *SYRC* 1991: 78–83; *SYRC* 1985: 88–95, Taipei: State Statistical Bureau; People's Republic of China, *China Statistical Yearbook* 1996: 770, Beijing: China Statistical Publishing House.

Indonesia, with the Philippines showing signs of joining this group in the 1990s. As an already industrialized country, Japan is not ordinarily included in this group; China, as a special case of a "transition economy" (from central planning to market-based), is not usually included either, although its 10 percent average annual growth since the start of its reform in 1978 is the fastest in the region. Table 4 provides an overview of the economic performance of the newly industrialized Asian nations and the new Asian tigers.

The growth in the region has been closely tied to rapidly rising exports which, with the notable exception of South Korea, were initially fueled by foreign direct investment. By the 1990s, the capital flows were being reversed, with Korea, Singapore and Taiwan becoming major investors abroad. The "model" for economic policy in the region is generally considered to be that of Japan, which promoted exports through a mix of industrial policies that protected domestic producers from competition (through tariff and non-tariff barriers to imports) and that channeled low-interest loans and scarce foreign exchange to successful exporters. We may refer to the mix of "market-friendly policies" (a World Bank phrase) and selective government interventions as the "East Asian model" of (capitalist) development.

## Approaches and models

The orthodox approach to development, typically spurred by economists trained in the USA and UK, stresses "getting the prices right" by minimizing government intervention in the economy, promoting privatization, and relying on market forces to spur economic growth. A "revisionist" approach, championed by Alice Amsden (1989) and others, emphasizes the key role the state must play (and has played in East Asia) in mediating market forces in late-industrializing countries. In *The East Asian Miracle*, a major report published in 1993, the World Bank finds explanatory value in elements of both approaches.

In analyzing the experience of the original four tigers, it is important to recognize the special characteristics of each of them. South Korea followed the Japanese model most closely, with giant business groups (the *chaebol*) dominating the economy with government support, foreign investment playing a relatively minor role. Development in Taiwan, by contrast, was initially spurred by many small entrepreneurial companies. Hong Kong and Singapore, both essentially city-states, also differed markedly; under British rule until July 1 1997, Hong Kong maintained the most pure free-market conditions while Singapore was heavily interventionist. All four tigers, however, were marked by extremely high levels of saving and investment, rapid growth in exports, and strong systems of public education focused on the elementary and middle school levels. With the exception of Hong Kong – a unique case as a British colony with strong ties to China prior to its 1997 return – the governments of each of the four tigers intervened selectively in the economy to favor selected industries and promote economic growth; the new Asian tigers share these general characteristics as well.

Government interventions include channeling credit to favored industries at subsidized rates through government banks or pressure on private ones, public investments in applied research, export marketing support and the formation of joint government–industry councils to share information. The East Asian development model differs from the continental European welfare states in that government welfare spending remains limited; welfare is generally considered a family responsibility. The major exceptions to this rule are the extensive expenditures on public housing in Singapore and Hong Kong.

Just as the economic interventionist policies of Japan provided the model for the old and new Asian tigers (Hong Kong excepted), the unprecedented stagnation that Japan experienced starting in 1990 was a precursor to serious problems that most of the Asian tigers began to experience in the mid-1990s, with the most serious problems appearing in South Korea, Thailand and Indonesia. Broadly speaking, it appears that the institutions most suited to helping nations "catch up" to the already industrialized countries begin to become counterproductive at some point in the process, although the precise reasons differ from country to country.

A combination of borrowed technology and low labor costs made a major contribution to rapid development in the Asian tigers. But as they caught up technologically and their labor costs rose, their export advantages diminished accordingly. Rapidly rising labor costs in South Korea led the *chaebol* increasingly to seek investment opportunities abroad. Also, government efforts to increase labor market flexibility by removing the protections of "lifetime" employment met massive popular resistance. Corruption in Indonesia and Thailand (where it was coupled with political instability) became a hindrance to rapid growth. Growing environmental problems and weak infrastructure (from power to transport) increasingly became problems in most of the region. And for the original tigers (again Hong Kong excepted), increasing investments in their own basic research became increasingly necessary as the pool of borrowed technology began to dry up.

## New institutions and strategies

State intervention gradually lost its power to generate rapid growth, amidst the sharply increasing competitive pressures generated by the globalization of production. The Asian tigers were thus forced in the 1990s to search for new institutions and strategies to sustain their exceptional economic performance. Hong Kong remained a special case, because it was able to shift its production to other parts of China, becoming a financial, commercial and management center for the rest of the country. Singapore sought to establish a comparable role for itself throughout South-East Asia (but with a special focus on nearby parts of Malaysia and Indonesia), and, like South Korea, sought to upgrade its educational and other institutions to accelerate technological progress. South Korea sought to enhance competitiveness by reducing protection and increasing labor market flexibility. Taiwan

differed from South Korea in that it was characterized by many smaller firms and greater flexibility in its markets, as well as by less protection and government intervention. Taiwan took the lead from the 1980s in establishing government-supported research parks, and thus may be in a better situation to respond to the challenges posed by a more competitive global economy.

The new Asian tigers continue to have some insulation from the forces of global competition, in that their labor costs are much lower than those of the original tigers. But even among them, countries such as Malaysia and Thailand are under severe pressure to upgrade the quality of their labor forces and improve productivity, since their (unskilled) labor costs are often as high as five times those of Indonesia and China. With the continued rapid growth of China and the sharp growth in intraregional trade partly insulating the Asian tigers from the sluggish growth experienced by much of the industrialized world in the 1990s, favorable regional performance continued through to the mid-1990s.

## Economic and financial crisis

Beginning in the summer of 1997, however, financial crises spread like wildfire throughout the region, hitting the new Asian tigers and South Korea with special severity. The financial crises, which continued into 1998, were marked by precipitously declining currency and stock market values, sharply rising interest rates and a drying up of confidence and credit availability (see Rosenberger 1997). In response to this situation, the International Monetary Fund (IMF) signed major loan agreements with Thailand, Indonesia and South Korea in the second half of 1997, agreeing to advance credit in stages in exchange for extensive institutional reform.

The reforms sought to target a number of the factors that underlay the financial crisis of the region. Following the extended period of rapid expansion, economies throughout the region had come to be characterized by a high degree of financial fragility. That is, banks and other firms had assumed debts well in excess of their ability to service them when unfavorable conditions arose; as they did with a vengeance during 1997. State officials had played a major role in directing the loan funds advanced by the banks and other financial firms; thus personal connections or payments to political figures rather than market forces often determined the allocation of capital.

Financial regulation was extremely weak and the accounts of firms marked by a lack of transparency. Firms were able to conceal their true levels of risk by transferring debts to subsidiaries at home or abroad, and by guaranteeing loans of related companies. Since financial authorities had intervened in foreign exchange markets to stabilize exchange rates, many companies throughout the region had found it profitable to borrow US dollars at low interest rates, expecting to repay interest and principal from domestic earnings. When the value of their own currencies fell sharply, they were unable to meet their foreign debt obligations, adding urgency to the IMF interventions.

The participation of the IMF and the financial reforms are expected to have the potential of limiting the extent of the Asian crisis of the late 1990s. However, success will be dependent on the willingness of the countries involved to undertake serious reforms, and even then a severe regional recession appears unavoidable. If corruption can be limited, transparency improved, financial regulation strengthened and market allocation of credit made the norm, the dynamic growth of the region can be expected to regain some of its momentum, given the sound underpinnings provided by high rates of saving and investment and the commitment to education.

## See also:

development political economy: major contemporary themes; human development index; markets; structuralist theory of development

## Selected references

Amsden, Alice H. (1989) *Asia's Next Giant: South Korea and Late Industrialization*, New York: Oxford University Press.

Bello, Walden and Rosenfeld, Stephanie (1990) *Dragons in Distress: Asia's Miracle Economies in Crisis*, San Francisco, CA: The Institute for Food and Development Policy.

Clark, Gordon L. and Won Bae Kim (eds) (1995) *Asia's NIEs and the Global Economy: Industrial Restructuring and Corporate Strategy in the 1990s*, Baltimore, MD: The Johns Hopkins University Press.

Kim, Eun Mee (1996) *Big Business, Strong State: Collusion and Conflict in South Korean Development, 1960-1990*, Ithaca, NY: State University of New York Press.

Rosenberger, Leif Roderick (1997) "Southeast Asia's Currency Crisis: A Diagnosis and Prescription," *Contemporary Southeast Asia* 19(3).

Stiglitz, Joseph E. (1996) "Some Lessons from the East Asian Miracle," (The World Bank) *Research Observer* 11(2): 151–78.

Wade, Robert (1990) *Governing the Market: Economic Theory and the Role of Government in East Asian Industrialization*, Princeton, NJ: Princeton University Press.

World Bank (1993) *The East Asian Miracle: Economic Growth and Public Policy*, New York: Oxford University Press.

VICTOR D. LIPPIT

# niches

The concept "niche" originates from biology and dates back to Grinell (1917) who originally coined the term to denote spatial characteristics of animal populations. Later Elton (1927) introduced a wider meaning by including also behavioral elements. For instance, there is the concept of "ecological niche," which means a particular link in a certain type of food chain. The same type of niche can be filled in different parts of the world by a similar, although unrelated animal. The "large carnivore niche" can house a lion in the African bush, crocodiles in the tropical swamps of northern Australia, and the killer whale in the ocean (see Vickrey 1993: 517).

## Economic origins

Economic origins of the term can be found in the works of Robinson (1933) and Chamberlin (1933), among others, who drew attention to market imperfections and heterogeneous preferences. They observed consumers "sticking" to their products, showing incomplete flexibility of moving from one market segment to another. Thus, each of the products occupies a specific market niche by serving characteristic needs of the consumers. Producers can capitalize on these market niches by satisfying and even creating a segment in the market which other producers have not exploited.

## Technical definitions and analysis

Consider an arbitrary state of a given "system," with all but a few elements having identical characteristics. If this small subset differs at least in one significant manner from the other elements, this subset is called a niche. This is a very general and static definition and means, at best, complete partitioning with no overlapping. Incorporating time and stability, we follow Hutchinson (1957) who defines a niche as "the $n$-dimensional resource space" within which a subsystem or subset exists.

The degree of homogeneity among the elements of a niche allows one to speak of a separate, autonomous part of the entire system. The niche concept necessitates internal homogeneity, whereas the external relationship affords heterogeneity. Niche size depends upon the amount of resources available. The more possibilities the niche provides to serve the members, the larger is its size. The niche width measures the range of environmental dimensions across which a population of a niche exists, and the niche distance describes the extent of the difference between the median of each niche.

Other, behavioral, attributes relate to interaction and competition. In the absence of any restriction, a niche can be completely occupied.

This so-called fundamental (potential, virtual, pre-competitive) niche comprises all circumstances under which the elements of the subset can survive. Environmental constraints imposed by competitors limit the niche's expansion, resulting in the realized (post-competitive) niche. Realized niches differ from fundamental niches by the loss of marginal elements/resources (May 1973). Wider niches favor occupation by generalists whereas specialists prefer to settle in smaller niches.

Often there is some overlapping of the niches, in which case the niche resources are utilized by members of both niches. It becomes evident that they must compete with each other. In general, the more the niches overlap the more competition will take place. The intensity of competition, then, depends upon the location and width of each habitat. Despite its promising features it took a long time for the niche concept to be adopted by economists. Marketers like Alderson (1957), however, recognized the potential of the ecological paradigm earlier. This is not surprising because terms like "brand," "market segmentation," "niche share," "strategic groups" and "positioning" are only different words for niche. Some economists, for instance, consider market segmentation to be a tool for the precise adjustment of product and marketing to the requirements of consumers. Markets, products and preferences are far from being homogeneous.

## Niches and consumers

The approach of Milne and Mason (1994) focuses on consumer segmentation in the US car market. Carroll (1990) studies the newspaper market, using the niche concept in order to measure the success of brands in capturing their target markets. This is an adequate understanding of the biological process, where individuals seek to become less dependent on a specific resource. The same is true for firms seeking independence from erratic disturbances and strengthening the producer–consumer link. Another promising field of application is in "voting patterns." The resources for which the politicians compete are votes. Thus it is crucial for their success that they design the content of party programs and election platforms as closely as possible to their voters' preferences, and, simultaneously, as far away as possible from competing parties. The observed tendency toward "median voter" programs and increasing political competition can be analyzed and explained by the niche approach.

Niches can be formed and created, especially through advertising. Consumers and voters can react and change their preferences, and a formerly well-adjusted firm will exit because of a vanishing niche. The exact identification of the boundaries of the niche is one of the major problems, both in theory and reality. The niche is not a crisp set, but rather a fuzzy set.

## Conclusion

Comprehensive theoretical models of niches are not yet well developed in economics. The existing approaches are often too close to biological terms and they lack distinct economic content. They offer, however, a better instrument for explaining competitive behavior in segmented markets than do "orthodox" economics. Market segmentation was formerly descriptive, and the concept of niches allows the identification of strategies and the prediction of future developments. Niche theory is a rather universal concept applying to marketing, product placement, spatial placement and even ideological platforms of politics. It is a strong analytical tool for all situations where we have to explain competition, why it takes place or not, and how one can evade it.

## See also:

evolutionary economics: major contemporary themes; producer and consumer sovereignty

## Selected references

Alderson, W.E. (1957) *Marketing Behaviour and Executive Action*, Homewood, IL: Irwin.
Carroll, G.R. (1990) "Concentration and Spezialisation: Dynamics of Niche Width in Populations of Organizations," *American Journal of Sociology* 90: 1262–83.
Chamberlin, E.R. (1933) *The Theory of Monopolistic Competition*, 7th edn, Cambridge, MA: Harvard University Press.
Elton, Charles (1927) *Animal Ecology*, London: Sidgwick & Jackson.
Grinell, J. (1917) "The Niche-Relationships of the California Thrasher," *Auk* 34.
Groenhaug, K. and Narapareddy, V. (1989) "Niche Changes and Population Strategies: Foreign Competition Revisited," *Scandinavian Journal of Management* 5(1): 49–61.
Hutchinson, G.E. (1957) "Concluding Remarks," *Cold Spring Harbor Symposium on Quantitative Biology* 22: 415–27.
Lambkin, M. and Day, G.S. (1989) "Evolutionary Processes in Competitive Markets: Beyond the Product Life Cycle," *Journal of Marketing* 53(July): 4–20.
May, R.M. (1973) *Stability and Complexity in Model Ecosystems*. Princeton, NJ: Princeton University Press.
—— (ed.) (1974) *Theoretical Biology – Applications*, Oxford: Macmillan.
Milne, G.R. and Mason, C.H. (1994) "A Niche Share Approach for Assessing Brand Performance and Identifying Competitive Groups," *Marketing Science Institute Report*, 94–107.
Robinson, J. (1933) *The Economics of Imperfect Competition*, London: Macmillan.
Vickrey, William Spencer (1993) "Ecology," in *Collier's Encyclopedia*, New York: P.F. Collier.

KARL-HEINZ WALDOW

# normative and positive economics

Virtually every mainstream textbook in economics begins with a brief discussion of the difference between positive and normative economics, made a dogma by those who slavishly followed Lionel Robbins in his *Essay on the Nature and Significance of Economic Science* (1932). For example, Schotter's *Microeconomics* states that:

Normative or welfare economics deals with what ought to be rather than what is and involves prescriptive statements that may be based on value judgments. Positive economics deals with what is rather than what ought to be and involves descriptive statements that are objective and verifiable.

(Schotter 1994: 4)

Schotter's emphasis is not unusual. Since positive economics is thought to be objective and verifiable, normative economics by implication is subjective and not subject to rigorous validation. This view is inherited from David Hume, who argued that a gulf exists between "is" and "ought"; and, more recently, from the 1930s logical positivists, who claimed both that scientific statements alone are rational and that scientific statements are those that are empirically verifiable. Mainstream economists, accordingly, claim that their work is scientific on account of its being value-neutral.

## Facts are theory-laden

Economic methodologists, however, deny that empirical evidence confirms a theory as scientific, because disconfirming evidence may always turn up in the future, and because any given set of facts may give support to conflicting theories. They also deny that theories that stand up to empirical tests designed to falsify theories must be scientific, because theorists can always add immunizing, auxiliary assumptions to protect core principles. Accordingly, it has not been shown that theories are scientific in virtue of their relation to facts and evidence. Indeed, philosophers of science since Norwood Russell Hanson (and later Thomas Kuhn) have argued that subjective factors are inevitably involved in the development of scientific ideas, and that facts are theory-laden because they are identified from the perspective of PARA-DIGMS. At the same time, many philosophers reject the notion that value judgments are inevitably subjective, and, indeed, often argue that widely accepted value judgments may possess as much or more "objectivity" as many scientific propositions.

## Values permeate economics

The mainstream view, then, that there exists a clear dividing line between positive and normative economics, is mistaken. Some traditional economists admit this when they allow that an individual's value judgments influence the views they develop. But this view is not widely supported in the mainstream of economics. Even when it is, value judgments are often understood as "individual motivation may shape theory," rather than as "the world views of economists in general influence the very questions they ask, the significance they attribute to some issues rather than others, and the concepts they select." For example, neoclassical economics focuses only upon instrumental rationality, and then characterizes decision making as rational when it is atomistic and self-interested. But this selective characterization of behavior has never been given any real scientific defense and, rather, represents a theoretical commitment one must have to be admitted to the ranks of neoclassical economists.

Thus, while it cannot be said that a clear dividing line exists between positive and normative economics, it is still unlikely that anyone would deny that there is a difference between positive and normative statements. This suggests that the important issue for heterodox economists is to understand how positive and normative economics are related and influence one another. Wilber (1996) puts this especially well by rejecting the notion that value neutrality makes sense, and by asking how our values come to permeate economic reasoning (see VALUE JUDGMENTS AND WORLD VIEWS).

## Characterizing and appraising value judgments

One proposal for how to do this, deriving from a reconsideration of the nature of values, is discussed by Blaug (1992). He draws attention to Nagel's (1961) distinction between two types of value judgments: characterizing value judgments and appraising value judgments. Characterizing value judgments concern the choice of subject matter, the mode of investigation to be followed and the criteria for judging results. Characterizing value judgments involve the sort of methodological judgments that are indispensable to any science. Appraising value judgments concern evaluative statements about the world, and are the basis for our claims about the relative desirability of different social outcomes. Appraising value judgments are usually considered to be normative economics, but it is obvious that characterizing value judgments are also normative and that they are essential to science.

Hence, Blaug recognizes that the methodological judgments or ground rules employed by any theory, when it makes various characterizing value judgments, are not free of the normative commitments and appraising value judgments the theory's practitioners hold. For example, the neoclassical treatment of agents as rational maximizers can well be argued to depend on the view that it is desirable or morally praiseworthy that individuals pursue their own restricted well-being in market contexts, and that doing so produces the greatest social good through an "invisible hand" process. At the same time, this view of economic agents can easily be argued to rule out the idea that individuals ought morally to put justice in relations with others above individual gain, and that failure to do so furthers an alienated life dominated by impersonal market relations. Thus, value judgments of the appraising sort enter into economists' selection of concepts and methods at the most fundamental level, and we seem not to have improved our understanding of "positive" and "normative" economics using Nagel's distinction.

## Reconstituting means and ends

A more promising approach, that also derives from a reconsideration of the nature of values, is to be found in institutionalist theory, which denies from the outset that positive and normative economics are mutually exclusive domains or categories. Dugger and Waller (1996), for example, accordingly argue that

the positive deals with our evaluating means and the normative deals with evaluating ends. More importantly, however, what counts as a means and what counts as an end is relative to the situation at hand. Indeed, something can be a means on one occasion and an end on another. Thus, an evolutionary approach, which views the economy as being concerned with historical processes and PATH DEPENDENCY, must be prepared to understand the continual reconstitution of means and ends.

This explains the value permeation of economic reasoning at a fundamental level, and ushers in an alternative to normative positive dualism in the form of Thorstein Veblen's split between instrumental and ceremonial knowledge. Instrumental knowledge is concerned with facts, getting things done and solving problems. Ceremonial knowledge is opposed to instrumental knowledge, and is concerned with prestige, getting credit for getting things done, and with exercising power (see INSTRUMENTAL VALUE THEORY). Since, throughout human history, the ceremonial has tended to prevail over the instrumental, a progressive economics aims at a critical apprehension of the use of power in the economy to gain position and prestige. Social problems – not social theories – should be the focus of economics. Since society will never be free of problems, the aims and ends of society are always evolving, thus suggesting the idea of "evotopia" (moving toward an evolving good society) rather than utopia as a guiding view of good economics (Hodgson 1995).

## Ideology and analysis

Finally, Dobb's Marxist appraisal of the positive and normative deserves attention. Dobb also begins with a re-characterization of values, and reconstructs the traditional Humean dualism between "is" and "ought" in terms of a distinction between IDEOLOGY and analysis. In contrast to Hutchison's view of values and ideology as an individual's personal predilections and commitments, Dobb defines ideology as "a whole *system* of thought, or coordinated set of beliefs and ideas, which form a framework, or higher-level group of related concepts, for more specific and particular notions, analyses, applications and conclusions" (1973: 1). As such, individuals are often unconscious of their ideological views, and tend to take many of their elements as having been established as "true" rather than "believed propositions." For example, Dobb takes the traditional fact–value distinction itself as being ideological in that most economists take it to be rooted in incontrovertible truths rather than an unexamined belief.

A view related to Dobb's needs to be distinguished. Schumpeter (1954) wrote of the difference between economic analysis and an economist's vision of the nature of reality and the problems at hand. The latter is ideological, and involves "a preanalytical cognitive act" which must precede "analytic effort in any field" and which may also "re-enter the history of every established science each time somebody teaches us to *see* things in a light of which the source is not to be found in the facts, methods, and results of the pre-existing state of the science" (Schumpeter 1954: 41). Yet, Schumpeter also claims that economic analysis can still be thought to be objective and independent of ideological views, indeed as a "box of tools" of a purely instrumental nature upon which scientific progress depends. Dobb rightly challenges this conception, arguing that this formal view of concepts as tools overlooks the way in which tools are developed for theoretical and ideological purposes.

Thus, if we are to employ a distinction between positive and normative economics, it must be with great caution and an awareness of the ways in which values inevitably permeate theories. It is true that descriptive and prescriptive language differ and that there are important differences between facts and values. However, economics is highly value-laden and, thus, understanding the role of values in economics is necessary to doing good economics.

## See also:

ethics and morality; modernism and postmodernism; natural rights; rhetoric

## Selected references

Blaug, M. (1992) *The Methodology of Economics*, 2nd edn, Cambridge: Cambridge University Press.

Dobb, M. (1973) *Theories of Value and Distribution since Adam Smith*, Cambridge: Cambridge University Press.

Dugger, W. and Waller, W. (1996) "Radical Institutionalism: From Technological to Democratic Instrumentalism," *Review of Social Economy* 54(2).

Hodgson, G. (1995) "The Political Economy of Utopia," *Review of Social Economy* 53(2).

Nagel, E. (1961) *The Structure of Science: Problems in the Logic of Scientific Explanation*, London: Routledge & Kegan Paul.

Robbins, L. (1932) *An Essay on the Nature and Significance of Economic Science*, 2nd edn, London: Macmillan.

Schotter, A. (1994) *Microeconomics*, New York: HarperCollins.

Schumpeter, J. (1954) *History of Economic Analysis*, New York: Oxford University Press.

Wilber, C. (1996) "Ethics and Economics," in Charles J. Whalen (ed.), *Political Economy for the 21st Century: Contemporary Views on the Trend of Economics*, Armonk, NY: M.E. Sharpe.

JOHN B. DAVIS

# North–South trade models

Models of North–South trade examine the interaction of two regions: the rich North (also called the metropolis, core or center) comprising "developed" economies, and the poor South (also called the periphery) comprising "less-developed" economies. Special reference is placed on international trade, factor movements, technology transfer and related factors. They consider the links between the two regions, and usually highlight the dynamic interaction between, and the structural differences between, the two regions. They can be seen as a reaction to the dominant microtheoretic Heckscher–Ohlin–Samuelson (HOS) models, which usually are static in nature and which make standard neoclassical market-clearing assumptions. They can also be seen as trying to formalize the arguments of those analysts of imperialism and dependency who have informally argued that North–South interactions lead to global UNEVEN DEVELOPMENT. In doing so, they draw from Marxian, Keynesian, Kaleckian, Sraffian and other political economy approaches (see Dutt 1990; Mainwaring 1991) in addition to neoclassical ones, including HOS, imperfect competition and endogenous growth models.

## Common framework

It is useful to describe North–South models in terms of a common framework which is shared by a number of such models (see Dutt 1990). They consider two regions – the North and the South – which produce one composite good each, where the Northern good can be used for both consumption and investment purposes while the Southern good – reflecting the relatively backward industrial structure of the South – is a pure consumption good. Each region produces with two inputs – labor and capital – using a given constant-returns-to-scale technology. Income in each region is allocated to workers as wages and capitalists as profits. The former consume all their income and the latter save a part of theirs; total consumption expenditure is allocated between the two goods, allowing for price response. Trade is assumed to be in balance.

## Specific models

Given this general framework, specific models make particular assumptions about the economic structures of the two regions. Most models assume that (a) surplus labor exists in the South; (b) the real wage of Southern workers is exogenously given at a level determined by alternative earning opportunities; and (c) Southern ACCUMULATION is determined by the saving supply, or equivalently under conditions of balanced trade by foreign

exchange constraints, which determine how much of the investment good can be imported.

The models differ in their characterization of the North. Findlay (1980), for instance, assumes a neoclassical structure with full employment of labor, which is determined by labor supply growth. Taylor (1983) assumes that excess capacity and unemployed labor exists and that growth is determined by EFFECTIVE DEMAND AND CAPACITY UTILIZATION in a Keynes–Kalecki fashion. Molana and Vines (1989), in a Kaldorian manner, assume that there is unemployed labor and a given real wage.

The models examine the determination of short-run equilibrium, given stocks of capital in the two regions. Some models, especially those interested in the short-run macroeconomic interdependence between the North and the South stop here, at times bringing interest rates into the analysis. However, most of the models also examine long-run dynamics in which each region adds to its capital stock through investment, possibly arriving at a long-run equilibrium in which there is balanced growth. The models are capable of analyzing the effects of changes in such things as TECHNOLOGY, Northern DISTRIBUTION OF INCOME (reflecting the increase in monopoly power in the North), spending patterns and savings rates.

Of particular interest are results which demonstrate that Southern growth is dependent on Northern growth, which is determined independently of Southern developments. Attempts by the South to grow faster imply a deterioration in its terms of trade, revealing the South's dependent status in the world economy. The relation between the Southern terms of trade and Southern growth, and the possibility of uneven development (reflected in the models by a rise in the ratio of Northern capital stock to Southern capital stock) can be due, for instance, to technological change, increasing monopoly power in the North, and changes in consumer preferences. Some of these mechanisms of uneven development have been endogenized in the North–South models to model processes of CIRCULAR AND CUMULATIVE

CAUSATION, due to such factors as international demonstration effects and technological change (see Dutt 1990). The long-run results of these models do confirm some of the informal ideas of authors such as Baran, Emmanuel, Singer, Prebisch and Myrdal, but the results depend on the specific assumptions made about the structures of Northern and Southern economies.

Most other models of North–South trade can be viewed as modifying one or more of the assumptions of these basic models; only a brief sample of such models can be discussed here and fewer can be mentioned by name. Some models introduce international capital mobility by allowing for foreign investment from the North to the South in search of higher profits, and find conditions under which capital mobility may reduce Southern growth or, alternatively, lead to more even development. Other models allow for debt accumulation by the South by introducing asset markets and interest payments, and model liquidity crises due to expectational factors as well as the structural explosive debt of the South (see DEBT CRISES IN THE THIRD WORLD).

Some models introduce incomplete specialization in production, thereby explaining the pattern of trade, rather than taking it as exogenously given. One such model assumes that both regions produce manufacturing goods with INCREASING RETURNS TO SCALE and agricultural goods with constant returns to scale (see Krugman 1990). This model shows that, if some historical accident makes one region (the North) export the manufactured good, it will grow faster with trade than under autarky, and over the long run there may be uneven development as the South becomes increasingly based on agriculture.

Yet other models incorporate additional factors of production in the analysis, for instance, primary intermediate goods (thereby modeling the implications of materials-saving technological change), and skilled labor embodying HUMAN CAPITAL (which is emphasized particularly in some recent HOS-type models). An important issue which can be analyzed using North–South models is the generation of technological innovation and its international diffusion through North–South technological transfers. Thus far, most of the contributions to this literature – despite work on technological change from an evolutionary political economy perspective – have used neoclassical models with full employment, and have typically concentrated on product rather than process innovations (see Krugman 1990). Finally, some models introduce a third region. When this region represents newly industrialized countries (or NICs), the models can be used to address whether the recent growth of the NICs reflects more even global development, or whether it implies that the gap between the North and the poorer regions in the South will widen over time as the more advanced parts of the South join Northern ranks (see NEWLY INDUSTRIALIZED ASIAN NATIONS).

## Conclusion

North–South models have proved useful for understanding the nature and consequences of the interaction between rich and poor countries, and for addressing central questions of political economy concerning international INEQUALITY and uneven development. They are more precise than earlier and less formal contributions to North–South relations, and make more explicit the structural differences between rich and poor regions. They are also less rigidly pessimistic about the implications of North–South interaction. Unlike many neoclassical models, they take into account structural differences between the North and the South, and depart from the assumption of smoothly-functioning markets which ensure full employment the world over, raising the possibility that North–South relations may not be mutually beneficial. However, as neoclassical models increasingly incorporate ideas such as increasing returns (as in neoclassical endogenous growth models and new trade theory), greater cross-fertilization between neoclassical and political economy North–South models can be expected to promote a better understanding of the informal ideas raised in the earlier informal political economy literature.

**See also:**

comparative advantage and unequal exchange; core–periphery analysis; foreign direct investment; free trade and protection; Kaldor's theory of the growth process

**Selected references**

Dutt, Amitava Krishna (1990) *Growth, Distribution and Uneven Development*, Cambridge: Cambridge University Press.

Findlay, Ronald (1980) "The Terms of Trade and Equilibrium Growth in the World Economy," *American Economic Review* 70(3): 291–9.

Krugman, Paul (1990) *Rethinking International Trade*, Cambridge, MA: MIT Press.

Mainwaring, Lynn (1991) *The Dynamics of Uneven Development*, Aldershot: Edward Elgar.

Molana, Hasan and Vines, David (1989) "North–South Growth and the Terms of Trade: A Model on Kaldorian Lines," *Economic Journal* 99(June): 443–53.

Taylor, Lance (1983) *Structuralist Macroeconomics*. New York: Basic Books.

AMITAVA KRISHNA DUTT

# North's theory of institutional change

Douglass Cecil North was educated at the University of California at Berkeley, receiving his BA in 1942 and Ph.D. in 1952. In 1993 he received the Nobel Prize for economics, together with Robert Fogel for work on economic history. His work can be divided into three or more stages, all of which deal with explanations of the history of ECONOMIC GROWTH. In that explanation, the role of institutions has always been important, but their role has evolved over time.

## Intellectual evolution

Initially North explained economic growth in the specific institutional context of the US capitalist economy (North 1955, 1961). In the second period, he explicitly analyzed the relationship between efficient institutions and economic growth (North and Thomas 1973). In the third stage of his academic life, North left the environment of a developed capitalist economy to study the Middle Ages and the Golden Age in the Netherlands, while at the same time addressing the issue of inefficient institutions (North 1981, 1990). In recent writings (for example, Denzau and North 1994), the importance of analyzing PATH DEPENDENCY, learning and "mental maps" of individuals is stressed.

The major contribution of Douglass North to POLITICAL ECONOMY is his analysis of the relationship between the institutional environment (belief systems, CULTURE, values, norms and legal ground rules), the institutional arrangements (the organizations that structure transactions in society), and the economic performance of nations. In analyzing these relations, Douglass North started as a neoclassical economist; then shifted in his second period to new institutional economics, in which TRANSACTION COSTS play a crucial role; and, in the third period, he can be characterized as a "neo-institutional" economist, because concepts like power, strategy and path dependency of the American institutional school are included.

In his neoclassical period, historical economic growth is analyzed in an exogenous environment of institutions. Institutions are data for fully-informed individuals who maximize utilities, resulting in equilibria. The engine of economic growth is to be found in cost advantages: relative prices are the central explanatory variables.

In his second period, Douglass North gave central stage to the process of efficient institutionalization and its consequences for economic growth. Institutions (property rights as well as political institutions) are efficient and lower the production and transaction costs for society. North and Thomas (1973) examine efficient institutionalization, based on transaction cost-minimizing individuals (who make rational choices) and efficient political and economic institutions (efficient institution hypothesis). Changes to the institutional environment which result in different relative prices are examined in different periods of economic history.

However, already in this period North had started to recognize the existence of inefficient institutions (institutions that hamper economic development and only serve the interest of a specific group). In his explanation, he not only points to free-rider problems, but also conflicting interests and differences in power. In doing so, North left the world of orthodox economics and entered the tradition of heterodox economics, like those working in the tradition of American institutionalists (see INSTITUTIONAL POLITICAL ECONOMY: MAJOR CONTEMPORARY THEMES). In the third period of his work, the efficient institution hypothesis was dropped and IDEOLOGY, power, bargaining and issues of information and motivation enter the explanatory framework.

## Inefficient institutions and transaction costs

North (1981, 1990) makes an attempt to explain the long-run existence of inefficient institutions. With his theory of the state, North tries to explain why property rights are often inefficient and why states are often unstable. The state tries to maximize tax receipts and, in exchange, provides society with services like legal rules, infrastructures and so on. In doing so, the state is confronted with internal and external rivalries, which have different opportunity costs, power bases and goals. The bargaining power of the state differs, depending on the position and power of different groups. Powerful interest groups are able to create special property rights, tax exemptions, voting privileges and the like. Instead of the efficient institution hypothesis, Douglass North refers to the institutional structure as a mixed bag. On the one hand, there are

institutions that promote activities that raise PRODUCTIVITY; on the other hand, there are institutions that provide barriers to entry, encourage monopolistic restrictions and impede the low-cost flow of information (North 1981: 64).

North thus replaces the neoclassical approach by one in which institutions play a crucial role. He is in search of a theory of institutional change which explains why efficient institutions are created, and why less than optimal structures continue to exist. The concept of transaction costs plays an important role. Actors create efficient institutions because they see opportunities to lower transaction costs, which improves competition and stimulates growth. On the other hand, actors are confronted with large uncertainties, resulting in high transaction costs, when they plan to change the institutional structure.

## Ideology

Along with the concept of transaction costs and economizing agents, Douglass North points to the importance of "ideology." Ideology can be described as the belief systems of society: cultural relations resulting in subjective perceptions (models, theories) all people possess in order to help explain the world around them. Because actors do not have complete information, ideology becomes important for making choices. In these cases, ideology and the so-called "mental maps" of the actors become important for explaining institutional change or institutional inertia.

## Integration, procedural rationality and power

Douglass North has gone through different stages in his academic career and he seems to try to combine elements of these different stages into one theoretical framework for explaining institutional change. This raises the fundamental question of whether Douglass North is not an arbitrary eclecticist, using concepts from different streams of thought when it suits him to explain specific historical developments. Or is he working on the integration of different concepts so that bridges are built between different schools of thought? History will judge, but his recent writings point to a fruitful attempt at integration.

He now seems to admit that there are limits to the applicability of neoclassical notions of maximizing agents, given environments, equilibrating forces and deductive explanations. The position is taken that the rational choice approach is only relevant when choices are simple and made in well structured environments. If choices are not simple and frequent, and the incentives for finding optimal solutions are weak, then uncertainty is high and procedural rationality becomes relevant. From that neoclassical world, he enters the new institutional world where the rational agent still plays a dominant role, but where institutions are endogenous and can be understood as the result of "economizing behavior."

Being confronted with many historical examples of the persistence of inefficient institutions, North was forced to cross the boundaries of traditional economic analysis and to enter the world of power relations, ideologies, learning and the like. The deductive approach is gradually being replaced by an interdisciplinary approach which is characterized by empirically established relationships and explanatory models, which are carefully designed to explain the process of institutional change. The transition from feudal labor relations to wage labor, for example, is explained in this manner.

### See also:

institutionalism: old and new; institutions and habits; knowledge, information, technology and change; rent-seeking and vested interests; Williamson's analysis of the corporation

### Selected references

Denzau, A.T. and North, D. (1994) "Shared Mental Models: Ideologies and Institutions," *Kyklos* 47: 3–31.
North, D. (1955) "Location Theory and Regional Economic Growth," *Journal of Political Economy*: 243–58.
—— (1961) *The Economic Growth of the United States, 1790–1860*, Englewood Cliffs, NJ: W.W. Norton & Co.
—— (1981) *Structure and Change in Economic History*, New York: Norton.
—— (1990) *Institutions, Institutional Change and Economic Performance*, Cambridge: Cambridge University Press.
—— (1994), "Economic Performance through Time," *The American Economic Review*, 84(3): 359–68.
North, D. and Thomas, R. (1973) *The Rise of the Western World: A New Economic History*, Cambridge: Cambridge University Press.

JOHN GROENEWEGEN

# nuclear energy and nuclear war

The dual nature of nuclear materials in weapons and energy production, and the link between reactor operations and the production of plutonium for bombs, have created both problems and opportunities for nuclear energy. All power reactors can be used in the production of military plutonium, the only difference between civilian power operations and military production being that the fuel is left in the reactor for a shorter period of time when military plutonium is being produced.

### History of nuclear energy

In 1955, US President Eisenhower launched the "Atoms for Peace" program, diffusing nuclear technology around the world while instituting stringent controls to guarantee that materials and technology would not be diverted to military uses. Over the following fifteen years, nuclear energy programs developed rapidly. The International Atomic Energy Agency (IAEA) was founded in Vienna with the dual roles of accurately accounting for nuclear materials to insure their peaceful use and promoting peaceful uses of nuclear energy.

In the 1960s, there was so much enthusiasm for nuclear energy that proponents felt it would eventually be "too cheap to meter." This never materialized, and even after the oil crisis of 1973 only Japan and France adopted large-scale nuclear energy plans. By the 1980s, nuclear energy was no longer seen as a cure for the energy crisis, for two interrelated reasons. The first reason is increased investment costs, due to more stringent licensing, design, construction and commissioning procedures. The second is public concern over the safety of nuclear energy after the Three Mile Island and Chernobyl accidents. Increased costs from both factors made production of nuclear energy a risky economic venture, as the bond default of the Washington Public Power System demonstrated.

The US nuclear power industry has been heavily subsidized since its inception. From 1950 to 1990, 20 percent or $96 billion of the $492 billion ($1990) spent to develop and obtain nuclear power was provided by the US federal government. Other sources of energy (oil, coal, etc.) received subsidies that stimulated product demand, but nuclear energy received almost all of its subsidies ($890 million in 1992) in RESEARCH AND DEVELOPMENT. The last US commercial nuclear reactor was started in 1978, but a few large companies still maintain commercial reactor research and development programs. The economic viability of commercial nuclear reactors in the US is unlikely to improve in the future, due to the costs of regulation, safety and raw materials.

## Nuclear war and weapons history

The forty-two year relationship in the USA between the Department of Defense (DOD) and the Department of Energy (DOE and its predecessors, the Atomic Energy Commission and the Energy Research and Development Agency) resulted from the Atomic Energy Act of 1946. This legislation came from the postwar debate over civilian versus military control of atomic energy and weapons programs. A key

requirement of the law is that the President retains control of all nuclear weapons and "special nuclear materials." Thus, while nuclear weapons are in the custody of military forces for readiness and operational reasons, control of these weapons is in the hands of a civilian Secretary of Defense and the President. The DOE is responsible for research, development, testing, production and retirement of all US nuclear warheads

Over the last fifty years, the US built about 70,000 warheads while the Soviets built over 50,000 (before the demise of the Soviet bloc). In the process, the US spent over $4 trillion on nuclear arms and the Soviets probably spent almost as much.

The primary goal of US nuclear strategy has always been deterrence. There were two important landmarks in this process. The first was the strategy of mutual assured destruction (MAD), where each side had sufficient nuclear weapons aimed at the other to insure that the destruction of any state that launched a strike against another was assured. The implications of this strategy – that both the US and the Soviet Union must remain at risk to assure that neither would launch an attack – gave birth to the Anti-Ballistic Missile (ABM) treaty. The second strategy was the countervailing strategy of the Carter Administration, as modified by the Reagan Administration. In this strategy, specific high-value targets – such as the Soviet elite – were selected as insurance against an attack.

Nuclear weapons spawned both a mind set and a dedicated production sector that make their passage from the arms inventory particularly difficult and prolonged. Nuclear arms caused an adversary to weigh carefully the costs of military adventures. However, as increasingly rapid, accurate and efficient methods were developed to deliver nuclear weapons, the US and the Soviet Union found themselves in a position where the use of nuclear weapons was becoming highly likely. Both countries found this condition to be untenable. This situation has been significantly eased by the Strategic Arms Reduction Treaties (START I and II). These treaties call for reductions in nuclear weapons on both sides to about 7,500 warheads.

## Deterrence

The real worth of nuclear weapons was assumed to be the deterrence they created, but the necessary components of nuclear deterrence could neither be clearly defined nor tested. Instead, domestic political and economic criteria often played decisive roles in the development and construction of nuclear weapon systems. The worth of nuclear weapons was often only measured in terms of their ability to promote technological development or income and jobs in specific regions. Similarly, the significant POLLUTION produced as a by-product of nuclear weapon production was unevenly shared by only a few of the regions in each nuclear nation.

## Proliferation

Vertical proliferation is the continued accumulation of nuclear warheads by states already in possession of nuclear arms. For example, at their maximum levels, US nuclear forces consisted of 32,500 warheads in 1967 while Soviet nuclear forces had over 45,000 warheads as late as 1986.

Horizontal proliferation is the acquisition of nuclear weapons by states that previously had no nuclear arms. It is widely assumed that several nations are on the threshold of developing nuclear weapons. India, Pakistan, Israel and South Africa are suspected of having already developed a nuclear weapon capability. Other non-European nations such as Iraq, Brazil, Argentina, Taiwan and South Korea have the sophisticated TECHNOLOGY necessary to build nuclear weapons within a relatively short period of time.

Nuclear proliferation is driven by national security, international diplomacy and domestic political incentives. International agreements limit access to nuclear weapons by nations that are not members of the nuclear weapons club. The primary agreement is the 1968 Non-Proliferation Treaty (NPT), which was indefinitely extended in 1995.

The treaty divides the world into nuclear weapon states (the United States, Russia, the United Kingdom, France and China) and non-nuclear weapon states (all other nations). The NPT promises full access to peaceful nuclear technology, subject to international safeguards, to all nations that promise not to build nuclear weapons. Article I bars parties to the treaty from helping non-nuclear nations obtain nuclear weapon materials. Article II prohibits non-nuclear member nations from building or acquiring nuclear weapons. Article III requires parties to the treaty to accept safeguards on fissionable material suitable for use in nuclear weapons and makes the IAEA responsible for monitoring compliance. Article IV guarantees the right of all parties to the treaty to develop facilities for the peaceful use of nuclear energy, obliges all parties to facilitate the exchange of nuclear equipment, materials and scientific information for peaceful uses, and extends the right to use nuclear energy – even nuclear explosives – for peaceful purposes. Article VI pledges all parties to the treaty to negotiate in good faith on measures to cease the nuclear arms race and to reduce and eventually eliminate all nuclear weapons. By 1995, most nations had ratified the treaty, with the notable exceptions of India, Pakistan and Israel.

## Site cleanup

In the USA, the Department of Energy is responsible for cleaning up the toxic legacy of Cold War nuclear weapons production facilities across the nation. In the race to build weapons, health and safety, plus environmental considerations, were often neglected, and DOE facilities are contaminated with some of the most lethal material in the world. A minimal cleanup has been estimated by the DOE to cost from $230 billion to $400 billion. Even at this level of expenditure, many sites and buildings will be closed to human access for the foreseeable future. Due to faulty containment and storage systems, the magnitude of the problem will increase if cleanup actions are deferred.

## Nuclear weapons testing

Except for a moratorium from 1958 to 1962, the United States and the former Soviet Union each conducted more than 1,000 nuclear tests over nearly fifty years, including 514 tests in the atmosphere or under water. Testing allowed scientists to design new nuclear weapons and to assure that older ones still worked. A Comprehensive Test Ban Treaty (CTBT) is a stated goal of the United States Government.

The United States still funds programs to increase the understanding of the remaining stockpile of nuclear warheads, to detect, anticipate and evaluate potential aging problems, and to plan for refurbishment and remanufacture of warheads, as required. Should the USA in future encounter problems that lead to unacceptable loss of confidence in the safety, effectiveness or reliability of a nuclear weapon type, it is possible that testing would resume to certify a specified fix. The DOE's current surveillance and maintenance program is intended to alert the nation to any such need that may arise, and a standard "supreme national interest" withdrawal clause in any CTBT treaty would permit the USA to respond appropriately, should such a need arise.

## See also:

military expenditure in developing countries

## Selected references

Forsberg, Randall (1992) "Defense Cuts and Cooperative Security in the Post-Cold War World," *Boston Review*, February.

Gertcher, Frank and Weida, William (1990) *Beyond Deterrence, The Political Economy of Nuclear Weapons*, Boulder, CO: Westview Press.

Isard, Walter (1993) "An Economic Analysis of the Costs and Benefits of Ending the U.S. Nuclear Testing Moratorium," *Peace Economics, Peace Science and Public Policy* 1(1): 1–6.

Lovering, John (1992) "Restructuring the British Defense Industrial Base after the Cold War: Institutional and Geographical Perspectives," *Defense Economics*.

Markusen, Ann and Yudken, Joel (1992) *Dismantling the Cold War Economy*, New York: Basic Books.

Shulman, Seth (1992) *The Threat at Home: Confronting the Toxic Legacy of the U.S. Military*, Boston, MA: Beacon Press.

Weida, William (1996) "The Disposition of Weapon-Grade Plutonium: Costs and Trade-offs," paper presented at the Conference on Utilization of Excess Weapons Plutonium, Como, Italy, March 17 1996.

WILLIAM J. WEIDA

# nutcracker theory of the business cycle

The basic hypothesis of the nutcracker theory – elements of which may be found in Karl MARX, J.M. KEYNES and W.C. Mitchell – is that the inner dynamics of CAPITALISM are such that in every expansion demand rises more slowly than costs near the peak of the cycle. Thus profit is squeezed in each cycle from two sides – limited demand and rising costs – like a nut in a nutcracker. For a formal model, and for a review of the literature, see Sherman (1991).

## Relational and historical approach

The nutcracker theory states that endogenous factors (limited demand and rising costs) lead to most cyclical downturns. The usual neoclassical view, on the contrary, proclaims that the economic system is always healthy and in equilibrium if left to itself. Thus, all cyclical downturns are caused by outside shocks. This tradition stretches from Say's Law around 1800 to the present approaches of the new classical economists, such as monetary shock theory and real shock theory.

The neoclassical analysis begins with individual psychology, so unemployment is an activity "chosen" by millions of workers. The nutcracker theory, however, begins with the relationships of classes within the institutions of capitalism. It explains unemployment as the result of a historical process which repeats itself, albeit with many differences, in each cycle.

## Previous Marxian theories

The two main Marxian theories that contributed to the nutcracker theory were the RESERVE ARMY OF LABOR theory and the underconsumption theory. The reserve army theory argues that in every expansion there is rising output and declining unemployment. As the economy nears full employment, workers are able to demand higher wages and less intensity of work. This means less profit per unit of output, which leads to less investment and a downturn.

Underconsumption theory says that in every expansion the exploitation of labor rises because wages do not keep pace with PRODUCTIVITY. Thus, the proportion of national income going to labor declines. But workers spend all of their income on consumer goods and services, whereas capitalists spend a much lower percentage of income on consumption. Therefore, there is a growing gap between output and consumer demand, resulting in a lower rate of profit.

## Premises of the nutcracker theory

The nutcracker theory uses elements of the previous Marxian theories to form an empirically defensible model. It uses the Marxian framework in which income is divided into wage income and profit income, where profit includes interest and rent in the first approximation. It also uses the Keynesian formulation that national income equals consumer demand plus investor demand, leaving aside government and international demand in the first approximation.

It is hypothesized that consumer demand is a function of all of workers' wage income plus a part of profit, with a certain time lag (note that time lags play a vital role throughout this theory). The workers are forced by economic necessity to spend all of their income on consumption, whereas capitalists are able to save some proportion of their income. This premise has been tested by many econometric studies, particularly by examining the correlation between the national propensity to consume and the national distribution of income between workers and capitalists (see discussion in Sherman 1991).

Second, it is hypothesized that investment demand is a function of profits and profit rates, with a considerable time lag. This hypothesis has been tested in several studies (see discussion in Sherman 1991). As noted earlier, the reasons are that profit expectations provide the incentive to invest, while total profits provide – directly and indirectly – the funds for investment.

Third, profit is defined as revenue minus cost. In the aggregate, revenue is defined as consumption plus investment, leaving aside government and net export revenues. Cost is defined as wages plus material costs, leaving aside depreciation, taxes and interest. The theory can be made far more realistic when the omitted items are included, but the first approximation is clearer with the simpler framework.

Fourth, wages enter the theory as a source of consumption revenue, but also as a cost to the enterprise. It is thus vital to specify the behavior of wages over the cycle. What is important in the model is the ratio of profits to wages, a crude version of Marx's EXPLOITATION ratio. The profit–wage ratio rises in every expansion. That is the same as saying that the wage–profit ratio (or wage–national income ratio) falls in every expansion. Wages plus profits are defined to equal all national income.

Why do wages fall as a percentage of profit – or of national income – in every cyclical expansion? As output rises, labor productivity – output per worker – is rising (there are many reasons for rising productivity at this point; see Sherman 1991). As the product of a capitalist enterprise rises, however, there is no automatic adjustment giving workers higher wages. They receive higher wages only after they have negotiated and fought for higher wages. Thus wages tend to lag behind profits and output for most of the expansion. Only after profit reaches a peak and begins to decline does the ratio of profit to wages begin to decline very slightly because employment still rises till the peak, so wages continue to rise. Thus in the key period before profits reach a peak, the profit–wage ratio is rising, or the wage–national income ratio is falling.

The implication of a rising profit–wage ratio is that the distribution of income is shifting, with a lower share to labor and a higher share to capitalists. Since workers must spend all of their income on consumption, while capitalists spend a smaller percentage on consumption, it follows that a smaller and smaller proportion of national income is going for consumer spending. Thus the gap between output and consumer demand grows. The effect on investment is twofold. On the one hand, the more limited growth of consumption means that much profit is not realized, that is, some consumer goods are not sold. The lack of realization of profit will harm investment, which means less employment and wages, causing still less consumer demand. On the other hand, the lower ratio of wage costs will help profits. In late expansion just before the profit peak, there is pressure on profits to drop because the falling ratio of consumer demand to output is quantitatively more important than the falling ratio of wage costs to output.

Fifth, in every expansion material costs rise rapidly. Theorists as diverse as Karl Marx, Wesley Mitchell and Friedrich Hayek have been concerned with this problem. Moreover, it is indeed a fact that prices of material goods rise faster in the average expansion than prices of consumer goods (see Sherman 1991). This rising ratio of material goods costs to output is another factor causing the decline of the profit rate at, or before, the cycle peak.

In the late expansion, the ratio of consumer demand to output is falling. At the same time, the ratio of material goods costs to consumer goods revenues is rising. In brief, the profit rate is squeezed – as in a nutcracker – by the limitations of consumer demand and the rising

cost of raw materials. Therefore the profit rate reaches a peak and declines. Some time later, usually with a considerable time lag, investment declines, thus setting off the cyclical recession.

It is important to stress the two-sided role of "wages" (wages are defined here to mean all labor income). Wages constitute the largest type of income and the largest component of consumer demand; the fact that wages lag behind profits in the expansion eventually limits demand. But wages are also the largest cost of production. For most of the expansion, wage costs fall as a proportion of output, so high wages cannot be singled out as a cause of the fall in the profit rate. However, once the profit rate starts to fall – even before the cycle peak – one consequence is that the profit–wage ratio falls; or wage costs rise faster than output. In other words, the profit rate fall is due to limited income and rising material costs, while wage costs are still a falling proportion of output; but the profit squeeze is immediately worsened by the fact that wages continue to rise slowly to the peak, while profits are already falling.

It is also important to stress that the five factors enumerated in this section lead to an endogenous downturn; but each of them is then reversed in the downturn, so the downturn is also ended endogenously. Only with an explanation of the upturn as well as the downturn can a cycle model be said to be complete. If the above behavioral hypotheses are each stated mathematically, a fully determined model of the cycle results (Sherman 1991). The model thus shows how capitalists, acting according to profit motivation, always cause a profit squeeze, resulting in a crisis and depression. Only after vast human misery – ranging from a brief recession to a vast depression lasting many years – are the conditions created (as Marx showed) for a new expansion. This is only a first approximation because it leaves out credit, government and international factors.

## A second approximation

In the first approximation, credit was ignored.

However, credit affects both consumer demand and investor demand. In every expansion the optimism generated by rising employment and rising profits leads consumers to increase their ratio of debt to income and also leads enterprises to increase their ratio of debt to income. As a result there are rising costs of interest, which help cause the downturn and which may lead to individual and firm bankruptcies after the recession begins.

Government was also ignored. But government is systematically affected by the economy, and systematically affects the economy. In every expansion, government spending rises slowly due to long-run increases in needs of the society as well as often the drive for more war spending. In every capitalist expansion, the amount of taxes also increases. Even if there is no tax rate increase, the amount rises because there is more income to generate income taxes, more sales to generate sales taxes and more wages to generate social security taxes. Since taxes rise faster than expenditures, the deficit decreases and sometimes there have been surpluses in late expansion. Deficit spending means higher demand, so the fiscal behavior tends to lower demand in late expansion, being another reason for declining profits. On the contrary, automatically rising deficits in every recession eventually help to stimulate demand, moderating the magnitude of the contraction. Further, usually in expansions, imports rise with national income, while exports are more sluggish. Thus, demand from net exports tends to decline in most expansions. This is another reason for limited demand.

Hence profit is squeezed in a nutcracker in the typical expansion because of limited demand (due to the declining wage–profit ratio, the decline in net exports, and the decline in deficit spending). At the same time, there are rising costs of raw materials and rising interest rates; and, after the initial decline, rising wage costs are also a problem. Note that the real private domestic factors are sufficient to generate a cycle, even though government behavior, money and credit, and international relations also influence it in reality.

Similarly, profit recovers and the nutcracker opens toward the bottom of a recession or depression. On the one hand, demand falls more slowly (due to rising wage–profit and consumption–income ratios, a rise in deficit spending, and an increase in the ratio of exports to imports). On the other hand, cost is falling rapidly (due to falling material costs and falling interest rates). Thus, sometimes after many long years of large-scale unemployment, eventually the combination of all of these factors usually leads to a recovery of profits and an eventual rise in investment.

### See also:

business cycle theories; cyclical crisis models; Mitchell's analysis of business cycles; profit squeeze analysis of crises; secular crisis

### Selected references

Sherman, Howard J. (1991) *The Business Cycle: Growth and Crisis under Capitalism*, Princeton, NJ: Princeton University Press.
—— (1995) *Reinventing Marxism*, Baltimore: Johns Hopkins University Press.
Sherman, Howard J. and Kolk, David X. (1996) *Business Cycles and Forecasting*, New York: HarperCollins.

HOWARD J. SHERMAN

# O

OBJECTIVES, CORPORATE: *see* corporate objectives

## Okun's Law

Okun's Law refers to a stable relationship between the annual change in the rate of unemployment and the growth rate of real gross national product (GNP) (see ECONOMIC GROWTH). Arthur M. Okun (1928–80), a long-time member of the (US) Council of Economic Advisers in the 1960s, estimated the gain (loss) of real GNP associated with a reduction (increase) in unemployment of one percentage point below (above) 4 percent to be 3 percent for the US economy in the period 1947–60 (Okun 1962). This relation is also called the Okun coefficient. Similar results were determined for many other countries so that today Okun's Law is regarded to be one of the most reliable empirical regularities in macroeconomics.

### Output–unemployment relationship

According to Okun, the relationship between output and unemployment can be demonstrated by three different methods:

(1) by the correlation of changes in the unemployment rate with the growth rates of real GNP;
(2) by the correlation of unemployment rates with deviations of potential from actual GNP;
(3) by using the assumption of a constant ratio between actual and potential GNP and a constant growth rate of potential GNP.

Whereas the estimation method (1) is relatively simple, (2) and (3) require assumptions about the development of potential GNP or the non-accelerating inflation rate of unemployment (NAIRU). The results of the regression coefficients then heavily depend on the specifications made in these variables (Perry 1977).

### Supply and demand

Although Okun's Law was formulated in the high tide of Keynesianism, it can be given a supply-side as well as a demand-side interpretation. If the unemployment rate is considered to be an independent variable, the law provides information about how much growth is reduced because of unemployment. If, however, the unemployment rate is considered to be the dependent variable, the influence of changes in effective demand on unemployment can be determined. Okun himself was not very clear about the chain of causation. Whereas he considered the rate of unemployment to be a measure of how unused resources can influence production, his estimation method follows the Keynesian interpretation.

Okun's Law basically covers the short-period PRODUCTIVITY gains (losses) associated with an increase (decrease) in output which reflect the economies gained (lost) from higher (lower) capacity utilization. The law can be used as a rule of thumb for the estimation of the unemployment rate or the output forgone. Moreover, in an integrated macro model, it can form the bridge between the labor and the goods markets thereby enabling the mapping of spillover and feedback effects between them. Both variables are endogenously determined in this case.

## Causality

Okun's Law clearly suggests that output and productivity are positively correlated in the short run. The overproportional reaction of GNP growth to changes in unemployment rates raises the question of the relevant causes. Okun mentioned three possible determinants. An increase (decrease) of the unemployment rate of one percentage point does not necessarily imply a corresponding change in the number of gainfully employed persons. An improvement of the labor market situation will also attract workers who hitherto had no jobs without being officially registered as "unemployed." Their employment will lead to an increase in output without a reduction in the unemployment rate. A second cause are induced reactions in the average working time, as, for example, an increase in the average weekly hours per worker in times of recovery. Procyclical movements of productivity per worker are the third cause. In general, it was expected that firms would displace more workers during recessions, and thus labor productivity would remain at least constant. In fact, however, the termination of labor contracts is not always possible (due to legal agreements) or sensible (requirements of production techniques, transaction costs or the danger of a loss in knowledge), particularly with regard to qualified workers of the primary segment of the labor market. The consequence is the procyclical variation of the growth rate of labor productivity (Okun 1962).

This phenomenon overlaps with VER-DOORN'S LAW, which states a close linear relationship between the growth rate of GNP and that of labor productivity in the long run, with increasing returns to scale as an important determinant. The increase in the working time of workers can mimic long-run increasing scale returns, if the period of observation is wrongly chosen and labor productivity is measured on a per capita basis.

## Labor market implications

Labor market implications can be drawn from the stability of Okun's Law and the level of the regression coefficients. The higher the growth rate of GNP which is necessary for a reduction of the unemployment rate by 1 percent, the higher is the probability that the labor market is characterized by small hire-and-fire activities. For economies like Germany with rather long-run employment contracts, the employment elasticities with regard to GNP growth are considerably smaller than for the USA. Furthermore, the phenomenon of an increasing basic unemployment must be reflected in a structural break of Okun's Law. The Okun coefficient should increase in the long run for those economies which show higher unemployment rates after each recession compared to those economies with a rather stable NAIRU (Gordon 1984; Kaufman 1988).

## Policy implications

The empirical results for Okun's Law have important implications for economic policy. On the one hand, they point to necessary reforms in the labor market. On the other hand, inferences on inflation potentiality can be drawn from the existence of Okun's Law, by comparing the actual with the potential GNP and by perceiving the attainment of full capacity utilization.

## Structural breaks

Although Okun's Law in principle is a reliable and stable relationship, its usefulness for prognostic purposes remains an open question. Since the developments discussed earlier can lead to structural breaks, extensions to the simple relationship are necessary. Changes in participation rates and the consequential composition of the labor force are particularly relevant. Furthermore, the development of prices and wages and price and wage expectations play a crucial role (Nourzad and Almaghrbi 1996). Okun's original law neglects the impact of investment activity on labor productivity and production potential. The nature and rate of technological innovation and endogenous technical progress influence output growth and unemployment. An exclusive concentration on labor as a production factor, therefore, is insufficient. Okun's Law represents an important building block in the explanation of cyclical phenomena. However, for a better understanding it is necessary to integrate it with long-run developments. The incorporation of potential output is a first step in the right direction, despite all difficulties in the empirical inquiry.

## See also:

productivity slowdown

## Selected references

Friedman, B.M. and Wachter, M.L. (1973) "Unemployment: Okun's Law, Labour Force, and Productivity," *Review of Economics and Statistics* 56(2): 167–76.

Gordon, R.J. (1984) "Unemployment and Potential Output in the 1980s," *Brookings Papers on Economic Activity* 2: 537–64.

Kaufman, R.T. (1988) "An International Comparison of Okun's Law," *Journal of Comparative Economics* 12: 182–203.

Nourzad, F. and Almaghrbi, Y. (1996) "Okun's Law and the Fulfillment of Wage and Price Expectations," *Journal of Post Keynesian Economics* 18(2): 293–308.

Okun, A.M. (1962) "Potential GNP: Its Measurement and Significance," *Proceedings of the Business and Economic Section*, Washington, DC: American Statistical Association, 98–104.

Perry, G.L. (1977) "Potential Output and Productivity," *Brookings Papers on Economic Activity* 1: 11–48.

Smith, G. (1975) "Okun's Law Revisited," *Quarterly Review of Economics and Business* 15(4): 37–54.

HARALD HAGEMANN
STEPHAN SEITER

**OLD INSTITUTIONALISM:** *see* institutionalism: old and new

**OVERDETERMINATION:** *see* determinism and overdetermination

# overhead costs

The first generation of neoclassical economists saw their task as a two-stage process. First, the static relations of the economy would be outlined. Then, when this was complete, it would be possible and necessary to proceed to a presentation of the dynamic relations. None of the originators of the neoclassical approach managed to progress to the dynamics of the economy, and of the second generation only John Maurice Clark (1884–1963) made a sustained effort to develop a dynamic theory on neoclassical principles. From his early paper "Business Acceleration and the Law of Demand," published in the *Journal of Political Economy* in 1917, through his books *Studies in the Economics of Overhead Costs* in 1923 and *Strategic Factors in Business Cycles* in 1934, to his last book, *Competition as a Dynamic Process* in 1961, Clark investigated the consequences of introducing TIME into neoclassical theory.

## Time, joint production and fixed costs

Clark's focus on the temporal component of economic decisions is directed to an analysis of the influence of past decisions upon current choices. Many decisions cannot be reversed, leading to a situation in which important costs of production cannot be assigned to particular units of output, and in which changes in output do not entail a change in these costs. Clark defines these two types of costs as "overhead costs." There are, of course, two different problems of economic theory included in the one concept: the problem of assigning costs in cases of joint production and the problem of fixed costs. Clark's insights on fixed costs have been incorporated into standard economic theory, but the problem of JOINT PRODUCTION still has not been adequately solved.

Usually in cases of joint production, costs are assigned in a somewhat arbitrary manner.

This has the advantage of introducing some flexibility into the actions of a firm, but the disadvantage of allowing multi-product firms to shift costs to products selling in non-competitive markets, and to engage in "cut-throat" competition in markets in which they have rivals. The result is a much more unstable economy.

## Excess capacity and social cost

The problem of fixed costs results in the now familiar analysis of fluctuations in output leading to situations of excess capacity, or to analysis of the overload capacity of the components of a production system. Clark, however, does not stop here. He extends the concept of overhead costs to the social level, and in doing this he is, with Pigou, one of the first to systematically investigate situations in which social and private costs diverge.

His discussion of the "overhead costs of labor" is particularly telling. Seen from the point of view of the firm, labor is a variable cost. It is relative easy to adjust the amount of labor to the level of output. From the point of view of the laborer or from the social point of view, the situation is quite different. The costs of maintaining labor do not vary with output: "When labor is laid off, no material human cost is avoided" (Clark 1923: 360). In addition, there are the costs of foregone output, and the costs associated with the deterioration of human skills during times of idleness; costs which cannot be avoided if the labor force is to maintain and reproduce itself. The policy prescriptions that flow from this analysis suggest that employers of labor should be required to pay more of the cost of idleness, thus bringing the social and private cost into a closer agreement. Clark has a number of suggestions for accomplishing this, including penalties for layoffs, guaranteed minimum employment for a given period, and the establishment of unemployment insurance schemes to which employers must contribute. The usual suggestions of increasing the flexibility of wages and prices to absorb unused resources is of no benefit if the equilibrium wages fall below the maintenance costs of labor. This situation would threaten the long-run viability of the economy as a going concern.

A viable economy also requires the "definition and maintenance of personal and property rights" (Clark 1923: 452) to create the social order necessary for business to be successfully carried on. It is of course impossible to trace the quantitative benefits of social order in order to assign the costs appropriately. Therefore, the expense of government can be defined as a social overhead cost. Clark was optimistic that business would recognize and accept these social overhead costs, and to some extent it has. But since social overhead costs, like private ones, can be assigned arbitrarily, periods of increased competition usually result in massive shifts of costs to those areas of society which cannot avoid them, thus allowing business to engage in damaging "cut-throat competition."

## Conclusion

This temporal social analysis leads Clark a long way from his traditional neoclassical starting point, and has led many to classify him as an "institutional" economist, despite his insistence that he was following closely in the footsteps of his father, J.B. Clark. However, if the rules for assigning overhead costs are arbitrary, the institutions for the distribution of those costs must themselves be somewhat artificial and temporary, subject to customs and conventions that change. The neoclassical view that sees institutions as the outcome of "laws of nature" is difficult to maintain in a dynamic analysis.

## See also:

business cycle theories; collective social wealth; effective demand and capacity utilization; human capital; hysteresis; institutional political economy: history; institutions and habits; neoclassical economics; social and organizational capital

## Selected references

Clark, John Maurice (1923) *Studies in the Economics of Overhead Costs*, Chicago: University of Chicago Press.
—— (1926) *Social Control of Business*, New York: McGraw-Hill, 1939.

ROD HAY

# ownership and control of the corporation

This subject deals with the question of whether owners or managers control the corporation, and the significance of this for corporate society and the functioning of the macroeconomy. It is related to the increasing size of industrial enterprises and the phenomenon of stock ownership in the twentieth century. The development of this concept is frequently associated with the work of Adolph Berle, Jr and Gardiner C. Means, *The Modern Corporation and Private Property*, which first appeared in 1932. In this work, Berle and Means describe the growth of corporations as producing concurrent centrifugal (decentralizing) and centripetal (centralizing) forces: fragmenting the ownership of industry into disparate shareholders while concentrating the effective control over corporate policy in the hands of professional management. In this way, the proliferation of the corporate form produces a system of managerial capitalism.

This scenario represents a significant break with the past. In the nineteenth century, the size of business was limited by the financial wealth of individuals or small groups who were also responsible for the management of the firm. With the rise of national markets and advances in mass production technologies, the corporate form emerged as a method of combining previously distinct firms. Following the initial attempts of consolidation through gentlemen's agreements, pools, associations and the short-lived trust period of the 1880s, this trend took a concrete form with the rise of corporations in the Great Merger Movement of 1895–1904. While the power of ownership over management could persist through majority or minority shareholdings, the continued growth of the corporation fragmented share ownership to the point that effective oversight of management by owners was lost. In this case the power of ownership, the foundation of all previous enterprise, was reduced.

## Berle and Means on managerial control

While Berle and Means carried this concept to the logical conclusion of the complete usurpation of ownership rights, other writers have also noted the divergence of ownership and control within the corporation. Even in its less developed state, where managerial control is maintained through the holding of majority or minority shareholdings, the disenfranchisement of owners still exists. This may occur through the use of holding companies or voting trusts, where control over management is concentrated with the largest shareholder. Because the block of securities necessary to control management may be only a small fraction of the total securities issued, the property rights of other shareholders is forfeited. Their ownership shares become merely a right to a portion of the earnings of the corporation. The influence of their ownership is minimal, as in the case of individuals who insist on voting in annual meetings, or they may turn over their voting rights to an independent body, as in the case of proxy committees (see INTERLOCKING DIRECTORSHIPS).

The most intriguing element of the Berle–Means theory is the managerial hypothesis. By describing the growth of the corporation as the owner's forfeiture of strategic or long-run policy, they argued that corporations ceased to follow the principle of profit maximization. This state of affairs would occur if all ownership holdings in the corporation are reduced to the point that no shareholder is capable of exercising control. The response to this hypothesis has been varied. Some writers (Zeitlin 1989; Baran and Sweezy 1966), utilizing a class-based analysis, have noted that professional managers come from the same community of interest as owners, and therefore still operate according to the goals of private property and profit maximization. From this perspective, the rise of the corporation is merely a further extension and concentration of the property owning interests. Coming to the same conclusion, although for a different purpose, efficiency theorists have compared the profitability of corporations with other business forms and concluded that corporations are more profit-oriented than smaller enterprises, thereby justifying the rise of the corporate form (see CORPORATE OBJECTIVES).

## Finance capital

In the early twentieth century, many authors recognized that financial and insurance companies began to hold controlling interests in industrial companies. This development of FINANCE CAPITAL is paradoxical because, while these financial-insurance companies increasingly had an ownership form of control throughout the corporate economy, the controllers within the financial companies are usually managers rather than "large" shareholders in the company. Hence, control is effectively held by those managers who do not own the corporations. Rudolf Hilferding (1910) and Thorstein VEBLEN (1923) were two notable political economists early in the century who studied finance capital. The financial managers themselves, however, often had a considerable portfolio of shares in their own right, and hence could be seen to be acting in the interests of maintaining the ownership rights of capital in general. The centralization of financial power was part of the process of concentration and collusion inherent in the dynamics of capitalism in the early and middle part of the twentieth century.

In the absence of collusion, independent corporations would be forced into a situation of destructive price competition that would initiate a crisis and undermine the artificially expanded values of the corporate assets, resulting in a contraction of credit and a decline in the earning capacity of the industrial

concerns. While legal developments of the early twentieth century lessened the influence of the financial community in the management of industry, the wider theme of the development of giant companies, and control being exercised by financial interests, still has much validity.

## Efficient stock markets?

The theory of efficient stock markets has little concern for the so-called division of ownership and control (see Jensen and Rubeck 1983). By assuming that stock prices efficiently represent the value of a firm, it is argued that management is conditioned to respond to the interests of owners. In this theory, the fluctuations of share prices are a signal of the quality of existing management. If the share price of a corporation is declining, this is proof of the poor policies of management and owners/investors will sell their shares, causing further stock price declines. Only by maintaining or increasing the profitability of the corporation can management be assured of retaining its position. While individual owners may not be capable of exerting direct authority over management, the efficiency of the stock market requires that management behave according to the principle of profit maximization.

## Corporate governance

Legal historians have added an additional element to the work of Berle and Means. They have argued that the situation of ineffectual ownership and independent management within the corporation is not inevitable, but is the result of a legal framework which limits the ability of owners to accumulate large share holdings and effectively control management policies. This perspective benefits from comparative analysis which refers to the issue of corporate governance, the structure of corporate ownership and the methods of governance existing in other countries. This literature describes the Anglo-American style of corporate governance, based on a large and active stock market and rapid turnover of shareholdings, the German system of Hausbanks and block shareholdings between finance and industry, and the interlocking Japanese system of the prewar *zaibatsu* or the later *keiretsu* (see Sykes 1994).

## Recent work on the managerial hypothesis

Despite the controversies surrounding the validity of the managerial hypothesis, the main point of the Berle–Means theory, that the corporate form divides ownership and management, is uncontested. Whether or not this situation occurred by design or by unregulated development, the adoption of the corporate form and shares of ownership allows the expansion of enterprise beyond the capacity of any single owner or group of partners. Depending on the laws regulating share ownership and the extent of ownership fragmentation, control over corporate policy may be centered among leaders of industry, finance or individual corporate management. While the notion of perfectly efficient stock markets has been used to minimize concern for the dissolution of ownership rights, writers in this tradition must refer to the influence of larger "market" forces that condition management to act in the best interests of share holders. The operation of speculative bubbles and fundamental UNCERTAINTY about the future question this framework.

The perspective of Berle and Means is implicit in much of the latest literature on corporate ownership and policy. During the most recent period of globalization and increased international competition, writers have argued about the efficacy of independent management. They have utilized the concepts of informational asymmetry, the short-term concern for maximizing share prices, and principal–agent conflicts. Buttressed by the observations of legal historians that diminish the inevitability of weak ownership rights, some writers in the United States and United Kingdom have speculated on the benefits of remov-

ing laws that force the diversification of ownership, so that financial institutions may regain effective control over management and implement strategies of long-term growth (see Roe 1994). The influence of these arguments has yet to be determined (see REGULATION AND DEREGULATION: FINANCIAL).

## Selected references

Baran, P.A. and Sweezy, P.M. (1966) *Monopoly Capital*, New York: Monthly Review Press.

de Vroey, M. (1973) "The Separation of Ownership and Control of the Large Corporations," *Review of Radical Political Economics* 7(2): 1.

Dimsdale, N. and Prevezer, M. (eds) (1994) *Capital Markets and Corporate Governance*, Oxford: Clarendon Press.

Hilferding, R. (1910) *Finance Capital*, repr. 1981, London: Routledge & Kegan Paul.

Jensen, M.C. and Rubeck, R.S. (1983) "The Market for Corporate Control," *Journal of Financial Economics* 11: 5–50.

Prasch, R.E. (1992) "Economics and Merger Mania: A Critique of Efficient Markets Theory," *Journal of Economic Issues*, June: 635–43.

Roe, M.J. (1994) *Strong Managers, Weak Owners: The Political Roots of American Corporate Finance*, Princeton, NJ: Princeton University Press.

Sykes, A. (1994) "Proposals for a Reformed System of Corporate Governance to Achieve Internationally Competitive Long Term Performance," in N. Dimsdale and M. Prevezer (eds), *Capital Markets and Corporate Governance*, Oxford: Clarendon Press.

Veblen, T.B. (1923) *Absentee Ownership*, New York: Augustus M. Kelley, 1964.

Zeitlin, M. (1989) *The Large Corporation and Contemporary Classes*, Cambridge: Polity Press.

ERIC R. HAKE

# P

## paradigms

The term "paradigm" is widely used, and it has a multiplicity of meanings. Masterman argued that Thomas Kuhn himself "uses 'paradigm' in not less than twenty-one different senses" (1970: 61) in the first edition of *The Structure of Scientific Revolutions*, published in 1962. In response to this perceived ambiguity in meaning, Kuhn (1977: xix–xx) has isolated the three principal definitions that the term "paradigm" has taken in the debates that followed that publication. The first is the notion that a paradigm is an exemplary problem solution. According to this definition, a paradigm is a model of behavior; a concrete illustration of how to "do good science." The second definition is associated with the classic books in which such exemplary problem solutions initially appear. Lastly, a paradigm has been taken to mean the global set of commitments shared by members of a scientific community. According to this definition, a paradigm is a world-view or belief system; an ideological framework.

### Paradigm as world view

Of these possible definitions of paradigm, the most commonly used in economics is that of paradigm as world view. For example, Paul Sweezy argues that a paradigm "is very close to what I have been referring to as a conception of reality" (1970: 2). A paradigm is thereby defined through the specification of a list of principles and values to which members of a school subscribe. Thus it has become commonplace to speak of the "neoclassical paradigm," the "post-Keynesian paradigm," the "institutional paradigm," the "Austrian paradigm,"

among others (Ward 1972). Eichner and Kregel (1975), for example, provide a checklist of criteria which they believe constitutes the post-Keynesian paradigm. The composition of such defining characteristics is to a large extent a matter for debate, and it is precisely because of its malleability that this definition of paradigm has come to be so widely used.

### Paradigm as exemplar

Yet Kuhn himself has stated that, of the three principal meanings that paradigm has taken, "world view" is not the one he wanted to assign to the term "paradigm." He has therefore suggested substituting the term disciplinary matrix (Kuhn 1962: 182) when referring to the overall world-view shared by members of a particular scientific community. To him, the term "paradigm" should be restricted to mean exemplary problem solutions, or exemplars. These exemplars are used to instruct members of a scientific community how to "do good science." In other words, they supply a model of behavior which, if followed, will lead to the solution of research puzzles. Although embedded in a broader world-view, these exemplars come to appear as simple technical means by which interesting puzzles can be solved. Indeed, most practitioners are unaware of the underlying theoretical framework within which a paradigm is nested, absorbing it as tacit knowledge; to most it is simply how "science" is practiced.

In their crudest form, such paradigms as exemplars are found in the problem sets and examinations that are assigned to students. In more high-brow form, they are found in the problem solutions published in the leading journals to which the members of a scientific community subscribe and in which they aspire to publish. For example, Argyrous (1992) has traced, within the pages of the *American Economic Review*, the development of the lifecycle/permanent income hypotheses as the paradigm for analysing consumption behavior.

## Evolutionary theory of scientific development

This narrower concept of paradigm as exemplar is the unit of selection Kuhn has described as an evolutionary theory of scientific development. This is because the paradigm provides the basis for "normal science." The incremental development and extension of the exemplar into novel areas leads to its constant modification and refinement. There are three ways in which this incremental process of normal science unfolds. The first is by extending the knowledge of those facts that the "paradigm" displays as particularly revealing. The second is by increasing the extent of the match between those facts and the paradigm's predictions. The third is by further articulation at the theoretical level of the paradigm itself (Kuhn 1970: 25–34). In all cases, the task of normal science is not to "test" the paradigm but rather to extend its field of applications. A failure to solve a particular puzzle that the paradigm deems to be interesting is a reflection on the scientist, and not the paradigm.

These periods of normal science, however, are interrupted when the paradigm confronts an anomaly. It must be a problem that the paradigm itself deems to be solvable on its own terms. It is only because the paradigm cannot solve a puzzle, which according to its own criteria should be soluble, that the paradigm itself comes into question. For example, the fact that Marxist economics does not supply the tools for analysing individual choice over scarce resources does not render this an anomaly, since Marxists do not consider such a question to be of interest. A failure to explain the class distribution of income, on the other hand, would be a crisis-generating anomaly because this is a problem that Marxism defines for itself as being important (see CLASS).

If a paradigm confronts such an anomaly, a scientific community passes into a period of revolutionary science in which alternatives are sought. The value system, which held the scientific community together, and permitted a general consensus to form over the appropriate tools of analysis, loses its cohesive force, and scientists increasingly look for more radical solutions. However, the ruling paradigm is not abandoned until an alternative that can provide the basis for a new puzzle-solving tradition is available. The new paradigm attempts to subsume the old one within its more "general" framework, giving the impression that there has in fact been a linear development of science. However, Kuhn argues that this is not the case; paradigms are incommensurable, and one paradigm cannot be completely subsumed within the terms of another.

This notion of incommensurability has created a great deal of confusion. It has been taken to mean that people who subscribe to different paradigms cannot communicate with each other. Kuhn, however, only meant by incommensurability that it is not possible to completely map the terms of one paradigm into the terms of another. There is always a loss of content in the translation. Indeed, Kuhn uses the analogy of language communities to illustrate his point: while speakers of different language can communicate there are always some elements that cannot be completely translated.

Thus, a paradigm allows for scientific progress through two mechanisms. The first is the linear evolution of a dominant paradigm during the process of normal science. The second is the abandonment of an outdated paradigm that no longer sustains a puzzle-solving tradition in favor of an alternative that holds out greater promise. The KEYNESIAN REVOLUTION has been considered by some to be such a paradigm shift (Mehta 1977).

The notion of paradigm is the core concept of an evolutionary theory of scientific development. Kuhn is careful to avoid any normative judgment and not to impose philosophical standards (as do Popper and Lakatos) on the factors governing the choice of paradigms. He is interested in the history and sociology of science (the way in which a paradigm takes hold and guides scientific practice for a time until it is replaced by another), rather than the philosophy of science. As an evolutionary theory of scientific development, the explanation of why a particular paradigm has been "selected" and dominates a professional community is not a justification of its innate superiority, according to some absolute criteria of assessment. It is simply an explanation of the reasons why, in a given historical situation, and according to the particular values, ideologies and pressures upon such a community, a given paradigm seemed to offer the most fruitful line of normal science. Unfortunately, writers have tried to use the notion of "paradigm" in a normative way: either through a relativist argument that any paradigm is as legitimate as another (Dow 1985), or in an absolutist way such that the dominance of a particular paradigm reflects the survival of the fittest and most superior alternative.

## Near unanimity of opinion over fundamentals

The last point to emphasize about the nature of a paradigm is that it should only be applied to scientific communities that possess a particular sociological structure; a point that Kuhn emphasized in the Postscript to the second edition of *The Structure of Scientific Revolutions*. Since the existence of a paradigm, as the basis of normal science, requires a near unanimity of opinion over fundamentals, only those societies which can enforce such a unanimity of opinion can sustain a paradigm. One needs to conduct a sociological analysis of the relevant group of professionals to gauge whether the use of the term paradigm is appropriate. It is only when a scientific community reaches a mature stage that the identification of a paradigm is relevant. In the pre-paradigm stage, there is too much disagreement and dissent; divergent schools of thought abound and the lines of communication are too open to external "interference." Thus, attempts

to identify a paradigm in economics before the late 1800s are pointless, since the tight sociological structure that binds a mature scientific community was not then evident.

## See also:

neoclassical economics; political economy; value judgments and world views

## Selected references

Argyrous, G. (1992) "Kuhn's Paradigms and Neoclassical Economics," *Economics and Philosophy* 8: 231–48.

Dow, S. (1985) *Macroeconomic Thought: A Methodological Approach*, Oxford: Basil Blackwell.

Eichner, A.S. and Kregel, J.A. (1975) "An Essay in Post-Keynesian Theory: A New Paradigm in Economics," *Journal of Economic Literature* 13: 1293–314.

Kuhn, T.S. (1970) *The Structure of Scientific Revolutions*, 2nd edn, Chicago: Chicago University Press; 1st edn, 1962.

Kuhn, T.S. (1977) *The Essential Tension*, Chicago: Chicago University Press.

Masterman, M. (1970) "The Nature of a Paradigm," in I. Lakatos and A. Musgrave (eds), *Criticism and the Growth of Knowledge*, Cambridge: Cambridge University Press.

Mehta, G. (1977) *The Structure of the Keynesian Revolution*, London: Martin Robertson.

Sweezy, P.M. (1970) "Toward a Critique of Economics" *Review of Radical Political Economics* 2(1): 1–8.

Ward, B. (1972) *What is Wrong with Economics?*, London: Basic Books.

GEORGE ARGYROUS

# paradoxes

According to the HOLISTIC METHOD, the whole is not necessarily just the sum of the parts. What may be true at the microeconomic level may become false at the macroeconomic level.

Fallacies of composition easily happen in economics. For neoclassical economists, who attach so much importance to methodological individualism in contrast to organicism or holism, these overall unintended results appear as paradoxical. They contradict mainstream views. This entry considers five instances of paradoxes, which are here designated as the paradoxes of thrift, costs, debt, liquidity and tranquillity.

Of course modern political economy does not have a monopoly on paradoxes. One of the oldest paradoxes, and one still held in high regard by most mainstream economists, is that of Adam Smith's invisible hand. Whereas one would have thought that letting individuals pursue their self-interest would have led to chaos, Smith argues that, under certain conditions, the search for private interest will bring order and maximum wealth for the nation as a whole.

## Paradox of thrift

The better known of the paradoxes of modern political economy is the paradox of thrift. This paradox is usually attributed to John Maynard KEYNES, but as Keynes himself mentions, many before him, notably Bernard Mandeville in his *Fable of the Bees* in 1723, have argued that prodigality is a social virtue while thrift is a vice, for if the latter helps to increase one's estate, it reduces overall employment and income. The paradox of thrift implies that an increase in the desire to save of individuals will not lead to any such rise at the macroeconomic level. Because people want to spend less, less is being produced and hence less employment is being offered and less income is being distributed. Causation has been reversed: instead of savings causing investment, Keynes argued that investment causes savings.

While Keynes's model was set in the short period, with no change in productive capacity, Joan Robinson extended the thrift paradox to a growing economy in her work, *The Accumulation of Capital*, in 1956. In such an economy, a higher desire to save leads to a lower rate of ACCUMULATION as well as to a lower profit rate, and presumably to a lower rate of technical progress. This is because more thrifty individuals or institutions reduce the demand for consumption goods, thus reducing profitability, and hence the desire to invest. This can be contrasted to the view popular among neo-conservatives, whereby higher savings are conducive to faster accumulation, and to the standard neoclassical model of growth, where higher savings rates lead to higher mechanization rates and higher output per head.

## Paradox of costs

Less general than the paradox of thrift, the paradox of costs is also based on the principle of EFFECTIVE DEMAND AND CAPACITY UTILIZATION. Mainstream economists usually presume, as do neo-conservative politicians, that high real wages are detrimental to the profitability of businesses and hence to labor employment (although partisans of EFFICIENCY WAGES, who can be found among both radical and neoclassical economists, deny this even on microeconomic grounds). Under some conditions however, higher real wages or higher overhead labor costs are conducive to higher macroeconomic profit rates, to higher rates of accumulation, and hence to higher employment. This is the paradox of costs. It arises as a result of wages playing a dual role in the economy; wages are costs to the firms but they are the main source of income of households.

These paradoxical positive relationships between real wages and employment, and between real wages and profitability, are often underlined in the KALECKIAN THEORY OF GROWTH, and the expression "paradox of cost" was first coined in such a model by Rowthorn (1981:18). The paradox of costs is a concrete example of the Marxist problem of profit realization. When real wages are set at a lower level, potential profits for firms increase, as common sense would tells us. Households, however, cannot consume as much as before, and as a result the rate of capacity utilization of corporations is driven down. This pushes down the actual profitability of firms, who then decide to reduce their rate of accumulation, which reduces further their profitability. In the wake of the "virtual corporation," with few permanent well-paid jobs, the paradox of costs implies that these virtual corporations are also creating virtual consumers, with no purchasing power. The actual profitability of an economy dominated by virtual corporations should thus soon decline way below its "virtual" profitability.

## Paradox of debt

The third paradox based on the principle of effective demand is the paradox of debt. It is usually assumed, on the basis of microeconomics, that it is always possible for firms to decrease their debt ratio, or their leverage ratio – the proportion of their assets financed by external debt – if they decide to do so. Similarly in expansion times, it is believed, along the lines of the FINANCIAL INSTABILITY HYPOTHESIS, that optimistic firms and their equally hopeful bankers will decide to increase their leverage ratio and automatically manage to do so. It has been pointed out, most notably by Joseph Steindl in his *Maturity and Stagnation in American Capitalism* in 1952, that while firms may decide to reduce their leverage ratio, they may not succeed in achieving this result.

To reduce the relative weight of their indebtedness, firms may decide to cut their investment expenditures and hence the amounts they borrow. If only a subset of corporations are pursuing this policy, this strategy will most likely accomplish its purpose. However if all companies are pursuing a similar scheme, cutting back on borrowing and investment might not put matters right, for the slowdown in capital accumulation reduces the profitability of businesses and hence the accumulation of the firms' own funds. Depending on the prevailing conditions, the rate of growth of these internal funds may drop below that of the rate of growth of borrowing. The actual leverage ratio would then move in a direction opposite to that wished by entrepreneurs. As a result, in times of expansion, debt ratios may drop or remain constant, although firms and banks are quite willing to increase

leverage, whereas in times of recession actual leverage ratios may rise, although firms desperately try to reduce their leverage vulnerability (Lavoie 1995).

## Paradox of liquidity

There are two other general paradoxes worthy of mention, although they do not necessarily involve the principle of effective demand. In the paradox of liquidity, developed by Dow (1993: 146–52), the attempt of individuals to become more liquid transforms previously liquid assets into not-so-liquid assets. Another way to put it is to say that "attempts to increase the stock of liquid assets only succeed in reducing it" (Dow 1993: 150). The frenzy of people to get rid of their assets to acquire safer ones will drive down the price of those assets and discourage others to purchase them. This paradox of liquidity may be applied both in space and time. In space, it can be likened to Myrdal's process of CIRCULAR AND CUMULATIVE CAUSATION, whereby residents of economically weak peripheral regions desire to hold the more liquid assets issued by the center region, thus weakening further the liquidity of their own peripheral assets. In time, during expansions, when liquidity is not really needed, liquidity will be abundant, whereas during recessions, when liquidity is badly needed, liquidity will hardly be provided: a phenomenon which can be linked to ANIMAL SPIRITS.

## Paradox of tranquillity

There is some similarity between the paradox of liquidity and the paradox of tranquillity. According to Minsky (1982), a stable growing economy is a contradiction in terms. A fast-growing free market economy will necessarily transform itself into a speculative booming economy. This is because a succession of periods with validated expectations of sales growth and high profitability will necessarily induce overly optimistic expectations. Because both entrepreneurs and their bankers tend to forget the hard-learned humbling lessons of the past, they are likely to launch into investment sprees and speculative bubbles. Their animal spirits, even in relative growth terms, will not remain constant when a tranquil situation lasts for any amount of time. "Stability is destabilizing," as Minsky (1982: 26) puts it. This is the paradox of tranquillity, as coined by Lavoie (1986: 7).

It should be pointed out that not all non-orthodox economists agree with the above paradoxes. In particular, many Marxist economists believe that while the paradoxes of thrift and of costs may be appropriate for short-run analysis, they are not valid descriptions of the long run.

## See also:

Kaldor–Pasinetti models of growth and distribution; Kaleckian theory of growth; liquidity preference; methodological individualism and collectivism; Robinson's contribution to political economy

## Selected references

Dow, Sheila (1993) *Money and the Economic Process*, Aldershot: Edward Elgar.

Dutt, Amitava K. (1995) "Internal Finance and Monopoly Power in Capitalist Economies: A Reformulation of Steindl's Growth Model," *Metroeconomica* 46(1): 16–34.

Lavoie, Marc (1986) "Minsky's Law or the Theorem of Systemic Financial Fragility," *Studi Economici* 29: 3–28.

—— (1995) "Interest Rates in Post-Keynesian Models of Growth and Distribution," *Metroeconomica* 46(2): 146–77.

Minsky, Hyman P. (1982) "The Financial-Instability Hypothesis: Capitalist Processes and the Behavior of the Economy," in Charles P. Kindleberger and Jean-Pierre Laffargue (eds), *Financial Crises: Theory, History and Policy*, New York: Cambridge University Press.

Robinson, Joan (1962) *Essays in the Theory of Economic Growth*, London: Macmillan.

Rowthorn, Bob (1981) "Demand, Real Wages and Economic Growth," *Thames Papers in Political Economy*, Autumn: 1–39.

Skott, Peter (1994). "On the Modelling of Systemic Financial Fragility," in Amitava K. Dutt (ed.), *New Directions in Analytical Political Economy*, Aldershot: Edward Elgar.

MARC LAVOIE

# participation in the labor force

## Definitions

In a market economy, participation in the LABOR FORCE is a distinguishing characteristic that is associated with selling one's labor power for remuneration (see LABOR AND LABOR POWER). Official statistics categorize individuals among the working age population as being either "in the labor force" or "not in the labor force." In the United States, the labor force is defined as all people sixteen years of age or older who are employed, plus all those actively seeking work. The proportion or percentage of the working age population who are in the labor force is labeled the "labor force participation rate." Prior to 1940, the US Census utilized the concept of "gainful worker," based on whether an individual claimed to have an occupation during the previous year. In many other countries, the term "activity rate" is also used.

## Problems with official statistics

Comparisons of labor force participation or activity rates across countries or regions must be interpreted with caution. Data collection techniques and categorizations of who is actively employed differ widely, especially between industrialized and developing countries. Goldin (1990) argues that official statistics undercount market-oriented home production. Women engaged in unpaid family work in agriculture and small enterprises are often omitted from official labor force counts. Economic fluctuations may also impact labor force participation. While prolonged recession may decrease labor force participation among "discouraged workers," some households provide "added workers" to compensate for lost wages.

Participation or non-participation is often confused with how the labor force is constituted by gender or race. For example, out of 100 percent of the US labor force, 46 percent are women and 54 percent are men. This is termed "labor force composition."

## Orthodox perspectives

Neoclassical economists have modeled the decision to participate in the labor force, legitimating the GENDER DIVISION OF LABOR between work in the market and in the home. Becker's theory of time allocation (1965) is based on the concept of COMPARATIVE ADVANTAGE AND UNEQUAL EXCHANGE, borrowed from international trade theory. Thus if one member of a household is relatively more efficient at domestic labor and another garners a higher wage in the labor market, it is rational for each to specialize.

Coupling this analysis with a theory of wage determination, HUMAN CAPITAL economists maintain that women's wages average less than men's, due to their lower labor force attachment. Labor force intermittency reduces experience and encourages the selection of jobs with less human capital investment in education and training. Therefore, both opportunity costs (market wages) and wage depreciation for time spent out of the labor force are reduced (see also LABOUR MARKET DISCRIMINATION).

The interaction of Becker's theory and human capital approaches results in a feedback effect. According to mainstream economists, women's lower wages result in interrupted and ultimately lower labor force participation rates. and women's planned intermittency results in lower wages.

## Political economy perspectives

Feminist political economists argue that this framework cannot adequately explain historical changes in women's labor force participa-

tion rates. Political economists emphasize the historical process of creating a waged labor force. Additionally, feminists have noted that GENDER is an essential category for understanding this process. Capitalist development separates market labor from the pre-existing family economy. Unmarried daughters are frequently among the earliest wage laborers as countries develop and industrialize, since they are often deemed most expendable from agricultural production. Thus, women's work has been integral to the development of capitalist economies, beginning with the transition from a "putting out system" to textile mills during British INDUSTRIALIZATION. Historically, being a "breadwinner" only became identified as a masculine pursuit in industrialized countries during the nineteenth century (see Matthaei 1982).

Modernization theorists have traditionally asserted a positive correlation between economic development and the level of labor force participation. However, recent attention to historical variations by RACE, ETHNICITY, GENDER AND CLASS, as well as age and marital status, indicate a more complex relationship. Compared with men, labor force participation rates for women tend to be relatively highest in the Nordic countries of Europe and lowest in sub-Saharan Africa and the Middle East. The "post-socialist" countries of Eastern Europe have inherited a legacy of high participation rates for women. Nevertheless, men's labor force participation rates have been declining in countries where service sector employment is replacing manufacturing.

In an empirical study of ninety-six countries, Cagatay and Ozler (1995) find a U-shaped relationship between long-term economic development and women's labor force composition. This pattern may also reflect changes in the gender division of labor, especially for married women. For example, Goldin (1990) indicates that married women's labor force participation resembles a U-shape over the course of US economic development. Their labor force activity was extensive but declining throughout much of the nineteenth century, as the locus of production shifted from the home to the factory. During this same period, the labor force participation of single, white, native-born women increased.

Gender and marital status are not the only significant categories for analyzing women's labor force participation. Black and immigrant women (regardless of marital status) also increased their labor force composition in the wake of slavery and mass immigration. However, compared with white women, they were segregated into lower-paid and less prestigious occupations and industries (Matthaei 1982; Weiner 1985). Thus, women's roles in the historical development of the US economy also depended upon their race, nativity, family class background, education, and other factors.

Much attention has been devoted to the global increase in married women's labor force participation and attachment during the post-Second World War period. While popular culture generally attributes this phenomenon to the women's liberation movement in various countries, most political economists focus on broader sectoral economic shifts toward female-intensive industries. This has led to the characterization of contemporary economic restructuring as a process of feminization. Increased demand for women's labor is viewed as a strategy to increase labor market flexibility in industrialized and developing countries. Economic liberalization and structural adjustment policies are credited with facilitating global feminization (Jenson *et al.* 1988; Standing 1989; Cagatay and Ozler 1995).

Is increased labor force participation beneficial for women? This issue has been relatively controversial between various schools of feminist economists. While Bergmann (1986) depicts women's "economic emergence" as the fruit of a beneficent industrial revolution, Marxist feminists view women's proletarianization with a more jaundiced eye. For example, Humphries (1977) asserts that the working class has historically defended traditional family structures in order to preserve a sphere of non-market relations (see FAMILY WAGE). The Marxist concept of a latent reserve army of labor has also been used to analyze women's proletarianization (transition from homemak-

ing to wage labor) during this period (see RESERVE ARMY OF LABOR: LATENT).

Further, married men's participation in domestic labor has not expanded at a comparable rate, leading to discussions of women's double day, that is, the pressure of combining paid and unpaid labor. Although the continued commodification of domestic labor has enabled some women to reduce this burden, reductions in state support for social services increases women's household responsibilities (Bergmann 1986; Jenson *et al.* 1988). Nevertheless, many political economists argue that, within a capitalist economy, earning a wage increases women's autonomy and contributes to undermining the gender division of labor within the household (Matthaei 1982; Hartmann 1987).

## See also:

feminist political economy: major contemporary themes

## Selected references

Becker, Gary (1965) "A Theory of the Allocation of Time," *Economic Journal* 80(2): 493–517.

Bergmann, Barbara R. (1986) *The Economic Emergence of Women*, New York: Basic Books.

Cagatay, Nilufer and Ozler, Sule (1995) "Feminization of the Labor Force: The Effects on Long-Term Development and Structural Adjustment," *World Development* 23(11): 1883–94.

Goldin, Claudia (1990) *Understanding the Gender Gap: An Economic History of American Women*, New York: Oxford University Press.

Hartmann, Heidi I. (1987) "Changes in Women's Economic and Family in Post-World War II United States," in Lourdes Beneria and Catharine R. Stimpson (eds), *Women, Households, and the Economy*, New Brunswick, NJ: Rutgers University Press, 33–64.

Humphries, Jane (1977) "Class Struggle and the Persistence of the Working Class Family," *Cambridge Journal of Economics* 1(September): 241–58.

Jenson, Jane, Hagen, Elisabeth and Reddy, Ceallaigh (1988) *Feminization of the Labor Force: Paradoxes and Promises*, New York: Oxford University Press.

Matthaei, Julie (1982) *An Economic History of Women in America: Women's Work, the Sexual Division of Labor, and the Development of Capitalism*, New York: Schocken Books.

Standing, Guy (1989) "Global Feminization through Flexible Labor," *World Development* 17(7): 1077–95.

Weiner, Lynn Y. (1985) *From Working Girl to Working Mother: The Female Labor Force in the United States, 1820–1980*, Chapel Hill, NC: University of North Carolina Press.

DEBORAH M. FIGART

# participatory democracy and self-management

Participatory democracy is a general term to describe a political-economic system, where democratic and participatory institutions govern not only political and social spheres but also economic and industrial, or work, spheres. Political democracy involves decision making in political life, economic (or industrial) democracy involves participation in decision making in economic and workplace life. These concepts have influenced most schools of political economy, especially from the 1960s to the present.

## Participatory democracy

The term "participatory," however, does not denote whether or not participation conveys any decision-making powers or the extent of such powers. In the economic/industrial sphere, participation includes two major cases. The first is where capital (private or state) controls and manages enterprises, but where labor shares to some degree in management and control, and/or in ownership. This includes quality circles, collective bargaining, job control, works councils, co-determination, employee participation on company boards, labor-controlled investment funds and employee stock ownership plans. The second is where decision-making powers reside solely with the workers and where ownership of capital entails no right to control or manage. This includes systems variously described as industrial democracy, worker (producer) co-operatives, workers' control, and worker, labor and socialist self-management.

A fully participatory economy includes the following principles (Vanek 1971: 8–12). First, at the level of the firm, control and management of economic activity must involve the active participation of all workers and employees on the basis of equality. Second, income must be shared on an equitable, democratically determined basis. Third, workers have the right to use, but not to destroy or sell, capital. At the level of the economy a market system must prevail, though policy levers may be utilized for economic planning and maintaining competition. Finally, in the labor market workers must have freedom of employment, the right to leave or accept any job.

## Self-management

Self-management, on the other hand, is a more specific term that describes a political–economic system where individuals, as part of democratically formed and controlled social collectives, are self-directed (or "managed") in all spheres of life including, more specifically, in their economic and industrial lives. Moreover, the institutions of control and management are subject to direct and participatory decision-making processes. Vanek distinguishes between worker self-management, where all income, including capital income, accrues to the workers, and labor self-management, where workers have complete control and management of the firm, but capital income is remitted to private or state "owners" of capital (Vanek 1975: 15). Socialist self-management, as perceived by Yugoslav theorists, involves worker self-management along with the elimination of the authoritarian state and the democratization and devolution of political power to the local community level.

## History of the movements: pre-1945

Historically, the idea of worker participation and self-management originated in the early years of the industrial revolution, particularly in Britain and France. In Britain, the pioneer was Robert Owen (1772–1837). His utopian vision of self-management led to the establishment of several cooperative communities in North America, and the foundation of a labor exchange and the Grand National Consolidated Trades Union in Britain, the aim of which was to replace capitalism with a worker-managed system. Similar ideas and experiments were developed by contemporaries in France, including Saint Simon (1760–1825), Charles Fourier (1772–1837), Phillippe Buchez (1811–65), Louis Blanc (1811–82) and Pierre-Joseph Proudhon (1809–65).

There are common themes among these utopians. The first theme is that there could be no meaningful political democracy without economic democracy which, in turn, required decentralized institutions practicing participatory management. This is related to the second theme, that the centralized state is not appropriate for managing a participatory society. Indeed, there was general acceptance of the necessity of the "withering away of the state," a theme later incorporated in anarchist, syndicalist and anarcho-syndicalist thought. The third theme is that workers should not be alienated from the means of production, but there was no common functional form of ownership advocated by all.

While the original experiments with cooperative communities and labor exchanges were largely failures, the ideal of participatory self-management kept re-emerging with every subsequent radical and revolutionary movement. Perhaps most significant in the earlier period was the Paris Commune in 1871, not because of the momentary appearance of worker

management, but because it influenced Marx to champion the ideas of a "free association of producers" and of self-management replacing the centralized state, ideas which a century later profoundly affected the Yugoslav experiment. Marx, however, rejected the idea that producer cooperatives, advocated by the German socialist Ferdinand Lassalle, could be the agent of social transformation or the basis of a new social system.

Self-management ideas also inspired the guild socialism movement, which emerged in Britain just before the First World War under the intellectual leadership of G.D.H. Cole. However, the movement, which advocated the administration of nationalized state property by national guilds of workers, collapsed in the 1920s.

Following the Russian Revolution of 1917, industrial soviets emerged spontaneously to take over management of the factories. Similar movements for workers' management sprang up in Germany, France, Italy and Spain after the war. However, all such institutions and movements were opposed, not only by capital but also by the communists and socialists who favored étatism (or statism), the control of the economy by a strong central authoritarian state. In Russia the soviets were quickly eliminated; the étatist model was extended to Eastern Europe following the Second World War, and maintained there by force against participatory reforms in Poland, Hungary and Czechoslovakia in the 1950s and 1960s. In Italy in the 1920s and Spain in the 1930s, self-management movements were crushed by fascism, a fate also accorded self-management after the fall of the Allende government in Chile a half-century later. Algeria also experimented with worker management in the wake of its independence revolution, but again the experiment was ended by an étatist government.

## Post-1945 experiments

Following the Second World War, works councils, experimented with in the First World War, were reinstated in Germany. This was combined with worker representation on company boards, first in the nationalized coal and steel industry in 1951 and later (1972) in all large-scale industrial employers, in a system labeled codetermination (*mitbestimmung*). Although codetermination extended participation in decision making beyond that in most other countries, it remains a capital-managed system in which the worker has limited power.

There have, however, been two major experiments in the postwar period with large-scale self-management. In Yugoslavia, the experiment began after Tito's victorious Communists broke with Stalin and the Cominform in 1948 over the issue of étatism. In its place, the Yugoslavs began the decentralization of planning and economic decisionmaking to the republic and commune level. In 1950, nominal management of state firms and social services was turned over to workers' councils. Then in 1952 the process of divorcing the Communist Party from the state apparatus was initiated; although, in the absence of any alternative political structure, the party's control remained.

In the mid-1960s further reforms were undertaken to "de-étatize" the economy and place more reliance on the market. This included the organization of self-managing communities (unions) of interest, composed of consumers and producers of social services to replace the state in the provision of these services. The final major reforms, the 1974 constitution and the 1976 Law of Associated Labor, embodied the utopian vision of the chief architect of Yugoslav socialist self-management, Edvard Kardelj, and ushered in the era of "total self-management" (Phillips and Ferfila 1992: 45ff).

At the political level, institutions of representative democracy were replaced by a complex delegational system of direct democracy. At the economic level, socialist firms were reorganized into Basic Organizations of Associated Labor (BOALs), giving small units of production labor direct control of social property (capital). BOALs would associate through self-management agreements with other BOALs and Work Communities (non-production workers) in work organizations (simple enterprises) governed by workers' councils, and in Complex Organizations of Associated Labor (COALs) (complex enterprises). At the same time, the banking system was made subordinate to the enterprises so as to accommodate financial self-management. To provide social services, self-managing communities of interest would negotiate social compacts with communes and local enterprises. Compacts and agreements between all parties would be coordinated through an economic plan.

The collapse of the Yugoslav Federation in 1991 has been attributed to a number of external and internal factors. Critical internal problems included the lack of integration of economic and political structures, and the movement away from a market-based economy. The result was the atrophying of real self-management, the monopolization of institutional and economic structures and the proliferation of bureaucracy (Phillips and Ferfila 1992: 101–8). Yet, despite the collapse, the positive experience with self-management has left a significant residual of support, perhaps best evidenced in Slovenia where privatization has been attempted, primarily through worker-management buyouts and direct distribution of shares to employees. However, the level of worker participation in management that will remain has yet to be determined.

The Mondragón experiment, in contrast, was based on the worker cooperative model. A five-person industrial cooperative, established in 1956 in Mondragón in the Basque region of Spain, grew into a complex of cooperatives and supporting financial, service and educational institutions. In the early 1990s these involved over twenty thousand worker-owners, which controlled the education planning systems for the region (see Whyte and Whyte 1991). The Mondragón model incorporates many participatory economy principles: limits on wage disparities between managers and workers; employment of managers by elected workers' councils, self-finance through retention of part of the profits as cooperative social capital, part as compulsory savings of the worker-owners, a no-layoff policy, continuous education, and internal research and development. Though not without problems, including developing the appropriate relationship between managers and the worker-owners and adjustment to globalization in the 1990s, the Mondragón experiment has to date been remarkably successful.

## See also:

labor-managed enterprises; social ownership and property; socialism and communism; Ward–Vanek model of self-management; worker participation in capitalist firms

## Selected references

Horvat, Branko (1982) *The Political Economy of Socialism*, Armonk, NY: M.E. Sharpe.

Phillips, Paul and Ferfila, Bogomil (1992) *The Rise and Fall of the Third Way: Yugoslavia 1945–1991*, Halifax: Fernwood.

Vanek, Jaroslav (1971) *The Participatory Economy*, Ithaca, NY: Cornell University Press.

—— (ed.) (1975) *Self-Management*, Harmondsworth: Penguin.

Whyte, William and Whyte, Kathleen (1991) *Making Mondragón*, Ithaca, NY: ILR Press.

PAUL PHILLIPS

# Pasinetti's analysis of structural dynamics and growth

Luigi L. Pasinetti (born in 1930 at Zanica, near Bergamo in Italy) is one of the leading representatives of the post-Keynesian school who, since the early 1960s, made constant efforts to renew economic theory. After obtaining his Ph.D. at Cambridge University, Pasinetti was a research fellow at the University of Oxford, lecturer and reader at Cambridge and at time of writing is professor of economic analysis at the Catholic University of Milan. He was a protagonist of the CAPITAL THEORY

DEBATES between the two Cambridges (UK and USA) and has made substantial advances in the field of income distribution (Pasinetti 1974). His model of structural change (first presented in 1965 and successively completed and published in 1981) is one of the most prominent contributions to economic theory of this century, a contribution comparable to the neoclassical general equilibrium model, to which it constitutes a valid alternative.

## General characteristics

Pasinetti's model is a multi-sector dynamic model which accounts for one of the most important features of industrial systems: structural change, that is, the permanent modification of the composition of macroeconomic magnitudes (GDP, overall employment, total consumption and investment) which results from technical change and new patterns of demand.

Four elements characterize the model: its classical inspiration, the pre-institution level of analysis (the "natural" system), learning as the general principle of economic rationality, and the analytical device of vertical integration. First, the model represents a return to the tradition of the "production" approach of CLASSICAL POLITICAL ECONOMY. With a view to studying the long-term dynamics of capitalist economies as well as income distribution and the relations between social classes, the classical economists deemed that, of the two main economic activities – production and exchange – the former was by far the most important. They thus emphasized the reproducibility of commodities instead of scarcity. Of course, exchange and the "scarcity" connected with natural resources were not ignored but, contrary to the marginalists who founded the totality of their analysis on exchange, the classical economists presupposed exchange and went into more depth by focusing on production phenomena.

Second, the classical tradition is the inspiration for the notion of a "natural" system. Pasinetti works out his model by studying "the 'primary and natural' determinants of the variables characterizing an economic system," which are prior to, and independent of, any institutional set-up (Pasinetti 1981: 149).

Third, economic rationality is defined not in the narrow sense of profit maximization but rather as the "intelligent" process of learning, the discovery of new and better methods on the production side, and the awareness of alternative patterns of consumption and the formation of new preferences on the demand side.

Finally, vertical integration is an algebraic transformation of the coefficients of the input–output table which focuses on the *final commodity* (instead of industry), showing what is directly and indirectly necessary in the whole economic system to produce it (Pasinetti 1973). The output of a final commodity is thus resolved into its two basic components: a flow of labor and a stock of productive capacity; all intermediate inputs are eliminated because they are subsumed by these two elements. For each final commodity there is a specific unit of (vertically integrated) productive capacity

## Structure and dynamic aspects of the model

The economy comprises three sets of sectors: (1) sectors $i$ ($i = 1, 2, \ldots, n-1$), concerning the production of *final commodities*; (2) sectors $k_i$, producing the capital goods required by final sectors $i$ as well as by the capital goods sector itself to replace the capital goods which wear out, and to increase productive capacity; (3) sector $n$, which is the households sector, providing the labor force for sectors $i$ and $k_i$ and receiving final commodities as well as capital goods for new investments.

In mathematical terms this is represented by two systems of equations – one for physical quantities, the other for prices. In the first system, the output of final commodities $X_i$ and the output of capital goods $X_{k_i}$ are expressed as a function of total labor force $X_n$; the system is closed by an equation describing the distribution of the labor force to sectors $i$ and $k_i$. In the price system, the prices of final commodities $p_i$ and the prices of capital goods $p_{k_i}$ are written as the products of two terms: a term concerning

the technical coefficients (labor coefficients, i.e. the quantity of labor required to produce one unit of $X_i$ or $X_{k_i}$; coefficients of depreciation) and the rate of profit, on the one hand, the wage rate, on the other.

The model accounts for structural change in a twofold manner. First, technical change takes place at a different pace in the various sectors of the economy. Second, the model is "open" in the sense that technical change implies the creation of new industries and the disappearance of others. Technical change is dealt with on the realistic hypothesis that its most important effect is to increase labor productivity. The labor coefficient of each sector thus diminishes at an exogenously given rate, which is different from one sector to another. This evolution is formalized on the basis of an exponential function. As an equilibrium condition of the model, wages are indexed to changes in the average productivity of the system.

Demand is explicitly introduced and plays a crucial role in determining the development of output. In fact, following the increase over time in productivity, real per capita incomes grow, and this has a double effect on per capita consumption: it adds to the size of the basket of consumer goods through the availability of new commodities, and it modifies the structure of consumption with respect to income, according to Engels's Law. Population is assumed to grow at a constant rate $g$, given exogenously.

## The main results

The model shows that the relative price of any commodity falls at a rate equal to that at which labor productivity increases in the corresponding vertically integrated sector. This rate of change is the weighted average of two productivity growth rates: that relating to the production of the commodity concerned (sector $i$) and that relating to the production of the corresponding capital goods (sector $k_i$).

Price movements can be measured with respect to a general level of prices which remains stable over time. This is obtained from Pasinetti's dynamic standard commodity, a composite commodity for which productivity is growing at the weighted average rate of the economic system (Pasinetti 1981: 101ff). It follows that, in terms of the dynamic standard commodity, the price of the commodities produced with above-average productivity growth will decrease, and that of the commodities with below-average productivity growth will increase (Pasinetti 1981: 105).

Assuming that the system tends to follow a dynamic equilibrium path, the change over time in physical output of any final commodity depends on the growth of its demand. This rate of growth comprises two elements: (i) a general term $g$ (the growth of population), which influences in a uniform way the demand for all commodities; (ii) a specific element $r_i$, the growth of demand for final commodity $i$ in question. This growth of demand for the final commodity also determines the evolution of output of the corresponding capital goods sector.

Employment is studied at two levels (sectoral and aggregate), in order to work out the macroeconomic condition for full employment. At sectoral level, the evolution of employment is the net result of two factors acting in opposite directions: (1) the increase in productivity, which reduces employment; and (2) the growth of demand $(r_i + g)$, which expands employment.

The macroeconomic condition for full employment is derived from either of the two systems of equations describing the economy, since it turns out to be the same whichever system is chosen. It appears that there is no guarantee that such a condition will be fulfilled automatically because the learning processes in production and consumption operate independently. In particular, the diversified impact of technical change entails a permanent shift in the structure of employment which calls for a continuous movement of workers from the contracting to the expanding sectors: when technical and structural changes are deep-seated, the most likely outcome is unemployment. Full employment can thus be attained only through an active economic policy.

Pasinetti (1988) shows that, in a natural system in which demand and output of each sector grow at the rate $r_i + g$, the "natural" price of commodity $i$ $(p_i, i = 1, 2, \ldots, n-1)$ is proportional to its labor value $(L_i)$:

$$p_i = L_i w \qquad \text{(where } w \text{ is the wage rate)} \qquad (1)$$

"Natural" prices include a "natural" rate of profit $\pi_i^*$, which is defined as what is required for the accumulation of capital in a growing economy:

$$\pi_i^* = g + r_i \qquad (2)$$

The result of formula (1), which is a generalization of Marx's TRANSFORMATION PROBLEM, yields a dynamic "pure" labor theory of value. It is obtained by defining labor value as the direct and indirect labor incorporated into a commodity plus the total labor incorporated into the additions to the stocks of means of production which, in each period, are required to meet the increased demand for the commodity in question.

## See also:

circular production and vertical integration; Kaldor–Pasinetti models of growth and distribution; post-Keynesian political economy: major contemporary themes

## Selected references

Pasinetti, Luigi L. (1973) "The Notion of Vertical Integration in Economic Analysis," *Metroeconomica*, reprinted in L.L. Pasinetti (ed.) (1980) *Essays on the Theory of Joint Production*, New York: Columbia University Press, 16–43.

—— (1974) *Growth and Income Distribution: Essays in Economic Theory*, Cambridge: Cambridge University Press.

—— (1981) *Structural Change and Economic Growth. A Theoretical Essay on the Dynamics of the Wealth of Nations*, Cambridge: Cambridge University Press.

—— (1988) "Growing Subsystems, Vertically Hyper-integrated Sectors and the Labour Theory of Value," *Cambridge Journal of Economics* 12(1): 125–34.

—— (1993) *Structural Economic Dynamics. A Theory of the Economic Consequences of Human Learning*, Cambridge: Cambridge University Press.

ANGELO REATI

# path dependency

Economic outcomes are path dependent when they are fashioned, not just by activities and decisions in the present, but also by events that took place in the past. An economic outcome that is path dependent is the product of the precise sequence of adjustments and changes that led up to it. Had this adjustment path been different, the specific outcome obtained would also be different.

## Centers of gravity versus evolution and change

In mainstream economics, it is typical to think of fluctuations and changes in the economy as being self-correcting temporary departures from predetermined, fully adjusted positions. For example, a recession appears as a temporary deviation from a long-run rate of growth and level of (un)employment, to which the economy will eventually return. The organizing concept on which mainstream models of the economy are based is that of determinate equilibrium, a position of rest defined and reached independently of the path taken towards it (Kaldor 1934). Determinate equilibria are "centers of gravity" towards which the economy is inevitably drawn, regardless of the activities and decisions that characterized any departures from these states in the past. They are path independent (see EQUILIBRIUM, DISEQUILIBRIUM AND NON-EQUILIBRIUM).

Many political economists, however, prefer to think of economic outcomes as the historical outgrowth of the sequences of events that preceded them. According to this view, economic activities do not inexorably tend towards determinate equilibria. Rather, outcomes are conceived as being the emergent properties of prior sequences of decisions and activities, to be interpreted as *ex post* historical facts rather than *ex ante* centers of gravity. For example, a series of long and deep recessions separated by weak economic booms might be seen as creating a poor long-run economic growth performance, that could have been different had the sequence of recessions and booms themselves been different. In this case, the trend rate of growth is not independent of short-run fluctuations but is, instead, a product of them. Economists who subscribe to this view eschew the static, atemporal and mechanical metaphor of gravitation in favor of the dynamic, temporal and biological metaphor of *evolution*, which stresses the potential for endogenous and ongoing change in a system as a result of its workings over time. The organizing concepts upon which they base their models embody the principle that earlier states of the world have a fundamental effect on later states, that is, the principle of path dependence.

## Feedback processes

Although a variety of path-dependent organizing concepts exist, all involve the critical notion of "feedback," from economic outcomes to the structural systems that determine them. For example, it is commonly believed that preferences influence consumption decisions. Feedback arises when consumption decisions contribute to a stock of consumption experience which, in turn, influences preferences and hence future consumption decisions. Feedback mechanisms set up a two-way interaction between outcomes and what would traditionally be conceived as the "data" determining them. They imbue economic systems with memories, by allowing current and future outcomes to be influenced by past experience.

Some concepts of path dependence involve strictly positive feedback. This is true, for example, of the "frequency dependency effects" that bring about lock-in (Arthur 1994). Frequency dependency effects promote the practice of activities in direct relation to the extent to which they have been practiced in the past. For example, use of a certain technique of production may result in learning by doing, making this technique preferable to others – which appear as "unknown quantities" – in future production decisions. Lock-in results when, in the context of past practice, deviation from a given activity either does not pay, or (in group situations) cannot be effected by an individual decision maker acting in isolation.

Although lock-in is a relatively new idea, the notion of positive feedback is not. Frequency dependency effects are essentially equivalent to Veblen's (1919) notion of cumulative causation. This involves a two-way interaction between economic variables, such that an increase (decrease) in one variable leads to supporting changes in other variables which subsequently give rise to a further increase (decrease) in the original variable, and so on. This recursive interaction continues indefinitely in the form of a series of non-equilibrium and non-equilibrating adjustments. For example, Kaldor's (1985) cumulative causation model of interregional trade and growth posits a direct relationship between the initial growth of output, subsequent gains in productivity and international competitiveness and, hence, the future growth of output. Once again, positive feedback is the key: path dependent change is characterized as being strictly self-reinforcing.

## Hysteresis

HYSTERESIS is perhaps the most general path-dependent organizing concept, because it does not necessarily involve positive feedback. For example, hysteresis might be used to describe a situation where changes in preferences which result in more consumption of a good or service today give rise to a consumption experience and impact on preferences which subsequently reduce consumption of the same good or service. Cornwall (1990) uses hysteresis to explain why macroeconomic institutions – such as industrial relations systems – may be eroded by the rapid growth and full employment to which they were originally favorable, resulting in a subsequent era of inferior macroeconomic performance. Positive or nega-

tive feedback due to hysteresis can be modeled in ways that emphasize either the endogeneity of a variable to its own past history (Setterfield 1997) or to the past history of exogenous shocks (Cross 1993). In either case, the emphasis is conventionally placed on the capacity for past events to create structural change in the underlying system that governs outcomes.

## Initial outcomes and uncertainty

As the plurality of path-dependent organizing concepts suggests, there is clearly scope for the whole phenomenon of path dependence to be treated in either more or less sophisticated ways. For example, systems with predetermined, locally stable, multiple equilibria might be described as path dependent, simply because the equilibrium towards which the system eventually converges depends on initial conditions. However, there is surely more to the belief that "history matters" than the idea that "initial conditions matter." (Note that this criticism can also be leveled at path-dependent organizing concepts involving strictly positive feedback.) A more sophisticated model of path dependence would permit events along a historical trajectory that are subsequent to initial conditions to exert an independent influence on future outcomes. Furthermore, the influence of the past on future outcomes can be conceived in a more or less deterministic fashion. To return to the earlier example, a knowledge of initial conditions allows perfectly certain prediction of final outcomes in systems with multiple equilibria, since these outcomes emerge mechanistically once initial conditions are specified. However, a more sophisticated vision of path dependence might conceive evolutionary change in the economy as being creative and therefore unpredictable a priori, resulting in conditions of fundamental UNCERTAINTY. This would link path dependence to the Robinsonian concept of historical TIME, according to which the present is a bridge between an immutable past and an as yet unmade future.

## Conclusion

The idea that "history matters" is not new, but it has been elevated by recent developments in the principle of path dependence. Whether or not economists will now abandon thinking in terms of gravitation towards predetermined outcomes, in favor of thinking in terms of historical process and emergent properties, remains to be seen. What is certain is that historical and evolutionary processes are critical to political economy.

## See also:

evolutionary economics: major contemporary themes; hysteresis; Kaldor's theory of the growth process; technological lock-in; Veblen

## Selected references

Arthur, W.B. (1994) *Increasing Returns and Path Dependence in the Economy*, Ann Arbor, MI: University of Michigan Press.

Cornwall, J. (1990) *The Theory of Economic Breakdown*, Oxford: Basil Blackwell.

Cross, R. (1993) "On the Foundations of Hysteresis in Economic Systems," *Economics and Philosophy* 9: 53–74.

Kaldor, N. (1934) "A Classificatory Note on the Determinateness of Equilibrium," *Review of Economic Studies* 2: 122–36.

—— (1985) *Economics Without Equilibrium*, Cardiff: University College Cardiff Press.

Setterfield, M.A. (1997) *Rapid Growth and Relative Decline: Modelling Macroeconomic Dynamics with Hysteresis*, London: Macmillan.

Veblen, T.B. (1919) *The Place of Science in Modern Civilization and Other Essays*, New York: Russell & Russell

MARK SETTERFIELD

# patriarchy

The original meaning of patriarchy was "rule by the father." Patriarchalism was an influential political philosophy in seventeenth-century Europe where, following on from the Reformation, male heads of households were increasingly perceived as society's moral guardians. Eighteenth- and nineteenth-century liberal philosophy replaced the notion of the "natural authority" of patriarchs with a model of free, equal and rational individuals. However, the liberal philosophers and political economists (with the exception of John Stuart Mill), were ambivalent about whether individual equality should extend to women (see Pujol 1992).

## Rule by the father

Marx and Engels adopted the "rule by the father" concept, but gave it a new economic and historical meaning. They identified a patriarchal mode of production as the dominant economic system over a particular phase of pre-capitalist history, when family households were property-owning and producing units. Ownership of property and direction of the production process was vested in male heads of household, and women and children were subordinate to male authority. Women had a dual economic value for their self-employed property-owning husbands, both as workers and as mothers of the next generation to inherit the business and provide its future workforce.

## Men's power over women

From the 1970s, feminists such as Kate Millett in *Sexual Politics* (1971), used patriarchy to refer to men's power over women in general, rather than the rule of the father. Patriarchy was no longer confined to analyzing power relations within the family, but was applied to the relations between men and women throughout all social institutions. Subsequently, feminists debated whether patriarchy as a concept could provide analytical and not just descriptive insights (Beechey 1979 and Rowbotham 1982). For patriarchy to explain rather than merely describe gender inequality, the specific social relationships and processes of patriarchy needed to be identified.

## Patriarchal relationships and processes

For some feminists, these were primarily economic; for instance, see Delphi (1977), Hartmann (1979) and Walby (1986). For others, such as Mackintosh (1977) and Folbre (1983), patriarchy was grounded in the social relationships of human reproduction and child-rearing. Mitchell (1975), argued that patriarchy was based on psycho-cultural factors. For other feminists, it was linked to women's biological reproductive role or men's use of sexual force.

## Patriarchal family and the labor market

Feminist socioeconomic writings on patriarchy can be divided into three broad strands. The first strand uses a broad definition of the patriarchal family, equating it with a household, which consists of a male breadwinner and dependent wife and children. This household is perceived to be the typical family structure in contemporary Western capitalism, across social classes, and to underpin a collective male interest in ensuring that women remain available to service men in the household. Within this strand, some writers identified marriage as the key institutional mechanism through which patriarchy was perpetuated (Delphy 1977). Others linked patriarchy to social relations in the public sphere, which sustained solidarity between men and enabled them to dominate women in both public and private spheres (Hartmann 1979; Walby 1986).

As women gained greater access to employment and other measures of social equality, and male authority within the family unit declined, gender segregation of jobs became an important mechanism for perpetuating women's economic dependence in the patriarchal family. The material underpinnings of gender inequality were perceived to be located less and less within the household and more and more in the labor market. Because capitalism and patriarchy were seen to be two distinct sets of social relations, sometimes mutually supportive (Hartmann 1979), sometimes in tension with each other (Walby 1990), this approach is referred to as "dual systems theory."

## Identifiable patriarchs

The second approach was to argue that patriarchy should be reserved for situations in which society is organized under identifiable patriarchs, and not weakened to include more socially diffuse systems of male dominance (Mackintosh 1981: 7). While there was a need to explore the relationship between the form and degree of women's subordination and the development of economic systems, Engels and other Marxists were criticized for their economic reductionism and overemphasis on the role of private property in the subordination of women. Patriarchal societies were characterized as those in which physical force and ideology combined with economic mechanisms to produce a systematic subordination of women (Young and Harris 1978: 51). Such societies were more likely to be found at particular levels of economic development, for example, peasant societies. The social relations of human reproduction were as important as the social relations of production in shaping the gender division of labor (Folbre 1983).

The essential elements of patriarchy were present where husbands/fathers were heads of households, wives/mothers were economically and legally dependent on the head of household, children were an economic resource and husbands controlled their wives' sexuality and fertility. In periods of patriarchal stability, all these elements would be present and patriarchal relationships would be sustained because all the different parties involved had an interest in sustaining them, not just men. Women also had an interest in marriage because it provided them with an economically supported and socially valued context in which to carry out what was perceived to be their natural reproductive role. The more children constituted an economic resource, the more highly valued motherhood would be. Women were able to play an active role in decisions about household labor and fertility (Folbre 1983).

However women who resisted male control would be punished. The wider society (religious and state institutions) also had an interest in sustaining patriarchy, because it provided a framework for inter- and intra-generational support which limited the incidence of poverty and dependence on social structures external to families.

## Race, ethnicity and culture

The third strand in the patriarchy debate represents the most important critique of patriarchy theory, that by black women, particularly African-American writers (see Hooks 1982; Collins 1990). They argued that white feminists' use of patriarchy failed to address the diversity of women's experience and the specific experiences of black women and men. For example African-American and African-Caribbean women's experience was shaped by the history of slavery and colonialism, in which black men were systematically denied positions in the white male hierarchy (Carby 1982: 215). For these black women, paid work was always a necessary adjunct to motherhood, since black men were denied access to a family wage. Full-time motherhood was uncommon in these communities and the opportunities available to white women to dedicate themselves to caring for their families were interpreted as a privilege to which many black women aspired (Hooks 1984: 133–4). Patriarchy could even exist as a cultural aspiration amongst men, and women, to whom racism or class had denied a stake in economic development (Hooks 1982: 92). Black feminists have developed an important historical analytical framework which takes into account ways in which race, ethnicity and culture are enmeshed with class and gender (see RACE, ETHNICITY, GENDER AND CLASS; CULTURE).

## Historically grounded analyses

Patriarchy has been an important concept for feminists because it made visible the material social relationships and institutional underpinnings of men's power over women. However,

in the course of the 1980s, in response to black women's critique and the growing influence of post-structuralism and post-modernism (Barrett and Phillips 1992), attention shifted away from attempts to find overall explanations for women's oppression towards more localized and empirically grounded research which looked at gender relations in clearly defined groups. The attention of feminists shifted away from a general analysis of the relationships between capitalism and patriarchy to specific instances of gender inequality which took account of difference among women. Patriarchal relations, rather than patriarchy, appeared a more appropriate concept, implying historical and cultural variation rather than universality (Smart 1983). There is a growing acceptance that patriarchy can contribute more usefully towards historically grounded analyses than to a universal explanation of gender relations.

## See also:

class structures of households; domestic labor debate; household labor; marriage; sexuality

## Selected references

Barrett, M. and Phillips, A. (eds) (1992) *Destabilizing Theory*, Cambridge: Polity Press.

Beechey, V. (1979) "On Patriarchy," *Feminist Review* 3: 66–82.

Carby, H.V. (1982) "White Woman Listen! Black Feminism and the Boundaries of Sisterhood," in Centre for Contemporary Cultural Studies, *The Empire Strikes Back*, London: Hutchinson, 212–35.

Collins, P.H. (1990) *Black Feminist Thought*, Boston: Unwin Hyman.

Delphy, C. (1977) *The Main Enemy*, London: Women's Research and Resource Centre.

Folbre, N. (1983) "Of Patriarchy Born: The Political Economy of Fertility Decisions," *Feminist Studies* 9(2): 261–84.

Hartmann, H. (1979) "Capitalism, Patriarchy and Job Segregation by Sex," in Z.R. Eisenstein (ed.), *Capitalist Patriarchy and* the Case for Socialist Feminism, New York: Monthly Review Press, 206–47.

Hooks, B. (1982) Aint I a Woman, Boston: South End Press.

—— (1984) Feminist Theory, Boston: South End Press.

Mackintosh, M. (1977) "Reproduction and Patriarchy," Capital and Class 2: 119–27.

—— (1981) "Gender and Economics: The Sexual Division of Labour and the Subordination of Women," in K. Young, C. Wolkowitz and R. McCullagh (eds), Of Marriage and the Market, London: CSE Books, 1–15.

Pujol, M.A. (1992) Feminism and Anti-feminism in Early Economic Thought, Aldershot: Edward Elgar.

Rowbotham, S. (1982) "The Trouble with 'Patriarchy'," in M. Evans (ed.) The Woman Question, London: Fontana.

Smart, C. (1983) "Patriarchal Relations and Law: An Examination of Family Law and Sexual Equality in the 1950s" in M. Evans and C. Ungerson (eds) Sexual Divisions: Patterns and Processes, London: Tavistock, 174–96.

Walby, S. (1986) Patriarchy at Work, Cambridge: Polity Press.

—— (1990) Theorizing Patriarchy, Oxford: Blackwell.

Young K. and Harris, O. (1978) "The Subordination of Women in Cross Cultural Perspective," in Papers on Patriarchy, Brighton: Women's Publishing Collective, 38–55.

JEAN GARDINER

**PHILOSOPHY OF SCIENCE, FEMINIST:** see feminist philosophy of science

# physiocracy

Physiocracy was the first school of modern economic thought, and one of the only schools perfectly delimited in time (1756–76) and place (France). François Quesnay (1694–1794), its founder and inspiration, saw his ideas spread by numerous disciples, the most famous being Mirabeau (1715–89), Le Mercier de la Rivière (1720–94), Dupont de Nemours (1739–1817) and Nicolas Baudeau (1730–92). The word économiste appears in French for the first time in a book by Baudeau describing the physiocrats, although opponents of physiocracy called it a "sect" with a rigid IDEOLOGY.

## Origins and influences

The name "physiocracy" comes from the Greek phusis (nature) and kratos (power). For the physiocrats, only agriculture can generate an ECONOMIC SURPLUS, which arises because of the productive powers of the land. In contrast, industry merely transforms already existing products, and creates no surplus. This is why the physiocrats generally called the manufacturing sector "sterile." Although these assumptions may seem unrealistic by contemporary standards, in mid-eighteenth century France industry was quite unproductive.

The main intellectual influences on the physiocrats were Pierre Boisguilbert (1645–1714) and Richard Cantillon (1697–1734), who emphasized both the circular flow of money and goods and the primacy of agriculture. The influence of William Harvey (1578–1657), who discovered the principle of blood circulation in 1628, was also strong on Quesnay, who had a medical degree and served as physician to Louis XV.

The physiocratic theories had their philosophical origins in the tradition of NATURAL RIGHTS, notably from John Locke (natural rights justifying private property), from Thomas Hobbes (ideas come from the senses), and from Nicolas Malebranche (sensations follow from God's action, as occasions offered by events). The main foundation of this philosophy is that moral and physical order is of divine origin and immutable. Human beings must discover this order by observation and by scientific thought, because violations are costly. Even if society is ruled by natural laws that transcend space and time, the monarch must assist them.

## Quesnay's model of reproduction

The most famous work by Quesnay is the *Tableau économique*, which was developed to depict the divine order of the economy. The *Tableau* graphically represents the monetary flows in the national economy between three social classes: landowners, farmers (the productive sector), and the sterile class (craftsmen, industrialists and merchants).

Below is one variant of the *Tableau*, where annual agricultural production is valued at 800 livres. This is produced with 400 livres' worth of inputs, thus yielding an economic surplus of 400 livres. This surplus is owed by the farmers to the landlords (see FEUDALISM). Annual output in the sterile sector is 400 livres, and is produced with 400 livres' worth of inputs, thus yielding no surplus.

With these assumptions, we can now turn to the *Tableau* itself. At the beginning of the reproduction cycle, the landowners hold all the money in the economy. They begin the reproduction process by spending their rent proceeds, half (200 livres) on agricultural goods and half (200 livres) on the output of the sterile CLASS. According to the zig-zags, half the receipts of the sterile class (100 livres) are spent on agricultural goods. Likewise, the agricultural class spends half its receipts on the goods of the sterile class. These expendi-

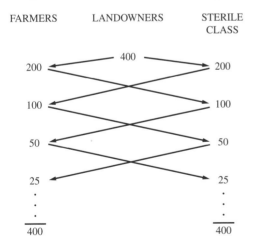

| FARMERS | LANDOWNERS | STERILE CLASS |

*Figure 9* A simple tableau

tures generate incomes of 100 livres for each producing class, which again are spent half on food and half on industrial goods. This process continues until inter-sector spending approaches zero. At this point we are ready for another production cycle to begin.

The sterile class has sold all of its previous output, 200 livres to the landowners and 200 livres to the agricultural class. It has bought 200 livres' worth of agricultural goods. The sterile class also holds 200 livres of money, received initially from the landowners, which it uses to buy raw materials from the productive sector (not shown in the diagram above). This returns all the economy's money to the agricultural class, where it will be used to pay rent and start the next production cycle. The sterile sector now has 200 livres of agricultural goods and 200 livres of raw materials bought from the productive sector. These 400 livres of inputs are then used to produce 400 livres' worth of output.

The productive sector holds 200 livres of manufactured goods bought from the sterile sector plus 200 livres of agricultural goods (the 800 livres they began with less the 600 sold to the proprietors and the sterile class). These 400 livres of inputs are used to produce 800 livres of agricultural goods. A surplus of 400 livres is created. The monetary value of this surplus must be paid to the landowners, thus allowing another production cycle to begin.

With this model, Quesnay has explained how money circulates throughout the economic system, and how reproduction takes place year after year. Quesnay then used his model for policy purposes. He used numerous *Tableaux* to show how savings would lead to economic decline. Also, he could show how high prices for agricultural goods, and spending geared more towards agriculture, result in ECONOMIC GROWTH. Finally, Quesnay demonstrated how taxes placed on the productive sector would lead to economic decline because they reduced productive advances or inputs (see Pressman 1994).

Quesnay produced his economic model for an agricultural nation managed by a *despote éclairé*, which was the system that he knew. He and his followers advocated a political project aimed at saving the endangered monarchy. Indeed, France at that time was searching for solutions to the social and economic problems linked to the ancien régime. The French economy was experiencing rising prices of wheat and rent, violent cyclical crises (notably 1752–5), and a political system grappling with violent conflicts between local parliaments and the royal administration. The budget was also paralyzed by the action of the *fermiers généraux* (the King's officers in charge of collecting taxes for him), who took a great share of the tax revenues destined for the State. The situation was so critical that Quesnay applied the word *crise* (crisis), used up to then only in medicine, to the state of the French economy.

Despite its descriptive pretensions, the *Tableau économique* represents a normative (optimal) state toward which the economy should aim, in the same way that human rights should mirror the divine natural right (Vaggi 1987). The economic system then appears to transcend human action, thus compelling the king to respect it.

## Assessment

Criticisms of the physiocrats have focused on the confusing nature of the *Tableau*, and the assumption that the industrial sector is sterile. However, we must credit Quesnay with discovering the role played by capital in increasing national income. A piece of land better cultivated by the addition of capital will increase the national revenue. The *Tableau* is also important because it was the first economic model ever developed. It shows the workings of the economy in motion through time, how this motion can be thwarted, and what can be done to improve economic performance.

The *Tableau* inspired MARX's reproduction schemes, the circulation approach (see MONETARY CIRCUIT), and Leontief's input–output diagrams. The light it has shed on monetary flows and the importance of investment for economic growth has triggered much debate on the role of the state in the national economy. Quesnay showed the importance of rational discussion about the organization of the economic system, and the economic policies necessary to reach normative goals.

## See also:

circuit of social capital; classical political economy; George's contribution to political economy; productive and unproductive labor; reproduction: simple and expanded

## Selected references

Blaug, Mark (ed.) (1991) *François Quesnay (1694–1774)*, Aldershot: Edward Elgar.

Cartelier, Jean (1991) "L'Economie Politique de François Quesnay: ou l'Utopie du Royaume Agricole," *Introduction to François Quesnay, Physiocratie*, Paris: Garnier Flammarion, 9–64.

Fox-Genovese, Elizabeth (1976) *The Origins of Physiocracy: Economic Revolution and Social Order in Eighteenth-Century France*, Ithaca, NY: Cornell University Press.

Hutchison, Terence W. (1988) *Before Adam Smith: The Emergence of Political Economy, 1662–1776*, Oxford: Basil Blackwell.

Meek, Ronald (1963) *The Economics of Physiocracy*, Cambridge, MA: Harvard University Press.

Pressman, Steven (1994) *Quesnay's Tableau Economique: A Critique and Reassessment*, New York: Augustus M. Kelley.

Vaggi, Gianni (1987) *The Economics of François Quesnay*, Durham, NC: Duke University Press.

IANIK MARCIL
STEVEN PRESSMAN

# Polanyi's views on integration

D.M. Goodfellow, in his *Principles of Economic Sociology* (first published in 1939) argued that "the concepts of economic theory must be taken as having universal validity, and that, were this not so, the result would be not only scientific confusion but practical chaos"; indeed "the proposition that there should be more than one body of economic theory is absurd." If modern economic theory "does not apply to the whole of humanity then it is meaningless." He goes on to add that: "Even if the savage, therefore, could be said to be "dominated by custom,' this is far from meaning that he did not dispose economically of his resources" (LeClair and Schneider 1968: 56–7, 64). Karl Polanyi (1886–1964), author of the famous *The Great Transformation*, published in 1944, was to take great exception to this view.

## Background and nature of integration

Polanyi was skeptical of the universal applicability of orthodox economic theory. Market-like activity does not automatically imply that decision making is based on profit or utility maximizing strategies. He believed that there are many possible ways to organize an economy; the rational economizing approach is only one, and only works where there is already considerable DIVISION OF LABOR, where relationships are impersonal and where MARKETS predominate. There are many other economies where these characteristics do not hold and where economies are not integrated through market exchange. Polanyi objected to the artificial identification of the economy with its market form. He formulated the concepts of reciprocity, redistribution and market exchange to describe different organizational patterns associated with social and political structures. Polanyi noted that these forms of integration do not represent "stages" of development and could coexist in time.

## Three forms of integration

Price-making markets, one of the main forms of integration, came into existence relatively late in cultural evolution, argues Polanyi. In ancient times, rarely did people depend for their livelihood on selling their labor power or producing for a market. Markets and trade were peripheral; they were of limited and marginal importance. Production, consumption and exchange were organized by the state or religion or tribal norms. Since Polanyi was an institutionalist, and sympathetic to Karl MARX (despite the views of George Dalton), the human economy was seen to be embedded and enmeshed in economic and non-economic institutions and habits. Political and social institutions and relationships conditioned economic activity, so that haggling over prices was not practiced; rather, exchange relations tended to be set fairly rigidly. In another context he talks about set-price markets and price-making markets, and that in the former traditional economic analysis loses most of its relevance.

His second form of integration, reciprocity, is often the dominant mode of integration in developing societies. Reciprocal transactions involve the exchange of material goods or services, and serve to create and maintain social relations. The long-term goal of people is to seek exchange partners who can provide them with the resources they lack, and thereby make provisions to cope with contingencies. Good exchange relations are the best guarantee for social security. If daily needs cannot be met by their own production, households try to obtain the goods from neighbors and relatives. What they have to give in return is often not specified in time or quantity.

The system of reciprocity in some societies takes the form of a general state of mutual indebtedness. Every person is involved in chains of reciprocal obligations. The strongest economic position is characterized by the ability to mobilize resources through reciprocity when necessary. The weakest economic position shows in the absence of credit relations. Usually, households are debtors and creditors at the same time. To be in debt is a sign of many good relationships, and one can be proud to be regarded as credit worthy.

A number of policy implications follow from this. First, credit programs are doomed to failure if there is no clear reason for the debtors to repay their debt. Second, people repay their debts according to the relationship with their creditor. The kind of relationship between the lender and the borrower affects not only the terms of credit, but also the chance of repayment.

The third form of integration, redistribution, involves the allocation of goods on the basis of custom, law or central decision. Sometimes it involves the physical collection of goods and their storage for later distribution; often it involves the assigned RIGHTS that people have to the produce, depending on rank or position. To be an effective form of integration, redistribution requires an allocative center in the COMMUNITY that determines entitlements. Polanyi regarded redistribution as the ruling method in tribal and archaic society, and finds parallels with the modern welfare state and the former Soviet Union.

## Modern followers of Polanyi

Modern followers of Polanyi argue that his work cannot be reconciled with orthodox economics. One, it is said, cannot integrate individual behavior with cultural analysis. Indeed, notions of universal principles or Pareto optimality and market efficiency are foreign to anthropology. Rothenberg (1992: ch. 2) has associated Polanyi with what she calls the "moral economy model." In this model, peasant, tribal or clan-based societies are seen as primarily collective arrangements for the economic and social security of all members of a group at risk, an arrangement which guarantees subsistence as a moral claim or as a social right to which every member is entitled. Others feel that this idealistic picture distorts Polanyi's views while the recent work by Humphrey and Hugh-Jones (1992) re-emphasizes the elements of strategy, calculation and self-interest common to both GIFTS and commodity exchange, and that indigenous groups are not passive victims but active and creative participants in the two-sided process of modernization.

Work in the Polanyi tradition stresses the importance of social relations in the economy. The kind of relationship that exists between two people determines how they should behave toward each other, which goods and services they can exchange, and what terms of exchange are appropriate. This largely explains why people prefer one mode of transaction over another, why they consider some people better exchange partners than others, and why some material goods cannot be exchanged at all or only in kind. The elaborate set of exchange arrangements demonstrate that economies can only be understood in the context of indigenous CULTURE, and any analysis of behavior should give room to cultural peculiarities and complexities.

## Conclusion

Hence, economic activities are embedded in social relations. People attempt to create long-term social exchange relationships and the terms of exchange in transactions depend on the quality of social relations between the exchange partners. Access to land, labor and food is organized along the lines of specific sets of social relations. The main message of the work of Polanyi's followers is that one cannot understand economic activities without the specific cultural context. This observation is lost in modern *traditional* economics.

## See also:

disembedded economy; economic anthropology: major contemporary themes; institutional political economy: history of

## Selected references

Dalton, George (ed.) (1967) *Tribal and Peasant Economies: Readings in Economic Anthropology*, New York: Natural History Press.

Ensminger, Jean (1992) *Making a Market*, Cambridge: Cambridge University Press.

Galenson, David W. (ed.) (1989) *Markets in History: Economic Studies of the Past*, New York: Cambridge University Press.

Humphrey, Caroline and Hugh-Jones, Stephen (1992) *Barter, Exchange and Value*, Cambridge: Cambridge University Press.

Lane, Robert E. (1991) *The Market Experience*, New York: Cambridge University Press.

LeClair, E.M. and Schneider, H.K. (eds) (1968) *Economic Anthropology: Readings in Theory and Analysis*, New York: Holt, Rinehart & Winston

Mayhew, Anne (1980) "Atomistic and Cultural Analyses in Economic Anthropology" in John Adams (ed.), *Institutional Economics*, Boston: Martinus Nijhoff, 72–81.

—— (1987) "Culture: Core Concept Under Attack," *Journal of Economic Issues* 21(2): 587–603.

Polanyi, Karl (1944) *The Great Transformation*, repr. 1957, Boston: Beacon Press.

Rothenberg, Winifred B. (1992) *From Market-Places to a Market Economy*, Chicago: University of Chicago Press.

Stanfield, James Ronald (1986) *The Economic Thought of Karl Polanyi*, London: Macmillan.

JOHN LODEWIJKS

# political business cycles

Political business cycle theorists claim that "stop–go" macroeconomic policies cause the boom-and-bust cycle of advanced capitalist economies. They make no claims about secular trends in the economy.

Mainstream political business cycle theorists are concerned that inflationary booms result from democratic governments using expansionary macroeconomic policies as part of their re-election strategies. In contrast, heterodox political business cycle theorists are concerned that, in the absence of a strong labor movement, big business and rentiers will use their market power to undermine democratic governments.

## Mainstream analysis

Mainstream political business cycle theorists are able to condemn cyclical booms caused by expansionary macroeconomic policies by assuming that free market forces bring about both the full employment and the most efficient allocation of resources, including the most efficient allocation of wealth and income. Since expansionary macroeconomic policies cannot increase the employment of resources that are, by assumption, already fully employed, they can only cause inflation. Mainstream theorists are then able to argue that, by causing inflation, the policy-induced booms redistribute income and wealth from the market participants that produce them to special-interest groups that are numerically large but make little contribution to the production of goods and services.

The two principal schools of mainstream economics – monetarism and new classicism – differ in their explanations of the contractionary macroeconomic policies that cause cyclical downturns. On the one hand, monetarists claim that contractionary policies are necessary after elections in order to regain control of the inflationary pressures unleashed by the expansionary policies prior to elections (see MONETARISM). On the other hand, new classical economists claim that contractionary macroeconomic policies are necessary after elections in order to reestablish the government's credibility as a hawk on inflation. New classical economists allege that expansionary macroeconomic policies will cause a cyclical expansion prior to future elections only if the implementation of them comes as a surprise to market participants.

Despite their different explanations of the causes of the contractionary phase of the political business cycle, both monetarists and new classical economists agree that the incomes and wealth of the market participants that produce them must be protected by authoritarian institutions. This includes, for instance, central banks that are not democratically accountable, protecting the economy from the inflationary policies of democratic governments seeking re-election (see, for example, Alesina and Rosenthal 1995; Persson and Tabellini 1994; Willett 1988).

## Heterodox analyses

In contrast to the mainstream concern that democratic governments impinge on the incomes and wealth of market participants, heterodox political business cycle theorists are concerned that big business and rentiers use their market power to undermine democratic governments. For example, in the first essay on political business cycles, KALECKI (1943) explains how the efforts of democratic governments to use expansionary macroeconomic policies to end the GREAT DEPRESSION in the 1930s brought big business and rentiers together into a powerful block supporting FASCISM. Boddy and Crotty (1975) extend Kalecki's analysis in order to explain US macroeconomic history from the late 1950s to the early 1970s.

That rentiers oppose expansionary macroeconomic policies should surprise no one. Rentiers do not need jobs, and they are hurt by the upward pressures on wages and prices caused by robust economic conditions. On the other hand, big business both gains and loses from expansionary macroeconomic policies. Under democratic governments, heterodox political business cycle theorists argue that big business must occasionally resort to contractionary policies in order to offset the costs of expansionary policies. But if big business aligns itself with rentiers to establish fascist regimes, then it can have the benefits of expansionary policies without having to occasionally resort to contractionary policies to offset its costs.

Big business is hurt by expansionary macroeconomic policies to the degree that the robust economic conditions that result from them reduce the COST OF JOB LOSS among workers. Discipline on the factory floor and in the office breaks down as the unemployment rate falls and workers become more secure in their jobs. The reduction in workers' fear of job loss also leads to more strikes, as the least advantaged workers demand, and receive, higher money wages and better working conditions. Consequently, the wage differentials between different types of workers begin to shrink, thereby undermining the artificial status divisions,

based on differences in income levels, that are the principal way in which big business prevents the development of class consciousness and working class solidarity (see for example Boddy and Crotty 1975: 9; Kalecki 1943: 141, 144).

In addition, expansionary macroeconomic policies weaken the link between the state of confidence of big business, the principal determinant of the level of private sector investments, and the level of output and employment. To the degree that big business loses its ability to cause recessions and rising unemployment rates by losing confidence, big business loses its control over the course of events (see, for example, Kalecki 1943: 139).

On the other hand, heterodox political business cycle theorists argue that there are two reasons why big business benefits from expansionary macroeconomic policies. First, the profits of big business rise with the rising incomes and sales which result from expansionary macroeconomic policies (and the profits of big business fall with the falling incomes and sales which result from contractionary macroeconomic policies). Second, big business needs expansionary macroeconomic policies because, as Boddy and Crotty put it, just letting the economy stagnate and keeping the unemployment rate high with contractionary policies would:

> effectively segment the labor force into those working, and those not only unemployed but, as time went on, increasingly unemployable because of deteriorating work skills and habits. The capitalists would once again be faced *de facto* with a militant, unfrightened work force and tight labor markets even though measured unemployment remained high.
>
> (Boddy and Crotty 1975: 10)

Fascist regimes solve the dilemma faced by big business, because the latter both gains and loses from expansionary macroeconomic policies. That is to say, if fascist regimes (rather than democratic governments) implement the expansionary policies, then big business can have the higher profits and sustain the work skills and habits of workers without undermining the discipline and docility of workers (Kalecki 1943: 141, 144).

If workers are strong enough to prevent the establishment of fascist regimes, then big business and rentiers must limit their activities to engineering a political business cycle. For example, Boddy and Crotty (1975: 1, 13) argue that the "unemployment engineered" by President Eisenhower's contractionary macroeconomic policies in the late 1950s weakened labor sufficiently for expansionary policies to then be used by the Kennedy and Johnson administrations to generate "the super profits... of the early to mid-1960s." But by late 1965, the robust economic conditions and falling unemployment rates had undermined workers' fear of job loss to the degree that "capital clearly required a recession" (Boddy and Crotty 1975: 13). Nonetheless, fear of galvanizing opposition to the Vietnam War prevented big business and rentiers from using contractionary macroeconomic policies to cause a recession until after the war was over (Boddy and Crotty 1975: 14).

## See also:

business cycle theories; fiscal crisis of the state; fiscal policy; monetary policy and central banking functions; profit squeeze analysis of crises

## Selected references

Alesina, Alberto and Rosenthal, Howard (1995) *Partisan Politics, Divided Government, and the Economy*, New York: Cambridge University Press.

Boddy, Raford and Crotty, James (1975) "Class Conflict And Macro-Policy: The Political Business Cycle," *Review of Radical Political Economics* 7(1): 1–19.

Kalecki, Michal (1943) "Political Aspects of Full Employment," in Michal Kalecki, *Selected Essays On The Dynamics of the Capitalist Economy 1933–1970*, Cambridge: Cambridge University Press, 1971, 138–45.

Persson, Torsten and Tabellini, Guido (eds) (1994) *Monetary And Fiscal Policy*, Cambridge, MA: MIT Press.

Willett, Thomas D. (ed.) (1988) *Political Business Cycles: The Political Economy of Money, Inflation, And Unemployment*, Durham, NC: Duke University Press.

EDWIN DICKENS

# political economy

## Introduction

Contemporary political economy and economics both grew out of an earlier and more underdeveloped body of knowledge known as CLASSICAL POLITICAL ECONOMY. In 1767, James Steuart produced the first book in English using the term "political economy" in its title. It took another half century, however, before the accumulated creative work of Adam Smith, Jean-Baptiste Say, David Ricardo and John Stuart Mill, in particular, helped to establish political economy as a discipline. Political economy became known as the study of how nations grow and what nations can do to increase the sum of material goods enjoyed by their citizens.

In the latter part of the nineteenth century, marginal analysis emerged and the phrase "political economy" fell into disuse in many circles. It was largely replaced by the term "economics," which appeared in the title of Alfred Marshall's *Principles of Economics* in 1890. For the next seventy years, political economy was treated as a descriptor of economics in its less scientific beginnings. The term was (and is) also sometimes used to describe a broader view of the economy than "economics," or a branch of economics, or as a synonym for economics (see Groenewegan 1987).

## Revival of political economy

In the latter half of the twentieth century, political economy experienced a major revival. One important reason for this was a growing dissatisfaction with the narrowness of economic analysis. Many political economists feel that there is more to economic activity than rational maximization by individuals as expressed in supply and demand. Institutions, political IDEOLOGY, cooperation, ECONOMIC POWER, human psychology and CULTURE also affect the production and distribution of goods in a society. Economics tends to ignore, or abstracts from, these factors; political economy takes them seriously (see Heilbroner and Milberg 1995).

A second important reason for the revival of political economy in the 1960s and the 1970s was a growing recognition of serious economic and social problems that standard economic analysis could neither explain nor solve. These include the problems of worker alienation, environmental degradation, race and gender discrimination, poverty and urban ghettos, and stagflation (see Lippit 1996: 1–5).

Political economy and economics, at base, are both attempts to understand how societies provide for their members and how goods and services are distributed. But the similarities end there. Political economy and economics represent two different perspectives on these processes. Each begins with a different focus and methodology; each employs a different set of assumptions; each adopts a different mode of analysis; and each comes to very different policy conclusions.

## Economic surplus

Political economy is primarily concerned with how to create an ECONOMIC SURPLUS. It attempts to analyze the nature of this surplus, and to understand how this surplus arises and gets distributed. SRAFFIAN POLITICAL ECONOMY, for example, ties the generation of a surplus to the TECHNOLOGY of production available at a given time, and ties its distribution to a struggle between workers and capitalists. Marxist political economy studies the production of surplus value in the exploitation process of capitalist business.

Political economy also focuses on how to increase the economic surplus. It is, therefore, concerned with the questions of ECONOMIC

GROWTH and development, and it emphasizes real world historical processes and institutional adjustment as being crucial to these processes (Whalen 1996: 7).

Economics ignores all questions surrounding the economic surplus, focusing instead on the allocation of given resources. It is primarily concerned with efficiency, or how some given output can be produced with the least cost or minimum effort. Economics also focuses on individual preferences and decision making, and how exchange among individuals can lead to an efficient allocation of resources if nothing hinders free exchange. Thus, unlike political economy, economics begins by focusing on the individual rather than the group (see INDIVIDUAL AND SOCIETY; CLASS).

## Methodology and philosophy

There are also important methodological differences between economics and political economy. Economics in general views itself as an objective, value-free science. It attempts to separate the normative from the positive, and to focus on only the positive aspects of economics. This, it is thought, creates an economics that is as scientific as the natural or hard sciences. Economists are thought to proceed with the same detachment as the scientist who devises rigorous, controlled experiments and professes no value judgments about the results of these experiments (see Friedman 1953).

Political economy rejects the view that any science can be value-free, either in how it views the world or in the types of questions it asks about the world (see Proctor 1991). Political economists hold that the normative and positive aspects of a science can never be divorced, and that one's beliefs and prejudices affect what one studies, how one proceeds to study production and the acceptable outcomes of this study. Therefore, one must study the psychological, sociological and political forces that affect individual behavior and economic performance (see NORMATIVE AND POSITIVE ECONOMICS; VALUE JUDGMENTS AND WORLD VIEWS). Going even further, radical political economists (see Lippit 1996) view traditional economics as producing analyses that support the interests of certain wealthy individuals and businesses.

The characteristic that most sharply distinguishes economics from political economy is the different assumptions employed by each perspective. For economics, hedonism is taken to be the unique and dominating factor affecting human behavior, and individual tastes are taken as given. Producers are assumed to desire more and more profit, and consumers to maximize their utility. The individual is assumed to know the satisfaction they would get from different bundles of consumption goods, and is assumed to buy the bundle that will yield the greatest utility. Individuals are also assumed to know the disutility that they would receive from working and the utility they would get from the goods consumed as a result of working and receiving income. Based on this knowledge, economists assume that people make rational decisions about whether they want to work or enjoy leisure.

In political economy, tastes are no longer assumed to be given. Rather, political economists seek to understand the forces that shape and try to control tastes. Thorstein VEBLEN, the father of institutional economics, sought to explain how the behavior of others can provide both a signal or emulating factor, and also a means of comparison for others to attempt to surpass. Galbraith (1967) has argued that tastes for goods are actually manufactured by producers in order to sell things.

## Society, class, conflict and inequality

Further, political economists see people acting because they belong to some group or class. They see individuals facing great UNCERTAINTY and thus making decisions based on habits, irrational beliefs and group pressures. Unlike neoclassical economics, which views economic activity as making both parties to all exchanges better off, political economy assumes that there will be conflicts among different groups and that these conflicts will create disorder. Workers and owners each want a larger share of the total output, and the battle for larger shares of this output gets carried out in battles over wage increases and price increases (see PROFIT SQUEEZE ANALYSIS OF CRISES; INFLATION: CONFLICTING CLAIMS APPROACH).

Economic analysis primarily studies how the interaction of individual agents leads to a stable set of relative prices. Economics sees these relative prices being determined by supply and demand. Supply is essentially how scarce a good is, or how hard it is to produce that good and yield profits for producers. Producers balance the cost of producing goods in different ways and select the method that is least costly and most profitable. Demand is determined by individual preferences, as consumers balance the marginal utility they expect to get from spending their money on different goods. Together, these two forces determine how much each good costs, and also determine wage levels. Individual utility maximization is then shown to lead to market clearing, so that firms do not produce goods they cannot sell and people get the goods they desire.

In contrast, political economists seeks to analyze the factors that help an economy produce goods and grow. They look to certain objective factors (like the available technology and social relationships in the workplace) rather than subjective utility as determining production. They look to political, social and institutional factors as determining the distribution of that output. Low taxes on the wealthy in conjunction with cuts in social spending, greater economic power for large businesses due to deregulation and globalization and a social ethics that encourages people only to "look out for number one," all contribute to sharply rising income INEQUALITY.

## Policy solutions

Finally, for economics the forces of supply and demand will solve almost all economic problems. People know what gives them the most utility, and they behave in ways that will maximize their utility. If everyone is given the freedom to make their own decisions, the utility of everyone will be maximized. Within this framework, economic problems can only arise when the forces of supply and demand are not allowed to function, either because of monopoly power by business firms or labor UNIONS, government intervention in the market, or because some aspect of life has not been subjected to the rule of supply and demand (for example, the environment). Policy solutions thus focus on reducing government intervention and enhancing the forces of supply and demand by promoting competition and MARKETS.

Political economists, in contrast, seek to understand the extra-economic causes of economic problems, and to devise solutions that might improve economic outcomes. Political economists frequently cite discrimination as a cause of lower wages for women and minorities. Post-Keynesians, as well as other political economists, identify uncertainty and insufficient spending as causes of high unemployment. Corporate power is pointed to as a major cause of environmental degradation (see ENVIRONMENTAL AND ECOLOGICAL POLITICAL ECONOMY: MAJOR CONTEMPORARY THEMES).

To solve these problems, political economists look to both popular and government action, rather than necessarily to the market. For example, they advocate laws prohibiting discrimination and pollution, as well as popular boycotts against firms that behave egregiously. Political economists also favor government deficits in order to increase aggregate spending if people and firms will not buy things, and redistributive policies to both increase spending and enhance the market power of lower and middle income families. They also tend to favor worker cooperatives as a way of helping to solve problems such as low PRODUCTIVITY, ALIENATION and the socioeconomic fragmentation (see MONDRAGÓN).

### Selected references

Friedman, Milton (1953) "The Methodology of Positive Economics," in Milton Friedman, *Essays in Positive Economics*, Chicago: University of Chicago Press, 3–43.

Galbraith, John Kenneth (1967) *The New Industrial State*, Boston: Houghton Mifflin.

Groenewegen, Peter (1987) "'Political Economy' and 'Economics'," in John Eatwell, Murray Milgate and Peter Newman (eds), *The New Palgrave: A Dictionary of Economics*, London: Macmillan.

Heilbroner, Robert and Milberg, William (1995) *The Crisis of Vision in Modern Economic Thought*, Cambridge: Cambridge University Press.

Lippit, Victor D. (ed.) (1996) *Radical Political Economy: Explorations in Alternative Economic Analysis*, Armonk, NY: M.E. Sharpe.

Proctor, Robert N. (1991) *Value-Free Economics? Purity and Power in Modern Knowledge*, Cambridge, MA: Harvard University Press.

Steuart, J. (1767) *An Inquiry into the Principles of Political Economy*, repr. 1966, ed. by A. S. Skinner, Edinburgh and London: Oliver & Boyd.

Veblen, Thorstein (1899) *The Theory of The Leisure Class*, London: Macmillan, 1979.

Whalen, Charles J. (1996) "Beyond Neoclassical Thought: Political Economy for the Twenty-First Century," in Charles J. Whalen (ed.), *Political Economy for the 21st Century*, Armonk, NY: M.E. Sharpe, 3–24.

STEVEN PRESSMAN
ROBIN NEILL

**POLITICAL ECONOMY, CLASSICAL:** *see* classical political economy

# political economy: history

In studies of the history of economic thought, the distinction between "political economy" and "economics" is of common usage, although there is no consensus as to the meanings of the terms. Here, the terms political economy and economics are taken to represent distinct approaches to economic theory which have existed side by side within the discipline. Political economy proposes an economic theory based on a socio-historical method. This assigns a central role to history, to institutions, and to the interaction between social classes. Economics bases its analysis on methodological individualism. It formulates an ahistorical theory, which is valid regardless of spatial-temporal limitations. Political economy has produced a science which examines levels of economic activity and income distribution from the point of view of the relationships between macroeconomic agents. In this entry, the history of economics, which finds its maximum expression in NEOCLASSICAL ECONOMICS from the 1870s onwards, is not examined.

## Mercantilism

Despite the theoretical attempts of Aristotle, Plato and scholastic philosophers, MERCANTILISM, which principally spread during the seventeenth century, represented the first current of thought directed at providing an interpretation of the entire working of the economic process. Mercantilism produced the economic theory of the new nation states, whose principal source of economic wealth lay in the exploitation of colonies. Mercantilist scholars maintained that a country's economic growth relied primarily on an active trade balance. Consequently, they theorized the need for a system of rules that protected the nation from international competition. The mercantilists assigned a central role to money as a symbol of power. They theorized a direct relationship between money stock and price levels and perceived the relations between the quantity of money, interest rate and the level of aggregate demand.

## Physiocracy

With PHYSIOCRACY, which constituted the first true school of economic thought, attention was shifted from exchange to production. The physiocrats, who took inspiration from the work of William Petty (1623–87) and Richard Cantillon (1697–1734), held that the economic surplus, or net product, could only originate from the agricultural sector. Consequently, the

manufacturing sector was defined as "sterile." The physiocrats laid out a circular representation of the economic process. François Quesnay (1694–1774) was the main exponent of this school of thought, and his analysis in the *Tableau économique* in 1758 is exemplary. In clear disagreement with the mercantilists, the physiocrats condemned many forms of state intervention in the economy, formulating the "doctrine of natural order." Moreover, they maintained, again in contrast to the mercantilists, that monetary variables could not affect real quantities.

## Classical political economy

The period from the publication of Smith's *Wealth of Nations* in 1776 to Mill's *Principles of Political Economy* in 1848 marks the age of CLASSICAL POLITICAL ECONOMY. The classical economists criticized the mercantilists for formulating a theory that gave pre-eminence to the role of politics in the economy and for having concentrated attention on circulation rather than on production. They were also critical of the physiocrats, particularly their theory of the exclusive productivity of agriculture. The classical economists described the working of the economy by means of the interaction of three social classes: landowners, industrial capitalists and waged workers. They raised the issue of the possibility of class conflict, although they generally held that the market was capable of ensuring, in Bentham's phrase, the "greatest happiness of the greatest number." They accepted the Malthusian population principle (that unchecked population growth tends to increase geometrically while food growth tends to increase arithmetically), and pointed to an increase in the division of labor as the means to economic growth. They held that the basis of commodity value was to be sought in the labor needed to produce it. However, there was strong disagreement among the classical economists over certain issues, for example, the question of the measure of value and monetary theory.

Adam Smith (1723–90) was the father of the classical school. He put forward his theory of the "invisible hand" of the market. Critically assessing Hume and Hobbes, he maintained that, in the economic arena, self-interest and the search for the greatest individual well-being (not cooperation) determined the greatest collective well-being. In his hugely influential work, *The Wealth of Nations*, Smith pointed to the increasing DIVISION OF LABOR as the driving force of development, and the labor "embodied" in commodities as the foundation of value. However, in capitalism the measure of commodity value was to be sought in the labor that this commodity can purchase in exchange (labor "commanded"). Only in this way was it possible to account for the existence of profit and rent, alongside wages. Whereas the "natural price" of a commodity was determined by the labor it commanded, the market price might differ from this only temporarily. Smith's thesis on distribution provided as much the starting point for theories of exploitation as for theories that link each income to the contribution of a factor of production.

David Ricardo (1772–1823) was the most acute exponent of the classical school. Employing the CORN MODEL in his *Essay on Profits* in 1815, Ricardo formulated the theory of differential rent. The continued growth of rent on better lands, with the consequent tendency of a fall in the rate of profit, was due to natural causes (scarcity of fertile land and population increase). In *The Principles of Political Economy* in 1817, Ricardo criticized Smith's theory of value and distribution: he maintained that embodied labor represented the cause and measure of value and stressed that profit and rent had to be considered as deductions from the produce of labor. Ricardo realized that, in the case of commodities produced by different relationships between direct and indirect labor, embodied labor could not function correctly as a measure of value. In this case, an "exception" to the "general rule" took place, where increased wages raised the relative price of goods produced with a high direct/indirect labor ratio. He tried to resolve this problem by looking for an INVARIABLE MEASURE OF VALUE. Ricardo agreed with Say's Law, according to which supply generates its own demand

and that there can be no question of a shortage of aggregate demand.

An extremely important role in classical political economy was played by Thomas Malthus (1766–1834). He is known above all for his "principle of population," where population tends to increase at a geometrical rate whereas agricultural production only increases at an arithmetical rate. In clear disagreement with Ricardo, Malthus put forward the first serious criticism of Say's Law, claiming that hoarding may determine a shortage of aggregate demand. Malthus deemed that, in order to increase aggregate demand, it was necessary to have the presence of unproductive workers.

Apart from Malthus, Ricardo's work was also criticized by Bailey and Torrens and by Ricardian socialists, primarily Hodgskin. But it was J. C. L. Simonde de Sismondi (1773–1842) who was to develop further the methodological base of classical political economy. Prior to Marx, Sismondi upheld the need to employ the "historically determined abstractions" method. With this, he came to define capitalism as an economy whose aim was the production of exchange value, as opposed to the working of an economy whose aim was the production of use value (see USE-VALUE AND EXCHANGE-VALUE).

John Stuart Mill (1806–73) was the last of the classical economists, and in some respects a forerunner of neoclassicism. In his thesis on method, set down in *Essays on Some Unsettled Questions in Political Economy* in 1844, it was deduced that political economy was to limit itself to the analysis of the basic relations between economic variables and was to be supported by psychology, ethology and political science in order to deal with questions of economic development and distribution. In his *Principles of Political Economy* in 1848, Mill linked value to exchange and set forth a value theory based on the contributions of more than one production factor. Both Ricardian and neoclassical elements may be found in his theory of distribution.

## Karl Marx

Eighteenth-century political economy reached

its high point with the theory of Karl MARX (1818–83). Marx's interest in economic theory arose from his materialistic conception of history. In *A Contribution to the Critique of Political Economy* in 1859 and later in *Das Kapital*, Marx defined value as abstract labor time objectified in commodities. In his famous theory of exploitation, the labor power purchased by industrial capitalists was capable of producing a value higher than that of wage goods necessary for the reproduction of the labor power itself. From this, surplus labor and then surplus value was derived. Surplus value became profit in the case of its realization in the market.

According to the Marxian view of capitalism as a monetary sequence, the economic process could be represented by the circuit Money–Commodity–Money, where money quantitatively increases (M–C–M′) (see CIRCUIT OF SOCIAL CAPITAL). Marx built up a theory of the economic cycle in which he showed the inverse relation between the size of the RESERVE ARMY OF LABOR and the average wage per worker. He theorized the growing poverty of the proletariat and the tendency of the rate of profit to fall (along with its counter-tendencies). The debate between Marx's supporters and his critics has most frequently concentrated on the TRANSFORMATION PROBLEM (see MARXIST POLITICAL ECONOMY: HISTORY).

## Thorstein Veblen

The publication of the first volume of *Das Kapital* barely preceded the work of Jevons, Menger and Walras, who in the 1870s laid the theoretical foundations of the neoclassical revolution. However, the unqualified success of neoclassical economics came to an end at the beginning of the twentieth century, when a number of critiques emerged which concentrated less on the internal coherence of the arguments than on the neoclassical method of analysis. Thorstein Bunde VEBLEN (1857–1929), for instance, developed a critique based on what he perceived to be the neoclassical preoccupation with teleological preconceptions of natural rights and equilibrium

tendencies. He castigated neoclassicists for accepting the prevailing distribution of resources, ignoring the importance of INSTITUTIONS AND HABITS in economic organization, and for assuming that economic forces settle towards stability rather than often working in a cumulative upward and downward motion characteristic of business cycles. In place of equilibrium economics, Veblen placed the emphasis on the economic organization of business enterprises, the socio-historical forces affecting the production and distribution of the economic surplus, and the historical evolution of capitalism through time. Many of these themes have been pursued by modern political economists, especially members of the institutional school (see INSTITUTIONAL POLITICAL ECONOMY: HISTORY).

## Wicksell, Schumpeter and the monetary circuit

Other critical responses to neoclassical economics also emerged. For instance, a series of attempts to formulate macroeconomic models came into being, characterized by the endogeneous nature of the money supply and by a rejection of the marginal theory of distribution. The debate began with the publication of *Interest and Prices* in 1898 by Knut Wicksell (1851–1926). Criticizing the quantity theory of money, Wicksell developed a macroeconomic model of the MONETARY CIRCUIT with endogeneous money and wage fund. Wicksell's work gave birth to the Stockholm School of Myrdal, Lindhal, Ohlin and Lundberg. The work of Joseph SCHUMPETER (1883–1950) moved even further away from neoclassicism. In his *Theory of Economic Development* in 1911, Schumpeter elaborated a "dynamic" model in contrast to the "static" Walrasian model. He maintained that the capitalistic economy was, at the same time, intrinsically monetary and dynamic. According to Schumpeter, money created by banks was the means by which innovative entrepreneurs were able to create new avenues for economic activity. The Wicksellian model was also taken up by, among others, R.G. Hawtrey (1879–1975), D.H. Robertson

(1890–1963) and M. Fanno (1878–1965). This new interest in monetary theory also influenced Marxist economists, such as Rudolf Hilferding (1877–1941).

## John Maynard Keynes

However, the main exponent of this new approach was John Maynard KEYNES (1883–1946). Keynes affirmed the need to go beyond the neoclassical approach in favor of a MONETARY THEORY OF PRODUCTION. In *The General Theory* in 1936, Keynes aimed to show that the capitalistic economy could fall into a depression without any endogeneous equilibrating mechanism propelling full employment. He showed how depressions came into effect following a fall in investment demand, due to a decline in the EXPECTATIONS of profit. This brought with it an accumulation of cash reserves and caused involuntary unemployment. Keynes's analysis revolved around a criticism of Say's Law. Whereas in the neoclassical tradition, supply generated demand, Keynes showed that in a monetary economy, firms took production decisions on the basis of aggregate demand. If demand was low, then production and employment rates were low. It was possible to have a macroeconomic equilibrium with involuntary unemployment, even in the absence of any market friction. Keynes stressed the necessity of the expansive fiscal policy in order to increase production and employment.

The new approach of the monetary theory of production defined by Keynes was subject to a number of attacks by the supporters of the neoclassical theory. The debate came to a head in the 1930s with the confrontation between Keynes and Hayek and with the formulation of the neoclassical synthesis of the *General Theory*. This formulation was opposed by Keynes's most faithful pupils, such as Joan Robinson (1903–83), Nicholas Kaldor (1908–86) and R.F. Kahn (1905–89), according to whom the "neoclassical synthesis" generated a kind of "bastard Keynesianism." A formulation close to the true Keynesian line was developed by Michal KALECKI (1899–1970). The Keynesian notions of effective demand

and uncertainty provided the foundations for post-Keynesian political economy (see POST-KEYNESIAN POLITICAL ECONOMY: MAJOR CONTEMPORARY THEMES).

## Piero Sraffa

Besides the current of the monetary theory of production and the institutionalist school, political economy reached a highpoint with Piero SRAFFA's *Production of Commodities by Means of Commodities*, first published in 1960. The aim of the work was to find a method of simultaneously determining relative prices and the profit rate, overcoming in this way the problems linked to the LABOR THEORY OF VALUE, which first Ricardo, then Marx, had come up against. Sraffa (1898–1983) developed the concept of "standard commodity" as a unit of measure invariable to changes in production, and re-affirmed that profits and wages were inversely correlated. He held that, because of the internal inconsistency of the neoclassical theory of capital, the orthodox doctrine of distribution must be rejected. It is due to Sraffa that there has been a renewed interest in classical political economy, and in Ricardo in particular.

## Modern political economy

Many of the scholars discussed in this article have contributed (directly or indirectly) to the development of modern political economy, which experienced a resurgence in the late 1960s, 1970s and early 1980s. The long boom of capitalism in the 1950s and 1960s contributed to the development of new, more holistic visions of socioeconomics processes, especially as the system itself started to experience instability along with high rates of unemployment and inflation. Political economists developed theories of inflation, unemployment, cyclical instability and the contradictory functioning of capitalism.

An array of different schools of thought emerged or developed further, including feminists, environmentalists, neo-Marxists, post-Keynesians, institutionalists, Sraffians and social economists. Some of them have more affinity with the classical economists, especially Ricardo, others are more in tune with Sismondi, others with Marx, Veblen or Keynes, and still others with Schumpeter or Sraffa. Many of these schools have much in common, while others are more disparate. They have developed their own associations and journals, and a considerable degree of cross-fertilization is beginning to emerge.

## See also:

feminist political economy: major contemporary themes; humanistic economics; political economy: major contemporary themes; political economy: schools; Schumpeterian political economy; Sraffian political economy

## Selected references

Dobb, M. (1973) *Theories of Value and Distribution since Adam Smith*, London: Cambridge University Press.

Graziani, A. (1982) "L'analisi Marxista e la struttura del capitalismo moderno," in *Storia del Marxismo*, Torino: Einaudi, vol. IV, 701–41.

—— (1994) *La teoria monetaria della produzione*, Arezzo: Banca popolare dell'Etruria e del Lazio.

Heilbroner, Robert (1980) *The Worldly Philosphers: The Lives, Times and Ideas of the Great Economic Thinkers*, 5th edn, New York: Simon & Schuster.

Hunt, E.K. (1992) *History of Economic Thought: A Critical Perspective*, 2nd edn, New York: HarperCollins.

Marx, K. (1963) *Theories of Surplus Value*, Moscow: Progress Publishers.

Napoleoni, C. (1970) *Smith, Ricardo, Marx*, Torino: Boringhieri.

—— (1976) *Valore*, Milano: Isedi.

Schumpeter, J.A. (1954) *History of Economic Analysis*, New York: Oxford University Press.

Zagari, E. (1991) *Storia dell'economia politica*, Torino: Giappichelli.

RICCARDO REALFONZO

**POLITICAL ECONOMY, ISLAMIC:** *see* Islamic political economy

**POLITICAL ECONOMY, JAPANESE:** *see* Japanese political economy

# political economy: major contemporary themes

The revival of interest in political economy, which began in the 1960s and continues into the present, recreated an array of interesting themes. A close study of the JOURNALS OF POLITICAL ECONOMY reveals both the commonality and heterogeneity of the themes. Five important themes are discussed here as good examples of debates that are ongoing in political economy: (1) a relatively common methodological outlook; (2) an analysis of phases of capitalist evolution; (3) a sociopolitical study of economic roles and contradictions; (4) an economic surplus and effective demand theory of growth, distribution and reproduction; and (5) a policy framework incorporating the "disembedded economy" and positive initiatives.

## A common methodology

The major schools of thought have begun to display a relatively common view of how to study political economy, although some differences remain. The basic method of political economy is orientated around the importance of historical time, institutions, instability and change, open systems, and endogenous explanations. Political economy seeks to be realistic, incorporating in its concepts a study of the economy operating through historical time. Historical analysis reveals that that there are trends and patterns within the economy which implies the operation of economic systems, such as SLAVERY, FEUDALISM and CAPITALISM. The main features of particular economic systems change over time and, therefore, the question of phases of metamorphosis arise. These different phases, such as "competitive," "monopoly" and "transnational" capitalism, influence the basic parameters of the economy and, therefore, need to be incorporated in the analysis.

Many of the changes that occur relate to the basic institutions: those social habits, norms and operational structures which condition how people think and behave in corporations, families, governments and the world economy. Political economists are concerned with how the institutions operate and change, how to theorize their structure and evolution, and what policies and political strategies to recommend or activate. Some political economists concentrate on the individual institutions (keeping in mind the linkages to the whole), while others specialize in analyzing the system. Major advances of knowledge have occurred at both of these levels.

Political economists try to understand the endogenous forces generating change. They attempt to model the changes, rather than assuming change to be determined exogenously "from without" (not explained). In order to do this, they incorporate an open-systems inquiry, one which looks at the interplay of many sub-systems – economic, social, political, environmental – and the coefficients of interaction between them. It is a broad, interdisciplinary field of inquiry. This is true since all economic problems, such as UNEMPLOYMENT AND UN-DEREMPLOYMENT, inflation, industrial fluctuations, underdevelopment, poverty and POLLUTION, are the result of forces which interact with all the sub-systems in the model.

However, political economy is not a deterministic study. DETERMINISM (in this context) is the view that causality is a relatively simple phenomenon, and that all factors can or should be explained and predicted with the precision of chemistry and physics. Hence, although endogenous explanation is the aim of most political economists, quite often the values of the variables and the manner of interaction cannot be specified precisely. The impact of many factors is often more qualitative than quantitative. In such cases, pattern models, storytelling, case studies, description,

and theoretical illustrations must replace precise empirical determination.

Historical analysis reveals that institutional parameters change, and that such change can be slow, moderate or radical, depending on circumstances. However, the basic fact of change, or dynamics, is critical to political economists. Of particular importance is the influence of change on human society, especially in relation to cycles and waves, QUALITY OF LIFE and development. Political economists see themselves as being in the service of humanity, especially concerned with the plight of the common person, or society as a whole. Hence, they recognize that change associated with recessions, labor-saving technology, insufficient demand, de-industrialization and industrial concentration – characteristics endemic to modern capitalism – may leave masses of people without (meaningful) employment. The problem of unemployment, therefore, constitutes a critical area of analysis.

## Phases of capitalist evolution

Modern political economists examine this theme of EVOLUTION AND COEVOLUTION in different contexts: phases of capitalist development and transformation, ENTROPY, NEGEN-TROPY AND THE LAWS OF THERMODYNAMICS, case studies of the labor process, technology, the corporation, the financial system, the world economy, the family and so on over time and changes in the cultural fabric of customs, institutions, conventions and morals. For instance, political economists recognize that in the early phases of Western capitalism, market structures were more competitive. The period from the early 1800s through to the 1870s is often called "competitive capitalism," being characterized by relatively small businesses and industries with few barriers to entry. This posed no major anomaly for capitalism as a whole until large-scale industry developed around the 1870s. The advent of large capital structures (machinery and factories) created difficulties, as there was a considerable expansion of output and labor productivity, without a commensurate increase in demand (but still with a moderately high level of competition). This promoted the periodic tendency towards overproduction, and the structural difficulties of the 1870s–1890s, when downswings were deeper than usual.

The merger movement, expansion of oligopolies, credit creation and the renewed era of imperialistic expansion in the late 1890s and early 1900s helped to solve the problem of low profitability for many advanced capitalist economies. This phase of "corporate capitalism," "imperialism," or "finance capital" was a boost to growth for a time. Two main problems remained, however: first, as before, a lack of demand on the part of workers; and secondly, the tendency for overspeculation and the domination of industry by financial considerations (business). These problems manifested themselves during the GREAT DEPRESSION of the 1930s and the associated FINANCIAL CRISES.

Many of the problems of insufficient demand and overspeculation were resolved through the Second World War and postwar institutional innovations associated with Fordism, the welfare and regulatory state and the recreation of HEGEMONY IN THE WORLD ECONOMY. Fordism provided high levels of productivity along with higher wages. The Keynesian WELFARE STATE helped to stabilize capitalism. Together, they solved the problem of effective demand for a time. US hegemony sought to stabilize the international economy through the making of agreements and leadership. The "age of the transnational corporation" was in motion, with large international companies dominating the world and national economies.

The greatest golden age of capitalist development occurred during the 1950s–1960s. However, this came to an end as the institutional innovations of the 1950s and 1960s developed CONTRADICTIONS and failed to propel sustained ECONOMIC GROWTH into the 1970s–1990s, when deep recessions prevailed. A new phase of capitalism may be developing in the late 1990s and into the twenty-first century, perhaps characterized by internationalization, privatization and the spread of the "flexible system of production." However, at present this has not on balance propelled sustained growth in most Western economies or in Africa, although much of Asia has been undergoing considerable expansion (often with a very active state apparatus and, recently, financial instability).

These changes from competitive capitalism to corporate capitalism to transnational capitalism and beyond are important processes which affect the nature of political economy (both as subject matter and theory). Political economy modifies its theory on the basis of an empirical examination of such changes, and such changes have implications for the workings of the dominant institutions of production, the financial system, the state, the family and the world economy. In addition, political economy has developed general concepts of change which are subject to continual reexamination and modification (see INSTITUTIONAL CHANGE AND ADJUSTMENT).

## Economic roles and contradictions

Political economists seek to understand the social-political foundations of the economy, and to situate problems within the framework of real agents and situations. They are dialectical in the sense of seeking a HOLISTIC METHOD, and also of attempting to comprehend the contradictions and opposing forces which impact upon economic processes. This social realism manifests itself in the concern for analyzing class, gender and ethnicity/race.

"Class" is a category which can be used for examining the main players in the economy according to their relationship to the production of surplus value or the means of production. For instance, under capitalism the main classes are workers and capitalists (or their functionaries). They are defined, according to one theory, according to whether they produce necessary and surplus labor (workers) or whether they reap the benefits of controlling the production and distribution of surplus labor (capitalists). Workers need to sell their labor power in return for wages because they lack alternative sources of income, while capitalists control the means of production and hence gain industrial profit as a return for such control.

There are, of course, other roles in the economy that may be termed a (subsidiary) class. For instance, consider the role of salary earners, such as teachers, corporate managers, state bureaucrats and other professionals. They tend to receive a part of the surplus value. Small business operators may both work (thus receiving the equivalent of a wage) and manage (also receiving surplus value). Other recipients of the surplus value include financiers and bankers (interest) and rentiers and entrepreneurs (rent) (see SURPLUS VALUE AS RENT, INTEREST AND PROFIT). Some of the taxes emanate from wages rather than surplus value.

The fundamental class contradiction emanates from the institutionalized conflict between workers and capitalists. The history of capitalism reveals a continual struggle between capital and labor over the distribution of income between wages and profits, workplace conditions, control of production and so on. This conflict is a major factor affecting inflation, unemployment, business cycles, economic growth and poverty. Political economists have espoused various means to moderate or counter this conflict, from incomes policies to various accords, worker cooperatives and worker control.

Two other roles of special significance to the economy are "gender" and "ethnicity/race." GENDER is related to the social construction of roles according to whether the agents are female or male. Ethnicity is related to cultural and historical differences between people, often emanating from particular regional variations. Race, however, does not exist as an objective phenomenon in the sense that, genetically, there are no significant differences between the ethnic peoples of the world. Race is therefore primarily subjective or superficial, based mainly on skin color or facial characteristics.

Gender and ethnicity/race are central to modern political economy. Together with class they provide the basis for the major roles that influence the distribution of income, quality of life and position of workers in the segmented labor market. For instance, the GENDER DIVISION OF LABOR predicates that women tend to do most of the household labor, including child care, while men tend to contribute only at the margins. Women thus produce most of the household output, without being much remunerated financially for these activities. This is important, since the asymmetric distribution of HOUSEHOLD LABOR differentially affects the ability of men and women to gain wages in the paid workplace. When women return to the waged workforce after bringing up children, it is often assumed that their HUMAN CAPITAL is low and hence that their income should be commensurately low. Men do not usually have this problem. For this and other reasons, men have received a far greater proportion of primary tier jobs than women under modern capitalism.

One's ethnicity has a major influence on the position one occupies in the labor market. Ethnicity predicates certain cultural traits and propensities, which influences one's choice of employment and also the ability to gain access to education and training. The color of one's skin or facial characteristics ("race") influence the perception of others as to the potential for work. For instance, people of a certain ethnicity and/or skin color may be stereotyped as being of inferior skill or workmanship, and this may affect many people from this group. Such behavior or discrimination affects the income of this group, which may be combined with an unsupportive environment for employment, which affects the attainment of skills and education, which in turn affects PRODUCTIVITY, and so on *ad infinitum* (as Gunnar Myrdal showed).

A major challenge to political economy is to develop an empirical analysis and theory which adequately incorporates class, gender and ethnicity/race (see Dugger 1996). Much progress along these lines has been made, but this process is ongoing.

## Economic surplus and effective demand theory

At the higher reaches of theory, various trends

in political economy have sought to integrate an analysis of the ECONOMIC SURPLUS with the theory of EFFECTIVE DEMAND AND CAPACITY UTILIZATION. This "surplus and effective demand theory" is related to the determination of economic growth, the distribution of income and the reproduction of capital.

The economic surplus is net national income minus the "essential consumption" requirements of the population. Under the influence of modern technology and increasing returns to scale, with the trend towards oligopoly industries, conditions are ripe for a large economic surplus over costs to be produced. As firms successfully innovate, the economic surplus transfers to them, and potential competitors must follow the leader, engage in non-price competition, change sectors or go out of business. Downward sloping supply curves for the high-technology producers lead to lower costs as output increases. An increase in demand and the search for markets leads to a greater surplus being distributed to the leading sectors.

However, a potential barrier to expansion is demand, especially if it is constrained by policy or corporate design. Historically, a combination of (a) expansion into new territories and markets, (b) continual innovation and reorganization, (c) advertising to enhance wants and demand, (d) efficiency salaries for upper segment workers, (e) state sector employment and (f) warfare and welfare, have periodically resolved the difficulties involved in realizing the surplus.

Given the political and economic trends of capitalism during the 1980s and 1990s, however, most of the emphasis in realizing the surplus is being given to expansion, innovation, advertising and high corporate salaries. Far less importance is being placed on state employment, welfare and higher wages. Demand constraining policies (along with labor shedding technology) are, however, resulting in an underclass of people with marginal attachment to the labor market and with few prospects for the future.

The Kaldorian, post-Keynesian perspective argues that the medium to long-term growth rate of production, and thus the economic surplus, is fundamentally affected by the growth rate of aggregate demand, both domestic and international (exports) in a CIRCULAR AND CUMULATIVE CAUSATION fashion. Productivity growth and economic surplus in turn is influenced by the growth of production, in particular due to dynamic increasing returns to scale, which includes endogenous learning and hence technical change (see VERDOORN'S LAW). The various sides of the cumulative model are interrelated, as shown in Figure 9.

Here, an expansion of output can arise from internal demand, external demand and innovation. First, an expansion of consumption or government spending (internal demand) leads to an increase in aggregate demand, which positively influences investment, and hence productivity, through dynamic returns to scale, and therefore exports, which increases demand,

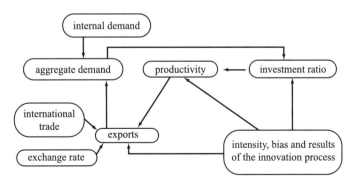

*Figure 10* Circular and cumulative growth (Pini 1995: 90)

and so on in a circular fashion. Second, a similar process results from an expansion of world income (external demand). Third, an expansion of innovation represents an increase in investment, which enhances productivity (directly and indirectly), thus leading to greater exports. The cumulative circle continues through several runs.

The growth rate of demand is thus propelled by the rate of productivity growth, and the rate of production is enhanced by greater effective demand. As a consequence:

> Sustained growth gives rise to effects which stimulate its own progress, thus setting off a virtuous circle of growth based on dynamic returns to scale. At the same time, low growth inhibits growth itself, setting off in this case a vicious circle of decline which progressively slows growth both in demand and in productivity.
>
> (Pini 1995: 187)

Hence, waves of high and low growth of GDP and economic surplus have been historically inherent in the long-term motion of modern capitalism. Current policies and structures, to the extent that they underplay demand, inhibit innovation or lead to industrial maturity, are adversely affecting economic performance.

## Critique and policy appraisal

Political economists tend not to adhere to Say's Law or Walras's Law, or believe in the full employment tendencies of modern capitalism. Hence they are reluctant to rely purely on a "level playing field" and monetary policy to provide the conditions whereby lower interest rates are supposedly able to enhance long-term confidence and investment. They see the need for positive initiatives to promote jobs and investment. These initiatives include, for instance, job creation schemes and fiscal stimulation for social capital, infrastructure and technological expansion.

Many political economists see a critical contradiction of modern capitalism to be the DISEMBEDDED ECONOMY. That is, purely market relations have a tendency to operate with

insufficient resources being directed to social safety nets, such as lender of last resort facilities, unemployment benefits, pensions, HEALTH AND SAFETY IN THE WORKPLACE legislation, discretionary FISCAL POLICY, environmental protection, child care, and various accords to moderate the conflict between capital and labor (see Stanfield 1995). Therefore, historically, political economists have been active in recommending the introduction of social safety nets and accords to reduce the degree of instability and UNCERTAINTY inherent in capitalist processes.

These public initiatives and safety nets are a form of social and organizational capital. Modern political economists tend to argue for a broad and heterogeneous perspective of capital, including durable social, organizational, institutional, human, technological, physical and NATURAL CAPITAL. The capital controlled by business needs to be balanced by social, technological and natural capital to protect the surrounding socio-ecological environment and structures of demand and innovation, especially during times of evolutionary stresses and strains (see CAPITAL AND THE WEALTH OF NATIONS).

The closer to the model of pure market capitalism the system becomes, the more lacking would be the protective balance (social capital), which potentially propels greater instability, uncertainty and fragmentation and hence problematical long-term economic performance. Researchers, however, recognize that state policies may overproduce safety nets and initiatives (for example, during the early and mid-1970s) from the view of the general interests of capitalism; and that major structural change is necessary before safety nets are institutionally engrained in the fabric of alternative liberal capitalist, social democratic, socialist or anarchist systems.

Political economists have shown great interest in the introduction of institutional innovations to promote a reconciliation or dissolution of the conflict between capital and labor. This has involved a redistribution or reorientation of ECONOMIC POWER. Incomes policies and accords are examples which may be successful for a time. INDUSTRY POLICY may help to develop technology and innovation necessary for international expansion. More PARTICIPA-TORY DEMOCRACY AND SELF-MANAGEMENT in the workplace and the other major spheres may have positive long-term benefits. For instance, the MONDRAGÓN experiment illustrates that participatory democracy (with suitable warranted knowledge and money capital) can enhance productivity, reduce ALIENATION, and question the foundations of EXPLOITATION simultaneously.

## Conclusion

All in all, modern political economy is a vast terrain of research and analysis into economic systems evolving through historical time. The approaches and perspectives are realistic, and suitable for critical analysis and policy making. Political economy is broad enough to be relevant to studying most social and economic problems, because it is interdisciplinary, evolutionary and subject to modification on the basis of reexamination. New research hypotheses are being generated in widely diverse fields. The five themes discussed here are examples of some of the contemporary concerns of political economy.

## See also:

capital theory debates; critical realism; evolutionary economics: major contemporary themes; feminist political economy: major contemporary themes; foundationalism and anti-foundationalism; institutional political economy: major contemporary themes; political economy; political economy: history; political economy: schools; post-Keynesian political economy: major contemporary themes; Schumpeterian political economy; social political economy: major contemporary themes; Sraffian political economy; surplus approach to political economy

## Selected references

Amott, Teresa L. and Matthaei, Julie A. (1991) *Race, Gender, and Work*, Boston: South End Press.

Arestis, Philip and Sawyer, Malcolm (eds) (1994) *Elgar Companion to Radical Political Economy*, Aldershot: Edward Elgar.

Dugger, William M. (ed.) (1996) *Inequality: Radical Institutionalist Views on Race, Gender, Class and Nation*, Westport, CT: Greenwood Press.

England, Richard W. (ed.) (1994) *Evolutionary Concepts in Contemporary Economics*, Ann Arbor, MI: University of Michigan Press.

Ferber, Marianne A. and Nelson, Julie (eds) (1993) *Beyond Economic Man: Feminist Theory and Economics*, Chicago and London: University of Chicago Press.

Hodgson, Geoffrey, Samuels, Warren and Tool, Marc (1995) *Elgar Companion to Institutional and Evolutionary Economics*, 2 vols, Aldershot: Edward Elgar.

Lavoie, Marc (1992) *Foundations of Post-Keynesian Economics*, Aldershot: Edward Elgar.

Norgaard, Richard B. (1994) *Development Betrayed: The End of Progress and a Coevolutionary Revisioning of the Future*, London and New York: Routledge.

Pini, Paoli (1995) "Economic Growth, Technological Change and Employment: Empirical Evidence for a Cumulative Growth Model with External Causation for Nine OECD Countries: 1960–1990," *Structural Change and Economic Dynamics* 6: 185–213.

Resnick, Stephen and Wolff, Richard (1987) *Knowledge and Class: A Marxian Critique of Political Economy*, Chicago: University of Chicago Press.

Sherman, Howard (1995) *Reinventing Marxism*, Baltimore, MD: Johns Hopkins University Press.

Shionoya, Yuichi and Perlman, Mark (1994) *Innovation in Technology, Industries, and Institutions: Studies in Schumpeterian Perspectives*, Ann Arbor, MI: University of Michigan Press.

Smelser, Neil J. and Swedborg, Richard (eds) (1994) *The Handbook of Economic Sociology*, Princeton, NJ: Princeton University Press.

Stanfield, James Ronald (1995) *Economics, Power and Culture: Essays in the Development* of *Radical Institutionalism*, New York: St Martin's Press.

PHILLIP ANTHONY O'HARA

# political economy: schools

## Introduction

Political economy, as distinct from "economics" which typically denotes NEOCLASSICAL ECONOMICS, takes a broad approach to the study of economy and society. It is characterized by the inclusion of historical and social context as part of the fundamental factors which shape and create economic activity. This contrasts with the neoclassical reliance on individualistic explanations and their progressive elimination of historical and social explanatory factors (Clark 1992). By adopting a broader perspective, political economy opens the door to a multitude of theories and approaches to explaining economic phenomena.

Economists working in the political economy tradition are often organized in schools of thought. Why there are multiple schools of thought in an intellectual discipline is a problem for the sociology of knowledge, and is well beyond the limited scope of this entry. However, it is helpful to note some common characteristics of the formation and persistence of particular schools. Most often a school of thought can be traced to the intellectual work of a single individual, even though that person frequently has nothing to do with the actual establishment of the school. What this singular individual does provide is a "vision," to use Schumpeter's term, by which the economy and society can be viewed and understood. This vision is adopted by a number of scholars who then start asking similar questions, use similar methods of investigation to arrive at the answers to these questions, and, not surprisingly, arrive at similar answers to these questions. These answers take the form of theories, which for the most part are in conformity, or are interpreted as being in conformity, with the

original work of the "visionary" who inspired their efforts.

The schools of thought considered in this entry are:

- Marxist political economy (MPE);
- Institutional political economy (IPE);
- Schumpeterian political economy (SCHPE);
- Post-Keynesian political economy (PKPE);
- Sraffian political economy (SRPE);
- Social political economy (SPE); and
- Feminist political economy (FPE).

These schools can be distinguished by their respective theories, and by their institutional or organizational affiliations. We will first briefly describe the essential elements of each school's view of the economy, and then examine the various linkages between the different schools.

## Marxist political economy

The oldest school in the political economy tradition is Marxist political economy. Karl MARX provided an alternative "vision" of economy and society, one which emphasized historical and social factors, and which attacked the "harmony of interests" view which pervaded classical economic analysis, in favor of a CLASS analysis. The essential ideas of Marxist political economy are threefold. The first main idea is historical materialism, the idea that economic relations are a fundamental force in history. Closely related to this is the DIALECTICAL METHOD. The second main idea is the LABOR THEORY OF VALUE. This is interpreted either as long run equilibrium prices being determined by their labor content, or (more correctly) that the social process by which surplus value is generated is the driving force in the economy. The third main idea is that a capitalist economy is riddled with numerous CONTRADICTIONS, making smooth economic development over time highly unlikely.

The formation of the UNION FOR RADICAL POLITICAL ECONOMICS (URPE) in 1968 established an organization which had as its primary goal the development of Marxian economics, although the URPE is also open to non-

Marxist radicals. The URPE sponsors the *Review of Radical Political Economy*. In Britain, the Conference of Socialist Economists performs a similar function, as do organizations in many other nations.

## Institutional political economy

Thorstein VEBLEN developed the original vision upon which institutional political economy (see INSTITUTIONAL POLITICAL ECONOMY: HISTORY) is based. Veblen saw that the key to understanding economic behavior was the understanding of the INSTITUTIONS AND HABITS which generated social behavior, and the evolutionary process by which these institutions are created. Veblen stressed the evolutionary process of INSTITUTIONAL CHANGE AND ADJUSTMENT as the most important aspect of economy and society. He rejected the idea of the existence of a "natural order" in the economy and society, emphasizing the fact that institutions are human creations. Furthermore, Veblen noted the inherent contradiction between business activities, which promote pecuniary gain, and industrial activities, which increase social output. This Veblenian dichotomy is an important cornerstone of institutional political economy (see COLLECTIVE SOCIAL WEALTH).

Even though many of the most important economists of the 1950s and 1960s were clearly working within the institutionalist tradition, with John Kenneth Galbraith and Gunnar Myrdal being the two best examples, the economics profession increasingly emphasized technique over substance. To combat the increasingly narrow perspective of the American Economic Association and of the leading mainstream economic journals, the Association for Evolutionary Economics (AFEE; see ASSOCIATION FOR EVOLUTIONARY ECONOMICS AND ASSOCIATION FOR INSTITUTIONALIST THOUGHT) was formed in 1965, with the *Journal of Economic Issues* following two years later. Since then, two other organizations committed to institutional/evolutionary economics have been formed: the Association for Institutionalist Thought (AFIT) and the EUR-OPEAN ASSOCIATION FOR EVOLUTIONARY POLITICAL ECONOMY (EAEPE).

## Schumpeterian political economy

Joseph SCHUMPTER (1883–1950) provided the "vision" upon which SCHUMPTERIAN POLITICAL ECONOMY is based. He was concerned to incorporate dynamics into economics, especially the dynamics of innovation, development and business cycles. The successful introduction of "something different" into economic life, according to Schumpeter, provides the foundation for "surplus value" (his words). This "something different" may be a new good, a new production process, a new market, a new source of raw materials and a new organizational structure. In reaping surplus value the innovations attract new entrants into the market and the surplus value may be spread more thinly to these firms, depending on the degree of monopoly. Innovations, within the framework of a credit-based capitalist economy, provide the foundation for the major business cycles and long waves which impact on the world. (See LONG WAVES OF ECONOMIC GROWTH AND DEVELOPMENT.)

Schumpeter's work on dynamics and market structure was eclipsed by the Keynesian revolution in the 1940s–1960s, and it wasn't until the onset of the most recent long wave downswing (which commenced in the 1970s and is still ongoing) that Schumpeterian themes began to seriously impact on theory and policy. Since then it has developed to great heights with a large following worldwide and an expanding research program. It is well recognized to have a good deal of relevance in a world of industrial and institutional change and metamorphosis. Examples of scholars who have extended the boundaries of Schumpeterian-evolutionary themes include G. Mensch, Chris Freeman, Nathan Rosenberg, Mark Perlman and W.B. Arthur. There is now an International Joseph Schumpeter Society and a *Journal of Evolutionary Economics* along with an innumerable number of books and articles being published on these themes.

## Post-Keynesian political economy

Post-Keynesian political economy has fewer of the characteristics of a school of thought than MPE, IPE and SCHPE (see POST-KEYNESIAN POLITICAL ECONOMY: HISTORY). In fact, it is often noted that post-Keynesians are defined more by what they are not than by what they are (Lawson 1994). Although post-Keynesians derived their name from John Maynard KEYNES, it is really from the interpretation given to Keynes's work by Joan Robinson and Nicholas Kaldor, as well as the independent work of Michal KALECKI, that we get the origins of post-Keynesian political ecomomy. It was as a reaction to the "bastardization" of Keynes (the grand neoclassical synthesis) as Joan Robinson often called it, that the post-Keynesians started to search for alternatives to neoclassical general equilibrium. Part of this dissatisfaction centered on the neoclassical theory of value, and the work to replace this theory led to Sraffian political economy. Post-Keynesians began to emphasize exactly what the neoclassicals left out: the existence of UNCERTAINTY, the problems caused by the concept of equilibrium, the importance of the institutional structure, particularly of the financial system, and the dominance of imperfect competition. Lavoie (1992) has attempted to synthesize the various aspects of post-Keynsian political economy and some other trends of heterodoxy (including Sraffian political economy) into a post-classical research project.

## Sraffian political economy

SRAFFIAN POLITICAL ECONOMY is also linked to a reaction to the grand neoclassical synthesis. Although Piero SRAFFA's book, *Production of Commodities by Means of Commodities*, is subtitled "A Prelude to a Critique of Economic Theory," followers of Sraffa quickly saw it as the basis of an alternative theory of value, one they hoped could be made consistent with Keynes's theory of effective demand (see Eatwell and Milgate 1984). Sraffa's analysis was seen as a rehabilitation of CLASSICAL POLITICAL ECONOMY and the SURPLUS APPROACH TO POLITICAL ECONOMY.

## Social political economy

As a school of political economy, social political economy is more diverse than any other. It lacks the "visionary" theorist to act as a center of gravity and inspiration, a coherent set of agreed upon theories or dogmas, and a monopolistic methodological outlook. Social economics has its roots in the Catholic Economic Association (CEA), the forerunner to the Association for Social Economics. The CEA, to a certain extent, fits closer our model of a school of thought than does modern social political economy. Today, social political economy includes a diverse collection of almost every branch of economic thought. Evidence of the diversity in social political economy is seen in the existence of many social economics associations (see SOCIAL ECONOMICS: ORGANIZATIONS).

What social economists share is the belief that the individual cannot be separated, even theoretically, from the COMMUNITY, and that all economics is necessarily normative. Thus the discussion of values must be open and at the beginning of any economic inquiry and not tacked on at the end of the discussion.

They see 'economic' phenomena as being heavily imbued with social, political and environmental forces which impinge on production, distribution and exchange.

## Feminist political economy

Perhaps the youngest school, if indeed it can yet be called a "school", of feminist political economy began to emerge out of the most recent feminist and political economy movements of the 1960s and 1970s (although of course it has older antecedents, such as the work of Charlotte Perkins GILMAN (1860–1935) and others). Notable in this respect was an ongoing dialogue with Marxists and socialists. A branch of FPE also emerged from the trend within neoclassical economics to expand its theory of production and choice to marriage, the household and social issues. More recently, institutionalists have enhanced the field of FPE. By the early 1990s the time was ripe for the creation of an official association and journal: the INTERNATIONAL ASSOCIATION FOR FEMINIST ECONOMICS (IAFFE) and *Feminist Economics..*

Feminists seem to have a threefold agenda in political economy. First, they seek to transform existing theories in order to accommodate questions of GENDER, inequality between the sexes, and the gender-blind nature of orthodoxy and much of political economy. Probably on this point both neoclassical and radical feminists would be in agreement; that economics/political economy should be free from androcentric bias and recognize the critical importance of gender relations in all the institutions. Radical feminists would go further by examining, second, the nature of and relationship between all the major "structures of collective constraint and conditioning": gender, race/ethnicity, class, nation and age. There is said to be no homogeneous agent in political economy, and hence theory should incorporate some semblance of the diversity and multidimensionality that exist in the real world. And third, radicals seek to comprehend the nature of socioeconomic reproduction as a whole: in the household, the labor market, and for society as a whole. Ultimately, political economy is seen as an interdisciplinary study of how the economy is necessarily embedded in a social and political fabric, the nature of which needs to be scrutinized and incorporated in theory. (See REPRODUCTION PARADIGM and FEMINIST POLITICAL ECONOMY: PARADIGMS.)

## Realism

One of the most common complaints made by all of the above schools is the lack of realism in neoclassical economic theory. This complaint is common to all those pursuing the political economy agenda, although there are often different emphases. MPE and SRPE feel that the lack of realism comes from neoclassical economic theory's emphasis on the "abstract-universal", concretely undefinable and unmeasurable phenomena of utility. The lack of realism here is the lack of attention given to historically specific and socioeconomic forces. Social political economy objects to abstracting away social concerns, such as value judgments and ethics. It emphasizes that these factors play a fundamental role in shaping economic activity. FPE argues this point more specifically, focusing on concerns with gender inequality and the influence of activities in the household on economic outcomes. PKPE objects to the unrealism with regard to the assumption of perfect competition and the treatment of money as neutral or exogenous. IPE agrees with many of these objections, but adds that the unrealism in neoclassical economic theory shields those with ECONOMIC POWER under the cover of the myths of consumer sovereignty and impersonal market forces. (See PRODUCER AND CONSUMER SOVEREIGNTY.)

Most schools of political economy tend to eschew the notion of "rational economic man" in favor of a method which recognizes the diversity of social groups and the realistic influence of institutions, habits, rules and routines (see RATIONALITY AND IRRATIONALITY). Economic agents are fundamentally influenced by the environment in which they operate and the relationships surrounding them. Whether they emphasize the relationship between capitalists and workers, men or women, production and reproduction, or entrepreneurial versus mainstream firms, the schools seek to isolate the social groups and forces which are central to the motion of the *system*. Increasingly, the schools are recognizing the multifarious nature of diversity and power, whether based on class, gender, race, or nation, or whether corporate in form. However, the analysis is to some degree indeterminate since the influence of family upbringing, schooling, the media, peer pressure and friendship is conditioned by novelty, imagination, specific goals and new ideas.

## Change and evolution

Another major issue which unites the various

schools of political economy (including influential trends in feminist and Schumpeterian political economy) is their concern to develop a dynamic and historically embedded (critical) analysis of capitalism. All the schools of thought seek to situate the economy in historical time, examining the evolution of various institutions and social groups, and centering on various factors which propel change or problems with the disruptive nature of change. They recognize the importance of history, TIME, and evolution. Hence their increasing interest in concepts which incorporate these phenomena, such as the notions of hysteresis, path dependency, increasing returns to scale, circular and cumulative causation, and chaotic dynamics. This follows from their concern to comprehend the complex processes associated with long-term growth and accumulation, technological and institutional change, and the nature of evolution within firms, households, the state, the world economy and the system as a whole.

While the schools are interested in these dynamic forces, some of them often emphasize the problematical nature of change, interested as they are in the social fabric underlying economic processes. While neo-Schumpeterians tend to be interested in various contradictions of capitalism, they *often* center on the nature of the technological or corporate changes rather than the social foundations which may deteriorate under the force of change. Institutionalists, social economists, feminists, Marxists, and some post-Keynesians, on the other hand, provide a critique of the destructive nature of change under modern capitalism. Whether it be the nature of unemployment, poverty, the de-industrialization of certain nations, or the destruction of culture, the concern here is also with how the dynamics adversely affect the common person, or minority groups or the environment.

## Normative economics and power

IPE and SPE have been most outspoken in attacking the neoclassical claim of a dichotomy between POSITIVE AND NORMATIVE ECONOMICS.

Following the work of Gunnar Myrdal, they have argued that all economic analysis, at all levels, is necessarily normative and that "positive" economics is just a smoke-screen economists use to hide their own political and ideological views. As Myrdal recognized, all observation must first start off with a point of view, and it is here that value judgments and philosophical preconceptions enter economic theory. Often these judgments are so deeply buried in the logic of the theory that the theorists and practitioners are unaware of their importance and lasting influence. Many of the assumptions relate to the desirable structure and form of power and authority in society.

One of the greatest weaknesses of neoclassical economic theory is its treatment (or lack of explicit treatment) of the phenomena of power. The doctrine of the "invisible hand," leading individual self-interested behavior to a socially optimum equilibrium, is the greatest of all enabling myths. All economists working in the political economy tradition have recognized that the economy is a system of power and control, far from the world of perfect competition and harmony of interests. At the very least, the unrealism of the perfect competition assumption is recognized, as is the reality of large corporations and other institutions and groups with significant economic power. This has implications for pricing, output, the distribution of income and long-term growth.

But most heterodox economists go beyond this. The existence of the economy as a system of power is more than the recognition of elements of monopoly power. It is a recognition that the market is an instituted process whose purpose is to yield power and control. The process of instituting a market includes: vesting the participants with collective powers; allocating costs; and exercising sovereignty (Dugger 1989). All of these are discretionary activities. The most important aspect of the economy as a system of control, noted first by Veblen, but hinted at by Marx and others, is the role of socialization, subservience, and acquiescence of the lower classes to the wishes of the elites (see HEGEMONY). These processes and activities are institutionalized today in the control of the mass media, educational systems and governments by large corporate interests, as well as the extensive interlocks between corporations (see CORPORATE HEGEMONY).

## Institutional linkages

Many economists working in the political economy tradition belong to more than one heterodox organization, and it is quite common for an individual scholar to publish in many of the journals affiliated with the different schools as well as in the non-affiliated heterodox journals (see JOURNALS OF POLITICAL ECONOMY). Moreover, there is often a significant overlap in the leadership positions in these organizations.

RADICAL INSTITUTIONALISM, a subset of institutional political economy, seeks to go back to the radical insights of Veblen, combining traditional institutional economics with aspects of MPE. It is, in fact, natural for institutionalists to find much common ground with Marxists, given that so much of Veblen's work was influenced and informed by Marx's writings.

Feminists have incorporated women's experiences into the study of the economy, contributing to empirical research in various schools of thought. Feminist political economists have also influenced theoretical developments in several schools, most notably Marxism and institutionalism. For example, the DOMESTIC LABOUR DEBATE of the 1970s contributed to more serious considerations of the role of social reproduction. Also, *feminist* radical *institutionalists* have emphasized the parallel methodological approaches of both schools.

Many seem to agree that institutionalists provide a general theoretical and methodological foundation to political economy, while post-Keynesians in many respects attempt to detail, empirically examine and add specificity to this analysis. Institutionalists also have a lot in common with Schumpeterians, in particular that they are both evolutionary and attempt to comprehend the nature of change, both in-stitutional and technological. Again, institutionalists tend to favor the general dimensions of analysis, including culture, while the Schumpeterians add specificity and rigor, perhaps placing more emphasis on the theory of the firm and technology more narrowly defined.

There are also many links between neo-Marxists and post-Keynesians. Michel Kalecki provides a good bridge between the two schools through the emphasis being placed on the demand-generated nature of profit (a Keynesian theme) and a class-defined analysis of distribution and accumulation (a Marxian theme). The Monthly Review School of Marxism (initiated by Paul Sweezy and Paul Baran) has a strong Keynesian flavor through the emphasis placed not simply on the production (supply) but also the realization (demand) of the ECONOMIC SURPLUS.

A critical theme which appears to permeate practically every school (post-Keynesian, neo-Marxist, institutionalist, Schumpeterian) is the notion of endogenous money and financial instability. In other words, money and credit growth is generated by business cycle upswings (economic activity), which often leads to financial instability as the credit boom over-extends the economy. Firms expand on the basis of unrealistic optimism and speculative activity begins to dominate industry. This eventually leads to a crash as costs rise and debt has to be repaid in an environment of low cash flow and prospective yield and pessimistic expectations of the future. (See ENDOGENOUS MONEY and FINANICAL INSTABILITY HYPOTHESIS.)

## Equilibrium or non-equilibrium analysis

The concept of equilibrium has long been "a central organizing idea" in economics, often giving the discipline credit for being a science (Clark 1987–8, 1992: ch. 7). It is through the concept of equilibrium that the natural law outlook continues to dominate the manner in which economists perceive the economy. Clearly the concept of equilibrium was central to classical political economy, which was openly working in the natural law tradition.

Within political economy schools today, Sraffian political economy holds equilibrium to be a central idea, while Marxist political economy is going through a debate on the subject. Analytical Marxism is clearly a general equilibrium theory, and Marx's transformation problem has traditionally been interpreted as a general equilibrium issue. However, the work of Andrew Kliman and Ted McGlone has called this whole approach into question. Their paper (reprinted in Freeman and Carchedi 1996) argues that Marx's method was dialectics and not general equilibrium. Thus the transformation problem is only a problem if one attempts to interpret Marx through Walrasian lenses (see DIALECTICAL METHOD). The Marxist-humanist approach suggested by Kliman and McGlone frees Marx from the general equilibrium straitjacket, and instead places emphasis on Marx's insights into the economic process. This approach also frees Marx's analysis from the teleological aspects which Veblen had criticized.

The rejection of equilibrium is central to post-Keynesian political economy, and is the main reason for the break with the Sraffians. Post-Keynesian objections to equilibrium go back to Keynes's own views on the limitations of equilibrium theory, particularly long-run equilibrium analysis (it was about this type of theorizing which Keynes made his famous "in the long run we are all dead" comment). The work of George Shackle, particularly his development of the importance of uncertainty, has also played a role in the post-Keynesian rejection of equilibrium, as has the recognition by Joan Robinson and Nicholas Kaldor that adherence to equilibrium theory forced one's theory to such high levels of abstraction as to cause such analysis to be irrelevant (Robinson 1974; Clark 1987–8). Starting with Veblen, institutional political economists have always held this view. To quote Galbraith, "The cost of believing in equilibrium – of seeing the study of economics as a search for improved knowledge of a fixed and final subject matter and thus as a hard science like physics or chemistry – is to be in an ineluctable march to obsolescence"

(Galbraith 1987: 129) (see EQUILIBRIUM, DIS-EQUILIBRIUM AND NON-EQUILIBRIUM).

## Theories of value

The differences between the schools center on their "vision" of society, and often this vision enters economic theory in the theory of value adopted by the school. The theory of value is a critical element for it provides the conception of what constitutes society and how it enters the analysis (Clark 1995). For instance, MPE (except for the humanist variety mentioned above) and Sraffians both adopt an objective theory of value. This holds that the economy is organized via a price system, which reflects the technical conditions of production.

PKPE does not hold an equivalent "theory of value." In its beginnings, the post-Keynesians shared the Sraffian approach to the theory of value, until it became apparent that the Sraffian approach had the same problems associated with general equilibrium theory discussed above. Now, most post-Keynesians follow some form of "cost of production" or "administered price" approach to price determination (see PRICING), usually remaining silent on the deeper question of value theory.

IPE, in their philosophical premises if not always in their practice, adhere to some form of the theory of social value (see INSTRUMENTAL VALUE THEORY), which is contrasted with theories of "natural value," and which emphasize the fully social character of "value" (that is, the social ordering process). This value theory is not directly related to price, but is rather a normative valuation of economic institutions according to whether they perform "instrumental" or "ceremonial" functions. Instrumental functions promote the general interest while ceremonial functions promote certain vested interests, and when the ratio of instrumental to ceremonial functions increases progressive institutional change is said to occur. Some social economists share this value theory as well.

Feminists have not yet developed a unique value theory, although some radicals have tried to modernize the labor theory of value, while neoclassical feminists adhere to the orthodox value theory with some modifications to include gender and related phenomena.

## Conclusion

All in all, the linkages between the schools are strong, although obvious differences remain. Perhaps the main differences emanate from the more conservative neoclassical feminists and some Schumpeterians; as well as on the general question of value theory. There is also a considerable gulf between some scholars who prefer a more substantivist analysis (history and institutions) and others who are more formalist in nature (mathematical and/or rational choice). In general, though, there is a remarkable degree of continuity which centers on the role of change and metamorphosis, history, institutions, technology and realism of analysis. In many journals and at conferences scholars of apparently different schools of thought are increasingly sharing perspectives on different facets of political economy and going beyond many of the limitations of the past.

## See also:

hysteresis, path dependency, increasing returns to scale, circular and cumulative causation; political economy: major contemporary themes; political economy; political economy: history.

## Selected references

Anderson, Esben Sloth Anderson (1994) *Evolutionary Economics: Post-Schumpeterian Contributions*, London and New York: Pinter.
Clark, Charles M.A. (1987–8) "Equilibrium, Market Process and Historical Time," *Journal of Post Keynesian Economics* 10(2): 270–81.
—— (1992) *Economic Theory and Natural Philosophy*, Aldershot: Edward Elgar.
—— (1995) "From Natural Value to Social Value," in Charles M.A. Clark (ed.), *Institu-tional Economics and the Theory of Social Value*, Boston: Kluwer Academic Publishers.
Dugger, William (1989) "Instituted Process and Enabling Myths: The Two Faces of the Market," *Journal of Economic Issues* 23(2): 607–15.
Dugger, William and Sherman, Howard (1994) "Comparison of Marxism and Institutionalism," *Journal of Economic Issues* 28(1): 101–27.
Eatwell, John and Milgate, Murray (eds) (1984) *Keynes's Economics and the Theory of Value and Distribution*, London: Duckworth.
Freeman, Alan and Carchedi, Guglielmo (eds) (1996) *Marx and Non-Equilibrium Economics*, Aldershot: Edward Elgar.
Galbraith, John Kenneth (1987) *Economics in Perspective*, Boston: Houghton Mifflin.
Lawson, Tony (1994) "The Nature of Post Keynesianism and its Links to Other Traditions: A Realist Perspective," *Journal of Post Keynesian Economics* 16(4): 503–38.
O'Hara, Phillip Anthony (1995) "The Association for Evolutionary Economics and the Union of Political Economics: General Issues of Continuity and Integration," *Journal of Economic Issues* 29(1): 137–59.
Robinson, Joan (1974) "History versus Equilibrium," *Thames Papers in Political Economy*, London: Thames Polytechnic.
Whalen, Charles J. (1996) *Political Economy for the 21st Century: Contemporary Views on the Trends of Economics*, Armonk, NY: M.E. Sharpe.

CHARLES M.A. CLARK

**POLITICAL STABILITY:** *see* democracy, political stability and economic performance

# pollution

Pollution generally refers to the unintentional effluents of human living and occupation. In the orthodox neoclassical perspective, pollution is the "unintended" byproduct of normal production or consumption activities.

Typically, a polluting firm generates an output – say, smoke – as a non-marketed spillover, due to producing some normal market product. Subsequently, the smoke becomes a direct element in the production or consumption functions of other agents in the economy, who suffer an increase in the cost of their production, for example, due to health problems.

## Varieties of pollution

Examining pollution at a more general level, human-initiated pollution needs to be distinguished from the emissions from natural sources, such as volcanos, thermal areas and highly erosive rivers, for example in northwest China or New Zealand. The worst excesses of pollution are often associated with some form of recent commercial development or industrial accident. Examples include mercury pollution from gold mining in many locations, acid rain from the fires of industry in Europe, China and the Americas, the accidents at Bophal, Minimata, and so on.

The lead pollution from the cauldrons of the bronze age can be found in the ice cores of Greenland, alongside the lead from the motor age. Pollution is evidenced in the most ancient of societies, and the Kooris of Australia appear to have changed their ecosystem dramatically with fire-related pollution 100,000 years ago (Singh and Geissler 1985). It seems that a range of other early communities went to the brink, or did in fact disappear, due to the negative consequences of their pollution (Flannery 1994). Thus, pollution cannot be said to be just a contemporary problem.

However, there are many pollution problems which are currently of grave concern. Some of the most important stem from carbon monoxide exhaust fumes, refrigeration with chlorofluorocarbons (CFCs), and weapons of war. It is at the global level that the problems of ozone loss, increased carbon dioxide concentrations and global warming need to be understood (Ehrlich and Ehrlich 1990).

## Pollution as an externality

Where polluting corporations are able to avoid the costs of their externalities, it is observed that the output of the finished product of such firms increases while the consumer price diminishes. The converse, of course, is true for industries which suffer from the pollution (Baumol and Oates 1975). In such circumstances, the neoclassical recourse is for the introduction of a Pigovian tax, applied as the difference between marginal social and private costs. Such a market internalizing tax, which is difficult to calculate, is perceived to contribute to the position of Pareto optimality in a manner consistent with normal self-seeking utility maximizing behavior.

## Market solutions

In the traditional neoclassical setting, pollution is regarded as some unintended, technical aberration of, for instance, an otherwise benign production process. The causes and consequences of pollution are generally interpreted in a straightforward panglossian manner, and the solutions usually favor some form of minor market tweaking (Baumol and Oates 1975). In this orthodox perspective, pollution is "simply" an issue of resource misallocation.

In some mainstream circles, the recourse for market solutions is carried further, such that the "problem" of pollution is directly attributed to governmental interference with benign market processes. This state of affairs is said to curtail the possibility of organizing mutually beneficial bargaining arrangements where pollutees buy out their polluters (Coase 1960; Buchanan and Stubblebine 1967). The inference is that getting government out of the market would solve the pollution problem by enabling affected parties to negotiate to a mutually more beneficial outcome. In this setting, it is also the case that the direct "policy failure" of government causes pollution. The worldwide subsidization of agriculture by many governments for certain domestic reasons, leading to some of the worst pollution on the planet, would be recognized to be a good demonstrative example. These views are convenient, since they avoid dealing with the ethical, moral and cultural relationship of humans to their environment in a negative waste repository and exploitative way.

## Modern and pre-modern societies

That some humans, as a product of the economic system, ideology or morality, could inflict great detriment on their neighbors (and themselves) would seem self-defeating and contradictory if individual utility maximization was the objective (Gauthier 1975). A critical response might be that the despoliation and human degradation of pollution is the inevitable consequence of inhumane capitalism and unfulfilled socialism. But the fact of the matter is that most societies, even indigenous communistic ones, share some blame for pollution and the environmental change which accompanies it (Flannery 1994). The features which minimize the affects of pollution in some primitive societies seem to have been their low populations and abundant assimilative capacity.

The most ancient and sustainable of societies, the Australian Kooris, came closest to solving the problem of pollution in a sustainable way by institutionalizing an ethic of responsibility and duty to the natural environment which, if performed diligently, might lead to environmental rewards and possibly human sustainability (Flannery 1994). While some ethicists have tried to articulate a contemporary perspective of this principle (Leopold 1966), contemporary Western society, with a blind rush for consumerism, has turned this ethic on its head. Nature is for dominating and hedonism rules (Agarwal 1992).

## Pollution as a social problem

Pollution is a social problem which is a function of educational, economic and institutional processes and structures. It is clear that existing institutional structures provide incentives for high levels of (over)consumption in most western societies, with significant detrimental consequences for the poor and uneducated (particularly women) in the underdeveloped nations of the south (Agarwal 1992), which are the quarries for cheap resources as well as the dumps for toxic refuse (Meuser and Szasz 1996).

Pollution is not simply a technical problem. It is a challenge for contemporary social and legal institutions to develop an environmentally empathetic ethic (Leopold 1966). Then they need to formalize this where some of the existing entitlements overlap, or where no clear entitlements exist at all. The problem then becomes Lockean: pitting the natural rights claims of one individual against those of another (Samuels and Schmidt 1976). There is no easy resolution to this conundrum, as was recognized by such philosophers as Hobbes and Bentham (see Commons 1959).

Pollution control does affect resource use efficiency and is costly to implement. Principally, the remediation of pollution relies on the specification of new institutions and legal structures and entitlements which ask questions concerning ethics, morality, equity, fairness and the distribution of income, within nations and internationally where the problems of pollution are now becoming more extreme and apparently unmanageable.

## Conclusion

The flake of chemical dust in the air of a city in some other country now has become ozone depletion, climate change, the wholesale depletion of human fertility and antibiotic resistance; all at the planetary level. Paretian possibilities for regional pollution abatement pale into insignificance in comparison to the planetary dimensions of the problem. There is a need for an equitable and fair international response which apparently needs to be achieved within a time frame of as little as a generation.

## See also:

environmental valuation; gross domestic product and net social welfare; institutions and habits; markets; property; rights

## Selected references

Agarwal, B. (1992) "The Gender and Environment Debate: Lessons from India," *Feminist Studies* 18(1): 119–58.

Baumol, W.J. and Oates, W.E. (1975) *The Theory of Environmental Policy*, Englewood Cliffs, NJ: Prentice Hall.

Buchanan, J.M. and Stubblebine, W.C. (1967) "Externality," *Economica* 29(November): 371–84.

Coase, R.H. (1960) "The Problem of Social Cost," *Journal of Law and Economics* 3: 368–91.

Commons, J.R. (1959) *Institutional Economics*, 2 vols, Madison, WI: University of Wisconsin Press.

Ehrlich, P.R and Ehrlich, A.H. (1990) *The Population Explosion*, New York: Random House.

Flannery, T.F. (1994) *The Future Eaters*, Chatswood: Reed Books.

Gauthier, D. (1975) "Reason as Maximisation," *Canadian Journal of Philosophy* 43: 411–33.

Leopold, A. (1966) *A Sand County Almanac*, Oxford: Oxford University Pres.

Meuser, M and Szasz, S. (1996) "Environmental Inequality Bibliography," 23 March, website address:
http://www.cruzio.com/~meuser/ejwww.html

Samuels, W.J. and Schmidt, A.A. (1976) "Polluters, Profits and Political Response: The Dynamics of Rights Creation," *Public Choice* 28(Winter): 99–106.

Singh, G. and Geissler, E.A. (1985) "Late Cenozoic History of Vegetation, Fire, Lake Levels and Climate at Lake George, NSW, Australia," *Philosophical Transactions of the Royal Society of London* 311: 379–447.

ANDREW K. DRAGUN

# population

Population size, growth and characteristics affect ECONOMIC GROWTH, the DISTRIBUTION OF INCOME and environmental conditions, all of which are relevant to standards of living. The policy issues most often discussed are control of fertility and mortality, migration and the distribution of income between the working and dependent populations.

## The stock of population

United Nations demographers estimate that the world population in 1991 was 5,292,000,000. The three largest countries by population size that year were China (1,115,790,000), India (849,638,000) and the United States (252,688,000). The populations of the world's most important industrialized regions on 1 January 1992 were: the European Economic Area (which does not include Eastern Europe), 379,121,200; North America (Canada, the United States and Mexico), 369,186,600; and Japan, 124,000,000.

Differences in the size of the population in a given economy can affect economies of scale in production. A larger population, when associated with a larger demand for products, makes more specialized production processes possible. It also allows the fixed or "overhead" costs of running the economy to be spread over a larger amount of output. An economy with a larger population can have lower unit costs of production, and, other things being equal, higher employment and a higher standard of living.

The economies of scale argument is predicated mainly on the scale of output of particular enterprises and industries, rather than on the size of the domestic population. Advocates of free trade cite the benefits of economies of scale as a reason for reducing tariff and non-tariff barriers to trade (see FREE TRADE AND PROTECTION).

Domestic producers who can compete successfully in international markets benefit from increased demand and the possibilities for economies of scale (see INCREASING RETURNS TO SCALE). The size and affluence of the domestic population would be a determinant of domestic demand for the product of protected industries that could be allowed to develop sufficiently in size to be able to compete in the larger unprotected market. This is the "infant industry" argument for domestic tariff and non-tariff protection against foreign competition.

There are also factors which tend to make larger output more costly per unit of output in real terms. Natural resource limitations and accompanying diminishing returns are often cited as an example. Some environmentalists have advocated limitations on population growth in order to preserve biological and physical natural resources that contribute to the QUALITY OF LIFE.

TECHNOLOGY has allowed for increasing production in primary industries with fewer workers per unit of output. As a result, there has been a relative reduction, and in many countries an absolute reduction, in population in rural areas, villages and small towns where primary production often takes place. Populations have grown in large urban areas where secondary and tertiary production, which benefit from economies of scale in production and marketing, tend to be located. These concentrations of population often result in urban congestion and dwindling access to green spaces and nature, and thereby pose economic costs and policy challenges (see ENVIRONMENTAL AND ECOLOGICAL POLITICAL ECONOMY: MAJOR CONTEMPORARY THEMES).

## Population characteristics

The age distribution of the population affects the size, mobility, and PRODUCTIVITY of the working population. The working population must produce the goods and services to support itself and the dependent population, that is, those in pre- and post-employment age groups and others unable to work. The ratio of the dependent population to the total population, and the ratio of the total population to the labor force, are dependency measures that indicate this relationship. At given levels of employment and productivity, a higher ratio of total population to dependent population or a lower ratio of total population to the labor force allows for higher standards of living.

In the developed industrial countries, low fertility rates and larger older populations are influencing dependency ratios and raising questions about the future adequacy and sources of retirement income. In many developing countries, high fertility rates are a major influence on dependency ratios and a drag on improving standards of living. The age distribution of the population also affects the nature of the demand for output and thereby the industrial and occupational distribution of market and non-market employment.

While birth rates of men and women are similar, the composition of a given population by GENDER can differ: war often reduces the size of the male population relative to the female population, immigration and emigration rates of men and women can be different, and the life expectancy of women is generally higher than that of men. Social policy must recognize these differences if it is to provide an equitable gender distribution of income.

## Population flows

Policies intended to manage the rate of growth of the population, and thereby the size of the population, must influence population flows that are determined by natural increases of population and net migration. Natural increases in the population are governed by birth rates and death rates. However, historical experience indicates that long-run fertility and mortality rates are difficult to predict and not easily influenced by public policy.

In developing countries, high fertility rates are often seen as a drag on living standards. China's current attempt to limit family formation to one live birth per family is a response to this perception. In the developed countries, low fertility rates are common and policies to stimulate higher birth rates by providing incentives in the form of money payments for additional births, better child care and more flexible working hours have been tried.

Mortality levels of countries are usually measured by death rates and expected life spans. In most parts of the world mortality rates are falling. In the developed countries, higher standards of living, improved lifestyle consciousness and better medical treatment are the usual explanatory variables. In the less developed countries, life-threatening illness has been reduced by more widespread use of inoculations against infectious diseases, and in some places more sanitary provisions for water supply and waste disposal. Declines in post-neonatal and child mortality rates typically account for a significant part of the increased expected life spans in these countries. Dramatic counter-forces to the general tendency towards reduced mortality levels are recent decreased expected life spans in the countries of the former Soviet Union, an increasingly threatening worldwide AIDS epidemic and a resurgence of genocidal war crimes.

Because natural increases in population are not easily influenced by public policy, those who are concerned about population size, characteristics and growth rates stress the importance of net migration as a policy variable. Net migration is the difference between immigration (incoming) and emigration (outgoing). Immigration is determined by the number of persons who want permanent residence in a country and the number of persons the government of the country allows such status. The inflow of immigrants is controlled by regulations provided by law, and also by the way that the regulations are administered. In some countries, immigration law and regulation is discriminatory with respect to race, color and national origin. In a number of countries, the economic attributes of immigrants, family ties and refugee status are relevant for entry.

The United Nations estimates that over 60 million people now reside in a country where they were not born. Over half of all immigrants typically go to the United States, Canada and Australia. Illegal immigration is significant in many countries. The willingness of countries to accept immigrants is often related to the state of the domestic economy. High levels of domestic unemployment tend to discourage potential immigrants, and domestic immigration policy tends to become restrictive. Persistent labor shortages tend to increase immigrant flows, available jobs attract potential immigrants and employers lobby government for less restrictive immigration policy.

Emigration offsets the effects of immigration on the size of population. Social, political and economic conditions affect emigration. Relatively few countries have direct controls on emigration. Differences in standards of living and employment opportunities among regions of a country are also factors in internal migration.

## See also:

labor force; marriage; sexuality; social structure of accumulation: family

## Selected references

Borjas, George J. (1994) "The Economics of Migration," *Journal of Economic Literature* 32: 1667–717.
Robinson, Joan (1957) "Population and Development," in *Joan Robinson, Collected Economic Papers*, vol. 2, Cambridge, MA: The MIT Press, 1980, 107–13.

SIDNEY H. INGERMAN

# post-Keynesian political economy: history

In the 1950s and early 1960s the term "post-Keynesian" was used by a variety of scholars (including Joan Robinson), but invariably only in a chronological sense, that is, to denote post-1936 work on Keynesian macroeconomics. Not until the publication in the December 1975 issue of the *Journal of Economic Literature* of the important survey article by Alfred Eichner and Jan Kregel was "post-Keynesian" firmly associated with opposition to the prevailing neoclassical interpretation of the *General Theory*, which is now the defining characteristic of post-Keynesian economics. Before then the work of Cambridge theorists like Robinson and Nicholas

Kaldor was sometimes described as "neo-Keynesian" or (to allow for the contributions of Piero Sraffa, Luigi Pasinetti and others) "Anglo-Italian."

A history of post-Keynesianism must therefore begin in 1936, with the initial controversy surrounding Keynes's book. The IS–LM formulation of the *General Theory*, which reduced it to a special case of Walrasian general equilibrium theory, was discovered more or less simultaneously by (at least) John Hicks, Roy Harrod, James Meade and Brian Reddaway. After further elaboration by Franco Modigliani and Don Patinkin in the 1940s, this neoclassical interpretation confined Keynes's message to the unexciting claim that sustained mass unemployment could be understood only as the result of "institutional rigidities," most especially in the labor market. According to this "grand neoclassical synthesis" (Arestis 1992: chaps 1–3), KEYNES had not produced a *general* theory at all. It was this "Bastard Keynesianism," as Robinson was later to describe it, which fell such easy prey first to the monetarists and then to the so-called "new classical" economists.

## Kalecki and Robinson

By 1939 the seeds of an alternative approach to macroeconomics had already been sown. The Polish neo-Marxist Michal KALECKI had published a model of the trade cycle which incorporated the principle of effective demand and went beyond the *General Theory* in deriving a theory of profits from the class nature of capitalist society and the prevalence of oligopoly, rather than the "perfect competition" on which Keynes had relied (Sawyer 1985). Although Kalecki was not entirely immune to the neoclassical virus, as his 1936 review of the *General Theory* reveals (Targetti and Kinda-Hass 1982), his early work pointed very clearly in a post-Keynesian direction.

So too did the contemporary writings of Joan Robinson, who befriended Kalecki during his brief, unhappy stay in Cambridge and became his staunch advocate. In her *Essays in the Theory of Employment,* published in 1937

but written in 1935–6, probably independently of Kalecki's influence, she attacked monetarism, New Keynesian economics and neoclassical growth theory decades before they identified themselves as such. Money wages and real wages were determined separately, money wages by trade union bargaining power and real wages by technical conditions of production and the degree of monopoly. Any relation between real wages and the level of employment was incidental. It was possible that no conceivable reduction in the rate of interest would establish full employment. Continuous inflation was impossible without a continuous increase in money wages. Five years later Robinson reinforced these striking assertions by arguing, in her *Essay on Marxian Economics*, that the best way to make sense of Keynes was to read Marx, and vice versa.

Kalecki spent the war years in Oxford, where his small but devoted following included the Austrian Joseph Steindl, himself a major influence on his fellow exile Kurt Rothschild. In 1952 Steindl published a major work, *Maturity and Stagnation in American Capitalism,* linking the rise of oligopoly to increased profit margins, declining capacity utilization and a weakening of the incentive to invest. There was, however, no Kaleckian school until the Polish economist's work was rediscovered, after persistent prodding by Joan Robinson, in the late 1960s and 1970s.

## Capital controversies

The first effective challenge to the grand neoclassical synthesis came, appropriately enough, from Cambridge where Sraffa was completing, with glacial slowness, his profound critique of orthodox value and distribution theory. It was Robinson, though, who initiated the (in)famous "Cambridge controversies in capital theory" with a series of articles, beginning in 1953–54, attacking the logical coherence of the neoclassical analysis of capital, distribution and growth (Harcourt 1972) (see CAPITAL THEORY DEBATES). At the same time, Kaldor was articulating a distribution model based on the (classical) assumption that capitalists have a greater savings propensity than workers. The marginal productivity approach to distribution theory was mortally wounded, as Paul Samuelson conceded in the 1966 *Quarterly Journal of Economics* symposium. Like Dracula, it has proved almost impossible to destroy, though Sraffa's 1960 *Production of Commodities by Means of Commodities* should already have administered the *coup de grace*.

## Weintraub, Davidson and Kaldor

Dissatisfaction with NEOCLASSICAL ECONOMICS was not confined to Cambridge, nor was it restricted to value and distribution theory. In the USA, Sidney Weintraub had begun to question the capacity of orthodox "Keynesians" to understand the inflationary tendencies of an economy manifestly operating at less than full employment. Weintraub became a tireless exponent of tax-based incomes policy as the only effective remedy for wage inflation. His student Paul Davidson went back to the *General Theory*, and in particular to the aggregate supply and demand model of Chapter 3, which formed the core of the first post-Keynesian textbook (Davidson and Smolensky 1964). Weintraub and Davidson were also early critics of the notion of an exogenously determined money supply, which was essential to Milton Friedman's resurgent monetarism. British economists too had begun to realize that money might be more effect than cause, a position implicit in the 1960 report of the Radcliffe Commission, itself profoundly influenced by two Cambridge economists, Kaldor and Richard Kahn. Kaldor in particular was a persistent and outspoken enemy of monetarist theory and policies.

## Developments in the 1970s

Originally the North American and Cambridge strands of resistance to the grand neoclassical synthesis developed very largely in isolation from each other. After 1970–1, the Atlantic proved much less of a barrier. This was the period when Davidson completed his important *Money and the Real World*, published in 1972 while on sabbatical in Cambridge, and Robinson harangued the membership of the American Economic Association in her 1971 Richard T. Ely lecture in New Orleans. There soon emerged an informal international network of post-Keynesians. It now included Hyman Minsky, whose FINANCIAL INSTABILITY HYPOTHESIS had roots in the ideas of Keynes and Kalecki, and Alfred Eichner, author of an extremely influential quasi-Kaleckian model of the determinants of oligopolistic mark-ups. The post-Keynesians were increasingly excluded from mainstream journals in the United States, publishing instead in the *Economic Journal* and in *Australian Economic Papers*, co-edited from 1963 to 1982 by Geoffrey Harcourt. Two significant milestones were the establishment of the *Cambridge Journal of Economics* in 1977 and the *Journal of Post Keynesian Economics* (jointly edited by Davidson and Weintraub) in the following year.

## Streams of post-Keynesians

The influential survey article by Harcourt and Hamouda (1988) gives a very clear picture of the state of post-Keynesian political economy in the late 1980s. They identify three distinct, and often bitterly opposed, sub-schools. The "fundamentalist Keynesians," led by Davidson, focused on the role of UNCERTAINTY in the *General Theory*, the essential properties of money and the economic implications of a non-ergodic universe. The Kaleckians included Eichner, Steindl and Athanasios Asimakopulos; they attempted to model a CLASS society dominated by great corporations with significant market power. Pierangelo Garegnani and John Eatwell led the Sraffians, who hoped to reconcile the principle of effective demand with the long-period analysis of (classical-Marxian) "prices of production." These three steams are no closer to convergence now than they were in 1988, although some writers have detected the beginnings of a new synthesis (Lavoie 1992). Meanwhile post-Keynesian economics has been enriched, both by the emergence of new problems (methodology, microfoundations, "endogenous growth") and by increasing contact with other dissident groups (institutionalists and evolutionary economists, radical political economists). Its past has been documented in some detail (King 1995), while its future remains very much an open question.

## Selected references

Arestis, Philip (1992) *The Post-Keynesian Approach to Economics*, Aldershot: Edward Elgar.

Davidson, Paul and Smolensky, Eugene (1964) *Aggregate Supply and Demand Analysis*, New York: Harper & Row.

Harcourt, Geoffrey C. (1972) *Some Cambridge Controversies in the Theory of Capital*, Cambridge: Cambridge University Press.

Harcourt, Geoffrey C. and Hamouda, Oscar M. (1988) "Post-Keynesianism: From Criticism to Coherence?" *Bulletin of Economic Research* 40(1): 1–33.

King, John E. (1996) *A Bibliography of Post Keynesian Economics*, Aldershot: Edward Elgar.

Lavoie, Marc (1992) *Foundations of Post-Keynesian Economic Analysis*, Aldershot: Edward Elgar.

Sawyer, Malcolm C. (1985) *The Economics of Michal Kalecki*, London: Macmillan.

Targetti, Ferdinando and Kinda-Hass, Bogulslawa (1982) "Kalecki's Review of Keynes' General Theory," *Australian Economic Papers* 21(3): 244–60.

JOHN E. KING

# post-Keynesian political economy: major contemporary themes

Post-Keynesian economics, like most other heterodox schools, has been subjected lately to a substantial amount of soul searching. While, on the one hand, the "broad church" approach of post-Keynesian political economy has attracted the attention of institutionalists, social economists, Marxists and Sraffians, on the other hand, the apparent multiplicity and vagueness of post-Keynesian fundamentals has led many observers to wonder whether there are any common characteristics to post-Keynesianism. These hesitations are best assessed by reading through the conversations which John King has held with various post-Keynesians. King (1995: 244) concludes his survey by noting that "there is substantially more agreement among post-Keynesians" than he had originally believed.

What, then, is post-Keynesian economics? Presumably, most post-Keynesians would agree with Victoria Chick (1995: 20) when she claims that the objectives of the post-Keynesian project are to recover the insights of KEYNES, KALECKI and their early disciples, and to go beyond these insights by extending them to new fields of research, and by taking into account modern realities. On economic policy, post-Keynesians would probably agree with Geoffrey Harcourt that the "purpose of economics is to make the world a better place for ordinary men and women, to produce a more just and equitable society" (Dow 1991: 188).

## Methodology

Quite a lot of work has recently been devoted to methodology. It has been argued that post-Keynesians share a belief in the diversity of methods (methodological pluralism) as well as an implicit approval of some version of realism (essential abstractions, Kaldor's stylized facts and the like), in contrast to the mainstream adoption of constrained maximization and of instrumentalism. While pluralism and realism certainly apply to post-Keynesianism, as would a weak form of organicism (in contrast to methodological individualism), it would be difficult to deny that they also apply to most other non-orthodox schools of thought. What then characterizes post-Keynesian economics from these other schools of political economy? What are the fundamental insights of Keynes and Kalecki?

## Specific features

It is submitted that *effective demand* and a *serious consideration of time* are the two specific features of post-Keynesianism. This can be seen at various levels. Post-Keynesians believe there almost always exists unemployed labor and excess productive capacity, that is, economies are demand-led both in the short and in the long period. This is to be contrasted to the beliefs of New Keynesians and of Marxists, who grant the relevance of demand-led phenomena mainly to short-run situations. This emphasis on demand-led economics is reflected in the well-known claim regarding causality, i.e. investment governs savings. This claim is backed by Sraffians, many of whom also see economies as being demand-led even in the long run. Post-Keynesians reject the standard neoclassical definition of economics as the science of scarcity analysis. For this reason, production and income effects are in the limelight, while substitution effects are seen as second-order effects. Post-Keynesians deny any relevance to the major tools of neoclassical scarcity analysis, such as the natural rate of unemployment or the natural rate of interest, or if these tools are of any help, their implications are subverted by such phenomena as PATH DEPENDENCY, HYSTERESIS and irreversibility.

## Time

This brings to the fore the importance of TIME in post-Keynesian analysis. Joan Robinson has highlighted the need to distinguish between historical and logical time. Whatever the strand of post-Keynesianism, time is to be taken seriously. For some, Kalecki for instance, the importance of time appears under the statement that long run trends are the *ex post* result of a series of short-period situations. The transition from one position to another – the problem of the TRAVERSE – must always be justified. For others, like Paul Davidson, the importance of time is reflected in the contention that the world is non-ergodic, meaning the world is not immutable and that calculations about past events are unreliable as statistical projections of the future. Post-Keynesians point out that production takes time and requires the issuance of debt and credit. This helps to understand why price and wage deflation may not be stabilizing. There is a MONETARY CIRCUIT, where money and LIQUIDITY PREFERENCE are the links between the past and the future – thus the emphasis among post-Keynesians on the necessity of providing a MONETARY THEORY OF PRODUCTION.

## Money, credit and finance

No one will be surprised, then, to learn that a major contemporary theme of post-Keynesian economics is the development of a non-orthodox theory of money, credit and finance. All post-Keynesians seem to agree that credit-money is endogenous, implying that the supply of money is demand-led, driven by the bank loans requested by firms (see ENDOGENOUS MONEY AND CREDIT). There are considerable discussions as to the best means to formalize and heuristically represent the above. Whereas, initially, most of the attention was assigned to an understanding of the processes that propelled the accommodation to money and credit demand, the attention has now turned to factors that are an impediment to this accommodation, such as credit-worthiness. Liquidity preference is now given more consideration. A considerable amount of attention, on both the theoretical and empirical fronts, is now given to the determinants of and the links between the various sorts of interest rates and the profit rates targeted and realized by firms.

The focus on monetary and financial matters has extended to dynamic models of business cycles. The FINANCIAL INSTABILITY HYPOTHESIS of Hyman Minsky, with its emphasis on debt–equity ratios and the weight of debt payments, as well as the evolving attitude of banks and firms *vis-à-vis* debt risk, along the lines of KALECKI'S PRINCIPLE OF INCREASING RISK, has given rise to a large number of contributions that attempt to combine real and financial phenomena. These insights have been particularly fruitful to apply the new tools of complex and non-linear dynamics.

## Kaleckian features

Also fruitful has been the extension of Kaleckian costing, pricing and investment behavior to long period analysis. The main features of the KALECKIAN THEORY OF GROWTH are the assumption of cost-plus pricing and the assumption that the rate of capacity utilization can be endogenous both in the short and in the long period. These have been adopted by non-orthodox economists of all persuasions, be they post-Keynesians, Marxists, structuralists or Sraffians. The diffusion of this common basic model has facilitated the identification of the assumptions which are specific to each school, and it has helped to build bridges between schools of political economy (see POLITICAL ECONOMY: SCHOOLS).

To a large extent, this new Kaleckian model of growth and distribution is overtaking the old Cambridgian model which was first developed in the mid-1950s. The problem with the old model, as was pointed out by critics such as Davidson, Harcourt and Peter Skott, is its failure to tackle time: no convincing traverse from the short to the long period could be provided. Nevertheless, there is still a considerable amount of energy being devoted to the original KALDOR–PASINETTI MODELS OF GROWTH AND DISTRIBUTION, extending the model in all directions, by taking into account firms and their retained earnings, taxation, government deficits, interest payments and exports, or by generalizing the model to a two-country economy.

Other strands of growth models continue to attract considerable attention. Whereas the Cambridge and Kaleckian models do not easily lend themselves to empirical verification, this is not the case for Kaldorian models of endogenous growth, inspired by VERDOORN'S LAW, and of Thirlwall's BALANCE OF PAYMENTS CONSTRAINT growth model, based on Harrod's export multiplier. A substantial amount of empirical work has been published along those lines, showing for the former that high growth rates of industrial output induce high growth rates of productivity, and for the latter that the growth rate of an economy can be explained to a large extent by the growth rate of its exports and by the income elasticity of its imports.

## Uncertainty

While some members of the post-Keynesian school are busy designing long run models, several post-Keynesians are involved in a revival of Keynesian fundamentalism. These new fundamentalists highlight the relevance of true UNCERTAINTY, as found in Keynes's Chapter 12 of the *General Theory*, as well as that of evidential weight, as found in Keynes's earlier *Treatise on Probability*. The new fundamentalists have brought to the fore the tight philosophical relationships that exist between uncertainty, social institutions, the acquisition of knowledge and bounded rationality. An interesting distinction has been drawn between epistemological uncertainty (agents lack the capacity to obtain enough appropriate information to predict the future) and ontological uncertainty (the world itself just cannot be predicted, as pointed out by those who emphasize non-ergodicity). Whatever the case, however, the consequence is that the hyper-rationality assumed in neoclassical models is meaningless; agents cannot but resort to conventions and reasonable rationality, of the sort made known by Herbert Simon's procedural rationality.

While all post-Keynesians agree on the necessity to incorporate a sensible form of rationality, there are some disagreements on the other consequences of uncertainty. The more radical view (almost a nihilistic one) would throw econometrics, mathematical formalization and equilibrium analysis, in the long and even in the short period, by the wayside. Some would deny relevance to long period analysis only. Others claim that the presence of uncertainty reinforces stable behavior, with individual or bureaucratic routines and social conventions, and hence that long run analysis is justified provided one remembers that parameters and functions will change in the real world. Within that view, it is also argued that complex dynamics are particularly appropriate tools to represent the insights of post-Keynesian economics, since they imply a lack of predictability, and hence justify fundamental uncertainty.

## Microeconomics

The other major source of controversy pertains to the appropriate microeconomic foundations of post-Keynesian political economy, notwithstanding the fact that many post-Keynesians would consider macroeconomics to constitute the foundations of microeconomics – the stylized facts evoked above. Two views seem to emerge. Some authors, mostly associated with Paul Davidson and Sidney Weintraub, endorse Marshallian foundations with diminishing returns and rising cost curves, as well as conditions generally associated with pure competition. This group takes the view that post-Keynesian economics is more general than neoclassical economics, and hence that it is helpful to maintain these standard assumptions which, incidentally, are to be found in Keynes. Other authors, closer to Joan Robinson, Nicholas Kaldor and Alfred Eichner (1991), favor Kaleckian foundations with administered cost-plus prices (simple mark-up, normal-cost or target-return pricing) and constant or near-constant unit direct costs, under conditions of imperfect competition. This latter group sees post-Keynesian economics essentially as a more realist alternative to neoclassical economics rather than an attempt at encompassing mainstream theory. The cleavage between these two views should not be exaggerated: many of those who would probably favor Kaleckian foundations have themselves built models with Marshallian foundations (Peter Riach, John McCombie and Amitava Dutt for instance). It should be pointed out, however, that the main message of post-Keynesian macroeconomics comes across more straightforwardly with Kaleckian foundations.

## Policy

While, on the one hand, a disproportionate number of post-Keynesians still devote much of their energy to the scriptures of past writers (a feature of post-Keynesian economics which has been of some concern to observers as diverse as Joseph Steindl and Robert Skidelsky), on the other hand, most post-Keynesians are concerned with the policy implications of their economic theories. Post-Keynesians generally agree that demand-side management is required to achieve full employment. There is also the realization that other policies are required to preserve full employment in the long run. There seems to be some consensus on the necessity of imposing long-term incomes policies, including the control of rentier income. These controls may have to be accompanied by some industrial policy that would have an impact on the allocation and size of private investment There is also a widespread belief that the deregulation of financial markets has not been beneficial to the world economy, resulting in an environment dominated by deflationary policies. As a result, many post-Keynesians would favor more regulation of the financial markets, including in some cases direct credit controls and permanent capital controls, being fully aware, however, that their effectiveness would be highly increased with worldwide cooperation (see REGULATION AND DEREGULATION: FINANCIAL).

## See also:

effective demand and capacity utilization; Kaldor's theory of the growth process; Keynesian political economy; money, credit and finance: major contemporary themes; post-Keynesian political economy: history; pricing; Robinson's contribution to political economy; structuralist theory of development

## Selected references

Arestis, Philip (1996) "Post-Keynesian Economics: Towards Coherence," *Cambridge Journal of Economics* 20(1): 111–35.

Chick, Victoria (1995) "Is There a Case for Post Keynesian Economics?," *Scottish Journal of Political Economy* 42(1): 20–36.

Dow, Sheila (1991) "The Post-Keynesian School," in Douglas Mair and Anne G. Miller (eds), *A Modern Guide to Economic Thought*, Aldershot, Edward Elgar, 176–206.

Eichner, Alfred S. (1991) *The Macrodynamics of Advanced Market Economies*, Armonk, NY: M.E. Sharpe.

King, John E. (1995) *Conversations with Post Keynesians*, Aldershot: Edward Elgar.

Lavoie, Marc (1992) *Foundations of Post-Keynesian Economic Analysis*, Aldershot: Edward Elgar.

McCombie, John S.L. and Thirlwall, Anthony P. (1993) *Economic Growth and Balance of Payments Constraint*, Basingstoke: Macmillan.

Palley, Thomas I. (1996) *Post Keynesian Economics: Debt, Distribution and Macro Economy*, London: Macmillan.

Reynolds, Peter J. (1987) *Political Economy: A Synthesis of Kaleckian and Post Keynesian Economics*, Brighton: Wheatsheaf Books.

MARC LAVOIE

# post-Keynesian theory of choice

Traditionally, there have been few attempts to form a systematized post-Keynesian theory of household choice, although recently one can detect an increasing interest with the appearance of works on the subject. In spite of this, there is a considerable degree of coherence concerning the elements that constitute what might be called a post-Keynesian theory of choice. These elements do not originate from post-Keynesian works only, but also from a number of economists broadly falling in the non-orthodox category. Thus, elements of a post-Keynesian oriented theory of choice can be found in the works of Robinson, Pasinetti, Georgescu-Roegen, Eichner, Nell, Earl, Lavoie and in KEYNES himself. The underlying framework can be described in terms of six principles as stated by Lavoie (1994): (1) procedural rationality, (2) satiable wants, (3) separability of needs, (4) needs hierarchy, (5) growth of needs, and (6) non-independence.

## Procedural rationality

This is also known as bounded rationality, as suggested by Herbert Simon (1959), and is one of the presuppositions of the post-Keynesian paradigm. The additional characteristic of the post-Keynesian approach is that rationality is also bounded by the essentially unknowable future. This type of rationality denies that the economic agent's decisions are characterized by optimizing in the sense of mainstream economics. Bounded knowledge, irreducible uncertainty and limited computational abilities undermine optimizing behavior. They also imply that agents avoid complex calculations and considerations and, therefore, base most of their decisions on rules of thumb, CONVENTIONS, customs and habits.

## Satiable wants

The principle of satiable wants implies that there are threshold levels of consumption beyond which a good gives no additional satisfaction. The standard theory has a similar view, with the idea of diminishing marginal utility, but satiation from that theoretical point of view occurs when incomes are infinite or prices are zero. The principle is connected to the view that some NEEDS are more basic than others (the principle of needs hierarchy). The important consequence here is that a distinction between wants and needs is necessary. Wants evolve from needs and they constitute the various preferences within a level of need (Lutz and Lux 1979).

## Separability of needs

The principle of separability of needs says that needs can be distinguished from each other.

The mainstream approach has implicitly recognized the existence of separate needs in ideas like the separability of the utility function. The principle can be associated with Lancaster's (1972) theory in which characteristics possessed by a good correspond to a specific need. The obvious consequence of need separability is the restriction of the degree of substitution between goods.

## Needs hierarchy

The fourth principle, needs hierarchy, states that given the separability of needs, needs are subordinate or that they exhibit a hierarchical structure. This idea is quite old and can be found in many economic writings and in Keynes (1936: 93, 97–8). Furthermore, one can find it in other disciplines, such as sociology, political science, and especially in psychology with the work of Abraham Maslow (for a general review, see Drakopoulos 1994). One can combine the principles of satiation, separability and hierarchy in a hierarchical preference ordering with thresholds levels. A special case of such an ordering is the lexicographic ordering that many orthodox texts mention as a perfectly rational system of choice but never develop further.

## Growth of needs

The next principle, growth of needs, implies that the needs of individuals will grow as their lower level needs are gradually fulfilled. This is mainly due to income effects, since in order to go from lower needs to higher ones, an increase in real income is necessary. Thus income effects seem much more important in explaining the change of expenditures on goods than are substitute effects.

## Non-independence

Finally, the principle of non-independence implies that decisions and preferences are not made independently of those of other agents. This is very similar to Keynes's idea that relativities matter. In particular, consumers of similar incomes fulfill their needs in the same order and have the same thresholds. Thus, norms of consumption will depend on past standards and on imitation as the consumer attempts to emulate those that belong to a higher social stratum or their reference group (Eichner 1986), in a manner similar to that of the relative income hypothesis and the work of Thorstein Veblen (see CONSPICUOUS CONSUMPTION AND EMULATION).

## Formal example

On the basis of the above six principles, it is possible to give a simple formal example which incorporates the basics of the post-Keynesian theory of choice. Suppose that $x$ and $y$ are commodities, or bundles of commodities, which satisfy the primary need to eat. The threshold level of this need is $e^*$ and this might involve a combination of both commodities. This implies substitution between the two commodities, as far as the first need is concerned, since $x + y = e^*$. But if $y$ satisfies better the secondary need which is assumed to be taste, then y will come into the picture when the primary need is satisfied. In symbols ($P$ means "is preferred to"):

$$(x_1, y_1) P(x_2, y_2) \text{ iff}$$
$$\text{either } x_2 + y_2 < x_1 + y_1 < e^*$$
$$\text{or } x_1 + y_1 = x_2 + y_2 \leqslant e^*; y_2 < y_1$$
$$\text{or } x_2 + y_2 < e^* < x_1 + y_1$$
$$\text{or } e^* < x_1 + y_1, x_2 + y_2; y_2 < y_1 < y^*$$

It is possible to extend the choice system to represent cases where there are more than two needs. Thus the existence of $y^*$ implies that there is a threshold for the second need after which a third need takes effect. The above system will produce quasi-indifference curves or behavior lines. It is also possible to express the above in "hierarchical" utility terms, if utility is represented as a components-ordered vector (Canterbery 1979).

There is also scope for connecting the above system to a conventional consumption savings framework. Let us introduce a hierarchical utility function for an individual, given as:

$$U = U(C_N, S, C_L)$$

where $C_N$ is consumption of necessary goods or threshold consumption, $S$ is savings and $C_L$ is consumption of luxuries. Taking $C_N$ as the first priority, $S$ as the second (because of risk aversion or other psychological reasons), and also income as being higher than $C_N$ expenditure with no borrowing, then it is possible to derive the familiar idea that the marginal propensity to consume is less than unity (Drakopoulos 1992).

## Further analysis

The post-Keynesian choice theory implies that price substitution effects are very modest, especially with reference to broad categories of consumption expenditures. Thus, non-substantial fluctuations of price will have an insignificant impact on quantities sold, given that goods respond to a need or set of needs. This means that there is a case for more attention to be placed on income effects and thresholds levels. Furthermore, macroeconomic models which deal with income classes and income effects are a natural consequence of post-Keynesian choice theory.

On a more theoretical side, the hierarchical choice model will give kinked demand curves with kinks representing the relative efficacy of goods in satisfying different needs (Earl 1986). Accepting that threshold levels will be similar for categories of goods (necessary and luxury goods) for large groups of population with similar incomes, then kinks will appear in the aggregate level as well. Apart from the obvious case of price rigidity, this might also imply a non-market clearing situation in the case of fixed capacity. In general, the post-Keynesian theory of choice can provide some of the microfoundations of the post-Keynesian approach.

## See also:

expectations; institutions and habits; methodological individualism and collectivism; post-Keynesian political economy: major contemporary themes; price theory, Sraffian; uncertainty

## Selected references

Canterbery, Ray (1979) "Inflation Necessities and Distributive Efficiency," in James Gapinski and Charles Rockwood (eds), *Essays in Post-Keynesian Inflation*, Cambridge MA: Ballinger.

Drakopoulos, Stavros (1992) "Keynes' Economic Thought and the Theory of Consumer Behaviour," *Scottish Journal of Political Economy* 9(3): 318–36.

—— (1994) " Hierarchical Choice in Economics," *Journal of Economic Surveys* 8(2): 133–53.

Earl, Peter (1986) *Lifestyle Economics: Consumer Behaviour in a Turbulent World*, Brighton: Wheatsheaf.

Eichner, Alfred ( 1986) *Toward a New Economics: Essays in Post-Keynesian and Institutionalist Theory*, London: Macmillan, and Armonk, NY: M.E. Sharpe.

Keynes, John M. (1936) *The General Theory of Employment, Interest and Money*, London: Macmillan.

Lancaster, Kelvin (1972) *Consumer Demand: a New Approach*, New York: Columbia University Press.

Lavoie, Marc (1994) "A Post Keynesian Theory of Consumer Choice," *Journal of Post Keynesian Economics* 16(4): 539–62.

Lutz, Mark and Lux, Kenneth (1979) *The Challenge of Humanistic Economics*, Menlo Park, CA: Benjamin Cummings.

Simon, Herbert (1959) "Theories of Decision-Making in Economics and Behavioural Sciences," *American Economic Review* 49: 253–83.

STAVROS A. DRAKOPOULOS

# poverty: absolute and relative

Poverty clearly is a matter of unmet human physical need. Even so, poverty has been difficult to define with any precision mainly because poverty is a normative concept, rooted in the value systems of its users. In a complex world, that makes for many different definitions. Consequently, it is virtually impossible to achieve universal agreement. What follows necessarily reflects the values of the author but, it is hoped, will contribute to wider agreement on a satisfactory definition.

Over the years, two general measures of poverty have emerged. One defines and measures poverty in an absolute sense, the other in a relative sense. Of the two, the absolute measure is the more widely accepted. Both are based on personal and family income but neither one determines unmet physical need with genuine specificity.

## Absolute standard

An absolute standard of poverty is built around the cost of the goods and services required to meet minimal human physical need. The most widely used absolute standard was developed by Mollie Orshansky of the US Social Security Administration in 1964, and is based on the current cost of the Department of Agriculture's 1961 Economy Food Plan. The cost of the other goods and services to satisfy physical need minimally is estimated on the basis of the Department of Agriculture's 1955 *Survey of Food Consumption*, which found that families spend almost one-third of their income on food. Thus, the total cost of the goods and services required to meet physical need minimally is fixed officially at three times the current cost of the Economy Food Plan. Critics point to this aspect of its construction as one of its main weaknesses.

## Relative standard

A relative standard of poverty is built around the economic resources that a person has in relation to the resources of others. To illustrate, a person with income that puts him/her in the lowest quintile of an income distribution or below one-half of the median income for the entire population might be classified as needy. According to the relative standard, the person

who does not have what others typically have, however much or little that may be, is needy. In principle, poverty can be eliminated when it is defined as a percent of the median income. However, it cannot be eliminated when the standard is defined in terms of the bottom fractile of the income distribution.

## Problems

There are two main problems with the conventional wisdom regarding absolute and relative standards. The first is a matter of semantics; the second is more substantial. Even though one standard is called absolute and the other relative, both in fact are relative. The relative standard defines need relative to the economic resources that people typically have at their disposal as compared to what others have. The absolute standard defines need relative to the cost of the minimum goods and services required. The second problem is that students of poverty do not agree as to which standard to use. Those students who use the absolute standard in effect ignore income distribution. Those who employ the relative standard disregard the critical minimum.

There is a simple resolution of this difference. Properly understood, physical need is both an absolute or minimal-living concept and a relative or income-distribution concept. This is because physical need is two-dimensional, reflecting both human individuality and human sociality. Physical need, therefore, incorporates both minimal living and income distribution. Thus, a person is needy if he or she (1) cannot afford the minimum market basket of goods and services, or (2) is separated from the company of others by a large difference in income. The needy person is one who is physically depleted or socio-economically segregated. The more severe the segregation or depletion, the greater the unmet need.

This controversy has persisted because students who use the absolute standard are not aware that they implicitly define human beings one-dimensionally as individuals alone. Similarly, those who use the relative standard are unaware that they implicitly construe human beings only as social beings.

## Criteria of poverty

Before either a minimal-living standard or income-distribution standard can be used empirically, it is necessary to express physical need in measurable form. This is done by assigning a critical value to the amount of unmet need that is incompatible with physical well-being. Whenever economic resources fall short of the critical value, unmet need is said to exist. We refer to that critical value which expresses unmet physical need in measurable form as a criterion of poverty ("threshold" according to the official US poverty standard).

The official poverty standard incorporates a two-way classification scheme – poor/non-poor – which operates arbitrarily. A family is poor if annual income is at or below a predetermined annual income threshold, but not poor if annual income is one dollar above the threshold. Accordingly, a three-way classification scheme – poor, near poor and not poor – is recommended which in effect demands a larger difference in annual income for a person to shift back and forth between poor and not poor.

Next it is necessary to fit the two-dimensional character of physical need – minimal living and income distribution – into the three-part classification scheme. The following prototype criterion of poverty demonstrates how that is done, blending the threshold or critical minimum from the official standard with the lowest decile from the income distribution.

A person is poor if income is below the official threshold *and* in the lowest decile of the income distribution. A person is not poor if income is above the threshold *and* above the lowest decile. A person is near poor if income is (1) below the threshold but not in the lowest decile, or (2) in the lowest decile but above the threshold.

Clearly, a large number of different criteria of poverty could be developed in similar fashion. Studies that apply the various criteria of poverty to the same population, develop poverty estimates for each one of the various criteria proposed, and compare those estimates with the official poverty estimates, will help us decide which criterion is best.

## A satisfactory criterion of poverty

A satisfactory criterion of poverty should be direct, comprehensive, consistent, convenient and, most especially, accepted. By "direct" is meant that the criterion measures unmet physical need rather than estimating it. A criterion is comprehensive if it encompasses every relevant aspect of unmet need; it is "selective" if it leaves out some aspect of need or resources. "Consistent" means that the criterion assigns everyone in the same circumstances with regard to unmet physical need into the same (poor, near poor, not poor) classification. A criterion of poverty ideally is "convenient," that is, it is relatively simple to apply it to the data and to generate estimates of poverty or unmet need.

The importance of public acceptance derives from the fact that need is a normative concept. Acceptance of a given criterion indicates that there is wide agreement that it conforms to the value systems of large numbers of persons. In 1965, Orshansky described the official poverty standard as "still relatively crude," and the food–income relationship as an "interim guide" to poverty thresholds. More than twenty years later, she confirmed that the poverty concept turns importantly on the absolute/relative question.

By conceptualizing poverty in terms of the duality of human nature and by selecting critical values that express that conceptualization in measurable form a better criterion of poverty will emerge. Such a criterion probes more deeply into the question: What does it mean to be poor?

EDWARD J. O'BOYLE

# poverty: definition and measurement

## Poverty line

Surprisingly, the attempt to define and measure poverty has had a relatively short history. Despite the widespread and deep poverty in nineteenth-century industrial England, no one, including Friedrich Engels (1845), who best described the problem, sought to calculate the extent of poverty. It was not until the beginning of the twentieth century that Charles Booth (1902–4), an English businessman, attempted to draw a boundary line between adequate family income and inadequate, or below poverty level, family income. Booth also surveyed London families in order to determine the percentage of families that were poor and by how much poor families fell short of the poverty line.

The work of Booth inspired the US Bureau of Labor to begin studying the income levels that would meet minimum family needs for food, clothing, shelter and health. From these studies, the poverty-level income for a family of five in the 1920s was placed at between $1000 and $1100 (Lamale 1958).

Mollie Orshansky (1969) of the US Social Security Administration expanded upon this work during the 1960s. Her methodology has become the standard practice for measuring poverty in the United States. Orshansky first calculated the cost of the minimum amount of food that a family would need to survive. Since Department of Agriculture surveys at the time found that families spent around one-third of their income on food, Orshansky multiplied by three the cost of an economy food plan for families of different types and sizes in order to arrive at poverty lines for each family type.

Every year the poverty line for each family type gets increased, based upon the annual rise in consumer prices. Poverty lines thus represent a fixed and constant real standard of living. In 1993, the poverty line for a family of four in the United States was $14,763. This represents the same purchasing power for a family of four as the 1962 poverty line of $3,100. The overall poverty rate is calculated as the percentage of families falling below the poverty line (for their family size and type) in a given year. In 1993, 12.3 percent of all families in the United States did not have sufficient income to bring them above their poverty line.

During the late twentieth century, poverty measurement became a contentious issue, and the Orshansky methodology has been criticized on a number of grounds. Many scholars believe the poverty rates calculated by using this method are far too low. For example, some authors note that the original food budgets used by Orshansky were designed for only short-term emergency situations, and could not meet the nutritional needs of a family for an entire year. Since the food budgets used by Orshansky were 80 percent of a permanent nutritional diet, these authors argue that the Orshansky poverty lines are 20 percent too low. It is also argued that, because food consumption has fallen from one-third to one-fifth of family spending, current poverty lines should be based upon a food multiplier of five rather than a food multiplier of three. This would lead to poverty lines that are 67 percent higher than the official poverty lines (consistent with public opinion about the amount of money a family requires if it is to escape poverty).

Taking a slightly different approach, Watts (1986) notes that, in the early 1960s, poor families paid no income taxes and virtually no social security taxes. But by the mid 1980s poor families in the United States were subject to considerable taxation. Computing poverty rates based upon pre-tax income ignores the fact that, because of higher taxes, incomes today buy less than a comparable (real) pre-tax income from the 1960s.

The poverty lines established by Orshansky have also been criticized as leading to poverty estimates that are too high. Friedman (1965) contends that families below the official poverty line still enjoy most of the amenities that Americans take for granted. For example, the poor have access to free education; they own televisions and automobiles; and they live in domiciles with indoor plumbing, central heating and electricity. Friedman also argues that low-income families probably consume too many calories. Since the Orshansky methodology is based upon family food and calorie consumption, according to this argument it overestimates the extent of poverty.

Others, including Browning (1975), criticize the Orshansky methodology because it looks only at money income. These authors point out that poor families have been receiving more and more income in the form of in-kind government benefits, such as Food Stamps (which provide free or subsidized food), Medicaid (which provides free medical care) and housing vouchers. Consequently, they contend that official poverty lines underestimate the living standard of low-income families and overestimate the number of families that are poor. In an attempt to deal with this problem, Paglin (1980) has added the value of in-kind transfers to family income and then recomputed the US poverty rate. He finds that the extent of poverty is dramatically reduced when the value of in-kind benefits gets taken into account.

## Relative poverty

Perhaps the most frequent criticism of the Orshansky poverty lines is that they establish an absolute, rather than a relative, measure of poverty. Since poverty lines are increased every year with the rate of inflation, the real standard of living necessary to escape poverty never increases. However, many authors argue that people are social animals. As a result, the standard of what is minimally necessary must change over time. For example, Appelbaum (1977) points out that prior to 1929 bathtubs were not considered a necessity, and standards of nutrition allowed for little consumption of fruit and vegetables. Today an indoor bath is a necessity, since there are no longer any alternatives, and fresh fruit and vegetables are regarded as an important part of a minimally acceptable diet.

For a more contemporary example, consider family needs for child care. In the early 1960s, when Orshansky developed her poverty lines,

child care was a luxury for almost all families. But in the 1990s, with single-parent and two-earner families becoming the norm, child care has become a necessity. Consequently, child care expenses should be added to necessary family expenditures and become part of the minimum income that a family requires.

Relative measures of poverty have become increasingly popular during the 1990s. This has been due partly to the many criticisms that have been raised against defining poverty in absolute terms; but this has also been a result of the Luxembourg Income Study, an international data base containing income and socio-demographic data for families in many developed countries (see Pressman 1991). The Luxembourg Income Study has allowed scholars to compare income distribution and poverty across countries, to examine the reasons some countries experience higher poverty, and to identify the sorts of policies that are effective in reducing poverty.

## International comparisons

In cross-nation studies, it is difficult to compare incomes denominated in different national currencies. Is 1 million yen really equal to $10,000 just because the current exchange rate is $1=100 yen? And do more Americans suddenly become poor while more Japanese families escape poverty because the dollar falls and the yen rises in value? Since families primarily consume goods and services produced in their own nation, family well-being usually changes little when exchange rates fluctuate. Thus, using exchange rates to compare income levels in different countries is inadequate; yet we still need some means of comparing poverty rates across nations.

One definition of poverty employed by many scholars using the Luxembourg Income Study is family income (adjusted for family size) below 50 percent of national median income. This definition of poverty is explicitly a relative one: any family receiving less than 50 percent of the national median is regarded as poor. This definition also allows a comparison of poverty rates among developed countries without having to depend on exchange rates to measure equal income levels in two different countries. This definition is also flexible in that the 50 percent figure can be easily increased or decreased. But such flexibility has led to further arguments concerning the minimum standard of living that is adequate in each country. Is 50 percent of median income enough? Is it too much? These questions are forcing every country to develop better measures of income adequacy and income poverty.

## See also:

collective social wealth; crime; distribution of income; ethics and morality; inequality; justice; needs; normative and positive economics; poverty: absolute and relative

## Selected references

Appelbaum, Diana Karter (1977) "The Level of the Poverty Line: A Historical Survey," *Social Service Review* 51(September): 514–23.

Booth, Charles (1902–4) *Life and Labour of the People in London*, New York and London: AMS Press.

Browning, Edgar K. (1975) *Redistribution and the Welfare System*, Washington, DC: American Enterprise Institute.

Engels, Friedrich (1845) *The Condition of the Working Class in England*, Moscow: Progress Publishers, 1992.

Friedman, Rose D. (1965) *Poverty: Definition and Perspective*, Washington, DC: American Enterprise Institute.

Lamale, Helen H. (1958) "Changes in Concepts of Income Adequacy Over the Last Century," *American Economic Review* 48(May): 291–99.

Orshansky, Mollie (1969) "How Poverty is Measured," *Monthly Labor Review* 92(February): 37–41.

Paglin, Morton (1980) *Poverty and Transfers In-Kind: A Re-evaluation of Poverty in the United States*, Stanford, CA: Hoover Institution.

Pressman, Steven (1991) "Frontiers of Economic Knowledge: The Luxembourg Income Study," *Eastern Economic Journal* 17.

Watts, Harold W. (1986) "Have Our Measures of Poverty Become Poorer?," *Focus* 9(Summer): 18–23.

STEVEN PRESSMAN

**POVERTY, FEMINIZATION OF:** *see* feminization of poverty

# pragmatism

The philosophical school of thought known as "pragmatism" is American in origin and arises from the works of Charles S. Peirce (1839–1914), William James (1842–1910) and John Dewey (1859–1952). Whereas Peirce and James offered the first formulations of pragmatism, it was John Dewey, by virtue of his longevity and voluminous scholarly output, who developed his "instrumentalist" version of pragmatism into the most important American philosophical school of thought in the twentieth century. Dewey's "pragmatic instrumentalism," as he referred to it, has had a profound influence on the philosophies of science, society, democracy, law, education and the methodology of American institutional/evolutionary economics, particularly the neoinstitutionalist literature (Bush 1993).

## Epistemology

Pragmatists ground their philosophy on a rejection of classical metaphysical notions of "essences," "foundationalist first principles," "ultimate ends," "eternal verities" and absolutistic formulations of any kind. Such constructs, they argue, are in their very nature prior to inquiry and therefore set arbitrary limits on inquiry by imposing constraints on it from without. They give rise to the "quest for certainty," which is based on the epistemological view that authentic knowledge must be indubitable (Dewey 1929). Pragmatists reject the quest for certainty on the fallibilist grounds that all knowledge claims are at best contingent, being subject to modification or refutation as inquiry moves forward. Thus, they reject the foundationalist belief that the validity of any given proposition must be referred back to some ultimate criterion of meaning or truth in order to establish its authenticity. Absolutisms are by definition beyond refutation; once accepted, they block the path of inquiry by insulating crucial assumptions and preconceptions from critical scrutiny. As Dewey observes (1938: 16), "there is no belief so settled as not to be exposed to further inquiry."

In contrast to foundationalist classical philosophy and Kantian idealism, pragmatists do not establish the meaning and truth of propositions by reference to universal epistemological standards established prior to the formulation of propositions. Pragmatists do not look to antecedents but to consequences in establishing the meaning and truth of propositions. They view ideas as plans for action, and they test their validity by the consequences that follow from acting on them. As Gouinlock puts it, "meanings, then, are not something antecedently given and intuited, but are determined by experimental operations. To find the meaning of 'glass' or of 'tree,' one must perform various operations with the things denominated" (Gouinlock 1984: x). Similarly, the truth (with a lower case "t") of a proposition is tested in its consequences by undertaking those actions set forth in the proposition and determining whether in fact the results are those entailed by its meaning.

## Ontology

With respect to ontological questions, pragmatism offers an alternative to the classical and contemporary formulations of both idealism and realism. Pragmatism adheres to a realist ontology in the sense that it "accepts things and events for what they are independently of thought" (Dewey 1925: 18). On the other hand, pragmatism is idealist "in so far as it contends that thought gives birth to distinctive acts which modify future facts and events in such a way as to render them more reasonable, that is to say, more adequate to the ends which we propose for ourselves" (Dewey 1925: 18). This ontological position lays the foundation for Dewey's pragmatic instrumentalist theory of knowledge.

## Scientific participation, doubt and community

Knowledge, according to Dewey, is "the product of competent inquiry" (Dewey 1938: 16). He calls such knowledge "warranted assertions." In spelling out his theory of inquiry, Dewey rejects the "spectator theory of knowledge," which results from the belief that "what is known is antecedent to the mental act of observation and inquiry, and is totally unaffected by these acts" (Dewey 1929: 19). "If knowing," Dewey says, "is not the act of an outside spectator but of a participator inside the natural and social scene, then the true object of knowledge resides in the consequences of directed action" (Dewey 1929: 157). Richard Rorty points out that Dewey's rejection of the spectator theory of knowledge constitutes a rejection of the idea that philosophy provides a "mirror of nature" (Rorty 1979).

According to Peirce, James and Dewey, inquiry itself has its origin in doubt. Doubt arises in response to what Dewey calls an "indeterminate situation," in which there is a sensed awareness that something is wrong, that what is the case ought not be the case. This sensed awareness is itself precognitive; it is an intuitive response to a real experience in which our habitual modes of thought and behavior are found not to have the expected consequences. Dewey lays stress on the point that it is the situation that is indeterminate; it is an existential condition, not a subjective state of mind. Inquiry comes into play when intelligence is utilized to transform the indeterminate situation into a "problematic situation." Inquiry into a particular problematic situation is brought to a successful conclusion with the "institution of conditions which remove the need for doubt." Dewey puts the matter as follows: "inquiry effects existential transformation and reconstruction of the material with which it deals; the result of the transformation, when it is grounded, being conversion of an indeterminate problematic situation into a determinate resolved one" (Dewey 1939: 161). In social inquiry, this leads to the view that the solution of social problems entails INSTITUTIONAL CHANGE AND ADJUSTMENT (Dewey 1929: 217–8).

Pragmatists view inquiry as a social process, requiring collaboration among a community of investigators. Accordingly, Dewey writes (1938: 484): "An inquirer in a given special field appeals to the experiences of the community of his fellow workers for confirmation and correction of his results." In consequence, inquiry involves "judgments of practice" which provide the values or norms by which the behavior of the community of investigators is correlated. Values direct the behavior of the investigator in the conduct of inquiry (Dewey 1929: 209). The only time that values pose a threat to "objectivity" is when "the values employed are not determined in and by the process of inquiry" (Dewey 1938: 496). Thus, contrary to the claims of the positivists, scientific inquiry is not value-free. The "objectivity" of science depends not on the absence of normative judgments, but rather on the use of instrumentally warranted normative judgments; that is, judgments of value that arise within inquiry and contribute to its continuity (see VALUE JUDGMENTS AND WORLD VIEWS; NORMATIVE AND POSITIVE ECONOMICS).

## Aversion to dualism

Pragmatists find philosophically barren the virtually endless array of philosophical dualisms which arise in both classical metaphysics and contemporary positivism. A partial list would include such dualisms as appearance/reality, mind/body, subjective/objective, normative/positive, fact/value, science/ethics, thought/action, means/ends and so forth. Pragmatists believe that such metaphysical constructs lead to philosophical cul-de-sacs by forging epistemological and ontological distinctions that distort our efforts to understand the relationship of thought to action in human experience. Positivism, in particular, relies on the cleavage between the analytic and the synthetic in formulating what Willard Quine calls the "dogma" of reductionism in *From a Logical Point of View* (1953: 41).

Dewey's aversion to dualism in philosophical thought is perhaps no better illustrated than in his rejection of the means/ends dualism. The means/ends dualism works in tandem with the normative/positive dualism to postulate the notion that "ends" as values are validated independently of the means by which they are accomplished (Dewey 1939). They are prescribed, for example, by the immemorial beliefs of the tribe, or the word of God, or given philosophically as some sort of categorical imperative. What lies in the realm of human discretion is the choice of the means by which to achieve a predetermined end. Thus, the legitimacy of the means of human action is determined by the authenticity of the ends of human action. Such a view reinforces the idea that "values" as "ends" are beyond rational consideration, critique, revision or rejection. In contrast, Dewey speaks of the "mean–ends continuum," in which "ends" are not ultimate but, rather, contingent and evolving "ends-in-view." With respect to inquiry, as organic elements of an evolving continuum, the ends-in-view of a given problem-solving process become the means by which newly discovered problems may be pursued. With respect to questions of ethics, the notion of the means-ends continuum requires that the ethical status of the ends-in-view cannot be considered independently of the ethical status of the means, and vice versa. As Gouinlock (1984: xii) observes, "Instrumentalism teaches the organic unity of thought, action, and the values of experience" (see ETHICS AND MORALITY).

## Hermeneutics

One of the most interesting and controversial developments in the recent literature of pragmatism is to be found in the works of Richard Rorty. John P. Diggins (1994: 492) has observed that "under Rorty the promise of pragmatism has moved from science and technology to script and vocabulary, from controlled experiment to constructed narration." Rorty has converted Dewey's rejection of philosophy as the mirror of nature into a quest for a hermeneutical alternative to epistemology (Rorty 1979: 315–56). In taking this philosophical stance, Rorty has attempted to align American pragmatism with the postmodern hermeneutics of continental philosophy. Many Deweyan instrumentalists have been highly critical of Rorty's intellectual strategy to update pragmatism in this fashion. The debate has spilled over into the literature of the social sciences where pragmatic instrumentalism has had a major influence on methodology, as in the case of neoinstitutional economics. The controversy over Rorty's effort to redirect pragmatism along the lines of hermeneutical philosophy promises to have a profound impact on the future evolution of this philosophical perspective.

## See also:

critical realism; institutional political economy: major contemporary themes; instrumental value theory; neoinstitutionalism

## Selected references

Bush, Paul D. (1993) "The Methodology of Institutional Economics: A Pragmatic Instrumentalist Perspective," in Marc R. Tool (ed.), *Institutional Economics: Theory, Method, Policy*, Boston: Kluwer Academic Publishers, 59–107.

Dewey, John (1925) "The Development of American Pragmatism," in Jo Ann Boydston (ed.), *John Dewey: The Later Works, 1925–1953, Vol 2: 1925–1927*, Carbondale, IL: Southern Illinois University Press, 1984, 3–21.

—— (1929) "The Quest for Certainty," in Jo Ann Boydston (ed.), *John Dewey: The Later Works, 1925–1953, Vol 4: 1929*, Carbondale, IL: Southern Illinois University Press, 1988.

—— (1938) "Logic: The Theory of Inquiry," in Jo Ann Boydston (ed.), *John Dewey: The Later Works, 1925–1953, Vol 12*, Carbondale, IL: Southern Illinois University Press, 1986.

—— (1939) "The Theory of Valuation," in Jo Ann Boydston (ed.), *John Dewey: The Later Works, 1925–1953, Vol 13*, Carbondale, IL: Southern Illinois University Press, 1988.

Diggins, John Patrick (1994) The *Promise of Pragmatism*, Chicago: University of Chicago Press.

Gouinlock, James (1984) "Introduction," in Jo Ann Boydston (ed.), *John Dewey: The Later Works, 1925–1953, Vol 2: 1925–1927*, Carbondale, IL: Southern Illinois University Press, 1984, ix–xxxvi.

James, William (1907) *Pragmatism*, New York: Longman, Green & Company, 1922.

Peirce, Charles S. (1877) "The Fixation of Belief," in Christian J.W. Kloesel (ed.), *Writings of Charles S. Peirce, Vol. 3: 1872–1878*, Bloomington, IN: Indiana University Press, 1986, 242–57.

—— (1878) "How to Make Our Ideas Clear," in Christian J.W. Kloesel (ed.), *Writings of Charles S. Peirce, Vol. 3: 1872–1878*, Bloomington, IN: Indiana University Press, 1986, 257–76.

Rorty, Richard (1979) *Philosophy and the Mirror of Nature*, Princeton, NJ: Princeton University Press.

PAUL D. BUSH

# precapitalist world-systems

Several theorists argue, contrary to conventional WORLD-SYSTEMS ANALYSIS, that world-systems existed in the ancient world. ("World" means a self-contained division of labor and is *not* a synonym for "global.") Precapitalist world-systems share many features with the modern world-system. The main ones include the division into core, periphery and semiperiphery; EXPLOITATION of peripheral areas by core areas, and different social structures in peripheral and core areas. Also, there were different degrees of technological and economic development, different kinds of production processes and different roles in trade. There are four sources for these claims.

## Interregional interaction systems

Pailes and Whitecotton (1979) used world-systems analysis to explain connections between development in Mesoamerica and what is now northern Mexico and south-western USA. Others have found world-system like structures in the ancient Near East, ancient Peru, Oaxaca and the Yucatan Peninsula in Mexico. Many, however, have found world-systems analysis inadequate in such settings (Schortman and Urban 1992; Hall and Chase-Dunn 1993). Specifically, Jane Schneider (1977) questioned world-systems analysis's emphasis on bulk goods exchange as a key process. She argued that the exchange of luxury goods (silk, precious metals or stones) often played a vital role in the social reproduction of early social systems.

## The East fell

Janet Abu-Lughod (1989) argues that the modern world-system has roots as far back as the twelfth century, and that "the West" did not rise, but that the "East fell." That is, that Chinese withdrawal from the South Seas left the field open to Portuguese and Dutch explorer/merchants. However, she is skeptical about tracing origins any further back (Frank and Gills 1993: ch. 9). Similarly George Modelski and William Thompson (1995) are pushing their analyses of the roles of technology, warfare and international relations in world-systems further into the past. David Wilkinson (Frank and Gills 1993: ch. 7; Sanderson 1995: chaps 2, 10) argues that central civilization (a form of world-system) has expanded steadily since it origins in Mesopotamia 5,000 years ago. Andre Gunder Frank and Barry Gills agree with Wilkinson on the origins, but emphasize oscillations between private and state ACCUMULATION over this period. Civilizationist Matthew Melko applauds this new attention to ancient empires, but criticizes world-systems analysis for under-

emphasizing CULTURE (Sanderson 1995: ch. 1). Wallerstein is cautious of these extensions of the world-systems analysis (Frank and Gills 1993: ch. 10; Sanderson 1995: ch. 9).

## Hegemonic cycles

Chase-Dunn and Hall (1997: ch. 11) consider whether current changes in the modern world-system (the decline of hegemony of the USA, the movement of financial power to Japan, and so on) are harbingers of a new form of world-system, or simply another round of the hegemonic cycle. They suggest the possibility of a future "socialist" world-system in which resources are used to promote collective egalitarian welfare through democratic practices. They propose that the study of major world-system changes in the past might shed light on current changes and future possibilities.

## Fundamental unit of analysis

Finally, there is a world-systems analysis explanation of social evolution. Explicitly disavowing teleological and unilinear approaches, Chase-Dunn and Hall (1997) argue that world-systems are the fundamental "unit of analysis" of social evolution. That is, the roles of states, groups or individuals in social evolution must be understood within their world-system contexts. To do this they convert many world-systems analysis assumptions into empirical questions. They raise questions such as "how and when do hierarchies arise?" "how and when does intersocietal domination arise?" and "what types of world-systems have existed?".

They argue that the first world-systems were composed of sedentary foragers, who interacted across cultural groups. Such systems had little or no hierarchy or domination. Trade and capital accumulation were embedded in the kinship and other normative relationships. When some groups began to dominate others, ranked lineage systems (chiefdoms) appeared. Eventually, as populations grew and competing groups were constrained within a limited territory, states were invented as a means of organizing hierarchy. In state-based world-systems, accumulation of capital occurred through coercion in any of several forms (FEUDALISM, helotry, SLAVERY, tribute and so on). The tributary world-systems contained pockets of capitalist production, typically in city-states that specialized in trade (for example, Phonecia). These pockets grew continuously, if sporadically. Only in the seventeenth century did capitalists gain control of the Dutch state. Capital was accumulated according to the logic of CAPITALISM (through the control of productive processes). This European based world-system became truly global in the late nineteenth century.

## Boundaries of the world-system

Chase-Dunn and Hall have modified world-systems analysis further. Based on the work of others, they argue that world-systems have boundaries formed by (1) information or cultural flows (civilizationists); (2) luxury or prestige goods exchanges; (3) political/military interactions; and (4) bulk goods exchanges (conventional world-systems analysis). Only rarely, such as in very small systems, or the modern world-system, do all four boundaries coincide. The first two boundaries, information and luxury goods, are the largest, although they typically do not coincide. Trade in luxury goods has always been important, but in "prestige" goods economies (Peregrine 1992) such trade plays a vital role in maintaining the authority and power of leaders. Political/military boundaries are usually nested within information and prestige goods boundaries. Bulk goods exchange networks are the smallest of the four. The effects of changes in one boundary on the others remain theoretical and empirical problems.

In this view, Eurasia has been linked at the information and luxury goods levels since at least early Roman times. The Mongol conquests in the thirteenth century linked most of it at the political/military level, albeit briefly. Only the modern world-system is linked globally at the bulk goods level. Indeed, the "rise of the West" was possible only because the Chinese withdrew from long-distance trade due to fear of another Mongol conquest and concerns about regime stability. Thus, explanations that rely solely on internal factors, whether Weberian rationality or Marxian CLASS competition, are incomplete: their effects can only be explained within a world-system context.

## World-system pulsations

Although empirical work is recent, there are some interesting findings (Sanderson 1995: ch. 4; Chase-Dunn and Hall 1997). All world-systems seem to pulse; that is, they expand and contract or have periods of faster and slower expansion. Hierarchical systems (those with chiefdoms or states) also have cycles of rise and demise of hegemonic states (they oscillate between what world-systems analysis calls world-empires and world-economies). While the modern world-system is one of the longest lived interstate systems, there have been others. Andrew Bosworth (Sanderson 1995: ch. 8) has found correlations in city size with these cycles. Semi-peripheral regions are a common seedbed of change. There has been a sporadic but steady increase in global inequality, size of systems, density of trade – especially in bulk goods – and cycles of warfare. While still tentative, these findings warrant further investigation.

## Continuous transformation

In contrast to Chase-Dunn and Hall, Frank and Gills stress the continuity of capital accumulation over the last 5,000 years. They do not see transformations, but one continuous transformation. Because they begin their account after states have appeared they do not address this major transformation. This debate notwithstanding, Frank has begun to rethink world-systems analysis altogether (Sanderson 1995: ch. 6). In his view, the recent resurgence of "the East" is not something novel, but a return to normalcy after a few centuries of aberrant Western domination. Pre-capitalist world-systems analysis, especially in Frank's hands, is a trenchant critique of Eurocentric social science (Sanderson 1995: ch. 7).

## See also:

core–periphery analysis; cycles and trends in the world capitalist economy; global crisis of world capitalism; hegemony in the world economy; world-system: incorporation into

## Selected references

Abu-Lughod, Janet L. (1989) *Before European Hegemony: The World System A.D. 1250–1350*, New York: Oxford University Press.

Chase-Dunn, Christopher and Hall, Thomas D. (1997) *Rise and Demise: Comparing World-Systems*, Boulder, CO: Westview Press.

Frank, A.G. and Gills, B.K. (eds) (1993) *The World System: Five Hundred Years or Five Thousand?* London: Routledge.

Hall, Thomas D. and Chase-Dunn, Christopher (1993) "The World-Systems Perspective and Archaeology: Forward into the Past," *Journal of Archaeological Research* 1: 121–43.

Modelski, George and Thompson, William R. (1995) *Leading Sectors and World Powers: The Coevolution of Global Politics and Economics*, Columbia, SC: University of South Carolina Press.

Pailes, Richard A. and Whitecotton, Joseph W. (1979) "Greater Southwest and Mesoamerican World-Systems," in W.W. Savage, Jr and S.I. Thompson (eds), *The Frontier: Comparative Studies*, vol. 2, Norman, OK: University of Oklahoma Press, 105–21.

Peregrine, Peter N. (1992) *Mississippian Evolution: A World-System Perspective*, Monographs in World Archaeology 9, Madison, WI: Prehistory Press.

Sanderson, Stephen K. (ed.) (1995) *Civilizations and World-Systems: Two Approaches to the Study of World-Historical Change*, Walnut Creek, CA: Altamira Press.

Schneider, Jane (1977) "Was There a Pre-Capitalist World-System?," *Peasant Studies* 6: 20–9; repr. in C. Chase-Dunn and T.D. Hall (eds), *Core/Periphery Relations in Precapitalist Worlds*, Boulder, CO: Westview Press, 45–66.

Schortman, Edward M. and Urban, Patricia A. (eds) (1992) *Resources, Power, and Interregional Interaction*, New York: Plenum Press.

THOMAS D. HALL

# price theory, Sraffian

Sraffa's formalization of prices in *Production of Commodities by Means of Commodities* (1960) is a modern interpretation of the classical theory of prices of production, as it appeared in the works of Ricardo and Marx. The stress is on the conditions of reproduction of the commodities which determine their long-period prices, with explicit reference neither to the "utility" of the commodities nor to their "scarcity." The formalization allows us to prove important properties stated by the classical economists and to study various economic problems, such as the incidence of distribution or taxation on prices.

## Characteristics of production

The two important characteristics of production at the basis of the formalization are reproducibility and uniform profitability.

According to the "circular" conception inherited from Quesnay and the classicals, commodities are reproduced from period to period by means of commodities and labor. This leaves aside the case of fine wines and master paintings, whose prices are mainly influenced by demand. A process of production is represented by a vector of quantities $a_{ij}$ of inputs $j(j = 1, \ldots, n)$ which, jointly with quantity $l_i$ of labor (assumed to be homogeneous for the sake of simplicity), produce $b_i$ units of commodity $i$. By setting the unit of measure of good $i$ appropriately, a method of production, or process, is formally written as

$$a_{i1} \text{ good } 1 \oplus \ldots \oplus a_{ij} \text{ good } j$$
$$\oplus \ldots \oplus a_{in} \text{ good } n$$
$$\oplus l_i \text{ labor} \rightarrow 1 \text{ unit of } i$$

A system of production is obtained by collecting $n$ such processes, one for the (re)production of every commodity $i = 1, \ldots, n$. One period of production separates the inputs and the production of the output.

The profitability of the $i$th process is based on the comparison of the value of the product with that of the inputs. Though the classical economists admitted that the wage is advanced from capital, we follow Sraffa's alternative hypothesis and assume that it is paid at the end of the period, when the product is obtained. For a nominal wage $w$ and a nominal price $p_i$ of commodity $i$, the rate of profit $r_i$ on the $i$th process is determined by the relationship

$$(1 + r_i)\left(\sum_j a_{ij}p_j\right) = p_i - wl_i \qquad (1)$$

The classical economists referred to competition to justify the hypothesis, which reflects a long-run tendency of capitalism, that all operated processes yield the same rate of profit $r$. Sraffa simply assumes the uniformity of the rate of profit. The price system thus satisfies the equality:

$$(1 + r)\mathbf{A}\mathbf{p} + w\mathbf{L} = \mathbf{p} \qquad (2)$$

where $\mathbf{A}$ is the $n \times n$ matrix of material input, $\mathbf{L}$ the $n \times 1$ labor vector, $\mathbf{p}$ the $n \times 1$ price vector and $w$ the nominal wage. For a given rate of profit $r$ and a given technique $(\mathbf{A}, \mathbf{L})$, the $(n+1)$ unknowns $(\mathbf{p}, w)$ are determined up to a factor as the solution to the $n$ equations (2). A *numéraire* is often chosen: the wage rate ($w = 1$; the prices are then expressed in terms of wage), or a specific commodity $j$ ($p_j = 1$), or a basket of commodities.

## Prices of production

These prices are called prices of production. They only depend on the conditions of production, as represented by the operated processes, and on distribution, as represented

either by the rate of profit (Sraffa's choice) or the real wage (the classical hypothesis), the other variable being endogenously determined. In Sraffa's conception, the minimum wage, considered as socially necessary, is incorporated into the input matrix, and variable $w$ only represents that part of wage above the minimum, which may depend on the state of the class struggle; with this convention, a zero level of variable $w$ is not unrealistic.

The circularity of production reflects itself in the fact that prices appear on both sides of equation (2). It is only for a "pure non-basic," i.e. a final consumption good which does not enter in any production process, that the price can be considered as a mere cost of production (see BASIC AND NON-BASIC COMMODITIES).

## Formal pricing solution

Prices are formally obtained by solving equation (2) as

$$\mathbf{p} = w(\mathbf{I} - (1+r)\mathbf{A})^{-1}\mathbf{L}$$

Their properties derive formally from the semipositivity of the input matrix, as expressed, for instance, by the Perron–Frobenius theorem. Sraffa uses arguments more closely related to economics. Here are three typical properties: the first one was suggested by Marx, the second by Ricardo, but the third goes against the intuition of the classical economists.

The price vector is positive as long as the rate of profit does not exceed a maximal rate of profit $R$, formally defined by the property that $(1 + R)^{-1}$ is the Perron–Frobenius root of matrix $\mathbf{A}$. The result $r = R$ is obtained for a null wage, and $R$ is positive as soon as a surplus can be produced in the economy.

There is a trade-off between the level of the rate of profit and the real wage, expressed in terms of any commodity. Or, equivalently, all prices in terms of wage increase with the rate of profit. When the rate of profit changes, the relative prices $p_i/p_j$ usually change in a very complex manner, which does not reflect the degree of capital intensity of industries $i$ and $j$.

For a zero rate of profit, the prices in terms

of wage and the labor values (see LABOR THEORY OF VALUE) both satisfy the condition: value (price) of the output = value (price) of the inputs + direct labor used. Hence they are formally equal (in Marxist terms, the labor values are the exchange ratios if there is no exploitation). The classical economists knew that this identity no longer holds for positive rates of profit, because the structure of relative prices is modified (except in the case of uniform organic composition of capital). The TRANSFORMATION PROBLEM examines whether the prices can be explained by referring to the labor values. Marx's answer is positive, but Sraffa simply ignores the problem.

## Technique and joint production

To assume that the technique of production is unique is only a first step. The choice of technique is considered in Part 3 of Sraffa's *Production of Commodities by Means of Commodities*. Its difficulty is due to the interactions between prices and techniques. Prices are determined by the operated methods, but the operated methods are themselves chosen because they are the cheapest, i.e. the prices must be known. It is possible to disentangle from this apparent difficulty and, eventually, define the prices and generalize the Ricardian trade-off property to the case of choice of technique. The study of multiple-product systems, when a process of production produces several goods simultaneously, is much harder.

According to Sraffa, production with fixed capital is the "leading species" of this joint production (an agricultural process using a tractor produces corn and, simultaneously, an older tractor). The modern analysis has basically succeeded in generalizing the properties of single-product systems to fixed capital. Joint production also includes production with land. In pure joint production, as represented by the familiar example of wool and mutton, some of Sraffa's statements are rejected by the Sraffian authors. The main difficulty was underlined by Jevons: the number of processes may fall short of that of commodities, hence prices are not determined by the conditions of production

alone (imagine the extreme case of one operated process only and $n$ produced commodities) and depend directly on demand. The analysis of joint production is presently an active field of research.

## See also:

competition and the average rate of profit; composition of capital; falling rate of profit tendency; Sraffian political economy

## Selected references

Kurz, H.D. and Salvadori, N. (1995) *Theory of Production*, Cambridge: Cambridge University Press.
Pasinetti, L.L. (1977) *Lectures on the Theory of Production*, London: Macmillan.
Schefold, B. (1989) *Mr. Sraffa on Joint Production and Other Essays*, London: Unwin Hyman.

CHRISTIAN BIDARD

# pricing

## Introduction

Political economy considers pricing as an integral part of the decision making process of the modern CORPORATION. Prices are set to advance CORPORATE OBJECTIVES, particularly survival and growth. Within this common orientation, a variety of pricing principles have been put forward, including administered pricing, full-cost pricing and markup pricing.

A characteristic common to all pricing principles in modern political economy is that prices are not directly affected by variations in product demand. These pricing principles are thereby distinguished from the market determination of prices through competitive supply and demand in neoclassical analysis. There is also a general tendency for price to exceed unit cost in the pricing principles of political economy, although this depends critically on the definition used for unit cost as is explained in the discussion below.

Adolph Berle and Gardiner Means, in their classic *The Modern Corporation and Private Property*, use the concept of the separation of OWNERSHIP AND CONTROL OF THE CORPORATION to explain their distinctive pricing behavior. Modern corporations are controlled by managers rather than individual proprietors, so that survival and growth supplant profit as the direct objective of activity. Imperfect competition in product markets allows prices to be set to support the achievement of these objectives.

## Administered pricing

Means (1962) develops the analysis of pricing by modern corporations into the principle of administered pricing. He argues in Chapter 4 that administered prices exhibit downward rigidity, and applies this notion to explaining price movements during the Great Depression. He also uses administered pricing in Chapter 5 to explain inflationary tendencies in highly concentrated US manufacturing industries during the 1950s. There is no role for an influence of product demand in the analysis of either depression or inflation.

## Full-cost pricing

Hall and Hitch (1939) provide an alternative explanation for the rigidity of prices during the Great Depression using the principle of full-cost pricing. Full-cost prices are set at a level sufficient to cover the sum of operating cost, overhead cost and an allowance for profit as a normal return to capital, provided that the firm is operating at its expected level of output. Short-run variation in product demand has no direct effect on price, as price is determined only with regard to the expected level of output. Also, while price is set to equal full cost, it exceeds the level of unit cost associated with variation in output (the operating costs of production labor and raw materials).

## Markup pricing

Andrews and Brunner (1975: ch. 2) extend the full-cost approach to a general framework for relating price to average cost. Price is determined by adding a margin (either net or gross) to a measure of average cost at normal output. The gross margin is added to average direct cost and is set to cover overhead cost and the allowance for profit at normal output. Alternatively, the net margin is added to average total cost at the normal output and is set to provide only the allowance for profit. Again, short-run variation in demand has no effect on average cost at normal output, so that price is invariant to demand (at least as long as input prices are unaffected by demand changes). Further, price can be described as cost determined in the sense that price moves proportionately with those costs that vary in the short run, namely average direct costs.

Adding a margin to some measure of standard unit cost to determine price has become known as the markup pricing principle. Markup pricing has been widely applied to determining price levels and, especially, to analyzing inflation in industrialized countries. The markup price is expressed as:

$$p = (1+m)u$$

where $p$ is price, $m$ is the markup and $u$ is the measure of unit cost to be marked up. If m is constant, we have

$$\Delta p = (1+m)\Delta u$$

Dividing the expression for $\Delta p$ by that for $p$, gives

$$\Delta p/p = \Delta u/u$$

Thus, the rate of price change is equal to the rate of cost change, so that inflation can be viewed as a cost-based phenomenon (see Coutts *et al.* (1978) for an empirical application of this approach and INFLATION: WAGE–COST MARKUP APPROACH).

## Explanations for the markup

The markup pricing principle is widely accepted in modern political economy. However, there is considerable disagreement over what determines the markup. In full-cost pricing the markup is determined to cover overhead cost and a normal profit, but other explanations for the markup have been offered as discussed below.

Lanzillotti (1958) suggests that most large US corporations use a variant of markup pricing, with the margin determined so as to achieve a target rate of return when operating at normal output. He links the adoption of the target rate of return to the investment plans of the corporation. A related linkage appears in the analysis of the new industrial state by Galbraith. Explicit models of pricing that determine the markup by investment opportunities are given by Eichner (1976) and Wood (1975), both of whom refer to the pioneering work of R. J. Ball in *Inflation and the Theory of Money*, first published in 1964. Harcourt and Kenyon (1976) summarize and extend investment-based models of determination of the markup. The markup determined according to these models varies in response to expected demand growth and other market opportunities, but is still insensitive to short-run demand fluctuation.

KALECKI (1971) derives an expression for the markup for manufacturing industry from pricing equations for individual firms. The coefficients in the firm pricing equations depend on the MONOPOLY, DEGREE OF in the firm's market position, so that the average markup for the industry expresses the average degree of monopoly for the industry. Kalecki relates this average degree of monopoly to industry concentration, union power and the level of selling costs, as well as to the level of overheads. Thus the markup is subject to change in the long run, due to changes in market power as well as changes in production and distribution methods.

It is important to note that Kalecki applies his markup pricing principle only to prices of finished manufactures. He treats prices of primary products as competitively determined and, hence, subject to demand as well as cost influences. Variation in demand affects the price of manufactures indirectly through the price of raw materials, providing a mechanism for altering income shares and obtaining macroeconomic equilibrium in response to supply or demand shocks. The distinction between demand-determined or competitive prices and cost-determined or oligopolistic prices is common in modern political economy and is used in explaining many phenomena (for example, Bloch and Sapsford (1991–2) use the distinction to explain cyclical movements in the international terms of trade between primary producers and manufacturers).

Whether the level of markup, as determined by Kalecki's analysis, differs from that implied by full-cost pricing is open to dispute. Cowling (1982: ch. 2) provides an interpretation of Kalecki's analysis that suggests different markups than with full-cost pricing. In particular, Cowling relates the degree of monopoly to the price elasticity of product demand and conjectures firms hold about the reactions of rivals to their own behavior. He thus provides a link between markup pricing and the neoclassical analysis of oligopoly, including a role for the strategic behavior of firms affecting conditions of entry into an industry. A view that rejects any interpretation of the markup based on the application of marginalism, including that associated with oligopoly, is put by proponents of the full-cost interpretation in a symposium on the marginalist controversy and post-Keynesian price theory in the *Journal of Post Keynesian Economics* in 1990–1.

## Conclusion

A clear link remains to be developed between the pricing principles of modern political economy, emphasizing the role of the markup, and the determination of prices according to costs of production in CLASSICAL POLITICAL ECONOMY. Price is not directly affected by demand and exceeds direct labor cost in both classical and modern analyses. However, the difference between price and cost in modern analysis allows corporations to advance their objectives, whereas in classical analysis the difference between price and direct labor cost provides the income of the capitalist and landlord classes. Kalecki's (1971) application of pricing analysis to the determination of income distribution in modern capitalism provides for comparison of classical and modern approaches, but the full potential of a linkage remains to be exploited.

## Selected references

Andrews, P. and Brunner, E. (1975) *Studies in Pricing*, London: Macmillan.

Bloch, Harry and Sapsford, David (1991–92) "Postwar Movements in the Prices of Primary Products and Manufactured Goods," *Journal of Post Keynesian Economics* 14: 249–67.

Coutts, Kenneth, Godley, Wynne and Nordhaus, William (1978) *Industrial Pricing in the United Kingdom*, Cambridge: Cambridge University Press.

Cowling, Keith (1982) *Monopoly Capitalism*, London: Macmillan.

Eichner, Alfred S. (1976) *The Megacorp and Oligopoly*, Cambridge: Cambridge University Press.

Hall, R.L. and Hitch, C.J. (1939) "Price Theory and Business Behaviour," *Oxford Economic Papers* 2: 12–33.

Harcourt, G.C. and Kenyon, Peter (1976) "Pricing and the Investment Decision," *Kyklos* 29: 449–77.

Kalecki, Michal (1971) *Selected Essays on the Dynamics of the Capitalist Economy*, Cambridge: Cambridge University Press.

Lanzillotti, Robert F. (1958) "Pricing Objectives in Large Companies," *American Economic Review* 48: 921–40.

Means, Gardiner C. (1962) *The Corporate Revolution in America*, New York: Crowell-Collier Press.

Wood, Adrian (1975) *A Theory of Profits*, Cambridge: Cambridge University Press.

HARRY BLOCH

# primitive accumulation

## Introduction

At any given time, capital ACCUMULATION presupposes that pre-accumulated capital has already been introduced into the process of production. Therefore it appears that capitalist production as a whole presupposes some "original," "primary" or "primitive" accumulation. Adam Smith in the *Wealth of Nations* claimed the accumulation of stock is a precondition for the enhancement of the productive power of workers and, therefore, that such an improvement is initiated by the accumulation process. According to CLASSICAL POLITICAL ECONOMY, this original accumulation of stock resulted from thrift and abstinence by a section of the population.

## Marx's analysis

In part 8 of Volume I of *Das Kapital* (chaps 26–33), Marx examines the forces which helped to propel the embryonic capitalist relations of production and reproduction onto the European (especially English) landscape. Special emphasis is placed on the role of the state in encouraging and forcing the dissolution of feudal relationships of land tenure, enhancing the supply of wage labor regardless of age and sex, extracting resources from the colonies and encouraging the continual supply of credit and funds for investment. The role of force, power, blood, death and destruction is critical to the creation of the new institutions of wage labor and capital; the class relations of capitalism.

For instance, Marx emphasizes the process whereby the institutions of serfdom, the guilds and feudal lordship relations dissolved when the agricultural population was expropriated from the land in England during the 1400s and 1500s. The landless moved into the towns at a greater rate than employment was available, creating numerous beggars, upper limits on wages, child labor and a large RESERVE ARMY OF LABOR. Turning small peasants (who usually supplied their own subsistence) into wage laborers created an important home market for capital in concentrated areas. Of critical importance was the process of global conquest, including the enslavement of indigenous populations, the plunder and monopoly marketing of colonies such as India, and commercial wars between Spain, Portugal, Holland, France and England. Primitive accumulation, as Marx saw it, was important to the fledging class relations of capitalism: as a ready supply of potential wage labor and a source of credit and riches for emerging capitalists.

## Traditional Marxist approaches

Within traditional Marxist literature, one main interpretative framework perhaps has its roots in Lenin's early study, *The Development of Capitalism in Russia*, in 1899. It sees primitive accumulation mostly as the historical premise of the capitalist mode of production and, therefore, focuses on the separation between people and means of production, as a moment in the transition between modes of production. Polemicizing against the populists, who believed that the absence of a developed market would prevent capitalist development in Russia, Lenin argues that the disappearance of the peasants and their communities was precisely the prerequisite for the creation of the capitalist market.

Lenin sees this process as inevitable and ultimately positive, although he often underlines its CONTRADICTIONS. However he does not envisage that the Russian peasantry could have resisted this process of expropriation, and thus shaped or indeed challenged the development of Russian CAPITALISM. He therefore does not foresee a Russian "bloody legislation" to meet that resistance, but emphasizes mostly the expropriation of the peasantry as the condition for the creation of a capitalist market.

A second interpretative framework seems to emerge from Rosa Luxemburg's *The Accumulation of Capital* in 1913. She formally accepts the understanding of primitive accumulation as a one-time, one-place phenomenon leading to capitalism (for a critique, see Rosdolsky 1977: 279). However, her theoretical framework points towards a different interpretation, in which primitive accumulation does not simply lead to capitalism, but is an integral part to it. Luxemburg regards Marx's schemes of expanded reproduction as a representation only of the mathematical conditions for accumulation in the case in which there are only two classes. In reality, she contends, capitalist production must rely on third parties (peasants, small independent producers and so on) to be commodity buyers. Thus, the enforcement of exchange relations between capitalist and non-capitalist production becomes necessary to realize surplus value.

However, this exchange relation clashes with the social relations of non-capitalist production. In order to overcome the resistance to capital that arises from this clash, capital must resort to military and political violence. Here Luxemburg introduces a crucial thesis that, independently of the validity of her reasoning and interpretation of Marx's schemes of reproduction, seems to open the way to consider primitive accumulation as an inherent, continuous element of capitalism; as such it encompasses the world as a whole, and implies political and military force.

## More recent approaches

Elements of Lenin's and Luxemburg's interpretations can be found in subsequent approaches. For example, in his classic studies on the development of capitalism, which have generated much debate on the transition from FEUDALISM to capitalism, Maurice Dobb (1963: 178) uses the category of primitive accumulation to denote a well defined "age of accumulation of property rights," better known as the "mercantile age," which predates capitalist production. Also, in the context of the early Soviet debate on the transition to socialism, Proeobrazhensky proposed the notion of primitive socialist accumulation in his book *The New Economics*. On the other hand, Samir Amin (1974) remains closer to the notion of inherent primitive accumulation which occurs through transfers of value within the world economy. Another interpretation within this general framework may include Wallerstein's (1979) WORLD-SYSTEMS ANALYSIS.

More recent literature has begun to emphasize other fundamental aspects all pointing toward an interpretation of primitive accumulation as an inherent and continuing element of capitalism. One new interpretation focuses on the class relation as a relation of struggle. and has suggested that primitive accumulation cannot be a one-time, one-place affair. Instead, "Whenever the profit rate tendentially falls and workers' power over the means of production and reproduction rises, the launching of a new phase of the primitive accumulation process is potentially at hand" (Caffentzis 1995: 18). Here, therefore, primitive accumulation is a strategy used to weaken workers' power and restore profitability.

A second approach is the recent emphasis on other aspects of primitive accumulation besides the expropriation of the land. In particular, it has been argued that the core of social reproduction is the reproduction of labor power, the great bulk of which is done by women. Therefore, the current attempt by states and international institutions to control demographic rates depends on the expropriation of the body, of the sexual and reproductive powers of women, for the purpose of accumulating labor power and thus promoting capital's valorization requirements. The witch-hunt terror in the sixteenth and seventeenth centuries opened the way for these state attempts to control demographic rates and the reproduction of labor power (Federici 1988; Mies 1986).

Finally, in his study on classic political economy, Michael Perelman (forthcoming) notes that the proponents of laissez-faire IDEOLOGY (for example, Smith and Wakefield) were actually disguising a strategy for state-implemented primitive accumulation to shape the social DIVISION OF LABOR, which includes both production and reproduction. Through the category of the social division of labor, Perelman interprets primitive accumulation as a contemporary phenomenon, encompassing the conditions of both production and reproduction, as do other current approaches.

## See also:

colonialism and imperialism: classic texts; slavery; Williams–Rodney thesis

## Selected references

Abdelkarin, Abbas (1992) *Primitive Accumulation in the Sudan*, London: Frank Cass.

Amin, Samir (1974) *Accumulation on a World Scale: A Critique of the Theory of Underdevelopment*, New York: Monthly Review Press.

Caffentzis, George (1995) "The Fundamental Implications of the Debt Crisis for Social Reproduction in Africa," in Mariarosa Dalla Costa and Giovanna F. Dalla Costa (eds), *Paying The Price: Women and the Politics of International Economic Strategy*, London: Zed Books.

Dobb, Maurice (1963) *Studies in the Development of Capitalism*, London: Routledge.

Federici, Silvia (1988) "The Great Witch Hunt of the Sixteenth Century," *The Maine Scholar* 1.

Linebaugh, Peter (1991) *The London Hanged: Crime and Civil Society in the Eighteenth Century*, London: Penguin.

Mies, Maria (1986) *Patriarchy and Accumulation on a World Scale*, London: Zed Books.

Perelman, Michael (forthcoming) *Classical Political Economy: Primitive Accumulation and the Social Division of Labor*, Durham, NC: Duke University Press.

Rosdolsky, Roman (1977) *The Making of Marx's "Capital"*, London: Pluto Press.

Wallerstein, Immanuel (1979) *The Capitalist World-Economy*, Cambridge: Cambridge University Press.

MASSIMO DE ANGELIS

# privatization

It has long been recognized that the provision of a number of basic services, such as electricity, gas, telecommunications, water and transport, constitute an integral part of a nation's infrastructure. Further, it is evident that there is a clear relationship between infrastructure investment in such services, advances in overall PRODUCTIVITY and ECONOMIC GROWTH. A public policy designed to raise the standard of living must assure that the benefits to be derived from the economies inherent in these networks of supply will be made available to all classes of customers at nonextortionist prices.

## History and recent trends

Since the late nineteenth century, electricity, gas, telecommunications and transport in Europe have been supplied primarily by public enterprises while investor-owned utilities and carriers (subject to price and earnings regulation) were much more common in the United States and Canada. Underlying both approaches was an implicit acceptance of the natural monopoly concept. In developing nations, public enterprises gradually replaced foreign ownership, beginning in the 1930s and continuing after the Second World War.

By the mid-1980s, however, there was a dramatic change in traditional patterns of ownership and control, as privatization of public enterprises and deregulation of investor-owned utilities became increasingly popular in both industrialized and developing nations. Whether measured in terms of the number of transactions or value of assets transferred from the public to the private sector, the magnitude of the privatization movement was impressive. Great Britain, New Zealand and Japan, together with many Latin American countries, were in the forefront of this change (Mody *et al.* 1995: chaps 1, 14). At the same time, there was a massive move toward partial or comprehensive deregulation in the USA and Canada. Approximately one-half of the state regulatory agencies abandoned traditional rate base/rate-of-return regulation (RB/ROR) by 1996 in favor of some form of light regulation, and the major federal agencies have moved in the same direction. Some industries, such as rail, motor and air trans-

port, were essentially removed from economic regulation.

## Motivating factors for privatization

There are at least four major factors promoting privatization and departures from traditional RB/ROR regulation. The first was growing dissatisfaction with the performance of public and privately owned firms in each of the major utility industries after 1970. In electricity, the combination of major cost overruns in nuclear power and general overbuilding resulted in pervasive excess capacity and price increases. Concurrently, the natural gas industry in the United States was plagued with alternate periods of shortage and curtailment followed by oversupply and price discrimination between different user groups. In telecommunications, the European postal telephone and telegraph systems (PTTs) were sluggish and slow to innovate, and when threatened by new technology they reacted by erecting barriers to new entry. As a consequence of this across-the-board record of price increases and service deterioration, there was a growing move to look for new supply options and pluralistic solutions.

A second factor promoting privatization and deregulation was the growing belief that economic efficiency was the primary goal of public policy. Achieving such efficiency, it was argued, assured lower prices, a higher standard of living and, by implication, an improved infrastructure. Earlier public policy concerns over equity, fairness and income distribution were relegated to a lower status in favor of attaining efficiency through privatization and deregulation.

A third pressure for privatization and deregulation came from those special interests that sought to benefit from the transfer of ownership to private enterprise or from the relaxation of price and earnings controls over private firms. This was a very diverse group, including the management of the former public enterprises which sought greater freedom to move into nonregulated activities and international markets. It also included new-era private utility managers who envisioned the utility as a cash cow that could finance diversification into deregulated or foreign utility markets. Such managers no longer regarded regulation as a source of protection, but rather viewed it as an impediment to swift adjustments in price and service that might be needed to retain market share.

There was also, of course, pressure from new entrants seeking to enter either niche or general markets, as well as pressure from large TRANS-NATIONAL CORPORATIONS wishing to exercise their oligopsony power to extract price and service concessions from the incumbent electricity, gas and telecommunications firms. Extracting such concessions would clearly be easier if the supplier were privatized or deregulated, and if successful, there would be a transfer of income and wealth to those capable of exercising such power. A more subtle consequence was the ability of the oligopsonist to affect the design of the supply network to its advantage (see Mansell 1993).

A fourth pressure for privatization came from the lending policies of the World Bank, as it sought to promote the shift from state-owned enterprises to private ownership in developing countries. The underlying assumption was that privatization would give local utilities access to foreign capital for needed plant investment, while negating the ability of governments to politicize pricing and employment practices, or to require the provision of subsidized services to special classes of customers.

## Conditions for success

Whether policies of promoting privatization and deregulation will yield both social and market efficiencies will depend in large part on the types of markets that emerge. If these markets are highly competitive, with low levels of concentration and virtually no social costs, then the prospects for success are good. The role of government could be confined to some form of interim light regulation during the transition. If, however, the emerging markets are highly concentrated, reflecting single-firm dominance or tight oligopoly, then the out-

come will be far different in both industrialized and developing nations.

## Likely outcome

Both the British experience since the mid-1980s in telecommunications and electricity, and patterns of change in the USA following deregulation strongly suggest that tight oligopoly will emerge. Twelve years after opening the telecommunications market in the UK, the dominant firm (British Telecom) still retains 85 percent of the market and its closest rival (Mercury) has only 10 percent. The divested British generating companies have been accused of holding prices at artificially high levels and moving to reintegrate by trying to take over local distribution systems. George Yarrow's conclusions seem to be particularly appropriate. He notes that the outstanding feature of British electricity privatization has been the transfer of wealth from consumers to the owners of networks and power stations (Yarrow 1992, 1995).

In the USA, AT&T continues to control over 60 percent of the domestic market and approximately 69 percent of the overseas market 12 years after divestiture in 1984. To further assure corporate dominance, it has entered into a series of alliances with PTTs in the Pacific Rim, Holland, Sweden, Switzerland and Spain (Trebing and Estabrooks 1995). The regional Bell operating companies have also tended toward merger (reducing their number from seven to five), and it is far from clear that the US Federal Communications Commission has the ability to prescribe cost-based access charges that will assure open entry into the local network. Indeed, whether one considers telecommunications, electricity or natural gas supply, new entrants who are independent resellers, brokers or marketers are vulnerable to a price squeeze because they must purchase capacity from the underlying utility or carrier while, at the same time, competing with these firms in retail markets.

On balance, any move toward pervasive competition in these industries will be confronted by factors that either promote or reinforce high market concentration. These include (1) inherent network economies that culminate in concentration and discretionary behavior; (2) industry specific barriers to entry, including long gestation periods, substantial sunk costs and implicit vertical integration; (3) common corporate control over differentiated markets of varying degrees of demand elasticity that facilitate price discrimination, cross subsidization and risk shifting; and (4) private control of monopoly focal points (such as the local phone loop and the power transmission grid). What emerges are markets characterized by definite patterns in pricing, corporate expansion and bilateral dealings which build upon these four characteristics to make market power a self-reinforcing force (Trebing 1994).

## Options for regulatory reform

The British model for reform, which was introduced in 1984, consisted essentially of three steps. The first was to challenge the incumbent privatized enterprise to open its market to new entry. The second was to protect captive customers from exploitative pricing by price cap regulation and by monitoring the quality of service during the transition to competition. The third called for regulators to fade away eventually, with the courts assuming responsibility for oversight of anticompetitive practices. Price cap regulation is particularly fallible in this process. Price caps will not promote price flexibility or experimental price reductions in markets perceived to be demand inelastic, nor will price caps control limit entry pricing, price leadership or tie-in sales. Price caps that combine monopolistic and competitive services within a given basket of services will do nothing to constrain cross subsidization. Finally, when price caps are combined with performance incentives, the results do little more than camouflage oligopolistic profits. The only option for the regulator confronted by unacceptable forms of oligopoly behavior will be to raise the productivity offset, thereby constraining price increases. (The ceiling price represents an adjustment for inflation minus a productivity offset.)

A far more effective constraint on market power would involve structural separation of the full network from the provision of potentially competitive marketing and procurement functions. The network would provide the essential infrastructure on a common carrier basis to all classes of customers. Administration of the network would have to be subject to separate financing, a separate board of directors and full regulatory oversight. The pricing of network services would have to be cost-based. This would not preclude peak/off-peak pricing, but it would preclude the adoption of price discrimination or opportunity cost pricing which would provide a strong stimulus to fragment the network into regulated and nonregulated functions. Properly priced, there would be no uneconomic bypass of the network as long as network direct and allocated overhead costs were less than the cost of providing the service on a stand-alone basis.

Structural separation would present a maximum opportunity for the largest number of competitive input suppliers and a large number of output buyers. Independent brokers or aggregators could prosper, since they would not have the direct threat of a vertical price squeeze. Residential and small business customers could either deal with an aggregator, thereby employing countervailing power, or they could request direct service from the network on a cost-plus basis. Problems would, of course, remain to be resolved, such as defining the boundary of the network, whether in telecommunications, electricity or natural gas.

## Conclusion

The prospects for structural separation appear to be greatest in those industries which are on the threshold of deregulation or privatization. It appears to be least favorable in those industries such as telecommunications, where the dominant firm or oligopolist has sufficient political influence to prevent any steps toward structural separation. In developing nations, local governments may be too weak to impose structural separation on a foreign firm which is moving to purchase the assets and service territory of the public enterprise. In such cases, any broadened realization of inherent network economies would seem to depend upon corporate discretion.

## See also:

economic rationalism or liberalism; fiscal crisis of the state; industry policy; regulation and deregulation: financial; rent-seeking and vested interests; structural adjustment policies; technology policy

## Selected references

Mansell, R. (1993) *The New Telecommunications – A Political Economy of Network Evolution*, London: Sage Publications.

Mody, B., Bauer, J.M. and Straubhaar, J.D. (eds) (1995) *Telecommunications Politics: Ownership and Control of the Information Highway in Developing Countries*, Mahwah, NJ: Lawrence Erlbaum Associates.

Trebing, H.M. (1994) "The Networks as Infrastructure – The Reestablishment of Market Power," *Journal of Economic Issues* 28(2): 379–89.

Trebing, H.M. and Estabrooks, M. (1995) "The Globalization of Telecommunications: A Study in the Struggle to Control Markets and Technology," *Journal of Economic Issues* 29(2): 585–644.

Yarrow, G. (1992) *British Electricity Prices Since Privatization*, Oxford: Regulatory Policy Research Centre.

—— (1995) *Power Sector Reform in Europe with Special Reference to Britain and Norway*, Oxford: Regulatory Policy Research Centre.

HARRY M. TREBING

# producer and consumer sovereignty

Consumer sovereignty refers to the idea that, in a market economy, the determination of what is to be produced is under the control of consumers rather than producers or government. This view is usually held by neoclassical economists. Producer sovereignty refers to the reverse, that control over what is produced is held by producers, who shape consumer sales and consumption. Producer sovereignty is more widely accepted in POLITICAL ECONOMY. Much of the controversy and conflict centers around two issues. The first is over which of the two, consumer or producer sovereignty, *actually* prevails. The battleground about which much of this controversy revolves is the role and function of marketing in a modern economy (see Benton 1987a). A second issue of controversy is whether or not consumer sovereignty should prevail.

## Consumer sovereignty

The terminology "consumer sovereignty" has been attributed to W.H. Hutt (1936, 1940). The idea is that in a market economy, consumers, in disposing of their income and wealth, determine how resources are used as producers compete for their patronage.

It might be said that consumers possessed complete sovereignty only in the days of the handicraft economy when goods were made to order and transactions were face-to-face. Today most goods are produced in anticipation of consumer demands. This, some hold, makes a world of difference. But adherents to the idea of consumer sovereignty argue that it makes no substantive difference at all. Producers usually act on their anticipations of consumer demand. If their anticipations are correct, they obtain a larger money return than if they are wrong; and if they are wrong, they change their plans to bring them into line with the wishes of consumers. Production is still ultimately controlled by demand. The metaphysical concept of consumer sovereignty is an expression of the liberal philosophy of the individual's determination of his or her own life and, as such, is an expression of the liberal concept of freedom.

## Producer sovereignty

The concept of producer sovereignty is a critique of the *realization* of that liberal philosophy. The concept is generally attributed to John Kenneth Galbraith. Although he did not use the term, others have used it to describe an element of his economic thought. Companies are said to start out with some idea of their desired level of output and transactions with the market. Thereafter, as Philip Kotler, the pre-eminent American marketer, recognizes, it is the task of marketing managers to influence "the level, timing, and composition of demand in a way that will help the organization achieve its objectives" (Kotler 1988: 12). Marketing management is thus "essentially demand management."

The management of demand is made necessary by the present institutional form of the economy; it is made possible by the fact of "abundance." In the presence of abundance, wants become increasingly psychological in origin. Not being grounded in any objective elementary physical sensation such as "hunger" or "cold," people are open to persuasion – or management – as to what they buy. In contrast to advocates of consumer sovereignty, Galbraith argues, "If the consumer can be reached and influenced by the producer, then much is changed and much that happens is at the behest of the producer, not the consumer" (Galbraith 1978: 217). Hence producers, not consumers, largely determine what is produced and, ultimately, how resources are utilized. This is especially the case in a system dominated by large corporations with large advertising budgets and considerable power in the marketplace (see GALBRAITH'S CONTRIBUTION TO POLITICAL ECONOMY).

Consumer needs and wants are part of the system of production in two ways. The first is through CONSPICUOUS CONSUMPTION AND EMULATION. As Galbraith expressed it, "One man's consumption becomes his neighbor's wish" (Galbraith 1984: 128). The direct link involves modern marketing activities: "Outlays for the manufacturing of a product are not more important in the strategy of modern business enterprise than outlays for the man-ufacturing of demand for the product" (Galbraith 1984: 129). To acknowledge such outlays is to recognize "that production, not only passively through emulation, but actively through advertising and related activities, creates the wants it seeks to satisfy" (Galbraith 1984: 130) (see ADVERTISING AND THE SALES EFFORT).

## Consumer sovereignty: does, should or could it prevail?

The neoclassical response to the challenge of producer sovereignty is either to ignore it, or to deny that producers can impact upon consumer preferences. Unlike contemporary neoclassical economists, who assume consumer sovereignty exists, Hutt argued that it *should* prevail, not that it does prevail. He argued that there are strong vested interests that prevent its fulfillment. He even suggested that those inhibiting the exercise of consumer sovereignty be bought out by the government (Reekie 1988: 23).

Conventional neoclassical economists argue that consumer sovereignty should prevail because free MARKETS increase society's production potential. In terminology strikingly similar to what Galbraith might use, Hutt argued that this idea of the market is misleading because of the circularity in defending a system which maximizes gross output as measured by the yardsticks the system itself generates (Reekie 1988: 21). What Hutt argued is that consumer sovereignty should prevail because it is in accord with "our ideas of justice. It is impersonal and, within the limits allowed by inequalities of income, an impartial force" (1936: 268).

In like manner, Galbraith argues that consumer sovereignty could prevail. The conditions under which he feels it could be realized are outlined in the final part of his *Economics and the Public Purpose* (1973). Its realization would involve, first, consumers contesting the belief that happiness and welfare depend on the consumption and production of goods; a belief propagated by corporations and the state. The second step is to emancipate the state from serving primarily the purposes of the corporation. In this, Galbraith's concept of "state" is that of impartial state, not unlike that of Hutt. Both agree that "Where industry is powerful, government responds strongly to its needs" (Galbraith 1973: 294) (see HEGEMONY; CORPORATE HEGEMONY).

## What about worker sovereignty?

Most discussions in neoclassical economics, as well as in political economy, present the producer and the consumer as two separate entities. But people are both producers and consumers, a point both Hutt and the neoclassical economist Milton Friedman acknowledge. In the neoclassical model, however, the only test of the desirability of a given flow of production is the utility products yield to consumers. The sacrifices and discomforts of the producers (or, for that matter, the happiness and satisfactions they derive from their work) are of no relevance to the current issue, according to neoclassical economists. However, it is never explained why sovereignty should be vested in the consumer rather than the worker.

Within the Western social science tradition, Karl MARX was the only writer to break with the liberal tradition by focusing on work, what people do at work, and what work does to people (see LABOR PROCESS; ALIENATION; EXPLOITATION). Most if not all religious traditions also place primacy of importance on work over consumption. It is only the liberal tradition of the West that reverses the ordering and gives pride of place to consumption over work, and in doing so it fails to distinguish between work (a creative activity) and labor (Benton 1987b). To redress this would be to argue for and institutionalize worker sovereignty, especially over how things are produced. Decisions as to how things are produced are important in political economy because of the question of quality of life and ethics in the workplace. But, in addition, how they are produced will have some impact on what is produced (including quality) and how much of particular goods are produced (see PARTICIPATORY DEMOCRACY AND SELF-MANAGEMENT; DEONTOLOGY).

To this, the neoclassical economist has a response: treat work the same as consumption. As Hutt expressed it:

In so far as the conditions of health and happiness in work are costly (i.e. to the extent to which they involve scarcity), they are products [and] healthy, attractive and psychologically satisfying conditions of work are attainable under effective consumer sovereignty if they are really wanted more than other things.

(Hutt 1940: 69)

To neoclassical economists, consumer sovereignty explains how the economy works. To consumers, it means freedom. As Gintis expresses it, "consumers experience their sovereignty as a form of personal power: the power to switch" (1989: 67). To many political economists, this camouflages the centers of power in the economic system and serves as an apology for the consumer society.

## Conclusion

There is no reconciliation between these views. Either consumer needs and wants are exogenous to the system and therefore their formation is of no concern or interest since individual motives do not need to be understood by economists (the position taken by most orthodox economics); or they are endogenous, in which case the origin and formation of consumer preferences are of concern and integral to understanding how the economy functions (the position taken by most political economists). In the first (exogenous) case consumers are sovereign; in the latter (endogenous) case producers are sovereign.

## Selected references

Baran, Paul (1970) "A Marxist View of Consumer Sovereignty," in David Mermelstein (ed.), *Economics: Mainstream Readings and Radical Critiques*, New York: Random House.

Benton, Raymond (1987a) "The Practical Domain of Marketing: The Notion of a

'Free' Enterprise Market Economy as a Guise for Institutionalized Marketing Power," *American Journal of Economics and Sociology* 46(4): 415–30.

—— (1987b) "Work, Consumption, and the Joyless Consumer," in A. Fuat Firat, Nikhilesh Dholakia and Richard P. Bagozzi (eds), *Philosophical and Radical Thought in Marketing*, Lexington, MA: D.C. Heath/Lexington Books, 235–50.

Fraser, L.M. (1939) "The Doctrine of Consumer Sovereignty," *Economic Journal*, 554–8.

Galbraith, J.K. (1973) *Economics and the Public Purpose*, London: Andre Deutsch.

—— (1978) *The New Industrial State*, 3rd edn.

—— (1984) *The Affluent Society*, 4th edn.

Gintis, Herbert (1972) "Consumer Behavior and the Concept of Sovereignty: Explanations of Social Decay," *American Economic Review* 62(2): 267–78.

—— (1989) "The Power to Switch: On the Political Economy of Consumer Sovereignty," in Samuel Bowles, Richard Edwards and William G. Shepherd (eds), *Unconventional Wisdom: Essays on Economics in Honor of John Kenneth Galbraith*, Boston: Houghton Mifflin, 65–79.

Hutt, W.H. (1936) *Economists and the Public Purpose*.

—— (1940) "The Concept of Consumer Sovereignty," *Economic Journal*, 66–77.

Kotler, Philip (1988) *Marketing Management*, 6th edn.

Lerner, Abba P. (1972) "The Economics and Politics of Consumer Sovereignty," *American Economic Review* 62(2): 258–66.

Reekie, W. Duncan (1988) "Consumer Sovereignty Revisited," *Managerial and Decision Economics*, special issue, 17–25.

Rothenberg, Jerome (1962) "Consumer Sovereignty Revisited and the Hospitality of Freedom of Choice," *American Economic Review* 52(2): 269–83.

Scitovsky, Tibor (1962) "On the Principle of Consumer Sovereignty," *American Economic Review* 52(2): 262–8.

RAYMOND BENTON, JR

# productive and unproductive labor

The notion of productive–unproductive activities has been with political economy at least since the time of the physiocrats and CLASSICAL POLITICAL ECONOMY. The revival of interest in political economy in the 1960s has seen a similar burgeoning of interest in this theme, not only among Marxists (see below), but also feminists (see DOMESTIC LABOR DEBATE) and even relatively conservative classical economists (see Bacon and Eltis 1976).

## Definitions

Marx's definition of productive labor and hence its differences from unproductive labor seem clear enough: "Productive labour is therefore – in the system of capitalist production – labour which produces surplus value" (Marx 1862–3: 396). Despite Marx's sharp demarcation – productive labor produces surplus value while unproductive does not – Marxists and others have encountered difficulties in using these categories for social analysis. Different concepts of productive/unproductive labor arose (in part because Marx too was sometimes inconsistent in his usage); see surveys in Resnick and Wolff (1987: 132–41) and Howard and King (1985: 128–32). Some defined the concepts in terms of the social usefulness of the products; productive labor yielded useful products while unproductive did not. Others made productive that labor whose product took a commodity or monetized form. Still others focused the distinction in terms of whether the labor was performed in a capitalist (hence productive) versus a non-capitalist (unproductive) class structure. Nor does this exhaust the list of different definitions.

Proliferating and often incompatible definitions have pushed the entire demarcation to the margins of most political economy discourse. Yet Marx's productive/unproductive distinction remains important to class analysis, to the identification of exploitation and its consequences, and to much of political economy.

Discarding the distinction would incur significant costs in terms of foregone social analysis. Because the stakes are high, the question to pose is: can we retain Marx's distinction between productive and unproductive labor, while recognizing the theoretical and political importance of the issues raised by the major alternative conceptualizations since Marx? The following examples try to answer this question.

## Productive labor

Consider a capitalist enterprise that produces and sells a security service (protecting property and/or persons). The economic processes occurring in the enterprise include: (a) the purchase of labor power for an equivalent value wage; (b) a labor process of working to produce the security service (a particular use-value); (c) the enterprise's sale of that produced service for a money equivalent; and (d) a class process in which the worker labors for six hours producing, say, $75 worth of security (assumed equal to his or her value wage) and two additional or surplus hours producing $25 worth. This latter surplus value is received by the enterprise's Board of Directors, acting as the consumer of the purchased labor power: "The only productive worker is one whose labour = the productive consumption of labour power" (Marx 1867: 1039).

The concrete labor of producing "security" is also, in Marxian terms, productive labor, for it produces a surplus value ($25) embodied in the sold capitalist commodity (worth $100). Thus, the definition of productive labor does not depend upon (a) what a buyer does with that purchased commodity; or (b) the revenue source out of which it is purchased. Nor does (c) the physical nature of the LABOR PROCESS or its output – a good or, as in this example, the service of providing security – determine whether or not the labor in question is productive (Rubin 1928: 260; Marx 1862–3: 401). Rather, it all depends on the context, especially the social relations of production.

This example of a capitalist firm, which specializes in the production and sale of security services can be extended to include a myriad of other services and material products produced in and by capitalist enterprises. These include services such as doctoring, accounting, advertising, cleaning and child rearing, and products such as armaments, narcotics, luxury goods of all sorts, and entertainment. Each of these different kinds of concrete labor and their respectively produced services and products may involve productive labor, depending upon the specific set of economic processes specified in each case.

## Unproductive labor

An example of unproductive labor illustrates this key conclusion. Consider a different enterprise, indeed any one not engaged in selling a security service as its business. We shall suppose that this new enterprise produces and sells automobiles. However, suppose as well that in this enterprise there also occurs the same labor process of working to produce a security service (the same use-value as in our first example), but this time security is used to protect the automobile factory from theft and damage. Once again, the security worker sells labor power for the same wage (of $75), and works the same eight hours producing the same service.

Because this enterprise does not produce security services for exchange (for any equivalent value), the security worker produces no value, surplus or otherwise. Although this worker performs the same concrete labor as in the first example, working the same number of hours and receiving the same wage, such labor is now classified as unproductive. While being unproductive of surplus value, the security worker does instead secure a condition for others inside this enterprise, the automobile workers, to produce surplus value. It is important to underscore that categorizing a particular labor as unproductive has nothing to do with the relative importance of that labor. While automobile labor produces surplus value, security workers are also required to provide capitalists with, say, protection of their factories, offices, records and so on. Without such protection, the surplus value produced by the automobile workers would be jeopardized.

The board of directors of the capitalist automobile corporation distributes a portion of the surplus value realized from automobile sales to purchase the unproductive labor power of these security workers. Consistent with our examples, this portion is $75. Thus, the automobile enterprise's productive labor produces the surplus out of which unproductive labor is paid. Productive and unproductive laborers enable and sustain one another: each provides conditions of the other's existence. The designations "productive" and "unproductive" refer to their locations within capitalist enterprises, according to their different relationships to the production and distribution of the surplus.

Other unproductive laborers located outside the enterprise may include those engaged in moneylending and the buying and selling of commodities (merchanting). Suppose workers in banks or merchant enterprises receive wages to produce, respectively, financial or merchanting services resulting in the loan of money to or the purchase of commodities from the automobile capitalist. If these respective services are not produced for sale, but rather as conditions enabling loans and purchasing to occur, then no value and no surplus value are produced: such labor is unproductive. The lending of money *per se* involves merely a change in the location of value from lender to borrower, while that of purchasing is merely a change in the form of value from money (command over exchange-value) to commodities. Hence the capitalist distributes surplus value in the form of interest to bankers and fees to merchants to secure access, respectively, to money and merchant-capital (see SURPLUS VALUE AS RENT, INTEREST AND PROFIT).

We may generalize this example to include still other forms of unproductive labor secured by distributions from the appropriated surplus value of capitalists. These include managing, advertising, researching, cleaning, accounting, legal work and so forth, in an enterprise which does not specialize in the production and sale of these activities. Each of such laborers also would receive a share of the surplus for providing these needed but unproductive labors.

## Productive bankers and merchants

However, a bank or merchant enterprise can also be a location in society in which productive labor does occur. For example, if security, insurance, money management and record-keeping or merchanting services of display, packaging, transportation, and storage are produced for (direct) exchange, then the labor in those respective enterprises would be productive of surplus value (see Rubin 1928: 271). Hence bank and merchant enterprises are locations in which both unproductive and productive labor may take place.

## State and government

Unproductive labor performed outside the enterprise may also receive distributed shares of the appropriated surplus of capitalists. Suppose security workers protecting the automobile plant are discharged in favor of relying instead on security provided to the automobile plants by the state police. Assume that the automobile capitalists distribute the same amount of value ($75) out of their appropriated surplus value as before, but they distribute it now to the state as taxes. The state uses these taxes to pay to state police workers (for an identical eight hours of work) the same wages as were formerly received by the automobile enterprise's own-employed security workers.

In this example, the state does not produce a security service commodity which it sells in the market. Hence, the state produces no value and no surplus value when it hires state police workers and provides security services. In this example, the state police are unproductive laborers. What this example demonstrates is merely a change in the location where unproductive labor is performed in society, from within to without the enterprise. Capitalists also may distribute portions of their appropriated surplus to other unproductive laborers located outside of the enterprise.

For example, our automobile enterprise might decide to stop employing a staff of unproductive workers engaged in accumulating and monitoring its needed cash reserves or merchanting its produced commodities. It might rely instead on a bank for cash loans when needed or a merchant enterprise for sale of its automobiles. Then, the bank's or merchant's employees, rather than the employees of the automobile enterprise, would be the unproductive laborers providing the respective financial or merchant conditions enabling the productive automobile laborers to produce their surplus value.

Another important aspect of Marx's conception of the productive/unproductive dichotomy emerges if we return to the state as provider of a good or service. A state could establish an enterprise that precisely paralleled a private capitalist enterprise, for example, a state automobile enterprise. Such a state enterprise would then buy and consume labor power and produce and sell automobiles as commodities in markets; its productive laborers would produce surplus value that the state enterprise's board of directors would appropriate and distribute. In this case, the state enterprise's automobile labor would be classified as state (rather than private) productive labor. Likewise, any security workers hired by such a state automobile enterprise would be state (rather than private) unproductive laborers. The point is that whether labor is productive or not depends on the processes occurring in the producing enterprise (who produces surplus, who provides conditions of existence for such surplus production, and so on). It does not depend on whether such an enterprise is located within the state or outside as a private entity (Marx 1862–3: 157).

## Small business

A final example considers a non-capitalist enterprise, in this case a self-employed individual business. He or she establishes an enterprise that produces and sells security services. Labor is performed and commodities are sold, but these processes occur without any capitalist class process consuming the purchased labor power of others and appropriating their produced surplus value. Instead, labor and commodity exchange occur together with a different class process. Suppose this individual labors for six hours producing $75 worth of security services which he/she sells and takes as his/her salary. Suppose, further, that this individual then works two additional hours producing $25 of additional security services sold in the market. This yields a surplus value of $25 which the individual distributes to secure his self-employed business (hiring an accountant, lawyer, and so on). In this case, the individual who produces this surplus also appropriates and distributes it. As Marx noted (1862–3: 407–8), this is not a capitalist class process – where surplus is produced by some people and appropriated and distributed by others – but rather something else.

## Growth and accumulation

A lively debate has begun as to how these notions of productive–unproductive labor may be applied to the question of the profitability, growth and ACCUMULATION of capital over the past fifty years. Moseley (1991), for instance, argues that the deteriorating profit on capital is due mainly to an increasing proportion of unproductive as against productive workers being employed in capitalist enterprises. Others, for instance Cullenberg (1994), argue that the question of profitability and growth is too complex to be reduced to a simple arithmetic ratio such as this. The debate is ongoing (see FALLING RATE OF PROFIT TENDENCY).

## Conclusion

Both productive and unproductive labor are employed by capital and receive a wage in exchange for their labor power. But whereas productive labor produces surplus value and is exploited by capital directly, unproductive labor reproduces the conditions of existence for others to produce surplus value and be exploited by capital. Unproductive workers may also indirectly reduce the TURNOVER TIME OF CAPITAL, and hence indirectly promote surplus value. Marx reserved the categories of productive and unproductive labor for capitalist and not for non-capitalist (self-employed, slave, feudal and still other) arrangements. A considerable scope exists for utilizing these concepts for an analysis of the dynamics of modern capitalism.

## See also:

advertising and the sales effort; circuit of social capital; class structures of households; economic surplus; finance capital; labor and labor power; monetary theory of production; monopoly capitalism; research and development; surplus approach to development; surplus approach to political economy; use-value and exchange-value

## Selected references

Bacon, R. and Eltis, W. (1976) *Britain's Economic Problem: Too Few Producers*, London: Macmillan.

Cullenberg, Stephen (1994) "Unproductive Labor and the Contradictory Movement of the Rate of Profit: A Comment on Moseley," *Review of Radical Political Economics* 26(2): 111–21.

Howard, M.C. and King, J.E. (1985) *The Political Economy of Marx*, London and New York: Longman.

Marx, K. (1862–3) *Theories of Surplus Value*, part 1, Moscow: Progress Publishers, 1969.

Marx, K. (1867) *Das Kapital*, published as *Capital, 1*, New York: Penguin Books, 1990.

Moseley, Fred (1991) *The Falling Rate of Profit in the Postwar United States Economy*, London: Macmillan.

Resnick, S. and Wolff, R. (1987) *Knowledge and Class*, Chicago and London: University of Chicago Press.

Rubin, I.I. (1928) *Essays on Marx's Theory of Value*, Detroit: Black and Red, 1972.

STEPHEN RESNICK
RICHARD D. WOLFF

# productivity

Productivity is the ratio of the output of goods and services to the input of the resources used to produce them. Measures of productivity attempt to describe the efficiency with which a system converts various resources – labor, capital, managerial ability, land, minerals and so on – into desired outputs. Most analysts identify the level and the rate of growth of productivity as the main factors governing material living standards in an economy. Moreover, differing levels and rates of growth of productivity are seen as the main causes of international differences in development. Intense interest is focused on the interplay among investment, TECHNOLOGY and productivity, and on facilitating policies for promoting sustained increases in productivity. Numerous inquiries have examined the sources of productivity in physical and intellectual capital, education, technology, services, differing organizational forms – and even in culture and geography. Yet a common model for analyzing productivity growth has yet to emerge (see McKinsey Global Institute (1993), and also the OECD report *Technology and Productivity: The Challenge for Economic Policy*, published in 1991).

## History and basic questions

Clay tablets unearthed in archaeological digs and parchments found in medieval abbeys, displaying calculations of crop yields and irrigation usage, attest to an ancient interest in productivity. The classics of political economy broach the subject early on. Adam Smith's account of the specialization of tasks and labor in a pin factory was foremost a description of how new forms of organization increased productivity (Cole and Mogab 1995).

Malthus's belief in the limits of agricultural productivity underpinned his influential population theory, which in turn inspired Darwin's theory of evolution. Ricardo's theory of rent was based in part on the concept of diminishing productivity in agriculture. The theoretical perspective of MARX led him to ask, using different terminology, "productivity for whom"? and to examine the nature of PRODUCTIVE AND UNPRODUCTIVE LABOR. By the time that neoclassical distribution theory had begun to solidify in the writings of Marshall, Clark, and Böhm-Bawerk, both the wages of labor and the value of capital were deemed to be determined by their respective marginal productivities.

However, numerous measurement problems on both the output and input sides have impeded the development of a common productivity model. There are difficulties with measuring real output in a precisely defined sector and with price data and deflation methods. Conventional methods overlook a range of externalities, as well as changes in quality and product attributes. Improvements in HUMAN CAPITAL, capital stock, SOCIAL AND ORGANIZATIONAL CAPITAL, RESEARCH AND DEVELOPMENT and public goods are also largely unaccounted for. A host of problems concerning the aggregation of heterogeneous individuals or industries, the use of index number formulae, shadow prices and weighting index components makes it clear that measuring productivity is difficult (Griliches 1987). Measurement problems are particularly challenging in the rapidly growing service sector (Gordon 1996). This is also true for HOUSEHOLD LABOR, given the diversity and complexity of the tasks. The CAPITAL THEORY DEBATES provide a critical point of departure for traditional views of capital and hence productivity.

Static equilibrium models use marginal productivity ratios, but average productivity relationships are the focus of the great majority of analyses. Output per unit of labor or per hour worked are among the common measures of average labor productivity. Because increased labor productivity leads to lower unit costs, *ceteris paribus*, many firms use various financial measures of cost per employee to assess labor productivity. Sales per worker is sometimes used as a common proxy for labor productivity. Total factor productivity (sometimes called multifactor productivity) is computed as some ratio of output to an index of both capital and labor inputs. By incorporating capital contributions, along with other factors, such a measure should yield a broader picture. However, despite the large amount of theoretical work done in this area, average labor productivity remains in greater use because of the difficulties in measuring capital contributions and the dearth of data on capital contributions to output.

## Labor productivity

At the national level, labor productivity is often computed by dividing the entire economically active population as an input into the total value of the goods and services as an output. Because labor is more geography-bound than other factors, particular attention is paid to differing levels and rates of growth of labor productivity among regions and nations. While labor productivity does not explicitly account for technology, scale, capital intensity, output mix, work organization and many other factors, it is clear these greatly influence this measure. These in turn are a function of management behavior – which is ultimately the primary determinant of productivity (Brinkerhoff and Dressler 1990; ILO 1969) (see X-INEFFICIENCY).

Since Adam Smith, labor productivity has been regarded as a function of task specialization. Scale economies demanded large numbers of specialized tasks and industrial engineering responded with work, such as Taylor's famed time and motion studies which prescribed a standardized division of tasks and responsibilities (see TAYLORISM). "Scientific management" separated the "thinking" of managers from the "doing" of workers within the framework of task specialization, large scale and production complexity. However, as organizational forms evolve so do views on productivity.

## Quality plus output productivity

A newer generation of global manufacturers compete based on a different process than traditional mass production, by harnessing all human resources to produce a continuous stream of improvements in every aspect that customers value. This includes the continuous improvement of quality, functional design and timely delivery, all without sacrificing low cost. These firms view productivity as including all such facets of quality plus output per worker. In such organizations, innumerable improvements yield the unit costs of mass production with the production flexibility of small job shops. Workers are generalized and tasks are specialized, and the Taylorist distinction between thinking and doing is blurred or completely eliminated (Cole and Mogab 1995; Aoki 1990; Best 1990) (see FORDISM AND THE FLEXIBLE SYSTEM OF PRODUCTION).

Measures of working capital productivity that are used in the newer generation of manufacturers reveal the efficiency of the entire production system, and serve to highlight managerial performance. In contrast, traditional mass production firms focus on labor productivity which appears to place the onus for performance on workers. How an organization views productivity affects its strategy. A firm which is based upon continuous improvement becomes "lean" via the continual elimination by all employees of non-value adding steps, and the streamlined design of products meeting or exceeding customer expectations. Innumerable improvements from design to delivery increase quality and productivity with no extra effort placed upon workers. Continuous improvement earns a reputation for quality which establishes a firm as a market leader. Because of perceived differences in the products, a competitor will have to offer a price that will lag the continuous improvement firm.

## Traditional versus new forms of work organization

In comparison, the traditional mass producer cannot increase productivity and quality while lowering costs. Instead, this firm seeks leanness and cost competitiveness through labor force reductions, labor-displacing technology, outsourcing and the relocation of production to low wage platforms. Conventional measures of labor productivity may reveal that productivity has increased, at least in the short term. However, such cost cutting can lead to deteriorating quality, customer satisfaction, market share, and ultimately profits. The mass production strategy focuses on only one aspect which customers value: price. Meanwhile, the continuous improvement competitor addresses all aspects that customers value simultaneously, while increasing its productivity and flexibility (Cole and Mogab 1995; Wilson et al. 1995).

New forms of work organization and technology may now be weakening the long observed link between productivity increases and real wages. In several countries – particularly in the USA and the UK – this relationship appears to be changing. For example, between 1973 and 1995 the output per person of all non-farm workers in the US private sector rose by 25 percent – yet the real hourly wages of production and non-supervisory workers declined over the same period by 12 percent. Official productivity statistics show that between 1990 and 1995 the productivity of all non-farm employees in the USA increased by 10.3 percent while real wages over the same period were unchanged. The explanations for this remain controversial, but a growing consensus among policy analysts points to the decline in union power, labor displacing technology, new forms of workplace re-engineering and the growing practice of slicing up the value chain through the outsourcing of production.

## See also:

increasing returns to scale; Kaldor's theory of the growth process; Maddison's analysis of growth and development; productivity slowdown; wage determination

## Selected references

Aoki, Masahiko (1990) "Toward an Economic Model of the Japanese Firm," *Journal of Economic Literature 28: 1–27.*

Best, Michael H. (1990) *The New Competition: Institutions of Industrial Restructuring*, Cambridge, MA: Harvard University Press.

Brinkerhoff, Robert O. and Dressler, Denis E. (1990) *Productivity Management: A Guide for Managers and Evaluators*, Applied Social Research Methods Series 19, Newbury Park, CA: Sage Publications.

Cole, William E. and Mogab, John (1995) *The Economics of Total Quality Management: Clashing Paradigms in the Global Economy*, Cambridge, MA: Blackwell.

Gordon, Robert (1996) "Problems in the Measurement and Performance of Service-Sector Productivity in the United States," National Bureau of Economic Research Working Paper 5519, Washington: NBER.

Griliches, Zvi (1987) "Productivity: Measurement Problems," *The New Palgrave Dictionary of Economics*, vol. 3, London: Macmillan.

International Labor Organization (1969) *Measuring Labour Productivity: Studies and Reports*, 75, Geneva: International Labor Organization.

McKinsey Global Institute (1993) *Manufacturing Productivity*, Washington, DC: McKinsey & Company, Inc.

United States Bureau of Labor Statistics (1996) *Report*, 29 January 1996, Washington, DC: Bureau of Labor Statistics.

Wilson, Steven R., Ballance, Robert and Pogány, Janos (1995) *Beyond Quality: An Agenda for Improving Manufacturing Capabilities in Developing Countries*, Aldershot: Edward Elgar.

STEVEN R. WILSON

# productivity slowdown

Productivity is the real value of output per unit of input used to produce that output. The most common measure is labour productivity, which is the real value of output per worker or per hour worked. The exponential growth of labour productivity is defined as the growth of output minus the growth of the labour input. The growth of a country's productivity is commonly taken as a measure of the rate of increase of its standard of living and league tables are often compiled in order to compare the relative economic performance of different nations. There are, however, substantial problems in measuring productivity growth, especially in the service sector where output often cannot be measured independently of the inputs. Moreover, productivity is only a very crude measure of per capita welfare because of a number of important conceptual problems in measuring output. Its valuation, for example, takes no account of such factors as leisure, POLLUTION and household labour (see HOUSEHOLD PRODUCTION AND NATIONAL INCOME). There have been some attempts, following the pioneering work of Nordhaus and Tobin (1973), to construct more comprehensive indices that attempt to take into account such factors (see GROSS DOMESTIC PRODUCT AND NET SOCIAL WELFARE).

## Total factor productivity

Total factor productivity growth, although subject to the above problems, is a more comprehensive measure and is defined as the growth of output less the growth of labor and capital, each weighted by its factor share. It is, however, a controversial concept, as it is derived from an aggregate production function and the marginal productivity theory of factor pricing (see CAPITAL THEORY DEBATES). Nevertheless, even though the capital stock grows much faster than employment, the relatively small size of its factor share (generally between a quarter and a third) means that labor productivity growth and total factor productivity growth move closely in line with each other.

## Nature of productivity slowdown

The early postwar period until 1973 saw a marked acceleration in productivity growth rates of all the advanced countries (with the exception of the US) to about double their historical norms. The productivity slowdown refers to the subsequent sharp decline in the trend rate of growth of productivity in most sectors of the advanced countries, which has lasted from 1973 until the present. For example, in the period 1945–73, the growth of labor productivity for the business sector of twenty-two OECD countries averaged 4.7 percent per annum: this fell to 2.1 percent per annum over the next growth cycle, 1975–9. There was no subsequent recovery, as labor productivity grew at 1.9 percent per annum from 1980 to 1993. Total factor productivity growth has shown a slowdown since 1973 of about two-thirds. (The term productivity will henceforth refer to labor productivity.) There was also a large downturn in output growth, which fell by one-half from the 5.1 percent per annum experienced during the Golden Age.

## Factors involved in slowdown

While the slowdown may be partly the response to an exhaustion of those factors which, during the Golden Age, were favorable to productivity growth, any comprehensive account must explain why the slowdown occurred simultaneously in all the advanced countries. There is evidence of the beginning of a slowdown in the USA, Germany and Japan in the 1960s, but even here there was a noticeable deterioration of productivity growth after 1973. Because of the timing, the quadrupling of oil prices in 1973–4 (followed by a doubling in 1979) was originally seen as a prime candidate. The substitution of capital and labor for energy and the increased obsolescence of the capital stock as a result of the energy price rise would lead to a fall in productivity. However, there is now a broad consensus that the oil price

increases had little direct effect on productivity growth, not least because energy is only a small fraction of total production costs. Moreover, surveys in both the USA and UK found that management did not perceive the energy price rises as being a significant factor in accounting for the slowdown. The econometric evidence is more mixed, with some studies finding an important explanatory role for the oil price rises (see Jorgenson and Olson, in Fischer 1988). Perhaps the most conclusive evidence is that, when the relative price of oil fell in the mid-1980s, there was no increase in productivity growth.

The indirect, or macroeconomic, consequences of the oil price rises were altogether more significant. In 1974, the advanced countries went into a prolonged recession from which they have never fully recovered (deep recessions in the early 1980s and early 1990s, interspersed by two short-cycle upswings, reinforced this malaise). The main cause was the deflationary policies introduced by monetarist governments, putatively to curtail the rate of inflation. A fast rate of growth of output induces a rapid growth of technical change and innovation, and, especially in the industrial sector, enhances productivity growth through the effect of economies of scale (VERDOORN'S LAW). Hence, the fall in output growth led to a decline in productivity growth. The importance of R&D expenditure is frequently cited as a key determinant of the rate of technical change. Nevertheless, notwithstanding the fact that there was a fall in R&D expenditure after 1973, this does not seem to have been a major cause of the productivity slowdown. There is also no evidence of a fall in the productivity of R&D expenditure (see Griliches, in Fischer 1988).

If the decline in output growth is the prime cause of the productivity slowdown, there is no reason why there should not be an eventual return to the growth rates of the Golden Age. However, if the output slowdown merely exacerbated the fading of factors favorable to productivity growth in the early postwar period, then this may be unduly optimistic. Certainly Japan and many of the countries of continental Europe in the early postwar period benefited from the substantial transfer of labour from the low productivity agricultural sector (where there was disguised unemployment) to the high productivity industrial sector. This led to an increase in GDP as the reduction in agricultural output due to the loss of a worker from that sector was more than offset by the increase in output which the worker contributed to industry. Furthermore, the elastic supply of labour to industry permitted industrial output to grow rapidly, further raising productivity growth through the Verdoorn effect. The rapid liberalization of trade in the early postwar period also led to a rise in productivity growth through the increase in both allocative and producer efficiency and through the benefits of greater specialization. It has also been suggested that productivity growth temporarily benefited from the commercial application of military inventions accumulated during the war.

Some commentators have argued that the international disparities in productivity growth rates observed in the Golden Age were due in large part to a technological "catch up" as innovations diffused from the technological leader (the USA) to the more backward countries and that these gains would become progressively smaller over time. This does not explain the slowdown in the productivity growth of the US itself. Consequently, it may be that the underlying rate of exogenous invention has declined, as there is less to discover and smaller scope for major technical change (Maddison 1991). While this may be true for individual industries, it is hardly plausible as a general explanation in a period that has seen major advances in information TECHNOLOGY, biotechnology, microelectronics and so on.

Other explanations stress institutional factors. Olson (1982) points out that, with the political stability of the postwar period, there has been a progressive accumulation in the advanced countries of special interest groups (trade unions, cartels, professional associations and so on). It is often rational for a special interest group to increase its share of income by rent-seeking practices, even though these reduce allocative efficiency and productivity growth for the nation as a whole. Hence, as the number of such groups increases over time, so there will be a decline in overall productivity growth. Olson attributes much of the spectacular growth of Japan and continental Europe in the period 1945–73 to the destruction of many special interest groups in these countries during the Second World War and its immediate aftermath.

Some other economists (Marglin and Schor 1990) argue, from a Marxist–Keynesian perspective, that the rapid productivity growth was partly a result of a long investment boom, the result of high profit shares. This was enhanced by Taylorization, the introduction of "scientific management" practices (see TAYLORISM). They argue that productivity growth began to decline in the late 1960s as fewer workers were left to Taylorize, or that scientific management became counterproductive. At the same time, the militancy of labor increased with the fall in the COST OF JOB LOSS. Profits were progressively squeezed, eventually leading to a dramatic fall in the rate of capital accumulation and a further decline in productivity growth.

To conclude, there is no dearth of theories explaining the slowdown. Maddison (1991), using the neoclassical growth accounting approach painstakingly to quantify some of the major factors, explains 71 percent of the slowdown of the six largest countries (see MADDISON'S ANALYSIS OF GROWTH AND DEVELOPMENT). However, the assumptions of this methodology are often controversial and there is no indication of the degree of confidence to be had in the estimates, unlike those of regression analyses. Econometric studies prove to be of limited help, since many of the possible explanatory factors showed major changes around 1973, so that the estimates are plagued by multi-colinearity.

## Conclusion

The fundamental causes of the productivity slowdown still remain somewhat of a mystery. There are still no conclusive answers to the questions of whether productivity growth rates can ever return to the rates experienced during the Golden Age or whether the Golden Age was an exceptional period of rapid growth that is unlikely to be experienced again.

## See also:

Fordism and the flexible system of production; regulation approach; reserve army of labor; social structure of accumulation: capital–labor accord; social structures of accumulation; transformational growth and stagnation

## Selected references

Fischer, S. (ed.) (1988) "Symposium on the Slowdown in Productivity Growth," *Journal of Economic Perspectives* 2: 3–99.

Maddison, A. (1991) *Dynamic Forces in Capitalist Development*, Oxford: Oxford University Press.

Marglin, S.A. and Schor, J.B. (eds) (1990) *The Golden Age of Capitalism, Reinterpreting the Postwar Experience*, Oxford: Clarendon Press.

Nordhaus, W. and Tobin, J. (1973) "Is Growth Obsolete?," in M. Moss (ed.) *The Measurement of Economic and Social Performance*, New York: National Bureau of Economic Research.

Olson, M. (1982) *The Decline and Fall of Nations: Economic Growth, Stagflation and Social Rigidities*. New Haven: Yale University Press.

JOHN McCOMBIE

# profit–squeeze analysis of crises

According to the profit-squeeze analysis, a crisis occurred in the advanced capitalist countries in the late 1960s and early 1970s because workers became strong enough to increase the value of their labor power and reduce the intensity of labor (see LABOR AND LABOR POWER). Profit-squeeze analysis helps to situate each new political and economic development in the ongoing CLASS struggles within the spheres of production, distribution, and the state. There are many theories of the factors precipitating the deteriorating economic conditions of the 1970s and beyond; the profit-squeeze analysis represents one important explanation offered in the literature (see Glyn and Sutcliffe 1972).

## Reserve army and accumulation

The value of labor power is the value of the part of the net national product that workers must receive in order to maintain the standard of living to which they have become accustomed (see Marx 1867: 275). Profits are the value of the net national product minus the value of labor power. If there is a large RESERVE ARMY OF LABOR, then usually the value of labor power is depressed (and the intensity of labor increases), and profits should start to rise for capitalists to accumulate (Marx 1867: 784). On the other hand, if there is full employment, then workers become strong enough to increase the value of their labor power, and reduce the intensity of labor, thus squeezing the profits available to be accumulated. "Crises" denote the stagnation in the rate of capital accumulation that thus ensues.

ACCUMULATION on a capitalist basis presupposes that there are large supplies of "disposable human material" to exploit (Marx 1867: 786). As capitalists churn profits back into the production process in order to make more profits, they tend to use up the disposable human material. Marx (1867: 769–71) argues that capitalists try to keep the demand for labor from increasing with the rate of capital accumulation by investing in labor-saving machines. But, according to Marx (1867: 763), a depletion of disposable human material still caused a crisis "in England during the whole of the fifteenth century, and the first half of the eighteenth." Profit-squeeze analysis argues that the same thing happened in the late 1960s and early 1970s in the advanced capitalist companies.

## Golden Age and crisis

Marx (1867: chaps 27–8) explains how capitalists, with the indispensable help of the state, resolved the crises in England by replenishing the reserve army of unemployed. In the same way, Armstrong *et al.* (1991: part 1) explain how capitalists, in the late 1940s, contributed to a Golden Age of robust profits and rapid capital accumulation by replenishing the reserve army of labor. They, too, emphasize the indispensable role of the state.

Armstrong *et al.* (1991: part 2) then show how, despite capital's sustained efforts to substitute machines for workers, the "accelerated accumulation" of the Golden Age finally caused a "labor shortage" in the advanced capitalist countries, and real wages grew significantly greater between 1968 and 1973 than over the period 1960–8. Consequently, there was a profit squeeze between 1968 and 1973 due to higher wages and reduced productivity. Armstrong *et al.* (1991: part 3) conclude with investigations of workers' efforts in the advanced capitalist countries to preserve the value of their labor power in the face of capital's efforts to restore the conditions for another Golden Age of capitalism.

Profit-squeeze analysis maintains that capitalist Golden Ages are possible if much of the consumption of workers during crises is transformed into the accumulation of capital. Profit-squeeze analysis also posits a "democratic socialist alternative" if the divisions of class, race, sex and so on can be reduced so that consumption and investment increase simultaneously. Unfortunately, the trend in the advanced capitalist countries during the 1970s, 1980s and 1990s, has not been toward socialist democracy but toward capital reorganizing itself to replenish the reserve army of labor, and thus reduce the value of labor power. And because of its relative insulation from democratic accountability, "monetary policy has been capital's weapon of choice against labor" (Epstein 1987: 248). However, as Epstein points out, "engineering depression levels of unemployment" with tight monetary policy may help to restore the conditions for another Golden Age of capitalism in the long run. In the short run, tight monetary policy exacerbates the profit squeeze by reducing sales revenues and thus capacity utilization rates.

For this reason, industrial capital prefers to respond to crises by passing on any nominal wage gains workers are able to obtain in higher prices (see Bowles *et al.* 1983: 119, 149). International competition has prevented many non-US based industrial capitals from responding to the crisis of the early to mid-1970s in this way (see Armstrong *et al.* 1991: 194). But the role of the US dollar as the principal means of exchange in international trade enabled US industrial capital to try and use inflation to undermine US labor's nominal wage gains. Since inflation originating in the United States caused the dollar to depreciate in the 1970s, US industrial capital came dangerously close to precipitating a replay of the competitive currency devaluations that exacerbated the crisis of the early 1930s: however, this failed to materialize.

## Cost of job loss

Schor's (1987: 177) data on the strength of US labor show that US industrial capital's inflation-depreciation strategy failed to resolve the crisis in the 1970s. She measures the strength of US labor in terms of the cost of job loss. During the Golden Age (1948–1966), the cost of job loss averaged 31 percent (see Schor 1987: 178). That is to say, workers who lost their jobs could expect to lose 31 percent of their annual earnings. This cost of job loss was high enough to corrode working class solidarity, make workers docile and thus make possible high profits and high rates of capital accumulation. But then "the advance of accumulation... came up against" what Marx (1867: 785) calls "a natural barrier in the shape of exploitable working population." This is reflected in the fact that the cost of job loss began a steady fall in 1962, reaching a low of 19 percent in 1969 (see Schor 1987: 177). Workers thus became strong enough to increase the value of their labor power, and the intensity of labor declined. The Vietnam War played some role in propelling such high demand for labor power, as did the high rate of accumulation especially during the 1960s.

The slowdown in capital accumulation from 1970–1 and US industrial capital's inflation-depreciation strategy caused the cost of job loss to rise into the 21 to 24 percent range for most of the 1970s. The ability of US workers to increase the value of their labor power was thus stymied. However, they remained strong enough to defend their earlier gains (see Schor 1987: 179). In 1979, when the cost of job loss fell back to 20 percent, US industrial capital abandoned its inflation-depreciation strategy in favor of tight monetary policy. Over the next three years, the US monetary authorities contributed to the worst recession since the Great Depression of the 1930s, and thereby replenished the reserve army of labor. By 1983, the Third World debt crisis emerged, which was itself in large part a result of tight US monetary policy. The Third World debt crisis forced the US monetary authorities to rethink their strategy. But by that time the "larger reserve army had lengthened the duration of unemployment, which increased the cost of job loss" back to 32 percent (Schor 1987: 180, 177; Bowles et al. 1983: 118–19, 149). It remains to be seen whether US capital's assault on US labor – spearheaded by the US monetary authorities – will be able to create the conditions for another Golden Age of capitalism as we head towards the twenty-first century.

## See also:

economic growth; long waves of economic growth and development; political business cycles; productivity slowdown; regulation approach

## Selected references

Armstrong, Philip, Glyn, Andrew and Harrison, John (1991) *Capitalism since 1945*, Oxford: Basil Blackwell.

Bowles, Samuel, Gordon, David M. and Weisskopf, Thomas E. (1983) *Beyond The Wasteland: A Democratic Alternative To Economic Decline*, Garden City, NY: Anchor Press/Doubleday.

Cherry, Robert et al. (eds) (1987) *The Imperiled Economy: Macroeconomics From A Left Perspective*, New York: Union For Radical Political Economics.

Epstein, Gerald (1987) "Federal Reserve Behavior And the Limits Of Monetary Policy In The Current Economic Crisis," in Robert Cherry et al. (eds) *The Imperiled Economy: Macroeconomics From A Left Perspective*, New York: Union For Radical Political Economics, 247–255.

Glyn, A. and Sutcliffe, B. (1972) *British Capitalism, Workers and the Profits Squeeze*, Harmondsworth: Penguin.

Gordon, David M., Weisskopf, Thomas E. and Bowles, Samuel (1987) "Power, Accumulation and Crisis: The Rise And Demise Of The Postwar Social Structure Of Accumulation," in Robert Cherry et al. (eds) *The Imperiled Economy: Macroeconomics From A Left Perspective*, New York: Union For Radical Political Economics, 43–57.

Kalecki, Michal (1971) "The Political Aspects Of Full Employment," in *Essays On The Dynamics Of The Capitalist Economies*, Cambridge: Cambridge University Press.

Marx, Karl (1867) *Das Kapital*, published as *Capital, Volume I*, London: Penguin Books, 1976.

Schor, Juliet B. (1987) "Class Struggle And The Macroeconomy: The Cost Of Job Loss," in Robert Cherry et al. (eds) *The Imperiled Economy: Macroeconomics From A Left Perspective*, New York: Union For Radical Political Economics, 171–82.

Weisskopf, Thomas E. (1979) "Marxian Crisis Theory And The Rate Of Profit In The Postwar U.S. Economy," *Cambridge Journal Of Economics* 3: 341–78.

EDWIN DICKENS

# profit in Sraffian political economy

In *Production of Commodities by Means of Commodities*, no theory for determining total profits can be found. Total profits equal the rate of profit times the price sum of total capital inputs. SRAFFA avoided assumptions about the "laws of returns" and took total production as given. Relative prices depend on income distribution, but the rate of profit is only represented as a declining function of the real wage rate. Because of this "openness," the Sraffa system (1) lent itself to a powerful criticism of neoclassical orthodoxy and (2) became a unifying framework for discussing heterodox approaches.

The far-reaching implications of Sraffa's theoretical system can be seen in an elementary representation of his system with single product industries. Let us consider a two-commodity system and let 1 be the index of the reproducible capital good, and 2 the index of the consumption good. The given quantities of commodities are $x_1$ and $x_2$. Suppose to have two alternative processes $\tau$ to produce the capital good, $\tau = \alpha, \beta$. Further, let $a_{11}^{\tau}$ and $a_{12}$ be the quantities of capital and $1_1^{\tau}$ and $l_2$ the quantities of labour, all of these necessary to produce one unit of commodities 1 and 2 respectively. The conditions for reproduction are $a_{11}^{\tau} < 1$ and $(a_{11}^{\tau})/a_{12} > x_2/x_1$. Let, finally, $r^{\tau}$ and $w^{\tau}$ be respectively the rate of profit and the nominal wage rate when process $\tau$ is adopted, $\tau = \alpha, \beta$ Sraffa's alternative systems are:

$$p_1^{\tau} x_1 = (1 + r^{\tau}) p_1^{\tau} a_{11}^{\tau} x_1 + w^{\tau} 1_1^{\tau} x_1$$
$$p_2^{\tau} x_2 = (1 + r^{\tau}) p_1^{\tau} a_{12} x_2 + w^{\tau} l_2 x_2$$

Total profits are $\Pi^{\tau} = r^{\tau} p_1^{\tau} a_{11}^{\tau} x_1 + r^{\tau} p_1^{\tau} a_{12} x_2$, which are maximized by choosing a technology. The change in relative prices resulting from a change in income distribution depends on relative capital-labour ratios, i.e.

$$\delta(p_1^{\tau}/p_2^{\tau})/\delta r^{\tau} \gtreqless 0 \quad \text{if} \quad a_{11}^{\tau}/1_1^{\tau} \gtreqless a_{12}/l_2$$

This is the price-Wicksell effect. The two wage-profit frontiers with commodity 2 as a *numéraire* are $r^{\tau} = r^{\tau}(w^{\tau}/p_2^{\tau})$. They are strictly declining, i.e. $\delta r^{\tau}/\delta(w^{\tau}/p_2^{\tau}) < 0$. Their shapes depend on the relative capital-labour ratios and the choice of the *numéraire*. When instead of $p_2^{\tau}$ the standard commodities belonging to the technologies $\alpha$ and $\beta$ are chosen to normalize prices, the wage-profit frontiers are strictly linear.

In 1960, many post Keynesians soon recognized the importance of Sraffa's work for the then ongoing capital theory debates concerning the neoclassical theory of income distribution. This theory holds that the macroeconomic capital–labour ratio is a strictly declining function of income distribution (r/w) and that in equilibrium the uniform rate of profit and the real wage are uniquely determined by the relative scarcities of capital and labour. Sraffa implicitly substantiated Joan Robinson's early criticism by showing that, as a result of the price-Wicksell effect, a macro-quantity of capital cannot be defined independently of income distribution. More damaging for neoclassical theory was that it could be shown that, with a choice of techniques, the wage-profit frontiers may intersect. In the elementary model, this happens when, for example, $r^{\alpha} = r^{\alpha}(w^{\alpha}/p)$ is concave and $r^{\beta} = r^{\beta}(w^{\beta}/p)$ is convex to the origin and none of the technologies to produce commodity 1 is strictly inferior. It may even happen twice. When the profit rate is high a profit maximizer selects technology $\beta$; rising wages induces him to switch over to technology $\alpha$, but at very high wages he reswitches to technology $\beta$. This implies that the capital–labour ratios cannot be strictly declining functions of income distribution.

In the background of the debates at the time was the post-Keynesian disbelief in an interpretation of the uniform rate of profit as a scarcity reward, a disbelief which was shared by the Marxists. Firstly, the idea of scarcity is not self-evident, as can be shown in the classical case of land with different fertilities. In joint production models it was brought out that, when land has alternative uses, the ranking of the land according to fertility, and hence the level of the rent for each piece of land, depends on the income distribution between profits and wages. Secondly, a uniform rate of profit can only come about in the long period, and precisely in this period the stock of reproducible capital goods is adaptable and depends on investment decisions. It was strongly believed that a theory of profits cannot be founded on "natural scarcity"; it requires a foundation in the behavioural characteristics of the social classes.

Sraffa's system became a unifying framework for discussing heterodox approaches to income distribution because of both its "openness" and its intellectual roots. By referring to ideas which were "long submerged and forgotten," Sraffa drew attention to the fact that a similar structure of economic reasoning can be found in classical political economy. Indeed, the insistence on the reproducibility of heterogeneous commodities is on the opening pages of Ricardo's *Principles* and the price-Wicksell effect was the reason why Ricardo engaged into a search for an invariable standard of value for the rest of his life. The first attempt to study relative prices mathematically in systems with reproducible commodities and a uniform rate of profit is found in Marx's third volume of *Das Kapital*. The core of the classical and Marxian analysis of value and distribution was, according to Garagnani, a simple framework which takes the level of accumulation, and hence net output and technologies, as given. The purpose of this framework was to define a surplus product as a residual income and to study the natural (or production) prices belonging to this state of the economy.

In Sraffa's outlook, total profit is not necessarily the residual income, as they were in the classical and Marxian surplus approach. In the old approach, real wages are determined by supply reactions in the labour market, which are caused by either the Malthusian population mechanism or Marxian class conflict. Sraffa left the matter undecided, except for the remark that "The rate of profit...is...susceptible of being determined...by the level of the money rates of interest." This remark implies, firstly, that labour income may be the residual category, and secondly, that real variables may be determined by monetary ones. It is entirely

at odds with both the classical intuition that the money rates adapt to the natural rate of interest and the Marxian idea that interest is nothing but redistributed surplus value. However, during the revival of classical political economy after Sraffa, this "double degree of openness" gave structure to the debates about a heterodox theory of income distribution.

Whatever the modern debates propose, it seems inconceivable that they will provide the "missing equation" which "closes" Sraffa's system. In that sense, a profit theory cannot exist in Sraffian political economy. This is true since, firstly, for many post-Keynesians and Marxists, unemployment is a long-run phenomenon and the normal state of the economy is not unique. Secondly and more intriguingly, a closure of Sraffa's system would require a once-and-for-all determination of whether wages or profits are the residual income. Not only will post-Keynesians and Marxists probably never agree on that, but it also seems to contradict a fundamental proposition of these approaches, which is that income distribution depends on the behavior of social classes. Marxists have always stressed the importance of class struggle, which puts the economy on a long-run roller coaster. This is reflected in modern Marxist theories of overaccumulation and the profit squeeze (see Itoh 1990). For many post-Keynesians, who stress ANIMAL SPIRITS and rely on the theory of effective demand, the center of the debate is the Cambridge equation $g = s_c r$, which, together with Kalecki's degree of monopoly, seems to close Sraffa's system. Other Keynesians have drawn attention to monetary phenomena and have argued that the rate of profit may depend on the money rate of interest set by monetary authorities or on financial instability (see Lavoie 1992; Pivetti 1991).

Attempts to integrate and extend these approaches theoretically (see Marglin 1984; Goodwin and Punzo 1987) have clearly emphasized that "openness" does not only mean an inverse relationship between the real wage rate and the uniform profit rate. It also means that a theory of profit can never be straightjacketed again. A heterodox theory has to rely on an extensive investigation of the various forces and institutions at work in the real world.

## Selected references

Abraham-Frois, G. and Bidard, C. (eds) (1987) *La Rente, Actualité de l'Approche Classique*, Paris: Economica.

Bharadwaj, K. and Schefold, B. (eds) (1990) *Essays on Piero Sraffa, Critical Perspectives on the Revival of Classical Theory*, London: Unwin Hyman.

Garegnani, P. (1984) "Value and Distribution in the Classical Economists and Marx," *Oxford Economic Papers* 36: 291–325.

Goodwin, R.M. and Punzo, L.F. (1987) *The Dynamics of a Capitalist Economy*, Cambridge: Polity Press.

Itoh, M. (1990) *The World Economic Crises and Japanese Capitalism*, Basingstoke: Macmillan.

Kurz, H. and Salvadori, N. (1995) *The Theory of Production: A Long-Period Analysis*, Cambridge: Cambridge University Press.

Lavoie, M. (1992) *Foundations of Post-Keynesian Economic Analysis*, Aldershot: Edward Elgar.

Marglin, S.A. (1984) *Growth, Distribution and Prices*, Cambridge, MA: Harvard University Press.

Pivetti, M. (1991) *An Essay on Money and Distribution*, Basingstoke: Macmillan.

Sraffa, P. (1960) *Production of Commodities by Means of Commodities, Prelude to a Critique of Economic Theory*, Cambridge: Cambridge University Press.

HENK W. PLASMEIJER

# property

Property plays a role in all theories of political economy. One the one hand, property in "factors" or "means" of production is often seen as central to how production is organized and its fruits distributed. On the other hand, accumulating property in natural resources and products is seen as a central goal of much economic activity. Since Marxian, Keynesian, neoclassical, institutionalist and other kinds of political economy all assign more or less importance to property and its distribution, albeit in different ways, a general definition of property is needed for an examination of its diverse usages and interpretations.

## Property is a kind of power

Property is one kind of power. To hold property in any object (land, resources, products or persons) is to wield the power to control access to that object. Like other sorts of power, property has been distributed in different ways at various moments of social history. Whole societies, different groups within society and individuals have all been propertied. Sometimes the power of property has been distributed only to individuals or groups or the society as a whole, while at other times various combinations of some or all distributions have occurred. Where state apparatuses exist within society, a differentiation between "state" and "private" (i.e. non-state) property emerges to overlap the distinctions among social, group and individual property.

However any society distributes property, those who obtain it thereby wield the power to control others' access to it. Propertied individuals or groups control the access of the propertyless. Society as a whole, in so far as it may be propertied (for example, as a "commonwealth"), controls the access of individual citizens to what the society as a whole owns. States and private individuals or groups can and often do contest the distribution of the power of property among them.

Property – like all other powers – is complex, contradictory, contested and forever changing. All manner of limits and qualifications typically attend property distributions within societies. For example, to control access to an object, say, fertile land, may but need not include the power to deny access under all circumstances. Depending on how property is effectively controlled, the owner may forfeit and lose the property to others. Those with little or no property may contest any particular social distribution of property demanding one or another alternative distribution. Those who favor any existing property distribution may take all sorts of steps – political, economic, and cultural – to protect and secure that distribution. The resulting maneuvers and compromises have often yielded social distributions of property that are inconsistent and internally contradictory.

For example, a historical compromise in the United States enables private individuals and groups to own land in cities and towns which is, at the same time, subject to these cities' and towns' right of "eminent domain." The latter thereby effectively wield a kind of ultimate power that coexists – often with great tension and struggle – with private power/ownership over the same land. Similarly, the distribution of "intellectual" property (ideas, artistic compositions, audio and video reproductions and so forth) has recently again become a topic of intense, shifting and contradictory legal and political disputation.

In many societies and for thousands of years, repeated attempts sought to encode property distributions in law. The goal was to have written definitions and rules for adjudicating disputes over the existing distributions of property in such societies. Property law became a central part of most legal systems; there the complexities and contradictions of systems of property distribution were encountered, debated and compromised. Of course, when conflicts over property became sufficiently socially divisive and explosive, the legal system could no longer contain or resolve them. Then other, non-legal forms of social conflict and conflict resolution became the sites where old distributions of property gave way and new ones arose (see Marx's famous "Preface" to his 1859 *Critique of Political Economy*).

## Property and political economy

In many kinds of political economy, property is essentialized. That is, the distribution of property in means of production (land and other natural resources, buildings, machinery, money and so on) is understood to define the basic classes in society: the more or less propertied versus the more or less propertyless. Class in this property distribution sense is seen to determine how (a) production is organized, (b) EXPLOITATION occurs, (c) MARKETS function, and (d) products are distributed (see DETERMINISM AND OVERDETERMINATION). In the traditional and still widespread interpretation of Marxism (for example, Paul Sweezy's *The Theory of Capitalist Development*, first published in 1942, and Barry Hindess and Paul Q. Hirst's *Pre-capitalist Modes of Production*, which appeared in 1975), the term "relations of production" refers chiefly to the distribution of means of production. Any society's particular relations of production (together with its technology or "forces of production") comprise the economic base which determines the superstructure (politics and culture) of that society. In countless political economic studies which stress other kinds of power, such as the power of state authority over commerce, money supply, foreign trade and so on, a close reading will show that those other powers are often presumed to derive from underlying distributions of property.

In political economies influenced by classical and neoclassical theory as much as by Marxian theory, property and its distribution likewise play central roles. For example, a pervasive presumption holds that the accumulation of property (wealth) dominates the objectives of market participants. Explanations for economic evolution flow from the presumed drive of enterprises and/or individuals to amass property. The availability of property (scarcity) in relation to the demand for it obtains a central position in shaping accounts of how and why economies develop. Relationships among individuals, other than those entailed in property distributions, occupy marginal positions when they do not disappear altogether from economic arguments. John Roemer (1986) also makes the distribution of productive property into the essence conditioning how individuals' preferences yield a specific, exploitative equilibrium set of prices and other economic outcomes.

While property and its distribution thus function as central determinants within a wide spectrum of political economic theories, that is not always the case. For example, one alternative kind of political economy accords a central determining role rather to the distributions of different kinds of social consciousness among members of a society. Indeed, they sometimes produce arguments that make the distribution of property as much an effect of such consciousness as its cause. Technological determinisms sometimes go so far as to make the development of technology into the cause and property distribution merely its effect; then economic structure and development flow ultimately from TECHNOLOGY, not from property. Finally, from an overdeterminist perspective, property and its distribution become some among a great variety of other aspects of society which cannot be ranked as to their quantitative impacts on economy or society. Rather, all play their qualitatively distinct roles in shaping one another as well as the unique structure and dynamic of any economy.

## Selected references

Hindess, Barry and Hirst, Paul Q. (1975) *Pre-capitalist Modes of Production*, London: Routledge & Kegan Paul.

Lange, Oskar (1963) *Political Economy*, vol. 1, *General Problems*, Oxford: Pergamon.

Marx, Karl (1859) "Preface" to *A Contribution to a Critique of Political Economy*, Moscow: Progress Publishers.

Resnick, Stephen and Wolff, Richard (1987) *Knowledge and Class: A Marxian Critique of Political Economy*, Chicago: University of Chicago Press.

Roemer, John (1986) *Analytical Marxism*, Cambridge: Cambridge University Press.

Sweezy, Paul (1942) *The Theory of Capitalist Development*, New York: Monthly Review Press.

Thompson, E.P. (1963) *The Making of the English Working Class*, London: Gollancz.

RICHARD D. WOLFF

**PROTECTIONISM:** *see* free trade and protection

# public choice theory

Public choice theory utilizes the assumptions and market model of mainstream economics to analyze the system of "democratic governance." Thus, humans are seen as rational, self-interested utility maximizers who behave in the political sphere as consumers, and politicians are seen as rationally pursuing policies likely to lead to their (re)election. Public choice theory elaborates the logical implications of these assumptions.

## Mainstream assumptions

Like mainstream economic theory, public choice theory rests on an atomistic, individualistic conception of society (Buchanan and Tullock 1962: 11). Individuals are the basic element of society, and government "is simply that complex of institutions through which individuals make collective decisions, and through which they carry out collective as opposed to private activities" (Buchanan 1968: 78). By applying the mainstream economic model to the political process, a democratic government becomes the equivalent of an economic market: both are merely devices through which individual desires are aggregated and reconciled. Generally, in this conception there is no "public interest," i.e. no values separate from the aggregation of individual values.

Public choice theory is so strongly rooted in methodological individualism that two of its founders practically disregarded the politician, instead – for the most part – assuming direct democracy (Buchanan and Tullock 1962: 8). This approach is closest to the model of the perfectly competitive goods market, but – like that model – fails to describe much of the real world. Other public choice theorists have considered representative democracy, a complication that allows the application of the paradigm to the phenomena of coalitions and party politics (Downs 1957: 17).

Public choice theory shares the behavioral assumptions of the mainstream economic model, in which the individual is assumed to be motivated by the desire to maximize "utility," defined as a subjective valuation of benefits or satisfaction. Thus, when faced with several alternatives, the voter will choose that which yields him or her the greatest net utility. In the model of representative democracy, the voter will choose the candidate who is expected to follow policies that lead to the voter's greatest possible net utility. Information thus becomes critical, as the voter must form a prediction of each candidate's likely policies and how those policies will affect the voter. This information is difficult to acquire, for several reasons. First, the public sector, with its system of public goods and taxation, does not represent a quid pro quo exchange in which the individual knows his or her personal costs and benefits. Second, in a representative democracy the voter must choose not policies but candidates, and (particularly with a non-incumbent) it is difficult to foresee all of the policies that a specific candidate will pursue. Third, given that many government expenditures will only create benefits far in the future (for example, basic science and medical research), the typical voter may be poorly equipped to assess rationally the present value of these benefits.

## Rational voter ignorance

It may not be rational for a voter to acquire much information on most proposals, as the cost of finding this information may exceed the expected benefits that come from casting a more well-informed vote. This phenomenon, called "rational voter ignorance," is analogous to the idea in economic theory that it may be more rational for a consumer to buy a product that gives less than maximum utility than to bear the cost of a search for the optimal good.

The voter will not be equally ignorant on all issues, however; rather, the individual will be relatively more informed on topics that have a large impact on his or her life (Browning and Browning 1979: 259–60).

## Self-interested politicians and voters

Politicians are not more altruistic or idealistic than the voters who put them in office. While acknowledging that people (even politicians) cannot accurately be described as being single-mindedly greedy, public choice theorists assume that people and politicians are self-interested in order to simplify the analysis (Downs 1957: 11, 27, 28). Politicians' primary desires are for the personal benefits that go with an elected office, and thus they aim all of their behavior toward maximizing their political support (Downs 1957: 11, 28). Some public choice theorists, however, theorize that the rational politician may not seek maximum support, but rather will seek to obtain the minimum amount of support necessary to win an election, as this will allow the gains from office to be spread over a smaller number of people (Holcombe 1985: 90). The latter view seems more in congruence with the rationality assumption, since the costs of getting support substantially beyond that necessary to win an election will probably outweigh the benefits (to the politician) received. Once elected to office, the politician will weigh every policy alternative with a calculating eye on the votes it will gain and those it will lose, just as the rational actor in mainstream economic theory assesses the utility foregone and the utility gained from a transaction.

## Origins and consequences

This conception of the politician, rooted as it is in the mainstream theory of the business firm, obviously has origins that may be traced back to Adam Smith's famous proverb about the butcher, the baker and the brewer. It has a more direct antecedent in the writings of Joseph SCHUMPETER, who noted that democracy is a collective decision-making process, not a factory for producing a common will; and that in the "competitive struggle for power and office...the social function is fulfilled, as it were, incidentally – in the same sense as production is incidental to the making of profits" (Schumpeter 1942: 282).

Since this model assumes that politicians' main desire is to be elected, the logical consequence is that they will give the voters what they want in order to gain support. Even if an expenditure could lead to vastly offsetting benefits, it will not be made unless the citizens can see these benefits and thus be in favor of the expenditure (Downs 1962: 81). Since there will be types of benefits of which the average voter will be rationally ignorant, many truly "rational" expenditures will not be made. This could result, as Anthony Downs argued, in a smaller government budget than would be optimal (Downs 1962: 80). Buchanan and Tullock, however, come to the opposite conclusion – that the government budget is too large in a democracy – by employing a methodology that is similar to that of Downs. The crucial difference is that Buchanan and Tullock assume direct democracy with a less than unanimity decision rule. In such a situation, special interests will be able to generate expenditures disproportionately through vote-trading, exploitation of minorities, and so on (Amacher et al. 1975: 105) (see BUDGET DEFICIT).

## Conclusion

Other areas of research within public choice theory include the implications of different democratic decision-making rules (under direct and representative systems), the provisioning of public goods, the role and impact of political parties, the place of models of bureaucracy, many issues of public finance/taxation, law and property rights, welfare policy and so on (see for example Mueller 1979: vii–ix; Gwartney and Wagner 1988: vii–viii).

The public choice approach represents a successful application of the mainstream market model to the democratic polity, and is thus an example of the "imperialism" of the economic approach into previously distinct fields. The acceptance of this approach was powerfully demonstrated by the granting of the 1986 Nobel Memorial Prize in Economic Science to James Buchanan, widely considered to be one of the seminal figures in public choice theory.

## See also:

Austrian school of political economy; economic rationalism or liberalism; free banking; free trade and protection; neoclassical economics; rent-seeking and vested interests

## Selected references

Amacher, Ryan, Tollison, Robert and Willett, Thomas (1975) "A Budget Size in a Democracy: A Review of the Arguments," *Public Finance Quarterly* 3(2).

Browning, Edgar and Browning, Jacquelene (1979) *Public Finance and the Price System*, New York: Macmillan.

Buchanan, James (1968) in Malcolm B. Parsons (ed.), *Perspectives in the Study of Politics*, Chicago: Rand McNally & Co.

Buchanan, James and Tullock, Gordon (1962) *The Calculus of Consent*, Ann Arbor: University of Michigan Press.

Downs, Anthony (1957) *An Economic Theory of Democracy*, New York: Harper & Row.

—— (1962) "Why the Government Budget is Too Small in a Democracy," in Edmund S. Phelps (ed.), *Private Wants and Public Needs*, New York: W.W. Norton.

Gwartney, James D. and Wagner, Richard E. (1988) *Public Choice and Constitutional Economics*, New York: JAI Press Inc.

Holcombe, Randall G. (1985) *An Economic Analysis of Democracy*, Carbondale, IL: Southern Illinois University Press.

Mueller, Dennis C. (1979) *Public Choice*, Cambridge: Cambridge University Press.

Schumpeter, Joseph A. (1942) *Capitalism, Socialism and Democracy*, New York: Harper & Row.

DOUGLAS KINNEAR

# public goods, social costs and externalities

Public goods (also referred to as social or collective goods), social costs and externalities are related concepts. Their uniting characteristic is that, when they are present, freely operating competitive markets fail to achieve Pareto's economic welfare maximum for a society. As a result, they are commonly used to define the circumstances when the state has a legitimate role in influencing the allocation of resources.

## Public goods

The classic "public goods" literature was published in continental Europe in the late nineteenth century. Important contributions were made by Emil Sax (Austria) and Ugo Mazzola (Italy), with a major critique by Knut Wicksell (Sweden), and subsequent consideration of the matter by Eric Lindahl (Sweden) in the early twentieth century.

In 1890, Mazzola defined public goods in terms of the "indivisibility of their use and the consolidation of need" (Mazzola in Musgrave and Peacock 1958: 42). This recognizes that individuals cannot be excluded from public good consumption. Also, the benefit to society from public good consumption is the sum of its individual members' subjective assessments of the value of the public good.

The classic literature explicitly recognized that there is no market mechanism associated with tax-funded provision of goods and services. Nevertheless, the consolidation of public good benefits enabled collective welfare to be reduced to a question of individuals' utility maximization, enabling principles from the new economics of the marginal revolution to be applied to public economics. In this framework, maximization of collective welfare from the public sector required equality between individuals' marginal utility from public good consumption and the price they pay in the form of taxes.

Controversy associated with the public goods concept centered on its public policy implications, rather than the concept *per se*. Mazzola advocated differential tax pricing of public goods, whereby individuals' tax contributions reflected their assessment of the marginal utility of public goods. However, this was rejected by Wicksell, because a utility maximizing individual will attempt to consume public goods without paying anything. Lindahl's proposed method of pricing public goods tries to address Wicksell's critique by dividing the community into two "parties," determining the share of the cost of public good provision that each party is willing to contribute at varying levels of public good provision, and pricing services at the point where the sum of the two shares is one. However, when the membership of each of the two parties grows and becomes more heterogeneous, the tendency towards equalization of individuals' marginal utility with the tax price paid for public goods weakens.

In the English-speaking world, the issue of public goods was developed further by Paul Samuelson (1954, 1955), and the series of articles that these seminal papers inspired. Samuelson established the conditions necessary for the efficient provision of public goods, namely that the marginal cost of producing a public goods equals the sum of individuals' marginal benefits from its consumption. He also sparked a debate which resulted in the deconstruction of the public good concept by claiming that decentralization of service provision will not enhance efficiency.

Charles Tiebout (1956) took the first step toward this deconstruction. It was contended that public goods need not be national in character, as the benefits may be localized. The local public goods concept that ensued applied to spatially constrained, or localized, public benefits in areas like municipalities, cities, provinces and so on. Tiebout claimed that competition among local authorities to attract residents to their area would lead to packages of local public goods and taxes that would ensure efficient service provision. Buchanan (1965) deconstructed the public good concept further with his discussion of club goods.

## Social costs and externalities

The origin and development of the related concepts of social costs and externalities predates Samuelson's influential work on public goods, but was developed subsequent to, and independently of, public good theory in continental Europe. In the 1920s, A.C. Pigou published the first editions of his influential works, *Economics of Welfare* and *A Study in Public Finance*, where two kinds of "maladjustments" (or externalities due to market failure, using contemporary terminology) are identified.

Maladjustments were characterized by Pigou as a divergence between the private marginal net product (or rate of return) and society's marginal net product from the economic use of productive resources. They constitute either a net benefit or a net cost to society from the consumption of goods or productive factors which are not sold or paid for. In the former case, currently referred to as a "positive" externality, utility maximization for members of society is not attained when suppliers of a particular good and service respond only to the demands of paying customers. As the marginal social benefit is greater than the marginal private cost, maximization of utility for the members of society requires an increase in provision of the particular commodity. In the latter case, currently referred to as a "negative" externality, the reverse applies. The marginal social benefit is less than the marginal private cost, and the particular commodity is over-provided for (see COST–BENEFIT ANALYSIS).

In both instances, maladjustments may be offset by public authorities through Pigovian taxes or subsidies to equalize social and private marginal net products. In the case of positive externalities, this is achieved by subjecting third-party beneficiaries to a bounty, with the proceeds or equivalent benefits being returned to the producers of the commodity associated with the externality. In the case of negative externalities, the reverse applies as producers are taxed and third parties compensated.

However, Ronald Coase (1960) denied that there was a prima facie case for public authorities to introduce Pigovian taxes or subsidies. He showed that, in the absence of transaction costs, economic activity which generates externalities can achieve a Pareto efficient outcome when property rights are clearly defined.

The externality literature has blossomed in economic sub-disciplines related to public policy. Environmental and ecological political economy (see ENVIRONMENTAL AND ECOLOGICAL POLITICAL ECONOMY: MAJOR CONTEMPORARY THEMES) examines environmental damage partly in terms of externalities. Public finance deals with government responses due to market failure, as well as the generation of fiscal externalities associated with fiscal activity itself. International economics and finance considers the impact of externalities related to asymmetric information problems in exchange and capital markets.

## Difficulties and controversies

The greatest practical difficulty with these related concepts concerns the measurement of social costs and benefits attributable to externalities/public goods. When there is no market value for an externality/public good, valuation issues may go beyond the bounds of agreed resolution. For example, valuing the extinction of a species or the destruction of an isolated wilderness can be very difficult. While questionnaires may be policy relevant, they are rarely uncontested. In relation to external benefits, practical concern focuses on making free riders pay for the social benefits they consume. The problem is that their actions may be strategically motivated to mask their valuation of social benefits.

At the conceptual level, controversy has centered on whether paternalistic views of distributive justice and community values are public benefits, and if so, whether such views justify overriding or modifying the preferences revealed by some members of the community.

Related to this is the question of whether some public benefits are actually "socially irreducible," in that they can only be considered collectively (Brennan and Walsh 1990).

## Selected references

Brennan, Geoffrey and Walsh, Cliff (eds) (1990) *Rationality, Individualism and Public Policy*, Canberra: Centre for Research on Federal Financial Relations.

Buchanan, James (1965) "An Economic Theory of Clubs," *Economica* 32(125): 1–14

Coase, R.H. (1960) "The Problem of Social Costs," *Journal of Law and Economics* 3(October): 1–44

Musgrave, Richard A. and Peacock, Alan T. (1958) *Classics in the Theory of Public Finance*, London: Macmillan.

Pigou, Arthur C. (1947) *A Study in Public Finance*, 3rd edn, London: Macmillan

—— (1972) *The Economics of Welfare*, 4th edn, London: Macmillan.

Samuelson, Paul A. (1954) "The Pure Theory of Public Expenditure," *Review of Economics and Statistics* 36(4): 387–9.

—— (1955) "Diagrammatic Exposition of a Theory of Public Expenditure," *Review of Economics and Statistics* 37: 350–6.

Tiebout, Charles M. (1956) "A Pure Theory of Local Expenditures," *Journal of Political Economy* 64(October): 416–24.

MICHAEL MCLURE

# Q

## quality of life

Despite Mahatma Gandhi's (1909) criticism, the faith in prosperity-generating economic growth and technological progress has spread around the globe. Increased material well-being, as measured by gross domestic product (GDP) or GDP per capita, food intake, housing, water quality, health care, education and physical security, have been cited as prime indicators of the success of continued ECONOMIC GROWTH and progress. Since 1970, however, critics who, like Gandhi, pointed to the tensions between human well-being and material progress, have again become vocal. Looming environmental disasters, income disparity, social decay, family breakdown and crime-ridden streets and the spread of new diseases such as AIDS and old ones long deemed eradicated have brought home to even the prosperous middle class in highly industrialized countries the proposition that material growth does not solve these problems. It may, in fact, contribute to their spread. The question as to what constitutes a quality of life, or lack thereof, is thus being raised in the midst of continued (albeit reduced) growth.

### History and measurement

The term "quality of life" was first used by John Kenneth Galbraith in his 1963 speech to the American Association for the Advancement of Science. While the expression became a motto for all manner of social movements critical of the infatuation with growth, consumerism and technological progress, it was quickly coopted by the social sciences. What ensued were numerous attempts to define and operationalize the "quality of life" in terms of quantifiable indicators. On the forefront of such measurement efforts was the search for objective, physical and material indicators like the ones listed above.

These efforts led to some rather paradoxical definitions of quality of life indicators, such as GDP per capita, TV sets per population or private cars per population, the very items which some felt contributed to a decline in the quality of life (Scheer 1980). Additional indicators such as leisure time, environmental and ecological conditions, income distribution, CRIME rates, education and recreational opportunities were added to correct some of the more obvious distortions. Yet the general categories of income, food, housing and health continue to be consulted regularly in both intra- and international comparisons of the quality of life.

A second set of objective measures has sought to address the sociocultural or socio-political conditions of the quality of life. These measures include categories such as the freedom of movement, freedom of belief, freedom of association, freedom of political determination, economic freedom and freedom from discrimination and denigration. Data collection and analysis of these measures is much less established. According to Inkeles (1994) this may be due to the fact that these categories are less easy to measure than material or physical indicators, but also because they raise exceedingly sensitive political and human rights issues for many governments. In addition, it has been argued that, as with much of the human rights discussion itself, socio-political categories of quality of life indicators are undeniably shaped by socio-cultural perceptions of the relationship between individual and social whole or individual and social quality.

The generally individualistic focus of today's

quality of life debate is taken to its extreme in much of the discussion of subjective indicators and subjective measures. These measures rely on surveys to assess the degree of individual satisfaction or displeasure with their own situation, as described by the same types of categories used in objective indicator analysis. In addition, surveys have also sought to assess an overall summary measure of satisfaction or happiness (Campbell *et al.* 1976; Converse 1980). Studies of international comparisons of individual satisfaction levels with working conditions, living conditions, environmental quality or overall satisfaction levels, however, show that such subjective expressions of the quality of live are significantly influenced by cultural factors. Other influential determinants are education, gender or so-called lifestyle associations.

## Individual or social quality?

This raises a fundamental question, namely, what quality of life do we mean – individual or social quality? The underlying assumption of the majority of quality of life studies is that individual expression or selection of measurement categories, based on individual achievement levels, are in fact an appropriate reflection of the quality of life. But as Arrow pointed out, the assumption that individual utility levels are an appropriate reflection of the level of social satisfaction is erroneous, particularly when individual satisfaction levels are vastly disparate. A similar point was raised by Bergson (1938) who pointed out that picking a single, uniquely optimal point (a constrained bliss point) on the Pareto optimal grand utility possibilities frontier from among the infinite "optimal" possibilities requires that a social welfare function is known which reflects the choices society deems "best." The construction of such a social welfare function needs to embody the welfare judgments of society as to the fairness or desirability of the distribution of goods among its members. Whether it be water quality standards, zoning regulations, income distribution, or attitudes toward health and safety in the workplace standards, such quali-

tative judgments move decidedly out of positive analysis (see NORMATIVE AND POSITIVE ECONOMICS).

The shift from a classical economic notion of welfare as the welfare of the collectivity, to today's predominant notion of an individualistically based understanding of welfare is only subtly hidden behind the selection of objective or subjective quantitative measures of the quality of life. It is thus all the more regrettable that so much attention in the quality of life debate has focused on a positive analysis of quantitative measures, while little attention has been given to the normative nature of the quality of life debate. Ammassari (1994), for example, stresses the embeddedness of the concept in relational categories. Quality of life may thus be defined not on the basis of individual but rather relational categories. A high quality of life may be defined as a state where one is at relative peace with (1) oneself, (2) one's social relationships and (3) one's natural environment (Diwan and Lutz 1985). Such a peaceful process requires health in all three constituent cycles, the individual, the social and the environmental. As our awareness about the interrelationships between ourselves, nature, economy and society becomes clearer, questions about what constitutes the "quality of life" will gain greater relevance and importance, challenging existing belief and knowledge systems. Such relational and decidedly normative definitions of the quality of life will become increasingly central to addressing the tensions between individual and social, material and environmental well-being, just as scientific methods and positive analyses have been at the center of our attention for the past two centuries.

## See also:

collective social wealth; community; distribution of income; Gandhian political economy; gross domestic product and net social welfare; human development index; limits to growth; needs; pollution

## Selected references

Ammassari, P. (1994) "Ecology and the Quality of Social Life," in W. D'Antonio, M. Sasaki and Y. Yonebayashi (eds) *Ecology, Society and the Quality of Social Life*, New Brunswick and London: Transaction Publishers.

Bergson, A. (1938) "A Reformulation of Certain Aspects of Welfare Economics," *Quarterly Journal of Economics* 52: 310–34.

Campbell, A., Converse, P. and Rodgers, W. (1976) *The Quality of American Life: Perceptions, Evaluations, and Satisfactions*, New York: Sage.

Converse, P. (1980) *American Social Attitudes Data Source Book: 1947–1978*, Cambridge, MA: Harvard University Press.

Diwan, R. and Lutz, M. (eds) (1985) *Essays in Gandhian Economics*, New Delhi: Gandhi Peace Foundation.

Gandhi, M.K. (1909) *Hind Swaraj, Ahemdabad*, Swaraj: Navjivan Trust Hind.

Inkeles, A. (1994) "Industrialization, Modernization, and the Quality of Life," in W. D'Antonio, M. Sasaki and Y. Yonebayashi (eds), *Ecology, Society and the Quality of Social Life*, New Brunswick, NJ and London: Transaction Publishers.

Scheer, L. (1980) "Experience with Quality of Life Comparisons", in A. Szalai and F. Andrews (eds), *The Quality of Life: Comparative Studies*, London: Sage.

SABINE U. O'HARA
ROMESH DIWAN

# R

## race, ethnicity, gender and class

### Race and ethnicity

Human social identity is constructed historically in complex inter-relationships of criteria of similarity and difference. Among the most ubiquitous modes of collective identification is ethnicity. The word derives from the ancient Greek *ethnos*, which referred to a collectivity of humans living and acting together; it is usually translated as "people" or "nation." In the twentieth century, the linked concepts of ethnicity and ethnic group have been taken in many directions, academically and politically. In everyday discourse they are central to the politics of group differentiation and advantage in the social democracies of Europe, North America and Australasia. With notions of "race" in a degree of public and scientific disrepute since 1945, ethnicity has stepped into the ideological breach to become central to the often bloody reorganization of the post-Cold War world: "ethnic cleansing" stands beside earlier euphemisms such as "racial hygiene" and "the final solution." Nor is "race" a uniformly disreputable notion. In the United States, which experienced the Holocaust at a greater distance than Europe, it still finds a place in much public debate.

The inverted commas around "race" indicate the concept's contested and problematic status. Following a coordinated program of research and education by UNESCO in the decade following the Second World War, it has become widely accepted that "racial" differences are historically and socially constructed, rather than being biologically fundamental. Differences of genotype between human populations are now held to be relatively trivial in degree and in substance. Phenotypical difference – visible "racial" differences that are a product of the interaction of genetic endowment and environmental influences – are real enough, but their consequences for individuals and groups are the product of social processes of categorization and racialization rather than biological determination. However, the school of thought that has argued that there are significant genetically-determined "racial" differences in intelligence and achievement – and which explains systematic disadvantage on this basis – has never gone away; it is, indeed, exhibiting signs of resurgence at the time of writing (Fraser 1995).

### Gender

The other globally ubiquitous social identification is arguably GENDER. The female–male polarity is one of the most basic, if not the most basic, model of similarity and difference that is available to human beings as a principle of classification and social organization. Here also biologically-rooted ideas are germane: sexual differentiation, grounded in the physiology of reproduction and nurture, is distinguished by social science from gender differences, which are socially- and culturally-constructed institutionalizations of female and male. The distinction between sex and gender is well understood, and decades of feminist debate and scholarship have established the arbitrary nature of much gender differentiation. However, there is some disagreement, within feminism and elsewhere, about whether the biology of reproduction and of male and female bodies has determining consequences and about whether men and women are, in any sense, fundamentally different (for example, Richardson 1993).

## Gender and ethnicity

Gender and ethnicity differ fundamentally in some important respects. Ethnicity is a collective social identity; it cannot exist in the absence of collective social organization based on ethnic attachments. Gender, however, has historically required political work and mobilization in order to materialize – and then only recently – as a potential basis for collective identification and mobilization (although it has always been a potent dimension of individual social identity). Another major difference is that gender identification is in all human societies internalized during the formation of selfhood in primary socialization. This is not necessarily true for ethnicity.

## Class

CLASS can be defined in two basic ways. First, it can be seen as a shared relationship to the means of production (following Marx). Second, it can be seen as social class, as a market position with respect to production, distribution and consumption (following Weber). In both models, private property is important; in both, economic differentiation and hierarchy are central; in both, there is no necessary political or organized awareness of class membership. MARX recognized this in his distinction between a class-in-itself and a class-for-itself; Lenin further acknowledged it in emphasizing the need for "vanguard" political activity. Even on the broadest of interpretations, class is not ubiquitous in the sense that gender and ethnicity are. Whether one accepts the arguments for the existence of classes before capitalism (for example, Anderson 1974), class as a core principle structuring social relations is essentially a phenomenon of capitalism.

## Relationship between categories

Ethnicity, "race," gender and class have historically all exhibited considerable potential as principles of stigmatization, exclusion and domination. Depending on local circumstances, each may or may not reinforce the other(s). From the point of view of the classic Marxist tradition, for example, the problem has been how to bring gender and ethnicity/ "race" into the same analytical framework as the basic dynamo of history, class struggle. To frame this in terms of practical politics, the labor movements of the United States and Europe have long histories of unresolved conflict in which workplace hierarchies of skill, ethnicity and "race," and gender have intertwined to the detriment of successful collective organization. And, as subsequent events have dramatically demonstrated, during the period of state socialist hegemony in Eastern Europe and central Asia, the "nationalities question" was institutionally and coercively contained rather than politically resolved.

For twentieth-century feminism the issues may, perhaps, be brought into focus by questioning whether one women's movement, uniting women of all "colors," cultures and classes in the pursuit of putative interests in common, is a realistic goal towards which to strive. In Britain and Europe, for example, one of the issues around which this question has crystallized concerns the stance of (white, often middle-class) feminism with respect to Islamic or African-Caribbean women, and vice versa.

Ethnicity and its ideological allotropes, RACISM and nationalism, have been among the most enduring, supposedly "primordial," identifications to conflict with the development of modern state structures and political systems, social democratic and socialist movements, trade unions, labor organizations and movements for the improvement of the social place of women. This can be seen in the often fraught relationship between national liberation, ethnic politics and left-of-center social reform in the ex-colonial world.

Something similar has also often been

observable in Europe, where nineteenth-century nationalist movements – grounded as they typically were in local bourgeois interests – tended, certainly once the nationalist project had been realized, to be unsympathetic if not utterly hostile to socialism. In the industrialized states of the North and West, the relationship between the struggles of the women's movement, seeking to reform or overthrow "traditional" patriarchy, and the struggles of the labor movement, seeking to reform or overthrow capitalism, has not always been easy. It has not been self evident that the two objectives are co-terminous.

## Marxist and feminist writings

Political considerations such as these have produced a steady stream of theorizing. Marxists and feminists, for example, have found it no easier to reconcile their positions in academic print than in other political arenas. Among the earliest examples, and perhaps the most famous, is Engels's *The Origin of the Family, Private Property, and the State*, first published in 1884, in which he argued that class antagonism and female–male antagonism developed historically together, alongside and as a consequence of private property and structured social hierarchy, the end result being capitalism. The working through of this approach in the context of twentieth-century feminism can be seen, for example, in Delphy's argument (1984) that women and men constitute different classes, the one subordinate to the other in the domestic mode of production.

Despite Lenin's writings on imperialism, Oliver Cromwell Cox's *Caste, Class and Race* was the first serious attempt at a Marxist analysis of "race," arguing that "race prejudice" was a product of capitalism. Cox's work has been subject to a wide range of criticism, as poor scholarship and, by radical Afro-American scholars, as bad politics. Subsequent attempts to square the circle of "race" and class (such as Bonacich 1980) have never been more than partly successful. Similar comment could, perhaps, be made about recent attempts to integrate "race" and gender into a unified theoretical framework (such as Anthias and Yuval-Davis 1992).

Yet the problem is not that these things are necessarily unrelated. It is, for example, uncontroversial to argue that imperialism, colonialism and racism are intimately bound up with each other; as indeed colonialism and imperialism are bound up with the development of capitalism and the management of class conflict in the metropolitan centers. Similarly, as already suggested, there are many cases of ethnic attachments and/or racism being deployed to subvert the organization of labor. It is equally clearly the case that class and ethnicity can each be influential in frustrating the political organization and mobilization of women. Once again, to refer back to an earlier point, the women's movement historically has had specific ethnic and class roots, and black women's critiques of feminism are well-known.

## Concluding comments

There are relationships between ethnicity, "race," gender and class. But what are they, and what is the problem? These questions converge on the same answer(s) (see Jenkins 1996, 1997). The first point is that ethnicity, "race," gender, and class – even if there were consensual social science definitions of these terms (and at the moment there are not) – are not the same kinds of things. Ethnicity and gender, different as they are, appear to be ubiquitous features of human social life, in the historical long term, unlike "race" or class. "Race" is very much more a matter of imposed, external categorization than ethnicity. Despite its pervasiveness as an index of lifestyle differentiation, class is a social identity the organizing capacity of which in everyday life is, on the historical evidence to date, weak.

The second point is that where there are relationships between these modes of social identification, those relationships have been historically contingent rather than theoretically specifiable. Much of the scholarship which has sought to establish such relationships has attempted to fit the contingencies of history into theory, rather than the other way around (and, although history may not be at an end, it is proving relatively impervious to anything other than *ex post facto* theorization). Since ethnicity, "race," gender and class are historical and local phenomena, we should be concerned with ethnicities and racisms, and with the local specificities of gender and class relations. Nor does the postmodern celebration of "difference" – which is arguably a species of historicism, masquerading under another sign – seem likely to provide a solution to the problem. We can only begin to understand better the complexities of these issues through the careful specification of concepts, in the light of the exploration of particular historical and contemporary instances and their interrelations, and in the absence of preconceptions about those relationships.

## See also:

capitalism; classes and economic development; domestic labor debate; gender and development; gender division of labor; labor market discrimination; Marxist political economy: contemporary varieties; race in political economy: history; race in political economy: major contemporary themes

## Selected references

Anderson, P. (1974) *Lineages of the Absolutist State*, London: New Left Books.

Anthias, F. and Yuval-Davis, N. (1992) *Racialized Boundaries: Race, Nation, Gender, Colour and Class in the Anti-Racist Struggle*, London: Routledge.

Bonacich, E. (1980) "Class Approaches to Ethnicity and Race," *Insurgent Sociologist* 10(2): 9–23.

Cox, O.C. (1959) *Caste, Class and Race: A Study in Social Dynamics*, New York: Monthly Review Press.

Delphy, C. (1984) *Close to Home: A Materialist Analysis of Women's Oppression*, London: Hutchinson.

Engels, F. (1884) *The Origin of the Family, Private Property, and the State*, New York: Pathfinder, 1972.

Fraser, S. (ed.) (1995) *The Bell Curve Wars: Race, Intelligence, and the Future of America*, London: HarperCollins.

Jenkins, R. (1996) *Social Identity*, London: Routledge.

—— (1997) *Rethinking Ethnicity: Arguments and Explorations*, London: Sage.

Richardson, D. (1993) *Women, Motherhood and Childrearing*, London: Macmillan

RICHARD JENKINS

# race in political economy: history

Economists have grappled with the meaning of race for over a century. In the 1800s, an era marked by the end of SLAVERY, the beginning of INDUSTRIALIZATION and mass migrations, economists asked "What difference does race make with respect to the individual?". In more recent years, the focus has shifted away from individual aspects of race and toward the differences in economic outcomes between races. The chief categories analyzed, in this context, have been "black and white," as the most persistent and obvious location of an "economic gap." There has also been discussion of other groups, requiring additional distinctions between race, caste, CLASS and ethnicity (see RACE, ETHNICITY, GENDER AND CLASS).

## Three perspectives on "race"

Race was originally a category used to describe various European groups (Celts, Normans and so on). Geographic origins were used to describe African and other non-European groups (see Banton 1987.) By the mid-nineteenth century, the debate over race had split into several distinct camps. One approach relied on essentialism and eugenics; a second looked at social environment and CULTURE; a third took an anti-racialist stance (see Cherry 1976).

The first group, essentialists and eugenicists, were more directly concerned with race. Essentialists believed that all humans belonged to distinct racial groupings, ranked with "whites" at the top and "non-whites" in various rankings below. Character traits were rated on a continuum across these groups and explained the difference between races. This focus on "biological traits" was a precursor to the eugenics movement, later adopted in its own way by economists (see Banton 1987). Early economists wrote often on the negative impact of what they termed "non-Nordic immigration." General Amasa Walker, founder of the American Economic Association (AEA), wrote of his fear that overpopulation by Negroes and immigrants would create a threat to public health, morals and living standards. He and his peers published frequently on this theme in the *Quarterly Journal of Economics*, the *Journal of Political Economy* and AEA sources. By the early twentieth century, some economists had concluded that black Americans would soon become extinct due to losing the competitive battle with whites in the marketplace, a theory that became known as the "disappearance hypothesis."

Having assumed blacks out of the picture, the focus then turned to immigrants of various races (see Cherry 1976). Eugenicists advocated stricter immigration laws out of concern that immigration from southern and eastern Europe would weaken the genetic stock. The decline in wages that coincided with international immigration to the USA was seen as harmful to ECONOMIC GROWTH, and became a key point of policy contention between groups of white racial theorists. Competitive, destructive underbidding of wages was thought to be a genetic instinct among immigrants. This line of reasoning is best represented by the early work of Irving Fisher. Themes from his early work on eugenics and social Darwinism resurface in his later works on differential ability and time preferences (see Aldrich 1975).

The second group, social environment or cultural theorists, believed that all humans originated from some point, but that differences between groups emerged due to differences in social environment or culture. Culture became indelibly linked to economics via the Marxist notion that relations of production contain the foundations of social organization. This linkage shifted the area of inquiry to social relations within work and other economic realms.

Nineteenth-century sociologists had observed that whites in industrial CAPITALISM increased discrimination to enhance their own status. Excluding minorities was utility maximizing because the differentiation of groups could lower wage costs (especially for minorities), a precursor to the discrimination theories of Becker and Mincer. The act of discrimination itself was considered by some to be based on social customs and the relative bargaining power of racial groups. Similar ideas were incorporated into later theories of imperfect competition, SEGMENTED AND DUAL LABOR MARKETS and the historical materialist approach (see Banton 1987).

Some social environment analysts, like essentialists, favored immigration controls. From their perspective, poverty, not genetic instinct, caused the underbidding of wages. They feared the cyclical nature of immigration would exacerbate US business cycles. John R. Commons, representative of this philosophy, advocated union membership for resocializing immigrants and keeping wages high, but he did not link his immigration theories to theories of racial discrimination. Instead, he advocated excluding blacks from UNIONS, claiming they lacked the traits to compete and underbid wages, and so were in no need of organizing (Cherry 1976).

The idea of the "black race" as a permanent inferiority, whether biologically or culturally determined, had taken hold as a defense of the slave trade by the early nineteenth century. In response, a third group, abolitionists (and others) began to look at discrimination from an anti-racialist approach. They identified prejudice and race-consciousness as important factors in the development of racial views, such as those described above. Anti-racialists used new demographic data and statistical techniques to prove that immigrants were not overpopulating or bargaining down wages. Instead, their presence helped ease severe labor shortages. Taking a wider view than other theorists, they tied lower wages to exogenous consumer demand and final prices for goods (see Cherry 1976). Even from this relatively enlightened perspective, anti-racialist policy proposals revealed a distinctly patronizing outlook. Attempts to overcome discrimination via welfare and social reform programs continued into the twentieth century (and often overlapped with social environment policy proposals). Within these programs, agency and power was seen as belonging solely to the dominant white group, who alone had the ability to improve the economic lot of those at the lower echelons. This issue of agency, or who would lead and define the course of change, is another issue that separates the historical work of "white" and "black" theorists.

## Black economic thinkers on race

Prior to the American Civil War, black economic thinkers focused their efforts on the abolition of slavery and the role of blacks in that society. Following the war and partly in response to the brutality of the Reconstruction era, writers within the black community turned to the economics of race, attempting to define the new role of blacks outside slavery but within a racist social system. They addressed the question of racial differences from a different perspective to that of white theoreticians. The latter viewed race as a factor in individual outcomes. Black writers, while often drawing on or responding to mainstream theories, located their work in the urgent need for public policy and COMMUNITY action. The source of black economic conditions was often attributed to white discrimination, conditions rarely acknowledged in the mainstream focus on race at the time.

Economic debate within the black community dealt mostly with experiences of African Americans. In the European colonies of Central and South America and the Caribbean, emancipation predated the American Civil War. The few exceptions (Cuba and Brazil)

outlawed slavery by the 1880s. But conditions in the USA differed from the rest of the hemisphere. Emancipated slaves outside the USA had relatively more freedom, particularly in property, labor and voting rights, and integrated communities gradually developed (see Franklin 1969). Within the USA, a deep emotional investment in racial inferiority, in the aftermath of the Civil War, resulted in legal restrictions on the economic development of freed blacks in both the northern and southern USA.

The most important debate within black economic literature is that of nationalism/ separatism versus integration. For example, an advocacy of black separatism is found in the late nineteenth- and early twentieth-century writings of Booker T. Washington (1865–1915). He placed less priority on blacks gaining civil rights in white society than on economic development. Washington believed equality could not come through forced integration. He advocated separate social spheres with intertwined economies. His emphasis on individual achievement was strongly influenced by CLASSICAL POLITICAL ECONOMY, and overlapped with the social environmentalist's emphasis on the attainment of HUMAN CAPITAL (Franklin 1969). Washington believed political agitation for equality would only serve to anger white society, increasing racial hostility and further impoverishing the black community (Grant 1968). In the 1920s, the separatist/ nationalist approach was taken up by Marcus Garvey (1887–1940) and the United Negro Improvement Association. He advocated the establishment of a separate black nation in Africa, and the development of separate economic institutions within black communities in the USA. Nationalism had thus begun as a defense against whites. By the mid-1920s it had taken on overtones of a culturally based movement (Grant 1968).

Integrationists advocated equality with whites and within white society. Political agitation was the main tool in this struggle. Like white anti-racialists, black integrationists relied heavily on demographic data and surveys to document their cause. Economic equality, in their view, is only one form of equality, and achievable only with the attainment of other rights. W.E.B. DuBois (1868–1963) is a prominent integrationist who responded to Washington's separatism, calling it too accommodating to white racists. DuBois, like Washington, was an advocate of education, but only in conjunction with legislative and judicial guarantees of suffrage, fair wages and civil rights (Robinson 1997). Economic institutions and the relations of production, not purely a lack of human capital, stood in the way of economic advancement. DuBois criticized employers for underpaying blacks and creating impoverished communities, while pitting black and white workers against each other. He also criticized labor unions for refusing to organize black workers, then castigating blacks who worked during strikes. Economic improvement, for DuBois, would come not only from individual attainment of human capital, but also through collective action. The leaders in this endeavor were to be "the Talented Tenth," DuBois' term for an elite group of intellectuals comprising ten percent of the black community. Along these lines, the NAACP (National Association for the Advancement of Colored People) and the Urban League were founded for political advocacy and to ease the transition of workers moving from the rural south to industrial north, providing job and housing assistance.

Support for nationalism or integration has historically broken down along class lines. Free blacks and later the urban northern professional class sought the privileges of non-blacks, including the attainment of economic goals. Southern ex-slaves were drawn to separatism. Garvey's black nationalism was immensely popular among rural sharecroppers and northern laborers, groups excluded by the elitism of integrationists (Robinson 1997).

In response to increasing support for Garvey's nationalist movement, integrationists became more accommodating, eliminating the call for development of a talented tenth. By the 1940s, Dubois had explicitly grounded his analysis of discrimination in Marxist theory and historical materialism (see Franklin 1969). He also integrated some aspects of nationalism

into his writings, essentially recognizing a separate black culture. However, the Communist Party and other left organizations united with Garvey's African Movement, advocating black separatism and self-determination (Robinson 1997).

Integrationists and separatists have shared one element of common ground from the start: all recognize in some way the influence of colonialism and imperialism on other communities of color in the world. This global perspective has been developed by others in more recent years, such as Oliver Cox in *Capitalism as a System*, in 1964.

## Postwar race theory

In the post-1945 era, race theory was concerned more with market mechanisms and ACCUMULATION and less with the influence of genetics or culture on the individual. A central issue was whether and how the market should be used to adjust outcomes between groups. Marxian-based theories dropped the assumption of competitive labor markets and explored racial discrimination as endemic to the accumulation process.

Gunnar Myrdal's *An American Dilemma* in 1944 influenced postwar public policy though recognizing the interdependencies between racial prejudice (based on ignorance), black poverty and education, and income inequality. Oliver Cox in *Caste, Class and Race*, published in 1948, criticized Myrdal's lack of attention to the conscious class use of power and force to perpetuate racial inequality. Both, however, believed in racial integration, albeit the former in a liberal and the latter in a socialist form. Integration as a policy was dominant in the postwar period.

The civil rights movement was strong in the 1950s and 1960s in the USA, and public policy became more concerned with the conditions and rights of blacks. Liberal variants of discrimination and human capital theory dominated the economics profession and integrationist organizations in the USA. Opposition came from more nationalist oriented groups, including Malcolm X and the Black

Power movement of the late 1960s. These groups often echoed Washington's philosophies of self-achievement and separatism, and tended to be more conscious of the effects of colonialism and apartheid. These newer movements split into several factions, including Pan-Africanism and Marxism. The anti-white, anti-capitalist stance of both groups left them outside the mainstream (see Marable 1981; Robinson 1983). Throughout the era of integration and civil rights there also remained an undercurrent of conservatism that focused on individual shortcomings and "blaming the victims." The resurgence of political economy in the 1960s, 1970s and into the present contributed much towards a coherent analysis of race, and the linkage of race/ethnicity with class and gender. In the 1980s, a political backlash brought conservative economists, both black and white, to the forefront of theory and policy.

## See also:

culture of poverty; race, ethnicity, gender and class; race in political economy: major contemporary themes; racism; Williams–Rodney thesis

## Selected references

Aldrich, Mark (1975) "Capital Theory and Racism: From Laissez-Faire to the Eugenics Movement in the Career of Irving Fisher," *Review of Radical Political Economics* 7(3): 33–42.

Banton, Michael (1987) *Racial Theories*, Cambridge: Cambridge University Press.

Cherry, Robert (1976) "Racial Thought and the Early Economics Profession," *Review of Social Economy* 34(2): 147–62.

Franklin, John H. (1969) *From Slavery to Freedom*, New York: Vintage Books.

Grant, Joanne (1968) *Black Protest: History, Document and Analyses*, New York: Fawcett.

Marable, Manning (1981) *Black Water: Historical Studies in Race, Class Consciousness and Revolution*, Dayton: Black Praxis Press.

Robinson, Cedric (1983) *Black Marxism: The Making of the Black Radical Tradition*, London: Zed Books.

—— (1997) *Black Movements in America*, New York: Routledge.

CHRISTINE D'ONOFRIO

# race in political economy: major contemporary themes

Most schools of political economy have shared a common tendency to undertheorize race. Theoreticians addressing the political economy of race and ethnicity increasingly refuse either to reduce race to CLASS or to insist on conceptualizing race as a historically invariant social practice. As an alternative to reductionist and essentialist thinking, these new projects explore the social production of racial meanings, race formations, and racial identities. The literature on discrimination in the labor market provides a perspective for viewing how alternative schools within political economy have conceptualized race and ethnicity. Within this literature, most political economists have not accorded sufficient significance to either the economic or extra-economic practices which create gendered, race-conscious workers or the historical specificity of those practices. In contrast, poststructuralist and feminist theories provide analytic means to the end of developing a richer theory of race and GENDER subjectification, agency, and "class interests."

## Mainstream Marxist theory

Marxist political economists agree that racial discrimination is a persistent feature of the daily operation of capitalist labor markets. However, they disagree as to the practices which reproduce racial inequality. Mainstream Marxist theory presents two forms of class-based models. The "divide and conquer" tradition argues that discrimination divides the working class, lowers workers' bargaining power relative to capitalists, increases profits, and is consistent with perfect competition

(Reich 1981). Divisions in the working class made possible capitalists' employment of black workers as strikebreakers between the two world wars. Strikebreaking increases capitalist profits (the new workers sell their labor power for less than the strikers) and reduces all workers' wages (divisions reduce bargaining power). Reich demonstrates a positive correlation between black–white family income inequality, on the one hand, and income and schooling inequality among whites, on the other. He reads this correlation as an affirmation of the hypothesis that racial inequality lowers workers' bargaining power and therefore their ability to shift income from profits to wages and community development.

Cherry (1988) amends the class-based model by noting that, in the post-Second World War era of segmented labor markets, capitalists rarely hire only African-Americans as strikebreakers. Moreover, gender-based occupational segregation limits the extent to which employers threaten their male workers with the specter of mass hirings of women. Still, contemporary capitalists use global wage hierarchies to reduce costs via the subcontracting of work to firms in secondary labor markets locally, nationally and internationally. Cherry argues that whites cling to "discriminatory attitudes" because of the perception that they benefit from RACISM. He explains a resurgence of white discriminatory attitudes in the post-Second World War period as the fault of an opportunistic union leadership that supported capitalist led foreign policy objectives, eschewed the formation of a labor party, and convinced white male union members to act against their class interest. White men's collaboration with racism and sexism undermined their class interests.

These traditional Marxist theories of discrimination construct white workers as the possessors of objective class interests which are determined by their relationship to the imposition and appropriation of surplus value. In other words, white workers are the bearers of a stable and non-contradictory class identity, grounded in the social relations of production. Radicals know what those interests are, and

discrimination is antithetical thereto. Mainstream radical theory yields a clear political strategy: radicals must convince working-class whites that they suffer from discrimination. If radicals can change white perceptions as to the benefits derived from discriminatory behavior, they will have achieved a necessary (but perhaps not sufficient?) step along the path toward ending racist behaviors and attitudes.

## Challenges to the mainstream

There are two schools of thought challenging the Marxist mainstream. Shulman (1990) rejects value theory and accords primacy to the analysis of SEGMENTED AND DUAL LABOR MARKETS and SOCIAL STRUCTURES OF ACCUMULATION. The classical camp employs Marxian theories of competition to conceptualize discrimination (Williams 1987; Darity 1989; Mason 1992). Both schools of thought agree with the traditionalists that discrimination persists in capitalist economies. However, these challengers posit different mechanisms for the continuation of discrimination, and challenge the notion that white workers always lose when they collaborate with or pursue racist practices.

Darity, Mason and Williams all ground their models of discrimination in Marx's analysis of competition and new theoretical work on noncompensating wage differentials. They argue that the competitive structure of capitals is consistent with recurring inter- and intra-industry wage differentials between comparable workers. The RESERVE ARMY OF LABOR, job-specific labor queues, and the wage hierarchies shape inter- and intra-class conflicts over the allocation of workers to jobs. Moreover, the classical school argues that labor market activities are a site for the construction, reproduction and disruption of race–gender subjects who define their interests in race and/ or gendered terms.

Discrimination's cost–benefit calculus is complex and contingent. One of the reasons that white workers discriminate is because of the absolute or relative benefits as "white people" from so doing. Even when racial divisions reduce workers' bargaining power

949

and lower labor's income relative to capital, dominant groups may still increase their absolute standard of living by controlling preferred industries, firms and occupations. To the extent that white workers are concerned with absolute income levels, their losses relative to capital are insufficient to render irrational the pursuit of racial inequality. We cannot take for granted the notion that white workers define their well being and status relative to capitalist or upper-income whites. Other interpretations of "interest" and the meaning and value of particular economic outcomes to workers are both plausible and historically observed.

Because discrimination's outcomes are complex, contradictory and contingent, challengers to the mainstream remain skeptical that there exists a set of economic outcomes that proves white workers lose from discrimination. The outcomes are complex because both continuing and ending discrimination are costly. They are contingent because these costs are mediated by political and aggregate economic conditions. Discrimination's outcomes are contradictory, in that occupational, wage and employment discrimination need not necessarily increase or decrease in tandem (Shulman 1991).

There is a symmetry to the new theories of discrimination. Both schools reject the notion that racism is something that capitalists impose on workers, even though employers sometimes benefit from racist practice. Yet the schools also resist the thesis that white workers are the only obstacle to ending discrimination. The main proposition of the new theories is rather more modest: white worker agency warrants inclusion in the social practices that reproduce discrimination. They are loathe to reduce racism and discrimination's persistence to false perceptions. On the contrary, they begin with the historically located and racially identified white workers for whom whiteness mediates notions of self, gender, community and class interest. Racial discrimination presupposes racial identity, and the creation of racial identities requires "racializing" socio-cultural relations and processes. Thus, "whiteness" is constitutive of identity, gender, community and interests.

## Dialogues with other theorists

In expanding conceptualizations of race, the new theorists of discrimination open a door to dialogues with a wide range of social theorists exploring the social and discursive construction of meaning and CULTURE. This community of scholars includes feminists, ethnic studies scholars, poststructuralists, historians, literary critics and philosophers (to name but a few) who are thinking about the social construction of race and racial representations, but do not take discrimination as their entry point. For example, in their important discussion of the formation of the racial state in the USA, Omi and Winant (1986) argue that individuals and groups contest the meaning of race, and that these struggles are not limited to the macrostructural world of state politics or the economic realm. In other words, we make racialized meanings and identities in the lifeworld – the everyday action contexts (workplaces, families, political organizations and so on) wherein we engage one another on the basis of an intersubjective consensus about community, values and objectives.

Feminists continue to theorize the gendering of race and class in capitalist social formations. The experience and meaning of race and class within families, workplaces, kinship systems, migratory communities, settler colonies, unions, clubs and political movements is deeply gendered. Many feminists now call for and conduct critical readings of class, gender, race, ethnicity and sexuality that historically, culturally, and materially locate the subjects and communities under investigation.

A new generation of Marxist and institutionalist economists has begun a dialogue with postmodern theories of subject formation. To date, political economists have eschewed a serious consideration of the social construction of discriminating subjects. Most have neither generated accounts that penetrate racialized and gendered self-understandings nor examined how such understandings inform the meaning of class interests and political possibilities. Yet these accounts are a necessary component of a fuller theory of political economy.

## See also:

culture of poverty; discrimination in the housing and mortgage market; race, ethnicity, gender and class; race in political economy: history

## Selected references

Cherry, Robert (1988) "Shifts in Radical Theories of Inequality," *Review of Radical Political Economics* 20(2–3): 33–57.
—— (1991) "Race and Gender Aspects of Marxian Economic Models," *Science and Society* 55(1): 60–78.
Darity, William, Jr (1989) "What's Left of the Economics of Discrimination," in Steven Shulman and William Darity, Jr (eds), *The Question of Discrimination*, Middletown, CT: Wesleyan University Press, 335–75.
Hooks, Bell (1990) *Yearning: Race, Gender, and Cultural Politics*, Boston: South End Press.
Mason, Patrick (1992) "The Divide-and-Conquer and Employer/Employee Models of Discrimination: Neoclassical Competition as a Familial Defect," *The Review of Black Political Economy* 20(4): 73–89.
Omi, M. and Winant, H. (1986) *Racial Formation in the United States from the 1960s to the 1980s*, New York, Routledge & Kegan Paul.
Reich, Michael (1981) *Racial Inequality: A Political-Economic Analysis*, Princeton, NJ: Princeton University Press.
Shulman, Steve (1990) "Racial Inequality and White Employment: An Interpretation and Test of the Bargaining Power Hypothesis," *The Review of Black Political Economy* 18(3): 5–20.
—— (1991) "Why Is the Black Unemployment Rate Always Twice as High as the White Unemployment Rate?," in Richard A. Cornwall and Phanindra V. Wunnava (eds), *New Approaches to Economic and Social Analyses of Discrimination*, New York: Praeger.
Williams, Rhonda M. (1987) "Capital, Competition, and Discrimination: A Reconsideration of Racial Earnings Inequality", *Review of Radical Political Economics* 19(2): 1–15.

RHONDA M. WILLIAMS

# racism

Racism refers to the ideology and practice of racial oppression. Racial oppression occurs when the social characteristics and abilities of ethnic, national, religious or tribal groups are differentiated and explained in organic or genetic terms, and when, on that basis, such groups suffer from systematic opprobrium, discrimination, EXPLOITATION and/or repression (Miles 1989).

## Race as a social category

Racism presupposes racial classifications and relationships. Unlike sex, race is a social category with little biological significance. Races are most often categorized in terms of visible physical characteristics (usually but not exclusively skin color), though the example of the Jews makes it clear that this rule is not without its exceptions. Although racial classifications vary from society to society, they consistently establish patterns of domination and subordination. These classifications define relationships among racial groups which are typically hierarchical, violent, exploitative and de-humanizing.

## Racial oppression

The forms of racial oppression also vary among societies, ranging from paternalistic systems such as the slave plantations and colonial regimes in Latin America, to segregationist systems such as the apartheid eras in South Africa and the southern USA, to genocidal systems such as Nazi Germany (van den Berghe 1978). All of these systems are characterized by the overt and dominant role of the state. The trend in the modern period is toward an open system in which the state professes neutrality (or even advocacy on the side of the oppressed) and racial oppression, albeit of a less vicious variety, becomes diffused into civil society and the ordinary workings of a capitalist economy. The paradigm case of an open system is that of the post-civil rights United States.

Racial oppression pre-dates CAPITALISM, but the globalization of capitalism coincided with the spread of the slave trade (see WILLIAMS–RODNEY THESIS), the genocide of native populations, the establishment of colonial empires, the fusion of anti-semitism and nationalism, and the doctrine of biological and civilizational inferiority which accompanied all of these events. Capitalism is clearly implicated in the remarkable spread of racism over the course of the last three centuries. At the same time, capitalism is also uniquely associated with the emergence of abolitionist and anti-racist movements, and its ethos of individualism, opportunity and democracy (the so-called "American Creed") has proven to be a potent counterweight to the classic forms of racial oppression. Capitalism has both reproduced and eroded racism, and it is this contradictory relationship which lies at the heart of the debates about the mechanisms, functions and trajectory of modern race relations (see CONTRADICTIONS).

## Gunnar Myrdal

The political economy analysis of racism is most explicitly indebted to the massive research project on African-Americans headed by the institutionalist Gunnar Myrdal (1944). Myrdal believed that racism was rooted in the tradition of economic exploitation which began with SLAVERY. At the same time, he explained prejudice as a psycho-sexual phenomenon linked to the fear of inbreeding with an allegedly inferior stock (the "anti-amalgamation doctrine"). He believed that economic forces tended to reproduce racism as a result of a vicious cycle: the exploitation of blacks

lowered their standard of living and so reinforced the prejudice of whites, which in turn rekindled exploitation (the "principle of cumulation").

On the other hand, he argued that the conflict between racism and the American Creed would eventually diminish the hold of racism on the popular imagination, and so would tend to reduce the practice of racism as well. He also thought that appropriate government policies could raise the standard of living of blacks, and by so doing reduce white prejudice and with it economic exploitation (the principle of cumulation in reverse). In the long-run he optimistically believed that the ideological and political forces working against racism would overwhelm the economic forces perpetuating it, a belief which appeared to be validated by the success of the civil rights movement two decades later (see CIRCULAR AND CUMULATIVE CAUSATION).

Although Myrdal was harshly criticized by many on the left, three of his basic perspectives – that the economy could reproduce racism, that capitalism had a contradictory relationship to racism, and that government activism was a necessary weapon in the fight against racism – became in various combinations the hallmark of the political economy analysis of racism.

## Racism as an economic phenomenon

Institutionalists inexplicably failed to follow in his footsteps, so the subsequent work in this tradition was primarily carried out by Marxists and an eclectic group of left-liberals. Their ideas were quite disparate, but (as time went on) they shared the goal of debunking the neoclassical argument that market mechanisms would automatically erode racism. They believed that racism was fundamentally an economic phenomenon and not just a psychological problem of whites. The modern view of political economists essentially represents a synthesis of the different conceptual approaches they took to this question.

The initial efforts of Marxists to argue that blacks were a "superexploited" sector of the working class proved unsuccessful since the relationship between wages and PRODUCTIVITY could not be shown to be different for black and white workers. Nor did efforts to describe the ghetto as an "internal colony" bear fruit. Instead of approaching racial analysis from the standpoint of describing blacks as a distinct class, caste or national group, the focus shifted to the processes which excluded blacks from desirable jobs or, all too often, from any jobs (but see Omi and Winant 1986). "Institutional discrimination" became the catch-all phrase for the persistence of implicit discriminatory barriers in the post-civil rights era.

Political economists analyze the institutionalization of discrimination in a variety of ways which are better viewed as complements than substitutes. They encompass the structure of occupations and labor markets, the behavior of unions, white workers and capitalists, and the economic and social context within which racism operates.

Employers must avoid offending the sensibilities of their workers, their suppliers or their customers if they are to function effectively in their social environment. They are particularly concerned that integrated work groups may experience conflict, which will reduce team productivity. Consequently, they tend to establish a division of labor which mimics existing social hierarchies (the same analysis has been applied to the GENDER DIVISION OF LABOR). Race relationships thereby become embedded in occupational definitions and structures.

The same is true with respect to the structure of the labor market as a whole. The theory of SEGMENTED AND DUAL LABOR MARKETS holds that qualified workers queue in the secondary sector as they compete for scarce job openings in the primary sector. Race becomes a cheap screening device which enables primary sector employers to reduce their perceived hiring risks. Because blacks as a group are purportedly less reliable and less skilled, they are culled out of the pool of job applicants and crowded in the secondary sector, where a smaller premium is placed on these attributes.

Both employers and white employees may also face incentives which cause them to behave in a discriminatory fashion. Employers may be able to lower their overall wage bill if racism enables them to reduce the solidarity and bargaining power of labor. In this case, white workers would also be hurt by racism, a claim which has been used to justify the optimistic belief that white and black workers share common interests in overcoming it (Reich 1981). This view is consistent with the orthodox Marxist interpretation of racism as a "divide-and-conquer" strategy of the capitalist class against all workers. However the empirical basis for this claim is weak, and white workers may also benefit from racism if it reduces job competition.

Other political economists have analyzed racism as a force which divides the labor market into racial/ethnic enclaves, as groups attempt to insulate themselves from job competition (Williams 1987). The distributional effects of racism vary with economic and political conditions, so the question "Who benefits?" cannot be answered in the abstract. Nonetheless, a functionalist connection is often drawn between the beneficiaries of discrimination and the blame for discrimination which can lay the basis for political judgments, particularly with regard to the role of white workers in the struggle against racism. The connection is tenuous, and conclusions concerning allies and enemies should be treated with care.

Political economists tend to argue that the context within which discrimination occurs may perpetuate it. In the short-run, the periodic recurrence of recessions tends to reignite racism as job competition intensifies. In the long-run, racism can become self-perpetuating as its effects stimulate perceptions and behaviors which reinforce it (for example, Myrdal's principle of cumulation). In this fashion, political economists treat discrimination as a dynamic phenomenon which can quantitatively and qualitatively vary with the circumstances it is in. Empirical research supports the contention that discrimination has changed but not disappeared (Turner *et al.* 1991).

Although political economists focus on the ability of capitalism to reproduce racism, their perspective contains some optimistic elements as well. Full employment can reduce racial discrimination, as can progressive changes in social attitudes, law and public policy. The government is considered to be a key player in achieving these outcomes. Political economists therefore tend to agree with Myrdal that racism is conditional, not inevitable, and can be reduced if the economic, political and ideological pressures are sufficiently strong.

## Limitations of political economy aproach to racism

The political economy analysis of racism has several limitations. First, it centers on the role of blacks as workers. It has had less to say about their wholesale exclusion from the economy, as evidenced by the long-run decline in labor force participation among the inner city poor. However, political economists have argued forcefully that the lack of opportunities are to blame for the problems of the "underclass" (Fusfeld and Bates 1984; Darity and Meyers 1994).

Second, the political economy analysis of racism often fails to place it in relation to other, more powerful forces affecting black Americans. Trends in marital and birth patterns, child rearing arrangements, educational attainment, labor market restructuring and inner-city turmoil have had more impact on black well-being than racism *per se*, especially over the past three decades (Wilson 1980). Political economists need to show how racism is situated within and responds to this larger set of forces.

Third, the patterns of inequality have become more complex. Blacks are no longer uniformly oppressed by racism. Compared to three decades ago, the black/white wage gap has narrowed while employment gaps have widened. Black occupational mobility has increased, and a substantial black middle class has emerged; at the same time, the desperation in the inner cities has intensified. The degree of racial inequality varies sharply with family structure, educational attainment and labor force participation. These patterns cannot be explained simply in terms of racism. The tendency of capitalism to erode as well as reproduce racism is clearly at work, and the effects of racism in an open system are in large part a function of the responses to it. Political economists should have more to say about these issues as well.

Finally, the political economy analysis of racism is too dependent upon the situation of African-Americans (as should be obvious from this review). It remains to be seen if it can be successfully extended to the experience of other minorities or synthesized with the analysis of other forms of oppression such as sexism (see RACE, ETHNICITY, GENDER AND CLASS).

## See also:

race in political economy: major contemporary themes

## Selected references

Darity, William, Jr and Myers, Samuel, Jr (1994) *The Black Underclass: Critical Essays on Race and Unwantedness*, New York: Garland Publishing.

Fusfeld, Daniel and Bates, Timothy (1984) *The Political Economy of the Urban Ghetto*, Carbondale, IL: Southern Illinois University Press.

Miles, Robert (1989) *Racism*, New York: Routledge.

Myrdal, Gunnar (1944) *An American Dilemma: The Negro Problem and Modern Democracy*, 2 vols, New York: Pantheon Books, 1972.

Omi, Michael and Winant, Howard (1986) *Racial Formation in the United States: From the 1960s to the 1980s*, New York: Routledge & Kegan Paul.

Reich, Michael (1981) *Racial Inequality: A Political-Economic Analysis*, Princeton, NJ: Princeton University Press.

Turner, Margery Austin, Fix, Michael and Struyk, Raymond (1991) *Opportunities Denied, Opportunities Diminished: Racial Discrimination in Hiring*, Washington, DC: The Urban Institute, Report 91–9.

van den Berghe, Pierre (1978) *Race and Racism: A Comparative Perspective*, New York: John Wiley.

Williams, Rhonda (1987) "Capital, Competition and Discrimination: A Reconsideration of Racial Earnings Inequality," *Review of Radical Political Economics* 19(2).

Wilson, William (1980) *The Declining Significance of Race: Blacks and Changing American Institutions*, Chicago: University of Chicago Press.

STEVEN SHULMAN

# radical institutionalism

Radical institutionalists combine the methodology of original institutional economics with the radical analysis of CLASS and consciousness provided by Karl MARX and some of his twentieth-century articulators. Building upon the ideas of Thorstein VEBLEN and J.K. Galbraith, in the late 1960s and early 1970s radical institutionalists such as Bill Dugger, Rick Tilman and Ron Stanfield began to develop explicitly radical interpretations of the modern liberal institutionalism they inherited from C.E. Ayres and Allan Gruchy, among others. A considerable number of radical institutionalists are now active in the institutionalist movement.

Radical institutionalists represent a trend within the ASSOCIATION FOR EVOLUTIONARY ECONOMICS AND ASSOCIATION FOR INSTITUTIONALIST THOUGHT, and have much in common with original institutional economics, especially the liberal institutionalists. However, they are in some respects more radical in that they engage in a thorough critique of the current forms of corporate and cultural HEGEMONY, and CLASS alienation in favor of more PARTICIPATORY DEMOCRACY AND SELF-MANAGEMENT in the firm, some measure of national planning, and cultural reform along lines of RACE, ETHNICITY, GENDER AND CLASS.

## Relationship to original institutionalists

Radical institutionalists accept many of the tenets of original institutional economics, which extends the scope of economic inquiry well beyond the conventional analysis of the efficient allocation of resources to attain maximum real income. Original institutional economics includes a consideration of the effects on the flow of real income of the exercise of power and the force of INSTITUTIONS AND HABITS which shape the wants of individuals and the resources available. Hence the focal point of original institutional economics is the process of INSTITUTIONAL CHANGE AND ADJUSTMENT. Change is seemingly irresistible, but it brings in its wake problems of maladjustment in the face of inertial ignorance or dedicated resistance from those with vested interests in potentially obsolete ways and means. Such institutional maladjustment can have dramatic consequences for the flow of real income.

The HOLISTIC METHOD of institutional economics differs from the conventional emphasis on positivist testing of deductions by means of sophisticated econometric procedures. To establish empirical correspondence, institutionalists rely on the comparative approach developed by anthropologists to collect information and pursue generalizations about the economic activities of human groups (see Arensberg, in Polanyi *et al.* 1971). In so doing, heavy reliance is placed upon qualitative empirical analysis of a historical and cultural nature, and descriptive rather than inferential use of quantitative information. Also central to the holistic method is the use of "participatory observation," in which the scholar attempts to get close to the institutional material under study, whether it be in the labor process, the state or the world economy. Interaction with economic agents, direct observation, and devising STORYTELLING AND PATTERN MODELS based on this direct analysis, are important for understanding the workings of groups of people within institutions and for positing agendas for institutional reform (Tilman 1987).

The significance of the institutionalist approach is that its evolutionary emphasis introduces social change and therefore power and CULTURE into the analysis. Treating human wants and technical capacities as variables introduces the question of the manner in which they evolve. Such issues cannot be addressed without attention to the issue of power and life chances that structure the differentiation of citizen input into these discretionary processes.

This tradition of original institutional economics is to some extent radical *per se* in that it undermines the habitual denial of power by the market and pluralist ideology, but the radical institutionalist thrust is much more explicit. Radical institutionalists find considerable evidence that powerful corporate capitalist interests dominate politics, culture, and economic processes (Galbraith 1973; Stanfield 1979, 1995; Tilman 1987; Dugger 1989a, 1989b). They insist that the administered economy and society necessitate radically new institutional responses if the political economy is to be reformed to operate more effectively in the service of humane social values.

## Influence of Marx, Veblen and Galbraith

The concern for cultural hegemony led radical institutionalists to incorporate into their analysis the critical theory of consciousness inspired by Marx, who insisted upon an analysis of the socialized individual in sharp distinction to CLASSICAL POLITICAL ECONOMY which tended to universalize bourgeois personality. This undermines an assumption that is the bulwark of capitalist ideology: "You cannot change human nature." Radical institutionalists use this insight and the concern for class power and CORPORATE HEGEMONY in examining the nature of contemporary capitalism.

The preferences and actions of individuals in modern capitalist society are influenced by an array of forces, some of them socially constructive and some destructive. The COMMODITY FETISHISM that permeates contemporary society engenders environmental deterioration and cultural disintegration. In examining these problems, and the basic issue of self-authenti-

city they imply, radical institutionalists have built upon an ample tradition within their own school. Veblen's scathing examination of invidious consumption rivals Marx's notion of commodity fetishism in driving home the point that the market mentality obscures the ways in which socially constructed inequality and consciousness reinforce problems of CEREMONIAL ENCAPSULATION and the DISEMBEDDED ECONOMY. Galbraith (1973) has underscored this theme in his trenchant examination of contemporary American capitalism which elaborates the institutionalist dissent from the conventional logic that price equals value (see GALBRAITH'S CONTRIBUTION TO POLITICAL ECONOMY).

## Critique of orthodox economics

Radical institutionalists insist that orthodox economic thinking obscures many critically important aspects of socially-structured inequality and ecological and social deterioration. Much ambiguity surrounds the validity of wants and costs, and the duality between the public and private sectors that NEOCLASSICAL ECONOMICS takes for granted. Allocating resources to reflect efficient outcomes in terms of the current pattern of wants and costs is cause for congratulation only if one celebrates the structure of power that determines wants and costs. The sharp duality between the public and private sectors loses much force if the business world possesses instruments of authority and persuasion that are tantamount to a "governing force."

## Policy questions

Fundamental institutional reform is needed that deepens the social control of business and popular participation in political processes. Examples include greater social auditing of corporate behavior, citizen input into corporate decision making, some measure of national economic planning, and aggressive extension of the social welfare state complex (Galbraith 1973; Bowles *et al.* 1983). Advocacy of these reforms is another distinct feature of radical institutionalism (see Brown 1988).

## Conclusion

Radical institutionalism is thus centered on the inequality of income, wealth and power and the psycho-cultural implications of the market capitalist economy. It abandons the original institutional economics disdain of Marx's analysis of class and alienation. Piecemeal reform is not seen as an adequate response to the pathology of late capitalism. Technocratic and meritocratic strategies are rejected in favor of strategies aimed at restructuring the cultural foundations of global capitalism. Radical institutionalists insist that only a fundamental and comprehensive repositioning of the place of economy within society can suffice in the effort to adjust the developmental trajectories of the industrial economies toward a more rational ordering of the global economy.

## Selected references

Bowles, S., Gordon, D. and Weisskopf, T. (1983) *Beyond the Waste Land*, Garden City, NY: Anchor Press.

Brown, D.M. (1988) *Towards a Radical Democracy*, London: Unwin Hyman.

Dugger, W.M. (1989a) *Corporate Hegemony*, New York: Greenwood Press.

—— (ed.) (1989b) *Radical Institutionalism*, New York: Greenwood Press.

Galbraith, J.K. (1973) *Economics and the Public Purpose*, Boston: Houghton-Mifflin.

Peterson, Janice and Brown, Douglas (1994) *The Economic Status of Women Under Capitalism*, Aldershot: Edward Elgar.

Polanyi, K., Arensberg, C.M. and Pearson, H.W. (eds) (1971) *Trade and Market in the Early Empires*, Chicago: Henry Regnery.

Stanfield, J.R. (1979) *Economic Thought and Social Change*, Carbondale, IL: Southern Illinois University Press.

—— (1995) *Economics, Power, and Culture: Essays in the Development of Radical Institutionalism*, New York: St Martin's Press.

Tilman, R. (1987) "The Neoinstrumental Theory of Democracy," *Journal of Economic Issues* 21(3): 1379–1401.

JAMES RONALD STANFIELD

# rationality and irrationality

## Rationality in neoclassical economics

The notion of rationality is one of the pillars of neoclassical economics. Within the mainstream, rationality is equated with maximization, but there are different versions of the maximization principle. Not many neoclassical economists seem to defend the descriptive version, according to which people do in reality deliberately maximize. More common are the "as if" version and the prescriptive version. In the former, people are seen as behaving "as if" they were maximizing (as in the example of a skillful billiard player), without actually performing calculations. The prescriptive variety examines what people "should do" in order to be rational. This version is the last resort of many neoclassical economists when faced with the empirical evidence against the two other versions.

Another important distinction within neoclassical economics is that between the approaches which identify self-interest as the objective being pursued, and the approaches which see maximization as a criterion for internal consistency (Sen 1987). The former case is the one typically underlying the association between neoclassical rationality and the selection of the best means to achieve a given end. In the latter case, the way is open to an association between rationality and maximizing an objective function, but the objective does not have to be straightforward self-interest.

Practitioners of political economy have criticized the mainstream treatment of rationality on several grounds. Two issues seem to be particularly noteworthy: (1) the relation between rationality and knowledge, and (2) the means–end framework.

## Rationality and knowledge

Regarding the first issue, an important critique points out people's limited computational capability relative to very complex situations. This argument is mainly associated with Herbert Simon's work, but it is made also by members of different schools of political economy. It has old institutionalist forerunners (see Rutherford 1994) and sympathizers in post-Keynesianism, neo-Schumpeterianism (especially in the Nelson–Winter strand), Austrian economics (especially in connection with Hayek) and in the new institutionalism. The argument supports Simon's alternative notions of bounded and procedural rationality, which rationalize rule-following behavior that yields satisfactory results.

However, factors such as TIME, surprise and entrepreneurship do not play significant roles in Simon's work (Loasby 1989), whereas all those schools have strands which emphasize the openness of the world and the indeterminacy of the future. The strong notion of UNCERTAINTY associated with these factors poses another challenge to neoclassical rationality on cognitive grounds. There is disagreement among economists who emphasize uncertainty concerning the extent to which rationality depends on knowledge and what kind of knowledge people can have under uncertainty. There exist two major options.

The first possible approach is to define rationality as something that has to be based on knowledge. This may be called the cognitive approach. It can be divided into two strands. The first defines irrationality as anything different from rationality. If uncertainty implies some lack of knowledge, then it implies that behavior is at least partly irrational. This may be called the dichotomic strand of the cognitive approach. For a second, non-dichotomic strand, irrationality is that which contradicts rationality. Under uncertainty, this implies rejecting a dichotomy between rationality and irrationality and introducing a third possibility: non-rationality or arationality, which applies to the case in which the lack of knowledge prevents us from determining what

is rational. Something cannot be said in this case to be irrational, since it cannot be said to contradict rational behavior. Factors such as ANIMAL SPIRITS and creativity have a role to play under uncertainty, as rationality does not dictate a particular course of action. Depending on which strand of the first approach one favors, these factors are seen as being irrational or arational.

The second approach is, of course, to define rationality as something that does not have to be based on knowledge. This does not necessarily imply that rationality requires no knowledge at all. It merely implies that something (such as animal spirits and creativity) that is not based on knowledge can be considered rational. In any case, creativity and animal spirits which differ from the average can lead people to break with existing rules, but this non-rule-following behavior may still be considered rational or at least not irrational.

Some elaboration is necessary, especially regarding the first cognitive approach and the role institutions may play in it. Some political economists (such as Joan Robinson and George Shackle) tended to adopt a notion of rationality close to the neoclassical, to admit the importance of uncertainty and/or of complexity, and to conclude that some types of behavior have to be irrational. However, alternative notions of rationality have been developed which are relevant not only to complex situations, as Simon's, but also under uncertainty. The notion of rationality can be broadened together with the notion of knowledge. First of all, people may be aware of uncertainty. This makes the cognitive approach compatible with the argument that it is rational to allow factors, such as animal spirits and creativity, to play an important part in economic behavior. Second, there are things about which people do have some kind of knowledge, which is not knowledge of completely reliable probability distributions. One of these things is the existence of institutions such as contracts and market-makers, typically emphasized by some post-Keynesians. An even broader notion incorporates the knowledge of institutions as socially shared standards of behavior.

The cognitive approach does not require conscious deliberation. It is compatible with considering at least some types of habitual behavior as an unconscious recourse to knowledge (tacit or not). This is emphasized by strands of old and new institutionalism, neo-Schumpeterianism, Austrian economics and, to a lesser extent, post-Keynesianism. To the extent that knowledge is involved, habitual behavior can be rational. Some habits become institutions. Thus, apart from their function of informing people of the likely behavior of others, institutions can be seen as embodying knowledge. Moreover, institutions have a deeper cognitive function, as they influence the very perception we have of reality. Thus, knowledge and rationality are institutionally conditioned in more than one way (see INSTITUTIONS AND HABITS).

## The means–end framework

Regarding the neoclassical means–end framework, several problems have been identified. First, old institutionalists have long insisted on the influence of the cultural environment on the definition of means and ends by economic agents. Given the connection between CULTURE and institutions, the relationship between rationality and means–ends reinforces the notion of rationality as being institutionally conditioned. Not only does this imply a dynamic and historical view of means and ends, but it also leads to the possibility that people pursue multiple and perhaps conflicting ends.

Against the view of ends as given, it has also been pointed out that rational people should assess and possibly change their ends (see Heap 1989). Another criticism refers to the interdependence of and the consequent difficulty in distinguishing between means and ends, as argued by Simon and others. Last but not least, the consideration of uncertainty in a strong sense represents another major blow to the neoclassical means–end framework. Uncertainty affects people's perception of means

and ends. If novelty is possible, means and ends cannot be all given (Langlois 1985).

All these criticisms do not prevent heterodox economists from seeing behavior as possibly being purposeful or even self-interested. For example, scholars in the tradition of Marx, Veblen, Keynes and Schumpeter do discuss some types of self-interested behavior pursuing, in a capitalist society, the end of pecuniary gain (in contrast with the neoclassical focus on "real" goods and utility). The two cognitive criticisms mentioned above, based on complexity and uncertainty respectively, are not restricted to the case in which self-interest is the end being pursued. Rather, they show that, even for a discussion of self-interested behavior, the neoclassical treatment is defective.

When discussing self-interested behavior, political economists can accept the weak version of the rational expectations hypothesis, if it means the reiteration of the postulate of self-interest in the context of expectation formation. However, the weak version of the rational expectations hypothesis has also been given a second meaning, which requires people to equate the expected marginal costs and benefits of obtaining information. This is problematic from a viewpoint that emphasizes uncertainty. Not only is there no way of knowing the benefit of additional information before having the information, but also some information does not exist, as the future is yet to be created. This latter point is also destructive for the strong version of the rational expectations hypothesis, which requires a convergence between subjective and objective probability distributions, and for standard subjective expected utility theory, which requires the assumption of completeness of states of the world, consequences and preferences.

Rationality can be assessed, at least for some purposes, in terms of the ends being pursued in some specific historical context. If so, the rationality of individual behavior does not necessarily depend on its consequences for the community or the system. For example, self-interested behavior can have negative consequences for other people and still be individually rational. Moreover, even for the individual the consequences may be negative without implying irrationality. Rationality can be assessed in the light of the knowledge that exists at the moment of acting, even if *ex post* results are not as expected.

Apart from the neoclassical notion of rationality itself and its use in economic discussions, political economists also criticize attempts to apply it to most or all spheres of human life. They (and in particular old institutionalists) insist on the impossibility of rationalizing some types of rule-following behavior. They also oppose treating all social and personal behavior as if it were economic behavior (see, for a Marxist example, Gorz 1989).

## See also:

collective social wealth; community; conventions; feminist political economy: major contemporary themes; instincts; knowledge, information, technology and change; transaction costs

## Selected references

Gorz, André (1989) *Critique of Economic Reason*, London: Verso.

Heap, Shaun Hargreaves (1989) *Rationality in Economics*, Oxford: Blackwell.

Hogarth, Robin and Reder, Melvin (eds) (1986) *Rational Choice*, Chicago: University of Chicago Press.

Langlois, Richard (1985) "Knowledge and Rationality in the Austrian School: an Analytical Survey," *Eastern Economic Journal* 9(4).

Lawson, Tony (1991) "Keynes and the Analysis of Rational Behavior," in Rod O'Donnell (ed.), *Keynes as Philosopher-Economist*, New York: St Martin's Press.

Loasby, Brian (1989) "Herbert Simon's Human Rationality," *Research in the History of Economic Thought and Methodology* 6.

Maki, Uskali, Gustafsson, Bo and Knudsen, Christian (eds) (1993) *Rationality, Institutions and Economic Methodology*, New York: Routledge.

Rutherford, Malcolm (1994) *Institutions in Economics: The Old and the New Institutionalism*, Cambridge: Cambridge University Press.

Sen, Amartya (1987) "Rational Behavior," in John Eatwell, Murray Milgate and Peter Newman (eds), *The New Palgrave: A Dictionary of Economics*, London: Macmillan.

Sugden, Robert (1991) "Rational Choice: A Survey of Contributions from Economics and Philosophy," *Economic Journal* 101.

DAVID DEQUECH

# Reaganomics and Thatcherism

Reaganomics and Thatcherism are terms that refer to the distinctive economic and social policies of the administrations of Ronald Reagan in the United States and Margaret Thatcher in the United Kingdom. Reagan served as President from 1980–88; and Thatcher as Prime Minister from 1979 to 1990. Indirectly, these terms also refer to similar New Right regimes that existed around the world in the 1980s, and which still dominate much of policy thinking in many countries despite some changes into the 1990s.

## Basis of the philosophies

Both Reagan and Thatcher shaped the development of New Right ideas in the 1980s, which called for reduced government intervention in economic affairs and a greater role for laissez-faire CAPITALISM, and influenced the spread of these ideas throughout the world. Both Reagan and Thatcher also accepted MONETARISM as a means of controlling inflation, and supply-side economics as a means to spur ECONOMIC GROWTH.

In the USA, tight monetary policy was first implemented by the Federal Reserve in 1979 during the Carter administration. This policy was initially supported by the Reagan administration as a means to end inflation. However, faced with the sharpest post-Second World War recession the USA had experienced, and the prospect of major electoral setbacks in the 1982 Congressional elections, the Reagan administration was forced to abandon monetarism and to go for growth. "Supply-side" policies therefore emerged as the dominant political economy of Reaganomics (Marshall and Arestis 1989).

Similarly, in the UK, rising unemployment due to tight monetary policy weakened the government's will to focus exclusively on inflation. As a result, interest rates were brought down, and the main focus of policy-making shifted to the politically more popular strategy of tax cuts and PRIVATIZATION. Privatization of course played a much bigger role in the UK, where the government sector was much larger than in the USA. Although support for privatization was justified by reference to the standard neo-conservative expectation of inefficiency in the public sector, its role in promoting the goal of a property owning democracy was at least as important.

Despite the claims of supply-side theory, significant and widespread increases in PRODUCTIVITY are unlikely to be achieved through a reduction of marginal rates of tax on the better off. More crucial is likely to be the ability to introduce new TECHNOLOGY and improved working methods and practices. Alongside the promulgation of supply-side rhetoric, therefore, significant changes took place in INDUSTRIAL RELATIONS. Given the differences in the nature of the labor markets of the two countries, it is not surprising that the focus on labor market restructuring was more forceful and direct in the UK than in the USA in the 1980s.

In the UK in the 1980s, the trade union movement was completely excluded from its earlier consultative role in the decision-making process. New trade union and industrial relations legislation affecting industrial action, picketing and the closed shop was introduced, and the state's role as model employer and industrial peacemaker was abandoned. There was a growing antipathy towards trade unionism; an increasing emphasis on management's right to manage; a predilection for local rather than national collective bargaining; and a general presumption that public sector indus-

trial relations should become more like those in the private sector. The aim was to create a decisive and permanent shift in ECONOMIC POWER from labor to capital.

## Culture of individualism and industrial relations

Indeed, one of the centerpieces of Thatcherite policy-making was the so-called de-politicizing of industrial relations. This was an audacious attempt to change the CULTURE of industrial relations in the UK, so that employees would more closely identify with a new enterprise culture. For this to be possible, commitment to trade unionism and belief in collectivism/socialism would have to be marginalized and, if possible, eliminated. The objective then, was no less than a transformation of the economy and the society. This was to entail the creation of a more individualistic, market-orientated, property-owning and, of course, politically more conservative working class.

The transformation of industrial relations was part of an overall package that included tax cuts, the sale of state-owned housing (council houses) and the privatization of state-run industries at prices that guaranteed immediate capital gains and hence encouraged, at least initially, a wider spread of shareholding (Hoover and Plant 1989). In short, Thatcher's industrial relations reforms were an integral part of her declared grand political strategy of "defeating socialism."

The changes in industrial relations in the USA were less marked than in the UK, and they were not, of course, on the declared agenda of the Reagan administration. However, given the rather weak conventional supply-side effects engendered by government policy, one might well conclude that the changes in industrial relations practices and systems constituted the real supply-side revolution of the Reagan years. Given the urgent stimulus of the depressed conditions of this period, which in turn provided the "softer" labor market necessary for the successful implementation of their reforms, the employers went on the offensive.

Increasing numbers of employers broke the law by sacking union activists; new, often twelve-hour, shift systems were imposed; two-tier wage systems were introduced; non-consolidated lump sum payments and wage freezes started to replace normal pay increases; the link between wages and profits and the performance of the company or plant was strengthened, and that between pay and cost of living rises weakened. The government's role here was not a neutral one. The Reagan administration's desire to undermine the SOCIAL STRUCTURE OF ACCUMULATION: CAPITAL–LABOR ACCORD seems clear. Moreover, its tight money policy of the early 1980s and its constant attacks on the welfare system seems to have increased the threat, and the perceived COST OF JOB LOSS (Marshall and Arestis 1991).

### Restructuring institutions

Both Reaganomics and Thatcherism can be understood as an attempt to construct a restructured set of institutional arrangements to foster a resumption of economic growth. In the USA, the growth of output was re-established, albeit inadvertently, via a Keynesian demand stimulus to the economy. It was a Keynesianism that was skewed towards the rich and the military-industrial complex: but it was Keynesian in effect nonetheless (Eichner 1988). In the UK, however, the situation was a little different in that the main impetus to the economy came from a dramatic increase in private consumers' expenditure, fueled by a credit boom provided by a deregulated financial sector (see REGULATION AND DEREGULATION: FINANCIAL). The policies pursued by the Reagan administration have been called right wing/militaristic Keynesianism. Thatcherism, on the other hand, can be dubbed Reaganomics without the fiscal stimulus.

Great claims have been made for supply-side policies (see Bartlett and Roth 1984). Both the Reagan and Thatcher administrations presided over growing output and falling inflation rates, but talk of "economic miracles" seems misplaced. Looking at the economic record of the Reagan administration it is hard to find compelling evidence of dramatic supply-side changes. While the administration's claims may have been colorful, the reality was more prosaic (Blanchard 1987; Modigliani 1988).

### Degree of success or failure

The Reagan and Thatcher administration policies did, eventually, produce economic recovery with falling unemployment and inflation rates in the 1980s. Given the circumstances and scale of their achievements, however, it would be foolish to conclude either that the successes were outstanding, or, indeed, necessarily achieved by design rather than by accident. Moreover, the promised gains in productivity never materialized. Also, a major feature of Reaganomics (and also of Thatcherism) was the resurrection of the fear of unemployment to discipline labor, raise productivity and hold wages in check. This is not a desirable way to raise productivity growth, nor is it an effective means of doing so.

### See also:

economic rationalism or liberalism; global liberalism; ideology; Keynesian revolution

### Selected references

Bartlett, B. and Roth, T.P. (eds) (1984) *The Supply-Side Solution*, London: Macmillan.

Blanchard, O.J. (1987) "Reaganomics," *Economic Policy* 5: 17–56.

Eichner, A.S. (1988) "The Reagan Record: a Post Keynesian View," *Journal of Post Keynesian Economics* 10(4): 541–56.

Hoover, K. and Plant, R. (1989) *Conservative Capitalism in Britain and the United States*, London: Routledge.

Marshall, M.G. and Arestis, P. (1989) "Reaganomics and Supply-Side Economics: A British View," *Journal of Economic Issues* 23: 965–75.

—— (1991) "The Myths and Realities of Conservative Economic Policy-Making in the US," *Review of Social Economy* 49(2): 218–42.

Modigliani, F. (1988) "Reagan's Economic Policies: A Critique," *Oxford Economic Papers* 40: 397–426.

Wells, J. (1993) "The Economy After Ten Years: Stronger Or Weaker?," in N.M. Healey (ed.), *Britain's Economic Miracle: Myth or Reality?* London: Routledge.

MIKE MARSHALL

# recognized interdependence

The principle of recognized interdependence, first formally stated by J. Fagg Foster (1981), is a theoretical construct that appears in the neoinstitutionalist theory of INSTITUTIONAL CHANGE AND ADJUSTMENT. It identifies one of two major noninvidious (non-ceremonial) constraints on the process of progressive institutional change. The other is the principle of MINIMAL DISLOCATION.

In this theory, institutions are defined as socially prescribed patterns of correlated behavior. Behavior is correlated within the institutional structure by the values of the COMMUNITY. The modes of valuation and behavior that compose the institutional existence of the individual are, for the most part, habituated as the individual is inculcated with the mores and folkways of the community into which he/she is born and raised.

## Statement of the principle

The theory advances the proposition that the dynamic force generating pressures for institutional change within the community is the process of technological innovation, which is generic to the pursuit of inquiry in arts and sciences. Technological innovations affect the institutional structure by bringing about changes in the tools/skills nexus upon which the life processes of the community depend. Thus, institutional adjustment requires changes in habitual patterns of thought and behavior (Veblen 1899: 190–2; Foster 1981: 933).

It is a characteristic of human rationality that in contemplating changes in their own behavior, individuals have the capacity to comprehend the impact such changes will have on the correlation of their behavior with that of others. "Persons simply cannot perform in any correlated manner unless they know at least the immediate points of correlation between their own behavior and that of others with whom they are brought into direct contact" (Foster 1981: 941). This is the principle of recognized interdependence.

## Knowledge, understanding and adaptation

This principle can be decomposed into two related propositions: 1) the availability of knowledge, and 2) the capacity for understanding and adaptation (Tool 1979: 173; Bush 1987: 1105–1106). Obviously, individuals cannot exercise their rational capacity to contemplate how changes in their behavior will impact on that of others if they do not possess adequate knowledge concerning the technological innovation and how it would require changes in their habitual modes of thought and behavior. It is clear, therefore, that the acquisition and dissemination of knowledge within the community is a vital determinant of the community's capacity to incorporate technological innovations into its problem-solving processes. The most vital knowledge in this regard is that which reveals the interdependent character of patterns of behavior within the community.

Correlatively, the capacity for understanding and adaptation is, without question, a function of the community's educational processes. If the educational system serves primarily to inculcate traditional (ceremonially warranted) values and practices, then habitual modes of thought and action will be treated as part of the natural scheme of things, and there will be a psychological predisposition to resist adapting behavioral patterns to accommodate technological innovations. On the other hand, if education teaches the skills of associated living in a changing world, the capacity of adaptation to new modes of behavior will be enhanced, and the community will have a higher potential for incorporating technological innovations in the problem-solving processes (see KNOWLEDGE, INFORMATION, TECHNOLOGY AND CHANGE).

## Policy implications

The principle of recognized interdependence helps to explain variations in rates of technological diffusion among different cultures. It also calls attention to the vital importance of universal education – particularly in democratic societies. Finally, the principle helps to understand why "revolutions from above" seldom succeed over the long term. Historically, efforts to impose institutional changes from the top (elite) down (to the common folk) are not undertaken through genuine educational processes, but are instead rationalized and mystified through propaganda. While the public and private use of force, fraud, fear and intimidation may indeed achieve a certain level of conformity within a broad cross-section of the population, such institutional arrangements tend to be highly unstable and subject to chaotic responses to relatively minor dislocations.

## See also:

ceremonial encapsulation;; culture; disembedded economy; evolutionary economics: major contemporary themes; innovation, evolution and cycles; institutional political economy: major contemporary themes; institutions and habits; instrumental value theory; neoinstitutionalism; pragmatism; social and organizational capital; technology

## Selected references

Bush, Paul D. (1987) "The Theory of Institutional Change," *Journal of Economic Issues* 21(3): 1075–1116.

Foster, J. Fagg (1981) "The Papers of J. Fagg Foster," *Journal of Economic Issues* 15(4): 857–1012.

Tool, Marc R. (1979) *The Discretionary Economy: A Normative Theory of Political Economy*, Santa Monica, CA: Goodyear Publishing Co.

Veblen, Thorstein B. (1899) *The Theory of the Leisure Class*, New York: Augustus M. Kelley, 1975.

PAUL D. BUSH

# regional economic integration in the world economy

Regional economic integration is the process by which a group of nation-states agrees on specific policies to reduce "the economic significance of national political boundaries" (Anderson and Blackhurst 1993: 1). The agreement may involve the reduction or removal of barriers to the mutual exchange of goods, services, capital and people. While the members of most regional integration agreements are normally located in a specific geographic area, this is not always the case. Examples of agreements extending beyond one region include the US–Israel Free Trade Agreement, and the proposed Asia-Pacific Economic Cooperation (APEC) free trade agreement.

## Stages of integration

Regional integration is viewed as occurring in "stages," as states agree to progressively more intense and complex levels of interaction. These stages, which were described by Bela Balassa and modified by others, include (successively) a free trade area, a customs union, a common market, an economic union and a political union. It should be noted that these stages are pure models, and that most regional agreements do not fit neatly within a single stage.

In a free trade area, member countries are to progressively eliminate tariffs on all or substantially all of their trade with each other. The members, however, retain the right to follow their own trade policies toward non-member states. Most economic integration agreements are free trade agreements. Members of a customs union, like those in a free trade area, remove their tariffs with one another; but they also develop a common external tariff toward outside countries. The European Economic Community (now the European Union) was formed as a customs union in 1957. A common market has the same characteristics as a customs union, plus provisions calling for the free mobility of factors of production (labor and capital) among the member states.

An economic union has all the characteristics of a common market, but it also involves the harmonization of industrial, transport, fiscal, monetary and other economic and social policies. A full economic union also includes a monetary union, with the adoption of a common currency by the members. The European Union is currently attempting to achieve a full economic and monetary union. It is possible that an economic union could eventually become a political union, which would be more akin to a federal political system than an agreement among sovereign states.

## Regional integration agreements

Although there is great variation among regional integration agreements, several points can be made about the general characteristics of regional integration. First, most successful regional integration has occurred in Europe, but regional integration agreements now also exist in many other regions. Second, most regional integration agreements call for reciprocal concessions among members, but some agreements between developed and less developed countries are non-reciprocal in nature. Examples of the latter include the association agreements of the European Union (EU) with former colonies in Africa, the Caribbean and the Pacific (the "ACP" countries), in which the EU does not expect full reciprocity.

Third, regional integration agreements limited to less developed countries (LDCs) are given special and differential treatment. Most regional agreements among LDCs today have more outward-looking policies than they did in the 1950s–60s, when developing countries were following import substitution policies. The World Trade Organization nevertheless continues to permit LDCs to make regional agreements that reduce rather than eliminate tariffs, and that apply to only a limited range of products. Fourth, Jagdish Bhagwati and others point to two major "waves" of regionalism in the postwar period, the first occurring in the late 1950s and 1960s, and the second in the 1980s and 1990s. While the United States refused to participate in regional integration agreements during the first wave, its policy changed in the 1980s and this gave a marked boost to regionalism. Thus, regional integration agreements have become extremely pervasive around the world.

In addition to the European Union, which now has fifteen full members (and many associate members), other important integration agreements include NAFTA (the North American Free Trade Agreement) established by the United States, Canada and Mexico in 1994, and Mercosur, formed by Argentina, Brazil, Paraguay and Uruguay in 1991. Furthermore, some existing agreements, such as the Andean Pact and the Central American Common Market, which had seemed moribund, have been revitalized in recent years. Formal initiatives to encourage regional integration have been far less important in Asia than in Europe and the western hemisphere.

However, the members of ASEAN (the Association of Southeast Asian Nations) have agreed to establish a free trade area by the year 2003, and APEC, which includes members from Asia, Australasia, and North and South America, has set a goal of establishing a free and open trade and investment area for developed country members by the year 2010 (and for less developed countries by 2020). In the Middle East, there are some regional integration agreements of note, such as the Gulf Cooperation Council formed in 1981. But integration efforts in sub-Saharan Africa have been hampered by problems with economic development and civil strife.

With the proliferation of regional agreements, many analysts have written about the development of three major trade blocs, centered in Europe, North America and East Asia. In Europe, the European Union is moving to both deepen and widen the integration process. In North America, political leaders have expressed commitments to extend the NAFTA to form a western hemisphere free trade agreement, but the US Congress has thus far resisted such efforts. Although formal institutional initiatives to encourage regional integration have been much less important in East Asia, trade and investment among these countries have demonstrated impressive ECONOMIC GROWTH rates.

East Asian linkages are particularly oriented toward a DIVISION OF LABOR to increase the competitiveness of the region's firms in global markets. Thus, Japan has provided capital and high-technology goods, the East Asian NICs (newly-industrializing countries) have provided goods and services with increasing levels of sophistication, and low-wage countries, such as China, Indonesia and Vietnam, have been involved with labor-intensive assembly operations. Whether the three major trading blocs in Europe, North America, and East Asia contribute to global trade liberalization or to increasing protectionism relates to debates over the effects of regional integration discussed below.

## Major issues and controversies

The most important controversy over regional integration is whether it contributes to, or detracts from, global trade liberalization. This controversy has many facets. The unconditional most favored nation (MFN) principle of the General Agreement on Tariffs and Trade (GATT) stipulates that every trade advantage that a GATT member gives to any country must be extended, immediately and unconditionally, to all other GATT members. Nevertheless, GATT Article XXIV provides an exception for customs unions and free trade areas which discriminate against other GATT members, if these regional agreements meet specific conditions. Many analysts point out that the proliferation of regional agreements in recent years poses a major threat to the MFN

principle, and therefore also to global trade liberalization.

Some liberal economists argue, however, that global free trade is an important but unrealizable objective at present. It is therefore necessary to examine "second best" routes to trade liberalization, such as regional agreements. Indeed, the growth of regionalism in the 1980s was closely related to dissatisfaction with the GATT's inability to regulate new types of protectionism, and with the protracted nature of the GATT Uruguay round negotiations. Despite the successful completion of the Uruguay round and the formation of the World Trade Organization, regionalism is still perceived to have some major advantages. These include the fact that regional integration agreements are usually composed of relatively small groups of like-minded states in geographically-focused areas. Regional integration agreement members are also likely to have a number of objective similarities, such as similar levels of income and development, which often make negotiations easier (Mexico's membership in NAFTA is a notable exception). Thus, regional integration agreements often achieve a deeper level of integration than multilateral agreements, and provide a positive demonstration effect for multilateral trade negotiations.

It may be best, therefore, to accept the existence of regional integration agreements as a "second best" option, and to attempt to ensure that they are more "trade creating" than "trade diverting" (these terms were first described in Viner 1950: 41–55). Trade creation results from liberalizing actions (for example, a reduction in tariffs among regional integration agreement members) that shift demand from less efficient domestic producers to more efficient regional integration agreement partner-country producers. Trade diversion results from protectionist policies that shift demand from more efficient third-country producers to less efficient regional integration agreement partner-country producers.

In free trade areas, rules of origin often have serious trade diverting effects. Since each free trade area member retains its own external tariff structure, free trade areas must have rules of origin to prevent importers from bringing goods into the free trade area through the lowest-duty member and shipping them to partner countries where duties are higher. Stiffer rules of origin, however, may become a source of trade protectionism against outsiders. In customs unions, such as the European Union, the threat or use of anti-dumping duties against outside countries has been another source of trade diversion. Efforts should be devoted, it is argued, to combat these forms of trade diversion.

Liberal economists assume that all regional integration agreement members will benefit if the regional integration agreement is more trade creating than trade diverting, and they are not inclined to view power disparities as a major problem for smaller states in regional agreements. Indeed, they often argue that small countries gain even more than large countries from regional trade liberalization. Nationalist and critical theorists, by contrast, often argue that the larger partner in a regional integration agreement would either not permit the smaller partner to receive disproportionate benefits, or would expect some "side payments" in return. These side payments would be greater than any economic benefits the smaller partner received from market access and INCREASING RETURNS TO SCALE. In the Canada–US Free Trade Agreement, for example, side payments included an easing of Canadian regulations on US foreign investment, greater US access to Canadian energy supplies, and an agreement on trade in services.

Critics also argue that regional agreements serve to perpetuate dependency relationships. For example, they believe that the European Union's association agreements with selected less-developed countries divide the Third World, and permit the EU to perpetuate its colonial linkages in modern form. Both critics and supporters of regional integration agreements, however, would agree that regionalism is very durable and will continue to be a major force in the world economy.

## See also:

comparative advantage and unequal exchange; core–periphery analysis; free trade and protection; hegemony in the world economy; industry policy; international competitiveness; international political economy; trade policy

## Selected references

Anderson, Kym and Blackhurst, Richard (eds) (1993) *Regional Integration and the Global Trading System*, St Alban's: Harvester Wheatsheaf.

Balassa, Bela (1962) *The Theory of Economic Integration*, London: Allen & Unwin.

Melo, Jaime de and Panagariya, Arvind (eds) (1993) *New Dimensions in Regional Integration*, Cambridge: Cambridge University Press.

Viner, Jacob (1950) *The Customs Union Issue*, New York: Carnegie Endowment for Peace.

World Trade Organization Secretariat (1995) *Regionalism and the World Trading System*, Geneva: WTO.

THEODORE  H.  COHN

# regulation approach

The regulation approach is a multi-disciplinary heterodox theory which attempts to explain the long term transformations of the industrialized capitalist economies. The approach was developed initially to account for the observed sustained economic growth of the post-1945 capitalist economies, especially that of the United States, and the economic crisis which emerged in the late 1960s and early 1970s. The approach has since been applied to studying the long-term changes in less-developed countries as well. The term *regulation* is borrowed from the French *régulation* and should not be confused with the term's usual English reference to government rules of microeconomic management. Specifically, regulation of the capitalist MODE OF PRODUCTION AND SOCIAL FORMATION refers to the control of its basic instabilities in order to generate overall systemic reproduction.

## Origin and nature

The development of the approach represented a specific attempt to formulate a theory of economic growth and economic stagnation, which opposed the static vision of Walrasian economics. In particular, it is counter to Walrasian general equilibrium and the fundamental axioms of economic rationality, equilibrium and exclusiveness of markets in economic relations, particularly labor relations. It was this general dissatisfaction with NEOCLASSICAL ECONOMICS, and its specific inability to explain the stagnation of the 1970s, which fostered interest in a theoretical approach which would combine elements of the Marxist tradition, focusing on reproduction, and the dynamics of socioeconomic structures plus Kaleckian and post-Keynesian political economy rooted in historical TIME.

Although adherents to the general approach are found in most countries, particularly among key neo-Marxist intellectual currents, founding theoreticians of this new heterodoxy are associated with two principal schools. The first group includes Aglietta and Boyer, of the Paris-based INSEE (the French national statistical agency) and CEPREMAP (a state planning commission applied research center). The term Parisian regulation school (École parisienne de la régulation) is often applied to its representatives. The second, called the Grenoble school, is associated with the work of de Bernis and Borelly. Basic differences between the two relate to their central focus. Whereas that of the Parisian school is centered on the nation-state, that of the Grenoble school, rooted more heavily in Marxist theory, is centered on an integrated multinational production system dominated by a hegemonic power.

## Accumulation regimes

According to the regulation school, the historical development of CAPITALISM can be analyzed as a succession of accumulation regimes. It is the historic changes in these regimes which lie at the core of the approach. An accumulation regime, a key regulationist concept, refers to the complex of regularities, notably between the consumption–investment division of spending and the wage–profit division of income, which insure a general and coherent progression of capitalist accumulation. Accumulation regimes find their origin, uniqueness and stability not in self-regulating market systems, but in a set of institutional forms whose mechanisms of regulation iron out distortions and absorb the imbalances generated by the accumulation process itself. In this context, it has many similarities with institutional political economy. The mechanisms are formalized and conceptualized in five basic institutional forms or structures. These structures bear a close affiliation to the theory of SOCIAL STRUCTURES OF ACCUMULATION, the originator of whom, David Gordon, was influenced by the regulationists.

## Five institutional structures or forms

Forms of competition describe basic market structures as they relate to successive accumulation regimes. In attempting to explain how relations between decentralized centers of accumulation are organized, regulationists distinguish between the competitive and monopolist (oligopolist) forms of competition. The competitive system is characterized by *ex post* price flexibility ensuring market balance, while the oligopoly system is permeated by *ex ante* rules ensuring correspondence between the structures of production and demand.

Forms of international regimes set the framework of nation-state relations within the international economy, including trade rules, investment rules and rules of currency exchange which insure stability and coherence. Forms of monetary regimes refer to the forms of money in existence and their links with credit creation. The regulationists here distinguish between a regime, based on metallic money only, within which credit is severely limited, and one where it is rather the volume of credit which determines the money supply in existence.

The fourth institutional form concerns state regimes. These identify the extent to which state organizations are incorporated in national economies and partake in the process of capital accumulation. A circumscribed state regime is contrasted with a state regime inserted in the economic and social realms, an example being that of the Keynesian WELFARE STATE. The fifth institutional form is central to the regulation approach's general analysis of long-term growth, instability, crisis and emergence of new accumulation regimes. It is the wage-relation, which summarizes the process under which production is socialized (capital–labor socioeconomic arrangements). Five socioeconomic components make up the wage relation: the rules of labor organization within the workplace; the forms of the social and technical division of labor, the worker's general way of life, the types of means of production in use, and the determinants of wages.

Regulationist analysis of capital–labor relations thus goes far beyond that of neoclassical orthodoxy, which reduces the wage-relation to the process of equilibrium wage determination. It also expands the Marxist theory of surplus value and exploitation, in that the capital–labor conflict, the centerpiece of Marxian analysis of capitalist crises, may evolve through class cooperation and institutionalized relations.

## Types of wage-relations

Four distinct historical types of wage-relations have been identified by the regulation approach. The first is the competitive wage-relation, in which labor consumption is not part of capitalist production (especially common in the nineteenth century). The second is the Taylorist wage-relation, in which the organization of labor is conducive to mass-production, but has little impact on living standards (especially common in the first half of the twentieth century; see TAYLORISM). The third is the Fordist wage-relation which coherently integrates consumption and production

norms (dominant in the 1940s–1970s). The fourth is the flexible system, in which quality circles, economies of scope and worker participation are common (especially influenced by Japanese companies in the 1980s and 1990s) (see FORDISM AND THE FLEXIBLE SYSTEM OF PRODUCTION).

## Accumulation regimes and modes of regulation

The regulation approach distinguishes between three historically determined accumulation regimes. The regime of extensive accumulation, associated with the period 1750–1914, rests on the extraction of absolute surplus value through increases in labor intensity; division of labor is simple and productivity gains are weak. The regime of intensive accumulation without mass consumption highlights the 1914–45 period. It is clearly distinguished from the former regime by its extraction of relative surplus value, through advances in productivity in capital goods industries; a Taylorist wage-relation produces these by spreading new norms of mass production. The regime of intensive accumulation with mass consumption describes the 1945–70 period. Here, high productivity gains occur particularly in consumption goods industries, thus allowing for relative surplus value extraction through the cheapening of labor reproduction. A Fordist wage-relation was established, providing workers with a share of productivity gains, thus growing real wages concurrent with employment stability. The flexible production system is making some headway in the 1980s and 1990s.

A theoretical concept central to the regulation theory's analysis of long-term capitalist development and economic crisis is the mode of regulation, which is specifically a set of procedures and behaviors, be they individual or collective, which sustain and guide an accumulation regime. Historical analysis has enabled theoreticians to distinguish between the competitive and the monopolist modes of regulation, the latter being subdivided into monopolist and state monopolist variants. These basic modes are separated essentially by differences in underlying forms of competition and state regimes.

The mode of regulation, in contrast to neoclassical static analysis, incorporates the notion of dynamic disequilibrium adjustment. In fact, the approach insists on the dynamic processes by which the distortions produced by accumulation regimes are stabilized, processes in which markets are merely part of a larger complex of institutional forms and mechanisms. The mode of regulation thus plays a key role in allowing an accumulation regime to produce long-term growth; it is the emergence of unchecked limitations to growth which cause their rupture.

Modes of regulation and accumulation regimes interact within the regulation approach so as to provide a general periodization of capitalist development, on the basis of specific historical correspondence between them. Thus, nineteenth-century capitalist growth was the product of a specific concordance, established between the competitive mode of regulation and regime of extensive accumulation. The post-Second World War period of unprecedented expansion corresponded to that between a state monopolist mode of regulation and a regime of intensive capital accumulation with mass consumption. The conjunction of an accumulation regime with a given mode of regulation is referred to as the mode of development. The mode of development will produce long-term growth, as long as underlying institutional forms regulate the process of accumulation so as to stabilize the periodic imbalances which expansions tend to produce.

## Economic crises

The analysis of economic crises centers prominently in the regulation approach's examination of the history of capitalist development. Two classes of crises are identified and ordered, according to the degree of involvement of key institutional forms. Minor crises, similar to recurrent contractions in classical business cycles, do not compromise an existing mode of development or mode of production. They occur within the mode of regulation and are its expression, as they allow accumulated tensions and distortions associated with given economic mechanisms and social relations, to dissipate without changing institutional forms. Major crises do involve such institutional changes, and these can successively disrupt the mode of regulation (when its mechanisms fail to reverse unfavorable cyclical developments), the accumulation regime (when key institutional forms, namely the wage-relation, collapse) and finally, the mode of production itself.

Mainstream regulationists identify two major crises in the twentieth century. The first is the crisis of the 1930s, the GREAT DEPRESSION. This is explained by the incompatibility between an emerging intensive accumulation regime and an unchanged competitive mode of regulation. The second is that beginning in the 1970s, the product of an exhaustion in the regime of intensive accumulation, and, in particular, of a rupture within its key institutional form, the wage-relation. If the crisis of the 1930s is one of the mode of regulation, that which emerged in the 1970s, more severe systematically, is one of the accumulation regime. The latter is referred to by regulationists as the crisis of the Fordist wage-relation, in recognition of the breakdown in the post-war pattern of real wage growth and employment stability. This crisis was initiated by the erosion in productivity gains, the cornerstone of the regime of intensive accumulation. Given its structural nature, thus unamenable to Keynesian counter-cyclical policies, the regulation approach points to a necessary reconfiguration of basic institutional forms, notably the wage-relation and the international regime, as requisite conditions of crisis resorption.

## See also:

global crisis of world capitalism; hegemony in the world economy; political economy: major contemporary themes; social structure of accumulation: capital–labor accord; social structure of accumulation: corporate; social structure of accumulation: family; social structure of accumulation: financial; social structure of accumulation: state–citizen accord

## Selected references

de Bernis, G. (1988) "Propositions for an Analysis of the Crisis," *International Journal of Political Economy* 18(2): 44–67.

Borelly, R. (1990) "L'articulation du national et de l'international: concepts et analyses," *Économies et Sociétés*, série "Théorie de la régulation."

Boyer, R. and Saillard, Y. (1990) *The Regulation School: A Critical Introduction*, New-York: Columbia University Press.

—— (eds) (1995) *Théorie de la régulation. L'état des savoirs*, Paris: La Découverte.

Jessop, B. (1990) "Regulation Theories in Retrospect and Prospect," *Economy and Society* 19(2): 153–216.

Lipietz, A. (1988) "Accumulation, Crises and Ways Out: Some Methodological Reflections on the Concept of Regulation," *International Journal of Political Economy* 18(2): 10–43

Noël, A. (1987) "Accumulation, Régulation and Social Change: An Essay on French Political Economy," *International Organization* 2(Spring).

Piore M. and Sabel, C. (1984) *The Second Industrial Divide*, New York: Basic Books.

PIERRE PAQUETTE

# regulation and deregulation: financial

## Definition and examples

Regulation of the financial system entails setting rules and establishing an enforcement mechanism designed to control the operation of the system's constituent institutions, instruments and MARKETS. Various forms of regulation include anti-trust enforcement, asset restrictions, capital standards, conflict rules, disclosure rules, geographic and product line entry restrictions, and interest rate ceilings, investing and reporting requirements. These rules may be set down in law with enforcement ensured by government officials (direct government regulation), or they may be set and enforced by either an association of financial institutions (self-regulation) or the firm itself (corporate governance). The longest standing objective of regulation has been to raise state revenue. Other objectives include minimizing the risk of FINANCIAL CRISES, and either limiting or channeling financial power to some advantage.

## Reasons for regulation

In less developed economies, the state relies heavily on seignorage for revenue. Seignorage is the excess of a currency's exchange-value over its production cost. A state monopoly on the issuance of currency, together with a law declaring the currency legal tender, ensures that the government reaps the profits. Requiring that banks obtain state charters in somewhat more developed systems is a means by which the state can limit competition among suppliers of money, and thus retain its control over seignorage as a revenue source.

Beyond the need to secure a revenue base, preserving the liquidity of the financial system and forestalling financial panic have been the principal concerns of financial regulation. In the nineteenth century this concern manifested itself in a prescription for a central bank with a lender of last resort power. Although the term lender of last resort originates with Bagehot (1873), the idea is of much earlier vintage. The first principal architect of this doctrine is Henry Thornton. In his classic treatise on paper credit (1802), Thornton recognized the potentially contagious nature of bank runs and recommended that the central bank stand prepared to grant aid to distressed banks. This aid, he suggested, should be judiciously extended. It should be given neither too slowly and scantily so as to jeopardize general interests, nor too promptly and liberally as to exempt banks from the consequences of their own misconduct.

More recently, Hyman Minsky (1986) highlights the critical role a lender of last resort can play in promoting the soundness and stability of the contemporary financial system. Alternatively, in a formal model of bank runs driven by existence of asymmetric information, Douglas Diamond and Philip Dybvig (1983) analyze the circumstances wherein either a lender of last resort or government provision of deposit insurance produces contracts which can prevent bank runs.

The mainstream view of financial regulation justifies it on the grounds that either (a) there is a market failure in need of correction or clear public sector advantage, or (b) it is necessary to control abuses of power and therefore protect the consumer. The latent threat of a financial crisis is an example of a market failure. In this context, the market failure refers to the market's inability to properly assess and price risk. The systemic risk inherent in a bank collapse introduces social costs not accounted for in private sector decisions. The implication is that firms, when constructing their portfolios, will assume more risk than is socially desirable; hence there exists a need for government control.

Regulation designed to limit the risk assumed by managers of financial institutions includes restrictions that limit the types and amounts of assets an institution can acquire. State-sanctioned measures designed to contain any distress should it occur include the aforementioned lender of last resort function of the central bank, and the creation of a government-administered system of retail banking deposit insurance.

Where public sector advantage explains the need for regulation, government intervention is again necessary. Regulation justified on these grounds include the reserve requirements imposed on depository institutions for the purpose of facilitating the conduct of monetary policy and the various ways in which governments direct credit to those sectors deemed important for some greater social purpose.

Regulation may also be justified on the grounds that it is necessary to control the concentration and abuses of power. American unit banking rules, whereby banks were limited physically to a single center of operation, were originally conceived of as a way of limiting the concentration of power. Rules designed to control its abuses and hence protect the consumer include rules such as interest rate ceilings – ostensibly designed to prohibit excessive prices – as well as the various reporting and disclosure requirements. Finally, there are rules, such as insider trading laws, that outlaw explicitly opportunistic producer behavior.

## Theories of regulation

Alternative theories of regulation applicable to the theory of financial regulation include the producer protection theory of regulation, and those theories based on Marxian value principles. In his construction of the former theory, Stigler (1971) argues that firms demand regulation to promote their own interests. Restrictions on either geographic or product line entry, for example, would certainly limit the degree of competition existing firms face.

Marxist theories of regulation claim, in essence, that those with power design regulation exclusively for the purpose of promoting their own acquisitive interest. Aglietta (1979) views financial regulation (using it here in the narrow sense of the term) as simply a part of the whole capitalist structure designed to promote the ACCUMULATION of capital. Reform of the monetary and financial system occurs whenever new structural features are needed to "regularize the expansion of a new long-term social demand." This in turn will support the new relations of exchange required by a new regime of regular accumulation (see REGULATION APPROACH).

Post-Keynesian contributions to the issue of financial regulation appear in broader treatments of money and credit. Here, money is a social convention that arises out of the creation of new liabilities in the process of expanding production. Regulation enters insofar as direct credit controls and various laws affecting interest rates enhance the central bank's ability to influence economic activity (see for example Moore 1988; Wray 1990).

## Forces of change

Forces of change affecting the financial system

include the decline in domestic capital controls, together with the technological advances affecting communication and computation (see FINANCIAL INNOVATIONS). These forces have contributed in no small way to the growth of new markets, institutions and instruments, many of which fall outside the purview of existing regulation by virtue of their location or definition or both. The result is that an increasing amount of financial activity escapes regulation of any kind. The national response has been largely to advocate and initiate deregulation of the domestic financial system.

The existence of unregulated markets and the INCREASING RETURNS TO SCALE afforded by new TECHNOLOGY lie behind the recommendation to relax or remove the various restrictions imposed on assets, centers of operation and the like. The elimination of such rules as the enforced separation of commercial from investment banking and interest rate ceilings should increase choice and competition, result in better and cheaper services for the customer, and increase the efficiency with which scarce funds are allocated (see Dale 1986).

The subsequent American savings and loan (S & L) crisis prompted some to reconsider just how far they were willing to take this argument. Others, however, remained convinced of its merits and argued simply that deregulation had not gone far enough. In particular, many argued that the deregulation of interest rates should have been coupled with a reform of the deposit insurance scheme. That many S&L owners assumed more risk, knowing that the insurance would reimburse the depositors if the firm failed, surprised no one believing that the existing system of deposit insurance posed a serious moral hazard problem.

In the international arena, these forces of change have fed the spectacular growth in international lending and cross-border equity flows in the last two decades. The high-profile collapse of Barings (in 1995), the Bank of Credit and Commerce International (in 1991) and the Banco Ambrosiano (in 1983), together with the international debt problem of the 1980s, have highlighted the inability of domestic regulation to control risk and supervise activity in this new environment. For many, these problems underscore the need at least to coordinate if not actually to legislate internationally rights of access, rules and supervision (see Herring and Litan 1995).

To date, international financial regulation is limited to the right-of-access rules negotiated by Canada, Mexico and the United States, as part of the North American Free Trade Agreement. The member countries of the General Agreement on Tariffs and Trade attempted to address the same issue in the recent Uruguay round of negotiations, but ultimately abandoned the exercise. The European Union continues to struggle with all three issues.

Instead, international efforts have been largely and significantly restricted to international agreements to incorporate proposed rules into national legislation. The 1988 Basle Accord, for example, recommended common capital standards for banks conducting international business. The twelve signatories gradually adopted these capital requirements as did several other countries. There remain, however, several markets and instruments in the international arena that have yet to be regulated, or at least have the relevant national regulation coordinated.

## See also:

endogenous money and credit; financial instability hypothesis; free banking; interest rates: risk structure; liability management; monetary policy and central banking functions; money, credit and finance: major contemporary themes; social structure of accumulation: financial

## Selected references

Aglietta, Michel (1979) *A Theory of Capitalist Regulation: The US Experience*, London: New Left Books.

Bagehot, Walter (1873) *Lombard Street*, Homewood, IL: Richard D. Irwin, 1962.

Dale, Richard (ed.) (1986) *Financial Deregulation*, Cambridge: Woodhead-Faulkner.

Diamond, Douglas W. and Dybvig Philip H. (1983) "Bank Runs, Deposit Insurance, and Liquidity," *Journal of Political Economy* 91(31): 401–19.

Herring, Richard J. and Litan, Robert E. (1995) *Financial Regulation in the Global Economy*, Washington, DC: Brookings Institution.

Minsky, Hyman P. (1986) *Stabilizing an Unstable Economy*, New Haven, CT: Yale University Press.

Moore, Basil J. (1988) *Horizontalists and Verticalists: The Macroeconomics of Credit Money*, Cambridge: Cambridge University Press.

Stigler, George (1971) "The Theory of Economic Regulation," *Bell Journal of Economics and Management Science*, Spring: 3–21.

Thornton, Henry (1802) *An Enquiry into the Nature and Effects of Paper Credit of Great Britain*, New York: Augustus M. Kelley, 1962.

Wray, L. Randall (1990) *Money and Credit in Capitalist Economies: The Endogenous Money Approach*, Aldershot: Edward Elgar.

BRENDA SPOTTON

# rent-seeking and vested interests

## Definition and nature

"Economic rent" is a technical term designating profits from the employment of resources well above the opportunity cost. According to economic theory, labor and capital will flow into this rent-generating activity until the returns become normal again. This market-created rent is not a problem when it is the result of ingenious entrepreneurship or of highly valued natural characteristics (as in the sport or entertainment industries).

However, individuals (usually organized in special pressure groups) often attempt to influence government policy in their favor, or to assure the preservation of their special economic status (their vested interests) at the expense of the rest of the population. This activity, called "rent-seeking" by Anne Krueger, is a typical characteristic of modern capitalist democracies and in some cases is even institutionalized. Almost all groups with common interests, including big business, try to influence government, legislators and administrative agencies into transferring wealth to them, using the correction of market failures, social JUSTICE or patriotism as an excuse. Leading in this "directly unproductive profit-seeking" are major corporations and powerful UNIONS. Rent seeking is, for example, one of the primary reasons of government failure, and it leads to both inequality and inefficiency.

Rent seeking and vested interests are neither new phenomena nor necessarily associated with modern democracies, as Frederic Bastiat's well-known satirical essay on candlemakers illustrates. They have been examined early in time by Aristotle and Xenophon. Another observer, Thorstein VEBLEN, stressed that the managers of industrial enterprises were the worst enemies of free competition and of society, since their behavior led to inefficient results. Their position in the market was transformed into vested interests ("free incomes") and was based on anti-competitive behavior and political power.

A number of political economists have engaged in a systematic scrutiny of the activities of these special interests, and developed theories which describe and analyze the phenomenon in a unified way. Their basic concern was monitoring the "rent-seeking activity." In a series of pathbreaking books, Anthony Downs (*An Economic Theory of Democracy*, published in 1957), James Buchanan and Gordon Tullock (*The Calculus of Consent*, in 1962) and Mancur Olson (*The Logic of Collective Action*, in 1965) used neoclassical economics and rational choice theory to study politics and developed a body of theory (see PUBLIC CHOICE THEORY) which investigates the behavior of voters, legislators and bureaucracies as rational actors pursuing their self-interest, most of the time at the expense of others.

Rent-seeking success is based on the small concentration of benefits and the wide dispersion of the costs of government action in favor of a group. Consequently, the few members of the group have a vital interest in the particular policy. But more importantly, it is profitable for them to exert expensive direct influence on the legislators and voters. This influence can range from a mere "endorsement" in the national or local elections (which works with larger groups) to substantial financial support. On the other hand, the dispersion of the costs to the rest of the citizens is usually so widespread as to render unprofitable not only the reaction to the rent-seeking activity, but also the very knowledge of it. Politicians (and administrators) have every reason (except for their consciences) to satisfy the requests of these groups, since their benefits are maximized in both money and votes (and often political power) and their cost is minimal. Additionally, these special interest organizations often manage to influence the media and public opinion by persuading them of their just cause.

## Methods of rent seeking

Rents can be created by the government in a variety of ways, the most usual being the regulation of certain activities in ways that restrict entry and/or ensure supracompetitive returns for the vested interests. Examples include licensing, minimum wage laws, rent control, price controls, artificially created monopolies and so on. Other typical government interferences in the market in order to create economic rents include:

- protectionism, as local corporations are protected with tariffs and quotas at the expense of local customers and other corporations and workers of foreign, usually poorer, countries (see FREE TRADE AND PROTECTION);
- subsidies in favor of professions, trades and specialties which should be obsolete or less profitable;

- unsatisfactory enforcement of antitrust laws, use of antitrust law against a new entrant who threatens not competition but "vested interests," or non-enforcement against well-established cartels and oligopolies.

The result of such regulation and favors is the formation of surpluses and shortages which lead to the creation of economic rents. The bottom line of rent seeking is the transfer of income from society at large to a specific group. This transfer is not the result of voluntary exchange or of the distributive justice concerns of society, but of the power of concentrated interests against powerless dispersed ones. As a result, the transfer is inefficient, arbitrary and not creative of valuable output (Tullock, in Buchanan *et al.* 1980). The total cost of the rent-seeking activity equals the sum of the cost of rent-seekers' efforts plus the cost of government and bureaucracy to attract or resist rent seeking plus the cost of third-party distortions induced in the process or especially following the success of rent seeking (see Buchanan, in Buchanan *et al.* 1980).

## Growth and democracy

This theory has been used by scholars of international economics to explain the low growth rates of countries with corrupted governments and organized special interests (Olson 1982). The welfare losses from rent-seeking-induced protectionism have been estimated (as a percentage of GDP) to be 7.3 percent for India, 15 percent for Turkey, (Krueger, in Buchanan *et al.* 1980), and 3 percent for the USA (Posner, in Buchanan *et al.* 1980). These figures are heavily disputed as being either too low or too high.

Neoclassical economists and public choice theorists offer a very dim image of modern constitutional democracy, which is sometimes very close to Marxian theories of the state. For them, the problem is so serious that only specialized constitutional rules can offer a solution. As a result, constitutional economics has been developed, which is interested in the design, examination and development of constitutional rules in order to control rent-seeking activity.

## Critique

Constitutional economics (based on rational choice) has been criticized by many, especially communitarians and the adherents of "civic republicanism." The critics believe that voters and legislators often behave contrary to their self-interest if they have a different conception of public interest. Recently, some scholars have stirred controversy by challenging the basic premises of rent-seeking theory. They have propounded that empirical research does not always justify the results of the theory (Green and Shapiro 1994); that democratic political markets are as efficient as economic markets (Wittman 1995); or that interests groups are not as powerful as they seem but that their activity is defensive, aimed at avoiding political disfavor (McChesney 1997).

However, it is generally accepted (and it is also a popular belief) that rent-seeking is one of the major problems of modern democracies. Practices like "logrolling" and "pork barrel legislation" undermine not only the economy but also democracy. Proposals like the balanced budget amendment in the USA and elsewhere may provide a solution to the problem of inefficiency, but there will still be other problems. One critique of such a big step is that its main target will be the welfare state and not the vested interests, since the theory of rent-seeking is ideological (see Samuels and Mercuro, in Colander 1984). The truth is that powerful groups will remain powerful, even under a balanced budget regime, and nothing can promise that rent-seeking activities will be contained. Nonetheless, further research is required to examine the effect of the limitation of government activity on the level of rent-seeking, as well as on monopolization and cartelization.

## Conclusion

Rent seeking (together with TRANSACTION

COSTS and UNCERTAINTY) is a significant critique of the mainstream (for the last fifty years) neoclassical model of perfect competition (with the "help of the government correcting market failures" caveat). Even though its analysis is usually categorized under the neoclassical heading, research by public choice and other scholars on directly unproductive profit-seeking behavior has proved that government is not an exogenous force but is "at least partially endogenous," making competitive equilibrium less stable than it appears in theory (Colander 1984: 2–3).

## See also:

Austrian school of political economy; budget deficit; corporate hegemony; economic rationalism or liberalism; economic surplus; neoclassical economics; ownership and control of the corporation; public choice theory; surplus approach to development; surplus approach to political economy; surplus value as rent, interest and profit; welfare state

## Selected references

Becker, Gary S. (1983) "A Theory of Competition among Pressure Groups for Political Influence," *Quarterly Journal of Economics* 98(3): 371–400.

Bhagwati, Jagdish N. (1982) "Directly Unproductive Profit-Seeking (DUP) Activities," *Journal of Political Economy* 90(5): 988–1002.

Buchanan, James M., Tollison, Robert D. and Tullock, Gordon (eds) (1980) *Toward a Theory of the Rent-Seeking Society*, College Station, TX: Texas A&M University Press.

Colander, David C. (ed.) (1984) *Neoclassical Political Economy: The Analysis of Rent-Seeking and DUP Activities*, Cambridge, MA: Ballinger Publishing Co.

Green, Donald P. and Shapiro, Ian (1994) *Pathologies of Rational Choice Theory: A Critique of Applications in Political Science*, New Haven, CT: Yale University Press.

McChesney, Fred S. (1997) *Money for Nothing: Politicians, Rent Extraction and Political*

*Extortion*, Cambridge, MA: Harvard University Press.

Olson, Mancur (1982) *The Rise and Decline of Nations*, New Haven, CT: Yale University Press.

Rowley, Charles K., Tollison, Robert D. and Tullock, Gordon (eds) (1988) *The Political Economy of Rent-Seeking*, Boston: Kluwer Academic Publishers.

Wittman, Donald A. (1995), *The Myth of Democratic Failure: Why Political Institutions Are Efficient*, Chicago: University of Chicago Press.

ARISTIDES N. HATZIS

# reproduction paradigm

## Introduction

Perhaps more than anything else, political economy is concerned with "reproduction." There are, however, many dimensions of reproduction, including, for instance, the reproduction of the social structure, the relations of production, institutions, social capital, the family, labor power, everyday life, and goods and services. Is there anything which all these dimensions have in common? The answer is positive. Reproduction means regeneration, continuation, preservation, organization, regulation and stability. Usually reproduction concerns an endogenous yet open-systems analysis of the forces at work propelling (or adversely affecting) regeneration and organization. However, it is not simply a matter of tranquil or equilibrium reproduction. Rather, political economy examines the CONTRADICTIONS and conflicts which render reproduction an anomalous process under most socioeconomic systems.

Reproduction in political economy, therefore, seeks to examine the forces propelling both stability and conflict in the fabric of human and environmental relationships associated with material provisioning. It is critical to recognize that:

reproduction implies differentiation, growth, change (continuous and discontinuous). However, there is something that does not change, which makes it reproduction. This "something" is the capacity of a system to preserve, *for a time*, its entirety in relation to its "environment" and to behave *as if* its aim were to preserve that entirety.

(Barel 1974: 93; emphasis added)

A challenge to political economy, however, is to eschew an entirely functionalist analysis of reproduction, in favor of one which is pragmatic, and interested in the real socioeconomic problems than emerge through historical time.

## Marx's analysis of reproduction

The history of "reproduction" in political economy can be traced back to the physiocrats and the classical economists. Quesnay, Ricardo, Marx and others sought to comprehend how the various classes of capitalism contributed (positively or negatively) to the production of an ECONOMIC SURPLUS. Marx's famous reproduction schemas were directed at studying the relationship between the reproduction of social classes and goods and services under both growth and steady state conditions. Many modern growth models, input–output systems and theories of business cycles have been developed on the basis of his reproductive schemas (see REPRODUCTION: SIMPLE AND EXPANDED).

Central to Marx's vision was the notion of the CIRCUIT OF SOCIAL CAPITAL, the movement of capital from its money forms to production and then to sale and reinvestment. Marx's work was unique in that he recognized the importance of comprehending both the human and material forces in interdependent motion. Marx argued that the reproduction of capital is permeated by contradictions. His dialectical method was used to show how the working class could propel the growth of capitalism, while simultaneously regenerating their alienated and exploited conditions of existence. Capitalism is a system predicated upon continual expansion of markets, use-values and output. However, this is typically linked to forces of instability underlying the business cycle, and the conflict between capital and labor in production and distribution. In addition, as it evolves the system qualitatively changes into new phases of evolution, and eventually a new mode of production through some combination of class conflict and evolutionary metamorphosis. Underlying these problems is the tendency of capitalism to destroy the reproductive foundations of sociality and community upon which stability is dependent.

## Reproduction of institutions

Throughout the history of political economy, the reproduction of institutions and the social fabric has been a critical area of investigation. The process of long-term change concerns modifications to the institutions of production, distribution and exchange, as well as broader concerns about ideology, the state and the family. When "long durations" are the subject of inquiry, the structural parameters of relationships change and evolve. Most schools of political economy are concerned with these phenomena.

Institutions include structured relationships associated with social values and behaviors. They also include clusters of organizations, such as banks, schools, firms, government departments, families and labor markets. The reproduction of institutions is a critical area of political economy. Institutions are the foundations of human relationships, and their durability affects the level of social stability. Fundamentally, institutions are the "social cement" which represent the real foundations of the economy (see Stanfield 1979).

Their reproduction is affected by many processes, such as hegemony, innovation and conflict. Hegemonic structures are means by which most of the population are persuaded to support the existing system through an elaborate network of dominant ideas and modes of socialization. Institutional or technological innovations and regressive modifications can modify the system, and often ensure continual reproduction through evolutionary adaptation.

Conflicts emerge in the process of change, especially in capitalism due to its inherent motion of change and dislocation (see INSTITUTIONAL CHANGE AND ADJUSTMENT).

Modern political economists have hypothesized that the reproduction of capitalism is fundamentally affected by institutions. A common concern for Karl Polanyi, the regulationists, social structure of accumulation theorists, feminists and institutionalists alike is the process by which capitalism often destroys institutions and thereby periodically obstructs its own growth and accumulation. A succession of networks of agreements and social supports have historically been necessary for the long-term growth process. But capitalism, in principle, is a revolutionary system, based on continual motion and change. Therefore, the double movement of the system (broadly speaking) is to both destroy and create social supports and institutions, which is hypothesized to be the basis of the unstable long-term growth path of the system (see DISEMBEDDED ECONOMY).

## The family and labor supply

One of the major developments in political economy has been in understanding the complex processes associated with family formation and labor power. Political economy is fundamentally concerned with people, material output and the surrounding socio-natural environment. Social relationships between people are critical to every aspect of the economy. The resurgence of interest in feminism has led, among other things, to major developments in comprehending the contradictory workings of the family. In order to live and work, people need at least a subsistence level of existence. But before they can work they need to undergo birth, childhood, adolescence and usually the early phases of adulthood. Workers need access to an adequate diet, clothing, shelter and emotional stability for their human capital to be of at least minimal quality for employment.

However, the market system does not automatically ensure that these processes are regenerated through time. Rather, the family, and to a more limited degree the state, have historically specialized in tasks linked to the continuation of "everyday life." In particular, household labor has been the main source of child and often worker support through the many tasks of pregnancy, labor, ante-natal care, psychological counseling, education, emotional bonding, nutrition and ensuring continuity in the home environment.

The family, therefore, has been a critical area of concern to political economists. It is a contested area, since while being of great importance, the labor performed there usually does not have the legal right to suitable remuneration. Historically, it has been dependent upon private arrangements between spouses. This has posed a problem, since women have been the main providers, which tends to adversely affect their conditions in the labor market. Many employers and conservative economists have tended to assume that women who perform household labor are not developing sufficient job-specific HUMAN CAPITAL. Marxist-feminists, on the other hand, have studied, in the DOMESTIC LABOR DEBATE, the question of whether household workers produce value, surplus value or contribute in some other fashion. Also, among many economists it is becoming more acceptable in principle for household production to be included in the national income accounts, either outright or as a supplementary account.

The family is thus a critical area of institutional reproduction. It should be emphasized, however, that the "family" is really a very heterogeneous set of relationships, as indeed is the wider economy. There are various classes, ethnic groups, sexes and nationalities involved in the economy. A modern notion of reproduction needs to address these differences in both theory and practice. The notion of *homo economicus* is of little use in political economy since, more than anything else, political economy seeks to recognize the real conditions of material life. Indeed, in this it specializes. This heterogeneous element is of particular concern in the so-called labor market and the conditions underlying work in the production process.

The critical commodity of capitalism is labor power, representing the skills, talents, knowledge and working *potential* of human beings sold on the market. The working potential of the various classes, sexes, ethnic groups and nationalities are created and reproduced in the family to varying degrees, plus in schools, and also the workplace. Of late, political economy has developed an account of the various ways in which labor power is developed, and especially of how labor is extracted in the production process (see LABOR AND LABOR POWER). This is a critical process, being the source of surplus value, and indirectly the basis of industrial profit, interest and rent (and, to some degree, state finances).

Indeed, to some political economists "reproduction" is equated with the reproduction of labor power and the conditions of labor supply, within the context of the production process and the associated institutions. Modern radical labor economics has examined various facets of discrimination in the labor process, and how it may in some cases be a rational step for capital to "divide and conquer" the working class, as well as more generally increasing the exploitation of labor. Also important is the DIVISION OF LABOR in the production process, and the creation of SEGMENTED AND DUAL LABOR MARKETS.

Perhaps the most important requirement for the reproduction of capital is to moderate one way or other the conflicts associated with capital and labor. Historically, this conflict has led to strategies ranging from "defeating" the working class (such as with Thatcherism and Reaganomics), to developing agreements between the main groups of capitalism (such as with the SOCIAL STRUCTURE OF ACCUMULATION: CAPITAL–LABOR ACCORD and incomes policies). The systemic conflict between the social classes is a source of much waste and discord, and is, therefore, critical to the manner in which capital is reconstituted historically. This is true not only within the sphere of distribution, but also at the point of production where commodities are produced.

## Conclusion

The question of reproduction in political economy thus has many dimensions. In essence, it is important because of the processual relationships between people, within the context of the physical environment. When the concerns center on historical processes, the question immediately arises as to how these processes are structured, activated and continued through real time. However, these dynamic questions are always situated within the context of conflicting tendencies and vested interests. Change and motion are central because reproduction is not identical replication, nor is it equilibrium tending. Rather, the political economy of reproduction concerns a whole series of heterogeneous relationships which are forever unfolding through various degrees of stability and instability.

## Selected references

Aglietta, Michel (1976) "1. Regulation, Equilibrium and the Concept of Reproduction," section 1 of the "Introduction" to Michel Aglietta, *A Theory of Capitalist Regulation: The US Experience*, London: New Left Books, 1979, 9–13.

Barel, Yves (1974) "The Idea of Reproduction," *Futures*, April: 93–102.

Biffl, Gudrun (1996) "Towards a Social Reproduction Model," *Transfer: European Review of Labour and Research* 2(1): 8–23.

Blumenfield, Emily and Mann, Susan (1980) "Domestic Labor and the Reproduction of Labor Power: Towards an Analysis of Women, the Family and Class," in Bonnie Fox (ed.), *Hidden in the Household: Women's Domestic Labor Under Capitalism*, Toronto: The Women's Press.

Giddens, Anthony (1979) "Institutions, Reproduction, Socialisation," in Anthony Giddens, *Central Problems in Social Theory: Action, Structure and Contradiction in Social Analysis*, London: Macmillan.

Lange, Oskar (1971) "Social Process of Production and Reproduction," trans. S.A. Klain and J. Stadler in Oskar Lange, *Political Economy*, vol. 2, Oxford and New York: Pergamon Press.

Oakley, Allen (1985) "Reproduction and the Immanent Crises of Capitalism," in Allen Oakley, *Marx's Critique of Political Economy: Intellectual Sources and Evolution. Volume II: 1861–1863*, London and Boston: Routledge & Kegan Paul, ch 12.

Passeron, Jean-Claude (1986) "Theories of Socio-Cultural Reproduction," *International Social Science Journal* 110: 619–29.

Picchio, A. (1992) *Social Reproduction: The Political Economy of the Labour Market*, Cambridge: Cambridge University Press.

Stanfield, J. Ron (1979) *Economic Thought and Social Change*, Carbondale, IL: Southern Illinois University Press.

PHILLIP ANTHONY O'HARA

# reproduction: simple and expanded

MARX's discussion of simple and expanded reproduction is to be found in Chapter 23 of Volume 1 of *Das Kapital* and in Chapters 18–21 of Volume 2. Good elucidations of Marx's treatment of this subject are to be found in Robinson (1951) and Mandel's Introduction to Volume 2 of *Das Kapital* (Marx 1885). Marx's reproduction schemes can variously be seen as

- an early model of balanced ECONOMIC GROWTH;
- providing the basis for G. Feldman's Soviet model of growth (see Domar 1957);
- a model which shows that balanced growth is possible, but highly improbable, and which can act as the basis for a theory of crises and/or colonialism and imperialism (as with the work of Tugan-Baranowski and Rosa Luxemburg);
- facilitating an investigation of the manner in which capitalist economic relations (and accompanying financial flows) serve to reproduce class relations.

## Nature of the models

Marx's includes a multi-sector analysis with two "departments." Department 1 is the sector producing new capital goods and Department 2 is the sector which produces consumption goods. This model links consumption and investment activity with production and distribution. Marx shows that, in the case of simple reproduction, all investment consists of replacement investment, so that there is no (net) ACCUMULATION of capital. In this simple case, there must be some connection between the value of consumption sector output and the value of wages paid in the economy (assuming no consumption out of profits). At the same time, the value of wages paid out and profits received (value added) in the capital goods sector will be related to the demand for replacement investment by the firms in the consumption sector.

Marx also models expanded reproduction, where net investment is positive, under a number of assumptions. These include (1) there being no technical progress and (2) capital accumulation in each sector – or at least in the capital goods sector – is a fixed proportion of that sector's current profits. Note that Marx did not give as much weight to problems of modeling investment demand as a modern author (and especially a post-Keynesian) would. He tended to assume that competition alone would force capitalists to reinvest their surplus. In this model, there is no borrowing and lending between sectors, no movement of capital in response to differences in rates of return between sectors. With the aid of these and other assumptions, Marx is able to solve the model arithmetically to show the conditions under which growth can occur with equilibrium flows persisting between the sectors.

His analysis of expanded reproduction is sketchy and incomplete. He did not complete the manuscripts which deal with the case where net investment is positive (see Engels's Preface to Volume 2 of *Das Kapital*). The assumptions of extended reproduction have been shown to be very restrictive. As Harris (1974) has shown, when capitalists are assumed to invest only in their own business, the actual rate of growth might not equal the equilibrium rate, except by accident. If, on the other hand, capitalists are freely able to move their capital between departments to take advantage of profit rate differences, equilibrium will result from the economic processes, and especially the capital mobility, embedded in the model.

## Equations of the models

Following Harris (1974), we may set up Marx's model as follows. In the case of simple reproduction, the demand for output for Department 1 (the capital goods sector) comes from its own replacement investment, as well as that from Department 2 (the consumption goods sector). So that:

$$c_1 + c_2 = c_1 + v_1 + s_1$$

which implies that

$$c_2 = v_1 + s_1$$

and so we may write

$$v_1 = c_2 - s_1$$

and

$$v_1/v_2 = (c_2/v_2) - (s_1/v_1)(v_1/v_2)$$

Thus:

$$v_1/v_2 = (c_2/v_2)/(1 + (s_1/v_1))$$

Hence, for equilibrium growth to occur, wages must be advanced in the two sectors according to a particular ratio determined by the organic COMPOSITION OF CAPITAL in Department 2 $(c_2/v_2)$ and the rate of surplus value (or exploitation) in Department 1 $(s_1/v_1)$. In the absence of any mechanism to ensure this, the right balance can only be achieved by accident.

In the case of expanded reproduction, we have:

$$c_1 + c_2 + \Delta c_1 + \Delta c_2 = c_1 + v_1 + s_1$$

and so we require

$$c_2 + \Delta c_1 + \Delta c_2 = v_1 + s_1$$

which implies that

$$v_1 = c_2 + \Delta c_1 + \Delta c_2 - s_1$$

and may be rewritten as

$$v_1/v_2 = (c_2/v_2)$$
$$+ (\Delta c_1/c_1)(c_1/v_1)(v_1/v_2)$$
$$+ (\Delta c_2/c_2)(c_2/v_2)$$
$$- (s_1/v_1)(v_1/v_2)$$

Therefore:

$$v_1/v_2 = [(c_2/v_2)(1 + (\Delta c_2/c_2))]$$
$$/[1 + (s_1/v_1) - (\Delta c_1/c_1)(c_1/v_1)]$$

Thus, for equilibrium growth with net capital accumulation, we require wages to be advanced in the two sectors according to a particular ratio determined by (1) the organic composition of capital in the two departments, (2) the rates of growth in constant capital in the two sectors and (3) the rate of exploitation in Department 1 (the capital goods sector). Again, since these various elements are independently determined, the "right" balance can only be achieved by accident.

## Effective demand

In Marx's own numerical examples of expanded reproduction (Marx 1885: ch. 21) it is the level of savings and investment undertaken by the firms in the consumption goods sector which vary in such a way as to guarantee that continued reproduction on an extended scale is possible. However, there is no warrant for presuming that this will be the case, and certainly Marx provides no justification for it. Once we recognize this artifice, a real puzzle emerges: where does the EFFECTIVE DEMAND AND CAPACITY UTILIZATION come from which keeps accumulation going? Such was the precarious nature of capitalist growth as revealed by, or at least as implicit in, Marx's analysis. Later writers such as Lenin and Luxemburg were to see the growth of exports accompanying imperialist expansion as necessary to sustain the rate of accumulation in capitalist economies.

## Class relations

Whatever else the reproduction schemes might represent and whatever other purposes they may serve, there can be no doubt that for Marx himself they were meant to throw light on the reproduction of class relations. Marx was well aware that it was not enough to study how classes were formed during the process of PRIMITIVE ACCUMULATION (this was the subject matter of Part 8, Volume 1 of *Das Kapital*), one also had to ask whether or not there was anything in the workings of the capitalist system which would serve to perpetuate the classes, and especially to ensure the economic dependency of the working class.

Marx believed that there was. At the end of the chapter on simple reproduction in Volume 1 of *Das Kapital*, for instance, he writes "Capitalist production, therefore, seen as a total connected process, i.e. a process of reproduction, produces not only commodities, not only surplus value, but it also produces and reproduces the capital-relation itself; on the one hand the capitalist, on the other the wage-labourer" (Marx 1867: 724). In conditions of equilibrium, firms receive as profits/income an amount of money equal to their current outlays on new capital goods. This implies that the total revenues received by firms will cover, in the aggregate, both their current outlays on wages (and materials) and their outlays on new investment (see Baumol (1974) for an exposition of this).

In other words, "the firms" or "the capitalist class" receive, as a result of the workings of the price system, an amount of money sufficient to restore their financial position to its original level. (This idea became the foundation for KALECKI'S MACRO THEORY OF PROFITS.) Thus:

On the one hand, the production process incessantly converts material wealth into capital, into the capitalist's means of enjoyment and his means of valorisation. On the other hand, the worker always leaves the process in the same state as he entered it – a source of wealth, but deprived of all means of making that wealth a reality for himself.
(Marx 1867: 716)

## See also:

balance of payments constraint; capitalism; circuit of social capital; class processes; classes of capitalism; falling rate of profit tendency; global crisis of world capitalism; reproduction paradigm; turnover time of capital; wage determination

## Selected references

Baumol, W. (1974) "The Transformation of Values: What Marx 'Really' Meant (An Interpretation)," *Journal of Economic Literature* 12: 51–62.

Domar, E. (1957) "A Soviet Model of Growth," in E. Domar, *Essays in the Theory of Economic Growth*, New York: Oxford University Press, 223–61.

Harris, D. (1972) "On Marx's Scheme of Reproduction and Accumulation," *Journal of Political Economy* 80: 505–22.

Howard, M. and King, J. (1985) *The Political Economy of Marx*, 2nd edn, London: Longman.

Marx, Karl (1867) *Das Kapital*, vol. 1, published as *Capital, Volume 1*, Harmondsworth: Penguin, 1976.

——(1885) *Das Kapital*, vol. 2, published as *Capital, Volume 2*, Harmondsworth: Penguin, 1978.

Robinson, Joan (1951) "Introduction," in Rosa Luxemburg, *The Accumulation of Capital*, London: Routledge.

Sweezy, P. (1970) *The Theory of Capitalist Development*, New York: Monthly Review Press.

ROBERT DIXON

# republicanism

## Introduction

In broad terms, republicanism is the notion that the people of a nation, locality or institution have the right to participate in the determination of the decisions, rules and regulations, or at least to elect representatives to act on their behalf in this capacity. Often "republicanism" is simply another word for "democracy." The history of the idea goes back at least as far as the Greek city states, which were in the height of their development in the fifth century BC.

Republican forms of national representation are usually a challenge to monarchies and oligarchies. A monarchy exists when a hereditary head of state (a king or a queen, for example) governs either absolutely or by constitution. An oligarchy is rule by a few, such as a class of nobles or the military. In some countries, essentially republican forms of government coexist alongside ceremonial monarchy.

Monarchies are essentially feudal forms of government. Therefore, it is not surprising that post-feudal systems and ideologies (such as capitalism and socialism) have been active in replacing monarchies with various supposedly "republican" forms of government. The French, American and Russian revolutions are examples. Generally, a monarchy represents a privileged source of power which is not justified on grounds of labor exerted, enterprise generated or electoral support. Republican governments, in contrast, are usually seen to be in the interests of "the people."

National republican forms of government can be based on presidential and parliamentary forms, which often coexist, such as in the USA. Some nations have a prime minister (along with a parliament) and a president, which act as a check and balance to each other. Other republics are based on a parliamentary system with a prime minister and no president, and some nations have a parliamentary system with a minimal monarchy playing not much more than a ceremonial function. Britain has not only a minimal monarchy but also a mainly hereditary House of Lords in addition to an elected House of Commons; it is far from being a republic. The Republic of Ireland has an elected president and parliament plus an appointed prime minister.

Yet other nations have the role of head of state played by an overseas monarch who is represented locally by a governor-general, such as in Australia. Despite this, the Australian system of government is in considerable measure republican. However, the sacking of the elected Labor government by the governor-general in Australia during 1975 created a storm which is still being played out. Currently in this country there is debate over whether or not to replace the last vestige of monarchy by a "president" (whether popularly elected or elected by parliament), along with other options.

## Classical republicanism

In general, there are three forms of republicanism: classical, direct and liberal (the first two being closely related). Classical republicanism developed out of the experience of the Greek city states, the Roman Republic (510–31 BC), and some of the ideas of Plato (427–347 BC), Aristotle (382–322 BC) and Cicero (106–43 BC). Basic to it is the notion of the "common good." People are seen to be naturally social, members of a community who come together to discuss and formulate public policy. The promotion of the common wealth or good of the community is the main function of the "polis" (city-state). Government is thus the concern of citizens who are not subject to the arbitrary abuse of power of tyrants and absolutists.

Political activity was seen by Aristotle to be one of the highest achievements of a community. By having a strong public spirit a republic could enhance the common good. Classical republicanism sought to promote virtue through association. Having the right of citizens to participate in the polis, however, also involved a responsibility to protect the republic through military service and patriotism. These early republics tended to be unstable, often engaging in warfare. Also, women did not have the right to participate in public affairs, nor did slaves.

## Direct republicanism

Classical republicanism was set in the shadows for many centuries through the dominance of Christian monarchism and feudalism. It re-emerged during late medieval times in the Italian city-states (such as Florence) and also to some extent during the Reformation and Renaissance periods (see Rohden 1934). Jean-Jacques Rousseau (1712–78) transformed classical republicanism into a form of "direct" or participatory democracy, elements of which are still strong today. Rousseau and Alexis de Tocqueville (1805–59) both saw danger in a society based on the absorption of its people in private concerns. They sought to promote freedom through greater involvement of citizens in public and community affairs. This idea of direct participation was strong throughout the French Revolution.

For Rousseau, people should be actively involved in public life, debating important issues and resolving problems. Underlying this is the assumption that there is a "general will," and that conflict can be resolved through debate and compromise. His radical form of democracy saw citizens having direct sovereignty as a legislature. Governments or the executive should be an agent of the popular will of the citizens. Laws should be enacted by sovereign citizens and be equally binding on all of them. Democracy is thus the active involvement of people in public decisions in all reaches of life. His main concern was for the creation of a democratic society rather than just a democratic state. In this respect, he has influenced modern conceptions of democracy, including anarchism and Marxism.

## Liberal republicanism

Liberal republicanism is less concerned with the common good and public participation and more with individual rights and liberties. It developed out of the ideas of people such as John Locke (1632–1704), Jeremy Bentham (1748–1832) and James Madison (1765–1832). Its central message is that countries should develop representative government, and that the aim of government is to protect the rights of citizens to assembly, property, expression and privacy. Governments should prevent vice and promote security rather than actively promote virtue.

Typically, liberal republicans seek to create a workable form of government for large nations with little or no direct representation. Danford (1995) has called this a "commercial republic," since it seeks to provide the legal and contractual framework for private citizens to engage in business and employment with few restraints on movement, association, property and the accumulation of capital. Private property and relatively free markets are the hallmark of the legal structure, which is the foundation of capitalism. The Dutch republic in the 1600s, the British republic soon after and the form in which the American republic eventually developed are early examples.

Commercial republics thus involve using "politics" as a means towards economic prosperity and trade. In political economy, David Hume (1711–76), Adam Smith (1723–90) and Jeremy Bentham were architects of this system of natural liberty and laissez-faire, with the government only supplying public goods such as legality, defense and a few other services. Abuses of self-interest could, it was thought, be tempered through electoral changes in government and checks and balances between the legislature, executive and judiciary. At the national level, commercial republicanism has been the dominant form of government in modern Western capitalist economies.

## Industrial republicanism

Republicanism can manifest at the global, national, regional, city or industrial level. Participatory democracy within the firm is an example of an "industrial republic" (see Reibel 1975). Worker cooperatives and the like are fundamentally republican in promoting the active involvement of workers in decision-making for the common good of the firm (and community) *à la* Rousseau. They challenge the rule of capital (the industrial equivalent of "supreme ruler" or monarch) in favor of democratic representation by the workers ("the people"). The Mondragón experiment in

Spain, for instance, is a contemporary and successful real-world example.

Industrial republicanism is of special interest to political economists because it reflects a concern to redistribute power from the wealthy owners of capital to the poorer members of the corporation or society. It is based on the assumption that those with little power can actively participate in the productive workings of the economy given sufficient knowledge, finance and motivation. Participation can promote productivity, community and general well-being.

This raises a critical issue usually lost in orthodox views of politics and economics. Namely, democratic politics is not simply about "representation," but also relates to questions of power, direct participation and decision making in all the main institutions of society, from the home to the corporation, the local community and the national and world stages. Politics thus concerns how a world, nation, community, household and so on distributes decision-making potential to its inhabitants; and the ability of those who are devoid of much power to rise in status in the community, thus reducing the degree of ALIE-NATION and poverty. It also concerns the ability of people to become informed in matters which affect their lives; and to participate directly in institutions so as to influence the outcome (see Arendt 1975).

## See also:

democracy, political stability and economic performance; exploitation; ideology; state and government; utopia

## Selected references

Arendt, Hannah (1975) *Crises of the Republic*, Harmondsworth: Penguin.

Danford, John W. (1995) "Commercial Republics," in Seymour Martin Lipset (ed.), *The Encyclopedia of Democracy*, London: Routledge.

Hudson, Wayne and Carrier, David (1993) *The*

*Republicanism Debate*, Kensington: New South Wales University Press.

Pateman, Carole (1970) *Participation and Democratic Theory*, Cambridge: Cambridge University Press.

Reibel, R. (1975) "The Workingman's Production Association, or the Republic in the Workshop," in Jaroslav Vanek (ed.), *Self-Management: Economic Liberation of Man*, Harmondsworth: Penguin.

Rohden, Peter Richard (1934) "Republicanism," in Edwin R.A. Seligman (ed.), *Encyclopedia of the Social Sciences*, New York: Macmillan, vol. 13, 317–21.

PHILLIP ANTHONY O'HARA

# research and development

Research and development (R&D) refers to the process undertaken by economic agents of (1) identifying new ideas, new TECHNOLOGY or scientific information through research, and (2) using these ideas, technology or scientific information to develop new products, innovate production methods or solve public problems. The term economic agents is appropriately used, because governments, universities, firms and industries, as well as individual entrepreneurs, engage in the process of research and development.

## Basic, commercial and hybrid R&D

Research and development can be categorized into three types. First, "basic" or "pure" research consists of research to further scientific understanding, such as advancing the state of scientific theory. The result of this type of research, knowledge, can by nature be defined as a public good, since it is both non-rival in consumption and non-excludable, and can be widely disseminated without decreasing its quantity or usefulness. The results of this type of research and development are quite often not easily adapted to commercial application, so only certain economic agents are motivated to undertake such research. Governments, either alone or through their university research programs, often fund such basic research, since private firms are less likely to do so, in general, because of the lack of profitability to such research. Nelson and Romer (1996) assert that public funding is critical in order to "feed" the commercial market's technological needs. Nelson also points out that the United States's technological and productivity hegemony after the Second World War was a result of the high level of public investment in this type of research in the USA (see also Mansfield 1990).

The second type of research and development consists of the adaptation of available knowledge for commercial application. For example, the data storage industry is performing research on blue laser technology in order to develop storage devices that can read data stored in denser capacities than currently possible. This type of research and development is most often undertaken directly by firms, industries or entrepreneurs, as it may result in either a new combination of inputs (land, labor, capital), a specific technological method in which to combine these inputs (process innovation), or a specific new product (product innovation). PROPERTY rights are an important factor in the determination of the level of research and development, since firms in general will only undertake the expense of research if they are legally guaranteed ownership of the results of the process. Given these property rights, profit-maximizing firms have an incentive to undertake such research. An issue with such research is that it tends towards PATH DEPENDENCY, relying on current institutional forces to determine the direction of the research.

The third type of research and development is a hybrid of the first two, since it consists of basic research undertaken to solve specific problems, such as the medical research to find vaccines for the human immunodeficiency virus (HIV). This type of research and development is undertaken by firms, universities and, increasingly, governments. In this case, the result is both a public and a private good, and consumption of the results are quite often protected through property rights to insure that the agent undertaking the expense is able to realize the resultant profits.

## Property rights and rate of return

As mentioned, who actually undertakes research depends on property rights, or the ability or desire of the researcher to have rights to the results of that research. Property rights serve as an incentive to the researcher to realize the fruits of the research process, since there is no inherent guarantee of success to the process. Of course, property rights do not preclude a competitor's desire and ability to copy other firm's research or products. However, property rights tend to slow down the diffusion of technology processes, or the time in which competitors can incorporate each other's new methods into their own production processes. Since pure research tends to be undertaken by governments, the issue of property rights is much less important as it is the government's goal to provide such new information to its productive industries (the provision of public goods).

Whether or not firms or industries decide to undertake research and development depends on the expected rate of return from research. As Mansfield (1990) points out, there is both a social rate of return and a private rate of return to consider. The private rate of return is the rate at which the agent undertaking the research process is able to realize a return. Given that knowledge is, by definition, a public good, results from research are quite often dispersed (diffused) within a relatively short amount of time, so that other firms and agents are able to profit. Therefore, the social rate of return includes not only the private rate of return, but the total rate of return to society as a result of the application of the new knowledge to other productive processes. Mansfield (1990) estimated the R & D private rate of return to average 24 percent across different industries, with high technology fields realizing a higher rate of return and relatively low technology fields realizing a lower rate of return. Mansfield also estimates that the social rate of return averages 52 percent across

different industries, although this return is not realized at the same time as the private return, but instead is realized as the diffusion of knowledge takes place.

## Public goods

Given that the end result of research and development is new or enhanced knowledge, the issue of public goods arises again. Knowledge cannot be exclusive in consumption by nature, so the process of knowledge diffusion occurs with any new knowledge. The existence of property rights can slow down the dissemination of new knowledge, but does not stop it. Diffusion overtly occurs as competing agents use reverse engineering or imitation. Imitation does increase costs for the imitator, thereby still allowing for a higher rate of return for the innovator. Regardless of the tendency for imitation, economic agents still undertake research and development in the quest for higher returns. According to Nelson and Winter (1982), firms still choose to undertake research and development in order to differentiate their product or their firm from competitors and allow for higher pricing.

## Path dependency and ceremonial encapsulation

Institutional and evolutionary political economy points out that there is an element of path dependency in research and development. For instance, during the 1950s and 1960s, due to cheap domestic oil, some US firms developed an expertise in petroleum, which led to the USA having an edge in petrochemicals. R&D in petrochemicals was a response to cheap oil. However, after the USA lost its advantage in cheap oil it continued to be successful in petrochemicals, and to engage in considerable R&D in this area. Thus, the historical workings of the US economy affected its pattern of R&D, and the decline in the USA's edge in oil has not reversed its fortunes in petrochemicals.

A similar process of path dependency occurs when, for instance, the vested interests controlling R&D in companies try and prevent new

R&D if it threatens their livelihood. Corporate managers, especially of some large firms, may decide to thwart competitive R&D in an attempt to continue receiving technological rents or economic surplus. They may engage in a takeover of the potentially competitive firm. Thus, the power structure behind the R&D and technological structures is often motivated by the private interests of managers and their ideologies. This R&D is thus dominated through a form of CEREMONIAL ENCAPSULATION by private or sectional interests, at the expense of the public interest (see Stanfield 1995).

This cycle can be broken when a new agent (one not vested in the old technology) is able to offer a new product or process to the market that is clearly better than the institutionally protected one. In this case, the new product or process breaks the institutional power of the old; new institutions are arranged to protect the new product and thereby renew the cycle. Thus, agents use technological change in order to gain or keep institutional advantage. SCHUMPETER expressed a similar point, referring to it as "creative destruction," in which certain research would lead to new designs and technologies that would destroy the old established methods (see Heertje 1977).

## Market structure and transaction costs

Market structure tends to be a critical determinant of the level of research and development occurring in firms. Nelson and Winter (1982) point out that, contrary to Schumpeterian theory, it is the more competitive firms that tend to engage in research and development in order to pursue higher levels of profit in the future. Schumpeter, on the other hand, asserts that it is the monopolistic firm that is able to generate the excess profits needed to engage in research and development. Nelson and Winter point out that monopolistic firms do not need to engage in such activity, except to deter competition. However, the competitive firm will engage in high levels of research and development in order to be able to reduce costs or differentiate their product from those of

competitors. If successful, these competitive firms will then be able to realize higher levels of profit due to the effects on demand of differentiated products. Oligopolistic firms tend to engage in research and development only in order to keep competitors from infringing on their market share or profitability (see MARKET STRUCTURES).

Williamson (1986) connected the research and development process to TRANSACTION COSTS, saying that firms experiencing high levels of transaction costs engage in research and development in order to eliminate costly steps in the production process. For example, if a firm must purchase a certain input from another firm in an imperfect market, this firm may undertake research and development to derive a replacement production method or input. Williamson saw institutions as leading to costly transactions, so firms wishing to maximize profits will eliminate costly transactions through research and development as well as through vertical integration (see WILLIAMSON'S ANALYSIS OF THE CORPORATION).

## Measurement of R&D

According to the Division of Sciences Resources Study (Organization for Economic Cooperation and Development), annual research and development among G7 countries increased between 1983 and 1993 from $198 billion to $276 billion (constant 1987 US dollars). Of these amounts, the United States and Japan comprised a fairly constant 68 percent of the total expenditure. Among the G7, an average of 2.5 percent of GDP was spent on research and development.

## See also:

human capital; innovation, evolution and cycles; knowledge, information, technology and change; Schumpeterian political economy; social and organizational capital

## Selected references

Heertje, Arnold (1977) *Economics and Technical Change*, London: Weidenfeld & Nicolson.

Mansfield, Edwin (1990), in Francis Rushing and Carol Ganz Brown (eds), *Intellectual Property Rights in Science, Technology and Economic Performance*, Boulder, CO: Westview Press.

Nelson, Richard (1987) "Roles of Government in a Mixed Economy," *Journal of Policy Analysis and Management* 6(October).

Nelson, Richard and Romer, Paul (1996) "Science, Economic Growth, and Public Policy," *Challenge* 23(March–April).

Nelson, Richard and Winter, Sidney (1982) *An Evolutionary Theory of Economic Change*, Cambridge, MA: Harvard University Press.

Stanfield, J. Ronald (1995) "Institutions and the Significance of Relative Prices," *Journal of Economic Issues* 29(June).

Williamson, Oliver (1986) *Economic Organization*, New York: New York University Press.

ARIC KRAUSE

# reserve army of labor

Marx argued in Volume 1 of *Das Kapital* that the "General Law of Capitalist Accumulation" is associated with the creation and recreation of a reserve army of labor, or relative surplus-population, along with an increase in relative poverty which accompanies the accumulation process. Marx's concept of the reserve army is often incorrectly assumed to include only "the unemployed." However, his analysis is much more dynamic and processual than this, since the reserve army of labor potentially relates not simply to (a) the number of workers who are officially unemployed, but also (b) the extent to which they are underemployed, (c) the extent to which they have become discouraged and left the active labor market, (d) the extent to which those not in the official labor market are latent members of it, (e) the extent of poverty, and (f) the nature and changing composition and segmentation of the LABOR FORCE according to age, sex and nationality.

Marx's analysis of the reserve army of labor examined the cyclical and structural forms in which these six dimensions become manifested in capitalist economies. The reserve army of labor tends to grow when constant capital (technology) is being substituted for variable capital (workers) at a specific rate (depending on population changes, etc.); when the economy is in a structural crisis of a long wave downswing (1970s–1990s); and during business cycle downswings (e.g. 1974–5, 1982–3, 1990–2).

The structural reserve army of labor relates to the introduction of new technology, especially that which is labor saving, plus secular and long-term changes adversely affecting labor. Marx recognized that new TECHNOLOGY is not chosen to increase the general welfare of the community by reducing working hours and increasing the standard of living. Rather, it is chosen primarily out of the desire for capitalists to reduce labor costs and increase the ECONOMIC POWER of capital over labor, through making workers redundant and having the threat of redundancy. The cyclical reserve army of labor, on the other hand, relates to "the general movements of wages [being] regulated by the expansion and contraction of the industrial reserve army, [which] in turn corresponds to the periodic alternations of the industrial cycle. ... The relative surplus population is therefore the background against which the law of the demand and supply of labor does its work" (Marx 1867: 790–92).

## Forms of the reserve army

There are, according to Marx, three main forms of the reserve army of labor: the floating, the latent and the stagnant (Marx 1867: 794). The floating form includes workers who tend not to have secure jobs and float from employment to unemployment, depending on labor market conditions. Included here are workers from the factories, workshops and services of capital, who have passed their youthful phase and are either not capable of performing to standard, or have been replaced by low-paid younger workers. Currently, this is especially prevalent in jobs demanding strong physical labor and in middle management positions (dominated by men) and in fashion, sales and checkout employments (dominated by women). The floating form also includes specialized workers whose skills are made redundant through technological change.

There are three main types of the latent reserve army of labor. First, feminist political economists have recently debated the question of (some) women in the home constituting a latent reserve army of labor to the extent that they are, from time to time, drawn into and out of the official labor market according to changing social and economic conditions (see RESERVE ARMY OF LABOR: LATENT). Currently, however, in many advanced nations women have a high rate of labor force participation and are starting to exhaust their role as a latent reserve army of labor; while in most developing and underdeveloped nations, the female latent reserve army of labor process is potentially or actually quite robust (see Humphries 1983).

The second relates to those workers who have become relatively redundant in agriculture with the rise of new technology, and are in the process of "passing over into an urban or manufacturing proletariat, and on the lookout for opportunities to complete this transformation" (Marx 1867: 796). The constant movement towards the cities and the regional towns creates a latent reserve army of labor in the countryside. This process has, perhaps, become exhausted in England, but in many developed, developing, and underdeveloped nations the process is still strong.

Also, the latent reserve army includes potential and actual migrants. Many countries solve some of their labor market supply and demand problems through incoming migration or guest workers when there is excess demand, and cuts in migration and the existence of guest workers when there is excess supply. This helps to segment the workforce through the availability of greater differentials in pay, conditions, and often human rights. Also, often

students and the elderly form part of the latent reserve army of labor.

The third main form of the reserve army of labor is the "stagnant population": workers employed in low-productivity industries who are competing with high-productivity industries. These people have extremely irregular employment, and when employed have the lowest wages (usually below the poverty level) and the longest hours of work. Generally, they are unskilled workers who are technologically redundant, and sometimes work at home on handicrafts or garments (for a discussion of such disguised unemployment, see Eatwell 1997). Below this third group is the "lumpenproletariat": the "vagabonds, criminals, prostitutes," long-term unemployed, street kids, the demoralized and the sick, many of whom have or will become paupers (Marx 1867: 797). They are a constant reminder to the employed of the worse threat that may arise if they lose their job and become an outsider.

## Cyclical reserve army

Modern political economy places much emphasis on the cyclical reserve army, and on how it influences the course of the rate of profit and hence investment over the business cycle (see Boddy and Crotty 1975; Sherman 1991: ch. 11). Generally, during business cycle upswings, unemployment can be reduced to lower levels, which increases the ECONOMIC POWER of workers in the spheres of both production and distribution. The intensity of labor (productivity) tends to decline when the threat of job loss is low, and the wage share of national income tends to increase as worker bargaining power is enhanced. Both of these factors reduce the rate of profit, investment and hence growth, resulting in recession (usually along with high interest rates and raw material prices). The recession then usually helps to restore conditions of profitability, as unemployment and poverty increase, capital has a large potential supply of labor to draw from, and workers feel compelled to increase PRODUCTIVITY and reduce wage demands (for example, during the recessions of 1974–5, 1982–3 and 1990–2 in Western economies).

The period since the 1970s in advanced capitalist economies has seen the pursuit of policies in business and government oriented to reducing the power of labor, since the recessions have not had the maximum required effect on profitability. The policies of labor market deregulation, privatization and reduced public services have the effect of increasing the army of casual, temporary, part-time, short-term and contracted labor (Michie and Wilkinson 1994). A measure called the subemployment index attempts to calculate the extent of the reserve army of labor. Indications are that it may be as high as two and one-half times the official unemployment rate in some nations, when including official unemployment, plus latent, discouraged and underemployed sections of the community (excluding "official paupers" and "low-paid full-time workers") (see Braverman (1974: ch. 17) for a discussion of relevant issues).

However, in no western nation has the reserve army substantially reversed economic decline (Kitson *et al.* 1997a, 1997b). The reserve army of labor may not have solved capitalism's problems, but the concept itself is a critical one for understanding the dynamic linkages between many processes affecting the lives of working people and the reproduction of capital.

## Selected references

Boddy, Raford and Crotty, James (1975) "Class Conflict and Macro-Policy," *Review of Radical Political Economy* 7(Spring): 1–17.

Braverman, Harry (1974) *Labor and Monopoly Capital*, New York: Monthly Review Press.

Collins, John (1984) "Marx's Reserve Army of Labor: Still Relevant 100 Years On", *Journal of Australian Political Economy* 16(March).

Eatwell, J. (1997) "Effective Demand and Disguised Unemployment," in J. Michie and J. Grieve Smith (eds), *Employment and Economic Performance*, Oxford: Oxford University Press.

Green, Francis (1991) "The Reserve Army Hypothesis: A Survey of Empirical Applications," in Paul Dunne (ed.), *Quantitative Marxism*, Cambridge: Polity Press.

Humphries, Jane (1983) "The 'Emancipation' of Women in the 1970s and 1980s: From the Latent to the Floating," *Capital and Class* 20(Summer).

Kitson, M., Michie, J. and Sutherland, H. (1997a) "The Fiscal and Distributional Implications of Job Generation," *Cambridge Journal of Economics* 21(1):103–20.

—— (1997b) " 'A Price Well Worth Paying'? The Benefits of a Full Employment Strategy," in J. Michie and J. Grieve Smith (eds), *Employment and Economic Performance*, Oxford: Oxford University Press.

Marx, Karl (1867) *Das Kapital*,Volume I, published as *Capital, Volume 1*, Harmondsworth: Penguin, 1976.

Michie, J. and Wilkinson, F. (1992) "Inflation Policy and the Restructuring of Labour Markets," in J. Michie (ed.), *The Economic Legacy: 1979–1992*, London: Academic Press.

—— (1994) "The Growth of Unemployment in the 1980s," in J. Michie and J. Grieve Smith (eds), *Unemployment in Europe*, London: Academic Press.

Sherman, Howard (1991) *The Business Cycle: Growth and Crisis Under Capitalism*, Princeton, NJ: Princeton University Press.

JONATHAN MICHIE
PHILLIP ANTHONY O'HARA

# reserve army of labor: latent

Marx introduced the concept of the latent reserve army of labor in Volume 1 of *Das Kapital* as part of his discussion of the industrial RESERVE ARMY OF LABOR. According to Marx, the process of ACCUMULATION generates a surplus population of wage laborers. There are three forms of this relative surplus population: floating, latent and stagnant reserves. Floating reserves are wage laborers who are able to obtain only marginal and transitory employment during labor shortages. Latent reserves are potential wage laborers; Marx's latent reserves consisted largely of the pre-capitalist agricultural population which was being absorbed through the expansion of CAPITALISM. The stagnant reserve is a composite of various impoverished groups.

Political economists have debated the contemporary relevance of these categories, especially the concept of a latent reserve. Most problematic has been the usefulness of class-based categories for analyzing the LABOR FORCE participation and immigration patterns of gender, racial and ethnic groups. For example, early Marxist-feminist theorists extended Marx's concept of the reserve army to account for women's lower attachment to the labor market. Women's employment and labor force participation were predicted to respond procyclically, as women were employed during labor shortages and expelled during economic downturns. However, this formulation of women as a floating (or cyclical) reserve has come under increasing criticism (see Bruegel (1979) for a summary and critique of this literature.)

## Cyclical and structural dimensions

This has led to two directions for empirical and theoretical work on women as a reserve army of labor. First, the cyclical reserve army hypothesis has been empirically tested against alternative hypotheses regarding women's employment over the business cycle. Second, political economists such as Humphries (1983) and Power (1983) have attempted to refine the notion of women as a reserve army by focusing on secular, rather than cyclical, changes in women's labor force participation. This second approach posits women as a latent reserve army of labor in the post-Second World War period.

The literature on women and recession suggests that there is some empirical evidence in the post-war era to support each of three hypotheses regarding women's cyclical employment patterns: (1) cyclical (floating) reserve army, (2) segmentation and (3) substitution. While the traditional reserve army hypothesis speculates that women's employment is more cyclically sensitive than men's, the two alternative hypotheses predict quite different employment patterns. (This literature focuses on the cyclical sensitivity of labor demand, rather than the "added worker" effects of women increasing their labor supply when male family members are unemployed.) Historians such as Milkman (1976) and Kessler-Harris (1982) have argued that labor market segmentation has tended to restrict women's employment into industries which, perhaps coincidentally, are less cyclically sensitive. This is the basis for a segmentation hypothesis, which posits that segmentation by industry and occupation shields women relatively more than men from economic fluctuations. The rigidity of these segmentations prevent employers from using women as a cyclical reserve army.

Political economists have also proposed a substitution hypothesis which suggests that the incentive for employers to use cheaper categories of labor, such as women and people of color, increases during economic crisis; it is also possible that recession weakens the ability of workers to resist these strategies. Under the substitution hypothesis, women's employment is predicted to respond counter-cyclically. Rubery (1988) suggests that substitution can be reconciled with the segmentation hypothesis by recognizing that substitution is unlikely to be cyclical. While a recession may instigate the substitution process, once feminization is accompanied by de-skilling and wage reductions the process is rarely reversed.

## History, culture and patriarchy

This recent research highlights the dangers in universalizing any thesis on the impact of business cycle fluctuations on women's employment. Historical evolution of the economy and GENDER relations, cross-cultural variations in institutions and social relations, as well as class, race and ethnic differences between women, may affect the cyclical sensitivity of women's employment. This has led to a second version of women as a reserve army which focuses on their secular incorporation into the labor force as a latent reserve army of labor.

Humphries (1983), for example, asserts that during the post-1945 period women are in the process of being fully assimilated into the labor force. Her argument draws an analogy between homemakers and the precapitalist agricultural laborers designated as a latent reserve by Marx. Humphries has theorized a specific historical trajectory leading to women's proletarianization. The expanding female-dominated sectors of the postwar economy initially drew homemakers into the labor force as latent reserves. This set in motion a process by which working-class families became dependent on women's labor to maintain their standard of living in the face of men's declining real wages. Employers were attracted by gender-based wage differentials and female employment during periods of employment stagnation. Thus, Humphries views substitution as a stage in the integration of women from a latent reserve (see Humphries' contribution in Rubery 1988).

Walby (1983) has critiqued Humphries and others for overlooking the systematic role of PATRIARCHY and the potential conflict between partriarchal and capitalist interests over women's labor force participation. Power (1983) provides an alternative formulation of married women as a reserve army which focuses on both capitalism and patriarchy. Power asserts the potential of women's increased economic autonomy for undermining the GENDER DIVISION OF LABOR within the family. However, Power is less optimistic that discrimination within the labor market will be undermined by women's greater participation.

## Conclusion

These alternative concepts of women as a latent reserve exemplify some of the problems which arise from relying exclusively on Marxist categories to analyze women's experiences. Labeling women a latent reserve in the postwar period often conflates the categories of women and homemakers, extrapolating from the experiences of primarily white, middle-class, heterosexual women to stand for all women. Further, even most married women historically spent part of their lives engaged in market work. Thus, unlike Marx's original latent reserves, women have not been living outside of capitalist social relations. Finally, when precapitalist agricultural workers were integrated (over several generations) from a latent labor reserve into the wage-labor force, they changed their class-based identity. However, CLASS is typically defined by a relationship to the means of production; GENDER (the social construction of a biological category) is not. Contemporary feminist political philosophy (see FEMINIST POLITICAL ECONOMY: MAJOR CONTEMPORARY THEMES) has articulated the importance of focusing on the relationship between RACE, ETHNICITY, GENDER AND CLASS (Beechey 1988).

## See also:

segmented and dual labor markets

## Selected references

Beechey, Veronica (1988) "Gender and Work: Rethinking the Definition of Work," in Jane Jensen, Elisabeth Hagen and Ceallaigh Reddy (eds), *Feminization of the Labor Force: Paradoxes and Promises*, New York: Oxford University Press.

Bruegel, Irene (1979) "Women as a Reserve Army of Labour: A Note on Recent British Experience," *Feminist Review* 3: 12–23.

Humphries, Jane (1983) "The 'Emancipation' of Women in the 1970s and 1980s: From the Latent to the Floating," *Capital and Class* 29: 6–28.

Kessler-Harris, Alice (1982) *Out to Work: A History of Wage-Earning Women in the United States*, New York: Oxford University Press.

Milkman, Ruth (1976) "Women's Work and the Economic Crisis: Some Lessons from the Great Depression," *Review of Radical Political Economics* 8(1): 73–97.

Power, Marilyn (1983) "From Home Production to Wage Labor: Women as a Reserve Army of Labor," *Review of Radical Political Economics* 15(1): 71–91.

Rubery, Jill (ed.) (1988) *Women and Recession*, London: Routledge & Kegan Paul.

Rubery, Jill and Tarling, Roger (1982) "Women in the Recession," in David Currie (ed.), *Socialist Economic Review*, London: The Merlin Press.

Walby, Sylvia (1983) "Women's Unemployment, Patriarchy and Capitalism" in Malcolm Sawyer and Kerry Schott (eds), *Socialist Economic Review*, London: The Merlin Press.

ELLEN MUTARI

# reswitching of techniques

## Definition and nature

Reswitching of techniques is a theoretical phenomenon which plays a key role in the CAPITAL THEORY DEBATES. The argument is merely logical. It considers the operating methods when several alternative techniques are available. For a given distribution, represented by the level of the rate of profit, $r$, the selection of the preferred technique is based on the principle of cost minimization. When distribution varies, different techniques are chosen. A switch point is a level $r^*$ at the divide between the ranges of use of two techniques. Reswitching is the fact that a technique can be used for low rates of profit, be abandoned at intermediate levels and then reappears at upper levels.

Reswitching is possible only because "capital" is made of heterogeneous capital goods. Its existence shows, in Sraffa's words, that "capital cannot be considered as a physical magnitude independent of prices and distribution." If capital is aggregated, it represents a value, not a factor of production as in the neoclassical "parables." The forerunners of these criticisms are David Champernowne, who explicitly mentioned the possibility of reswitching, and Joan Robinson, who dubbed it a "Ruth Cohen curiosum" (she later minimized the importance of the phenomenon). Both intended to criticize the logical grounds of the neoclassical concep-

tions of capital after Clark or after Fisher. But it is mainly after Sraffa's book, followed by Levhari and Samuelson's unsuccessful attempt to discard reswitching, that this phenomenon has been fully recognized and regarded as one of the most theoretically significant paradoxes of capital theory (only a "paradox" for the neoclassical conception of things). At variance with CAPITAL REVERSING which considers values, it describes a real phenomenon (substitution of techniques).

If capital were a physical factor of production, it could be considered as a homogeneous magnitude $K$, and the relationship between production $Q$, capital $K$ and labor $L$ could be written $Q = f(K, L)$, $f$ being the production function. A technique of production is then characterized by the amount of capital per worker. The choice of technique depends on the relative price of capital (the interest rate) and labor (the wage rate): when the wage increases, capital is progressively substituted for labor.

## Illustrative models

Let us simplify the framework by assuming a CORN MODEL and the existence of two methods of production only, which are written as

$$a_i \text{ corn} \oplus l_i \text{ labor} \to 1 \text{ unit of corn}$$

with $i = 1, 2$. Let $a_1 > a_2$ and $l_1 < l_2$, i.e. method 1 is more capital intensive than method 2. For a given rate of interest or profit $r$, the real wage $w_i$ when method $i$ is used is determined by relationship

$$(1+r)a_i + w_i l_i = 1 \tag{1}$$

Corn is chosen as the *numéraire* and the wage is paid *post factum* (these choices are not crucial). At the same level of $r$, method $j$ is preferred to method $i$ (by the capitalists) if it is cheaper, i.e. if inequality

$$(1+r)a_j + w_i l_j \leqslant 1 \tag{2}$$

holds. A simple manipulation of relationships (1) and (2) shows that the capital intensive method 1 is chosen up to the rate of interest $r^*$ defined by $1 + r^* = (l_2 - l_1)/(a_1 l_2 - a_2 l_1)$ and method 2 is preferred above this rate. In other words, the capital intensive technique is chosen at low rates of interest (corresponding to high levels of the wage rate) and the labor-intensive technique at high rates of interest (or low levels of the wage rate). The limit value $r^*$ is a switch point between the two techniques, and the only value at which both methods are used simultaneously: at $r^*$, the profitability of the two methods are identical.

Consider alternatively a simple multi-sector model of SRAFFA's type. There are two capital goods, say corn and iron. The physical data are described by $(\mathbf{A}, \mathbf{L}) \to \mathrm{I}$ with

$$\mathbf{A} = \begin{bmatrix} a_{11} & a_{12} \\ a_{21} & a_{22} \end{bmatrix}, \mathbf{L} = \begin{pmatrix} l_1 \\ l_2 \end{pmatrix} \to \mathbf{I} = \begin{bmatrix} 1 & 0 \\ 0 & 1 \end{bmatrix}$$

$a_{ij}$ being the amount of commodity $j$ used in the production of one unit of $i$, jointly with labor $l_i$. For a given rate of interest, the price and wage vector $(p_1, p_2, w)$ is a solution to the homogeneous equation $(1+r)\mathbf{A}\mathbf{p} + w\mathbf{L} = \mathbf{p}$ (see PRICE THEORY, SRAFFIAN). Introduce an alternative method $(a'_{21}, a'_{22}, l'_2)$ for iron. This method is preferred if and only if it yields extra profits at these prices, i.e. if inequality $(1+r)(a'_{21}p_1 + a'_{22}p_2) + wl'_2 \leqslant p_2$ holds (with equality at a switch point). The choice of technique depends on prices, hence on distribution. Let us first identify switch points. At such a point $r^*$ the above price relationships can be rewritten in a matricial form as:

$$\begin{bmatrix} 1-(1+r^*)a_{11} & -(1+r^*)a_{12} & -l_1 \\ -(1+r^*)a_{21} & 1-(1+r^*)a_{22} & -l_2 \\ -(1+r^*)a'_{21} & 1-(1+r^*)a'_{22} & -l'_2 \end{bmatrix} \begin{pmatrix} p_1 \\ p_2 \\ w \end{pmatrix} = 0$$

Therefore the $3 \times 3$ matrix on the left hand side is singular, hence its determinant $\Delta(r^*)$ is zero. Since $\Delta(r)$ is a second-degree polynomial in $r$, it may have two positive roots $r_1^*$ and $r_2^*$, which are switch points between the two techniques. For an adequate choice of the numerical data, the reswitching phenomenon is observed: the first technique is preferred to the second for "low" rates $r < r_1^*$ and for high ones $r > r_2^*$, but the second technique is preferred on the intermediate range $r_1^* < r < r_2^*$. Hence, at variance with the one-good model, these techniques cannot be ranked according to an alleged

degree of capital intensity, when the substitution between techniques would follow monotonously the change in distribution.

The reswitching phenomenon can also occur in one-good intertemporal models, even in the neo-Austrian framework: it is then closely related to the multiplicity of the internal rates of return. Some properties are suggested by a generalization to $n$ commodities of the above calculations. First, the choice of technique depends on the sign of the determinant $\Delta(r)$. Second, the number of switch points is that of the feasible roots of $\Delta(r)$. Since $\Delta(r)$ is a polynomial of degree $n$, it is equal to $n$ at most. This number can be reduced to the degree of regularity of system $(\mathbf{A}, \mathbf{L})$, i.e. to the maximal number $s$ such that vectors $\mathbf{L}, \mathbf{A}\mathbf{L}, \ldots, \mathbf{A}^{s-1}\mathbf{L}$ are independent. As a particular case, there is no reswitching if the organic composition is uniform (vectors $\mathbf{L}$ and $\mathbf{A}\mathbf{L}$ are proportional).

## Can reswitching be excluded?

Can there be significant cases where reswitching is excluded? Some assumption on the "regularity" of the economy must be introduced (Burmeister 1980). A general idea is that an easy substitution between techniques avoids reswitching. For instance, differentiability avoids reswitching, though not a continuum assumption (Garegnani 1970). It can also be showed, by choosing data at random, that the a priori probability of reswitching between two techniques is some few percent at most. However, the point of the reswitching phenomenon is primarily theoretical and, whatever the restrictions on its empirical validity, the crucial lesson to be reminded of is that capital cannot be considered as a factor of production.

## See also:

capital theory debates; heterogeneous capital and labor; invariable measure of value; joint production; Sraffian political economy

## Selected references

Burmeister, E. (1980) *Capital Theory and Dynamics*, Cambridge: Cambridge University Press.

Garegnani, P. (1970) "Heterogeneous Capital, the Production Function and the Theory of Distribution," *Review of Economic Studies* 37: 407–10.

Harcourt, G. and Laing, N.F. (eds) (1971) *Capital and Growth*, Harmondsworth: Penguin.

Sraffa, P. (1960) *Production of Commodities by Means of Commodities*, Cambridge: Cambridge University Press.

Symposium in the *Quaterly Journal of Economics*, November 1966.

CHRISTIAN BIDARD

**RETURNS TO SCALE:** *see* increasing returns to scale

# rhetoric

The introduction of "rhetoric" into economics debates is the result of pioneering work by McCloskey (1985, 1990, 1993a) who has argued that economics functions rhetorically just as other discourses do. McCloskey draws on a western European tradition extending from classical Greece and Rome, through Renaissance humanist scholarship, to contemporary debates in literary criticism and post-analytic philosophy, in which rhetoric is not devalued as the opponent of reason but is seen as an indispensable characteristic of any reasoned discourse which aspires to be persuasive to a particular audience.

## Metaphor, storytelling and anti-foundationalism

Arguing against what she sees as a blinkered attachment to an unfounded positivist scientism inherited from defunct epistemological arguments, McCloskey argues that facts and logic have been overvalued by economists at the expense of metaphor and story, whereas properly all four function together in the "rhetorical tetrad." She has thus sought to forge links between an increasingly technical economics and the humanist tradition of western Europe by restoring economics to the civilized "conversation" of mankind in which tolerance and the ability to listen attentively are more important than knock-down proofs which silence opponents.

In arguing against foundationalism, i.e. the theory that there are basic beliefs which provide the grounds for knowledge, McCloskey argues that the "Big-T truth," which is grounded on such beliefs, is simply unattainable. A rhetorical theory of truth does not pretend to deliver the impossible and so it is a theory of "small-t truths." These truths emerge as the product of a social process of inquiry and persuasion in which protocols of debate, evidence and reasoned argument all play their part within any given institutional context. This anti-foundationalist argument has led to a number of critiques by methodologists and philosophers of economics who measure the rhetorical approach against their own conceptions of truth and realism, and so criticize what they see as rhetoric's preference for persuasion at the expense of Big-T truth (see the extensive bibliography of these debates in McCloskey 1993a).

McCloskey's celebration of rhetoric has stimulated a number of collected readings which have critically considered the contribution of rhetoric to understanding the nature of economic theorizing and economic debate (e.g. Klamer *et al.* 1988; Henderson *et al.* 1993). It has, for example, made economists more aware of the power of the deep metaphorical structures inscribed in economic theorizing, and the effects of these structures for the development of economics as an autonomous discipline and its relationship with other disciplines such as physics and biology.

## Significance for political economy

For political economy, however, there is also a

question of the substantive implications for economics of adopting a rhetorical approach. In spite of the apparently disruptive potential of McCloskey's arguments, some aspects of her work have been self-confessedly conservative and even non-substantive. McCloskey extols mainstream (i.e. old Chicago) neoclassical economics on the whole, and asks mainly that economists rename their analytical techniques in rhetorical terms that would bring them in from the cold world of incoherent positivist methodology to the warm, humane and civilized conversation of mankind which literary types have tended to monopolize in the past. This conservative inflection of the significance of rhetoric has also been noted in the market metaphors driving her rhetorical analysis, in which economic imperialism has been extended to the rhetorical analysis itself and in which neoclassical competitive markets become metaphors for a humane moral order (Stettler 1995).

In adhering to the norms of democratic conversation, however, McCloskey has also listened to a range of heterodox voices which are not normally heard in mainstream economics, and this raises the question whether rhetorical analysis may also contribute to the development of political economy broadly construed. McCloskey has likened the distinction between scientism and rhetoric to that between masculine and feminine attributes; in this comparison, fact and logic are the hard masculine properties while metaphor and story are the soft feminine ones. In this gendered metaphor, feminist economics is rhetoric's ally in attempting to overcome these gendered dualisms by transcending the objective–subjective dichotomies with a new "conjective" economics which is produced as part of social processes of conversation (McCloskey 1993b).

## Human agency

This connects with current debates outside economics which challenge the atomistic and privatized subject of classical liberalism by reformulating the notion of human agency in terms of social and historical processes of communication. Quinn (1996), for example,

draws on these debates to counterpose a rhetorically rich conception of individual agency against both the instrumental rationality of rational choice theory and McCloskey's liberal view of the self which, Quinn argues, is inconsistent with her anti-foundationalism elsewhere. A similar concern with the social and symbolic construction of subjectivity is also evident in some Marxist theory (Milberg and Pietrykowski 1994).

A rhetorical approach may, however, facilitate a rereading of the history of economics where the textual resources of rhetoric and literary theory may be used in reading historical texts. Brown (1994), for example, questions the canonic meaning of Adam Smith's works by a reading which shows how style, figuration and rhetorical techniques can contribute to a different construction of their meaning.

## Conclusion

Future research in rhetoric and political economy (and economics more broadly) depends on the extent to which economists think they can learn from areas such as post-analytic philosophy, history, sociology and post-structuralism. It remains to be seen whether such a project can produce different economic knowledge and whether this would transcend existing divisions within the economics profession.

## See also:

foundationalism and anti-foundationalism; modernism and postmodernism

## Selected references

Brown, V. (1994) *Adam Smith's Discourse: Canonicity, Commerce and Conscience*, London: Routledge.

Henderson, W., Dudley-Evans, T. and Backhouse, R. (eds) (1993) *Economics and Language*, London: Routledge.

Klamer, A., McCloskey, D. and Solow, R.M. (eds) (1988) *The Consequences of Economic Rhetoric*, Cambridge: Cambridge University Press.

McCloskey, D. (1985) *The Rhetoric of Economics*, Madison, WI: University of Wisconsin Press.

—— (1990) *If You're So Smart: The Narrative of Economic Expertise*, Chicago: University of Chicago Press.

—— (1993a) *Knowledge and Persuasion in Economics*, Cambridge: Cambridge University Press.

—— (1993b) "Some Consequences of a Conjective Economics," in M.A. Ferber and J. Nelson (eds), *Beyond Economic MAN: Feminist Theory and Economics*, Chicago: University of Chicago Press.

Milberg, W.S. and Pietrykowski, B.A. (1994) "Objectivism, Relativism and the Importance of Rhetoric for Marxist Economics," *Review of Radical Political Economics* 26(1): 85–109.

Quinn, K. (1996) "A Rhetorical Conception of Practical Rationality," *Journal of Economic Issues* 30(4): 1127–42.

Stettler, Michael (1995) "The Rhetoric of McCloskey's Rhetoric of Economics," *Cambridge Journal of Economics* 19(3): 391–403.

VIVIENNE BROWN

# rights

A right is by definition a capacity, condition of existence or possession which entitles either an individual or group to the enjoyment of some object or state of being. For example, the right to free speech is a condition of existence which entitles individuals to express their thoughts as they see fit.

These rights are secured either by nature, laws (positive or moral), a grant or a purchase. Philosophers and jurists split on the issue of what secures these rights. Positivists who deny the existence of natural or moral law necessarily claim that there are only legal rights, rights which are the result of legislation. Hence the rights apply only to those whom the laws designate. The difficulty with this positivist position is that every system of rights is self-legitimating and there can be no claims of moral rights by which we can evaluate the soundness of the system.

## Objective moral code

Those who claim that there are universal rights and that some legal systems, such as those which permit SLAVERY, are immoral and violate moral rights must maintain that rights are grounded somehow in the nature of things or in some sort of objective moral code. The most basic grounding would be in the NEEDS of human beings. One is entitled or has a right to those things which are necessary for a quality existence. This was the method of philosophically grounding rights in Western cultures, from the time of Socrates to the modern era, called natural law theory.

For example, Thomas Aquinas (1265–73), with respect to the right of property, asserts that "Whatever is held in superabundance is owed by natural right to those in need." John Locke in the seventeenth century echoed Aquinas and argued for the NATURAL RIGHTS to life, liberty and property. But Locke added to the right to property argument a consideration of fairness. It is only fair that people be entitled to that for which they work. The notion of a right to property based on need begins to fade with the development of CAPITALISM. In line with the theories of Locke, the writers of the American Declaration of Independence claim basic rights to life, liberty and the pursuit of happiness. For them, as for Locke, these rights were grounded in the fact that our dignity arises from our being children of God. Further, the existence of these rights and the equality of all "men" is a self-evident truth.

The Enlightenment, however, is skeptical of the self-evidence claim and attempts to ground rights without an appeal to God. This leads to a more modern approach from a deontological or from a utilitarian perspective. Either rights flow from the basic equality and dignity of humans (Immanuel Kant grounds them in the fact that rational beings are ends in themselves), or they flow from the natural needs of humans which must be met to maximize happiness.

Of course, Jeremy Bentham refers to rights as "nonsense on stilts," since from his point of view, the word "right" is just shorthand for securing those actions which will bring about that greatest happiness. From Bentham's perspective one finds rights, not by consulting a catalog of rights, but by examining whether behavior, such as respecting peoples' property, leads to more pleasure than pain. His successor, John Stuart Mill, grounds rights in the same way. Mill defends the existence of a right to liberty by demonstrating that a society which allows its members to freely express themselves will be a society that is better off (happier) than a society which does not allow such self-expression.

Deontologists, following Kant, would maintain that the difficulty with this position is that it makes rights susceptible to revocation if they no longer serve the needs of society. This is incompatible with the notion of inalienable or indefeasible rights, where inalienable means those incapable of being surrendered or transferred, and indefeasible means not capable of being annulled, voided or undone. Sides of this debate can be seen by contemporaries, such as Hart and Dworkin (see DEONTOLOGY).

## Positive and negative rights

Whatever the grounding of rights, there are certain other aspects of rights theory that must be mentioned. It is often held that for every right there is a correlative duty. Hence, if I have rights to life and liberty, others have a duty to respect that right and not interfere with my life and liberty; and I have the same duty toward others. The reciprocity of rights and duties leads to a distinction between positive and negative rights. Thus, if every right has a corresponding duty and rights are based on needs, the question arises as to who has the duty to meet positive rights. Positive rights are rights of recipience. They are claims to entitlement to receive certain goods or services. For example, the right to an education is a positive right. The right to employment is a positive right. Whether such rights exist is a subject of debate. Given the law of reciprocity of rights and duties, if I have a right to education, someone has a correlative obligation to provide the education. If I have a right to employment, someone has the obligation to provide the employment.

The last is a difficult kind of claim in a free market society, for how can it be claimed that anyone has an obligation to start a business so that others have employment? If one lays the obligation on the state, then the free market is compromised. So it only makes sense to claim such rights when there are facilities to provide the goods involved. What sense would it make to claim a right to health care in a society that had no health care delivery systems? It certainly would make sense to claim a need for health care, but that underlies the difference between a right and a need.

Accordingly, some claim that there are only negative rights, for negative rights do not require others to provide the goods or the needs. They are rights that protect those goods or needs. Hence the rights to life, liberty and property are negative rights, for no one has the obligation to provide those goods, but all have an obligation not to violate them.

## Inalienable rights?

Are rights inalienable? Is not some interference justifiable? The classic case against free speech is that one is not free to shout fire in a crowded theater. Issues of killing in self-defense and in war, and issues of capital punishment, require working out the limits of the indefeasibility. It is helpful to remember that the modern working out of rights was for the purpose of securing a justification for rebelling against governmental authority. One of the primary functions of government was to secure the rights of its citizens.

## Extension of rights

Besides the traditional doctrines on rights, the number of rights articulated have expanded. For example the United Nations Declaration of

Human Rights, in Article 22, claims that everyone has a right "to a standard of living adequate for the health and well-being of himself and his family, including food, clothing, housing." (This echoes the "right to a living wage" enunciated in the Papal Encyclical *Rerum Novarum* in 1891.) Others claim a right to adequate health care for everyone. There are contemporary concerns for animal rights. In such contexts, we see clearly that these rights claims are statements of basic needs or interests, either of humans or other animals. They rest on criteria for the quality of life, which become a standard by which to judge existing governments and policies.

### See also:

ethics and morality; human dignity; inequality; justice; social economics: major contemporary themes

### Selected references

Aquinas, Thomas (1265–73) *Summa theologica* II–II, q. 66, a.7, New York: Oxford University Press, 1975.

Bentham, Jeremy (1789) *Introduction to the Principles of Morals and Legislation*, London: Athlone Press, 1970.

Dworkin, Ronald (1978) *Taking Rights Seriously*, New Impression with a Reply to Critics, London: Duckworth.

Hart, H.L.A. (1955) "Are There Any Natural Rights?," *Philosophical Review* 64: 212–13.

Locke, John (1690) *Two Treatises of Government*, ed. Peter Laslett, Cambridge: 1960.

RONALD F. DUSKA

# Robinson's contribution to political economy

Joan Robinson's (1903–83) career as a political economist can be said to have begun during the Great Depression of the 1930s. Her theoretical work is extensive, but can be broadly and chronologically divided into two categories. The first category is that of the short-period, which characterizes her work in the 1930s, namely, imperfect competition and her involvement in the KEYNESIAN REVOLUTION. Long-period analysis, however, is the category which demanded her intellectual energy throughout the remainder of her life, as her dissent from neoclassicism intensified. It is in the context of this interest in the long-period that her contributions to the CAPITAL THEORY DEBATES and to questions of ECONOMIC GROWTH, ACCUMULATION and structures of reproduction can be situated.

## Imperfect competition and capacity utilization

Analyzing her own book *The Economics of Imperfect Competition* Robinson credited Sraffa for his "pregnant suggestion that the whole theory of value should be treated in terms of monopoly analysis" (Robinson 1933: v). The major problem facing perfect competition theory was its prediction that less efficient firms would close down as a result of a sustained fall in demand, similar to the one that was being experienced in the 1920s and 1930s. Under the assumption of perfect competition, each firm faces a perfectly elastic demand curve, setting output where price is equal to marginal cost and selling all that it produces at the prevailing price without affecting the price. In the depth of the economic slump of the 1930s, Robinson found it harder and harder to accept this orthodoxy, since she could see that the real world was made up mostly of imperfectly competitive markets, with large firms and restricted entry. Moreover, most firms were operating below capacity rather than closing down. In *The Economics of Imperfect Competition*, Robinson showed that large firms face downward sloping demand curves and thus falling marginal revenue curves, and maximizing profits at output levels where marginal revenue is equal to marginal cost at a price above marginal cost. She therefore found the explanation for firms operating below capacity during the depression rather than closing down as perfect competition theory had predicted (see MARKET STRUCTURES).

The GREAT DEPRESSION was ultimately responsible for Robinson's abandonment of imperfect competition itself, as she became more and more involved in the Keynesian revolution. In 1930 she was one of a group of five economists known as the Circus who began to discuss Keynes's ideas, which led to the development of *General Theory*. She interpreted the Keynesian revolution as the acknowledgment of the historical specificity of the capitalist system, and the consequent recognition that economic life in this system is the result of the decisions of individuals based on CONVENTIONS and guesswork.

## Effective demand and wages

The concrete historical issue with which Keynesians were concerned was unemployment. Keynes had shown that output depends on demand, which itself is both determined by and determines income in the sense that "One man's expenditure provides other men's income and one man's income is derived from other men's expenditure" (Robinson 1937: 3). Individuals, however, only spend part of their income, while also saving a portion. If saving went directly into a demand for capital goods, then the fact that individuals save a portion of their income would not result in unemployment. "But the demand for capital goods comes, not from saving, but from business concerns who use them in production, and no entrepreneur is inclined to acquire goods unless he can see a profit by doing so" (Robinson 1937: 4). Moreover, since "the profitability of capital goods depends upon the demand for the consumption goods which they produce," individual saving in fact "does nothing to encourage entrepreneurs to expect a greater profit from capital" (Robinson 1937: 4). If individual saving is higher than the demand of entrepreneurs for capital then unemployment will result, while employment can rise as a result of either an increase in investment or a decrease in private saving.

However, a change in money wages will not lead to any significant change in employment. Money wages are rather the primary determinant of the level of prices and are themselves the result of the relative bargaining power between workers and employers. Robinson referred to the recognition of the primary role of money wages in governing the level of prices in industrial economies as "the other half of the Keynesian revolution" (Robinson 1972: 173). She argued that this "was a greater shock to notions of equilibrium even than the concept of effective demand governed by volatile expectations" (1972: 174).

## Accumulation and growth

With the postwar boom, Robinson's interest moved away from analyzing the role of effective demand in the determination of output and employment, to examining the conditions necessary for accumulation and growth. This period saw her intense interest in the causes and consequences of long-period development, her initiation of the capital controversies with her famous 1953 article "The Production Function and the Theory of Capital," as well as her careful reconsideration of Marx in works such as *An Essay on Marxian Economics* (1942) and *On Re-reading Marx* (1953), as well as her magnum opus, *Accumulation of Capital*, in 1956.

For Robinson the question of the measurement and, even more importantly, the meaning of capital was a long-period question. This is because in the short period there is a fixed and specific set of capital equipment in use, so that it is possible to talk of a specific quantity of capital and a specific rate of profit. But in the long period, "capital equipment changes in quantity and in design. So the question arises: What is the quantity of capital?" (Robinson 1973: 261). What was particularly confusing for Robinson was the lack of a distinction in the neoclassical production function between capital as the means of production and capital as the "command over finance." Moreover, for Robinson, the concept of the marginal productivity of capital – the relative share of profits in distribution – was itself incoherent if a meaningful quantity of capital could not be identified. Neoclassical theory's view of prices as an index of scarcity implies that the rate of profit would be high or low depending on the degree of scarcity of capital. Therefore, a measure of capital must exist before the rate of profit can be determined. Yet NEOCLASSICAL ECONOMICS does not have a measure of capital independent of the rate of profit. Moreover, by defining the return of capital as "the reward for waiting," the ideological justification for income from property in capitalism is accomplished by neoclassical theory. Finally, for Robinson, the marginal productivity theory of distribution was not descriptive of a real world phenomenon, since it was based on an "error in methodology" which ignores attention to real historical processes.

Robinson identified two distinctions between Marx and neoclassical economics, and sympathized with Marx. First, there was Marx's historical approach versus the ahistoricism of orthodox theory. Secondly, "the orthodox economists argue in terms of a harmony of interests between various sections of the community, while Marx conceives of economic life in terms of a conflict of interest" between the classes (Robinson 1942: 1). Theoretically, what was of particular interest to her in Marx was his long period employment analysis, his emphasis on effective demand, and his schema of expanded reproduction. Following her interest in structures of reproduction, in *Accumulation of Capital* she explored the dynamic long-run consequences of capital accumulation brought about by short-run investment. She attempted to discover and explore the "principles of coherence" embedded in the fundamental confusion of the capitalist system. But she rejected Marx's LABOR THEORY OF VALUE as a theory incapable of providing an analysis of prices, and found his explanation of the FALLING RATE OF PROFIT TENDENCY confused. She reserved, however, her most piercing critique not for Marx but for "Marxists." She found Marxists' dogmatic and uncritical idolization of Marx as anathema to Marx's historical vision, since, for her, a

historical perspective requires the theorist to adapt the method and tools of analysis to changing circumstances.

## Methodology and philosophy

Robinson's long-period analysis culminated in the methodological distinction she made between logical and historical TIME in her article, "History versus Equilibrium" (1974). Specifically, in the simultaneous equations model of neoclassicism, general equilibrium is the outcome of a long-run process (a sequence of short-run equilibria at the end of which all markets clear), and as such needs a satisfactory analysis of how the economy can in fact get into equilibrium. Robinson observed, however, that this neoclassical process moves in logical time in that it is only able to account for the differences and not changes in the underlying variables. Moreover, this methodology is mechanical in its use of a space metaphor to describe a process through time (see EQUILIBRIUM, DISEQUILIBRIUM AND NON-EQUILIBRIUM).

In *Economic Philosophy* (1962), Robinson gives her views on the nature of economic knowledge by expounding on the relationship between science and IDEOLOGY. While arguing that the hypotheses, concepts and the very process of scientific investigation are value-laden, Robinson also argued that, given a particular economic system, it is possible to describe the main features of its operation fairly objectively. Thus, by arguing that it is not possible to have a value-free science of economics, Robinson implies that "to look at a system from the outside implies that it is not the only possible system; in describing it we compare it (openly or tacitly) with other actual or imagined systems. Differences imply choices, and choices imply judgement" (Robinson 1962: 14). Indeed, for Robinson it is essential that the practitioner of science be far more comfortable with doubt and uncertainty than with certainty. This description of scientific practice, while modest relative to the neoclassical aim of pure objectivity, is nevertheless quite ambitious, since it includes the notion of change through the use of our objective capacities as well as moral reasoning.

## See also:

Cambridge revolution; normative and positive economics; post-Keynesian political economy: major contemporary themes; Sraffian political economy; value judgments and world views

## Selected references

Robinson, Joan (1933) *The Economics of Imperfect Competition*, 2nd edn, London: Macmillan, 1969.

—— (1937) *Introduction to the Theory of Employment*, 2nd edn, London: Macmillan, 1969.

—— (1942) *An Essay on Marxian Economics*, 2nd edn, London: Macmillan, 1962.

—— (1953–4) "The Production Function and the Theory of Capital," *Collected Economic Papers*, 2: 114–31.

—— (1956) *Accumulation of Capital*, London: Macmillan.

—— (1962) *Economic Philosophy*, Chicago: Aldine Publishing Company.

—— (1972) "What Has Become of the Keynesian Revolution?" *Collected Economic Papers*, 5: 168–77.

—— (1973) *After Keynes*, Oxford: Basil Blackwell.

—— (1974) "History versus Equilibrium," in Joan Robinson, *Contributions to Modern Economics*, New York: Harcourt Brace Jovanovich.

ZOHREH EMAMI

# S

## Scandinavian model

Within the Scandinavian countries there has developed, since the economic crisis of the 1930s, a distinct political, economic and social commitment to the idea of shaping a welfare society. The specific form that it took differed somewhat between the various Scandinavian/Nordic countries. The common feature is an acceptance by all relevant parties that society should evolve toward further equalization of social opportunities.

### Foundations of the model

The guiding force of the Scandinavian model, for instance in Sweden, has been the two wings of the labor movement, the Social Democratic Party and the Trade Union Confederation (LO). They sought to create a prosperous and equal society, and were empowered, historically speaking, by being the largest political party and by the LO having organized 80 percent of wage earners.

The basic goals in the economic sphere were high ECONOMIC GROWTH, low unemployment, a large public service and a considerable redistribution of income. The theoretical content of the Scandinavian model is mainly established by Swedish economists related to the labor movement (see Hedborg and Meinert 1984). Before the Second World War it was Ernst Wigforss and Gunnar Myrdal who established the ideological background and carried out the political implementation. The model was further elaborated by economists within the LO as the "Rehn–Meinert model" (Rehn 1988: 219).

Within this theoretical tradition of a negotiated economy the model (Edgren *et al.* 1970) was developed to stipulate the acceptable range for wage increases, with an emphasis being placed on the external competing sectors (for instance, manufacturing, wood and pulp). The basic idea was that the private sector should be given optimal conditions, from the allocative point of view, to secure high growth. Private ownership of firms and a free market approach should be a guiding principle. The condition of the external competing sectors was given particular attention, in close collaboration with the labor movement, to lessen the constraint on growth.

A properly functioning labor market was given high priority. An essential part of the Scandinavian model was for centrally controlled bargaining of collective wage agreements. Due to the high number of wage earners being unionized, wage agreements could be (at least in the high days of the model) pre-arranged between employers' organizations, the labor movement and government. There was a certain element of corporatism or tripartite agreements within the model. Labor accepted a moderation of wage increases, in accordance with productivity gains in the external competing industries. Employers agreed to invest excess profits in new plants where labor from declining/ailing industries could be employed. Government promised to provide macroeconomic stability, a competitive exchange rate, and a moderation of domestic demand.

A solidaric wage policy became an integrated part of the model, where wage differentials (between skilled and unskilled women and men) became compressed. This policy would simultaneously squeeze low productivity jobs and facilitate job shifts from wage-leading but ailing firms to rising industries. The centrally negotiated wages and the small wage differentials made skilled workers in excess demand, while unskilled jobs were deliberately squeezed through labor saving investments.

In Sweden, an active and selective labor market policy has always been an integrated part of economic policy. Unemployed workers were relatively quickly involved in job training programs, with the specific aim of upgrading their work abilities. Unemployment benefits can be gained for not much longer than a year. In Denmark, until recently, unemployment benefits could be secured by individual workers for between five and seven years. Also, the size of the benefit differs between the two countries. In Sweden the general rule is that the benefit is fixed at 75 percent of the previous wage. In Denmark there is a flat rate for all unemployed persons, mostly independent of the former income.

## Assessment and future of the model

Until the mid-1980s, it seemed that the labor market did function surprisingly well in Sweden, when measured by the unemployment–wage trade-off (see Bosworth and Rivlin 1987: 172–4). Since then it has become increasingly disputed as to whether the compressed wage structure does impede the mobility and flexibility of the labor market. In Denmark, wage settlements have become more and more decentralized during the 1980s, and Sweden has followed the same route.

The precondition for a well-functioning labor market in a society aiming at equality is a high supply of public goods. In addition to the labor market policy, a generous social security system makes labor more willing to accept job mobility even when it implies a period of involuntary unemployment. An important aspect of creating equal job opportunities in a longer perspective, the public sector is supposed to provide households with basic public goods (education, health care and social care) in adequate supply and free of charge, independently of the current income. Especially with regard to equal employment opportunities on the basis of gender, child care

institutions and kindergartens have been created in a vast number, trying to catch up with the seemingly never-ending waiting lists.

These high public expenses have to be financed. That requires as a general principle tax receipts of an equal size. Until the mid-1980s personal income tax was the main source of public income, which was also used as a tool for further equalization. That resulted in quite high marginal tax rates of 70–80 percent (in some cases above 100 percent when means-tested social benefits were included), creating disincentives in the labor market.

Due to the extended welfare system, the public sector is financially fragile. Any unexpected increase in unemployment immediately causes a (larger) budget deficit. Denmark in the early 1980s and Sweden in the 1990s experienced a budget deficit surpassing 10 percent of GDP. Thus the public debt grew with considerable speed. These events, in conjunction with rising unemployment, have initiated the debate as to whether the Scandinavian model has become obsolete (Ekonomikommissionen 1993).

The question arises as to the future of the social democratic model, in the light of declining political fortunes, the deregulation of financial markets, more flexible international capital flows, more decentralized wage negotiations, and privatization of public property. The deregulation of the financial system seems to have been the immediate cause of the boom and collapse of stock and property prices, which all Scandinavian countries experienced (along with many others) in the late 1980s and early 1990s. Also, productivity gains have been relatively small, which could be a consequence of centrally fixed wages. It appears that a renewed vision and a reworked model are necessary for the Scandinavian experience in the light of these major changes (see SOCIAL DEMOCRACY).

## See also:

budget deficit; collective social wealth; fiscal policy; justice; market socialism; needs; rights; social economics: major contemporary themes;

social and organizational capital; socialism and communism; welfare state

## Selected references

Amoroso, B. and Jespersen, J. (1992) *Macroeconomic Theory and Policies for the 1990s*, Basingstoke: Macmillan, ch. 6.

Bosworth, B.P. and Rivlin, A.M. (1987) *The Swedish Economy*, Washington, DC: The Brookings Institution.

Ekonomikommissionen (1993) *Nya villkor för ekonomi och politik* (Assar Lindbeck-rapporten), Stockholm: SOU, 16.

Edgren, G., Faxén, K.-O. and Odhner, C. (1970) *Lönebildning och samhällsekonomi*, Stockholm.

Hedborg, A. and Meinert, R. (1984) *Folkhemsmodellen*, Rabén & Sjögren.

Mjøset, L. (1996) *Does the Nordic Model Still Exist?*, Oslo: Universitetsforlaget.

Mogensen, G.V. (ed.) (1995) *Work Incentives in the Danish Welfare State – New Empirical Evidence*, The Rockwool Foundation Research Unit, Copenhagen: Danmarks Statistik.

Rehn, G. (1988) *Full sysselsättning utan inflation*, Stockholm: Tidens förlag.

JESPER JESPERSEN

# Schumpeter, Joseph Alois

## Time in Europe

Joseph Schumpeter (1883–1950) was born in Triesch in Moravia, in what was then the Hapsburg Empire and is now part of the Czech Republic. His grandfather, Alois, founded a textile factory, which his father, Joseph Sr, expanded and mechanized. Joseph Sr died four years later, and the family moved to Graz, where his mother, Johanna Grüner, married Sigismund von Kéler, a high-ranking officer in the Austro-Hungarian army. When his stepfather retired, the family went to Vienna. There, from 1893, Joseph attended a school for the upper class, the Theresianum. In 1901 he enrolled in the law faculty of Vienna University.

Schumpeter studied economic theory under Friedrich von Wieser, Eugen von Philippovich and Eugen von Böhm-Bawerk. In 1905 he took part in Böhm-Bawerk's seminar, where the latter's criticism of Marx was one of the topics debated, and where he met Marxists such as Otto Bauer and Rudolf Hilferding, as well as Ludwig von Mises. A year later he took the degree *doctor utriusque iuris*.

In his first book, *Das Wesen und der Hauptinhalt der theoretischen Nationalökonomie* (*The Nature and Essence of Theoretical Economics*) in 1908, he referred with admiration to Walras's general economic equilibrium approach as an adequate analytical scheme of the pure logic of the interdependences among economic quantities. He also refrained from a frontal assault on Marxism. Schumpeter has indeed often been depicted, both by friends and foes, as a "bourgeois Marx," who thought CAPITALISM was doomed and socialism was an interesting experiment to try out, and whose last work was significantly entitled the "March into Socialism." Nevertheless, he was also to some degree a conservative, disdainful of the New Deal, and would choose to side with Franco – or even, according to some of his pupils, with Hitler – rather than "give in" to communism.

During 1906 and 1907 Schumpeter spent a year in England, and married Gladys Ricarde Seaver, the daughter of a high dignitary of the Church of England. The marriage was ill-starred, and ended in divorce some years later. Afterwards, he worked for almost two years as a junior partner in a law firm in Cairo. He returned to Vienna in 1909 to become a *Privatdozent*, which gave him the right to lecture. Thanks to Böhm-Bawerk, Schumpeter soon obtained his first academic appointment as an associate professor teaching both economics and sociology in Czernowitz. It was there that Schumpeter lectured and gathered notes on method in the social sciences and on the theory of social classes. In 1911 he became a full professor and moved to Graz, nearer to Vienna, when he published his masterpiece, the

*Theorie der wirtschaftlichen Entwicklung* (the *Theory of Economic Development*).

The following decade saw a quick burst of publications. Among the most important were *Epochen der Dogmen- und Methodengeschichte* (*Economic Doctrine and Method: A Historical Sketch*) in 1914; *Das Sozialprodukt und die Rechenpfennige: Glossen und Beiträge zur-Geldtheorie von heute* (*Money and the Economic System*) in 1917–18; *Die Krise des Steuerstaates* (*The Crisis of the Tax State*) in 1918; and *Zur Soziologie der Imperialismen* (*The Sociology of Imperialism*) in 1919.

In these years, however, Schumpeter was lured by the siren of politics and by the offers of his old Marxist friends. In 1918, he became a member of the German Socialization Commission, signing the majority report pleading for socialization as a means to increase economic efficiency. The next year he accepted the office of Finance Minister in the Austrian government led by Karl Renner, and supported by a coalition in which the Social Democrats had the relative majority. He tried to impose a capital levy, to stabilize the currency, and to open the country to capital imports. Having upset everybody, he was fired. In 1921 Schumpeter took up the presidency of the Biedermann bank, which collapsed in 1924, the first in a series of Austrian and German banks to do so. If his political interlude was a failure, his spell as a banker was a catastrophe, especially for his personal finances. He had to work hard for more than a decade to pay off his debts.

A chair in public finance allowed Schumpeter to restart his academic career in 1925. In 1926 his second wife, Annie Reisinger, twelve years his junior and the daughter of the caretaker of Schumpeter's mother's apartment, died in childbirth along with their child. For a number of years, Schumpeter worked on a volume on money and banking activity, but the work was not published in his lifetime.

## Time in the USA

In 1932 Schumpeter left Europe for the United States, at the invitation of Harvard University.

In his American years, Schumpeter was no longer the *enfant terrible* and the most brilliant of the younger generation of European economists. Instead, he was respected as an established master, but he felt increasingly isolated. He was often overtaken by long periods of depression, finding some relief in his third marriage with Elizabeth Boody, an economic historian who specialized in Japan. *Business Cycles*, the two-volume update of Schumpeter's view on economic development, appeared in 1939 but was overshadowed by Keynes's *General Theory* (it had to await the 1970s and 1980s to become widely acclaimed with the ascent of neo-Schumpeterianism). The 1940s were, nevertheless, years marked by occasional editorial and academic successes. *Capitalism, Socialism and Democracy*, published in 1942, was widely acclaimed, though he saw it as a minor diversion. In 1949 he became President of the American Economic Association, and only his death in the night of 7–8 January 1950 stopped him becoming the first President of the International Economic Association.

## Core of his work

The core of his analytic system is SCHUMPETER'S THEORY OF INNOVATION, DEVELOPMENT AND CYCLES (for a detailed reference guide on Schumpeter, see Augello 1990). As Schumpeter himself wrote in the introduction to the Japanese translation of *The Theory of Economic Development*, he wanted to show that capitalist accumulation cannot be understood unless it is recognized that "there was a source of energy within the economic system which would of itself disrupt any equilibrium that might be obtained. If this is so, then there must be a purely economic theory of economic change which does not merely rely on external factors," and according to which economic development is "a distinct process generated by the economic process itself." Later he realized "that this idea and this aim are exactly the same as the idea and the aim which underlie the economic teaching of Karl Marx," though Schumpeter's "intention and results are much too different" to those of Marx (see Schumpeter 1989:166–7).

Indeed, Schumpeter's legacy may be summarized through a comparison with Marx. Schumpeter, like Marx, viewed economic theory as part of a unified social science. Sociology and history enter into the definition of the same economic notions and processes, and the whole of social science is more than the sum of the parts constituted by the separate perspectives of the individual disciplines. Moreover, Schumpeter's theory, like Marx's, is evolutionary in that it uncovers the processes by which each state of the economy gives way to another. However, Schumpeter and Marx divide on a number of issues, especially on the nature of classes in capitalism and the forces propelling the system towards socialism (see EVOLUTIONARY ECONOMICS: MAJOR CONTEMPORARY THEMES).

According to Schumpeter, technological change in the capitalist process is both incessant and discontinuous. It is propelled by the entrepreneurial introduction of new combinations, which may be implemented only thanks to the "monetary complement" of bank-credit creation. Within capitalism, upward mobility is possible when individuals do something exceptional, opening up new ways of doing things (innovating). A remarkable feature of the capitalist CLASS structure is the unceasing exit of old families from, as well as the entry of new ones into, the "higher" strata, with the ascent of temporarily successful entrepreneurs into the class of the bourgeoise.

However, the very success of capitalism as an engine of production and of rationalization, on the one hand, and the metamorphosis of competitive capitalism into monopoly "trustified" capitalism, on the other, reduce the need for the entrepreneurial function and the motives to fulfill it. So Schumpeter gives a breakdown theory, even if it does not appeal – as in Marx – to economic but rather to ideological and political contradictions inherent in the capitalist process, which erode (some of) the institutional prerequisites of capitalism.

According to Schumpeter, in monopoly capitalism the threat of dynamic competition and the process of "creative destruction" are more powerful than ever. Imperialism, rather than being the inevitable outcome of pure capitalist tendencies, is a reversion to feudal military habits and/or the fruit of protectionist practices resembling absolute monarchies. On the other hand, for Schumpeter, trust-dominated capitalism, where innovation itself becomes routine, paves the way for bureaucratic socialism (see Schumpeter 1942 and SCHUMPETERIAN COMPETITION). He saw the latter to be quite a feasible mode of production (against Mises and Hayek), though it amounts essentially to nothing other than guided capitalism (see SOCIALISM AND COMMUNISM).

The monetary aspects of the Schumpeterian system are the most fascinating. Schumpeter succeeded in reviving the Marxian theme of money as capital, and of the necessary prior role of finance to start production. As the manuscripts of Schumpeter's treatise on money and banking activity testify (see Schumpeter 1996), he saw banks as the "social accountants" of the economic system (the idea has been taken up again by Stiglitz and Weiss (1988)). He saw credit creation *ex nihilo* to finance entrepreneurs as the equivalent of the setting by a planning agency of "orders," removing from the path of the entrepreneurs obstacles arising from the private ownership of resources (similar to the MONETARY CIRCUIT approach).

## Conclusion

In a broad sense, Schumpeter is also the forerunner of much of the contemporary analysis of TECHNOLOGY as developed by modern Schumpeterian political economy (see Freeman 1994). A fair assessment, however, cannot fail to note that Schumpeter's challenging task was to build an evolutionary monetary theory of the capitalist process, where "all economic propositions are relative to the *modus operandi* of a given monetary system," but at the same time monetary processes "never carry their explanation in themselves" (Schumpeter 1939: 548). Nowadays this idea has been almost completely deserted. Maybe for Schumpeter, the best is yet to come.

## See also:

business cycle theories; evolutionary political economy: history; innovation, evolution and cycles; long waves of economic growth and development; monetary theory of production; Schumpeterian competition

## Selected references

Allen, R.L. (1991) *Opening Doors: The Life and Work of Joseph Schumpeter*, 2 vols, New Brunswick, NJ: Transaction Publishers.

Augello, M.M. (1990) *Joseph Alois Schumpeter. A Reference Guide*, Berlin: Springer Verlag.

Freeman, C. (1994) "The Economics of Technical Change," *Cambridge Journal of Economics* 18(5): 463–514.

Schneider, E. (1970) *Joseph A. Schumpeter. Leben und Werk eines Grossen Sozialökonomen*, Tübingen: J.C. Mohr; trans. *Schumpeter: Life and Work*, Lincoln, NB: Bureau of Business Research, University of Nebraska, 1975.

Schumpeter, J.A. (1939) *Business Cycles*, Philadelphia: Porcupine Press, 1982.

—— (1989) *Essays on Entrepeneurs, Innovations, Business Cycles and the Evolution of Capitalism*, ed. R.V. Clemence, New Brunswick, NJ: Transaction Publishers.

—— (1991) *The Economics and Sociology of Capitalism*, ed. R. Swedberg, Princeton, NJ: Princeton University Press.

—— (1996) *Trattato della moneta: capitoli inediti*, ed. Lapo Berti and Marcello Messori, Naples: Edizioni Scientifiche Italiane.

Stiglitz, J.E. and Weiss, A. (1988) *Banks as Social Accountants and Screening Devices for the Allocation of Credit*, NBER Working Paper no. 2710.

Stolper, W.F. (1994) *Joseph Alois Schumpeter. The Public Life of a Private Man*, Princeton, NJ: Princeton University Press.

Swedberg, R. (1991) *Joseph A. Schumpeter: His Life and Work*, Cambridge: Polity Press.

RICCARDO BELLOFIORE

# Schumpeter's theory of innovation, development and cycles

According to Joseph SCHUMPETER, the capitalist process is marked by qualitative endogenous change. Development proper, which must be distinguished from mere quantitative ECONOMIC GROWTH, is the outcome of the spontaneous and incessant, though discontinuous, introduction of innovations by entrepreneurs. To be carried out, innovations need the monetary creation of purchasing power by the banking system. Since entrepreneurs, backed by bank credit, appear in groups or clusters, capitalist development exhibits a cyclical pattern. Entrepreneurial action gives way to the "prosperity" phase, in which innovations emerge, and the "recession" phase, a lapse of time during which the system adapts to creative destruction.

The essentials of the theory of economic development are sketched out in Schumpeter (1911, 1939) (for a general assessment, see Egidi 1981; De Vecchi 1995). Schumpeter's model of cycles and development uses a system of successive approximation to a "real economy," which means starting with a simple model and then becoming increasingly complex as the model tries to approximate a more realistic view of capitalism. He starts with an economy of unchanging structures of production and circulation (the "circular flow"), followed by the introduction of changing methods, markets and credit, followed by the use of credit for general accumulation, and finally new production methods of differing durability.

## Circular flow and equilibrium

In Schumpeter's system, the economy starts in

the circular flow, which is identified by routine behavior: agents act following habitual past experience. This steady-state economy is characterized by perfect competition, perfect adjustment to equilibrium, absence of stocks and futures markets, two social classes, of workers and landlords, and money functioning only as a means of simple circulation (no net savings or credit). Economic processes merely reproduce themselves on the same scale with constant flows. Any changes in economic data occur continuously, being absorbed by the system without any disruptions.

In each period, firms are assumed to repeat the same decisions about their demand for the services of the original factors of production (labour and land) and about their own supply. Money incomes (wages and rents) are spent on consumption goods produced in the previous period. Production takes time and needs to be financed. But since production processes are synchronized, each supply finds its own demand at the expected prices just covering unit costs. Money may be entirely neglected without losing anything essential of what is going on in the economy. In the stationary flow, firms are making neither economic profits nor losses. The system of prices and quantities is well-known to agents.

## Innovation and credit

In the "first approximation" to the real economy, Schumpeter introduces innovations and credit into the system. Innovations are defined as the production of "other things," or of the "same thing by a different method." They are "new combinations" put forward by "new men" through the creation of "new firms" (see SCHUMPETERIAN COMPETITION). The new combinations may include (a) introduction of a new method of production, (b) production of a new good, (c) opening up of a new market, (d) capturing of a new source of raw and semi-manufactured materials, and (e) reorganisation of an industry. Sustained changes in these qualitative conditions over time are referred to as "development" (see Schumpeter 1911: 63–6).'

Innovation (commercial application) and invention (discovery) are not synonymous. The technical possibilities for new combinations are always available. What has to be endogenously explained is the discontinuous path of innovation and development under capitalism. Entrepreneurs are radicals whose motive to innovate pertains to their strong desire to enter the capitalist class: becoming an entrepreneur is the way to becoming a member of the bourgeoisie (Schumpeter 1927). However, once they join the establishment they usually lose their radical flair; therefore, entrepreneurs cannot constitute a static and continuous class of persons. Innovations are embodied in new firms which question the established practices of economic life.

Potential entrepreneurs do not individually have available the purchasing power to command the productive resources required to implement new combinations. In a social arrangement where private ownership of means of production and private production for the market are typical features, the essential function of banks is to create credit in favor of the entrepreneurs so as to overcome the monetary obstacle to innovation. The inflow of new purchasing power increases the demand for labor (and land), hence putting upward pressure on money wages (and rents).

Managers of the old firms face a relative squeeze in purchasing power and, ultimately, suffer a transfer of resources in favour of new firms. Credit creation to entrepreneurs is granted before they contribute to the stream of goods. The consequent endogenous increase in the money supply (see ENDOGENOUS MONEY AND CREDIT) starts an inflationary process, in which the rise in the general price level accompanies that restructuring of relative prices which only allows the carrying out of the innovation. Finance to entrepreneurs, however, is burdened with a short-term money rate of interest. New firms will be able to pay interest, which is perceived as a tax on entrepreneurial profit, if and when their new supply enters the market and they start realizing money profits. Old firms are now displaced by the new ones, unless they try to copy the leaders. Since the first innovators lessen the social resistance to novelty and force a restructuring of firms still working along traditional lines, they induce a wave of secondary innovations, which is followed by imitators.

The economic system cannot adapt gradually to qualitative change and moves further away from equilibrium. The partial disequilibrium, introduced from within by entrepreneurs, cannot but degenerate into a general disequilibrium marked by a radical upsetting of prices and quantities, by UNCERTAINTY, and by the impossibility of calculating costs and receipts from "doing new things." As entrepreneurial action and dynamic competition decline, adaptive behavior and static competition take the field. The economic system approaches once again a new circular flow, where profit and interest disappear.

We have referred so far to the fundamental two-phase cycle of prosperity or upswing (the movement away from equilibrium caused by innovation) and of recession (the diffusion and reabsorption process eventually leading to a new equilibrium). This simple two-phase first approximation business cycle represents the essential core of the capitalist process. Discontinuous innovation and credit creation are both part of the dynamic motion of capitalism in the two-phase cycle. As Schumpeter says: "capitalism is that form of private property in which the innovations are carried out by means of borrowing money, which in general... implies credit creation" (1939: 223) and credit is "nothing but a means of diverting the factors of production to new uses, or of dictating a new direction to production" (1911: 116).

## Four-phase cycle

Schumpeter, however, also considers a "second approximation," the four-phase cycle where the "recovery" leads to "prosperity," while the "recession" leads to "depression." Here, credit is used not only for innovation but also for general capital accumulation, speculation and over-indebtedness, which leads to a high level

of uncertainty and instability of the cycle, leading to a crisis, followed by recession and depression. The cause of the depression is prosperity and the endogenous use of credit beyond innovation for unproductive uses.

## Innovations of different durabilities

The "third approximation" is based on the bunching of innovations of different durabilities (linked to the endogenous use of credit for innovation and unproductive uses). Schumpeter introduces major process innovations which propel the 45–60-year Kondratieff cycle, medium-term innovations which instigate the 8–11-year Juglar cycle, and the 3–5-year Kitchin cycle based on changes in inventories. Major depressions occur when all three cycles are in a downswing simultaneously, with the resultant cumulative uncertainty and negative expectations of the future. Government action may be necessary to break the vicious circle of negative expectations.

Schumpeter's theory of innovation and development was eclipsed in the 1930s–1950s by the KEYNESIAN REVOLUTION and in the 1950s–1960s by aggregate growth theory of the Solow and Harrod–Domar varieties. However, in the 1970s–1990s there has been a marked revival in Schumpeterian themes, as the industrial nations experience major economic problems, innovation and market dynamics become major social concerns, and long waves of capitalist development become a popular topic of debate. However, a critical part of Schumpeter's contribution, concerning the role of money and credit in economic evolution, seems to have escaped attention (see Bellofiore 1985), except in relation to the modern theory of the MONETARY CIRCUIT.

## Schumpeter's heterodoxy

Schumpeter's approach breaks with mainstream theorizing on virtually each step of the argument. Though his circular flow resembles neoclassical general equilibrium, the interest rate is absent and therefore cannot be seen as the remuneration of "capital" following the marginalist theory of distribution. Rather, it is a wholly monetary and conventional phenomenon along Keynesian lines. Economic development is the outcome of previous waves of entrepreneurial action made possible by credit creation. In Schumpeter, producer sovereignty rather than consumer sovereignty rules the roost. Loans make deposits; and purchasing power, endogenously provided by banks to entrepreneurs, is the essential lever of qualitative change. There is thus no money neutrality (Schumpeter 1917–18, 1970; for Schumpeter's credit theory of money, see Messori 1996).

The capitalist development process is not an adaptation to exogenous shocks but it arises endogenously by its own initiative "from within," and is structurally unstable (Vercelli 1986). On the one hand, after the boom the system will once again come to approach a new equilibrium, but only as a transient and temporary resting point. On the other hand, the prosperity necessarily causes a slackening of entrepreneurial action. Thus, the long run is a sequence of short period positions, and the trend is conditioned by cyclical movements. There are clear macroeconomic foundations to individual entrepreneurial behavior in the Schumpeterian system.

## See also:

animal spirits; business cycle theories; expectations; innovation, evolution and cycles; Schumpeterian political economy

## Selected references

Bellofiore, R. (1985) "Money and Development in Schumpeter," *Review of Radical Political Economics* 17(1&2): 21–40.

De Vecchi, N. (1995) *Entrepreneurs, Institutions and Economic Change: The Economic Thought of J. A. Schumpeter (1905–1925)*, Aldershot: Edward Elgar.

Egidi, M. (1981) *Schumpeter. Il Capitalismo Come Trasformazione Morfologica*, Milan: Etas.

Messori, M. (1996). "The Credit Theory of Money of J. A. Schumpeter," mimeo.

Schumpeter, J.A. (1911) *Theorie der Wirtschaftlichen Entwicklung*, Leipzig: Duncker & Humblot; trans. Redvers Opie as *The Theory of Economic Development: An Inquiry into Profits, Capital, Credit, Interest, and the Business Cycle*, Cambridge, MA: Harvard University Press, 1934.

—— (1917–18) "Das Sozialprodukt und die Rechenpfennige: Glossen und Beiträge zur Geldtheorie von heute," *Archiv für Sozialwissenschaft* 44: 627–715; trans. (1956) as "Money and the Social Product," *International Economic Papers* 6: 148–211.

—— (1927) "Die Sozialen Klassen in Ethnisch Homogenen Milieu," *Archiv für Sozialwissenschaft* 57: 1–67; trans. as "Social Classes in an Ethnically Homogeneous Environment," in R. Swedberg (ed.), *The Economics and Sociology of Capitalism*. Princeton, NJ: Princeton University Press, 1991.

—— (1939) *Business Cycles: A Theoretical, Historical and Statistical Analysis of the Capitalist Process*, New York: McGraw-Hill.

—— (1970) *Das Wesen des Geldes*, Gottingen: Vaderhoeck & Ruprecht.

Vercelli, A. (1986) "Keynes, Schumpeter, Marx and the Structural Instability of Capitalism," *Cahiers d'économie politique* 10–11: 279–304.

RICCARDO BELLOFIORE

# Schumpeterian competition

SCHUMPETER argued in *Capitalism, Socialism and Democracy* (1942) that the kind of competition that "counts" is that associated with:

the new commodity, the new technology, the new source of supply, the new type of organization (the largest-scale unit of control for instance) – competition which commands a decisive cost or quality advantage and which strikes not at the margins of the profits and the outputs of the existing firms but at their foundations and their very lives.

(Schumpeter 1942: 84)

## Dynamic duality of competition

Schumpeter's focus on the innovative aspects of competition was in no small part an attack upon the neoclassical theory of perfect competition, but not a wholesale rejection of neoclassicism as such. Dismissing the idea of "an entirely golden age of perfect competition" as mere "wishful thinking" (1942: 81), Schumpeter nevertheless wanted it both ways. If the competition that really counted was destabilizing (or "disequilibrating" in neoclassical terms), disrupting a prevailing equilibrium state or requiring that a new equilibrium state be established, his vision of capitalism nonetheless also called for the stabilizing ("equilibrating") actions of imitative or emulative competitors to bring markets back towards equilibrium.

This duality of competition is the very essence of Schumpeter's heroic, if unsuccessful, attempt to reconcile the crisis-ridden dynamics of MARX with the disciplined order of Walras's general equilibrium statics (Dennis 1970, 1977). This duality is especially evident in his massive *Business Cycles* (1939), but more vividly sketched in *Capitalism, Socialism and Democracy* (1942) as the "perennial gale of creative destruction" (1942: 87).

Schumpeter's appeal to this dynamic version of competition had already been outlined earlier in his *The Theory of Economic Development* (1911). Here, Schumpeter referred to innovations as "new combinations" (1911: 66). Even in his earlier work, he acknowledged the "progressive 'automatisation' of development" through the growth of "great combines" (1911: 67, 155). But a major idea of his – that "new combinations are, as a rule, embodied in new firms" and that "the vast majority of new combinations will not grow out of the old firms" (1911: 66, 225–6) – stands in sharp contrast to his outlook in 1942.

## Large corporations and anti-trust

In Schumpeter (1942), his critical weaponry was trained as much upon America's experience with anti-trust policy as upon the theory of perfect competition. By then, the "large-scale establishment" had become "a necessary evil," being inseparable from economic progress, indeed being "the most powerful engine of that progress," whereas perfect competition was "not only impossible but inferior, [having no title] as a model of ideal efficiency" (1942: 106). Granting that large firms may well engage in some "restrictive practices," these were but "incidents, often unavoidable incidents, of a long-run process of expansion which they protect rather than impede" (1942: 88). Given their superior innovative performance (or "dynamic efficiency," as it is now often called), Schumpeter therefore asked: "Why then all this talk about monopoly?" (1942: 99). Giving small allowance for exceptional cases, he concluded: "There is no general case for indiscriminate 'trust-busting' or for the prosecution of everything that qualifies as a restraint of trade" (1942: 91).

In terms of pedagogy, Schumpeter's efforts to "dim the halo" of perfect competition (1942: 103–6) must be judged a failure. Entry-level and intermediate textbooks accord his ideas on competition only a passing mention at best, no doubt because economists have been unable to devise ways of incorporating what are essentially qualitative and dynamic notions about innovation into their simple mathematical models about static market equilibrium. Yet, his thesis that the large-scale enterprise has replaced the small in promoting dynamic efficiency has prompted much subsequent, if inconclusive, empirical research (Baldwin and Scott 1987; Scherer and Ross 1990). More significantly, in the broader arena of policy debate, Schumpeter's defense of corporate giantism has enjoyed a strong revival since the 1980s with the emergence of neo-conservative schools of thought.

## Empirical and institutional research

Empirical research on the firm size–innovation hypothesis has been bedeviled from the outset by the fact that innovation itself is a qualitative act or process, not to be confused with its presumed effects on productivity, profits or utility. It is difficult enough just to individuate the "units" of innovative activity to be counted, without having to further identify a suitable dimension as the magnitude for measuring innovative activity. Thus, quantitative researchers have been willing to posit such things as RESEARCH AND DEVELOPMENT (R&D) spending, or even investment, as a "dummy" variable for innovative activity, construing its costs (or inputs) as its benefits (or outputs) to test Schumpeter's hypothesis.

More interesting are historical and institutional studies of the innovative process (Lazonick 1991), pointing to a wide variety of patterns in which both small and large enterprises play different roles. For example, Schumpeter's original schema for innovation and imitation has been analyzed into more complex sequences involving the initial invention of basic new ideas, ongoing R&D into potentially marketable applications, the eventual investment and profit-making realization of these new ideas, and the ensuing diffusion (whether as imitation or as modification) by competitors.

## Critical aspects

Schumpeter reasoned that large-scale enterprises were more likely to achieve dynamic efficiency because they had both the motive and the ability to do so. As to motive, innovation by other firms is "an ever-present threat [that] disciplines before it attacks," that is, as potential competition that "will in the long run enforce behavior very similar to the perfectly competitive pattern," even in markets dominated by single firms (1942: 85). In relation to capability, the large firm may possess both the financial resources to engage in costly long-term research, and some measure of market power to reap sufficient reward from that costly research to justify its risk (1942: 87–90).

Of course, such arguments run both ways (as Schumpeter was no doubt aware). Research activity by dominant firms may be no more than cosmetic and defensive, aimed at creating only costly barriers to entry for potential

competitors. Superior financial capability may lead only to defensive strategies, such as preemptive purchases of new ideas from smaller enterprises to protect vested interests in past research and existing investments (see RENT-SEEKING AND VESTED INTERESTS).

Stimulating though Schumpeter's ideas on competition may be, they have engendered a serious anomaly in conventional economic wisdom. The mainstream textbook teaches beginners that, whereas monopoly profits signal allocative inefficiency, "normal" profits (linked to marginal-cost pricing in perfect competition) signal allocative efficiency. But Schumpeter's rationale for the dynamic efficiency of large-scale enterprise supports a conventional wisdom that conflicts with this textbook orthodoxy: accepting profitability *per se* as a measure of enterprise performance, a measure that draws no distinction between the effects of efficiency and those of market power.

## See also:

corporate hegemony; evolutionary economics: major contemporary themes; innovation, evolution and cycles; market structures; Schumpeterian political economy; Schumpeter's theory of innovation, development and cycles

## Selected references

Baldwin, William L. and Scott, John T. (1987) *Market Structure and Technological Change*, Newark, NJ: Harwood.

Dennis, K. (1970) "Schumpeter on Competition," MA thesis, University of Manitoba.

—— (1977) *Competition in the History of Economic Thought*, New York: Arno Press.

Lazonick, William (1991) *Business Organization and the Myth of the Market Economy*, Cambridge: Cambridge University Press.

Scherer, F.M. and Ross, D. (1990) *Industrial Market Structure and Economic Performance*, 3rd edn, Boston: Houghton-Mifflin.

Schumpeter, Joseph (1911) *The Theory of Economic Development: An Inquiry into Profits, Capital, Credit, Interest, and the*

*Business Cycle*, New York: Oxford University Press, 1934.
—— (1939) *Business Cycles*, 2 vols, Philadelphia: Porcupine Press, 1982.
—— (1942) *Capitalism, Socialism and Democracy*, New York: Harper & Brothers.

KEN DENNIS

# Schumpeterian political economy

## Introduction

Since its emergence in the 1970s, neo-Schumpeterian political economy has developed and now come of age. Numerous journals and books include modern Schumpeterian themes. The home base of this school is the Joseph A. Schumpeter Society, which publishes the *Journal of Evolutionary Economics*. Many of the themes discussed below are examined in this and other journals, such as the *Cambridge Journal of Economics*, *Structural Change and Economic Dynamics*, the *Journal of Economic Issues* and a host of others.

Inspired by American industrial developments in the early part of the twentieth century, SCHUMPETER in *Capitalism, Socialism and Democracy*, first published in 1942, would come almost grudgingly to acknowledge the role of large, oligoplistic firms successfully institutionalizing innovation through the establishment of RESEARCH AND DEVELOPMENT laboratories. He went on to describe how these new institutions were at the center of the innovation process, in association with other financial, production, marketing and distribution capabilities. They had come to operate as a vehicle for the accumulation of knowledge and the exploitation of economies of scale, presented as a significant barrier to the entry of would-be rivals (see Freeman 1994: 466–9). It is this complex institutional reading of economic development which probably most serves to distinguish neo-Schumpeterian political economy from its neoclassical counterparts.

## Evolutionary metaphor

Metcalfe (1995) suggests that, for the evolutionary theorist, competition is not seen to be based primarily on price and primarily determined by optimizing behavior, nor viewed in terms of adjustment to equilibrium under a variety of market structures. Competition is rather more concerned with endogenous dynamic processes of adaptive learning and open-ended unpredictable novelty. To reassure the policy maker, who fears a descent into the abyss of ignorance and uncertainty, Metcalfe (1995: 28) responds that: "Nonetheless, although the emergence of novelty is unpredictable, the processes which translate novelty into coherent patterns of change are not, and it is on this distinction that the role of technology policy hinges."

It must be emphasized that biology is only one of many applications of evolutionary analysis. Economic notions of EVOLUTION AND COEVOLUTION differ from their biological counterparts in recognizing that processes generating variety are rarely "blind" in the sense of acting randomly and independently of selective advantage. Rather, they are guided by experiential learning and are anticipative and intentional. In addition, processes of environmental selection in the market environment of suppliers and users is supplemented by internal selection within organizations. Moreover, there is feedback from selection processes to the processes generating variety. The downside of this realization is that innovation is also constrained by institutional limitations and inertia.

This heterodox, evolutionary perspective investigates the structures, institutions and processes which determine the range of innovations generated at any location or point in time, and their contribution to economic welfare. It is based on a rich understanding of strategic, cognitive and organizational aspects of firm behavior and cumulative, path-dependent processes. These are associated with the emergence of new design configurations, the internal development of existing configurations through sequences of innovations, and the comparative diffusion of competing alternatives (see Freeman 1994).

## Globalization and national policy

The world is being subjected to ever-diminishing costs of transport and communication (in terms of both resources and time) and rapidly receding barriers to the free flow of trade, finance and know-how. In such a world, certain evolutionary theorists have suggested that national borders are becoming less relevant. Nelson and Wright (1992) are advocates of this view. They argue three main points: first, that all nations are now exposed to a common TECHNOLOGY; second, that processes of rapid diffusion have been assisted by the growth of dynamic TRANSNATIONAL CORPORATIONS; and third, that scientific knowledge (widely and freely disseminated) now dominates over learning by doing in the creation of new technology.

A contrasting view is presented by authors such as Michael Porter. He argues in *The Competitive Advantage of Nations* (1990) that home nations' skills and technology are the source of their competitive advantage. In support, Fagerberg (1995) cites a range of studies to demonstrate that large firms conduct most technological activity in their home rather than host nations, and are more influenced by the characteristics of home nation in the choice of research profiles. Technological spillovers are said to be geographically localized. In the competitive strategies of large firms, domestic R&D is more important than foreign sourced R&D, while for firms in small countries, international technology flows are more important.

Fagerberg also reviews the empirical findings of the technological activity literature which finds that growth rates in GDP per capita are influenced by technology activities, as reflected in published national data on the number of patents granted and levels of R&D expenditure. It seems that the importance of these activities rises as nations come closer to the global technological frontier. Nevertheless, Fagerberg emphasizes that technological activities in non-frontier nations cannot be ignored,

because the evidence suggests that more successful imitation is guaranteed when national levels of R&D exceed certain thresholds. Also, imitation and innovation tend to be combined in follower nations, and are governed by the size of the GDP per capita gap. This offers more scope for the exploitation of overseas know-how and the volume of investment, which affords more scope to exploit available technology. In addition, convergence or slowdown in rates of GDP per capita growth tend to be strongly correlated with convergence or slowdown in the extent of technological activity (see *Journal of Evolutionary Economics*, 1995, 269–296).

## National systems of innovation

Detailed institutional studies of the national innovation systems demonstrate the way in which national policy can direct, guide, and heighten the process of technological change and diffusion. Innovative policies are ones which tend to center on three dimensions. The first is building stronger bridges between science and industry. The second dimension is making university and government research bases stronger and more relevant to the institutional needs of technological knowledge and application. The third is fostering horizontal and vertical networks and clusters of firms, through the provision of bureau services and other resources. Lastly, an important dimension is encouraging interactions between users and producers of technology (including those within the public business enterprise sector).

Fransman (1995) provides a recent overview of changes in Japan's national system of innovation. He shows how it has adapted over time to exploit the opportunities afforded by international collaborative research, immigration of skilled labor, international strategic technological advance, foreign transplanted R&D laboratories, direct foreign investment, and the trade and imitation of technology. Building on the seminal ideas of Michael Porter, Fagerberg (1995) presents an empirical model of user–producer interaction, learning and comparative advantage. In this model, the development of new technology requires close interaction and communication between both the users and the producers of technology. Establishment of channels and codes of communication involve fixed costs. Stable relationships imply costs per transaction are decreasing over time, leading to both a higher volume of transactions and preventing the immediate diffusion of benefits to others.

Unlike the new growth theory, which emphasizes externalities associated with activities internal to firms, the evolutionary theorists focus on interactions between different firms. Fagerberg's arguments and empirical findings confirm that user–producer interactions are more important for industries that are characterized by complex and user-specific technology.

At a more fundamental epistemological level, this integrative process is being facilitated by studies which reveal the commonality between neo-Schumpeterian and post-Keynesian views about UNCERTAINTY and unpredictability. In a foundational inquiry, Vercelli's *Methodological Foundations of Macroeconomics: Keynes and Lucas* (1991) finds common links between the notions of dynamic instability at play in the work of Rene Thom, the notion of autopoesis in the works of Ilya Prigogine and Isabelle Stengers (see their *Order Out of Chaos*, 1984), and post-Keynesian notions of fundamental uncertainty.

The "national systems of innovation" framework was developed in a European context by the early work of Ferdinand List and others. More recently, evolutionary theories have been applied by writers such as Amsden (1994) to developing economies, particularly to the rapidly growing East Asian nations. As these nations evolve from being technological imitators to innovators and inventors, their systems of innovation must undergo profound transformations.

## Long waves and business cycles

One area of current activity involves the development of (sometimes chaotic) dynamic models that formally integrate both the shorter frequency business cycles and long wave Kondratieff cycles driven by clusters of innovation (see Freeman and Perez 1988; Goodwin 1991). As more detailed data become available, this may assist in resolving the on-going controversy over their existence.

Much work remains to be done to achieve a synthesis of Schumpeterian models of innovation clustering with post-Keynesian models of financial instability and endogenous business cycles. Antonelli (1996) has attempted to develop models of localized technological change based on tacit skills and the exploitation of learning-to-learn externalities, which are amenable to integration with P*Capitalism, Socialism and Democracy* (1942 post-Keynesian macroeconomic theory. He argues that macroeconomic policy can play a major role in promoting technological change over the cycle by sustaining levels of aggregate demand during the recessions, and easing financial constraints on firms searching for new localized technological breakthroughs.

## Regulationists and Schumpeterians

Dic Lo (1995) has described the recent merging of evolutionary economic approaches with those informed by flexible specialization theory and the REGULATION APPROACH. This includes the burgeoning literature on "after-Fordist" systems of accumulation and the pressing need for the development of new modes of social regulation (statist, corporatist or neo-liberal) to curb the excesses and inefficiencies of unbridled neo-liberal programs.

## See also:

business cycle theories; chaos theory; evolutionary economics: major contemporary themes; Fordism and the flexible system of production; hysteresis; increasing returns to scale; innovation, evolution and cycles; long waves of economic growth and development; path dependency

## Selected references

Amsden, Alice (1994) "Why Isn't the Whole World Experimenting with the East Asian Model to Develop?: Review of *The East Asian Miracle*," *World Development* 22(4): 627–33.

Antonelli, Cristiano (1996) "Localised Technological Change and Schumpeterian Growth Regimes," *The Manchester School* 64(4): 351–70.

Fagerberg, J. (1995) "User–producer Interaction, Learning and Comparative Advantage," *Cambridge Journal of Economics* 19: 243–56.

Fransman, M. (1995) "Is National Technology Policy Obsolete in a Globalised World? The Japanese response," *Cambridge Journal of Economics* 19: 95–119.

Freeman, C. (1994) "The Economics of Technical Change," *Cambridge Journal of Economics* 18: 463–514.

Freeman, C. and Perez, C. (1988) "Structural Crisis of Adjustment: Business Cycles and Investment Behaviour," in G. Dosi, C. Freeman, R.R. Nelson, G. Silberberg and L. Soete (eds), *Technical Change and Economic Theory*, London: Pinter.

Goodwin, Richard M. (1991) "Economic Evolution, Chaotic Dynamics and the Marx–Keynes–Schumpeter System," in Geoffrey Hodgson and Ernesto Screpanti (eds), *Rethinking Economics: Markets, Technology and Economic Evolution*, Aldershot: Edward Elgar.

Lo, Dic (1995) "Techno-economic Paradigm Versus the Market: on Recent Theories of Late Industrialisation," *Economy and Society* 24(3): 443–70.

Metcalfe, J.S. (1995) "Technology Systems and Technology Policy in an Evolutionary Framework," *Cambridge Journal of Economics* 19: 25–46.

Nelson, Richard R. and Wright, Gavin (1992) "The Rise and Fall of American Technological Leadership: The Postwar Era in Historical Perspective," *Journal of Economic Literature* 30(4): 1931–64.

Porter, Michael (1990) *The Competitive Advantage of Nations*, London: Macmillan.

JAMES JUNIPER

# secular crisis

The foundation of Marx's social and political philosophy is his view of CAPITALISM as a historical, time-bound system. A long social evolution created the preconditions for capitalism to exist. Capitalism in turn becomes increasingly contradictory and crisis-laden as it matures, and it sets the stage for its own replacement by higher forms more suited to continuing human development (see SOCIALISM AND COMMUNISM). The theory of secular (meaning long-term, or tendential) crisis of capitalism is therefore at the heart of Marxist political economy. It is all the more surprising that so little attention has been paid to the explicit elaboration of this theory.

What, then, prevents capitalism from going on forever? In the classical texts, the primordial answer focuses on conflict between the social classes. The bourgeoisie of the *Communist Manifesto* (Marx and Engels 1848) creates its own gravediggers in the form of the proletariat in their in-built struggle to accumulate capital. To industrialize, concentrate, centralize and expand, capitalists create a property-less working class, shaped by its growing numbers, increasing misery and collective experience in production and struggle. The workers are seen as the agent both able and willing to overthrow their oppressors. In this vision, there is no separation between objective tendency and political consciousness; both are embedded in the evolution of the major socioeconomic classes.

A famous passage from Volume 1 of *Das Kapital* reads:

> Along with the constantly diminishing number of the magnates of capital, who usurp and monopolise all advantages of this process of transformation, grows the mass of misery, oppression, slavery, degradation,

exploitation; but with this too grows the revolt of the working-class, a class always increasing in numbers, and disciplined, united, organised by the very mechanism of the process of capitalist production itself. The monopoly of capital becomes a fetter upon the mode of production, which has sprung up and flourished along with, and under it. Centralisation of the means of production and socialisation of labour at last reach a point where they become incompatible with their capitalist integument. This integument is burst asunder. The knell of capitalist private property sounds. The expropriator is expropriated.

(Marx 1867: 836–7)

This vision is, however, vulnerable: there appears to be no reason why capital ACCUMULATION, involving as it does technical change and ECONOMIC GROWTH, cannot lead, given sufficient working-class pressure, to higher living standards and social differentiation, such that the revolutionary will of the proletariat is blunted.

Such considerations apparently motivated Marx's investigations into the FALLING RATE OF PROFIT TENDENCY. A falling rate of profit would certainly qualify as a basis for secular capitalist crisis. This notion, however, has been mired in controversy ever since the publication of Volume 3 of *Das Kapital*. The theory underlying it is by no means certain; the empirical evidence is inconclusive and the link between a falling rate of profit and crisis has not been adequately developed. There is a clear need for a fresh approach to the theory of long-term tendencies in capitalist accumulation.

A general model of secular crisis may be built up out of three elements: immanent critical tendencies, barriers and sites (see Laibman 1997). Crisis is manifest at multiple sites. Four such sites may be identified: the workplace, consumption, central and financial sites. At each site, a critical tendency is at work, and barriers are in place. The barriers generate chronic or "nonreproductive" crisis when encountered. Chronic crisis points at one site may define barriers at another site. Barriers may thus be fundamental (not determined at other sites and therefore not capable of further causal analysis), or derivative.

## Workplace site

In the capitalist workplace, continual struggle occurs over authority, discipline, and the pace of work. Top management has a single, central problem: to provide incentive, while maintaining control. The composite variable describing a top management strategy is the degree to which both creative and managerial functions are exercised at lower levels of the hierarchy of command: this can be called the devolution ratio. At a given level of the real wage rate, there is a range of devolution possibilities, high enough to ensure adequate incentive in the modern, high-tech environment, but low enough so that dominant capitalist authority is not called into question. As the wage rises, however, the minimum devolution ratio consistent with sufficient workplace incentive rises; and the maximum ratio consistent with maintaining authority falls.

These, then, are the barriers associated with the workplace site: an incentive floor that rises and a control ceiling that falls, as the real wage rate rises. The rising real wage rate is the critical tendency (it is actually a derivative critical tendency, driven by rising productivity). The barriers meet at a single devolution ratio and a maximum real wage rate. At this point, incentive and control become completely incompatible within the antagonistic limitations of the capitalist workplace. The maximum real wage rate becomes a derivative barrier at the central site. Although this may seem contrary to Marx's "increasing misery" doctrine, rising real wages appear here as a critical (crisis-inducing) process, linked to power relationships between capital and labor (see EFFICIENCY WAGES).

## Consumption site

This centers on the share of profits in net output (the profit share). Profits are either consumed or saved and invested (saving out of wages being negligible). The profit share is thus the sum of the capitalist consumption share and the investment share (or investment/income ratio). Each of these components has a maximum, which constitutes a barrier in the sense of the term used here. The conspicuous and luxury consumption of capitalists and their functionaries cannot rise above a certain critical level without provoking a crisis of legitimacy. After all, working people can tolerate the sight of only so many stretch limos without feeling a sense of revulsion requiring political action. At the same time, the investment share finds an upper limit at the point where a cyclical realization crisis occurs; consumption is limited, and investment demand collapses due to the perception of constricted markets. The critical tendency is the rising profit share, which reduces the region of mobility between the maximum consumption share and the maximum investment share. The sum of the two maxima determines a maximum profit share, which is a derivative barrier at the central site.

## Central site

The central site, then, has two barriers: the maximum real wage rate and the maximum profit share, determined at the workplace and consumption sites, respectively. The critical tendency is rising PRODUCTIVITY of labor, or output per unit of labor. This tendency is of course inherent in capitalist competition; its ubiquitous presence has never been doubted theoretically or questioned on empirical grounds. As productivity rises, either the profit share or the real wage rate or both must rise. Eventually, the two barriers – the maxima of the profit share and real wage rate – must be encountered simultaneously, implying both workplace (discipline) and consumption (legitimation, realization) crisis.

## Financial site

The maximum profit share also appears as a derivative barrier at the financial site. The other barrier at this site is the minimum rate of profit at or below which chronic (non-repro-ductive) financial instability sets in. The critical tendency at this site is the controversial rise in the ratio of the value of the capital stock to current labor (the organic composition of capital), which can be shown to be equivalent to the (physical) capital to net output ratio. If capitalism-driven technical change raises this ratio, the profit rate and profit share are pushed toward their barrier levels (minimum and maximum, respectively). This is where the long-debated falling rate of profit tendency retains its significance.

The theory of the sites, tendencies and barriers requires much further development. The challenge is to build into the theory all of the many interactions among these elements, without losing determinacy and the ability to prioritize. But capitalism itself is like that: it is a complex process occurring at multiple sites, which are irreducibly distinct, yet interrelated. The model suggests ways of interpreting the experiences of different countries. A country may have a tendency to push toward one sort of barrier, and therefore crisis, instead of another. It also urges us to look for fruitful interchange among investigators working at the various sites: labor process theory, the financial sector, demand-limited accumulation, legitimation and so on.

Finally, the multiform quality of the process described serves as protection against any simple unilinear or overly determinist understanding of capitalist crisis. Ever-increasing human possibilities press in many ways against a system based on private accumulation and social irresponsibility. Moreover, the ultimate source of all the barriers lies in the question "How much will the working class tolerate?". This does not prevent us from tracing objective tendencies in capitalist development that force the working class to tolerate more and more as time passes.

## See also:

capitalist breakdown debate; contradictions

## Selected references

Laibman, David (1992) *Value, Technical Change and Crisis: Explorations in Marxist Economic Theory*, Armonk, NY: M.E. Sharpe.

—— (1997) *Capitalist Macrodynamics: A Systematic Introduction*, London: Macmillan.

Marx, Karl (1867) *Das Kapital*, vol. 1, published as *Capital, Volume I*, Chicago, Charles H. Kerr & Company, 1906.

Marx, Karl and Engels, Friedrich (1847–48) *The Communist Manifesto*, published in *The Birth of the Communist Manifesto*, ed. Dirk J. Struik, New York: International Publishers, 1971.

DAVID LAIBMAN

# segmented and dual labor markets

## Definition of segmentation

Labor market segmentation refers to the persistence of different rewards for workers with comparable skills and abilities, independently of their preferences for job characteristics. Accordingly, a labor market is segmented if observed differences in wages and other job rewards cannot be fully explained by differences in workers' performance traits or in their job preferences. Juxtaposed with this outcomes-based definition, many authors also explain it with reference to "segments" or parts of the labor market structure with distinct characteristics or behavioral rules (e.g. the informal sector).

## Duality

A dual labor market is the simplest variant of segmentation. Critical to labor market duality is the notion of segmentation, not the number of segments. The stylized facts of segmentation are usually described in terms of "duality." Jobs in the primary segment are characterized by high wages, good working conditions, stable employment, long tenure and opportunities for advancement into higher-paying positions, while jobs in the secondary segment have the opposite characteristics. The process of WAGE DETERMINATION differs across segments. The pricing and allocation of primary jobs are governed by administrative rules and procedures within the firm – the INTERNAL LABOR MARKETS – such as the attachment of wages to jobs, established career ladders, and the hiring of outsiders only for port-of-entry positions.

It is also accepted that there exists persistent involuntary unemployment (or non-market-clearing), that primary jobs are rationed and that their occupants enjoy rents (that is, rewards in excess of their opportunity wage). The secondary segment is composed disproportionately of women, blacks and other disadvantaged groups. It is also marked by pervasive underemployment, because workers who could just as easily be trained for primary jobs are confined to secondary jobs. Relevant to both segments is the endogenous formation of tastes, as in the case of the negative feedback effects of unstable secondary jobs on the attitudes and motivations of their occupants.

## History and origins

The segmented labor market debate can be traced back to distinguished political economists beginning with Adam Smith, whose theory of the equalization of net advantage across jobs in *The Wealth of Nations* is now considered the fundamental market equilibrium construct in mainstream labor economics. He stipulated that, through competition, wages perform the role of equalizing net, monetary and nonmonetary, advantage across jobs with different nonwage characteristics. John Stuart Mill's response in his *Principles of Political Economy* is equally important as a precursor of the institutionalist challenge to neoclassical orthodoxy. He contended that wage differentials are generally noncompensating in character: "the really repulsive labors, instead of being better paid than others, are almost invariably paid worst of all, because performed by those who have no choice" (1848:

388). He also noted the limited mobility between noncompeting occupational groups, each tending to recruit from its offspring, resulting in inter-group wage differentials unrelated to group differences in skills and abilities.

In its current form, the segmented labor market literature emerged from the post-war institutionalist tradition in labor economics, which drew attention to the "balkanization of labor markets," due to Clark Kerr, and the presence of job clusters and wage contours in wage determination. Neoclassical theory at the time ruled out the existence of segmentation, treating the prediction of compensating differentials as deliberately beyond question. With the failure of mainstream economics and HUMAN CAPITAL theory in particular to explain the persistence of low pay and high unemployment among disadvantaged groups, the 1960s witnessed the first wave of research on segmented labor markets directed at understanding the problems of black workers in US urban ghettos.

Drawing on case studies, surveys, open-ended interviews and other participant--observer techniques, and on the historical and qualitative aspects of labor markets, early segmented labor market research explained pay inequalities in terms of three characteristics (Doeringer and Piore 1971):

- skill specificity, with wage premiums being used to reduce employee turnover;
- product markets and technology, with jobs in the lower tier of the primary segment being based on capital intensive technology catering to products with stable demand; and jobs in the secondary segment and the upper tier of the primary segment being based on labor intensive techniques for products with unstable demand patterns;
- social class, with the labor supply to each segment being rooted in different subcultures. The lower class is hired for secondary jobs, the working class being drawn into lower-tier primary jobs, and the middle class being recruited for the upper tier.

Secondary workers were deemed unable to get primary jobs due to their unstable work patterns and high turnover rates. These behavioral traits are not intrinsic to workers, but are, instead, acquired unwittingly due to the scarring effect of secondary jobs on the attitudes and work habits of their occupants.

## Other strands of segmentation theory

Several other strands of segmented labor market research can be identified, all of which reject the neoclassical position of perfectly compensating wage differentials. The radical strand of segmented labor market research emphasizes employer and managerial strategies for differentiating between groups of workers through control of the LABOR PROCESS (Edwards et al. 1975). A Kaleckian strand characterizes the US economy as a dual structure with a core of oligopolistic firms with high productivity, high profitability, capital-intensive techniques and trade unions, and a competitive periphery of small firms with low productivity, low profitability, labor-intensive techniques and little unionization. The low productivity of peripheral firms arose from their inability to invest in improved technology, given their low profitability and lack of product market power. Yet another connected strand emerged from the post-Keynesian literature, emphasizing the non-market nature of labor transactions and the macroeconomic and social policy implications of segmentation (see Seccareccia 1991).

Segmented labor market research uncovered a wealth of stylized facts about institutional and qualitative aspects of labor markets, many of which were either unexplained or at odds with the predictions of neoclassical theory. With the exception of the work of Edwards et al., the first wave of the segmented labor market literature was open to mainstream criticism that it was lacking theoretical foundations, particularly for not explaining how segmented labor markets arise from individual or collective behaviors. Segmented labor market research had not clearly demonstrated why firms do not replace primary jobs with secondary jobs (or unemployed workers) if that reduces unit labor costs or why firms cannot otherwise extract the job rents from workers in the presence of excess labor supply.

New institutionalism provided a neoclassical rebuttal to segmented labor market research (see INSTITUTIONALISM: OLD AND NEW). Proponents such as Oliver Williamson put forth efficiency explanations for several features of INTERNAL LABOR MARKETS, arguing that if jobs are idiosyncratic, perfect competition no longer holds, giving rise to problems of bilateral monopoly. In this context, stylized facts such as collective bargaining agreements, internal promotion ladders, seniority provisions and the attachment of wages to jobs rather than to workers, may result in the economization of monitoring activities and on TRANSACTION COSTS resulting from workers' opportunistic behavior. Yet, this approach failed to recognize, among other things, the presence of workers' market power and fairness considerations in the development of segmented labor market institutions and practices. It is also unclear whether these efficiency explanations allow for workers to earn rents in selected jobs.

## Second wave of segmentation literature

The second wave of segmented labor market research has devoted more attention to theoretical issues. Product market conditions remain central. For instance, high fixed cost/low variable cost TECHNOLOGY caters to the stable portion of product demand, and low fixed cost/high variable cost technology responds to the unpredictable component of demand. However, recent segmented labor market research emphasizes the interaction and mutual conditioning in historical time of supply and demand determinants of labor market outcomes. Thus, in explaining the relative autonomy of social reproduction, Humphries and Rubery (1984) argue that, rather than being exogenous, current gender differences in labor supply behavior are more plausibly the product of family organization, which is itself the product of historical gender differences in earning opportunities. The same interaction

between supply and demand parameters, including social and political factors, led Wilkinson (1983) to underline the need for a dynamic and interactive analysis to take account of the historically contingent nature of labor market outcomes.

Recent developments in mainstream labor economics made a significant contribution to the microfoundations of segmented labor markets. EFFICIENCY WAGES models explain why firms may find it unprofitable to cut wages when they knowingly confront an excess supply of qualified labor. These (mainly neoclassical) models indicate that firms may pay above market-clearing wages in order to minimize turnover costs or to minimize the labor cost per unit of work effort elicited (e.g. Bulow and Summers 1986). Insider–outsider models attempt to explain how turnover costs – costs of replacing an incumbent (insider) with an unemployed worker (outsider) – enable workers to gain the labor market power required to extract job rents (Lindbeck and Snower 1988). These costs may be production-related when due to hiring, screening, training, and negotiation activities; or rent-related when due to statutory provisions (such as severance pay), or to workers' own rent-generating activities such as strikes.

However, both efficiency wage and insider–outsider (neoclassical) models do not *per se* provide any rationale for the groups of workers found in the primary and secondary segments. Nor can they generally explain why some workers can earn rents in equilibrium, because firms can in theory devise more sophisticated employment contracts – such as entrance fees, posting performance bonds, or deferred compensation schemes – to extract the job rents from applicants. This suggests that both types of models require an infusion of institutionalist considerations, such as wage contract norms or fairness rules, in order to explain why some firms may not have access to the type of employment contracts which extract all workers' rents.

## Conclusion

Despite these neoclassical segmented labor market models, institutional research on segmented labor markets will continue to make significant contributions. This is because it provides a coherent alternative to the methodology of neoclassical labor economics, which is based on the unquestioned tenets of utility maximization and methodological individualism and whose implications are derived through deduction and appraised using the criteria of predictive instrumentalism. In contrast, institutional segmented labor market methodology is based on critical realism, which is predicated on a search for, and understanding of, the causal mechanisms responsible for generating the observed phenomena of interest (Iacobacci 1991).

## See also:

labor market discrimination; labor markets and market power; social structures of accumulation

## Selected references

Bulow J.I. and Summers, L.H. (1986) "A Theory of Dual Labor Markets with Application to Industrial Policy, Discrimination and Keynesian Unemployment," *Journal of Labor Economics* 4.

Doeringer, P. and Piore, M.J. (1971) *Internal Labor Markets and Manpower Analysis*, Lexington, MA: Heath/Lexington Books.

Edwards, R.C., Reich, M. and Gordon, D.M. (1975) *Labor Market Segmentation*, Lexington, MA: D.C. Heath and Company.

Humphries, J. and Rubery, J. (1984) "The Reconstitution of the Supply-Side of the Labor Market: the Relative Autonomy of Social Reproduction," *Cambridge Journal of Economics* 8.

Iacobacci, M. (1991) "The Institutionalist Approach to Segmented Labor Markets: A Realist Interpretation," paper presented at the 1991 Annual Meeting of the European Association of Evolutionary Political Economy, Vienna.

Lindbeck, A. and Snower, D.J. (1988) *The Insider–Outsider Theory of Employment and Unemployment*, Cambridge, MA: MIT Press.

Seccareccia, M. (1991) "An Alternative to Labor-Market Orthodoxy: The Post-Keynesian Institutionalist Policy View," *Review of Political Economy* 3(1).

Wilkinson, F. (1983) "Productive Systems," *Cambridge Journal of Economics* 7.

MARIO IACOBACCI

# sexuality

## Introduction

An analysis of sexuality, based in Marxist-feminist economic theory, builds on the recognition that individuals are constructed by the economic and social relationships that they enter into with other members of their society. This contrasts sharply with a neoclassical economic analysis, which explains MARRIAGE and sexuality as the result of biological and preference differences between utility-maximizing individuals (Becker 1991; Posner 1992). Thus, Marxist-feminist theory rejects biological explanations of sexual desire, behavior and identity. Sexuality is neither genetically/naturally determined, nor a purely self-conscious moral choice. Social institutions and practices not only direct and restrict one's sexual behavior, but give this behavior its content and meaning. Theorizing about sexuality involves studying the social construction of a constellation of possible sexual behaviors at a particular place and time.

Thus, neither heterosexuality nor homosexuality is either "natural" or universal; both are in large measure socially produced. Even if biologists were able to identify a genetic marker which appeared to be correlated with homosexual behavior of some sort (which they have not), this marker could not in any way be understood to determine or create homosexuality as a culturally specific set of social concepts and practices (see CULTURE).

The growth of the gay liberation and feminist movements in the West in the 1970s engendered the development of the field of lesbian and gay history. The earliest studies were essentially searches for the lesbians and gays that had been "hidden from history," as one collection called itself. However, as the field developed breadth and sophistication, the rising social constructionist school criticized such studies as "essentialist" for incorrectly positing a cross-historical lesbian or gay identity. Indeed, historians of sexuality have criticized the very idea of "gay history," since the concepts which construct sexuality have varied so greatly across time.

## Absence of universals

There are no universals about human sexuality that hold true for all time periods and societies. For example, in the United States, sexual practices have changed very rapidly over the past 150 years, with capitalist development. The concepts of heterosexual and homosexual persons – that is, sexuality as an identity – did not arise until the early twentieth century. Before then, it was considered natural for individuals to be sexually attracted to members of the same sex, but sinful for them to indulge these attractions.

Neither is homophobia/heterosexism – prejudice against and fear of homosexuals/homosexual behavior – a universal. Consider, for example, the oft-admired Greeks, who viewed man–boy love (including sex) as one of the highest forms of love; or consider certain Native American nations, including the Kaska and Navajo, in which lesbians were highly valued (Amott and Matthaei 1996: 37). Finally, there is no unambiguous one-to-one correspondence between the economic system which characterizes a society and its sexual practices; compare the tolerance for homosexuality of the Netherlands with the repression presently practiced in Great Britain. These historical and cross-cultural differences make any historical study of sexuality (or indeed, of any social

construct, be it the family, gender or whatever) difficult.

Sexuality, even within a particular historical period and place, varies across race-ethnicity, GENDER and CLASS. A person's sexuality is not a discrete entity, taking the same form regardless of the gender, class or race-ethnicity it is combined with. The interconnections between sexuality and gender are viewed, in most societies, as self-evident; indeed few would presume to discuss sexuality without specifying the genders of the participants. However, race-ethnicity and class also differentiate sexuality in important ways. For example, in the nineteenth-century United States, white middle- and upper-class women were constructed as relatively asexual, endangered by the lust of black men (for which the latter were lynched), while free black women, viewed by the dominant white society as oversexed and "loose," were not allowed to protest against their rape by white men (Hooks 1981: ch. 2).

## Role of economic institutions

Economic institutions have played an important role in the social construction of family and sexuality. In particular, the organization of work into men's and women's work – the gender division of labor – makes the sexes into genders that need the "opposite sex" to be complete, and as such underlies heterosexual marriage and sexuality. This division of labor is, however, only one part of the social construction of gender and sexuality, which begins at birth with sex role socialization, such that gender identities are usually firmly established before adulthood. The gender division of labor plays a key role in constructing gender identity and marriage, because preparation for and involvement in different and complementary work activities makes the sexes into different and complementary genders.

Thus, an essential part of gender identity has been the social requirement to marry and form a family with a member of the opposite sex and gender. Women marry only men, and men only women. The gender division of labor has provided much of the incentive for marriage, as well as the "glue" keeping these marriages together, since it makes the genders economically and socially complementary and in need of one another. In this way, gender and the sexual division of labor which accompanies it can be seen as involving "compulsory heterosexuality," i.e. as forcing males and females to marry and procreate with one another (Rich 1980). Sexuality within heterosexual marriage can have the result of biological procreation, and this procreation is equated with the social activities of mothering and fathering.

## Sexual and gender relationships

So strong are the social constructs of gender that those few who, for a variety of reasons, take on the gender role of the opposite sex – i.e. masculine females or feminine males – usually take on the sexuality associated with that gender. That is, they form heterogenderal (cross-gender) but homosexual (same-sex) relationships: a masculine female marries a feminine female, or an effeminate male would be attracted to a masculine male. Much homosexuality thus takes a heterogenderal form.

While the gender division of labor creates a basis for heterosexuality within marriage, sexuality is rarely restricted completely to marriage, or to heterosexual relations. For example, the construction of sexuality among the white middle classes in the US and Europe in the nineteenth century restricted married women's participation in sexuality, even with their husbands, because of the lack of birth control, risks of venereal disease and conception of women as sexless. At the same time, a "double standard" for men and women and the concentration of income in the hands of men meant that extra-marital sex thrived for men, through the purchase of the services of both female and male prostitutes.

The extreme restriction on women's economic activities, especially their exclusion from living wage jobs, caused a number of females to choose to "pass" as men in order to be able to gain economic independence. Such "passing" (male) women often married other (female)

women. Further, the chasm between the sexes created by the gender division of labor made same-sex, homo-emotional and homosexual relationships more intimate and satisfying for many, and in some cases brought the construction of same-sex relationships and households, such as "Boston marriages" between professional women.

## Conclusion

Married women's increasing entrance into the paid labor force in many countries is bringing a partial breakdown of gender division of labor in the family and in the workplace, and thus of gender roles. Feminist and "lesbigay" movements have actively taken up the task of criticizing these institutions as sexist and heterosexist. Some put forward notions of marriage as a partnership between similar and equal adults, of the same or opposite sexes.

## See also:

class structures of households; feminist political economy: major contemporary themes; household labor; patriarchy; race, ethnicity, gender and class; social structure of accumulation: family

## Selected references

Amott, Teresa and Matthaei, Julie (1996) *Race, Gender and Work: A Multicultural Economic History of Women in the United States*, Boston: South End.
Becker, Gary (1991) *A Treatise on the Family*, Cambridge, MA: Harvard University Press.
Duberman, Martin, Vicinus, Martha and Chauncey, George (eds) (1989) *Hidden from History: Reclaiming the Gay and Lesbian Past*, New York: Penguin Books.
Escoffier, Jeffrey (1992) "Generations and Paradigms: Mainstreams in Lesbian and Gay Studies," in Henry Minton (ed.), *Gay and Lesbian Studies*, New York: Haworth Press, 7–88.
Gottlieb, Rhonda (1984) "The Political Econ-

omy of Sexuality," *Review of Radical Political Economics* 16: 143–66.

Hooks, Bell (1981) *Ain't I A Woman: Black Women and Feminism*, Boston: South End Press.

Matthaei, Julie (1995) "The Sexual Division of Labor, Sexuality, and Lesbian/Gay Liberation," *Review of Radical Political Economics* 27(2): 1–37.

Posner, Richard A. (1992) *Sex and Reason*, Cambridge, MA: Harvard University Press.

Rich, Adrienne (1980) "Compulsory Heterosexuality and the Lesbian Existence," *Signs: A Journal of Women in Culture and Society* 5(4): 631–60.

Weeks, Jeffrey (1991) *Against Nature: Essays on History, Sexuality and Identity*, London: Rivers Oram Press.

JULIE MATTHAEI

# short-run cost curves

The behavior of short-run costs has long been of interest to economists. It is fair to say, however, that this interest lies not so much in the behavior of costs *per se*, but in their immediate connection with theories of the firm and PRICING and, ultimately, the perception of the role of theory and view of the world held by the economist. It is in this context that the empirical behavior of short-run costs is examined.

## Textbook and empirical approaches

The textbook presentation of cost behavior is typically an assumption of rising short-run marginal costs. It follows that average variable costs must eventually rise and that average total costs must be U-shaped once the spreading of overheads is allowed for. Rising marginal costs and associated average cost behavior are essential to the theory of perfect competition. This theory is the "epistemic ideal" of NEO-CLASSICAL ECONOMICS. Rising marginal costs, combined with assumptions such as fully informed optimizing atomistic agents, homo-genous products and so on produce a determinate solution to firm size when price-taking firms face a horizontal demand curve.

Historically, various theorists have produced more realistic notions of cost behavior and the firm in rejecting this deductive emphasis in theory. With similar conclusions to Hall and Hitch's seminal investigation into pricing, and based on case studies, Andrews (1949) argues that average direct costs, and hence marginal costs, are constant over the relevant range of output. Prices are set by applying a mark up to average variable costs. The mark-up includes allowances for overheads and profits calculated on the basis of the firm operating at a normal, standard, or long run, level of output. The mark-up is thus set with the expectation of meeting the long-run threat of competition.

Such work has spawned a large empirical literature examining cost behavior. There are, of course, countless problems with all empirical work. Case study research is always open to difficulties of interpretation. Econometric work is also problematical. Joel Dean pioneered econometric work in examining a furniture factory, a leather belt factory and a large department store. In the latter case, Dean found that both linear and non-linear curves could be fitted to the data, although the non-linearities were small. The problem is finding an example in which output varies over sufficiently large ranges for changes in productivity to occur, yet at the same time leaving products and technology unchanged. This is notwithstanding problems of cost definition and measurement. In essence, the "logical" emphasis of neoclassical work belies its applicability. Not surprisingly, the evidence remains ambiguous.

Mansfield's (1994) survey of the literature is, however, not unrepresentative of the traditional balance of opinion. He argues, in light of the problems above, that marginal costs, and hence average variable costs, are constant over the relevant range of output. This is despite the implied defense of the traditional theoretical presentation of costs offered by Friedman's famous essay in 1953 on positive economics. Friedman implies that the actual behavior of costs is irrelevant in testing the theory's general predictions about price behavior (see NORMATIVE AND POSITIVE ECONOMICS).

As a direct challenge to the deductive emphasis of textbook theory, therefore, a "microeconomic–neoclassical" synthesis has emerged. Once average direct costs are constant they are equivalent to constant marginal costs and, as a result, one can formally demonstrate the logical equivalence of pricing by setting a mark-up on constant average variable costs, and pricing through maximizing profits by equating marginal revenue and costs. One cannot dispute this logical equivalence and, conventionally, managerial economics textbooks (Douglas 1992) and microeconomics textbooks (Mansfield 1994) conflate the two pricing explanations.

## Post-Keynesian mark-up approaches

These empirical findings and inductively driven theoretical developments have also been capitalized on in post-Keynesian political economy. Kalecki, Kaldor and Eichner each develop pricing theories which share the view that prices are determined as a mark-up on constant average direct costs. They do differ in some respects, for example, in the explicit references to types of costs marked up and the basis by which firms identify their output level. In this context, Lee (1986), as the first in a number of pieces of work on pricing and costs, has added a new twist to the debate.

Lee cites a large number of studies on actual cost behavior to suggest that, at both the level of plants and across plants in multi-plant firms, average direct costs will not necessarily be constant. One can view Lee's work as stemming from concern that post-Keynesian and neoclassical work can be conflated in the light of the neoclassical–microeconomic synthesis. Early replies to Lee's work are offered by Eichner (1986) and Yordon (1987). Eichner suggests that Lee's evidence does not preclude the researcher from presenting average direct costs as constant. The researcher may wish to do this to abstract from technical progress to

permit the use of input–output analysis and constant returns to scale.

Yordon essentially stresses that the evidence is against average direct costs increasing. However, it is clear that these criticisms do not directly confront the thrust of Lee's argument, which is that it is misleading in general to assume that average direct costs are constant. More recently, Lee (1994) argues that theories which appear to invoke a mark-up on constant average direct costs alone should be avoided by post-Keynesians in favor of normal-cost pricing as presented by Hall and Hitch and by Andrews.

This precludes the possibility of the microeconomic–neoclassical synthesis mentioned above in explicitly allowing for overheads in pricing decisions, thus making the post-Keynesian presentation of pricing more representationally accurate. An additional advantage is that, for any given mark-up, the normal-cost pricing procedure, by making prices independent of current costs, helps to explain the relative insensitivity of prices to changes in demand without relying on the assumption that firms face constant average direct costs. As Downward et al. (1996) have recently pointed out, however, the distinctions drawn by Lee are more apparent than real.

## Conclusion

The empirical shape of average direct costs is, thus, both a thorny and important issue. This is particularly so for political economists trying to emphasize the descriptive and explanatory relevance of their theories. In terms of evaluating the evidence on average direct costs in the context of political economy, as a problem of induction, the issue will not be resolved by appeal to the number of observed cases of cost behavior. It is clear that a variety of possibilities of cost behavior exist at the microeconomic level.

The implications of this hinge on the purported use of theory. On the one hand, for macroeconomic analysis, the simplification of constant average direct costs may be, to all intents and purposes, innocuous. On the other hand, in conceptualizing the microeconomic processes underlying pricing, attention should be paid to average direct costs not always being constant.

Having said this, attention should also be paid to the other processes involved in pricing. For example, prices changing more in response to cost changes than demand changes – as emphasized in the post Keynesian literature – can rely on prices being set with reference to current costs as in the normal cost approach. Mark-ups should be recognized as a behavioral parameter in their own right. They may be constrained, for example, by the desire for price stability as a normal objective of business as emphasized by Andrews and by Hall and Hitch. This means that much of the concern over specifying the "correct" representation of actual cost behavior is misplaced.

## See also:

corporate objectives; increasing returns to scale; supply and demand: microeconomic; time

## Selected references

Andrews, P.W.S. (1949) *Manufacturing Business*, London: Macmillan.

Douglas, E.J. (1992) *Managerial Economics*, London: Prentice-Hall.

Downward, P.M., Lavoie, M. and Reynolds, P.J. (1996) "Realism, Simulations and Post Keynesian Pricing Models," *Review of Political Economy* 8(9): 427–32.

Eichner, A.S. (1986) "A Comment on Post Keynesian View of Average Direct Costs," *Journal of Post Keynesian Economics* 9.

Lee, F.S. (1986) "Post Keynesian View of Average Direct Costs: A Critical Evaluation of the Theory and the Empirical Evidence," *Journal of Post Keynesian Economics* 8(3): 400–24.

—— (1994) "From Post Keynesian to Historical Price Theory, Part 1: Facts, Theory and Empirically Grounded Pricing Model," *Review of Political Economy* 6(3): 303–6.

Mansfield, E. (1994) *Applied Microeconomics*, London: Norton.

Yordon, W.J. (1987) "Evidence Against Diminishing Returns in Manufacturing and Comments on Short-Run Models of Price-Output Behavior," *Journal of Post Keynesian Economics* 9(4): 593–603.

PAUL DOWNWARD

# slavery

Slavery as a status and consequently as an institution has existed in many societies in different times and places (see Patterson 1982). Political economy has, however, generally been concerned with slavery not as a status but primarily as it has existed as a MODE OF PRODUCTION AND SOCIAL FORMATION. We find many concrete examples of slavery and slave societies in history.

MARX makes frequent reference to slavery in his writings, but it is usually mentioned along with other forms of unfree labor (as in the *Grundrisse* (1857–8)) or in drawing a contrast between slave labor and wage labor. Nevertheless, Marx does identify the relationship between slave and slaveholder as a CLASS relationship and refers to Greek and Roman antiquity as slave economies.

Engels's discussion of slavery is more direct and ascribes to slavery a greater importance in the history of civilization:

> With slavery, which reached its fullest development in civilization, came the first great cleavage of society into an exploiting and exploited class. This cleavage has continued during the whole period of civilisation. Slavery was the first form of exploitation, peculiar to the world of antiquity; it was followed by serfdom in the Middle Ages, and by wage labour in modern times. These are the three great forms of servitude, characteristic of the three great epochs of civilisation; open, and, latterly, disguised slavery, are its steady companions.

(Engels 1884: 223)

Engels had earlier in the same work compared slavery's role in the ancient world to Marx's analysis of CAPITALISM in the modern world. Forced slave labor "formed the basis on which the superstructure of all society was reared" (Engels 1884: 227).

## Slave mode of production

The question of conceptualizing the slave mode of production has been taken up most explicitly by Hindess and Hirst (1975). They identify slavery with chattel slavery, which they define as "a form of bondage in which human beings are a form of property and in which the owner has all of the rights of property over the slave" (1975: 110). They argue that the developed form of chattel slavery presupposes the existence of private property as a general institution, which is supported by the legal and repressive apparatus of the state.

The key aspect of property which pertains to the slave is his/her alienability (see ALIENATION). The slave can be sold and ownership transferred from one person to another. In consequence of this, the slave is deprived of all legal ties, both to the larger community and to kin, away from whom he or she may be sold. The slave was always a deracinated outsider, originating outside the society in which he or she was enslaved, and denied the most elementary of social bonds (Finley 1980: 75).

The Roman division of forms of property into *instrumentum mutum*, *instrumentum semivocale* and *instrumentum vocale* captures the contradictory character of slave status. On the one hand, the slave is an *instrumentum*, a mere property. In some ways the slave is the paradigmatic property, as it is only in comparison to the slave that objects are mute. Yet it is the human attributes of the slave, understanding, judgment and so on, which make the slave valuable.

The existence of property in slaves is insufficient to constitute a slave mode of production. In a slave mode of production, the acquisition of slaves is made with a view to their potential for productive activity. Crucially, slaveholders must also be able to access the means of production, raw materials and sustenance for the slaves. The slaveholder must be able to combine his slaves with the other elements of the production process.

## Necessary and surplus labor

By virtue of ownership of the direct producers, the entire product of the slave laborer falls to the slaveholder. "The master owns the product of the slave's labour just as he owns the slave" (Hindess and Hirst 1975: 127). While there is no obvious distinction between the labor necessary to reproduce the slave and the surplus labor which ultimately accrues to the slaveholder, such a division must be made when a part of the slave's labor or its equivalent is returned to the slave as subsistence. In this way, it is the legal relation of ownership which constitutes the specific form in which surplus labor is extracted from slaves as individuals and as a class. It is this particular process of EXPLOITATION which constitutes both slaves and slaveholders as classes in the Marxist sense.

The extraction of surplus labor from the slave is rendered problematic because the slave has value both as a commodity and as a direct producer. Even in the absence of productive work, the slave retains value through his potential sale. This sale value must be conserved through the provision to the slave of the means of subsistence. Thus, the slave is not forced to labor in order to reproduce himself. The slave must be compelled to work through IDEOLOGY, threat of force or incentives. In addition, the slave is separated from the means of production. He cannot own them and must have them provided by the slaveholder (Hindess and Hirst 1975: 129–34).

## Division of labor and market

Because the slave must be combined with the means of production, and because the slave is not compelled to work through physical necessity, the slave must be closely supervised. The necessity of such detailed supervision directs the LABOR PROCESS towards simple cooperation. Such cooperation involves the concentration of the slaves in a single area, and a minimal division of labor. Working slaves in gangs on single tasks minimizes the cost of supervision. Supervision under these conditions leads to the emergence of a third class between slaves and slaveholders, that of overseers and other functionaries (Hindess and Hirst 1975: 134–39).

Economic institutions which are necessary to slave production prominently include the slave market. The alienability of slaves implies the existence of markets where slaves can be bought and sold. The distribution of labor power to the different units of production is then mediated by this market. Slaves can be most cheaply provided to this market through capture outside of the mode of production, although "slave breeding" remains as a more expensive and less flexible alternative.

While it does not strictly follow that commodity markets in slaves must imply the production of commodities for market exchange, the creation of the preconditions of the one will also create the preconditions for the other. Indeed, the purchasing power necessary to acquire slaves on the market will most likely come from the exchange of commodities. Because of problems in the generation of balanced demand for both consumer and producer goods, commodity producing slave societies find it easier to reproduce themselves in trade with societies based on other forms of production (Hindess and Hirst 1975: 144–8)

## Slave societies in history

The institution of slavery and the acquisition of slaves for the purpose of production has been widespread in human societies. Identifying a slave society, containing within it the fullest development of the slave mode of production, involves identifying a social formation within which the slave mode of production is dominant (Anderson 1974: 22). De Ste. Croix (1981) takes up this question in *The Class Struggle in the Ancient World*. He argues that it is correct to speak of a slave economy when slavery is the main way in which the dominant propertied

classes obtain the fruits of surplus labor. This is the case regardless of what fraction of the total share of production is due to slave labor (1981: 52).

Applying something like this criterion, Anderson (1974: 21) finds "the slave mode of production was the decisive invention of the Graeco-Roman world, which provided the ultimate basis for its accomplishments and its eclipse." He finds that slavery was "massive and general" during the great classical epochs, Greece in the fifth and fourth centuries BC and Rome from the second century BC to the second century AD.

Finley (1980: 9) identifies just a further three instances of slave societies. These were the slave economies of the New World. They included northern Brazil in the colonial era, the colonial Caribbean basin (see WILLIAMS–RODNEY THESIS), and the slaveowning South of the United States prior to the Civil War. Interestingly, Barbara Solow (1987) identifies a direct connection between the slavery of antiquity and New World slavery. After the fall of the Roman empire, slavery persisted in the Mediterranean world. Significantly, it became the basis for sugar plantations organized in the Levant by Italian colonists following the Crusades. This "slave–sugar complex" spread from East to West and became "the bridge over which European civilization crossed from the Old World to the New" (Solow 1987: 52). A significant distinction between Old and New World slavery is that New World slavery was African slavery. Henceforth, the ideological basis of slavery would rest on a radical distinction justified by "racial" difference.

Marxist analyses of slave societies have attempted to discover whether they contain an inherent dynamic similar to the drive towards ACCUMULATION which powers capitalist development. It is widely agreed that accumulation within the slave mode of production is not technologically dynamic, and consequently such accumulation consists in the linear addition of units of production. This is because of simple cooperation in the labor process, the lack of competition and the general opprobrium which tends to attach itself to productive labor. As a result, in an agricultural economy, accumulation takes the form of geographical expansion.

The major source of disagreement is whether or not soil exhaustion necessarily adds a further impetus to geographical expansion. Genovese (1967) argues that the limitation of slave labor to simple cooperation and the resistance of slaves to the performance of even simple tasks, let alone skilled operations, inhibited crop rotation, fertilization and other soil restoration techniques. For these reasons, the slave mode of production was forced by soil exhaustion to expand at its uncultivated margins. This was one of the dynamics which led to the American Civil War. Similar arguments can be advanced as to why slaves were a poor source of industrial labor.

Historians of ancient society tend to reject these arguments, observing that slaves in the ancient world performed all the functions performed by free labor, including imperial administration (Finley 1980; Anderson 1974). Hindess and Hirst (1975) contend that simple cooperation says nothing in itself about the level of skill involved in the task. They argue that the soil exhaustion of the slave South was conditioned primarily by the availability of virgin land at the frontier, and that plantation agriculture in antiquity did not suffer from declining fertility.

### See also:

economic anthropology: major contemporary themes; feudalism; hunter–gatherer and subsistence societies; socialism and communism

### Selected references

Anderson, Perry (1974) *Passages from Antiquity to Feudalism*, London: NLB.
Engels, Friedrich (1884) *The Origin of the Family, Private Property, and the State*, London: Lawrence and Wishart, 1972.
Finley, M.I. (1980) *Ancient Slavery and Modern Ideology*, London: Chatto & Windus.
Genovese, Eugene D. (1967) *The Political Economy of Slavery*, New York: Vintage.
Hindess, Barry and Hirst, Paul Q. (1975) *Pre-capitalist Modes of Production*, London: Routledge & Kegan Paul.
Marx, Karl (1964) *Pre-capitalist Economic Formations*, London: Lawrence & Wishart.
Patterson, Orlando (1982) *Slavery and Social Death*, Cambridge, MA: Harvard University Press.
Solow, Barbara L. (1987) "Capitalism and Slavery in the Extremely Long Run," in Barbara L. Solow and Stanley L. Engerman (eds), *British Capitalism and Caribbean Slavery*, Cambridge: Cambridge University Press.
Ste. Croix, G.E.M. de (1981) *The Class Struggle in the Ancient World*, London: Duckworth.

TERRENCE MCDONOUGH

# social capabilities and convergence

Neoclassical theory predicts that, at least in the long run, economies will converge towards similar levels of real per capita gross domestic product (GDP) with like mean factor prices. Convergence occurs through the process of interregional and international trade and factor mobility and is facilitated by the unfettered working of the marketplace. In other words, it is expected that the laggard economic performers or the less developed economies will catch up with the leaders who are operating at, or close to, the frontier of technology. The greater the gap between the leader and the laggards, the greater the potential for catch-up and greater is the expected rate of growth of per capita GDP amongst the less developed economies. It is implicitly assumed that those factors responsible for the leaders' high per capita GDP performance, inclusive of best practice technology, can and will be adopted by laggards in short shrift.

Conventional wisdom begs two sets of related questions. First, is convergence a stylized fact of the world economy? In other words, is the process of economic development an inevitable product of the free market? Second, if convergence has not occurred over the long run, what factors might have thwarted the catch-up process? Moses Abramovitz's concept of social capability – the term itself is borrowed from Kazushi Ohkawa and Henry Rosovsky – addresses the important question of the necessary conditions for convergence which lie outside of the simple domain of the price mechanism.

The empirical debate on convergence became a substantive one with the publication in 1982 of Angus Maddison's detailed and comparable time series estimates of real per capita GDP for the now developed economies which reach back to the late nineteenth century and forward as far as the 1970s. William Baumol (1986) launched the first noticeable salvo in the debate, arguing that convergence had actually taken place, from 1870 to 1979, amongst the currently industrialized countries of the world in terms of real per capita GDP and labor productivity. However, Baumol's results were immediately challenged by Bradford DeLong (1988) as being a product of sampling selection bias, whereby the countries tested for convergence were exactly those countries which successfully converged. If the sample is expanded to include those nations expected to converge, given their relatively high real per capita GDP in 1870, the empirics would no longer support the case for convergence since there are countries in this expanded sample, such as Argentina, Chile, Spain and Portugal, which actually diverged. Baumol accepted the essence of DeLong's results, but adds that if the sample is further expanded to include less developed countries, for the post-Second World War period, there is no evidence for convergence except among the highest income countries (Baumol and Wolff 1988).

Little attention has been paid to Paul Bairoch's less detailed estimates for real per capita GDP for the Third World and the now developed economies (1981). They suggest that per capita real GDP was marginally higher in the less developed economies in 1750, just at the beginning of the industrial revolution, only to fall to 12 percent of the developed world's per capita GDP by 1990, in spite of Third World per capita income more than doubling over this period: unequivocal evidence for long-run divergence between these two blocks of nations. Although, Bairoch's 1750 estimates are not beyond debate (Bairoch 1995; Maddison 1983), and it is possible that at this time the now developed economies already bettered the per capita GDP of the future Third World countries by at least a 2:1 margin, the overall finding of Bairoch on long-run divergence is supported by the most detailed recent estimates of Maddison (1995) for the period 1820–1992.

Indeed, in terms of blocks of countries, the wealthiest regions, Western Europe and its offshoots, Australia, Canada, New Zealand and the USA (the world's lead economy), have experienced the fastest growth, seeing their real per capita income rise by a factor of 13 and 17 respectively. The relatively poorer regions experienced lesser rates of growth, with Africa at the bottom of the list, only tripling its real per capita GDP in 170 years. In the process, the real per capita income gap increased dramatically between the richer and poorer regions of the world. For example, this gap increased from $837 to $20,227 (1990 US dollars) from 1820 to 1992 between Africa and the United States. Comparing China and the United States, where China has most recently undergone significant growth, the income gap has increased from $764 to $18,460.

In relative terms, the rich regions have remained rich and the poor have remained poor. However, this conclusion must be qualified. Especially since the Second World War, there has been some catch-up with the United States by other relatively well-to-do countries and also between Western and Southern Europe. Moreover, in Asia, Japan, South Korea and Taiwan are quickly catching up to their Western counterparts. Nonetheless, the stylized facts of the global economy do not sit well with the general predictions of convergence emanating from mainstream theory; there appears to be no tendency towards convergence even in the long run.

Abramovitz argues that convergence is not inevitable and that the absence of convergence which, in turn, is related to technological backwardness, can be largely explained by the absence or dearth of appropriate social capability. He writes: "Tenacious social characteristics normally account for a portion, perhaps a substantial portion, of a country's past failure to achieve as high a level of productivity as economically more advanced countries" (Abramovitz 1986: 387). He here refers specifically to the capacity of government and firms to facilitate the adoption of best-practice technology (Abramovitz 1986, 1994). And, speaking to the twentieth century experience, this relates to developing the necessary experience: "with the organisation and management of large-scale enterprise and with financial institutions with markets capable of mobilising capital for individual firms on a similarly large scale" (1986: 388).

However, social attitudes toward growth and development and related incentives and opportunities can also be of importance. The free market, in and of itself, is no guarantee of convergence. The appropriate social infrastructure must be in place if the laggard economies are to catch up with the leaders and if today's leaders are not to become tomorrow's relatively backward economies. Abramovitz's analysis, however, leaves unanswered the larger question of what factors drive the development of those social capabilities necessary to the process of convergence and economic development (Altman 1996).

## Selected references

Abramovitz, M. (1986) "Catching Up, Forging Ahead, and Falling Behind," *Journal of Economic History* 46: 385–406.
—— (1994) "Catch-up and Convergence in Post War Growth Boom and After," in William J. Baumol, Richard R. Nelson and Edward N. Wolff (eds), *Convergence of Productivity: Cross-National Studies and Historical Evidence*, New York: Oxford University Press.
Altman, Morris (1996) *Human Agency and Material Welfare: Revisions in Microeconomics and their Implications for Public Policy*, Boston: Kluwer Academic Publishers.
Bairoch, Paul (1981) "The Main Trends in National Economic Disparities Since the Industrial Revolution," in P. Bairoch and M. Levy-Leboyer (eds), *Disparities in Economic Development Since the Industrial Revolution*, New York: St Martin's Press, 86–125.
—— (1995) *Economics and World History: Myths and Paradoxes*, Chicago: University of Chicago Press.
Baumol, W.J. (1986) "Productivity Growth, Convergence, and Welfare: What the Long-Run Data Show," *American Economic Review* 76: 1072–85.
Baumol, W.J. and Wolff, E.N. (1988) "Productivity Growth, Convergence, and Welfare: Reply," *American Economic Review* 78: 1155–9.
DeLong, B.J. (1988) "Productivity Growth, Convergence, and Welfare: Comment," *American Economic Review* 78: 1138–54.
Maddison, Angus (1982) *Phases of Capitalist Development*, New York: Oxford University Press.
—— (1983) "A Comparison of Levels of GDP Per Capita in Developed and Developing Economies, 1700–1980," *Journal of Economic History* 43: 27–41.
—— (1995) *Monitoring the World Economy:1820–1992*, Paris: OECD.

MORRIS ALTMAN

# social democracy

Social democracy is a political IDEOLOGY focusing on an evolutionary road to socialism or the humanization of CAPITALISM. It includes the parliamentary process of reform, the provision of state benefits to the population, agreements between labor and the state, and the revisionist movement away from revolutionary communism. It has been historically associated with the ideas of Eduard Bernstein in Germany, the Fabian Society in England, the

Menshevik Party in Russia, the Social Democratic Party in Sweden and Holland, the socialist party in France, India and Japan, and Labor Parties in many countries.

Social democracy is actually a multifarious beast, variously concerning itself with helping the poor and the working class, extending public benefits such as education, health and utilities, utilizing Keynesian policies, having industrial agreements between unions, government and business, and promoting industrial democracy in the firm. Essentially it concerns reform of some of the dominant institutions of capitalism over long historical time in the pursuit of greater stability, equality and consensus.

## History

Historically, social democracy grew out of the European union of liberalism and socialism. During the late 1800s, the working class of many European nations was becoming materially better off and their access to the parliamentary process was improving, especially in England and Germany. Socialists and liberals, therefore, sought to institute moderate changes to capitalism to benefit the working class, and stabilize capitalism in the "general interest." Initially, in many countries, social democratic parties included reformers and communists, but in the early 1900s communists started their own parties and differentiated themselves from social democracy.

Eduard Bernstein wrote the classic text of early social democracy, *Evolutionary Socialism* (1898). In this work, he argued that the revolutionary road to socialism was unnecessary since there was a considerable degree of heterogeneity in the social structure (rather than class polarization), and the standard of living of the working class had increased (rather than being subject to immiserization). Trade unions could work alongside labor and social democratic parties for the institutionalization of reform, rather than await the tumultuous revolution. In Germany, this led the way for "revisionism" of classical Marxism within the Social Democratic Party, which has

been a dominant party in parliament and formed the government for many years during the 1950s–1980s.

In England, the Fabian Society and the Labor Party were the principal architects, while George Bernard Shaw and Sidney and Beatrice Webb were the main exponents of social democracy. Fabian socialism is committed to an extension of the state's regulatory, administrative and industrial activities, based on the efforts of the most capable rather than the most fortunate. Wealth was seen to be at least in part collectively generated (see COLLECTIVE SOCIAL WEALTH), and this justified the use of the state as the collective's representative, with the Labor Party being the chief parliamentary reformer. In the 1980s, when some in England viewed the Labor Party as too radical, a relatively conservative Social Democratic Party was instituted, but support for this party waned as the Labor Party became more reformist into the 1990s.

In Russia, the Russian Social Democratic Labor Party, originated in 1898, was a Marxist party committed to the overthrow of the monarchy and capitalism. It was divided into two factions, the evolutionary (Mensheviks) and revolutionary (Bolsheviks) socialists. The Bolsheviks went on to split from the party, eventually becoming the Communist Party of the Soviet Union, while the Mensheviks continued to advocate evolutionary change. Some of the greatest Marxist economists were Mensheviks, including Plekhanov and I.I. Rubin. Stalin purged the Mensheviks from important positions of power and subsequently killed off the potential for social democracy in Russia for many decades. The future may see a return of social democracy in Russia and the former Eastern bloc.

One of the classic and most successful forms of social democracy was in Sweden, where the Social Democratic Party was in government for most of the 1960s, 1970s and 1980s. Traditionally, Scandinavian social democracy has followed the European model of WELFARE STATE capitalism and Keynesian economic policies. However, in the late 1980s and 1990s, the New Right policies of ECONOMIC RATIONALISM OR

LIBERALISM led to a decline in traditional social democratic policies, and the need for a new agenda.

## Economic foundations

The economic foundations of social democracy are similar to socialism and progressive liberalism in seeing the need for a balance between private capital and SOCIAL AND ORGANIZATIONAL CAPITAL. The difference is one of degree. Free market capitalism has a tendency towards unstable business cycles, vast INEQUALITY of income, wealth and power, and the destruction of the environment. Once the majority of the population achieved the franchise, the tasks ahead were of stabilizing capitalism and redistributing income to promote equality of opportunity, community, health and mass education. This, of course, led to the rise of the welfare state and Keynesian discretionary policies, and questioned the DISEMBEDDED ECONOMY of free market policies.

During the 1950s, 1960s and 1970s, the welfare state, Keynesian economic policies and industrial relations agreements to balance the power of capital and labor were the defining features of social democracy. Big government helped to stabilize capitalism and prevent a major depression, welfare policies improved the material welfare of the working class, and industrial agreements resolved some of the CONTRADICTIONS between capital and labor. Keynesian policies were said to reduce the depth of recessions and provide a safety net for the unemployed.

## Present and future

However, with the onset of deep recessions during the 1970s–1990s in advanced capitalist nations, much of the economic logic of social democracy was questioned. This provided a foundation for a renewal of conservative and liberal as well as radical POLITICAL ECONOMY. The conservatives were elected to government in many nations, notably under Thatcher in the UK and Reagan in the USA. The revival of Marxism and radical political economy in the 1960s and 1970s was based in part on their stringent critique of the redistributive state and bastard Keynesian policies. Social democrats needed to change their policies or be seen to be left in the past.

As a response to the structural crisis of capitalism, in the 1970s and 1980s a new trend of social democracy emerged, not only in Sweden, but also in Austria, Germany, Australia and elsewhere. This trend saw the introduction of some combination of neocorporatist accords, industrial agreements and industrial democracy. Typically, the accords were social contracts between the party and the union movement institutionalizing wage moderation and productivity increases in return for increases in the SOCIAL WAGE. The industrial agreements were means of introducing new TECHNOLOGY along with retraining schemes for workers. And industrial democracy included cooperative work agreements, profit sharing, and worker representation on the board. (More recently, such as with Tony Blair and New Labour in Britain, a minimalist program has been instigated. This includes such piecemeal reforms as reducing class sizes and cutting hospital waiting lists.)

This new wave of social democracy attempts to link the spheres of production, distribution and exchange within the context of the technological and market needs of modern capitalism into the twenty first century. Thus, it represents the latest phase of social democracy in attempting to balance the needs of social stability and economic performance in an era of greater INTERNATIONALIZATION OF CAPITAL, deregulation and technological change. This new phase may be viewed not only as a more holistic approach to capitalism away from mere redistributive policies, but also as a more thorough acceptance of the logic of capitalism given the constraints involved. The crisis of social democracy is still with us, however, and the agenda for the future needs to be worked on further if the social democratic vision is to be seen to be relevant to the forces of modern capitalism into the twenty first century.

## Selected references

Apter, David E. (1993) "Social Democracy," in William Outhwaite and Tom Bottomore (eds), *Blackwell Dictionary of Twentieth-Century Social Thought*, Oxford: Blackwell.

Bernstein, Eduard (1898) *Evolutionary Socialism*, New York: Schocken, 1961.

Milner, Henry (1990) *Sweden: Social Democracy in Practice*, Oxford: Oxford University Press.

Nettl, J.P. (1973) "Social Democracy in Germany and Revisionism," in *Dictionary of the History of Ideas, vol. 4, Studies of Selected Pivotal Ideas*, ed. Philip P. Wiener, New York: Charles Scribner's Sons.

Pierson, Christopher (1991) *Beyond the Welfare State: The New Political Economy of Welfare*, Cambridge: Polity Press.

Pimlott, B. (ed.) (1984) *Fabian Essays in Socialist Thought*, London: Heinemann.

PHILLIP ANTHONY O'HARA

# social economics: organizations

In the contemporary scene, social economics tends to center around three main organizations: the Association for Social Economics (ASE), the International Center for Social Economics (ICSE), and the Society for the Advancement of Socio-Economics (SASE). Each of these is discussed below.

## Association for Social Economics

The Association for Social Economics was founded in 1941 as the Catholic Economics Association, with a membership drawn largely from US Catholic colleges and universities. Its journal, the *Review of Social Economy*, was first published in 1942. Early papers focused on the application of Catholic social doctrine to economics, the role of social values in the economy and in economics, social justice and contemporary issues of socioeconomic organization (such as labor relations, unions, employment, social security, credit policy, the Federal Reserve and postwar reconstruction). Though early contributors were influenced by neoclassical economists, solidarism, a theoretical orientation critical of neoclassical economics with origins in the work of Heinrich Pesch and Goetz Briefs in interwar Germany, became increasing influential. Members of the ASE tended to reject liberalism and laissez-faire, and argued for a social market economy and an economic process embedded in the larger living context of society.

In 1970 the members of the Association elected to give up their strict identification with Catholic social thought, and gave the organization its current name to reflect the increasingly pluralistic character of its membership. The organization grew to include institutionalists, Marxists and secular humanists, who favored an emphasis on social values in economics and who developed new arguments regarding the socially-embedded and value-laden character of the economy and economics. In the Association's new constitution, the organization's objectives are to "foster research and publication centered on the reciprocal relationship between economic science and broader questions of human dignity, ethical values, and social philosophy... to consider the personal and social dimensions of economic problems... and to assist in the formulation of economic policies consistent with a concern for ethical values a... pluralistic community and the demands of personal dignity."

The quarter-century of publication in the *Review of Social Economy* and the *Forum for Social Economics* since 1970 has continued an emphasis on social values and pluralism. More recent contributors include post-Keynesians, feminists, environmentalists, cooperativists, methodologists and behaviorialists. Since 1995 the *Review* has been published quarterly by Routledge in London, which also sponsors the "New Developments in Social Economics" book series.

## International Center for Social Economics

The ICSE was founded in 1986, and supports

research examining the relationship between income distribution and economic growth, as well as the manner in which they influence and are influenced by cultural factors and social institutions. The Center was founded by Y.S. Brenner (Utrecht University), H. Deleeck (University of Antwerp/UFSIA), A. Hirsch (Brooklyn College/CUNY), H. Kaelble (Free University of Berlin), W.J. Samuels (Michigan State University), P. Scholliers (Free University of Brussels), I. Stone (Baruch College/CUNY), T. van Tijn (Utrecht University) and the late J. Tinbergen.

The ICSE cooperates with Brooklyn College/CUNY, Baruch College/CUNY, The Center for Social Policy/University of Antwerp/UFSIA and the Center for Contemporary Social History/Free University of Brussels. The Center has hosted a number of conferences, among them several together with the Belgian–Dutch Association of Post-Keynesian Studies, and the founding meeting of the International Confederation for the Reform of Economics (ICARE).

The ICSE coordinates research to structure the efforts of participating scholars from the social and cultural sciences. Issues focused upon include empirical analyses of income distribution, income distribution theories, linkages between income and wealth distribution, empirical testing of distribution theories, the significance of income distribution to social policy, economic growth and the role of institutions, technological choice in relation to income distribution, the international distribution of income, and ethical aspects of income distribution. The results of some of these studies have been published in the *Journal of Income Distribution*, which was founded for this purpose in 1990. The editors at time of writing are Y.S. Brenner, M. Bronfenbrenner and W.J. Samuels. The publisher is JAI Press/UK, and the managing editor is J.T.J.M. van der Linden.

The *Journal of Income Distribution* aims to facilitate communication and discussion of research in the field of social economics and particularly in the sphere of the distribution of income and wealth. Its intention is to provide an international forum for the dissemination of the results of scholarly work in this field.

## Society for the Advancement of Socio-Economics

SASE (founded in 1989) is an international, interdisciplinary organization with members in over 50 countries. The academic disciplines represented in SASE include economics, sociology, political science, management, psychology, law, history and philosophy. The membership of SASE also includes business people and policy makers in government and international organizations. SASE's honorary fellows include Pierre Bourdieu, Mary Douglas, Amitai Etzioni, John Kenneth Galbraith, John Gardner, Albert O. Hirschman, Rosabeth Moss Kanter, Amartya Sen, Herbert Simon and Neil Smelser.

The purpose of SASE is threefold: (1) to advance an encompassing understanding of economic behavior across a broad range of academic disciplines; (2) to support intellectual exploration and policy implications of economic behavior within the context of psychological, societal, institutional, historical, philosophical and ethical factors; and (3) to balance inductive and deductive approaches to the study of economic behavior at both micro and macro levels of analysis.

Socioeconomics is an emerging meta-discipline. Socioeconomics begins with the assumption that economics is not a self-contained system, but is embedded in society, polity and culture. Socioeconomics regards competition as a subsystem encapsulated within a societal context that contains values, power relations, and social networks. The societal context both enables and constrains competition. Socioeconomics further assumes that individual choices are shaped by values, emotions, social bonds and moral judgments rather than by narrow self-interest. There is no a priori assumption that people act rationally or that they only pursue self-interest or pleasure.

Methodologically, socioeconomics regards inductive studies as co-equal in standing with deductive ones. Socioeconomics is both a positive and a normative science. That is, it openly recognizes its policy relevance and seeks to be self-aware of its normative implications rather than maintain the mantle of an exclusively positive science. Socioeconomics does not entail a commitment to any one ideological position, but is open to a range of positions that share a view of treating economic behavior as involving the whole person and all facets of society.

## See also:

community; ethics and morality; humanistic economics; justice; social economics: history and nature; social economics: major contemporary themes; value judgments and world views

JOHN B. DAVIS

# social economics: history and nature

Economics is a child of the Enlightenment. Social economics is an alternative to it, and older. Mainstream economics is a mixture of philosophical assumptions and scientific devices originating out of the social philosophy of seventeenth- and eighteenth-century France and Britain. For example, in the elementary principles courses teachers use the analytic geometry of Descartes to explain supply and demand; the intermediate and higher levels use the calculus of Leibniz and Newton. Its philosophical assumptions imply that the whole economy works effectively and harmoniously because it is an equilibrating stationary flow mechanism governed by natural physical laws analogous to Newton's solar system. Assumed also is the natural social law mentioned by Adam Smith that individuals making economic decisions are motivated by self-love, and that this self-interested behavior is held in check by another natural phenomenon, effective competition.

These assumptions and heuristic devices

help to form an Enlightenment-based conception of an economy that is believed to be efficient and equitable if property claims to land and resources are equitable to begin with. Conventional economists will admit that this model may not always work well in the real world; there may be serious obstacles such as "market failures" (externalities and public goods) and imperfections due to interferences from monopolists and governments. But, with all its limitations, they accept it as a benchmark for public policy. The ideal is delineated as one leading to Paretian optimality, a state of maximum economic utility or welfare.

Social economists' complaint against this conventional viewpoint is not so much that the assumptions are false; most social economists would admit that there are natural physical laws applicable to social phenomena. What is wrong with it is that it is narrow, incomplete and too individualistic. Completely unacceptable is the assumption that the final cause or end of the economy is the maximization of utility: that is, the purpose of an economy is to achieve the greatest amount of material welfare. Most social economists assume a different end, as did the ancient Greeks who were the first to study the economy seriously.

## Provisioning of the community

The very terms "economy" and "economics" as used by Xenophon and Aristotle in the second century BC indicate a substantive difference in social philosophy. The word "economics" was derived from two Greek words, *oikos* (household) and *nemein* (to rule). The study of the economy to the Greeks was one of ruling or managing a household writ large, a view radically different from the prevailing one of effective markets operating by impersonal forces of supply and demand. To Aristotle, the purpose of an economy is to control the provisioning of the community. As summarized by Karl Polanyi, Aristotle's assumptions pre-ordering the direction of economic activity were COMMUNITY ("man's economy is, as a rule, submerged in his social relations"), self-sufficiency (first priority is the provisioning of the polis or urban community) and JUSTICE (fairness for all, for example, prices should conform to the rule of right ordering) (see Polanyi 1968: 65, 97).

## Positive and normative branches

Thomas O. Nitsch (1990) sketches aspects of the history of social economics. While compressed into only eighty-six pages, the treatment is monumental in its grasp and breath. He shows that social economists have employed both positivist and normative approaches in their emphasis upon society rather than the individual, and that some normative approaches are secular and some religious (see NORMATIVE AND POSITIVE ECONOMICS). Max Weber is an outstanding example of a positivist practitioner; his social economics is very broad, being inductive and institutional (unlike mainstream economics that is deductive and narrow), but it is positivist in that he makes no attempt to elicit reform or improvement. The older Karl Marx fits into this category to some extent as well. Most social economists are secular/normative practitioners, however; they include, among many others, P.J. Proudhon, Adolph Wagner, Leon Walras, Alfred Marshall, J.A Hobson, Knut Wicksell and most American institutionalists, including John Maurice Clark.

In this normative group is William Dugger, who believes that social economics differs from mainstream economics in many ways, the most significant being that it is value-directed: "Value premises, carefully selected and used, direct research into the problems of the economically disadvantaged" (Dugger 1977: 309–10) (see VALUE JUDGMENTS AND WORLD VIEWS). A religious/normative group includes Charles de Coux, Alban de Villeneuve-Bargemont, Heinrich Pesch, Goetz Briefs and the twentieth-century Jesuits G. Gundlach, O. von Nell-Breuning and B. Dempsey. A discussion of other important social economists of the twentieth century, including KEYNES, SCHUMPETER, Sen, Georgescu-Roegen, Herman Daly, Bruyn and Ray Marshall, is found in Waters (1993).

## Work of Simonde de Sismondi

The work of the early nineteenth-century Swiss economist Simonde de Sismondi is pivotal to the development of social economics. He carries forward the Greek/medieval tradition of focusing upon the community, but, at the same time, integrates the social approach with the more modern individualist economics. As explained by Lutz, "instead of teaching how to increase national wealth, or the 'wealth of nations' he sought to increase [the] human well-being *of all*" (Lutz 1990: 237; italics added). Social economics contends that utility maximization does not describe adequately how people behave. Proposed instead is the more realistic and humane judgment that people also act deontologically, that is, according to their perceived duty. Different social economics treatises draw upon different inspirations as the source of this behavior, including Christian, Kantian, Marxian and, for insitutionalists such as Lewis Hill, that of Charles Pierce.

## See also:

deontology; humanistic economics; Polanyi's views on integration; quality of life; social economics: major contemporary themes

## Selected references

Briefs, Goetz (1983) "The Solidarist Economics of Goetz Briefs," *Review of Social Economy* 41(December).

Danner, Peter L. (1994) *Getting and Spending*, Kansas City, MO: Sheed & Ward.

Davis, John B. and O'Boyle, Edward J. (eds) (1994) *The Social Economics of Human Material Need*, Carbondale, IL: Southern Illinois University Press.

Dugger, William L. (1977) "Social Economics: One Perspective," *Review of Social Economy* 35(December).

Hill, Lewis E. (1978) "Social and Institutional Economics: Toward a Creative Synthesis," *Review of Social Economy* 36(December).

Lutz, Mark (1990) "Social Economics: A

Humanistic Tradition," in Mark Lutz (ed.), *Social Economics: Retrospect and Prospect*, Boston: Kluwer.

Lutz, Mark and Lux, Kenneth (1988) *Humanistic Economics: The New Challenge*, New York: The Bootstrap Press.

Nitsch, Thomas O. (1990) "Social Economics: the First 200 Years," in Mark Lutz (ed.), *Social Economics: Retrospect and Prospect*, Boston: Kluwer.

Polanyi, Karl (1968) *Primitive, Archaic and Modern Economies: Essays of Karl Polanyi*, ed. George Dalton, New York: Doubleday, chaps 1, 4–5.

Schumpeter, Joseph A. (1954) *History of Economic Analysis*, New York: Oxford University Press.

Waters, William R. (1993) "A Review of the Troops: Social Economics in the Twentieth Century," *Review of Social Economy* 51(3): 262–86.

WILLIAM R. WATERS

# social economics: major contemporary themes

Social economics is concerned with the role and nature of social values in economics and economic life. The principal assumption of a social economic approach is that all economics is strongly influenced by social values that operate in economic life, and that all economic explanation makes (usually implicit) use of social values. Economics, that is, is inescapably value-laden. Thus a social economic approach rejects the fact–value distinction as it is generally understood by neoclassical economists. Moreover, social economists argue that the effect of neoclassical economists' claim that they produce a value-free, positive economics is to legitimate and reinforce their own social values at the expense of other social values by: (1) generally discouraging examination of the diversity of values that operate in economic life, and (2) suppressing debate over the nature and importance of the liberal values favored by neoclassical economists (see VALUE JUDGMENTS AND WORLD VIEWS).

## *Homo economicus* versus *homo socio-economicus*

Thus, neoclassical economists suppose that individuals – in economic life, *homo economicus* – in fact act to maximize self-interest, and that individuals are accurately described in economics as atomistic rational maximizers. Social economists characterize this as a value assumption, because the pursuit of self-interest reflects only one dimension of human personality, and neglects the whole person, better labeled as *homo socio-economicus*. In particular, basing economics on self-interest alone requires (among other things) that individuals' cooperative behavior, their altruism and regard for others, and their sense of having responsibilities and duties be explained away or reduced to self-interest.

Heterodox economists in general take a social economic approach in rejecting the fact–value distinction, and in developing explanations of economic life that rely upon a wider range of social value assumptions than that involved in neoclassical economics. Neoclassical economics, in addition to assuming that individuals are atomistically self-interested, includes among its other value assumptions that wants alone explain choice, that interpersonal comparisons of well-being cannot be made, that competition fully characterizes economic life, that the economy reduces to a market process, that markets work reasonably well, that markets are impersonal, and that more is always preferred to less.

Heterodox economists, in contrast, often begin by explaining individual behavior in terms of richer social-historical frameworks that help explain a variety of types of individual motivation in economic life. Individuals may emulate one another, cooperate, act as members of a class, follow conventions and rules, act in non-market economic contexts and so on. This enables heterodox economists to place greater weight on concepts excluded from the neoliberal value framework: NEEDS, power, equity, market failure, DISTRIBUTION OF IN-COME, history, the production process, GENDER, CULTURE, the family, institutional context, custom and other dimensions of economic life left out of the narrow neoclassical focus on exchange. Heterodox economists thus typically work in terms of value frameworks that make reference to social JUSTICE, fairness, equality, HUMAN DIGNITY, human RIGHTS, and the common good.

The major contemporary themes of social economics, then, range not surprisingly across a very wide variety of topics and subjects. In addition, these topics and subjects shift and change over time, with the emergence of new historical social value challenges. In more recent research, five general and often over-lapping social value frameworks have domi-nated the principal social economic publications, including the *Review of Social Economy*, the *Forum for Social Economics*, the *Journal of Income Distribution*, the *Interna-tional Journal of Social Economics* and the *Journal of Socio-Economics*. They may be distinguished roughly as follows: (1) family and community relationships, (2) the work-place and its social organization, (3) the social nature of market relationships, (4) macroeco-nomic social policy issues, and (5) the metho-dology of economics, especially normative themes in economics, and the history of economic thought, especially as these impinge on social economics. What follows represents a selection of recent themes in these five cate-gories.

## Family and community relationships

To understand the social-historical frameworks in which individuals operate, and the impact these frameworks have on individual behavior, social economists have studied the economics of non-market social networks. Recent social economic research on the family investigates household relationships as gendered relation-ships, as in work on divorce, the FEMINIZATION OF POVERTY, and the nature and incidence of domestic violence. COMMUNITY has been investigated in terms of the role of those institutions that tend to foster it, such as credit unions, non-profit organizations, churches, and labor UNIONS. One special focus in this connection has been the network of coopera-tive institutions developed in the Basque region of Spain in MONDRAGÓN. Community-specific issues include housing discrimination and red-lining (see DISCRIMINATION IN THE HOUSING AND MORTGAGE MARKET), inter- and intra-racial income distribution, schooling and child care. Public policy, as it specifically impacts on families and communities – welfare, social security, unemployment insurance, health, the urban environment, and the living wage – have all received regular attention. General themes operating across family and community are the nature and extent of poverty, fairness and equity across classes and ethnic divisions, and how to address material need. One particular cross-cutting research project that falls in this area is the character of consumption, especially in terms of the social constitution of taste, meta-preferences, consumption as a form of communication, and the place of emulation and status (see CONSPICUOUS CONSUMPTION AND EMULATION).

## The workplace and its organization

Though production is a pre-eminently eco-nomic activity, social economists see the work-place as having a range of organizational forms that are thought to be necessary to any understanding of the economics of firms. Long-standing and continuing areas of interest in this category are worker participation and worker rights, the democratically operated firm – sometimes characterized in terms of PARTICIPATORY DEMOCRACY AND SELF-MANAGEMENT – and the labor theory of property. Central is cooperation as a principle of workplace organization. Organizational capital is seen to be essential to firm behavior to give human capital analysis a social dimen-sion (see SOCIAL AND ORGANIZATIONAL CAPITAL). Critical perspectives toward contem-porary firms have been developed in terms of the post-Fordist flexible work specialization (in Japan, North America and Europe), control and inefficiency in the capitalist firm and X-INEFFICIENCY in the tradition of Leibenstein. Labor-related themes include workweek and workday length, underemployment and over-employment, labor discrimination and earnings inequality.

## The social nature of market relationships

Social values – both with ethical overtones and as they reflect culture and custom – form a backdrop to market transactions that social economists emphasize for understanding those transactions. General perspectives on the nature of the exchange process include an emphasis on trust and personal relationships in contract formation and execution, workable competition, the social significance of externalities, markets as socially and institutionally-embedded, and exchange as a form of communication. At the same time, social economists have been particularly interested in the appearance of power in markets. Thus an examination of the monopoly-type firms and criticism of markets as atomistically competitive is standard. In connection with the former, attention is given to mark-up PRICING practices, the sales effort, the social control of business, and CORPORATE HEGEMONY. Another topic is how markets impose social stratification, especially in connection with employment relationships that lead to SEGMENTED AND DUAL LABOR MARKETS. Policy perspectives include AFFIRMATIVE ACTION and COMPARABLE WORTH, the corporate income tax, revisiting the Santa Clara Supreme Court decision treating corporations as individuals, and laissez-faire as an ideology.

## Macroeconomic social policy issues

Social economic research on the macroeconomy is especially focused on the current historical conjuncture, how it came about, and what the prospects are for a more humane economy. The "silent" depression, as both systemic malaise and as a result of conservative economic policy dating from Reagan, constitutes a shared perspective for most social economists. Supply-side economics, monetarism and income redistribution toward the wealthy have all come in for critical examination. In addition, monopoly capital theory in the neo-Marxist surplus tradition has been used to explain the GREAT DEPRESSION and more recent experience. One specific focus has been the causes and consequences of the savings and loan crisis as they impact on the macroeconomy. More general themes include the social costs of macroeconomic instability, Schumpeterian innovation, the importance of COLLECTIVE SOCIAL WEALTH and public goods in growth, the status of the WELFARE STATE, poverty and income distribution, and the centrality of Keynesianism in understanding the macroeconomy. Increasingly, the relationship between the environment and the economy, BIOECONOMICS and the principle of sustainability have been given valuable attention. Specifically international issues include the transition from socialism to capitalism, development in poor nations, and international income inequality.

## Methodology, normative themes, and history of thought

Sorting out the relationship between ethics and economics, including explaining the nature of value judgments and the value-ladenness of economics, represent fundamental preoccupations for social economists. Normative values regularly stressed are equity and fairness, social justice, human dignity and the common good (see NORMATIVE AND POSITIVE ECONOMICS). There is also broad commitment among social economists to communitarianism, egalitarianism and the idea of a human-centered economy. Naive COST–BENEFIT ANALYSIS and Pareto efficiency analysis come in for criticism. Theoretically, social economists begin with a rejection of atomistic individualism, emphasize the whole person, and often use holistic forms of reasoning to explain the relationship between individual and society. Important empirical work is associated with analyzing the extent of poverty, and determining measures of QUALITY OF LIFE and well-being. Important

normative orientations are HUMANISTIC ECO-
NOMICS, pragmatism, solidarism and deonto-
logical Kantianism. New methodological/
philosophical strategies include discourse ana-
lysis, CRITICAL REALISM and postmodernism.
Individuals whose thought has received parti-
cular attention from social economists, past
and present, are (in no particular order)
Herman Daly, Nicholas Georgescu-Roegen,
Joseph SCHUMPETER, Kenneth Boulding,
Adam Smith, Karl MARX, Amartya Sen, Joan
Robinson, J.M. KEYNES, Mark Lutz, J.S. Mill,
Amitai Etzioni, Bill Dugger, Charlotte Perkins
GILMAN, Heinrich Pesch, Bernard Dempsey,
David Ellerman, John M. Clark, Karl Polanyi,
Thorstein VEBLEN, John Rawls, Alasdair
McIntytre, Ron Stanfield, Alfred Marshall,
Edward O'Boyle and Severyn Bruyn. Consti-
tuencies that have been active under the banner
of social economics include institutionalists,
humanists, feminists, solidarists, post-Keyne-
sians, Marxists, radical political economists,
cooperativists and behaviorists.

## Conclusion

The fluidity and dynamic character of social
economics should be emphasized. Because
social economics is co-extensive with the
investigation of social value in its diverse
respects in economic life, very different substantive orientations in economics incorporate
social economic themes, and examine social
economic issues. Also, because the development of human society continually generates
new questions regarding social values, the ways
in which different orientations in economics
approach the interface between society and the
economy is always changing. Neoclassical
economics today may be identified by the
closed character of its social value investigation. Social economics, in contrast, is by nature
pluralistic. It defends as a necessity open
discussion of social values, and presupposes
intellectual tolerance. In an important sense,
pluralism is the underlying method of social
economics.

## Selected references

Bürgenmeier, Beat (1992) *Socio-Economics: An
Interdisciplinary Approach: Ethics, Institutions, and Markets*, Boston: Kluwer.

Davis, John. B. (1994) "Pluralism in Social
Economics," *History of Economic Ideas* 2(3):
119–28.

Davis, John B. and O'Boyle, Edward (eds)
(1994) *The Social Economics of Human
Material Need*, Carbondale, IL: Southern
Illinois University Press.

Eatwell, John, Milgate, Murray and Newman
Peter (eds) (1989) *The New Palgrave: Social
Economics*, New York: Norton.

Henderson, Jim and Davis, John (1993) "The
Challenges Facing Social Economics in the
Twenty-First Century," special issue of the
*Review of Social Economy* 51(4).

Lutz, Mark (ed.) (1990) *Social Economics:
Retrospect and Prospect*, Boston: Kluwer.

Lutz, Mark and Lux, Kenneth (1988) *Humanistic Economics: The New Challenge*, New
York: Bootstrap Press.

O'Boyle, Edward (1996) *Social Economics:
Premises, Findings and Policies*, London:
Routledge.

Waters, William (1993) "A Review of the
Troops: Social Economics in the Twentieth
Century," *Review of Social Economy* 51(3):
262–86.

JOHN B. DAVIS

# social fabric matrix

## Institutionalist concerns

The social fabric matrix is the tool-kit for
articulating and integrating the various categories of concern to institutionalists for the
study of real world contexts. The first set of
categories of concern are those of (1) philosophy, (2) theory, (3) statistical and mathematical techniques and (4) policy. The social fabric
matrix allows for the expression of a philosophical context that is holistic, normative,
deontological and systemic. It is constructed to

allow for the expression of institutionalist theories and principles and to encourage the collection of data in a manner to both utilize and test those theories.

The cell upon cell of data collection is not determined by mathematical techniques, but rather cells are determined by what is found in reality. Yet, the social fabric matrix allows for the application of a broader and more diverse range of statistical and mathematical techniques, especially Boolean techniques, than in neoclassical economics. Finally, the social fabric matrix is designed for policy analysis. This is so because it allows for the description of a "what is" matrix in order to define the problem, as well as a comparative "what ought to be" matrix to determine the policy and programs needed to move from what is to what ought to be.

A second set of categories of concern that institutionalists emphasize are (1) criteria, (2) transactions and (3) transformations. These concepts are expressed by social institutions. The application and enforcement of the diverse array of social, legal, economic, financial and religious criteria help shape and structure institutions. Our life is a series of transactions among institutions, persons, agencies, and between all of these and the elements of the ecological system. In addition, the criteria, institutions and ecological systems regularly undergo evolutionary transformations. The social fabric matrix expresses these concerns through the integration of flows and deliveries. Changes in the entries, flows and deliveries in the social fabric matrix also provide us with real time evolutionary clocks, based on events of the real world.

The third set of institutionalist concerns is drawn from anthropology, social psychology, economics and ecology. They are (1) cultural values, (2) societal beliefs, (3) personal attitudes, (4) social institutions, (5) technology and (6) the ecological system. These serve as the components of the social fabric matrix.

## Diagramatical illustration

The social fabric matrix is an integrated process matrix designed to express the attributes of the parts, as well as the integrated process of the whole (see Figure 10). The rows

| Receiving Component / Delivery Component | | Households | Water Aquifier | Goods Producer | Chemical Processor | River | Farmers |
|---|---|---|---|---|---|---|---|
| | | 1 | 2 | 3 | 4 | 5 | 6 |
| Households | 1 | 0 | 0 | 0 | 0 | 0 | 0 |
| Water Aquifier | 2 | 1 | 0 | 0 | 0 | 0 | 0 |
| Goods Producer | 3 | 1 | 0 | 0 | 0 | 0 | 0 |
| Chemical Processor | 4 | 0 | 1 | 1 | 0 | 0 | 0 |
| River | 5 | 0 | 0 | 0 | 0 | 0 | 0 |
| Farmers | 6 | 0 | 0 | 0 | 1 | 1 | 0 |

*Figure 10*  A simple social fabric matrix

represent the components which are delivering, and the columns represent the components which are receiving. It is a nonequilibrium, noncommon-denominator process matrix, which is read from left to right, with the *i*th row and the *j*th column being the same entry. The terms "delivering" and "receiving" convey the idea that there is no final demand, absolute requirement, or end to the process. Delivering and receiving suggest analysis in terms of processing or functioning.

This figure is a simplified example of a social fabric matrix, that is presented to help define and explain the nature of social fabric matrices (the largest the author has seen is one with 400 rows and 400 columns). Assume that after initial research, it is found that the main components of a problem area are (1) farmers, (2) a river, (3) a chemical processor, (4) a goods producer, (5) a water aquifer and (6) households. There is a 1 in the cells where deliveries are made and a 0 where there is no delivery. The deliveries are as follows: cell (6, 4) is the delivery of soybeans from farmers to the chemical processor and cell (6, 5) is the delivery of eroded soil from farmers to the river. Cell (4, 2) is the delivery of pollution from the chemical processor to the water aquifer, and cell (4, 3) indicates the delivery of plastics to producers of goods. Cell (3, 1) is the delivery of goods to households while cell (2, 1 ) is the delivery of water and the processor's pollution from the water aquifer to the households.

Research for the matrix begins by accumulating a broad scientific base with an emphasis on field observation for the problem area of interest. From this research, the components and elements of the components can be determined for the rows and columns. In this way, a row component can be followed across the matrix to discover the columns to which it makes deliveries, based on the research. Deliveries in the cells are both qualitative and quantitative. They can include criteria, court rulings, POLLU-TION emissions, goods production, services and so forth. Thus, it is necessary to develop many different kinds of numerical modalities in order to capture the essence of various flows and relationships. This means that standard matrix

algebra is not appropriate to the matrix and that all the information in the rows and columns are not summative (as in an input–output matrix).

The social fabric matrix becomes a thinking tool. As researchers are forced to deal with each cell, linkages among elements are discovered that otherwise would have been overlooked. The number and kinds of entries in each cell depend on the problem being studied.

## Sequence and real time

The social fabric matrix can be converted to a sequence digraph in which the matrix components are referred to as nodes and the directed lines between the nodes, which indicate the deliveries among the components, are referred to as edges. The digraph is useful for conveying to researchers and policy makers the structure of the system. The digraph can be used to organize the different kinds of expertise needed. With the digraph, the different scientists will not see themselves as isolated and disconnected specialists. In addition, the digraph rendition allows for a quick identification of gaps. If the nodes in the digraph are not fully connected, then it is not fully defined.

The social fabric matrix is consistent with activity sequencing as required in real-time systems. Traditional TIME concepts and clocks are not sufficient for the space–time coordination which is needed to solve social and ecological problems. The timing system needs to internalize events in a socially relevant sequence. Such sequencing places social problems into a context which is ideally timed by the succession of events and deliveries relevant to that socio-ecological context. This kind of system-timing makes universal or clock time secondary to the internalized timing which is defined by the activity of the system being investigated.

The social fabric matrix can be utilized to represent the sequence of relations and the direction of deliveries among the components of the social and ecological system. Such an approach can be used to plan communication networks, or transportation systems, or pollution controls, or whatever needs to be coordinated in a timely manner. Events and flows need to follow one another in an order prescribed by the system. Sequence is essential to temporal order. The rate and frequency of events for a duration of real time is critical for understanding a system and making policy for a system. Timing is the necessary temporal coordination of the components and elements in a collective context. Without real-time ordering, real world activities can have no order at all. The social fabric matrix approach is crucial for accomplishing such timing and coordination of all the belief, institutional, technological and ecological components.

## Spatial analysis, coordination and policy

Likewise, the social fabric matrix approach allows for spatial analysis and coordination. The receiving and delivery nodes of the social fabric matrix digraph can be placed on a map, or integrated with many of the available geographical and remote sensing computer softwares.

Since the social fabric matrix is used to detail all the entities that contribute to a system, it can serve as the basis for valuing a system and its parts. As clarified above, there is no common denominator which provides a measuring mechanism for a system. The relationships and components of a socio-ecological system call for an array of different kinds of measures in order to define and evaluate the system. This array can be captured by the social fabric matrix; thus, it allows for the evaluation of alternative policies. The purpose of policy is to apply criteria and norms in order to change systems. The social fabric matrix can be used to measure the effectiveness of such normalization by defining the system, before the application of new policies, and comparing the pre-policy social fabric matrix to the post-policy social fabric matrix.

## Further research

A more complete explanation of the social fabric matrix, along with an indication of the relevant literature upon which it is built, can be found in Hayden (1993a, 1993b) and in the other references below. The other references are important for exploring various ways in which the social fabric matrix has been utilized. The institutional economics tradition has been one concerned with theory, describing systems, and policy making. The social fabric matrix allows for the integration of those concerns.

## See also:

culture; holistic method; institutional political economy; institutions and habits; technology

## Selected references

Gill, Roderic (1996) "An Integrated Social Fabric Matrix/System Dynamics Approach to Policy Analysis," *System Dynamics Review* 14(2): 554–80.

Groenewegen, John and Beije, Paul R. (1989) "The French Communication Industry Defined and Analyzed through the Social Fabric Matrix, the Filere Approach and Network," *Journal of Economic Issues* 23(4): 1059–74.

Hayden, F. Gregory (1993a) "Institutionalist Policymaking," in Marc R. Tool (ed.), *Institutional Economics: Theory, Method, Policy*, Boston: Kluwer.

—— (1993b) "Order Matters and Thus So Does Timing: Graphical Clocks and Process Synchronicity," *Journal of Economic Issues* 27(1): 95–115.

Mesiter, Barbara (1990) "Analysis of Federal Farm Policy Using the Social Fabric Matrix," *Journal of Economic Issues* 24(1): 189–224.

Stephenson, Kurt and Hayden, F. Gregory (1995) "Comparison of the Corporate Decision Networks of Nebraska and the United States," *Journal of Economic Issues* 29(3): 843–69.

F. GREGORY HAYDEN

# social and organizational capital

The essence of capital, as defined by economists, is lasting productive capacity that is produced and, subsequently, used by economic entities to achieve their purposes. Until relatively recently, almost everyone simply took this to mean tangible assets (factories, equipment, etc.) possessed by enterprise owners seeking profit. In the light of the increased recognition of the role that intangibles play in determining productive capacity, the term capital has been extended more and more to intangible factors such as HUMAN CAPITAL, in which the productive capacity is embodied in individuals due to education, training and so on. During the last decade or so, analyses focusing on the concepts of social and organizational capital have continued this trend.

Both terms refer to the features of social relationships that enable economic entities to accomplish their purposes. Organizational capital, which can be considered a type of social capital, is a concept that has been used primarily by economists to denote the productive capacity that derives from the qualities of an organization's "people relationships." Social capital, on the other hand, has been used, typically by economic sociologists, not simply to refer to productive capacity but more generally to denote a social resource that enables actors to attain their ends.

## Organizational capital

The concept of organizational capital was developed by John Tomer in his 1973 Ph.D. thesis and later as an article and book (1981, 1987). Working separately, Edward Prescott and Michael Visscher (1980) also wrote about "organization capital."

Investment in organizational capital uses up resources in order to bring about lasting improvement in PRODUCTIVITY, worker well-being, or social performance through changes in the functioning of the organization (Tomer 1987: 24). It involves (a) changing the formal and informal social relationships and patterns of activity within the enterprise, or (b) changing individual attributes important to organizational functioning, or (c) accumulating information useful in matching workers with organizational situations. This third aspect is the one on which Prescott and Visscher focus.

Organizational capital is embodied either in organizational relationships, particular members of organizations, the organization's repositories of information, or some combination of the above. Pure organizational capital provides the best contrast with human capital because it is vested entirely in the relationships among workers, not in the workers themselves. It is these relationships, for example, particular organizational structures, that enable desired worker behavior to be evoked or fostered. Another type of organizational capital is a hybrid of organizational and human capital, called H–O capital; it is embodied in workers in the form of attitudes and knowledge created through socialization processes. A second hybrid, known as O–H capital, consists of information about the actual and desired characteristics of current and prospective employees. This type is embodied in formal organization repositories as well as the memories of managers and personnel people (Prescott and Visscher 1980: 446–8; Tomer 1987: 24–9).

## Organizational capital and productivity

The organizational capital concept has great value in that it links organizational behavior insights regarding the contribution of organizational structure, culture, climate, patterns of interaction, socialization, etc. to the economic concepts of capital and productivity. The organizational capital concept has found useful application as (a) an explanation of the rate of economic growth, (b) a factor explaining increases in worker effort levels and cooperation and thus X-efficiency, and (c) a factor in understanding the high productivity of Japanese manufacturing companies as well as other high performance companies (Tomer 1987). Organizational capital has important implications for INDUSTRY POLICY, that is, for understanding when government ought to act to foster industry investment in critical types of organizations. Investment in organizational capital can also contribute to increasing an organization's socially responsible behavior, the rationality of its decision-making, and the citizenship behavior of its members.

Prescott and Visscher (1980) have used organizational capital to explain important facts concerning constraints on the growth rate of firms and the size distribution of firms. Tremblay (1995) conceives of the firm as an "evolutionary learning engine" in which its capacity to learn is determined by its investment in organizational capital. Embodied in the firm's organizational capital is a learning strategy involving communication codes that allow for efficient communication and prevent rapid diffusion of the firm's distinctive competencies.

## Social capital

In contrast to organizational capital, social capital is a broader term that has been developed largely by sociologists, most notably, James Coleman. Social capital refers to the social-structural resources that are embodied in families, institutions, civic communities, and the larger society. The capacity provided by social capital inheres in social relationships, not in individuals (Coleman 1990: 304). Because of the social capital available to them, economic entities such as individuals, social groups, businesses, and governments, as well as the national or regional economies of which they are a part, are able to accomplish more than would be possible in the absence of these capital endowments (Coleman 1988: 98). In some cases, social capital is created intentionally by persons who view it as an investment from which they hope to profit. However, it is more often created as a by-product of activities engaged in for other reasons (Coleman 1990: 312, 317).

In contrast to the main intellectual currents in economics and sociology, "revisionist" socioeconomics views economic actors as being partially embedded in society. Orthodox econ-omists, on the one hand, have tended to view the actor as behaving independently, rationally and entirely self-interestedly. Sociologists, on the other hand, have tended to see the actor as behaving in accord with social norms, rules and obligations. However, with partial embeddedness, economic actors, who are rationally striving to achieve their ends, respond in part to economic incentives and in part to social influences. The concept of social capital is particularly important in this context as a theoretical tool that explains both how social relationships influence actors and how actors can utilize social organization to attain their ends.

Regardless of the intentionality involved in its creation, social capital can be a resource of great value when its functioning enables actors to realize their interests. Among the social features that can serve as social capital are (a) obligations and expectations, (b) norms and effective sanctions, (c) authority relations, (d) family and friendship bonds and (e) voluntary social organizations (Coleman 1990). Social scientists' use of the social capital concept provides explicit recognition of the inherently social nature of economic processes. With regard to the productivity of a nation or an industry, it is useful to conceive of a capital system comprised of the tangible, human, social/organizational and other forms of capital required for production. This perspective enables us to understand better, first, how the different types of resources combine to produce system-wide outcomes, and second, how these different resources can either substitute for or complement each other.

Social capital is a key concept in the research of a number of leading sociologists. For example, Coleman (1988) finds that school drop out rates are inversely related to the endowment of social capital available to children, the latter reflecting the strength of the relationships between parents and their children as well as the strength of COMMUNITY relationships, especially parents' relations with institutions in the community. Secondly, Putnam (1993) finds that, in Italy, regional differences in both economic strength and the effectiveness of government performance are directly related to regional differences in social capital, i.e. differences in the activity of community organizations and the quality of the norms and networks of civic engagement. Finally, according to Fukuyama, a key to a nation's economic well-being and its ability to compete is the level of trust in the society, which reflects a society's social capital in the form of shared norms and values and ability to subordinate individual interests to those of the larger group. Without such trust, business costs, especially transaction costs, are higher, less organizational innovation occurs and spontaneous cooperation is lower.

Few economists have utilized the social capital concept. Among the exceptions are several economists from Michigan State University who have incorporated social capital insights into neoclassical economic theory in a way permitting the quantification of its importance (see, for example, Schmid and Robison 1995). Their model utilizes social capital weights reflecting the strength of the relationship between two parties as perceived by one of the parties. An important finding of their research is that the social relationship between the two parties to a transaction makes a significant difference with regard to important transaction outcomes such as price.

## See also:

accumulation; capital theory debates; capital and the wealth of nations; capitalism; circuit of social capital; collective social wealth; cultural capital; disembedded economy; finance capital; institutions and habits; knowledge, information, technology and change; natural capital; reproduction paradigm; social structures of accumulation

## Selected references

Coleman, James S. (1988) "Social Capital in the Creation of Human Capital," *American Journal of Sociology* 94(Supplement): 95–120.

—— (1990) *Foundations of Social Theory*, Cambridge, MA: Belknap Press, 300–21.

Prescott, Edward C. and Visscher, Michael (1980) "Organization Capital," *Journal of Political Economy* 88(3): 446–61.

Putnam, Robert D. (1993) *Making Democracy Work: Civic Traditions in Modern Italy*, Princeton, NJ: Princeton University Press, 163–85.

Schmid, A. Allan and Robison, Lindon J. (1995) "Applications of Social Capital Theory," *Journal of Agriculture and Applied Economics* 27(1): 59–66.

Tomer, John F. (1981) "Organizational Change, Organizational Capital and Economic Growth," *The Eastern Economic Journal* 7(January): 1–14.

—— (1987) *Organizational Capital: The Path to Higher Productivity and Well-being*, New York: Praeger.

Tremblay, Pascal (1995) "The Organizational Assets of the Learning Firm," in *Human Systems Management* 14: 7–20.

JOHN F. TOMER

# social ownership and property

In the modern world, the concept of social ownership can be traced back to Philippe-Joseph-Baptiste Buchez, one of the utopian reformers of early nineteenth-century France, who in 1831 advocated the establishment of "workmen's associations." These associations would be made independent of control by capital and the state by the accumulation of a permanent stock of "social, inalienable and indivisible capital" which would be the PROPERTY of the association in perpetuity (see Reibel 1966: 40).

The concept of social ownership, like its related concept "self-management," languished with the triumph of the "statist model" following the Russian Revolution. However, with the progressive abandonment of that model by Yugoslavia after its break with the Soviet bloc in 1948, and the adoption of the self-management model, social ownership and social property became the dominant form of property relations in that country until its disintegration in 1991. A few other countries have experimented with limited social property sectors; the most common form is in worker cooperatives, such as the MONDRAGÓN experiment in Spain, Israel's *kibbutzim* and not-for-profit non-government organizations (NGOs).

## Definitions

The concepts "social property" and "social ownership" refer to productive property collectively owned by a "society" or "group." The use and management RIGHTS associated with this property are exercised by workers or consumers or both. The society or group also constrains the right of its users to destroy, consume or alienate the property and, in some cases, to withhold it from use (Phillips 1992: 67).

The concept is defined not so much by legal title to property, but by the economic rights to manage and use (see Bajt 1968). Horvat, a leading theorist of social ownership and self-management, has defined social property specifically in relation to access to the means of production, entitlement to property income, and the right of workers to participate as equals in management (Horvat 1982: 235–9). Hence, with social property there is no class of owners of the means of production, or private property holders to appropriate property income. In this sense, social ownership implies distribution of income according to work performed.

Social ownership is similar to what in Canada is referred to as community ownership, which involves the creation of not-for-profit organizations governed by volunteer boards and dedicated to the provision of sports, performing arts and non-governmental health and social service agencies (see Quarter 1992). Property accumulated by such organizations remains the property of the community, in trust to the board.

Social ownership is also used to refer to the collective, non-transferable portion of cooperative property in the Mondragón group of companies in Spain, and other cooperative and worker self-managed systems (Thomas and Logan 1982). None of the workers in Mondragón, for instance, can take a portion of the productive assets at any time, including when they leave. With the Mondragón cooperatives, a significant portion (between 20 and 60 percent) of any surplus of income over costs is allocated to social capital. This portion of the surplus is retained by the co-ops for reserves, investment and expansion of the collectively owned and managed means of production, and is inalienable and indivisible. Thus, while wages are paid as a cost of production in relation to work performed, only a part of the ECONOMIC SURPLUS is allocated to the accounts of individuals in proportion to their work, and even that allocation is only paid out at retirement or when a worker leaves the co-op. Similarly, for most community ownership organizations (NGOs and not-for-profits companies) any surplus is normally retained for reserves or used to expand services.

## Economic basis of the concepts

Property involves a bundle of rights. Horvat has established a schema of property rights, obligations and conferred individual rights associated specifically with social productive property (or social capital). The property rights are the right to use, change, or sell for the benefit of the collectivity, and the right to reap benefits from the use of property. Social property, however, brings the obligation to maintain undiminished the value of the social capital. The existence of social capital confers on individuals the rights to work; to compete for any job consistent with a person's capabilities; to participate in management; and to derive economic benefits solely from work but not from property (Horvat 1982: 236–8).

The essence of social ownership, as expressed by Bajt (1968: 158), is the "socialist principle of distribution of income according to work" with the value of work being determined by supply and demand (see SOCIALISM AND COMMUNISM). Social ownership, Bajt maintains, requires self-management at the macro level as well as at the micro or enterprise level. The "macro" part of this definition, however, would seem to be rather limiting in its applicability to the modern world at present.

Ownership of monetary capital does not convey rights to manage or to expropriate the economic surplus to entrepreneurship (see Bajt 1968: 163). These surpluses belong, rather, to self-managing labor. Thus, social ownership is associated with the money capital advanced to the enterprises being turned into means of production by work collectives. The physical means of production may be bought and sold freely as long as the capital value is maintained.

Bajt distinguishes between the right to own social capital (which he labels ownership) and the right to manage (which he labels entrepreneurship). The right of ownership of social capital resides with society or some other social agency or collective body, and takes the form of "monetary capital." The right to employ and manage that social capital involves the purchase and utilization of the means of production (entrepreneurship), a right that resides with self-managing labor. The economic surplus so produced under self-management, after remitting to society a rental payment for the use of the (monetary) social capital, belongs to the workers as a return to their entrepreneurship.

This concept of social property allows Bajt and Horvat to defend individual farm and artisanal production as individual social ownership. This is so because, given the competitive nature of these markets, prices tend to fall to a level such that individual proprietors receive only a return to their labor and entrepreneurship and not property income, rents or profits.

## Criticism

Criticism of the notion of social ownership comes from both the right and the left of the political spectrum. Critics on the right argue that social ownership is inefficient because of the attenuation of ownership from management. This is implied by the criticism that social property is "owned by everybody and by

nobody." Everybody has access to it but nobody takes responsibility for it. This, they argue, leads to underinvestment, a problem referred to as the "horizon problem." In other words, since there is no individualized claim on the net worth of the enterprise, the workers have the incentive to distribute all earnings rather than retaining all, or part, of the surplus for reinvestment. Since investment of retained earnings would benefit only those workers who remained employees for the productive life of these assets, older workers and those with a high discount rate (i.e. those with a short horizon) would have a strong incentive to underinvest (Ellerman 1986: 62–5). Critics on the left, on the other hand, point out that initial differences in productivity allow for widening income disparities, particularly where investment in social property is financed from internal funds.

There is little empirical support for either of these criticisms in the evidence from Yugoslavia or Mondragón. If anything, Yugoslavia was plagued by overinvestment. Also, wage dispersions in the Mondragón cooperatives, both within and between the individual cooperatives, as well as in Yugoslavia, were generally smaller than in capitalist enterprises and countries (Thomas and Logan 1982: 145–6).

## See also:

anarchism; labor-managed enterprises; market socialism; participatory democracy and self-management; Ward–Vanek model of self-management

## Selected references

Bajt, Aleksander (1968) "Social Ownership – Collective and Individual," in Branko Horvat, Mihailo Markovic and Rudi Supek (eds), *Self-Governing Socialism*, vol. 2, White Plains, NY: International Arts and Sciences Press, 1975.

Ellerman, David P. (1986) "Horizon Problems and Property Rights in Labour Managed Firms," *Journal of Comparative Economics* 10: 62–78.

Horvat, Branko (1982) *The Political Economy of Socialism*, Armonk, NY: M.E. Sharpe.

Phillips, Paul (1992) "Functional Rights: Private, Public and Collective Property," *Studies in Political Economy* 38(Summer): 61–84.

Quarter, Jack (1992) *Canada's Social Economy*, Toronto: Lorimer.

Reibel, R. (1966) "The Workingman's Production Association, or the Republic in the Workshop," in Jaroslav Vanek (ed.), *Self-Management*, Harmondsworth: Penguin, 1975.

Thomas, Henk and Logan, Chris (1982) *Mondragón*, London: Allen & Unwin.

PAUL PHILLIPS

# social structure of accumulation: capital–labor accord

The capital–labor accord was a central aspect of the "golden age" of SOCIAL STRUCTURES OF ACCUMULATION in the United States (and some other nations) that underpinned rapid economic growth during the period 1945–73. At the heart of capitalist relations is the extraction of work effort from workers. Firms must secure the cooperation of workers in the production process, and this may generate conflict over control of the labor process and over the division of income between profits and wages. Rapid capital accumulation, therefore, requires a set of institutions to stabilize capital–labor conflict.

## Nature of accord

The postwar capital–labor accord is described as an implicit contract or "invisible handshake" between monopolistic firms and unionized labor that defined a new approach to industrial relations. In the face of a growing threat of industrial conflict, coercive forms of labor control – such as Taylorism, the "drive system" and anti-union policies – gave way to a more consent-based system and positive incentives as a means of influencing the intensity of work. The evolution of INTERNAL LABOR MARKETS replaced the arbitrary authority of foremen on the shop floor, with "due process" governing employment matters, and collective agreements with negotiated job postings and seniority provisions encouraging greater work effort and bolstering productivity. Diligent work could get an employee up the job ladder and pay scale. This tended to limit the firm's flexibility in assigning work; however, hierarchical job structures replaced some of the need for costly supervision of worker effort.

While management retained effective control over the organization of work, workers gained the power to share in the productivity gains by bargaining collectively over wages and benefits. Union recognition and the right to collective bargaining were tangible victories for working people: they gained the legal right to strike, under specific conditions, in order to back wage demands. This did not, however, require capital to relinquish its dominant position. Restrictions on union membership, picketing, secondary boycotts and strikes during the life of a collective agreement constrained the actions of workers, and firms retained the ultimate power to discipline workers through the threat of dismissal.

## Contradictions and slowdown

Forging a degree of consensus between capital and labor in the workplace contributed to rapid PRODUCTIVITY growth, capital accumulation and rising profits, while workers enjoyed higher real wages. However, after some twenty years of steady growth, economic performance worsened in the late 1960s and, with the significant PRODUCTIVITY SLOWDOWN of the 1970s, it was apparent that the conditions necessary for rapid capital accumulation were undermined.

The dissolution of the capital–labor accord stemmed from its inherent CONTRADICTIONS. Demands by organized labor for a more equitable distribution of income contributed to the "creeping" inflation of the 1960s. According to Bowles, Gordon and Weisskopf

(1983), unions were "emboldened to press for higher wages," while firms with monopoly power sought to raise prices in order to protect their profit margins. Growing conflict over the distribution of income led to increasingly adversarial industrial relations, evident in the growing frequency of strikes and lockouts.

Capital's leverage over workers also declined. As unemployment fell to historically low levels and the welfare state expanded, the expected COST OF JOB LOSS was significantly reduced. The threat of dismissal thus became a less effective means of discipline. By the late 1960s, downturns in the business cycle were no longer "reproductive": as the cost of job loss declined, recessions did not lower wage demands and restore the conditions for rapid capital accumulation. The result was a "squeeze" on profits.

The success of collective bargaining had other contradictory effects. As wages rose and unemployment declined, concern with material insecurity lessened. Workers' attention turned to shop floor concerns such as health and safety (see HEALTH AND SAFETY IN THE WORKPLACE), workplace decision making, and opportunities for meaningful and creative work. The frequency of wildcat strikes and of strikes over working conditions indicate growing rank-and-file militancy during the 1960s and 1970s over issues outside of the postwar settlement.

Concurrent changes in the structure of the labor force also eroded the capital–labor accord. The increasing segmentation of the labor market left a large number of workers who entered the labor force after the Second World War – particularly women, African-Americans and new immigrants – without the collective bargaining rights necessary to protect relative incomes and working conditions. This led to greater demands upon the state to ameliorate the economic hardships experienced by those left outside of the accord (see SEGMENTED AND DUAL LABOR MARKETS).

## New social order

Observers of industrial relations in North America have since proclaimed the arrival of a new social order. Experiments in Japanese systems with flexible job assignments, reductions in job classifications, greater part-time and casual employment, and subcontracting to non-union firms have diminished the role of formal job structures. Two-tiered wage systems and profit-sharing schemes permit less rigid forms of remuneration, and management initiatives aimed at the "quality of working life" and "work circles" are designed to usurp the role of unions in the everyday life of workers (see FORDISM AND THE FLEXIBLE SYSTEM OF PRODUCTION).

The search for greater flexibility in the labor process is paralleled by more repressive labor legislation and an erosion of the principle of free collective bargaining. The state has assumed an increasingly coercive stance with the use of back-to-work legislation, rescinding the right to strike for many workers, having greater restrictions on industrial action, and the imposition of wage controls. The dismantling of key aspects of the welfare state has led to a sharp increase in the cost of job loss and in capital's leverage over workers. With terms like "outsourcing" and "downsizing" entering into popular vocabulary, it is evident that the corporate agenda is in the ascendancy. The trade union movement and progressive groups appear ill-equipped at present to resist these changes in order to define a new, more democratic social structure of accumulation.

## See also:

hegemony in the world economy; profit-squeeze analysis of crises; regulation approach; social structure of accumulation: corporate; social structure of accumulation: family; social structure of accumulation: financial; social structure of accumulation; state–citizen accord

## Selected references

Bowles, Samuel, Gordon, Don and Weisskopf, Tom (1983) *Beyond the Wasteland: A Demo-*

*cratic Alternative to Economic Decline*, Garden City: Anchor Press/Doubleday.

—— (1990) *After the Waste Land: A Democratic Economics for the Year 2000*, Armonk, NY: M.E. Sharpe.

Kochan, Thomas A. *et al.* (1986) *The Transformation of American Industrial Relations*, New York: Basic Books.

Marglin, Stephen and Schor, Juliet B. (1990) *The Golden Age of Capitalism: Reinterpreting the Postwar Experience*, Oxford: Oxford University Press.

HUGH GRANT

# social structure of accumulation: corporate

The SOCIAL STRUCTURES OF ACCUMULATION (SSA) approach argues that long periods of ECONOMIC GROWTH and stagnation in CAPITALISM are the result of the construction and disintegration of sets of institutions which underpin the profit rate. The approach has been used to describe the effect of institutional change on the ACCUMULATION process. Conversely, it can also be applied to the history of the component institutions which constitute the SSA. Writing the history of particular institutions from an SSA perspective seeks to comprehend the transformations in these institutions in relation to the changing role they have played in the construction and breakdown of successive SSAs. The corporate structure is one of a number of such institutional relations.

## Market relations and management structure

Changes in the corporate structure have played a prominent part in the explanation of successful accumulation, and in the development of the contradictions which eventually undermined these periods of expansion. Such changes can be viewed from the perspective of the market relations between corporations or,

alternately, from the perspective of the internal management structure and organization of the CORPORATION. Most SSA accounts of the history of the corporation have examined the internal structure of the firm primarily in terms of capital–labor relations (see SOCIAL STRUCTURE OF ACCUMULATION: CAPITAL–LABOR ACCORD). A partial exception is the multinationalization of the American corporation after the Second World War. Even here the discussion has had less to do with the internal structure of the firm than with the changing fortunes of American firms, in competition with European and Japanese TRANSNATIONAL CORPORATIONS.

Emphasis has been placed on the corporate market structures in explaining the transition from one SSA to another. This is not surprising, as the SSA framework originally arose as an extension of the American monopoly capital school (see MONOPOLY CAPITALISM), analyzing the rise of the postwar system in a way analogous to the work of Baran, Sweezy, Magdoff and Huberman. These authors had in turn based their analysis on that of Lenin in *Imperialism, the Highest Stage of Capitalism* where Lenin asserted that "imperialism is the monopoly stage of capital" (see McDonough 1995; COLONIALISM AND IMPERIALISM: CLASSIC TEXTS).

## Competitive capitalism: 1840s–1890s

The changing market structure has been central to the analysis of the SSAs in American history. Bowles and Edwards (1985: 97) identify the first SSA, extending from the 1840s through the 1890s, as "competitive capitalism." This SSA was characterized by, among other institutions, "small businesses, which competed with each other in the widening markets mainly by price cutting."

The price-cutting process which was endemic to a competitive market structure gives a clue to the nature of the breakdown of this SSA, which started in the mid-1870s. The SSA school argues that the competitive process eventually caught the corporations in a profit squeeze (see Reich 1994; PROFIT-SQUEEZE

ANALYSIS OF CRISES). Competition intensified towards the end of the nineteenth century, partially because of the breakdown of regional market barriers as a result of improvements in transportation. Corporations were caught between falling prices and a labor force able to raise its real wage through increasingly effective direct action on and off the shopfloor. This improvement in the fortunes of labor was at least partially conditioned by the competition for labor among firms. At the same time, competitive expansion led to chronic excess capacity, a further drag on the profit rate. Investment, driven by competition, initially continued in the face of the profit squeeze, intensifying the crisis which manifested itself in wild swings in the business cycle rather than intense stagnation during the 1880s and 1890s (see BUSINESS CYCLE THEORIES). Some nations, however, experienced a depression in the early to mid-1890s.

## Monopoly capital: 1890s–1940s

The crisis of the late nineteenth century was resolved with the advent of a new SSA, based on monopoly reorganization of the market. The developing crisis had produced pressures toward consolidation. Various barriers to consolidation began to wear away at the end of the century. A market in industrial securities took shape. New Jersey legalized the "holding company." Court interpretation of the Sherman Act, while outlawing informal pools and cartels, seemed to allow the creation of monopoly by merger. With the cyclical upturn in 1898, finance capital unleashed a wave of mergers which ended around 1904 in the US (Edwards 1979).

It was now possible to overcome the ruinous price wars through cooperative pricing behavior. Corporations were able to plan their market share, eliminating excess capacity. Monopoly would also be important in strengthening the capitalist class in conflict over the establishment of the other conditions of renewed accumulation. McDonough (1994) argues that the establishment of the monopoly market structure provided the lynchpin around

which the other institutions of the SSA were organized. In the USA, the increasingly monopolistic structure of capital led to a consolidation of political support for the Republican Party, the party of tariffs, for the gold standard, and for imperial expansion. The replacement of the anti-monopoly tradition in government was necessary if the new market structure was to survive. This was accomplished through a regime of mild regulation, bolstered by the development of corporatist ideology. Increasing corporate power enabled large firms to break unionizing efforts and to institute TAYLORISM and machine pacing on the shopfloor. Bigger corporations needed bigger markets and supplies of raw materials. This led to America's entry into the international imperialist sweepstakes around the turn of the century.

The monopoly market structure was to contribute to the next long run crisis of capitalism. Low wages dampened consumer demand. Competing imperialisms made the expansion of foreign markets difficult. Monopolized industries restricted the scope for investment. These factors, along with growing financial instability (see FINANCIAL INSTABILITY HYPOTHESIS), helped to promote the GREAT DEPRESSION of the 1930s.

## Postwar corporate system: 1940s–1990s

The resolution of the Great Depression involved profound institutional changes, including the Democratic Coalition, the Keynesian state, bureaucratic unionism and US international hegemony. Gordon et al. (1987) call the postwar corporate structure the "moderation of inter-capitalist rivalry." In the period after the Second World War, two interrelated structures evolved into place (see Bowles and Edwards 1985). One was a system of large-scale oligopoly production, with considerable monopoly rents and greater than average profits (core firms). The other was a more competitive system of small-scale producers, which in some measure lived off the contracts of the larger firms and had a much smaller rate of profit (peripheral firms).

Inter-capitalist rivalry was thus moderated through the emergence of the oligopoly system, with US-based TRANSNATIONAL CORPORATIONS dominating the world and large profits leading to high rates of accumulation. This worked well through the 1950s and the 1960s; but into the 1970s, 1980s and 1990s, such monopoly rents were challenged by firms from Europe and Japan, and eventually from Asia more generally. The intensification of competitive pressures have eroded profits and thus contributed to the erosion of profitability and accumulation (see HEGEMONY IN THE WORLD ECONOMY).

## A new corporate system?

Any new SSA in the twenty-first century will emerge in an environment of increasing globalization of capital. This development will lend greater importance to the study of the internal structure of the global corporation. Perhaps this will also provoke a closer examination of the internal organization of the corporation in the history of SSAs.

## See also:

pricing; regulation approach; social structure of accumulation: family; social structure of accumulation: financial; social structure of accumulation: state–citizen accord

## Selected references

Bowles, S. and Edwards, R. (1985) *Understanding Capitalism*, New York: Harper & Row.

Edwards, R. (1979) *Contested Terrain*, New York: Basic Books.

Gordon, David, Edwards, Richard and Reich, Michael (1982) *Segmented Work, Divided Workers*, Cambridge: Cambridge University Press.

Gordon, David, Weisskopf, Thomas and Bowles, Samuel (1987) "Power, Accumulation and Crisis: The Rise and Demise of the Postwar Social Structure of Accumulation," in Robert Cherry *et al.* (eds), *The Imperiled Economy Book 1*, New York: Union for Radical Political Economics, 395–400; repr. in Samuel Bowles and Richard Edwards (eds) (1990) *Radical Political Economy Volume II*, Aldershot and Brookfield, VT: Edward Elgar.

McDonough, T. (1994) "The Construction of Social Structures of Accumulation in US History," in D. Kotz, T. McDonough and M. Reich (eds), *Social Structures of Accumulation*, Cambridge, Cambridge University Press, 72–84.

—— (1995) "Lenin, Imperialism, and the Stages of Capitalist Development," *Science & Society* 59(4): 339–67.

Reich, M. (1994) "How Social Structures of Accumulation Decline and are Built," in D. Kotz, T. McDonough and M. Reich (eds), *Social Structures of Accumulation*, Cambridge: Cambridge University Press, 29–49.

TERRENCE MCDONOUGH

# social structure of accumulation: family

A workable family social structure of accumulation (SSA) is a set of domestic institutions and hence relationships which contribute to long-term macroeconomic performance by facilitating important family and systemic socioeconomic functions. A family SSA can facilitate communication, proper nutrition, emotional maturity, preparation for work, population growth, consumption and a potential LABOR FORCE, which may facilitate employment, HUMAN CAPITAL and growth. SSAs perform systemic functions which generally lie beyond the normal realm of individual firms (see SOCIAL STRUCTURES OF ACCUMULATION).

In the postwar era of Western capitalist development, the family SSA, along with other SSAs, contributed markedly to growth and ACCUMULATION during the 1940s–1960s, but CONTRADICTIONS emerged which reduced the positive role of the family (and many other institutions) in the late 1960s–1990s. A broadly similar pattern seems to have emerged in the USA, Canada, Western Europe, Australia and New Zealand.

The early years of the postwar era saw the emergence of a qualitatively new social structure of the family, through the baby boom phenomenon, a stable nuclear family, a child-centered ideology, the importance of the sphere of consumption and the emergence of the double day for women. A new era of optimism emerged in the family.

## Postwar functions of household labor

The family SSA, including household labor, promoted macroeconomic performance through four principal means. First, there was the reproduction of potential labor power, or children who in their teenage or later years contribute to gross domestic product and ECONOMIC SURPLUS (over and above consumption costs). For instance, the population of the United States increased from around 140 million people in 1945 to 213 million in 1974 and then to 249 million in 1990. This is a sizable increase in terms of demand, family organization and potential labor power, which contributed towards economic performance over the long run.

Second, household labor contributed to the reproduction of economic agents: actual labor power, workers, capitalists, rentiers, financiers, government workers, other household laborers, members of the RESERVE ARMY OF LABOR and the like. The workforce in the USA increased from around 65 million in 1950 to 92 million in 1973, and then to 129 million in 1992. This is a sizable increase, which necessitates constant attention to adequate nutrition, sleep and education/training in order for a nation to have an adequate supply of healthy, well-adjusted and skilled people to contribute to accumulation and growth.

Third, household labor contributed to the expansion of the sphere of consumption, through the promotion of emulation, mass consumption and management of household functions (see CONSPICUOUS CONSUMPTION AND EMULATION). There was a major shift from housework as production to housework as consumption activity, in which "shopping and managerial tasks" increased fivefold between 1935 and 1966 (Vanek 1974). The expansion of unwaged consumption work contributed to the cheapening of the value of labor power through the lower price of the product, and also to the expansion of demand and hence profitability.

Fourthly, the "double day" was a phenomenon of growing importance during the postwar era: women participated in paid employment, but also performed most of the domestic chores. For instance, US data for white, married, employed persons for 1977 shows that total labor time per week for women (including child care) was 87 hours while that of men was 77 (Coverman 1983). The double day is important because many women were expected to perform adequately both in the home and in paid employment, without the normative expectation that men would adequately share household duties.

Through these four functions, household labor and the family became critical to postwar stability and economic performance through the 1950s and 1960s. However, problems arose, especially from the late 1960s onwards. A major problem is that private capitals are as a general rule unable to secure the collective and social wealth necessary for institutional stability, and have no direct control over household labor to ensure a steady supply of the right type of labor power at the right price, place and time.

## Family instability in the 1970s–1990s

As Popenoe (1993) recognizes, since the late 1960s the HEGEMONY of the nuclear family has declined; families lost functions, power and authority over their members, and they became more unstable, smaller in size and shorter in duration. People now invest more time and money in themselves than in families. Nuclear family instability rose in the late 1960s, accelerated in the 1970s, and remained at a high level through the 1980s and 1990s. A landmark occurred in 1974 when, for the first time, more marriages ended in divorce than in death in the USA.

Families with the greatest threat of MAR-RIAGE disruption include those with low-income wives who average 35–40 hours at work per week. These working-class women had the lowest levels of support from husbands in household labor; hence the women's double day and dissatisfaction in marriage. Also, they often worked in enterprises which were sub-ordinating, uncreative and physically demand-ing. Both of these conditions promoted family disunity and divorce. During the early 1970s in the USA, the vast majority of separated or divorced women did not receive any alimony, and many children in such families lacked access to basic essentials (despite some degree of state support).

## Macroeconomic uncertainty and instability

Systemic family instability contributed to macroeconomic problems at three levels. First, the instability tendencies of unstable or broken families have a negative influence on the ability of children (and parents) to develop effective human capital and to engage in sustained levels of PRODUCTIVITY. This may have contributed in some measure to the PRODUCTIVITY SLOW-DOWN which has been taking place since the 1970s in most advanced capitalist nations.

Second, as the postwar era evolved, the tendency for labor, capital and consumers to relocate in search of market opportunities led to a breakdown in traditional social safety networks, and hence to a decline in the ability of people, on balance, to reproduce stable relationships of stability, friendship, love and community (see DISEMBEDDED ECONOMY). The ideology and practice of individualism, increas-ingly dominant in the USA (and many other nations), failed to sustain the social capital necessary for long-term stability, leading to an increase in systemic uncertainty which ad-versely affected capital accumulation.

The third factor concerns the latent industrial reserve army. As their labor force participation grew, the proportion of women in the potential reserve army by definition declined, which exerted upward pressure on the wage share of gross domestic product (GDP) and adversely affected the profit share. This may also have contributed in some measure to the declining profit rate since the 1970s in most advanced capitalist nations.

It is hypothesized that these three problems contributed to the uncertainty and instability associated with lower levels of expected profit and growth. The degree of fragility of the family environment influences the state of long-term expectation upon which long-term economic performance rests. At the general level, capital tends periodically to underinvest in the social capital and HUMAN CAPITAL necessary for long-term institutional stability, leading periodically to the demise of institu-tions, greater systemic uncertainty and macro-economic instability (which lowers the floor of business cycles). It is necessary to transform towards a non-patriarchal family SSA which is more stable, communal and participatory.

## See also:

class structures of households; domestic labor debate; patriarchy; reserve army of labor: latent; social and organizational capital

## Selected references

Coverman, S. (1973) "Gender, Domestic Labor Time, and Wage Inequality," *American So-ciological Review* 48(October): 633–7.

O'Hara, Phillip Anthony (1995) "Household Labor, the Family and Macroeconomic In-stability in the United States: 1940s–1990s," *Review of Social Economy* 53(1): 89–120.

Popenoe, D. (1993) "American Family Decline, 1960–1990: A Review and Appraisal," *Jour-nal of Marriage and the Family* 55(August): 527–41.

Vanek, J. (1974) "Time Spent in Housework," *Scientific American* 231(July): 116–20.

PHILLIP ANTHONY O'HARA

# social structure of accumulation: financial

The concept "financial social structure of accumulation" (FSSA) must be placed within a uniquely American paradigm developed recently by left-wing economists grouped in the UNION FOR RADICAL POLITICAL ECONOMICS (URPE). Their theoretical framework, often referred to as the SOCIAL STRUCTURES OF ACCUMULATION (SSA) approach, elucidates the historical evolution of institutions and the social organization of CLASS relations to analyze postwar CAPITALISM in the United States (Bowles *et al.* 1990).

Among the various social relations shaping our economic system the SSA approach identifies credit as one of fundamental importance in the processes of capital formation and income creation/distribution. Its modalities are an integral part of any economy's structure and can be conceptualized in terms of a "financial social structure of accumulation." This notion comprises credit's linkage to money, the financial institutions and markets organizing the interactions between lenders and borrowers, as well as the management of money and banking by the state's monetary authorities.

## Post-Depression financial SSA

Following the collapse of the gold standard during the GREAT DEPRESSION, Roosevelt's "New Deal" reforms put into place a new financial SSA based on ENDOGENOUS MONEY AND CREDIT. Protagonists of the SSA approach have analyzed this postwar financial SSA in terms of MONETARY POLICY AND CENTRAL BANKING FUNCTIONS involving regulation of the endogenous money supply and interest rates (Dymsky *et al.* 1993), the strategic position of commercial banks (Kotz 1978), as well as global capital transfers and exchange-rate determination under the BRETTON WOODS SYSTEM (Wachtel 1993).

## Decline of the financial SSA

The thrust of this tri-dimensional analysis has been to argue that, while the postwar financial SSA initially contributed to rapid economic expansion during the 1950s and 1960s by sustaining ample credit supplies at low interest rates, its evolution over the last couple of decades has been counterproductive and costly for our economy. URPE economists, such as Epstein, Pollin and Wachtel, like to point in this context to the prohibitively high interest rates caused by the Federal Reserve's conversion to MONETARISM and an excessive propensity for destabilizing SPECULATION in the aftermath of financial deregulation (see Wolfson 1994). These conclusions have led to recommendations for a more democratically representative central bank and a new regulatory framework for financial institutions capable of encouraging affordable credit for productive investments.

## Contribution of the regulation approach

Another variant of the financial SSA concept has been developed by the French REGULATION APPROACH (Aglietta 1976; Lipietz 1985; Guttmann 1996) the roots of which predate the SSA theory. Obvious similarities between the two approaches notwithstanding, the regulationists extended the financial SSA concept in two ways that have made an important contribution to our understanding of money, credit and finance. First, they have given us an unusually rich picture of the operations of "credit-money," with special emphasis on the postwar management of the tensions between its private commodity and public good aspects by the state's monetary authorities. Second, regulation theory has also helped to clarify the monetary and financial underpinnings of STAGFLATION as a new form of structural crisis which emerged in full force during the early 1970s.

The regulationist argument can be briefly summarized as follows: credit-money, our contemporary form of money, involves the creation of new funds by the banking system in acts of credit extension. Bank loans are thus automatically backed by liquidity injections. Such debt monetization facilitates continuous financing of excess spending, provided this process is managed by central banks in accommodating fashion through a combination of financial regulations, "easy money" policies and timely lender-of-last-resort interventions. That kind of "monetary regime" supported various pillars of the postwar boom: the widespread adoption of mass production technologies, oligopolistic administration of prices and wages, social consumption norms based on car and home ownership, chronic budget deficits in support of income maintenance programs or public sector investments, and large-scale capital transfers from the United States to the rest of the world.

When the boom ended in the late 1960s, due to a breakdown in the balance between wage increases and productivity growth, the institution of state-managed credit-money prevented the kind of debt-deflation adjustment that had characterized earlier depressions. Instead, there was a more moderate and gradual form of structural crisis that came to be known as stagflation. This crisis form, however, ended up destroying each of the constituent elements of the postwar monetary regime: Bretton Woods in 1971, domestic regulation of private bank money after 1975, low-interest monetary policy in 1979, and limited lender-of-last-resort guarantees aimed at crisis prevention by 1982.

## National differences

Another possible application of the financial SSA concept concerns national differences in the organization of credit and their effects on domestic economic performance. While the postwar regime of credit-money established commercial banks as the most important financial institutions, and indirect finance in the form of bank loans as the primary channel of credit in all industrial nations, two markedly different versions emerged. One was the model adopted in the United States which kept commercial banks small, limited in scope and separated from financial markets. This decentralized structure encouraged rapid growth of other financial institutions (e.g. investment banks, pension funds, mutual funds) and tradable securities (in lieu of bank loans) whose markets those non-bank institutions helped to organize. The other model, developed above all in Germany and Japan, consisted of much larger banks that were allowed to form close ties with industrial enterprises as both their creditors and principal shareholders. This more centralized structure may have played a crucial role in the rapid postwar recovery of the German and Japanese economies, but was ultimately hampered by relatively underdeveloped financial markets.

## Future research

Future research concerning the financial SSA concept will necessarily have to focus on trends that are currently transforming the financial structure of the economic system. Having been destroyed by the decade-long stagflation crisis, the postwar financial SSA is now giving way to something qualitatively different. The proliferation of new forms of private bank money has complicated monetary policy, with "electronic money" (especially cybercash on the Internet) marking the appearance of an entirely new money form. The deregulation of interest rates and EXCHANGE RATES has made those prices of money much more volatile, spurring FINANCIAL INNOVATIONS in so-called "derivatives" and feeding speculative activity on a massive scale. "Securitization" of credit threatens the position of commercial banks and forces their extensive restructuring while benefiting those intermediaries engaged in the organization of securities markets. Financial institutions and markets are increasingly global in nature, and this globalization encourages huge cross-border flows of capital. A greater propensity toward FINANCIAL CRISES must be contained by reforming existing lender-of-last-resort mechanisms.

## Conclusion

These trends do not necessarily produce a coherent financial SSA capable of sustaining growth at high employment levels. That objective requires additional reform initiatives toward a new regulatory framework for money and banking, including international policy coordination and harmonization of financial regulations. In their absence, the anti-inflationary obsessions and speculative proclivities of financial asset-holders have come to dominate our economy, subjecting its growth pattern to a great deal of instability and potentially dangerous deflationary pressures.

## See also:

finance capital; financial instability hypothesis; hegemony in the world economy; interest rate–profit rate link; international money and finance; social structure of accumulation: capital–labor accord; social structure of accumulation: corporate; social structure of accumulation: family; social structure of accumulation: state–citizen accord

## Selected references

Aglietta, M. (1976) *A Theory of Capitalist Regulation: The US Experience*, London: NLB, 1979.

Bowles, S., Gordon, D. and Weisskopf, T. (1990) *After the Wasteland: A Democratic Economics for the Year 2000*, Garden City, NY: Anchor Press/Doubleday.

Dymsky, G., Epstein, G. and Pollin, R. (eds) (1993) *Transforming the U.S. Financial System: An Equitable and Efficient Structure for the 21st Century*, Armonk, NY: M.E. Sharpe.

Guttmann, R. (1994) *How Credit-Money Shapes the Economy: The United States in a Global System*, Armonk, NY: M.E. Sharpe.

Kotz, D. (1978) *Bank Control of Large Corporations in the United States*, Berkeley: University of California Press.

Lipietz, A. (1985) *The Enchanted World: Inflation, Credit and the World Crisis*, London: Verso Books.

Wachtel, H. (1993) *The Money Mandarins: The Making of a Supranational Economic Order*, Armonk, NY: M.E. Sharpe.

Wolfson, Martin H. (1994) *Financial Crises: Understanding the Postwar U.S. Experience*, Armonk, NY: M.E. Sharpe.

ROBERT GUTTMANN

# social structure of accumulation: state–citizen accord

## Introduction

The state–citizen accord is one of the institutional pillars of the 1940s–1990s advanced capitalist SOCIAL STRUCTURES OF ACCUMULATION (SSA). According to the SSA theoretical approach, capitalist economies perform satisfactorily in the long-term when and so long as an appropriate set of socioeconomic institutions that collectively constitute a particular SSA has been firmly established. However, after some period of time they necessarily fall into a state of crisis and stagnation, due to the inherent CONTRADICTIONS within the SSAs. Many of the supporting institutions of each SSA inevitably turn from propellers to fetters of accumulation. The construction of a new SSA, based on a different set of institutions, becomes necessary for a new period of sustained economic growth to emerge.

## Definition and dimensions

The state–citizen accord (or "capital–citizen accord" as it is sometimes called) is meant to describe the process of mediation by the state in stabilizing the power relations between capital and the citizenry (or popular movements). Of critical importance is the role of the state, especially its role in affecting the SOCIAL WAGE as well as private profitability and capital ACCUMULATION. The state–citizen accord is characterized (like the other SSAs) as providing some element of harmonic coexistence, during which it exerted a positive contribution to profits (late 1940s to early 1970s), and then by a phase of erosion that seriously undermined corporate profitability (early 1970s to 1990s) (see Bowles *et al.* 1986, 1990).

There were three main dimensions of this accord. First, government macroeconomic stabilization policy, that kept unemployment rates at relatively low or politically acceptable levels. An example of this novel postwar role of the state was the Employment Act of 1946 in the USA. Secondly, direct subsidies and guaranteed markets for capital through state purchases that bolstered profitability, plus infrastructure expenditures that lowered the costs of operation for capital. And thirdly, the development of a rudimentary WELFARE STATE that socialized (to an extent) the reproduction of labor power and provided some kind of economic security for low-income families. The Social Security Act of 1935, one of the most enduring and popularly supported government programs, was an example of state action in this field. With a few qualifications (for instance, relatively less military expenditure and more social spending), the structure of state expenditures was similar in all advanced capitalist countries (see Gough 1975).

## Terms of the accord

The terms of the accord were such that the increased state intervention in economic and social reproduction left capitalist supremacy in resource allocation untouched. Furthermore, the accord helped to promote profitability and accumulation, by controlling capital–citizen conflict during the consolidation and rise of the postwar SSA in the 1940s and 1950s. But during the 1960s, popular reaction to the terms of the accord resulted in government intervention, in the form of more regulation on occupational health and safety, consumer safety and the environment. This challenged capitalist control and the logic of profitability to some degree, and eventually contributed towards undermining corporate profits and the entire SSA (Bowles *et al.* 1990: 57–61; 72–5).

## Assessment of the accord

While it is relatively straightforward to describe the postwar state intervention in the economy, it is more difficult to assess the overall economic and social impact of this intervention. It has been especially difficult to establish, empirically, the pattern of the relationship (first positive then negative) between the terms of the state–citizen accord and profitability that the SSA approach claims has characterized the postwar SSA. The degree of government regulation of business, and capital's tax share in total taxes, have been used in order to quantify the content of this power relationship and capture the effect of this particular accord on corporate profitability Those two indices were moving in the opposite direction, and they have contributed, on balance, to an increase in profitability throughout the entire period because of the continuous decline in capital's tax share (Bowles *et al.* 1986: 154).

Furthermore, in some SSA writings there is a degree of ambiguity regarding the nature of the state and the impact of state policies on interclass distribution, profitability and accumulation. In Bowles (1982), and especially in Bowles and Gintis (1982), it is argued that "the current articulation of the liberal democratic state and capitalist production renders the social whole a contradictory rather than a functional totality" (1982: 52). One of the results of this development was a large increase in the "citizen wage": the working class was able to redistribute economic surplus from capital through state policies, which was a major factor in producing the crisis of profitability. This argument has been empirically challenged in the SOCIAL WAGE debate by Shaikh and Tonak (1987) and Miller (1989), where it has been argued that the net transfer from the state to the working class was negative for most of the years of the postwar period; and the existence of a "welfare state" in the USA has been questioned. As a result, in the most recent works on the SSA approach, the direct state effect on distribution has been downplayed.

Other problems with the SSA account of the

state–citizen accord have to do with the fact that Keynesian demand management was first applied in a consistent manner only in the 1960s (Kotz 1987), while military expenditure was declining as a share of state expenditures and GDP after the early 1950s (Gough 1975; Miller 1987). Thus their effect on demand during the boom may not have been as strong as is implied in the analysis.

Developments in state policy and their effects after the late 1970s are less controversial. The Republican administrations in the 1980s directly attacked organized labor, initiated a wave of deregulation reforms and attempted through restrictive monetary policies to reduce demand and employment in a successful effort to redistribute income from labor to capital. The increases in military expenditures, plus the tax cuts for capital and the wealthy, resulted in public deficits, despite the cuts in social spending which have threatened a crisis in the reproduction of labor power. These trends not only were not reversed by the Democrats in (limited) power during the 1990s but, on the contrary, attacks on welfare and social spending have been intensified. However, so far it does not appear that a stable institutional relationship, involving the state and the economy, has been re-established in order to support the construction of a new SSA.

## See also:

cost of job loss; fiscal crisis of the state; hegemony in the world economy; Reaganomics and Thatcherism; social structure of accumulation: capital–labor accord; social structure of accumulation: corporate; social structure of accumulation: family; social structure of accumulation: financial

## Selected references

Bowles, Samuel (1982) "The Post-Keynesian Capital-Labor Stalemate," *Socialist Review* 65: 44–72.
Bowles, Samuel and Gintis, Herbert (1982) "The Crisis of Liberal Democratic Capital-

ism: The Case of the United States," *Politics and Society* 11(1): 51–93.
Bowles, Samuel, Gordon, David and Weisskopf, Thomas (1986) "Power and Profits: The Social Structure of Accumulation and the Profitability of the Postwar US Economy," *Review of Radical Political Economics* 18(1 & 2): 132–67.
—— (1990) *After The Waste Land*, Armonk, NY: M.E. Sharpe.
Gough, Ian (1975) "State Expenditures in Advanced Capitalism," *New Left Review* 92: 53–92.
Kotz, David M. (1987) "Long Waves and Social Structures of Accumulation: A Critique and Reinterpretation," *Review of Radical Political Economics* 19(4): 16–38.
Kotz, David M., McDonough, Terrence and Reich, Michael (1994) *Social Structures of Accumulation: The Political Economy of Growth and Crisis*, Cambridge: Cambridge University Press.
Miller, J. (1987) "Accumulation and State Intervention in the 1980s: A Crisis of Reproduction," in R. Cherry *et al.* (eds), *The Imperiled Economy*, New York: URPE.
—— (1989) "Social Wage or Social Profit? The Net Social Wage and the Welfare State," *Review of Radical Political Economics* 21(3): 82–90.
Shaikh, A. and Tonak, A. (1987) "The Welfare State and the Myth of the Social Wage," in R. Cherry *et al.* (eds), *The Imperiled Economy*, New York: URPE.

THANASIS MANIATIS

# social structures of accumulation

Social structures of accumulation (SSA) theory is a radical approach to economic growth and crisis under capitalism, initiated in the wake of the deteriorating economic conditions of the 1970s. It was first developed by David Gordon (1944–96) in a Union for Radical Political Economics (URPE) special education project volume entitled *U.S. Capitalism in Crisis* (Gordon 1978). A detailed theory of the SSA approach was developed by Gordon two years later (Gordon 1980). Since then the SAA concept has been developed and applied by Gordon with his colleagues Samuel Bowles, Tom Weisskopf, Michael Reich and Richard Edwards, to be followed by a host of other scholars (see for example Kotz *et al.* 1994). The theory operates at a middle-level between abstract Marxian historical materialism and theory-free, narrative accounts of historical development. It is perhaps best thought of as a radical theory of institutional change in capitalist society. Many similarities (and some differences) exist between the SSA and regulation approaches to the evolution and unstable growth of capitalism.

## SSA theory and hypotheses

The SSA approach begins by embracing LONG WAVES OF ECONOMIC GROWTH AND DEVELOPMENT. This is the idea that there have been recurring 40–60-year waves of capitalism, each wave of which includes an initial period of rapid capital accumulation followed by structural crisis during which accumulation and growth are subdued. SSA theory offers a new explanation for long waves which is grounded in social conflict and changing institutional arrangements (see INSTITUTIONS AND HABITS).

Institutional arrangements which are beyond the control of individual capitalists are viewed by the SSA approach as being important to the process of capital accumulation. Labor laws and collective bargaining agreements, the laws of incorporation and franchise arrangements, central banking and private bank lending practices, international agreements and conflict, and even relationships within the family are critical to the accumulation process, and too often ignored in more abstract theoretical formulations. Institutional arrangements facilitate accumulation in a variety of rather obvious ways; making it easier, for example, to acquire finance capital, to market products, and to ensure a steady supply of workers for production. The basic purpose of institutions is

to reduce uncertainty, especially the uncertainty associated with conflict over the distribution of rewards and decision making authority in society. Stable institutional arrangements allow capitalists to formulate reasonable expectations of the future, thereby promoting growth and ACCUMULATION.

However, institutional arrangements also contain the seeds of their own CONTRADICTIONS. Thus, while a given institutional structure – or SSA – facilitates growth and accumulation, it does so only temporarily. Internal contradictions eventually emerge which hamper accumulation, foster economic crises, and require resolution through the emergence of new institutional arrangements before capital accumulation and growth can resume at a healthy level. Contradictions may emerge, for example, because the dynamic process of capital accumulation renders older, more stable institutional arrangements no longer useful in facilitating growth; or because the evolution of institutions leads them to become relatively incompatible.

During crisis periods, capital and labor and other groups with conflicting interests seek to work out new institutional arrangements that may, once again, temporarily resolve distributional struggles and allow for renewed growth. Historical contingency and government action may be particularly important in influencing the path of institutional change during these periods, suggesting that the new institutional arrangements are not historically predetermined.

## History of successive SSAs

A brief treatment of SSA theory, as applied to the changing institutional arrangements of the US labor market and labor process (and extending beyond this for the 1970s–1990s explanation), gives a flavor of the approach. The US economy has experienced three long waves of accumulation (see Gordon *et al.* 1982): the 1850s–1890s, the 1890s–1930s, and the 1940s–1990s.

The period of "proletarianization" from roughly the 1850s to the 1870s was followed by relative decline until the mid-1890s. Growth and accumulation during the period of proletarianization was premised on the extension of proletarian status to a greater number of American workers. It followed upon years of experimentation with arrangements for fostering a wage labor force, and it went into crisis (1880s–1890s) when new technologies made it possible for, and indeed imperative that there be, a transfer of control in the labor process from workers to management. Capital accumulation and technological change had rendered the old institutional arrangements, premised on untransformed wage labor, dysfunctional.

The period of "homogenization" from roughly the 1890s to the First World War (or into the 1920s) was followed by the GREAT DEPRESSION of the 1930s. The rise of mass-production, and with it the de-skilling and homogenization of workers and Taylorist approaches to shopfloor control by management, brought forth the era of monopoly capitalism and the semi-skilled machine tender system (1890s–1920s). With a new wave of immigration providing fodder for the machine system, and large firms treating labor as a homogeneous and disposable commodity, wages were low, labor turnover was high, and profits and accumulation were robust. However, the poor treatment of labor, combined with its homogenization, provided the basis for a contradiction in this SSA. Homogenization fostered solidarity, and led to greater worker cooperation in demanding unions and even bolder forms of change. High rates of EXPLOITATION, worker solidarity, and of course instabilities associated with finance capital, helped to promote the crisis of the 1930s.

The period of "segmentation" from roughly the Second World War to the 1970s was followed by the structural crisis of the 1970s–1990s. Most SSA research has centered on this era, in the United States. The resolution of the crisis of the 1930s was in part due to the rise of independent unions and progressive government labor policies in the 1930s and early 1940s. Although divided, workers and citizens were granted a moderate degree of power through certain postwar institutional arrangements, such as the capital–labor accord

and the state–citizen accord. In addition, the existence of US HEGEMONY IN THE WORLD ECONOMY promoted stability for world capitalism in the 1950s and 1960s. Three other institutional spheres of importance in this period were the financial SSA, which propelled credit and banking security; the corporate SSA, segmented between oligopoly and competitive sectors; and the family SSA, which stabilized relations in the home and ensured a steady supply of quality labor power for business.

However, problems arose within all the major institutional relations. The growing gap between the earnings of the privileged and dispossessed segments of the labor market fostered demands by women and minorities for equal employment opportunities in the 1960s. Rising international competition and challenges to US hegemony during this period led to increased pressure on workers in the form of machinery speedups and rising injury rates, to which unions responded by bidding up wages and the government by introducing workplace health and safety regulations. However, after some time this put a squeeze on profits and propelled a PRODUCTIVITY SLOWDOWN, leading to declining investment and the emergence of the third period of economic crisis in US history, beginning in the late 1960s and early 1970s and following on to the present (see Weisskopf et al. 1983; Naples 1986). The onset of crisis was due to institutional arrangements impinging on profits and accumulation.

One response to the current long wave downswing has been the conservative policies of the Reagan and Bush administrations, which shifted power from workers and citizens back towards capital in the 1980s and early 1990s. However, this was done by raising real interest rates and dampening economic activity, and thus capacity utilization, thereby giving little incentive for a sustained resurgence of capital investment in the economy (see Bowles et al. 1989). An alternative approach to the present crisis would be to further workers' and citizens' roles in economic decision making, including investment decisions, as organizing principles for progressive social action (see Bowles et al.

1990). SSA analysis does not encourage us to wait for the crisis of capitalism in the hope that socialism will emerge from the ashes, but rather to act on the current institutional crisis of capital accumulation in the hope that "non-reformist reforms" might be instituted which move us closer to the goals of justice and economic democracy.

## Further research

SSA theory is still very much in its infancy and requires a rich understanding of the institutional features of an economy. Several elements of the theory are in need of further research to bring the theory to maturity. First, the existing account of the rise of a new SSA – i.e. coalition building around coherent proposals leading to compromise – is not terribly satisfying, as it fails to do justice to the subtle ways in which institutional arrangements actually do emerge. Second, the precise character of an SSA as a unified whole – i.e. beyond a laundry list of its constituent institutional elements – needs to be spelled out more clearly. For instance, is it necessary to have a completely new SSA, or is the notion of "core components" being reconstituted adequate? Third, the meaning of "internal contradiction" in the set of institutional arrangements that compose an SSA, and the links more generally to Marxian crisis theory, need further clarification. And fourth, extending the analysis further into areas of race and gender, developing nations, other advanced economies, and the world economy as a whole is needed in order to supplement the traditional SSA interests of class, labor and the US economy (see Kotz *et al.* (1994) for some initial work in some of these areas).

## Selected references

Bowles, Samuel, Gordon, David M. and Weisskopf, Thomas E. (1983) *Beyond the Wasteland: A Democratic Alternative to Economic Decline*, Garden City, NY; Anchor Press/Doubleday.

—— (1986) "Power and Profits: The Social Structure of Accumulation and the Profit-ability of the Postwar U.S. Economy," in *Review of Radical Political Economics* 18 (1–2): 132–67.

—— (1989) "Business Ascendancy and Economic Impasse: A Structural Retrospective on Conservative Economics, 1979–1987," in *Journal of Economic Perspectives* 3(1): 107–34.

—— (1990) *After the Wasteland: A Democratic Economics for the Year 2000*, Armonk, NY: M.E. Sharpe.

Gordon, David M. (1978) "Up and Down the Roller Coaster," in *U.S. Capitalism in Crisis*, an education project produced by the Union for Radical Political Economics, New York.

—— (1980) "Stages of Accumulation and Long Economic Cycles," in *Processes of the World System*, ed. Terence Hopkins and Immanuel Wallerstein, Beverley Hills, CA: Sage Publications.

Gordon, David M., Edwards, Richard and Reich, Michael (1982) *Segmented Work, Divided Workers: The Historical Transformation of Labor in the United States*, New York: Cambridge University Press.

Kotz, David M., McDonough, Terrence and Reich, Michael (1994) *Social Structures of Accumulation: The Political Economy of Growth and Crisis*, New York, Cambridge University Press.

Naples, Michele I. (1986) "The Unraveling of the Union–Capital Truce and the U.S. Industrial Productivity Crisis," in *Review of Radical Political Economics* 18(1–2): 110–31.

Weisskopf, Thomas E., Gordon, David M. and Bowles, Samuel (1983) "Hearts and Minds: A Social Model of U.S. Productivity Growth," in *Brookings Papers on Economic Activity* 2: 381–450.

DAVID FAIRRIS

# social wage

## Broad and narrow definitions

The social wage can be defined as government expenditure and tax measures which affect living standards through both direct income transfers and the provision of services (Baldock and Cass 1988). This definition sees the social wage as comprising: (1) income replacements for those unable to be in paid work; (2) money income supplements such as payments towards the care of children, universal or targeted to families on low incomes; (3) money income, vouchers or subsidies, universal or targeted to those on low incomes and tied to particular expenses, such as food, housing or the purchase of superannuation; and (4) the provision of free or subsidized services, such as health and education. It also sees the social wage as applying to all citizens, not just those in paid work, and being provided by governments out of taxation revenues, although contributory social security schemes may also be involved.

When used in this broad sense and set at a generous level, it is only a short step to the notion of a citizen's or universal basic income, based not on social insurance or a categorical benefit system, but on the concept of social citizenship. Organizations in Europe, New Zealand and elsewhere are currently advocating various versions of this, financed from one or more taxes on income, land or financial transactions. The concept can also be traced back to the notion of the "national dividend of social credit" (Hutchinson 1995).

However, the notion of social wage has alternatively come to be used for the "full" wage, including the wage plus benefits of the types (2) to (4) above, to wage earners. In this narrower framework, some elements may accrue to all citizens and be paid from tax revenues, but others will apply only to those in waged work. Social citizenship, based on the economic citizenship of the supposed universal wage earner, is inevitably gender and race biased (Pateman 1988). Hence, some feminist analyses of welfare systems also suggest a guaranteed universal income (Funiciello 1993). Generous provisions under either concept of the social wage have come under increasing scrutiny in the reduction in government expenditure of the 1980s–1990s, for example in Scandinavian countries. Many business interests lobby to cut non-wage labor

costs in order to reduce elements of regulation and social wage provisions.

## Trade-off social wage for wage constraint

Under either usage, increases in government or employer expenditures towards the social wage (and in the second usage government imposed expenditures by employers) may be invoked as a rationale for wage restraint. Reduced taxes as a trade off against low wage increases are used similarly. The Australian experience with the Government/Trade Union Accord was an example of cases where such tradeoffs were explicitly bargained at a centralized level. The Australian Labor Party, in government from 1983 to 1995, considered initially that it could achieve macroeconomic objectives by obtaining union support for wage restraint in return for social wage gains, including the introduction of Medicare and a role in decision making. However, later in its term of office the real value of the broad social wage declined, with a consequent increase in the COST OF JOB LOSS.

In addition, where only wage-earners benefit, adverse effects on groups with a relatively marginal position in the labor market, including women, result. This is often part of a deliberate government strategy to increase the gap between those in paid work and those on benefits. Benefits and services to those not in paid work will then tend to become a residual safety net at an inadequate level, increasing poverty in this group. It also exacerbates the binary divide into superior and inferior strata for social policy, social insurance or employer provided benefits against government provisions, rights-based against needs based, independent against dependent, entitlements against welfare, and even deserving against undeserving. This divide is also evident in the United States, with federal against state/local governments and contributory against noncontributory. These divides are gendered and racialized, and create two classes of social citizenship (Gordon 1994).

## Family wage policies

Countries which place importance on the wage-earners' social wage are also inclined to place emphasis on FAMILY WAGE policies to ensure that minimum earnings and benefits available to all male employees should be sufficient to support a family. While this has the advantage of securing adequate subsistence for the families of employed lower paid men, it puts in sharp focus the separate spheres of men and women and increases the divide between the employed and others in poverty. Countries in this category tend to have highly targeted support through social security, with benefits residual and flat-rate, and child support low and not universal. New Zealand is an example of this conjunction.

## Examples: New Zealand and Australia

For instance, the first Labor government in New Zealand, elected in 1935, combined aspects of both a universal and wage-earner social wage. This included progressive implementation of policies aimed at low income earners: free hospital care, maternity benefits, free prescriptions, state housing, plus minimum wages and other labor market policies (Du Plessis 1995). However, the broader social wage was later eroded and the wage earner social wage became predominant (Castles 1985).

In Australia, the family wage principle dates back to the 1907 Harvester case. As late as 1949–50, Justice Foster ruled that the male basic wage was a social wage for a man, his wife and family and that equal pay for women would put an intolerable strain on the economy (Isaac 1989). The later years of the Australian Accord into the early–mid 1990s were again based more on the wage-earners' than the universal social wage. Employer-provided superannuation as part of award wage settlements became a part of wage policy under the Accord in 1985. However, collective bargaining over its implementation resulted in not all part-time and casual staff, predominantly women, benefiting. Despite extended coverage from 1991 a gender gap remains (Sharp 1995).

## See also:

collective social wealth; community; economic rationalism or liberalism; feminist political economy: major contemporary themes; fiscal crisis of the state; inequality; needs; rights; Scandinavian model; social structure of accumulation: state–citizen accord; welfare state

## Selected references

Baldock, C. and Cass, B. (1988) *Women, Social Welfare and the State in Australia*, Sydney: Allen & Unwin.

Castles, F.G. (1985) *The Working Class and Welfare: Reflections on the Political Development of the Welfare State in Australia and New Zealand 1890–1980*, Wellington: Allen & Unwin.

Du Plessis, R. (1995) "Women in a Restructured New Zealand: Lessons for Australia," in A. Edwards and S. Magarey (eds), *Women in a Restructuring Australia*, St Leonards, NSW: Allen & Unwin.

Funiciello, T. (1993) *Tyranny of Kindness – Dismantling the Welfare Sytem to End Poverty in America*, New York: Atlantic Monthly Press.

Gordon, L. (1994) *Pitied But Not Entitled: Single Mothers and the History of Welfare 1890–1935*, Cambridge, MA: Harvard University Press.

Hutchinson, F. (1995) "A Heretical View of Economic Growth and Income Distribution," in E. Suiper and J. Sap (eds), *Out of the Margin: Feminist Perspectives on Economics*, London and New York: Routledge.

Isaac, J.E. (1989) "The Arbitration Commission: Prime Mover Or Facilitator?," *Journal of Industrial Relations* 4(3): 407–27.

Pateman, C. (1988) "The Patriarchal Welfare State," in A. Gutman (ed.), *Democracy and the Welfare State*, Princeton, NJ: Princeton University Press.

Sharp, R. (1995) "Women and Superannuation: Super Bargain or Raw Deal?," in A. Edwards and S. Magarey (eds), *Women in a*

*Restructuring Australia*, St Leonards, NSW: Allen & Unwin.

PRUE HYMAN

**SOCIAL WEALTH, COLLECTIVE:** *see* collective social wealth

# socialism and communism

The terms socialism and communism have never had single, universally agreed meanings. The range of their modern meanings emerged in the late eighteenth and nineteenth centuries as names taken by various reformist and revolutionary groups. The root notions of "common" and "social" reflected these groups' differing antipathies to the private property individualism increasingly dominant across those centuries and since. Socialist and communist thinkers constructed critical analyses of private property, individualism and the societies committed to them. The latter came increasingly to be called CAPITALISM. When those analyses focused attention on the economic structures and effects of capitalism, and when they sometimes sketched desired alternative economic structures, we may speak of the emergence of "political economies of socialism and communism." Where CLASSICAL POLITICAL ECONOMY and then NEOCLASSICAL ECONOMICS emerged largely to celebrate capitalism and criticize socialism and communism, the political economies of the latter variously pursued the reverse agenda.

## Marxian views of socialism and communism

While the political economy of socialism and communism includes a diverse collection of theories, those associated with Karl MARX have been the best known, the most thoroughly worked out, and the most widely disseminated globally. Indeed, the different interpretations of Marx's work have yielded several different Marxian political economies of socialism and communism alongside the non-Marxian. Any complete discussion of the issue would have to account for all the theories, not just the few discussed here because of space limitations (Howard and King offer a survey in their two-volume *A History of Marxian Economics*, published in 1989 and 1992).

The most influential (although not the first) early statement of a Marxian political economy of socialism was Engels's *Socialism: Utopian and Scientific*. For Engels, capitalism had outlived its historical usefulness. Where it had once represented an advance over the FEUDALISM which preceded it – especially in terms of the quality and quantity of production it made possible – its evolution had transformed it into the enemy of further advances. While private entrepreneurs hiring free laborers and operating in MARKETS broke through the limitations of feudal economy, once dominant they also displayed the limitations of their capitalist system. On the one hand, they had developed technologically, amassing masses of hired laborers in huge factories yielding vast outpourings of use-values. On the other hand, they also interacted in markets in ways that seemed increasingly irrational and socially disastrous.

First, their interactions yielded recurring, serious macroinstability: the business cycles or crises. Vast wastage of human and material resources attended these regular downturns. Second, centralization and concentration of capital made the production process increasingly social (disciplined, coordinated production systems driven to maximize productivity) even as it positioned fewer and fewer private corporate boards as a dominant economic and also political elite. Their private profit calculations had social consequences, yet they were not responsible for them. Capitalism was, in short, the scene of a deepening contradiction between its socialized production system and its privatized ownership and control systems (see CONTRADICTIONS).

Engels and Marx sometimes wrote that this social/private (or collective/individual) contradiction at the heart of capitalism would be its inevitable undoing, exploding as its costs rose to socially intolerable levels. Their political

1071

economy of socialism represented in part a critique of classical and neoclassical economics for their blindness to this contradiction. Yet it also formulated a positive counterpart to its negative critique of pro-capitalist theories. The political economy of socialism affirmed the desirability and argued the viability of a collective economic system which, instead of being capitalist, would be socialist.

## State socialism

What this meant has been interpreted and debated ever since, a good hundred years of diverse understandings. The dominant line of thinking took socialism to mean that productive PROPERTY should be owned collectively, not privately, and managed by the state as custodian for the collectivity. However, those who thought this way also disagreed among themselves about (a) whether all or only some productive property should be collectivized, and (b) whether the state should manage markets or eliminate them in favor of state planning and administration of the production and distribution of goods and services. Often the term communist attached to those who went the furthest toward collectivization and state planning and administration. The term socialist (or social democrat) then referred to those more inclined to allow some private property and some role for (state managed) markets. Despite these disagreements, which often ran deep and were sometimes expressed in violent ways, both socialists and communists shared a fundamental allegiance to Engels's basic analysis. They therefore focused on capitalism's injustices and inefficiencies as fruits of its historically anachronistic combination of private property and socialized production systems (Lenin 1967; Nove and Nuti 1972; Bottomore 1990).

## Worker-control socialism

There were always significant dissents from this dominant strain (and its variants) of the political economy of socialism and communism. Typically, these either added other features of capitalism (beyond property ownership and markets) that had to be radically altered to achieve socialism, or else they made such other features more central to the definition of socialism and displaced property and markets to matters of lesser or even marginal importance. For example, advocates of "workers' control" opposed state ownership in favor of direct worker ownership and control of production facilities. Among them, some supported state planning of the distribution of resources and products, while others advocated letting markets mediate among such worker owned and controlled enterprises (Vanek 1975; Sirianni 1982). Still other workers' control groups favored state ownership but worker control of production facilities (see PARTICIPATORY DEMOCRACY AND SELF-MANAGEMENT).

## Communism, class and surplus

Another dissenting group – sometimes called the "new Marxian economists" and increasing over recent years – approaches the political economy of socialism and communism in quite different terms. It focuses the critique of capitalism not on its typical property ownership nor on its typical reliance on markets. The critique concerns rather the particular CLASS organization of production. By "class" is meant, not who owns productive property nor who controls production and distribution (important as these social conditions are) but, rather, the arrangement whereby some people – productive laborers – produce more in output than is returned to them as payment for that work. This labeled "surplus labor" – following Marx's formulation – passes automatically to others who did not themselves participate in producing it. These first recipients of this surplus are, by this class definition, capitalists. The capitalists then distribute portions of the surplus, realized in money form, to others as interest, dividends, rentals and so on and to themselves as profits and retained earnings (see EXPLOITATION AND SURPLUS VALUE).

Such a political economy of socialism and communism has some arresting differences from the traditionally prevalent view described above (Resnick and Wolff 1987; Callari and Ruccio 1996, part 3; Fraad *et al.* 1994). First, it objects most to that aspect of capitalism – the production of surplus by some and its appropriation by others – which it calls exploitation. This is seen to be fundamentally intolerable on grounds of ETHICS AND MORALITY, commitments to democracy and so on; but it is also seen to be a major contributor to many of capitalism's other unwanted qualities (inequality of income, wealth and power, inefficiencies of business cycles, DISEMBEDDED ECONOMY and so on). The critical arguments of such a political economy of socialism and communism thus focus on the class (in terms of surplus production and distribution) aspects of capitalism.

The positive sides of this alternative political economy are likewise rather new. The terms socialism and communism are radically recast. Capitalism is no longer seen as removed if and when collective replaces private property, if and when state planning replaces markets as mechanisms of distribution. Instead, if the structure of production remains one where the productive laborers produce a surplus appropriated by others, it remains capitalist whether the ownership is private or collective, whether distribution is planned or marketed. The defining issue for the arrival of a non-capitalist class structure is the presence or absence of the collective appropriation of the surplus by those who produced it. This is called "communism" and affirmed to be what Marx had in mind and what remains on the agenda for basic social change today. To stress their point, this group uses the term socialism for all those concrete social experiments and theoretical visions that couple capitalist class structures in production with collective property ownership and planning. In short, socialism is redefined as "state capitalism," and while it is sometimes a far more humane and desirable form of capitalism (as against private capitalisms), it is no longer what the Marxist-inspired revolution against capitalism seeks (Resnick and Wolff 1994). The latter is reserved as communism – the radically different, non-

capitalist organization of the class structure of production.

## Future of socialism and communism

The older tradition of political economy of socialism and communism – based on property ownership and private market versus state economic power – continues to fade. The rise of alternative political economies of socialism and communism are part of the rethinkings and repositionings among the critics of capitalism following upon the end of that remarkable experiment in anti-capitalist social organization called the USSR. It is not yet clear whether a consensus will soon emerge or what it will be. However, there is little doubt that political economies of socialism and communism, however differently defined, will develop and contest with increasing sharpness in the future.

For as long as capitalism has existed, it has provoked its devotees to formulate political economies that celebrate its virtues and debunk the possibility or desirability of alternatives. That will continue. Likewise capitalism has always provoked its critics to formulate political economies of socialism and communism as critiques of and alternatives to capitalism. Crises continue to beset capitalisms around the world. They display strong tendencies now to exacerbate unequal distributions of wealth, income, and power within and across national boundaries. Indeed, the old slogan of socialists and communists – "Workers of the world, unite" – may have more relevance now than it ever had. All these and still other features suggest that fertile ground and interested audiences for political economies of socialism and communism remain very much in place.

## See also:

alienation; capitalist breakdown debate; labor-managed enterprises; market socialism; Marxist political economy: major contemporary varieties; Mondragón; social democracy; social ownership and property

## Selected references

Bottomore, Tom (1990) *The Socialist Economy: Theory and Practice*, New York: Guilford Press.

Callari, Antonio and Ruccio, David F. (eds) (1996) *Postmodern Materialism and the Future of Marxist Theory*, Hanover, NH and London: Wesleyan University Press.

Fraad, Harriet, Resnick, Stephen and Wolff, Richard (1994) *Bringing it all Back Home: Class, Gender, and Power in the Modern Household*, London: Pluto.

Howard, M.C. and King, J.E. (1989–92) *A History of Marxian Economics*, 2 vols, Princeton, NJ: Princeton University Press.

Lenin, V.I. (1967) *On Socialist Economic Organization*, Moscow: Progress Publishers.

Nove, Alec and Nuti, D.M. (eds) (1972) *Socialist Economics*, Harmondsworth: Penguin.

Resnick, Stephen and Wolff, Richard (1987) *Knowledge and Class: A Marxian Critique of Political Economy*, Chicago: University of Chicago Press.

—— (1994) "Between State and Private Capitalism: What Was Soviet 'Socialism'?," *Rethinking Marxism* 7(1): 9–30.

Sirianni, Carmen (1982) *Workers' Control and Socialist Democracy: The Soviet Experience*, London: Verso.

Vanek, Jaroslav (ed.) (1975) *Self-Management: Economic Liberation of Man*, Harmondsworth: Penguin.

RICHARD D. WOLFF

# socialist calculation debate

## Mises and Barone

The issue of "economic calculation in socialism" was brought to the attention of economic theorists by the Austrian economist Mises in 1921. In this paper, Mises argued that, in an economy with state-owned production means, it was impossible to determine the value of capital goods and, consequently, to achieve an efficient use of the economic resources of society. However, the problem of economic calculation in socialism had been thoroughly discussed by the Italian economist Enrico Barone (1908) many years before Mises launched his "challenge." In this article, Barone showed that (when pursuing a rational use of resources) the problem of price formation was to be posed in the same way in a socialist economy as in a capitalist system. According to Barone, the problem with which the ministry of production of a socialist state had to cope was how to collect all the information needed in determining the prices of capital goods. Once this information had been collected, prices could be determined by solving the general equilibrium equations "on paper."

In Barone's view, however, the solution to the problem of determining equilibrium prices in a socialist system was at hand only in theory, but not in practice. If production coefficients were given, he argued, the ministry might succeed in collecting the huge body of data needed to establish the quantities of each good that would be demanded for each set of prices by setting up a colossal organizational structure. But as production coefficients are not fixed, he added, economic calculation in socialism is impracticable because it is impossible to identify *a priori*, i.e. on paper, the combinations of production coefficients that will minimize production costs.

## Taylor and Lange

In a 1929 contribution, which has often been misinterpreted, Taylor reached different conclusions (see Lange and Taylor 1938). He was the first to show how the trial and error procedure would have to be implemented. In his opinion, at the outset the ministry of production would have to fix prices for all production goods plus services and incomes for families. Based on these prices, the families would decide what consumer goods to buy and firms would choose production combinations capable of minimizing production costs. Monitoring the choices made, the ministry of production would then change those prices until demand equalled supply in all markets.

The merit for having solved the problem of economic calculation in socialism is usually attributed to Lange (see Lange and Taylor 1938). According to Lange, prices can and must be fixed in the same way in a socialist system as in a capitalist one with perfect competition. Individuals and firms make their choices based on given market prices for consumer goods or labor services, and on accounting prices which the ministry attributes to capital goods as scarcity indexes. Setting out from the levels of demand and supply which are observed at these prices, the ministry will then increase prices in every market where demand exceeds supply and vice versa, after the manner of Walras's *tâtonnement*.

But what rules will firms follow in making their choices? Lange made it clear that the socialist planner would have to impose two rules upon firms. The first rule is that factors must be combined in such a way as to level out weighted marginal productivities. The second rule is that the marginal costs of goods must equal prices everywhere (the so-called "Lange and Lerner rule"). As is well known, both of these are rules of maximum profit in perfect competition capitalism and lead to a Pareto optimum. From this perspective, Lange argued that, in his socialist model, there was not only planning but also a better market mechanism than the capitalist one (where perfect competition does not exist). In relation to planning, he contended that the task of the State was mainly to choose the accumulation rate in the long run by equating it with the level at which the marginal efficiency of capital is zero. Thus, Taylor and Lange's greatest merit was to have shown that the authorities of a socialist state would be in a position to tackle the economic calculation problem without having access to the technologies of firms and without solving "hundreds of thousands of equations" on paper.

## Dobb and Hayek

Nonetheless the Taylor–Lange model is open to a number of criticisms. Dobb, in particular, found fault with Lange's analyses, owing to their static nature. He emphasized that the problem needs to be addressed from a dynamic perspective, since only dynamic analyses will throw adequate light on the defects of the market. In Dobb's view, whenever investment decisions are left to the market they turn out to be thoroughly arbitrary and short-sighted, and they will systematically underestimate future needs.

Important criticisms of the Lange model were set forth by Hayek in 1940 (see Hayek 1948), who identified three distinct stages in the socialist calculation debate. The first stage addressed the question of whether a socialist economy could do entirely without value calculations. The second explored the problem of whether the central planner could determine value in a socialist system by simply relying on mathematical techniques. The third stage, the one in which Lange's contribution appeared, addressed the problem of whether a socialist economy could be expected to function by re-introducing some measure of competition. Hayek had criticisms at all the stages, especially the third.

When pricing is centralized, he observed, prices can only be fixed for large categories of goods and changed at long intervals of time (if they must be reviewed all together). Consequently, when pricing is centralized, the determination of prices may be made only in an approximate way. As for the prospects that the instructions of the planner are obeyed, if managers are prevented from inducing a supplier to offer them the quantities of a good they need, they would have obvious difficulties in manufacturing their products and would be, therefore, forced to adopt higher-cost techniques.

But let us assume that a manager about to run short of a tool expects a short-term price rise. Will she or he have to balance out price and marginal cost by basing calculations on the prices anticipated in the future? And if so, how will the manager convince the central bureau that she or he is behaving correctly if expected prices have not yet been fixed in any price list?

In other words, to control the actions of managers the planning authority would have to ascertain not only what managers have actually done, but also what they might or should have done; which Hayek thought was impossible in practice.

On the subject of risk-taking and investment choices, Hayek argued that the Lange model fails to make it clear how responsibility for decision-making and rewards and penalties for the consequences of such decisions would have to be apportioned between central authorities and firm managers. In Hayek's opinion, such crucial decisions cannot be vested in managers since these are not the owners of the firms' capital goods. However, such decisions cannot be left to central planners either, because economic information is dispersed and every individual is merely conversant with what is happening in the immediate vicinity. A planner, called upon to make all investment choices, would need a huge body of data concerning a myriad of facts which no single operator will ever be able to collect.

## Conclusion

One shortcoming of Hayek's contribution is that it seems to cling to the idea that the planning bureau would have to collect the data for the general economic equilibrium equations. Taylor and Lange had already made it clear that the planner did not need to solve a complex system of equations on paper. Nevertheless, historically the socialist calculation debate was formally brought to a close by Hayek's contribution. On occasion it was resumed in more recent years, for instance by Roberts (1971) and Don Lavoie (1985), but these later approaches do not seem to have changed the basic terms of the debate. Of course, questions of pricing under socialism have also been discussed by planners and theorists linked with the economies of the former Eastern bloc (see, for instance Bettelheim 1975: ch. 6), but these are not the terms of the debate discussed under the present heading.

## See also:

labor-managed enterprises; market socialism; Mondragón; participatory democracy and self-management; socialism and communism; Ward–Vanek model of self-management

## Selected references

Barone, E. (1908) "The Ministry of Production in the Collectivist State," in A. Nove and D.M. Nuti (eds), *Socialist Economics*, Harmondsworth: Penguin, 1972; also repr. in Hayek (1935).

Bettelheim, Charles (1975) *The Transition to Socialist Economy*, Brighton: Harvester Press.

Hayek, Friedrich A. (ed.) (1935) *Collectivist Economic Planning*, London: Routledge.

—— (1948) *Individualism and Economic Order*, Chicago: The University of Chicago Press.

Lange, Oskar and Taylor, Fred M. (1938) *On the Economic Theory of Socialism*, ed. Benjamin E. Lippincott, New York: McGraw-Hill, 1964.

Lavoie, Don (1985) *Rivalry and Central Planning*, Cambridge: Cambridge University Press.

Mises, L. von. (1921) "Economic Calculation in a Socialist Commonwealth," in A. Nove and D.M. Nuti (eds), *Socialist Economics*, Harmondsworth: Penguin, 1972; also repr. in Hayek (1935).

Roberts, P.C. (1971) "Oskar Lange's Theory of Socialist Planning," *Journal of Political Economy* 79.

BRUNO JOSSA

# speculation

Nicholas Kaldor defined speculation succinctly as:

the purchase (or sale) of goods with a view to re-sale (or repurchase) at a later date, where the motive behind such action is the expectation of a change in the relevant prices... and not a gain accruing through their use, or any kind of transformation effected in them or their transfer between different markets.

(Kaldor 1939: 1)

Speculative activity contrasts with what John Maynard KEYNES termed "enterprise," or long-term investment activities. The latter are driven by efforts to accumulate wealth via interest earnings or the accrual of long-term capital gains (Chick 1992). Long-term investors engaging in enterprise activities do not attempt to exploit short-term financial market volatility, but to forecast "the yield of assets over their whole life" (Keynes 1936: 158). While defining speculation remains uncontroversial, the causes and economic consequences of speculation remain a site of theoretical dispute.

## Speculative excesses

Spectacular speculative episodes have been documented over the past three centuries (Kindleberger 1989). Among the most widely analyzed are the Dutch "tulipmania" of 1634–7, the "Mississippi Bubble" of 1716–20, the "South Sea Bubble" of 1711–20 and the dramatic fluctuation of asset values throughout much of the world in the late 1980s. These (and other) cases are generally classified as speculative excesses because the behavior of boom-euphoric investors resulted in an appreciation of asset values beyond any fundamental or "rational" basis (see SPECULATIVE BUBBLES AND FUNDAMENTAL VALUES; RATIONALITY AND IRRATIONALITY). However, some contributions to neoclassical political economy theorize these episodes of asset price fluctuation as the result of "rational" decisions by informed investors reacting to new or inside information (Garber 1994).

## Heterodox and orthodox views

Keynesian and post-Keynesian theorists argue that speculation arises from the condition of "fundamental uncertainty" under which market participants make forecasts of future economic events. Given that the future is unknowable, speculators seek to arbitrate by "anticipating what average opinion expects average opinion to be" concerning future asset values (Keynes 1936: 156). What Keynes called "market psychology" is therefore central to Keynesian and post-Keynesian analyses of speculative activity.

Institutionalist political economy reaches similar conclusions: Thorstein VEBLEN in *The Theory of Business Enterprise*, first published in 1904, identified the same phenomenon as "folk psychology." The degree to which speculation occurs at any given time will depend on the state of investor sentiment and the matrix of institutional pressures, opportunities and incentives to speculate, such as the degree of liquidity of the market (see Carter 1991–2; Grabel 1995; FINANCIAL INNOVATIONS).

In neoclassical political economy, speculative activity is driven by two circumstances. The first is the opportunity to exploit divergences between the market price of a financial asset and its fundamental value which results from market imperfections, asymmetric information and so on (Friedman 1953). This price distortion creates opportunities for informed investors to garner speculative returns from a subsequent market correction. The second factor is a variance in risk preferences across agents. Financial innovation and deregulation allow for the creation of financial markets (such as futures markets) and instruments (such as derivatives) that allow relatively risk-averse agents to enter into contracts with agents willing to assume greater risk. These markets and instruments create opportunities for agents to enter into risk-shifting arrangements, and create new secondary markets for trading these instruments.

In monopoly capital theory, speculative activity flourishes in the context of economic stagnation which results from the concentration and overaccumulation of capital that characterize mature capitalist economies. Given that in times of stagnation there is a paucity of opportunities to extract surplus value via labor EXPLOITATION, capitalists must search for alternatives to generate profits

(Magdoff and Sweezy 1987). Speculation is one such activity.

## Similarities and differences in views

Note the following points of divergence and convergence among these schools of thought. Keynesian, post-Keynesian, and institutionalist theorists seek to embed the actions of speculators in the institutional context in which they operate. Facing fundamental uncertainty, they rely on conventional wisdom and best guesses in forming expectations of the future. In contrast, speculators in neoclassical political economy make rational decisions based on their true knowledge of economic fundamentals, their degree of risk-aversion and their probabilistic knowledge of the future. Monopoly capital theory largely abstracts from the question of knowledge and expectations formation, emphasizing, instead, the economic conditions that give rise to the speculative imperative.

These schools of thought differ substantially with regard to the effects that speculative activities have on the economy. Keynesian and post-Keynesian theorists contend that speculation destabilizes and distorts the economic activity of the real sector (such as manufacturing and high-tech industries). Active trading by speculators engenders financial asset price volatility and financial instability, which trigger real sector turbulence via direct linkages between the financial and real sectors. Speculation can, therefore, induce a contagion scenario in which the macroeconomy is destabilized and rendered vulnerable to economic shocks and crises (see FINANCIAL CRISES; FINANCIAL INSTABILITY HYPOTHESIS). Moreover, in that the opportunities to earn short-term capital gains by exploiting asset price volatility may induce agents to abandon enterprise in favor of speculation, there may be a general biasing of overall economic activity toward the latter and away from the former. Given that speculation – especially when it dominates enterprise – has such adverse economic effects, Keynes argued that "when the capital development of a country becomes the by-product of the activities of a casino, the job is likely to be ill-done" (Keynes 1936: 159). It follows that post-Keynesians call for the curtailment of speculation through transfer taxes and other means. Monopoly capital theory shares these insights, while emphasizing that disparities in income, wealth and especially ECONOMIC POWER may be aggravated in those societies where speculation dominates enterprise activities.

In contrast, neoclassical theorists have traditionally viewed speculation as being unambiguously beneficial to the economy (Friedman 1953). Speculation closes the gap between market and fundamental prices and hence restores the information content of asset prices. Moreover, assuming that the fundamental values of assets are relatively stable, speculation serves to stabilize market prices and, thereby, the macroeconomy.

These perspectives differ also with respect to the effects of speculation through the use of risk-shifting instruments. For Keynesians and post-Keynesians, the trading of risk-shifting instruments provides the illusion of safety, creating inducements for agents to assume greater risk and generating higher ambient risk levels in the economy. In neoclassical theory, on the other hand, risk-shifting instruments stabilize the economy while enhancing the welfare of risk-averse and risk-taking agents.

## Tension between neoclassical views

A notable tension has developed recently in neoclassical political economy. In contrast to the traditional view, some neoclassical theorists draw on the rent-seeking framework to argue that speculation is economically and socially wasteful, and may result in price distortions or destabilization. For example, Hart and Kreps (1986) show that speculation is price stabilizing only under very restrictive conditions. Others argue that speculation may actually reduce the information content of asset prices, and/or waste real resources in the pursuit of returns that do not directly result in increased output. There are some obvious affinities between this new work in neoclassical political economy and the critical stance toward speculation associated with the other perspectives surveyed here. To date, however, this new work has not supplanted the traditional view within neoclassical thought.

## Conclusion

The controversy over the causes and consequences of speculation is not likely to yield to empirical resolution. For one thing, the distinct paradigms surveyed here imply different measures of volatility. For example, Keynesians refuse the neoclassical presumption that observed asset prices reflect underlying fundamentals, and so object to neoclassical measures of divergences between market and fundamental prices. It follows, then, that controversy also surrounds the effort to measure the degree to which price volatility reflects changing fundamentals versus changing perceptions of market participants. Hence, the project of measuring the aggregate macroeconomic effects of price instability that speculation is seen to induce remains mired in empirical disagreement that follows from theoretical dispute.

## See also:

finance capital; money, credit and finance: major contemporary themes

## Selected references

Carter, Michael (1991–2) "Uncertainty, Liquidity and Speculation: A Keynesian Perspective on Financial Innovation in Debt Markets," *Journal of Post Keynesian Economics* 14(2): 169–82.

Chick, Victoria (1992) "Some Methodological Issues in the Theory of Speculation," in Philip Arestis and Sheila Dow (eds), *Money, Method and Keynes*, New York: St Martin's Press, 181–92.

Friedman, Milton (1953) "The Case for Flexible Exchange Rates," in *Essays in Positive Economics*, Chicago: University of Chicago.

Garber, Peter (1994) "Famous First Bubbles," in Robert Flood and Peter Garber (eds),

*Speculative Bubbles, Speculative Attacks, and Policy Switching*, Cambridge, MA: MIT Press, 31–54.

Grabel, Ilene (1995) "Speculation-Led Economic Development: A Post-Keynesian Interpretation of Financial Liberalization in the Third World," *International Review of Applied Economics* 9(2): 127–49.

Hart, Oliver and Kreps, David (1986) "Price Destabilizing Speculation," *Journal of Political Economy* 94(5): 927–52.

Kaldor, Nicholas (1939) "Speculation and Economic Stabilization," *Review of Economic Studies* 7(1): 1–27.

Keynes, John Maynard (1936) *The General Theory of Money, Interest and Employment*, New York: Harcourt Brace Jovanovich, 1964.

Kindleberger, Charles (1989) *Manias, Panics and Crashes*, New York: Basic Books.

Magdoff, Harry and Sweezy, Paul (1987) *Stagnation and the Financial Explosion*, New York: Monthly Review Press.

ILENE GRABEL

# speculative bubbles and fundamental values

Speculative bubbles describe a process denoting movements in asset prices that cannot be justified on any reasonable economic grounds, and are not sustainable. The idea behind bubbles is not new (see, for instance, Mill 1826; Keynes 1936). Historically, many assets, both real and financial, have been the object of intense speculation. But the higher profile events have most often involved highly liquid, financial assets. The stockmarket crashes of 1929 and 1987 are perfect examples.

## Definitions

Speculative bubbles occur when competitive bidding, motivated by repetitive and self-fulfilling expectations of capital gains, drives up asset prices in excess of any reasonable value

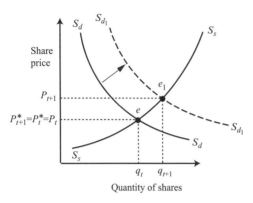

*Figure 12*

for the asset. At some point the speculative bubble "bursts," causing the process of accelerating price increases to halt and a round of distress selling to replace the bidding excesses. The result is that price fluctuations are greater than they would have been in the absence of a speculative bubble, and such bubbles are evidence of destabilizing speculation.

An asset's fundamental value is related directly to the stream of income that the asset is expected to generate over its lifetime. In competitive markets, an asset's price should just equal this stream of expected income discounted to the present. Acknowledging the presence of a speculative bubble, then, is the same as allowing for the possibility that, at times, this correspondence between prices and fundamental values does not hold.

According to the theory of efficient markets (strong form), asset prices "fully reflect" all available public and private information. If this hypothesis is correct, asset prices are not shifted durably away from fundamental values, and prices are then reliable signals of an asset's relative economic worth. As such, markets are said to be efficient. Prices provide accurate signals for resource allocation, and the consequent production and investment decisions are "optimal." If, however, a bubble exists in asset prices, the quality of price signals is distorted and the market's ability to transfer

command over resources in any efficient manner is inhibited.

## Illustration of bubbles

Examine Figure 12, for the share market, with supply ($S_s$) and demand ($S_d$) for shares. Imagine a situation in the 1980s, before the stockmarket crash of October 1987. After the deep recession of the early 1980s, a growing economy led to a higher level of confidence in the macroeconomy and the share market. By early 1986, both fundamentals ($P^*$) and share prices ($P$) were buoyant, and approximately equal around equilibrium point $e$. However, as the demand for shares rose from $S_d$ to $S_{d_1}$, share prices escalated to $P_{t+1}$ at point $e_1$ by mid-October 1987, while fundamentals were at the lower level of $P^*_{t+1}$. Share traders began to realize that the dynamics of the sharemarket can become quite autonomous from the real economy, especially during times of economic boom, when euphoria prevails. However, very suddenly this bubble reversed itself during late October 1987, since the speculative price bubble (equal to $P_{t+1}$ minus $P^*_{t+1}$) crashed as the demand for shares plummeted. Eventually, share prices and fundamentals became more equal again at the lower point $e$.

There are three main contemporary theories of speculative bubbles: (1) irrational bubbles, (2) endogenous or systemic bubbles, and (3) rational bubbles.

## Irrational bubbles

Some orthodox theorists explain bubbles as mean-reverting deviations from fundamentals. Deviations stem from the actions of a set of uninformed traders who adopt "feedback trading" strategies. De Long *et al.* (1990), for example, describe traders who are ignorant of fundamentals and whose behavior is guided instead by the most primitive of feedback trading strategies: buy after prices have risen (in the expectation of further rises) and sell after prices have fallen (in the expectation of further falls). The presence of these traders alters market dynamics. It becomes profitable for some sophisticated investors to disregard the intrinsic value of the asset, follow the herd and contribute to the irrationality of the asset bubble that results. Eventually, however, the dominance of smart traders selling overvalued stock and buying undervalued stock overtakes the feedback traders' actions, and the average value of shares reverts back to fundamentals over time.

## Endogenous bubbles

Friedman and Laibson (1989) have examined the endogenous nature of share market instability, in a model which is similar to the work of Hyman Minsky. Stockmarket crashes are thought to be systemic. The most recent economic or financial crisis becomes a more distant memory, the risk aversion of speculators declines as they presume that market risk is low. They then engage in more (endogenously generated) debt to finance their share purchases, since they are optimistic, and waves of euphoria pervade the market. However, a critical paradox emerges, since the lower the *perceived* risk, the higher is the *true* nature of the risk. Crises tend to occur when they have not occurred for some time, and they are not necessarily expected in accordance with the true underlying risk.

Thus, for instance, in early–mid 1987 speculators were optimistic about the future, and quite happy to engage in extravagant ventures in the light of their optimism, despite their recognition of the existence of bubbles. However, when the expected rate of growth of the bubble declined, such as in late October 1987, the crash was much greater than expected, because of the chain of credit linking speculators with banks and the true riskiness underlying the bubbles. While speculators may know of the existence of the bubbles, they have a distorted view of the potential ramifications of a crash.

## Rational bubbles

The idea of a "rational bubble" has been applied to the stockmarket crash of 1987 by Hardouvelis (1988). He hypothesized that bubbles may be initiated by extraneous events that are independent of fundamental values. One group of speculators buy shares, prices rise, and other speculators follow. Speculators know that share prices at period $t$ $(P_t)$ are greater than fundamentals at period $(P_t^*)$, to an extent equal to the bubble premium in this period $(b_t)$:

$$P_t = P_t^* + b_t$$

But they also know that they can make large profits by trading in the euphoric market. They realize that the bubble may crash, but continue to buy so long as trading brings them large returns (in line with Figure 12). Specifically, they continue trading in a buoyant market so long as their rate of return $(R_t)$ equals the risk free rate $(rf_t)$ plus the risk premium $(rp_t)$, plus the bubble premium $(bp_t)$, plus a return for unanticipated unforeseen circumstances $(e_t)$:

$$R_t = rf_t + rp_t + bp_t + e_t$$

During the stockmarket boom of 1986 and through to late 1987, the bubble premium was supposedly positive. Under these conditions, current expectations $(E_t)$ about the bubble next period $(b_{t+1})$ are that it will equal $(1+r)b_t$:

$$E_t(b_{t+1}) = (1+r)b_t$$

If stock prices rise less than the increasing level of "$r$," then there is a crash. In other words, the bubble continues only so long as $r$ keeps rising along with the probability and depth of the crash, and as long as speculators are compensated for the likely capital losses. When they think they are not being fully compensated, speculators make massive selloffs and the crash happens. Such is the explanation posed for the crash of October 1987 (and possibly the Japanese crash of the early 1990s), when stock prices dropped by over 40 percent in some countries (such as Australia, Hong Kong and Singapore). Perhaps the 1997/8 Asian financial crisis had some link to speculative bubbles?

## Conclusion

In general, there exists much debate about whether or not a given price increase at a given time in a given asset market is indeed justified by changes in the asset's fundamental value. Never is the debate more intense than when a sudden market collapse follows a given run-up in price. The significance of speculative bubbles is considerable, because they tend to foreshadow financial crises and depression, as occurred in the wake of the 1929 crash. Depression did not follow from the 1987 crash probably because of a number of factors, including accommodating monetary policy (see MONETARY POLICY AND CENTRAL BANKING FUNCTIONS).

## See also:

financial instability hypothesis; regulation and deregulation: financial

## Selected references

De Long, J.B., Schleifer, A., Summers, L.H. and Waldman, R.J. (1990) "Positive Feedback Investment Strategies and Destabilizing Rational Speculation," *Journal of Finance* 45(2): 375–95.

Friedman, B.M. and Laibson, David (1989) "Economic Implications of Extraordinary Movements in Stock Prices," *Brookings Papers on Economic Activity* 2.

Hardouvelis, Gikas A. (1988) "Evidence on Stock Market Speculative Bubbles: Japan, the United States, and Great Britain," *Federal Reserve Bank of New York Quarterly Review*, Summer: 4–16.

Keynes, John Maynard (1936) *The General Theory of Employment, Interest and Money*, London: Macmillan.

Kindleberger, C.P. (1978) *Manias, Panics, and Crashes*, New York: Basic Books.

Kompos, T. and Spotton, B. (1989) "A Note on Rational Bubbles," *Economic Letters* 30: 327–31.

Mill, J.S. (1826) "Paper Currency and Commercial Distress," in vol. 4, *Collected Works of John Stuart Mill*, ed. J.M. Robson, Toronto: University of Toronto Press, 1967.

Shiller, R.J. (1990) *Market Volatility*, Boston: MIT Press.

BRENDA SPOTTON
PHILLIP ANTHONY O'HARA

# sport

The "economics of sport" was given its first credentials when, forty years ago, Sam Rottenberg (1956) published his "trailblazing" article on the economics of the baseball labor market, in a leading mainstream journal of economics, the *Journal of Political Economy*.

## Traditions and main themes

Two traditions have emerged in the field, a North American or Anglo-Saxon tradition, and a continental European tradition. The Anglo-Saxon tradition generally has a microeconomic focus, often applying the standard supply and demand tools of microeconomics in an attempt to formally model the behavior of the various participants in the world of sport. North Americans, and their Anglo-Saxon colleagues from Britain and Australia, usually focus their attention on professional sport, more specifically men's team sports, as will be seen below. They use, whenever they can, econometrics and regression analysis.

On the other hand, economists from continental Europe usually rely on descriptive statistics, with the computation of various ratios. Their work is usually more of an institutionalist variety, i.e. more descriptive, sometimes relying on more unorthodox economic theories. Although they are also concerned with the implications of professional teams, continental Europeans mainly study the economics of amateur and recreational sport and the economics of the sport industry. For instance, they identify and assess the importance of private sponsors and government subsidies; they compute market shares, export and import ratios, and so on (Andreff *et al.* 1995).

One could argue that four main themes have

attracted the attention of economists of sport. These are (a) the impact and the causes of restrictions on players' mobility, (b) whether or not sport teams maximize profits, (c) exploitation of players, salary discrimination and entry discrimination, and (d) the economic impact of franchises in professional sport.

## Player mobility and income distribution

Since Rottenberg (1956), economists have systematically objected to the reserve clause or other similar restrictions on player mobility, for instance, in the "draft" of amateur players, whereby clubs own the rights to these players. Rottenberg's claim is that profit-maximizing club owners will behave in such a way that the distribution of talent will remain the same, whether restrictions are kept in place or removed. Thus, whether there are restrictions or not, big-city franchises should have winning teams while small-city franchises should have losing teams. The competitive imbalance is invariant to the restrictions designed to alter it. A similar result occurs with league-wide revenue sharing: competitive imbalance is not diminished whatsoever: small-city franchise owners do not use the additional financial resources to hire star players; instead they keep the extra money.

Thus the issue is about the DISTRIBUTION OF INCOME: who gets the rent (the extra profits) generated by extraordinary athletic ability, athletes or club owners, and if the latter, which club owners? This is most obvious in European soccer, where huge cash transfer payments are pocketed by the club when it still owns the rights of the player, whereas they are collected by the player as a signing bonus when the contract has expired.

## Do clubs maximize profit?

While the statements in the above paragraph constitute the representative opinion of economists, there has always been a minority current of contrary opinion on some of these statements. It has been pointed out that Rottenberg's claim assumes the standard profit-maximizing behavior. What if club owners have other objectives? Késenne (1996) has shown that Rottenberg's claim still holds if club owners maximize winning under a zero-profit budget constraint. However, if owners are content with some "satisficing" behavior, if they accept heavy losses, or if the league forbids the sale of players and unfair trades, Rottenberg's claim does not hold any more: restrictions to players' mobility will make the league more balanced. In addition, once the profit-maximizing hypothesis is dropped, revenue sharing will in all cases lead to improved league balance. Thus the debates that occur in the general economic literature, between proponents of profit-maximizing, growth-maximizing and objective-satisfying firms, find their equivalent form in the economics of sport, between proponents of profit-maximizing and victory-maximizing teams (see CORPORATE OBJECTIVES).

## Exploitation and discrimination?

Many economists attracted to the economics of sport are labor economists. Their main fascination with the sport industry is that there are reliable measures of output and PRODUCTIVITY per individual, in contrast to other industries. In sport, the reliable measures of individual output are, of course, the numerous individual performance statistics. In addition, over the last fifteen years or so, complete salary sets have become available. This has allowed economists to claim that performance has been increasingly unequally distributed, but that the inequality in the earnings of athletes has increased much faster (Scully 1995: 79). This phenomenon is setting major league sports on the road to SEGMENTED AND DUAL LABOR MARKETS (Bourg 1989).

There have been two approaches to the issue of salary determination in professional team sports. The first approach attempts to verify whether or not players are exploited by their employers, or it attempts to estimate which sort of player is being most exploited: star players or journeymen, free agents or those subjected to a reserve clause. This normative approach is based on the neoclassical concept of the marginal revenue product. The degree of EXPLOITATION is then defined as the ratio of the actual salary of the player to his marginal revenue product. This approach was first put in operation by Scully for baseball in 1974. It has been used in the arbitration hearings between the Major League Baseball Players Association and the Major Leagues, when the union filed grievance against the owners, accusing them of colluding to restrain the salaries of free agents in the mid-1980s. However, the results are highly sensitive to the technique used: conclusions about free agents having been "shafted" by the owners have been overturned.

Things are different with the second approach, more positive than normative, which purports to explain how salaries are actually determined. In this second approach, salaries are explained by the location characteristics of the team, as well as the characteristics and the past performance of players. Pascal and Rapping – the same Rapping who started new classical economics (along with Lucas) and who later turned to non-orthodoxy – were the first to proceed with this approach in 1972. It was shown repeatedly that salaries depend on various measures of performance and on experience. This approach has also been used to assess the presence of salary discrimination. It seems there is no salary discrimination against blacks or Hispanics in baseball or football, and salary discrimination against blacks in basketball seems to have recently subsided. These results are symmetric to those designed to assess entry discrimination, based on performance differentials by origin. There is some evidence of entry discrimination against blacks in basketball, and against French-Canadians in ice hockey (Kahn 1991).

## Impact of franchises

With the advent of free agency, and with the increase in popularity of professional team sport, the salaries of professional athletes have skyrocketed. As a result, the viability of several small market franchises has been questioned. Small market teams attract fewer spectators than big market ones; smaller attendance prevents poor teams from keeping or hiring productive free agents; and weak performance on the field worsens attendance figures (an instance of CIRCULAR AND CUMULATIVE CAUSATION). This has induced the owners of small market teams to favor league-wide revenue sharing and payroll caps, but also to pressure local public authorities in the hope of getting public subsidies or local tax exemptions. The renovation, construction, siting, and use of public sports stadiums or arena has become an issue on the political agenda.

While economic consultants, hired to assess the economic impact of sport teams and their stadiums on host communities, systematically find a positive impact, this is not so with academic economists. The latter are usually highly skeptical of the economic benefits associated with a new franchise and a new or renovated stadium. The consensus among academic economists is that most of the benefits, if they exist, are intangible and related to civic pride. The most recent studies are those of Baade (1996) and Rosentraub (1997). Looking at major leagues, they show that a new franchise or a new stadium has no impact on the level of metropolitan income or retail sales. Other studies have shown that the multiplicand in the multiplier formula is often near zero. In other words, the direct benefits assessed by sport consultants are grossly exaggerated, by omitting the fact that major league athletes save a large proportion of their revenues while their consumption expenditures are often made out of town. Subsidies to professional sport teams are thus money taken away from the median local taxpayer, and help rich franchise owners to pocket more profits while paying higher salaries to athletes who earn over one million dollars a year on average (in the four major North American sports).

## Conclusion

The economics of sport is thus a vibrant field of inquiry, with many interesting hypotheses and areas of concern. Different methods are being employed, and the range of publications is expanding. Many of the questions associated with the increasing link between sport and big business are being explored. Much scope exists for political economy type methods and analysis in this relatively new area of study.

## Selected references

Andreff, W., Bourg, J.F., Halba, B. and Nys, J.F. (1995) *Les enjeux économiques du sport en Europe: financement et impact économique*, Paris: Dalloz.
Baade, R.A. (1996) "Professional Sports as Catalysts for Metropolitan Economic Development," *Journal of Urban Afffairs* 18(1): 1–17.
Bourg, Jean-François (1989) "Le marché du travail sportif," in W. Andreff (ed.), *Économie politique du sport*, Paris: Dalloz.
Kahn, L.M. (1991) "Discrimination in Professional Sports: A Survey of the Evidence," *Industrial and Labor Relations Review* 44(3): 395–418.
Késenne, Stephan (1996) "League Management in Professional Team Sports with Win Maximizing Clubs," *European Journal for Sport Management* 1(4).
Rosentraub, Mark S. (1997) *Major League Losers: The Real Costs of Sports and Who's Paying for It*, New York: Basic Books.
Rottenberg, Sam (1956) "The Baseball Player's Labor Market," *Journal of Political Economy* 64(3): 242–58.
Scully, Gerald W. (1995) *The Market Structure of Sport*, Chicago: University of Chicago Press.

MARC LAVOIE

# Sraffa, Piero (1898–1983)

Piero Sraffa was the only son of a professor of commercial law, Angelo Sraffa, later Rector of Bocconi University. Following his family, he attended elementary schools in Parma, secondary schools in Milan, upper secondary schools and the University in Turin. During his secondary studies he was influenced by socialist ideas, and in 1919 he became a friend of Antonio Gramsci, the Italian Communist leader.

## Early work

As an economist, Sraffa started his career working on applied, mainly monetary and financial, issues. His degree dissertation, discussed with Luigi Einaudi in November 1920 (and simultaneously published for private circulation), was on the topic of *Monetary Inflation in Italy During and After the War*. Sraffa then worked for a few months in a bank, becoming familiar with the various duties of a bank clerk. In 1921–2 he visited the London School of Economics and met KEYNES in Cambridge. At the latter's request, he wrote an article on "The Bank Crisis in Italy" (published in the *Economic Journal* in June 1922), which shows a deep understanding of the problems involved in the relationships between banks and manufacturing firms. Another article, "The Present Situation of the Italian Banks," (*Manchester Guardian Supplement on the Reconstruction of Europe*, 7 December 1922), provoked a quarrel with Mussolini and the chairman of the Banca Commerciale. Two letters on the revaluation of the lira are then published in 1927 in *Stato operaio*.

In November 1923, Sraffa began an academic career as lecturer in public finance and political economy in the faculty of law at Perugia University. In January 1926 he became a full professor of political economy at Cagliari University. Then from 1927 he was on leave from his Cagliari chair to research and teach at Cambridge, and he left Italy just a few months after Gramsci's arrest.

## Returns to scale

Teaching a first-year, general course in economics induced Sraffa to critically reconsider the then-prevailing Marshallian approach. The result was "On the Relations between Cost and Quantity Produced," published in Italian in the *Annali di economia* during 1925. In this article, Sraffa attacks both the Marshallian method of partial equilibria, and the use of "laws of returns to scale" for establishing a (U-shaped) functional relationship between cost and quantity produced (see NEOCLASSICAL ECONOMICS). As for partial equilibrium, Sraffa showed that there is a contradiction between assuming perfect competition and using supply and demand curves in determining the price-quantity equilibrium. Supply and demand curves are not independent, since the reasons behind changes in average unit costs in the industry under consideration simultaneously cause unit average cost changes in other industries.

More generally, Sraffa criticized the attempt at unifying the "laws" of increasing and decreasing returns into a (U-shaped) supply curve. In classical political economy, decreasing returns stem from land, a scarce means of production, and are associated with rent; that is, with the theory of distribution. INCREASING RETURNS TO SCALE, instead, stem from the DIVISION OF LABOR, and in the framework of production theory explain economic development accompanying over TIME the expansion of markets. The different "laws of return" thus refer to a different kind of analysis, and cannot be coordinated in a single functional relationship connecting cost to quantity produced.

These criticisms are summarized in the first part of an article, "The Laws of Returns under Competitive Conditions," again written at the instigation of Keynes, published in the *Economic Journal* in December 1926. The second part of the article proposes a theory of imperfect competition, presented as a general case of which perfect competition and monopoly are but the extreme cases. As a result of the imperfections of real markets, in each industry every firm has before it a specific decreasing demand curve, even when the number of firms is large (see MARKET STRUCTURES).

The theory of imperfect competition attracted considerable attention, and was later developed by Joan Robinson and others. However, Sraffa is from the start conscious of the limits of this line of analysis. In particular, it neglects "the disturbing influence exercised by the competition of new firms attracted to an industry the conditions of which permit of high monopoly profits." This is precisely the element behind the classical theory of competition, and the assumption of a uniform rate of profits in all industries. This element was central to Sraffa's famous work *Production of Commodities by Means of Commodities* (1960), a first draft of which he showed to Keynes in 1928. Sraffa's explicit rejection of the Marshallian approach is evident in his contributions to the symposium on "Increasing Returns and the Representative Firm," in the *Economic Journal* for March 1930.

## Further Cambridge activities

In Cambridge Sraffa also gave lectures on the theory of value, and on German and Italian banking, between 1928 and 1931. Later he become Director of Research at King's College, then a Fellow of Trinity College and then Marshall Librarian. Sraffa also took part in the so-called Cambridge Circus, and in the discussions following the publication, in 1930, of Keynes's *Treatise on Money*. He also published a critique of Hayek's *Prices and Production* in the *Economic Journal* in March 1932, followed in the subsequent issue by a short note replying to Hayek's rejoinder. In these articles, Sraffa stressed the crucial differences between the monetary theory of Keynes and Hayek. He also developed an analytical tool, the "own rate of interest," which Keynes was to use in Chapter 17 of his *General Theory of Employment, Interest and Money*. In collaboration with Keynes, Sraffa also edited *An Abstract of a Treatise on Human Nature*, a learned introduction to Hume's book, which was published in 1938.

In 1930, on behalf of the Royal Economic Society, Keynes entrusted Sraffa with the editorship of the critical edition of Ricardo's *Works and Correspondence*. After many years of work (and a *coup de théâtre* in July 1943 when important manuscripts of Ricardo were discovered in Ireland), ten volumes appeared between 1951 and 1955, followed by a volume of indexes in 1973. With unrivaled philological rigor, Sraffa rescues Ricardo from a century of marginalist misinterpretations (Marshall, Cannan, Hollander), bringing to new light the CLASSICAL POLITICAL ECONOMY approach based on the notion of the surplus.

## Production of Commodities

Parallel to the work of Ricardo, Sraffa proceeded with his theoretical research, culminating in his book *Production of Commodities by Means of Commodities*. Here, Sraffa solves the classical problem of value by the simultaneous determination of relative prices and the rate of profit. TECHNOLOGY and production levels, and one of the two distributive variables (wage rate or rate of profits) are data. Uniform profit rates in the different sectors of the economy are assumed, following the classical idea that the unity of a capitalist economic system is ensured by the freedom of movement of capital in search of the most remunerative employment.

The classical representation of an economy, based on the division of labor, is also assumed. In such a system, at the end of the productive process, each sector has to rebuild its own stock of means of production in order to be able to start up a new cycle of production. This it does by selling its own product to the other sectors and acquiring from them its own means of production. Relative prices must be such as to guarantee the "reproduction" of the economic system. Each sector must be able to replenish the capital advanced and have the necessary profit incentive to continue production. Since commodities are simultaneously products and means of production, the price of each commodity cannot be determined independently of the others.

Exchange relations are thus determined within what has been called "the conceptual framework of reproducibility," representing a break from the marginalist "scarcity approach." The latter defines prices as indicators of scarcity, while Sraffa concentrates on the relative "difficulty of production." Sraffa's analysis provides the foundations for a critique of marginalist value theory, especially the notion of the rate of profit as the "scarcity price" of a "factor of production" called capital. Sraffa also critiques the idea of a direct functional relationship between the wage rate and the capital–labor ratio, with negative consequences for the marginalist adjustment process which is supposed to lead to full employment equilibrium in the long run (see SURPLUS APPROACH TO POLITICAL ECONOMY).

Sraffa thus isolates *in vacuo* a specific problem, the relationship between relative prices and distributive variables, and considers only the factors directly relevant to the problem. The analysis concerns a "photograph" of an economic system at a given moment of its development. Other issues, concerning levels of production, absorption of production, distribution, investment, technical change and so on, are left aside to be dealt with separately, possibly with different kinds of analyses and different analytical tools.

## Influence of Sraffa

Sraffa had considerable influence on the Austrian philosopher Ludwig Wittgenstein, whom he met at Cambridge in 1929. He influenced Wittgenstein's transition from the logical atomism of his book, the *Tractatus logico-philosophicus*, to the *Philosophical Investigations* published posthumously in 1953. In the *Tractatus*, Wittgenstein argues for a logical, axiomatic system of propositions, each describing a "fact" and in their totality describing the world, or rather everything in the world which can be described in rational form: in short, a "general theory." Wittgenstein later abandons this position, developing a theory of "linguistic games" or ideal models that concentrate on particular aspects, each one capable of being considered a general language for a given situation: that is, a specific analytical treatment of each issue.

More generally, Sraffa exerted an extraordinary influence on the culture of the twentieth century. This is true not only of political economy but also in politics and philosophy, through his friends Gramsci and Wittgenstein. Within economics, he set himself a gigantic task of shifting the pattern of research from the dominant marginalist approach towards a modern revival of the classical tradition, which was open to Keynes's insights. To this gigantic task he provided the main pillars, in his role as the "founding father" of SRAFFIAN POLITICAL ECONOMY. He contributed to a critique of traditional marginalist value theory; a revival of the classical conceptual framework, based on the notion of the surplus; and an analytical solution to crucial issues left unsolved by classical authors. It is now up to modern political economists to bring to full fruition this line of research.

## Selected references

Ricardo, David (1951–55) *Works and Correspondence*, 10 vols, ed. Piero Sraffa, Cambridge: Cambridge University Press.

Roncaglia, Alessandro (1978) *Sraffa and the Theory of Prices*, New York: Wiley.

Sraffa, Piero (1925) "Sulle relazioni fra costo e quantità prodotta," (On the Relations between Cost and Quantity Produced), *Annali di economia* 2: 277–328.

—— (1926) "The Laws of Returns under Competitive Conditions," *Economic Journal* 36: 535–50.

—— (1960) *Production of Commodities by Means of Commodities*, Cambridge: Cambridge University Press.

ALESSANDRO RONCAGLIA

# Sraffa's critique of atomism

## Sraffa's critical perspective

Piero Sraffa's *Production of Commodities by Means of Commodities* (1960) is subtitled *Prelude to a Critique of Economic Theory*. One important aspect of the book is the demonstration that knowledge of consumer preferences is not necessary to the derivation of relative prices. Given knowledge of (1) the technical alternatives of production, (2) the size and composition of the social product, and (3) the real wage rate, one can determine a system

of relative prices and the rate of profit (see PRICE THEORY, SRAFFIAN).

Since Marshall, neoclassical economists have explained prices in supply and demand terms, utilizing consumer preferences to explain the demand side of markets. Indeed, Marshall coined the idea that supply and demand are like the blades of a pair of scissors, both being necessary to the determination of prices. The critical thrust of Sraffa's book, then, was aimed at Marshall's general view of prices as supply and demand determined, as well as NEOCLASSICAL ECONOMICS subsequently based upon it.

Earlier, however, SRAFFA (1926) developed a related but somewhat different critique of Marshall's partial equilibrium analysis. Marshall assumed that the conditions of production and the demand for any commodity could be considered essentially independent both of one another and of the conditions of production and demand for other commodities. Ruling out constant costs, which would have eliminated a role for demand in determining prices, Marshall supposed that the effects on costs of diminishing and increasing returns in any industry were confined to the industry under examination.

Sraffa showed that this involved a misrepresentation of the nature of diminishing and increasing returns. He also showed that a variation in the quantity produced in an industry generally creates forces which act not only on costs in that industry but also on the costs of other industries. Industries, then, are generally interdependent in relation to costs. Athough the subject was complex, it was necessary to forgo partial equilibrium analysis, and "examine the conditions of simultaneous equilibrium in numerous industries" (Sraffa 1926: 541).

Sraffa thus rejected Marshall's view that the laws of supply and demand could be explained in terms of symmetrically opposed, atomistically independent forces. Indeed, not only did the different forces acting on costs operate across industries, but these also interacted with demand factors. For Sraffa, the theory of competitive valuation departed from the actual state of things in two important respects. The first is in supposing that producers could not affect market prices; and the second is in supposing that they normally produce in circumstances of individually increasing costs. Everyday experience, rather, showed that most producers experienced diminishing costs, and that they found it necessary to reduce prices if they were to sell larger quantities of their products. This created conditions for the emergence of monopoly, and further showed that Marshall's model of many autonomous undertakings was inconsistent with an interdependence of supply and demand forces both within and across industries.

## Association with Wittgenstein

Sraffa's critical perspective on atomistic independence was also indirectly exhibited in connection with his interaction with Ludwig Wittgenstein after 1929. Wittgenstein's early logical atomist philosophy (1921) assumed that elementary statements "pictured" facts about the world, and that the logical form of true statements mirrored the actual configuration of objects. According to Norman Malcolm's memoir of Wittgenstein (1958: 69), Sraffa shook Wittgenstein's confidence in this view when he asked Wittgenstein to explain the logical form of a gesture.

That gestures take on meaning according to context suggested that meaning could not be explained simply as a correspondence between individual statements and sets of objects. On the model of a gesture, the meaning of a statement involved lateral relationships with the meaning of other statements, which together were understood in terms of the context or practice in which they were used. Wittgenstein developed this latter conception in his influential *Philosophical Investigations* (1953), where he explained meaning in terms of use rather than correspondence. In the book's preface he credited Sraffa for criticism "for many years unceasingly practiced on my thoughts" and "for the most consequential ideas of this book" (Wittgenstein 1953: x).

Thus, just as Sraffa rejected Marshall's view

that prices could be explained market-by-market in partial equilibrium terms to reflect underlying configurations of autonomous supply and demand forces, so he also rejected Wittgenstein's early view that language meanings could be explained statement-by-statement in logical atomist terms to reflect underlying configurations of objects in the world. In a word, the world in both domains, meaning and price determination, exhibited interdependence. This did not imply that everything affected everything equally, or that the world is organic. Wittgenstein (1953) went on to explain interdependent meaning in terms of overlapping but relatively distinct social practices, such as how the language associated with working with stone overlapped with a language involved in different types of building practices.

## Basic and non-basic goods

Sraffa, in *Production of Commodities*, distinguished for a surplus economy between BASIC AND NON-BASIC COMMODITIES, with the former being used in the production of the latter but not the reverse. The prices of both types of goods depended on the prices of basic goods – a manifestation of interdependence – but the ultimate destination of non-basic goods, as luxury consumption, reflected discrete relationships between distinct economic classes contesting the distribution of the economy's surplus. Sraffa, then, reasoned in terms of systems of interdependence that internally generated qualitative distinctions significant for the explanation of the respective social practices investigated.

## Interdependency and relative autonomy

The origins of Sraffa's philosophical thinking date back to his contact with Antonio Gramsci. Gramsci, as other turn-of-the-century revolutionary Marxists, rejected inevitabilist historical materialism framed in terms of the dominant forces of production, and gave superstructural politics and IDEOLOGY causal effectiveness in a process of historical change. This substituted a system of interdependent effects for the monocausal logic of the Third International, yet reserved relative autonomy to spheres of practice in which revolutionary activity was pursued by CLASS agents (communist and fascist). In outline, it was essentially this vision of the nature and dynamic of society that Sraffa brought to his critiques of Marshallian economics. Marshall, in a mixture of nineteenth-century physics metaphors and eighteenth-century NATURAL RIGHTS politics, saw society as constituting collections of atomistic individuals. Sraffa's critiques of atomism presupposed a more subtle philosophical grasp of historical socioeconomic processes.

## See also:

determinism and overdetermination; dialectical method; holistic method; individual and society; methodological individualism and collectivism; Sraffian political economy

## Selected references

Davis, J. (1988) "Sraffa, Wittgenstein and Neoclassical Economics," *Cambridge Journal of Economics* 12: 29–36.
Malcolm, N. (1958) *Ludwig Wittgenstein: A Memoir*, London: Oxford.
Marshall, A. (1920) *Principles of Economics*, 8th edn, London: Macmillan.
Sraffa, P. (1926) "The Laws of Returns Under Competitive Conditions," *Economic Journal* 36: 535–50.
—— (1960) *Production of Commodities by Means of Commodities*, Cambridge: Cambridge University Press.
Wittgenstein, L. (1921) *Tractatus logico-philosophicus*, London: Routledge & Kegan Paul, 1961.
—— (1953) *Philosophical Investigations*, 3rd edn, New York: Macmillan, 1958.

JOHN B. DAVIS

# Sraffian political economy

## Introduction

The obvious starting-point for an account of the history of "Sraffian political economy" would seem to be the publication of Piero Sraffa's *Production of Commodities by Means of Commodities* in 1960. However, as SRAFFA indicated in his sub-title, *Prelude to a critique of Economic Theory*, and explicitly stated in his preface (1960: v–vii), his purpose was to provide the basis for a critique of the marginal theory of value and distribution (see NEOCLASSICAL ECONOMICS: CRITIQUE), and to revive the standpoint adopted by the old classical economists, that is, the surplus approach to the theory of value and distribution.

It has been demonstrated that the basis provided by Sraffa was sound. This implies, of course, that there is no such thing as Sraffian political economy. What exists is rather a logically coherent formulation of the theory of value and distribution in capitalist economics under conditions of universal free competition. While many authors have contributed to its development, its modern reformulation is mainly due to Piero Sraffa's seminal contributions to economic theory.

## Reconstruction of the surplus approach

Sraffa's work on the reconstruction of the surplus approach was begun already in the 1920s, immediately after his early critique of Marshallian partial equilibrium analysis (Sraffa 1925). It further involved his masterful edition of *The Works and Correspondence of David Ricardo*, in the Introduction to which he clarified the basic analytical structure of the surplus approach, and the particular formulation it was given by Ricardo.

However, the surplus approach itself can be traced back to the writings of Petty, Cantillon and the physiocrats, authors who had put forward land, land and labor, and material-based value theories. The labor-based value theory adopted by Smith, Ricardo and Marx, in order to determine the general rate of profit, was thus merely a particular formulation of the surplus approach. Major analytical contributions to its modern reformulation, prior to Piero Sraffa's analysis in 1960, had been made by authors such as V.K. Dmitriev, L. von Bortkiewicz, G. von Charasoff and J. von Neumann (see Kurz and Salvadori 1995: ch. 14).

The most important difference between the surplus approach to the theory of value and distribution and the neoclassical one concerns the treatment of capital in the analysis. The surplus approach starts from the following data: (1) the size and composition of the social product, (2) the technical alternatives from which producers can choose, and (3) the ruling real wage rate (or the rate of profits). From this data, it determines long-period commodity prices and the normal rate of profit (or the real wage rate) compatible with cost minimization in conditions of free competition.

A fundamental characteristic of the surplus approach is the asymmetric treatment of the distributive variables, which is in sharp contrast to neoclassical analysis. Neoclassical economists take as given (1) the initial endowments of the economy with respect to goods and factors of production and their distribution among agents, (2) the preferences of economic agents, and (3) the available technical alternatives. These differences in the data reflect, of course, a fundamental difference between the two approaches with regard to the determination of the distribution of income in capitalist economies under conditions of full competition.

Traditional neoclassical theory has generally viewed the distribution of income to be determined by the relative scarcity of the "factors of production," labor, "capital" and land. It thus sought to treat capital in full symmetry with labor and land; i.e. to extend the scarcity principle, which the classical economists had only applied to non-reproducible inputs like land, symmetrically to all factors of production. However, the formidable problem for traditional neoclassical theory was to find an expression for the given endowment of capital which is independent of the distribu-

tion of income. As the controversy in the theory of capital of the 1960s has shown, this is not possible except in very special cases. The initial endowment of capital goods produced means of production can, therefore, only be taken to be given in kind. This implies, however, that only short-period equilibria can be determined.

## The capital critique

Until the 1950s, it was commonly taken for granted that a lower rate of interest (that is, a higher real wage rate) can be associated with the choice of relatively more "capital-intensive" methods of production. This principle is known as capital deepening. It was shown to be not generally valid in contributions by Joan Robinson, Pierangelo Garegnani and Luigi Pasinetti to what has later been dubbed the "Cambridge capital controversies" (see Harcourt 1972).

The first target of criticism was the concept of a "quantity of capital" and the aggregate production function. Joan Robinson demonstrated that the value of capital depends on the distribution between wages and profits. In constructing a "pseudo-production function," she found the possibility of reverse capital deepening, i.e. that a technique which minimizes cost at a higher real wage rate may be more labor-intensive than that which is chosen at a lower wage rate. Therefore one cannot, in general, suppose a monotonic inverse relationship between the rate of profit and the capital/output (or the capital/labor) ratio.

In an attempt to support Solow's growth theory (and possibly counter Robinson's "perverse relationship"), Paul Samuelson constructed a "surrogate production function," which allowed for heterogenous capital goods, but exhibited all the properties required for the validity of the neoclassical "parables." Pierangelo Garegnani (1970) then demonstrated that Samuelson's results are not valid in general, but only for the special case of a uniform "organic composition of capital," i.e. equal proportions of labor and capital in all sectors. The basis for this critique was laid in Sraffa's 1960 book.

Sraffa demonstrated that a technique can be (a) cost-minimizing at a low level of the rate of profit; (b) replaced by another technique which is less costly at a higher rate of profit; and then (c) become cost-minimizing again with a further increase in the rate of profit. This RESWITCHING is a sufficient but not a necessary condition for the existence of "reverse capital deepening" (CAPITAL REVERSING). These findings are relevant to economic theory whenever capital is involved. For example, they destroy the general validity of the Heckscher–Ohlin–Samuelson trade theory (as authors such as Sergio Parrinello, Stanley Metcalfe, Ian Steedman and Lynn Mainwaring have demonstrated); the Hicksian neutrality of technical progress concept (as Steedman has shown); neoclassical tax incidence theory (as Steedman and Metcalfe have shown); and the Pigouvian taxation theory applied in environmental economics (as Gehrke and Lager have shown).

## Implications for Marxian analysis

A theme that occupied political economists during the 1960s and 1970s has been the clarification of the implications of Sraffa's analysis for Marx's theory of value and surplus value. The single most important contribution to this debate was Ian Steedman's *Marx after Sraffa* (1977). Here it was argued with impeccable logical rigor that, in the further development of the surplus approach, the LABOR THEORY OF VALUE must be dispensed with.

## Recent developments

Apart from spelling out the implications of Sraffa's analysis for neoclassical and Marxian theory, economists working in the Sraffian tradition have also been concerned with extending, generalizing, and (where necessary) correcting Sraffa's analysis. Important recent developments concerned particularly the analysis of joint production, fixed capital and rent.

In the case of joint production the problem of overproduced commodities and negative prices may arise. Whereas von Neumann (1945–6) adopted the rule of free goods, Sraffa (1960) assumed that, by an appropriate combination of processes, the proportions in which commodities are demanded can always be met by those in which they are produced. In other words, he based his analysis on square systems of production. Justifications for Sraffa's (indirect) approach were provided for the special cases of (1) "all-productive" systems (by Schefold) or (2) for an economy which grows steadily at a rate which is equal to the rate of profit (by Steedman).

However, in the general case, Sraffa's assertion of square systems cannot be sustained. Salvadori stressed that a system of production can be defined only with respect to given requirements of use, since "demand" will generally influence which processes will and which will not be operated. Hence the "non-substitution theorem" (i.e. demand does not affect prices) does not, in general, hold in the presence of joint production. Following the direct approach provided by von Neumann, Salvadori proved the existence of cost-minimizing systems of production. For a survey of joint production analysis see Salvadori and Steedman (1988).

Sraffa's approach to the analysis of fixed capital was based on the simplifying assumptions that (1) every industry utilizes only one type of fixed capital good and (2) that the efficiency of this capital item remains constant throughout its life. Sraffa's model has been generalized in various contributions by Baldone, Varri and especially Schefold (1989) to allow for increasing, decreasing or varying efficiency of capital.

In the case of changing efficiency, a choice of technique problem arises; one has to determine the optimal life (or optimal truncation period) of a capital good. It was shown that appropriately truncated systems exhibit positive prices. The return of the same truncation period appeared as a special case of reswitching of techniques. The device of the "plant," a composite fixed capital good, allows for the utilization of more than one machine. Salvadori generalized this concept to account also for intra-sectoral transferability of used fixed capital items.

Sraffa (1960) was also concerned with the reformulation of the classical theory of differential rent on land. Discussing extensive as well as intensive diminishing returns, Sraffa stressed that the scarcity of land is reflected in the coexistence of two or more processes to produce the same commodity. In a "square" system – a system where the number of processes equals the number of qualities of land plus the number of products – the rent on land and the prices of the commodities can be determined. Thus Sraffa concluded that more complex cases, such as the multiplicity of agricultural products, would not give rise to any complications. Recent contributions have demonstrated that this proposition cannot be sustained and that, in the case of many agricultural products, a long-period position need not exist or need not be unique.

Additional interesting cases of rent on land were found by Abraham-Frois and Berrebi (external rent) and by Salvadori (singular rent). Salvadori proved the existence of a cost-minimizing system for a general model which exhibits all forms of rent as well as a multiplicity of agricultural products. Other important contributions to the theory of rent can be found in several publications by Quadrio-Curzio, Bidard, D'Agata, Kurz and Montani.

### Effective demand and surplus approach

A topic that still ranks highly on the research agenda of Sraffian economists is the attempt to integrate Keynes's principle of effective demand and the surplus approach to value and distribution. An immediate outcome of the work done in this area has been a movement away from the "old" post-Keynesian theory of growth and distribution developed by Kaldor, Pasinetti and others. In this theory, the (normal) rate of profit was taken to be determined, via the "Cambridge equation," by the rate of ACCUMULATION. The argument that the rate of accumulation, in order to be compatible with the normal or natural rate of profit, cannot be regarded as being given exogenously, determined by "animal spirits" or

suchlike, was taken on board also by authors working in the post-Keynesian or Kaleckian tradition. Consequently, economists working in the Sraffian and in the post-Keynesian tradition have recently started to investigate the implications deriving from the possibility of varying degrees of capacity utilization for short- and long-period analysis. Clearly, this research is closely related to and, indeed, inseparably intertwined with attempts to develop a coherent theory of growth and distribution. Some authors (Rogers, Pivetti and Panico) have discussed the significance of the classical approach for monetary theory (see, for instance, Rogers 1989).

### Depletable and renewable resources

Another contemporary theme is to fit depletable and renewable resources into the classical concept. Following Ricardo, Sraffa thought that mineral deposits could be treated like land and that both resources will generally pay a rent to their owner. Whereas Schefold provided some rationalizations for the Sraffian–Ricardian approach, Parrinello questioned the method of long-period positions for the treatment of exhaustible ressources. Going beyond the long period, Kurz and Salvadori (1995: ch. 12) developed an intertemporal linear programming model. Other formulations were provided by Roncaglia and Quadrio-Curzio. A model for renewable resources and a survey of the existing literature is contained in Kurz and Salvadori (1995).

### General theory or special case?

Another major concern is with refuting Hahn's claim that the classical model, as exemplified by Sraffa's analysis, is but a special case (characterized by appropriately adjusted endowments) of the neoclassical model of intertemporal general equilibrium. Against Hahn, the following arguments were put forward by authors, including Garegnani, Kurz and Salvadori, Schefold and Duménil and Lévy.

First, since endowments of produced means of production are given at the beginning of the first period, it seems that the "problem of capital" has been successfully circumnavigated: all productive inputs, including capital, have the character of primary factors that can be dealt with according to the principle of scarcity. However, the problem of capital and its reproduction is still present. It finds its expression in the form of unstable equilibria caused by perversely shaped investment demand functions, due to reverse capital deepening.

Second, prices of production are not simply prices of a short-run equilibrium model, assuming short-run clearing of markets and appropriate endowments, as viewed by Hahn. Rather, as defined by the classical economists, they are results of a process of gravitation of actual market prices towards a long-run equilibrium position. Consequently the classical concept is not a special case of the general neoclassical model, but is a different concept. Whereas the classical model deals with the long period the neoclassical model concerns the short period.

Third, intertemporal general equilibrium is the result of a dynamic process of market clearing, the Walrasian *tatônnement*, which is very particular, highly unrealistic and, above all, will not work in the case of instabilities. Lastly, it has been demonstrated that, under fairly general conditions, the intertemporal models converge to long-run positions. Consequently, the classical concept is not a special case. Rather, intertemporal equilibrium can be viewed as a special case of the classical process of gravitation.

Particular formalizations of the classical gravitation process have been developed by Nikaido, Boggio, Duménil and Lévy, Franke, Kubin, Steedman and others. For a detailed discussion of single production systems see Pasinetti (1977). Kurz and Salvadori (1995) provided a comprehensive account of modern classical political economy. Collections of important articles in that field were edited by Steedman (1988) and Bharadwaj and Schefold (1990).

## See also:

Cambridge revolution; capital theory debates; circular production and vertical integration; gravitation and convergence; heterogeneous capital and labor; international trade in Sraffian political economy; invariable measure of value

## Selected references

Bharadwaj, Krishna and Schefold, Bertram (eds) (1990) *Essays on Piero Sraffa: Critical Perspectives on the Revival of Classical Theory*, London: Unwin Hyman.

Garegnani, Pierangelo (1970) "Heterogeneous Capital, the Production Function and the Theory of Distribution," *Review of Economic Studies* 37: 407–36.

Harcourt, G.C. (1972) *Some Cambridge Controversies in the Theory of Capital*, London and New York: Cambridge University Press.

—— (1986) *Controversies in Political Economy: Selected Essays of G.C. Harcourt*, New York: New York University Press.

Kurz, Heinz D. and Salvadori, Neri (1995) *Theory of Production: A Long-Period Analysis*, Cambridge: Cambridge University Press.

Neumann, John von (1945–6) "A Model of General Economic Equilibrium," *Review of Economic Studies* 13: 1–9. (Originally published in 1937.)

Pasinetti, Luigi L. (1977) *Lectures on the Theory of Production*, London: Macmillan.

Rogers, Colin (1989) *Money, Interest and Capital: A Study of the Foundations of Monetary Theory*, Cambridge: Cambridge University Press.

Salvadori, Neri and Steedman, Ian (1988) "Joint Production Analysis in a Sraffian Framework," *Bulletin of Economic Research* 40: 165–95; repr. in Neri Salvadori and Ian Steedman (eds), *Joint Production of Commodities*, Aldershot: Edward Elgar, 1990.

Schefold, Bertram (1989) *Mr. Sraffa on Joint Production and Other Essays*, London: Unwin Hyman.

—— (ed.) (1988) *Sraffian Economics*, 2 vols, Aldershot: Edward Elgar.

Sraffa, Piero (1925) "Sulle relazioni fra costo e quantità prodotta," (On the Relations between Cost and Quantity Produced), *Annali di economia* 2: 277–328.

—— (1951) "Introduction," *The Works and Correspondence of David Ricardo*, vol. 1, Cambridge: Cambridge University Press.

—— (1960) *Production of Commodities by Means of Commodities*, Cambridge: Cambridge University Press.

Steedman, Ian (1977) *Marx after Sraffa*, London: New Left Books.

CHRISTIAN GEHRKE
CHRISTIAN LAGER

# Sraffian and post-Keynesian linkages

Many of the authors who do surveys of post-Keynesian political economy include the Sraffian school as one of the strands of post-Keynesian political economy. There are historical reasons for this association, since the early Sraffians and post-Keynesians were mostly located at the University of Cambridge. While all agreed that full employment, if left to market forces, could only occur occasionally, substantial theoretical disputes arose between the two schools. The Trieste Summer School during the 1980s gave the main actors of these two schools an opportunity to vent their opinions and differences, resolve their disagreements and build a coherent synthesis that would become an alternative to neoclassical theory.

Since the School has now disappeared without having brought the dominant views of the two schools any closer, it would appear that the Trieste Summer School project has been a failure. This assessment, which is endorsed by many observers, appears to be both partial and mistaken. It arises from an unfair reading of the positions arising from an undue focus on the dominant views of the two schools rather than on their dissident views (Arena 1992). In addition, even the discrepancies between the dominant views may not be as large as they are usually held to be, according to some well-known topological depictions, such as that of Carvalho (1984–5).

## Dominant views

The dominant views are associated, on the Sraffian side, with Pierangelo Garegnani and John Eatwell, and on the post-Keynesian side with Paul Davidson and Hyman Minsky. For reasons which can be linked to their personalities and to the sociology of science, the opinions of these authors and their followers have become the respective dominant views. Things on the post-Keynesian side are, however, a bit more complicated, for Sraffians sometimes consider the KALDOR–PASINETTI MODELS OF GROWTH AND DISTRIBUTION, and those associated with Joan Robinson, to constitute the dominant post-Keynesian view on output and distribution. Indeed, the tensions between the Sraffian and post-Keynesian approaches can be understood almost through the sole study of the works of Robinson, as she went through various phases supporting one or the other method.

The usual account of crystallized positions is as follows. The dominant post-Keynesian view is associated with the notion of fundamental UNCERTAINTY and subjectivism, the instability of the economy, the importance of monetary and financial markets, the primacy of short period analysis, and the presence of Marshallian foundations (e.g. diminishing returns). The dominant Sraffian view has been associated with the primacy of comparative statics based on long period analysis, the importance of real analysis based on objective magnitudes, and the gravitation towards prices of production and normal levels of output.

## Dissident views

Within both the Sraffian and post-Keynesian schools, however, there have always been other authors disputing the dominant views. Most of these dissidents have questioned the validity of the analytical distinction between the short and the long period. The validity of the notion of gravitation has also been questioned by dissident Sraffians (for example, Parrinello, Pasinetti, Roncaglia, Schefold), while dissident post-Keynesians have turned away from Marshallian foundations (for example, Kaleckian authors). Dissident Sraffians and post-Keynesians authors have recently produced models of growth and distribution that have similar implications with regard to demand-led economies. On this last issue, as we shall see, there seems to be a convergence of views, among all strands of Sraffians and post-Keynesians, be they dissidents or part of the dominant school.

## Disagreements

Indeed, the major disagreements between Sraffians and post-Keynesians seem to arise more from their criticisms of neoclassical analysis than from their potential positive contributions. Sraffians and post-Keynesians seem to disagree most about how the KEYNES AND THE CLASSICS DEBATE should be perceived. For Sraffians the flaws of neoclassical theory are mostly due to their adoption of continuous downward demand curves for investment or for labor, based on diminishing marginal productivity. For post-Keynesians, the flaws are to be found in the neoclassical school's avoidance of fundamental uncertainty, the instability of expectations, and the non-neutrality of money. Both schools agree, however, on the fact that flexible money wages, or the elimination of market imperfections, would not automatically bring back the economy to full employment in the long period. Indeed, both schools reject the relevance and operation of the neoclassical principle of substitution. Members of both schools also generally agree on the independence of investment from savings, and on the fact that demand forces drive the economy both for short-run cycles and for long-run growth.

## Similarities

In addition, and this may seem quite ironic to some observers, both dominant post-Keynesians and dominant Sraffians recognize that a lack of deterministic results can prevail: Sraffians express this by referring to the lack of clear results that can be obtained outside the core (i.e. outside the determination of prices of production), while post-Keynesians refer to systemic uncertainty and non-ergodicity. Thus, in contrast to what has been claimed repeatedly, Sraffians and post-Keynesians have commonalities that go beyond their dislike of neoclassical economics. This dislike, as reflected in their divergent critique of neoclassical economics, is more a source of tension than a source of unity. Despite appearances to the contrary, Sraffians and post-Keynesians are brought together by the similitudes in their positive contributions.

The similarity in the views between Sraffians and post-Keynesians is surprisingly clear in the field of money. Members of both schools underline the relevance of ENDOGENOUS MONEY AND CREDIT, whereby the causality of the quantity theory equation must be read in reverse, and short-term rates of interest must be taken as the exogenous variable under the control of the central bank. This has led, under the leadership of Panico and Pivetti, to a theory of the normal rate of profit ($r_n$) which would depend on the rate of interest ($i$), adjusted by a normal entrepreneurial profit or premium (*nep*): $r_n = i + nep$ (see INTEREST RATE – PROFIT RATE LINK). The rate of interest is the average rate observed for the current monetary regime. The entrepreneurial premium can be linked to a liquidity premium, required by entrepreneurs (or by their bankers) to enter into real capital expenditures, rather than remaining liquid in financial markets. Relative prices are thus directly affected by monetary factors and liquidity premiums, as emphasized by post-Keynesians. Uncertainty and liquidity preference, along with class struggle, thus indirectly enter into the determination of relative prices.

While one may or may not wish to accept this view of the normal rate of profit (Joan Robinson proposed it in 1952 only to reject it later), there are obvious tight links between the dissident Sraffian versions of normal prices and the administered cost-plus prices, to be found in many empirical studies and endorsed by most Kaleckians. This is most obvious in Lanzillotti's version of full-cost pricing, which is based on target-return PRICING. Prices are based on the normal unit costs of the price leaders, assessed at the standard rate of capacity of utilization, on the basis of a target rate of return. There is no presumption that this target rate of return will be the realized rate of profit: the former will be achieved only if sales are equivalent to the standard rate of utilization.

Dissident Sraffians give a similar interpretation of prices of production. Such prices may be defined on the basis of a stable system of profit rate differentials. They are based neither on the best available nor the average technique, but rather on the dominant technique, that of the price leaders; and on the normal degree of utilization of the existing productive capacity, rather than on actual output levels (Roncaglia 1990). While Sraffians generally believe the normal rates of profit will tend towards uniformity because of competition, they have also recognized from the onset that there may be a stable system of profit rate differentials, due to imperfect competition and barriers to entry, thus being in agreement here with Kaleckians.

## Contentious issues

A major subject of contention between Sraffians and post-Keynesians is the issue of the GRAVITATION AND CONVERGENCE of market prices towards prices of production. Dominant Sraffians, such as Garegnani and Eatwell, assume convergence to occur, following the arguments of Adam Smith. While there are still debates as to whether such convergence needs to be shown, several models now provide conditional demonstrations. In the so-called classical model of gravitation, the evolution of market prices (i.e. actual prices) is essentially regulated by excess demand, while the evolution of output and capacity is regulated by profit rate differentials. Various models have shown that convergence towards prices of production, at normal rates of utilization of capacity, could be achieved with appropriate

behavioral functions and restricted reaction parameters. There are a number of drawbacks to these models, which has led a number of Sraffian authors to argue that the concept of gravitation is self-destructive; that it reasserts the importance of neoclassical constructs (Schefold 1984; Lee 1994). These dissident authors view prices of production (with profit rate differentials) not as something that would be eventually realized in the long period, but rather as full-cost prices that are realized in the short-period, but which are affected by imperfections and time lags in pricing decisions (Nell 1994: 330). These more realist full-cost prices can also be studied in a multi-sector framework, as they have been by Alfred Eichner, Frederic Lee and Luciano Boggio.

Perhaps the most crucial issue is that of effective demand. Initially, most Sraffians, along with many Marxists and Cambridgian authors such as Joan Robinson, associated the long period with fully adjusted positions only, that is, those positions that correspond to normal use of capacity or normal output. Most Sraffians now have explicitly abandoned this claim. The present Sraffian view is that, even in the long period, the realized rate of utilization will generally be different from its normal level. The rate of capacity utilization is thus flexible, even in the long run, and this flexibility allows savings to adjust to a higher rate of investment, as the post-Keynesians would have it, but without profit margins having to rise or real wages to fall. This rejection of the necessary link between higher growth rates and higher profit margins constitutes the main Sraffian critique of the old Cambridgian model of growth, which we called the dominant post-Keynesian view of output and distribution (Garegnani 1992).

It should be noted that the very same critique against the Cambridgian model of growth had been made by Davidson in his 1972 book, *Money and the Real World*. Both Kaldor and Robinson, in the mid and late 1960s, had themselves recognized the deficiencies of their own models in that regard, noting that actual profit rates could be modified through changes in the rate of utilization, without modifying profit margins. The endogenous view of the actual degree of utilization is also fully compatible with the growth models constructed by dissident post-Keynesians in the Kaleckian tradition, and it extends Keynesian income effects beyond the short-run, where it had been contained until then (Kurz 1994). Dominant Sraffians will express this by saying that, on average, there is no reason for the actual rate of capacity utilization to equal its normal rate. This is perhaps the clearest instance where there occurs a convergence of views between the various dominant and dissident strands.

The main issue of contention remains the relationship between the short and the long period, as emphasized by Carvalho. Extreme views on this matter, such as the belief that determinate destinations are fully independent of short-run results, or that short-run situations are impervious to long-run forces, clearly cannot be reconciled. As pointed out above, dissidents from both the Sraffian and post-Keynesian schools have gone beyond this short run/long run dichotomy. For instance, if the long-run rate of capacity utilization can diverge from the normal or standard rate of utilization, the question immediately arises about how these two variables can consistently diverge. The possibility that normal rates of utilization (or normal rates of profit) are influenced by actual levels is now being explored. Actual values during the TRAVERSE influence the definition of long-period positions, it being understood that economies are usually in transition rather than at these long-period positions, and that these long-period positions are constantly being modified. Effective demand and the SURPLUS APPROACH TO POLITICAL ECONOMY are thus tightly linked.

## See also:

classical political economy; effective demand and capacity utilization; Kaleckian theory of growth; money, credit and finance: major contemporary themes; Sraffian political economy

## Selected references

Arena, Richard (1992) "Une synthèse entre post-keynésiens et néo-ricardiens est-elle encore possible?," *L'Actualité économique* 68(4): 587–606.

Carvalho, Fernando (1984–5) "Alternative Analyses of Short and Long Run in Post Keynesian Economics," *Journal of Post Keynesian Economics* 7(2): 214–34.

Dutt, Amitava K. and Amadeo, Edward J. (1989) *Keynes's Third Alternative? The Neo-Ricardians and the Post Keynesians*, Aldershot: Edward Elgar.

Garegnani, Pierangelo (1992) "Some Notes for an Analysis of Accumulation," in Joseph Halevi, David Laibman and Edward J. Nell (eds), *Beyond the Steady State: A Revival of Growth Theory*, New York: St Martin's Press, 47–71.

Kurz, Heinz D. (1994) "Growth and Distribution," *Review of Political Economy* 6(4): 393–420.

Lee, Frederic S. (1994) "From Post-Keynesian to Historical Price Theory, Part I: Facts, Theory and Empirically Grounded Pricing Model," *Review of Political Economy* 6(3): 303–36.

Nell, Edward J. (1994) "Minsky, Keynes and Sraffa: Investment in the Long Period," in Gary Dymski and Robert Pollin (eds), *New Perspectives in Monetary Macroeconomics*, Ann Arbor, MI: University of Michigan Press, 311–35.

Roncaglia, Alessandro (1990) "Is the Notion of Long-Period Positions Compatible with Political Economy?," *Political Economy: Studies in the Surplus Approach* 6(1–2): 103–11.

Schefold, Bertram (1984) "Sraffa and Applied Economics: Are There Classical Supply Curves?," Center for Advanced Economic Studies, Trieste Summer School.

MARC LAVOIE

# stagflation

Stagflation is quite simply the simultaneous occurrence of high rates of inflation and unemployment. Until the 1970s, stagflation was unknown to the developed nations of the world. These countries either experienced high inflation and low unemployment, or high unemployment and low inflation. Moreover, whenever inflation increased, unemployment would normally fall, and vice versa. Economists even thought that stagflation was impossible because inflation and unemployment were mutually exclusive alternatives: inflation was the result of too much demand, while unemployment was the result of too little demand. This tradeoff was expressed in the notion of the Phillips curve, which depicted unemployment and inflation as being inversely related.

## Stagflation in the 1970s

Things changed, however, in the early 1970s. Inflation and unemployment both increased in virtually every developed country. For example, unemployment averaged 4.8 percent and inflation averaged 4.6 percent in Canada from 1963 to 1973; but from 1974 to 1979, Canadian unemployment averaged 7.2 percent while the Canadian inflation rate doubled to 9.2 percent. In France, unemployment averaged 2 percent and inflation averaged 4.7 percent from 1963–1973 period; but in the 1974–9 period, unemployment grew to 4.5 percent of the labor force, while the inflation rate soared to 10.7 percent. Even Japan, one of the most successful developed economies in the second half of the twentieth century, suffered from stagflation during the 1970s. Japanese unemployment averaged 1.9 percent in the 1974–9 period, up from 1.2 percent in 1963–73; similarly inflation in Japan increased from 6.2 percent in the early time period to 10.2 percent in the later period.

The term "stagflation" was coined in the 1970s to denote this new economic reality, the conjunction of economic stagnation (leading to high unemployment rates) and high rates of inflation. Economists then began to seek the causes of this new phenomenon and propose policies to remedy it. Four different approaches to the problem of stagflation can be identified.

## Supply siders and New Keynesians

The standard account of stagflation comes from supply-side economics (see Evans 1983). According to this view, stagflation is the result of a reduction in the aggregate supply of goods and services businesses are willing to produce. A decline in aggregate supply results from higher business costs to produce goods and services. Supply-side economists stress two main factors which increased business costs in the 1970s: greater government regulation of business and higher taxes on business. Under these circumstances, businesses would want to produce the same output and hire the same number of workers only if they could pass these costs onto consumers (thus generating inflation); at the same time, businesses would want to produce less under the burden of heavy taxes and regulations (thus leading to higher unemployment). For supply-siders, the solution to the problem of stagflation follows directly: a reduction in business taxes and a reduction in government regulation of business firms.

One question left unanswered by the supply-side analysis is why wage rates do not fall in the presence of high unemployment, thus mitigating both the unemployment and inflationary pressures. This question has been addressed by the New Keynesian school of macroeconomics, which views rigid wage rates as the main cause of stagflation. Bruno and Sachs (1985) present stagflation as a phenomenon caused by supply-side shocks in conjunction with worker resistance to real wage cuts. In addition, EFFICIENCY WAGES theory argues that employers have incentives to pay workers more than the going wage if they want loyal and productive employees. This provides another explanation for why wages do not fall in the presence of unemployment, and why employees may be given wage increases that keep up with inflation despite the presence of high unemployment.

## Marxian political economy

A second attempt to explain stagflation comes from Marxian political economy. According to Bowles *et al.* (1990), high demand and low unemployment in the late 1960s led to rising wages and reduced business profits. As a result, beginning in the 1970s, business launched a counterattack against labor, becoming aggressively anti-union. Firms reduced employment by investing overseas, especially in less developed countries where labor costs were much lower. They also engaged in union busting and sought to defeat all attempts to unionize workers. Government joined the anti-union efforts by also fighting unions. For example, in 1981 President Reagan destroyed the US air traffic controllers' union. Government also sided with business by refusing to use their economic policy tools to keep unemployment rates down and add to the bargaining power of unions (see FISCAL POLICY; MONETARY POLICY AND CENTRAL BANKING FUNCTIONS). This explains the high unemployment beginning in the 1970s.

To explain the high inflation, Bowles *et al.* point out that with less output (due to both higher unemployment and productivity problems), the claims on national income exceed the national income itself. Thus, the demand for goods is greater than the supply of those goods, and inflationary pressures rise. To solve the stagflation problem, Bowles *et al.* call for an end to union busting and deliberately creating high unemployment.

## Post-Keynesians

Post-Keynesians have argued that stagflation can be explained by the fact that unemployment and inflation are determined by different factors. Unemployment depends on the level of effective demand in the economy; while inflation depends upon the costs of production (especially wage costs and the mark-up over costs). Whenever effective demand is low, an economy will experience unemployment. On the other hand, if workers are pushing for higher wages, or if more monopolistic business firms seek to increase their PRICING mark-up inflation will be the result. When these two events occur together, the result is stagflation.

According to post-Keynesian economists, the way to combat inflation is a consensual incomes policy, where workers agree to wage increases in line with productivity (thus keeping costs from rising), and business firms agree to keep their mark-ups and their prices constant. With an incomes policy keeping inflation in check, expansionary fiscal and monetary policies can be used to keep unemployment under control (Cornwall 1994; Weintraub 1978).

## Structuralists

Finally, the structuralist hypothesis (Baumol 1967; Pasinetti and Lloyd 1987) views stagflation as the consequence of divergent development in different economic sectors. Kaldor (1976) looked at the economy as comprised of two different economic sectors: a primary sector that produces food and raw materials, and a secondary sector that produces manufactured goods. In the primary sector, price shocks are frequent and lead to macroeconomic fluctuations. So, when oil prices and food prices rose in the 1970s, developed economies experienced inflationary problems. Higher raw material prices led to higher prices in the industrial sector, which therefore reduced demand for these goods. In addition, the inflation in the primary sector led to restrictive economic policies to try to control inflation, further hurting the industrial sector and leading to unemployment problems there.

Structuralists propose to solve the problem of stagflation by stabilizing primary commodity prices. Kaldor (1976) proposed developing buffer stocks of primary commodities which would be released in times of shortages and added to in times of surpluses. Following this advice, the US government began accumulating a vast stock of oil reserves during the 1980s. Another way to stabilize primary commodity prices would be to reduce national demand for energy, thereby making countries less susceptible to energy shocks.

## Decline in stagflation

In the mid to late 1980s, stagflation disappeared almost as quickly as it appeared in the early 1970s. Inflation rates declined in almost every developed country, and economic growth resumed, although at lower rates than in the golden era following the Second World War. This turn of events was helped by declining energy prices as well as by high unemployment rates and the threat of businesses moving production facilities to less developed countries. Both of these events reduced inflationary pressures in the world economy, and changed a stagflation problem into a stagnation problem.

## See also:

budget deficit; inflation: wage–cost markup approach; supply and demand: macroeconomic; unemployment and underemployment; unemployment: policies to reduce

## Selected references

Baumol, William (1967) "Macroeconomics of Unbalanced Growth: The Anatomy of Urban Crisis", *American Economic Review* 57(June): 415–26.

Bowles, Samuel, Gordon, David M. and Weisskopf, Thomas E. (1990) *After the Wasteland: A Democratic Economics for the Year 2000*, Armonk, NY: M.E. Sharpe.

Bruno, Michael and Sachs, Jeffrey (1985) *Economics of Worldwide Stagflation*, Oxford: Basil Blackwell.

Cornwall, John (1994) *The Theory of Economic Breakdown*, New York: Basil Blackwell.

Evans, Michael (1983) *The Truth about Supply-Side Economics*, New York: Basic Books.

Kaldor, Nicholas (1976) "Inflation and Recession in the World Economy," *Economic Journal* 86(December): 703–14.

OECD (various years) *Economic Outlook*, Paris: OECD.

Pasinetti, Luigi and Lloyd, P. (eds) (1987) *Structural Change, Economic Interdependence and World Development*, vol. 3, London: Macmillan.

Weintraub, Sidney (1978) *Capitalism's Inflation and Unemployment Crisis*, Reading, MA: Addison-Wesley.

MARCO MUSELLA
STEVEN PRESSMAN

# staple theory of growth

The staple theory analyzes the ECONOMIC GROWTH and INDUSTRIALIZATION of national economies in general and of economies with colonial backgrounds in particular. The theory, which evolved from the "staple approach," attempts to explain the growth of newly settled regions by pointing to their interactions with the international economy. In essence, exports of staple products, generally defined as primary products, are considered to be pre-conditions for growth which, in this context, takes the form of industrial diversification around resource exports. The original formulation of the staple framework is attributed to Canadian economic historians H.A. Innis and W.A. Mackintosh. They are referred to as the early staple writers by reference to their pioneering work in the 1920s, 1930s and 1940s on that country's first export staples, namely cod, fur, timber and wheat. Further historical analysis by Innis, Mackintosh and others such as V.C. Fowke, K. Buckley and W.T. Easterbrook, added to the staple approach literature and fostered analytical refinement, ultimately leading to a synthesis and theoretical formalization particularly by M.H. Watkins.

## Export staples

Watkins, writing in the 1960s, was the first to propose a staple theory of growth. In his formulation, the staple theory is considered to be a variant of a more general growth model, articulated by C.P. Kindleberger, in which external trade is the leading sector. The large scale production of export staples determines the growth of incomes in the export sector and induces economic spin-offs in the form of infrastructure investment. There is a territorial expansion of economic activity (extensive growth) and diversification of the economy (intensive growth). Sustained external demand is the key determinant. However, the growth-inducing capability of staples is ultimately rooted in their intrinsic characteristics, as these delineate the scope of input production and resource transformation.

## Production linkages

Borrowing from the field of economic development, and especially from A.O. Hirschman, Watkins integrated into his staple theory formulation the multi-dimensional concept of economic linkage, specifically forward, backward and final demand linkages. This was done in order to clearly identify and differentiate the nature and potential of the growth processes induced by competing export staples. The forward, backward and final demand linkages respectively refer to induced staple transformation, input production and consumption good production. Hirschman added an important political dimension by drawing attention to the role of the state, as owner of property rights in resources, in either hindering or initiating staple production, and industrial diversification via staple development and resource taxation policies. The concept of fiscal linkage, the ability to generate and appropriate resource rents, was coined in reference to the state's general impact.

The staple theory has been the subject of numerous literary and quantitative analyses of staple development in Canada, the United States and Australia. Many writers concur with the theory's explanatory power in accounting for the growth experience of these areas. In so doing, however, staple analysts and commentators have generated significant controversy regarding the industrialization potential of staple extraction, which can be traced back to the respective writings of Innis and Mackintosh themselves.

## Stagnationist perspective

The Innis perspective on staple development, pursued in the post-1960 period by what have been called the neo-Innisian historians, is referred to as the stagnationist perspective. It highlights the dependency aspects of international staple product specialization: on foreign markets, on unstable world raw material prices and on foreign finance. These dependencies, along with the complementary structural obstacle of a weak local entrepreneurial class, or one subservient to foreign interests, limit economic linkages and tend to produce export enclaves cut off from other sectors of the staple exporting economy.

Viewing the Canadian experience, Innis argued that the growth potential of staple exports, initiated from more industrialized economies, was determined by the nature of the latter's political and economic relations with the staple areas. The locus of political power among the staple areas' economic interest groups was fundamental, as it determined the nature of state-supported development strategies. Herein lies a potential danger: externally dominated local political elites developing a resource-owner rentier ideology whereby staple-induced or staple-supported industrialization is set aside in favor of a symbolic share of staple profits. R.T. Naylor, a contemporary proponent of this view, concluded that the historical strength of the Canadian commercial capitalist class reproduced a state-initiated pattern of overinvestment in staple exports, at the expense of national industrial diversification. Such a development bias was termed a "staple trap".

## Staple industrialization

The opposite perspective, initially expounded by Mackintosh and pursued by Buckley and Fowke, viewed staple development in newly settled regions as a necessary and sufficient condition for industrialization. Reasoning from the international trade principle of comparative advantage, the growth of staple exports, it was argued, would tend to have not only pervasive economic effects, but also to influence social and political systems, and ultimately generate a mature industrialized society. From a political angle, staple development reflected more the strategies of autonomous local elites, rather than those of dominating imperial powers as Innis feared. In the Canadian and North American context, the Mackintosh perspective was favorable to the idea of economic continentalism, a concept rejected by the neo-Innisian Anglo-Canadian nationalists.

## Contemporary controversies

Contemporary controversies between neoclassical and Keynesian economists have spilled into the field of the staple theory debates. Following the Innis tradition, neo-Innisians have favored, both on efficiency and distributional grounds, the active exercise of state property rights in resources. This would increase fiscal linkages, namely resource rents, and promote diversification via industrial strategies incorporating public enterprises and nationalizations if so required. On efficiency grounds, public planning in resource development can yield broader long-term impacts. On distributional grounds, the active exercise of state power will increase the ability to capture economic rents associated with staple extraction.

The contemporary neoclassical economic historians, in line with the Mackintosh tradition, take an opposing non-interventionist policy view. They believe that interventionist staple development policy is predicated on the exercise of collective property rights, producing market distortions which dissipate resource rents and compromise growth. The neoclassical implication is that government support of market-induced comparative advantages and privatization of resource property rights will generate growth.

## See also:

agrarian question; classes and economic development; colonialism and imperialism:

classic texts; core–periphery analysis; development political economy: major contemporary themes; uneven development

## Selected references

Buckley, K. (1958) "The Role of Staple Industries in Canada's Economic Development," *Journal of Economic History* 18: 439–50.

Easterbrook, W.T. and Watkins, M.H. (eds) (1967) *Approaches to Canadian Economic History*, Toronto: McClelland & Stewart.

Fowke, V.C. (1957) *The National Policy and the Wheat Economy*, Toronto: University of Toronto Press.

Hirschman, A.O. (1977) "A Generalized Approach to Development with Special Reference to Staples," *Economic Development and Cultural Change* 5, supplement.

Innis, H.A. (1957) *Essays in Canadian Economic History*, Toronto: University of Toronto Press.

Mackintosh, W.A. (1923) "Economic Factors in Canadian History," *Canadian Historical Review* 4(March):12–25.

—— (1936) "Some Aspects of a Pioneer Economy" *Canadian Journal of Economics and Political Science* 2(November): 457–63.

Naylor, R.T. (1972) "The Rise and Fall of the Third Commercial Empire of the St-Lawrence," in G. Teaple (ed.), *Capitalism and the National Question in Canada*, Toronto: University of Toronto Press.

Pomfret, R. (1981) "The Staple Theory as an Approach to Canadian and Australian Economic Development," *Australian Economic History Review* 21(2): 133–46.

Richards, J. (1985) "The Staple Debates," in D. Cameron (ed.), *Explorations in Canadian Economic History: Essays in Honour of Irene M. Spry*, Ottawa: University of Ottawa Press.

PIERRE PAQUETTE

# state and government

Government, or the state, has come to play a major economic role in the twentieth century. In the early 1900s, government expenditures were a mere 5–10 percent of GDP in most developed countries. During the Second World War, Western governments increased their take of national income to around 25 percent, and the size of the state continued to increase after the war. By 1980, government spending exceeded 40 percent (on average) of GDP for the developed countries of the world (Tanzi and Schuknecht 1996). This trend is likely to continue. Many economists estimate that government spending will reach 50 percent of GDP in the first decade of the twenty first century. What is all this money spent on?

## Purchase of goods and services and transfers

First, all governments directly purchase goods and services produced by private business firms. They buy military equipment, buses and subway cars, and new school and office buildings. Government expenditures also go to pay for services like education, health care, national defense, air traffic control, fire and police protection. In addition, government transfer payments redistribute income, through programs such as child allowances, unemployment insurance and old age pensions (social security). Interest payments on the national debt also count as government transfers. State spending and income redistribution programs, of course, must be financed. This will require greater taxation and/or large budget deficits, both of which will have an impact on economic activity. Finally, governments spend money and affect the economy through the laws they enact and the rules they impose on economic activity. For example, occupational health and safety and minimum wage laws restrict the ways that goods are produced and how little firms can pay their workers.

Despite the large presence of government activity in modern economies, there is little agreement among economists regarding what role the state should have in economic affairs. There is even less agreement on whether the state affects economic performance positively or negatively.

## Neoclassical perspective

Neoclassical economists generally favor a minimal role for the state. Market economies are seen to be efficient, and are thought to lead to the greatest happiness for the inhabitants of a country. This conclusion follows logically from the basic principles of neoclassical theory: non-coercive trade benefits both parties, since neither party would take part in trade if they did not gain from it. Going even further, neoclassical economists see state involvement in economic affairs as reducing individual freedom (Friedman 1962) and bringing a nation down the road to serfdom (Hayek 1944). Consequently, neoclassical economists generally support the principle that "the government which governs least, governs best" as well as laissez-faire policy prescriptions.

Neoclassical economists, however, usually accept three reasons for state intervention into economic affairs, and see these actions as improving economic performance. First, government action is justified to reduce the monopoly power of individual firms or to prevent firms from acquiring monopoly power. According to neoclassical theory, trade is beneficial only if it is non-coercive. Firms with great market power can extort high prices from consumers, or force workers to accept low pay and dangerous working conditions. Consequently, government must ensure that firms do not attain such power.

Second, government action is warranted in cases with important externalities or spillover effects. When large gains or losses go to individuals not taking part in the market transaction, we do not get the best possible outcome. For example, if some production costs can be imposed on third parties via air and water pollution, these goods sell below their true cost and too many polluting goods get produced. On the other hand, too few goods get produced (like public transportation) that benefit third parties (because of reduced congestion for those driving automobiles). In these cases, government must prohibit or internalize the negative externality (make the polluting firm pay to clean up the environment), and must provide those goods where positive externalities exist.

Finally, government action is warranted whenever consumers cannot obtain adequate information about the goods and services they buy. If it is impossible for consumers to be knowledgeable about the most recent medical advances, they can easily become the dupes of someone claiming medical expertise. As a result, the state needs to make sure that both medical practitioners and certain types of medical treatment are sanctioned by professional experts.

## Political economy perspectives: demand

In contrast to the neoclassical view, political economists view the state as an integral part of economic activity. The term itself – "political economy" – indicates the close linkage between political and economic factors. Political economists, however, do not agree on the effect that the state has on economic performance and activity. Many political economists see the state as a potentially positive force, for instance by improving economic performance. John Maynard KEYNES and post-Keynesian economists believe that laissez-faire policies will not lead to desirable economic outcomes. They thus look to the state as a means to improve economic outcomes.

According to Keynes, capitalist economies do not generate sufficient demand and employment, and government policy must fill the breach. Keynes (1936) favored both money creation and government spending and tax cuts to increase EFFECTIVE DEMAND AND CAPACITY UTILIZATION and reduce unemployment. Keynes also wanted the government to stabilize the level of investment. When private investment is low, the government should borrow money (i.e. run a BUDGET DEFICIT) and engage in public investments such as building new roads, bridges and other infrastructure, and

creating an educated work force. In contrast, when business investment is high due to great optimism, government should stop borrowing and cut back on its public investment.

## Political economy perspectives: state and corporations

John Kenneth Galbraith has set forth another role for the state. In contrast to neoclassical economists, Galbraith sees large, monopolistic firms as having more benefits than costs. State policy seeking to keep monopoly power from arising is thus a mistaken policy, one which will worsen economic performance. Rather than limiting monopoly power, the state must counteract the economic power of business interests. Galbraith (1958) argues that years of favoring private production and neglecting the provision of public goods has led to private affluence and public squalor. To redress this imbalance, funds must be diverted from private hands, where they will purchase less needed commodities, to the public treasury, where they will satisfy important public needs.

The state must also counter the political power of the large corporation. Large firms have developed the power to control prices. They have resources to mold public opinion through advertising, and influence the political process to their advantage. In contrast, small firms have little ability to sway public opinion or the political process. They are thus at a competitive disadvantage. The result is unequal economic development: the planning system produces too many goods and the market system produces an inadequate supply of goods.

Power between the planning and the market systems must be made more equal, according to Galbraith (1973), and this function must be performed by the government. Income must be redistributed from the planning system to the market system. Price controls, minimum wage legislation, guaranteed minimum incomes, protective tariffs and support for small businesses all need to be enacted (see GALBRAITH'S CONTRIBUTION TO POLITICAL ECONOMY).

1105

## Political economy perspectives: worker and citizen rights

Going further than either Keynes or Galbraith, a number of political economists have looked to the state to help plan economic output. These economists see the market as producing only goods for people who start out with the income and wealth to purchase things. As a result, many important needs remain unmet.

Greater government involvement thus improves economic decision making by making it more democratic. For example, Bowles *et al.* (1988) suggest that "needs surveys" be taken and used to make decisions about what sorts of goods will be produced. In addition, these surveys can help determine the sort of working conditions that people desire. If people want to have more a flexible working week, or if they want to be able to take time off for family emergencies without putting their job at risk, and if "the labor market" fails to produce these outcomes, then the government must step in and guarantee workers these rights.

## Political economy perspectives: contradictory role of the state

Not all political economists, however, see the state as a positive force. Karl MARX has been the main proponent of the view that the state under capitalism could produce problematical outcomes because it would be controlled by the capitalist CLASS. With their vast wealth, Marx thought that capitalists would be able to buy political influence. Government officials and policymakers would be beholden to capitalists for their jobs. For the same reason, Marx did not think government action could be counted on to keep unemployment down in a sustained fashion, or to provide legal recognition for labor and greater bargaining power to labor unions.

Similarly, many radical political economists hold that, under capitalism, the state acts primarily to benefit members of the capitalist class. This can be done directly by bestowing benefits on them, or indirectly by preserving class inequalities. On the radical view, the state might pass minimum wage laws or social insurance programs if this helps reduce disruptive forces from jeopardizing the privileges of the wealthy. But once the danger of mass rebellion has passed, spending will be cut back, and government programs will languish.

Another political economist skeptical of the ability of the state to improve economic outcomes is James O'Connor. O'Connor (1973) sees the problem as there being too many problems to solve. He argues that every special interest group will want the government to provide those goods that benefit it. As a result of logrolling or favor trading, one group will support more state spending on pollution control, education and mass transit in exchange for other groups supporting greater spending for the elderly. At the same time, no one wants to pay the higher taxes necessary to support all this spending. The result is that large government deficits arise. Eventually, this develops into a FISCAL CRISIS OF THE STATE. With great debt and so much debt service, the government cannot afford to do the things needed to improve economic performance.

## Conclusion

At the end of the twentieth century, few issues are more hotly debated than the role of the state. Does a larger government help or hinder economic performance? What kinds of government expenditure are more efficient in improving economic performance? Are government deficits too large and do they hurt the economy? These are the questions that political economists will be grappling with in the twenty first century.

## See also:

disembedded economy; economic rationalism or liberalism; environmental policy and politics; fiscal policy; industrial relations; industry policy; monetary policy and central banking functions; social structure of accumulation: state–citizen accord; state and internationalization; technology policy; trade policy; welfare state

## Selected references

Bowles, Samuel, Gordon, David M. and Weisskopf, Thomas E. (1988) *Beyond the Wasteland*, Garden City, NY: Anchor Press/ Doubleday.

Friedman, Milton (1962) *Capitalism and Freedom*, Chicago: University of Chicago Press.

Galbraith, John Kenneth (1958) *The Affluent Society*, New York: New American Library.

—— (1973) *Economics and The Public Purpose*, New York: New American Library.

Hayek, Friedrich (1944) *The Road to Serfdom*, Chicago: University of Chicago Press, 1994.

Keynes, John Maynard (1936) *The General Theory of Employment, Interest and Money*, New York: Harcourt Brace & World, 1964.

O'Connor, James (1973) *The Fiscal Crisis of the State*, New York: St Martin's Press.

Olson, Mancur (1965) *The Logic of Collective Action: Public Goods and the Theory of Groups*, Cambridge: Harvard University Press, 1971.

Tanzi, Vito and Schuknecht, Ludger (1996) "The Growth of Government and the Reform of the State in Industrial Countries," IMF Working Paper.

STEVEN PRESSMAN

# state and internationalization

There has been a renewed interest in conceptualising the place of the nation-state in the international economy within radical political economy. The impetus for this has been the apparent transformation of the institutional order of the global political economy since the mid-1970s. The key element has been the INTERNATIONALIZATION OF CAPITAL, especially that driven by the transnationalisation of capital and the increased mobility of financial capital. In addition, the increasing regulatory authority of international economic organizations, such as the OECD, the Bank for International Settlements, the IMF and the World Bank, have contributed to this changing institutional order.

The early classical Marxist critiques of capitalist imperialism, especially those by Lenin and Bukharin, have influenced the terms of the debate on the role of the state. Their forays into analysing the role of the state in capitalism's imperialist era were essentially concerned with nationalist agendas entailing the assertion of the authority of the state beyond national borders to enhance capital accumulation. The distinctive feature of these contributions was the theorisation of the nation-state in essentially political terms, with the state performing a range of administrative functions to serve the needs of capital. Inscribing this political or administrative function to the state influenced the context in which subsequent theorisations of the state in the global political arena were constructed.

Two particular emphases or tendencies evident in these interventions have come to dominate the debate. The Leninist conception posited the state in terms of a role that reflected and represented a particular CLASS interest in which national monopoly capital assumed the dominant influence. The internationalization of monopoly capital became bound up with the state asserting its authority internationally. This linking of state and national capital formed the basis of the more popular contention that the internationalization of capital, in severing the state–capital nexus, undermined the capacity of states to manage the national economy as a coherent, integrated and independent system.

The alternative perspective defined the state's role of governance in more general terms. The role of the state in advancing capitalist imperialism was regarded as being structural, a product of its role as the institution formed to secure the conditions for expanded accumulation and not a role that was functionally defined in terms of the interests of a particular class. This thesis has informed the critique of the state posed in terms of the state being one administrative element in a capitalism that has always been global in character. Accordingly, the transformations in the institutional organisation of capital and inter-state and transnational state structures evident from the 1970s onwards effects changes in, rather than undermines, the role of the state.

The first serious articulation of the thesis that internationalization of capitalism eroded the authority of the state drew upon the classical Marxist(-Leninist) theories of imperialism to focus on the economies of the South, the less developed countries (the LDCs), invaded by the metropolitan capitalist powers. The critique was essentially concerned with the development of underdevelopment. But, in considering how the LDCs were drawn more systematically into the globally-organised trading and production system, dependency theorists reckoned that the force and independence of the state as an instrument of governance was weakened. In endeavoring to attract the capital of the transnationals of the advanced industrial economies the states assumed a subservient role. The states were transformed into the instruments of international capital and international capital's subordinate indigenous partners, assuming what has been referred to as a *comprador* role.

The state in LDCs in this thesis, a hallmark of the neo-Marxist tradition, is envisaged as an instrument facilitating the transmission of economic surplus from the economies of the South to the metropolitan economies. This approach has been adapted by institutionalist and other neo-Marxist political economists to explain dependent development in the former white settler colonies and now more advanced industrial economies. Here the sovereignty of the state was held to have become subsumed by the necessity to meet the accumulation demands of foreign metropolitan transnational capital.

The Marxist critique of the role of the nation-state in advanced industrial economies has been broader and more abstract in focus. Attention has focused on the "internationalness" of capital, with capital's mobility, rather than the nationality, or "foreignness," of capital. In the Marxist critique, the dilemma confronting the authority of the state is posed in terms of the lack of correspondence between the spatial terrain over which the nation-state is constituted to regulate and underwrite the accumulation of capital, and the global domain of international capital.

The argument which attracted most support in the 1970s, and one which has a continuing purchase, stressed the way in which the internationalization of capital had emasculated the state's ability to cohere the national economy and regulate accumulation within the national economy. The internationalization of capital frustrated the state's ability to pursue Keynesian economic management policies within the national economy. The scope for an autonomous capitalist strategy was held to be impaired by the increasingly global or transnational organisation of production, the increasing mobility of financial capital and accumulation patterns that has become internationally orientated (Radice 1984). With different spheres of production and exchange influenced or defined in terms of international forces, there was a disarticulation of the national economy, and the capacity of the state to govern the economy in classical Keynesian ways was frustrated.

More recently, other interventions have argued that new forms of international state structures or mechanisms of regulating accumulation have assumed a dominant role in the global political economy. These international economic institutions increasingly dictate the parameters within which nation-state policy must be conducted, and this compromises the authority of the nation-state. It has also been argued that the role of the nation-state has been further emasculated by the globalisation of a whole range of political struggles that contribute to defining the social and political contexts in which capital is organised and accumulated. Perhaps the most significant is the organisation of international finance capital and transnational industrial capital and their influence in shaping the liberalisation of world commodity and capital markets. The globalisation of the economic, political and institutional edifices of capitalism dramatically diminishes the importance of the nation-state and has, according to socialist critics, major ramifications for the conduct of a socialist politics and makes nonsense of any social democratically defined nation-based economic recovery program.

The counter thesis has stressed the structural role of the state in terms of globally defined accumulation processes. This thesis reiterates the contention that the nation-state is a product of the evolution of the global political economy and its authority is inscribed in its being a constituent element in the international polity. Accordingly, the nation-state has a continuing role as the principal institutional vehicle for regulating class relations, for securing the terrain upon which the politics of exploitation and accumulation is organised, as fractured elements of a global system. The state functions to regulate class relations, organise infrastructure and capital, and the social and physical plain in which production is established, in order to articulate the national economy into the global economy. In this conception, the role of the state is premised on the construction of a state that is internationalised. While the territorial boundaries of the nation defines the physical space over which the state has formal jurisdiction, the authority of the state is not necessarily restricted to this territory, as the theories of imperialism have made clear.

The debate on the state and internationalization of capital has been framed within the context of assuming that the role of the nation-state is structurally determined. Although most contributors would recognise the contingent form and organisation of individual nation-states, there is a tendency to downplay the nation-state's active constitution within and shaping of the international polity and political economy in the face of the globalisation of capital. This proposition, that the nation-state is imprisoned, or subsumed within an international accumulation process and consequently debilitated as a managerial apparatus, is premised on quite a static conception of the state. It is also one that is founded upon the false dichotomy of the state being defined within the political realm while capital is defined within the sphere of the economy.

Accepting that the role of the nation-state is contingent, the place of the state in the global political economy cannot be dismissed *a priori* as being increasingly problematic or ineffectual simply on the grounds that the nation-state is bound by territorial contingencies. The classical Marxist theories of imperialism provided considerable insight into the extra-territorial assertion of the authority of the nation-state. Contemporary political developments highlight a range of ways in which the authority of the nation-state reaches beyond territorial boundaries. Unilateral displays of extra-territorial authority can be set alongside the assertion of a political will through the institutions of the international economy, in informal and formal inter-state cooperative arrangements, as well as in the building of regional and global institutional vehicles through which the interests of individual nation-states can be advanced.

It is also necessary to move beyond the notion of the state as being politically constituted, an administrative apparatus whose principle function is to secure the conditions for capital accumulation and/or reconcile competing class interests, to consider a conception of the state as being integral to and existing within the accumulation process. The state is essential to the accumulation process insofar as it helps to constitute the conditions of production and establish the concrete foundations for accumulation. Moreover, particular compartments of the state contribute directly to the accumulation process. Just as accumulation is not constrained by territoriality, so the state or particular divisions within the state can assume extra-territorial functions of regulating, administering and contributing to accumulation. This denotes the possibility of a comparable shift in the form and character of the state as that evidenced with capital. It amounts to what might be regarded as the possibility of the transnationalisation of the state.

## Selected references

Holloway, John (1994) "Global Capital and the National State," *Capital and Class* 52(Spring).

McGrew, Anthony and Lewis, Paul (eds) (1992) *Global Politics: Globalization and Nation-States*, London.

Picciotto, Sol (1991) "The Internationalization of the State", *Capital and Class* 43(Spring).

Pooley, Sam (1991) "The State Rules OK? The Continuing Political Economy of Nation-State," *Capital and Class* 43(Spring).

Radice, Hugo (1984) "The National Economy – a Keynesian Myth," *Capital and Class* 22(Spring).

STUART ROSEWARNE

# steady-state economy

A steady-state economy is one where the stocks of people and artifacts are constant and the rate of throughput is minimized. Advocates of a steady-state economy argue that continued ECONOMIC GROWTH is both impossible and undesirable. The difference between quantitative growth and qualitative development is emphasized. While a steady-state economy would not grow, a steady-state society would hopefully continue to develop and improve.

## History

For the classical economists, the stationary state was viewed with trepidation. Falling profits would put an end to capital accumulation, and the stationary state with its stagnate wages and negligible profits would ensue. John Stuart Mill was unique in seeing a bright side to these dismal prognostications. In his *Principles of Political Economy* in 1848, he suggests it would be "a very considerable improvement on our present condition." Foreshadowing Keynes (1932), he eschewed the notion that "the normal state of human beings is that of struggling to get on" and argued "the trampling, crushing, elbowing, and treading on each other's heels" were the "disagreeable symptoms of one of the phases of industrial progress." In modern times, the steady state has been viewed, not as a consequence of falling profits, but as a necessary and desirable response to social and environmental concerns. John Kenneth Galbraith's 1958 classic *The Affluent Society* challenged the preoccupation with production, and by the late 1960s and early 1970s writers such as Boulding, Georgescu-Roegen, Meadows and Meadows, and Daly had drawn attention to the economy's biophysical constraints. With the 1977 publication of Daly's *Steady-State Economics*, the arguments for a steady state were becoming widely known, though not widely accepted, by economists.

## Arguments for a steady state

Advocates of a steady-state economy argue that continued growth is both impossible and undesirable. Booming populations, exponential industrial growth, and the constraints of the laws of thermodynamics gave rise to arguments that current trends were not only unsustainable, but could lead to disaster and ruin by the next century if not checked. Exponential growth in population has been a concern since Malthus. While dramatic improvements in agricultural and medical sciences have accommodated an enormous increase in population, scientists still point to the same dilemma: population can be controlled humanely by reducing the birth rate or disastrously by hunger and disease. Rates of growth reveal only part of the picture. Never before have billions of people been added to the planet in a single generation. At the same time, dramatic increases in the standard of living exacerbate the problem and lead to worries that the law of entropy will become increasingly pressing.

Biophysical constraints, rooted in ecology and the laws of thermodynamics, make unlimited growth impossible. Additionally, social, ethical and ecological concerns have led to arguments that continued growth is undesirable as well. As humanity's impact on the environment continues to grow exponentially, many have voiced concerns about non-human nature. Daly (1991: 188), for example, argues that society's concern for the environment should not be limited to nature's sustaining role of providing sources and sinks for the economy. Attention must also be given to the intrinsic value of non-human species. Social malaise in the midst of unprecedented affluence has also led to questions about the desirability of unchallenged growth. Growth cannot satiate relative wants. Moving ahead of the crowd, whether for invidious or practical reasons, is a zero-sum game. As relative wants grow in significance compared to more basic needs, tacit polices of growth in lieu of redistribution become less and less satisfactory.

## Service, throughput and stock

In addition to enumerating reasons for a steady-state economy, a good deal has been written on the nature and structure of such an economy. The following identity (Daly 1991) is useful in determining the desiderata of a steady state as well as highlighting the difference between growth and development:

$$\frac{service}{throughput} \equiv \frac{service}{stock} \times \frac{stock}{throughput}$$

The first ratio, that of service to throughput, is the benefit–cost ratio of the economic system. Service is the satisfaction or Fisherian "psychic income" (Daly 1991: 35) yielded by stock. Throughput is "the entropic physical flow of matter-energy from nature's sources, through the human economy and back to nature's sinks" (Daly and Townsend 1993: 326). Throughput is viewed as the ultimate cost of economic activity (Daly 1991: 25) because its inevitable and irreversible consequence is increased entropy. Stock refers to physical things capable of satisfying human wants. It includes the human population as well as producer and consumer goods. Daly (1991), in keeping with Boulding (1949–50), emphasizes that service is yielded by stocks rather than flows. It is the radio itself, not its wearing out, that brings enjoyment. The ratio of service to stock is the service efficiency. Similarly, the ratio of stock to throughput indicates the efficiency of throughput in maintaining stock. Improved durability will increase this "maintenance efficiency" ratio.

The identity shows that growth has an ambiguous effect on development. The left-hand side of the identity is the amount of service per unit of throughput. Development can be thought of as an increase in this ratio (Daly 1991: 37). Growth, on the other hand, is the increase of stock. This affects the two ratios on the right-hand side of the identity. Stock itself, great or small, will divide out. And while greater stock may accommodate greater service, it also, *ceteris paribus*, requires greater throughput. It is possible, however, to develop without growth. This can be accomplished by reducing the amount of throughput required to maintain a given level of stock, or by changing the use and composition of this stock so as to produce more service per unit of stock. That is, development occurs by improving service efficiency and maintenance efficiency. It is possible, Daly (1991) acknowledges, that there may even be a limit to development. Maintenance efficiency is constrained by the Second Law of Thermodynamics (entropy). Specifically, the tendency towards higher entropy prevents stocks from being infinitely durable. It is also conceivable, he argues, that the limits of time and human physiology may ultimately constrain service efficiency.

The identity shows a clear distinction between throughput, service, and stock. Steady-state policies require treating each differently: minimizing throughput, maximizing service (subject to a given stock) and satisficing with regard to stock. Steady-state economics, therefore, challenges not only the habitual policy of economic growth, but calls into question measures used to track economic progress. Rather than making such distinctions, national income accounts add together "three very unlike categories: throughput, additions to capital stock, and services rendered by the capital stock" (Daly 1991: 30).

## Morals and ethics

Often, policies championed by steady-state advocates revolve around moral issues. In fact, it has been argued that the only arguments against continued growth and material accumulation are ethical and religious ones (Daly and Townsend 1993: 155). Because of this explicitly moral orientation, steady-state discussions often attract controversy. For example, zero growth would demand a more even distribution of wealth within and among nations, as well as institutions for controlling population (Daly 1991: 53). Yet policy recommendations advocating birth control or redistribution raise counter arguments by people concerned with such issues as religion, gender and nationalism.

## Critique of steady state

The urgency of a steady-state economy has also been challenged by some radical and neoclassical economists. Generally, these economists are optimistic about technological advance empowering society to stay ahead of biophysical constraints: allowing, for example, for the discovery of new resources and the more efficient use of old ones. Many are quick to point to falling prices of a variety of resources as evidence that the constraints imposed by the laws of thermodynamics are not so pressing. In the end, focusing on the unsatisfactory nature of habitual growth may be more relevant and produce more agreement – at least among heterodox economists – than debates about technological possibilities.

## Further research

Arguments for a steady-state economy are now widely known by economists. Acceptance has been slower. To progress in their uphill struggle against convention, steady-state theorists will have to bolster their arguments about the limits to growth. This includes conducting further inquiries into the social limits to growth (see Hirsch 1976). Determining guidelines for the innumerable policies to facilitate a steady-state economy also provides abundant opportunity for further research. In addition, steady-state economics draws attention to a host of other issues. Steady state or not, issues such as distributive justice, sustainable development, population control, environmental ethics, and the disillusionment with affluence will very

likely be widely debated while continuing to grow in importance.

## See also:

bioeconomics; development and the environment; entropy, negentropy and the laws of thermodynamics; environmental and ecological political economy: major contemporary themes; quality of life

## Selected references

Boulding, Kenneth E. (1949–50) "Income or Welfare?," *Review of Economic Studies* 17(2): 77–86.

Daly, Herman E. (1991) *Steady-State Economics*, 2nd edn, Washington, DC: Island Press.

Daly, Herman E. and Townsend, Kenneth N. (eds) (1993) *Valuing the Earth*, Cambridge, MA: MIT Press.

Hirsch, Fred (1976) *Social Limits to Growth*, Cambridge, MA: Harvard University Press.

Keynes, John Maynard (1932) "Economic Possibilities for Our Grandchildren," in John Maynard Keynes, *Essays in Persuasion*, New York: Harcourt, Brace & Company.

TERREL GALLAWAY

# storytelling and pattern models

## Storytelling

All economic theory involves storytelling. The use of the term is not meant pejoratively. Rather it is an accurate description of most work in the social sciences. In the harder, natural sciences there is little need for such an approach. The economist, like other social scientists, must contend with a situation where there are a large number of relevant variables, where there is an inherent paucity of data, and where human behavior is unlike electron behavior. Storytelling is an attempt to provide a coherent account of a situation where fact, theory and values are all mixed together in reality and in the telling.

One way to assess the benefits of formalism in economic theory is the pressure it exerts for systematic storytelling. For example, the introduction of linear programming models led to the systematic collection of data, and the models themselves function as the outline of a story one wants to tell about optimizing economic agents.

Political economists, particularly institutionalists, have developed a special form of storytelling known as pattern modeling. Instead of using a pre-existing theoretical framework, such as rational choice theory, to logically construct a story, this type of story is constructed empirically from the bottom up through the use of case studies. As part of the HOLISTIC METHOD, the investigator functions as a participant–observer with the primary subject matter being a single, self-maintaining social system. Although there are varying conceptions of how whole the system needs to be, one thing is clear. It is not the sheer magnitude of the whole that is important, but that the particular system under investigation constitutes a unified whole. The magnitude of the selected system may vary from the culture on the shop floor in industrial society to a village in the developing world, or perhaps from a formal organization or institution such as the business corporation to a whole economic system. In any case, the emphasis is upon the individuality or uniqueness of the particular system.

## Socialization of the investigator

The first step in constructing a pattern model via case studies using the participant–observer approach is the "socialization" of the investigator. As a participant, the investigator allows the studied group, such as workers on the shop floor, to impress upon him or her their norms and to instill within him or her their categories and point of view. Many of the best-known institutional political economists – John R. Commons, Gardiner Means, John Kenneth Galbraith, Gunnar Myrdal – have developed

their ideas while working on public utility regulation, price control, economic planning and antitrust. In effect, the participant–observer studies from the inside what is going on, using the insider's categories and norms to understand what is going on.

In getting close to the concrete reality of the system studied, the investigator is in a unique position to perceive a wide variety of recurrent themes, such as target profits, markup PRICING, INTERNAL LABOR MARKETS and so on, that appear in a variety of contexts. A theme is more important the more links it has with other themes, because the investigator wants to construct a model which emphasizes the interconnectedness or unity of the system (the coherence of the story). The investigator, as an observer, looks for themes which illuminate the system's wholeness, that is, which contribute to its individuality or oneness.

The next step is to make explicit this information which, as a participant, the investigator is now able to perceive. Initially, this process may be rather haphazard. The investigator constructs tentative hypotheses about parts of the system out of the recurrent themes that become obvious in the course of the socialization process. These hypotheses or interpretations of themes are tested by consulting a wide variety of data (previous case studies, survey data, available statistics, personal observations and so forth). Evidence in support of a hypothesis is evaluated by means of contextual validation. This technique is a process of cross-checking different kinds and sources of evidence, and it serves as an indirect means of evaluating the plausibility of one's initial interpretations. If the investigator is unable to secure evidence in support of earlier hypotheses, or if the validity of the evidence or its sources prove to be questionable, the hypotheses are revised or discarded.

Gradually, as socialization proceeds, the investigator becomes increasingly attuned to accurate perception and interpretation of the recurrent themes and formulation of validated hypotheses. The investigator uses this experience and the various pieces of evidence to build up a many-sided, complex picture of the subject matter. Unfortunately, this technique of contextual validation can never produce the rigorous certainty espoused by formalist mainstream economists; it can only indicate varying degrees of plausibility. It is a process not unlike the one that a good police detective uses to construct a story to explain what happened and who did it. The process can be better understood by reading Bolch and Miller (1978), Salmen (1987), Stake (1995), Ullman and Colbert (1991) and Yin (1994).

## Pattern model

After several themes or hypotheses have been validated, the investigator proceeds to the last step of the approach: putting the elements of the story together or building what is called a pattern model. This is constructed by linking validated hypotheses or themes in a network or pattern. The account of each particular part of the system emphasizes the multiplicity of connections between that part with the other parts and with the whole system. It is in this way that the investigator attempts to capture the interactive relationship between part and whole. As the investigator constructs the system model (puts together the story), earlier descriptions of the parts are continually tested by how well they fit together in a pattern, and to what extent new evidence can be explained within the pattern. The investigator is constantly seeking to obtain a finer and finer degree of coherence between his or her account of the system as a pattern of interconnections and the real system. However, since new data are constantly coming in, and since the system itself is evolving, the model is continually being revised and can neither be completed nor rigorously confirmed.

Verification of the pattern model or story as a whole consists of expanding it further and filling in more details. That is, the investigator is reasonably certain that an explanation is the correct one if new data and different kinds of evidence tend to fall into place in the pattern. Consequently, verification of the accuracy of the explanation lies not in any one component but in the whole. This is due to the low level of

reliability that the investigator attaches to any particular interpretation of a specific part (since the parts are only contextually validated). It is more likely that the explanation is correct if, as the pattern becomes more complex and detailed, a greater variety of evidence easily falls into place. At this point, it is more difficult to imagine an alternative pattern or explanation which manages to include the same themes. As a consequence, the explanation of the whole system is tentatively held as correct until an alternative or revised pattern is able to supersede the old story by incorporating an even greater variety of data.

Ben Ward offers a check-list for verifying a story (1972: 189):

- Are the facts and theories correctly stated?
- Are important facts or theories omitted?
- Can one find other stories which use the facts and theories employed in the given story?
- Are the facts and theories relevant or essential to the story; that is, can no other hypotheses be used to tell a good story about the facts?
- Do experts in the various parts of the story believe the story itself?
- Are values correctly stated?
- Are all relevant values included?

The stronger the yes to each of these questions, the stronger is the verification of the story.

## Understanding and explanation

From the viewpoint of holism, the primary function of pattern models is to promote understanding. From the viewpoint of mainstream economics, the purpose of models is to allow predictions. Within the context of the pattern model form of story, the pattern which provides the explanation does not uniquely determine the parts. Thus, knowledge of the whole pattern and of some of the parts does not necessarily enable the investigator to predict any or all unknown parts. The explanation still explains even though it leaves open a range of possibilities. The theory of evolution explains highly specialized forms as produced by natural selection, but they are predictable only in a general way. Use of pattern model storytelling appears appropriate when an explanation involves many diverse factors, each of which is important; and when these factors can be observed in the particular case under study.

## See also:

culture; institutional political economy: major contemporary themes; methodology in economics; pragmatism; value judgments and world views

## Selected references

Bolch, Judith and Miller, Kay (1978) *Investigative and In-Depth Reporting*, New York: Hastings House.

Diesing, Paul (1971) *Patterns of Discovery in the Social Sciences*, Chicago: Aldine-Atherton.

Salmen, Lawrence F. (1987) *Listen to the People: Participant-Observation Evaluation of Development Projects*, New York: Oxford University Press.

Stake, Robert E. (1995) *The Art of Case Study Research*, Thousand Oaks, CA: Sage Publications.

Ullmann, John and Colbert, Jan (1991) *The Reporter's Handbook: An Investigative Guide to Documents and Techniques*, New York: St Martin's Press.

Ward, Benjamin (1972) *What's Wrong with Economics?* New York: Basic Books.

Wilber, Charles K. and Harrison, Robert S. (1978) "The Methodological Basis of Institutional Economics: Pattern Model, Storytelling, and Holism," *Journal of Economic Issues* 12(1): 61–89.

Yin, Robert K. (1994) *Case Study Research: Design and Methods*, 2nd edn, Thousand Oaks, CA: Sage Publications.

CHARLES K. WILBER

# structural adjustment policies

The term "structural adjustment" comes from the World Bank lending window, which was created in the 1980s to offer quick-disbursing balance of payments financing based on economy-wide conditionality. Structural adjustment programs, based on such financing from the BRETTON WOODS SYSTEM international financial institutions (IFIs), i.e. the International Monetary Fund (IMF) and the World Bank, were introduced in at least sixty nations during the period 1980–92.

## Propelled by three crises

Structural adjustment programs emerged from the historical conjuncture of three interrelated crises. First, many countries experienced grave BALANCE OF PAYMENTS imbalances in the 1970s and 1980s. The etiology of those imbalances varied markedly across countries, with some attributable almost entirely to global shocks (e.g. oil and other commodity prices) and others ascribable principally to domestic mismanagement. Regardless of the cause of their crisis, developing countries generally requested exceptional balance of payments financing from the IFIs. Since commercial credit dried up due to contemporaneous DEBT CRISES IN THE THIRD WORLD, and bilateral donors were fatiguing of what they perceived as ineffective FOREIGN AID, this left the multilateral IFIs as the primary source of financing. This gave the IFIs unprecedented power to influence policymaking in developing countries (Mosley *et al.* 1991). The IFIs' newfound power over sovereign states, and their default perspective that policy errors were at the root of all countries' problems, led to sometimes acrimonious struggles over economic policymaking in the 1980s and well into the 1990s.

Secondly, institutional crisis beset the World Bank (and other development agencies) in the 1970s, as their core portfolio of project finance came under increasing attack for economic inefficiency, environmental profligacy and human RIGHTS insensitivity. Mounting evidence indicated that microeconomic and sectoral interventions had limited positive effects, and sometimes negative returns, in the absence of macroeconomic stability and prices that reasonably accurately reflected relative scarcities. The internal experiences of development institutions thus induced a radical reorientation of administrative priorities, toward a decidedly more macroeconomic focus and an emphasis on quick loan disbursement. This administrative reorientation prompted deference to the IMF's supposed macroeconomic expertise in establishing which countries needed and deserved financing and how much. More than 90 percent of World Bank structural adjustment loans and commercial and government debt reschedulings through the London and Paris Clubs, respectively, were preceded or accompanied by an agreed stabilization program with the IMF.

Thirdly, an intellectual crisis emerged within the social sciences as the post-Second World War Keynesian orthodoxies in development economics, macroeconomics and political economy were subjected to sharp empirical and theoretical attack by monetarist, public choice, rational expectations, and new classical macroeconomic theorists. While these challenges responded to genuine deficiencies in theory and achievement, none of them constituted a coherent, empirically defensible approach on which to found development strategies. By diminishing hopes for generalizable macroeconomic theory, the conservatives of the 1970s empowered the use of neoclassical microeconomic rules of thumb in policy design. In this intellectual vacuum, structural adjustment programs advanced in the 1980s on the basis of a relatively atheoretical dogmatism (see Killick 1989). By the mid-1990s, a decade of sometimes vitriolic debate had leavened the neoliberalism of the Washington-based institutions with a touch of structuralism, as evidenced by greater attention being paid to structural impediments to the efficient working of markets, and the evolution of structural adjustment program policy instruments (see STRUCTURALIST THEORY OF DEVELOPMENT).

## Basis of the policies

Macroeconomic reforms have been fundamental to structural adjustment programs. The first generation programs (to the mid-1980s) were inextricably linked to macroeconomic stabilization efforts, led by the IMF. This emphasized expenditure reduction and expenditure switching policies (for example, exchange rate devaluation, fiscal and monetary contraction) to restore macroeconomic balances. The emphasis of structural adjustment programs was on market-oriented reforms, based on three main assumptions. The first assumption was that it is important to reduce the size of government through fiscal contraction and asset privatization to minimize distortions associated with *ad valorem* taxation, agency problems and rent-seeking. The second was that market prices (including exchange rates and interest rates) provide appropriate information signals for resource allocation, investment and innovation. The third assumption was that free domestic and international trade leads to efficiency-enhancing specialization according to comparative advantage. This was largely an agenda based on IDEOLOGY.

From the mid-1980s, sectoral initiatives, especially in agriculture and finance, became additional important components of most structural adjustment programs. By the early 1990s, structural adjustment programs began to include efforts to improve the delivery of education and health services and the provision of basic infrastructure, and to cushion the adverse effects of adjustment on the poor. The evolution of the instruments commonly involved in structural adjustment program design now reflects the gradual realization that adjustment is a long-run undertaking fraught with considerable risk of social dislocation, and that the structural context for macroeconomic and sectoral policy heavily conditions outcomes.

While little attention was paid to the plight of the poor in the course of first generation structural adjustment programs (Cornia *et al.* 1988; Stewart 1995), the task of poverty alleviation in adjustment became prominent in the rhetoric, if not often the substance, of structural adjustment programs in the 1990s. The idea that state-led INDUSTRIALIZATION would benefit the poor fell into disfavor. A weak consensus emerged behind the belief that growth in low-income economies is likely to disproportionately benefit laborers, and thus the poor, since the poorest members of society have only their labor, not other assets from which to derive income (Lipton and Ravallion 1995). Still, little attention has yet been paid in practice to public action necessary to protect, much less empower, the poor, or to advance either environmentally SUSTAINABLE DEVELOPMENT or GENDER equity.

## Results of structural adjustment programs

The results of structural adjustment programs have been mixed but generally disappointing, both in terms of ECONOMIC GROWTH and poverty alleviation. Protracted contractionary adjustment programs made the 1980s a "lost decade" of negative per capita economic growth, rising poverty and deteriorating social indicators in virtually all adjusting economies in Africa and Latin America. However, adjustment by and large coincided with accelerated growth and poverty reduction in Asia. Moreover, while, by the mid-1990s, the Latin American economies had largely resumed strong economic growth and employment creation, with some reduction in poverty and improvement in social indicators, African nations continued to show little sign of durable recovery (Cornia and Helleiner 1994; Stewart 1995).

The efficacy of structural adjustment programs seems to have depended on the initial structural conditions of the adjusting economies, and on the commitment of the donors and governments involved to protect the poor and rectify imprudent policies. But without much prior empirical research to motivate the design and sequencing of reforms, and in the context of intense international and domestic political struggles, it is perhaps not surprising that the countries most in need of growth-oriented adjustment and poverty alleviation

had few positive results to show from structural adjustment programs after a decade of reform efforts. Moreover, widespread decline over the era of structural adjustment programs in fixed capital formation rates and education and health indicators raise ominous portents for future development in the poorest adjusting economies. While it was not a necessary outcome, the costs of structural adjustment programs seem to have been borne disproportionately by the poor.

## See also:

development political economy: major contemporary themes; gender and development; human development index; world hunger and poverty

## Selected references

Barrett, C.B. and Carter, M.R. (1998) "Does It Take More Than Liberalization? The Economics of Sustainable Agrarian Growth and Transformation," in M. Carter, J. Cason and F. Zimmerman (eds), *Rebalancing Market, State and Civil Society for Sustainable Development*, Madison, WI: University of Wisconsin.

Cornia, G.A. and Helleiner, G.K. (eds) (1994) *From Adjustment to Development in Africa: Conflict, Controversy, Convergence, Consensus?* New York: St Martin's Press.

Cornia, G.A., Jolly, R. and Stewart, F. (1988) *Adjustment with a Human Face*, 2 vols, Oxford: Clarendon Press.

Killick, Tony (1989) *A Reaction Too Far: Economic Theory and the Role of the State in Developing Countries*, Boulder, CO: Westview.

Lipton, Michael and Ravallion, Martin (1995) "Poverty and Policy," in Jere Behrman and T.N. Srinivasan (eds), *Handbook of Development Economics, Vol IIIB*, Amsterdam: Elsevier Science.

Mosley, Paul, Harrigan, Jane and Toye, John (1991) *Aid and Power: The World Bank and Policy-Based Lending*, 2 vols, London: Routledge.

Stewart, Frances (1995) *Adjustment and Poverty: Options and Choices*, London: Routledge.

CHRIS BARRETT

# structuralist theory of development

The structuralist theory of development is often considered to be one of three main approaches to development economics (along with neoclassical and Marxian theories). It can be defined as a theory of development which gives attention to the specific structure of the particular economy it examines. In line with structuralism in other disciplines, it emphasizes interactions between various components of the economy, and its overall macroeconomic structure, in contrast to a focus on individual components as in neoclassical theory. Since it is not obvious how focusing attention on specific structural characteristics can constitute a coherent theory, and since the aproach was initially developed as a critique of neoclassical growth and development theory, the "theory" has come to encompass a wide range of views which emphasize structural rigidities in less-developed countries (LDCs).

## Origins

The origins of structuralism as a theory of development can be traced back to the analysis which developed in the 1930s and 1940s of market failures which prevent the price mechanism from efficiently allocating resources, especially due to the immobility of factors of production (Arndt 1985). Proponents of the view included Rosenstein-Rodan, KALECKI, Balogh, Seers and Kaldor, many of whom participated in the debates on planning and direct controls in the postwar British economy. The vast majority of the pioneers of development economics – Nurkse, Myrdal, Singer and Chenery, in addition to Rosenstein-Rodan – subscribed to this broad structuralist view, being skeptical of the ability of the price mechanism in LDCs to guide resource allocation efficiently in a static and especially in a dynamic sense, and to bring about greater equality, and favoring state intervention through planning and direct controls.

More specific structuralist theories evolved in the 1950s and 1960s, primarily in Latin America under the auspices of ECLA (United Nations Commission for Latin America) and its first director, Raúl Prebisch (see Palma 1987). The approach emphasized the differences between the homogeneous, integrated and diversified production structure in the center or developed countries, on the one hand, and the heterogeneous, disjointed and specialized structure of the periphery or LDCs, on the other; and the need to understand the development in LDCs in terms of its interaction with the center (see CORE–PERIPHERY ANALYSIS).

## Implications for LDCs

This overall framework had some more specific implications for LDCs. First, it pointed out that the structure of most LDCs was dualistic, in the sense that they have a traditional sector, which has surplus labor, and a modern industrial (primary import-substituting) sector, which has a limited amount of productive capital. The small and stagnant size of the modern sector implies structural unemployment in the economy, as formalized by Lewis's (1954) dual economy model (see LEWIS'S THEORY OF ECONOMIC GROWTH AND DEVELOPMENT).

Second, it pointed out that LDCs were plagued by chronic BALANCE OF PAYMENTS problems due to the income-inelastic world demand for their mostly primary product exports and their price-inelastic demand for manufactured imports, especially for essential investment purposes. The early two-gap models of Chenery and others formalized these issues. The problem was exacerbated – according to Prebisch and Singer – by the secular deterioration of the terms of trade of the periphery *vis-à-vis* the center due to the pattern of international specialization in which the center exports income-elastic goods, which made it more difficult for the former to obtain foreign exchange for its imports.

Third, it argued that high inflation in LDCs is caused by the inelastic supply of agricultural goods, balance of payments problems and the conflict between social classes over the DIS-TRIBUTION OF INCOME. This approach, pioneered by Juan Noyala and Osvaldo Sunkel, who cited the authority of Kalecki, was opposed to the monetarist theory of inflation which stresses the role of poor macroeconomic management which leads to excessive money supply growth (see MONETARISM). The policy implication drawn from these ideas was that active state intervention was necessary to mobilize saving and investment for capital accumulation in the modern sector, to promote import-substituting industrialization for diversifying the production structure of LDCs and reducing the dependence of LDCs on imports, and to remove supply rigidities through policies such as LAND REFORM.

## Criticism of structuralism

These early structuralist theories were criticized by both Marxist and neoclassical development economists. There was criticism from Marxists, because the structuralists were said to divert attention away from the basic exploitative structures within LDCs; and there was criticism from neoclassical economists for overemphasizing structural rigidities, and underestimating the potential of individual economic agents to take advantage of market opportunites presented to them. In the late 1970s and early 1980s, structuralist development theory was to be associated primarily with short-run aspects of development economics dealing especially with stabilization policies in heavily indebted and high inflation economies of Latin America. The focus was on criticizing orthodox contractionary stabilization policies for their distributionally regressive and recessionary effects, and the earlier emphasis on long-run development issues was lost.

## Revival of structuralism

Structuralist development theory has recently experienced a revival, with the development of macroeconomic models, pioneered by Taylor (1983, 1991), drawing on the contributions of early structuralist development economists and of MARX, KEYNES, Kalecki and Kaldor, among others. The general characteristic of this approach is to start with a skeleton comprising basic macroeconomic identities (such as commodity balance, income decomposition, and balance of payment accounts), and add to it hypotheses regarding the behavior of groups (drawing on stylized facts based on micro-level empirical analysis rather than merely optimizing microfoundations), and the nature of specific markets.

Some of the models have only one sector, where relevant sectoral distinctions are taken into account, such as those between industry and agriculture, traded and non-traded sectors, basic and luxury goods sectors, and consumption and investment goods sectors. The industrial sector is usually characterized by an oligopolistic structure with markup pricing and excess capacity, due to deficient aggregate demand. It is recognized that, in some cases, output can be constrained by other factors such as capacity or balance of payment constraints. The agricultural sector, on the other hand, is usually assumed to be supply constrained due to institutional rigidities. Differences between different classes (such as capitalists, workers, landlords, and peasants) regarding saving and patterns of consumption are usually taken into account.

Appropriate assumptions are used to model investment behaviour in different sectors, giving particular emphasis to financial factors and the determinants of expected profitability and market prospects. Asset markets are modeled by taking into account the important assets relevant for the economy – sometimes including informal curb-side markets – and the characterstics of the banking and financial sector.

Adding assumptions about imports, exports and other external relationships, and government finances, the models are used to examine the short-run implications of government policy (such as contractionary fiscal and monetary policies and devaluations) and other socio-political changes (such as changes in income distribution), given the productive capacity of each sector. The models are also extended to deal with medium-term issues such as wage and price inflation and distributional changes (thereby formalizing the conflict approach to inflation) and long-run issues relating to capital ACCUMULATION, technological change and sectoral balance. On long-run issues, for instance, closely scrutinized are the income distribution between social classes, long-run growth, and agricultural and industrial growth under alternative assumptions about economic structure.

The models have been used to characterize a number of different constraints on long-run growth, including demand constraints, savings constraints, constraints arising from the slow growth of stagnant sectors (such as an agriculture which is stagnant due to institutional obstacles), foreign exchange constraints, and fiscal constraints. The approach has also been extended to deal with the economic relations between the advanced countries and LDCs, using North–South models which often emphasize the structural differences between rich and poor countries.

## Conclusion

Unlike early structuralist development theory, this newer approach does not have an overall view of the development process. Altough this makes it less attractive to those who prefer a grand overall "vision" of development, it appears to have a greater degree of methodological coherence than earlier structuralist theory. This is because it starts with accounting identities which show the interconnections between different components of the economy and builds on them, by choosing from a set of behavioral and institutional assumptions to reflect the specific characteristics of the economy being considered. This has made structuralist development economics not only a productive area for theoretical research, but

also for policy analysis using empirical models (see Taylor 1990).

## See also:

balance of payments constraint; development political economy: major contemporary themes; economic growth; import substitution and export-oriented industrialization; structural adjustment policies

## Selected references

Arndt, H.W. (1985) "The Origins of Structuralism," *World Development* 13(2).

Lewis, W. Arthur (1954) "Economic Development with Unlimited Supplies of Labour," *The Manchester School of Economic and Social Studies* 22.

Palma, Gabriel (1987) "Structuralism," in J. Eatwell, M. Milgate and P. Newman (eds), *The New Palgrave: A Dictionary of Economics*, London: Macmillan.

Taylor, Lance (1983) *Structuralist Macroeconomics: Applicable Models for the Third World*, New York: Basic Books.

—— (1990) (ed.) *Socially Relevant Policy Analysis: Structuralist Computable General Equilibrium Models for the Developing World*, Cambridge, MA: MIT Press.

—— (1991) *Income Distribution, Inflation and Growth: Lectures on Structuralist Macroeconomic Theory*, Cambridge, MA: MIT Press.

AMITAVA KRISHNA DUTT

# substantivist–formalist debate

## Definition

The substantivist–formalist debate refers to a controversy that raged in economic anthropology during the 1960s regarding the application of conventional economics to primitive and peasant societies. The formalists defended economics as being universally applicable and truly cross-cultural, and argued that substantivist concepts were merely descriptive and unsystematic. The substantivists argued that conventional economics was particularist and ethnocentric and not cross-culturally applicable, and that only substantive concepts were cross-culturally applicable because they truly dealt with patterns of variability in the processes of material livelihood. Edward LeClair and Harold K. Schneider's *Economic Anthropology: Readings in Theory and Analysis*, published in 1968, contains many of the important contributions and Raymond Firth's *Themes in Economic Anthropology* from 1967 has several interpretive essays that impinge on the debate.

## Background

Few early ethnographers explicitly studied primitive economics, and those that did presented descriptive accounts of TECHNOLOGY or subsistence patterns in the context of larger studies of the society as a whole. Raymond Firth's *Primitive Polynesian Economy* in 1939 and Melville Herskovits's *The Economic Life of Primitive Peoples* in 1940 broke new ground. Both turned to the discipline of economics for constructs and theories, seeking to establish the respectability of economics in the eyes of anthropologists while at the same time respecting the anthropological caution against ethnocentric interpretations and the commitment to cross-cultural comparative studies. They paid particular attention to situations where conventional economics did not apply because primitive economic life diverged sharply from "our" own. They were both committed to the emergence of a science of comparative economics, in the broadest sense of the word, and interested in the making of contextualized "generalizations."

## Polanyi and the substantivists

In 1957, Karl Polanyi and his associates published *Trade and Market in the Early Empires*, ushering in the substantivist–formalist debate. Polanyi's primary dispute was with economists who claimed to have defined the universal principles of economic

rationality, and to have constructed a foundation for a general theory of the economy. However, Polanyi also implicated anthropologists like Firth and Herskovits, who had begun to develop an economic anthropology upon the basis of conventional economic postulates. In this book, and in a series of articles that followed, Polanyi and his colleagues argued that, by definition, formal economic analysis eliminates from consideration any material means of want satisfaction that are not scarce, and any non-material means of want satisfaction whether scarce or not. They also took issue with psychological assumptions underlying economics, including the assumptions of rational choice making behavior, which they believed were culturally and institutionally determined and hence particular, not general.

Polanyi argued that the term "economic" embraces two meanings, a "subsistence" or "substantive" meaning and a "scarcity" or "formal" meaning. The substantive meaning permits of economics the study of how different societies institute the processes of material livelihood, and a study of the shifting place occupied by the economy in society. The formal meaning, the scarcity definition of neoclassical economics, evolved within an economy dependent upon market elements not generally found in the societies studied by anthropologists and historians. Since contemporary economic theories have no general historical scope, Polanyi argued, they cannot be applied outside the particular institutional and historical context within which they evolved, and cannot constitute the basis for a general theory of economic institutions.

The formalists countered that any attempt "to discover or validate economic laws by inductive investigation" is a "wild goose chase" because economic principles "have little more relation to empirical data of any sort than do those of elementary mathematics" (Knight 1941). Formalists also asserted that anthropologists did not understand what economics is about, either because they had not read Lionel Robbins' *Nature and Significance of Economic Science*, or because they had not understood him, or they had failed to apply him consistently.

## The formalists

The formalists chided the substantivists for claiming that economics dealt with the material side of life. They argued that economists do not restrict human wants to material wants in market societies, and that they do not assume they are so restricted in any society. Burling (1962) suggested that Polanyi was the only recent economist to seriously suggest the material side of life has any distinctive claim on economic theory.

What economists study, the formalists maintained, is rational choice making behavior, which is universal regardless of the institutional framework within which it occurs. To this, the substantivists replied that everybody, everywhere economizes. To live is to economize. However, that does not tell you anything about how a people organize their economy.

Formalists also suggested the substantivists' position implicitly condemned to the anthropological wastebasket a number of studies of simple societies which utilize conceptual scaffolding derived from sociology and psychology. The burden of proof, they argued, rests with the substantivists to demonstrate that what has been done with recognized success by anthropologists with sociological and psychological theory cannot also be done with economic theory.

The debate became polemical and rhetorical and at times heated; eventually it faded away, with neither side having won (although others may argue in favor of either side). During and immediately after the debate, many students of non-industrial economic systems escaped to ecological analysis or historical and regional approaches. Those wanting to apply formal analyses in economic anthropology treated economics as one of many formal models, each potentially useful in the study of non-western economic systems.

## Political economy and economics

The substantivist–formalist debate embraced all the methodological disputes of, and was an anthropological version of, the larger and older "economics versus political economy" debate (see POLITICAL ECONOMY). From the perspective of political economy, the polemic unfortunately centered around the question of whether economics could be used to solve anthropological problems. In the beginning, in the writings of Malinowski, Firth and Herskovits, there was hope that an anthropological perspective would serve to improve economic science, either by restricting the applicability of models based on scarcity and maximizing assumptions, or by insisting that cultural and historical perspectives be accommodated within economic science. That hope has never materialized. The neglect of anthropology in economics is as evident today as it was then.

## See also:

disembedded economy; economic anthropology: major contemporary themes; historical school; hunter–gatherer and subsistence societies; institutional political economy: history; neoclassical economics; Polanyi's views on integration

## Selected references

Burling, Robbins (1962) "Maximization Theories and the Study of Economic Anthropology," *American Anthropologist* 64: 802–21.

Kahn, Joel S. (1990) "Towards a History of the Critique of Economism: The Nineteenth-Century German Origins of the Ethnographer's Dilemma," *Man* (new series) 25(June): 230–49.

Knight, Frank H. (1941) "Anthropology and Economics," *Journal of Political Economy* 49(2): 247–68.

Malinowski, B. (1921) "The Primitive Economics of the Trobriand Islanders," *The Economic Journal* 31(121): 1–16.

Polanyi, Karl (1957) "The Economy as Instituted Process," in Karl Polanyi, Conrad Arensberg and Harry W. Pearson (eds), *Trade and Market in the Early Empires*, Glencoe, IL: The Free Press, 64–94.

RAYMOND BENTON, JR

# supply and demand: aggregate

## Heterodox foundations in Keynes

Aggregate demand and supply analysis was created by John Maynard Keynes in *The General Theory of Employment, Interest, and Money* in 1936 in order to explain the equilibrium determination of employment, output and income in a modern monetary production economy. By specifying the aggregate demand function as not being coincident with the aggregate supply function at all levels of employment, Keynes does three things:

- he explicitly rejects Say's Law that holds that these two functions are coincident at all levels of employment (Keynes 1936: 25–6);
- he positions aggregate demand to make an independent and dominant contribution to the determination of employment, output and income levels (Keynes 1936: 27–8); and
- he allows for the revolutionary conclusion that, in general, aggregate supply and demand equilibrium occurs at employment levels well below full employment (Keynes 1936: 28, 254). This occurs due to the relatively high minimum acceptable rate of return imposed on real investment by the liquidity preferences of firms and households causing the investment component of aggregate demand to be insufficient to maintain full employment (Keynes 1936: 248–53).

Because of its relative novelty, Keynes devoted Books III and IV of *The General Theory* to the details of the aggregate demand function, explaining the propensity to consume, the inducement to invest and the monetary influences on the latter. An unwanted byproduct of this comparative empha-

sis is that the aggregate supply component of Keynes' MONETARY THEORY OF PRODUCTION has been perpetually ignored by many authors. Consequently, the standard interpretation of Keynes' theory fails to recognize that his aggregate supply and demand model (1) is fully capable of incorporating an extensive range of technology, cost, firm structure and other supply considerations; (2) includes a comprehensive theory of inflation; (3) has an explicit social theory of the DISTRIBUTION OF INCOME; and (4) forms the basis for a theory of ECONOMIC GROWTH and long-term dynamics. Only a minority of authors have persistently highlighted both the aggregate supply and demand components of Keynes' analysis (Weintraub 1958, 1966; Davidson 1978, 1994; Davidson and Smolensky 1964; Wells 1977; Casarosa 1981; Dutt 1987; King 1994; Deprez 1996).

## Aggregate supply function

Keynes derived the aggregate supply function directly from competitive Marshallian micro-foundations, "involving few considerations which are not already familiar" (Keynes 1936: 89). Aggregate supply is a function between Keynes's two fundamental units, "quantities of money-value and quantities of employment," and can be constructed for the firm, industry or economy. The aggregate supply function for the individual firm is a direct mapping of the short-run Marshallian flow-supply schedule, presented in price–quantity space, into employment–money–value space. $Z_r$ represents the minimum value of sales that would lead the firm to employ a certain amount of labor, $N_r$. The aggregate value of supply of the specific firm, $Z_r$, is equal to the product of the physical quantity of output, $O_r$, produced with a particular amount of employment, $O_r = \psi_r(N_r)$, and the unit supply price, $P_{s,r}$, associated with that output level, $P_{s,r} = \lambda_r(O_r)$. Formally, following Keynes (Keynes 1936: 44–5):

$$Z_r = P_{s,r} O_r = \lambda_r(O_r)\psi_r(N_r) = \phi_r(N_r) \quad (1)$$

The aggregate supply function of a homogenous output industry is the summation of the aggregate supply functions of the individual firms of that industry. The economy-wide aggregate supply function presents the minimum value of sales for all firms in the economy, $Z$, that is needed for the whole of industry to offer to employ a certain amount of labor, $N$:

$$Z = \phi(N) \qquad (2)$$

Keynes uses quantities of money-value that are homogeneous by definition and aggregate heterogeneous labor into a common labor unit, paid the wage unit, on the basis of constant relative money wages. By doing this, Keynes avoids the common problems of aggregating heterogeneous physical goods and unit supply prices that persist in today's orthodox aggregate demand and supply models. By assuming a given structure of employment, the aggregate composition of output and employment is examined.

## Aggregate demand function

Keynes' aggregate demand function is made up of two components: $D_1$, which is the amount expected to be spent on consumption, and $D_2$, which is the amount expected to be spent on new investment. The former is a function of the level of employment while the latter is not:

$$D = f(N) = D_1 + D_2 = \chi(N) + D_2 \qquad (3)$$

Davidson (1994: 24–7) points out that all that is necessary for the basic Keynesian argument is that some portion of spending is independent of current (and past) employment and income, no matter what the specific source or function thereof may be.

A central demand-side confusion appearing in the literature is that between the expected and actual magnitudes of aggregate demand (Casarosa 1981; Dutt 1987; King 1994). A clearer exposition is arrived at by explicitly distinguishing between expected and actual aggregate demand functions (Wells 1977; Casarosa 1981).

A particular level of output and employment is chosen by the profit-maximizing competitive firm, when its expected sales proceeds are equal

to the value of aggregate supply (Keynes 1936: 25). The equality of the aggregate (expected) demand function of the firm and its aggregate supply function is equivalent to the unit expected demand price, being equal to the unit supply price (and marginal prime cost) in the more common microeconomic analysis (Casarosa 1981: 189–90). The aggregate (expected) demand function is the product of the output level and the expected unit sales price:

$$ED_r = P_r^e O_r = \pi_r(O_r)\psi_r(N_r) = \theta_r(N_r) \qquad (4)$$

By the same aggregation process used on the supply-side, an industry's aggregate (expected) demand function can be derived. For the given structure of employment used on the supply side, the corresponding economy-wide aggregate (expected) demand function can be derived:

$$ED = \theta(N) \qquad (5)$$

The equality of the aggregate (expected) demand function of the firm sector as a whole and the economy-wide aggregate supply function, generates the actual employment and output level, on the basis of profit maximization, and is the point of effective demand (Keynes 1936: 25). At this point, the unit expected demand prices in each industry and of each firm are equal to the unit supply prices (and marginal prime costs) of the respective industries and firms. Formally:

$$Z = ED \qquad (6)$$

$$\phi(N) = \theta(N) \qquad (6')$$

The actual aggregate demand function or aggregate expenditure function (Casarosa 1981: 190–93) captures actual spending from the different units in the economy. This incorporates the idea that demand depends partially upon employment and income, but increases in smaller increments as income rises:

$$AD = f(N) = AD_1 + AD_2 = \chi(N) + AD_2 \qquad (7)$$

The Marshallian demand curve is drawn on the assumption of a given level of income, that is independent of the amount of output and employment in the industry/market under consideration. However, Keynes (1936: 259) recognized that changing employment and output levels change the levels of actual and expected income, so that this Marshallian assumption would not do for macroeconomic models. Each point on the aggregate supply curve has associated with it a particular Marshallian demand curve. The aggregate (actual) demand curve takes the points that are relevant from the full set of Marshallian demand curves that would otherwise exist. Weintraub's demand–outlay function (1958: 30–9) explicitly captures this idea in price–quantity space, and shows how this builds into Keynes' aggregate (actual) demand function in employment–money–value space.

## Equilibrium, disequilibrium and employment

Short-period equilibrium is, consequently, the situation where the three functions that make up the aggregate demand and supply model coincide and the short-term expectations of firms are exactly realized:

$$Z = ED = AD \qquad (8)$$

$$\phi(N) = \theta(N) = f(N) \qquad (8')$$

Full employment is just one of the possible equilibrium situations, one not likely to exist because liquidity preference tends to generate insufficient investment. Full employment for a firm, industry or the economy as a whole exists only when the elasticity of employment with respect to demand is zero (Keynes 1936: 306). Market-clearing can be consistent with disequilibrium positions and thus – contrary to orthodox thinking – is not a condition uniquely correlated with full employment equilibrium.

Keynes' demand curve for labor is derived from the aggregate supply and demand results, and is not equal to the marginal product of labor curve (Weintraub 1958: 109–17). Similarly, labor supply conditions may depend on the demand for output and monetary conditions. As a consequence, it is possible to have a market-clearing situation in the labor market that is not at the same time a full employment situation – an impossibility with a "classical"

model – and this is consistent with either short-period equilibrium or disequilibrium (Deprez 1996).

It should also be recognized that Keynes' aggregate supply and demand model has built into it, right from the start, unit prices. Hence, inflation is analyzed as arising from changes in money-wages, pricing markups and technology (Weintraub 1958; Davidson 1978: 338–57; Davidson 1994: 142–63), and not from the quantity of money in the economy upon which the orthodox pseudo-aggregate demand curve is based. Integrated with this is a theory of income distribution, where the shares and amounts of profit and wage income depend upon a number of variables. They depend upon technical conditions, but – more importantly – also upon the level of aggregate demand, the degree of competition and the socially-generated expectations that influence both supply and demand conditions, including user cost and liquidity preference.

## Dynamics, growth and open economies

By the application of Keynes' theory of shifting equilibrium (Keynes 1936: 293), the model is able to go beyond the short period to deal with questions of dynamics, including theories of growth and technical change (Weintraub 1958: 80–5; Weintraub 1966). The realized equilibrium or disequilibrium results of one period influence and change the factors determining the aggregate supply and demand functions for the next period, creating a historical chain of events. For example, the investment purchases of one period change the capital stock that can be utilized in the next period, shifting the aggregate supply curve.

Recent overall elaboration of the model is focused in the area of open economies (Davidson 1994: 213–19; Deprez 1997). Extensions of the supply side of the model include the incorporation of user cost, alternate cost structures (Davidson and Smolensky 1964: 126–35) and different degrees of competition (Weintraub 1958: 65–75). The explicit inclusion of the fixed income of rentiers (Davidson and Smolensky 1964: 139), money-wage rate variation (Davidson 1994: 175–93; Deprez 1996), and extended monetary considerations (Davidson 1978: 246–81) are certain demand-based extensions of the model.

## Conclusions

Some controversial areas have been touched upon above. General issues include the structure of the different functions, the role of expectations, the method of long-period analysis and the ability to accurately capture Keynes's ideas (King 1994). Among heterodox economists, the dependence of the model on aggregate production functions, on Marshallian cost conditions and on particular competition assumptions are key areas of confusion and debate. Nevertheless, this is a central macroeconomic model still ripe with many crucial insights.

## See also:

animal spirits; effective demand and capacity utilization; Keynesian political economy; post-Keynesian political economy: major contemporary themes; short-run cost curves; supply and demand: microeconomic; uncertainty

## Selected references

Casarosa, Carlo (1981) "The Microfoundations of Keynes's Aggregate Supply and Expected Demand Analysis," *Economic Journal* 91(361): 188–94.

Davidson, Paul (1978) *Money and the Real World*, 2nd edn, London: Macmillan.

—— (1994) *Post Keynesian Macroeconomic Theory*, Aldershot: Edward Elgar.

Davidson, Paul and Smolensky, Eugene (1964) *Aggregate Supply and Demand Analysis*, New York: Harper & Row.

Deprez, Johan (1996) "Davidson on the Labour Market in a Monetary Production Economy," in Philip Arestis (ed.), *Keynes, Money and the Open Economy: Essays in Honour of Paul Davidson*, Cheltenham: Edward Elgar, 123–43.

—— (1997) "Open-Economy Expectations, Decisions, and Equilibria: Applying Keynes' Aggregate Supply and Demand Model," *Journal of Post Keynesian Economics* 19(4): 599–615.

Dutt, Amitava Krishna (1987) "Keynes with a Perfectly Competitive Goods Market," *Australian Economic Papers* 26: 275–93.

Keynes, John Maynard (1936) *The General Theory of Employment, Interest, and Money*.

King, J.E. (1994) "Aggregate Supply and Demand Analysis since Keynes: A Partial History," *Journal of Post Keynesian Economics* 17(1): 3–31.

Weintraub, Sidney (1958) *An Approach to the Theory of Income Distribution*, Philadelphia: Chilton.

—— (1966) *A Keynesian Theory of Employment, Growth & Income Distribution*, Philadelphia: Chilton.

Wells, Paul (1977) "Keynes' Disequilibrium Theory of Employment," in Sidney Weintraub (ed.), *Modern Economic Thought*, Philadelphia: University of Pennsylvania Press.

JOHAN DEPREZ

# supply and demand: microeconomic

Supply and demand analysis has its origins in two different arenas. The classical political economists sought to analyze the costs of production, and the early marginalists undertook an analysis of the demand for goods and services. Alfred Marshall then weaved these two strands together and developed a theory showing how costs of production and demand jointly determined both the price of a good and the quantity of that good bought and sold.

## Marshallian analysis

In order to study individual markets, Marshall developed the tools of supply and demand curves. The upward sloping supply curve shows that as prices rise firms produce more and bring to market greater quantities of any good. The downward sloping demand curve shows the law of demand: as price falls, consumers buy greater quantities of a good. The "two scissors" of supply and demand together determine an equilibrium price for each good.

Marshall argued that competition would force actual prices towards the equilibrium price. If prices were set above the equilibrium level, firms would not be able to sell what they produced and would see their inventories pile up. This would provide a signal to the firm that it must lower prices and cut production (see MARKET STRUCTURES). On the other hand, if prices were set below the equilibrium level, shortages would result. People would line up to buy a limited stock of goods, or consumers would have to be told that some good was "sold out." Businesses would take this as a sign that prices could be increased and production should be expanded. Only at equilibrium would firms sell all they produced and only at equilibrium would prices tend to remain the same, barring any change in either supply or demand (see Figure 13).

Marshall noted that these "two blades" were complex constructions. He then went on to analyze both supply and demand in greater detail. Demand was governed by the utility (or satisfaction) that consumers received from consuming a particular good. Rational consumers were forever attempting to get the greatest utility from what they purchased and consumed. They would compare the additional satisfaction from buying one good with the additional satisfaction that would result from all alternative purchases. When priced highly, consumers could buy very little of any particular good and thus would get more satisfaction from using their money to buy other goods.

Marshall (1989: 97) defined a change in demand as the desire and ability to purchase more (or less) of some good at the same price. Changes in the demand relationship, or shifts in the demand curve could result from several causes – changes in wealth, population changes, changes in tastes, the price of other goods, or changed expectations about future

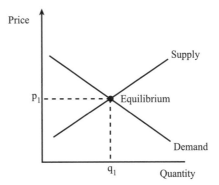

*Figure 13*

prices (III, ch. IV). Greater wealth and a larger population would increase demand, or shift the demand curve to the northeast in Figure 13. This would push up prices. Advertising could change consumer tastes and cause demand to increase. Likewise, expectations of greater prices in the future would push up demand and prices.

The impact of a change in the price of other goods was a bit more complicated. Normally, when the price of some good, like gasoline, increases, people buy less gasoline and spend their money on other goods. Thus demand for goods other than gasoline should rise. However, there are some cases when the reverse is true. Complementary goods are sets of goods usually consumed together. Any good normally consumed with gasoline, like automobiles (especially gas guzzlers), would experience reduced demand if the price of gasoline rose.

Supply, in contrast to demand, was governed by the costs of production. Producers, like consumers, were always trying to maximize; but the producers wanted to maximize profits from production. Due to diminishing returns and the rising cost of parts and labor, greater output could be produced only at rising costs. Businesses would therefore only produce more goods if they received a higher price. Hence the Marshallian supply curve was positively sloped.

Like demand, the supply relationship could shift; and like shifts in demand, this means more (or less) of the good produced at each price. The main factor causing supply to shift is a change in the cost of production. Higher wages, for example, would raise the costs of production – no matter how much was produced. Business could make the same amount of profits only if they pass this higher cost on to consumers in the form of higher prices. An increase in wages would therefore shift supply up in the above figure, thereby raising prices. In contrast, improved technology, by reducing the amount of labor necessary to produce goods, would lower unit costs and shift supply down (Marshall 1890: V, ch. III).

A second important factor causing supply to shift is the number of firms producing some good. If firms in a particular industry are making above normal profits, this will cause new firms to enter the industry in order to earn these profits. This will increase the supply of goods being produced. Prices and profits will thus tend to fall. In contrast, when firms incur losses, some firms will leave the industry. Supply now falls, thereby raising price.

## Critique

This Marshallian perspective on price and output determination has been criticized by political economists on a number of grounds. The most important critiques came from the pen of Joan Robinson. One problem with supply and demand analysis according to Robinson (1974) was that it ignored time and expectations; instead, a timeless notion called "equilibrium" took center stage. Robinson thought that the notion of stability inherent in equilibrium analysis was inappropriate for a discipline like economics, which deals with growing and changing economies. Contrary to standard economic theory, consumers and businesses do not respond to current prices in ways that move the economy towards an equilibrium price. Rather, consumers and businesses respond to prices today based upon what they think prices will be in the future.

Moreover, changing prices can change expectations. Lower prices can lead to expectations of even lower future prices, making

consumers less willing to buy some good despite the drop in price. Under such conditions no equilibrium, or market clearing, price is possible; and supply and demand analysis cannot illuminate what is going on in the real world. To understand real economies requires a new theoretical orientation, one which focuses on how prices change over time rather than on equilibrium analysis.

A second problem with supply and demand analysis for Robinson concerned the nature of capital. Robinson began the CAPITAL THEORY DEBATES with her critique of the marginalist theory of distribution. According to this theory, the returns to capital equipment used in production were determined by the marginal productivity of capital. The question raised by Robinson (1953–4: 4) was how to measure capital in order to find its marginal productivity. This relatively simple and innocuous question sparked a heated debate between the two Cambridges, England and Massachusetts (see Harcourt 1972). This debate has important consequences for supply and demand analysis. If the marginal productivity of capital cannot be determined within marginalist theory, then there can be no supply curve: for the supply curve was based on the costs of production, and returns due to the owners of capital equipment comprise one important cost of production.

A third problem with supply and demand analysis involved imperfect competition. Here too, Joan Robinson made many of the seminal contributions. Robinson (1933) showed that with imperfect competition one could not derive a supply curve for either the firm or the industry. Firms would produce goods at the level where their marginal revenue (derived from a demand curve) equaled their marginal cost; but once a particular level of output was determined, firms had considerable leeway in the price they could charge. Thus no supply curve, relating price and firm output, could be constructed for the firm. Likewise no industry-wide supply curve, and no supply curve for some specific good, could be constructed. Consequently, some theory other than supply and demand analysis was needed to explain prices in a world of large firms and imperfect competition. Moreover, as Robinson and others have pointed out, imperfect competition was the rule rather than the exception in developed economies.

Despite these many flaws, supply and demand analysis remains an integral part of economic analysis and gets taught to most students of economics. Part of its survival value stems from its usefulness for analyzing the impact of various changes in a particular market. Another part of its survival value probably stems from inertia. Political economists have sought to replace the supply and demand model with mark-up and cost of production models of pricing, and with CONSPICUOUS CONSUMPTION AND EMULATION theories of firm-generated demand, in order to explain levels of output produced by the firm.

## See also:

equilibrium, disequilibrium and non-equilibrium; neoclassical economics; neoclassical economics: critique; supply and demand: aggregate; traverse; value foundation of price

## Selected references

Harcourt, Geoffrey C. (1972) *Some Cambridge Controversies in the Theory of Capital*, Cambridge: Cambridge University Press.

Marshall, Alfred (1890) *Principles of Economics*, 8th edn, London: Macmillan, 1920.

Robinson, Joan (1933) *Economics of Imperfect Competition*, London: Macmillan.

—— (1953–4) "The Production Function and the Theory of Capital," *Review of Economic Studies* 21: 81–106; repr. in Robinson (1980), vol. 2.

—— (1974) *History Views Equilibrium*, London: Thames Polytechnic; repr. in Robinson (1980), vol. 5.

—— (1980) *Collected Economic Papers*, 5 vols, Cambridge, MA: MIT Press.

STEVEN PRESSMAN

# surplus approach to development

Discussing development in low-income countries without taking the ECONOMIC SURPLUS into account is like discussing *Hamlet* without the Prince of Denmark: surplus is the key to growth and development. This insight was part and parcel of mainstream economic theory from the physiocrats in the mid-eighteenth century up to the transition to marginalism in the 1870s. Hence, most attempts to revitalize the surplus approach to development consist in reformulating the classical economic theory of growth (see CLASSICAL POLITICAL ECONOMY). This is as true for dual economy approaches such as Lewis (1954) as for more Marxian approaches such as Baran (1957). A critical survey may be found in Danielson (1994: chaps 2–3).

## Baran's legacy

In the literature inspired by Baran's work, there are two central issues. First, how do we measure surplus? Second, what is the analytical significance of surplus? Although Baran's approach concentrates on the potential surplus – so questions of actual measurement may be regarded as less important – Stanfield (1973) makes an attempt to measure the potential surplus for the USA. Ignoring the actual measurement problems encountered by Stanfield, it is not clear how potential surplus should be interpreted. Baran (1957) defines it as resources that would be available for consumption and investment in a more rationally ordered society, so it seems that it measures "the anarchy of capitalist production" (Baran 1957: 24) and hence the gains to be made from the transition to a different economic organization called "socialism."

## Measuring actual economic surplus

Danielson (1990) argues that a more fruitful approach would be to measure the actual surplus and to study how this is actually used.

The proposed method is as follows. Define subsistence as the amount of resources necessary to replicate this year's production next year. Then, actual surplus is defined as the difference between actual output and subsistence. Consider the national account definition for GDP:

$$Y = W + P + dK + T_i - Z \qquad (1)$$

where $Y$ is GDP, $W$ is the wage bill, $P$ is profits, $dK$ is capital depreciation, $T_i$ is indirect taxes and $Z$ is subsidies. Assume that the annual subsistence wage rate can be measured and call this $s$. Then, actual surplus, $S$, is defined as

$$S = Y - sL - dK = eL + P + T_i - Z \qquad (2)$$

where $L$ is employed labor and $e \equiv w - s$ is the "excess wage rate." Of course, $W \equiv wL$.

How do we measure $s$? Baran (1957: 30) argues that $s$ should represent "the amount and composition of real income necessary for what is socially considered as necessary" and Stanfield (1973) devotes considerable space discussing whether, for instance, payment of mortgage principal or insurance costs should be included. As argued by Danielson (1994: 30–13), this approach is hampered by lack of reliable data and it makes international comparisons of the size and use of surplus difficult. As long as the study concerns low-income countries, Danielson (1994) argues that the average annual wage in agriculture represents a reasonable proxy for $s$. The argument is that most low-income countries are characterized by surplus labor in the sense of Lewis (1954), so if everyone has access to land, $s$ represents the opportunity cost of not working in agriculture.

A related problem concerns the fact that all labor may not add to the value of production, that is to say, some labor may be unproductive. Danielson (1994: 39) argues that the amount of unproductive labor may be approximated by the amount of publicly employed labor. This procedure, however, is not entirely free of objections since it ignores the indirect impact of public activities on the surplus (for example, more teachers in public schools may raise productivity and thereby the surplus), and it ignores other "unproductive" areas, such as the financial and sales activities. Denoting productive and unproductive labor by subscripts $p$ and $u$, respectively, gives

$$\begin{aligned} S &= Y - sL_p - dK \\ &= wL_u + eL_p + P + T_i - Z \end{aligned} \qquad (3)$$

and the surplus is distributed between labor $(wL_u + eL_p)$, capitalists $(P)$ and the government $(T_i - Z)$ (see PRODUCTIVE AND UNPRODUCTIVE LABOR).

## Areas of research

The classical theory of growth focuses on the size and use of the surplus. The size of the surplus defines the upper limit to investments and hence to growth; the use of surplus determines how much is actually invested. Using the definition of actual surplus expressed in (3) above, the classical theory of growth may be subjected to tests. There are three particular areas which merit further empirical analysis: formation of the surplus, distribution of the surplus and use of the surplus.

If surplus as a share of GDP increases over time, this may be caused either by growth of productivity in non-agricultural activities or by stagnation in agricultural wages. Hence, the conflict between agricultural workers (or the peasantry) and the rest of the economy is acknowledged and issues of exploitation and intersectoral resource transfers enter the picture naturally. Indeed, as has been argued by Mamalakis (1971), the classical struggle between labor and capital is sometimes less relevant for an understanding of what is going on in an economy. In certain instances, "sectoral clashes" may be more appropriate. Danielson (1989) shows how the situation in Jamaica during the 1970s fits well into Mamalakis's framework, when the government systematically exploited agriculture in order to generate resources to finance industrialization. One important point here is that it is not only agricultural capitalists who gain from stagnating wages in agriculture; workers and capitalists in the manufacturing sector gain too, and as shown by Mamalakis (1971), a sectoral perspective makes it sometimes easier to see the rationale of government actions.

Expression (3) divides the surplus into three parts according to recipient. This is particulaly convenient when, for example, savings behavior is assumed to be different for different groups. Danielson (1994: ch. 6) shows that Jamaica's economic stagnation in the late 1970s may be explained by a government-orchestrated redistribution of surplus from high-saving capitalists to the high-spending middle class. The mechanism identified in this paper appears to be present in other stagnation episodes as well (for example, Tanzania in the early 1980s, Togo and Cameroon in the late 1980s and Peru in the 1980s). Falling profits meant falling investments and hence lower growth and this was exacerbated by higher imports of consumer goods which tightened the foreign exchange constraint. This mechanism clearly deserves further empirical investigations.

If surplus is not invested, it is used for what conventionally is denoted "luxury consumption" and even countries with low per capita incomes waste surplus on such activities (building pyramids or fighting wars). Policy issues deserving further research here include the following. What is the effect on the use of aggregate surplus of income redistribution? How is surplus disposal (and thus growth) affected by trade liberalizations associated with World Bank reforms? What is the proper role of the state in a situation where surplus is consumed rather than invested?

## Problem areas

The approach outlined above is not free of objections. Here, I mention only three of the most important. First, as shown by Eltis (1984), the classical theory of economic growth is a case of capital fundamentalism: investments, and only investments, affect the rate of growth. Clearly, research and development, or marketing, may also be important determinants, as would exogenous factors, such as trade policy in rich countries. One important issue in the future is to reformulate the simple classical growth model to take these considerations into account. Second, formation, distribution and use of surplus are not independent of each other and one important reasearch topic is to investigate precisely how they hang together. In particular, the distribution of the surplus between classes is an important determinant of surplus disposal, and the sectoral distribution of surplus affects surplus formation. Third, the classical theory of growth assumes that markets are always supply constrained. For low-income countries trying to achieve growth via exports to the rich world, this is not necessarily the case. One important topic is to investigate the consequences of demand-constrained markets for the formulation of the surplus approach (see Jamal and Weeks 1993).

Understanding development dynamics is impossible without understanding class relations in society. Frequently these relations are manifested in conflicts over the use and distribution of resources. The surplus approach to development breaks away from conventional economic development theory by, albeit tentatively, allowing for the incorporation of class conflicts in the study of growth and development.

## See also:

classes and economic development; development political economy: major contemporary themes; surplus approach to political economy

## Selected references

Baran, P.A. (1957) *The Political Economy of Growth*, New York: Monthly Review Press.

Danielson, A. (1989) "Struggle for the Surplus: Jamaica, 1970–84," *METU – Studies in Development* 16: 127–52.

—— (1990) "The Concept of Surplus and the Underdeveloped Countries: Critique and Suggestions," *Review of Radical Political Economics* 22: 214–30.

—— (1994) *The Economic Surplus: Theory, Measurement, Applications*, Westport, CT: Praeger.

Eltis, W. (1984) *The Classical Theory of Economic Growth*, London: Macmillan.

Jamal, V. and Weeks, J. (1993) *Africa Misunderstood or Whatever Happened to the Rural-Urban Wage Gap?*, London: Macmillan.

Lewis, W.A. (1954) "Economic Development with Unlimited Supplies of Labour," *Manchester School of Social and Economic Studies* 22: 139–91.

Mamalakis, M. (1971) "The Theory of Sectoral Clashes and Coalitions Revisited," *Latin American Research Review* 6: 103–41.

Stanfield, J.R. (1973) *The Economic Surplus and Neo-Marxism*, Lexington, MA: Heath.

ANDERS DANIELSON

# surplus approach to political economy

The "surplus approach" is a frontal attack on the scarcity approach of NEOCLASSICAL ECONOMICS. The fundamental problem of economics here is not defined as the problem of optimization, as in neoclassical economics, it is rather the determination of the "surplus production" and the conditions for the reproduction of the relations that give rise to surplus production (see ECONOMIC SURPLUS). Instead of rooting the problem of economics in the human individual with unlimited wants and limited resources, as in neoclassical economics, it divides the society into various classes with their income categories being determined by different principles (see CLASS; INDIVIDUAL AND SOCIETY). Instead of production being seen as an earlier phase of consumption, as in neoclassical economics, it is seen here as a circular process, being an instance of reproduction (see REPRODUCTION PARADIGM). The idea of production as a circular process rejects the idea of "scarcity."

## Core of the theory

In 1960, Sraffa presented the basic theoretical framework of the surplus approach, which, according to him, was the approach of CLASSICAL POLITICAL ECONOMY from Adam Smith to Ricardo. Although Sraffa's reading of "classical" economists is somewhat controversial, the logical propositions he put forward as the theoretical foundation of surplus theory have been, up until now, accepted as quite sound by friends and foes alike. In a classic paper, Garegnani (1984) presented the basic problematic of the surplus approach in a diagrammatical form (see Figure 14).

The core of the theory takes the TECHNOLOGY, real wages and total social product as given, being determined by the socio-historical factors, at any point in TIME. One fundamental aspect of the theory is to determine the size of the social surplus and its distribution among the non-working classes. Although the size of

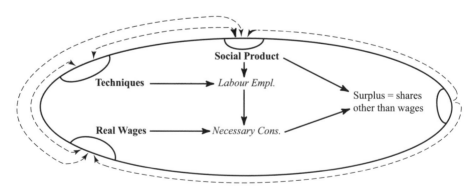

*Figure 14*

the surplus is known in physical terms, given the data, its size in economic terms is still indeterminate; the appropriation of the surplus by the non-working classes must follow certain rules. In the simplest case of a capitalist economy with only two classes, the workers and the capitalists, the whole of the social surplus must be appropriated as profits by the capitalists. The competitive nature of capitalism requires that the rate of profit that is appropriated by all the capitalists must be equal. However, the rate of profit cannot be calculated given the physical data, because the physical ratio of surplus to cost would be a ratio of heterogeneous goods.

Thus, to determine the rate of profit one needs to reduce the heterogeneous goods to a single homogeneous unit. A theory of price or value comes into the picture at this stage. If all the commodities could be reduced to their prices, then the rate of profit could be calculated (see PRICE THEORY, SRAFFIAN). Sraffa (1960) showed that competitive prices are directly determined by the given technology and a distributive variable. Given that wages could be taken to be historically given, the production technology, along with wages, would simultaneously determine the prices that would guarantee an equal rate of profit across sectors in the economy. (Conversely if one thinks that the rate of profit is determined by the monetary institutions; then the system would determine prices and wages simultaneously.)

## Demand and natural resources

Thus, contrary to orthodox economics, competitive prices are independent of demand: demand only affects the allocation of labor, but has no effect on either market clearing prices or the DISTRIBUTION OF INCOME. The reader should note that these competitive prices are not the "market prices" at which the commodities at any given time are bought or sold. They are rather the gravitational points toward which "market prices" tend to gravitate due to the pressure of competition. "Market prices" would diverge from competitive prices as long as

supply diverges from "effectual" demand in the specific market (Garegnani 1976) (see COMPETITION IN SRAFFIAN POLITICAL ECONOMY).

These "effectual" demands are the demand points, as opposed to the demand schedules of the orthodox theory. The effectual demands are determined by such factors as: (1) the level of aggregate income and activity, (2) the technical conditions of production (governing, among other things, the outputs of means of production), and (3) the distribution of social product among the social classes (and therefore, in terms of the classical theories, the level of the independent distributive variable), since different classes generally spend their income on different commodities (Garegnani 1990).

At this stage, one objection could be raised: the above propositions are correct for an economy that produces commodities by means of commodities and labor, but what about production that requires natural resources such as land? Are these not limited by "nature"? How can one escape the problem of scarcity and the influence of demand on prices of these commodities? This problem was tackled by Ricardo (1821) early on within a surplus approach framework. Ricardo argued that, with capital accumulation and the growth of population, production would eventually be extended to lands with relatively lower fertility. In this case, the cost of agricultural production would rise, leading to a new set of competitive prices as well as income distribution for the non-working classes.

This, however, should not be confused with the role of demand in the orthodox theory. First of all, in the surplus framework, the idea of nature's "scarcity" is not assumed *a priori* as in the orthodox theory. Here the supposed scarcity is the result of the level of social output (see Kurz and Salvadori 1995). Second, the influence of a change in demand here does not directly affect the market for "factors of production," thus simultaneously determining both prices and income distribution. In the surplus framework, the effect of growing demand, due to accumulation and the growth in population, is a change in technology, an effect taking place in a loop outside of the core. Given this change in the total social product and technology, a new set of relative prices and the rate of profit are determined in the core of the theory. Thus, the analysis is conducted sequentially in two stages (for further details on the question of demand in the surplus theory, see Caravale 1994; Garegnani 1990; Schefold 1990) (see SRAFFIAN AND POST-KEYNESIAN LINKAGES).

## Market and socio-historical forces

The most interesting aspect of the surplus approach is that it minimizes the role of the market in a capitalist economy. The orthodox theory, on the other hand, determines all its economic variables in the market; the variables that are not determined in the market are put in a "black box". The role of the market in the surplus approach is only to allocate labor in the production of different goods. All the other economic variables are determined by socio-historical forces, with the market having a minor effect (see MARKETS).

The theoretical distinction between the core and "outside the core" is not to suggest that the core is more important to the theory. Rather, the distinction is only to suggest that the relationship between variables within the core is of definite quantitative nature. The relationship obtaining between the variables outside the core, and the second order effect of the variables within the core on the variables outside the core, do not form any definite quantitative relation. This opens up the scope of economics greatly. The determination of economic variables must be understood in the context of history, CULTURE and politics. Marx was one surplus approach theorist who brought these aspects to economic analysis most forcefully (see Sinha 1996).

## See also:

capital theory debates; circular production and vertical integration; Pasinett's analysis of structural dynamics and growth; Sraffian political economy

## Selected references

Caravale, G.A. (1994) "Demand Conditions and the Interpretation of Ricardo," *Journal of the History of Economic Thought* 16(Fall): 229–47.

Garegnani, P. (1976) "On a Change in the Notion of Equilibrium in Recent Work on Value and Distribution," in M. Brown, K. Sato, and P. Zarembka (eds), *Essays in Modern Capital Theory*, Amsterdam: North Holland, 25–45.

—— (1984) "Value and Distribution in the Classical Economists and Marx," *Oxford Economic Papers* 36(2): 291–325.

—— (1990) "Sraffa: Classical versus Marginalist Analysis," in K. Bharadwaj and B. Schefold (eds), *Essays on Piero Sraffa*, London: Routledge, 112–140.

Kurz, H. and Salvadori, N. (1995) *Theory of Production*, New York: Cambridge University Press.

Ricardo, D. (1821) *Works and Correspondence of David Ricardo*, vol. 1, ed. P. Sraffa, Cambridge: Cambridge University Press, 1951.

Schefold, B. (1990) "On Changes in the Composition of Output," in K. Bharadwaj and B. Schefold (eds), *Essays on Piero Sraffa*, London: Routledge, 178–202.

Sinha, A. (1996) "A Critique of Part One of *Capital* Vol. One: The Value Controversy Revisited," *Research in Political Economy* 15: 195–222.

Sraffa, P. (1960) *Production of Commodities by Means of Commodities*, Cambridge: Cambridge University Press.

AJIT SINHA

# surplus value as rent, interest and profit

The total value of production in excess of what is necessary for the historically specific subsistence of the productive workforce is termed surplus value. Surplus value can include wages above subsistence levels. In this entry the concern is with that portion of surplus value which accrues as PROPERTY income, and for simplicity we shall assume no surplus wages, no state apparatus, and no unproductive workers. Under these assumptions, the aggregate surplus value is equivalent to the total property income of the economy. Thus, if the aggregate labor income (wages, salaries and benefits) is taken as an approximation of the total output necessary for the subsistence of the productive workforce, then the rest of aggregate income must be equivalent to the excess of output above the "necessary product." This excess includes industrial profit, interest and rent.

## Property income and productive labor

Yet there is more here than a mere accounting equivalence. Property income is, by definition, received by virtue of owning property. Rent is received from the ownership of land or natural resources; interest is received by virtue of owning financial assets; and profit is received from the ownership of production capital. Property income is not received in return for any productive activity performed by its recipients. Although mainstream economists have studiously avoided confronting this fact, even the US Internal Revenue Service refers to property income as unearned.

Since such income is not an equivalent return for any productive activity, it amounts to an entitlement to a portion of the aggregate output of others' productive activity. The workforce produces the output, but surrenders part of it to people who have nothing directly to do with production. Arguably, this occurs by virtue of a social system to which those in the workforce have never given their full consent, i.e. that of private property. Alternatively, it occurs by virtue of a structure of social power to which the workforce is subject (see also ECONOMIC POWER): property income is the fruit of EXPLOITATION. The fact that it is essential to CAPITALISM makes the latter a CLASS system akin to such other historical cases as SLAVERY and FEUDALISM.

Of course, in part the issue is not one of property income *per se* but of its distribution.

For example, if income-earning property were to be distributed among people in proportion to their labor incomes, then property income would be received roughly in proportion to people's productive labor and would not be the result of exploitation. Assuming that labor incomes are received in accordance with people's contributions of productive activity, each person would receive in addition a share of the economic surplus in proportion to that contribution. Alternatively, suppose that shares in the aggregate of income-earning property were instead equally distributed among the population. This may be the result, for example, of a democratic state owning all such property and distributing a dividend of surplus value on it to all citizens equally (perhaps in the form of public goods). Then also property income would not be the result of exploitation. In practice, of course, income-earning property is privately owned and extremely unevenly distributed in most capitalist economies (see INEQUALITY).

## Rationalizing property income

Attempts at rationalizing property income on the grounds that property owners make other kinds of "productive contributions" besides labor are simply of no avail (Schweickart 1993: ch. 1). For example, it is often argued that profit recipients provide organizational and supervisory contributions. Yet it is clear that these activities are rewarded not by profit but by labor income, specifically, managerial salaries. Similarly, entrepreneurial innovation is rewarded by profit income only when the innovator owns the productive capital involved. A large proportion of innovative activity that today yields profit to firm owners merely returns routine salary income to the innovators (who undertake RESEARCH AND DEVELOPMENT activities).

Risk-bearing, another argument for property income to be considered a "productive contribution," is "rewarded" by an interest premium above the risk-free interest-rate. This, however, cannot at all rationalize the risk-free portion of interest income itself. While rent and interest income do serve as an effective mechanism for rationing land and capital use, by no means does that imply that land and financial asset owners make any productive contribution for which they are receiving a return (nor that this particular rationing mechanism is the best available). Property income is received for owning property, not for performing productive services, as any honest heir may attest.

## Categorization problems

This and related issues arising from the concept of surplus value are often obscured by the complexities of property income in reality today. For one thing, conceptual distinctions among rent, interest and profit often do not conform neatly with their real-world counterparts. For example, a considerable portion of the "profit" income of real-estate and development, resource extraction and agricultural and forestry firms is actually rent income. Similarly, the "profit" received as dividends by corporate share-holders who have no control in their firms is better understood to be merely interest income, since such owners are, in effect, merely providing finance.

More critical, of course, are complexities in the basic categorical distinction between labor and property income. For example, given that many top-level managers control the productive capital of their firms, the income-earning property they receive as bonuses (in the form of stock options) represents a portion of their firms' profits. Yet, for the same reason, some portion of their "salaries" too ought to be considered "profit" rather than labor income. And because, at the same time, middle and lower-level managers and other employees do not have control over their firm's productive capital, most of the "profit-sharing" income sometimes paid to these groups is actually labor income. Similarly, a portion of the "proprietors' income" of small-business owners who work in their own firms is actually labor income rather than profit.

## Measuring components of surplus value

Such complexities make the empirical measurement of surplus value quite difficult. There is, moreover, the problem of PRODUCTIVE AND UNPRODUCTIVE LABOR. For example, a large portion of the activities involved in ADVERTISING AND THE SALES EFFORT is plainly unproductive, being devoted not to the provision of goods or services but to inducing people to purchase commodities they would not otherwise purchase. Thus all the incomes received in the associated industries and occupations of advertising ought to be treated as entitlements to a portion of the aggregate economic surplus created elsewhere by productive labor.

On reflection, there is perhaps a great deal of unproductive labor in modern capitalism. A large part of business management is concerned not with organizing production, but with extracting labor from employees who lack work incentives on account of the ALIENATION of working life in capitalism. Some portion of legal and judicial activity should be treated similarly, insofar as these serve merely to bolster the capitalist system by moderating some of the social problems of class and pervasive "pecuniary emulation." Government WELFARE STATE activities similarly exist to moderate the social problems of class, and many government-provided "public goods" are similarly better understood as mitigating various other "bads" that arise from capitalist industry, such as crime prevention and control and environmental pollution clean-up. Much military spending too, of course, would seem to have more to do with bolstering the nation's capitalist class than with providing generally useful products or services.

Measuring the extent of these unproductive economic activities is clearly problematic, and has made empirical estimations of aggregate surplus value enormously difficult. There have been some important successes, however (for example, Shaikh and Tonak 1994). Despite the difficulties, the concept of surplus value is crucial, not merely for substantiating the general perspective of critical political economy, but for comprehending the specific functioning of the capitalist economy as well.

## Conclusion

Surplus value is both the source of the investment capital needed for economic growth, and the result of that growth in capitalism. Surplus value and exploitation are basic determinants of the economy's growth prospects and the profitability of capitalist investment. Forms of appropriation of surplus value importantly determine the rate of its reinvestment back into capital accumulation and the directions which that accumulation takes. For example, the appropriation of surplus value primarily in the form of rent income is arguably a major cause of under-development in the Third World. And in advanced economies, the division of corporate profit between dividends, top managerial compensation, retained earnings, taxes and unproductive expenditures is a major determinant of the rate and directions of corporate capital accumulation (for example, Pitelis 1987). An analysis of the nature and determinants of surplus value, including its division between profit, interest and rent, is thus absolutely essential for comprehending the real nature and logic of the capitalist economy (Heilbroner 1985).

## See also:

economic surplus; falling rate of profit tendency; labor theory of value; surplus approach to development; surplus approach to political economy

## Selected references

Foley, Duncan K. (1986) *Understanding Capital*, Cambridge, MA: Harvard University Press.

Heilbroner, Robert L. (1985) *The Nature and Logic of Capitalism*, New York: W.W. Norton.

Pitelis, Christos (1987) *Corporate Capital:*

*Control, Ownership, Saving and Crisis*, New York: Cambridge University Press.

Schweickart, David (1993) *Against Capitalism*, New York: Cambridge University Press.

Shaikh, Anwar M. and Tonak, E. Ahmet (1994) *Measuring the Wealth of Nations: The Political Economy of National Accounts*, New York: Cambridge University Press.

ERIC SCHUTZ

# sustainable development

Sustainable development is a broad term that signifies attempts to reconcile economic development with conservation of natural resources and protection of environmental quality. The term first appeared in the early 1970s (Redclift 1987), then gained importance through the World Conservation Strategy that was presented by the International Union for the Conservation of Nature and Natural Resources (IUCN) in 1980. By the end of the decade, the term had become a staple in the development-environment literature. This resulted from its use by the Brundtland Commission as a platform for global action (WCED 1987). The idea of sustainable development, as articulated in the Brundtland Report, has become the dominant perspective among mainstream economists and international development agencies such as the World Bank. Nevertheless, the concept is not generally accepted, partly because it lacks clarity and specificity.

## Standard definitions

According to the World Conservation Strategy, development – interpreted as ECONOMIC GROWTH with desirable improvements in social conditions – can be sustained if it takes into account social and ecological as well as economic factors. Conservation was defined as the management of the biosphere to maximize benefits to current generations, while maintaining its potential to benefit posterity (IUCN 1980). This statement became the basis for all subsequent definitions of sustainable development. The Strategy identified three objectives: to maintain essential ecological processes and life support systems; to preserve genetic diversity; and to ensure sustainable utilization of ecosystems. Thus, the Strategy focused primarily on ecological aspects. The Brundtland Commission extended the World Conservation Strategy to address the economic aspects of development. The Commission defined sustainable development as: "development that meets the needs of the present without compromising the ability of future generations to meet their own needs" (WCED 1987: 43).

The basic premise of this definition is that poverty is a major cause of environmental degradation. The Commission argued that a "world in which poverty is endemic will always be prone to ecological and other catastrophes" (WCED 1987: 8). The poor are perceived to be destroying their environment in their struggle for survival, for example, by cutting trees to obtain firewood. The World Conservation Strategy had earlier argued that this pattern creates a vicious cycle that can only be broken by development. This view can be contrasted with the view held by others, such as Barry Commoner, that overconsumption is the main cause of POLLUTION and resource depletion.

Sustainable development is related to the concept of sustainability, generally meaning economic, ecological, or social continuity. Solow defines sustainability of growth as a non-declining capital stock (Pezzey 1989). Ecological sustainability, which refers to the continuity of ecosystems and bioresources, can be accommodated within Solow's formulation by extending the definition of capital to include NATURAL CAPITAL. What ecological sustainability implies for the management of individual ecosystems and bioresources is unclear, but it is generally accepted that "every ecosystem everywhere cannot be preserved intact" (WCED 1987: 45). Calls for ecological sustainability are partly motivated by a concern for inter-generational equity, that is, equal access to resources by each generation. In the mainstream literature, this is expressed as non-declining utility, or a constant consumption path. Social sustainability refers to distributive justice as a basis for social stability. This element is apparent in frequent calls for intra-generational equity. According to the UN Environment Program, sustainable development encompasses help for the poor, self-reliance, and a people-centered approach (Pezzey 1989). The Brundtland Commission noted the "neglect of economic and social justice within and amongst nations" (WCED 1987: 49). Nevertheless, the relationship between social equity and ecological sustainability is controversial. In the absence of specific institutional provisions, social equity in access to resources may not lead to ecological sustainability. The dominant interpretations of sustainable development, however, suggest that the two are symbiotic.

## Poverty and environmental degradation

Another controversial aspect of sustainable development is the relationship between poverty and environmental degradation. The emphasis of the dominant conception on this relationship discounts the environmental damage inflicted by members of rich countries or affluent constituencies in poor countries. Indeed, the emphasis on the role of poverty in environmental degradation results in a villainization of the poor. In cases where certain social groups are disproportionately poor, for example, women, these groups bear more than their share of the blame for environmental destruction. If poverty is the problem, then clearly the solution is growth. The Brundtland Commission proposed a global annual growth rate of approximately 5 percent to achieve the goal of sustainable development. It is a matter of debate whether a world population of over 5 billion people can grow indefinitely at such a rate. A thorny issue in this regard is inequality in the current international economic system. The export-led growth model of the World Bank and the IMF fuels the massive exploitation of natural resources in less developed countries faced with declining terms of trade, foreign debt, and protectionism in developed countries (Redclift 1987). The Brundtland

Commission has acknowledged that international disparities in wealth and power force poor countries to rely on exports of natural resources to obtain foreign exchange, thereby threatening sustainability (WCED 1987).

## Critiques

Critiques of sustainable development come from mainstream as well as opposing sources. Mainstream critiques usually focus on the breadth and vagueness of the term. Most definitions of sustainable development are so broad that the concept is non-operational. For instance, NEEDS are not specified in either quantitative or qualitative terms. Sustainable development is sometimes defined in a generic sense: development that can be sustained. This reduces the idea of sustainable development to a mere triviality (Lele 1991). At other times it is defined as survivability, turning the idea into an insignificant tautology. Norgaard (1994) argues that the dominant conception of sustainable development is non-operational because it is defined within the same philosophical framework that has created the prospect of the unsustainability of the biosphere. For example, the perceived solution for environmental problems in the dominant view of sustainable development is further technological progress and economic growth.

Sustainable development is also critiqued as being thoroughly anthropocentric, i.e. its concern for the natural environment is driven by utilitarian interests (for example, the World Conservation Strategy's emphasis on "satisfying human needs"). Extreme examples define sustainability as the "indefinite survival of the human species" (Pezzey 1989). This character of sustainable development is certainly at odds with biocentric perspectives, such as deep ecology, which define sustainability on ethical grounds, requiring equal treatment of all species. (See ECOLOGY.)

The Marxist critique of sustainable development points out that sustainability can be defined only within a specific politico-economic context. The context favored by mainstream proponents of sustainable development is the neo-liberal combination of free markets and multi-party democracy. However, critics point out that the inherent CONTRADICTIONS of CAPITALISM make it both socially and ecologically unsustainable (O'Connor 1994). Economic and social sustainability is threatened by recurrent demand crises as a result of the advanced EXPLOITATION of labor. But, moreover, ecological sustainability is threatened by the "second contradiction" of capitalism, where the cost of production rises as a result of the destruction of the material conditions of production, including the environment and natural resources. Another factor that contributes to crisis is the growth of social movements organized by labor, women, and environmentalists.

## Alternative views of sustainable development

Other views on sustainable development include those of Herman Daly, who defines the term as: "a cultural adaptation made by society as it becomes aware of the emerging necessity of nongrowth" (1993: 268). Daly suggests that the idea of sustainable development is plausible only if defined as a qualitative improvement in the economic base maintained by a steady-state throughput. This means a constant level of population and physical output supported by a minimum withdrawal of energy and materials. Daly's concept has its origins in the stationary state idea discussed by John Stuart Mill over a century ago (see STEADY-STATE ECONOMY). Another view is offered by Richard Norgaard (1994). Rejecting the dichotomy between man and nature, Norgaard sees development as a co-evolutionary process involving the environment, knowledge, technology and social organization. Ecological and social processes interact and determine a particular co-evolutionary path that may or may not be sustainable (see EVOLUTION AND COEVOLUTION).

Views like those of Daly and Norgaard have made some inroads into the literature, but are not the conventional wisdom. The persistence of mainstream interpretations of sustainable development has led many scholars and activists to see this concept as an instrument for co-opting genuine environmental concerns and radical critiques of industrial society (Esteva 1991). For the moment, most notions of sustainable development allow policy makers to revamp the idea of development rather than seek a radical transformation in human ethics toward the protection of the biosphere, based on necessary social transformations.

## See also:

development and the environment; development and underdevelopment: definitions; environmental and ecological political economy: major contemporary themes; Marxist political economy: contemporary varieties

## Selected references

Daly, Herman (1993) "Sustainable Growth: An Impossibility Theorem," in H. Daly and Kenneth Townsend (eds), *Valuing the Earth: Economics, Ecology, and Ethics*, Cambridge, MA: MIT Press.

Esteva, Gustavo (1991) "Preventing Green Redevelopment," *Development* 2: 74–8.

IUCN (1980) *World Conservation Strategy: Living Resource Conservation for Sustainable Development*, Gland: IUCN-UNEP-WWF.

Lele, Sharachchandra (1991) "Sustainable Development: A Critical Review," *World Development* 19: 607–21.

Norgaard, Richard B. (1994) *Development Betrayed: The End of Progress and a Coevolutionary Revisioning of the Future*, London and New York: Routledge.

O'Connor, Martin (ed.) (1994) *Is Capitalism Sustainable? Political Economy and the Politics of Ecology*, New York: The Guilford Press.

Pezzey, John (1989) *Economic Analysis of Sustainable Growth and Sustainable Development*, Environment Department Working Paper 15, Washington, DC: World Bank.

Redclift, Michael (1987) *Sustainable Development: Exploring the Contradictions*, New York: Methuen.

World Commission on Environment and Development (WCED) (1987) *Our Common Future*, Oxford and New York: Oxford University Press.

EIMAN ZEIN-ELABDIN

# systems approach

A systems approach or general systems theory is an interdisciplinary approach to formally describing and analyzing the features of all kinds of natural, social, and technical systems. The basic idea of systems theory is to identify the interdependencies between the internal structure of a system and its performance. In political economy, for instance, the "economic system" is seen to be inextricably linked to the social, political, cultural, psychological and biospheric processes, and the pattern of symbiotic interaction and change is a critical part of inquiry.

## History and example

A systems approach is a conceptual research program rather than a compact theory. The roots go back to the debate between the so-called reductionists and the vitalists. The debate began with the discovery of the principles of functioning of smallest entities like cells. Since the observed principles of metabolism were universal, the reductionists concluded that, if one knows the specific behaviour of the smallest unit, one can also derive the system-performance by a mechanistic summing up. The vitalists (Aristotle) denied this, emphasizing that an aggregation forms a "superstructure," with a system being "more than the sum of its parts." This qualitatively different outcome results from interaction and environmental feedback. Systems theory is in the vitalist tradition. Bertalanffy (1956), Boulding (1966) and Rapoport (1971) were early protagonists of an incorporation of systemic holism into scientific thinking.

Easton's (1953) systems analysis of political life is an example. In his model, there is a total environment (encompassing social, ecological, personality systems and so on) that stimulates the political system (government, administration, parties) by a steady flow of effects. In particular, these flows of demand (subsidies) and support (resources) are converted within the political system into outputs (laws, decrees) that respond to the initial wants. Feedback processes may alter the environment as well as the original effects, propelling new wants, subsystems and rules.

## Definition and main concepts

The definition of a system is crucial. Hall and Fagen (1956) give a general description of the notion of "system," meaning "a set of objectives together with relationships between the objects and their attributes." Thus, any system can be described by its resources, and the underlying processes of control. Entities are not independent from each other, but together form a coherent organizational form. The duration of that cooperation is essential. Only long-term interaction and feedback stimulate the development of a system's identity. Short-term meetings, such as cocktail parties, are quasi-systems and not systems in their true sense. What kind of identity emerges and how this process proceeds depends on the coevolutionary interaction with other systems (see EVOLUTION AND COEVOLUTION).

There are three main concepts associated with systems theory. The first is the "functional concept." It, for instance, treats the (political) system as a black box analyzing only the effects of various inputs to system outputs. The second is the "hierarchical concept," which focuses on the coexistence of different systems at varying levels of importance. The third is the "structural concept." This is the most critical, stressing the degree of interdependency of the components of the system.

If there were no degree of interdependency, then this equates with an isolated system with no exchange with other systems. Here, the processes are programmed and the resources are given at the genesis of the system. Both the development and the final state are completely determined by this initial state, as in a closed loop model (see GAME THEORY). Few if any of these "closed systems" exist in real historical TIME. By its very nature, systems analysis is primarily concerned with open systems, where neither the future path nor the final state are exactly predictable by the mere knowledge of the initial data. This indeterminacy (equifinality) is due to all forms of mutual interaction, such as adaption, incorporation, and rejection.

## Endogenous processes

In contrast to mainstream economic theory, which focuses on, for instance, how the political system reacts to environmental changes, the systems approach takes into account endogenous processes that are provoked by the very action of politics. Additionally, with systems theory, people are not seized with the goal of maximization, as *homo economicus* might suggest. In systems theory, individuals act within an institutional environment of rules and norms, which helps to shape their preferences and behavior, which in turn impinge on the institutions, in a circular and usually cumulative fashion (see CIRCULAR AND CUMULATIVE CAUSATION).

For instance, the "Eastonian systems approach model" examines the embedded political system within the social fabric, and investigates how the network of INSTITUTIONS AND HABITS affect overall performance. The search for typical, stable relationships dominates, and the observed principles help to understand the behavior of similar constellations as well as deviant behavior in a more realistic way. Consider, again, Easton's political system and its capacity to respond to disturbances, such as increasing demands on the social security system, or the opposition of taxpayers. What repertoire of mechanisms is available to prevent the political system from being torn apart? What are the strategies available to cope with external threats and what should the optimal design of the system's structure look like in order to attain stability?

## Survival of systems

The systems approach provides two basic strategies that help systems survive. First, systems tend to try and manage disturbances through reducing levels of interaction during potential crises. Dictatorship systems exert pressure upon the environment or cut themselves off from (hostile) wants in order to leave their internal status quo unaffected for as long as possible. Democratic governments want to escape from increasing demands of interest groups. As a consequence, politics may restrict group access to resources. This strategy affords special laws and decrees that either deter interest groups or hamper their influence. In both cases, the battle takes place at the edge of the system and demands a permanent consumption of governmental resources.

The second strategy is the system's adaptation to new environmental conditions. This presupposes the system's ability and willingness to alter essential parts of its organization, and means a reformulation of policy in such a way as to accommodate the interest groups. Rent-seeking interest groups spend resources in order to get artificial rents from state regulation and subsidies. By declaring the private interests as public interests the groups enter the inner system like viruses to manipulate the original mandate; they capture the system.

Snow (1993) stresses this point, arguing that inflexible institutional systems perpetuate the status quo, sticking to their traditional habits as long as possible and strengthening their defense mechanisms. Notwithstanding these efforts, in the long run they will surrender because they have been unable to adapt to societal changes. That is one of the major reasons why "constitutional economics" (Brennan and Buchanan 1985) is primarily concerned with the nature of rules. Institutions should be designed to be as stable as possible and as flexible as necessary.

## Holistic method

The existence of reciprocal relationships in nearly all systems poses a problem for mainstream economic "*ceteris paribus*" analysis. In a world of growing complexity and transition, it is necessary to apply a HOLISTIC METHOD to properly examine the underlying processes. Reality shows multidimensional conflicts, ambivalent behavior and intra-societal contradictions. The systems approach, being an open theory, can incorporate these aspects better than conventional mechanistic theory. To understand the systems' behavior we must analyze the details as well as their interrelations and joint operations. They, in turn, altogether influence individual behavior, so that every partial analysis would be incomplete and, possibly, misleading.

It is promising that today one can find the holistic idea of systems being revitalized in many fields working on dissipative structures, CHAOS THEORY, game theory, information theory, self-organizing systems and evolutionary economics (see EVOLUTIONARY ECONOMICS: MAJOR CONTEMPORARY THEMES). Of special interest is the analysis of complex systems at the Sante Fe Institute (see Arthur 1994), the ecosystem approach of Henry Regier and Buzz Checkland, the study of hierarchies by Tim Allen, the work of Ilya Prigogine on self-organization and the social system, and Georgescu Roegen's study of ENTROPY, NEGENTROPY AND THE LAWS OF THERMODYNAMICS.

## See also:

environmental and ecological political economy: major contemporary themes; hysteresis; path dependency; regulation approach; social structures of accumulation; technology

## Selected references

Arthur, W. Brian (1994) *Increasing Returns and Path Dependency in the Economy*, Ann Arbor, MI: University of Michigan Press.

Bertalanffy, L.V. (1956) "General Systems Theory," *General Systems* 1: 1–10.

Boulding, K. (1966) *The Impact of Social Sciences*, New Brunswick, NJ: Transaction Publishers.

Brennan, G. and Buchanan, J.M. (1985) *The Reason of Rules*, Cambridge: Cambridge University Press.

Buckley, W. (ed.) (1968) *Modern Systems Research for the Behavioral Scientist: A Sourcebook*, Chicago: Aldine.

Easton, D. (1953) *The Political System: An Inquiry into the State of Political Science*, New York: Knopf.

Hall, A.D. and Fagen, R.E. (1956) "Definition of System," *General Systems*, vol. 1, 8–28.

Parsons, T. (1969) *Structure and Process in Modern Societies*, Glencoe, IL: Free Press.

Rapoport, A. (1971) *The Big Two. Soviet-American Perceptions of Foreign Policy*, New York: Pegasus.

Snow, R.M. (1993) "Crisis as Status Quo: A Systems Approach to Understanding Institutional Organizations During a Period of Societal Transformation," *Human Systems Management* 3: 179–91.

KARL-HEINZ WALDOW

# T

# Taylorism

## Definition and nature

Taylorism or "scientific management" is a body of thought derived from the work of the American engineer and management consultant Frederick Winslow Taylor (1856–1915). Taylor believed that the productivity and well-being of society would be greatly enhanced if the managers of organizations would replace their traditional reliance on fiat and rule of thumb with systematic analysis and the generation of friendly cooperation between worker and manager. By the detailed analysis of production and distribution methods, Taylor and his followers sought to develop planning mechanisms that would enhance the efficiency of resource utilization and flows both within the firm and across the various sectors of the economy.

Planning had always been utilized within industry, but a key factor that distinguished Taylorism from previous systems of management was that Taylor and his inner circle endeavored to bring this aspect of the management process to the level where one could speak of a science of management. As Harlow Person observed: "Planning generally had not been effective because it had been based on too many chance factors. Now, with the aid of standardization, calculations could be made with a fair degree of certainty" (Person 1929: 81). The significance of the planning element in Taylor's system was also highlighted by the institutionalist Rexford Tugwell, who saw in Taylorism an approach to the allocation and utilization of economic resources that could enable society to gain greater influence over market forces, and thus enhance the capacity of

human beings to control their own history and economic well-being.

## Nature and critique of the degradation thesis

The foregoing depiction of Taylorism is at odds with much of the political economy literature, which tends to reduce scientific management to work measurement and techniques designed to systematically de-skill and disempower labor. In recent years, the wide acceptance of this demonized depiction has been furthered by the highly influential work of Braverman (1974). He argued that employer use of these techniques has induced a general degradation of labor skills within the industrialized nations. Aglietta encapsulated Braverman's perspective when he defined Taylorism as:

> the sum total of those relations of production internal to the labor process that tend to accelerate the completion of the mechanical cycle of movements on the job and to fill the gaps in the working day. These relations are expressed in general principles of work organization that reduce the workers' degree of autonomy and place them under a permanent surveillance and control in the fulfillment of their output norm.
> (Aglietta 1976: 114)

Braverman's depiction of Taylorism has not gone without criticism. It has been observed repeatedly that he failed to capture the complexity of workplace change and gave inadequate attention to worker resistance. The degradation thesis has also been subjected to sustained criticism. An examination of the trajectory of skill change over the twentieth century reveals that, if the working class is defined as that sector of society that lives primarily by the sale of labor power, then skill enhancement rather than degradation is the dominant trend within modern capitalism (see WORK, LABOR AND PRODUCTION: MAJOR CONTEMPORARY THEMES).

As vocal as has been the criticism of Braverman, however, the essence of his depiction of Taylorism has gone largely unchallenged. Most political economists continue to equate the Taylorist management system with the use of work study techniques, the domination of labor and the separation of mind and hand. In the late 1980s this orthodoxy came under challenge by management historians who found they were unable to locate convincing evidence for Braverman's depiction of Taylorism in Taylor's writings. The critique of the degradation thesis was reinforced by their resuscitation of the 1950s literature that detailed the close alliance forged by members of the Taylor Society (very close to Taylor) and organized labor through the period 1915–50. At the heart of the program developed by the Taylorists was a commitment to the notion that workers should play a major role in all areas of management, and a bitter opposition to those industrialists and technicians who sought to utilize tools, such as time study and job analysis, to exclude workers from the decision making process and destroy their skills.

## Taylorist alliance with organized labor

Together with organized labor the Taylorists fought against industrialists, such as Henry Ford, who expected workers to "learn their jobs within a few hours or a few days" (Ford 1923: 79). They also campaigned against the system of worker representation promoted by industrial relations theorists associated with John R. Commons, generally known as the Wisconsin School. Where the Taylorists advocated a system of worker representation that ceded workers an active role in all areas of management, Commons believed employees should limit their involvement in the management process to questions relating to the determination of conditions of employment,

with all other issues, and particularly those relating to investment and production, being acknowledged the prerogative of the employer.

The Taylorists and the leadership of the union movement in the USA campaigned for what they termed "co-determination" (sharing of power between managers and labor) for over three decades. However, they were eventually defeated in the late 1940s by an employer and government campaign that was fought under the banner of "managers must have the right to manage." As a consequence of this defeat, the Ford–Commons approach to labor management became the accepted norm in the Anglophone world. Thanks largely to the writings of scholars influenced by the Wisconsin school, this system came to be credited to the Taylorists. This was made possible by three major factors. First, labor historians, even those on the left, accepted that workers should not accept any responsibility for maintaining production; their concern was industrial conflict and its management. Secondly, political economists and others have generally not distinguished between the liberals of the Taylor Society, conservatives such as Henry Ford and fascists such as Charles Bedaux. And thirdly, Taylor's critics tended to ignore the fact that Taylor's thought became more concerned with the managerial potential of labor as it matured.

The result was an alliance between capital and labor that existed not only within the workshop. By the early 1920s, the Taylorists became convinced that the single greatest cause of waste and inefficiency within the American economy was not how hard workers labored but rather that they often did not labor at all because of instability in the business cycle. Their concern with this issue intensified as it became clear that the wealth they believed their movement was helping to generate was not being distributed in a manner compatible with long-term economic stability. This led them to emphasize the need for effective instruments for scientifically managing the demand side of the business enterprise and the economy as a whole. As a consequence the Society became an important component of the political and economic network that promoted a proto-

Keynesian strategy within the New Deal Administration.

## Conclusion

Political economists must reconsider the assumptions behind their use of terminology, in which Taylorism is equated with management control of labor, de-skilling, and the degradation of labor. The essence of the work of Taylor and Taylorism is towards enhancing the skills and managerial role of labor.

## Selected references

Aglietta, Michel (1976) *A Theory of Capitalist Regulation*, London: NLB, 1979.

Braverman, Harry (1974) *Labor and Monopoly Capital*, New York: Monthly Review Press.

Ford, H. (1923) *My Life And Work*, Sydney: Angus & Robertson.

Jacoby, S. (1985) "Union–Management Cooperation in the United States During the Second World War," in M. Dubofsky (ed.), *Technological Change And Workers' Movements*, Beverly Hills, CA: Sage Publications.

Nadworny, M. (1955) *Scientific Management And The Unions 1900–1932: A Historical Analysis*, Cambridge, MA: Harvard University Press.

Nelson, D. (1991) "Scientific Management and the Workplace 1900–1935," in S. Jacoby (ed.), *Masters To Manage: Historical And Comparative Perspectives On American Employers*, New York: Columbia University Press.

Nyland, C. (1987) "Scientific Management and Planning," *Capital And Class* 33.

—— (1996) "Taylorism, John R. Commons and the Hoxie Report," *Journal Of Economic Issues* 30.

Person, H.S. (ed.) (1929) *Scientific Management In American Industry*, New York: Harper & Brothers Publishers.

Taylor, F.W. (1914) "Scientific Management and Labor Unions," *Bulletin Of The Taylor Society To Promote The Science Of Management* 1(1).

CHRIS NYLAND

# technical change and measures of technical progress

By technical change, one means technical progress: the development of new – not switches among known – techniques of production. Though the distinction can be questioned (Hicks 1973: 120), measures of technical progress refer to the former and consist fundamentally of measures of the improvement in the competitive efficiency of "factors of production." These are three basic measures of technical progress, or "residuals": Hicks–Solow, Harrod and Sraffa–Pasinetti measures. All three have different concepts of capital.

## Hicks–Solow measure

The Hicksian or Solovian residuals measure the rate of improvement in the efficiency with which labor (or all non-reproducible noncapital inputs) and reproducible capital inputs are combined to produce output. In a simple one commodity competitive equilibrium model, with standard notation, $PY = WL + RPK$, $P$ is the money price of the net product, $Y$ is the money wage rate, $W$ is the price of the quantity of labor, $L$ (and land), $R$ is the real rate of return and $K$ is the net stock of reproducible capital (the same stuff as $Y$), so that the net product equals the wages bill and net returns to capital.

One has, in Divisia index number form:

$$\alpha(y - l) + \beta(y - k) = y - [\alpha l + \beta k] = t$$
$$= \alpha w + \beta(r + p) - p$$
$$= \alpha(w - p) + \beta(r + p - p)$$

where lower case letters represent proportionate rates of change and $\alpha, \beta$ represent partial production elasticities or shares. The Hicks–Solow residual, $t$, measures the weighted growth rates of output per unit of labor and capital identical to the weighted growth of the "real" prices of labor and capital (e.g. $w - p$ is the growth rate of the real wage rate). The Hicks–Solow residuals are simply illogical (Steedman 1985). They treat capital and output as the same stuff (Bliss 1975), and they fail to take into account that, as technical progress occurs, capital as an input, because it is simultaneously output, is itself being produced more efficiently. With technical progress, the primary inputs involved in the production of capital goods are improving in their efficiency (Rymes 1971; Hulten 1979, 1992). If technical progress is neutral in Harrod's sense, then $y = k$ and $r = 0$ and the Hicks–Solow residual would be $\alpha(y - l) = t = \alpha(w - p)$.

If some of the labor inputs are capitalized, that is, human capital and research and development expenditures are introduced, then it follows that as $\alpha$ is reduced as returns to capital become larger as a share of net income, the measured residuals are lower (more of technical progress is said to be accounted for). Such results are artifactual (see Rymes 1989).

## Harrod measures

Harrod measures of the rate of technical progress, where the capital concept is waiting done by individuals and where account is taken of the fact that capital as a commodity is produced more efficiently, are obtained as solutions from:

$$\alpha(y - l) + \beta(y - k + h) = y - [\alpha l + \beta(k - h)] = h$$
$$= \alpha w + \beta(r + p + h) - p$$
$$= \alpha(w - p) + \beta(r + h)$$

So that, for Harrod neutrality, solving for $h$ one has $y - l = h = w - p$. It appears, with Harrod neutrality, that the rate of technical progress equals the growth rate of labor productivity. (Harrod technical progress is said to be labor augmenting!) The concept means, however, that the efficiency of "working and waiting" are rising at the same rate. Thus the growth rate of the real returns to waiting, $r + h$, equals the growth rate of real wage rates under Harrod neutrality.

There is, in general, no reason to expect, with given propensities to work and to wait, for technical progress necessarily to be Harrod neutral. For non-neutrality (with shares remaining unchanged):

$$y - l + \frac{\beta}{\alpha}(y - k) = h = w - p + \frac{\beta}{\alpha}(r)$$

So that, for instance, given that $h > 0$, if $h > y - 1$ and $h > w - p$, where $y - k > 0$ and $r > 0$, the efficiency of waiting is increasing relative to that of working.

The Harrodian residuals show then that technical progress is both labor and capital, that is, waiting, augmenting. The capital concept is the flow of waiting, that is, non-consumption, done to carry, maintain (to offset depreciation) and augment the stock of capital conceived of as intermediate inputs (or durable machines) so that, in a technically progressive world, given flows of waiting result in the appearance of larger and larger flows and of stocks of capital inputs.

Harrodian measures of technical progress can be developed for multisectoral models of economies with interactivity flows of heterogeneous intermediate inputs and capital goods and the many difficulties of disaggregation which the Hicks–Solow residuals face can be overcome with the Harrod measures (Cas and Rymes 1991).

## Sraffa–Pasinetti measure

The third concept of technical progress, what may be called the Sraffa–Pasinetti concept, is akin to the incorrect interpretation of the Harrod residuals. It shows all productivity increase as advances in labor productivity only. It accords no role to capital productivity increase, either in the form of reproducible capital inputs as intermediate or fixed capital inputs or as waiting (Sraffa 1960; Pasinetti 1993). If real rates of return exceed the rate of Harrodian technical progress, exploitation is taking place. Natural rates of return (or natural real interest rates), determined by the state, should equal the rate of technical progress. Waiting may be done collectively and there is no need for private rewards for waiting with rates of return in excess of rates of Harrod technical progress.

## Conclusion

The three measures of technical progress employ different concepts of capital. The Hicks–Solow measures treat capital as intermediate inputs but fail to account for the way in which technical progress itself increases the output of such inputs. The Sraffa–Pasinetti measures eliminate capital as a primary input of any kind and reduce technical progress to labor productivity advance only.

The Harrod measures treat "working and waiting" as primary inputs and show productivity advance as increases in the efficiency of these basic primary inputs. While the Harrod measures are the only ones rooted in intertemporal economy theory, they have a drawback (as do the others) on which fundamental research is necessary. Keynes argued that, *ceteris paribus*, an increase in waiting might see the "waiting" lost in terms of greater unemployment of "working" and excess capacity of capital goods or unemployment of waiting. If the system exhibits Keynesian underemployment equilibria, then the Harrod measures would show lower measured rates of technical progress. In short, Harrodian measures of the rate of technical progress are not independent, nor should they be, of the underlying Keynesian equilibria in which all measurement takes place.

## Selected references

Bliss, Christopher J. (1975) *Capital Theory and the Distribution of Income*, Amsterdam: North Holland.

Cas, Alexandra and Rymes, Thomas K. (1991) *On Concepts and Measures of Multifactor Productivity in Canada, 1961–1980*, New York: Cambridge University Press.

Hicks, J.R. (1973) *Capital and Time*, Oxford: Clarendon Press.

Hulten, Charles R. (1979) "On the 'Importance' of Productivity Change," *American Economic Review* 69: 126–36.

—— (1992) "Accounting for the Wealth of Nations: the Net Versus Gross Output Controversy and its Ramifications," *Scandinavian Journal of Economics, Supplement* 94: 9–24.

Pasinetti, Luigi (1993) *Structural Economic Dynamics*, Cambridge: Cambridge University Press.

Rymes, Thomas K. (1971) *On Concepts of Capital and Technical Change*, Cambridge: Cambridge University Press.

—— (1989) "Technical Progress, Research and Development," in George R. Feiwel (ed.), *Joan Robinson and Modern Economic Theory*, London: Macmillan.

Sraffa, P. (1960) *Production of Commodities by Means of Commodities*, Cambridge: Cambridge University Press.

Steedman, Ian (1985) "On the 'Impossibility' of Hicks-Neutral Technical Change," *Economic Journal* 95(September): 746–58.

THOMAS K. RYMES

# technological lock-in

## Introduction

Why is it so costly to develop or drive an electric car? Why are more than 70 percent of personal computers running on MS-DOS? Why does the top row of letters on your computer keyboard read QWERTY? These are examples of technological lock-in. If the use of technology *x* causes positive feedback, then the use and development of alternative technologies is impeded and *x* becomes increasingly dominant in the market, even though an alternative is potentially just as efficient or superior.

There are two major types of positive feedback effects, and each type is the subject of a separate literature. One type of positive feedback increases the benefits to users of a product without changes in the technology or in related knowledge. This type is the subject of neoclassical network externalities models. The second type of positive feedback arises from a dynamic process of learning and ongoing innovation, topics that are mostly treated in the technical change literature. Within each of these broad categories there are different feedback mechanisms, which can operate simultaneously and reinforce each other.

## Network externalities

Network externalities exist when the benefit of the product to one user increases with the number of users. This additional benefit is not due to technological progress.

First, there are the direct effects. The benefit of a telephone or fax machine to one user increases with the number of users of compatible telephones or fax machines. This positive feedback in communications networks is confined to the demand side of the market. It magnifies any small advantage when there are two incompatible products that serve the same function. For example, MS-DOS had an initial advantage because it was adopted by IBM, and this created the expectation that it would become the prevalent operating system. The benefits of file compatibility and readily available information, due to the larger number of expected users, "tipped" the market in favor of MS-DOS.

Then there are the indirect effects. The size of the market may be inversely related to production costs. There may be increasing returns to scale for the product itself, or for complementary goods or services. Due to economies of scale, applications software for MS-DOS have lower costs than applications for the Macintosh operating system, further tipping the market against Macintosh computers.

## Learning effects

The above mechanisms operate in the choice between given technologies. By contrast, historical and institutionalist studies trace paths of technological and organizational evolution during which the lock-in occurs. Not only do the characteristics of competing products change over time, but also knowledge and skills adapt to the more successful competitor.

Products are improved and refined through learning-by-doing. Larger cumulative output over time can lead to higher quality and/or lower average costs, compared to an alternative product with smaller market share. For example, automobiles with internal combustion engines have come a long way over the past hundred years. Electric cars, however, remain at an early stage of development, with numerous quality problems yet to be ironed out and relatively high costs. The two products are at different points on their respective learning curves.

Complementary goods or services are also subject to learning effects. Setting up additional gas stations is a well-developed routine, but setting up battery recharge stations for electric cars would be a major and highly uncertain innovation. In his pioneering study, Paul David (1985) points out that as the number of typists trained on QWERTY increased, so did the benefits to employers of using machines with this keyboard. Conversely, as employers increasingly did so, the benefit to typists of training on QWERTY increased. (This is despite the fact that QWERTY was introduced in order to slow typing speed to prevent locking of keys on the old mechanical typewriters.)

Research and development skills become adapted to successful products, increasing the cost of developing alternative technologies. It is cheaper for auto makers to design new cars with internal combustion engines than with electric engines, because engineers are experienced in and know more about the former.

## Conclusion

If there are increasing returns to consumers or producers for any of the reasons described above, then lock-in is likely. This does not imply that all existing technologies are locked in, or that a lock-in is necessarily universal or that it will last forever. A new discovery may meet needs that existing products cannot. An industry elsewhere may take another route. Noble (1986) argues that US automated machine tools were designed to use numerical control because of the need for extreme precision in military airplanes and the research interests of MIT engineers. This did not stop Japanese machine toolmakers from developing alternative systems and producing technically less sophisticated but cheaper and commercially more successful tools.

Economists analyze network externalities as "market failures." But many lock-ins, as in the above example, were caused by government action and hence are more accurately described as "government failures." Studies of lock-in point to the danger of premature standardization. Since the full potential of competing designs is not known at the early stage of development, action favoring one over the other may produce a white elephant.

### See also:

circular and cumulative causation; hysteresis; knowledge, information, technology and change; path dependency; technology policy

### Selected references

Arthur, W. Brian (1990) "Positive Feedbacks in the Economy," *Scientific American*, February: 92–9.

David, Paul (1985) "Clio and the Economics of QWERTY," *American Economic Review: Papers and Proceedings* 75(2): 332–7.

Katz, Michael and Shapiro, Carl (1994) "Systems Competition and Network Effects," *Journal of Economic Perspectives* 8(2): 93–116.

Noble, David (1986) *Forces of Production: A Social History of Industrial Automation*, Oxford: Oxford University Press.

CHIDEM KURDAS

# technology

Technology, more specifically technological change, is the most important feature of the real world which influences both macro- and microeconomic processes. It includes product technology – the characteristics of a good or service – and process technology – the methods by which the good or service is produced. Process technology subdivides into technology narrowly defined (e.g. robots); techniques and procedures (e.g. just-in-time methods); and work organization (e.g. multi-skilling). At the micro level, it is the key determinant of competitive success for firms, and of the characteristics of competition in each industry. At the macro level, it is accepted as the most important determinant of the economic growth rates and levels of national income of individual states, and of their trading and other relationships. Its effect on employment and unemployment has long been hotly debated by economists and the lay public.

Mainstream economics has, however, tended to neglect technology or treat it as an exogenous variable. One reason for this is that (treated as a factor of production alongside capital, labor and land) it "misbehaves badly." One essential assumption of most neoclassical models of the macroeconomy is that factors of production become less and less abundant, and thus rise in price, the more they are used. Technology is not like that: the more it is used, the more it improves ("learning by doing"; "learning by using"). This characteristic also falsifies the usual neoclassical assumption of decreasing returns to scale (see INCREASING RETURNS TO SCALE). As Arthur (1989) shows, increasing returns to adoption mean that whole industries, world wide, can be "locked in" to "inferior" technologies. Similar effects lead individual firms (like IBM in mainframe computers) and whole industrial districts (like "Silicon Valley" in some areas of information technology) to acquire an advantage which is cumulative (see CIRCULAR AND CUMULATIVE CAUSATION).

## Technological progress at global and national levels

Technology is more manageable as a determinant of the proportions of capital, labor and land (and natural resources) used to produce a given output. The usual mainstream assumption is that there is a "menu" of various alternative technologies which together define an isoquant line joining different least cost combinations of factors. The choice of technology from this menu will then depend on relative factor prices. Technological "progress" can, then, be defined as a movement inward – towards lower cost – on all or part of the line.

In practice, it is difficult to distinguish a menu of possibilities from the technologies used. Even the fact that a given technology is being used somewhere by firm $x$ does not establish it as an item on the menu being available, at the same price, to firm $y$. Sometimes, to some extent, this is due to patent protection and other legal restrictions on imitation, or to secrecy. More important is that only part of any given technology can be "codified" as a "blueprint," and even less usually will be so codified at any given time. The rest is in the form of "tacit knowledge," which is often "team specific" and (partly for that reason) is generally only acquired by experience. It is, thus, safer to refer to technological progress as an improvement in the technology actually in use. At a global level, this would have to mean producing a given output with less labor and land, since these are in some sense in fixed supply. Since investment can increase the quantity of capital *ad infinitum*, an increase in capital use might be acceptable. (For the difficulties of defining and measuring capital see KNOWLEDGE, INFORMATION, TECHNOLOGY AND CHANGE; CAPITAL THEORY DEBATES).

In practice, technological change has often involved an increase in labor productivity, with less use of labor inputs and increased use of natural resources (including "sinks" for pollution as well as "sources" of raw materials). This is because these natural resources have been underpriced, if priced at all, while the price of labor has continued to rise, in the advanced countries. This has led to the development of "state of the art" technology, which is often inappropriate in at least two senses. First, it is inappropriately "land using" (extravagant in natural resources) generally. Second, it is, for the less advanced countries, inappropriate in its use of the other factors. Simplifying in mainstream style, one may say it uses too little labor and too much capital for these countries' "factor endowments." In fact, the problem is rather, or also, that these countries have, for the most part, not yet mastered the technologies involved. (However many engineers India has, however much equipment it buys, it cannot make a jumbo jet like Boeing or Airbus.) Nonetheless, for various political, cultural and economic reasons these countries seek to imitate the new or recent technologies of the advanced countries, rather than to find or develop ones more appropriate to their own needs and resources (see Kaplinsky 1990). This exacerbates the dependence on the North, and causes inequality of income, mass unemployment and slow growth.

What technological "catch up" requires is two things. Firstly, appropriate technological change is needed in the mass of existing enterprises: building on their existing capabilities and resources; being small in scale and simple in operation. And secondly, the adoption of modern technology in a "spearhead" of leading firms is required. The "spearhead" has to accumulate skilled labor and capital (as well as technological capability) at a great rate and, at the same time, adapt the technology it is adopting to its own needs and resources. This is the course followed by those countries which have succeeded in joining the North in the last half-century: Japan, followed by Taiwan and Korea (Morris-Suzuki 1994; Hobday 1995).

## A taxonomy of innovation by scale

Freeman and Perez (1988) distinguish between four categories of innovation (whether product or process).

*Incremental innovations.* These are particularly likely to occur through learning by doing and learning by using. They lead to a steady growth of productivity, which is easily measurable, and improvement of quality which is not easily measurable (and leads to underestimation of economic growth). They naturally tend to confirm and increase the advantage of established firms, regions and economies.

*Radical innovations.* These are discontinuous and nowadays likely to arise from deliberate research and development (R&D) in and outside firms. They may provide an opportunity for new firms to challenge the incumbents. Not only do the incumbents find much of their existing expertise and equipment devalued, but the uncomfortable implications of this for powerful groups and individuals may make their firms slow to recognize the advantage of the innovation.

*Changes in technology systems.* These are far-reaching changes in technology which affect several branches of the economy and create entirely new sectors.

*Changes in the techno-economic paradigm (or "technological style").* These are changes in one or more technology systems which have a pervasive effect throughout the economy. Once established as the dominant influence on engineers, designers and managers, the new "meta-paradigm" guides the trajectories of innovation for several decades. Thus "Fordism" centered on assembly line mass production engineering and continuous flow production in chemicals. This technological style became dominant in the United States in the 1920s; spread from there to the rest of the North; and remained dominant until in the 1970s it was challenged by the information and communication technology paradigm (Tylecote 1992).

New systems and (still more) new paradigms do not only devalue existing technology, narrowly and broadly defined. They also require, for their successful adoption, an appropriate "socio-institutional framework." In every country, to put such a framework in place will necessitate reform; in many, it would have to be far reaching. Thus, just as radical innovations give lagging or new firms their chance, so new paradigms give backward countries – suitably reformed, as the East Asians were – an opportunity to catch up, or even in some sectors overtake the leaders. The only advantage in backwardness is that it means low wages. This may allow a newcomer a chance to break into an industry where advanced countries are not yet entrenched. This happened in the case of the East Asian economies in electronics.

## How technological innovation takes place

Recent surveys, standardized across countries, have done much to improve our understanding of how technological innovation takes place in practice. There is a wide range of sources and promoters of innovation: not only R&D, but other departments inside the firm, suppliers of equipment and materials, customers, exhibitions and trade fairs. Science-based industries make heavy use of internal sources, mainly R&D, design, and university research. More traditional industries make more use of sources external to the firm, and often acquire innovations which are embodied in capital goods. In terms of expenditure, the data for Italy, for instance, indicate wide variations among industries in the importance of R&D, design and engineering, capital investment, and marketing. R&D ranged from 39.3 percent in pharmaceuticals to 2.3 percent in aircraft; while design and engineering was 16.2 percent in pharmaceuticals and 50.2 percent in aircraft. In both food and textiles, on the other hand, capital investment exceeded 80 percent and no other category reached 10 percent (Evangelista, in OECD 1996: ch. 6).

What virtually every industry has in common, on the other hand, is a preference for retaining all the functions required for innovation – R&D, design and engineering, production, marketing – within the firm, however much their efforts might be supplemented externally. There is little or no tendency to vertical disintegration in which (for example) an "innovation supplier" does the R&D and hands over the developed product to another firm to produce and sell it.

There are at least two reasons for this. The

first is "appropriability" due to "those properties of technological knowledge and technical artifacts, of markets, and of the legal environment that protect... innovations, to varying degrees, as rent yielding assets against competitors' imitation" (Dosi 1988). Lead times and learning curve advantages are key methods of appropriation, combined with secrecy (for process innovations) and marketing (for products). Only for product innovations in pharmaceuticals, and to a lesser extent mechanical engineering and chemicals, do patents play a central role – and even there, not on their own. But an innovation supplier which does not produce or market has little but patents to protect its returns.

The second reason for retaining innovation functions in the firm is that innovation is better done through the close interaction of the different functions involved (which, while possible between firms, is obviously easier within them). Not only functions need to interact: so, in a large and divisionalized firm, do divisions. Teece (1986) put forward the idea, popularized and developed by Prahalad and Hamel (1990), that the appropriate boundaries for firms are defined by the scope of their "core competences": related skills in development, production and marketing which feed into, and off, their output of "core products," and need to be controlled at the firm, not divisional, level.

## See also:

evolutionary economics: major contemporary themes; innovation, evolution and cycles; institutions and habits; long waves of economic growth and development; technology policy

## Selected references

Arthur, W. Brian (1989) "Competing Technologies, Increasing Returns and Lock-In by Historical Events," *Economic Journal* 99: 116–31.
Dosi, Giovanni (1988) "Sources, Procedures and Micro-economic Effects of Innovation," *Journal of Economic Literature* 26(September): 1120–71.
Freeman, Christopher and Perez, Carlota (1988) "Structural Crises of Adjustment, Business Cycles and Investment Behaviour," in G. Dosi, C. Freeman, R. Nelson, G. Silverberg and L. Soete (eds), *Technical Change and Economic Theory*, London: Pinter, 38–66.
Hobday, Michael (1995) *Innovation in East Asia: the Challenge to Japan*, Aldershot: Elgar.
Kaplinsky, Raphael (1990) *The Economies of Small: Appropriate Technology in a Changing World*, London and Washington DC: IT Publications in association with Appropriate Technology International.
Morris-Suzuki, Tessa (1994) *The Technological Transformation of Japan: From the Seventeenth to the Twenty-First Century*, Cambridge: Cambridge University Press.
OECD (1996) *Innovation, Patents and Technological Strategies*, Paris: OECD.
Prahalad, C.K. and Hamel, G. (1990) "The Core Competences of the Corporation," *Harvard Business Review*, May/June.
Teece, D.J. (1986) "Profiting from Technological Innovation," *Research Policy* 15(6): 285–306.
Tylecote, Andrew (1992) *The Long Wave in the World Economy: The Current Crisis in Historical Perspective*, London and New York: Routledge.

ANDREW TYLECOTE

# technology policy

Governments usually intervene because MARKETS fail to allocate resources efficiently from a social point of view. One of the issues at stake is the "competitiveness of nations." The comparative advantages of nations, regions and sectors change over time. For instance, labor cost advantages disappear because of rising wages, a natural resource advantage disappears because of changing TECHNOLOGY. In market economies, entrepreneurs should anticipate these changes so that firms, regions, and nations continue to be competitive (see INTERNATIONAL COMPETITIVENESS).

## Different perspectives

Technology and innovation policies are controversial in economics. Neoclassical and new institutional approaches consider the market mechanism to be capable of efficient structural adaptation. Government policy, in this view of the world, should be restricted to cases of public goods, externalities and regulation of natural monopolies. The market can allocate efficiently and in some cases needs government to get the prices right.

Neo-institutionalists (original institutionalists) have a different perspective on the market: competition is not a neutral selection process in which the fittest survives, but power is involved, and markets are fundamentally short-sighted. Markets operate, not in a vacuum, but in specific institutional contexts of which history, CULTURE and social-political structures are crucial elements. Instead of the neoclassical belief that markets, competition and selection automatically result in efficient structural adaptation, neo-institutionalists consider technology and innovation policies to be useful in promoting structural adaptations after which competition may perform its short-term tasks (see INSTITUTIONALISM: OLD AND NEW).

In the process of structural adaptation of the economy, technological change is crucial. Such change is largely initiated by firms which attempt to improve their competitive position via product and process innovations. However, firms may fail to initiate change or to adapt efficiently: R&D investments can be postponed or not undertaken at all because of the costs, uncertainties and risks involved. One of the issues firms are confronted with is the so-called appropriation problem. Because competitors can often easily imitate innovators, it is not always clear how firms can extract or appropriate technological rents from the end results of R&D investments. Imitators have a free ride and government policy can prevent this by allowing the innovating firm a temporary monopoly by means of a patent. Then the innovator has the exclusive property right to apply the innovation in a new product or production process and to reap technological rents.

However, patents have their costs, as a temporary monopoly reduces competition, and an exclusive right prevents the diffusion of the new technology. Nevertheless, patents are generally considered an important element of government policy to stimulate investments in R&D. However, patents are no guarantee against imitation, and technology policy should do more than simply protect property rights.

## Stimulation of innovation and R&D

In general, technology policies of governments seek to stimulate the production, application and diffusion of product and process innovations. Firms underinvest in RESEARCH AND DEVELOPMENT (R&D) because of costs, risks, and a lack of complementarities. In principle, firms can solve these problems to varying degrees by strategic alliances and joint ventures. When costs are too high for individual firms to bear they can create a mutual fund or merge their laboratories. In the case of lack of complementary knowledge, firms can combine knowledge in joint ventures; and when the risks involved are too high, firms can organize long-term agreements with customers or engage in vertical integration. Governments should encourage such efficient types of market organization because uncertainties are reduced and innovations stimulated.

However, the private organization of markets can result in low levels of R&D expenditure. In this case, public institutions should complement the market in order to facilitate the production, application and diffusion of new technologies. With respect to the cost issue, governments can facilitate innovation by subsidizing R&D. In the case of basic research, where application in commercial products is not immediately clear, governments can organize R&D in public research institutes, where the knowledge is made available to firms as a collective good. Governments can also stimulate the production of basic research by facilitating private research associations, bringing parties together and supervising projects. The transfer of technology to small and medium sized enterprises is an important area of technology policy.

## Cultural and socio-political environment

Governments in market economies can play an important role in the production, application and diffusion of new technologies. Government can be initiator and facilitator with financial instruments as well as organizational instruments. What role of government is necessary and effective largely depends on the initiative taken by private firms. If private actors easily cooperate and operate in environments in which long-term commitments are fostered, then the role of government should be different compared to environments in which firms are used to cutthroat competition. In other words: the cultural and socio-political environment in which firms are embedded largely determines what kind of technology policy is necessary and effective

For instance, the role of the Japanese Ministry of International Trade and Industry (MITI) in organizing basic research and facilitating the organization of research associations is embedded in a cultural environment in which government is expected to play such a role. In France, government plays a similar role in specific projects like nuclear energy, telecommunications and high speed trains. However, copying such technology policy is questionable and demands careful analysis of the specific institutional environment at hand.

## See also:

industry policy; innovation, evolution and cycles; institutional political economy: history; neoinstitutionalism; structural adjustment policies

## Selected references

Dosi, Giovanni, Freeman, Christopher, Nelson, Richard, Silverberg, Gerald and Soete, Luc (eds) (1988), *Technical Change and Economic Theory*, London and New York: Pinter.

Nelson, Richard (ed.) (1992) *National Innovation Systems: A Comparative Study*, New York: Oxford University Press.

JOHN GROENEWEGEN

# technology: globalization of

New technologies play a crucial role in economic and social globalization. Airplanes, media and satellite-based communications make possible an exchange of information, commodities and relationships which are dramatically superior (at least in quantity) to those of the past. The so-called "global village" could not exist without the microelectronics technological revolution. "Technological globalism" is used to describe and explain how and why the process of economic and social globalization is affecting the production, distribution and transfer of technology. Strategies developed by both government and business to generate technology are no longer based on a single country. Rather, firms face the competition of foreign as well as domestic firms, and they have increased their dealings in international business (see INTERNATIONAL COMPETITIVENESS). This has major consequences for the organization of innovative activities.

There are three main dimensions to technological globalism: the international exploitation of national capabilities, the role of transnational corporations, and international collaboration (see Archibugi and Michie 1995). This entry is structured around these three dimensions.

## International exploitation of national technological capabilities

Profit-seeking firms try to exploit innovations

in foreign markets by exporting products which embody new technology, by licencing the know-how and by installing production facilities in host countries. Although the returns associated with technological innovations are sought in global markets, the bulk of innovation is still national in scope.

Once firms have undergone successful innovation in their home market, they tend to try to enter foreign markets. Exports are one way to benefit from technological expertise. This is implicit in the "technology gap" theory of international trade, which assumed that the leading country would export high-tech products to the lagging country until the latter caught up through imitation. However, there is more to the question than simply imitation. Globalization of technology has substantially increased over the last twenty years, in tandem with the growth of international trade flows, foreign direct investment and the exchange of information.

While technology is shaped more and more by global phenomena, nation-specific factors have increased in importance. A new body of literature (Lundvall 1992; Nelson 1993) has emphasized the role of national systems of innovation in shaping the technological and economic performance of countries. Education, research and development, and innovation are still largely nation-based. How is it possible to reconcile the relative importance of national and global forces in innovation? The answer should be searched for in the increased international division of labor, which has produced a specialized form of integration, relying very much on the existing capabilities of nations to foster technological advantage.

## Transnational corporations

Innovative products and processes are increasingly generated by firms operating in more than one country, the TRANSNATIONAL CORPORATIONS (TNCs) which are active in host as well as home countries. Already in the 1960s and 1970s a substantial share of US-based TNC research and development activities were performed in host countries. The quantitative importance of innovations produced by TNCs in host countries is still controversial (see Patel 1995; Cantwell 1995).

There is, however, a consensus on three things. First, the nations mostly affected by technological globalization are the industrially advanced ones, while the developing countries do not host any significant portion of TNC research and development or technology-intensive activities (see TRANSNATIONAL CORPORATIONS AND DEVELOPMENT). Second, although a significant number of very large TNCs have their own innovation networks, the global generation of technology is not widespread. Third, the main dimension of R&D in host countries is the adaptation of products to local needs.

Bartlett and Ghoshal (1990) identified three main innovation strategies being used by multinational companies:

- R&D and technology-intensive activities are highly concentrated at corporate headquarters, being distributed to subsidiaries in host countries according to a centralized strategy;
- for highly diversified corporations lacking a common strategy, subsidiaries tend to independently develop technological capabilities to serve local markets;
- each subsidiary participates in the development of the innovation strategy by supplying its own inputs and expertise.

## International technological collaboration

Both government and business collaborate with counterparts based in other nations in the exchange and development of knowledge. Firms are expanding their non-equity agreements to share the costs and risks of industrial research. However, profit-seeking institutions were not the first to implement this strategy, as the academic community and other non-profit organizations have for much longer been international in scope.

Global technological collaboration falls into a gray area between the international exploitation of technology and the global generation of innovation. On the one hand, there is a bilateral flow of knowledge and expertise which does not occur under the exploitation of technology. On the other hand, absent is the question of a single corporation as in the global generation of innovation. Collaboration covers intentional knowledge-sharing by economic agents in which they preserve their ownership autonomy. Business firms have an incentive to share technology with other firms when this leads to lower cost and risk. They are generally keener to collaborate with firms which do not compete in the same product market, either because they are based in different regions or because they develop different product lines. A large and growing proportion of these strategic alliances cross national borders, especially in new technologies (see Hagedoorn and Schankenraad 1990).

Profit-seeking firms are not the only actors involved in international collaboration. Public and non-profit institutions, including universities and research centers, have for long been international in scope and willing to share knowledge with foreign-based individuals and institutions. The available evidence suggests that global technological collaboration is increasing substantially between public and business institutions. Moreover, mixed collaborations involving government-sponsored and profit-seeking organizations are becoming significant. Bilateral and multilateral inter-government agreements have also fostered collaboration. The most significant case of publicly-induced global collaboration is represented by the European Community's science and technology policy.

### See also:

core–periphery analysis; global corporate capitalism; innovation, evolution and cycles; international political economy; knowledge, information, technology and change; uneven development

### Selected references

Archibugi, Daniele and Michie, Jonathan (1995), "The Globalization of Technology: A New Taxonomy," *Cambridge Journal of Economics* 19(1): 121–40.
—— (eds) (1997) *Globalization of Technology: The End of the Nation State?* Cambridge: Cambridge University Press.
Bartlett, C.A. and Ghoshal, S. (1990) "Managing Innovation in Transnational Corporations," in C.A. Bartlett, Y. Doz and G. Hedlund (eds), *Managing the Global Firm*, London: Routledge.
Cantwell, John (1995) "The Globalization of Technology: What Remains of the Product Cycle Model?," *Cambridge Journal of Economics,* 19(1): 155–74.
Dunning, John (1992) *Multinational Enterprises and the Global Economy*, Workingham: Addison-Wesley.
Hagedoorn, John and Schankenraad, John (1990) "Inter-firm Partnership and Co-operative Strategies in Core Technologies," in Christopher Freeman and Luc Soete (eds), *New Explorations in the Economics of Technical Change*, London: Pinter.
Lundvall, Bengt-Åke (ed.) (1992) *National Systems of Innovation: Towards a Theory of Innovation and Interactive Learning*, London: Pinter Publishers.
Nelson, Richard (ed.) (1993) *National Innovation Systems: A Comparative Analysis*, New York: Oxford University Press.
Patel, Pari (1995) "Localised Production of Technology for Global Markets," *Cambridge Journal of Economics*, 19(1): 141–53.

DANIELE ARCHIBUGI

# time

Time is central to economics because economic activity – production, consumption, exchange and so on – takes time to conduct, while the planning of such activity necessarily involves attempts to anticipate future events. Conceptions of time in contemporary economic analysis are traditionally differentiated into two broad categories: analytical or logical time, and historical time. Appeal to historical time frequently distinguishes political economists (with their emphasis on the changing, evolutionary nature of capitalism) from orthodox neoclassical economists (whose models typically embody logical time).

## Logical time

Although some economic models are formally static, claiming only to explain events at a point in time, frequent appeals to adjustment and change over time are made even in the context of these models. This is the case, for instance, when convergence towards equilibrium or comparative statics are discussed. Sometimes, models are made formally dynamic by the introduction of $t$-subscripts to explicitly date variables and by the functional dependence of some variables on others with earlier dates. Analyses of this nature are based on logical time, which permits an ordinal ranking of events according to $t$-values that are conventionally interpreted as denoting "earlier" and "later" states.

In fact, such interpretation is highly problematic. Logical time has the characteristics of a mathematical space, and does not even begin to approximate time as it is actually experienced by real world social agents. First, in logical time, events occur as if they were instantaneous and simultaneous. Changes over time occur in the context of models whose structure is time invariant, and whose results are therefore unaffected by whether or to what extent dynamic adjustments actually occur. There is no sense of prior cause and subsequent effect, final outcomes being quite independent of the adjustment path taken towards them. This, therefore, provides a purely nominal characterization of the concrete historical functioning of a system according to the conventional ordinal ranking of $t$-values.

Secondly, the time invariance of the structure of logical time models means that it is possible (and, indeed, quite common) to speak of events unfolding in such a manner that restores initial conditions entirely. For example, models with unique, stable equilibria will always return to their original equilibrium position following any arbitrary disturbance. No trace of the disequilibrium adjustment experience will remain. This means that in logical time, it is essentially possible to move from the present into the future and from the present back into the past. Finally, the ahistorical structure of logical time models grants analytical omniscience to the economic decision maker. Agents can, in principle, learn the relative likelihoods of the complete set of possible outcomes associated with past, present, and future economic events.

A good example of logical time analysis is the neo-Walrasian Arrow–Debreu–MacKenzie model. In this model, agents optimally plan all present and future economic activity, so that all economic outcomes are determined simultaneously at a single instant in time. The system can also change back and forth with no trace of the processes involved. From a position of equilibrium, the introduction and removal of a shock to the system is supposed to fully restore the pre-shock position.

## Historical time

If logical time is an essentially spatial/mechanical concept, then historical time is innately social and behavioral. Historical time comprises a strictly uni-directional sequence of events, in which the present occurs in the context of the given and immutable series of prior events that make up the past. Putting the present in the context of what has gone on beforehand draws attention to the possibility that "history matters," in the precise sense that the past has an indelible influence on the subsequent outcomes of a system. Hence, the concrete historical functioning of a social system will always be associated with path dependent change, at least insofar as movement through historical time results in changes in stocks of experience which, through learning, impact behavior and, as a result, subsequent outcomes (see PATH DEPENDENCY).

Furthermore, experiential changes of this kind cannot easily (if at all) be eradicated; the trace of past experience is even evident in the act of forgetting exactly what has happened (Bausor 1986: 95). In historical time, then, the impact of past events on the present cannot be completely undone in such a way that restores the initial conditions prevalent before a concrete historical experience. Unlike logical time, historical time is irrevocable (Georgescu-Roegen 1971); we move strictly from the present to the future.

The notion that history matters obviously implies that current actions and events can impact on future outcomes. Unlike logical time, then, the determinants of future outcomes in historical time are not extraneous, time invariant laws or rules of behavior. Rather, these determinants are partly constituted in a historical (sequential) fashion, and include innovative behaviors which, by their very nature, cannot be known about (or even correctly anticipated by the use of certainty equivalents) in advance. The analytical omniscience that is possible in logical time is thus denied in historical time, and instead decision making is subject to UNCERTAINTY.

## Importance of historical time

There continues to be serious debate in economics about the incorporation of time into economic theory. Most neoclassical models embody logical time, but some heterodox economists attempt to incorporate historical time into their models. Introducing historical time into economic theory is important for a variety of reasons. First, the concept of historical time underpins the basic vision of capitalism as a changing, evolutionary system that is favored by schools of thought such as post-Keynesianism, Institutionalism and Marxism. Second, the principle that "history matters" forces economic theorists to take account of path dependence. Instead of specifying outcomes independently of the adjustments that lead up to them (as in conventional equilibrium models), a recognition of historical time demands that we characterize "long run" or "final" outcomes as emergent properties of the sequences of events that precede them. A recognition of path dependence also demands that a premium be placed on concrete historical and institutional knowledge of actually existing

economic systems in the pursuit of applied economics.

Third, historical time is necessary for choice to be truly meaningful. If possible future states are predetermined by immutable economic laws, then the most that choice can achieve is to select between otherwise exogenously given outcomes. In historical time, however, the future is as yet unmade; current choices contribute to the causal sequence of events that will create future outcomes. Finally a consideration of historical time raises the issue of whether or not plans based on EXPECTATIONS are likely to be reconciled with actual future outcomes, and how this will impact individual and aggregate economic behavior. These considerations are central to Keynes's and post-Keynesians' thinking about money and the principle of EFFECTIVE DEMAND AND CAPACITY UTILIZATION.

Clearly, any economic model that is entirely faithful to the properties of historical time must embody path dependence, irrevocability, and uncertainty. The past must be shown to influence the present, in a manner that cannot subsequently be completely undone, while some aspects of the future must be unknowable in principle. This is easier said than done. Nevertheless, a number of techniques have emerged for modeling in a manner that is broadly confluent with the concept of historical time.

## Modeling with historical time

First, structural models of economic processes can be based on path dependent organizing concepts, such as HYSTERESIS and CIRCULAR AND CUMULATIVE CAUSATION, rather than traditional equilibrium constructs which remain anchored in logical time (Setterfield 1995). Secondly, it is possible to take advantage of the fact that not all features of a capitalist economy evolve and change continuously. If it is possible to identify periods during which some elements of the economy – such as capital, institutions or states of confidence in long run expectations – are unchanging, then conditional or *ceteris paribus* analysis of the other elements can be performed (Vickers 1994). This approach, associated with Marshall and Keynes, involves "locking up without ignoring" features of an economic system which are known to be changing over time, in order to facilitate an explicitly contingent analysis of other features.

Finally, there exist microeconomic models of individual choice under uncertainty inspired by the work of G.L.S. Shackle (Bausor 1986; Vickers 1994). These models posit expectations and hence actions based on imagined rather than known future possibilities. Individual behaviors may consequently be quite incompatible, the upshot being a nonequilibrium sequence of creative and adaptive behaviors that Shackle calls Kaleidics.

## Conclusion

Economics incorporates two broad categories of time: analytical or logical time, and historical time. Logical time, however, is an essentially spatial/mechanical concept. It abstracts from the social/behavioral dynamics of historical time. Historical time, on the other hand, is consistent with a more processual and institutionally specific analysis of economic systems. Historical or real time is important to incorporate into political economy in order to comprehend real world problems such as growth, accumulation, poverty, unemployment and inflation.

## See also:

culture; equilibrium, disequilibrium and non-equilibrium; evolution and coevolution; hysteresis; increasing returns to scale; institutional change and adjustment; institutions and habits; knowledge, information, technology and change; traverse

## Selected references

Bausor, R. (1986) "Time and Equilibrium," in P. Mirowski (ed.), *The Reconstruction of Economic Theory*, Boston: Kluwer-Nijhoff.

Currie, M. and Steedman, Ian (1990) *Wrestling with Time*, Ann Arbor, MI: University of Michigan Press.

Davidson, P. (1991) "Is Probability Theory Relevant for Uncertainty?," *Journal of Economic Perspectives*, 5(1): 129–43.

Georgescu-Roegen, N. (1971) *The Entropy Law and the Economic Process*, Cambridge, MA: Harvard University Press.

Hood, W.C. (1948) "Some Aspects of the Treatment of Time in Economic Theory," *Canadian Journal of Economics and Political Science* 14: 453–70.

Marshall, Alfred (1920) *Principles of Economics*, 8th edn, London: Macmillan.

Robinson, J. (1974) "History Versus Equilibrium," *Thames Papers in Political Economy*, London: Thames Polytechnic.

Setterfield, M. (1995) "Historical Time in Economic Theory," *Review of Political Economy* 7(1): 1–27.

Shackle, G.L.S. (1958) *Time in Economics*, Amsterdam: North-Holland.

Vickers, Douglas (1994) *Economics and the Antagonism of Time: Time, Uncertainty, and Choice in Economic Theory*, Ann Arbor, MI: The University of Michigan Press.

RICHARD P.F. HOLT
MARK SETTERFIELD

# trade policy

At its most fundamental level, trade policy embodies, with INDUSTRY POLICY, a political ambition to direct a country's level and structure of trade towards rapid national economic development.

## Strategic underpinnings

Implicit in the typical use of the label is the presumption of a strategic underpinning. A narrow example is provided by Japanese resources policy, deemed necessary for the desired industrial take off for which the meager domestic supply was inadequate. The strategy first took the form of colonial expansion and has since involved a ruthless commitment to ensuring security of supply at minimum prices. Historical examples of more overarching strategic visions through trade policy can be found in Alexander Hamilton's wide-ranging *Report on Manufactures* as a basis for sustained development of the post-revolutionary American colonies (Hamilton 1791); and in Friedrich List's 1840s agenda for German development (List 1885).

The strategic character of trade policy is reflected in its perennial enmeshment with foreign policy. Trade concerns may be a dominant consideration in foreign policy – as in the West's sustained influence in the Middle East, first to ensure access to the "Far East" and later to access oil supplies. Trade policy may also be dictated by foreign policy considerations. The fight in seventeenth-century England over trade policy between the Whigs (protectionist) and Tories (free trade) was fought over divergent positions on relations with France. After 1950, the USA was tolerant of access by its Asian anti-Communist allies to its valued domestic market, in spite of the adverse impact on its trade balance.

## Colonial and imperial preferences and treaties

In the era of MERCANTILISM, which gave birth to the European powers and to capitalism, trade policy was indistinguishable from war and colonialism. An atypical respite occurred in the cooperative Anglo-French treaty of 1786. The treaty was uncharacteristic for its time, and it lapsed in 1793, to be followed again by war. The era of civility in trade policy dates from the Anglo-French Treaty of Commerce of 1860 (Fuchs 1893). Here was a bilateral agreement for reciprocal reductions on key commodities. The Treaty was inconsistent with Britain's prevailing unilateralist approach to trade. Britain generalized its French concessions to others on non-discriminatory principles. France considered the Treaty strictly as a bilateral one, making bilateral treaties with other trading partners.

Britain's unilateralist trade policy contrasted with the protectionist stance of the second-rank industrializing countries. Britain was thus incapable of exercising leverage over the trade policies of these countries. Britain's white settler colonies also sought more "balanced" economic development behind protectionist barriers. Britain survived the divergence in national trade policies for as long as its earnings from services exports and overseas investments compensated for its growing deficit on merchandise trade. When the returns from Empire diminished, Britain belatedly turned to the Empire for help. Thus was Imperial Preference born at the Ottawa Conference in 1932, though conceived fifty years previously.

Trade policies which have been devised by countries to remedy perceptions of their inequality of opportunity have been, in turn, perceived by other countries as generating an inequality of opportunity for themselves. The USA saw the imperial networks of Britain and France as significant impediments to its own expanding interests. The ascendancy of the USA to dominant imperial power during the Second World War found a powerful administration committed to a policy of "open door" for trade and investment flows. The turning point for this ambition was the 1934 Reciprocal Trade Agreements Act, coupled with the movement of formal authority for trade policy making from Congress to the Executive.

## General Agreement on Tariffs and Trade

The ultimate outcome of this thrust was the General Agreement on Tariffs and Trade. The GATT's formal procedures were those of non-discrimination, transparency (a preference for tariffs over alternative protectionist or support measures), stability (the binding of negotiated liberalization), and the resolution of disputes within the GATT regulatory structure (Salvatore 1992: chaps 1–2).

Thus from 1948, trade policy has been embedded within a multilateral framework; a historically unprecedented, if compromised, phenomenon. Signatories to the GATT increased from 23 at its inception to 90 during the Uruguay Round of 1987–93. Bilateralist practices continued; indeed, bilaterally negotiated reductions (generalized through "most favored nation") were the centerpiece of trade liberalization until the Kennedy Round (1964–7). However, bilateralism was sometimes elevated to a preferred strategy because of the perceived limitations of multilateralism. For example, in 1965 Australia and New Zealand negotiated a Free Trade Area Agreement, contrary to GATT principles.

The multilateral framework itself was compromised from its inception (Shutt 1985). The perceptions by the original signatories to GATT that a purely open trading regime would be detrimental to national interests, led to the insertion of opting out facilities, not the least being the escape provisions of Article XIX of the GATT. Those facilities have since been complemented by practices which have merely ignored the spirit of the GATT framework. The USA continued with a unilateralist trade policy, a product of both a nationalist Congress and the power to carry it out. This thrust has been reflected in the use of Voluntary Export Restraints, imposed on a variety of products, starting with cotton textiles in the late 1950s (Salvatore 1992: ch. 5).

## Trading blocs

The other significant development in the post-1945 period has been that of trading blocs. The short-term motivation for and effect of trade blocs has involved divergences from the liberalization ideal. The European Economic Community was a product of Cold War politics; the GATT structure had no choice but to accommodate its imperatives. The North American Free Trade Agreement is a defensive measure on the part of the USA facing endemic current account deficits, and of two countries being effectively semi-colonized by their powerful neighbor.

## Current trade policy

Current trade policy is thus an incoherent blend of multilateralism, bilateralism, unilateralism and trade blocs. Underlying that blend is a tension between national interest and inter-

national obligations. The novelty of the post-1945 period is the multilateralist infrastructure. This was buoyed by the internationalist executive arm of the US government, and supported by globally-oriented US capital. It has since been structurally underpinned by a substantial personnel of interlinked bureaucrats and intellectuals with a religious commitment to the multilateralist ideal.

Governments of necessity live by norms more pragmatic and occasionally more strategic. The most surprising element of post-1945 developments is not the many divergences from free trade but the degree to which freer trade has been achieved. It is a salutary lesson for multilateralism that the divergences from the ideal have been necessary for the survival of the system as a whole. The USA has entrenched this dualism in that Congressional agreement for US participation in successive GATT Rounds has been formally acquired by means of concessions to domestic interests.

The completion of the Uruguay Round of GATT in December 1993 was the trigger for the creation of the GATT's successor, the World Trade Organization (Cline 1995). It is intended that the WTO shall be more comprehensive in coverage (adding services, intellectual property and investment) and more demanding of rules compliance than was the GATT. However, the competition between nation states is a constant; mercantilist practices survive behind the rhetoric of free trade. In the context of a heightened global competition between capitals, the more ambitious pursuit of the multilateralist ideal of minimally restricted global trade will inevitably contribute to making the multilateralist infrastructure more brittle.

## See also:

colonialism and imperialism: classic texts; comparative advantage and unequal exchange; free trade and protection; global liberalism; hegemony in the world economy; international political economy; mercantilism

## Selected references

Cline, William R. (1995) "Evaluating the Uruguay Round," *The World Economy* 18(1): 1–23.

Fuchs, Carl Johannes (1893) *The Trade Policy of Great Britain and Her Colonies Since 1860*, London: Macmillan, 1905.

Hamilton, Alexander (1791) "Report on Manufactures," in Robert Birley (ed.), *Speeches and Documents in American History*, vol. 1, London: Oxford University Press, 1944.

List, Friedrich (1885) *The National System of Political Economy*, New York: Augustus M. Kelley, 1966.

Salvatore, Dominick (ed.) (1992) *National Trade Policies: Handbook of Comparative Economic Policies*, vol. 2, Westport, CT: Greenwood Press.

Shutt, Harry (1985) *The Myth of Free Trade*, Oxford: Blackwell.

EVAN JONES

# transactions costs

An exchange or transaction is the primary unit of analysis in economics. This is a first principle of heterodoxy and orthodoxy alike. These alternative streams of economic thought handle the conceptualization of the transaction very differently, a divergence that reflects essential features of their rival epistemologies. In economics, exchanges are the equivalent of social interactions in sociology. Transactions that encompass significant economic content are a subset of all possible social relations. Economic interchanges comprise finished goods, services, and factors of production. Trading dried fish for salt, a hen for a ride to town, or grain for crop weeding are representative. Monies greatly facilitate exchange and are used to acquire commodities, services, inputs, and other monies.

## Approaches

Orthodox economists look at a transaction by positing two rational, self-interested individuals who settle upon an exchange ratio, or agree on a price if money is involved. They engineer a voluntary contract, or in non-market cases, a contract equivalent. The heterodox treatment is more complex. First, every transaction is assumed to occur in a dynamic institutional context. The parties bring considerable knowledge and experience to the compact, which is predicated on customs and values. Those engaged are aware that they may interact in the future, so reliability and not taking unfair advantage are considerations. Secondly, the agents possess limited information and rely upon practical shortcuts in reaching acceptable, but rarely ideal, outcomes. They are neither strictly rational maximizers nor wholly self-interested. Thirdly, every transaction is not an isolated private contract between two agents, but is a social and legal event in which participate many interested witnesses and parties, including neighbors, family members, rulers, and judges. No exchange ever eventuates outside a facilitating and potentially corrective social and political context. Fourth, transactions are not limited to the market mode, but occur in such non-market forms as reciprocity, redistribution and intrafamilial household arrangements.

A frequently silent presupposition in the orthodox analysis is that transactions are frictionless and costless, or that institutions do not matter. In the heterodox framework, arranging transactions always necessitates social negotiations, requires time, uses resources, conduces individually and collectively borne risks, and incurs potential enforcement burdens. Economic history and anthropology provide rich examples of the political and social support systems required to sustain material exchanges. Periodic fairs in medieval times operated under the sanction of nobles or prelates. Flows of goods and services in the traditional Indian village were channeled along the networks of relations between landed and non-landed castes, such as potters, barbers and blacksmiths.

When applying the comprehensive heterodox viewpoint, it is direct and natural to consider how existing institutional conventions interact with the stream of ongoing market and non-market transactions being effected by individual participants. In contrast, when employing the stripped down orthodox vision, it is difficult to consider how atomistic exchanges are connected to institutions or organizational systems. Orthodox practitioners have customarily presumed, implicitly more often than explicitly, the normative, legal and institutional setting of commercial capitalism as the context for economic exchanges. Taking this historically unique background for granted precludes the concern for how people might engage in economic transactions in other institutional surroundings; retards an investigation of the symbiosis of market exchange and commercial society; and deflects diagnosis of how the capitalist economy and its integrative institutions co-evolved to their present point (see EVOLUTION AND COEVOLUTION).

## Problems with the orthodox approach

The limited scope of vision inherent in the orthodox way of looking at transactions severely restricts attempts to explain obvious phenomena. For instance, why are large, modern corporations the dominant form of industrial enterprise? A corporation is a non-market transactional space in which move factors and semifinished products. How do managers determine which corporate transactions shall be internal to the firm and which will involve external market contracting? Why are many potentially rewarding economic transactions not consummated, most noticeably across international borders? When property rights are ill defined, what special encumbrances complicate the arrangement and enforcement of exchange contracts?

## Institutional economics

Answering these important questions in the framework of standard neoclassical economics is very difficult. Although the deep importance of the transaction was not fully appreciated until recently, the cognizance of transactions

costs opened creative avenues of thought that broke fetters that are organic to orthodoxy. A few orthodox proponents began to reintroduce notions that were akin to, but not identical with, those of institutional economics. The nearness of this convergence is evidenced by the designation of transaction cost economics, and related arenas of thought, as the new institutional economics (NIE), which has been exaggeratedly distinguished from the old or original institutional economics (OIE) (see INSTITUTIONALISM: OLD AND NEW). The key overlap of NIE with OIE followed the admission that exchanges do not occur in a frictionless vacuum. Rather, the content and range of transactions are heavily influenced by the social, political, and legal setting in which they are contrived. A crucial distinction between NIE and OIE is that the former treats the social and legal appurtenances of transactions as costs, frictions, or burdens, while the latter construes the institutional matrix as sustaining or facilitating.

## Transaction cost economics and John Commons

To respect the tenets of neoclassicism, the founders of transaction cost economics rely upon their existing vocabulary and reduce all the dimensions of the setting in which a transaction occurs to the common denominator of costs, although they concede that not all costs are monetized. Transactions costs are defined as the real resource costs, including the opportunity cost of time, entailed in negotiating, completing and enforcing an act of economic exchange. The immediate implications are that the higher are such costs, the more difficult it is to exchange, the fewer transactions occur and the more constricted is the orbit of mutually beneficial trade. The ultimate prospect is that the range and volume of privately contracted market agreements are severely limited. This implies that market economies never come close to attaining the full efficiency gains postulated in the competitive general equilibrium case; they operate suboptimally, a daunting discovery.

Contributions to transaction cost economics burgeoned in the 1980s and 1990s. Three economists are usually credited with giving strong impetus to this new orthodox field, Ronald Coase, Oliver Williamson and Douglass North, the first and third of whom earned Nobel Prizes for their ideas. The much-heralded NIE invention of transactional analysis cannot be regarded as a novelty by anyone familiar with John R. Commons's earlier work on the nature of transactions. His *Legal Foundations of Capitalism* (1924), for instance, is devoted almost entirely to developing an innovative and cogent theory of exchange.

Commons identifies at least five persons involved in any economic or social transaction. Using a market example, he specifies $B$, a buyer; $S$, a seller; $B^*$, a buyer who offers slightly less than $B$; $S^*$, a seller who would have sold for slightly more than $S$; and, crucially, $J$, a fifth party who arbitrates or adjudicates any of the "indefinite number of possible disputes between the parties to a transaction that may arise before or after the completion of the transaction" (the letters are added by the present writer). In various places, the $J$ personage may be "a judge, priest, chieftain, paterfamilias, arbitrator, foreman, superintendent, general manager... acting within the limits of the group's, or going concern's... common rules, or working rules, the 'laws' of the concern" (Commons 1924: 67). A going concern is a government, church, business firm, or other organization. Commons distinguished clearly between a firm's internal sphere, where its own working rules govern transactions, and the external market sphere in which the firm transacts with other going concerns according to commercial principles (Commons 1924: 134–53).

Ronald Coase criticizes the standard microeconomic theory of markets, saying of it that "exchange takes place without any specification of its institutional setting" (Coase 1988: 3). He echoes Commons in remarking that "...the crucial role of the law in determining the activities carried out by the firm and the market has been largely ignored" (1988: 5; see also Coase 1937). Against this backdrop of orthodox darkness, Coase poses a momentous question that is as deceptively simplistic as it is radiantly profound: Why do firms exist? The answer can be given in one pregnant sentence: "The limit to the size of the firm is set where its costs of organizing a transaction become equal to the cost of carrying it out through the market." He adds, "this determines what the firm buys, produces, and sells" (Coase 1988: 7). With zero transactions costs, there are no firms. Furthermore, in a world of zero transactions costs, law and property rights could take any form at all, and exchanges could be negotiated that would lead to the optimal outcome of welfare economics. This so-called Coase Theorem, he laments, has been misapplied by orthodox economists in "disappointing" fashion to excuse them from weighing transactions costs or property rights in policy analysis, although his intent was entirely the reverse (1988: 15; see also Coase 1960).

Oliver Williamson (1975, 1985) has extensively applied transaction cost theory to the economics of the firm and used NIE to consider the institutional system of capitalist economies. Douglass North (1981) attempted to argue that powerful economic incentives to reduce transactions costs impelled the reform of European feudal institutions so that they became more favorable to commercial capitalism. He later (North 1990) admitted that his case was overstated and that institutional inertia and path dependence are tenacious. This volte-face brings him very close to alliance with Clarence Ayres's contention that the intermittent rhythms of economic history are best understood as the product of forward-pushing technologies and past-binding institutions. Some economists have appraised the effects of transactions costs on other areas, such as, for instance, international trade flows (see Adams 1996).

## Conclusion

Transaction cost economics reintroduces institutions into orthodox thought. Although unresolved differences remain, older and contemporary heterodox ideas afford many antecedents and parallels. Transactions costs are now agreed to matter and to derive from institutional arrangements such as governance, the legal system, and property rights. Frequently, transactions costs may be estimated by empirical work. The emerging field of transaction cost economics contains powerful ideas and opens many intriguing lines of inquiry. It is certainly a domain where orthodox and heterodox economists can participate in a dialogue and a common advance.

## See also:

Ayres's contribution to economic reasoning; Commons's contribution to political economy; culture; institutional political economy: history; institutional political economy: major contemporary themes; institutions and habits; North's theory of institutional change; path dependency; Williamson's analysis of the corporation

## Selected references

Adams, John (1996) "Institutional Coordination, Transactions Costs, and World Trade," in John Adams and Anthony Scaperlanda (eds), *The Institutional Economics of the International Economy*, Boston: Kluwer Academic Publishers, 1996.

Coase, R.H. (1937) "The Nature of the Firm," *Economica* 4(November): 386–405.

—— (1960) "The Problem of Social Cost," *The Journal of Law and Economics* 3(October): 1–44.

—— (1988) *The Firm, the Market, and the Law*, Chicago and London: University of Chicago Press.

Commons, John R. (1924) *Legal Foundations of Capitalism*, Madison, WI: University of Wisconsin Press, 1959.

North, Douglass C. (1981) *Structure and Change in Economic History*, New York: W.W. Norton.

—— (1990) *Institutions, Institutional Change, and Economic Performance*, Cambridge: Cambridge University Press.

Williamson, Oliver (1975) *Markets and Hierarchies*, New York: Free Press.

—— (1985) *The Economic Institutions of Capitalism*, New York: Free Press.

JOHN Q. ADAMS

# transfer pricing

Transfer prices are the prices at which an enterprise transfers physical goods and intangible property or provides services to associated enterprises. Enterprises are said to be associated if one of them participates directly or indirectly in the management, control or capital of both enterprises (OECD 1995). There are two reasons why firms use transfer pricing. The first is to provide managers with the information and incentives necessary to achieve the most profitable (after tax) use of resources within the larger organization. The second reason is that it is necessary for reporting purposes to tax authorities. Policy issues arise because an enterprise may misreport transfer prices with the aim of reducing total taxation liabilities. This further opportunity to increase after tax profit typically arises from the differences in tax and tariff rates between countries. In addition, enterprises may also misreport transfer prices to counter the impacts of investment and exchange rate controls.

With a few exceptions, up until the late 1960s transfer pricing was largely a neglected field of study. After a seminal paper by Lall (1973), the related issues of profit shifting and tax revenue losses attracted greater interest from researchers and policy makers. Empirical research since then (for example Stewart 1989; Gurbert and Mutti 1991) has confirmed that tax and tariff variations between different countries have also had significant impacts on international trade patterns, and the distribution of real capital and location of manufactures.

### Intra-firm trade

Transfer pricing is an increasingly important issue, given the volume of intra-firm trade between countries, especially intra-firm trade by TRANSNATIONAL CORPORATIONS (TNCs). Due to the nature of intra-firm trade, data are difficult to obtain. Bonturi and Fukasaku (1993) have estimated that, in the 1980s, the share of US intra-firm trade to total trade was around 35–40 percent. With increasing trends toward the globalization of trade and integration of international capital markets, transfer pricing is a particularly pertinent issue for most governments as they strive for internationally competitive tax regimes. As well as losses to governments through the erosion of their tax bases, profit shifting through misreported transfer prices can also impose welfare costs on other parties. For example, costs may be imposed on local shareholders (through reductions in their share of profits), on workers (through lower wages), and on consumers (through higher prices).

## Arm's-length principle

Many tax jurisdictions have attempted to detect misreporting by adopting the "arm's-length" principle. This principle states that the intra-firm transfer prices that should be adopted when determining tax liabilities are the prices that would have prevailed between two unrelated parties in otherwise similar situations. This principle has the advantages of often being simple to apply and of reducing the risk of double taxation. Another attractive feature is that resource misallocation is diminished, because competitive neutrality is maintained by providing a broad parity of tax treatment between TNCs and independent enterprises. The principle may be readily applied where a comparable transaction can be found between independent enterprises in analogous situations; for example, in transactions involving the provision of financial services, or the supply of metals, minerals and many agricultural commodities (OECD 1995).

In some cases, however, it can be difficult to identify comparable transactions between unrelated parties. This is particularly so where intellectual property or intangibles (such as the expected fruits of research, use of brand names,

tacit knowledge, and other property whose value is difficult to impute) are involved, or in the integrated production of specialized goods or services. In the pharmaceutical industry, for example, because most products are produced by TNCs and protected by patents, few comparable transactions take place between unrelated parties, so it is difficult to apply the arm's-length principle (Collins 1993).

## Incentive compatibility approach

The arm's-length approach may be considered to depend upon tax authorities being fully informed, particularly on being able to impute sufficient information about the TNC's product costs. When a comparable transaction between unrelated parties exists, with complete information, arm's-length regulation can be optimal. However, where the authority cannot adequately infer product costs, then regulatory difficulties arise from asymmetric information. With information asymmetry, a more appropriate policy is a regime in which the tax authority induces the TNC to voluntarily report its true costs and pay the appropriate level of tax by making it in the TNC's best interests to do so. This is called the incentive compatibility approach. This approach seeks to create an environment in which the TNC will behave in a similar manner to an independent enterprise (see Prusa 1990; Gresik and Nelson 1994).

## Harmonized tax–tariff regimes

Another policy, that has elements of the incentive compatibility approach, is for governments to agree on and implement harmonized tax and tariff regimes. When this is achieved the economic incentive for profit shifting is removed. Less satisfactory devices include controls on royalties and dividends remitted overseas, price controls, and foreign investment controls.

## Is regulation necessary?

Some have questioned whether the regulation

of transfer prices reported to tax authorities is even necessary or advisable. For example, TNCs often use shadow transfer prices at marginal cost to clear transactions amongst their divisions. According to this view, the transfer prices set by TNCs are efficient and any attempt to regulate them will create inefficiency and misallocation. The optimal policy under this approach is to remove all distortions and to permit TNCs to set efficient transfer prices. However, this view is naive. In a world in which there are no economic incentives to profit shift (and no penalties for doing so) there can still remain strategic, social and patriotic reasons for choosing to pay tax in one jurisdiction rather than another. Also, in the world in which we live, the absence of harmonized taxation and tariff regimes mean that incentives remain which encourage TNCs to maximize their after tax profits in ways which do not maximize global welfare (see Rugman and Eden 1985). In any case, that any regulation must lead to significant distortions and resource misallocations is overstated. After all, TNCs can always maximize after-tax profits by using one set of transfer prices to coordinate their intra-firm transactions while simultaneously using the transfer prices acceptable to the regulator to determine tax liabilities.

## Conclusion

While it may seem that, on the face of it, there are two opposed approaches to the regulation of transfer pricing by TNCs, practical economic policy most probably requires that each country adopt a mixture of the arm's-length principle, the incentive compatibility approach and some harmonization of tax regimes. As harmonization can involve some loss of sovereignty, an appropriate transfer pricing policy has to be balanced with numerous other policy objectives.

## See also:

corporate objectives; economic power; pricing; transnational corporations and development

## Selected references

Bonturi, M. and Fukasaku, K. (1993) "Globalisation and Intra-Firm Trade: An Empirical Note," *OECD Economic Studies* 2(Spring): 145–59.

Collins, M.H. (1993) *International Transfer Pricing in the Ethical Pharmaceutical Industry*, Amsterdam: IBFD Publications.

Gresick, T.A. and Nelson, D.R. (1994) "Incentive Compatible Regulation of a Foreign-owned Subsidiary," *Journal of International Economics* 36(3/4): 309–30.

Lall, S. (1973) "Transfer-Pricing by Multinational Manufacturing Firms," *Oxford Bulletin of Economics and Statistics* 35(3): 173–95.

Organisation for Economic Cooperation and Development (1995) *Transfer Pricing Guidelines for Multinational Enterprises and Tax Administrations, Part I: Principles and Methods. Report*, Paris: DAFFE/CFA/TPA (95)3/REV3.

Prusa, T.J. (1990) "An Incentive Compatible Approach to the Transfer Pricing Problem," *Journal of International Economics* 28(1/2): 155–72.

Rugman, A.M. and Eden, L. (eds) (1985) *Multinationals and Transfer Pricing*, London: Croom Helm.

MALCOLM COOK
PETER CRIBBETT

# transformation problem

## Introduction

One of the central theses of MARX in *Das Kapital* is that the basic structural variables of a capitalist economy are determined by socio-historical factors rather than market forces. The appearance of the dominance of market forces in a capitalist economy was characterized by Marx as COMMODITY FETISHISM. Though commodity fetishism is an important aspect of capitalist culture, Marx attempted to penetrate through this appearance and reveal the real relations of capitalism that hide behind market appearances. The relation of "values" to "prices of production," which has come to be known as the transformation problem, was simply an attempt to show how the real capitalist relations of exploitation, expressed by the concepts of "value" and "surplus value," hide behind the market appearances of "prices" and "profits."

Marx's contention was that the total gross output produced in a "year" could be reduced to a homogenous measure in terms of labor time. This total labor time, $W$, could be divided into three specific parts, $W = C + V + S$, where $C$ stands for constant capital, meaning the labor time needed to produce the raw materials, machines and so on used in the production process; $V$ stands for variable capital, meaning the labor time needed to produce the wage goods consumed by the workers during the "year"; and $S$ stands for surplus value, meaning the total live labor time over and above $V$ performed by the workers during the "year." All the individual commodities constituting this gross output of the "year" will have their counterpart of this aggregate division as $\lambda_i = c_i + v_i + s_i$, where $\lambda_i$ is defined as the "value" of the commodity $i$. These three divisions of value are supposed to be independent of the price ratios of commodities. The size of the constant capital is determined by the prevalent technology; the size of the variable capital (i.e. the real wage basket) by the social and historical factors; and the size of the surplus value by the length of the working day or the class struggle. The three determinants are, however, interdependent.

## Exchange and competition

The next stage in the analysis was to introduce exchange, since reproduction of the system from year to year is made possible by the exchange of commodities. In the first two volumes of *Das Kapital*, Marx conducted a structural analysis of the system on the assumption that commodities exchange in proportion to their values. This proposition was already made by Ricardo as the best possible approximate theory of prices, which came to be known as the LABOR THEORY OF VALUE. As long as the labor theory of value holds, the income of the capitalist would be equal to the surplus value produced in his/her enterprise, making the exploitation of the workers by the capitalists transparent.

In a competitive capitalist economy, however, the labor theory of value in general will not hold. For, as long as the organic composition of capitals ($OCC = c_i/v_i$) are different in different sectors, the exchange of commodities in proportion to their values would imply that the rate of profit in the lower OCC sectors would be higher than the rate of profit in the higher OCC sectors. This would instigate a migration of capital from higher OCC sectors to lower OCC sectors, thus raising the prices of commodities produced by the higher OCC sectors *vis-à-vis* the commodities produced by the lower OCC sectors. Therefore, the exchange ratios of commodities must diverge from their value ratios to bring about the condition of the equal rate of profit across sectors. What exchange ratios would guarantee the equal rate of profit across sectors, and how are they related to value and surplus value was the problem Marx tried to solve in Chapter 9 of *Das Kapital*, Volume 3 (see COMPETITION AND THE AVERAGE RATE OF PROFIT).

## Marx's solution

Marx's solution to the problem of prices and the equal rate of profit was simple. He defined the average rate of profit, $r = S/(C + V)$ ([the sum of $s_i$]/[sum of $c_i + v_i$]). He then calculated the prices of production ($p_i$) by marking up the sector's capital investment in terms of its value (i.e. $c_i + v_i$) by its average share in the total profit, i.e. $p_i = (c_i + v_i) + r(c_i + v_i)$. Marx's method ensured that the sum of prices would be equal to the sum of values, and the sum of profits would be equal to the sum of surplus values in the system (i.e. sum of $p_i$ = sum of $\lambda_i$, where $\lambda_i = (c_i + v_i + s_i)$, and sum of $r(c_i + v_i) = $ sum of $s_i$). These two results confirm Marx's basic proposition that bourgeois accounting, in terms of prices and profit, only obfuscates the fundamental relations expressed by the accounting in labor-value terms. The deviation of prices and profit from values and surplus values is thus caused by a redistribution of surplus within the capitalist class which leaves the relation between capital and labor untouched.

## The "problem": Bortkiewicz

However, in 1906–7, Bortkiewicz pointed out a major problem in Marx's formulation (which Marx recognised but did not rectify). The inputs are calculated as labor values $(c_i + v_i)$, whereas the outputs are calculated as prices of production $(p_i)$; which implies an inconsistent accounting practice. A consistent formulation of the problem must use the same accounting procedure on both sides of the equations; because capitalists buy their inputs by paying the equivalent of prices, not values. Thus, Marx's average rate of profit was wrong because the total capital investment cannot be taken as equal to the sum of $(c_i + v_i)$ a priori. Therefore, the average rate of profit is an unknown in the system.

Moreover, Bortkiewicz showed that once the problem is consistently formulated, the system turns out to be short of one equation for the complete determinacy of the prices of production. And when an invariance condition, i.e. some postulate about the relation of value to prices of production, is added to the system, then Marx's two aggregate results, in general, would not hold simultaneously. In other words, there are $n + 1$ unknowns in the system and only $n$ independent equations, and the system has one degree of freedom. The imposition of $S/(C + V)$ as the rate of profit on the system amounts to the imposition of two conditions on the system, thereby overdetermining it. Since Marx had presented his two results as a sort of proof of the correctness of his value analysis, Bortkiewicz's results inevitably turned it into a "problem."

## First round of the modern debate

After this, the first round of debate examined which invariance postulate between value and prices of production should be added to the system, i.e. whether total value equals total prices or total surplus value equals total profit should be added to the system (see Laibman (1992) for a detailed discussion on various invariance postulates). At the culmination of this round of debate, Seton proclaimed that the transformation of values to prices of production cannot be relied upon because there is no objective basis to the selection of one invariance postulate from many good candidates: "...and to that extent the transformation problem may be said to fall short of complete determinacy" (Seton 1957: 153).

Soon after this, in 1960, Sraffa, not intending to solve the transformation problem, presented a physical input–output system that simultaneously solved for the relative prices and the average rate of profit, given the real wage rate from outside the system. From Sraffa's physical input–output system, one could directly derive the commodity values as well as the solution for prices and the average rate of profit. This gave rise to the charge by Steedman (1976) that labor-value accounting is redundant for a theory of prices and distribution in a SURPLUS APPROACH TO POLITICAL ECONOMY.

Marxists have resisted the redundancy charge on the ground that Marx's notion of exploitation is rooted in the idea of forced surplus labor performed by the workers due to their lack of control over the means of production. Labor time is the variable in which the exploitative relation of the system is expressed; that is, exploitation is defined at the level of production and not at the level of distribution, as is the case in the Sraffian system (Sinha 1991).

## Fundamental Marxian Theorem

Many scholars have argued that the divergence of total profit from total surplus value or total prices of production from total value is not all that damaging to Marx's basic proposition about exploitation. This is because it can be proven that positive profit is possible if and only if there is positive surplus value, what has been called the Fundamental Marxian Theorem (see Morishima 1973). Moreover, it has shown that the rate of profit is a monotonic increasing function of the rate of surplus value $(S/V)$ (see Petrovic 1987). Sinha (1991) has argued in favor of using the condition that total value is equal to total prices of production as an outside constraint on the system, given that values are substance and it is neither created nor destroyed in the process of exchange.

If the system is in a balanced state and growing at the rate of profit then, as Morishima (1973) has shown, Marx's average rate of profit will come out to be the correct solution, and thus both his conditions would be met. Otherwise, total surplus value and total profit would diverge. But this is not a problem, because total surplus product is only a part of the total gross output and, as long as prices diverge from values, any part of the total value and prices need not stay the same.

## "New" solution

Many Marxist scholars, however, have taken a different line. They argue that wages are given in money terms and not in real terms. So the value of labor power, or the variable capital, should be redefined in terms of money in some sense. In the early 1980s, a new group of scholars (Duménil, Foley, Lipietz, see Laibman 1992) argued that the equality of total value and prices of production should apply to net output, not gross output as Marx had done. On this basis, the "value of money" can be calculated by dividing the total living labor spent in the production process by the total money value of the net output. Given the "value of money" so calculated, the value of variable capital can be calculated by multiplying the given money wages with the "value of money." Once these definitions are in place, Marx's two invariance conditions turn out to be a tautology.

Their "solution," however, has drawbacks (Sinha 1991). Not only do we lose the notion of "commodity value," defined as $c + v + s$, given that $c$ is determined differently than $v$ and $s$,

but it also dilutes the notion of exploitation significantly. In this case, the rate of surplus value becomes dependent on the subjective consumption patterns of the capitalists. This problem can be taken care of by the use of Sraffa's "standard commodity." Eatwell (1975) has shown that with the aid of the standard commodity, one can always translate a given money wage to its share in the total living labor time spent in the production process. Exploitation, so defined, then becomes independent of the composition of the net output. A direct relation between the rate of exploitation (i.e. the rate of surplus value so defined) and the rate of profit could then be established. The concept of commodity value becomes redundant in this approach nevertheless.

## *Rethinking Marxism* solution

Independently of the "new solution", Wolff *et al*. (1984), contributors to the journal *Rethinking Marxism*, came up with a similar solution. They also argued in favor of using the equality of the net value and prices as the outside constraint on the system, as well as identifying the value of variable capital with its prices of production. They, however, overcame the problem of an inconsistent definition of commodity value by redefining value as the prices of production of its constant capital plus the living labor time spent on its production. Thus, in their scheme the commodity value is determined by the prices of production, rather than the other way round as was the case with Marx. It is not clear what significance remains of the concept of "commodity value" in this approach.

## Disequilibrium solution

In the end, a highly unorthodox but interesting interpretation deserves mentioning. Farjoun and Machover (1983) have argued that Marx's attempt to derive the prices of production was a mistake. The nature of capitalist competition is such that there is no real tendency for the rate of profit to equalize. This is the case because, as prices change to bring about equal rates of profit across sectors, simultaneously some other parameters of the system, such as technology of production, income distribution and so on, also change, throwing the system continuously into disequilibrium. They go on to claim, on the basis of the method of statistical mechanics, that the labor theory of value gives a better estimate of empirical prices than the prices of production.

This may be true, but this by no means appears to be a criticism of Marx's "deterministic method" or its explanatory power. The deterministic method only claims that, given the technology and the rate of surplus value, there would be a tendency for the relative prices to gravitate toward the prices of production. If, in the meanwhile, the technology or other parameters change then the prices of production or the gravitational point itself would change.

## See also:

labor and labor power; surplus value as rent, interest and profit; value foundation of price

## Selected references

Bortkiewicz, A. von (1907) "On The Correction of Marx's Fundamental Theoretical Construction in the Third Volume of *Capital*," in P. Sweezy (ed.) *Karl Marx and the close of His System*, New York: Augustus M. Kelly, 1949.

Eatwell, J. (1975) "Mr. Sraffa's Standard Commodity and the Rate of Exploitation," *Quarterly Journal of Economics* 89(November).

Farjoun, E. and Machover, M. (1983) *Laws of Chaos*, London: Verso.

Laibman, D. (1992) *Value, Technical Change, And Crisis: Exploration in Marxist Economic Theory*, New York: M.E. Sharpe.

Morishima, M. (1973) *Marx's Economics: A Dual Theory Of Value And Growth*, Cambridge: Cambridge University Press

Seton, F. (1957) "The 'Transformation Problem'," *Review of Economic Studies* 24(3): 149–60.

Sinha, A. (1991) "The Concept of Value in Marx's Economic Writings: A Critique,"

Ph.D. dissertation, State University of New York at Buffalo.

Sraffa, P. (1960) *Production of Commodities By Means Of Commodities*, Cambridge: Cambridge University Press.

Steedman, I. (1976) *Marx after Sraffa*, London: NLB.

Wolff, R., Callari, A. and Roberts, B. (1984) "A Marxian Alternative to the Traditional Transformation Problem," *Review of Radical Political Economics* 16(2/3): 115–35.

AJIT SINHA

# transformational growth and stagnation

The theory of transformational growth, most closely associated with the work of Edward Nell, explains the deterioration in the performance of the US economy since the late 1960s. Efforts are underway to use the theory of transformational growth to also explain the performance of other advanced capitalist economies (see, for example, Nell and Phillips 1995).

There is a family resemblance between Nell's (forthcoming) *General Theory of Transformational Growth* and Keynes's *General Theory of Employment, Interest and Money* (1936), in the sense that the multiplier relationship between investment expenditures and the level of output and employment provides the formal structure of both theories. However, Nell parts company with Keynes by developing the contents of the theory of transformational growth in terms of Marx's analysis of the nature of capital as self-expanding value.

For both Keynes and Nell, capitalist economies tend to stagnate because of long-run dampening forces on both investment expenditures and the propensity to consume. As far as the propensity to consume is concerned, Keynes and Nell would agree that, since people save more of larger incomes, the growing affluence of the American people has reduced the multiplier to a little less than 2 (see Nell

1987: 94; 1988: 164–5). However, the core of both Keynes's theory and Nell's theory is their respective explanations of the determinants of investment expenditures.

For Keynes, investment expenditures are determined by the interaction of the interest rate and the marginal efficiency of capital. Keynes defined the marginal efficiency of capital as the discount rate that sets the expected returns from investment projects equal to their supply prices. New investments are undertaken, causing increases in output and employment, so long as the marginal efficiency of capital is greater than the interest rate.

Keynes argued that capitalist economies tend to stagnate because expenditures on investment projects do two things. First they increase the demand for capital goods, and thus put upward pressure on their prices; and secondly, they increase the supply of consumer goods, thereby dampening expected returns from investments in facilities to produce more of them. For Keynes, during the nineteenth century, "the growth of population and invention, the opening up of new lands, the state of confidence and the frequency of war" kept the marginal efficiency of capital greater than the interest rate. In the twentieth century, however, as capital has increased relative to labor, the marginal efficiency, or PRODUCTIVITY, of capital has fallen below "a rate of interest high enough to be psychologically acceptable to wealth owners." Keynes concluded that capitalist economies will thus stagnate unless investment expenditures are socialized (Keynes 1964: 307–9, 320, 375–6).

Like Keynes, Nell argues that capital ACCU-MULATION runs up against an internal barrier in the form of rising prices of capital goods, which cannot be passed on in higher prices for consumer goods. However, whereas for Keynes the diminishing marginal productivity of capital ultimately undermines inducements for wealth owners to invest, Nell takes for granted a large pool of entrepreneurs seeking investment opportunities. Nell thus rejects the idea of a diminishing marginal productivity of capital, as capital increases relative to labor, and instead derives the determinants of investment expenditures from Marx's analysis of the nature of capital as self-expanding value (see, for example, Nell 1987: 94; 1994: 77; forthcoming).

The purest expression of value is money (M). Therefore, self-expanding value, or the nature of capital, is expressed as $M - M'$, where $M' > M$ (see CIRCUIT OF SOCIAL CAPITAL). Despite the illusions created by both interest and profits apparently made from unproductive labor, value can only expand if there is an intermediate stage, between M and M', when money is thrown into the production of useful products. Traditionally, the production of useful products was largely done by households. Nell argues that the growth of capital has thus taken the form of arrogating traditional household activities, "that were formerly carried out through non-market procedures," to the monetary circuit, M–M' (Nell forthcoming: ch. 1; also see Nell 1987: 97–8; 1988: 168–9, 172, 230; 1994: 81–2).

For Nell, capitalist economies tend to stagnate because there are a limited number of non-market procedures to be transformed into market processes. Yet, at the end of each MONETARY CIRCUIT, there is a larger value (M') that can only realize itself as capital by being thrown into the production of more useful products. Nell attributes the deterioration in the performance of the US economy to the fact that, by the late 1960s, the opportunities for capital to realize itself, by arrogating non-market procedures to the monetary circuit, were more or less exhausted (see, for example, Nell 1987: 99; 1988: 170; 1994: 64).

Indeed, Nell (1988: 170; 1994: 80) argues that stagnation would have set in during the late 1940s and early 1950s, if it were not for the GI Bill of Rights, which entitled twelve million ex-GIs "to college tuition, federal and medical services," and thereby created "a major new market for homes, automobiles and all consumer durables."

It is often argued that, "just as crafts gave way to industrial mass production, so the latter is giving way to automated and computerized systems of production" that have the potential for setting off another era of transformational growth (Nell 1988: 162; 1994: 64). But Nell is skeptical. For investments in automated and computerized systems of production, like the production of cars with less steel and more electronics, do not cause "the transference of activities and functions from the household to industry and the market" in the same way that such activities and functions were transferred when the production of automobiles displaced craft-based industries, like harness-making and carriage-making (Nell 1988: 230; 1987: 94–5; 1988: 160–1).

The current effort to privatize government services, like welfare and social security, may temporarily counterbalance the dampening forces on both investment expenditures and the propensity to consume. But, for Nell, "the great market development of the industrial economy seems to have drawn to a close." This is because "for both the middle classes and large parts of the working class there is little, if anything, left to transform" from a non-market to a monetary process. Nell argues that the only alternative to stagnation is for the government to provide more purchasing power to the poor, who have not yet been completely integrated into the monetary circuit, through "high and rising [minimum] wages." However, if the government is going to succeed in generating "investment and technical progress" through higher wages, then, as Nell points out, it will be necessary to prevent businesses from passing the higher wages on in higher prices, and from migrating elsewhere (Nell 1987: 101–2; 1988: 230–1).

## See also:

budget deficit; economic growth; effective demand and capacity utilization; household labor; household production and national income; Marxist political economy: major contemporary varieties; post-Keynesian political economy: major contemporary themes; wage determination

## Selected references

Keynes, John Maynard (1936) *The General Theory of Employment, Interest and Money*, New York: Harcourt Brace, 1964.

Nell, Edward (1987) "Transformational Growth and Stagnation," in Robert Cherry *et al.* (eds), *The Imperiled Economy: Macroeconomics from a Left Perspective*, New York: The Union for Radical Political Economics.

—— (1988) *Prosperity and Public Spending: Transformational Growth and the Role of Government*, Boston: Unwin Hyman.

—— (1993) "Transformational Growth and Learning: Developing Craft Technology into Scientific Mass Production," in Ross Thompson (ed.), *Learning and Technical Change*, London: Macmillan.

—— (1994) "On Transformational Growth: Edward Nell Interviewed by Steven Pressman," *Review of Political Economy* 6(1): 63–87.

—— (forthcoming) *The General Theory of Transformational Growth: Keynes after Sraffa*.

Nell, Edward and Phillips, Thomas F. (1995) "Transformational Growth and the Business Cycle," *Eastern Economic Journal* 21(2): 125–45.

EDWIN DICKENS

# transnational corporations

## Introduction and definition

The first decades of the twentieth century were marked by the rapid growth of the modern transnational corporation (TNC), which emerged as a powerful entity playing important roles in international economic, political and cultural relations. The number of TNCs increased dramatically after the Second World War, reaching some 40,000 parent companies and over 260,000 foreign affiliates in the 1990s. Their total sales were estimated to be over $5 trillion in 1992 (two-thirds of world trade) and the stock of their foreign direct investment was close to $3 trillion in 1995 (10 percent of world GDP) (World Investment Report 1995–6). Because of their great power to influence economic activity worldwide, TNCs have been a subject of controversy since the beginning of the century.

The United Nations defines a TNC as an enterprise which controls assets such as factories, mines, sales offices and so on in two or more countries (UNCTC 1988). The term "transnational" is apparently intended to make a distinction between foreign-owned affiliates (which specifically link with TNCs) and those joint ventures aimed at achieving regional integration between neighboring countries. Others prefer to use the term "multinational corporations" or "international companies" in order to describe the overseas activities of such firms. Some writers prefer to focus on firms which are engaged in international industrial production and ignore those which supply foreign markets through exports. Critics argue that this view is incomplete, since it ignores the importance of trade and the role of banking and finance in the expansion of international industrial production.

## Mercantilism and colonialism

Historians maintain that "international [trading] companies have a long history, and that...banking has been conducted on international lines since the middle ages" (Tugendhat 1974: 30). Indeed, as early as the ninth century, Arab traders established important commercial routes linking Asia with Africa and parts of Europe. From the sixteenth century onward, several companies from Britain and other colonial powers engaged in long distance trade and other profitable overseas operations, such as railways and gas and electricity supplies. They therefore became a symbol of wealth and power of their country of origin.

During this period of MERCANTILISM, merchant capital acted as the most loyal representative of colonialism. For example, the East India Company ruled India for many years and later annexed it to the British Empire. The Hudson's Bay Company participated in the treaty negotiations with the North American indigenous peoples, and helped in paving the way for the establishment of British power in North America. Other companies, such as the Royal African Company, played similar roles in other continents (see COLONIALISM AND IMPERIALISM: CLASSIC TEXTS).

The overseas trading operations of these companies were very profitable, not only because they brought back gold and consumer goods to the metropolis, but also because they secured ownership over the land and its riches for many years to come. By the nineteenth century, finance had also become internationalized so that all the wealth that had been accumulated so far could now be invested abroad in government bonds, shares in rail and tramways, gas and electricity and other public utilities. Although portfolio investment was predominant during this period, FOREIGN DIRECT INVESTMENT (FDI) was not negligible. Companies from the USA and Europe were involved in the exploitation of raw materials and natural resources of Latin America, Africa, Asia and Australia and later started establishing overseas production facilities as we know them today. The late nineteenth century marks the beginning of many of today's major transnational corporations. Tugendhat (1974: 33) reports that Singer, the US sewing machine company, built its first overseas factory in Glasgow in 1867. At the turn of the century, other giants, such as General Electric, ITT, Nestlé and Siemens, had established manufacturing plants and begun operating in several countries. Foreign direct investment during this period was mainly in primary production and a large share of it was located in developing countries. But as manufacturing production gained importance, industrially advanced countries increased their wealth substantially so that today they account for the lion's share of all TNC activities.

## Old and new international division of labor

There is a general consensus that during the colonial era and until recently, developing countries provided cheap sources of food, energy and raw materials and served as markets for manufactured products from the industrial countries. This corresponds to what some call the old international division of labor. However, when advanced industrial countries entered a period of slow growth in the last quarter of the twentieth century, firms responded by rationalizing and restructuring their operations. As a result, manufacturing production started moving offshore, primarily in search of more profitable conditions. In this new international division of labor (Frobel *et al.* 1980), advanced industrialized countries (the core) retain high-level knowledge and skill-intensive activities, but low-skilled, standardized production processes are decentralized to developing countries (the periphery). According to this line of analysis, foreign investment and overseas operations by TNCs are seen primarily as a defensive reaction to problems of profitability and competitiveness in the core.

## Modern theory of the firm

The reasons why firms invest abroad are numerous and more complicated than those given by the new industrial division of labor model (see UNCTC 1992). Understanding the complexity and diversity of organizational models of the modern corporation has been a central task that has attracted the interests of researchers from various schools of thought. Ronald Coase (1952) is often cited as having provided the key insight on which the modern theory of the firm is built. He observed that firms arise because of the costs involved in using the price system. He argued that economic activity can be coordinated either directly within the firm or outside of it, through exchange transactions on the market. The boundary between internal (direct) coordination and external (arm's length) coordination is determined by TRANSACTION COSTS, that is, the costs of internal coordination and control on the one hand, and the costs of market transactions on the other. The optimal level of internalization is reached when "the

costs of organizing an extra transaction within the firm become equal to the costs of carrying out the same transaction by means of an exchange in the open market" Coase (1952: 341).

Following Coase, Williamson (1986) also noted that product and firm-specific assets (technology, human capital and so on) create coordination problems that cannot be solved by market transactions. The firm, thus, emerges as an organization which is capable of managing these problems. Williamson went on to observe that these coordination problems can sometimes be solved through cooperation between firms, such as in the case of joint ventures, sub-contracting and so on. However, others consider that the strategy of inter-firm agreements is in itself a rejection of the internalization principle since it involves market transactions (Delapierre and Michalet 1989). They argue that competitive considerations are the driving force behind organizational change, and that firms are forced to externalize some of their activities in order to remain competitive. The externalization process may result in new entities, such as autonomous affiliates, or it may bring together already existing firms in order to form a strategic business network (Ouchi 1980) (see WILLIAMSON'S ANALYSIS OF THE CORPORATION).

Business network structures are common in Japan and other Asian countries, and have recently spread to North America and Europe. There are various types of business networks, but they can generally be considered as a form of economic organization that lies somewhere between MARKETS and hierarchies. The rationale for such an organization is that transactions can be carried out at a lower cost than through open market mechanisms or an integrated, hierarchical firm.

## Expansion of capital on a world scale

Marxist inspired critics (Palloix 1975) reject the idea that firms arise because of transaction costs. They argue that capital is a social relation whereby the capitalist is constantly seeking to expand and extract maximum profits. The transnational corporation is nothing but the manifestation of the expansion of capital on a world level. The basis of this approach is found in the notion of CIRCUIT OF SOCIAL CAPITAL discussed by MARX in Volume 2 of *Das Kapital*. Marxists maintain that capital assumes different forms during the various stages of production and circulation: commodity capital, money capital and productive capital. The geographic expansion of capital led to the internationalization of these aspects, which correspond, respectively, to the expansion of world trade since the seventeenth century, the rapid growth of international capital movements during the first decades of the twentieth century, and more recently, the internationalization of production through foreign direct investment.

In this respect, the transnational corporation has proved to be an efficient institution in physically separating the different functions of the firm and locating them in various parts of the world in order to maximize its global profits. Technological improvements have been instrumental in this internationalization process, since they helped to break down all barriers and make even the most remote areas seem very close, therefore bringing geographically dispersed markets into an ever more integrated world economy (Kobrin 1995).

## Impact on host economies: positive

The controversy over TNCs becomes somewhat passionate when we consider their impact on the economies of host countries (Dunning 1994). Neoclassical economists have been traditionally the main supporters of TNCs. They maintain that there are substantial net benefits to be derived from the activities of these corporations. For example, investments by such corporations are assumed to have a positive impact on the local economy because they contribute to employment creation, improve the quality of the labor force through training, and stimulate new investments through backward and forward linkages. Concerning trade, it is often argued that, in addition to availing consumers with cheaper products and a wider choice, international exchange of commodities by TNCs increases the transmission and diffusion of TECHNOLOGY and know-how. TNCs, therefore, contribute to reducing the duplication of research efforts, and allow resources to be allocated towards the pursuit of new and distinctive technological frontiers.

According to this view, TNCs are efficient allocators of resources on a world level, and they make important contributions to ECONOMIC GROWTH and standards of living in both home and host countries. They, therefore, are said to reduce the gap between the rich and the poor. Moreover, if there are no obstacles, such as government control of trade, foreign investment and exchange markets, the theory predicts that free mobility of commodities and factors of production contributes to increased international integration and globalization of economic life. This in turn is said to lead to a progressive convergence across countries in income levels, costs and growth rates.

## Impact on host economies: negative

This unrealistic image of TNCs has angered not only non-neoclassical academics but also trade unionists, environmentalists and even politicians. Conscious of the impact such corporations have on their livelihood, leaders of the labor movement have been actively trying to mobilize public opinion and focus the debate on the contribution of TNCs to employment creation. For example, they point out that TNCs often rely on capital-intensive production techniques and imported skilled labor, and tend to use local labor only for low-skilled, non-unionized, low-paying jobs. This criticism is generalized by several writers who argue that, unless they are closely monitored, the activities of TNCs can be detrimental to the host economies.

The most notorious debate is obviously that concerning the contribution to economic growth and development. Critics argue that transnational corporations and their affiliates enjoy a tremendous market power, which enables them to earn and repatriate monopoly profits. Their technological superiority, in addition to ensuring low cost production, also gives them easy access to information, finance, and other valuable resources. TNCs tend to borrow extensively from local financial institutions, and by doing so, they use up local capital that otherwise would be available for locally owned businesses. Suppressing local entrepreneurship is synonymous with both economic retardation and the creation of a monopolistic market structure which ensures the continuation of dominance by a few powerful corporations.

The situation is made worse when the TNC is to a large degree independent of the domestic market of the host country. Low wages in certain countries may attract foreign capital, but since they are associated with weak effective demand and narrow markets, foreign investors tend to target high wage countries to sell their products. The extreme case is when foreign investment takes the form of an enclave producing mostly for exports and operating with almost no linkages to the rest of the local economy. But foreign subsidiaries operating in "Export Processing Zones" can never really be considered completely isolated from the rest of the domestic economy, because such operations are bound to have some kind of effect on their environment, such as water and air pollution, exhaustion of non-renewable resources and so on (see Chapter 9 of World Investment Report 1992). Such environmental degradation represents a very high cost which may offset the short-term economic benefits that can be derived from their operations.

In order to evade exchange controls and take advantage of differences in taxation, TNCs often resort to such techniques as TRANSFER PRICING, by under or over-invoicing the goods sold by one subsidiary to another. The use of transfer pricing is widespread in developing countries, because of the loopholes and inefficiency of their institutions. Another feature which is criticized is that, in addition to being able to extract extremely favorable concessions and agreements from host countries, TNCs are also used by governments of their country of origin in order to assert political domination. For example, the laws of the USA may require that General Motors forbids its subsidiary in Canada or elsewhere from exporting certain equipment to Cuba or China, but Canadian law cannot require the local subsidiary to make similar demands on the parent company. Such interferences are deeply resented by nationalists and, at times, have contributed to straining international relations (Stopford 1994).

However, it must be noted that nationalists tend to exaggerate the loyalty of national capital, because it is not obvious that national capitalists behave differently from foreign investors when faced, for example, with the choice of technology or the issues of local re-investment of profits versus their expatriation, serving local markets versus exports and so on. Capital, whether national or transnational, is governed by opportunities for its expansion, and for this reason it must generally behave like its competitors by cutting costs and seeking new markets.

## See also:

corporate hegemony; corporate objectives; corporation; economic power; ownership and control of the corporation; pricing

## Selected references

Coase, R.H. (1952) "The Nature of the Form," in G.J. Stigler and K.E. Boulding (eds), *Readings in Price Theory*, Chicago: Irwin.

Delapierre, M. and Michalet, C.-A. (1989) "Vers un changement des structures des multinationales: le principe de l'internalisation en question," *Revue d'Economie Industrielle* 47: 27–43.

Dunning, J. (1994) "Re-evaluating the Benefits of Foreign Direct Investment," *Transnational Corporations* 3(1): 23–51.

Frobel, F., Heinrichs, J. and Kreye, O. (1980) *The New International Division of Labour: Structural Unemployment in Industrialized Countries and Industrialization in Developing Countries*, Cambridge: Cambridge University Press.

Kobrin, S.J. (1995) "Regional Integration in a Globally Networked Economy," *Transnational Corporations* 4(2): 15–33.

Ouchi, W.G. (1980) "Markets, Bureaucracies and Clans," *Administrative Science Quarterly* 25: 129–42.

Palloix, C. (1975) *L'internationalisation du capital*, Paris: Maspero.

Stopford, J.M. (1994) "The Growing Interdependence between Transnational Corporations and Governments," *Transnational Corporations* 3(1): 53–76.

Tugendhat, C. (1974) *The Multinationals*, Harmondsworth: Penguin.

United Nations Center on Transnational Corporations (UNCTC) (1988) *Transnational Corporations in World Development: Trends and Prospects*, New York: United Nations.

—— (1992) *The Determinants of Foreign Direct Investment: A Survey of the Evidence*, New York: United Nations.

Williamson, O.E. (1986) *Economic Organization: Firm, Markets and Policy Control*, Sussex: Wheatsheaf Books.

World Investment Report (1992) *Transnational Corporations as Engines of Growth*, New York: United Nations.

—— (1995) *Transnational Corporations and Competitiveness*, New York: United Nations.

—— (1996) *Investment, Trade and International Policy Arrangements*, New York: United Nations.

HASSAN BOUGRINE

# transnational corporations and development

## Nature and size

Transnational corporations (TNCs) are hierarchical organizations with subunits located and operating in different countries, but with a home base in one country (rarely two) in which most of the equity holders reside. Their strong economic role in their home country's economy means that they often have substantial lobbying power there. US trade policy and the US position in the GATT Uruguay Round negotiations, for example, strongly reflect the interests of US-based TNCs.

It is often stated that the top hundred TNCs are each comparable in economic size to many medium-sized developing countries. For instance, the sales of General Motors are larger than the GDP of Indonesia (Todaro 1995: 529). This overstates the case somewhat, as gross, rather than value-added, sales of TNCs are being compared to GDPs of countries. It is, however, hard to exaggerate the importance of TNCs in world trade, with intra-TNC flows accounting for about a third of all trade, rising to effectively all for some commodities.

Foreign direct investment in developing countries, most of it through TNCs, increased rapidly in the 1960s and 1970s, from \$2.4 billion in 1962 to \$17 billion in 1980. In the 1980s, the focus of attention of TNCs shifted away from developing countries, whose share of global foreign direct investment fell from over 30 percent in the 1960s to 17 percent in the late 1980s. In the 1990s investment flows to Latin America and Asia have recovered.

## Approaches

The role of TNCs in economic development has been the subject of controversy for several decades. Attitudes have ranged from those of the "modernization" theorists, who saw the TNC as the most dynamic agent promoting development, through to "underdevelopment" theorists, who saw them as the main agent preventing development. However, both supporters and opponents of TNCs have been found amongst Marxists and non-Marxists alike. Jenkins (1987: 17) has proposed a useful four-fold taxonomy (see Table 5).

The neoclassicals (for example Vernon 1972) argue that TNCs act as efficient allocators of resources internationally, thereby helping to maximize world welfare. They assume that they provide resources which supplement domestic resources in closing savings, foreign exchange and revenue gaps; that markets are competitive, except insofar as government interventions

*Table 5*

|              | *Pro TNCs*         | *TNC Critics*   |
|--------------|--------------------|-----------------|
| *Non-Marxist* | Neoclassical       | Global Reach    |
| *Marxist*    | Neo-fundamentalist | Neo-imperialist |

have introduced imperfections; and that, furthermore, TNC activities result in the generation of additional local resources. This occurs through their provision of other factors in short supply, including technology, skilled labor, management, subcontracting and access to markets. More recent theoretical variants introduce technology, through product cycle theory, and argue that TNCs seek to internalize transactions as a response to market imperfections.

By contrast, many other non-Marxists (such as Lall and Streeten 1977) argue that the market power of TNCs introduces an oligopolistic element into what might otherwise be fairly competitive markets. Some believe that the main motivation for foreign investment is precisely the control of markets and a reduction of competition. This "global reach" approach is also known as the "industrial organization approach" because of its focus on TNCs as institutions. It emphasizes the negative aspects of their impact, such as their exploitation or abuse of market power, restrictive business practices and their inhibiting effect on local capital. Economic costs are identified in terms of profit, interest, royalty and management fee payments made abroad (so that in the long run they result in net outflows of capital); the costs of TRANSFER PRICING; the costs of importing intermediates and capital goods available locally, the lowering of domestic savings and investment, and the excessive concessions needed to attract investment in a global economy. In addition sociopolitical costs are also involved in inappropriate technology transfer and demonstration effects, the inhibition of domestic capital; the pre-emption of local resources, and the takeover of local initiatives. State control of TNCs, or intervention on behalf of local capital, tend therefore to be advocated.

The "neo-imperialist" Marxists accept most of the above criticisms. But, following Lenin, they tend to oppose TNCs, primarily for the additional reason that they see them as the main agents of capitalism. Hence, they are driven to invest overseas by a rising ECONOMIC SURPLUS, caused by monopoly rents in their home economies. Their inhibiting effect on local capitalists blocks the route to development through national capitalism, or actively helps to produce underdevelopment. The political conclusion is that TNCs must be attacked as part of a wider attack on capitalism.

In complete opposition to this picture, the neo-fundamentalist Marxists view capitalism as still performing a progressive role in poor countries, and they support TNCs as agents of this process (Warren 1973). They accept many of the assumptions of the neoclassical approach, but are less concerned as to whether the local bourgeoisie are strengthened or weakened by the actions of TNCs.

A fifth approach, dubbed the INTERNATIONALIZATION OF CAPITAL approach by Jenkins has become ever more relevant with the progress of "globalization." Whereas the first three approaches are primarily concerned with exchange relations, and while the neo-fundamentalist approach is mainly concerned with production, the new approach seeks to understand TNCs as institutions in a way that integrates their exchange and production relations. Thus TNCs are seen as the main institutional expression of the increasing global integration of capitalist production and exchange. They therefore have the power to counter attempts by other institutions (such as states) to challenge the logic of their geographical distribution of economic activity. A related aspect of TNCs' behavior is their attempt to control the market by bringing areas of economic activity inside the firm (Murray 1981).

## Resolution of the debate

Resolution of the debate on the role of TNCs in development has not been helped by the fact that some of the most successful developed/developing countries (Japan and the new industrializing countries), as well as some of the least successful (some African countries), have been severely restrictive towards foreign capital, while there have also been successes and failures amongst countries most open to TNCs. These facts are most easily understood through the fifth approach.

Numerous statistical studies (see Bornschier and Chase-Dunn 1985) of the impact of TNCs on developing countries broadly support the following generalizations:

- TNC investments bring immediate increases in the economic growth rate and employment. This is unsurprising as new capital and productive plant are usually introduced during the initial investment.
- Over longer periods, the higher the share of stock of capital owned by TNCs the lower the growth rate. Although this will appear counter-intuitive to many, it is well supported by a number of studies, and is most easily explained in terms of the socio-political costs listed above under the "global reach" approach.
- The higher the share of foreign capital in investment, the higher the level of inequality in the economy.

We may conclude by making two points. Firstly, development strategies based on the promotion of investment by TNCs, and assuming the existence of a free world market, are likely to meet with serious problems. Secondly, strategies which assume the sovereignty of the nation state, and its ability to substitute for the lack of domestic capitalists (or locally based TNCs), will be disappointed.

## Selected references

Bornschier, Volker and Chase-Dunn, Christopher (1985) *Transnational Corporations and Underdevelopment*, New York: Praeger.

Jenkins, Rhys (1987) *Transnational Corporations and Uneven Development: The Internationalisation of Capital and the Third World*, London: Methuen.

Lall, Sanjaya and Streeten, Paul (1977) *Foreign Investment, Transnationals and Developing Countries*, London: Macmillan.

Murray, Robin (ed.) (1981) *Multinationals Beyond the Market*, Brighton: Harvester.

Todaro, Michael P. (1995) *Economic Development*, 5th edn, London: Longman.

Vernon, Raymond (1972) *The Economic and Political Consequences of Multinational Enterprise*, Cambridge, MA: Harvard University Press.

Warren, Bill (1973) "Imperialism and Capitalist Industrialisation," *New Left Review* 81 (September–October): 3–44.

COLIN STONEMAN

# traverse

The traverse was first defined by John Hicks (1965: ch. 16) to describe the passage between two semi-stationary states. Hicks was interested in whether it was possible for an economy to move from a given full employment rate of accumulation to another rate of growth, while preserving full employment of labor and capacity during the transition. Hicks's first model was a two-sector model, with a fixed capital good sector and a consumption good sector. This model employed BASIC AND NONBASIC COMMODITIES and fixed coefficients, similar to those often used by Sraffians to highlight the Cambridge CAPITAL THEORY DEBATES. Hicks showed that such a full-employment traverse is possible only if the consumption good industry is more capital intensive than the investment good industry. This result is akin to the condition required in the earlier models describing GRAVITATION AND CONVERGENCE towards prices of production.

## Relevance of traverse

What is the specific relevance of traverse

analysis? Some authors argue that traverse analysis is no different from stability analysis. Although there is some truth in that statement, proponents of traverse analysis contend that stability analysis focuses on the end result of the traverse (the convergence process), whereas traverse analysis goes beyond the asymptotic long-run properties of the model, studying the path taken by the various variables of the economy immediately after the change occurs (Magnan de Bornier 1980: 9). Traverse analysis thus covers the short-run and medium-run consequences of the change as well as the long-run ones. In some models, traverse analysis is also concerned with how the economy can actually proceed from using old techniques to using new ones (producing and using new machines), a process about which stability analysis has little to say. An additional reason for focusing on the traverse is a more practical one. In the real world, economies are seldom at or around their terminal equilibrium points, the stationary or semi-stationary states. Economies are usually on some transition path; they are in the traverse, with capital stocks and employment slowly readjusting themselves to the new conditions.

The concept of the traverse is closely associated with the concept of historical TIME. In steady states, although some variables may be growing faster than others (because of technical progress), there is no change in the proportion of capital in each industry. With new conditions, however, the existing composition of capital and labor employment is incompatible with the proportions needed for the new long-run equilibrium. The traverse is thus the study of the reproportioning of the stocks of capital in each industry, along with the appropriate distribution of employment. Those few who have analyzed the traverse have shown that the reproportioning of the capital stocks and of the labor force usually cannot be done without encountering severe difficulties. Traverse analysis thus gives credence to those who, in the past, have claimed that an overall control of aggregate demand may not be sufficient to maintain the economy at full employment (authors in the Hayekian tradition

for instance, or the young Kaldor). The difficulties associated with a successful traverse are also closely linked to the proportionality problem put forth by MARX, as well as the critique by Marxists of indiscriminate Keynesian demand management. Even Ricardo's famous chapter 31 of his *Principles*, on the possible negative effects of introducing new machinery, can be reinterpreted as an unsuccessful traverse.

## Types of traverse analyses

There are two main sorts of traverse analyses: the sectoral traverse, as illustrated above and presented by Hicks (1965); and the neo-Austrian traverse, later developed and favored by Hicks (1975). In the sectoral model, or horizontal approach, the circularity of capital is fully taken into account. This is particularly the case of the three-sector model developed over the course of forty years by Adolph Lowe (1976). In Lowe's model, there is a consumption good and two investment industries. The first investment good is produced only to be used in the consumption good industry. The second investment good is used for its own production and for the production of the other investment good; it is the basic good of the system. Conditions similar to those identified by Hicks (1965) can be deduced from Lowe's model, but of course additional problems arise in his more complicated structure. Lowe concludes that, in general, market forces alone cannot lead the economy towards a successful traverse. Market signals can misguide the economy (see LOWE'S INSTRUMENTAL METHOD).

Lowe's model was initially conceived within the so-called Kiel School, which included the modern father of input–output analysis, Wassily Leontief. The School arose in reaction to Austrian capital theory (Clark 1984). In Austrian theory, as in Hicks's (1975) neo-Austrian model, the relation between capital and consumption is linear. Production is said to be vertically integrated; capital goods are not physically specified, but time appears explicitly in production as the duration of the process by which the original labor inputs are converted into final consumption goods. Besides time appearing explicitly, the main advantage of this approach is that the evolution of each vertically integrated sector can be analyzed independently of the changes in the other such sectors. This approach is particularly effective in dealing with innovations, since reduced values in technical coefficients are sufficient to take these innovations and their required new machines into account.

The main drawback of the neo-Austrian approach is that it cannot handle basic goods (Hagemann 1992). A similar drawback afflicts Pasinetti's model, to be found in his book *Structural Change and Economic Growth* (see PASINETTI'S ANALYSIS OF STRUCTURAL DYNAMICS AND GROWTH). Pasinetti's hyper-vertically integrated model can be considered to be a Sraffian variant of the neo-Austrian approach to the traverse. Pasinetti's model can be understood as a continuous traverse, since growth keeps proceeding at different rates in each independent subsystem, with relative sectoral stocks of capital growing at diverging rates. Pasinetti's device is to assume that, within each subsystem, the supply constraints are compatible with the given sectoral demand growth. If the growth rate of a given vertically integrated sector were to change, then the analysis and the conditions of the traverse pursued by Hicks (1965) would need to apply to this sector.

## Capacity utilization and the long period

Traverse analysis need not be limited to fully-utilized capacity or full employment of labor. It was pointed out early on, notably by Hicks (1965: 193), that traverse would be facilitated by spared capacity or a RESERVE ARMY OF LABOR. The question then arises as to what determines the rate of capacity utilization. While traverse analysis is traditionally conducted by assuming changes in supply side conditions, one can conceive of traverses being initiated by changes in demand conditions. Kaleckians have explored this avenue, replacing the full employment assumptions with investment functions and variable rates of capacity

utilization. It has been shown, within the context of two-sector models, with a basic good and a non-basic one, that a successful traverse does not depend on the technical conditions identified by Hicks (1965). If the model is stable in the short run, meaning that saving reacts more to changes in rates of utilization than does investment, then a traverse from one steady state of growth to another will always be successful (Lavoie and Ramírez-Gastón 1997).

The issue of the traverse has also been brought up in the discussions surrounding the validity of the long-period approach. Many post-Keynesians believe that comparative statics based on normal positions (i.e. positions with uniform rates of profit at normal capacity utilization) are not acceptable unless some coherent adjustment process can trace the traverse from one normal position to another (Halevi and Kriesler 1991). Ironically, most at fault here is Joan Robinson's *Accumulation of Capital*, where economies growing at various rates are being compared, but where no traverse is being provided between short-run analysis, based upon changes in the rates of capacity utilization, and long-run analysis, where fixed normal rates of capacity utilization are being assumed.

## Hysteresis

Some adjustment processes have now been provided by authors in the classical tradition. However, a further problem, also mentioned by Halevi and Kriesler, has now arisen; that of HYSTERESIS. While there may exist a traverse, the transition itself may be a determinant of the new normal position. The end result of the process cannot be determined without knowing how the traverse proceeds. Reaction parameters of the dynamic adjustments that occur in the short period thus help to determine the new normal position. The equilibrium is path determined and hence the possibility of an infinite number of equilibria arises (Lavoie 1996). It thus becomes impossible to separate long-run analysis from short-run forces. The long run cannot but be considered as a succession of short runs. As reflected by the traverse, history matters.

## See also:

circular production and vertical integration; Kaleckian theory of growth; path dependency; Sraffian and post-Keynesian linkages; time; transformational growth and stagnation

## Selected references

Clark, David (1984) "Confronting the Linear Imperialism of the Austrians: Lowe's Contribution to Capital and the Growth Theory," *Eastern Economic Journal* 10(2): 107–27.

Hagemann, Harald (1992) "Traverse Analysis in a Post-Classical Model," in J. Halevi, D. Laibman and E. Nell (eds), *Beyond the Steady State*, London: Macmillan, 235–63.

Halevi, Joseph and Kriesler, Peter (1991) "Kalecki, Classical Economics and the Surplus Approach," *Review of Political Economy* 3(1): 79–92.

Hicks, John (1965) *Capital and Growth*, Oxford: Clarendon Press.

—— (1975) *Capital and Time*, Oxford: Clarendon Press.

Lavoie, Marc (1996) "Traverse, Hysteresis, and Normal Rates of Capacity Utilization in Kaleckian Models of Growth and Distribution," *Review of Radical Political Economics* 28(4): 113–47.

Lavoie, Marc and Ramírez-Gastón, Pablo (1997) "Traverse in a Two-sector Kaleckian Model of Growth with Target Return Pricing," *Manchester School of Economic and Social Studies* 65(1).

Lowe, Adolph (1976) *The Path of Economic Growth*, Cambridge: Cambridge University Press.

Magnan de Bornier, Jean (1980) *Capital et déséquilibres de la croissance*, Paris: Économica.

MARC LAVOIE

# turnover time of capital

Karl MARX developed his theory of capitalist production and accumulation in Volume 2 of *Das Kapital*. The fundamental concept in developing his reproduction schemes is the CIRCUIT OF SOCIAL CAPITAL. The basic formula for the circuit of money capital is $M \rightarrow C \ldots P \ldots C' \rightarrow M'$ (Marx 1885: 25).

In stage 1 ($M \rightarrow C$), M represents the stock of money capital which is utilized as capital outlays on commodities, C, consisting of labor power and means of production. In stage 2, $\ldots P \ldots$, the sphere of production, there is a break in the sphere of circulation. In this process of production, labor power is applied to the means of production, resulting in the flow of finished commodities, C'. This is sold in stage 3 ($C' \rightarrow M'$) of the circuit, and thereby value is transformed back into the money form of capital, M'. This is followed by a repetition of the circuit through the further spending of money capital, and so on.

## Production and circulation

During stage 2, the transformation of C into C' through $\ldots P \ldots$, surplus value is created within the sphere of production. The value of C' exceeds the value of C by the amount of new production of surplus value, c. Stages 1 and 3 of the circuit of money capital consist of commodity exchanges within the labor and commodity markets, and as such are within the sphere of circulation. The capital investment, M, returns to the capitalist firm in its monetary form, M', after it completes one circuit of capital. The money capital returned, M', exceeds the capital advanced, M, by the monetary equivalent of the surplus value, m. In general, the reproduction and accumulation of capital is characterized by the endless repetition of this process.

## Number of turnovers and value

Each stage of this process takes time. The production process requires a certain period – the time of production – between the time when inputs to production are purchased and the time when the finished product emerges. It also takes some time for the commodity to realize its value through its sale. Finally, the recommittal of the realized value from sales to the production process as capital advances also takes time. The two delays are the realization and recommittal delays respectively, which together constitute the time of circulation. The entire "time of turnover of a given capital is equal to the sum of its time of circulation and its time of production. It is the period of time from the moment of the advance of capital value in a definite form to the return of the functioning capital value in the same form" (Marx 1885: 156). Thus, the turnover time of capital is the time it takes for the capital to complete one circuit. One could equivalently speak of the number of turnovers. "If we designate the year as the unit of measure of the turnover time by $T$, the time of turnover of a given capital by $t$, and the number of its turnovers by $n$, then $n=T/t$" (Marx 1885: 159).

The description of motion of value through the stages of the circuit of social capital reveals that, within this framework of analysis, the flow of value from one stage to the next is the underlying force which propels the self-expansion of capital. Thus, for capitalist firms to maximize the rate of capital accumulation, it would be desirable to maximize the rate of capital flows, or to minimize any delays in the processes of production and circulation of commodities. However, stocks of value arise inevitably because the processes of production, sales, and investment require time for completion. The value tied up for the duration of each of these processes is a stock of productive, commodity, or money capital.

## Foley's model

In recent years a formal model of the circuit of capital has been developed by Duncan K. Foley (1982, 1986b). Each stage of the circuit of capital is modeled with a stock of capital value in a form corresponding to that stage (i.e. stocks of money, productive or commodity capitals), and between each stage a continuous flow of value moves from one form of capital to the next. The stock variables in the circuit of social capital correspond to the categories on the asset side of the balance sheet of a firm, while the flow variables correspond to the categories on the income statement of a firm (Foley 1986a). Thus, given the aggregate financial statements of firms, this model makes it possible to measure the parameters of the circuit of social capital, including the turnover time of social capital.

## Rate of profit and business cycles

A number of different issues are associated with the turnover time of capital. Within the Marxist tradition, the FALLING RATE OF PROFIT TENDENCY is affected by turnover times of capital. If, as in the above, we designate a year to be the unit of measure of the turnover time, and if, for example, the turnover time is three months, then the number of turnovers would be four. If the quantity of capital is fixed and its rate of return in a single turnover is fixed, then capital which turns over four times a year accumulates twice as much surplus value as capital which turns over twice a year. Therefore, faster turnover times, *ceteris paribus*, exert upward pressure on the rate of profit. Theoretically, turnover time may fall on the account of more "energetic" production processes (e.g. speedier assembly lines, higher pressure fluid flows, shorter or quicker transport between inter- and intra-plant processing location), firms switching to just-in-time inventory management, improved financial instruments and so on.

The framework of the circuit of social capital provides a particular way of looking at business cycles. In this view, the very nature of a downturn in the economy would be a slowing of the circulation of capital, and a lengthening of the delay times associated with various stocks of capital. The elongation of the turnover time appears primarily as the result of longer circulation times associated with the realization of value in the money form and its recommittal to production process in the form of capital advances. The former delay appears as accumulation of inventories of finished goods by firms as a result of a deficient aggregate effective demand. The latter delay may be associated with scarce profitable capital outlays. Finally, recent studies (Azari-Rad 1996) show that, although production times in US industries have been experiencing secular declines over the past two decades, the circulation times associated with the realization and recommittal of value have not exhibited such downward trends.

## See also:

effective demand and capacity utilization; labor and labor power

## Selected references

Azari-Rad, Hamid (1996) "Turnover Times of Capital in the United States (1976–1994)," Ph.D. dissertation, University of Utah.

Fitchenbaum, Rudy (1988) "'Business Cycles,' Turnover and the Rate of Profit: An Empirical Test of Marxian Crisis Theory," *Eastern Economic Journal* 13(3): 221–8.

Foley, Duncan K. (1982) "Realization and Accumulation in a Marxian Model of the Circuit of Capital," *Journal of Economic Theory* 28(2): 300–319.

—— (1986a) *Understanding Capital: Marx's Economic Theory*, Cambridge, MA: Harvard University Press.

—— (1986b) *Money, Accumulation and Crisis*, Volume 2 of *Fundamentals of Pure and Applied Economics*, New York: Harwood Academic Publishers.

Marx, Karl (1857–8) *Grundrisse: Foundations of the Critique of Political Economy*, trans. Martin Nicolaus, New York: Random House, 1973.

—— (1885) *Das Kapital*, published as *Capital: A Critique of Political Economy*, vol. 2, New York: International Publishers, 1967.

HAMID AZARI-RAD

# U

## uncertainty

Taken in conjunction, the three terms "uncertainty," "probability" and "long-term expectations" are usually associated with the writings of J.M. Keynes, particularly Chapter 12 of his *General Theory of Employment, Interest and Money* (1936) and his *Quarterly Journal of Economics* defence of the same book (1937). What follows is a sketch of the relationship between these three categories, concentrating on Keynes's own contributions.

### Probability

A good deal of the recent interest in Keynes's views on probability and uncertainty in economics may be attributed to his earlier authorship of *A Treatise on Probability* (Keynes 1921). In this work, Keynes analyzes probability as a relation of partial entailment between some hypothesis $h$ and some set of evidential propositions $e$. This "probability relation" is written $h/e$ and read "$h$ relative to $e$." The probability relation is presented as a logical and therefore objective entity, the apprehension of which warrants some rational degree of belief between certainty and impossibility. Certainty is where $h$ is a logical consequence of $e$ and $h/e = 1$, while impossibility is where $\neg h$ is a logical consequence of $e$ and $h/e = 0$. The theory that Keynes presents is essentially one of comparative probability building on binary comparisons of the form $h_1/e_1 \geqslant^* h_2/e_2$ (where $\geqslant^*$ denotes the relation "at least as probable as" and what we would now call a partially ordered set of probability relations).

Keynes's logical probabilities generally do not bear numerical values and are often not even pairwise comparable. But comparison may sometimes be possible, and Keynes shows how further comparisons of probability relations may be deduced from comparisons of probability relations already given. Only under special conditions, in this framework, is it possible to assign numerically definite probabilities. What is required here is that the hypothesis to which a numerical probability is to be assigned be one from an exhaustive list of $n$ mutually exclusive $h_i$'s. These $h_i$'s are both "indivisible" (i.e. incapable of being split into sub-alternatives of the same form) and equally probable (i.e. $h_i/e =^* h_j/e$). Judgements of equiprobability are based on the "principle of indifference," that equal probabilities should be assigned to each of several hypotheses in the absence of positive grounds for assigning unequal ones.

The numerical probability of any one $h_i$ is then equal to $1/n$, an epistemic version of what is sometimes called the classical or *a priori* interpretation of probability. Keynes also allows that numerically definite probabilities may sometimes be assigned on the basis of a knowledge of the relative frequency of a certain kind of event in a suitably defined series or group of similar events. But he stresses that this assumes both the existence, and the validity of our empirical knowledge, of such series or groups (Keynes 1921: 103). The situations in which these assumptions are met, in Keynes's view, are however very special cases and he accordingly rejects the frequency theory as a general theory of probability (for a modern interpretation and exposition of Keynes's *Treatise* as a theory of comparative probability, see Kyburg 1995).

## Uncertainty

It has become conventional, following Knight (1921), to define uncertainty in opposition to risk. A situation of risk is characterized as one in which the decision maker is guided by a knowledge of *a priori* probabilities or statistical frequencies. Situations of uncertainty, then, are defined as ones in which the decision maker does not have such knowledge and, accordingly, cannot assign numerically definite probabilities. (Knight was writing prior to the emergence of the personalist or Bayesian interpretation of probability associated with Ramsey 1926 and Savage 1954). This convention has led some authors to define Keynesian uncertainty as corresponding to situations in which the decision maker does not have knowledge of the relevant Keynesian probability relation, either because it does not exist or because he or she cannot perceive it (for example, O'Donnell 1989).

As we have seen, however, it is quite possible for a decision maker to have knowledge of probability relations and even to compare them, on Keynes's account, without their bearing numerically definite values. To avoid confusion on this point, it is therefore better to follow the Knightian convention and to define situations of Keynesian uncertainty also as ones in which the decision maker's choices are not guided by *a priori* probabilities or a knowledge of frequencies. In terms of this definition, it is possible for a decision maker to have knowledge of the relevant Keynesian probability relations and yet still be choosing in a situation of uncertainty in the Knightian sense.

The distinctive conception of evidential "weight" that Keynes introduces in chapter 6 of *A Treatise on Probability* may also be interpreted as a measure of uncertainty. What Keynes has in mind here is that, when using probability as a guide to conduct, the decision maker is typically interested in, not only the strength of the probability relation between hypothesis and evidence, but also, and in some sense, the amount, degree of completeness or what he calls the "weight" of that evidence. Note that in terms of Keynes's theory, evidential weight is a measure of the quantity of (usually qualitative) evidence for and against the truth of some hypothesis. It is quite different from more familiar distributional measures, such as variances or confidence intervals. As with judgments of probability *per se*, Keynes suggests that it is generally only possible to make qualitative comparisons of probability relations in terms of evidential weight. Other things being equal, he argues, when using probabilities as a guide to conduct, we should prefer those based on the greater body of evidence or that which is relatively "more complete" (for more on evidential weight, see Runde 1990).

## Long-term expectation

By long-term EXPECTATIONS, Keynes means expectations "concerned with what the entrepreneur can hope to earn in the shape of future returns if he purchases (or, perhaps, manufactures) 'finished' output as an addition to his capital equipment" (Keynes 1936: 47). Long-term expectations are distinct from short-term expectations, which are "concerned with the price which a manufacturer can expect to get for his 'finished' output at the time when he commits himself to starting the process which will produce it" (1936: 46). The "state of long-term expectation," which Keynes refers to in Chapter 12 of the *General Theory*, is defined as "the state of psychological expectation concerning future events that inform investors' anticipations of yields, and which can only be forecasted with more or less confidence: future changes in effective demand, type and quantity of the stock of capital goods, consumer demand, and so on" (1936: 147–8).

## Linkages between uncertainty, probability and expectations

It is now possible to spell out the links between probability, uncertainty and long-term expectation in Keynes's thought. We have seen that, according to his theory of probability, it is only rarely possible to determine numerically definite probabilities (namely only in games of chance or when statistical frequencies can be determined). This same position provides the point of departure in his later writings on long-term expectations. In Chapter 12 of the *General Theory*, for example, he argues that investors are generally not able to determine numerical probabilities of yields, by invoking the principle of indifference (1936: 152). In the *Quarterly Journal of Economics* article (1937: 113), he goes on to say that the knowledge investors have at their disposal typically does not extend to a knowledge of statistical frequencies (such as might be available in the cases of a lottery ticket being drawn or life expectancy or the weather). It then follows that "existing knowledge [held by potential investors] does not provide a sufficient basis for a calculated mathematical expectation" (Keynes 1936: 152). Keynes, therefore, denies at one stroke that investment decision makers act as subjective expected utility maximizers, or are able to form rational expectations, a denial that forms a key theme in modern post-Keynesian thought (e.g. Shackle 1972).

But this is not to say, as is sometimes claimed, that Keynes fails to provide a theory of long-term expectations and their formation. In fact he provides a rich account, according to which investors form expectations by falling back on CONVENTIONS. Depending on conventions is the practice of (a) assuming that the existing situation will continue indefinitely, except in so far as there are definite reasons to expect a change; (b) taking current market valuations as "correct" relative to existing knowledge; and (c) copying the behavior of other market participants who find themselves in a similar situation (see Davis 1994). The fact that investors often adopt conventions of this kind is quite consistent with their making judgments of probability about the possible outcomes of the courses of action open to them, although these judgments will typically be qualitative rather than quantitative in nature. Moreover, in an explicit reference to the weight of evidence, Keynes argues that the state of long-term expectation depends not only on the most probable forecasts that investors make, but also on the confidence

with which they make those forecasts. The idea here is that investors lack confidence in their judgments of probability because they are lacking in evidential weight.

The dominant themes in Keynes's *General Theory* account of investor behavior are the causes and the consequences of the precariousness of the state of long-term expectation. There are three main reasons for this precariousness. The first is the fact that investment expectations are informed, in a sense disproportionately, by the facts of the existing situation and are therefore unduly sensitive to changes in the "news" and swings in confidence. The second is that the self-referential nature of the conventional methods of calculation leads to bubble phenomena and, if everyone is following everyone else's lead, to the possibility of dramatic fluctuations in asset prices (see SPECULATIVE BUBBLES AND FUNDAMENTAL VALUES). The third links to the short-termism that follows as a consequence of the liquidity provided by stock markets; and the subconscious and possibly irrational motivations of investors. The consequences, of course, are that a collapse in the state of long-term expectation may have a strongly negative impact on investment demand, and hence on the level of employment and the rate of ECONOMIC GROWTH.

## See also:

animal spirits; business cycle theories; financial crises; financial instability hypothesis; monetary theory of production; post-Keynesian political economy: major contemporary themes; post-Keynesian theory of choice

## Selected references

Davis, J.B. (1994) *Keynes's Philosophical Development*, Cambridge: Cambridge University Press.

Keynes, J.M. (1921) *A Treatise on Probability*, London: Macmillan, 1973.

—— (1936) *The General Theory of Employment, Interest and Money*, London: Macmillan, 1973.

—— (1937) "The General Theory of Employment," *Quarterly Journal of Economics* 51: 209–23; repr. in *The Collected Writings of John Maynard Keynes*, vol. 14, *The General Theory and After, Part II*, London: Macmillan, 1973, 109–23.

Knight, F.H. (1921) *Risk, Uncertainty and Profit*, Chicago: Chicago University Press.

Kyburg, H.E. (1995) "Keynes as a Philosopher," annual supplement to *History of Political Economy* 27: 7–32.

O'Donnell, R.M. (1989) *Keynes: Philosophy, Economics and Politics*, London: Macmillan.

Ramsey, F.P. (1926) "Truth and Probability," in R.B. Braithwaite (ed.), *The Foundations of Mathematics*, London: Routledge & Kegan Paul, 1931, 156–98.

Runde, J.H. (1990) "Keynesian Uncertainty and the Weight of Arguments," *Economics and Philosophy* 6: 275–92.

Savage, L.J. (1954) *The Foundations of Statistics*, New York: John Wiley.

Shackle, G.L.S. (1972) *Epistemics and Economics: A Critique of Economic Doctrines*, Cambridge: Cambridge University Press.

JOCHEN RUNDE

# unemployment: policies to reduce

The current orthodoxy amongst policy makers is that further deregulation is still the way to more jobs, and that there is no likely demand-side macroeconomic policy route to higher employment in the long run. The recommended cures which follow seem to be either to get the low skilled to accept low-paid jobs or to train them so they can compete more effectively for the high-paid ones. It is not obvious how such an increase in the supply of people willing and/or able to take jobs can affect the overall level of employment, unless there is an increase in demand for goods and services and hence an increase in the number of jobs available. Although it might be argued that either higher skills or lower pay will increase competitiveness, this is unlikely to do any more than reshuffle world employment unless there is a stimulation through macroeconomic policy (Michie and Grieve Smith 1995).

## Deflationary bias and employment costs

High levels of unemployment can rather be explained by the deflationary bias in macroeconomic policy since the mid-1970s (Michie and Wilkinson 1994). Even so, there can be little doubt that there is no easy route to full employment in most countries through demand management alone, because the effect of years of high unemployment has been to leave most economies with insufficient industrial capacity to fully employ the workforce (Michie and Grieve Smith 1996). Also, many economies are being balance-of-payments constrained (Kitson and Michie 1996).

The European Commission is currently considering two different but related policy programs for reducing indirect employment costs as a way of gaining INTERNATIONAL COMPETITIVENESS and reducing unemployment. First is the idea of a general reduction in the employment taxes and other charges which fall on employers for each worker employed. The argument is that such indirect costs (that is, in addition to the direct wage costs) are higher on average in the European Union than in the US or Japan, and that a reduction would allow a concomitant reduction in prices, boosting international competitiveness, world market shares, output and employment. However, there are a number of questions begged by this hoped-for virtuous circle. First, would the entire reduction in employment costs feed directly through into lower output prices, or might some go in higher profit margins? Alternatively, by reducing market pressure on the firms to pursue international competitiveness through PRODUCTIVITY gains and quality improvements, might these tax reductions be accompanied by lower gains in productivity than might otherwise have occurred, resulting in no net gain in unit costs?

Second, from where would the lost tax revenue be recouped? There are, of course, arguments against increasing income tax, VAT or any of the other possible candidates. If the lost revenue is not to be made good, then what would the implications be for the government budget deficits which are already greater than allowed by the convergence criteria of the Treaty on European Union (the "Maastricht Treaty") which requires fiscal deficits to be cut to under 3 percent of GNP. If the fall in employer taxes is to be matched by government spending cuts, then this could exacerbate the unemployment problem.

The second policy program for reducing indirect employment costs, being considered by the European Commission, is to reduce costs particularly on low-paid, low-skilled employment. The idea is to encourage the sort of employment creation witnessed in the US in the 1980s, through a combination of expanding the sectors of the economy in which such labor is employed, and encouraging the further substitution of labor for capital in such sectors. However, the idea that labor–capital substitution follows changes in relative prices does not, at that general level, enjoy any empirical (or indeed theoretical) support. More generally, the idea of differential cuts in indirect employment costs is a type of labor subsidy towards low wage and skill labor, and as such there are various associated dangers. First, there may be a disincentive to upgrade the productive system if this would involve the associated labor losing its subsidy. Second, there is the risk that the economy might be diverted towards the low-skill, low-investment sectors which are subsidized.

## Historical perspective

Much of the industrial world is in the grip of an unemployment crisis which bears some resemblance to the situation in the 1920s and 1930s. In the 1920s, the world economy was highly volatile with unprecedented stock market and currency speculation. Organized labor was on the retreat and wage cutting and labor market deregulation were the order of the day, especially in the USA and the UK. The consequent underconsumptionist tendencies were exacerbated by the collapse of commodity prices in the early 1920s, which benefited industrial profits but ruined agriculture. This unstable economic base collapsed in 1929 when the world financial system was completely disrupted by the Wall Street crash, and industry was undermined by the GREAT DEPRESSION against which national governments proved individually and collectively powerless.

Economic orthodoxy, then as now, held trade unions, state labor market regulation and social welfare payments responsible for unemployment, and preached balanced budgets; opposing state intervention to counter joblessness. When translated into policies these notions, by deepening the recession and multiplying social deprivation, had an effect opposite to that predicted; and the consequent widening of the credibility gap led to weak and vacillating governments. In Britain, the Labor Government split over policies which cut pay, reduced unemployment benefit levels and introduced means testing, policies which were insisted on by international bankers and finally implemented by the National Government led by Ramsay MacDonald. Germany had six million people unemployed. This, in association with widespread poverty and cuts in unemployment pay, paved the way for the rise of fascism and ultimately to the Second World War.

The lessons learned from this debacle, at the level of economic theory and public policy, laid the groundwork for postwar prosperity. National governments committed themselves to full employment and a WELFARE STATE policy which included expanded health, social security, education and housing spending. In the labor market, collective bargaining was encouraged, minimum employment rights guaranteed and industrial training strengthened. At the international level, agreements on finance and trade were concluded which were designed to encourage international commerce, but which were targeted at currency SPECULATION and the problems of chronic surplus countries. These were reinforced at the national level by controls on international capital movements. Contingency plans were made for the stabilization of commodity prices, but these made little headway after the end of the Korean War crisis when the collapse of raw material prices turned the terms of trade in favor of industrial countries. The purpose of these policies was to create a framework of rules for encouraging free enterprise creativity whilst prohibiting the strong predatory and exploitative tendencies in CAPITALISM.

This national and international collectivist effort created the promise that for some small proportion of the world's working class, poverty would at last be eliminated. This promise was most fully realized in those countries of Northern Europe which most completely adopted the cooperative state model. A classic example was Sweden, where the Social Democratic Party embraced "wage solidarity," with "active labor market" policies formulated by trade unions so that labor effectively managed capitalism (see SOCIAL DEMOCRACY).

The real failure of the postwar period was at the international level. This can be explained by the dominant economic power of the USA, and that country's continued adherence to the notion that capitalism operates at its best when completely unrestricted. This philosophy came to pervade the workings of the international agencies (the IMF, World Bank and GATT), and subverted their role as agents working for world economic stability. The cost to the USA itself was great. Its own unrestricted capital moved the production base of the US economy offshore and came increasingly to be dominated more by short term speculation on the stock market than long term industrial investment. This, and the fact that the degenerating industrial relations and labor market conditions in the USA made it incapable of meeting the quality competition from abroad, undermined American competitiveness so that it joined the UK as a newly deindustrializing economy.

## Pre-Keynesian orthodoxy

A lack of any effective stabilizing international

institutions, and the progressive decline in the economic power of the USA, played a major part in recreating the sort of financial and trade volatility last seen in the interwar years. This undermined the ability of national governments to exercise control and destroyed the credibility of the policies which formed the basis for postwar economic prosperity. The return to pre-Keynesian orthodoxy in macro-economic management completed the circle. Restrictive monetary policies, intensified competition for shares in markets which were growing more slowly than productive potential, and unrestricted currency speculation interacted to recreate world recession.

Unemployment today is not therefore the result of the working of mystical economic laws regulating wages. There is no substance to the claim that if the worst off in society accept a cut in their living standards, long term prospects would be magically restored; the opposite is more likely to be the case. Both private need and public squalor are on the increase. The physical environment needs to be improved; more work should go into education, health and public services generally; housing and other infrastructure work would in almost all countries be welcome. The problem is not a shortage of things which need doing. It is a shortage of political will to do them (Glyn and Rowthorn 1994; Kitson et al. 1997a, 1997b).

## See also:

business cycle theories; cost of job loss; economic rationalism or liberalism; effective demand and capacity utilization; fiscal policy; human capital; long waves of economic growth and development; monetary policy and central banking functions; reserve army of labor; state and government; unemployment and underemployment

## Selected references

Glyn, A. and Rowthorn, B. (1994) "European Employment Policies," in J. Michie and J.

Grieve Smith (eds), *Unemployment in Europe*, London: Academic Press, ch. 12.

Kitson, M. and Michie, J. (1996) "Britain's Industrial Performance since 1960: Underinvestment and Relative Decline," *Economic Journal* 106: 196–212.

Kitson, M., Michie, J. and Sutherland, H. (1997a) "The Fiscal and Distributional Implications of Job Generation," *Cambridge Journal of Economics* 21(1): 103–20.

—— (1997b) "'A Price Well Worth Paying'? The Benefits of a Full Employment Strategy," in J. Michie and J. Grieve Smith (eds), *Employment and Economic Performance*, Oxford: Oxford University Press.

Michie, J. and Grieve Smith, J. (eds) (1995) *Managing the Global Economy*, Oxford: Oxford University Press.

—— (eds) (1996) *Creating Industrial Capacity: Towards Full Employment*, Oxford: Oxford University Press.

Michie, J. and Wilkinson, F. (1994) "The Growth of Unemployment in the 1980s," in J. Michie and J. Grieve Smith (eds), *Unemployment in Europe*, London: Academic Press.

JONATHAN MICHIE

# unemployment and underemployment

## Basic issues

Unemployment refers to the state of being part of the labor force, looking for work and without a job. The stock of measured unemployment can be defined in any given period as the product of three factors. The first factor is the incidence of unemployment, or the proportion of those in the labor force experiencing unemployment spells. The second factor is the frequency of unemployment as measured by the average number of spells of the unemployed. The third is the duration or average length of these spells.

Except for exclusions due to social norms regarding working age, statistical conventions by which unemployment is measured do not account for workers in a state of underemployment. For instance, no adjustments are normally made to the official measures of unemployment to take account of workers employed below their productive potential because they hold jobs which do not make adequate use of their labor market skills and/or which offer fewer hours of employment than desired on a regular basis. Potential labor market participants may also have given up job search on the expectation that no job is available. These pools of discouraged workers constitute an additional category of underemployed that are excluded from official measures of unemployment by virtue of job search inactivity.

In 1995, measured unemployment for the OECD countries totaled over 33 million, with a growing proportion experiencing longer term unemployment. An additional 15 million workers held involuntary part-time work, of which women constituted over two-thirds. Finally, approximately 4 million were also directly estimated as discouraged workers, with the largest incidence of this phenomenon affecting prime-age males (OECD 1995: 43–96).

Various types of unemployment have been discussed over the postwar period, both in terms of their characteristics and their underlying causal mechanisms. Seasonal unemployment has received little attention in recent years, with the declining proportion of workers employed in seasonal industries such as agriculture, and with new technologies allowing for winter operations in other seasonal industries such as construction. Frictional unemployment is considered a short-term phenomenon, resulting from labor turnover in the presence of search costs. Structural unemployment continues to be the subject of much debate, regarding underlying causes and policy remedies. It differs from the frictional type as a matter of degree, entailing longer spells of unemployment, greater search and mobility costs and the eventual reallocation of labor across industries, occupations and regions. It is also characterized in terms of mismatch between skills required and those supplied in the workforce. Cyclical unemployment arises due to the deficiency of aggregate demand and as such has been at the center of the controversy between (post) Keynesian and new classical macroeconomics.

It is generally recognized, however, that these various types of unemployment are not watertight compartments analytically, because both frictional and structural unemployment are not independent of cyclical demand factors. Expanding these unemployment concepts to incorporate the underemployment dimension would further heighten the importance of cyclical factors. Indeed, it is well known that both the proportion of involuntary part-time employment and the number of discouraged workers (or hidden unemployed) generally move in tandem with official measures of the unemployment rate. All this points to the significance of aggregate demand considerations in affecting various measures of labor under-utilization.

## Neoclassical conception

The neoclassical conception of labor markets has generally sought to minimize the importance of unemployment, particularly involuntary unemployment arising from aggregate demand deficiencies. It focuses, instead, on the market-clearing function of wage flexibility. It posits that the substitutability of labor and capital, combined with flexible wages and interest rates, is sufficient to preclude any involuntary unemployment other than that of a transitory nature. The rationale is that firms can choose among a wide range of technologies consisting of alternative combinations of labor and capital, thereby ensuring that firms will substitute labor for capital in the presence of excess labor supply and an equilibrating reduction in real wages. In this context, involuntary unemployment is attributed to a failure of the real wage to adjust to its competitive equilibrium value, be it due to workers' wage bargaining power or to statutory impediments such as minimum wage rates. Any unemployment over and above the level of

involuntary unemployment is treated as voluntary in that it is assumed to be the product of individual choice.

## Keynes and Kalecki on unemployment

In the *General Theory*, KEYNES rejected the neoclassical view of a self-regulating, equilibrating labor market. He showed that involuntary unemployment did not hinge on real wage inflexibility and that it would persist even if real wages were to fall via "a small rise in the price of wage-goods relatively to the money-wage," for the "aggregate supply of labor willing to work for the current money-wage...would be greater than the existing volume of employment" (Keynes 1936: 15). As was also emphasized by KALECKI at the time, this is because both the real wage and the level of employment were assumed to be largely dependent on conditions in the product market. In Chapter 19 of the *General Theory*, Keynes further elaborated his concern and argued that a policy of wage flexibility would exacerbate unemployment through a negative feedback on aggregate EFFECTIVE DEMAND AND CAPACITY UTILIZATION.

One of Keynes's achievements was in explaining why full employment can be attained primarily through long-term aggregate demand management and policies of income redistribution away from rentier income (see FISCAL POLICY; MONETARY POLICY AND CENTRAL BANKING FUNCTIONS). However, the postwar neoclassical synthesis came to rest on the erroneous interpretation of involuntary unemployment in terms of wage inflexibility due to workers' money illusion. The upshot was a distorted picture of the determinants of Keynesian involuntary unemployment, and it was only in post-Keynesian political economy and especially among followers of Kalecki that Keynes's explanation remained intact. While acknowledging the ability of governments to counteract the vagaries of cyclical unemployment, Kalecki, however, pointed to the incapacity of capitalist economies to maintain permanent full employment. This incapacity was due to two factors. The first is due to the inherent stagnationist tendencies of MONOPOLY CAPITALISM later emphasized by Steindl. And the second is related to socioeconomic factors: a coalition of business and rentier interests would act to preserve a normal long-term rate of unemployment well above the full employment level.

## Postwar neoclassical perspectives

The postwar revival of the neoclassical labor market construct was first marked by Friedman's (1968) natural rate of unemployment. The natural rate was defined as "the level that would be ground out by the Walrasian system of general equilibrium equations, provided there is imbedded in them the actual structural characteristics of the labor and commodity markets, including market imperfections, [and]...costs of gathering information..." (Friedman 1968: 8). While similar in its steady state nature to Kalecki's long-term "normal" rate of unemployment, Friedman's concept precluded equilibria with involuntary unemployment. It did not allow for cyclical or demand-deficient unemployment, other than in the form of temporary deviations of actual unemployment from the natural rate of unemployment. In this framework, Keynesian aggregate demand policies could only achieve temporary reductions in unemployment.

New classical macroeconomics ruled out even temporary bouts of involuntary unemployment. Under the twin assumptions of rational expectations and perfect information, it posited that money wages will always be set, given the expected rate of inflation, to achieve market-clearing real wages. Only unanticipated inflation can lead to non-market clearing real wages, but this is not a relevant outcome because the twin assumptions preclude systematic expectational errors. Moreover, rational agents will also learn to anticipate the effects of any systematic rule to expand aggregate demand, thereby ruling out any impact on employment and output, according to the policy impotence result first put forth by Sargent and Wallace. However, once informational imperfections are introduced into these models, the role of aggregate demand policies is restored even while retaining the full force of the rational expectations assumption.

Other strands of equilibrium macroeconomics have been equally pernicious in denying the existence of persistent involuntary unemployment. The seminal paper by Lucas and Rapping in 1969 sought to explain observed fluctuations in unemployment using a model with market-clearing prices, where workers are always on their labor supply curve. Employment varies due to shifts in the labor supply curve, caused by intertemporal substitution of labor supply in response to temporary actual or perceived fluctuations in the real wage. These models have developed into their current form based on real business cycle theory, which ignores monetary factors and generates employment fluctuations through technology shocks. However, these models require very high labor supply elasticities to generate employment fluctuations – a feature inconsistent with the results of microeconometric studies (Killingsworth 1983).

The new classical work that has come closest to explaining unemployment is that of David Lilien, which posited in 1982 that technical change may vary over time, implying variations in the desirable level of interfirm and interindustry mobility of labor and, hence, variations in unemployment as workers seek out new jobs. The novelty of this labor reallocation view lies in identifying interindustry dispersion of employment growth rates as the cause of variations in aggregate unemployment. All factors or policies which discourage labor mobility (for example, skill mismatch, income security) are deemed to contribute to the natural rate of unemployment. However, this theory has been severely criticized on empirical grounds for mistaking cyclical unemployment for structural unemployment (Osberg 1988). Not surprisingly, there is no role here for involuntary unemployment or activist aggregate demand policies.

The emergence of New Keynesian models in the last decade has restored the view that fluctuations in aggregate demand can have considerable effects on employment. This was accomplished through models where firms have small fixed costs of changing nominal prices or nominal wages, thereby generating significant non-neutralities of money. Efficiency wage models have tried to explain why labor markets do not clear by examining informational imperfections and social institutions specific to labor markets. Whether these models are based on issues of adverse selection, effort elicitation, or fairness considerations, the general insight is that wages cannot clear the market when achieving multiple objectives (for example, labor allocation as well as retaining the most able workers, eliminating shirking, reducing turnover costs) (Solow 1990). One objection to these models is that there exist other instruments such as entrance fees, or employment contracts incorporating other bonding mechanisms, which would eliminate the need for wage premiums as an incentive device. However, the more serious problem with the New Keynesian and efficiency wage models is that they have so far contributed little to explaining the changes in unemployment observed in the last few decades. The same can be said of insider–outsider models (see Bean 1994).

### Hysteresis models

Perhaps the most promising avenue for explaining the persistence of high levels of involuntary unemployment are HYSTERESIS models, which explain that changes in aggregate demand can have a permanent impact on the unemployment rate through mechanisms such as skill deterioration among the long-term unemployed. It follows that an expansionary demand policy in the presence of hysteresis effects reduces not just the current unemployment rate but also contributes to a lower "natural" rate of unemployment, thereby debunking the steady-state properties long associated with such equilibrium concepts (Hargreaves-Heap 1980). As Galbraith (1997: 101) points out, if estimates of the natural rate track the actual rate of unemployment, albeit sluggishly, why not ditch the former?

### See also:

business cycle theories; cyclical crisis models; long waves of economic growth and development; regulation approach; reserve army of labor; social structures of accumulation; unemployment: policies to reduce

### Selected references

Bean, C. (1994) "European Unemployment: A Survey," *Journal of Economic Literature* 32.
Friedman, M. (1968) "The Role of Monetary Policy," *American Economic Review* 58.
Galbraith, James K. (1997) "Time to Ditch the NAIRU," *Journal of Economic Perspectives* 11.
Hargreaves-Heap, S.P. (1980) "Choosing the Wrong 'Natural' Rate: Accelerating Inflation or Decelerating Employment and Growth?," *Economic Journal* 90.
Keynes, J.M. (1936) *The General Theory of Employment, Interest and Money*, repr. in *The Collected Writings of John Maynard Keynes*, vol. 7, London: Macmillan, 1971.
Killingsworth, M. (1983) *Labor Supply*, Cambridge: Cambridge University Press.
OECD (1995) *Employment Outlook*, Paris: OECD.
Osberg, L. (1988) "The 'Disappearance' of Involuntary Unemployment," *Journal of Economic Issues* 22.
Solow, R.M. (1990) *The Labor Market as a Social Institution*, Oxford: Basil Blackwell.

MARIO IACOBACCI
MARIO SECCARECCIA

UNEQUAL EXCHANGE: *see* comparative advantage and unequal exchange

# uneven development

### Introduction

A useful summary of the process of uneven development, as a necessary aspect of CAPIT-

ALISM, comes from Volume 1 of Marx's *Das Kapital*. Here he states that a major contradiction of capitalism is the simultaneous emergence of concentrations of wealth and capital (for capitalists) on the one hand, and poverty and oppression (for workers) on the other. This "general law of capitalist accumulation," as Marx termed it, highlights capital--labor conflict, and is one way to ground a theory of uneven development. But thinking about uneven and combined development dates further back, at least to Marx's *Grundrisse* (1857-8), where unevenness represents the condition for a transition from one declining MODE OF PRODUCTION AND SOCIAL FORMATION to another rising, more progressive mode. In general terms, then, uneven development can relate to differential growth of sectors, geographical processes, classes and regions at the global, regional, national, subnational and local level.

The differing conceptual emphases are paralleled by debate surrounding the origins and socioeconomic mechanisms of unevenness. Neil Smith (1990: ch. 3) rooted the equalization and differentiation of capital – the fundamental motions of uneven development – in the widespread emergence of the DIVISION OF LABOR. But Ernest Mandel (1962: 210) searched even further back, to "private production" among different producers within the same community; insisting that "differences of aptitude between individuals, the differences of fertility between animals or soils, innumerable accidents of human life or the cycle of nature," were responsible for uneven development in production.

## Political implications

However, it is less the definitional roots of the concept, and more its political implications and contemporary intellectual applications, for which uneven development is known. Leon Trotsky's theory of combined and uneven development – established in his book *Results and Prospects* in 1905 – served as an analytical foundation for "permanent revolution." Given the backward state of Russian society in the early twentieth century, due to structured unevenness, both bourgeois (plus nationalist or anti-colonial) and proletarian revolutions could and must be telescoped into a seamless process, led by the working CLASS (see Howard and King 1989).

In more measured, less immediately political terms, the debate was revived when Marxist social science regenerated during the 1970s. Here the phenomenon of uneven and combined development in specific (peripheral or semi-peripheral) settings was explained as a process of "articulations of modes of production." In these debates, the capitalist mode of production depends upon earlier modes of production for an additional "superexploitative" subsidy by virtue of reducing the costs of labor power reproduction (Wolpe 1980), even if this did not represent a revolutionary or even transitional moment. Smith (1990: 141, 156) insists, however, that "it is the logic of uneven development which structures the context for this articulation," rather than the reverse.

That logic entails not only the differential (or "disarticulated") production and consumption of durable goods along class lines (de Janvry 1982). It also embraces the disproportionalities (Hilferding 1910) that emerge between departments of production, especially between capital goods and consumer goods, and between circuits and fractions of capital (see CIRCUIT OF SOCIAL CAPITAL). For example, the rise of financial markets during periods of capitalist overproduction crisis amplify unevenness (Bond 1998: ch. 1). Or, as Aglietta remarks: "Uneven development creates artificial differences in the apparent financial results of firms, which are realized only on credit. These differences favor speculative gains on the financial market" (1974: 359). Tendencies towards sectoral unevenness are manifest periodically in financial crisis.

In spatial terms, unevenness has been associated with theories of unequal exchange and forms of core–periphery dominance. This is in part because of their grounding in progressive Third World nationalism. Such debates have had the effect of overemphasizing interstate relations and underemphasizing the flows of capital and social struggles that have more decisively shaped local "underdevelopment."

But as David Harvey (1996: 295) has argued, historical-geographical materialism entails a consideration of the process of unevenness in more general ways. The fulcrum of geographical unevenness is the differentiated return on investment that creation and/or destruction of entire built environments – and the social structures that accompany them – offer to different kinds of investors with different time horizons. Meanwhile, different places compete endlessly with one another to attract investment. In the process they tend to amplify unevenness, allowing capital to play one local or regional or national class configuration off against others.

## Conclusion

Comprehending the uneven development of sector, space and scale is ambitious enough. But there must be, as well, future opportunities to explore systematic unevenness in spheres as diverse as the production and destruction of the environment, social reproduction, and human domination along lines of class, gender and race/ethnicity. Can the theory of uneven development move from political economy through politics and culture, all the while stressing the social damage associated with uneven capitalist development? If so, uneven development analysis should inform activists intent on reversing unevenness, not because – as Smith points out – "our goal is some rigidly conceived 'even development.' This would make little sense. Rather, the goal is to create socially determined patterns of differentiation and equalization which are driven not by the logic of capital but genuine social choice" (1990: 159).

## See also:

business cycle theories; comparative advantage and unequal exchange; development and underdevelopment: definitions; development political economy: major contemporary themes; distribution of income; environmental and ecological political economy: major contemporary themes; hegemony in the world economy; urban and regional political economy: major contemporary themes

## Selected references

Aglietta, Michel (1974) *A Theory of Capitalist Regulation*, London: New Left Books, 1979.

Bond, Patrick (1998) *Uneven Zimbabwe: A Study of Finance, Development and Underdevelopment*, Trenton: Africa World Press and Harare: University of Zimbabwe Press.

de Janvry, Alain (1982) *The Agrarian Question and Reformism in Latin America*, Baltimore, MD: Johns Hopkins University Press.

Harvey, David (1996) *Justice, Nature and the Geography of Difference*, Oxford: Basil Blackwell.

Hilferding, Rudolf (1910) *Finance Capital*, London: Routledge & Kegan Paul, 1981.

Howard, Michael and King, John (1989) *A History of Marxian Economics*, vol. 1, Princeton, NJ: Princeton University Press.

Mandel, Ernest (1962) *Marxist Economic Theory*, vol. 1, London: Merlin Press, 1968.

Smith, Neil (1990) *Uneven Development*, 2nd edn, Oxford: Basil Blackwell.

Wolpe, Harold (ed.) (1980) *The Articulations of Modes of Production*, London: Routledge & Kegan Paul.

PATRICK BOND

# Union for Radical Political Economics

The Union for Radical Political Economics (URPE) was founded in mid-1968, when graduate students and faculty from Michigan, Harvard, Radcliffe College, Berkeley, Columbia, and others held a working meeting in Ann Arbor just a few weeks before the National Democratic Party Convention in Chicago. Some of the early active members included Sam Bowles, Marilyn Power, Barry Bluestone, Lourdes Beneria, Gene Coyle, Herb Gintis,

Paddi Quick, Arthur MacEwen, John Pool, Michael Reich, Laurie Nisonoff, Tom Weiss-kopf and Howard Wachtel. URPE's core purpose was and is to be an alternative professional organization for left political economists and an intellectual home for academics, policy makers and activists who are interested in participating in a left intellectual debate on theoretical and policy issues.

## Objectives and activities

The prospectus of URPE, developed in the first few weeks of its inception, included the following objectives (URPE 1968). First, to promote a new interdisciplinary approach to political economy, which includes also relevant themes from political science, sociology and social psychology. Second, to develop new courses and research areas which reflect the urgencies of the day and a new value premise. Such areas include the economics of the ghetto, poverty, imperialism, interest groups, and the military-industry complex. And third, political economics should be sensitive to the needs of the social movements of our day, and have more group research, with an approach that links issues to a broad framework.

The organization opposes all exploitation on the basis of class, race, gender, ethnicity, sexual orientation and other social/economic/cultural constructs. URPE presents constructive critical analyses of the capitalist system and supports debate and discussion on alternative left visions of a socialist society. URPE was founded by activist-oriented individuals who realized the need for coherent strategy and theory. It has often experienced a tension between theory and activism. Those interested in theory see URPE as an intellectual community to discuss and develop research in left political economy. Those interested in activism see URPE as an organization that can be a proactive resource for non-economists to understand economic issues from a left perspective. Organizational efforts to wed these divergent views has focused on the preparation and dissemination of publications and other activities that present alternative left visions of economic analysis.

URPE's main activities include publications, annual meetings, and associated projects. The publications include a journal which is published four times a year, special education projects, and a newsletter. The journal is called the *Review of Radical Political Economics*, and is run by an elected editorial board and a managing editor. Many special issues of *RRPE* have emerged, including five on the political economy of women. Over the years, URPE has published a number of special projects in book form, such as *U.S. Capitalism in Crisis* (1978); two volumes on *The Imperiled Economy* (one on micro and macro, respectively) (1987, 1988); and volumes on political economy courses and readings. The *URPE Newsletter* is also published quarterly and includes news of the organization and short articles on current topics from members. The most prolific period of publication activity was the 1970s, when URPE was organized in research collectives, and published the results of this research in the areas of, for instance, food policy, energy, public sector spending and women's issues. The URPE home page on the World Wide Web includes information on the journal and on activities in the organization (organized by Eric Nilsson in 1995).

There are two main annual meetings of URPE. First there is the academic conference held in January of each year in a prominent US city, as part of the Allied Social Science Association (ASSA). In this forum, URPE members present papers in a collegial environment (usually about thirty URPE sessions are held), and socialize at dinners and other gatherings. Second, there is the annual summer camp conference, where both academics and activists informally participate in discussions, classes, work-in-progress, networking and social activities. Topics are chosen to reflect relevant policy debates in the news, as well as other themes.

Research groups have been active in URPE, including the Political Education and Action Project and the Economics Education Project. The Women's Caucus was formed in 1971 to protest the white male domination in the organization that tended to mute women's and feminists' voices. Members of this caucus fought to ensure representation by white women and people of color on both the URPE steering committee and the *RRPE* editorial board. The Gay, Lesbian and Bi-Sexual Caucus was formed in the early 1980s, and has actively participated in sponsoring workshops and panels on issues such as sexuality, family policy and AIDS, as well as presented the concerns of gays, lesbians and bisexuals to the organization as a whole. Also, the Third World Caucus was founded in the late 1980s, in order to bring a representative voice of people of color and from countries of the South into the organization and onto the Steering Committee.

## Organization, linkages and influence

The struggle within the organization for representation and participation in the radical debate not only led to a greater heterodoxy of views in the organization, but has also re-inforced a non-hierarchical structure. URPE has attempted to maintain a broad community of left academics and intellectuals among its membership, despite individuals' diverse political and theoretical perspectives. Through overlapping membership and similar goals, URPE has connections with other left political economy organizations. These include, for instance, an exchange of information and ideas with the Conference of Socialist Economists in the United Kingdom (which publishes the journal *Capital and Class*); sponsorship of the magazine *Dollars and Sense* when it first began in the mid-1970s; and help in the organization of the Committee for the Status of Women in the Economics Profession. Serious efforts are made to keep the journal, *RRPE*, accessible to low-income students and the unemployed with a multi-tier system of subscription rates and a special membership rate without a journal subscription. URPE membership has always run the whole gambit of heterodox schools of thought, from neo-Marxist to institutional, to post-Keynesianism, feminism and social economists (although Marxism has been dominant, especially in the earlier years).

URPE's influence in the economics profession is concentrated in the USA, although the journal and conference meetings have an international showing. The period of greatest prominence ranged from its inception through the 1970s, at a time when graduate and under-graduate students were clamoring for alternative, left, and Marxian teachings in an atmosphere of broader social change in the United States. The organization served as a recruitment center for many universities and colleges that were searching for academics in political economy to fulfill the demands of their students. In the late 1980s and 1990s, however, reduced interest in Marxian economics and radical economics; an increased number of interdisciplinary programs that incorporate radical social theory; an escalation in the number of other political economy organizations and journals; and a rise in the significance of conservative political economy, have reduced the importance of URPE in the political economy debate among academics. The shrinking space for radical political economists' voices in the public debate makes the existence of an organization like URPE as important as previously, but more difficult as well.

Perhaps the most promising development for radical political economy has been increasing linkages between the schools of thought. Many members of URPE have been active in the commencement of new organizations and journals. For instance, the International Confederation of Associations for the Reform of Economics (ICARE) seeks to build bridges between the various strands of heterodoxy. Some members of URPE became active in the formation of the Association for Social and Economic Analysis (which publishes the journal *Rethinking Marxism*), and the International Association for Feminist Economics (which publishes *Feminist Economics*). Also, in the 1990s, URPE has a stronger membership base among post Keynesian economists and institutionalists. On the Internet, and at conferences, there are stronger links between the schools of radical or heterodox economics. And many more publishers are active in soliciting manuscripts in political economy.

Some of these activities negatively impact on URPE, but at the same time emanate to some degree from the very successes of URPE in helping to revive political economy in the late 1900s into the next century.

## Selected references

Attewell, Paul A. (1984) *Radical Political Economy Since the Sixties: A Sociology of Knowledge Analysis*, New Brunswick, NJ: Rutgers University Press.

Cherry, R., D'Onofrio, C., Kurdas, C., Michl, T., Mosley, F. and Naples, M. (eds) (1987) *The Imperiled Economy: Macroeconomics from a Left Perspective*, New York: Union for Radical Political Economics.

—— (eds) (1988) *The Imperiled Economy: Through the Safety Net*, New York: Union for Radical Political Economics.

O'Hara, Phillip Anthony (1995) "The Association for Evolutionary Economists and the Union for Radical Political Economics: General Issues of Continuity and Integration," *Journal of Economic Issues* 29(1): 137–59.

Steinberg, B. *et al. (Editorial Collective)* (1978) *U.S. Capitalism in Crisis*, New York: Economics Education Project of the Union for Radical Political Economics.

Union for Radical Political Economics (1968) "The Union for Radical Political Economics: A Prospectus," *Conference Papers of the Union for Radical Political Economics*, Ann Arbor, MI: URPE, December.

SUSAN FLECK

# unions

## Definition, rights and ideology

Despite the passage of a century which has seen massive variations in the role and fortunes of trade unions, the definition provided by Sidney and Beatrice Webb back in 1894 remains satisfactory. A trade union is "a continuous association of wage earners for the purpose of maintaining or improving the conditions of their working lives." It applies to any sustained attempt by employees to organize themselves in order to regulate or otherwise influence their contractual relationships with their employers.

Their right to do so is widely acknowledged, in principle, as a necessary condition of a democratic society. All major industrialized countries are publicly committed to the International Labor Organization's Convention 98 of 1949 which upholds rights for trade unions to organize, requiring them to be financially independent of both employers and other non-union organizations, such as political parties. The reality of trade unionism is far more controversial. From their earliest stirrings before the Industrial Revolution, trade unions have provoked bitter debate about their purposes, their conduct, and their economic and social consequences. These debates will now be outlined in turn.

All manner of political and social movements have attributed purposes to trade unions in order to enlist them to their cause. At the start of the twentieth century, syndicalists argued that the route to the true socialism of workers' control would not be achieved through conventional political means but by trade unions' strategic use of industrial action. MARX had ascribed to trade unions the double purpose of, first, reducing divisions within the working classes so that, second, they could challenge the capitalist class. A more cynical view of motives caused Lenin to warn that trade union leaders could be captured by the CAPITALISM with which they necessarily compromised. Only the presence of a separate communist party could prevent their settling for mere reformism.

Reform, rather than revolution, has been the central purpose of trade unionism for many Christian activists, who saw trade unions to be vital to the improvement of industrial working and living conditions. Trade unions were important to strands of Protestant thinking which espoused socialism and worker cooperation. A tradition of social Catholicism, reinforced by papal encyclicals in 1891 and 1981, upheld the view that capital and labor are not naturally hostile, and that trade unionism is a force for social order. A brutal parody of this has been manifest in many totalitarian regimes of the mid-twentieth century, defining the role of trade unions as one of maximizing production, and firmly subordinating them to the state. For all these disparate movements, trade unions have been seen as providing unique access to the mass of working people and, for the more extreme, to the potent weapon of the strike (Martin 1989).

## Objectives, functions and activities

Stripped of ideological rhetoric, trade unions are most fruitfully conceived in a pluralist framework, as pressure groups alongside other pressure groups in a society where conflicts of interest are endemic, and where success comes through the pursuit of negotiable compromise rather than outright victory. The Webbs observed how unions pursued their objectives through three distinct sorts of activity. The first was mutual assurance, aiding their members as friendly societies. The second was political action, aimed at encouraging the state to introduce laws and regulations to protect the interests of working people. The third was collective bargaining, dealing directly with employers in order to regulate the conduct and terms of work.

These three means of "maintaining or improving the conditions of their [members'] working lives" have experienced fluctuating fortunes. Mutual assurance, while still a feature of unions in developing countries with limited public services, was largely eclipsed elsewhere, partially through the success of political action. Such action can claim substantial achievements in most developed countries. But it generally depends upon a close collaboration with political parties which, in most mature democracies, has weakened as confrontational approaches to capitalism have declined. Collective bargaining is now the dominant function of trade unions although its future, as we shall see, is far from assured.

The Webbs conceived of collective bargain-ing as an essentially economic activity, in which workers substitute a group negotiation for individual bargains (see INDUSTRIAL RELATIONS). Subsequent theorists have embraced a much broader political conception which encompasses any involvement of unions in the management of the employment relationship. For Flanders (1975) trade unions were involved in rule making: the conclusion of a collective bargain does not bind anyone to buy or sell any labor, but rather sets out the terms and conditions that apply when a worker is employed.

The success that a trade union can achieve in collective bargaining depends in large part upon the pressure it can bring to bear upon its members' employers. The strategy adopted for this had fundamental implications for its structure. For traditional craft unions and for many professional associations, the main objective was to control labor supply by regulating the definition of occupational competence and the numbers of trainees. Other unions which could not achieve this tried to win comprehensive coverage of an occupation in order to achieve monopoly power in the labor market. Another strategy that became important later was to try to organize a whole industry in order to cover all the employers within a given product market; there being no benefit in extracting a favorable settlement from just one firm if it thereby became uncompetitive and closed down. Western Europe in the mid-twentieth century, the period when trade unions were most secure, was characterized by national, industry-wide collective agreements through which employers' associations and trade unions effectively shared the rents that they could extract from national product markets.

Such strategies are confounded by rapid technical change, increased geographical mobility, and the massive increase in international competition that they have unleashed. Controlling a particular skill is increasingly as forlorn an objective for a union as controlling a product market is for an employers' association. International competition is peculiarly damaging to unions because they have been effectively incapable of mobilizing international collective action. Solidarity stops at the frontier. Employers are increasingly responding to international competition by weakening or abandoning industry-wide agreements in favor of enterprise-based bargaining, usually at the level of sub-units of the enterprise. In countries where legislative structures provide little union security, the response of employers to competitive pressure is often to withdraw recognition from trade unions altogether. For much of employment in most countries, the century is ending with unions' having to accept an increasingly compliant, consultative, enterprise-based role if they are to survive at all (Kochan *et al.* 1986).

## Economic effects

The economic effects of trade unions have long been a source of controversy. There is ample evidence that they generally achieve an improvement in their members' wages and do much to protect their terms and conditions of employment. But by so doing, their critics argue, unions act against the public interest because they force up wage costs and reduce managerial discretion to use labor flexibly and to introduce new technology. This, the counter-argument goes, is a short-term view. Freeman and Medoff (1984) are among those who have demonstrated that employers unchallenged by trade unions tend to manage labor poorly and to rely more than would otherwise be the case on labor-intensive techniques. They tend to react more slowly to sources of employee discontent, lacking the advantages of an articulate representative structure. It is certainly possible to manage labor humanely and efficiently without trade unions, through the use of what are generically termed "human resource management" techniques. But the evidence suggests that firms that are unchallenged by unions are less likely to do so, and that they find it more difficult to sustain a relationship of trust when sharpened competition calls for job losses.

## Future of unions

In so far as trade unions have a future, it is likely to be more consultative and less combative than in the past. Many would argue that it is important that they do have a future, and that they have a key role in the democratic framework from the nation down to the workplace. It should be recalled that the victorious Allies after the Second World War placed a high priority on the installation of a robust trade union movement in the defeated countries as a defence against future totalitarian regimes. At the level of the firm, a structure of employee representation is widely seen to be an important means of helping employees to adapt to changing circumstances. However difficult the intensification of competition makes the role of trade unions, they are likely to continue to be valued as a source of industrial democracy.

## See also:

efficiency wages; health and safety in the workplace; internal labor markets; labor markets and market power; wage determination; work, labor and production: major contemporary themes

## Selected references

Flanders, A. (1975) *Management and Unions*, London: Faber.

Freeman, R.B. and Medoff, J.L. (1984) *What Do Unions Do?* New York: Basic Books.

Kochan, T.A., Katz, H.C. and McKersie, R.B. (1986) *The Transformation of American Industrial Relations*, New York: Basic Books.

Martin, R.M. (1989) *Trade Unionism: Purposes and Forms*, Oxford: Clarendon Press.

Webb, S. and Webb, B. (1894) *History of Trade Unionism*, London: Longmans.

WILLIAM BROWN

# urban and regional political economy: history

Competing currents in the analysis of urban and regional development have mirrored the major schools of thought in the discipline of economics. Applications based on NEOCLASSICAL ECONOMICS vie with contributions of a more institutional or Marxian character. The situation has been made more complicated by the influence of other disciplines in what is essentially an interdisciplinary area of inquiry. However, to the extent that there is a distinctive economic analysis of urban and regional issues, it has reflected the general state of that discipline. Thus, the dominant paradigm throughout most of the twentieth century has been applied neoclassical economics, using the familiar apparatus of marginal analysis to analyze locational choices and the functioning of urban land, labor and property markets. Dissident voices have been increasingly heard, particularly in the last three decades, leading to an alternative political economy of cities and regions, drawing particularly on Marxian and institutional political economy and forming a radical challenge to orthodoxy (see, for example, the survey by Stilwell 1992).

## Urban and regional economics

The foundations of the subject were laid in the nineteenth century by von Thunen in some eminently practical concerns with the allocation of agricultural land. Here was the parallel with the more general concerns of David Ricardo about the use of land and its role as a source of surplus payments. Alfred Weber, brother of the more famous sociologist Max, then developed a more general theory of the least-cost location of business enterprises, paving the way for subsequent analysts to develop a neoclassical focus on transport costs, location choice and allocative efficiency. Pushed along by US economists Hoover and Isard, this culminated in the elegant but pedestrian synthesis by Greenhut (1970), showing the optimum location conditions for profit maximization by individual firms. This narrow interpretation of how a spatial dimension can be injected into economic analysis provided one of the principal targets for political-economic critics, paralleling the more general critique of the neoclassical theory of the firm as a hopelessly inadequate starting point for analyzing modern corporations (Massey 1973).

Alongside these applications of neoclassical economics, a quite different school of thought had developed in urban sociology, albeit with characteristically similar political implications. The Chicago school of "urban ecologists" sought to model urban development in terms of biological analogies having their origins in the work of Charles Darwin. The focus on evolutionary change (e.g. resulting from rural–urban migration and subsequent processes of socioeconomic adaptation) ties into the analytical orientation of institutional political economy, but the political implications of the Chicago school were more in sympathy with a laissez-faire approach, natural selection and survival of the fittest. Notwithstanding the useful contribution of urban ecology in stimulating a wealth of empirical research on the socioeconomic structure of cities, this too came to be a particular target for critique by radicals seeking an alternative means of analyzing capitalist cities (for example, Castells 1976).

Alongside these influences, regional economic analysis had also been shaped by policy-oriented concerns. Formulating systematic regional policies requires a measure of the impact of an expenditure injection on a regional economy. Similarly, regional policy practitioners need to know how much stimulus to regional growth is likely to result from the development of a particular set of industries. Such policy-oriented concerns led to the widespread application of a distinctive set of quantitative tools, such as:

- regional input–output analysis, applying the Liontieff methodology at the regional rather than national scale;
- shift-share analysis for studying the impact of industry structure on regional economic growth;

- an estimation of regional economic multipliers, extending the Keynesian multiplier concept from the national to the regional level.

Such developments had come to be well established by the 1960s, and were widely seen to constitute defining features of regional economics as a discipline.

## Turning point

The 1970s were a major turning point in urban and regional political economy. The mainstream economic perspective had become consolidated into textbooks, such as the classic work by Richardson (1969), including not only location theory and models derived from the urban ecology school, but also other extensions of neoclassical price theory. Keynesian theory had also come to be applied, rather mechanistically, at the regional level as a means of understanding regional economic inequalities and the problems of regional economic stabilization. Three "bombshell" contributions changed all that, laying the foundations for modern urban and regional political economy. These were books by Manuel Castells, David Harvey and Stuart Holland.

Manuel Castells's *The Urban Question* (1977) adapted Althusser's then fashionable structuralist interpretation of Marx to the reformulation of urban studies. Rejecting the existing corpus of urban analysis as ideological rather than scientific, Castells sought to show how urban phenomena are shaped by the social structuring of space arising out of the systemic needs of capital. His later work put further emphasis on the role of "collective consumption" as a key feature of the modern capitalist city. The provision of items of collective consumption, such as public transport and housing, are seen as typically involving the state as a key player in its provision, thereby politicizing the urban question. Urban social movements then emerge as agents of progressive change. The analysis of these movements, responding to the CONTRADICTIONS of the modern capitalist city, makes for a strong

contrast with the more traditional Marxian focus on the role of the working class and the capital–labor relationship.

David Harvey's *Social Justice and the City* (1973) provided a similarly dramatic, but more accessible, critique and launching pad for modern urban political economy. Harvey set out to demonstrate that the capitalist urban system impedes progressive redistribution in the elusive pursuit of "social justice," but that the tools of liberal social science, including neoclassical economics, are inadequate for the task. Hence his declaration of the need for a socialist reformulation of the whole issue. A mixing of ideas from Karl Polanyi, as well as MARX and Engels, paves the way for an analysis of the city as one part of a broader study of economy and society. As further developed in later works, this involves an analysis of how capitalist interests shape patterns of urban land use, how interacting circuits of capital shape the flow of investment into the built environment, and how urban form shapes class struggle and class consciousness. This is a grand project of integrating urban analysis with a modern Marxian political economy.

Stuart Holland can be credited with extending political economy to the study of regional economic imbalance and, in particular, with signalling the importance of drawing from the traditions of institutional economics and J.M. Keynes as well as Marx. His twin publications *Capital Versus the Regions* (1976a) and *The Regional Problem* (1976b) thereby played an important role in the development of modern urban and regional political economy. Alongside Holland's work, Myrdal's principle of CIRCULAR AND CUMULATIVE CAUSATION has been acknowledged as being of particular relevance in understanding the causes of divergence in regional economic performance. With transnational corporations "striding the globe in seven league boots," as Holland puts it, the propensity is for such imbalances to become more pronounced. The characteristically different spatial distributions of "leader," "led" and "laggard" firms give rise to pronounced regional inequalities. As Hymer

(1972) had earlier argued, the spatial division of labor, interregionally and internationally, comes to reflect the hierarchical structure of the corporation.

## Challenges of regional political economy

Such analytical issues have been the focus of much lively debate among urban and regional political economists in the last quarter of the twentieth century (see URBAN AND REGIONAL POLITICAL ECONOMY: MAJOR CONTEMPORARY THEMES). Many articles continue to be published in the tradition of mainstream economics, but the rupture of the 1970s generated by the works of Castells, Harvey and Holland pitched urban and regional studies more directly into the realm of radical political economy. The challenge now is for political economy to integrate the spatial dimension with other aspects of the study of capitalist economic development. In this respect, the concerns of urban and regional political economists are not sharply distinct from the more general concerns of political economists – to understand the forces generating structural change in the world economy, precipitating new patterns of social conflict and political responses.

## Selected references

Castells, M. (1976) "Theory and Ideology in Urban Sociology," in C.G. Pickvance (ed.), *Urban Sociology: Critical Essays*, London: Methuen.
—— (1977) *The Urban Question: A Marxist Approach*, London: Edward Arnold.
Greenhut, M.L. (1970) *A Theory of the Firm in Economic Space*, New York: Appleton-Century-Crofts.
Harvey, D.M. (1973) *Social Justice and the City*, London: Edward Arnold.
Holland, S. (1976a) *Capital Versus the Regions*, London: Macmillan.
—— (1976b) *The Regional Problem*, London: Macmillan.
Hymer, S. (1972) "The Multinational Corporation and the Law of Uneven Development," in H. Radice (ed.), *International Firms and Modern Imperialism*, Ringwood, Victoria: Penguin.
Massey, D. (1973) "Towards a Critique of Industrial Location Theory," *Antipode* 6.
Richardson, H. (1969) *Regional Economics: Location Theory, Urban Structure and Regional Change*, London: Weidenfeld & Nicolson.
Stilwell, F. (1992) *Understanding Cities & Regions; Spatial Political Economy*, Sydney: Pluto Press.

FRANK STILWELL

# urban and regional political economy: major contemporary themes

Urban and regional political economy is commonly characterized as being problem-oriented. Certainly, there is no shortage of socioeconomic problems associated with cities and regions. Worldwide, most large cities face a familiar array: transport congestion, atmospheric POLLUTION, long journeys to work, poor access to public facilities, substandard housing, pockets of UNEMPLOYMENT AND UNDEREMPLOYMENT and a rising fear of CRIME. Concurrently, there are major tensions associated with unevenness in regional economic development – the tendency for regional inequalities to impede "trickle down" processes and to become intensified over time. Given that these urban and regional problems also typically give rise to political pressures, their political-economic character is likewise inescapable. There are recurrent demands for amelioration of urban and regional problems through policies of reform.

## Problems, policies and spatial dimensions

Much contemporary research and writing in urban and regional political economy focuses on these problems and policy issues. However, there are more fundamental analytical concerns. These involve developing an understanding of the spatial dimension of economy and society. Of course, all economic activity takes place in TIME and space. Economic analysis has had difficulty coming to terms with these dimensions, most obviously because of the dominance of equilibrium analysis (see EQUILIBRIUM, DISEQUILIBRIUM AND NON-EQUILIBRIUM) and the methodology of comparative statics. The difficulties of formulating a historically-based economic dynamics have been at least matched by the difficulties of injecting a spatial dimension into economics. To quote one frequent jibe, much of orthodox economics treats the economy as if it were located on the head of a pin. The development of urban and regional economics as a branch of the discipline (see URBAN AND REGIONAL POLITICAL ECONOMY: HISTORY) has been largely concerned to rectify this deficiency.

## Major journals

In the last couple of decades these analytical and problem/policy–oriented concerns have been reflected in a substantial academic literature. The leading international journals emphasizing a political economy perspective are *Environment and Planning: Society and Space* and the *International Journal of Urban and Regional Research*, but articles have appeared in a wide range of other publications, including interdisciplinary journals such as *Regional Studies*, *Urban Studies* and *Comparative Urban Research*. The *Journal of Urban Economics* and *Regional Science and Urban Economics* are principal outlets for mainstream economics applications. Geography journals are also an important reference point for this subject, given that the topic straddles the two disciplines. Indeed geographers, more than economists, are notable for their flexibility in embracing and developing such themes. Also notable is the role played by the Regional Science Association (RSA), which organizes numerous conferences around the world and publishes the *Journal of Regional Science*, in addition to its own *Papers and Proceedings*. Begun initially by Walter Isard as an interna-

tional forum for a formal mathematical modeling approach to the study of spatial phenomena, the RSA exists today at least equally as a focal point for regional policy practitioners. Finally, it is pertinent to note that this is a field which, by its very nature, tends towards a national/regional orientation in research and publication, illustrated in Australia for example by journals such as the *Australasian Journal of Regional Studies* and *Urban Policy and Research*.

## Spatial forms and change

What concerns feature in this literature? Issues range from theoretical questions about the conceptualization of space to down to earth treatments of particular problems of urban unemployment, transport and land use planning. At the core is a concern to understand the two-way relationship between spatial form and socioeconomic change. A recurrent theme, particularly strongly emphasized in Doreen Massey's work, such as *Spatial Divisions of Labour*, published in 1984, has been the interactive character of this relationship. In other words, spatial form shapes structural economic change, just as structural change impacts on spatial form. This is what can be called the social–spatial dynamic or, to impart a more distinctly Marxian flavor, the social–spatial dialectic.

## Cities and suburbanization

As with political economy in general, a historical focus is important in understanding the development and functioning of cities and regions. The growth of cities as focal points for commerce and industry, and their changing form during different phases of capitalist development, are common themes in the literature on the processes of urbanization. Studies of suburbanization in the United States, for example, recurrently stress that, while it was made possible by advances in transport technology, it was driven by "white flight" from the inner city areas which had become increasingly characterized as "ghettoes." The suburbanization process also served to reproduce and extend the conditions for capital accumulation – the demand for cars, housing and the associated consumer durable expenditures being key elements in the realization of surplus value. The persistent fiscal crises of some cities have been intensified by these patterns of capital accumulation which have seen spectacular waves of urban growth give way to relative stagnation of the older urban cores.

## Deindustrialization and unemployment

Meanwhile, at a regional scale, the processes of industrial change have generated chronic problems of deindustrialization and localized unemployment. These various sectoral–spatial imbalances and adjustment problems have become of growing analytical and political concern. There are also sources of dynamism in urban and regional change. Gentrification, for example, continues to transform the physical and socioeconomic character of many inner city areas, the very areas which had commonly been vacated by more affluent population groups earlier in the twentieth century. Modern urban political economy, particularly in the United States, lays particular stress on these themes, emphasizing the complex dynamics of space, CLASS and race (see, for example, Tabb and Sawers 1984; Bluestone and Harrison 1982; Davis *et al.* 1990).

## Gender, housing and transport policies

Feminist contributions to urban political economy have also grown significantly in a number of countries, typically emphasizing how spatial form interacts with uneven GENDER relations. Disadvantages of access to housing and transport are a recurrent theme (see DISCRIMINATION IN THE HOUSING AND MORTGAGE MARKET). More generally, housing and transport studies may be regarded as distinct sub-themes within urban political economy, each with established practitioners and specialist journals. What gives these sub-themes particular status is their direct connection with

particular fields of public policy: housing policy and transport policy. This leads to a recurrent concern with the development of practical policy instruments for helping to build better cities. That, of course, is easier said than done. Indeed, one recurring lesson from the study of urban political economy is that the local state is not substantially less problematic as an instrument of social amelioration and reform than is the capitalist state apparatus in general. The constraints imposed on the urban reform process by the various fractions of capital are persistent.

## Globalization

A particularly important development in modern urban political economy is the focus on urban and regional aspects of globalization (for example, Allen and Hamnett 1996). The integration of the world economy through trade, investment, labor movements and finance is proceeding apace, although the concept of "globalization" remains disputed. The structural economic changes associated with these processes are having major impacts on patterns of urban and regional development. The emergence of global cities as focal points for the orchestration of transnational capitalist interests is one such development (Sassen 1991). So too is a rapidly changing international and interregional division of labor (Fagan and Webber 1994). Intensified spatial competition has major implications for the role of the state too. The tendency to promote particular urban centers as "national champions" in this competitive situation is tempered by competition within nation-states for mobile capital, particularly where a federal structure of government pertains, as in Australia and Canada. Beggar-thy-neighbor outcomes are predictable, fueling the redistribution of income from labor to capital.

## Fordism and post-Fordism

David Harvey's influential work treats these tendencies as particular manifestations of a tendency toward "time–space compression"

(Harvey 1989). Many modern urban political economists also link the issue in to the debate around post-Fordism (for example, Storper and Scott 1989). Increased "flexibility" in the use of space can be seen, according to this view, as one aspect of a more general breakdown of the previously dominant Fordist system and the transition to a post-Fordist system (see FORDISM AND THE FLEXIBLE SYSTEM OF PRODUCTION). "New industrial spaces" as diverse as Silicon Valley in California, the Emilia region of Italy, Baden-Wurttemburg in Germany and the M4 corridor in England evidently have characteristics enabling them to achieve impressive regional economic growth, contrasting with the demise of the more traditional heartlands of industrial capitalism. Yet it is not obvious what they have in common or to what extent they form normative models for regional economic planning. These are contentious issues in modern urban and regional political economy, illustrative of linkages into broader debates about the trajectory of contemporary capitalist development.

## Other questions

Analysis of these themes has burgeoned alongside more traditional concerns with location theory, urban land use and the role of urban and regional planning. Evidently, there is no shortage of questions for urban political economists in the current period of rapid structural/spatial change. Given the general tendency for increased polarization in the DISTRIBUTION OF INCOME in capitalist societies, for example, does that mean the promotion of increasingly divided cities? Does the increased importance of information technologies generate spatial–social cohesion or lead to further fracturing of our cities between "winners" and "losers" (Castells 1989)? And what, if anything, can the state, either nationally or locally, do to address these processes? The "manageability" of cities, long a concern of the more pragmatic contributors to this field, comes increasingly into question.

The analysis of the political responses to these urban and regional problems necessarily extends the subject beyond the narrowly economic. It also goes beyond the dominant reformist concerns to a consideration of more dramatic change in social structure and political organization. Inspired by the work of Castells, there is a considerable literature on the significance of the "urban social movements" which have developed to confront capital and the state in the cities (Lowe 1986). Here, too, the work of urban and regional political economists has obvious linkages with the work of sociologists, political scientists and geographers in dealing with important issues of an essentially interdisciplinary character.

## Selected references

Allen, J. and Hamnett, C. (1996) *A Shrinking World? Global Unevenness and Inequality*, Oxford: The Open University in conjunction with Oxford University Press.

Bluestone, B. and Harrison, B. (1982) *The Deindustrialisation of America*, New York: Basic Books.

Castells, M. (1989) *The Informational City*, Oxford: Basil Blackwell.

Davis, M., Hiatt, S., Kennedy, M., Ruddick, S. and Sprinker, M. (1990) *Fire in the Hearth: the Radical Politics of Place in America*, London and New York, Verso.

Fagan, R. and Webber, M. (1994) *Global Restructuring: The Australian Experience*, Melbourne: Oxford University Press.

Harvey, D.M. (1989) *The Condition of Postmodernity*, Oxford: Basil Blackwell.

Lowe, S. (1986) *Urban Social Movements: The City After Castells*, London: Macmillan.

Sassen, S. (1991) *The Global City: London, New York, Tokyo*, Princeton, NJ: Princeton University Press.

Storper, M. and Scott, A. (1989) "The Geographical Foundations and Social Regulation of Flexible Production Complexes," in J. Wolch and M. Dear (eds), *The Power of Geography: How Teritory Shapes Social Life*, Boston: Unwin Hyman.

Tabb, W.K. and Sawers, L. (1984) *Marxism and the Metropolis: New Perspectives on Urban*

*Political Economy*, 2nd edn, Oxford and New York: Oxford University Press.

FRANK STILWELL

# use-value and exchange-value

## Introduction

In Marxian economics, the use-value of a commodity or product of nature is its objective usefulness, which depends upon the application made of the good by the purchaser, but not upon the purchaser's subjective valuation of the good. This contrasts with neoclassical economics, where the corresponding concept of utility is the subjective valuation of a good, which necessarily can vary from individual to individual. While in NEOCLASSICAL ECONOMICS, the utility of a commodity directly influences its price, in Marxian economics the exchange-value of a commodity is seen as completely independent of its use-value.

The justification for this proposition is the argument that, whereas under previous social systems, goods were produced primarily for their use, under CAPITALISM, goods are not produced for their use to the direct producer, but for their exchange-value. In pre-capitalist societies, when exchange was "no more than an occasional incident wherein superfluities only are exchanged" (Hilferding 1904: 126), perceptions of use-value may well have motivated the consideration paid. But under capitalism, commodities are produced specifically for exchange, and exchange itself involves one party giving what is for them a non-use-value in return for exchange-value.

In this capitalist circumstance, "the distinction becomes firmly established between the utility of an object for the purposes of consumption, and its utility for the purposes of exchange. Its use-value becomes distinguished from its exchange-value" (Marx 1867: 91). Use-value, then, plays no role in determining exchange-value. Instead, since commodities are produced specifically for exchange, "the quantitative proportion in which the articles are exchangeable, becomes dependent on their production itself" (1867: 91). As a consequence, "the exchange of commodities is evidently an act characterized by a total abstraction from use-value" (1867: 45).

Thus, while neoclassical economics focuses upon exchange and the maximization of utility, and describes capitalism as a system for deciding the allocation of scarce resources between competing wants, Marxian political economy puts the primary emphasis upon production and exchange-value, and views capitalism as a system driven by the accumulation of capital. As MARX put it:

> It must never be forgotten, that in capitalist production what matters is not the immediate use-value but the exchange–value, and, in particular, the expansion of surplus value. This is the driving motive of capitalist production, and it is a pretty conception that – in order to reason away the contradictions of capitalist production – abstracts from its very basis and depicts it as a production aiming at the direct satisfaction of the consumption of the producers.
>
> (Marx 1861–2, part II: 495)

## Critical role of use–value

Traditionally, Marxists argued that use-value was as irrelevant to political economy as it was to capitalism itself (Hilferding 1904: 130; Sweezy 1942: 26). However, modern access to *Grundrisse* (Marx 1857–8), and a re-examination of the classic texts, has revealed that the concept of use-value was essential to Marx's analysis (Rosdolsky 1977; Groll 1980; Keen 1993). Its most important role was in explaining the origin of surplus value.

As is well known, Marx rejected explanations for surplus value which were based upon unequal exchange (1867: 154), arguing that to understand the origins of profit under capitalism one must explain it on the basis of the fundamental assumption that commodities are sold at their values, as an equivalent exchange in proportion to the quantity of labor realized in them. Therefore, he had to provide an explanation for surplus on the assumption that the exchange-value of a commodity was its value (where this, according to Marx, was the socially necessary abstract labor time embodied in it).

Since exchange, and therefore exchange-value, could not of itself provide the answer to the riddle of how a capitalist could "buy his commodities at their value... sell them at their value, and yet at the end of the process... withdraw more value from circulation than he threw into it at starting" (1867: 163), Marx concluded that surplus-value must originate in the use-value of a specific commodity: "We are, therefore, forced to the conclusion that the change originates in the use-value, as such, of the commodity... our friend, Moneybags, must be so lucky as to find... a commodity, whose use-value possesses the peculiar property of being a source of value" (1867: 164).

Marx argued that this commodity was labor power. He identified the means of subsistence as the exchange-value of labor power (measured in terms of the labor time needed to produce the subsistence bundle of commodities), and the work that a laborer could perform in a day as its use-value (also measured in terms of labor time). Just as in general the use-value of a commodity is unrelated to its exchange-value, so with this specific commodity. Therefore "the value of labor power, and the value which that labor power creates in the labor process, are two entirely different magnitudes." This difference between the value of labor power – its exchange-value – and the use-value of labor power – its use-value – is the source of surplus value. Thus, "this difference of the two values was what the capitalist had in view, when he was purchasing the labor power" (1867: 188) (see LABOR AND LABOR POWER).

This is the most important application of the concept of use-value, but far from its only application (see Groll 1980). Marx himself passionately attacked the misconception that use-value plays no role in his economics in his acerbic commentary upon a critic's interpretation of *Das Kapital* in his "Marginal Notes on A. Wagner," where he concludes that "only an obscurantist, who has not understood a word of *Capital*, can conclude: Because Marx, in a note to the first edition of *Das Kapital*, overthrows all the German professorial twaddle on "use-value" in general... therefore, use-value does not play any role in his work" (Marx 1879: 198–9).

## Conclusion

However, as Rosdolsky argued many years ago, the role of use-value in Marx's economics has yet to be fully appreciated by Marxist economists. This is despite the fact that it is "one of the most fundamental discoveries of Marx's economics, the neglect of which makes his conclusions in the theory of value and money appear utterly distorted" (1977: 133).

## See also:

dialectical method; exploitation and surplus value; labor theory of value; Marx's methodology of political economy

## Selected references

Groll, S. (1980) "The Active Role of 'Use-Value' in Marx's Economics," *History of Political Economy* 12(3): 336–71.

Hilferding, R. (1904) "Böhm-Bawerk's Criticism of Marx," repr. in Sweezy (1942).

Keen, S. (1993) "Use-Value, Exchange-Value, and the Demise of Marx's Labor Theory of Value," *Journal of the History of Economic Thought* 15(Spring): 107–21.

Marx, K. (1857–8) *Grundrisse: Foundations of the Critique of Political Economy (Rough Draft)*, Harmondsworth: Penguin, 1973.

—— (1861–2) *Theories of Surplus Value, Part II*, Moscow: Progress Press, 1963.

—— (1867) *Das Kapital*, Volume I, published as *Capital Volume 1*, Moscow: Progress Publishers, 1954.

—— (1879) "Marginal Notes on A. Wagner," in T. Carver, *Karl Marx: Texts on Method*, Oxford: Basil Blackwell, 1975.

Meek, R.L. (1973) *Studies in the Labor Theory*

*of Value*, 2nd edn, London: Lawrence & Wishart.

Rosdolsky, R. (1977) *The Making of Marx's Capital*, London: Pluto Press.

Sweezy, P.M. (1942) *The Theory of Capitalist Development*, New York: Oxford University Press.

STEVE KEEN

# utopia

"Utopia" refers to images of an ideal society; its opposite is "dystopia," visions of the worst society. Utopian visions make moral principles more concrete in a way that can guide us in creating new and different ways of organizing society and economy. Thus, utopianism represents a radical extension of normative economics.

## Nature of utopias

As Geoffrey Hodgson (1995) argues, utopian visions have been central to the putatively anti-utopian economics of Friedrich Hayek, Karl MARX and Thomas Malthus. Most modern economists adopt a utopian vision based on principles of laissez-faire, a descendant of Adam Smith's conception of the natural liberty of isolated individuals working harmoniously through markets and exchange, with little positive role for government. Though the Arrow–Debreu general equilibrium model indicates that the assumptions necessary to the existence and stability of this ideal are unrealistic, laissez-faire forms the intellectual basis of the dominant school of normative economics and of current neo-liberal ideology. On the other hand, most utopian thinking (with exceptions, such as *The Moon is a Harsh Mistress*, by Robert Heinlein) is collectivist, emphasizing values of reason, justice and solidarity.

When Thomas More coined the word "utopia," he merged two Greek words meaning "good place" and "no place." A typical utopia is thus a morally ideal situation seen as unobtainable given current political, economic, societal and technological conditions. A serious utopian goes beyond fanciful visions of the "Garden of Eden" variety, pre-utopian images of the "Golden Age" of the past, and satire such as Samuel Butler's *Erewhon* and tries to explain how his or her vision would be feasible if these given conditions were to change. The more useful utopias rely not on unreal technology or on radical alterations of human character, but on reorganized societal arrangements which can spawn improved techniques, incentives and personalities. Despite their unreachability, utopian visions have been used as yardsticks for judging actually existing societies, as guides to policy and practice, or as inspirations for changing the world.

What follows is an incomplete survey of some utopian contributions to political economy. As Kumar (1986) points out, almost all developed utopian thinking comes from the "Western" tradition. This may be because utopian dreams are encouraged by the disruption of tradition and the injustices arising from modernization and commercialization, a process that has gone further in the "West."

## Plato and More's utopias

Plato's *Republic*, the first known utopia, is also the earliest to argue the idea that people can benefit from the DIVISION OF LABOR. However, rather than representing a mode of cooperation amongst atomistic individuals, his division of labor represents internal relations of an organic whole. Plato aimed to make that whole healthy, to embody his ideal of JUSTICE. The social and political structure (involving hierarchy, censorship, and an artificial civic religion, among other things) fostered the development of moral character in its governing guardians. This character insured the reproduction of the system over time. Following Plato, and in stark contrast to neoclassical economics, the endogeneity of human character is a common utopian theme, implying the need for an ideal social organization to foster personal development.

Thomas More's *Utopia*, in 1516, updates the

*Republic*, presenting a more concrete picture of a society that serves all basic needs. Though written as a satire, it was a critique of the society of his time, specifically of the British enclosure movement and the replacement of feudal agrarian society by commercial capitalism. Need and the workday were reduced by more efficient organization, partly via the abolition of unemployment and unproductive work. Goods are produced by all in a collectivist way and distributed freely; scholarly learning is emphasized. This system was organized in a relatively egalitarian and democratic way (for More's time), idealizing traditional village or monastic life. Making it successful was the assumption of a wise Founder and a religion that abolished the sin of pride. Symbolizing More's anti-commericalism, gold is used to make chamber pots.

More's image of a small faraway island ideal has been the dominant image, even as utopians embraced Rousseau's republican ideas, visions of non-capitalist progress and modern technology. For recent examples, see Theodor Hertzka's imperialist but innovative *Freeland* (1890), Charlotte Perkins GILMAN's feminist *Herland* (1915), B.F. Skinner's social-scientific *Walden Two* (1948), or Aldous Huxley's Buddhist and drug-using *Island* (1962).

## Utopian socialists

In the nineteenth century, utopians attempted to put their ideas into practice, mostly in the Americas. First came the agrarian and uniformitarian tradition of religious colonists and the followers of Etienne Cabet. Later, Robert Owen proposed and set up paternalistic and social reforming industrial "Villages of Unity and Mutual Cooperation" based on his success at New Lanark. The followers of Charles Fourier tried to put into practice his ideas of rural phalansteries that promised to liberate human passions, including sexual ones, and to make work a joyful activity. William Lane attempted to set up a rural communist utopia in Paraguay in the 1890s. Though most of these efforts failed, a small number of the utopian colonies survive until the present.

Going beyond small-scale colonization was Edward Bellamy's best-selling *Looking Backward* (1888), which envisioned a "nationalist" utopia for the United States as a whole. Translated into many languages, its technocratic vision (akin to that of Henri de Saint-Simon) provoked a large spate of utopian and dystopian thinking. This book portrays a large-scale planned economy with no money or private property in physical goods, centered on serving each person "from cradle to grave" according to his or her needs. Bellamy suggested practical solutions to class strife in a way that, bolstered by patriotic pride, would motivate workers to labor from each according to their abilities. Products were distributed using a system of central disbursement and debit cards (which had an equal value per year per person). Unlike most utopians, Bellamy suggested that his utopia was not only possible but likely, as an automatic result of the centralization of capital. Because of Karl Marx's refusal to provide utopian "recipes for the cook-shops of the future" and the similarities of many of Bellamy's ideas to those of crude Marxism, Bellamy's undemocratic planned economy may have influenced the Bolsheviks' grasping for ways to organize the Soviet economy. Aspects of Bellamy's utopia influenced the work of Thorstein VEBLEN.

If Bellamy represents the undemocratic "socialism from above" tradition, William Morris's response, *News from Nowhere* (1891), exemplifies the ideal of "socialism from below." It finds its roots in utopian popular uprisings, such as those of the Levelers and Diggers during the English Civil War. Morris posits his utopia as arising from a process of workers' class struggle (violently resisted by the capitalists). Its political system is that of grassroots community democracy, while the Parliament building is used to store dung. Most interesting to economists is the abolition of scarcity: the pleasure inherent in doing craft-type work under one's own control increases the supply of commodities, while the pleasure of working cooperatively with one's friends makes even the drudge work pleasant. Yet more obnoxious tasks would be done with automated technology or abolished. On the other hand, the demand for products is lower, since people no longer have to consume to fill psychological voids imposed by alienation, to compensate for their boring and dominated working lives (see CONSPICUOUS CONSUMPTION AND EMULATION). In effect, prices are zero. Finally, Morris's emphasis on the aesthetic dimension of life produces one of the first ecological utopias, preserving not only nature but beautiful old buildings.

## Twentieth-century dystopias and utopias

While the nineteenth century evoked a wave of utopian dreams, most of the twentieth century elicited dystopian nightmares, from Jack London's *The Iron Heel* (1907), to Aldous Huxley's *Brave New World* (1932), to George Orwell's *1984* (1948). The first predicted the rise of fascism; the second critiques Henry Ford-style capitalism; the third lambastes Stalinism and Bellamy-style socialism. But the New Left of the 1960s sparked utopias concerned with ecology, sexism, racism and authoritarianism. Notable here are Ernest Callenbach's *Ecotopia*, Marge Piercy's *Woman on the Edge of Time*, and Ursula LeGuinn's *The Dispossessed*. Though such novels have broadened the concerns of utopians beyond narrow "industrial" issues, they stand on the shoulders of the giants discussed above.

## See also:

anarchism; liberation theology; Mondragón; participatory democracy and self-management; socialism and communism

## Selected references

Bellamy, Edward (1888) *Looking Backward*, New York: New American Library, 1960.

Claeys, Gregory (1987) "Utopias," in John Eatwell, Murray Milgate and Peter Newman (eds), *The New Palgrave: A Dictionary of Economics*, London: Macmillan, 783–6.

Geoghegan, Vincent (1987) *Utopianism and Marxism*, London: Methuen.

Hodgson, Geoffrey M. (1995) "The Political Economy of Utopia," *Review of Social Economy* 53(2): 195–213.

Kumar, Krishan (1986) *Utopia and Anti-Utopia in Modern Times*, Oxford: Basil Blackwell.

Levitas, Ruth (1990) *The Concept of Utopia*, Syracuse, NY: Syracuse University Press.

Loubier, Leo (1974) *Utopian Socialism: Its History Since 1800*, Cambridge, MA: Schenkman.

Morris, William (1891) *News from Nowhere*, London: Routledge & Kegan Paul, 1970.

JAMES DEVINE

# V

## value foundation of price

From the eighteenth century onwards, all the major schools of economic thought gave a central role to value theory in their analytical system and world-view. Up until the 1930s, value theories all made the distinction, explicitly or implicitly, between the "price" (or "exchange-value") of a commodity and the "value" element(s) that was the source and regulator of price. A commodity was seen to have a price precisely because it was valuable in some other sense. The price of a commodity is a reflection of its value, as well as its expression. It was considered to be an essential task of any value theory to provide a value foundation for price, by explaining the determination of relative prices in terms of the influence of underlying value elements. A "value theory" which made no attempt to explain prices in terms of an underlying value substratum was regarded as vacuous.

### Underlying value substance

All major value theories, from classical to early neoclassical, attributed the source of a commodity's exchange-value to one or more underlying value elements. The underlying value element has been variously identified as the "real costs" of production (exertions of labor, sacrifices in abstaining from consumption in order to provide financial capital), the marginal utility from satisfaction in consumption, labor values, and so on. For MARX, a commodity's price reflected the amount of socially necessary abstract labor time embodied in its production. For Jevons, the price reflected the intensity of the marginal wants satisfied by consuming the commodity. For Ricardo, price was related to the pain cost of the labor required to produce the commodity.

Most of these value theories also attempted (not always successfully) to explain the determination of relative prices in terms of differences between commodities in the quantities of the underlying value element(s) that they possessed, embodied or elicited in consumers. These value elements were not only believed to be the source of exchange-value, but were also seen as the regulators of relative prices. Relative prices were viewed as the outcome of the pursuit, avoidance or expression of various human values and "disvalues" – wants, needs, dislikes, efforts, sacrifices – and were viewed as being commensurate with the intensity of these values and disvalues.

In some of these theories the distinction between value and price was made explicit. Marx gave possibly the clearest definition of the distinction between the two, using the very words "value" and "price." Jevons also gave a clear definition of the distinction between price and his value substance (utility). In some other cases, the distinction was implicit. However, all value theorists recognized that price theory needed to be given a satisfactory value foundation if it was to perform adequately as an explanation of how prices were determined. This value foundation had to link prices to the human processes of valuation that motivate or accompany all labor, production, exchange, consumption and other forms of economic activity.

The distinction between value and price is an important one. Price is the appearance and value the underlying essence, to use a Hegelian distinction. Value theory enables us to make sense of the empirical world of relative prices, costs, wages and other monetary magnitudes, by relating these back to the underlying human values and disvalues that drive everything. The value foundation of price provides the link between the objective realm of prices and the subjective realm of human values. This also reflects an epistemology and methodology more in tune with the method of *Verstehen*, which provides an interpretive understanding of the social realm, based on the values, motives, purposes and intentions of individual agents.

## Purge, conflation and separation of value from price

Important though this distinction between value and price is, the concept of an underlying value substance came under attack earlier this century. The attack initially focused on utility, but broadened out to become an attack on all underlying value substances: the real cost notions of the late classical economists, Marshall and the early neoclassicists, as well as the labor value concept of Marx and his followers.

Hicks (1939: ch. 1), Samuelson (1938: 62) and others set out to purge value theory of all its real value (utility and real cost) elements. The notion of utility, particularly its cardinal version, came under attack, as did disutility/ real costs on the production side of value theory. But neoclassical value theory was not the only target of attack. Samuelson (1971), Steedman (1977) and others attacked Marx's value analysis as an unnecessary detour in his price theory. These attacks were all a reflection of a growing positivism in economics that regarded utility, real costs, labor values and other value elements as redundant, tautological, unobservable and/or metaphysical constructs, with no useful role to play in price theory or in economic theory in general.

More recently, the attitude of neoclassical economists to the value/price distinction has been one of indifference, rather than hostility. As Heilbroner (1983: 253) and Gramm (1988: 225) note, value theory is virtually synonymous with price theory and many economists would be hard pressed to explain the difference between the two. In fact, the two terms are widely conflated by neoclassical economists.

Some Marxist political economists separate value and price theory and treat them as independent theories, performing different roles in their analytical system. Some restrict the use of the LABOR THEORY OF VALUE to CLASS analysis and to an explanation of the process of extracting surplus value. Others use value analysis in their theory of justice and exploitation. Similarly, for institutional economists, the INSTRUMENTAL VALUE THEORY is a normative analysis which is independent to some degree from price theory.

Some theories of price have no underlying value theory (in the sense explained here). For instance, the energy theory of prices attempts to explain the relative prices of commodities in terms of the quantities of direct and indirect energy resources embodied in their production. Post-Keynesian price theory, a hybrid of classical cost of production and neoclassical price theories, is purely an empirical price theory. It has no underlying value substance explaining price determination (see PRICING).

## Value, price and welfare

Paralleling the purge of cardinal utility and real costs from value theory, that occurred in the 1930s, was a rejection of the assumptions of interpersonal comparison of utility and diminishing marginal utility of income. The devaluation of welfare theory that occurred with the "new welfare theory" went hand in hand with the devaluation of value theory. A similar devaluation of policy-oriented, normative economics occurred when neoclassical economists were exhorted to be "value free" and to restrict their professional activities to the realm of positive economics.

There are important linkages between price theory, value theory, welfare theory, the measurement of aggregate economic welfare, and the methodology and framework for carrying out normative (evaluative) economics (see Kerr 1996). These linkages cannot be adequately understood and utilized for the benefit of society unless economists subscribe to a price theory which is also a value theory in the fullest and richest sense of the term. Such a theory explains prices in terms of underlying values and disvalues and is integrated with a welfare theory couched in these terms. It also provides a measure of aggregate economic welfare, as well as a framework of analysis that permits and encourages the evaluation of economic policy in terms of the promotion of the underlying values.

Such a value theory imbeds price theory in a variety of dimensions of value, valuation and evaluation, and provides an adequate value foundation for price. Classical value theory, Marx's value theory and early neoclassical value theory satisfy these requirements in varying degrees. However, further progress is necessary in order to imbed modern price analysis in a value framework.

## See also:

classical political economy; Marxist political economy: major contemporary varieties; neo-classical economics; normative and positive economics; transformation problem; use-value and exchange-value; value judgments and world views

## Selected references

Gramm, Warren S. (1988) "The Movement from Real to Abstract Value Theory, 1817–1959," *Cambridge Journal of Economics* 12: 225–46.

Heilbroner, Robert L. (1983) "The Problem of Value in the Constitution of Economic Thought," *Social Research* 50(2): 253–77.

Hicks, John R. (1939) *Value and Capital*, Oxford: Clarendon Press.

Kerr, Ian A. (1996) "The Linkages between Real Value and Economic Welfare: From Classical to Neoclassical Economics," paper presented at the 1996 Annual European Conference on the History of Economics, Lisbon, Portugal.

Lowe, Adolph (1981) "Is Economic Value Still a Problem?," *Social Research* 48(4): 786–815.

Samuelson, Paul (1938) "A Note on the Pure Theory of Consumers' Behaviour," *Economica* 5: 61–71.

—— (1971) "Understanding the Marxian Notion of Exploitation: A Summary of the So-Called Transformation Problem Between Marxian Values and Competitive Prices," *Journal of Economic Literature* 9(2): 399–431.

Steedman, Ian (1977) *Marx After Sraffa*, London: New Left Books.

IAN ALEXANDER KERR

# value judgments and world views

In recent years there has been a flurry of literature on METHODOLOGY IN ECONOMICS, much of it calling into question its supposed scientific character. Part of that literature deals explicitly with the impact of value judgments on economics as a science. Of this literature, a greater amount argues in favor of the value permeation thesis than defends the idea of value neutrality. However, value neutrality of economics as a science is the dominant position in the day-to-day work of contemporary mainstream economists. It seems expedient to begin by laying out its arguments.

## Value neutrality

There are two pervasive tenets to the value neutrality argument. The first is a reliance on the Humean guillotine, which categorically separates fact ("what is") from value ("what ought to be"), also known as the distinction between NORMATIVE AND POSITIVE ECONOMICS. The second basic tenet strongly supports the first by claiming that, since we have objective access to the empirical world through our sense experience, scientists need not concern themselves with "what ought to be." This second tenet is the crucial point, and the one which post-positivist philosophy of science has sought to undermine.

The value neutral position argues that scientific economics is comprised of three separate components: pre-scientific decisions, scientific analysis and post-scientific application. However, there is a difference between the value judgments of pre-science and of post-science. Hume's guillotine is protected by drawing a distinction in social science between two types of value judgments. The first is "characterizing" value judgments, involving the choice of (a) the problem to be investigated; (b) the theory to be used; (c) the criteria for verification, such as the use of formal logic; (d) the selection of data in terms of definite standards of reliability and so on; in short, everything that can be classified as a methodological judgment. The second is "appraising" value judgments, which express approval or disapproval either of some moral (or social) ideal, or of some action (or institution) because of a commitment to such an ideal. "Characterizing value judgments" are thus not really value judgments of any ethical significance, but judgments that merely allow one to carry on the scientific enterprise (see Nagel 1961: 492–5; Blaug 1992: 114–16).

In other attempts to reconcile value judgments and objective science, the notion of "brute fact" is often used. This is the claim that facts are in some sense "out there" for all to see, independent of scientific theory. Unfortunately for the value neutral position, the idea of brute fact has fallen on hard times in the philosophy of science literature. Today it is generally recognized, even by sophisticated logical empiricists, that facts are theory laden and that theories are tested by the facts designated as of interest by the theory. The more important question then becomes whether theory itself is, in part, value determined, for if it is, then theory laden facts would also appear to be value laden. The defence of value neutrality still stands, but the pillars seem to be weakening. Blaug concedes that both "factual" and "moral" arguments rest "at bottom . . . on certain definite techniques of persuasion, which in turn depend for their effectiveness, on shared values of one kind or another" (Blaug 1992: 115).

## Value permeation

Let us now consider recent criticisms of the value neutrality thesis. One value permeation argument holds that while science is driven by a search for truth, it is not interested in just any truth. The relevant truth must be both "interesting" and "valuable," and thus all science is goal directed activity. Further, the criteria for a "good" or "acceptable" scientific theory cannot be ranked in terms of their intrinsic importance, but only in relation to the degree to which they serve particular goals of the scientific community

Theory choice is not, therefore, based objectively on non-controversial criteria (for example, degree of verification or corroboration), but on criteria that are inevitably value laden (that is, the extent to which each theory serves specific ends). The scientists' search for "valuable truth" is directed by what they think society (and science) ought to do. Since no amount of evidence ever completely confirms or rejects any empirical hypothesis, but only renders it more or less probable, the scientist's values inevitably play a role in theory construction.

Another line of reasoning, Kuhnian in character, is more convincing to many. Kuhn, referring to the natural sciences, speaks of PARADIGMS, characterized by the shared values of a given scientific community (Kuhn 1970). It is Kuhn's rejection of the tenet that we have objective access to the empirical world through our sense experience, that is important for those opposed to the value neutrality position. He argues that the empirical world can be known only through the filter of a theory; facts are, therefore, theory laden. Thus, a major argument of those who build on Kuhn's approach runs as follows: a world view greatly influences the scientific paradigm out of which one works; value judgments are closely associated with the world view; theories must remain coherent with the world view; facts themselves are theory laden; therefore, the whole scientific venture is permeated by value judgments from the start. This world view, or *Weltanschauung*, shapes the interests of the scientist and determines the questions asked, the problems considered important, the answers deemed acceptable, the axioms of the theory, the choice of "relevant facts," the hypotheses proposed to account for such facts, the criteria used to assess the fruitfulness of competing theories, the language in which results are to be formulated, and so on.

## The neoclassical world view: a case in point

At this point let me illustrate the world view argument with neoclassical economics (see Wilber and Hoksbergen 1986). The world view of mainstream neoclassical economics is closely associated with the notion of the "good" imbedded in its particular scientific paradigm.

Neoclassical economics is founded on a world view made up of the following propositions. First, human nature is such that humans are both self-interested and rational. That is, they know their own interest and choose from among a variety of means in order to maximize that interest. Second, the purpose of human life is for individuals to pursue happiness as they themselves define it. Therefore, it is essential that they be left free to do so. Third, the ideal social world is a gathering of free individuals who compete with each other under conditions of scarcity to achieve self-interested ends. As in the natural world with physical entities, in the social world too there are forces at work which move economic agents toward equilibrium positions.

Neoclassical economists either accept the preceding empirically unverifiable and unfalsifiable statements or, barring overt acceptance, conduct scientific inquiry with methods based thereon. To state it simply, neoclassical economists believe that humans are rational maximizers of their own self interest, and that humans act in a rational world characterized by forces which move things toward equilibrium. The belief in rationality survives contrary evidence. Experimental studies by psychologists and economists indicate that people are concerned about cooperating with others and with being fair, not just preoccupied with their own self-interest (see Frank et al. 1993).

It seems fairly clear that judgments of value, of a particular notion of the good, are directly implied by propositions one and two of this neoclassical world view. If the purpose of life is that individuals pursue happiness, and if they do so self-interestedly, then it certainly would be good for individuals to receive what they want. Here is the basic notion of the good permeating all of NEOCLASSICAL ECONOMICS: individuals should be free to get as much as possible of what they want. That this basic position is in fact a judgment of value, or of "the good," is a point willingly granted by many economists.

Thus any use of economic theory, such as cost–benefit analysis, is founded on two basic value judgments. The first of these is that individual preferences should count. The second is that a system of competitive markets is the preferred economic institution in which to satisfy those preferences.

The second value judgment derives from elements one and three of the neoclassical world view and from the first value judgment that individual preferences should count. If one takes the core ideas of individualism, rationality and the social context of harmony among diverse and conflicting interests, along with a number of limiting assumptions, it can be shown that competitive market equilibrium maximizes the value of consumption and is therefore the best of all possible economic situations. The second value judgment is thus a different sort than the first, because it is conditional on the first. It does not stand alone. Competitive markets are good, in part, because they allow the greatest number of individual wants to be satisfied.

The notion of competitive equilibrium carries out two basic functions: it serves as an ideal and as a standard by which to measure the real value of current economic conditions. Because it serves as an ideal for which we strive, it leads directly to the value judgment that wherever competitive markets do not exist or are weak, they should be instituted or promoted. Wherever markets do not exist, the natural competitiveness of human beings will be channeled in other nonproductive directions. It would be better to establish markets where this competitiveness and self interest seeking behavior could be channeled into mutually satisfying activities. Wherever markets are weak and distorted due to monopoly power or government interference there is sure to be a reduction in actual consumption. Therefore, competitive markets should be promoted so that the ideal competitive equilibrium can be achieved (but see WILLIAMSON'S ANALYSIS OF THE CORPORATION).

## Conclusion

The paradigm or research program of any scientific community is circumscribed by boundaries laid out in a world view which, while not perhaps individually subjective, is nevertheless empirically untestable or metaphysical, as Boland and others would say (see Boland 1982; McCloskey 1985). How then do value judgments about the good, the just and the right enter into scientific analysis? Such value judgments are themselves entailed by the same world view which gives rise to theoretical and factual analysis. "What is" and "what ought to be" are thus inextricably linked in the data, the facts, the theories, the descriptions, the explanations, the prescriptions, and so on. All are permeated by the a priori world view.

There is no alternative to working from a world view. Making explicit the values embodied in that world view will help keep economics more honest and useful. For example, many institutional economists see the social world as characterized by interdependence of economic actors with the result that "externalities" are ubiquitous. The assignment of rights by the political and legal systems, therefore, determines "who gets what." The DISTRIBUTION OF INCOME, wealth and rights that results from economic transactions and public policies becomes as important as efficiency. Therefore, economists with this world view believe every policy should be evaluated for its impact on distribution as well as on efficiency (see Schmid 1978).

## See also:

critical realism; ethics and morality; holistic method; ideology; methodological individualism and collectivism; modernism and postmodernism

## Selected references

Blaug, Mark (1992) *The Methodology of Economics: Or How Economists Explain*, Cambridge: Cambridge University Press.

Boland, Lawrence (1982) *The Foundations of Economic Method*, London: George Allen & Unwin.

Caldwell, Bruce (1982) *Beyond Positivism: Economic Methodology in the Twentieth Century*, London: George Allen & Unwin.

Diesing, Paul (1991) *How Does Social Science Work? Reflections on Practice*, Pittsburgh: University of Pittsburgh Press.

Frank, Robert H., Gilovich, Thomas and Regan, Dennis T. (1993) "Does Studying Economics Inhibit Cooperation?," *Journal of Economic Perspectives* 7(2): 159–71.

Kuhn, Thomas S. (1970) *The Structure of Scientific Revolutions*, Chicago: University of Chicago Press.

McCloskey, Donald N. (1985) *The Rhetoric of Economics*, Madison, WI: University of Wisconsin Press.

Nagel, Ernest (1961) *The Structure of Science: Problems in the Logic of Scientific Explanation*, New York: Harcourt Brace & World.

Schmid, A. Allan (1978) *Property, Power, and Public Choice: An Inquiry into Law and Economics*, New York: Praeger.

Wilber, Charles K. and Hoksbergen, Roland (1986) "Ethical Values and Economic Theory: A Survey," *Religious Studies Review* 12(3/4): 208–14.

CHARLES K. WILBER

**VALUE THEORY, INSTRUMENTAL:** *see* instrumental value theory

# Veblen, Thorstein Bunde (1857–1929)

Thorstein Bunde Veblen has been described, with some justification, as the last man who knew everything. He is clearly America's most original social theorist, and arguably its most important. Much of Veblen's great originality came from his willingness to go beyond the narrow boundaries of orthodox economics and to examine economic life as cultural and social activity. This interdisciplinary approach, along with his irreverent analysis and devastating critique of neoclassical economic theory, are the reasons why Veblen continues to be relevant to political economy.

Veblen was born on July 30 1857, two years before Charles Darwin published *The Origins of Species*, and died in August 1929, two months before the great crash in the stock-market. Both events nicely illuminate Veblen's place in the history of political economy, for two of Veblen's most important contributions to political economy are his application of the evolutionary perspective to the understanding of economic phenomena and his analysis of the conflict between business principles and in-dustrial efficiency (which was a primary cause of the Great Depression).

## Life and background

Born and raised in a Norwegian farming community in the mid-west, Veblen's upbring-ing was certainly not typical. Education was highly stressed in the Veblen household, with most of the children who survived to adult-hood attending higher education. Much has been made of Veblen's outsider or marginal status. However, the stories of the Veblen family's social isolation are now seen to be gross exaggerations, vigorously disputed by many of his brothers and sisters. Much has been written on Veblen's personal life and habits, no doubt containing as much exaggera-tion as the Icelandic sagas Veblen would translate towards the end of his life. Yet we should remember that Veblen's rejection of the

orthodoxy of his day came not from his unorthodox lifestyle, but from his adopting an evolutionary vision of social life.

Veblen studied under many prominent thin-kers during the course of his formal education, including John Bates Clark at Carleton Col-lege, Richard Ely and Charles S. Peirce at Johns Hopkins University and William Gra-ham Summer at Yale University. All were to leave their mark on Veblen's thought, although as is characteristic of Veblen, their influence was frequently negative.

Unable to obtain a teaching position upon completion of his Ph.D. in philosophy from Yale in 1884, Veblen eventually (1891) went to Cornell on a economics fellowship. A year later he followed J. Laurence Laughlin to the newly founded University of Chicago. Veblen spent fourteen years at Chicago, teaching and serving as managing editor of the *Journal of Political Economy*, although never rising above the position of assistant professor. Veblen also held teaching positions at Stanford, the Uni-versity of Missouri and the New School for Social Research. His unorthodox views, coupled with the generally poor quality of his teaching and his nonconformist personal life, made it difficult to obtain a permanent university position.

## Major works and evolutionary economics

Veblen's most famous work is *The Theory of the Leisure Class: An Economic Study of the Evolution of Institutions*, first published in 1899, which owed much of its initial success to its being incorrectly reviewed as purely a work of satire. Other important books include *The Theory of Business Enterprise* in 1904, *The Instinct of Workmanship and the State of Industrial Arts* in 1914, *Imperial Germany and the Industrial Revolution* in 1915, *The Vested Interests and the Common Man* in 1919, and *Absentee Ownership and Business Enterprise in Recent Times: The Case of America* in 1923. His study of the influence of business on colleges and universities entitled *The Higher Learning in America: A Memorandum on the Conduct of Universities by Business Men* was published in 1918, and the originally intended sub-title was *A Study in Total Depravity*. A collection of his more important essays, *The Place of Science in Modern Civilization*, was published in 1919, demonstrating that Veblen was one of the most profound historians of economic thought, and in many ways a postmodern thinker (see MODERNISM AND POSTMODERNISM).

More than anyone before him, and more than most after, Veblen consistently applied the evolutionary perspective in his analysis of the social world and social theory. This allowed him to gain numerous insights into the economic process which remained hidden to adherents to the mechanistic perspective that has dominated economic theory since the time of Adam Smith. Veblen's evolutionary perspective was derived from the evolutionary biology of Charles Darwin, the most important intellectual influence on Veblen. Veblen contrasts the pre- and post-Darwinian view of science in the following passage:

> Before that epoch [of the Darwinian Revolution] the animus of a science was, on the whole, the animus of taxonomy; the consistent end of scientific inquiry was definition and classification.... The scientists of that era looked to a final term.... The center of interest and attention... was the body of natural laws governing phenomena. [Post-Darwinian theory is] substantially a theory of the process of consecutive change, which is taken as a sequence of cumulative change, realized to be self-continuing or self-propagating and to have no final term.
> (Veblen 1919: 36–7)

Other important influences on Veblen's ideas included Edward Bellamy, Charles S. Pierce and John Dewey (Edgell and Tilman 1989).

Veblen's importance in the history of political economy comes equally from his devastating critique of NEOCLASSICAL ECONOMICS theory and from his positive contributions to an evolutionary and institutional approach to economics. Veblen's critique of neoclassical economics centered on the limitations that the equilibrium view of the economy placed on the

scope and depth of economic analysis. This equilibrium approach was a hold over from the natural law philosophy to which economic theory owes much of its origins. The search for natural laws forced the economists of Veblen's day (much like today) to concentrate on unrealistic assumptions of human behavior and hypothetical models with little real world application, and to ignore (or underplay) the active force in an evolutionary approach to institutions. The evolutionary perspective advocated by Veblen highlights INSTITUTIONAL CHANGE AND ADJUSTMENT, complex processes, history and CULTURE, exactly what the natural law/mechanistic approach must ignore (Clark 1992).

## Veblenian dichotomy

Unlike the German Historical School, to which he is often erroneously linked, Veblen's analysis is underpinned by a theory of institutional change. According to Veblen, there are two dominant forces in the process of cumulative change, two types of institutions that can and do shape the process of institutional change: institutions of acquisition and institutions of production, institutions serving either invidious or non-invidious economic interests (Veblen 1899: 143). This distinction has become known as the Veblenian dichotomy, and it is one of Veblen's most important contributions. By employing this distinction, to give one example, Veblen was able to offer an original analysis of the role of consumption in a social order. Breaking free of the narrow marginal utility approach, Veblen was able to distinguish consumption that meets actual human needs and that which merely communicates the status of the affluent leisure class to the rest of the community. Veblen's analysis of CONSPICUOUS CONSUMPTION AND EMULATION, the main thesis of *The Theory of the Leisure Class*, is crucial to any understanding of the acquiescence of the lower classes to the power of the upper classes.

The Veblenian dichotomy also provides the underpinning of Veblen's analysis of business. According to Veblen, the dynamics of an industrial economy and technological change frequently run counter to the vested interests of business enterprise. Therefore, Veblen argued, there is a conflict between the goals of the engineers who design and build the apparatus of modern production systems, and the goals and aims of the businessmen who manage them; between pecuniary and industrial employments. Engineers seek maximum efficiency, which translates into maximum output at minimum costs. The pecuniary aims of businessmen promote industrial sabotage; the restriction of output to keep prices artificially high. Veblen frequently noted that there was no force of nature to harmonize the goals of business with the goals of social well-being.

## Veblen's influence

Veblen's lasting influence in political economy is felt through institutional political economy, which developed out of the ideas of Veblen and John R. Commons, and especially in the writings of the radical institutionalists, whose central theme is a return to the critical approach of Veblen. Many scholars working within these traditions have developed ideas which originated in Veblen. Clarence Ayres expanded on the Veblenian dichotomy, as have other institutionalists. Much of John Kenneth Galbraith's work has its roots in Veblen, especially his critical analysis of the role of consumption in affluent societies, his analysis of the large corporation as the dominant institution of modern capitalism and his analysis of the formation of the conventional wisdom. The institutionalist theory of social value, especially as developed by Marc Tool, and the critical role power and ideology play in institutionalist thought, best exemplified in the works of William Dugger and Ron Stanfield, are further examples of Veblen's lasting influence. Veblen's analysis of the history of economic thought, particularly the role of preconceptions, metaphors and the influence of natural law philosophy, forms the basis of Philip Mirowski's important contributions to this field, as well as others (see Clark 1992). Geoffrey Hodgson has shown how important

Veblen is to both the American and European traditions of evolutionary economics. Mainstream economists have, for the most part, ignored Veblen's ideas, with the exception of the occasional reference to Veblen goods and conspicuous consumption.

## Conclusion

Thorstein Veblen's ideas and theories are, in many ways, as relevant today as they were a century ago. Veblen is the model of a scholar who ignores artificial disciplinary boundaries, combining philosophical, social, cultural and economic analysis to grasp the full interrelatedness of social phenomena. But most important of all, Veblen's singular concentration on the role of institutions in shaping economic activity, and on the continual evolutionary process these institutions are subject to, is what is needed most to counter the fixation of neoclassical economic theory on the futile search for equilibrium states and the natural laws that produce them.

## See also:

circular and cumulative causation; collective social wealth; Galbraith's contribution to political economy; individual and society; instincts; institutional political economy; history; institutional political economy: major contemporary themes; institutions and habits; radical institutionalism

## Selected references

Clark, Charles M.A. (1992) *Economic Theory and Natural Philosophy*, Aldershot: Edward Elgar.

Diggins, John P. (1978) *The Bard of Savagery: Thorstein Veblen and Modern Social Theory*, New York: The Seabury Press.

Dorfman, Joseph (1934) *Thorstein Veblen and His America*, New York: Augustus Kelley.

Edgell, Stephen and Tilman, Rick (1989) "The Intellectual Antecedents of Thorstein Veblen: A Reappraisal," *Journal of Economic Issues* 23(4): 1003–1026.

Mirowski, Philip (1989) *More Heat than Light*, Cambridge: Cambridge University Press.

Tilman, Rick (1992) *Thorstein Veblen and His Critics 1891–1963*, Princeton, NJ: Princeton University Press.

CHARLES M. A. CLARK

# velocity and the money multiplier

Velocity describes the total amount of spending, in a set period of time, per unit of the money stock. If velocity is stable and if the money supply is exogenous and if the monetary authorities are both willing and able to control it, then a discretionary change in the money supply causes a predictable change in spending. If velocity is more than one, as is usually the case, then we have a relationship between changes in money and changes in total spending which is analogous to the Keynesian expenditure multiplier.

The assumption of a stable velocity, and the other conditions listed above, lies at the heart of MONETARISM and new classical economics, where the traditional monetary/real dichotomy is accepted. Changes in money cause predictable changes in spending which cause changes only in the price level. Such a relationship is, however, rejected in Keynes's own work and, for quite different reasons, in the neoclassical synthesis.

As defined above, velocity looks a simple concept, but it is not without ambiguity. Consider the expression $MV = PT$, where $M$ is money supply, $V$ is velocity, $P$ is average price level and $T$, number of transactions per period. This equation is an identity since $PT$ is the total value at current prices of all goods and services sold, while $MV$ is total spending, also at current prices. Current spending (and total sales) are both carried out with a stock of money, $M$, which can be numerically related to total spending by making it the denominator. The result is $V$.

## Quantity theory of money

The expression $MV = PT$ is the "equation of exchange" and was familiar to Locke (1632–1704) and Hume (1711–76), but it is better known now as the basis of the Quantity Theory of Money, which links changes in the money stock causally to changes in the price level. Moving from identity to theory requires that we place restrictions on the terms by virtue of a priori reasoning. The best known of early writers to do this was Irving Fisher in 1911 in *The Purchasing Power of Money*. The restrictions were that $M$ was controlled by the monetary authorities, and was thus independent of $V$ and $T$ which were determined by "habit" and "convention" in the former case, and by physical quantities in the latter. Notice that $T$ refers to *all* transactions, that is to transactions in finished goods and services as well as financial, intermediate and secondhand transactions.

Following Fisher, velocity became linked with the demand for money in the "Cambridge" equation. This was developed in the early twentieth century by Pigou, Marshall, Keynes and Robertson and can be written as $M = kPR$. This states that the quantity of money people wish to hold, $M$, is proportionate ($k$) to nominal ($P$) income, wealth, or transactions (the precise definition of $R$ varied). Algebraically, the Cambridge equation is identical to the equation of exchange if $k = 1/V$, Indeed, the determinants of $k$ were very similar to those discussed by Fisher for velocity. Furthermore, the same predictions (as those of the Quantity Theory) followed a change in money supply, if $k$ is stable and $R$ is limited in the same way as total transactions.

In its most modern form (for example, Friedman 1956), the Quantity Theory is most frequently expressed by placing restrictions on terms in the identity $MV = PY$. $V$ is seen (following Cambridge) as the inverse of the demand for money. It is stable because, in Friedman's famous phrase, "the demand for money is a stable function of a small number of variables." $Y$ is real income, or final output. If the Phillips curve is vertical in the long run (a monetarist claim), then, in the long run, $Y$ can grow at a rate limited by increases in labor force and productivity. Increases in the money supply in excess of this rate can only increase prices in the long run. If the short-run Phillips curve is also vertical (a new classical proposition), then excessive increases in money supply can only ever cause increases in prices. A vertical long-run Phillips curve has dominated monetary policy making for the last twenty years and lay behind the monetary growth targets adopted by many administrations in the 1980s.

## Critiques of stable velocity

The best known rejections of a stable velocity come from three directions. The first group originates in empirical work on the demand for money where variables proxying financial innovation are introduced to explain shifts in the quantity of money held, relative to spending.

The second is associated with the neoclassical synthesis. This is that the demand for money is highly interest elastic (see for example Modigliani 1977). Thus, a small rise in interest rates produces a large fall in the quantity of money people wish to hold relative to income (velocity rises).

The third stresses the non-ergodic nature of the world and the importance of liquidity preference in the face of genuine uncertainty (see for example Davidson 1994). Faced with a threat of high levels of non-quantifiable uncertainty, people will rush to hold money balances on a scale which may bear no relation to any previous fluctuation in the demand for money (velocity falls). The demand schedule is fundamentally unstable. This is a more accurate representation (than high interest elasticity) of the ideas of Keynes in *The General Theory of Interest, Employment and Money* in 1936. But it is not often noticed that it contrasts with Keynes on velocity in the *Treatise on Money* in 1930. In this earlier work, Keynes explicitly excludes changes in the holding of idle balance ("hoards," as he called them) as explanations of velocity; "otherwise

an increase (or decrease) in the amount of hoards would appear as causing a decrease (or increase) in velocity of money whereas what they were really causing was a change in the supply, or quantity, of effective money" (Keynes, *Treatise*, p. 17). Keynes's treatment of velocity in the *Treatise* yields a number of valuable insights which have only been partially explored. They hinge on a distinction between what we might call income velocity, $V_Y (= PY/M)$, and transactions velocity, $V_T (= PT/M)$.

## Transactions and income velocities

It is one thing to argue that velocity is determined by institutional factors, and is stable, when the relevant definition of spending is total spending, i.e. $T$ (or even $R$), and another thing altogether to argue that it is stable when it is the inverse of a demand for money function which tries to link the demand for money to spending only on final output, or $Y$. $PT$ and $PY$ are not equivalent expressions. $PT$ is larger than $PY$ by some multiple. And hence, $V_T > V_Y$. It is true that $PT$ and $PY$ can be made equivalent for many purposes by assuming that $Y$ is a constant fraction of $T$ and that the price of $Y$ does not behave differently from the price of $T$. (The growth rates of $PT$ and $PY$ are then equal and $V_T$ and $V_Y$ maintain a constant relationship.) However, assuming this relationship between $T$ and $Y$ is highly problematic.

Four years before Keynes wrote the *Treatise*, in the second edition of Fisher's *Purchasing Power of Money*, Fisher recognized that $MV = PT1 + PT_2$ where $T_1$ were income transactions and $T_2$ were financial transactions. The distinction is only worth making if one thinks they may behave differently. Keynes in the *Treatise* made this more explicit. Some of the transactions encompassed by $T$ (but not $Y$) will change slowly over time and will follow $Y$ closely (intermediate transactions are an obvious example), but some (non-$Y$) transactions:

need not be, and are not, governed by the volume of current output. The pace at which a circle of financiers, speculators and investors hand round to one another particular pieces of wealth, or title to such, which they are neither producing nor consuming but merely exchanging, bears no definite relation to the rate of current production. The volume of such transactions is subject to very wide and incalculable fluctuations.

(Keynes, *Treatise*, p. 42)

Clearly then, for Keynes, $T$ could vary widely with respect to $Y$ and in those circumstances, we should note, $V_T$ will diverge from $V_Y$.

If $T$ and $Y$ diverge, the behavior of $V_T$, compared with $V_Y$, will depend upon whether the money supply follows $T$ or $Y$ more closely. Some years ago, Bain and Howells (1991) showed that $T$ diverged sharply upward from $Y$ in the UK from the mid-1970s, and that broad money aggregates followed $T$ more closely than $Y$, with the result that $V_T$ was fairly stable while $V_Y$ fell sharply. The evidence is updated in Howells (1996). This result is entirely predictable for ENDOGENOUS MONEY AND CREDIT since there is no reason to suppose that the demand for new loans, the source of new deposits, depends only on plans to buy finished output ($Y$), rather than on housing and financial assets as well ($T$). Howells and Biefang (1992) found the UK personal sector's demand for bank loans was better explained by $PT$ than by the more conventional $PY$.

In a world of endogenous money, in other words, the behavior of $V_Y$, depends upon the $PT/PY$ relationship.

## Selected references

Bain, K. and Howells, P.G.A. (1991) "The Income and Transactions Velocities of Money," *Review of Social Economy*, Fall: 383–95.

Davidson, P. (1994) *Post Keynesian Macroeconomic Theory*, Aldershot: Edward Elgar.

Fisher, I. (1911) *The Purchasing Power of Money*, 2nd edn, New York: Macmillan, 1926.

Friedman, M. (1956) "The Quantity Theory of Money – A Restatement," in M. Friedman, *Studies in the Quantity Theory of Money*, Chicago: Chicago University Press, 3–21.

Howells, P.G.A. (1996) "Endogenous Money and the State of Trade," in P. Arestis (ed.), *Keynes, Money and the Open Economy: Essays in Honour of Paul Davidson*, vol. 1, Aldershot: Edward Elgar.

Howells, P.G.A. and Biefang, I. (1992) "The Recent Behaviour of Income and Transactions Velocities in the UK," *Journal of Post Keynesian Economics* 14(3): 367–88.

Modigliani, F. (1977) "The Monetarist Controversy or, Should We Forsake Stabilization Policies?," *American Economic Review* 69: 1–19.

PETER HOWELLS

# Verdoorn's Law

Verdoorn's Law is the empirical generalization that there is a close linear relationship between the rate of growth in industrial output ($q$) and that of labor productivity ($p$) in the long run. This relationship is specified as:

$$p_t = a + bq_t$$

where $a$ is the autonomous rate of productivity growth and $b$ is the Verdoorn coefficient. This concept goes back to the pioneering study of Verdoorn (1949), who looked for a method to estimate the future level of labor productivity. Using cross-country data for Canada, Japan, the USA and twelve European countries, mostly for the period 1924–38, Verdoorn found a mean value of 0.45 for the elasticity of productivity with respect to industrial production; with a range of 0.41–0.57.

## Origins of the law

Verdoorn's Italian article of 1949 did not attract much attention until Kaldor (1966) focused on the broader implications of Verdoorn's results in his Cambridge inaugural lecture. Here they formed an important part of his thesis that economic maturity is a major cause of the UK's slow rate of growth relative to other countries in the postwar period. In particular, Kaldor observed that the faster the rate of output growth in manufacturing, the faster will be the rate of growth of labor productivity. Thus a substantial part of productivity growth is endogenous to the economy's growth process, with the manufacturing sector functioning as the engine of growth, owing to economies of scale or INCREASING RETURNS TO SCALE in the widest sense. These account for Verdoorn's Law or Kaldor's Second Growth Law as it is also called (see Thirlwall 1983).

The existence of production-induced productivity effects was already interpreted by Verdoorn as an indicator of increasing returns to scale occurring in industry due to an increase in the DIVISION OF LABOR. Stimulated by the work of Allyn Young (1928), his early teacher at the LSE who had elaborated the ideas of Adam Smith and Alfred Marshall on the role of economies of scale, Kaldor distinguished between static economies of scale in mass production and dynamic economies of scale due to learning effects. These learning effects are the result of an increasing division of labor, internal and external to the firm. The division of production processes into several working performances does not only cause an increase in the dexterity of laborers but also allows for the invention of machines. Likewise the introduction of more capital intensive methods of production becomes profitable only with a sufficiently high number of products being produced. New industries arise due to the invention and introduction of new machines. An increasing division of labor is not exclusively a firm-internal phenomenon but takes place also on the industrial level, for example, between firms and whole industries.

## Production-induced productivity

Verdoorn derived an equation for the relation between output growth and productivity growth from a Cobb–Douglas production function to elucidate possible determinants of production-induced productivity effects. This equation comprises elasticities of production as well as parameters of the labor supply function. It does not allow a clear-cut quantification of the scale effects, which in Verdoorn's model are of a purely static kind since it abstracts from technical progress. The same holds for a direct determination of the Verdoorn relationship from a Cobb–Douglas function, because the Verdoorn coefficient, $b$, depends only on the production elasticity of labor (see Rowthorn 1979). This derivation of the Verdoorn relation contains several problems. It records the growth of capital stock only in the absolute term $a$, and thereby does not take into account possible distortions of the Verdoorn coefficient (see McCombie 1982). Moreover, the dynamic estimation of Verdoorn's Law (growth rates) reveals significant differences in scale effects, in contrast to the static version (changes in absolute terms).

Although this paradox can be generated by statistical errors, it is widely seen as an indicator for the fact that the standard neoclassical production function does not represent the true cause of Verdoorn's Law. Several authors (for example, Dixon and Thirlwall 1975), therefore, have proposed the technical progress function as an alternative. Here, the Verdoorn coefficient covers the effects of embodied and disembodied technical progress, as well as the effects of demand-induced capital accumulation. The reduction of Verdoorn's Law to a simple functional relationship is too narrow an interpretation. Rather it has to be grasped as a "productivity regime," with several functions that determine how an increase in demand can lead to productivity growth (see Pini 1995). Besides scale effects, the diffusion of new technologies, demand-induced technical progress in the sense of Schmookler, as well as institutional and social aspects play an important role (see Boyer and Petit 1991).

## Implications for growth processes

Verdoorn's Law has far-reaching implications for growth processes. Since an increase in output leads to an increase in productivity, countries, regions or firms will gain in international competitiveness, with a consequential further increase in output growth and so on, or in other words, a virtuous circle. Verdoorn's Law thus allows for CIRCULAR AND CUMULATIVE CAUSATION. In contrast to the traditional neoclassical growth model, Verdoorn's Law thus explains divergence instead of convergence in per capita income of regions or countries over time. It contributes to a clarification of the same questions which are at the center of the so-called "new" growth theory.

The demand-oriented approach hypothesizes that the limits to growth do not lie on the supply side, such as labor supply (neither Verdoorn's nor Kaldor's measure of labor input is quality adjusted). Rather the main limit is in the level and structure of demand, whose development over time determines the growth process. Verdoorn's Law has a great importance for economies with export-led growth. McCombie and Thirlwall (1994) have shown the consequences of the external equilibrium condition within these models. Cumulative processes also contain feedback effects from productivity growth to demand ("reverse causation").

## Employment consequences

The existence of Verdoorn's Law has important consequences for the development of employment. According to Kaldor's cross-country study of OECD countries, an increase in the growth of output of 1 percent results in an increase in productivity growth and in employment growth of about half a percentage point each. Whereas the double-sided nature of induced productivity growth might have been welcome in the full employment years of the 1960s, it looks different in phases of high unemployment. The higher the productivity effects of growth the higher is the growth rate of production that is required to keep employment constant. On the other hand, productivity growth is necessary to sustain international competitiveness. Verdoorn's Law thus makes a contribution to explaining the phenomenon of jobless growth (see Pini 1995).

## Stability of the Verdoorn relation

A further aspect refers to the stability of the Verdoorn relation, which has been examined in cross-country as well as in time series analyses. In the first case, the problem arises that the Verdoorn relation can be generated by great differences in exogenous productivity growth and associated production growth without increasing returns being necessary (Rowthorn 1975). Empirical studies have to consider cyclical phenomena like OKUN'S LAW, since the development of labor productivity is affected by the degree of capacity utilization. There is some empirical evidence that the Verdoorn relation was particularly strong in manufacturing in the 1960s and 1970s, whereas from the late 1970s onwards the autonomous component $a$ has increased and the Verdoorn coefficient $b$ has diminished (see, for example, Boyer and Petit 1991). However, the empirical results also depend on the sample of countries. Furthermore, a stable Verdoorn coefficient cannot be expected, since it would require a stable productivity regime.

## See also:

Kaldor–Pasinetti models of growth and distribution; Kaldor's theory of the growth process; reserve army of labor; unemployment: policies to reduce; unemployment and underemployment

## Selected references

Boyer, R. and Petit, P. (1991) "Kaldor's Growth Theories: Past, Present and Prospects for the Future," in E.J. Nell and W. Semmler (eds), *Nicholas Kaldor and Mainstream Economics*, London: Macmillan, 485–517.

Dixon, R. and Thirlwall, A.P. (1975) "A Model of Regional Growth-Rate Differences on Kaldorian Lines," *Oxford Economic Papers* 27(2): 201–14.

Kaldor, N. (1966) *Causes of the Slow Rate of Economic Growth in the United Kingdom*, Cambridge: Cambridge University Press.

McCombie, J.S.L. (1982) "Economic Growth, Kaldor's Laws and the Static-Dynamic Verdoorn Law Paradox," *Applied Economics* 14: 279–94.

McCombie, J.S.L. and Thirlwall, A.P. (1994) *Economic Growth and the Balance-of-Payments Constraint*, London: Macmillan.

Pini, P. (1995) "Economic Growth, Technological Change and Employment: Empirical Evidence for a Cumulative Growth Model with External Causation for Nine OECD Countries: 1960–1990," *Structural Change and Economic Dynamics* 6: 185–213.

Rowthorn, R.E. (1975) "What Remains of Kaldor's Law?," *Economic Journal* 85: 10–19.

——(1979) "A Note on Verdoorn's Law," *Economic Journal* 89: 131–3.

Thirlwall, A.P. (1983) "A Plain Man's Guide to Kaldor's Growth Laws," *Journal of Post Keynesian Economics* 5(3): 345–58.

Verdoorn, P.J. (1949) "Fattori che regolano lo sviluppo della produttività del lavoro," *L'Industria*, 45–53; trans. in L.L. Pasinetti (ed.), *Italian Economic Papers*, vol. 2, Oxford: Il Mulino Oxford University Press, 59–68.

Young, A.A. (1928) "Increasing Returns and Economic Growth," *Economic Journal* 38: 527–42.

HARALD HAGEMANN
STEPHAN SEITER

**VERTICAL INTEGRATION:** *see* circular production and vertical integration

# W

## wage determination

Questions pertaining to wage determination are generally of two types. One focuses on the general level of wages; the other on the wage structure. The answers supplied over the years have been many and varied, but, in general, either emphasize market forces, institutional factors, or class conflict.

### Brief history of approaches

Adam Smith's *Wealth of Nations* (1776) reveals the variety of ideas developed in England and on the Continent by the mid-eighteenth century. Supply and demand received Smith's special attention, with demand playing the larger role in the short run and supply in the long run (a theme carried forward by classical and neoclassical economists). Smith's emphasis on market forces did not, however, preclude him from explicitly recognizing the important role of institutional factors – customs, laws, and traditions – in the determination of both the general level and structure of wages. In addition, while acknowledging that in theory, and under certain conditions, market forces would equalize wages across occupations (the "law of one price"), he conceded that, in practice, this would never happen since occupations differed with respect to:

> the agreeableness or disagreeableness of the employments themselves...the difficulty and expense of learning them...the constancy or inconstancy of employment in them...the small or great trust which must be reposed in those who exercise them; and...the probability or improbability of success in them.
>
> (Smith 1776: 202)

Classical economists after Smith generally de-emphasized the role of institutional factors as they moved toward abstract theorizing. Two classical theories of note are Ricardo's iron law of wages and the wages fund doctrine.

Writing in the same period, Marx took essentially the same position as the classical economists in asserting that the price of labor power under capitalism, like the value of all commodities, is determined by the cost of producing it. The cost of reproducing labor power was postulated to equal the socially determined level of subsistence necessary for the maintenance, education, training, and propagation of the worker (Marx 1847). For Marx, the value of labor power, which on average equals the wage, is determined by cultural and historical factors. What distinguishes Marx most from the classical economists is his analysis of wage determination in the dynamic context of class struggle. According to Marx, as capitalists compete with one another through the reduction of commodity prices, they seek out ways to reduce that part of the workday given to the production of individual commodities.

One strategy is to increase labor PRODUCTIVITY through the introduction of machinery and the DIVISION OF LABOR. This strategy results in the de-skilling of the labor force and hence reduces its cost of production, which in turn reduces its exchange-value or wage. Furthermore, competition among workers increases as skilled workers are replaced by the unskilled, men by women, and adults by children, thus further reducing the cost of reproducing any one laborer (the wage) and creating a RESERVE ARMY OF LABOR (Marx 1847). However, Marx also recognized the importance of linkages between the capital and consumer goods sectors, and in this context aggregate profit may be expanded by higher wages in some instances.

The marginal productivity theory, developed at the turn of the nineteenth century, provided an alternative to the Marxian notion of wage determination under capitalism. According to the marginal productivity theory, a firm will hire workers up to the point where the value of the output produced by the additional worker is just equal to that which must be sold in order to pay the individual. Because real wages will always equal the marginal product of labor, and because every worker in the firm can be conceived of as the marginal worker, each worker is said to be paid what she or he is worth.

## Modern marginalist and Keynesian aproaches

Today, marginal productivity theory forms the foundation of the neoclassical theory of labor demand. The supply of labor, which is analyzed in terms of a labor–leisure trade-off, together with demand determines the general level of wages as the two interact in ways congruent with an aggregate price-auction model. As labor productivity increases in the aggregate, the marginal product of labor and hence the demand for labor rises, increasing the general level of wages.

Despite its wide acceptance, the neoclassical view has not gone unchallenged. KEYNES, for example, rejected the whole notion of an aggregate labor market and argued that money wages are not as flexible as the price-auction model presumes. Workers, he maintained, are concerned not just with their absolute level of wages but also with their relative wages. Consequently, they will resist a cut in money wages because of its effect on their relative socioeconomic position. Furthermore, Keynes asserted that unemployment (excess supply) cannot be eradicated even if workers acquiesce to a lower money wage.

This latter argument has been taken up by modern day post-Keynesians with their theory of markup PRICING, the idea that firms set prices by taking the money costs of production (of which wages constitute the largest share) and adding a generally accepted profit margin. If money wages do fall, prices will fall along with them. Consequently, real wages change little, if at all. This is not to say that real wages will never change over the business cycle. In fact, real wages change in a procyclical fashion, a phenomenon post-Keynesians explain in terms of temporal differences in the demand for workers in the capital goods sector (which generally pays higher than average wages) and in the consumer goods sector (which generally pays lower wages).

Unlike the post-Keynesians, New Keynesians accept the validity of an aggregate labor market as a theoretical construct. Their challenge to the neoclassical price-auction model is one that stems from the existence of sticky money wages. This stickiness may be due to worker concern with relative wages, union wage contracts being imperfectly indexed for inflation, the TRANSACTION COSTS associated with changing money wages, and game-theoretic pricing decisions by firms. Wage determination may be due to societal conceptions of what is just and fair; the payment by firms of above market wages (see EFFICIENCY WAGES) in order to secure a greater amount of effort from workers; and implicit contracts between employers and workers, whereby workers accept a certain degree of employment instability in return for higher than market wages (Solow 1980).

## Approaches to wage structure

Most contemporary theoretical work in the area of wage determination has focused not on the general level of wages, but on the structure of wages across occupations and individuals. The neoclassical model explains occupational differences in terms of compensating wage differentials which equalize net utility across occupations (similar to the arguments put forward by Adam Smith). Individual wage differentials are explained in terms of human capital investment in education and training, the returns to which are affected by such factors as labor force intermittency and occupational choice. Discrimination plays no role in the determination of wages in the long run. In the long run, the law of one price applies to workers of similar human capital characteristics.

Alternative models of the structure of wages emphasize either institutional factors or class. Of those that emphasize institutional factors, theories of labor market segmentation have been the most influential. These theories, which derive from the ideas presented by the US institutionalists of the late nineteenth and early twentieth centuries, emphasize the institutional barriers – such as discrimination, internal labor markets, union work rules, and licencing requirements – that prevent workers from competing in certain labor markets.

The most widely known of the segmentation theories is that of dual labor markets. According to this theory, workers are separated into two distinct labor markets, identified as primary and secondary. Jobs in the primary labor market are relatively high paying with decent working conditions, employment security, and chances for promotion. These jobs are typically found in firms with well-established internal labor markets. Within the internal labor market of a firm, there exist well-established rules which govern the allocation of labor among specific jobs and job ladders. While market forces do play some role in the setting of wages, most jobs are firm-specific and thus have no exact counterpart in the market. Consequently, wages are set by prescribed rules, in order to achieve goals such as internal equity and labor force continuity. Because of the significance of equity considerations, the value placed on the jobs that people do is often reflective of society's valuation of those who do them. INTERNAL LABOR MARKETS are linked to the external labor market through entry level positions, via ports of entry. Wages paid for these jobs tend to be more highly susceptible to the forces of supply and demand, although internal equity concerns do play a role.

According to dual labor market theorists, most women and minorities are relegated to low-paying, dead-end jobs within the secondary labor market. These jobs are found in smaller firms, or in industries such as retail trade and services, where workers do not require much firm-specific, on-the-job training. Because of limited training and short job ladders, the wages paid are low. Coupled with the poor working conditions and arbitrary work rules, which often characterize these jobs, workers have no incentive to remain at the job for any length of time, for developing good work habits, or for placing a high value on education or skill enhancement. Consequently, as workers adapt to jobs in the secondary market, and employers in this market adapt their jobs to the workers in this market, the conditions become self-perpetuating.

While empirical evidence does not support the view of two separate sectors with little to no mobility between them, evidence does suggest that there exist different and distinct sets of rules governing the allocation and remuneration of labor in different segments of the labor market. The challenge is to construct a theoretical framework within which to understand the processes that lead to the segmentation of labor markets, in spite of the mobility of workers between them (Gordon *et al.* 1982) (see SEGMENTED AND DUAL LABOR MARKETS).

Radical political economists also understand the determination of the wage structure in terms of segmentation, but emphasize the Marxian notions of class and class conflict as they are played out within the firm. Capitalists, in their efforts to extract from labor the greatest amount of surplus value possible, can succeed only as long as workers do not identify themselves as a class in opposition to the capitalist class. Consequently, capitalists are motivated to keep the working class divided. They do this by creating institutions that perpetuate the social DIVISION OF LABOR. In the labor market itself, this is done by the segmentation of the labor market and the introduction of internal labor markets. This is done by the introduction of specific forms of technology that foster divisions among the working class, and by the exploitation of sex, race, and ethnic antagonisms that exist in society at large. The structure of wages both reflects and supports this social division of labor and thus keeps workers from recognizing their common class interests.

## Conclusion

Historically, theories of wage determination were developed to answer questions raised by the labor market issues of the day (Tolles 1964). Today, wage theories must address such problems as persistent GENDER and race-based wage differentials, rising income INEQUALITY, and falling real wages in the face of rising productivity and profits. Despite the failure of neoclassical wage theory to provide adequate explanations of these phenomena, it continues to dominate the way Western economists think about these issues. Possibly the current infusion of feminist analysis into institutional and class-based theories will provide the next major challenge.

## See also:

comparable worth; discrimination in the labor market; family wage; gender division of labor; labor and labor power; women's wages: social construction of; wage and profit share

## Selected references

Edwards, Richard C. (1979) *Contested Terrain: The Transformation of the Workplace in the Twentieth Century*, New York: Basic Books.

Gordon, David M., Edwards, Richard and Reich, Michael (1982) *Segmented Work, Divided Workers*, Cambridge: Cambridge University Press.

Marx, Karl (1847) *Wage-Labour and Capital*, New York: International Publishers, 1976.

McNulty, Paul J. (1980) *The Origins and Development of Labor Economics*, Cambridge: The MIT Press.

Smith, Adam (1776) *An Inquiry into the Nature and Causes of the Wealth of Nations*, Harmondsworth: Penguin Books, 1979.

Solow, Robert M. (1980) "On Theories of Unemployment," *American Economic Review* 70(1): 1–11.

Tolles, N. Arnold (1964) *Origins of Modern Wage Theories*, Englewood Cliffs, NJ: Prentice Hall.

ELIZABETH A. PAULIN

# wage and profit share

## Introduction

In their DISTRIBUTION OF INCOME theories, post-Keynesian economists divide income into two categories. First there are "wages," which includes all income received from employers in return for allocating time to work. Second, there are "profits," a residual to encompass all income derived by those who own and/or control property. This division derives from the belief that the wage share is conditioned by entrepreneurial power affecting the profit mark up on costs in imperfectly competitive markets, and/or by differential savings propensities out of these two categories of income.

Published data do not correspond precisely with the theoretical categories, and care is required in constructing meaningful time series for the wage share. This is particularly so when the incidence of self-employment and government activity is changing over time (King and Regan 1976: 9–15). The distribution between wages and profits plays a central role in the theories of income determination and ECONOMIC GROWTH propounded by the founders of post-Keynesian political economy: Nicholas Kaldor, Michal KALECKI, Joan Robinson and Sidney Weintraub.

## Kalecki's influence and work

Theoretical endeavors to explain the determination of the wage share date back to the classical economics of Ricardo and MARX (see WAGE DETERMINATION). In twentieth-century political economy, Kalecki was certainly the originator of post-Keynesian wage/profit share analysis. His degree of monopoly theory of the profit share is based on a manufacturing firm in an imperfectly competitive product market

(Kalecki 1971: 43–77). This firm is assumed to operate with excess capital capacity, so that factor proportions can be maintained when output expands. The firm is not a strict profit maximizer, and sets its price by reference to its own average direct costs of production, and the weighted average price of its competitors (see PRICING). The size of the profit markup on direct costs which can be obtained is determined by the "degree of monopoly".

Kalecki aggregates from the firm to the industry, and then to the overall manufacturing sector. With the degree of monopoly determining the ratio of profits to direct costs, it follows that the ratio of profits to wages will also be influenced by the proportion which wages represent of direct costs. Also, inter-industry differences in profit shares mean that the aggregate profit share can vary under the impact of changes in the composition of total output. Consequently, the profit share is dependent on three variables: the degree of monopoly, the ratio of wage costs to material costs, and the industrial composition of value added.

Several economists, including post-Keynesians such as Davidson and Kaldor, have criticized "the degree of monopoly" notion as a tautological formulation, which is defined simply as the price-average direct cost relationship. However, Kalecki makes it clear that the price-average direct cost relationship is determined by the degree of monopoly. This, in turn, is dependent upon the extent of industrial concentration and cartelization, the extent to which price competition is replaced by advertising and product differentiation, and the strength of trade union resistance (Kalecki 1971: 49–52). Kalecki may well have produced an empirically awkward independent variable, but it is not one which is tautological. Certainly, it is an intuitively plausible hypothesis that the relative shares of wages and profits are influenced by the power which comes when market participants are concentrated or collectivized, rather than being perfectly competitive.

The other foundation of post-Keynesian distribution theory which Kalecki laid was the assumption of differential savings propensities out of wages and profits. In Keynes's *General Theory*, the multiplier process ensures, in circumstances of unemployment, that total income adjusts sufficiently to maintain a flow of savings which matches investment demand. In KALECKI'S MACRO THEORY OF PROFITS, Kalecki assumed that there was no saving out of wages. Consequently, it is profit which must now adjust sufficiently to maintain a flow of savings which matches investment demand. In conditions of UNEMPLOYMENT AND UNDEREMPLOYMENT, the absolute volume of profit is determined by the level of investment and the reciprocal of the savings propensity out of profit. In effect, this is Kalecki's version of the Keynesian multiplier.

## Kaldor and other contributions

Kaldor (1956) generalized this by assuming a positive savings propensity out of wages, but one which was less than the savings propensity out of profits. He also assumed full employment. Consequently, it is the profit share which must now adjust sufficiently to maintain a flow of savings which matches investment demand. For instance, if investment demand rises there must be a redistribution towards profits, in order to establish a higher aggregate savings propensity. Kaldor is using the multiplier principle to explain the distribution rather than the level of income (see KALDOR–PASINETTI MODELS OF GROWTH AND DISTRIBUTION).

Some scholars, such as Wood (1975), have proposed models with a direct microeconomic linkage between profit margins and investment demand, based on the self-financing objectives of firms. This was not Kaldor's position, however, at least until his mature years. Kaldor relies on the general level of prices varying relative to the general level of wages, in response to the impact which changing investment plans have on aggregate demand (but see his later work for a different perspective). As in Kalecki, it is profit takers as a class who benefit from increased investment demand.

If we relax Kaldor's full employment assumption, but retain differential savings propensities, the profit share becomes a determinant of aggregate demand. For instance, a fall in the profit share will increase the aggregate propensity to consume, so that, provided investment remains unchanged, output and employment will rise (Kalecki 1971: 156–64). This possibility, that a higher wage share (and real wage) could be associated with increased employment, is obviously in direct contrast to the neoclassical position. Of course investment may be deterred by the squeezed profit share, which Kalecki notes (see KALECKI'S PRINCIPLE OF INCREASING RISK). This dependence of both consumption and investment demand, and therefore the level of income, on the distribution of income is a central feature of post-Keynesian economics. It is encompassed in several eclectic theories of income distribution, which allow for interdependence between the level and the distribution of income. By far the most impressive of these theories is that of Sidney Weintraub (1958).

In Weintraub's theory, the distribution of any given level of income is determined by the relationship of marginal product to average product (the M/A ratio), and by the degree of monopoly: this is contained within his aggregate supply function. Weintraub's aggregate demand function incorporates the impact of distributional changes on aggregate consumption demand (see SUPPLY AND DEMAND: AGGREGATE). The interaction between these two functions provides an explanation for the wage/profit share, in which the demand side emphasis of Kaldor is complemented by the supply side forces of wages rates, productivity and pricing. Here the two branches of post-Keynesian distribution theory are reconciled (see Weintraub 1958: 104–107; Weintraub Symposium 1985: 557, 576).

### Selected references

Hicks, J.R. (1963) *The Theory of Wages*, London: Macmillan.

Kaldor, N. (1956) "Alternative Theories of Income Distribution," *Review of Economic Studies* 23: 83–100.

Kalecki, M. (1971) *Selected Essays in the Dynamics of the Capitalist Economy*, Cambridge: Cambridge University Press.

Keynes, J.M. (1939) "Relative Movement of Real Wages and Output," *Economic Journal* 49: 34–51.

King, J. and Regan, P. (1976) *Relative Income Shares*, London: Macmillan.

Phelps Brown, E.H. (1957) "The Meaning of the Fitted Cobb–Douglas Production Function," *Quarterly Journal of Economics* 71: 546–60.

Weintraub, S. (1958) *An Approach to the Theory of Income Distribution*, Philadelphia: Chilton.

Weintraub Symposium (1985) *Journal of Post Keynesian Economics* 7: 504–606.

Wood, A. (1975) *A Theory of Profits*, Cambridge: Cambridge University Press.

PETER A. Y. RIACH

# waged household labor

Waged household labor is HOUSEHOLD LABOR – cleaning, cooking, laundry, etc. – performed for payment, usually to replace otherwise unpaid household labour. Waged household labor has two defining features: (1) it entails the direct purchase of labor time, and (2) it is performed in the home of the purchasing householder.

### Nature of the market

In recent years, social theorists have predicted strong growth in the market for household labor services. Accurate and comprehensive data about the size and composition of this market are extremely difficult to obtain, because much activity probably takes place in the unrecorded cash economy. However, it is safe to assert that waged household labor is overwhelmingly a female occupation.

Because women's primary responsibility for household labor has so profoundly affected their LABOR FORCE participation, the existence of a significant market for domestic labor services would be an important development for political economists interested in the GENDER DIVISION OF LABOR in the home.

Moreover, employment in social reproductive labor is divided along racial as well as gender lines, and is disproportionately undertaken by racial-ethnic women in both private household and institutional settings (Glenn 1992). Thus, waged household labor is important in the analysis of RACE, ETHNICITY, GENDER AND CLASS relations. Finally, waged domestic labor is also implicated in debates about structural change and the future of work.

## History

The incidence, economic significance, organization and employment relations of waged household labor differ with time and place. During the nineteenth century in industrializing countries, more women worked as "domestic servants" than in any other occupation, doing a variety of indoor household tasks in the homes of their employers, for whom they worked full-time and with whom they usually lived. Servants received board and lodging in addition to money wages, and their private lives were circumscribed by their servitude and place of residence.

In Western countries, changing domestic technologies and emerging alternative employment opportunities saw numbers in domestic service decline after the turn of the twentieth century, and collapse after the Second World War. Paid household workers today rarely live with their employers, and are likely to work part-time in more than one household, resulting in very different kinds of employment relationships. "Nannies" or private childcare workers are a frequent exception to this new pattern, and their experience may resemble that of some "domestic servants" more closely; so too does that of waged domestic laborers in developing countries, where waged household labor on the "domestic service" model remains a significant source of employment.

Modernization theory argued in the 1970s that employment in "domestic service" first increases, then decreases with economic development, as commodity production and state provision progressively replace domestic production of the necessities of daily life (Boserup 1970: 103). Sociological variants of the modernization thesis claimed that the master–servant relation was premodern in character, and so "obsolete" in the modern occupational structure (Coser 1973). More recently, feminist writers have pointed to the existence of waged household labor as a refutation of modernization theory, and theorists of "post-industrial society" have located waged household labor within the growing service sector, analyzing it as a potential source of jobs as manufacturing employment declines.

## Inequality and the division of labor

Responses to this potentiality vary. Some view domestic and personal services as an untapped mine of commercial opportunity, and believe that growth in the new domestic services industry will herald in a new Golden Age of full employment. Others, notably André Gorz (1994), argue that grave inequalities in the distribution of work and income generate "new servants" as money-rich, time-poor elites pass the menial tasks of daily reproduction to the time-rich and income-poor masses displaced by labor saving technologies in other areas of the economy.

Feminist theorists, too, are ambivalent. On the one hand, the "socialization," "professionalization" or "industrialization" of housework have figured in feminist idealizations of the good society. Yet, some feminists argue, waged household labor is an occupation at the bottom of the social DIVISION OF LABOR, in which middle class women employ working class women, typically from racial-ethnic minority groups, in isolated, privatized and inappropriately personalized employment relationships. Women's participation in the labor force has increased, and the women's liberation movement has contributed to increased access to well-paid full-time employment for some women. Thus a GENDER dimension is added to Gorz's general theory of demand for private domestic services: some women are able to avoid the double day (where women work for wages and then undertake most of the unpaid household chores as well) by replacing their own household labor with that of other women.

Feminists also argue that the practice of employing domestic workers leaves the GENDER DIVISION OF LABOR unchallenged. Men are left relatively free of responsibility for household labor, which remains feminized and essentially private. Moreover, householders may be purchasing deference as well as time from waged domestic laborers (Romero 1992: ch. 5), particularly when the women of color they so often employ "function better as contrast figures for strengthening employers' egos and class and racial identities" (Rollins 1985: 156). Thus, the household worker–employer relationship may reproduce and reinforce existing unequal social relations of race, class and gender.

On the supply side, international migration, legal and illegal, is frequently cited by feminist writers as an important source of waged domestic laborers. Women from poor countries migrating to rich ones in search of work and emigration opportunities take up waged household labor – often because it is isolated and privatized and so available "off the books," or because they experience discrimination in markets for other kinds of labor. Here the dimension of international inequality is taken into account (see Sanjek and Colen 1990).

## Cycles, policy and location

Although supply and demand for waged household labor are clearly correlated with secular changes in economic structures – as modernization theory suggests – the size and composition of the market is also profoundly affected by cyclical, political and cultural factors. Demand for waged domestic labor tends to fall and its supply increases in times of economic downturn. Immigration policy in some industrialized countries (the United States, Canada, Hong Kong) allows the importation of paid household workers from poor countries, in others (Australia) it does not. Geographical location may facilitate or hinder large scale illegal immigration, inhibiting the development of a large, cheap and vulnerable migrant labor force available for waged household labor. The level of public provision of childcare affects demand for private childcarers also.

## Conclusion

Whether the market for waged household labor will significantly increase its share of employment remains to be seen. If it does, it will represent an important change in the social division of labor, and may displace unpaid domestic labor from its central place in the agenda of much feminist political economy.

## See also:

class structures of households; domestic labor debate; feminist political economy: major contemporary themes; reserve army of labor: latent; women's wages: social construction of

## Selected references

Boserup, Esther (1970) *Women's Role in Economic Development*, London: George Allen & Unwin.

Coser, Lewis A. (1973) "Servants: The Obsolescence of an Occupational Role," *Social Forces* 52(September).

Glenn, Evelyn Nakano (1992) "From Servitude to Service Work: Historical Continuities in the Racial Division of Paid Reproductive Labor," *Signs* 18(1).

Gorz, André (1994) "The New Servants," in *Capitalism, Socialism, Ecology*, London: Verso.

Gregson, Nicky and Lowe, Michelle (1994) *Servicing the Middle Classes: Class, Gender and Waged Domestic Labour in Contemporary Britain*, London: Routledge.

Rollins, Judith (1985) *Between Women: Domestics and Their Employers*, Philadelphia: Temple University Press.

Romero, Mary (1992) *Maid in the U.S.A*, New York: Routledge.

Sanjek, Roger and Colen, Shellee (eds) (1990) *At Work in Homes: Household Workers in World Perspective*, American Ethnological

Society monograph series 3, Washington, DC.

GABRIELLE MEAGHER

# wages theory, Sraffian

## Introduction

SRAFFA sought both to provide a critique of marginal economics and to contribute towards a revival of the classical theory of value and distribution. On the critical side, Sraffa showed that the marginalist theory of wages, as determined by the intersection of labor supply and a downward sloping demand curve, is logically flawed. The Sraffian critique undermines the theoretical foundations of the marginalist "supply and demand" explanation of distribution and prices and the tendency of a competitive market economy to full employment (or "natural unemployment") in the traditional long-period framework of analysis; while the short-period framework of analysis cannot provide a sound alternative foundation for marginalism (see Roncaglia 1988).

## Renewal of the classical theory of value and distribution

Sraffa (1951, 1960) contributed to the revival of the classical approach by rediscovering its logical structure and solving some analytical problems, such as the demonstration of the inverse relation between the rate of profit and the real wage.

In the classical approach, wages are regarded as being determined by two main factors: (1) the bargaining position of the parties, and (2) the habitual, historically determined living standards of the workers. The latter determine what the classical economists used to call the subsistence minimum, a "floor" under which actual wages cannot persistently fall. If circumstances are favorable to workers, the normal wage rate can be established above this minimum. Thus wages may include part of the surplus product, besides the subsistence component (Sraffa 1960: 9).

The factors influencing the bargaining position of workers can be of an institutional, political and economic nature. An important role is played by labor market conditions: especially the number of unemployed or underemployed workers (the RESERVE ARMY OF LABOR). This is why the pace of capital ACCUMULATION (and hence employment trends) and POPULATION growth were regarded as having a major influence on the course of wages over time. In the classical view, unemployment is a common feature of a market economy because there is no inherent tendency of capitalist economies to operate at or near full employment (see Stirati 1994).

The classical theory of prices and distribution is compatible with the Keynesian principle of EFFECTIVE DEMAND AND CAPACITY UTILIZATION, which is taken as the point of departure for the theory of output and accumulation by contemporary economists working in the surplus approach (see Garegnani 1983; Eatwell and Milgate 1983; Mongiovi 1991). The criticism addressed by Sraffa and others of the marginalist capital theory not only discards the neoclassical demand curve for labor, but also the notion of investment as a negative function of the rate of interest. This is the ground for criticism of the neoclassical argument that investment will tend to equal full employment savings. Hence employment and its trends crucially depend on effective demand.

In the classical approach, it was generally recognized that population may fail to grow as much as employment, thereby enhancing workers' bargaining position. Wages can be above their minimum, even for long periods of time, and "subsistence" itself can change as a result. Population theory mainly had the role of rendering labor supply endogenous in the very long run.

The latter view can be supported also on different grounds. One explanation rests on Marx's reserve army of labor created through technical innovation and the expulsion of workers from the pre-capitalist sectors of the economy (which may be regarded as including domestic production of goods and services). During this century, changes in female participation rates have been a major determinant of labor supply in advanced economies. Although this process is intertwined with major social and institutional changes, there is evidence that female activity rates have tended to increase more in those countries in which the demand for labor has increased further. This lends support to the view that labor supply tends, in the long run, to (roughly) adjust to the requirements of accumulation.

## Habits, norms and institutions

Ideas often found in contemporary literature appear to be close to classical views. For example: the idea that workers resist reductions in real wages, and that their target real wage is related to habitual living standards, which is central in the literature on "real wage resistance," and "cost-push" inflationary processes; the importance of notions of fairness in causing wage stickiness, stressed in some versions of the efficiency wage models; and the role of unions and bargaining processes in wage determination, which points to the importance of institutional factors.

It should be emphasized here that attempts to explain the emergence of institutions or norms which render wages "sticky" tend not to be very convincing when a high elasticity of employment to wages is affirmed, as traditionally done by neoclassical economists (see Solow 1980). By contrast, in the classical approach a fall in the real wage rate cannot be expected to bring about an increase in employment, but would only cause a fall in workers' income. This may help explain why wage norms or institutions tend to emerge as a safeguard for the working class, and also to preserve social stability.

The classical approach to distribution appears to provide a framework consistent with the role of custom, power relations and institutions in determining wage differentials, which has been highlighted in SEGMENTED AND DUAL LABOR MARKETS. It is also consistent with recent empirical findings on the inverse relationship between the unemployment rate and the real wage level. A similar case holds for evidence that rising minimum wages have not negatively affected employment. HYSTERESIS in employment supports the importance of effective demand and the notion that large levels of unemployment cannot be re-established through normal market forces.

## Role of the money interest rate

Until now we have discussed factors that appear to affect the real wage level directly, following the idea prevalent among classical political economists that the real wage should be regarded as the given variable when determining prices and the rate of profit. However, Sraffa suggests that when the wage cannot be regarded as a set of "specified necessaries determined by physiological or social conditions" independent of prices, it may be more appropriate to regard the rate of profit as the given distributive variable, "susceptible of being determined outside the system of production, in particular by the level of the money interest rate" (1960: 33). So, while the "ever present element of subsistence" would still establish a floor of the real wage (and "subsistence" is used by Sraffa in the same way as the classical economists), the surplus component of the wage might be determined residually, given the rate of interest.

This suggestion by Sraffa has been followed up in several contemporary contributions (see Panico 1988; Pivetti 1991), which regard the nominal interest rate as a cost component of normal money prices. This implies that the rate of interest can affect real wages by altering the price level.

## See also:

Cambridge revolution; capital theory debates; classical political economy; heterogeneous capital and labor; neoclassical economics: critique; Sraffian political economy; wage determination

## Selected references

Eatwell, J. and Milgate, M. (eds) (1983) *Keynes's Economics and the Theory of Value and Distribution*, London: Duckworth.

Garegnani, P. (1983) "Two Routes to Effective Demand: a Comment on Kregel," in J.A. Kregel (ed.), *Distribution, Effective Demand and International Economic Relations*, London: Macmillan.

Mongiovi, G. (1991) "Keynes, Sraffa, and the Labour Market," *Review of Political Economy* 3(1): 25–42.

Panico, C. (1988) *Interest and Profit in the Theories of Value and Distribution*, London: Macmillan.

Pivetti, M. (1991) *An Essay on Money and Distribution*, London: Macmillan.

Roncaglia, A. (1988) "Wage Costs and Employment: The Sraffian View," in J.A. Kregel, E. Matzner and A. Roncaglia (eds), *Barriers to Full Employment*, London: Macmillan.

Solow, H. (1980) "On Theories of Unemployment," *American Economic Review* 70(1):1–11.

Sraffa, P. (1951) "Introduction," in *The Works and Correspondence of David Ricardo*, Cambridge: Cambridge University Press.

—— (1960) *Production of Commodities by Means of Commodities: Prelude to a Critique of Economic Theory*, Cambridge: Cambridge University Press.

Stirati, A. (1994) *The Theory of Wages in Classical Economics: A Study of Adam Smith, David Ricardo and their Contemporaries*, Cheltenham: Edward Elgar.

ANTONELLA STIRATI

# Ward–Vanek model of self-management

The economic theory of the worker-managed firm was first formulated by Ward in 1958. It was subsequently developed above all by Domar, Vanek and Meade (see Vanek 1970, 1977; Meade 1972). These contributions, and those of other writers on the subject over the period 1958–79, gave life to the Ward–Vanek model of self-management. In more recent years, the discussion of self-management has taken a rather different form under the heading LABOR-MANAGED ENTERPRISES.

## Assumptions

Ward analyzed the short-run equilibrium conditions for a worker-managed firm. There are two main assumptions to the theory. First, decisions of the firm are guided by the criterion of maximizing income per worker. This is a fundamental assumption, which serves as a basis for all the theoretical analysis. Second, profits are distributed equally among workers. This is a simplifying condition which can be removed in a more general analysis.

## Producer cooperative economy

A production cooperative may be thought of as a firm in which it is not capital which hires labor, but rather labor which hires or borrows capital. It is reasonable to suppose, as Ward does, that the cooperative must periodically pay a fixed "rent" for the use of plant and machinery. In his pioneering analysis, Ward assumed that the firms are nationalized and that, consequently, the cooperative has to pay an annual fixed rent to the state. This is justified in a subsequent theoretical analysis, which shows that externally financed cooperative firms must be publicly owned.

Ward further assumed that a firm may freely increase or decrease the number of its partners, but not their working hours (which are assumed to be fixed). One may further assume, for purposes of exposition, that the institutional wage rate, $w$, is fixed by the state, even though this does not affect the incomes of workers, which depend on the firm's earnings.

## Maximization conditions

The production function for the firm is given by:

$$X = f(L) \qquad (1)$$

where $L$ is the quantity of labor (the only variable factor); $X$ is the output obtained; and one usually assumes a diminishing marginal product of labor. If one ignores other costs and assumes perfectly competitive markets, the maximum income for workers ($y$) is consequently:

$$y = w + \frac{\pi}{L} = w + \frac{p_x X - (R + wL)}{L}$$
$$= \frac{p_x X - R}{L} \qquad (2)$$

where $\pi$ is profit, $p_x$ is the price of the good, $R$ is the rent paid to the state and $y$ is consequently average income per worker, being the sum of the wage rate ($w$) and profit per worker ($p/L$). We suppose that $R$ is equal to the product of the value of the means of production, $Kp_k$, and the marginal product of capital, $r$.

Given the institutional salary, the cooperative firm will seek to maximize profit per worker, which is the difference between average output and average cost per worker:

$$\frac{\pi}{L} = \frac{p_x X - rKp_k - wL}{L} \qquad (3)$$

The first order condition for maximizing (2) or (3) gives:

$$\frac{\partial X}{\partial L} p_x = \frac{p_x X - rKp_k}{L} \qquad (4)$$

This states that, assuming that the second order conditions are satisfied, workers' incomes are maximized when the value of the marginal product of labor is equal to the average income of workers. In other words, in a self-managed firm, partners have an incentive to coopt a new member when the value of the marginal product of labor, which is the increment to income that all partners earn, is greater than the income that the existing partners earn. This is also the income which must be paid to the new arrival.

It is easy to demonstrate (a) that in comparing a self-managed firm and its capitalist "twin," the equilibrium position is the same only in the case in which the capitalist firm makes no profit; and (b) that the self-managed firm produces less (more) and em-

ploys fewer (more) workers when the capitalist firm makes positive (negative) profits.

Given that under perfect competition, in the long run the capitalist firm does not make supernormal profits, this brings one intuitively to a conclusion which has been formally demonstrated by Drèze: this is that, in long-run equilibrium, the two systems arrive at identical equilibria.

One may rewrite (4) as:

$$\frac{X}{L} - \frac{\partial X}{\partial L} = \frac{rK}{p_x L} \qquad (5)$$

This shows that, if $r$ increases or $p_x$ falls, the difference between average and marginal product must increase. Given that equilibrium requires that the average product is greater than the marginal product, this implies that output and employment will increase. One thus arrives at Ward's celebrated "perverse" result: that with a fall in the price of output, the self-managed firm will increase its output; which gives rise, obviously, to a problem with the stability of equilibrium.

## Later contributions

This result has, however, on more than one occasion been refuted by later contributions. The first situation in which the result does not hold is when there is more than one variable factor. In which case, every increase in the output price sets in motion an impulse in the opposite direction. This is because the value of marginal product of all factors increases, thus inducing the firm to employ more factors and to raise output. Analogously, one can show that, in the case of a multi-product firm, an increase in the price of some of the products can lead to an increase in employment if the products whose prices rise are highly labor intensive. Furthermore, Domar has demonstrated that, if one also takes into account labor supply, the "perverse" result disappears when the firm cannot hire as many workers as it would like. This is because the movement occurs along the labor supply schedule, which one supposes is, as a rule, upwardly sloping.

However, the principal reason for even

cooperative firms having, as a rule, an upwardly sloping supply schedule is the potential for varying working hours. In fact, as the price of output rises, partners of a cooperative earn more and will tend to alter their labor--leisure choice, working longer hours (because labor is better rewarded).

The other "perverse" result in Ward and Vanek's model concerns "underinvestment." In cooperatives, by assumption, a partner who leaves the firm cannot take his or her share in the firm. Consequently, partners will be less willing to make investments in firms which will continue to bear fruit even after the partner leaves the firm (Furubotn and Pejovich 1970).

In order to discuss this proposition, it should be observed that the worker-managed firm, by its very nature, must attribute all surplus to the workers. This implies that the firm must reward capital in a way that does not depend on the surplus. That is, the firm (whether it is exclusively externally financed or whether there is some investment by partners) must finance itself by borrowed capital. However, when the firm is financed by borrowed capital, the problem of underinvestment tends to disappear. Although partners leaving the firm have no rights over future earnings accruing to past investment, neither do they have the burden of having to continue to repay the financiers of the investment.

## See also:

alienation; exploitation; market socialism; Mondragón; participatory democracy and self-management; socialism and communism

## Selected references

Furubotn, Erik G. and Pejovich, Svetozar (1970) "Property Rights and the Behaviour of the Firm in the Socialist State: The Example of Yugoslavia," *Zeitschrift für Nationalökonomie* 30.

Ireland, Norman J. and Law, Peter J. (1982) *The Economics of Labour-Managed Enterprises*, London: Croom Helm.

Meade, James E. (1972) "The Theory of Labour Managed Firms and Profit Sharing," *Economic Journal* 82(March), supplement.

Vanek, J. (1970) *The General Theory of Labor Managed Market Economies*, Ithaca, NY: Cornell University Press.

—— (1977) *The Labor-Managed Economy: Essays by J. Vanek*, Ithaca, NY: Cornell University Press.

Ward, B. (1967) *The Socialist Economy*, New York: Random House.

BRUNO JOSSA

# welfare state

The welfare state emerged in response to the high social costs created by nineteenth century laissez-faire capitalism. During the GREAT DEPRESSION it was seen as providing a "middle way" to the totalitarian alternatives of communism and FASCISM. The welfare state is something of a social and economic hybrid, often being labeled a "mixed economy," reflecting the mix of public and private involvement in the economic process. Among its primary objectives, the welfare state has sought to increase economic and social security, reduce income INEQUALITY, and achieve sustainable economic growth and development. It has done so through a range of policies, including welfare or anti-poverty programs; state ownership or regulation of industry; universal education, health care and social security; trade management; and Keynesian aggregate demand management targeted at sustained full employment. From the 1960s on, demonstrating rising concern with ecological damage and inequalities based on race and GENDER as well as CLASS, welfare state policies were expanded in the areas of civil rights, affirmative action and environmental protection.

## History

Early experiments in welfare state institutions may be seen in Otto von Bismarck's Imperial Germany, which introduced old age pensions and other social programs in the 1880s; the New Zealand liberals of the 1890s who introduced universal suffrage, pensions, labor protection and arbitration, and expanded public health care; and the British Liberals who enacted workers' compensation, pensions, and unemployment and health insurance during 1906–11.

Despite broadly similar patterns, the welfare states emerged in specific historical contexts in particular countries. In the USA, the Great Depression shifted the tide of political allegiance to the Progressive movement, which had been established in particular states and localities prior to the 1930s. This movement had been supported by many prominent original institutional economists (OIE), such as John R. Commons, whose work in the state of Wisconsin on social and labor legislation became in many ways the model for subsequent national reform (Fine 1957) in the New Deal era and thereafter. The American welfare state took shape in the New Deal tradition that continued to be the dominant coalition in American politics until the late 1970s.

The Great Depression emerged as a consequence of the financial consolidation around the turn of the century, that heavily concentrated market structure and ownership of American manufacturing industry (Veblen 1923). Continuing technological change coupled with oligopolistic pricing led to a decisive shift of income distribution toward the very wealthy, away from workers, farmers, and small business operators. Rexford Tugwell and other old institutional economists viewed the New Deal as an attempt to re-balance the flow of income and in order to keep the machines running (Sternsher 1964; Ayres 1944). This is apparent in such New Deal legislation as institutionalizing collective bargaining, establishing agricultural price and income parity, supporting small businesses with loans and other assistance, protecting income with unemployment compensation, workman's compensation, social security, and boosting demand by public works projects. These and subsequent programs that came to comprise the American welfare state placed a floor under the income of the population at large, and therefore operated to maintain aggregate demand and prevent the worsening of income inequality.

Also in the New Deal era and beyond, regulatory formats were established or extended to pursue consumer product safety, truth in advertising, workplace safety, affirmative action and anti-discrimination in industrial relations, and environmental protection. The social regulatory complex became an important part of the welfare state apparatus.

In Sweden, the influence of a unified labor movement in the political process led to the emergence of one of the most aggressive welfare states. The labor organizations and the social democratic political parties pursued "cradle to grave" social security, full employment, equality, and solidarity (see SOCIAL DEMOCRACY; SCANDINAVIAN MODEL).

In New Zealand, the first Labor government implemented a range of welfare state policies between late 1935 and 1949. Initial steps by Gordon Coates, the Minister of Finance in the previous coalition government (1932–5), had helped clear the path for the Labor program by the creation of a central bank, reform of agricultural finance, introduction of orderly agricultural marketing and public works programs. The Labor government took the greater steps toward the creation of a welfare state. Incomes were stabilized and macro balances restored by the introduction of guaranteed pricing of farm exports, along with industry regulation and the use of import controls to deal with balance of payments problems. Greater security and equity was achieved by the rapid expansion of public provision of housing, education, and health care as well as the adoption of universal social security "as of right, not of privilege." Collective bargaining and unionization were expanded. Along with the Swedish experiment, New Zealand became known as one of the "social laboratories of the world."

Similar programs were developed in Australia, with the introduction of the basic wage (1904), age and invalid pensions (1908), war widow pensions (1914), civilian widow pensions (1942), plus child endowment, unemployment and other benefits. The Australian Labor Party has historically been the group most committed to extending welfare benefits, especially during its tenure in government during the 1940s and the early to mid-1970s (somewhat less so during the 1980s and 1990s).

In the United Kingdom, the Beveridge Plan, along with Keynes's macroeconomics, provided the blueprint for the postwar welfare state. Comprehensive social insurance was to provide a social safety net, including the National Health Service, free public education, and a system of family benefits. As in a number of other welfare states, welfare and pension benefits were never set at a level sufficient to eliminate poverty, and benefits were means-tested, undercutting the universality principle and stigmatizing the poor.

The diversity of the "general welfare state" experience is very important but so are the similarities (Furniss and Tilton 1977). The underlying values of equality, solidarity, security, democracy, and freedom were only occasionally explicit and seldom if ever formed an integrated popular ideology. Hence the widely noted tendency to *ad hoc* programs and policy drift.

### Polanyi and the protective response

Perhaps the most cogent expression of these paradoxical phenomena is that of Karl Polanyi. The evolution of laissez faire capitalism in the nineteenth century was characterized by a "double movement." As the market system spread to impact wider areas of social life it was met by a socially protective response aimed at limiting the cultural dislocation caused by market shocks. The protective response focused on immediate experiences, pragmatically setting about remedying the apparent problems, usually by *ad hoc* interventions (see DISEM-BEDDED ECONOMY).

The welfare state emerged in the twentieth century as one institutional form of this socially protective response. In the 1930s, the responses of emerging welfare states to the Great Depression were to the immediate circumstances of massive unemployment, lost output, and collapse of the financial and trading systems. Planning was not a key element in the response to the crisis of capitalism. Instead the character of welfare state intervention can best be described as an "interventionist drift," reflecting the spontaneous, uncoordinated reactions of the protective response (Stanfield 1986).

The continuing force of the market mentality accounts for these uncoordinated reactions to the market. Even those who argue the case for intervention to offset the excesses of the market must base their arguments for social control in terms of improving upon the achievements of the market system, e.g. in offsetting the effects of externalities and public goods. The state itself is so subject to the influence of the market mentality that its performance is often assessed in terms of its ability to achieve market efficiency, an objective only relevant to markets.

### State of crisis

By the late 1970s, the welfare state and the capitalist economic structure in which it was placed were in a general state of crisis. There had never been a well articulated vision or ideological foundation of the welfare state. The modern liberal vision of a reformed capitalism that utilized the efficiency properties of the market economy, as well as the participatory and egalitarian thrust of the democratic state, was clear enough. J.S. Mill and English "new liberalism" had forged the way in this regard and laid the basis for the political alliance of the intelligentsia and working class (Stanfield 1996: ch. 8). But many issues with regard to the compatibility of widespread public intervention, with the operation of capitalist markets and the liberal state form were neglected (Clarke 1989).

Eventually this ideological neglect proved to be critically problematic. The floor placed under popular income sustained aggregate demand and weakened the ability of capital to maintain the profitable intensity of labor. Structural inflation became rampant. Social movements arose to press their case on the public purse and business interests took advantage of the violation of the liberal state form to advance their cases for what came to be known as "corporate welfare" in the American idiom. The idea of *civitas* or citizen responsibility and solidarity was sadly lacking in the culture of the welfare state. This is not surprising given the absence of an articulate ideology of the nature of the welfare state that could guide popular understanding of its mission and requirements, including the responsibility of citizens to participate in the democratic process on the basis of reasoned inquiry into the public interest (Offe 1984; McClintock and Stanfield 1991).

The critical issues were perhaps revealed most clearly in the Swedish case. Among the most advanced of the social welfare states, Sweden in the early 1980s faced a pivotal choice between CAPITALISM and the transition to socialism. In the discourse focused upon its nagging problems of international imbalances, declining competitiveness, and capital flight, two polar solutions emerged. Olaf Palme supported an aggressive use of workers' funds, by which capital formation would have been largely collectivized in two generations. The funds would have come to own predominant stakes in Swedish corporations on behalf of workers. The other alternative was to retrench the welfare state and provide conditions favorable to private capitals formation. Palme's proposal appears never to have garnered widespread popular support and was left with no champion in the wake of his assassination.

Sweden eventually became part of the Great Capitalist Restoration of the 1980s and 1990s. In all the industrial democracies and beyond, this recent era has seen the retrenchment of the welfare state by reduced social spending in real terms, tax cuts, deregulation and privatization, and a weakening of the influence of organized labor. The Great Capitalist Restoration includes the "conditionality" governed development of the emerging market economies and the transition of the formerly "state socialist" economies to capitalism. The crisis of the welfare state is, at least for now, being resolved by a return to capitalist domination of society that would have been largely unthinkable during the 1940s to 1960s.

## See also:

budget deficit; economic rationalism or liberalism; fiscal crisis of the state; fiscal policy; Polanyi's views on integration; social structure of accumulation: state–citizen accord; social wage; state and government

## Selected references

Ayres, C.E. (1944) *The Theory of Economic Progress*, 3rd edn, Kalamazoo, MI: New Issues Press, 1976.

Clarke, S. (1989) *Keynesianism, Monetarism and the Crisis of the State*, Brookfield, VT: Gower.

Fine, S. (1957) *Laissez Faire and the General-Welfare State*.

Furniss, N. and Tilton, T. (1977) *The Case for the Welfare State*, Bloomington, IN: Indiana University Press.

McClintock, B.T. and Stanfield, J.R. (1991) "The Crisis of the Welfare State: Lessons from Karl Polanyi," in M. Mendell and D. Salee (eds), *The Legacy of Karl Polanyi: Market, State, and Society at the End of the Twentieth Century*, New York: St Martin's Press, 50–65.

Offe, Claus (1984) *The Contradictions of the Welfare State*, London: Hutchinson.

Stanfield, J.R. (1986) *The Economic Thought of Karl Polanyi*, London: Macmillan.

—— (1996) *John Kenneth Galbraith*, London: Macmillan.

Sternsher, B. (1964) *Rexford Tugwell and the New Deal*, New Brunswick, NJ: Rutgers University Press.

Veblen, T.B. (1923) *Absentee Ownership and Business Enterprise in Recent Times: The Case of America*, New York: Augustus M. Kelley, 1964.

JAMES RONALD STANFIELD
BRENT MCCLINTOCK

# Williams–Rodney thesis

The intimate relationship between Caribbean plantation SLAVERY and the development of industrial CAPITALISM in Europe is the subject of the Williams–Rodney thesis. The thesis contends that the European industrial revolution was at least partially dependent on Europe's involvement with the African slave trade and slave production in the Caribbean. Conversely, the continuing underdevelopment of Africa is partially explained by the deleterious effects of European commerce. Specifically, the slave trade had a profoundly adverse impact on Africa's economic and social development.

Eric Williams was born in Trinidad in 1911. His Oxford Ph.D. dissertation work became the book *Capitalism and Slavery*, published in 1944. Williams eventually served as Prime Minister of Trinidad and Tobago. Walter Rodney was born in British Guyana in 1942. Rodney received a doctorate in African History from the University of London and studied with C.L.R. James. Rodney's most influential work, *How Europe Underdeveloped Africa*, was published in London and Tanzania in 1972. Rodney returned to Guyana in 1974 and founded the Working Peoples Alliance. Amidst escalating government repression, Rodney was assassinated with a car bomb in 1980.

## Development, underdevelopment and slavery

The Williams–Rodney thesis contends that there is reciprocal causation between the early development of capitalism in Europe, particularly in Britain, and the underdevelopment of Africa. At the center of this mutual relationship is African slavery. Williams argues the first part of this relationship in *Capitalism and Slavery*.

Williams sees the fundamental reason for the creation of the slave plantation in the Americas in the shortage of free labor. "The great problem in a new country," he writes, "is the problem of labor" (1944: 12). This problem was especially severe in sugar, cotton and tobacco growing areas, where extensive production required large gangs of inexpensive labor. African slavery was eventually settled on as the cheapest solution.

The slave plantations of the New World provided the market for a highly organized African slave trade. Much of the commerce of cities like Liverpool, Bristol, and Glasgow consisted of the highly lucrative business of selling human flesh. Williams quotes a local annalist of Bristol as saying, "There is not a brick in the city but what is cemented with the blood of a slave" (1944: 61). This slave trade was a vital link in a "triangular trade" involving sugar from the islands, and British manufacturing goods. Williams argues that this trade played a vital role in the ACCUMULATION of capital in metropolitan Britain. His summary is worth quoting at length:

> The triangular trade thereby gave a triple stimulus to British industry. The Negroes were purchased with British manufactures; transported to the plantations, they produced sugar, cotton, indigo, molasses and other tropical products, the processing of which created new industries in England; while the maintenance of the Negroes and their owners on the plantations provided another market for British industry, New England agriculture and the Newfoundland fisheries. By 1750 there was hardly a trading or manufacturing town in England which was not in some way connected with the triangular or direct colonial trade. The profits obtained provided one of the main streams of that accumulation of capital in England which financed the Industrial Revolution.
>
> (Williams 1944: 52)

As British capitalism grew it became much less dependent on the West Indies, and more dependent on open trading relations with the rest of the world. The slaveowners, an anachronistic agrarian elite dependent on protected trading relationships with the mother country, became a drag on the rising capital's freedom of political maneuver. Capital joined the movement for the ending of slavery, and this shift swung the balance. Slavery was abolished in the British empire in 1833.

Williams's work was one of the inspirations for the emergence of dependency theory, based in the work of Paul Baran and Andre Gunder Frank. Rodney applied the development of underdevelopment theory to Africa in his *How Europe Underdeveloped Africa*. As part of a larger argument about the effect of trade, colonialism, and capitalist investment on African development, Rodney examines the impact of the slave trade. As Europe opened up a system of international trade in the sixteenth and seventeenth centuries, "European decision-making power was exercised in selecting what Africa should export – in accordance with European needs" – slaves (Rodney 1972: 77).

## African underdevelopment

Rodney identifies the European slave trade as a basic factor in African underdevelopment. Assessing the effect of the slave trade entails "measuring the effect of social violence rather than trade in any normal sense of the word" (1972: 95). In the most direct sense, the slave trade represented a diminution of the African LABOR FORCE. This was compounded by the fact that "slave sellers" concentrated on the young and able-bodied. While every other continent showed a steady increase in POPULATION during the era of the European slave trade, the African population stagnated. The dynamic effects of a rising population on both supply and demand were absent from the African economy.

Slave raiding increased the insecurity of those left behind. The violence practiced between African communities was inconsistent with most other economic pursuits. Existing agriculture and industry declined. Rodney argues that "the orientation of large areas of the continent towards human exports meant that other positive interactions were thereby ruled out" (1972: 100). In this way, the deleterious effects of the slave trade rippled throughout the continent. The orientation of trade to the coastal areas and sea routes, dominated by European shipping, prevented the regional integration of the African economy.

European goods in trade strangled local production. They consisted overwhelmingly of consumer goods rather than capital goods. Entrepreneurial energies were diverted into trade rather than production. Requests for technical assistance from African leaders were ignored.

## Divergence between Africa and Britain

Williams and Rodney together construct a complex argument linking capitalism and slavery during the crucial period of the industrial revolution. This linkage would initiate a growing divergence in the development of Europe and Africa, the consequences of which cascade down to the present day. It is Williams's part of the thesis which has attracted the most controversy. Subsequent historians have taken issue with the importance Williams gives to slavery in the industrial revolution and to the role of capitalist development in the ultimate success of British abolitionism. It is argued that the profits from slavery constituted only a small portion of the capital available during the industrial revolution, and that it is difficult to trace fortunes from their origin in the plantation economy to particular industrial innovations.

Nevertheless, it is undeniable that slave profits made their way into the eighteenth century British economy. Solow and Engerman argue that "if the technical change of the Industrial Revolution is put into the context of an increasingly rich, commercial, manufacturing society, then the connection holds. For slavery helped make eighteenth century England more rich, more commercial, and more industrial" (1987: 10).

Williams's argument was not limited to investment. Slavery supplied raw materials to the industrial revolution as well as a substantial portion of its market. Richardson finds that "West Indian demands, directly and indirectly, may have been responsible for almost half of the growth of Britain's domestically produced exports between 1748 and 1776" (1987: 131).

Industrial exports led to industrial growth and industrial growth led to structural change. While slavery may not have "caused" the industrial revolution, it certainly played an important role in its pattern and timing (Solow 1987: 72).

## Critics

Some historians have taken issue with Williams' economic interpretation of abolition. It is nevertheless undeniable that the relative importance of the plantation economy to British prosperity fell sharply after 1776. Davis (1975) has extended Williams' argument contending that the anti-slavery movement reinforced capitalist HEGEMONY in British society by establishing the virtue of the free labor contract and the market allocation of labor. Critics of Williams have asked why British capitalism should have wanted to cripple an active, commercially driven trading partner producing complementary products within the British empire (Drescher 1977).

## Conclusion

While Williams saw the plantation economies as capitalist in nature, this issue may be illuminated by understanding industrial capitalism and plantation slavery as separate modes of production. As such, their relationship to one another was both potentially complementary and contradictory. It is not surprising that in a period of rapid change, the balance of complementarity and CONTRADICTIONS should change over time. In this light, the Williams–Rodney thesis can be seen as a dynamic and sophisticated historical analysis of the articulation of two modes of production, capitalism and slavery.

## See also:

development and underdevelopment: definitions; development political economy: major contemporary themes; race, ethnicity, gender and class; race in political economy: major contemporary themes; racism

## Selected references

Davis, David Brion (1975) *The Problem of Slavery in the Age of Revolution*, Ithaca, NY: Cornell University Press.

Drescher, Seymour (1977) *Econocide: British Slavery in the Era of Abolition*, Pittsburgh.

Richardson, David (1987) "The Slave Trade, Sugar, and British Economic Growth," in Barbara L. Solow and Stabley L. Engerman (eds), *British Capitalism and Caribbean Slavery*, Cambridge: Cambridge University Press.

Rodney, Walter (1987) *How Europe Underdeveloped Africa*, Washington, DC: Howard University Press.

Solow, Barbara L. (1987) "Capitalism and Slavery in the Extremely Long Run," in Barbara L. Solow and Stanley L. Engerman (eds), *British Capitalism and Caribbean Slavery*, Cambridge: Cambridge University Press.

Solow, Barbara L. and Engerman, Stanley L. (1987) "British Capitalism and Caribbean Slavery: The Legacy of Eric Williams: An Introduction," in Barbara L. Solow and Stanley L. Engerman (eds), *British Capitalism and Caribbean Slavery*, Cambridge: Cambridge University Press.

Williams, Eric (1994) *Capitalism and Slavery*, Chapel Hill, NC: University of North Carolina Press.

TERRENCE MCDONOUGH

# Williamson's analysis of the corporation

## Foundations in Coase's analysis

Williamson's analysis of the corporation is drawn from and extends the classic work of Ronald Coase (1937), which examines the rationale for the existence of, and changes in the size of, the firm in a market economy. Coase was concerned with the development of a theory and definition of the firm that were realistic as well as tractable in terms of neoclassical marginal analysis. Coase asks the critical question: why does the firm exist in a market economy, if the price mechanism is the most efficient means of organizing and co-ordinating transactions, where the firm sup-presses the price mechanism and substitutes for it administrative or entrepreneurial organiza-tion of transactions?

Coase argues that the firm is a product of the fact that it is costly to use the price mechanism: TRANSACTION COSTS exist in the discovery of relevant prices and in negotiating and concluding separate contracts for each and every exchange. By shifting some transactions into the firm, transaction costs are reduced. Nonetheless, firms do not completely subsume all transactions under their domain, because entrepreneurs are characterized by diminishing returns in organizing transactions. Ultimately, one would expect the firm to substitute for the marketplace up to the point where the marginal costs of so doing equal the marginal benefits. The size of the firm is determined by marginal considerations and the relative costs of orga-nizing transactions inside and outside of the firm. Coase's transaction cost approach to the firm is not only consistent with marginal analysis but also with the neoclassical proposi-tion that economic agents are driven by efficiency considerations and that, in equili-brium, costs are minimized. Coase simply introduces the reality of transaction costs into the analytical framework.

## Corporate integration

Williamson draws upon Coase's theoretical insights to explain not simply traditional economies of scale arguments, but also how vertical, horizontal and conglomerate integra-tion can be economically beneficial to society. The key to his thesis is that corporate integra-tion or "bigness" is a product of transaction cost economizing. Such economizing has the effect of cutting unit costs by reducing the cost of developing, signing, enforcing, and adjusting contracts between independent economic agents. Like Coase, Williamson emphasizes that the typical firm searches for ways and means to minimize transaction costs, and that the pursuit of efficiency is central to the

behavior of the firm and to members of the firm hierarchy in general.

## Policy and antitrust

The policy-related significance of this proposi-tion is that, even if mergers cannot be justified by any savings in production costs through economies of scale, or by downward shifts in the upward sloping marginal cost curve, they can be justified for transaction cost reasons. This challenges the policy recommendations of economists who tend to ignore transaction costs, and see mergers as a source of economic inefficiency due to the generation of classic deadweight losses. Williamson argues that by incorporating transaction cost economizing into one's analytical framework, corporate bigness would be recognized as a source of transaction cost savings, which typically out-weigh any resulting deadweight losses.

Williamson's analysis of the corporation has seriously weakened, from a theoretical perspec-tive, economic arguments favoring vigorous antitrust activity. This is because one might predict, from Williamson's modeling of the firm, that the private market typically generates firms of efficient size and organization. The pursuit of market power and rent-seeking behavior in general is not considered to be of central importance to an understanding of the evolution of the firm. Williamson also argues that his modeling of the firm best explains the changing organizational structure of the firm. A critical assumption made by Williamson is that, over the long run, market forces enforce efficient, cost-minimizing behavior by the firm: the market will not tolerate inefficient organi-zational structures.

## Competitive pressures

Economic agents might prefer leisure and other non-pecuniary benefits in preference to the pursuit of lower costs and higher profits. Such preferences might delay the development of efficient organizational structures, but such behavior cannot persist in the market. Thus, it is assumed that corporate bigness does not affect the extent of competitive pressures on the firm. Hence, there should be little difference in the extent of competitive pressures generated by a perfectly competitive or oligopolistic market structure. This assumption has been bolstered, theoretically, by recent work on contestable markets (Baumol 1982), which argues that, no matter what the market structure, the threat of competition will enforce efficient behavior.

## Deadweight losses and X-inefficiency

To the extent that larger corporations reduce competitive pressures, Williamson's efficiency arguments need no longer hold and deadweight losses become a possibility. In addition, corporate bigness need not be the most efficient transaction cost economizing organizational structure, since relatively inefficient firms can survive under conditions of imperfect competition. To the extent that the larger corporation reduces transaction costs, one would have to estimate the gains here as compared to any deadweight losses produced.

Williamson also ignores the possibility that corporate bigness can generate X-INEFFICIENCY: economic agents working less hard or less well than their potential. This follows from his assumption that corporate size has no effect on competitive pressures. Harvey Leibenstein (1966) finds, on the other hand, that, to the extent that market pressures are diminished, economic agents tend to behave X-inefficiently, thereby reducing output and increasing unit costs. Therefore, to evaluate the costs of corporate bigness one must add to the traditional deadweight losses the x-inefficiency costs which, Leibenstein argues, are much greater than any deadweight losses. Unless integration or merger result in cost savings, stemming from scale economies, downward shifts in the marginal costs curve, or from savings in transaction costs, which exceed the costs in allocative and X-inefficiency, increasing firm size is not economically beneficial (Altman 1991).

## Conclusion

The evidence does not exist to support the view that mergers, by and large, result in a reduction of unit production costs or that competitive pressures remain severe no matter what the market structure (Shepherd 1984, 1986). These stylized facts open the door to the traditional view that corporate bigness may do more harm than good. Although the revisions to economic theory presented by Williamson enrich our understanding of the development of the firm, they do not and cannot prove that integration and merger necessarily generate net economic benefits, as most mainstream economists would have it. As in the past, such a determination can only be made empirically, where the empirics are informed by the possibility that corporate bigness generates both positive and negative economic effects.

## See also:

corporate objectives; corporation; institutionalism: old and new; market structures; transnational corporations

## Selected references

Adams, Walter and Brock, James W. (1991) *Antitrust Economics on Trial: A Dialogue on the New Laissez-Faire*, Princeton, NJ: Princeton University Press.

Altman, Morris (1991) "A Critical Appraisal of Corporate Size and the Transaction Cost-Economizing Paradigm," *Handbook of Behavioral Economics*, Volume 2A, 1991, 217–32.

Baumol, William J. (1982) "Contestable Markets: An Uprising in the Theory of Industry Structure," *American Economic Review* 72: 1–15.

Coase, Ronald A. (1937) "The Nature of the Firm," *Economica* 4: 386–405.

Leibenstein, Harvey (1966) "Allocative Efficiency vs. 'X-Efficiency'," *American Economic Review* 56: 392–415.

Shepherd, William G. (1984) "Contestability

vs. Competition," *American Economic Review* 74: 572–87.

—— (1986) "On the Core Concepts of Industrial Economics," in H.W. de Jong and W.G. Shepherd (eds), *Mainstreams in Industrial Organization*, vol. 1, Boston: Kluwer Academic Press, 23–67.

Williamson, Oliver E. (1975) *Markets and Hierarchies: Analysis and Antitrust Implications*, New York: Free Press.

—— (1980). "Emergence of the Visible Hand: Implications for Industrial Organization," in Alfred D. Chandler and H. Daemes (eds), *Managerial Hierarchies: Comparative Perspectives on the Rise of the Modern Industrial Enterprise*, Cambridge, MA: Harvard University Press, 182–202.

—— (1981) "The Modern Corporation: Origins, Evolutions, Attributes," *Journal of Economic Literature* 19: 1537–68.

—— (1985) *The Economic Institutions of Capitalism: Firms, Markets, Relational Contracting*, New York: Free Press.

—— (1986) *Economic Organization: Firms, Markets and Policy Control*, New York: New York University Press.

MORRIS ALTMAN

# women's wages: social construction of

The wages of women in capitalist countries are consistently lower than men's wages, and are in many cases below a living wage, inadequate to support a woman and those dependent on her for survival. Bare subsistence wages for women have been the norm since the beginnings of capitalist production, and were observed by the mercantilist writer Cantillon, cited approvingly by Adam Smith in *The Wealth of Nations*. Karl Marx, in Volume 1 of *Das Kapital*, documented the low wages paid to women, as well as their long hours and poor working conditions. The poor conditions and low wages of women in factories and in home work became the focus of social reformers in the United Kingdom and the United States in the late nineteenth and early twentieth centuries, culminating in a range of reform legislation, including the instigation of industry-specific minimum wages. (In the UK, as well as New Zealand and Australia, these laws applied to men in low wage industries as well; in the United States, they applied only to women.)

## Natural exogenous forces?

While low wages for women were lamented, most political economists of this period understood them to be the outcome of "natural" forces, exogenous to the economic process. Custom and biology both prescribed women's economic dependence on men; men needed family wages while women, at most, needed only to support themselves (Picchio 1992, Kessler-Harris 1990). Women's inherent docility and timidity, and their primary duty to their children and domestic responsibilities, guaranteed that this dependence would be perpetuated, although state intervention might be needed to prevent women's wages from sinking below the level that would assure a healthy new generation.

## Socially constructed inequality

Political economists of the last few decades have challenged this emphasis on women's "natural" characteristics, arguing that wages for men and women under capitalist production are determined in a complex fashion by a combination of market, institutional, and political forces resulting in discriminatory treatment of women (see LABOR MARKET DISCRIMINATION). Labor market segmentation theorists have pointed to the GENDER DIVISION OF LABOR as part of a "divide and conquer" strategy on the part of capitalists intent on weakening working-class resistance (see SEGMENTED AND DUAL LABOR MARKETS). Feminists argue that a historically specific, socially-constructed sex–gender system has been central to the subordination of women; and that women's place in wage labor cannot be understood separately from an analysis of their role in the home. Recognizing the central importance that women's role in social reproduction has played in relegating them to low wage labor, feminist political economists argue that this interaction is socially constructed, not biologically determined.

## Patriarchy and capitalism

Theoretical disagreements developed in the 1970s and early 1980s over the specification of PATRIARCHY as an ideology or a mode of production with a separate material base, and over the relative importance of patriarchy and CAPITALISM in determining women's economic position and wages (see Barrett 1980). Heidi Hartmann argued that women's economic position was the outcome of the mutual accomodation of capitalism with the pre-existing system of patriarchy, which resulted in the segregation of women into female-dominated, low-wage occupations. Male workers' struggles to exclude women from skilled occupations and achieve family wages for themselves had the intention of keeping women economically dependent on men, subordinate to them and providing domestic services in the home. In turn, women became a source of cheap labor for capitalists (see Hartmann 1981).

## Reproductive and productive labor

Humphries and Rubery argued that analyses of women's role in social reproduction by neo-classical and political economists alike over-simplified its relationship to the system of production, theorizing it either as absolutely autonomous or wholly integrated and functional to production. They advocated a methodology that viewed the system of social reproduction as being relatively autonomous from the system of production, with a historically specific, non-functionalist relationship to it. For example, Humphries and Rubery argued that demands for a family wage were part of an attempt to shield the working class family from the continuous driving down of wages; but that at the same time, particularly in conjunction with women's role in social reproduction, the

concept of a family wage served to legitimize wages lower than subsistence for women (Humphries and Rubery 1984). Although these arguments were never entirely resolved, feminist political economists are in agreement over the central role played by occupational segregation by sex and the relegation of the vast majority of unpaid reproductive labor to women in explaining women's continued low wages.

## Policy-oriented studies

Since the mid-1980s, the analysis of women's wages by feminist political economists has largely shifted to concrete policy-oriented studies of women's economic position in advanced and developing economies, in the face of conservative victories and economic restructuring (see Rubery 1988) Analyses of advanced capitalist economies over the past two decades deepened in complexity, pointing to the differences as well as similarities in the economic experiences of women across countries, by race and by class (see RACE, ETHNICITY, GENDER AND CLASS; RACE IN POLITICAL ECONOMY: MAJOR CONTEMPORARY THEMES). In the United States, for example, predominately white college-educated women have achieved unprecedentedly high wages, largely through their movement into traditionally male occupations (albeit with persistent inequalities). Most women, however, continue to labor at bare subsistence in traditionally female occupations. A growing group of poor single mothers, frequently women of color, live marginalized lives cycling between low wage labor and government relief, all below the level of subsistence for themselves and their families. Feminist political economists studying the developing world have demonstrated that women's unpaid labor provides the bulk of subsistence for their families, but leaves them vulnerable to oppression by men who control the money economy and the political structure (see GENDER AND DEVELOPMENT).

A number of policy proposals, not necessarily mutually exclusive, have developed in response to women's persistent low wages.

Feminist political economists have pointed out that women are, in fact, in need of a "family wage," as they are often the sole wage earners, or have partners whose earnings are insufficient to support a family. Advocates of AFFIRMATIVE ACTION argue that the dismantling of occupational segregation by sex and race is necessary for achieving living wages for women. Advocates of COMPARABLE WORTH argue that most women cannnot realistically expect to move out of their traditionally female occupations, and that many of these occupations are skilled and socially useful work, but that they are underpaid relative to their skill levels. They argue that the notion of "skill" is itself socially determined, and that capabilities associated with women have been systematically undervalued (Steinberg 1990). A properly conducted reevaluation of women's occupations would be a significant step toward achieving a living wage for women workers (Figart and Lapidus 1995).

Additional strategies advocated in the United States have included an increased emphasis on unionization for women and an improved system of government support. This includes an increased minimum wage, continuing income support for low wage working women, universal medical coverage and subsidized, quality child care (see Hartmann 1995). A growing number of feminist political economists have called for studies to account for the value women's non-wage labor contributes to the national product, particularly but not exclusively in the developing countries, with the goal of a more equitable distribution of income and wealth (see HOUSEHOLD PRODUCTION AND NATIONAL INCOME).

### See also:

feminist political economy: major contemporary themes; household labor; reproduction paradigm; reserve army of labor: latent; wage determination; waged household labor

### Selected references

Barrett, Michele (1980) *Women's Oppression Today: Problems in Marxist Feminist Analysis*, London: Verso.

Figart, Deborah M. and Lapidus, June (1995) "A Gender Analysis of U.S . Labor Market Policies for the Working Poor," *Feminist Economics* 1(3): 60–81.

Hartmann, Heidi (1981) "The Unhappy Marriage of Marxism and Feminism: Towards a More Progressive Union," in Lydia Sargent (ed.), *Women and Revolution*, Boston: South End Press.

—— (1995) "The Recent Past and Near Future for Women Workers: Addressing Remaining Barriers," Washington, DC: Institute for Women's Policy Research.

Humphries, Jane and Rubery, Jill (1984) "The Reconstitution of the Supply Side of the Labour Market: the Relative Autonomy of Social Reproduction," *Cambridge Journal of Economics* 8: 331–46.

Kessler-Harris, Alice (1990) *A Woman's Wage: Historical Meanings and Social Consequences*, Lexington, MA: University Press of Kentucky.

Picchio, Antonella (1992) *Social Reproduction: the Political Economy of the Labour Market*, Cambridge: Cambridge University Press.

Rubery, Jill (ed.) (1988) *Women and Recession*, London: Routledge & Kegan Paul.

Steinberg, Ronnie J. (1990) "Social Construction of Skill: Gender, Power, and Comparable Worth," *Work and Occupations* 17(4): 449–82.

MARILYN POWER

# work, labor and production: major contemporary themes

As we move into the twenty-first century, political economy is facing new challenges from the transformation in production. This transformation may be best illustrated by the shift from Fordism to post-Fordism which subsumes a number of new production systems, such as "flexible specialization" and "lean production" (see FORDISM AND THE FLEXIBLE SYSTEM OF PRODUCTION).

## Post-Fordism: general

These new production systems are a combination of both new technological applications and organizational changes. Their characteristics have many dimensions. In relation to production and products, these systems include high quality production; rapid changes in product mix; the application of new technologies such as computer-aided design; and just-in-time production. In relation to issues of work, there is the expansion of on-the-job training, multi-skilling and job rotations, and the compression of job categories. In management systems, there are changes such as eliminating some layers of traditional management, decentralizing production decisions within smaller and less hierarchical units, and greater integration between management and production activities. At the firm level, there is a greater degree of specialization of enterprises, networking among firms, and more horizontal inter-firm links.

Other trends associated with the flexible mode include the recomposition of production, the global optimization of productive flows, and close and long-term ties between producers and users. New production systems have also intensified enormously the already dual character of the workforce, labor market and production: for example, skilled versus unskilled labor, UNEMPLOYMENT AND UNDEREMPLOYMENT versus employment, and globalization versus localism.

## Impact on skill

The impact of production systems, particularly TECHNOLOGY applications, on skill has been an inconclusive and controversial issue. Optimists argue that technology is upgrading the skill levels of work because of the application of multi-skilling and continuous training. According to them, new technologies support loose networks of autonomous producers and create a workplace populated by autonomous and skilled workers.

Pessimists argue that work is being de-skilled, due to technological developments whose main aim is to lower production costs and increase control over the LABOR FORCE. Supporters of this argument point out that the increase in the number of tasks does not necessarily imply an upgrading of skills, but the intensification of work accompanied by the growth of contingent and insecure employment.

In reality, jobs and skills are not uniform. Hence, the impact may vary depending on the characteristics of jobs and skills. Even though the level of skill may be questionable, the existence of changes in the nature of skill and the LABOR PROCESS itself is not (Wood 1989). Some skills are being destroyed, while others are created and some others are transformed. Also, many manual skills are being replaced with skills involving the manipulation of data. Production activities are becoming more integrated, resulting in new forms of work organization and career patterns. As teams become a more important organizational form, individuals learn new roles and skills. Additionally, labor are trained more, since firms realize that technology and labor are not separable and the successful application of technologies depends on the quality of labor. This necessitates more labor involvement in production as well as training. The new work structure also brings more responsibility to the employee because of the increased intensification of work.

## Gender and race

It is also important to note that Fordism was never as rigid as the stereotype suggested, nor is post-Fordism always flexible. Indeed, some studies identify the Japanese production system as an intensified extension of Fordism (Wood 1989). While different types and dimensions of flexibility may reinforce management's overall control, the concepts of control, autonomy and cooperation need further clarification in order to observe the actual impact of new production systems on skills and labor process. This is especially important for the impact of new production systems on GENDER and race, since while restructuring for men may mean flexible production, it may imply something quite different for women and colored workers. For example, it is not uncommon to observe that when both men and women experienced an upgrading of their skills, only men had more control over decision making about the task (Crompton *et al.* 1996).

## Employment impacts

The impact of new production systems on employment varies also. While this impact may have job-creating effects, it may well be job destroying too (OECD 1996). According to the job-creating view, job losses following the introduction of new labor-saving processes are compensated both by the job creation associated with the output growth following the decline in prices, and by the formation of additional employment in other sectors. Furthermore, it is expected that the possible substitution of labor for capital will create new jobs. This argument assumes the existence of unsatisfied needs in the economy as well as the flexibility of both labor and product markets. The expected increase in employment also hinges upon two implicit assumptions, namely that markets are competitive and increasing returns exist. Moreover, the actual impact of technology on employment is determined by macroeconomic conditions and institutional characteristics of the economy.

The job-destroying view highlights the labor-saving feature of new technologies and illustrates the actual changes in many countries which clearly have shown a significant reduction in employment (Rifkin 1995). Besides the direct impact of new production systems on employment, new production systems also have a profound impact on the type of employment by increasing the use of part-time employment (OECD 1996). This, in turn, means a reduction both in job security and compensation.

It is also argued that rising PRODUCTIVITY makes many firms, particularly small and medium sized firms, more competitive, thereby allowing them to grow and create jobs, off-setting the job losses in big firms. However, US data show that the gains in small and medium sized firms cannot offset the increase in unemployment arising from the recent down-sizing of large firms (Harrison 1994).

## Geography of production

Finally, new production systems have an impact on the geography of production. On the one hand, they strengthen regional and local dimensions of production by increasing the outsourcing to local contractors in order to ensure just-in-time delivery. Thus, new production systems tend to reinforce regional and local specialization, and this has important implications for the quantity and quality of local production structures. This is sometimes referred as a "global mosaic of regional economies" where, regardless of which state they belong to, local economies become a node within a global network of inter-industrial linkages (Storper and Scott 1992). On the other hand, the application of new production systems increases globalization, eliminating national boundaries and local dimensions. Strong evidence shows a long-term trend towards a greater role for TRANSNATIONAL CORPORATIONS.

Overall, then, this discussion makes it clear that new production systems are not easy to characterize. Both the application of new production systems and their results may follow several alternative paths due to the struggle between labor and capital. It is, therefore, necessary to consider the specificity of each dimension and the developments related to it. The transformation of work is a dynamic process and it is not purely endogenous to an industry. It is a product of a complex array of organizational and societal factors, such as the industrial structure, the political environment, and regional characteristics.

## Institutions, the labor market and the state

The interactions among technology, people, and organizations can, therefore, be analyzed only in a broader framework by incorporating the social institutions and cultural characteristics associated with this process (Storper and Scott 1992) (see CULTURE; INSTITUTIONS AND HABITS). As such, the state will continue to be an important element in the restructuring of production, since it influences labor markets through many institutional factors, such as training systems and labor–management–government cooperation

New studies indicate that the labor market is not a simple system, based on a demand and supply mechanism, but that it is a complex series of social institutions. Even mainstream economists have started accepting this view. For instance, the World Bank economists call for governments to help workers, not only by providing a social safety net, but also by helping them to cope with production changes (World Bank 1995). Based on HUMAN CAPITAL theories, many economists have started acknowledging the increased role of government in educating labor for high-skilled jobs.

New production systems and the global competitive pressures have had impacts on labor markets. But more importantly, the theoretical understanding of labor markets has changed. Recent studies have shown that most of the traditional and New Keynesian arguments concerning labor markets do not explain the actual mechanisms in these markets. For example, evidence shows that increasing the minimum wage does not reduce employment (Card and Krueger 1995). Even though wages and the power of unions have declined, unemployment has still risen in advanced countries. Another argument, concerning the non-accelerating inflation rate of unemployment (NAIRU), is also being challenged by real-life experiences of the relationship between inflation and employment. This argument suggests that a portion of the labor force must be kept unemployed in order to keep the inflation rate low. After enforcing NAIRU by reducing minimum wages, benefits, and the social safety net, many advanced countries faced reduced demand and this, in turn, led to more (long-term) unemployment in these countries (see HYSTERESIS). This shows that unemployment insurance and social welfare do not necessarily cause a rise in UN-EMPLOYMENT AND UNDEREMPLOYMENT.

Another failed argument concerning labor markets is the impact of fiscal policies on the labor market. It is shown that increases in unemployment lead to budget deficits, due to a loss of tax revenues and a rise of unemployment benefits. As fiscal policies, including tax cuts and government spending, are not being applied much in the 1980s and 1990s, many advanced countries could not create sufficient demand to expand their economies and thus often failed to induce much employment in the long term (Pressman *et al.* 1995) (see FISCAL POLICY).

In short, new studies argue that government macroeconomic policies need to be applied, including investing in infrastructure, supporting industrial investment by low interest rates, supplying education, applying progressive taxes, and employing fiscal policies (Pressman *et al.* 1995).

## Conclusion

In sum, political economy needs to meet the challenge by focusing more on the dynamics of the transformation of production and labor markets. In this regard, new findings stemming from studies on evolutionary economics, institutional political economy, social political economy, the REGULATION APPROACH and economic geography may help political economists come to a better understanding of both the nature and consequences of the transformation of production. This is because they show the internal mechanisms of firms and the structures of cooperation and social governance outside the bounds of firms (Sayer and Walker 1992). These approaches will take into account the diverse units and levels of analysis involved in the organization and experience of production. This, in turn, will facilitate the concern of political economy to understand the changes in the power structure in terms of shifting balances among capital, labor, states, and regions.

## See also:

industrial relations; labor process; regulation approach; reserve army of labor; social and organizational capital; Taylorism; technology; unemployment and underemployment; wage determination

## Selected references

Card, David and Krueger, Alan B. (1995) *Myth and Measurement*, Princeton, NJ: Princeton University Press.

Crompton, Rosemary, Duncan, Gallie and Purcell, Kate (eds) (1996) *Changing Forms of Employment: Organisations, Skills and Gender*, New York: Routledge.

Harrison, Bennett (1994) *Lean and Mean: The Changing Landscape of Corporate Power in the Age of Flexibility*, New York: Basic Books.

OECD (1996) *Technology, Productivity and Job Creation, vol 2, Analytical Report*, Paris: Organization for Economic Cooperation and Development.

Pressman, Steven, Seccareccia, Mario and Lavoie, Marc (1995) "High Unemployment in Developed Economies," *Review of Political Economy* 7(2): 125–32.

Rifkin, Jeremy (1995) *The End of Work: the Decline of the Global Labor Force and the Dawn of the Post-Market Era*, New York: Putnam.

Sayer, Andrew and Walker, Richard (eds) (1992) *The New Social Economy: Reworking the Division of Labor*, Oxford: Blackwell.

Storper, Michael and Scott, Allen J. (eds) (1992) *Pathways to Industrialization and Regional Development*, New York: Routledge.

Wood, Stephen (ed.) (1989) *The Transformation of Work? Skill, Flexibility and the Labour Process*, London: Unwin Hyman.

World Bank (1995) *Workers in an Integrating World*, Oxford: Oxford University Press.

DILEK CETINDAMAR
KARAOMERLIOGLU

# worker participation in capitalist firms

The notion of "worker participation in capitalist firms" strikes many political economists as an oxymoron. Capitalist management is typically undemocratic and hierarchical, with a heavy emphasis on controlling workers due to the inherent conflict of interest between capitalists and workers (Braverman 1974; Edwards 1979). Meaningful worker participation would allow the interests of workers to control managerial decisions (Pateman 1970), and hence is antithetical to capitalist management.

Part of the socialist movement developed around the notion that capitalist management is for the purpose of exploiting workers, and degrades and subordinates workers in the process. Only alternative ownership forms can alleviate exploitation, and permit PARTICIPATORY DEMOCRACY AND SELF-MANAGEMENT in the workplace. This line of logic explains Yugoslavian experiments with MARKET SOCIALISM, and also the MONDRAGÓN experiment.

Three events forced political economists to entertain the possibility of worker participation in capitalist management. First was the dissemination of Marx's *Economic and Philosophical Manuscripts of 1844* during the 1960s, with an emphasis on worker ALIENATION within the capitalist LABOR PROCESS. This led some political economists to become less macro-oriented and to undertake more research on workplace conditions. Second, trade unions, particularly through the processes of codetermination in Northern Europe, and the shop stewards movement in the UK, demonstrated that workers were not powerless in the face of capitalist management, and that the shopfloor was a contested terrain. Third, beginning with the Tavistock Institute experiments in the 1950s and proceeding through the 1990s, capitalists began experimenting voluntarily with processes whereby workers took over supervisory and limited engineering functions through autonomous workgroups, quality of working life programs, quality circles, employee involvement teams, etc. (see FORDISM AND THE FLEXIBLE SYSTEM OF PRODUCTION).

Political economy provides several interpretations of worker participation in capitalist management, each yielding different policy conclusions. First, worker participation can have a radicalizing effect on workers, permitting them to get a glimpse of what true workers' control entails and engendering solidarity against capitalism (Andre Gorz in Hunnius *et al.* 1973). To the extent that worker participation unleashes workers' knowledge and abilities in this process, capitalists are caught between the lure of the productivity benefits of worker participation and the trap of the unprofitable radicalizing effect, so will ultimately reject worker participation (Marglin 1978; Edwards 1979). The policy conclusion of this view is that worker solidarity and SOCIAL DEMOCRACY will flow from sustained support for worker participation. The increasing prevalence of worker participation programs in the 1980s and early 1990s, in conjunction with the emergence of REGANOMICS AND THATCHERISM, seemed to contradict this view.

A second view holds that worker participation is a logical extension of capitalist management and a method for maintaining HEGEMONY (Ernst Mandel in Hunnius *et al.* 1973; Parker and Slaughter 1994). Drawing on Pateman's (1970) distinction between high and low-level managerial decisions, it can be argued that challenges to capital necessarily involve high-level managerial decisions (for example, investment and overall employment). Worker participation in low-level decisions, historically made by supervisors, provides workers with a sense of involvement without endangering the profit objective of the firm. Indeed, workers may become more closely identified with the firm and de-skill their own jobs (Parker and Slaughter 1994). Somewhat differently, to the extent that de-skilling reduces possibilities for worker solidarity, then as jobs are deskilled, employers may find the motivational gains of low-level participation outweighing any potential radicalizing effects (Braverman 1974).

A third view, from the political economy spectrum, identifies the extent and possibilities for worker participation in capitalist management as flowing from larger decisions regarding macroeconomic policies and general managerial strategies (David Levine and Laura D'Andrea Tyson, in Blinder 1990). Levine and Tyson argue that successful capitalist experiments with worker participation are part of an overall managerial strategy (often labeled "workplace transformation") involving job security, gain or profit-sharing, egalitarian wages, and worker rights. Such strategies can generate high levels of productivity and quality via low-level participation so that high wage operations can effectively compete with low wage counterparts. Job security, in particular, requires full employment policies at the macro level. Government policies consistent with this strategy also fit comfortably with social democracy. This strategy is also compatible with union/management cooperation or high-level participation (Appelbaum and Batt 1994; Adrienne Eaton and Paula Voos, in Mishel and Voos 1992).

Technological choices by firms and governments can also influence the opportunities for participation (Appelbaum and Batt 1994). To the extent that technologies are chosen or implemented in ways which fragment and de-skill the labor process, firms will have less interest in implementing Levine and Tyson's preferred strategy. Conversely, technologies which effectively re-skill and empower workers will tend to favor the strategy. High levels of worker training and skills can similarly promote (and low levels discourage) firms pursuing Levine and Tyson's strategy.

A fourth view holds that increases in capitalist power improve the opportunities for profitable low-level worker participation in capitalist management. Persistent or increasing levels of unemployment can undercut any radicalizing effects of worker participation. In conjunction with mass production technologies, capitalists may be able to involve workers in implementing lean production techniques which improve quality and reduce employment at the workplace (Appelbaum and Batt 1994; Parker and Slaughter 1994). Capitalists may be able to generate high levels of worker cooperation and motivation by making workplaces disposable, or by making collective rather than individualistic threats to job security (Drago 1996). Worker participation under lean production or in disposable workplaces is favored by non-existent or weak unions, the absence of worker rights, and governmental policies promoting high levels of unemployment and wage deflation.

Over the last thirty years, opportunities for low-level participation have grown while the possibilities for high-level participation – such as that provided by unions or systems of codetermination – have diminished. Low-level participation in capitalist firms, up to and including autonomous workgroups, does not appear in general to induce worker solidarity against capitalism, though such participation may be a useful (if minor) element in trade union strategies to strengthen their shopfloor presence and for social democratic political movements. High-level participation in issues such as investment and employment continues to offer greater promise for creating and sustaining worker solidarity.

## Selected references

Appelbaum, Eileen and Batt, Rosemary (1994) *The New American Workplace*, Ithaca: NY: ILR Press.

Blinder, Alan S. (ed.) (1990) *Paying for Productivity*, Washington, DC: Brookings Institution.

Braverman, Harry (1974) *Labor and Monopoly Capital*, New York: Monthly Review Press.

Drago, Robert (1996) "Workplace Transformation and the Disposable Workplace," *Industrial Relations* 35(4): 526–43.

Edwards, Richard C. (1979) *Contested Terrain*, New York: Basic Books.

Hunnius, Gerry, Garson, G. David and Case, John (eds) (1973) *Workers' Control*, New York: Vintage Books.

Marglin, Stephen (1978) "Catching Flies with Honey," *Economic Analysis and Workers' Management* 13(4): 473–87.

Mishel, Lawrence and Voos, Paula (eds) (1992) *Unions and Economic Competitiveness*, Armonk, NY: M.E. Sharpe.

Parker, Mike and Slaughter, Jane (1994) *Working Smart*, Detroit: Labor Notes.

Pateman, Carole (1970) *Participation and Democratic Theory*, Cambridge: Cambridge University Press.

ROBERT DRAGO

# world hunger and poverty

Hunger stunts physical and mental growth, saps the strength of the hungry to protest their plight, and makes people vulnerable to disease and untimely death. Both hunger and poverty have absolute and relative dimensions; although hunger does have a more absolute aspect to it. Famines grab headlines as the crisis of survival is revealed through scenes of dying people, but endemic hunger afflicts more people, approximately 800 million in the mid-1990s: almost one-fifth of the world's POPULATION.

Analysts have essentially reached consensus on the idea that hunger and poverty are intertwined, but still disagree on the influence of different variables and policies to address the problems. Was Malthus right: does the rate of population growth doom millions to lives of poverty and hunger? Is the problem of feeding the world's people related more to inadequate food supply or inadequate access to the food that is available? Are women and men affected similarly by the problems and policies that address them? Should policies focus on promoting market solutions, such as correcting distorted prices and providing economic incentives, or is direct government intervention required?

## Dimensions of the problem

Since the publication of Malthus' *Essay on Population* in 1798, people's "breeding behavior" has been blamed for keeping them poor and hungry. Although Malthusian predictions have not been borne out, because food supply per capita has risen on a global scale, they have been fueled in recent years by the rapid growth of world population and falling per capita agricultural production in some African countries. Population growth and poverty work together to strain marginal environments and contribute to problems such as desertification, deforestation and overfishing of coastal waters. The poor, however, are often small contributors to environmental degradation associated with modernization (see Tinker 1994).

The reduction in global stocks of fish, for example, has resulted from large vessels from rich countries fishing the waters near their own and developing countries. Technologies designed to augment food production, such as the Green Revolution, while being praised for helping avoid the Malthusian trap, often produce undesired side effects of increasing income disparity by benefiting the rich more than the poor. In the late 1990s, global food production remains adequate for feeding the world's current population, but the 800 million malnourished do not have access to it. Analysts vary in their estimates of when rapid population growth could bypass world food production; the more optimistic forecasts suggest that, although destruction of the environment is a serious problem, with current trends world population is likely to level off before the critical point is reached (see ENVIRONMENTAL AND ECOLOGICAL POLITICAL ECONOMY: MAJOR CONTEMPORARY THEMES).

## A.K. Sen and entitlements

A turning point in the economic analysis of hunger and poverty occurred with the publication of A.K. Sen's *Poverty and Famines* in 1981. "The focus on population and food supply would have been innocuous but for what it does to hide the realities that determine who can command how much food" (Sen 1981: 150). In this volume, Sen presented empirical evidence from several major famines that food availability per capita was not the most significant factor in the crisis. Often governments were exporting food grains at the same time that thousands of their citizens were starving to death. Sen's analysis presented the concept of "entitlements," which represent a person's command over commodity bundles influenced by laws, customs, traditions, and transfer programs in the society. Entitlements are based on both production and exchange, given a person's endowments (for the poor, labor power is often the only endowment) (see Sen 1981).

The famine in Bangladesh in 1974 illustrates how the focus on food production and use of averages, such as food availability per capita, can be misleading. In the main year of the famine, food availability per capita was higher than average. Millions of landless laborers, however, lost their source of income when the floods hit. Although the stock of food from the previous year was still there, the poor with no savings and now no jobs were no longer part of the effective market demand for food. They lost their entitlement to the food stocks, and this entitlement failure was the main reason for starvation (see Dreze and Sen 1989).

## Gender

Throughout the world, discrimination against women has resulted in an imbalance in entitlements that is clearly evidenced in problems of poverty, hunger and famine. Presently women comprise 70 percent of the world's poor. They are major actors in the production and preparation of the family's food. They are increasingly responsible for the financial support of themselves and their children: female-headed households have become more prevalent, both because of growing divorce rates and *de facto* separation when husbands migrate to the city or abroad in search of economic opportunity (see Summerfield 1997). STRUCTURAL ADJUSTMENT POLICIES, advocated by the World Bank, have accelerated the pace of urbanization and caused transitional problems in access to food, health care and employment as governments reduce their direct involvement in the economies and cut subsidies. At the Fourth World Conference on Women in Beijing in 1995, World Bank officials acknowledged that the structural adjustment policies had paid too little attention to the suffering of the poor, especially that of poor women.

Policies designed to alleviate hunger also are often not gender-neutral. For example, food stamps, direct food subsidies and direct feeding programs have different effects. Food stamps and subsidies that are used in the home may permit traditional forms of bias in a girl's share of the food. Direct feeding programs in India had better results with respect to girls' nutrition than home subsidies, but such policies reduce the family's ability to make decisions about when and what to eat. Targeted feeding programs in famine stricken African countries that require the family to show at least one severely malnourished member have sometimes resulted in one child, usually a girl, being deprived so that the family can qualify for the program.

## Markets and government

The structural adjustment policies referred to above, and the economic transition policies of post-socialist countries during the 1980s and 1990s, have been strikingly similar in their emphasis on reduction of government intervention in the economy, including privatization of firms and property and trade liberalization strategies. The emphasis on market solutions and the legacy of waste, associated with inefficient and corrupt forms of government intervention earlier, have led to some resistance to government intervention. MARKETS, however, do not determine a particular type of income distribution, and crises that threaten people's basic entitlements can be expected to occur at intervals. The array of policies proposed to address hunger and famine now includes a combination of market solutions and interventions by government agencies and nongovernmental organizations.

## Program of action

Participants in the "World Conference on Hunger and Poverty" in Brussels in 1995 were able to agree on a program of action that includes: (1) policies to empower the poor, such as reviving agrarian reform efforts; (2) establishing a knowledge network; (3) increasing public awareness and political will in the North; (4) setting up a program for preventing and addressing emergencies whether caused by nature or human warfare; and (5) augmenting efforts to combat desertification (see Programme of Action 1995). These policies at times combine government intervention with greater use of the market. Public works projects, for example, can restore the entitlements of those unemployed because of a natural disaster, and with the wages earned, they can support the local market for grain (see Dreze *et al.* 1995). While some efforts for prevention of hunger and famines focus on expensive satellite technology, Dreze and Sen have promoted the use of democratic institutions, such as elections and a free press, to achieve this goal. In India, for example, newspapers have been effective in eliciting actions from politicians who must face future elections. The proposals also note the need to pay special attention to bias against women and groups such as indigenous peoples.

## See also:

agrarian question

## Selected references

Dreze, J. and Sen, A. (1989) *Hunger and Public Action*, Oxford: Clarendon Press.

Dreze, J., Sen, A. and Hussain, A. (1995) *The Political Economy of Hunger: Selected Essays*, Oxford: Clarendon Press.

Programme of Action (1995) *World Conference on Hunger and Poverty*, Brussels: IFAD.

Sen, A.K. (1981) *Poverty and Famines: An Essay on Entitlement and Deprivation*, Oxford: Clarendon Press.

Serageldin, I. and Landell-Mills, P. (eds) (1994) *Overcoming Global Hunger*, Proceedings of a Conference on Actions to Reduce Hunger Worldwide, Washington, DC: World Bank.

Summerfield, G. (1997) "Economic Transition in China and Vietnam: Crossing the Poverty

Line is Just the First Step for Women and Their Families," *Review of Social Economy.*

Tinker, I. (1994) "Women and Community Forestry in Nepal: Expectations and Realities," *Society and Natural Resources* 7: 367–81.

GALE SUMMERFIELD

# world-system: incorporation into

The modern world-system, or capitalist Europe (and its extensions), has for the last five centuries been a singularly successful social predator. European states have absorbed states, as well as many smaller, less complex non-state societies. This absorption has produced varied results. WORLD-SYSTEMS ANALYSIS of such absorption has tended to focus on colonial EXPLOITATION and development. This absorption, called incorporation, is "the integration of its production process into the interdependent network of production processes that constitute the world market" (Wallerstein and Martin 1979: 193). This is called effective or *real* incorporation, which is "a situation in which the patterns of production and reproduction typical of external arenas have ceased to be dominant within the region and tend to disintegrate qua systems" (Arrighi 1979: 162). Familiar examples are the replacement of subsistence agriculture with commercial crops for export. This distorts the local economy and forces a dependency on international trade for goods that were formerly produced locally.

When "political domination by an external power and/or economic relations with the capitalist world-economy have been established but the dominant patterns of production and reproduction within the region are still those typical of external arenas," (Arrighi 1979: 161) this is called nominal or *formal* incorporation. Furthermore, "should for any reason political domination cease and/or economic relations with the capitalist world-economy be severed, there would be a tendency toward the re-

establishment of those patterns" (Arrighi 1979: 161–2). Thus, the early spice trade constituted formal incorporation, since production techniques were not transformed. Arrighi (1979) argues that, for conventional world-systems analysis, incorporation involves only real incorporation.

## The problem of plunder

Although this conceptualization works well for describing what happened when areas were colonized and exploited (see Hopkins *et al.* 1987), it has several problems at other levels. The first concerns the problem of plunder. Wallerstein (1989: ch 3) argues that, even though an area has been plundered by a core power, it is not yet incorporated and peripheralized until local production has become integrally linked in to the "commodity chains" of the larger world-system. However, plundering can have profound consequences for local groups, especially stateless societies, as can be seen in the early impacts of European expansion globally. The most dramatic example is the impact of the slave trade on west Africa.

## The problem of local conditions

Alvin So (1984) argues that incorporation has political as well as economic components. He shows how the Opium Wars in the 1840s prompted a lessening of incorporation for Canton, and an increase for Shanghai. For Canton this generated unemployment, peasant uprisings and rebellions. He also argues that these local actions and conditions strongly shaped the incorporation process.

## The problem of formal incorporation

Another criticism focuses on Arrighi's claim that, if "formal" incorporation is severed, local conditions will tend to return to the *status quo ante*. This conceptualization makes it difficult to study the impact of formal incorporation and tends to turn those peoples incorporated into passive victims. Empirically, such return to prior conditions is rare.

## The problem of focusing on core activities

This conceptualization of incorporation leads to a radical misreading of sociocultural evolution. Brian Ferguson and Neil Whitehead (1992) have shown that contact between states and nonstate societies (a common type of incorporation) raises the general level of violence which spreads well beyond the contact zone. Early observers often mistook the heightened violence for normal conditions among nonstate peoples. Given these impacts of even minimal incorporation, the reports of the earliest observers seldom reflected pre-contact conditions. When these observations are assumed to reflect ancient conditions, conclusions about evolutionary processes are distorted considerably. Ferguson and Whitehead criticize world-systems analysis for failing to come to grips with these issues due to an overly strong focus on core activities and processes. This criticism is, in the main, correct. However, some world-systems analysts have addressed these issues.

## Incorporation as a continuum

Based on a detailed study of the Spanish impact on indigenous peoples in what was northern New Spain and is now the southwestern area of the United States, Hall (1989) reconceptualized incorporation as a continuum. At the weakest pole are areas where contact has been slight, which he calls *contact peripheries*. Areas with middle level of incorporation he calls *marginal peripheries*. At strongest pole are *full-blown peripheries*. Conventional world-system analyses have addressed only effective or full-blown incorporation.

Hall argues that world-system expansion necessarily entails incorporation of new areas and peoples, and thus creates frontier zones where the degree of incorporation is highly variable. Conceptualizing incorporation as a continuum facilitates systematic study of these variations. His analysis of northern New Spain/southwestern USA shows that: (1) local actors play active roles in incorporation; (2) world-

system processes set the context for that local action; (3) while incorporation is to some degree reversible, it is a "sticky" process that is easier to increase than to decrease; and (4) even slight degrees of incorporation can have massive effects on the groups and regions incorporated into the world-system.

## The example of Native Americans

Thus, several of the southwestern US Native American groups we know today were created from loosely connected groups of nomadic hunter–gatherers at the time of Spanish colonization: they were incorporated into the Spanish, Mexican and American states. Some, like the Comanches, were pushed toward a more unitary tribal organization. Others, like many Apache groups, were fragmented by similar pressures. Groups on the fringes of occupation, like the Navajo, were able in later years to selectively adopt and "Navajoize" European practices such as sheep-herding and silversmithing. In the late nineteenth century, all these groups along with others and the erstwhile Spanish/Mexican conquerors were transformed into ethnic minorities as the entire region was incorporated into the American capitalist state. Only in the twentieth century, when oil and uranium became valuable, did incorporation of Native American lands generally reach full-blown or effective incorporation. Throughout these four centuries, Native American adaptations, adoptions, resistance and rebellion to Europeans shaped the process and trajectories of incorporation (Hall 1989).

## Example of the fur trade

Research by other scholars has extended and elaborated these findings. The early fur trade in northern North America is an example of weak incorporation. Furs were not vital to European economies, yet the trade produced major social and economic changes among indigenous societies (Kardulias 1990). As metal products replaced more frangible indigenous products, the desire for European goods turned into a need, and more furs were required for trade. In the search for furs, men often went on long hunting expeditions and families often scattered in the winter. This led to major shifts in household structures and gender roles. Even in instances where the fur trade was severed, conditions did not return to precontact conditions.

Wilma Dunaway (1996) notes that, in the southeastern USA, Cherokees became extensively involved in commercial fur gathering which changed hunting and fighting techniques, and began to create a unified tribal government in the seventeenth and eighteenth centuries. Later, in the nineteenth century, incorporation via forced settlement on reservations transformed traditional Anishinaabe (Chippewa/Ojibway) clan structures into "mixed-blood" and "full-blood" factions (Meyer 1994).

Incorporation processes and consequences are far from fully understood, either empirically or theoretically. The study of incorporation, however, offers abundant opportunity to examine the roles and effects of local actors in world-systems analysis.

## See also:

colonialism and imperialism: classic texts; core–periphery analysis; hegemony in the world economy; international political economy

## Selected references

Arrighi, Giovanni (1979) "Peripheralization of Southern Africa, I: Changes in Production Processes," *Review* 3: 161–91.

Dunaway, Wilma A. (1996) *The First American Frontier: Transition to Capitalism in Southern Appalachia, 1700–1860*, Chapel Hill, NC: University of North Carolina Press.

Ferguson, R. Brian and Whitehead, Neil L. (eds) (1992) *War in the Tribal Zone: Expanding States and Indigenous Warfare*, Santa Fe, NM: School of American Research Press.

Hall, Thomas D. (1989) *Social Change in the Southwest, 1350–1880*, Lawrence, KS: University Press of Kansas.

Hopkins, Terence K., Wallerstein, I., Kasaba, Resat, Martin, William G. and Phillips, Peter D. (1987) "Incorporation into the World-Economy: How the World System Expands," special issue of *Review* 10(5/6): 761–902.

Kardulias, P. Nick. (1990) "Fur Production as a Specialized Activity in a World System: Indians in the North American Fur Trade," *American Indian Culture and Research Journal* 14: 25–60.

Meyer, Melissa L. (1994) *The White Earth Tragedy: Ethnicity and Dispossession at a Minnesota Anishinaabe Reservation, 1889–1920*, Lincoln, NE: University of Nebraska.

So, Alvin Y. (1984) "The Process of Incorporation into the Capitalist World-System: The Case of China in the Nineteenth Century," *Review* 8: 91–116.

Wallerstein, Immanuel (1989) *The Modern World-System III: The Second Era of Great Expansion of the Capitalist World-Economy, 1730–1840s*, New York: Academic Press.

Wallerstein, Immanuel and Martin, William G. (1979) "Peripheralization of Southern Africa, II: Changes in Household Structure and Labor-Force Formation," *Review* 3: 193–207.

THOMAS D. HALL

# world-systems analysis

World-systems analysis is a term invented in the 1970s. World-systems analysis is not a theory but a perspective on social analysis which permits one to view critically existing theoretical frameworks. The key issue revolves around what is the appropriate unit of analysis, both for concrete empirical work and for theoretical construction in social science.

## States and traditional social science

Most of social science, including the theorizing, the disciplinary categories, and the historiography, was put into place in the nineteenth century. This was also the century, par excellence, of the construction of modern states. It seemed virtually self-evident to most scholars that the unit of analysis was the state (or what some asserted was the nation-state). It was the states that had juridically defined boundaries and state apparatuses, and were therefore considered to have histories, economies, modes of production, and societies. It was the states that, in twentieth-century terminology, were thought to "develop." It was therefore the states that had crises, movements, revolutions. It is not that it was necessarily thought that the state was always the responsible agent, but simply that the various concepts of modern social science all referred to processes that occurred within the multiple states, separately and in parallel fashion.

The various disciplines that emerged within the universities all studied these processes within the framework of states. This is true for at least, the four disciplines of history, economics, political science, and sociology, which for a long time concentrated their attention entirely on the "civilized" or "industrialized" world (that is, essentially, Western Europe and North America). History was the history of the "historic" national states. Economics studied enterprises which operated within states or, at a "macro level," so-called national economies. Political science studied governments of these same states, and sociology looked at societies, whose boundaries were usually defined as being the same as those of the states (see STATE AND GOVERNMENT).

This divisioning of knowledge about processes within states then became the basis of the so-called fundamental methodological quarrel between those who emphasized the uniqueness of each particular (that is, national) construction, the idiographic historians, and those who emphasized the universality of the laws of behavior, the nomothetic economists, political scientists and sociologists.

Underlying this model was liberal IDEOLOGY, which recognized the fundamental importance to the capitalist system of the modern state. But as Marxism developed into the "Marxism of the parties," first with the German Social Democratic Party, and later with the Communist Party of the Soviet Union, it was transformed into a statocentric form of theorizing as well, in which its analyses also presumed the centrality of the state as a basic analytic construct, the unit within which social action occurred. Thus, in the post-1945 period, there emerged two formally parallel versions of "developmentalism" – the liberal and the "Marxist" – which, while using different historical models of development, shared epistemological premises, and hence drew many parallel conclusions in terms of practical action.

## Capitalism as a singular system

Over the past two centuries there have been a number of important intellectual voices protesting against this framework, and seeing in CAPITALISM a singular system, which contained states but didn't occur primarily within states. There was, first of all, Karl MARX himself, but there were also Joseph SCHUMPETER, Karl Polanyi, Oliver Cox and Fernand Braudel, among others. While it had often been sensed that, beneath their obvious differences, all these thinkers shared something, it was not until the 1970s that world-systems analysis made the argument that this something was their common insistence on the historical singularity of capitalism.

World-systems analysis built on this heritage to argue that the theorizing and the historiography of the modern world had to be looked at with a fresh eye, and then went on to question the methodologies that were being used, and finally opened up the question of the meaningfulness of the existing disciplinary boundaries. World-systems analysis insisted that history was not a study apart, since all of social science was necessarily and always historical. But world-systems analysis also rejected the concept that economics, political science and sociology were separate arenas of study.

## Unidisciplinarity

Liberal ideologues had always insisted that the modern world was built on three relatively independent pillars: the market, the state, and civil society. From this intellectual position and political proscription, liberal ideologues had erected the virtue, indeed the necessity, of studying separately the inherent logic of each arena of social action. From this it followed that there should be three separate disciplines: economics, political science and sociology. The alternative view was that these three so-called arenas of social action were part of a seamless skein, totally and constantly interacting, and indivisible analytically. World-systems analysis was not the only perspective that made this point. All those who, within the Marxist tradition, protested against the economism of the "Marxism of the parties," and the concept of "ultimate determining factors," were making the same point.

World-systems analysis is often confused with certain mutants of liberal ideology. The emphasis on a world-system is not at all the process referred to as "globalization." Most explanations of globalization presume two elements which are precisely the inverse of the arguments of world-systems analysts: that the process is recent rather than fundamental to the historical existence of capitalism; and that it has radically changed the way in which the capitalist system operates. Here the emphasis on totalities is not a call for multidisciplinarity, but rather for unidisciplinarity. Multidisciplinarity assumes the continuing legitimacy of the disciplinary constructs. Historicity is not a call for social science history, since social science history accepts the idiographic–nomothetic distinction, and merely calls for the testing of nomothetic propositions with non-contemporary data. Holism is not a demand for general education, but rather questions the meaningfulness of the structure–agency divide, and therefore of the divide between the sciences and the humanities (see HOLISTIC METHOD).

World-systems analysis, therefore, is not easy to pigeonhole. Its practitioners can be found located in all the social science disciplines. The range of empirical materials and methods that have been used are drawn from all of social science. When writing about the history of the capitalist world-economy, the writings seem to resemble sometimes economic history, sometimes geopolitics, sometimes the history of ideologies. When writing about the contemporary world, the writings seems to resemble sometimes studies of Third World development, sometimes studies of finance capital, sometimes long wave analysis, and sometimes imperialist politics and rivalries. When writing about the structures of knowledge, the writings seem to resemble sometimes the sociology of knowledge, sometimes the history of university systems. Of course, when writing about the unequal development of the capitalist system, the writings seem to resemble simultaneously traditional class analysis and both race and gender analysis.

## Tendencies

The variety of subject matter and styles makes clear that neither the topic nor the data collection method distinguishes world-systems analysis. Nor is world-systems analysis limited to the study of the modern world-system. What distinguishes it is the underlying premises about the nature of social scientific activity. There are two major tendencies within this intellectual movement that have begun to concentrate on pre-modern data, though each is controversial within the field.

One tendency argues that it is important to study comparatively various kinds of world-systems, and specifically the differences between a capitalist world-economy and pre- or non-capitalist historical systems. This kind of work has attracted many archaeologists into world-systems analysis. The second tendency has been to see the creation of the contemporary world-system as the result of a plurimillennial construction, in which the modern world-system seems either a minor variation or a culminating point. The former, comparative, tendency has been criticized on the grounds that it is too nomothetic in method and extends the concept of a world-system to too large a gamut of empirical situations. The latter tendency, concerning the contemporary world system, has been criticized because it is too idiographic in method, and effaces the crucial distinctiveness of the capitalist mode of production. The debate within world-systems analysis has remained a lively one.

## Critics

World-systems analysis has not been without its critics. They have come from all camps. Mainstream social scientists have considered it too Marxist, too historicist, too Third Worldist. In certain Marxist circles, it has been deemed too "circulationist," too little rooted in class analysis, insufficiently useful for political action. Traditional methodologists have attacked it as being insufficiently rigorous or scientific. Proponents of cultural studies have attacked it as neglecting agency, as being one more grand narrative, and as neglecting the centrality of GENDER or race to an understanding of the modern world. Obviously, these criticisms go in opposite directions.

## Conclusion

World-systems analysis arose at a particular moment of recent history, as a mode of criticizing the dominant tendencies in world social science. Its primary utility has been that of opening to question many of the traditional and seemingly self-evident verities of social science, in both its liberal and Marxist variants. World-systems analysis is not a field within social science, but the prolegomenon to an alternative way of doing social science. It stands or falls on its claim to providing greater coherence and greater relevance to social science in the contemporary transformation of the world-system.

## See also:

class analysis of world capitalism; core–periphery analysis; cycles and trends in the world capitalist economy; global corporate capitalism; global crisis of world capitalism; global liberalism; world-systems: incorporation into

## Selected references

Amin, Samir (1974) *Accumulation on a World Scale*, New York: Monthly Review Press.

Braudel, Fernand (1984) *Capitalism and Civilization, 15th–18th Century*, 3 vols, New York: Harper & Row.

Chase-Dunn, C. and Hall, T.H. (eds) (1991) *Core/Periphery Relations in Precapitalist Worlds*, Boulder, CO: Westview.

Cox, Oliver C. (1964) *Capitalism as a System*, New York: Monthly Review Press.

Frank, A.G. and Gills, B.K. (eds) (1993) *The World System: Five Hundred Years or Five Thousand?*, London: Routledge.

Polanyi, K., Arensberg, C.M. and Pearson, H.W. (eds) (1957) *Trade and Market in the Early Empires*, New York: Free Press.

Schumpeter, Joseph A. (1939) *Business Cycles: A Theoretical, Historical, and Statistical Analysis of the Capitalist Process*, 2 vols, New York: McGraw-Hill.

Wallerstein, Immanuel (1995) "Hold the Tiller Firm: On Method and the Unit of Analysis," in S. Sanderson (ed.), *Civilizations and World Systems*, Walnut Creek, CA: Altamira, 239–47.

—— (1996) *Historical Capitalism, with Capitalist Civilization*, London: Verso.

IMMANUEL WALLERSTEIN

**WORLD SYSTEMS, PRECAPITALIST:** *see* precapitalist world-systems

**WORLDLY PHILOSOPHY:** *see* Heilbroner's worldly philosophy

# X

## X-inefficiency

In 1966, Harvey Leibenstein published a classic article which not only challenged the very foundations of conventional neoclassical microeconomic production theory, but also represented a methodological break with what had come to be the traditional deductive approach in the construction of economic theory. It was in this paper that Leibenstein first introduced the revolutionary concept of X-efficiency, and its mirror image X-inefficiency, and planted the seeds for their further development. X-inefficiency, most simply stated, exists when people and organizations do not work as hard or as well as they could: when firms and economies do not operate along the most outer-bound production possibility surface or along the innermost production isoquant (Leibenstein 1966). As a firm becomes more X-efficient, less inputs are used to produce a given level of output. One has, in effect, less unused capacity determined by supply-side as opposed to the traditional demand-side factors.

### Cooperation in organizations

X-inefficiency represents the missed opportunities in realizing the potential of productive organizations. It represents a failure in organization, but one which is avoidable given the present state of knowledge, information and technology. Leibenstein argues, however, that X-inefficiency is the normal state of affairs and represents a most significant cost to society in terms of both the quantity and quality of output forgone. Leibenstein goes on to argue that this failure in organization is, in effect, the failure of hierarchy as an organizational

structure, where workers, managers and owners find themselves immersed in a world of conflict and mistrust. Only in a relatively cooperative organizational structure would X-inefficiency be eliminated and unit costs minimized: "if firm members attempted to interpret their jobs in such a way that they made effort choices which involved cooperation with peers, superiors, and subordinates, in such a way as to maximise their contribution to output" (Button 1989: 346).

In essence, therefore, the concept of X-inefficiency assumes that the organizational structure will not inevitably be the one which yields the most efficient results. Thus, what occurs inside the black box of the firm of conventional 'microeconomics' is critical to an understanding of the economy. For this reason, analyses of firm organization and the behavior of economic agents inside the firm – Leibenstein's "micromicroeconomics" – becomes a pertinent area of economic discourse. However, for organizations to be of substantive importance, effort discretion must be a variable in both the short and long run. Unlike conventional microeconomics, economic agents are assumed to be able to choose to work less hard and less well than they potentially can, since it is not assumed that the market will automatically or inevitably generate X-efficient behavior. It is presumed that individuals are not cogs in a machine, and that some freedom of choice exists in the realm of work.

### Organizational capital

Unlike conventional microeconomics, X-efficiency theory assumes that, not only is the quantity and quality of effort a discretionary variable in the process of production, but also that there is no unique equilibrium level of effort input which can somehow be mechanically induced by simply creating the "right" set of pecuniary incentives. For X-inefficiency to be eliminated, the overall organizational structure of the firm must be appropriate (X-efficient), as must be the personal preferences of the relevant economic agents in the firm, from workers to managers. In this sense, the organizational structure and work culture of the firm become part of the capital which must be invested for the firm to realize its productive potential and for unit costs to be minimized (see Tomer 1987; SOCIAL AND ORGANIZATIONAL CAPITAL). For this reason, unlike much of the EFFICIENCY WAGES literature, X-efficiency theory does not assume that wage rates alone determine effort levels. Wage rates must be seen as but one component of a larger organizational and incentive package.

## Protected markets

Effort discretion becomes a possibility in a world of imperfect contracts, transaction costs, imperfect and asymmetric information, and bounded rationality. Nonetheless, according to Leibenstein, X-inefficiency is an important feature of the typical economy, largely as a consequence of the prevalence of imperfect product markets which affords X-inefficient firms the protection necessary for them to operate continuously and consistently inside of the outer-bound production possibility surface. In a highly competitive product market, the X-inefficient firms would be driven into bankruptcy. This line of argument has become common in the contemporary game-theoretic literature, which Leibenstein (1982) contributed to, where the prisoner's dilemma solution to the PRODUCTIVITY problem is approached in an environment of conflict and mistrust.

In other words, in a protected market individuals tend to opt for behavior which minimizes their potential losses given that they expect their colleagues to behave in an opportunistic fashion. Such behavior tends to reduce productivity way below its potential, shifting the production possibility curve inward and production isoquant outward. In addition, Leibenstein has argued that X-inefficiency is a product of individuals behaving in only a selectively or quasi-rational manner.

## Perfect product markets

The fundamental critique of X-efficiency theory maintains that Leibenstein's assumptions of long term imperfect product markets and quasi-rational behavior are unreasonable. However, both assumptions are not necessary to explain the existence of X-inefficiency in either the short or long run. Even under the extreme assumption of perfect product markets, X-inefficiency can persist if wages and working conditions can be kept at a low enough level to keep unit costs in the low productivity X-inefficient firms competitive. On the other hand, higher wages and improved working conditions can serve to encourage the development of a more X-efficient (cooperative and trusting) organizational structure. Moreover, individuals who are quite rational, in the neoclassical sense of attempting to maximize their utility given the multifarious constraints which they face, need not be behaving X-efficiently.

Making a firm X-efficient requires that individuals invest in the firm's organizational capital in terms of time, effort and money, at least in the short run. Given the pecuniary and non-pecuniary costs involved in making firms X-efficient, members of the firm hierarchy, for example, may very well be maximizing utility in an X-inefficient environment if they can get away with it either in a protected market or through the shelter afforded by a low wage regime. This is especially true when their economic decision-making process is largely governed by a myopic world view (Altman 1996). In addition, the available empirical evidence weighs heavily in favor of the view that effort is a discretionary variable and that X-inefficiency exists (Frantz 1988; Leibenstein and Maital 1994; Altman 1996).

## Research and policy

X-efficiency theory has sparked a large and growing literature examining the significance of organizations and motivational systems to productivity: a subject which had been given short shrift in the traditional literature. In addition, X-efficiency theory has triggered research addressing a variety of theoretical and empirical questions from this different theoretical perspective. Indeed, the growing literature touched by Leibenstein's theoretical breakthrough has profound implications for public policy, based on theories which flow from a world of effort discretion. The concept of X-inefficiency offers different explanations and predictions than the standard neoclassical fare.

## Conclusion

What appears to be one thing through the visors of conventional microeconomics turns out to be quite another through the better focused lenses of X-efficiency theory. For example, in a world with X-inefficiency, the costs of monopoly are much higher than traditional theory suggests (Leibenstein 1966; Frantz 1988; Altman 1996). Higher wages might stimulate, as opposed to deaden, productivity increases and ECONOMIC GROWTH. Cultural factors can play an important role in determining the level of material well-being realized in an economy (Altman 1996). In addition, in a world where effort is a discretionary variable, and where X-inefficiency exists, microeconomic theory becomes more complex and more consequential than it has been. It becomes much more than a mathematical or purely deductive exercise. X-efficiency theory builds upon a combination of inductive and deductive reasoning, wherein theory is continuously enriched by our ever-changing understanding of the reality of economic life.

## Selected references

Altman, Morris (1996) *Human Agency and Material Welfare: Revisions in Microeconomics and their Implications for Public Policy*, Boston: Kluwer Academic.

Button, K.J. (ed.) (1989) *The Collected Essays of Harvey Leibenstein, vol. 2, X-Efficiency and Micro-Micro Theory*, New York: New York University Press.

Frantz, R.S. (1988) *X-Efficiency: Theory, Evidence and Applications*, Boston: Kluwer Academic.

Leibenstein, H. (1966) "Allocative Efficiency vs. 'X-Efficiency'," *American Economic Review* 56: 392–415.

—— (1979) "A Branch of Economics is Missing: Micro-Micro Theory," *Journal of Economic Literature* 17: 477–502.

—— (1982) "The Prisoner's Dilemma in the Invisible Hand: An Analysis of Intrafirm Productivity," *American Economic Review* 72: 92–7.

—— (1987) *Inside the Firm: The Inefficiencies of Hierarchy*, Cambridge: MA: Harvard University Press.

Leibenstein, H. and Maital, S. (1994) "The Organizational Foundations of X-Inefficiency: A Game-Theoretic Interpretation of Argyris' Model of Organizational Learning," *Journal of Economic Behavior and Organization* 23: 251–68.

Tomer, J.F. (1987) *Organizational Capital: The Path to Higher Productivity and Well-Being*, New York: Praeger Publishers.

MORRIS ALTMAN

# INDEX

# Index

social costs: excess capacity, 822; maladjustments, 935
social Darwinism: evolutionary economics,
291; feminism, 401
social democracy: capitalist breakdown, 70, 71,
72, 1037; economic foundations, 1037; history, 1036–7; ideology, 1035–6; new wave,
1037; Scandinavian model, 1005–7, 1246
social economics: associations and journals,
870, 1038–40; contemporary themes,
1042–5; family and community, 1043; health
care, 427–9; history and nature, 1040;
macroeconomics, 1044; markets, 1044;
methodology, 1039–40, 1044–5; positive and
normative branches, 1041, 1044–5; provisioning the community, 1040–1; workplace,
1043–4; *see also* ethics
social expenses, 355
social fabric matrix, 1045–8
social ownership: definition, 1052; property,
1051–4
social political economy, 870
social problems: crime, 163–4
social property, 1052–3
social sciences: biology, 37–9
social structures of accumulation: capital–labor
accord, 1054–6; competitive capitalism,
1056–7; contradictions, 1054–5; corporations, 1056–8; family, 1058–60; finance,
1061–3; history, 1066–8; homogenization,
1067; long waves, 676; monopoly capital,
1057; postwar corporate system, 1057–8;
productivity, 1054–5; proletarianization,
1066–7; segmentation, 1067; state–citizen
accord, 1063–5; theories, 1065–8
social wealth: collective, 111–12
social welfare: Islamic thought, 719–20
socialism: associations and journals, 592–3;
calculation debate, 1074–6; capitalism, 68–9;
class, 94, 95; contemporary models, 684–6;
feminism, 329–30; future, 1073; markets,
684–7; Marxist theories, 1071–2; states,
1072; utopias, 836, 1215; worker-control,
1072
society and individuals, 493–6
Society for the Advancement of Socio-
Economics (SASE), 1039–40
South Africa: land rights movements, 655–6
sovereign risk: interest rates, 551

Soviet Union: 208, Stalinism, 703, 710, 711,
713–14; centralized private sector planning,
69; dialectics, 208
Spain: anarchism, 15; Mondragón experiment,
639, 685, 748–50, 837–8, 867, 985, 1052,
1053, 1260
spatial analysis: circuit of social capital, 89;
urban and regional political economy, 1209
speculation: definition, 1076–7; endogenous
bubbles, 1081; exchange rates, 46, 303;
irrational bubbles, 1080–1; monopoly capital
theory, 1077–8; neoclassical theory, 1077–9;
post-Keynesian theories, 1077, 1078;
rational bubbles, 1081; speculative bubbles,
303, 1077, 1079–82, 1191; speculative
finance, 435, 738
Spencer, H.: evolution, 290, 291; natural
causation, 38
sport, 1082–5
Sraffa, P.: atomism, 1088–9; capital reversing,
60, 1092; capital theory, 64, 1091–2;
commodities, 35–7, 91, 860, 870, 1087;
competition, 133–5; corn model, 148; early
work, 1085; effective demand, 1093;
increasing returns to scale, 1085–6; influence, 1087–8; interdependency and relative
autonomy, 1089–90; international trade,
577–80; invariable measure of value, 584;
political economy, 133–5, 577–80, 1090–8;
price theory, 900–2, 1132–3; rate of profit,
927–9; renewable resources, 1093; surplus
approach, 1090–1, 1093; technical progress,
1148–9; wages theory, 1241–3
Sraffian political economy: capital critique,
1091–2; competition, 133–5; effective
demand, 1093; general theory or special
case, 1093–4; international trade, 577–80;
post-Keynesian theories, 1095–8; recent
developments, 1092–3; resources, 1093;
surplus approach, 1090–1, 1093; wages,
1241–3
stability: exchange rates, 31, 44–7; hegemony,
440–1; political, 186–7; velocity, 1226–7;
*see also* instability
stagflation, 1099–1101
stagnation, 1173–5
staple theory of growth, 1101–3
states: contradictions, 1106; corporations,
1105; economic policy, 531; fiscal crisis,

# Index

# AMERICAN THEATER

*THE UNITED STATES, CANADA, AND
MEXICO: FROM PRE-COLUMBIAN
TIMES TO THE PRESENT*

# Felicia Hardison Londré
# and Daniel J. Watermeier

CONTINUUM / NEW YORK

1999

The Continuum Publishing Company
370 Lexington Avenue
New York, NY 10017

Printed in the United States of America

Library of Congress Cataloging-in-Publication Data

Londré, Felicia Hardison, 1941–
        The history of North American theater : the United States, Canada,
    and Mexico : from pre-Columbian times to the present / Felicia Hardison
    Londré and Daniel J. Watermeier.
            p.   cm.
    Includes bibliographical references and index.
    ISBN 0-8264-1079-0
    1. Theater—North America—History. 2.Drama—History and criticism.
    I. Watermeier, Daniel J. II. Title.
    PN2219.5.L66   1998
    792'.097—dc21                                        97-51387
                                                            CIP

Frontispiece photographs, clockwise from left: *Porgy and Bess,* courtesy Lawrence and Lee Theatre Research Institute, Ohio State University; traditional Aztec ritual, photograph by Felicia Londré; Scene from *World of Wonders,* courtesy Stratford Festival (Ontario). All other photo and artwork cedits are given with the captions.

# Contents

# Preface

This volume was conceived at about the same time that the North American Free Trade Agreement was being debated in the United States Congress. In the years since then, whenever we have mentioned to colleagues that we were working on the first theater history book devoted to all of North America—Canada, Mexico, and the United States—a frequent response was "Oh, a NAFTA history of theater." Important as economic considerations are to the theater, however, our real motives were much simpler. We wanted to learn more about our neighbors and sharpen our long-standing appreciation of their respective cultures. Given the suspicions and hostilities that exist among many neighboring nation states in the world today, we Americans must count ourselves very lucky to have such a long tradition of friendly borders both north and south. From Canadian students who have occasionally taken our classes, we've learned that they generally know far more about our history, geography, and culture than we know about theirs. We are confident that the same condition prevails regarding our intercultural understanding of Mexico. We wanted to play fair with our nation's best friends by making it possible for others to learn about the theater culture of Canada and Mexico in an accessible, readily available volume. And we hoped that in so doing colleagues might be stimulated to teach American theater history in a larger, continental context. We also find it somehow appropriate that our book begins and ends with North America's native people.

We have aimed our history mainly at students of theater, both those engaged in formal university study and those—in the broader sense of "student"—with a keen interest in an ancient and absorbing artistic expression. Indeed, the history of theater, filled with colorful personalities, stirring events, lively dramas, a range of activities that flow and ebb within larger social and political currents, is intrinsically interesting. The history of theater in North America, taken as a whole, is at least as compelling as the theater histories of other countries or continents.

By no means did we plan to tell the whole story. To date, there is no definitive history of theater in the United States, although the three-volume *Cambridge History of Theatre in America,* edited by C. W. E. Bigsby and Don Wilmeth, the first volume of which has been published, is a giant leap forward in that direction. Clearly, a definitive history of theater in all of North America would encompass many more pages than we had at our disposal and would undoubtedly be beyond the scope of even two authors. *The History of North American Theatre* is intended primarily as a survey of the subject. We have tried to be comprehensive and thorough, covering major theatrical developments, events, and important, influential figures. But we did not aim to be all-inclusive. We trust that our survey might be useful as a text and that it will sufficiently inform the general reader interested in theater history.

We have tried to strike a balance among the several national theaters, providing fair coverage of their respective histories. Still, the theater of the United States looms larger than the others, in part because of our greater familiarity with its history, but also because it is the largest and most complex theater culture on the continent. We have arranged the story of theater in the United States around a series of topics: theatrical organization and management, theater buildings, actors and acting, playwrights and plays, designers, directors and choreographers, critics, and certain popular entertainment forms—minstrel shows, vaudeville, and musical theater. Not every chapter, however, addresses each of these topics. In the colonial period and in the early nineteenth century, for example, the arts and crafts of scenic design in the United States were not as well-developed as they would later become. Thus, our coverage of this topic is more cursory in the earlier than in the later chapters. In a like vein, stage direction and theatrical dance and choreography, as we know it today, grew out of developments in the late nineteenth and early twentieth centuries, so this topic is only touched on, if mentioned at all, in the chapters dealing with the colonial and romantic eras.

A few other organizational and stylistic decisions might be briefly explained. The order in which each section appears varies somewhat from one chapter to another. For the colonial period, it was simple enough to move from south to north: historically, the theater of New Spain developed far in advance of that of the American colonies or New France. Later, the decision became a more intuitive process of achieving the best "fit" for our writing. In chapters 2 through 6, Quebec refers to the city of Quebec. In chapter 7, Québec (with an accent) is the province, while the city becomes Quebec City. Similarly, México (with accent mark) refers to the capital of New Spain or the capital of the Mexican nation in chapters 2 through 6, but México D.F. is used for the city in chapter 7, while Mexico (without accent mark) denotes the country throughout.

Although we have been informed by several historiographical approaches from empiricism to feminism, our "point of view" is eclectic and practical, shaped by the intended purpose of our book and its probable readership. Our focus is primarily on mainstream, professional theater. When warranted, however, we have steered out of the mainstream to explore important and influential theatrical tributaries. Thus, for example, in chapter 7 we have not neglected the significant avant-garde theater artists and companies that emerged in the United States beginning in the 1960s. We did not attempt to incorporate the history of puppet theater; still, certain practitioners of that art could not be ignored: Don "Chole" Aycardo, Peter Schumann, Julie Taymor. We faced similar judgment calls in areas like community theater and pageantry, musical theater, variety entertainment, dinner theater, and children's theater. Perhaps the most glaring of these boundary disputes is in the area of performance as opposed to formal or traditional theater. Our chapter on the pre-Columbian era necessarily focuses on performance, but the treatment must be acknowledged as unavoidably colored by the filter of "western" perceptions. If objectivity is an impossible goal to achieve in any historiographical discourse, then distortions are certainly inevitable in material apprehended at such cultural remove from the original intent of the creators. Yet the attempt must be made. As Steve Wilmer has commented in an unpublished paper on "The Ghost Dance: Re/deeming the Authors' Intentions":

> the theatre historian needs to examine the artifacts remaining from the performance, as well as the interpretation of the performance by eye witnesses of the event (while questioning their reading positions), and investigate the general social context in which the event is set. The theatre historian will recognize that the interpretation of all of these elements will be full of pitfalls.

Generally throughout our narrative, we have given special attention to the contributions of women and various ethnic minorities, especially in our increasingly multicultural modern age. We have also given more consideration than is customary to the business and organizational infrastructure of the theatrical enterprise. Appreciating that among the new historiographies it may not be fashionable, nonetheless we have been oriented to *people,* if not to a *great* woman/man approach. Believing that theater is made by individuals, usually working in collaboration, we have focused on the activities and contributions of numerous actors, playwrights, producers, architects, and designers who have left a distinctive mark in the annals of the North American stage. We know that many names have been omitted, but we hope that we have not consciously neglected any signal achievement.

As the length and scope of the book escalated beyond our original estimates, coverage of Caribbean theatrical activity had to be restricted; we acknowledge that our treatment of the theaters of Cuba, Santo Domingo, and Puerto Rico is superficial and trust that other scholars will make up for our lacunae. The section on Canadian theater since 1945, though relatively lengthy, could scarcely do justice to that vast subject. The international prestige of Canada's cultural presence in recent decades testifies to the power of government funding of the arts and of a citizenry imbued with patriotic pride in its own national and multiethnic identity and history.

One of Felicia's particular pleasures in working on this book was a reawakened awareness and appreciation of her own ancestry. Felicia's maternal grandmother, Georgiane Césarée Gagnon (Mrs. Roy Charles Lemach Graham), was born in Sainte-Anne de la Pocatière, Province of Québec, and grew up speaking only French. According to a yellowed newspaper clipping (*Le Soleil,* Québec, May 31, 1940), in June 1940 the "illustrious family" of numerous Gagnons could celebrate three hundred years in America. In 1960, after attending the École Française d'Été (French Summer School) at McGill University in Montreal, Felicia took a three-day side trip to Sainte-Anne de la Pocatière to trace her ancestors. She recalls:

> I had written in advance a letter blindly addressed to the postmaster of the town, in which I explained my quest and supplied all the family names I knew. My

grandmother's parents were Louis Gagnon (b. 1874) and Léontine Bérubé (1872–1921), but the family had moved to Epping, New Hampshire, early in the century. Fifty years later I couldn't realistically expect to find anyone who remembered them. My search captured the interest of the elderly postmaster, who introduced himself in a letter as Ti-Georges Dionne. It turned out that his nephew was a Bérubé, and Ti-Georges put me in the Bérubé family's care as soon as I arrived in town. M. et Mme Bérubé had a daughter, Raymonde (about twelve), a younger son, and a dog named Beauté. If by some remote chance Raymonde should read this, I hope she will contact me. I remain deeply grateful for her family's generous hospitality and I cherish the memory of those lovely days with them as they took me to various local cemeteries where I copied names and dates from tombstones. And we were taken into many a farmhouse kitchen where extended families gathered around the table to look at the genealogical charts I was tentatively filling out. On my final day with the Bérubé family, we followed our strongest lead. They drove me across the river to Rivière Ouelle and found a man who may have been my great-uncle Louis Gagnon. He was dozing on a bench in the sun and did seem mildly interested when I was presented to him as an American descendent of his family. Of course, there was little to be said to each other, but I remember being moved by the encounter. Ti-Georges and I kept up a correspondence for several years. I still have the thirty or so turn-of-the-century classic paperbacks he sent me: Shakespeare, Goethe, and others translated into French, some bearing Ti-Georges's notation on the cover: "Très beau."

Another great reward for Felicia was the opportunity to learn much about Mexico's history and culture in the course of writing about its theater. She found herself compulsively reading books on the Maya, on Cuauhtémoc and Cortés and Malinche, on Maximillian and Carlotta, on Benito Juárez. A good read she especially recommends is Fanny Calderón de la Barca's *Life in Mexico*. The perfect culmination to these studies came in June 1997 when she attended the International Federation for Theatre Research conference hosted by the Universidad de las Américas–Puebla in Cholula, Mexico. The excursions arranged by the conference organizers, Domingo Adame, Octavio Rivera, and Bárbara Padrón–León, included Cacaxtla, Xochitectl, Tlaxcala, the archeological site at Cholula, Acatepec, Teotihuacán, and México D.F. It was thrilling for Felicia to walk on the spot in Tlaxcala where the earliest ecclesiastical dramas were performed, and to see two different troupes perform the ancient folk-drama *Los Moros y los cristianos* and to attend Sor Juana's *loa* to *El Divino Narciso*, which was very movingly performed by UDLAP students under the direction of Octavio Rivera. Felicia was also very gratified to meet legendary scholars like María Sten, Giovanna Recchia, and Daniel Meyran.

We appreciate that NAFTA is, for better or worse, an economic, political, and cultural reality. The countries of North America are more intricately interconnected than ever through bonds of heritage, commerce and trade, common languages, and shared national ideals and aspirations. Perhaps *The History of North American Theatre* will in a small way contribute to furthering cultural understanding and comity among all the peoples of our continent.

A book of this scope relies heavily on the work of other scholars. The last fifteen years or so have been particularly rich in scholarship about North American theater. Our bibliographies list the numerous monographs and articles on which we depended, but we take this opportunity to single out a few works to which we repeatedly returned. The general bibliography lists works that served as important resources for two or more chapters. For Mexican theater history, Manuel Mañon's *Historia del Teatro Principal de México* (1932) strongly informs chapters 2 through 6. Jean Laflamme and Rémi Tourangeau's *L'Église et le théâtre au Québec* (1979) proved similarly helpful for French–Canadian theater history. Among the pioneering histories that informed us are Arthur Hornblow's two-volume *A History of Theatre in America: From Its Beginnings to the Present Time* (1919) and Arthur Hobson Quinn's two-volume *A History of American Drama*, first published in the mid-1920s and then in a revised edition in the late 1930s (vol. 1) and early 1940s (vol. 2). We found Oral Summer Coad and Edwin Mims's *The American Stage* (1929) filled with factual tidbits and some unique illustrations. Special mention should be made of theater historian and educator Barnard Hewitt (1906–87). Through his *Theatre USA* (1959), a documentary history of American theater, his numerous articles, and a score of dissertations on American theater and drama completed under his mentorship, Hewitt inspired an entire generation of younger scholars to explore their national theatrical history. The fruits of Hewitt's tutelage are evident in *The Cambridge Guide to American Theatre*, edited by two of his former students, Don Wilmeth and Tice Miller. The *Guide* was a faithful writing companion, a trustworthy map to the territory, and an authoritative source of abundant information and insight. Garff B. Wilson's *Three Hundred Years of American Drama and Theatre* (1973; second edition, 1982) and his *A History of American Acting* (1966; reprinted 1980) were also helpful surveys. Charles H. Shattuck's (1910–92) gracefully written two-volume *Shakespeare on the American Stage* (vol. 1, *From the Hallams to Edwin Booth*, 1976; vol. 2, *From Booth and Barrett to Sothern and Marlowe*, 1987) not only sketches the careers of numerous actors but illumines the entire history of nineteenth-century American theatrical taste. Sam Leiter's monumental calendars to the New York stage from the 1920s through the 1940s, his study of New York theater in the 1970s, and his several books on modern directors, including many American stagesmiths, were invaluable to us. Mary C. Henderson's seminal *The City and the Theatre* (1973) and her lavishly illustrated *Theatre in America* (1986; revised edition 1996) were treasured volumes. Gerald Bordman's several books on the development of the American musical theater and his recent *American Theatre: A Chronicle of Comedy and Drama* in three volumes (to date), covering the century from 1869–1969, were immensely useful. The labor of many other fellow historians of American theater have inspired us. In addition to those mentioned above, we are especially indebted to Rosemarie K. Bank, Weldon Durham, Ron Engle, Richard France, Errol Hill, Foster Hirsch, Richard Moody, Benjamin McArthur, Bruce McConachie, Douglas McDermott, Brooks McNamara, Walter Meserve, Laurence Senelick, and Barry Witham.

For their help in tracking down information, defining terms, providing illustrations or other materials, Felicia would like to thank Stephen Archer, Rose Bank, Ian Borden, Reverend Dwight Frizzell, Frank Higgins, Dolores Kaptain, Venne-Richard Londré, Anne Nothof, Marc Plowman, Richard Poole, Jason Pollen, Tim Richards, Octavio Rivera, Robert A. Schanke, Steve Wilmer, Barry Witham, George Woodyard, and Phyllis Zatlin. She is especially grateful to Claudia Jasso of the Biblioteca de las Artes, Centro Nacional de las Artes, for her kind assistance with photographs of Mexican theater, and to Mark Kelty for reading the sections on twentieth-century Mexican theater. She also thanks André Bourassa for reading the sections on early Canadian theater history.

Securing illustrations proved more complicated and expensive than we originally anticipated. For their help in providing illustrations, Dan thanks Joseph Benford, head of the Print and Picture Collection, and Geraldine Duclow, head of the Theatre Collection, the Free Library of Philadelphia; Lisa Brant, archivist of Canada's Stratford Festival; Marsha Camera of the New York Power Authority; Tisa Chang, artistic/producing director, and Jodi Lin, administrative assistant, the Pan Asian Repertory Theatre; John Grafton of Dover Publications; Martha Hayes, collection supervisor of the unique Theatre Museum of Repertoire Americana in Mt. Pleasant, Iowa; Lorenzo Mans, literary manager of INTAR Hispanic American Arts Center; Steve Martin, managing director, and Laura E. Laing, marketing associate, The Virginia Stage Company; Sheryl Padula, curator of the Curtis Theatre Collection at the University of Pittsburg; Maureen V. Reagan, assistant marketing and public services director of the Krannert Center for the Performing Arts at the University of Illinois at Urbana-Champaign; Denny Reed, business manager of the Showboat Majestic and Cara Matho, director of the Cincinnati Recreation Commission; Cindy Reynolds, marketing director of Penumbra Theatre; John and Jennifer Rockwood of Toledo; Jana Scharhorst, marketing director of St. Louis's Fabulous Fox Theatre; Robert Shaddy, director of the Ward M. Canaday Center for Special Collections at the University of Toledo Library; Jo Ann Schmidman, artistic director of the Omaha Magic Theatre; Jeanne Somers, curator of special collections and archives at the Kent State University Libraries; Bart Swinnall, historian for the Auditorium Theatre Council; David A. Tucker III, associate director of public relations, the Old Globe Theatre; Ray Wemmlinger, curator and librarian of the Hampden–Booth Theatre Library at The Players; Patricia Willis, curator of the Yale Collection of American Literature; and Fredric Woodbridge Wilson, curator, and Michael Dumas, curatorial assistant of The Harvard Theatre Collection. Dan singles out for special thanks Kathryn Beam, special collections librarian at the University of Michigan. Nena Couch, curator, John Taylor, curatorial assistant, and Professor Alan Woods opened the resources of Jerome Lawrence and Robert E. Lee Theatre Research Institute at Ohio State University solely for Dan on a Sunday afternoon and then graciously shared their intimate knowledge of the institute's iconographic holdings. Marguerite Lavin was particularly cooperative and helpful in providing at reasonable cost a dozen superb photographs from the Museum of the City of New York. Indeed, the museum's extensive collection of primary theatrical materials is an outstanding treasure-trove for American theater scholars. Dan also owes a debt to Stephen Archer and to the students in Professor Archer's graduate American theater course for reviewing the United States sections of the manuscript and suggesting numerous improvements. Roberta Kane also read the sections on theater in the United States and contributed a series of refinements and changes. He is especially grateful to Gigi Boyle who typed and retyped the manuscript more times than she undoubtedly cares to remember. Without her patience and assistance, the task would have been far more demanding and time consuming. The Department of Theatre at the University of Toledo tacitly absorbed the costs of numerous phone calls, faxes, and photocopying.

We both acknowledge and appreciate the confidence and patience accorded us by the Continuum Publishing Company, and especially by our editor Evander Lomke, as they allowed us to take the time we needed for work that was originally to have been completed two years earlier. The two additional years, a mere blip in the grand scheme of history, to us meant over seven hundred more days of continuous research, thought, and writing devoted to this work.

Felicia Hardison Londré
Daniel J. Watermeier

# 1 Pre-Columbian Performance

Conjectures about the origin of theater generally fall into three broad categories: dance, shamanism, and ritual enactments to propitiate the forces of nature. Among the native populations of North America we find evidence that all three kinds of performance activities were practiced before the arrival of the first Europeans. Such enactments were tied to religious beliefs and tended to remain fixed in form over many generations. Although religion permeated virtually all aspects of pre-Columbian life, there seems also to have been, in some instances, a pre-Columbian equivalent to "theater" as westerners traditionally conceive it: that is, performance events at which there is a clear distinction between the roles of performer and spectator, and which are intended more for entertainment than for ritual purposes. The gaps in our knowledge of both the religion and theater of the era exist largely due to the systematic destruction of evidence by the bringers of Christianity and other elements of Old World culture. With motives ranging from the lofty (salvation for the heathen) to the base (profit and aggrandizement), the invaders set about obliterating the existing culture as a concomitant to implanting their own. It is inevitable that contact between any two alien cultures will effect changes in both. That process rapidly accelerated in the sixteenth century and after, as the imported culture prevailed over the indigenous; thus what was not wiped out was altered, often beyond recognition. Because most Native American tribes were not literate (the Maya were a notable exception), we must seek clues to past performance traditions in pictorial artifacts, oral narratives, and surviving tribal practices. Written eyewitness accounts by early Western explorers, conquerors, missionaries, and settlers are also helpful, although those observers stood outside the native cultural context and necessarily imposed their own perceptions on what they were seeing.

The Americas have been home to aboriginal peoples since at least 9000 B.C.E., and most scientists trace their presence as far back as twenty-five to forty thousand years ago. The North American native population peaked around C.E. 1200 with up to ten million inhabitants north of the Río Grande, while urbanized Mesoamerica supported (estimates vary widely) from twenty-five to one hundred million. It is in the ruins of those ancient, magnificent cities of the land we know today as Guatemala, the Yucatán peninsula, and the highland basin of Mexico that we find the earliest evidence of Native American performances. The Olmecs, whom some archaeologists believe to have been the "mother culture" of the region, left as evidence of performance only some stone carvings that probably represent dancers. The Maya, however, combined ritual and spectacle in their dances, shamanistic practices, and other enactments, as is evident from various sources. Theater history on the North American continent must begin with them.

## THE MAYA

Maya civilization divides into two phases. The Classic Maya flourished in cities like Tikal, Palenque, Bonampak, and Copán in the Guatemalan lowlands from C.E. 300 to 900. These Maya developed a system of writing that combined hieroglyphs and phonetic symbols. They invented the earliest known mathematical system using the concept of zero. They were also accomplished astronomers who worked out complex interlocking calendars for the solar year (365 days) and the ritual cycle (260 days). For reasons that remain unclear, those great cities were abandoned in the tenth century, and most Maya peoples immigrated to the Yucatán peninsula where—merging with the Náhuatl-speaking Toltecs who invaded from the north—they built the capital city of Chichén Itzá. These post-Classic Maya explored new patterns of social organization, but continued the ritual and commercial practices of their ancestors for about two centuries, after which the cities of the Yucatán were abandoned.

Although the Maya were a rural people by the time of the Spanish conquest, their ancient beliefs persisted for centuries, even after the destruction of the "books" in which their myths and historical data were recorded. (Only about seventeen preconquest books have survived, four Maya and the rest Aztec. These codices are composed of screenfold panels made of deerhide or bark paper and coated with lime plaster on which colorful and intricate pictures and symbols are painted on both sides; a wooden cover at each end encases the folded panels.) The Spanish missionaries of the mid-sixteenth century, in their zeal to replace the traditional cosmology with Catholicism, made bonfires of most of these books. In teaching Christianity, the Spaniards took advantage of some readily apparent resemblances between imported and indigenous religious concepts—the Maya depiction of the tree that supports the sky, for example, takes much the same form as the Christian cross—without realizing that often they were merely grafting some outer trappings onto an unchanging core of native beliefs. When the Náhuatl-speaking Dominican friar Diego Durán wrote of the native dances he witnessed in the 1570s, he mentioned the native proclivity to preserve hidden meanings in performance. Beyond the obscure metaphors contained in the words of songs that sometimes even referred obligingly to Christian saints, there lay more complex aboriginal meanings conveyed in gesture and movement. That is, nonverbal aspects of performance were often highly inflected, their symbolic connotations understood only by those who had grown up in the culture.

Diego de Landa (a Franciscan, in the Yucatán from 1549 to 1564 and, as bishop, from 1573 to 1579) recorded his observations in his *Relación de las cosas de Yucatán.* He reported, without attempting to contextualize the practice within its system of belief, what is probably the most renowned—and certainly the most horrific—form of Maya spectacle: the sacrifice of human beings (usually the most admirable of those taken captive in ritual wars with other tribes) whose hearts were cut out of their living bodies as they lay across altars elevated high above the spectator-filled plaza. After the body was thrown down the steep flight of steps, the skin was removed in one piece, so that a naked acolyte could step into the skin as if it were a costume and dance in it. Apparently the main temple at Chichén Itzá was still used for sacrifices in Landa's time, though the rest of the city was overgrown with vegetation.

Landa noted that the Maya had "over a thousand kinds" of dance performances. All were essentially religious in context. One category of ritual dance known as *okot* was penitential in nature and incorporated supplicatory prayer. Among the specific Maya dances described by Landa was one done in a large circle surrounding two dancers who tossed and caught a bundle of reeds. Another was a day-long, warlike dance of about eight hundred Indians with little streamers. Landa also watched shamanistic healing rituals and ecstatic dances that culminated in walking barefoot on hot coals. Such performances probably fall into the category of *ez yah*, involving sleight of hand and tricks of illusion. Toward these, the Spaniards were particularly hostile (Sahagún, for example, condemned such conjuring because it passed off fakery as if it were truth).

This temple at Tusapan near the eastern coast of today's Mexico exemplifies the pyramidal structures constructed of stone by the Maya and other ancient indigenous peoples. Their ritual human sacrifices often took place, visible to the large crowds gathered below, at the top of such steep flights of steps. From Brantz Mayer, Mexico, As It Was and As It Is, 1847.

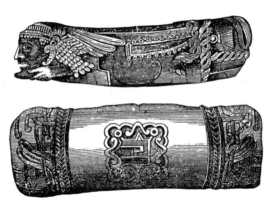

*The carved wooden* tun *provided drum accompaniment for the dance–dramas of the ancient Maya. From Brantz Mayer,* Mexico, As It Was and As It Is, *1847.*

Landa further hinted tantalizingly at some kind of dramatic performances which he called "farces" or "comedies for the pleasure of the public." He was told that they were performed on the "two small stages of hewn stone, with four staircases, paved on top" opposite the temple at Chichén Itzá. In his discussion of Maya feasts, Landa noted: "These Indians have very agreeable amusements, and especially have players who act with a great deal of wit." He may have been referring to a form of ritual buffoonery known as *baldzamil,* which the Spanish regarded indulgently despite its vulgarity, because the content apparently resembled that of their own comic playlets about husbands and wives and servants. These probably also included animal characters. Elements of the *baldzamil* survive in the present as folklore.

Since the 1960s, as scholars have learned to decipher the Maya glyphs found in the codices and carved on rock, there have been rapid advances in our understanding of the Maya world view and way of life. In addition to the four surviving preconquest Maya codices, there is a version of the creation story or sacred book of the Maya, the *Popol Vuh,* which was written down in the 1550s. Having studied this and countless other Maya texts in stone, in books, and on pottery fragments, David Freidel and Linda Schele see in Maya myth, ritual, and patterns of daily life (including the horribly violent sports for which the famous ball courts were built) a remarkably unified conception of man's place in nature's endless cycles of birth and death. They demonstrate that Maya reenactments of the myth of creation through festivals, pageantry, and dance were integral to the life of the community.

The creation myth recounted in the *Popol Vuh* animates the ritual *Dance of the Giants,* which is now overlaid with the Biblical story of David and Goliath as well as references to the martyrdom of Saint John. Thus it survived into the twentieth century, performed annually on June 13 and 24, at the sun's zenith, by the natives of the town of Tisipe. The dance's antiquity is indicated in that it contains elements common to both Maya and Quiché cultures before their separation in the tenth century. Performed by eight actor–dancers and a master of ceremonies plus musicians, *Dance of the*

*Giants* incorporates calendrical and directional principles in homage to the sun. The mythic Hero Twins, one representing the young sun, the other the young moon, are called the Two Gavites (the indigenous version of David); those roles are danced by boys no older than twelve. They battle the forces of darkness represented by the Black Giant (or One-Death), who has killed their father, the White Giant (Seven-Deaths). The Gavites dance on an east–west line and the Giants on a north–south line, a manifestation of the importance of the four cardinal directions in all Native American ritual. In a crucial episode, the Gavites demonstrate their magical powers by killing and dismembering each other (the separated body parts represented by a handkerchief) and then coming back to life.

Another important, exceptional survival of Maya culture is a dramatic text known as *Rabinal Achí* (Rabinal warrior), which had been passed down from one generation to the next, apparently through performances in the Quiché language, in the vicinity of the remote Guatemalan village of San Pablo de Rabinal, perhaps since the thirteenth century. Records dating back to 1685 show that a rapid turnover of parish priests was the norm for Rabinal; thus, the priests' lack of opportunity to learn the languge and local customs may account for the dance-drama's survival. As Anita Brenner has explained, the natives of Mexico obstinately preserved their ancient idols behind the Christian altars they were conscripted to build. The missionaries succeeded only in making the original culture "invisible," not destroying it completely. Although the church finally suppressed performances of *Rabinal Achí* in the 1820s, one Indian, Bartolo Sis, remembered the words well enough to dictate them in 1855 to an interested parish priest, Charles Etienne Brasseur de Bourbourg (1814–74).

Brasseur was a French priest who had worked in the Vatican library in Rome. A remarkable scholar, he financed his collecting of rare manuscripts by writing historical novels, several of which remained in print as late as the 1890s. In Guatemala, he learned the Náhuatl, Quiché, and Kaqchikel languages. In his 1862 *Grammaire de la langue quichée,* he included *Rabinal Achí* in both his Quiché transcription and his own French translation, along with musical notations and an account of his discovery of the text. According to Brasseur, it was shortly after his arrival in Rabinal that he met Bartolo Sis, the village's elderly *holpop* (a kind of *magister ludi,* who functioned as the living repository of the performance tradition). Under Brasseur's ministrations, Sis recovered from an illness and, in gratitude, spent twelve days dictating the text that he had memorized under the tutelage of his father and grandfather. Brasseur transcribed it with the help of two Indian servants. Important research conducted on the site in the 1950s and 1960s by René Acuña suggests that Sis may well have made his own prior transcription from memory.

Brasseur was told that when *Rabinal Achí* had been performed on a regular basis more than thirty years earlier, the village had been wealthier and had spent a great deal on feathers and fabrics for the costumes and masks. Bartolo Sis himself had been a leading actor–dancer in it. Brasseur urged Sis to mount a performance of *Rabinal Achí,* and this was done in January 1856.

The twelve-day cycle of performances involved about a hundred people and demonstrated that the complex work could not be fairly understood on the basis of the text alone. Music, dance, masks, make-up, and ceremonial objects were integral components. Unfortunately, Brasseur described neither the masks nor the choreography. It is known, however, that the musical accompaniment was provided by a *tun* (a yard-long hollow wooden drum that was struck on its side) and two trumpets. The use of the *tun* and trumpets in the pre-Columbian era is documented in the codices and in the mural paintings (showing musicians and masked dancers) of the ancient Maya city of Bonampak. Indeed, the authentic name for what we know as *Rabinal Achí* was *Xahoh tun* or *Aj tun* (*tun* dance). Similar dance–dramas in the Guatemalan highlands were the *Tun Teleche* described by Prieto de Villegas in 1624, and the *Quiché Vinac* reported by Francisco Ximénez in the eighteenth century. Twentieth-century survivals of *bailes del tun* (dances accompanied by the *tun*) have been witnessed by S. K. Lothrop in the 1920s and Francisco Rodriguez Rouanet in the 1960s. The costume elements they described provide clues to what may have been used for *Rabinal Achí*. Of particular interest are the carved wooden "shields" worn on the back of the shoulders of certain dancers. On each of these "shoulder plaques" (as Lothrop calls them) is "a hollow tube supported by two heraldic-like figures. The dancers go in pairs united by an arched sapling, the ends of which are inserted in the tubes. . . . [The arch] is adorned with twenty or thirty bunches of feathers dyed a brilliant crimson." The heraldic figures shown in Lothrop's photographs appear to be monkeys on one plaque and men on another. However, Rodriguez Rouanet described a plaque with two jaguars facing outward, and another carved with a two-headed eagle. This is significant in that *Rabinal Achí* calls for two groups of dancers: jaguars and eagles.

*Rabinal Achí* is, according to Georges Raynaud, "the only ancient Amerindian theatrical text that comes down to us" uncontaminated by "the slightest trace of word, idea, or fact of European origin." He conjectures, however, that the version we have may be somewhat abbreviated in that it contains neither religious references nor recitations of the lineage and titles of the Rabinal and Quiché chiefs (both of whom speak the Quiché language). Yet the speeches are long and contain much repetition. Most of the text is spoken by only three characters: the Rabinal Warrior, the Quiché Warrior, and Five Rains, the Rabinal chief. A Rabinal servant has a few short speeches. Although she does not speak, the Rabinal "princess"—whose titles include Mother of the Feathers, Mother of the Little Green Birds, and Precious Gem—has a featured role in the action. Besides those individual characters, the cast includes twelve yellow Eagles and twelve yellow Jaguars, as well as extra dancers representing warriors, servants, and women of Rabinal. The Eagles and Jaguars were warriors who had earned by their valor the right to wear the skins of those creatures, and the color yellow seems to have been a distinction of highest rank.

The central figure in *Rabinal Achí* is not the eponymous Rabinal Warrior, but his captive, the Quiché Warrior, with whose sacrifice the action culminates. Because this is a unique work on which we must rely for much of our understanding of Maya dramatic conventions, it is necessary to recount the action in some detail. The drama begins with a circle dance by the Rabinal Warrior and his men. Suddenly the Queché Warrior appears and dances to the center of the circle, thrusting his lance toward the Rabinal Warrior's head. The dance accelerates. The Queché Warrior taunts the Rabinal Warrior, but at the same time uses certain courteous locutions that will be repeated in virtually every speech thereafter: "Those are my words before the face of the sky, before the face of the earth. And thus I will not speak many words to you. May the sky and the earth be with you, most eminent of warriors, warrior of Rabinal." The Rabinal Warrior responds: "Indeed! Brave warrior, man of the Cavek Queché. These were your words before the face of the sky, before the face of the earth." The Rabinal Warrior then repeats verbatim the Queché warrior's insults, followed by the verbal formula to indicate a closed quotation: "Were not those your words?" The Rabinal Warrior tells how he will use his rope to lasso and bind the Queché Warrior "before the face of the sky, before the face of the earth." Presumably, he accomplishes this by the time he reaches the formula that ends his speech: "May the sky and the earth be with you, brave warrior, captive man, prisoner." The Rabinal Warrior pulls the lassoed Queché Warrior to him. The music and dancing stop. There is a long silence while the two warriors stand face to face. The remainder of this scene is the Rabinal Warrior's interrogation of the Queché Warrior, in the course of which the speeches become quite long as each repeats the words of the other's preceeding speech. Given the time devoted to demonstrating polite attention and verbal memory on the part of both warriors, the dramatic action unfolds slowly. For Maya audiences, the visual context of those poetic, mesmerizing speeches must have greatly enhanced the interest.

The interrogation proceeds with musical and dance underscoring. The Rabinal Warrior ascertains that it was the Queché Warrior who made animal cries outside the walls of the Rabinal fortress to lure the hunters. He confirms that his chief had sent a message to Queché that resulted in the Queché Warrior's coming alone and bravely into Rabinal territory. The Queché Warrior admits to having made mistakes. The Rabinal Warrior exits to inform his chief of the capture.

The second scene takes place inside the Rabinal fortress. The Rabinal chief, Five Rains (Hobtoh in Quiché, a name perhaps derived from the weather on his day of birth), sits on his throne, surrounded by servants, women, warriors, Eagles, and Jaguars. The Rabinal Warrior approaches and describes his capture of the Queché Warrior who had imitated animal cries to lure Rabinal hunters and then killed them; furthermore, the Queché destroyed two or three villages. Five Rains thanks the Rabinal Warrior formulaically and orders that the captive be brought inside the fortress in a dignified manner as it is imperative that one worthy of sacrifice be "loved and admired." Five Rains mentions the honors in store for the captive: he will sit on benches of precious metals and gems, he will drink twelve superb liquors, he will drape himself in the finest cloth, he will dance with the princess and perhaps touch her virgin face. After a further exchange of formalities, the Rabinal Warrior goes to get his captive.

*Carved wooden shoulder plaques like these were part of the* tun *dance costume of the Quiché Indians and may well have been worn in performances of* Rabinal Achí. *Courtesy of the National Museum of the American Indian Smithsonian Institution (negative #11073).*

*The Quiché-language play* Rabinal Achí *includes dances by Eagle warriors and Jaguar warriors. Eagles and jaguars are often carved on ceremonial drums as depicted here. Reprinted from* Dances of Anáhuac: The Choreography and Music of Precortesian Dances *by Gertrude Prokosch Kurath and Samuel Martí (Viking Fund Publications in Anthropology #38, Aldine Publishing Co., Chicago, 1965) by permission of the Wenner–Gren Foundation for Anthropological Research, Inc., New York, New York.*

In the very brief third scene, the Rabinal Warrior unbinds the Queché Warrior (who was tied to a tree), while repeating the chief's words about the honors in store for the captive as long as he makes a dignified entrance and kneels before Five Rains. The Queché Warrior repeats the instructions at which he takes offense. As a brave warrior he refuses to bow his head; however, he will lay down his arms and shield. Angered, he is on the point of attacking the Rabinal Warrior, but a Rabinal servant steps between them, and the sequence comes to an abrupt halt.

The fourth scene brings the Queché Warrior before Five Rains. The Queché recounts the essence of the previous scene and asks for a bench worthy of the station he held in his own mountains and valleys. Five Rains then reviews the Queché Warrior's various acts of aggression against people of Rabinal. The Queché Warrior repeats the chief's accusations against him, admits to having done these things, and asks to drink the twelve liquors as a sign that he will be sacrificed. Five Rains gives his servants an order, and they carry in a table laden with food and drink. The Queché Warrior eats and drinks disdainfully, then dances. Again addressing Five Rains, the Queché Warrior boasts of how much better the food and drink are in his own mountains and valleys. He recognizes his drinking cup as the skull of his ancestor and hopes that his own skull will be put to such noble use, so that his descendents may be honored by drinking from it. He also offers the bones of his arms and legs to be used as drumsticks. Now he reminds the chief that he was to be given fine cloth to wear. At the chief's order, servants bring the cloth and drape it on the Queché Warrior. Each request is granted formulaically "within the walls, within the fortress, as a supreme sign of my [your] death and disappearance from this place beneath the sky, upon the earth."

The Queché Warrior asks whether the Rabinal trumpets and drums can produce sounds as sweet as Queché music. He dances in the midst of the court, giving his war cry in each of the four corners. His next request is to dance with the princess, to touch her face and mouth that have never been touched. Five Rains orders that the young woman be brought in. The warrior and the princess dance together, after which the Queché Warrior again approaches Five Rains and asks to practice his skills at arms with the Eagles and Jaguars. After dancing a war dance with the twelve Eagles and twelve Jaguars, the Queché Warrior disparages them, telling Five Rains that these Eagles and Jaguars—unlike the ones of his own mountains and valleys—have no teeth or claws.

Finally, the Queché Warrior asks for thirteen times twenty days and thirteen times twenty nights in which to go and say goodbye "to the face of my mountains, to the face of my valleys." (Thirteen times twenty yields 260, the number of days in the Maya ritual cycle.) There is no reply to this. The Queché Warrior dances away and remains out of sight for a moment. Reentering, he crosses directly to the Eagles and Jaguars who are grouped around a central altar. He tells them that he has said goodbye to his mountains and valleys, and now he knows he must die. He asks that his weapons be returned to his homeland and that the news of his death be relayed to his chief. His final words are: "O Eagles! O Jaguars! Come now and carry out your duty, accomplish your mission. May your teeth and claws kill me in an instant, because I am a warrior and have come from my mountains, from my valleys. May the sky and the earth be with you, O Eagles, O Jaguars!" The Eagles and Jaguars surround the Queché Warrior. Although Brasseur does not say so, they probably stretch him on the sacrificial stone and mime cutting out his heart, which is then held up to the sun and to the four cardinal directions.

## THE AZTEC EMPIRE

After the decline of the Maya, the Aztecs began their rise to predominance. If Maya civilization is sometimes regarded as analogous to that of classical Greece, then the Aztecs represent Mesoamerica's Romans. The Aztec empire encompassed various Náhuatl-speaking tribes spread over a vast area of central Mexico. It was the Mexica people specifically who settled on the site selected according to the prophesied sign of an eagle perching on a cactus (the symbol that appears on the Mexican national flag today) and in 1325 founded the city of Tenochtitlán on an island in Lake Texcoco in the Valley of Mexico. Over the next two centuries until the arrival in 1519 of the Spanish conqueror Hernán Cortés, Tenochtitlán grew to legendary magnificence, incorporating the town of Tlatelolco on the northern end of the island. The island was connected to the mainland by three causeways; goods were transported to the city's enormous, bustling market by human carriers and by canoe. The temple precinct, Tenochtitlán's ritual center, included a steep-sided pyramid topped by twin towers, a ballcourt, palaces, temples, and a plaza that could accommodate thousands of spectators. Under Moctezuma II (reigned 1502–20), Tenochtitlán as a seat of government with a population of 300,000 extended its rule over ten million people and regularly exacted tribute from them. Thus it was easy for Cortés to win the allegiance of the various tributary tribes in his campaign that led to the destruction of Tenochtitlán in 1521. Fortunately, many of the Franciscan friars who arrived shortly after the conquest made the effort to learn Náhuatl and record the native reminiscences; the work of Bernardino de Sahagún and Diego Durán is invaluable. For that reason, the Mexica (or Aztec) way of life before the coming of Europeans is the best documented of any indigenous population in North America.

Like the Romans, the Mexica assimilated the traditions of the people they conquered. The Mexica were particularly eager to be recognized as the heirs of Toltec culture. Hence we see many aspects of Toltec–Maya culture—such as the eagle and jaguar warrior ranks—adopted by the Mexica. Like the Maya, the Mexica and other Aztec tribes believed in the necessity of blood-letting to repay the earth for its bounty. Because human sacrifice was central to the Aztec system of belief, numerous ceremonies were built around it. (It has been conjectured that parallels between Maya and Aztec sacrificial practices resulted from a reverse influence, the late Maya having adopted elements of Mexica culture.) With the object of taking high-ranking captives to be ritually sacrificed, the Mexica regularly engaged in "flower wars" with other tribes.

The theatricality of the sacrifice itself was heightened by many performance events building up to it, such as the *mitotes* or combinations of song, dance, pantomime, creation myth, and tribal history. (It should be noted that a similar form of collective ritual performance, called *areito,* was found among the Arahuaks of the Antilles when Christopher Columbus landed there in 1492.)

The earliest form of Náhuatl-language performance seems to have been a religious procession of priests decked out in elaborate finery to represent

*This drawing based upon the reports of an early eyewitness, Fray Diego Durán, depicts Mexica dancers and musicians, including a Jaguar dancer at left and an Eagle dancer at right. From Désiré Charnay,* The Ancient Cities of the New World, *1887.*

*Some sacrificial victims of the Aztecs were allowed to go down fighting, as shown here. The victim, tethered to the sacrificial stone and equipped with a mock weapon (feathers in place of blades), is shown here under attack by a Jaguar warrior while priests look on. From Désiré Charnay,* The Ancient Cities of the New World, *1887.*

*The Codex Magliabecchiano contains a depiction of Mexica gladiatorial combat in which the captive is tied to a stone for his mock battle with the elaborately costumed Jaguar warrior. Reprinted from* Dances of Anáhuac: The Choreography and Music of Precortesian Dances *by Gertrude Prokosch Kurath and Samuel Martí (Viking Fund Publications in Anthropology #38, Aldine Publishing Co., Chicago, 1965) by permission of the Wenner-Gren Foundation for Anthropological Research, Inc., New York, New York.*

various gods. The costume itself was a major element of spectacle and could be read metaphorically by everyone. Each god had his own sacred hymn, the singing of which was punctuated with dance. Diego Durán noted that performers rehearsed their songs and dances for many days before the festival while putting together their ritual dress of feathers, masks, and shawls as well as costumes representing eagles and other birds, jaguars, serpents, soldiers, hunters, and a thousand other disguises. During the festival itself, the action of the priests and the general public gave visual form to the religious doctrine.

Besides the priests and citizens, performers of another kind participated in the ritual spectacles, playing roles they would never repeat. These were the sacrificial victims whose culminating moment in the public eye brought them to a mystical unity with the gods. They too had been rehearsed. During the period leading up to the festival, they were honored with the best of food and clothing; attended by servants as well as a "pleasure girl"; allowed to roam freely during the daytime. They were also shown the sacrificial stone, the stage upon which the final episode would be played—for real. Inga Clendinnen has analyzed the Mexica psychology of "victim management," whereby the admiration of the public, the conditioning through rehearsal, and probably also the administration of drugs, all induced the victim to perform well in his final climb up those steep steps to the sacrificial stone where he would be laid on his back and held down while a priest plunged an obsidian blade into his chest and pulled out his heart. Certain highly ranked captives were permitted a more active role in their final performance; their stage was a "gladitorial" stone on a central platform that was more visible to the public than the sacrificial stone on the flat-topped pyramid. The warrior victim would be tethered by one foot to the center of the flat, circular stone on which he stood. Given a dummy weapon (a club with feathers stuck in it), he would defend himself as long as possible against four Mexica warriors whose clubs were studded with flint or obsidian blades. Motivated by the hope of winning renown and having his name remembered in his home city, the warrior would fight until loss of blood from "the striping" caused him to fall. He would then meet the gods by the same method as the other victims.

The Mexica ritual calendar meant that there was a nearly continuous cycle of ritual events of a quasi-theatrical nature. Each of the eighteen "months" (twenty days) was dedicated to a particular seasonal theme and group of gods; the five remaining days in the 365-day year were considered an unlucky transition period during which no festivities were held. One of the most solemn festivals was that in honor of the rain god Tláloc; it was celebrated annually in the fourth month (late April) at several auxiliary sites in addition to the great temple of Tenochtitlán. A priest representing Tláloc sang in dialogue with a chorus of supplicants asking the god for rain to grow the maize so that man might live. The sacrificial victim at this festival was a girl

*Traditional costume, dance, and ritual of the Aztecs are kept alive by their descendants on the site of the great pyramid of Tenochtitlán adjacent to the Cathedral of Mexico. Photograph by Felicia Londré.*

*Left, this seventeenth-century engraving depicts Aztec "flyers." Accompanied by the musician at the top, four voladores would "fly" around a pole, making sixteen turns around it to reach the ground. Reprinted from* Dances of Anáhuac: The Choreography and Music of Precortesian Dances *by Gertrude Prokosch Kurath and Samuel Martí (Viking Fund Publications in Anthropology #38, Aldine Publishing Co., Chicago, 1965) by permission of the Wenner-Gren Foundation for Anthropological Research, Inc., New York, New York.*

*Right, the Mexica performed amazing acrobatic feats, which, however entertaining, always carried religious significance. Reprinted from* Dances of Anáhuac: The Choreography and Music of Precortesian Dances *by Gertrude Prokosch Kurath and Samuel Martí (Viking Fund Publications in Anthropology #38, Aldine Publishing Co., Chicago, 1965) by permission of the Wenner-Gren Foundation for Anthropological Research, Inc., New York, New York.*

of seven or eight, dressed in blue, with a blue-tufted garland on her head; she was taken by canoe to the middle of the lake, knifed, and allowed to bleed for a short while into the waters that finally swallowed up her corpse. Both Durán and Sahagún described similarly the costumes, ceremonies, and ritual intentions of the festivals for each of the eighteen months of the Aztec year.

Other festivals occurred only rarely. The one honoring Atamalqualiztli, for example, came around only once every eight years. For this celebration, people dressed as birds, butterflies, flies, and beetles to dance in the marketplace throughout the night. With the coming of dawn, the god Quetzalcóatl arrived; his impersonator sang of his gifts to humanity, sunlight, and the fruits of the earth. Everybody danced to the hymn sung as a stirring finale to this festival, its words describing a "football" game that the god played with the sun. On the feast of Tezcatlipoca, which occurred every four years, the impersonator of the god was a slave who had been adorned and honored as the deity for a year and whose sacrifice brought a general remission of sins.

The religious myths of the Náhuatl-speaking peoples served as the basis for other forms of performance too. For example, it was the function of the *tlaquetzque* (narrator or minstrel) to visit various public sites where he would recite ancient narrative poems recounting stories of the gods and heroes. There people would crowd around to listen. The "good narrator," Sahagún was told, has "flowers on his lips, . . . flowers bursting from his mouth." Sahagún was further told of a popular entertainer named Teuquiquixti who carried puppet figures of the gods in a huge sack and gave shows in the marketplace and in the central plaza. He would shake his sack and call to those who were within. The tiny figures would then come out of the sack to dance, sing, or perform at the puppeteer's bidding. The costumes of the women and the warrior puppets were especially fine, the latter having gemstone collars. Finally, the puppeteer would again shake the sack and the puppets would go back into it. Thus, Teuquiquixti was known as "he who could make the gods come out and jump."

One of the most spectacular forms of ritualistic performance was that of the "flyers," later called *voladores*. After days of purification rites, five men would dance on a small platform at the top of a pole sixty to ninety feet high. Then four of the dancers, each attached by a rope to the top of the pole, would fling themselves headfirst into space and whirl around the pole before landing on their feet, all to the musical accompaniment of the fifth dancer at the top. While the entertainment value of such events is readily apparent, it is important to note that every aspect was invested with religious significance, even to the number of rotations around the pole. The marvels performed by sleight-of-hand artists undoubtedly also carried ritual meanings. There is a reference to one who cut off his hands and feet and limbs, then (covered by a red blanket) grew them back again, stood up, and uncovered himself, a whole man again. Another specialized in setting fire to other people's houses; after the realistic blaze attracted a crowd, the magician showed the flames to be a trick. He even performed this stunt at the palace and was rewarded with some shelled maize.

While it is impossible to make any distinction between religious and secular performance among the Mexica, for whom religion permeated every aspect of daily life, some kinds of preconquest performance appear to have featured entertainment values above all else. One example is the enactment of situations from ordinary life using the texts of dramatic poems, some fragments of which have survived in a manuscript of *Cantares Mexicanos*. These Náhuatl poems include passages in dialogue as well as choral sections interspersed with descriptions of pantomimic dance. It is possible that they were performed by ensembles of actors who also sang and danced. One piece seems to have been a humorous one-man show. With rapid changes of mask and costume, and a song to go with each incarnation, the comedian played in succession a human being, a deer, a rabbit, a redthroat thrush, a quetzal (the long iridescent blue-green tailfeathers of this exotic bird were highly prized), a parrot, and finally a buffoon again. Apparently, he was well recompensed by the spectators in the old Tlatelolco market.

Unfortunately, there is no surviving play text as such. However, Durán described what he perceived in terms of Spanish culture as *farsas y entremeses* (farces and interludes). According to Durán, "farces" were performed on a whitewashed platform of about thirty square feet on the plaza before Quetzalcoatl's temple in Cholula. That stage sounds not unlike the one in the Tlatelolco marketplace, as described by Hernán Cortés in his third *Carta de relación*, a long narrative letter from the New World to Emperor Carlos V. (Cortés set up a catapult on the platform during his final assault and destruction of Tenochtitlán in 1521.) It was a squared structure made of lime mortar and quarry stone, about thirty paces in diameter and high enough so that "when they have some festival or games, the performers can be seen there by everyone in the market."

Durán's testimony affords a glimpse of what sounds like a theater of pure entertainment in Aztec culture, although the proximity to the temple was undoubtedly relevant. The players he saw in Cholula provoked gales of laughter by their portrayals of comically afflicted persons seeking cures from the gods. Other actors came on stage costumed as insects, frogs, and lizards, and described their lives. There were skits blending comedy and dance: one with masked dancers playing elderly hunchbacks, another in which a simpleton pretended to hear the opposite of what his master ordered, and other dances in which the men smeared themselves with black or white or green, stuck feathers on their heads and feet, and surrounded some women, who—along with the men—mimed drunkenness. All this was done, Durán wrote, "to give pleasure and amusement to the citizens, delighting them with a thousand kinds of very satisfying playful inventions of dances and farces and interludes and songs."

Another early eyewitness account is provided by Fray Jerónimo de Mendieta:

> Sometimes they play their trumpets and little out-of-tune flutes, others blow on little bonewhistles, others disguise their appearance and voice to play people from different tribes speaking other languages. These are actually clowns who attract attention to themselves, making a thousand faces, and saying a thousand clever comments to elicit laughter from anyone who sees or hears them. Some go about like old women, others like bumpkins.

An especially elaborate and popular dance drama reported by Durán was performed at Huitzilipochtli's temple, where artificial trees covered with roses were placed around the patio. Boys from the temple, costumed as brightly colored butterflies and birds, entered and climbed the trees, sipping dew from the roses as they clambered from branch to branch. Then the priests entered and began shooting at the birds and butterflies with blowguns. The priests, representing gods, were dressed like the idols on the altars. To the delight of the audience, the boys and the priests engaged in witty repartee until a performer representing the goddess Xochiquetzalli took away the blowguns. She then honored the "gods" with roses and incense. All the performers joined in the dance finale.

Náhuatl-language performances continued after the fall of the Aztec empire and the arrival of contingents of Spanish missionaries, but their much-altered form and content places them in the category of colonial drama.

## REPRESENTATIVE NORTH AMERICAN PEOPLES

Farther north, in what is today the United States and Canada, hundreds of native tribes practiced a range of performance activities, few of which were documented or have survived. The following survey will cover only a small, somewhat representative sampling of the dances and other ritual enactments. The Pueblo peoples, who have inhabited the area between the Río Grande and Colorado Rivers in Arizona and New Mexico for two millennia or so, include several linguistic groups, each with its own ritual and dance practices. Notable among them are the Hopi, the Zuñi, and the Tewa. The Spaniards, who arrived in the 1540s, called the southwestern Native Americans by the Spanish name for "villages" (*pueblos*), because of their settled, communal lifestyle. Although they share some beliefs with the Indians of Mexico (creation myths involving twins, reverence for corn, activities based upon the four cardinal directions, among others), the Pueblo have never practiced human sacrifice; indeed, their cosmology stresses respect for all living things as equal components of a harmonious whole. Fundamental to the Pueblo worldview is a sense of duality. Thus, the inhabitants of each Tewa pueblo divide themselves into two classifications, the summer people and the winter people, and each group is responsible for seasonal ceremonies in their portion of the year. Other ceremonies are staged by the various secret societies that exist in each pueblo. Notable among the many such events are the Deer Dance, Buffalo Dance, Corn Dance, and Blue Lake Dance of the Taos; the Basket Dance, Cloud (or Corn Maiden) Dance, and Raingod Dance of the Tewa; the Snake Dance, Corn Dance, and Eagle Dance of the Hopi; the Koko dances and Shalako ceremonies of the Zuñi.

Although the ritual purpose is paramount in the Pueblo dances, most ethnographers do not hesitate to call them ritual dramas or prayer dramas. The entertainment value of their costumes, masks, and clowning often draws outside observers to the villages. The concept of duality is carried out in the juxtaposition of sacred and profane elements, and in the distinction between the secret rites performed indoors and the quasi-theatrical activities on public view in the plaza. Preparations for Pueblo enactments begin inside a *kiva,* an interior chamber that serves as a clubhouse, rehearsal room, and ceremonial center for a society within the pueblo; each pueblo has at least two kivas. For the most sacred of the Pueblo ceremonies, the kachina dances, the men who are scheduled to perform must retreat to the kiva for four days of purification during which they repaint the ceremonial masks that are stored there.

*Left, the Hopi Natacka man, with his long snout made of gourds hinged together and studded with pointed teeth, frightens children who have misbehaved. From Virginia Roediger,* Ceremonial Costumes of the Pueblo Indians: With a New Introduction *(plate 33), used by permission of the University of California Press and Carl S. Johnson. Copyright 1991 Regents of the University of California (Introduction). Copyright 1941, 1969 Virginia More Roediger Johnson.*

*Right, the Hopi Eagle kachina is supposed to be so completely disguised that even members of his family would not recognize him. From Virginia Roediger,* Ceremonial Costumes of the Pueblo Indians: With a New Introduction *(plate 24), used by permission of the University of California Press and Carl S. Johnson. Copyright 1991 Regents of the University of California (Introduction). Copyright 1941, 1969 Virginia More Roediger Johnson.*

The highly stylized, fantastically decorated masks fit over the head like helmets, completely disguising the wearer, who is believed to assume the spirit of the kachina as soon as the mask is put on. It is imperative that the performer not be recognizable, nor may he be touched while he is a kachina. The kachinas (or *koko* among the Zuñi) are powerful spiritual beings or rain gods. Their dances are solemn.

In contrast to the kachinas are the clowns (*koyemci* for the Zuñi) whose free-wheeling antics extend to mocking the kachinas, perhaps by putting buckets over their heads like helmets and wielding brooms as spears. The clowns also single out spectators to mock, perhaps with gossipy comments on the state of the victim's marriage—a striking departure from the normally inhibited social behavior of the Pueblos. Much of the clowns' humor is physical and scatological, serving a function apparently analogous to that of the earthy satyr play following the intensity of Greek tragedy in classical

*Left, the* chiffoneti *are an order of clowns among the Pueblo peoples, characterized by the horizontal stripes of black and white body paint. From Virginia Roediger,* Ceremonial Costumes of the Pueblo Indians: With a New Introduction *(plate 39), used by permission of the University of California Press and Carl S. Johnson. Copyright 1991 Regents of the University of California (Introduction). Copyright 1941, 1969 Virginia More Roediger Johnson.*

*Right, the Zuñi and Hopi clowns known as mudheads cover their bodies with pink clay and wear bag-like masks made of cloth. From Virginia Roediger,* Ceremonial Costumes of the Pueblo Indians: With a New Introduction *(plate 40), used by permission of the University of California Press and Carl S. Johnson. Copyright 1991 Regents of the University of California (Introduction). Copyright 1941, 1969 Virginia More Roediger Johnson.*

Athens. In the Pueblo performances, however, the clowns are ultimately punished for their transgressions by the kachinas.

For outdoor performances, the clowns often make their entrance in a humorous manner by rope from a housetop. For performances inside a kiva, they enter through a hole in the roof. They announce the arrival of the kachinas and keep the spectators entertained when the kachinas go off to rest after several hours of dancing. One order of clowns is the *chiffoneti*, whose entire bodies are painted with horizontal black-and-white stripes. They wear no masks but paint their faces white with black circles around the mouth and eyes. Their hair is made to stand up in two tall "horns" trimmed with cornhusks. Another order of clowns is the mudheads, whose bodies are coated with pinkish clay gathered during a summer solstice pilgrimage to a sacred lake. A matching pink cotton bag is worn over the head; bunches of seeds tied into the cloth form grotesque lumps on the head.

The patterns of performance vary considerably among kiva societies, among villages, and according to the season. Understanding the complex ceremonial life of the Pueblos is also complicated by the secrecy that is vital in Pueblo thinking. Some dance dramas are offered publicly except for the culminating prayer of thanksgiving inside the kiva. In contrast, the mythic drama of the Hopi Powamua or Snake Dance is performed inside the kiva over a sixteen-day period, and only the final episode, the Bean Dance, is seen in public. In general, the various animal dances are the most theatrical of the Pueblo performances. In these, the elaborateness of the animal costume does not completely conceal the identity of the dancer; thus, the performer remains an impersonator rather than an actual avatar of the god. Somewhat less sacred still are the various Corn Dances in which women often participate, the dancers forming long straight lines across the plaza.

Moving northward to the great plains and eastward to the area around the Great Lakes, among the Siouan and Algonquian tribes we again find certain recurring patterns of belief such as the role of twin brothers in the creation myth, social structures reflecting the concept of dualism in nature, the mystical significance of the number four, and an obsession with secrecy. However, it may not be accurate to refer to "pre-Columbian" performance among these peoples, for the plains were settled by nomadic tribes only after horses had been introduced to North America by the Spanish. The sacred Medicine Rite of the Winnebago, for example, is dated by Paul Radin no earlier than the latter part of the seventeenth century, long after the coming of the French to the Great Lakes region. Nevertheless, that "ritual drama," which Radin transcribed in 1908 and published as *The Road of Life and Death,* preserves in dialogue form a wealth of material that must have been based upon an ancient cosmology. It includes reference to the four hero spirits of the Winnebagos: Hare, Coyote (or Trickster), Turtle, and Bladder. Although much of the Winnebago Medicine Rite's symbolism is lost to the modern reader, it exhibits certain features in common with the *Rabinal Achí* of the Quiché Maya: repetitions, respectful formulae of address, incorporation of song and dance, the enactment of death (followed in the Winnebago rite by rebirth), and a sense of closeness to the land.

Among the characteristics shared by numerous native tribes of the northern plains and forests were the existence of many different warrior societies, each with its own ritual costume elements, songs, and dances. All ritual performance, including the War Dance and even the late-nineteenth-century Ghost Dance, somehow reified the people's relationship with the unseen spirits and forces of nature. Particular mention must be made of the most important ceremony of the Lakota (Sioux), the Sun Dance. In actuality, dance comprised only a small portion of this complex eight-day sequence of rituals. Performed in early summer, the Sun Dance brought together the tribal bands that had scattered for the winter. Only those selected as dancers did not join in the spirit of merrymaking, but prepared themselves, guided by the shaman, to endure a painful rite as a form of sacrifice to the sun. The first four days of the ritual were devoted to purification. The remaining four days brought

*The Ghost Dance brought different tribes together, as shown in this 1891 colored-ink drawing on buckskin. The Arapaho women (with their hair loose) and Cheyenne women (with braids) participate in the dance that they hoped would restore a fast-disappearing way of life. From James Mooney,* The Ghost Dance Religion and the Sioux Outbreak of 1890: Fourteenth Annual Report of the Bureau of Ethnology to the Secretary of the Smithsonian Institution, 1892–93, *Part 2, 1896.*

a variety of ceremonies, some involving "dramatic" enactments of battle, and culminating, on the eighth day, in the sun-dancers' ordeal by torture during which they were bound by leather thongs drawn through the flesh. Gazing continuously at the sun during the four movements of the dance, they pulled against their bonds. During the fourth movement, the dancers would actually tear themselves free, if possible, at the cost of considerable pain and bloodshed. Those who did not succeed in releasing themselves through torn flesh would be cut free after dawn on the day following. The suffering of the Sun Dance warriors was expected not only to bring blessings upon the tribe but also to induce in the dancer a vision that would put him in close touch with the spirit world. Warriors of the Plains tribes could gain further honor by counting coup against their enemies, and it was expected that the warrior would describe his deeds in tribal ceremonies, thus providing both entertainment and inspiration to others.

The Iroquois performed dances with a strong pantomimic component. Fortunately, the Jesuit missionaries who witnessed them took the trouble to document the practices they sought to suppress. In addition to ritual dances performed on religious festival days, there were social dances (usually a circle of dancers around the musicians) and dances of imitation or parody in which an event (hunting, war, domestic life) was pantomimically enacted. In addition, each man had his individual song or autobiographical chant which might include pantomime. Joseph Lafitau, who lived among the Iroquois at Kahnawake in the early eighteenth century, noted both the spiritual and the entertainment values in their dances. The Kahnawake Mohawks drew upon those traditions and kept them alive in public performances throughout the nineteenth and early twentieth centuries.

Of all the native peoples of North America, the most distinctive, according to anthropologists, were those of the Pacific Northwest coast. Seven major linguistic groups occupied the area along the coast from what is today Alaska to northern California; these were, from north to south: Tlingit, Tsimshian, Haida, Kwakiutl, Bella Coola, Nootka, and Coast Salish–Chinook. Their distinctive characteristics—strong consciousness of rank and lineage, clan legends based upon an ancestor's encounter with a spirit, artistry with wood (manifested especially in carved masks and totem poles), and potlatches—were perhaps derived from the area's natural abundance of food. Because it was possible in only a few days to catch and smoke enough salmon to feed a family for months, these tribes had the leisure to devote to the arts. Their ritual dances incorporate such elaborately rigged effects and illusions to awe the uninitiated that anthropologists do not hesitate to call them "theater."

A particular clan's ancestor legend, songs, dances, names, and masks were revered as gifts from the supernatural being and were passed down through the family as its prize possessions. An individual took special pride in his song to his own guardian spirit who was represented by a symbolic mask; the individual also owned certain activities in the esoteric rituals of the secret society into which he was initiated. The performance of certain dances dramatizing the ancestral experience comprised the process of initiation into one of the tribe's dancing societies. Within a dancing society, each family's hereditary dance was ranked in relation to the others. While the Kwakiutl dancing societies were the most numerous and complex, all northwestern tribes practiced variations on the winter ceremonial which was the major occasion for religious and artistic expression by the societies.

Preparations for performing in a winter ceremonial—like the Hamatsa rituals of the Kwakiutl—involved fasting and purification. During a dancer's four-day sequence, he would remain hidden during the day and reappear only at night to dance. In some cases, commemorating an ancestor's having been kidnapped by a spirit, the dancer might disappear entirely for four days and then reappear as the supernatural spirit, wearing the mask and skin of the bear or whatever other animal embodied the spirit. Possession by a monstrous spirit involved a frenzied dance that might be aggressively violent or self-mutilating. The fourth night of dancing often featured elaborate sleight-of-hand tricks that could be powerfully effective in the dimly lit lodge. Curtains and dangling masks could be raised and lowered. The Raven dancer could open and close the long beak on his mask by pulling strings hidden under his costume. (The Raven was the Trickster figure for these tribes.) When the Fool dancer drew his knife across his neck, blood flowed from a bladder hidden beneath the feather ruff. Or he could slice his stomach and release the dog entrails hidden in his costume.

A beheading could be simulated using a wooden head carved to resemble the dancer's face, along with some codfish bladders filled with animal blood that would spatter when the bladders were punctured. A dancer could disappear into a ditch that had been secretly dug on the far side of the fire. Ghostly voices that seemed to come from the ditch were actually supplied by initiates hidden in adjoining rooms and speaking through hollow tubes that opened into the ditch. The series of dances would culminate in a potlatch; that is, feasting and gift-giving by which the gift-giver confirmed his preeminent status. The winter ceremonial was often followed by the burning of the spirit masks.

The Trickster—known as Coyote to the Plains Indians and Raven to those of the Pacific Northwest—appears also among other peoples. Among the Cree of the Canadian northwoods, the Trickster is called Weesageechjak. To the Ojibway "he" is Nanabush. Of indeterminate gender, the clownish Trickster embodies both human and divine characteristics. As a bungling "superhero," the Trickster is a favorite figure in Native American mythology and frequently turns up in storytelling and other performance activities.

The rituals of the Alaskan Inuit (formerly called by the pejorative "Eskimo") resembled those of the Northwest Pacific coast in their theatrical contrivances and in their highly stylized wooden masks representing spirits. In place of the latter's propensity for the monstrous and the violent, however, the Inuit love jokes and humor. The missionaries' 1908 banning of their ceremonials as a pagan religious activity also meant suppression of seasonal occasions for communal fun. Recordings of Inuit *katajjait* or "throat games" (nonmusical vocal repetitions, some inspired by animal sounds, performed by players whose faces are virtually nose to nose) often capture the sound of those unusual vocalizations dissolving into laughter.

While most Inuit dances were religious in nature, they were also performed for enjoyment and at some point everyone participated. Accompanied by drums, clappers, and rattles, Inuit dancers used pantomimic movement to tell stories. Male dancers were naked except for their masks and glove-like hand coverings. The athleticism of their dances was enhanced by the undulating feathers on some of the masks. Some masks had movable eyes and jaws. A single male dancer might portray both the hunter and the animal, including animal vocalizations. The women, whether dancing in pairs alongside the man or as a group in unison, usually swayed in place, conveying narrative elements with hand gestures.

The Inuit shaman functioned as master of ceremonies at the festivals; he also went into trances to visit the spirit world and—with the help of unseen assistants—performed amazing tricks, including feats of survival after being speared or thrown into the fire. Among the Inuit, stage effects that have been described by eyewitnesses include mechanical figurines representing animals and humans. Animated by hidden cords, a wooden owl could flap its wings or a tiny oarsman in a kayak could paddle vigorously. Whalebone springs could make the stuffed skins of a fox and a raven jump at each other. A puppet could be made to move jerkily on strings across the ceiling to grasp the bladder that hung at center.

Chief among the various hunting festivals held in the Inuit ceremonial houses each winter was the Bladder Festival. The bladders of the animals killed for food—seal, caribou, sea lion, walrus—were saved all year to be inflated, decorated, and hung in the ceremonial house for the festival. The Bladder Festival honored the animal's spirit (which resided in the bladder) and insured successful hunting in the coming year. Indeed, the bladders were returned to the water after the four-day festival, at which time the dancers' masks were destroyed.

Another type of performance event was reported by a Russian visitor among the Aleuts early in the nineteenth century. The Aleuts had a "play" called *Kugan Agalik* (The appearance of the devils), which was intended to keep the women submissive. The conditions of performance were kept secret among the men, with a death sentence for anyone who violated the trust. At a time when some of the village men were off "hunting" for several days, the men at home would express a sense of nervous foreboding. Sure enough, nightfall would bring terrible noises outside the lodge. Finally, a tall devil in grass raiment would drop through the ceiling hole. The men would rally to fight and drive away the devil. After the scuffle, one of the men would be missing, so a woman would be carried out of the lodge as an offering. The man's corpse would be brought back along with the frightened woman. Beating the "dead man" with inflated bladders resurrected him. A few days later, the returning hunters would complete their performance responsibilities by listening to the story in pretended amazement.

Coverage of the numerous and complex pre-Columbian ritual and performance activities of the five hundred or so native nations of North America is not possible in a work of this scope. Those few mentioned here can serve only as indications of rich and relatively neglected cultures. Recent years have seen a strong movement to preserve our continent's aboriginal cultural heritage. The remarkable survival of so many native mythic elements despite centuries of forced conversions is in some sense a tribute to the lasting impact of performance traditions, for it is in dance and storytelling that those elements have been kept alive.

# 2 *Theater in New Spain, the American Colonies, and New France*

## NEW SPAIN

The colonial periods in the lands that were later to become Mexico, the United States, and Canada all began in the sixteenth century and lasted through most of the eighteenth century or longer. The theater, however, developed quite differently in each colonized country. Of the three, it was New Spain that boasted the earliest, most abundant, and most varied theatrical undertakings. There, too, we find the most systematic involvement of the indigenous peoples in the creation as well as in the enjoyment of theater.

Once the *conquistadores* had done their work, the missionaries set about educating and converting the aboriginals, quickly realizing that the Indians' love of song and dance could be channeled to religious ends. The Franciscan Pedro de Gante (one of the first three missionaries arriving in 1523) was particularly successful at fusing Catholic doctrine with native verse forms and imagery. Those whom he instructed at the church and school of San José de los Naturales in the capital then assisted in the creation of religious compositions that mingled musical segments and dialogue, Spanish and the indigenous language. Undoubtedly, the performers also incorporated their own meanings through gesture and inflection.

Cortés himself staged a public ceremony with theatrical flair designed to impress the people he had subjugated. A contingent of twelve Franciscans (their number intended to evoke the twelve apostles of Christ, their religious order chosen for its acceptance of poverty) had landed in May 1524 at the site of today's Veracruz. Barefoot, they walked the five hundred or so kilometers to the capital, where Cortés awaited them. Virtually the entire population was gathered to watch Cortés ride out, splendid in his military regalia, to meet the Franciscans, dismount, and fall to his knees before them. He kissed their hands and feet and the hems of their rough robes, then ordered the astonished Mexica chiefs to do the same.

New Spain's receptiveness to performance activities is evident in the fact that in less than five years after Cortés's destruction of Tenochtitlán (August 13, 1521), Corpus Christi processions had begun to be organized in the new

*This sixteenth-century Holy Week procession typifies the earliest form of religious spectacle organized by the Franciscan friars in New Spain. From Luis González Obregón,* México viejo: epoca colonial, *1900.*

*The Corpus Christi procession with its masked figures and tableau scenes on carros prefigured the performance of short plays on stationary platforms in New Spain's early colonial period. From Luis González Obregón,* México viejo: epoca colonial, *1900.*

capital city of México that arose on the site. Those annual religious festivities, like the ones in the mother country, featured decorative *carros* with *tableaux vivants* drawn through the streets in procession. Soon there were added stationary platforms called *tablados,* erected in the plazas or in front of the churches, for performances of playlets. These short plays on religious subjects, or *autos,* were medieval in form and content because Spain was still a medieval country, its renaissance lagging a century behind the rest of Europe due to Spain's intense involvement in driving out the Moors who had occupied it since 711. Completing the unification of Spain in 1492, the Catholic monarchs Ferdinand and Isabella turned to the propagation of the faith. The *autos* and the *autos sacramentales* (thematically specific to Corpus Christi) were tools of the Church, reinforcing dogma in Holy Spain and serving its evangelical ends in the New World.

The leap from the earliest known Corpus Christi procession (1526) to performances of *autos* must have been short. However, the evidence for pinpointing the earliest *auto* in the New World remains ambiguous. A Náhuatl-language piece, *The Conversion of St. Paul,* complete with devils represented as Aztec priests, was apparently performed by natives in 1530 in the atrium of the church of San José de los Naturales. More significant was an *auto* of *The Last Judgment* presented in Tlatelolco in 1531 or 1533 under the guidance of the much-loved Franciscan friar Andrés de Olmos (1500–1571), who arrived in New Spain in 1528 and became fluent in at least four native languages. There were undoubtedly a number of *autos* on the theme of the Last Judgment, some adapted from Spanish originals, others written to fit immediate educational needs. The latter seems to be the case in the surviving Náhuatl-language text, *Nexcuitilmachiotl motenhua juicio final* (*nexcuitili* was the Náhuatl term for *ejemplo,* a form of *auto* that taught a moral lesson), which warns of the torments of hell awaiting those who practice polygamy or concubinage (as the Mexica nobility did). This particular version of *The Last Judgment,* attributed to Olmos, combines allegorical figures (Penitence, Death, Time, Confession) with supernatural characters (St. Michael, Christ, Lucifer, Satan, Antichrist) and a host of angels and devils, plus two mortals: the sinner Lucia and the kindly priest. Lucia, the only female character (no doubt played by a male native), is scourged to damnation wearing a snake of flames about her neck, while the righteous carry garlands of flowers as they follow Christ up the stairway to heaven. Enhanced by fireworks, trumpets, and singing, the Tlatelolco presentation was mentioned by Sahagún as "something worthy to see." Either this production was revived or another was created in 1535 in the chapel of San José de los Naturales, where Bartolomé de la Casas saw it and was inspired to encourage the use of evangelical song and drama among the Dominican missionaries who followed the Franciscans into New Spain.

The next milestone in the theater of New Spain occurred in Tlaxcala, a city (about seventy-five miles east of the capital) that had allied itself with Cortés against the Mexica overlords of Tenochtitlán. In 1538, these early converts presented a series of performances for which we have eyewitness

*The site in Tlaxcala where Corpus Christi processions and* autos *were presented as early as 1538 can still be seen in front of the church where Motolinía preached. Photograph by Felicia Londré.*

*The earliest surviving* capilla abierta *(open chapel) in Mexico is in Tlaxcala, just below the entrance to the* atrio *where the earliest performances were held. The potential theatrical use of the open chapel is evident in the architecture. Photograph by Felicia Londré.*

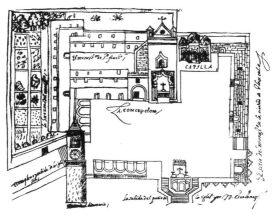

*This drawing from about 1580 shows the layout of Tlaxcala's Franciscan church and monastery with walls surrounding an* atrio *where early performances of evangelical drama were given. Tlaxcala's famous* capilla abierta *is in the lower center surrounded by flights of steps. From Diego Muñoz Camargo,* Descripcion de la ciudad y provincia de Tlaxcala.

accounts by Friar Toribio Paredes de Benavente, a.k.a. Motolinía (d. 1568), one of the twelve Franciscan missionaries who arrived in 1524. Indeed, Motolinía may well have been involved in the productions, which began with a Corpus Christi procession—and first display of the city's coat of arms granted by Carlos V—on June 20, 1538. Motolinía reports that the procession was enlivened with a great variety of dancers, singers, instrumentalists, images of saints made of gold and feathers, over a thousand arches decked with multicolored flowers, and four tableaux scenes of natural elements. Four days later, on the feast of St. John the Baptist (June 24), the Tlaxcalans presented four *autos,* which had apparently been written (or translated into Náhuatl from Spanish sources) and memorized during the three intervening days. The first was the *Annunciation of the Nativity of St. John the Baptist* to his father Zacharias. The hour-long "devoutly presented" piece culminated in a lovely motet sung in parts. *The Annunciation of Our Lady* was then performed on another stage, followed by *The Visitation of Our Lady to Saint Elizabeth* on yet another stage in the church courtyard. After mass came the performance of *The Nativity of St. John,* incorporating a crowd-pleasing comic sequence in which the mute Zacharias gestures that he wants writing materials, while his servants pretend not to understand and bring him all sorts of other things. Mass baptisms of the natives followed.

Later that year, for the Feast of the Assumption in August, the Indians of Tlaxcala enacted the ascent of the Blessed Virgin (*La asunción de Nuestra Señora*). On a visit to the Franciscan mission in Tlaxcala, Bartolomé de las Casas witnessed that event in the church's *atrio* (patio or courtyard), where the native playing the title role was rigged to rise, to the accompaniment of singers and flute-players, "from a platform to another level that had been made for the heavens." Las Casas emphasized that no Spaniard had been involved in putting on the performance. The *atrio* in which that piece was staged evolved perhaps from similar spaces, designed to accommodate thousands of spectators, in front of pre-Hispanic pagan temples. The large, enclosed space in front of the church became a standard architectural feature in New Spain, where churches could not be built large enough to hold the multitudes of converts, and it was also a logical space in which to set up a *tablado* for theatrical performance. Another New World innovation in church architecture was the *capilla abierta* (open chapel). José Juan Arrom conjectures that performance needs actually influenced the design of these chapels under the arcade that opened onto the *atrio*. Because these chapels were not fully enclosed, they could not be consecrated and thus were not off limits for theatrical activity. Some were even elevated above the level of the *atrio*. With the flanking walls of the *atrio*, the hard floor, and the roof over the small nave, the *capillas abiertas* offered excellent acoustics, so that the priests' (or performers') voices were projected clearly and without echo to those assembled in the *atrio*. The earliest known *capilla abierta* was built in Tlaxcala in 1539, and the spread of this architecture coincided with the period of greatest concentration of evangelical drama in New Spain, from the 1530s to 1570s.

Tlaxcala continued its extraordinary theatrical activity with a spectacular Náhuatl-language production of *The Fall of Adam and Eve* during the week after Easter in 1539. Motolinía recorded many details of the realistic scenic environment created near the Tlaxcala hospital, claiming that "for all who saw it, it was one of the most noteworthy things ever done in New Spain." The setting for the Garden of Eden was created of natural trees and an abundance of flowers, with a great variety of live and artificial birds in the trees. Motolinía counted fourteen live parrots in one tree, and wrote that the gold-feathered artificial birds were "a wonder to behold." There were in addition many small wild and domestic animals as well as two fierce jaguars on tethers. At one point Eve inadvertently brushed up against a jaguar, but "luckily this was before she had sinned, so she escaped unhurt." The setting also included a mountain, four rivers, and a tableau scene of a lion devouring a deer. Before Eve would eat the forbidden fruit and Adam consented to it, she went back and forth between Adam and the serpent three or four times, a sequence that may have been improvised, as there is no equivalent in any Spanish *auto*. Adam resisted, but she cajoled him. When God called Adam to account, he blamed his sin on Eve, and she in turn blamed the serpent. After God pronounced their penance, angels came and dressed them in animal skins. Three angels carried Adam and three carried Eve, placing them in a very different setting, one with brambles, thorns, and snakes (but including rabbits, just as in Eden), while a cherubim guarded the entrance to the garden paradise with sword in hand. This expulsion was very well acted and very moving, so that none who watched it could hold back tears. Although Motolinía does not say so, he must have sensed an element of recognition among spectators who had so recently lost their own traditional way of life and symbiotic relationship with nature. The performance ended with the singing of a *villancico* (carol), the text of which Motolinía recorded: *Para qué comió / la primer casada, / para qué comió / la fruta vedada? / La primer casada, / ella y su marido, / a Diós han traído / en pobre posada / por haber comido / la fruta vedada?* (Why did the first wife eat the forbidden fruit? Why did the first wife and her husband betray God in their humble home by eating the forbidden fruit?)

To celebrate the signing of a French–Spanish treaty of alliance against the Turks, a magnificent drama, *The Conquest of Rhodes* (*La conquista de Rodas, o La conquista de México*), was staged in the central plaza of México in March or April of 1539. With substantial underwriting by the *cabildo* (city council), towers and ramparts were erected to represent the city of Rhodes. Bartolomé de las Casas estimated that over a thousand Indians took part as performers or musicians, and he noted the use of simultaneous settings. A highlight of the production was the appearance of four realistic-looking ships that "sailed" around the plaza carrying natives dressed as friars.

Determined to outdo the Mexicans, the Tlaxcallans staged a similar spectacle, *The Conquest of Jerusalem,* as well as a procession and three *autos,* for Corpus Christi (June 5, 1539). The main event, *La conquista de Jerusalén,* attributed to Motolinía, was a mixture of military reenactment, religious invocation, myth, allegory, political commentary, and spectacle. It evoked *Los moros y los cristianos,* the ceremonial enactment of a battle between Moors and Christians, which was popular on the Spanish stage and which, transferred to New Spain, would live on as folk drama. Performed by a huge, elaborately costumed cast of natives, *The Conquest of Jerusalem* featured simultaneous action in and around five towers and walls representing the contested city. The action conflated battles between eleventh-century crusaders and Turks with battles for the conquest of New Spain. Somewhat confusingly, Motolinía recorded that Hernán Cortés played the infidel sultan (who is conquered and converted at the end of the play). While it is true that Cortés was in New Spain at the time of the production, most scholars believe that it was an Indian playing Cortés playing the sultan, a double-layered performance. Several battles over the city were staged, one of which involved setting fire to it. To add to the realism of the battles, red ochre was used as stage blood. According to Motolinía, "grenades of sun-dried mud filled with damp red ochre were thrown and whoever was hit by them appeared to be badly wounded and bleeding." The presence of the Holy Eucharist at the end defines this play as an *auto sacramental*. The finale also incorporated an actual mass baptism which segued into the Corpus Christi procession. Fourteen hundred arches of roses and other flowers decorated the route in adddition to ten large triumphal arches. Three natural-looking mountains were constructed along the route to serve as settings for the three *autos*. The first, *The Temptation of Our Lord,* featured a band of lively devils. *St. Francis Preaching to the Birds* combined a horrifying hell scene and a homily against drunkenness. *Abraham's Sacrifice of Isaac* may have been chosen to excoriate the Aztec practice of human sacrifice.

Sixteenth-century evangelical theater in the New World seems to have peaked with *The Conquest of Jerusalem*. The Franciscan practice of capping off such performances with the simultaneous baptism of thousands of Indians by aspersion came under fire from the Pope. By 1544 Juan de Zumárraga, first archbishop of Mexico, fearing that dance and drama performed by natives served to perpetuate their old pagan beliefs and practices, published a tract condemning any theatrical performance done in conjunction with religious observances: "It is disrespectful and shameful that in the presence of the Holy Sacrament men go about wearing masks and women's clothing, dancing and cavorting with immodest and lascivious gestures, making noise and drowning out the church hymns. . . ." After Zumárraga's death in 1548, the restrictions were reinforced by his successor, Alonso de Montúfar, a Dominican who was not disposed to acknowledge Franciscan successes. Still, evangelical drama could not be completely suppressed, as numerous records of performances attest.

While the second half of the sixteenth century saw nothing so elaborate as the earlier dramatic spectacles in Tlaxcala and México, there was a proliferation of activity in smaller and more distant towns. Two manuscripts have survived of a Náhuatl-language drama *Tlacahuapahualiztli* (On the education of youth), which was probably written and performed around 1555. For the Corpus Christi festivities in Etla, Oaxaca, in 1575, Friar Alonso de Anunciación wrote an *auto,* but its performance turned to tragedy when a poorly constructed viewing gallery collapsed, killing 120 people, including the friar. Particularly popular with the natives (perhaps because of certain parallels with Mexica myth) was the Bible story of the three kings following a star to give gifts at the Nativity. When Friar Alonso Ponce visited Tlaxomulco in 1587, he was told that performances of the *auto* of the *Adoration of the Three Kings* had been an annual tradition on the Feast of the Epiphany there for over thirty years. Another version, *Play of Kings (La comedia de los reyes),* has been attributed to the native translator Agustín de la Fuente (d. 1596). Agustín de la Fuente served at least ten years as secretary to the Franciscan friar Juan Bautista at the College of Tlatelolco and may well have contributed to the three books of religious *comedias* published under the latter's name in 1599. Closely related to Epiphany plays were *autos* of the Nativity, including *pastores* (shepherds' plays) or *pastorelas*. These dramatizations of the birth of Christ and of the shepherds who visit the stable exist in numerous variations (and many others must have gone unrecorded); often, comic stock characters, Bato and Gila, appear along with the Biblical characters. With simpler staging than that demanded by the episodic *autos sacramentales* of Corpus Christi, the pastorelas became traditional fare in hundreds of villages and, transmitted orally across the generations, survived into the twentieth century as folk drama throughout Mexico and in Spanish-speaking areas as far north as Colorado.

Religious drama was boosted anew in the city of México in 1565 when the ecclesiastical council voted to award a prize of "gold or silver, of value up to thirty crowns, for the best play composed or arranged for performance on Corpus Christi." The city council followed suit with similar prizes, such as fifty gold pesos to Diego Juarez for *The Fall of Man (La cayda del hombre)* in 1575.

Records of the *cabildo* show regular allotments of money for Corpus Christi presentations, going as high as thirteen hundred gold pesos in 1593. Although a court ruling in Mexico in 1574 called for censorship of *autos, comedias,* and other dramatic works, and the Third Church Council (1585) seemed to reinforce earlier restrictions, in actuality enforcement was lax enough that performances of religious plays continued unabated. Indeed, it was during these decades that Francisco de Gamboa instituted at San José de los Naturales the Spanish custom of having a religious auxiliary sponsor theatrical performances as a charitable endeavor. Encouraged by the Cofradía de la Soledad, the natives would make the stations of the cross on Fridays and then enact, perhaps pantomimically, an episode from Christ's passion. On Sunday mornings they would listen to Father Gamboa's sermon and that afternoon present an *ejemplo* on the subject. These performances regularly filled the *atrio* to capacity, and their popularity was such that Juan de Torquemada, in his chronicle of the period, shamelessly credited them to his own initiative.

During the final decades of the sixteenth century, other forms of theater began overtaking the evangelical drama. On December 5, 1574, for example, a Spanish-language play was presented as part of the festivities honoring Pedro Moya de Contreras upon his consecration as archbishop. Although religious in content, *Spiritual Contract between the Shepherd Peter and the Mexican Church (Desposorio espiritual entre el pastor Pedro y la Iglesia Mexicana)* echoed the Italian pastoral in form. The action centers upon the marriage of shepherd Peter (representing the archbishop) with shepherdess Iglesia Mexicana (the Catholic Church of Mexico) amidst a group of well-wishers: shepherdesses Faith, Hope, Charity, and Grace, and shepherds Prudence, Justice, Steadfastness, and Modesty. Divine Love officiates as priest, and there is even a *bobo* (traditional Spanish rustic buffoon) for comic relief. The author, Juan Pérez Ramírez (b. 1545?), was a *criollo* (born in the New World) and a *mestizo* (son of an Indian woman and a Spanish conquistador), fluent in Náhuatl and Latin as well as an excellent poet in Spanish; he is generally recognized as the first Mexican dramatist. On December 8 the continuing festivities included a *coloquio* (humanist dialogue) by Fernán González de Eslava; it was performed with three *entremeses* (interludes) by other authors. The third *entremés* was a hilarious piece about tax collectors, and this offended the civil authorities, who had recently instituted a new tax. Although the play was actually an old work imported from Spain (and, as a nonreligious play, was not particularly subject to censorship), its performance probably carried an element of malice on the part of the archbishop, whose relationship with the viceroy had long been openly hostile. On August 9 the viceroy called a halt to all planned performances of plays during the archbishop's festivities. On August 18, several of those who had been involved in presenting the *entremés* were arrested and imprisoned (though the viceroy was unable to pin anything on the archbishop). The trial brought no convictions, but the archbishop received a letter of reprimand from Philip II, king of Spain, with instructions to exercise greater control in future. The 1574 festivities were noteworthy also in Mexican theater history in that the role of the *gracioso* (clown) in the *entremés* was played by the earliest known professional actor in New Spain, a mulatto whose name has not come down to us.

Another major festival that featured theatrical performances took place in México in November 1578, to celebrate the arrival in New Spain of some holy relics sent by Pope Gregory XIII to the Jesuits, whose first missionaries had arrived in 1572. In the New World as in Europe, the Jesuits presented school dramas, which were aimed at smaller and better-educated audiences than the evangelical dramas of the Franciscans and Dominicans. (Adam Versényi offers several reasons for the decline of influence of those mendicant orders, including their loss of power base as the native population was first decimated by disease and then integrated, at least linguistically, into a larger social structure.) The Jesuits experimented with tragicomedy even as comic and tragic forms were still being defined by European humanists. A number of plays and *coloquios* were presented during the eight days of festivities in 1578, but the most important was a five-act tragedy, *El triunfo de los santos*, in Spanish, using what was then an avant-garde poetic form, and probably written by several Jesuits in collaboration. Performed by students as a demonstration of intellectual and histrionic capabilities, *The Triumph of the Saints* dealt with religious persecutions suffered under Diocletian as opposed to the church's prosperity under Emperor Constantine. It mingled allegorical and historical characters, including several saints, all richly costumed. According to one eyewitness, it "affected audiences as never before in this city . . . and instigated many conversions, with much credit to the Jesuits." By popular demand, the performance was repeated the next day.

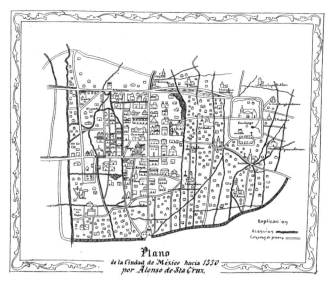

*This 1550 map of the city of México, less than three decades after the conquest of Tenochtitlán over which the new capital was built, shows numerous churches and canals. From Luis González Obregón,* México viejo: epoca colonial, *1900.*

COLOQVIOS
ESPIRITVALES Y SACRAMENTALES
y Canciones Diuinas, compueſtas por el Di
uino poeta Fernan Gonçalez de Eſla
ua Clerigo Presbitero.

Recopiladas por el R.P. Fr. Fernando Vello de
Buſtamante; de la Orden de S. Auſtin.

¶ Dirigido al muy Reuerendo padre Maeſtro
Fr. Iuan de Guzman, Prouincial digniſsimo
de la Prouincia del Santiſsimo nombre
de Ieſus de la Orden de San
Aguſtin.

Año de                                  1610.

EN MEXICO.
¶ En la Emprenta de Diego Lopez Daualos y a ſucoſta

*Left, Fernán Gonzálex de Eslava (1534–1601?) might be considered the first impor-
tant dramatist of North America. The title page of his* Coloquios *indicates that they
were collected and published in 1610 by Fray Bustamente.*

*Right, sor Juana Inés de la Cruz (1648?–95) became a nun in hopes of devoting her
life to scholarship and literature. Her poetry and plays are among the finest works in
the Spanish language.*

Besides the *entremés,* several other dramatic forms were introduced in
the latter part of the sixteenth century with entertainment as their primary
purpose. The *paso* was a short piece, a form invented by the early Spanish
actor–manager Lope de Rueda. The *loa,* a monologue in praise of some person or event, often served as a curtain-raiser. *Comedias* were three-act plays
of any genre, most often mingling serious and comic elements, best exemplified by those of the prolific Spanish dramatist Lope de Vega. This was the
genre of choice at the palace of the viceroy, where the Spanish nobility pat-
terned their amusements after those at the court of the king of Spain, celebrating special dates (such as birthdays of the king or viceroy, or births of
their children) with private performances of *comedias.* And the local governors of small towns followed suit. For example, in the town of Puebla in
November 1673, to honor a visiting dignitary, the governor had *comedias*
presented in his home on two consecutive evenings. The *coloquio,* like the
*auto,* might use allegorical, historical, or everyday characters, but the characters narrated their story in the *coloquio,* as opposed to acting it out as they
did in the *auto.* The *coloquio,* according to George C. Barker,

had the advantage of enabling the liturgical authors to insert much moral and doctrinal material in the lengthy dialogues of the chief characters. Such recitatives, therefore, were limited by the ability of the Indian and mestizo actors to memorize their lines. But the clerical playwrights met this obstacle by writing in well-rhymed verses which were easily learned.

The leading author of *coloquios*—and now recognized as the first major dramatist in North America—was Fernán González de Eslava (1534–1601?). Arriving in New Spain at twenty-four, he was ordained a priest in the New World, where he remained the rest of his life. In the aftermath of the 1574 performance of the *entremés* about tax collectors, González de Eslava spent seventeen days in prison. His *coloquio* that had framed the notorious interlude was his third and his longest, *A la consagración del Doctor Don Pedro Moya de Contreras, primer inquisidor desta Nueva España y arzobispo desta Santa Iglesia Mexicana;* its audience appeal is indicated by the fact that it was repeated the following day and, before the viceroy intervened, was scheduled for other performances. Although González de Eslava's contemporaries labeled his poetry "divine," his work might not have survived if a friend had not published it posthumously. *Coloquios espirituales y sacramentales y Canciones Divinas* (1610) contains 16 *coloquios*, 4 *entremeses*, 8 *loas*, and 157 poems, all written between 1567 and 1600. Father Bustamente, who collected and published the work, wrote that he intended to publish also a volume of González de Eslava's secular writing, but none is extant. According to records of the city council of México, for example, a *comedia* by González de Eslava was performed with enormous success in 1588, but no copy has been found. González de Eslava's dramatic writing is characterized by an abundance of local color, a humanist sensibility, fluid verse, and lively, realistic characters. José Juan Arrom sees also traces of indigenous influence in the treatment of natural elements in *coloquios* such as the sixteenth, *In the Garden of Paradise with God's Birds and Animals* (*Del bosque divino donde Dios tiene sus aves y animales*).

With increasing numbers of *criollo* (American-born, but of European descent) and Spanish inhabitants of New Spain (only 3,000 in 1574; more than 1,040,000 in 1810), there was a solid audience base for public performances of secular plays. A steady supply of *comedia* texts arrived from Spain where the seventeenth century saw a Golden Age of the arts with dramatic poetry as its crowning glory. At the same time, the New World did produce some writers who tried their hand at dramatic forms. Although Juan Ruíz de Alarcón (1580?–1639) has generally been classed as a Spanish Golden Age dramatist, he was actually a *criollo*, who wrote several plays before settling permanently in Madrid in 1613. His twenty-four plays, the best known of which is *The Truth Suspected* (*La verdad sospecha*), exhibit certain characteristics that might be identified as distinctively Mexican: elaborate courtesy typical of New World manners as influenced by the natives, sharp views expressed with brevity, more logical and reflective action than in Spanish *comedias*. Similarly, Agustín de Salazar y Torres (1642–75) spent his youth in New Spain, but returned to the mother country to write the plays which perhaps bear some traces of his Mexican education. Matias de Bocanegra (1612–68) won a following with his poetry, but his plays are unfortunately lost, except for one, *Comedia de San Francisco de Borja* (1640). Francisco de Acevedo wrote a play about the life of St. Francis of Assisi that premiered at the Coliseo de México in 1684, but the Inquisition ordered it withdrawn— specifying further that the author was not to keep a copy—because the treatment of the saint was too secular. The same play would not have faced any difficulty in Spain.

One dramatist stands apart from all others for the lasting value of her work. Sor Juana Inés de la Cruz (née Juana Inés Ramírez y Asbaje, 1648?–95) has been called one of the most extraordinary minds of all time and "the Mexican muse." At three she was precociously learning to read, and at eight she wrote her first *loas*. Failing to win her mother's permission to dress as a man in order to attend the university in México, she studied on her own. At sixteen she became a lady-in-waiting at the viceroy's palace. There the viceroy tested her extraordinary learning by inviting forty professors from the university to question her on all subjects. In the viceroy's opinion, she defended herself "as a royal galleon would against a few canoes." In 1667 she took her religious vows. In the convent, she served as archivist and continued her studies, motivated solely by intellectual curiosity. In 1691, in response to a letter from the bishop of Puebla, Sor Juana wrote her one important prose work, *Respuesta a Sor Filotea*, which is both an autobiography and a defense of women's right to learn. Most of her writing, however, was lyrical or dramatic verse, and she has been judged one of the greatest poets of all time in the Spanish language. Her secular plays (two *comedias*, two *sainetes*, fourteen *loas*) are very much in the Spanish tradition of Calderón de la Barca. In October 1683 the *comedia* called *The Trials of a Noble House* (*Los empeños de una casa*) was produced in México along with some of her shorter pieces for a festival honoring the viceroy and also welcoming a new archbishop. Her religious plays (three *autos sacramentales* with their introductory *loas,* and a fourth *loa*) include her masterpiece *Divine Narcissus* (*El divino Narciso*, 1690). The mythical figures of Echo and Narcissus function allegorically as Satan and Christ. Striving to be worthy of Narcissus, Human Nature is left, after his death, with Grace, who offers the hope of the resurrection. The poetic dialogue between Narcissus and Human Nature, while religious in content, achieves remarkable lyric beauty. *Saint Hermenegild, Martyr of the Sacrament* (*El mártir del sacramento San Hermenegildo*) and *Joseph's Sceptre* (*El cetro de Joseph*) are historical and allegorical *autos*. In 1989 Guillermo Schmidhuber discovered what has been verified as an additional play by Sor Juana, published under Agustín de Salazar's name. This *comedia, The Second Celestina* (*La segunda Celestina*, 1676), whose title character is a strong, intelligent woman, is then Sor Juana's earliest known play.

Some plays were still being written in indigenous languages as late as the seventeenth and early eighteenth centuries. The anonymous *Loa satírica en una comedia en la fiesta del Corpus hecha en Tlayacapa* (1682) uses a mixture of Náhuatl and Spanish. Agustín de la Fuente's *Comedia de los reyes* was

*The interior of the Teatro Principal de Puebla, which was reconstructed in 1940 with the same plan as the 1761 playhouse on the site, shows the circular arrangement of boxes in a* coliseo-*style structure. Photograph by Felicia Londré.*

composed in Náhuatl. Manuel de los Santos y Salazar wrote *Invención de la Santa Cruz por Santa Elena* (1714), a *coloquio* in the Mexica language. The anonymous Náhuatl-language *An Old Woman and Her Young Nephew* (*Entremés entre una vieja y un mozo su nieto*), surviving in an eighteenth-century manuscript, recalls pre-hispanic performance in its incorporation of animal cries and dance along with the buffoonery. Records from various regions show many such endeavors encompassing a range of dramatic forms and indigenous languages.

While the *criollos* preferred dramatic texts imported from Spain, they welcomed theater created in the New World, adhering to European traditions but imbued with American sensibilities. Such theater grew out of Corpus Christi entertainments that were entrusted to professional theater people. Perhaps as early as the 1570s the *cabildos* may have initiated the practice of contracting with an individual to take charge of all festivities. An actor–manager who functioned as impresario and "director" was known as an *autor;* numerous references to *autores* appear in documents by 1600. The earliest of such records is from 1586, when Alonso de Buenrostro (who had recently brought the first theater company to New Spain from Spain) was appointed to run the festival in the city of México that year. Luis Largarto was paid one thousand pesos for three *autos* in 1593, and thirteen hundred pesos to run the entire Corpus Christi festival of 1594. Similarly, records of the city council of Puebla show that the festival was put in the hands of *autores*: Diego Loçano in 1588, Joan de la Cruz in 1589, and Diego Díaz in 1590.

In 1589 the scholar Arias de Villalobos (1568–1637?) was accused of not having fulfilled his contract as *autor* of that year's Corpus Christi festival in México. Nevertheless, Villalobos came back to the city council in August 1594 with a proposal to organize all entertainment, including three new plays, for the eight days of Corpus Christi and for the feast of Saint Hippolytus (patron saint of New Spain) the following spring, all for two thousand pesos. The request was granted, but was withdrawn in March 1595 when Gonzalo de Riancho (b. 1566?) offered to provide similar events for fifteen hundred pesos. Although Riancho spent over three thousand pesos and was not reimbursed, he continued to be a presence in the theater of New Spain until 1620. In 1596 and 1598 he staged the annual August 13 reenactment of Cortés's conquest of Tenochtitlán (but in 1599 the city had no funds for it, and the event was cancelled). By 1601 Riancho headed a professional company of actors, and he himself was perhaps the finest actor of his time. Meanwhile, Villalobos turned to teaching and writing, and it is through his published poetry that we know (as reported by Rodolfo Usigli) that "in 1621 there were in México three companies of actors who performed in two different theatres plays from Castile."

There is no record of the opening of the first public playhouse in New Spain. Some vague references suggest that a wooden "house in which *comedias* are presented" existed in Puebla de los Angeles as early as the 1550s. In 1602 a Puebla carpenter successfully petitioned for a six-year monopoly as provider of the town's performance facility. He boasted that his building, where plays had been presented during the previous year, would offer reserved seating for any officials who wanted to see the comedias. The carpenter, Juan Gómez Melgarejo, ran his playhouse so successfully that the monopoly was several times renewed and passed to his widow when he died in 1639; indeed, as late as 1666 a Melgarejo was operating the *corral de comedias* in Puebla. Today's Teatro Principal de Puebla was inaugurated during Easter week of 1761, used as an arsenal during the war for Independence, and was largely destroyed by fire on July 27, 1902. Reconstructed on the site in 1940, it typifies the eighteenth-century baroque *coliseo*. Another provincial playhouse is recorded as having existed in New Veracruz in 1660. As in Spain, a portion of the revenue from each playhouse was directed to charitable institutions, often to hospitals for the poor.

The most important public playhouses were those in the capital city of México. The first was probably one established by Francisco de León and located near the Royal Hospital of Our Lady. Villalobos referred to it in a poem as the "*Casa de oficiales del contento*" (house of offices of enjoyment). Gonzalo de Riancho seems to have been using it by 1597. A second theater—constructed in the patio of the Royal Hospital of the Indians—was in

 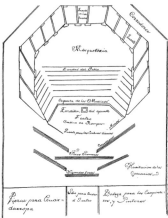

*Left, this newspaper photo of the Teatro Principal de Puebla the day after the 1902 fire shows the interior configuration of* coliseo-style *playhouse architecture. It appears that there was enough remaining of the 1761 structure to justify calling the reconstructed building the oldest surviving theater in North America.*

*Right, México's Coliseo Viejo, built in 1725, was a rectangular structure with a coliseum-style auditorium. This surviving ground plan shows fifteen* aposentos, *surrounding a patio where* mosqueteros *could stand behind the rows of seating. The location of the prompter's box is indicated down center on the stage. From Luis González Obregón,* México viejo: epoca colonial, *1900.*

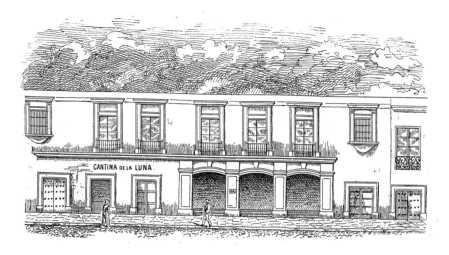

*Built in 1753, the first stone playhouse in México survived fires, earthquakes, and remodelings until a tragic fire razed it in 1931. Originally called the Coliseo Nuevo, it became the Teatro Principal in 1826. From Luis González Obregón,* México viejo: epoca colonial, *1900.*

operation shortly after that, as indicated by a 1602 reference to Cristóbal Pérez as manager of "the two houses in which plays are performed in this city." The viceroy granted Pérez a monopoly: no *autos* or *comedias* could be performed anywhere other than at the two designated playhouses; the penalty for doing so would be at least one hundred gold pesos and ten days in jail. (It should be noted that a 1600 ordinance had already prohibited performances in churches, monasteries, and convents.) But in 1603 a new viceroy asked that the players come to the Guadalupe hermitage to present two plays, and the *cabildo* granted its permission. Once the viceroys showed interest in the theater, the city officials became active playgoers. In 1626 the *cabildo* ordered that both playhouses be installed with special "appropriately ornate" seating, equivalent to the *aposentos* (boxes) used by important personages in the theaters of Madrid, Seville, and other cities of the mother country.

Flooding in 1629 caused the playhouse at the Royal Hospital of the Indians to deteriorate, but planning for its reconstruction did not begin until 1638. The new playhouse's dimensions, determined by its location in the hospital patio, were approximately eighty-one feet by sixty-seven feet. The contract specified fifty *aposentos*. Probably inaugurated in April 1640, the Theatre of the Royal Hospital got twenty-five years of hard use before major repairs were necessary in 1665. It was probably this structure that was destroyed by fire in 1722. The theater was immediately rebuilt, but the noise of performances disturbed the patients. Thus, another rectangular wooden playhouse was erected in 1725 on nearby hospital property. The latter structure—eventually known as the Coliseo Viejo (Old Coliseum)—included a stage door, so that, for the first time, the actors did not need to use the same entrance as the public. The location also enabled the viceroys to attend the theater in style; they could leave the south side of the viceregal palace in a luxuriously appointed canoe that carried them along a system of drainage canals (which, during the next century or so, became blacker and fouler smelling until finally paved over) to the very door of the theater. Even with constant repairs, the wooden Coliseo Viejo lasted little more than twenty-five years.

In 1752 a larger tract of land was acquired for construction of a new playhouse—the first stone theater in México—that would be worthy of the growing city. Inaugurated in December 1753, the Coliseo Nuevo (New Coliseum) boasted seventy-five orchestra seats with standing room for 350 behind them, three iron-reinforced balconies (eighteen boxes on each level), and a top gallery with separate sections (*cazuelas*) for men and women as well as a machinist's loft. The ceiling and walls were painted blue and white, embellished by mythological paintings and the royal coat of arms. The Coliseo's administrative and financial ties to the Royal Hospital continued despite their physical separation; in the 1760s the Coliseo was generating forty-four hundred pesos a year for the hospital. For the remainder of the colonial period, the Coliseo was the authorized playhouse in the capital. (Renamed Teatro Principal in 1826, this structure continued in use until it was destroyed by fire in 1931.) The site, on today's Bolívar street, a few blocks from the zócalo, is commemorated by a plaque on a wall.

The business management of the playhouses was handled by hospital administrators or other appointees of the viceroy. They kept meticulous financial records, but unfortunately did not always record the titles of the plays presented. The playhouses in México and other cities were rented by various companies. Besides Gonzalo de Riancho, early seventeenth-century *autores* included Juan Corral, Alonso Velásquez, Juan Ortiz de Torres, Juan de Santiago and Francisco Maldonado. After the floods of 1629 in the capital, all the theater companies moved to Puebla de los Angeles. Thus, in 1630 an *autor* had to be invited from Puebla to stage the Corpus Christi festivities in México. Juan Antonio de Sigüenza took the job, but later returned to Puebla, which seems to have had a livelier theater scene than the capital until the 1640 opening of the new playhouse at the Royal Hospital of the Indians. In fact, Puebla was home to a woman theater company manager, Anamaría de los Angeles, who became embroiled in a rivalry with another Puebla *autor,* Fernando Ramos. In 1632, when both wanted to remain in Puebla, the *autora* was given no choice but to take her company to México. There the flood season caused poor attendance at her performances. She hoped to recoup her losses by being put in charge of a January festival, but Ramos showed up and applied to the *cabildo* for the job. Anamaría de los Angeles appealed to the viceroy and won her case; Ramos was sent back to Puebla and ordered not to return to the capital without the viceroy's express permission. It is worth noting that one who spoke up on Anamaría's behalf was Gonzalo Jaramillo (b. 1601), the first professional actor born in the New World. From the latter half of the seventeenth century the names of many more managers and actors have been preserved, including that of another *autora,* María de Celi, wife of actor José Corona. In 1683, both were employed by Bartolomé de la Cueva to perform at the playhouse of the Royal Hospital of the Indians. In 1687 she petitioned the viceroy for official designation as *autora,* citing her years of exemplary performance in leading roles. Her request was granted on the grounds that there was no qualified man to do the job.

Not until the early eighteenth century does an *autor* of exceptional abilities stand out from the many who kept theater alive in the capital over the decades. Eusebio Vela (1688–1737) belonged to a theatrical family from Toledo, Spain. By 1713 he was performing in New Spain, in a company managed by his brother José (Eusebio as leading man, José as the comic *gracioso*). Vela later took charge of the company, and from 1718 to 1736 was the principal lessee and star actor of the major playhouse in México, working harmoniously with the hospital administrator, Augustín Vidarte. The ups and downs of Vela's colorful professional life have been chronicled by J. R. Spell. Three plays written by Vela have survived. *If Love Exceeds Art, Be Prudent in Neither (Si el amor excede al arte, ni amor ni arte a la prudencia)* is a dramatization of the adventures of Telemachus on the island of Calypso, which relies heavily upon magical effects. *The Loss of Spain (La pérdida de España)* is a patriotic historical drama. *Apostleship in the Indies and Martyrdom of a Chief (Apostolado en las Indias y martirio de un cacique)* is the most interesting in that it focuses on Mexican history. Considerably fictionalized, this treatment of Cortés, the first Franciscan missionaries, and converted natives versus natives who maintain their pagan beliefs includes three *graciosos,* a martyrdom by fire while angels descend from above, and a Demon mounted on a dragon.

With the opening of the Coliseo de México (Coliseo Viejo) in 1725, the capital of New Spain entered a period of intense theatrical activity, although quantity did not mean quality. Sustained only by his faith in the possibilities of art, Eusebio Vela weathered many setbacks, both economic and bureaucratic, during his tenure at the helm of the Coliseo Viejo. The company usually performed four or five different *comedias* a week, averaging twenty a month, thus necessitating extensive prompting of actors. Maya Ramos Smith has counted 142 different plays presented between April 1786 and January 1787 (the season actually ran through February 1787, but the records for that month are missing). By the end of the century, the Coliseo was required to offer performances every day of the year except during Lent. Feast days called for the presentation of five comedias as well as dances. Furthermore, the company leasing the Coliseo obligatorily provided entertainment at the viceroy's palace on special occasions like the king's birthday. That exhausting regimen—as well as the low esteem with which the profession was regarded—resulted in a dearth of talented performers and considerable instability in the maintenance of a company.

Theater companies were formed and dissolved rather frequently. A company was generally composed of five to twelve actors and four to six actresses, each having a particular line of business, in addition to singers and dancers. Maya Ramos Smith's compilation of names of performers at the Coliseo during this period includes a rare example of a company for which we have a complete listing: that of Manuel Lozano in 1786–87, which comprised sixteen women (four actresses, three singers, nine dancers) and twenty-seven men (fifteen actors, nine dancers, three prompters). For more than a decade, beginning in 1780, the Coliseo's leading lady was Antonia de San Martín, who came from Spain with her husband Antonio Pizarro and quickly won renown for her beauty as well as her acting talent. Realizing that her popularity with the public contributed much to the fortunes of the theater, the imperious San Martín demanded a higher salary and, when refused, was stricken with a sudden "illness" that prevented her from performing; only the viceroy's intervention could restore her to the stage. In 1783 she wrote the viceroy a long letter detailing the abuses she suffered from her husband and appealing for a separation; such was her worth to the Coliseo that Pizarro was expelled from the city. Antonia de San Martín later tried again to use illness as a ploy for missing performances, but was destined to lose the prolonged power struggle. In 1793 the hospital administrator José del Rincón won the viceroy's consent to drop the difficult actress from the company and to contract new actors and dancers from Spain.

Despite the abundance of theatrical offerings available to the growing and heterogeneous population, the artistic development of the theater in New Spain was undoubtedly retarded during the final decades before the achievement of Mexican independence in 1821. One reason for this may well have been the rigorous censorship which covered a lot of bases: political, theological, moral, artistic, and even mundane matters like scheduling. In general, theater censorship was designed to mirror that of the mother country as well as actively to promote the moral, social, and political values that allowed the colonial regime to function smoothly. *Comedias de magia* (fairy extravagnzas) employed mechanical effects and enjoyed great popularity until prohibited in 1794 on the grounds that fantasy subjects were incompatible with the dissemination of Christianity. Translations from the French (Molière and Racine) satisfied the convictions of the governing class that neoclassical plays provided the best examples for upholding the moral order as well as furthering the secularization of the theater. The incorporation of popular songs and dances broadened the appeal of those works for theatergoers of all classes. Indeed, neoclassical drama regularly shared the stage with *loas, entremeses,* and *sainetes* about daily life among the humble. The demand for such popular fare sometimes led to flouting of the prohibition against performances in private venues—an injunction purportedly intended to guard against riots in unpoliced locations, but which probably had more to do with shielding the Coliseo from competition. By 1768 the Coliseo effectively held a monopoly on everything from kite-flying, puppets, and acrobatics to *coloquios.* Among the violations documentated by Germán Viveros was a house known in 1796 as the Mesón de las Animas (Showcase of Spirits). A loosening of restrictions in 1808 merely signalled acquiescence to existing practice.

In his analysis of the 1790 theater season at the Coliseo in México, Irving A. Leonard notes that the fare was largely *comedias* by minor Spanish writers or adapters, while local writers contributed only the shorter pieces that filled out a bill. (We know, for example, that 503 plays were shipped from Spain in 1713 for use in the New World playhouses.) Given the abundance of plays available from the dramatists of Spain's Golden Age and after, perhaps there was little incentive for *criollo* writers. Nevertheless, a few names are worthy of note. José Agustín de Castro (1730–1814), a functionary who lived in Puebla, wrote a number of *loas* that have survived, as well as some *autos* and two short pieces. Tomas de Torrejón y Velasco composed the first opera in the Americas, *Blood of the Rose* (*La púrpura de la rosa,* 1701). Juan de Medina, a comic actor, wrote *Eglea's Game* (*Los juegos de Eglea*), a "heroic pastoral dance in one act," for performance on the name-day of the viceroy's wife (June 13, 1796); outlines of this and two other largely nonverbal pieces by him were published that year: *The Tragic Death of Muley Eliacid, Emperor of Morocco* (*Muerte trágica de Muley Eliacid, emperador de Marruecos*), a "tragical-comical-pantomimical dance in six acts," and *Ircana in Yulfa,* a "heroic pantomimical dance in four acts." Titles of plays that have come down to us (though the texts are lost) indicate a number of historical dramas about Hernán Cortés and the conquest.

In addition to the censorship of play texts, production values were also closely regulated. It was the *autor*'s responsibility to see that the nonverbal aspects of performance were "pure and decent." Concern about such matters was expressed in 1786, when a theater subscriber, Silvestre Díaz de la Vega, addressed a "Discourse on Dramas" to the viceroy. Following a lengthy statement of lofty principles, Díaz de la Vega noted that "some of our actors at the playhouse of México employ their talent in actions, movements, and expressions that are scarcely modest, motivated by the wrongful intention of eliciting general applause through these punishable means." The response from the viceroy, the Count of Galvez, stands as the first surviving official decree devoted to the theater in New Spain. That "Reglamento y Ordenanzas de Teatros" (Regulation for the economic and administrative direction of the Coliseo, 1786) reiterated the king of Spain's 1765 prohibition of plays on religous subjects, emphasized the importance of setting good examples in the theater, and affirmed the viceroy's right to make changes in the theater's proposed repertoire. Its forty articles also tell us something of the theatergoing experience; for example, article 17 stipulates: "The boys who sell sweets and water must do so without calling out, and only between the acts of the main piece; it suffices that they are visible at the ends of the rows or in the aisles."

A wealth of subsequent documents cited by Germán Viveros, by Manuel Mañon, and by Armando de María y Campos demonstrate a variety of concerns about the operations of the Coliseo during the latter part of the eighteenth century. Juan Manuel de San Vicente's "Notice to the Public Concerning the General Reform of the Coliseo" (ca. 1786) lists thirty improvements; among these are: careful selection of the best available actors to form the "most perfect" company possible, a repertoire of the best plays that had not become overfamiliar through frequent revival, rearranged seating for better sightlines, the option of personal redecoration of boxes rented by the year, and the presentation of puppet plays on the three days a week that the actors would have off. Article 10 gives us another insight into conditions: "At the special request of his excellency the viceroy, we have prohibited begging for alms at the entrances or other spots around the Coliseo, and this includes actors as well as nuns and others." In 1790 a company manager named

*The second Count of Revillagigedo, viceroy of New Spain from 1789–94, took a lively interest in the theater. From Luis González Obregón,* México viejo: epoca colonial, 1900.

Mariani posted a public notice, an "Advice to the Public," affirming the theater's mission of moral instruction and laying out behavioral expectations for the theater audience.

As viceroy from 1789 to 1794, the second Count of Revillagigedo took an active and benevolent interest in the theater (and is generally regarded as one of the greatest of the sixty-one viceroys of New Spain). In a message to the Coliseo players, dated May 7, 1794, he criticized theatrical productions he had witnessed:

> It is to be noted that the performances contain certain defects and improprieties that should be avoided and which I consider easily remedied. For example, some of those playing servants and other inferiors passed in front of those playing the principle roles; the former also wore their hats in the presence of the latter; and some were in a place where nobody should ever see them, for example, inside houses; for actors to conclude a *comedia* or *entremés* by asking the public to pardon its mistakes destroys the illusion, a quality so essential in theatre, without which it is reduced to nothing; and finally, for those playing poor or common people to come on stage in such rags and tatters, bordering on indecency, seriously undercuts the visual effect and shows disrespect for the audience.

A regulation of 1796 dealt with such matters as the Coliseo's payments to the hospital, frequency of performance, selection of plays and short entertainments, and the Coliseo's right to draw upon the resources of other theater companies in New Spain in order to fulfill its educational and entertainment mandate. Manuel del Campo y Rivas's "Regulation for the Interior of the Theater and Its Actors" (1806) affirmed that theater—although it could be used as a "school of corruption" as easily as a "workshop for the reformation of manners"—is necessary to human life. While Campo y Rivas certainly recognized the Coliseo's shortcomings, his document extolling "delight and instruction," according to Germán Viveros, planted "on the eve of the Independence movement an idea of what the Mexican theatre might be."

## THE CARIBBEAN

The island of Cuba was one of the first North American shores to be visited by Europeans (Columbus stopped there on his first voyage) and one of the last to achieve independence from its European colonizers (in 1902). Although the Taino (or Arawak) and Siboney tribes that populated the island in 1492 built no great cities as did the Maya and Aztecs, they participated as whole communities in ritual entertainments called *areitos*. These were choral festivals that incorporated dance, pantomime, prayer, recitation of tribal history, masks, libations, and a great variety of musical instruments to celebrate a success or to memorialize a deceased chief. European contamination of the *areitos* occurred as early as 1512, according to José Juan Arrom, when a peaceful tribe near today's Santiago cared for a Spanish sailor who had fallen ill; the Spaniard then persuaded the natives to include the "Ave Maria" in their singing. A cross-cultural influence in the other direction is often detected in the rhythms and melodies that became characteristic of later Cuban music, which also displays elements of African music. With the drastic decline in the native population, the colonizing Spaniards began in 1523 to import black Africans to work as slaves on the sugar plantations. (Slavery was finally abolished in Cuba in 1886.) One of the most characteristic expressions of Afro–Cuban culture was the *diablitos* or "devil myths," a range of allegorical ritual dances that invoke magical spirits of various African ancestries.

During the sixteenth and seventeenth centuries, theatrical activity on Cuba progressed from Corpus Christi processions to Spanish secular dramatic forms with little evidence of intervening evangelical performance. In 1588 Francisco Moxica was paid by the Havana city council for the Corpus Christi performance of a farce he wrote. The next significant event occurred on a midsummer's night in 1598, as recorded by historian Hernando de la Parra:

> In honor of our governor, the young men of this community put on a *comedia* for Saint John's Night, for which they built a cabin near the fort. This play was called *The Good in Heaven and the Bad Below (Los buenos en el cielo y los malos en el suelo)*. It was the first show of this kind in Havana, and it attracted all the residents. There was a lot of disturbance during the performance, because the people, not accustomed to plays, conversed aloud and would not be quiet, to the point that the governor threatened them with the stocks if they could not behave in an orderly fashion. The play ended after one o'clock in the morning, and the people found it so enjoyable that they insisted on its being started over from the beginning.

Cuban dramatic literature takes as its point of departure a play by Santiago Pita y Borroto, a native of Havana. *The Gardener Prince Alias Cloridano (El príncipe jardinero y fingido Cloridano*, 1730–33)—a palace intrigue drama with conventional character types—irritated conservatives, but enjoyed enormous popularity with the general public, many of whom knew long sequences by heart. Apart from that landmark, Cuba existed largely in a state of cultural deprivation (relying for entertainment on dances, cockfights, and widespread gambling) until the arrival of the most progressive of its governor generals. Field Marshal Felipe Fondesviela, Marques de la Torre (ruled 1771–77) not only embarked upon a program of municipal beautification in the capital, but included construction of a playhouse among the public works that brought the island a measure of prosperity. The Coliseo, an elegantly decorated wooden structure, opened in 1776. Renovated in 1792, renamed Teatro Principal in 1803, weakened by a cyclone in 1844, the historic theater finally closed its doors forever in 1846. While the Coliseo remained the only theater in Havana until the end of the eighteenth century, private houses were often used for additional dramatic presentations. Set up in a private home by two "mechanical artists" from New Orleans, a Teatro Mecánico caused a sensation in 1794. Even the governor general came to see the two-hour spectacle in which "automated dolls" moved mechanically through events depicting the seven wonders of the world and the destruction of Jerusalem. Theatrical performances of any kind were usually canceled during rainy seasons, because the available modes of transportation—the *quitrín* (curricle, a two-wheeled open carriage) or the sedan chair—were affordable only to the wealthy.

The nineteenth century saw the construction of many other theaters on Cuba. Those in Havana included the Teatro del Circo (1800, renamed Teatro de Villanueva in 1853), the Diorama (used as a theater 1829–46), and Teatro Cervantes (1867). In other towns were the Teatro Principal in Camagüey (1849), Teatro de la Reina in Santiago (1850), Teatro de la Avellaneda in Cienfuegos (1860), Teatro Esteban in Matanzas (1863). Above all, Havana's luxurious Teatro Tacón (1838), named after Governor General Miguel Tacón, garnered encomiums as one of the finest theaters in the world. As an incentive to construct such a monumental building, Tacón granted entrepreneur Francisco Marty y Torrens the right to use the theater for up to six masquerade balls (very lucrative events) each year in carnival season. Besides the elegance of the white and gold auditorium, the Tacón was celebrated for its good ventilation (twenty-two doors and eighty windows), its boxes fronted with graceful latticework "so open that the dresses and pretty feet of the señoras are seen to best advantage," its magnificent cut-glass gaslit chandelier, its huge stage, its patio with cafés along the side, and a portico that allowed theatergoers to descend from their *quitrines* under cover from the rain. With 2,287 seats and standing room for 700, the Tacón boasted a capacity of 3,037.

At the Coliseo, a Compañía de Cómicos under the management of Lucas Sáez performed on Thursdays and Sundays. This long-lived company, to which the great Francisco Covarrubias belonged, was performing at the Circo in 1803 when it changed its name to Cómicos Havaneros. José Juan Arrom's tabulation of their eighty-six performances in 1791 demonstrates

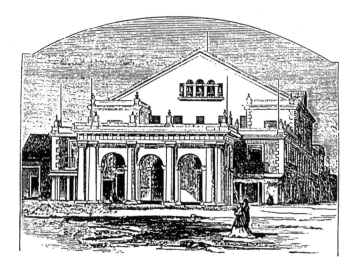

*The monumental Teatro Tacón, built in Havana in 1838, was regarded at the time as one of the world's grandest theatres. From Samuel Hazard,* Cuba with Pen and Pencil, *1871.*

*This drawing of the interior of Havana's famous Teatro Tacón shows its large capacity and attractive design. Fanny Calderón de la Barca described it as "remarkably pretty and airy, and the pit is remarkable for its cleanness and respectability. All the seats are red leather armchairs, and all occupied by well-dressed people." From Samuel Hazard,* Cuba with Pen and Pencil, *1871.*

that the repertoire was very much the same as what was being presented in Spain: fifty-one classic works (mostly Spanish Golden Age), twenty-three eighteenth-century Spanish plays, four non-Spanish plays in translation, one by a Cuban author, and one unidentified. In the Spanish style, musical numbers filled the intermissions of a central dramatic work. Cuba's location as an obligatory stop for ships between Europe, the United States, and Mexico meant that numerous foreign companies visited Havana and performed there. Actors like Diego María Garay and Andrés Prieto, who later made their careers in México, first spent several seasons in Havana. However, musical entertainment strongly dominated Havana's theater scene from the 1830s. Habaneros loved opera and saw many Italian opera companies as well as some French ballet companies.

Theater on Puerto Rico during the early colonial era followed a pattern similar to that on Cuba, with a mingling of festival traditions from the *areitos* of the soon-decimated Taíno population and the songs of the African slaves imported to replace them on the plantations. The island of Santo Domingo (Hispaniola) can probably be signaled as having the earliest European play performed in North America. The governor's wife, María de Toledo, brought with her some Spanish works that were performed at the seminary founded there in 1510. In 1588 university students performed in the atrium of the cathedral an *entremés* written by a Santo Domingan, Cristobal de Llerena (c. 1540–1610). Llerena may have composed additional plays drawing upon Latin sources and speaking to local concerns, but the survival of that one is due to its satirical audacity, for which Llerena was punished and a copy of the play was sent with a report of its production to authorities in Spain, where it was discovered in 1921.

The French who colonized the western part of Santo Domingo (today's Haiti) brought in many French touring companies, while their African slaves performed voodoo ceremonies. Similarly, theatrical activity on Martinique, Guadaloupe, and other islands of the French Caribbean might be characterized as split between imported French culture for the *créoles* (born in America of French ancestry) and an oral Creole-language (Caribbean dialect of French) culture of storytelling and carnival festivities enjoyed by those of African descent. For purposes of this book, the latter islands are outside the scope of what we have identified as North American. Among the British colonies (West Indies), only Jamaica is more closely associated with North— rather than South—America. Its theater history has been the subject of numerous studies, most notably those of Errol Hill.

## THE AMERICAN COLONIES

The earliest recorded performances of plays in the territory that is now the United States were offshoots of the theatrical activity in New Spain. In 1567, two plays were performed under the auspices of the Spanish missionaries at Tequesta, Florida, for the soldiers there; the subject matter seems to have been intended to encourage that audience to resist temptations of the flesh. In 1598 Don Juan de Oñate led an authorized colonizing expedition north of the Río Grande to the province (today the American state) of New Mexico. Because a 1573 ordinance prohibited conquest by violence, the colonization of the land inhabited by the Pueblo Indians had to be accomplished by persuasion. Oñate's strategy, according to Ramón A. Gutiérrez, was to create obvious parallels between himself and the conquistador Hernán Cortés, and to reinforce the notion of Spanish supremacy with theatrical reenactments of events related to Cortés's 1521 conquest. Oñate not only traveled with a native mistress just as Cortés had been accompanied by Malinche (also known as Malintzin), but he also included in his contingent twelve Franciscan friars. The significance of the friars' presence was underscored in that first known theatrical performance on American soil, a play about the arrival of the original twelve Franciscans in 1524. Written by Captain Marcos Farfán de los Godos, *Comedia del recibimiento que hizo la Nueva España a la Iglesia* (Play about New Spain's welcome of the Church) was performed by the soldiers after mass and a sermon on April 30, 1598 near today's El Paso. Subsequent performances, as the expedition journeyed inland, included the ever-popular allegorical drama of conflict between pagan and Christian, *Los moros y los cristianos,* a demonstration of the inevitable triumph of the Spaniards' religion.

On the eastern seabord, encounters between indigenous Americans and the colonials also gave rise to ceremonial enactments, but in these instances it was the natives who determined the format. Their "treaty ceremonies" of the late sixteenth and early seventeenth centuries, many of which were recorded by the colonials and later published, incorporated speeches, dialogue, dance-drama, and formal gift-giving. From a Western European perspective, such one-time occasions served a political purpose and thus were not considered entertainment. For the natives, however, aesthetic pleasure could not be divorced from social utility. The natives' profound respect for oral eloquence, for example, often meant the conferral of leadership roles on the most talented speakers, and the exercise of their art endowed the people with an oral literature even as it negotiated tricky cross-cultural encounters.

From New England to Virginia, those who colonized America in the seventeenth century came largely from the middle and lower-middle classes of England, and—at least initially—they brought an English mindset based upon their previous circumstances. Thus the early Puritans fleeing religious persecution held the same sober-minded views as those who closed down all London playhouses during the Commonwealth (1642–60). Later-arriving Puritans, Quakers, and others who settled the northern regions remembered the licentiousness of the Restoration theater (1660–1700) and maintained their strong antipathy toward an activity they regarded as wasteful of time and money, and even, by its depiction of vices, detrimental to public morals. The territory further south, heavily promoted by the Virginia Company and other commercial interests, drew those who came seeking wealth, who proved to be more open to theater as a pleasant diversion. These general attitudes persisted throughout the eighteenth century and, in some manifestations, into the 1800s. Yet there was also, almost from the beginning, an indefinable break with English views and habits. For example, English village traditions like maypole dancing, local fairs, and holiday folk customs—incompatible with the greater mobility of the colonial population and the daily hardships they faced—quickly disappeared.

The earliest known English-language performance of a play in America seems to have been—judging by its title—on a subject of local American interest. *Ye Bare and Ye Cubb* was probably written by William Darby, one of the three men who performed it in Cowle's Tavern, Accomac County, Virginia, on August 27, 1665. Although the play's text has not survived, the event is recorded for posterity in the county records, as a result of the three having been brought to court by the king's attorney and ordered by the justices to repeat their performance in costume at the next session. Not only did the justices find the performers "not guilty of fault," but their accuser had to pay the court costs. In Boston, tavernkeeper John Wing did not get far as a purveyor of entertainment, though his idea of presenting a "stage-fight" along with a magician does sound peculiarly American. In 1687 Wing had prepared a separate room in his tavern for the purpose, but bowed to pressure against it by a committee under the leadership of the civic-minded and wealthy businessman (later chief justice of Massachusetts) Samuel Sewell.

For at least a century after that, theatrical activities in America continued to meet pockets of resistance or outright hostility. Under the leadership of William Penn, for example, the Quakers of Pennsylvania began in 1682 to enact a series of injunctions against "rude or riotous sports" like prizefighting, cockfights, bull-baiting, revels, and stage-plays. Each time the mother country's monarchs, William and Mary, disallowed the colony's antitheatrical law, Pennsylvanians would pass new restrictions, only to be again overruled by the Crown. Antitheatrical laws were passed also in Massachusetts, New Hampshire, Rhode Island, and, indeed, all of the colonies at one time or another, except Virginia and Maryland. Social and religious pressures were also brought to bear, yet the players—amateurs at first, and later professionals—gradually made inroads. Meanwhile, various colleges harbored student performances of dramatic dialogues, pastoral colloquys, and even plays like *Gustavus Vasa* by Benjamin Coleman at Harvard in 1690.

Professional acting in the English colonies might be traced back to the brief presence of Anthony Aston (ca. 1682–1753). Aston had been a law student, poet, and strolling player in England, then decided to try his fortune in Jamaica, where a playhouse had been built as early as 1682. Disappointed by the opportunities there, Aston joined a military expedition led by South Carolina governor James Moore. In January 1703 the soldiers returned to Charles-Town (today's Charleston) "full of Lice, Shame, Poverty, Nakedness and Hunger." Aston added cryptically that he "turn'd Player and Poet, and wrote one Play on the Subject of the Country," but nothing else is known of the play and little else of his brief American career. He spent the winter in New York "acting, writing, courting, fighting," perhaps thus contributing to the low regard in which the acting profession was held. In Virginia that spring he may have done some acting before he sailed back to England, where he achieved a degree of success as a performer of variety material or medleys, for which he took the stage name Matt Medley.

The next milestone was the first publication of a play in America. *Androboros; A Biographical Farce in 3 Acts, viz: the Senate, the Consistory, and the Apotheosis* (1714), written by Robert Hunter, governor of New York and New Jersey from 1710 to 1719, satirized Hunter's political enemies, taking particular aim at General Francis Nicholson, a royal commissioner empowered to investigate colonial affairs. The title character, Androboros or "Man-eater," lampooned the unpleasant Nicholson. Indeed, most of the fifteen characters corresponded to recognized public figures. The printing of the work served its satirical purpose; it was not performed. The fifty years between *Androboros* and the next American play to be published, the anonymously written farce *The Paxton Boys* (1764), did bring some colonial writing for performance—albeit, primarily intended as moral instruction—in the form of "dramatic dialogues." Among those short, plotless oratorical exercises for students were the anonymous "Dialogue between Christ, Youth, and the Devil" (1735), "Dialogue between a Minister and an Honest Country-man" (1741) by John Checkley, an adaptation of *The Masque of Alfred* (1756) by College of Philadelphia provost William Smith, and "An Exercise Containing a Dialogue and an Ode, Sacred to the Memory of His Late Gracious Majesty George II" (1761) by Smith and Francis

Hopkinson. As the Revolution neared, such pieces took on patriotic content, as in "Poem on the Rising Glory of America" (1771) by Hugh Henry Brackenridge and Philip Freneau.

With the help of his indentured servants Charles and Mary Stagg, William Levingston erected the earliest known playhouse in the colonies. In 1716 Levingston had begun by operating a dancing school in a building at the College of William and Mary in Williamsburg, which was then the capital of Virginia. Perhaps encouraged by the talents of the Staggs, Levingston decided to expand his activities, sent to London for additional performers, and purchased the land where he laid out a bowling green and built a house, a separate kitchen, a stable, and a theater. Few records survive to attest to the fare presented in the eighty-six-by-thirty-foot theater, and even its opening date—sometime between 1716 and 1718—is not known. A 1718 letter written by Governor Spotswood mentions a play presented there to solemnize the birthday of His Majesty George I. In any case, Levingston soon faced financial difficulties and lost the property in 1723. The building seems to have continued in use as a theater, if only for occasional amateur performances, at least until 1745, when it was remodeled to serve as a community center. By 1770 America's first theater had been torn down.

The first half of the eighteenth century saw only sporadic references to isolated theatrical initiatives in many locales. In New York, for example, amateur actors led by Dr. Joachimus Bertrand presented *Romeo and Juliet*—the first recorded staging of Shakespeare in America—at the Revenge Meeting House in 1730. Dr. Bertrand himself played the Apothecary, noting that this must be regarded as "a rare act of condescension in a physician." Two years later the second floor of a lower Manhattan warehouse owned by Rip Van Dam served as a theater for a group of players about whom nothing is known. Local recognition of the facility as the "new Theatre" or "Play-house" as well as the fact that three performances a week were given in 1732, with performance announcements appearing as late as 1734, suggest that the actors may have been professionals. In any event, the plays they presented—*Cato, The Recruiting Officer, The Beaux' Stratagem,* and *The Busy Body*—are the same popular works that are recorded as having been presented at the Williamsburg theater in September 1736 by "young Gentlemen and Ladies of the country." Boston's first public performance, a presentation of *The Orphan* organized by two Englishmen and some Bostonians of their acquaintance at the Coffee House in State Street, led to the March 1750 passage of "An Act to Prevent Stage-Plays, and Other Theatrical Entertainments" by the General Court of Massachusetts. The preamble of that act sums up the views that typically animated antitheatrical prejudices wherever they occurred in the colonies: "For preventing and avoiding the many and great mischiefs which arise from public stage-plays, interludes, and other theatrical entertainments, which not only occasion great and unnecessary expenses, and discourage industry and frugality, but likewise tend generally to increase immorality, impiety, and a contempt of religion."

Charleston proved receptive to the arts, at least until the influence of certain evangelical preachers began to take a toll around 1737. On January 24, 1735, a courtroom served as venue for *The Orphan,* the popularity of which led to three additional performances. This production brought another "first": the earliest known American prologue introducing a play. The anonymous poet (whose contribution was published in the South Carolina *Gazette*) invoked how far along the colonists had brought their civilizing influence to the wilderness that Columbus once faced, and then noted:

> *Hence we presume to usher in those Arts*
> Which oft have warm'd the best and bravest Hearts.

February brought *Flora; or, The Hob in the Well,* a ballad opera, often touted as the first musical play presented in America. After a third Charleston production (John Dryden's *The Spanish Friar*), pledges were given to finance construction of the "new Theatre in Dock Street," which opened on February 1, 1736 with *The Recruiting Officer.* As the Theater in Queen Street (the street name changed that year), it drew audiences to new productions and revivals, as well as concerts and a ball, until 1737.

Philadelphia's well-known antipathy toward the theater did not deter players from trying their luck there. One means of getting around the Quaker prohibitions was to create a performance space just outside the city limits, as did those who advertised variety entertainments like rope-dancing at "The New Booth on Society Hill" in 1724. Legitimate theater inside the city limits began with performances at Plumsted's Theatre in 1749. The liberal-minded William Plumsted (later elected mayor of Philadelphia) installed a stage, pit, boxes, and gallery in his three-story brick warehouse on Water Street for use by the company of Thomas Kean and Walter Murray. The company's origins are unknown, but they could have been performing there for several months before the mention in a private journal of their August 1749 presentation of *Cato.* A formal protest against their activities (possibly put forward when Nancy George joined the company over the community's objections) elicited strong antitheatrical language from Philadelphia's Common Council in January 1750. In February the Murray–Kean "Company of Comedians" moved on to New York, where they opened *Richard III* on March 5 in a Nassau Street warehouse that had belonged to the late Rip Van Dam. There, supported by a population of only seven thousand, they presented twenty-four plays in seventeen months, closing their remarkable run on July 8, 1751. In Williamsburg in October they performed in a new playhouse built expressly for them, and then toured to other Virginia towns. In Fredericksburg in June 1752, young George Washington attended a Murray–Kean production. The brevity of their stay in Virginia might be attributed to reports of "loose behavior" by some of the company. Later that month they were performing at the New Theatre in Annapolis, which remained their base of operations for a few months, after which the Murray–Kean company apparently disbanded.

The history of professional theater in the American colonies begins in earnest with the arrival of the Hallam company in Yorktown, Virginia, in

June 1752. The Hallams were lured to America by the glowing reports of John Moody, an Irish actor who had been performing Shakespeare in Jamaica since 1745. On a return visit to London to recruit actors for his theater in Kingston, Moody brought back David Douglass, an actor whose talents further stimulated the demand for theater in Jamaica—and who would eventually combine forces with the Hallams. The bruited opportunities available in the New World held strong appeal for William Hallam when the New Wells Theatre he managed in Goodman's Fields in London was closed by the authorities for violation of the licensing laws. William Hallam organized and backed a company to be managed on the road by his brother Lewis Hallam under a commonwealth scheme for sharing responsibilities and profits. The Hallams employed Robert Upton to travel ahead to the colonies as an advance man who would secure performance permissions and sites. Upton, however, betrayed his employers not only by joining the Murray–Kean company as an actor, but also by giving Murray and Kean the seven new plays and four new farces that the Hallams were rehearsing. Upton managed to evade the Hallams, returning to England before they arrived in America.

In Williamsburg from June until their September 15, 1752 opening, the twelve adult actors and three young Hallam children found non-theater-related work in the community by which they proved their good intentions and reliability. They also busied themselves refurbishing the facility that had been built for Murray and Kean, while Lewis Hallam repeatedly petitioned the reluctant Governor Dinwiddie for permission to perform. Clearly intending to set a respectable tone while drumming up interest, Hallam published a series of announcements in the Virginia *Gazette,* promising scenery and costumes that would be "entirely new, extremely rich, and finished in the highest taste" and ensuring that "the Ladies and Gentlemen may depend on being entertain'd in as polite a Manner as at the Theatres in London." For its inaugural program, the "select Company of Comedians" presented Shakespeare's *The Merchant of Venice* and a farcical afterpiece, *The Anatomist; or, The Sham Doctor,* and were rewarded "with great Applause" by "a numerous and polite audience." Residing in Williamsburg until the following spring, the company performed two or three times a week. At a November performance attended by the "Emperor of the Cherokee nation" along with his "Empress," their son, and several warriors as guests of Governor Dinwiddie, *Othello* was followed by "a Pantomime Performance which gave them great surprise, as did the fighting with naked Swords on the Stage, which occasioned the Empress to order some about her to go and prevent them killing one another."

In June 1753 the "Company of Comedians from London" arrived in New York with a certificate of good behavior signed by Governor Dinwiddie, but the legacy of bad feelings left by the "tricks and mischief" of the "roystering young men" of the Murray–Kean company frustrated the Hallams' expectation of a ready welcome. Hallam wrote a thoughtful petition that candidly explained his aims and difficulties. Permission granted him, Hallam built "a very fine, large and commodious new theater" in Nassau Street, which he opened on September 17 with *The Conscious Lovers* and the ballad-farce *Damon and Phillida.* During their six-month season in New York, the Hallams presented twenty-four different plays.

Moving on to Philadelphia in the spring of 1754, Hallam's Company of Comedians again faced opposition but overcame it by guaranteeing that nothing indecent would be performed, tendering security for any debts, and offering one of their twenty-four performances for the benefit of the poor. The troupe undoubtedly provided a stimulus to the local economy by its remodeling of Plumsted's Theatre as well as the hiring of local hairdressers, play copyists, and musicians to accompany performances; printing of handbills, tickets, and advertisements; purchase of candles and other necessities. Yet some Philadelphians persisted in seeing the theater as detrimental to trade because it would "encourage idleness." The two-month season there brought a visit by William Hallam from London to settle accounts with his brother Lewis.

After constructing a new playhouse in Charleston and offering a fall season there (October 3 to December 27, 1754), the Company of Comedians sailed for Jamaica. There they soon merged with the remnants of a company managed by David Douglass (d. 1789). Lewis Hallam died in 1755, and his widow eventually married Douglass, who took over the combined company's management. Nineteen-year-old Lewis Hallam Jr., began to play the leading male roles opposite his still-beautiful mother. During the next fifty years, Lewis Hallam Jr. (1740–1808) would establish himself as one of the favorite performers of the growing American theatergoing public. In 1758 the Company of Comedians returned from Jamaica to the mainland. Arriving in New York in October, they encountered resistance by local authorities, who felt it would be imprudent to offer the frivolity of theater during a period of economic slump. Douglass, having already incurred the expense of preparing a sail-loft to serve as a "new theatre on Cruger's Wharf," published a plea for tolerance of his "moral, instructive, and entertaining" art. Finally, the company was allowed to open on January 1, 1759. The moralistic *Tragedy of Jane Shore* proved wildly popular, initiating a five-week run of an eighteen-play repertoire. In Philadelphia Douglass built the Theatre in Society Hill, where the company performed from June to December 1759, beset by constant opposition. In 1760–62 they toured to Annapolis, Williamsburg (where the young planter George Washington was often in the audience), back to New York (where Douglass had a theater built in Chapel Street), Newport, and Providence. In the face of lingering prejudice against theater throughout New England, the company touted its plays as "moral dialogues." For example, *Othello* was advertised as "a series of MORAL DIALOGUES in five parts/ Depicting the Evil Effects of Jealousy and other Bad Passions, and Proving that Happiness can only spring from the Pursuit of Virtue."

Beginning with a 1763 Charleston engagement, Douglass cannily renamed the Company of Comedians from London in response to a rising tide of public opinion; henceforth they would be the American Company. Among several new actors joining the company there, the charming Nancy Hallam, a cousin of Lewis Hallam Jr., won a wide following. Douglass had begun the Charleston residency, as usual, by constructing a theater. The need to build a new playhouse virtually every time they returned to a given city strained the company's resources, but it did lead Douglass to build permanent facilities, beginning in 1766 with the Southwark Theatre in Philadephia. This first permanent theater in America had a foundation and first-story exterior of brick, while the upper floor was a red-painted frame construction with three windows. The roof leaked and there was no heating, so theatergoers brought their own small foot stoves. Oil lamps over the stage area provided illumination much improved over the standard candles stuck on barrel hoops. An important innovation was storage space for the Southwark's own painted scenery, which would remain there rather than be transported to other playhouses on the Douglass theater circuit. The following year Douglass constructed a similar brick building in New York, the John Street Theatre.

The inaugural season at Philadelphia's Southwark included the first professional production of a play by an American author. Thomas Godfrey (1736–63) was a promising Phildelphia-born poet who died suddenly at twenty-seven; his friends honored Godfrey's memory by publishing his only play, *The Prince of Parthia*, a five-act heroic verse tragedy. Douglass hoped vainly that the production would ingratiate the American Company with the antitheatrical contingent, but the play, presented on April 24, 1767, was not successful enough to merit a second performance. Godfrey's work had been a last-minute substitute for another play the company had been rehearsing: *The Disappointment; or, The Force of Credulity,* a comic opera by Colonel Thomas Forrest (using the pen-name Andrew Barton). A Pennsylvania *Gazette* announcement stated that the latter had been withdrawn because it contained "personal reflections" that were "unfit to be played." Perhaps it was the satire of recognizable Philadelphians that prevented this work—which also features the first Negro character in American drama—from taking "first" place. Another interesting play of the period—though not produced in its author's lifetime—was *Ponteach; or, The Savages of America* (1766), a sympathetic portrayal of the tragic–heroic Native American title character (pronounced Pontiac). Written by Major Robert Rogers, commander of Rogers's Rangers during the French and Indian War, *Ponteach* initiated a long tradition of dramas on indigenous themes.

New York's John Street Theatre, the second permanent playhouse in America, opened on December 7, 1767, with *The Beaux' Stratagem.* This wooden, red-painted facility—with a pit, a gallery, two rows of boxes, and a large stage above some dressing rooms and a green room—served as the city's leading theater for thirty years. In its inaugural season, which ended June 2, 1768, the American Company presented thirty-eight plays, including eight by Shakespeare. That season also brought the American debut of a new leading man: the tall, handsome, Irish-born John Henry (1738–94). Douglass showed some clever marketing skills when a group of Cherokee delegates to a treaty negotiation passed through New York and asked to see a play. Douglass advertised the evening as a command performance, which quickly sold out. According to the newspaper report, the Cherokees watched *Richard III* with "seriousness and attention," but seemed to get more enjoyment from the

*Left, the Southwark Theatre, built by David Douglass in 1766 in Philadelphia, was the first permanent (brick) playhouse in the American colonies. From Arthur Hornblow,* A History of the Theatre in America, *vol. 1, 1919.*

*Right, Mercy Otis Warren (1728–1815), a well-educated young woman, wrote topical satires in support of the American antiroyalists during the Revolutionary period. From Arthur Hornblow,* A History of the Theatre in America, *vol. 1, 1919.*

*Left, this drawing supposedly represents the actor–manager Thomas Wignell (1753– 1803) lighting the way to a theater box for President George Washington. From Arthur Hornblow,* A History of the Theatre in America, *vol. 1, 1919.*

*Right, Fanueil Hall was used by the British forces occupying Boston for theatrical performances, including General Burgoyne's* The Blockade of Boston *in 1776. From Arthur Hornblow,* A History of the Theatre in America, *vol. 1, 1919.*

pantomime-ballet afterpiece *Harlequin's Vagaries*. The John Street Theatre prospered after that, and the Cherokees, on their return trip three months later, attended another performance, after which they performed "a war dance" on the stage to reciprocate for "the friendly Reception and civilities they have received in this city."

Despite such successes, the life of the players was never easy. Between engagements or while a new theater was under construction, they earned income as best they could, some by giving fencing or musical lessons, others by giving free-lance lectures or song and dance performances. And rival entertainers appeared with increasing frequency, notably, in the spring of 1768, the Virginia Company of Comedians, which reconstituted itself the following season as the New American Company. Furthermore, the 1770s brought growing political unrest as American patriots sometimes carried their demonstrations for the cause of liberty from the streets into the theater. The debt-burdened American Company built yet another theater in Charleston for the 1773–74 season (which marked the first production of *Julius Caesar* in America, aptly chosen to show "the Noble Struggles for liberty of those renowned Romans"), after which Lewis Hallam sailed for London to recruit new actors. The most important of these, Thomas Wignell (1753–1803), was a cousin of Hallam and had acted with David Garrick at Drury Lane. Scarcely had Wignell sailed for the colonies when the Continental Congress met in Philadelphia and, in view of the prospect of war against the mother country, passed a resolution on October 20, 1774 to "encourage frugality, economy, and industry," which, of course, necessitated the banning of "every species of extravagance and dissipation, especially all horse-racing, and all kinds of gaming, cock-fighting, exhibitions of shews, plays, and other expensive diversions and entertainments." With the closing of the theaters, the American Company removed to Jamaica. There David Douglass, mourning the recent death of his wife, retired from the theater and became a prosperous printer. Under the management of Lewis Hallam Jr., the company settled into a new six-hundred-seat Kingston theater, opening on July 1, 1775 with *Romeo and Juliet*. Touring occasionally to Spanish Town and elsewhere on the island, the company enjoyed a steady following during its ten years in Jamaica.

Despite the 1774 resolution against entertainments, the Revolutionary years actually brought an increase in the extent of theatrical activity, as Jared Brown has shown, and this paved the way toward general acceptance of theater in America in the nineteenth century. On the whole, it was the British soldiers who engaged in the performance of plays as a morale-building diversion, while American patriots largely contented themselves with the publication of propagandistic or satirical dialogues. Most important in the latter category were the sharp political satires written by Mercy Otis Warren (1728–1814) and published anonymously: *The Adulateur* (1772), *The Defeat* (1773), *The Group* (1775). Warren sent the manuscript of the latter work to her husband James Warren, who was paymaster general for George Washington, and thus it may have been presented as a dramatic reading by soldiers in the American camp. Other published plays in support of the American cause included Hugh Henry Brackenridge's five-act verse drama *The Battle of Bunker Hill* (1776) and John Leacock's five-act tragicomedy (in which George Washington appears as a character) *The Fall of British Tyranny* (1776).

On the British side, General John Burgoyne encouraged the production of plays in Faneuil Hall during his army's occupation of Boston in 1775 and 1776. Burgoyne himself wrote a farcical afterpiece, *The Blockade of Boston*, ridiculing American patriots, but its performance on January 8, 1776 was interrupted by a panicked soldier bringing news of an American attack. At first the audience applauded what they thought was a very intense performance, but once the reality of it hit them, there was "fainting . . . confusion, terror, and tumult." The perfect American riposte came in the form of an anonymous parody, *The Blockheads; or, The Affrighted Officers,* published in 1776, but probably not performed.

During the seven-year British occupation of New York, the John Street Theatre—renamed Theatre Royal—served as an entertainment center for the troops who had little to do during the winter months. Officers acted in the plays, performing at least once a week. Similarly, the occupation of Philadelphia by twenty-three thousand British troops during the winter of 1777–78 provided an opportunity for at least thirteen performances by British officers in Southwark Theatre, most spectacularly a pageant titled *The Meschianza*. That event was supervised by Major John André, who had earned praise for his scene-painting at the theater (and who would later be immortalized in William Dunlap's popular play about him). During that same winter, George Washington's army created some diversion from the hardships of Valley Forge by indulging in theatricals. When the American troops entered Philadelphia in the spring of 1778, they too staged plays at the Southwark—until October 16, 1778, when the Continental Congress passed a law that strengthened the 1774 injunction and firmly prohibited play-acting and play-going. So suddenly did this occur that General Washington had to cancel his theatergoing plans for that evening.

Maryland seems to have disregarded the law. Although Baltimore's recorded theater history had not begun until 1772, when the American Company had presented an evening of theater in an old stable, the city's first theater was under construction even before Washington's defeat of General Cornwallis at Yorktown in October 1781 (the final peace treaty to end the American Revolution was signed on September 3, 1783). Indeed, Thomas Wall, who had previously acted with the American Company, won permission on June 8, 1781, from the State Council of Maryland "to exhibit Theatrical performances." Wall organized the Maryland Company of Comedians, which opened the New Theatre in Baltimore on Christmas Day 1781, and continued its operations until September 1785. In 1782 the company was considerably strengthened by the addition of Mr. and Mrs. Dennis Ryan among several other recruits. Dennis Ryan (d. 1786) soon became sole manager of the Maryland Company of Comedians, overseeing its tours to other towns as well as the American premiere of *The School for Scandal.*

As the war drew to a close, colleges began presenting dialogues again. At Dartmouth College, for example, professor John Smith (1752–1809) wrote pieces for student performance: *A Dialogue between an Englishman and an Indian* (1779) and *A Little Tea-Table Chitchat* (1781). Recitations on patriotic themes also served as an entering wedge against lingering antitheatrical prejudices in Philadelphia and New York when the American Company prepared for its return from Jamaica. When the Pennsylvania Assembly denied his 1784 petition to resume theatrical production in Philadelphia, Lewis Hallam Jr., presented a series of "lectures" instead. At the Southwark he performed a "Monody to the Memory of the Chiefs who have fallen in the Cause of American Liberty," which—enhanced by scenery and songs—must have blurred the distinction between a lecture and a theatrical performance. Clearly, it was possible simply to ignore the 1778 law, which was finally repealed in 1789.

In 1785 Hallam and several actors from the American Company reopened New York's John Street Theatre, repeating the pattern of escalating production values. Later that year John Henry arrived with his own contingent of actors from the American Company, including Thomas Wignell. Hallam and Henry formed a partnership, taking the name Old American Company and introducing the concept of reserved seating. Wignell quickly emerged as the leading comic actor. The peripatetic performer John Durang (1768–1822) joined the company in 1785 and won a following as a dancer–acrobat–pantomimist. "Durang's hornpipe" was a virtuoso piece danced in a sailor costume. His talents extended to violin-playing, puppetry, and scene-painting, and he left a series of watercolor sketches of himself in various costumes. Thus did the first fully professional theater company of the American colonies make its comeback after the Revolution and embark upon a second phase of its existence in the United States of America.

## NEW FRANCE

Despite Jacques Cartier's claiming of the land around the Gulf of St. Lawrence for the king of France in 1534, the French colonization of the land that would become Canada did not begin in earnest until Samuel de Champlain established a *habitation* of a few dozen people in 1608. Thus it is even before the actual settlement of New France that Canadian theater history begins. November 14, 1606, was the date of the historic event: an aquatic masque enacted by the men at Port Royal, a temporary post in Acadia (on today's Annapolis River in Nova Scotia). The one-time performance of *The Theatre of Neptune in New France (Le Théâtre de Neptune en la Nouvelle France)* welcomed the return of the ship carrying the men's leader, Baron Jean de Biencourt de Poutrincourt, after a ten-week absence. Poutrincourt and his navigator Champlain, along with the group's surgeon, apothecary, carpenter, and others, had been exploring the coast as far south as Cape Cod, seeking a prime location for a base of operations for the fur trade. The men remaining in camp were nervous about their ability to survive the winter on their own if the mother ship failed to return, and they might have turned mutinous had not Marc Lescarbot, who was left in charge, come up with a morale-building distraction. The classically educated Lescarbot penned some verses in preparation for the hopefully anticipated arrival of the leaders, and he presumably conducted a few rehearsals. The costumed Frenchmen who rowed out to meet Poutrincourt and his crew thus playfully vented their pent-up anxieties even as they celebrated the occasion and reaffirmed their loyalty to King Henri IV.

Marc Lescarbot (1570–1634?) had already published some poetry and translations, and had practiced law in Paris before accepting an invitation from his friend Poutrincourt to join the expedition to the New World. They sailed from La Rochelle on May 13, 1606, spent that winter in Acadia, and, following the revocation of their sponsor's fur-trading monopoly, headed back to France on July 30, 1607. In 1609 Lescarbot published his *History of New France,* with a supplement including the text of his *Theatre of Neptune* as well as his impressions of the country. He noted, for example, that "there are certainly no violins, no masquerades, no dances, no palaces, no towns, and no goodly buildings as in France." Of his own play he noted: "I beg the reader to excuse me if these rhymes are not as well polished as an educated man would wish," but the work was composed in haste in order to greet the returning party with "some jovial spectacle."

Dropping anchor in the bay near Port Royal, Poutrincourt and the returning crew boarded their shallops to row ashore, and there on the water suddenly encountered Neptune, costumed in a blue cloak with trident in hand, seated on his "chariot," a barge pulled by six Tritons. Once this floating stage was coupled to the landing craft, Neptune delivered the play's longest speech, addressing the captain as "Sagamos," the Micmac word for "leader." In rhymed couplets, the mythological god of the sea recited instances of his aid to the French in their overseas ventures and predicted a prosperous empire for France in the New World. Trumpet flourishes introduced the second sequence: speeches by the six Tritons. The first three Tritons invoked the powers of nature and the glory of discovery. The fourth praised the courage of explorers who advanced the cause of the French monarch. The fifth, speaking in Gascon dialect, waggishly hinted at his own amorous exploits, a none-too-subtle allusion to Henri IV (who had Gascon connections and was known as a womanizer). The sixth Triton praised Henri IV with a vision of a great future for New France.

Then a canoe brought four Frenchmen impersonating Indians with gifts for Poutrincourt. The first presented a quarter of a moose, offering to employ his hunting skills in service to the civil way of life exemplified by the French. The second briefly and humbly gave some beaver skins. The lovesick third Indian spoke mostly of his sweetheart while presenting some bracelets and necklaces she had made of porcupine quills. The fourth explained his failure to bring a gift as the result of an unsuccessful hunt, but he hoped that by transferring his allegiance from Diana to Neptune he would enjoy better luck as a fisherman.

Speaking extemporaneously, Poutrincourt then thanked all the characters for their good wishes and invited the real Micmacs witnessing the event to join the Frenchmen for a meal at Port Royal. The various boats made their way to shore to the accompaniment of song, trumpets, and cannon volleys. Finally, "a companion of jolly disposition" greeted Poutrincourt as he stepped ashore, speaking a humorous epilogue to the performance—or prelude to the evening's banquet. R. Keith Hicks's 1926 loose translation captures the flavor of the original:

> *Pour your flagons, fill our glasses,*
> *Drinks for everyone that passes.*
> *Let them swill all they can swallow,*
> *Throats are dry and bellies hollow.*

A number of Micmac Indians (also known as Souriquois), including their elderly chief Membertou, joined the festivities. Communal feasting by natives and would-be colonizers apparently became a habit that winter, while the French high spirits led to their creation of the Order of Good Cheer (*L'Ordre du Bon Temps*).

Twelve speeches (called *harangues*) spoken by twelve characters comprise *The Theatre of Neptune*. Simple in structure it may be, but this dramatic poem incorporates classical allusion and wry wit, the immediacy of the occasion with a global and timeless sensibility, allegorical elements and deft touches of characterization. It even intersperses several words in the language of the Micmacs; for example, *caraconas* (bread) and *adesquidés* (friend). It might well be tied to the Renaissance tradition of the royal entry, the ceremonial public honoring of a visiting dignitary, but it could also be described as a nautical extravaganza or an allegorical masque. Furthermore, it bears similarities to the *réceptions* (dramatic dialogues geared to specific occasions) that were often performed in Jesuit schools like the one Lescarbot had attended in Paris.

Most scholars believe that performances in New France were far more extensive than the historical record indicates. In terms of documented activity, however, a thirty-four-year hiatus follows *The Theatre of Neptune*. In 1640 a double bill marked the birthday of the future Louis XIV. In addition to the tragicomedy chosen for the entertainment of the colony's social leaders (this was not long after the heyday of Alexandre Hardy's *tragicomédies* in Paris), the governor invited the Jesuits to present a mystery play that would appeal to the Native Americans who would be present. A Jesuit later wrote of the production: "We had the soul of an unbeliever pursued by two demons, who finally hurled it into a hell that vomited forth flames." For the indigenous spectators, "the struggles, cries, and shrieks of this soul and of these demons, who spoke in the Algonquin tongue," achieved such a fearful effect that at least one native was having nightmares two days later. The paired performances represented an all-too-rare cooperation between civil and religious authorities in New France.

The governor and other titled nobility in New France undoubtedly enjoyed tragicomedies on a number of occasions, either performed by themselves as a diversion or by administrative staff and citizens of the town of

Quebec. Tragicomedies by Pierre Corneille are known to have been performed in 1651, 1652, and 1693, and perhaps also in 1646. In 1694, Count Frontenac, who served twice as governor in New France (1672–82, 1689–98), mentioned dramatic pieces "which it has always been the custom to stage in this country" as well as "tragedies and comedies which were performed during the *Carnaval* in previous years." Seventeenth-century performances of secular theater in New France seem to have clustered under the governorships of three who enjoyed cultural activities (Montmagny, Lauzon, Frontenac), whereas there is no record of any such performance under the very pious governors Mézy and Denonville.

Thanks to Jesuit record-keeping, theatrical activities that took place under religious auspices can be chronicled with somewhat greater frequency than the society performances. Quebec's Jesuit secondary school was founded in 1635, and a group of Ursuline nuns arrived three years later to found a seminary for girls. Both institutions used theater for educational as well as evangelical purposes. Recitation of dramatic texts gave the students practice in memorization and elocution. Often, these exercises also served political ends, as on July 28, 1658, when a dozen students aged ten to sixteen presented a *réception* to welcome the new governor, Monsieur d'Argenson. A stage was set up in the garden of the Jesuit school, and rustic benches arranged in a semicircle could seat the entire population of Quebec (approximately two thousand). Although the author is not known, the text miraculously survived. The *harangues* of the first four children paid their formal respects to the governor in French verse. Then a student representing the Huron nation addressed the governor. As translated by Angus J. Macdougall, S.J., the speech began: "My Lord, I am aware today that I am condemned to perpetual tears. I have wept till now the loss of our country, ruined by our common enemy, by the loss of the most beautiful lake and of the most beautiful lands in the world; behold me an exile forever." But the speech culminates in his expression of loyalty to a benevolent governor. The Algonquin nation, represented by the next performer, declared that the "war, sickness, and famine" he had known since childhood had been alleviated by his embrace of the faith of the French, and thus he would shed his blood in service to the governor. Next, a student functioning as a kind of master of ceremonies, allegorically named the Universal Genius of New France, introduced four Indians (presumably also played by students) who spoke in four different native dialects which were translated into French by the Genius of the Forests. The last two of those portrayed a Huron and a Nez Percé who had been held captive by the Iroquois and appealed to the governor for protection. The clincher came near the end: the governor's reward for suppression of the cruel, rampaging Iroquois would be "immense riches in beaver skins." Other Jesuit or Ursuline-supervised *réceptions* or plays with religious content are known to have been performed in 1648, 1651, 1659, 1661, 1668, 1691, and 1727.

Theater became the catalyst for a clash between religious and civil authority in 1694. The "*Tartuffe* affair" was, in fact, the most notorious theater-related episode in the one-hundred-fifty-year history (1608–1760) of the French colony. By the end of the seventeeth century, the population of Quebec had reached seven thousand, and the prosperity brought by the fur trade encouraged the nobility in their enjoyment of cultivated pleasures. If the ladies of Quebec were only six months behind Paris in wearing the latest dress styles, as Roquebrune has noted, then intellectual and cultural fashions would have been closely followed as well. Molière's controversial comedy *Tartuffe* (1664) had been revived for the 1680 inaugural season of the Comédie-Française, and by the end of the century it had achieved 172 performances there (far more than any other Molière revival), including 14 performances in 1694. Thus it is not surprising that, after having hosted performances of Corneille's *Nicomède* and Racine's *Mithridate* at Château Saint-Louis (the governor's residence in Quebec) during the winter of 1693–94, Governor Frontenac scheduled a performance of *Tartuffe*. In fact, Frontenac had attended his sister's Paris salon when Molière himself read the play there. Although Frontenac had often performed in society theatricals, at seventy-four he preferred to watch young people presenting a play, and there were plenty of amateur actors among the members of his staff, military officers, and upper-class citizens of Quebec.

The Bishop of Quebec, Jean de la Croix-Chevrière de Saint-Vallier, a severe moral watchdog, already in 1691 had issued an "Order for the Correction of Several Abuses," in which he condemned "dances and other dangerous recreations practiced by people of different sexes, as experience has shown that they are the likely occasions for a great number of sins." Saint-Vallier had several causes for concern when he heard that *Tartuffe* was in rehearsal. First, the play itself, while mocking false piety and religious hypocrisy, somehow still carried anticlerical overtones. Moreover, certain lines in the play would trigger associations with Saint-Vallier's 1685 "Notice to the Governor and his wife concerning their obligation to set a good example for the people," which had forbidden women to bare their shoulders and neck— or to think they could get away with merely covering them with a transparent fabric. The edict was reinforced five years later when priests were asked to refuse absolution to women who still showed bare bosom despite "ample warnings of danger in this immodest fashion." Tartuffe, addressing the servant Dorine in act 3, says: "Cover that bosom which I ought not see. Such forms endanger the soul and conjure unclean thoughts." She replies: "Are you so easily tempted? Is your flesh so weak?" If playing those lines would have made a joke of Saint-Vallier's interdiction, cutting them from such a well-known play would also have called undue attention to the bishop's obsession.

Saint-Vallier's most serious objection to the planned performance of *Tartuffe* concerned the character of the man who had been put in charge of the production and was set to play the title role. Lieutenant Jacques-Théodore Cosineau de Mareuil not only bore a reputation for dissolute conduct, but he had also blasphemed, which was both a civil and religious offense. On January 16, 1694, Saint-Vallier signed two pastoral letters, one of which— "Letter on Impious Discourse"—condemned Mareuil's scandalous behavior. The other, "Letter on the Subject of Plays," reinforced an earlier directive concerning the problems associated with different kinds of comedies, but specifically named *Tartuffe* as one of the "impious" and "injurious" sort. It emphatically forbade any person in the diocese to attend a performance of it at the Château Saint-Louis. Mareuil was excommunicated and imprisoned, but eventually gained his freedom and made his way back to France.

The final showdown between bishop and governor was witnessed only by the governor's intendant, Champigny. Saint-Vallier, during a chance encounter with Frontenac and Champigny, who were out for a stroll, offered to pay a hundred *pistoles* if Frontenac would cancel the performance of *Tartuffe*. There is no question that Frontenac accepted and that Saint-Vallier paid him, but what motivated such an exchange is not clear. It has been conjectured that the money was intended to cover expenses already incurred by the cancelled production. Or perhaps Frontenac never intended to go through with the production, but took the money as a way of getting the best of Saint-Vallier. Some have even suggested that Frontenac accepted payment, then went ahead and did the play anyway in a more private location than the château. In any event, Saint-Vallier's 1694 injunction against public performances, reiterated in 1699, effectively suppressed theater in Quebec for about two centuries.

The few exceptions to the rule during the remainder of the colonial period can be briefly noted. In 1706, while Saint-Vallier was abroad, a new intendant, Jacques Raudot, had a four-act light opera performed at his residence. The reprimand that this elicited seems to have taken effect; no other such venture is known. Some school plays were excepted from Saint-Vallier's ban; for example, in 1727 a biblical pastoral written by a Jesuit was recited by seven schoolgirls who boarded at the Hôpital Général in Quebec—and Saint-Vallier himself attended! A play was performed during Carnival in Montreal in 1749, according to a surviving letter by a resident named Elisabeth Bégon. Finally, in 1757 the French troops under Captain Pierre Pouchot at Niagara indulged in play-acting as recreation. When bad weather prevented the soldiers from working on fortifications, they created a comedy sketch, *Le Vieillard dupé* (Taking advantage of the old man). Thus, the military might be credited with Quebec's first original "play" outside of an educational institution.

It was a military presence that also spurred what little English-language theatrical activity occurred during the French colonial period. Even before Champlain's permanent settlement, the English explorer Sir Humphrey Gilbert, arriving in 1583 to claim Newfoundland for Queen Elizabeth I, had brought along his own entertainers (musicians, Morris dancers, mummers) "to delight the Savage people, whom we intended to winne by all faire means possible." Not until the winter of 1743-44 was a full play performed in English: British garrison officers celebrated Christmas at Fort Anne (the former Port Royal) with a presentation of Molière's *The Misanthrope* translated into English by Paul Mascarene, lieutenant governor of Nova Scotia. Only after the British victory over the French—General James Wolfe defeating the Marquis de Montcalm on the Plains of Abraham in 1760—and the 1763 Treaty of Paris, making Britain the supreme colonial power in North America, does the history of anglophone theater in Canada begin in earnest.

# 3 *National Stages*

## THE UNITED STATES

The Treaty of Paris (1783) secured the peace, but the republican experiment continued to be torn by political tensions as Revolutionary leaders struggled to organize an effective government and to assert America's sovereignty. Not until the conclusion of the War of 1812 would independence be firmly secured. On the whole, however, the period between the 1790s and 1820s was an optimistic, increasingly prosperous era for many Americans who were buoyed by a growing sense of individualism and national identity.

Changes to the land laws promoted a rapid expansion in the settlement of the trans-Alleghany West. The Louisiana Purchase in 1803 more than doubled the size of America. New towns and cities were established and interconnected by a growing system of roads and canals. Steamboats improved travel and trade along the Mississippi and Ohio Rivers. By 1820, eleven more states had been added to the Union. Population steadily mounted from about seven million in 1810 to almost ten million in 1820 The cities of the East especially became increasingly industrialized and populous. New York, for example, went from a city of about 33,000 in 1790 to one of 124,000 by 1820.

Peace, general prosperity, and the increase in population and settlement contributed significantly to the growth of theater in the immediate postcolonial era.

BY THE 1790s, the largest American cities—New York, Boston, Philadelphia, and Charleston—had become major theatrical centers with one or more theaters in operation, each housing its own resident stock company. Many other cities—Baltimore, Savannah, Hartford, Providence, New Orleans—also had permanent theaters to host companies touring from the theatrical centers. The number of theaters and theater companies increased with the rapid expansion of population and settlement in the decades immediately after the American Revolution.

Typically, American theaters in this period were designed after eighteenth-century English theaters with circular, tiered auditoriums arranged in the standard box, pit, and gallery configuration. Like their English counterparts, they also had stages with the standard apron, proscenium arch, proscenium doors and boxes, raked stage, and orchestra space between the pit and the front of the apron. A row of iron spikes frequently separated the orchestra from the pit, though this feature disappeared in the new theaters built at the end of the eighteenth century. Lighting was provided in the auditorium by

*Left, Chestnut Street Theatre, Philadelphia (1794), showing the portico designed by Benjamin Henry Latrobe. Courtesy Free Library of Philadelphia.*

candle chandeliers that hung above the pit and candelabra attached to the fronts of boxes. The apron was illuminated by candle footlights; scenery and the upstage area were lit by candle ladders in the wings. Toward the turn of the nineteenth century, oil lamps with shades (patent lamps) began to replace candles. Dripping wax and oil fumes were a normal, expected hazard for playgoers. Theaters were heated by open fireplaces or stoves in the lobbies; some theaters also had stoves in the boxes. With the presence of so many open flames and flammable scenery and curtains, theater fires were a frequent occurrence.

Toward the end of the eighteenth century, a number of new, substantial and well-fitted playhouses were built including the Charleston (South Carolina) Theatre (1793), the Chestnut Street Theatre in Philadelphia (1794), the Federal Street Theatre in Boston (1794), and the Park Theatre in New York (1789).

The Charleston Theatre, designed by James Hoban (1762–1831), architect of the White House, and built by Thomas Wade West (1745–99), seated twelve hundred. Each box had its own rear window and venetian blind to provide appropriate ventilation in Charleston's frequently sultry weather. The theater was lit by patent lamps in glass chandeliers and was elegantly painted in French white with silver gilding. In 1804–5, it was completely repainted and ornamented, and the ceiling altered to improve the acoustics. In 1812, to provide swift exits in case of fire, thirteen doors opening directly into the street were added.

The Chestnut Street Theatre, modeled after the Theatre Royal in Bath, England, was hailed as the finest theater in America. With frequent refurbishings and remodelings over the next two decades, the Chestnut Street Theatre (also known to locals as the New Theatre) maintained its reputation as the country's best equipped and most lavishly decorated playhouse. In 1805, for example, Benjamin Henry Latrobe (1764–1820), the first professional architect in America, designed a new façade for the theater. Latrobe also reconfigured the stage apron from straight to semicircular. Above the proscenium an inscription reaffirmed the value of theater: "For useful mirth or salutary woe." In 1808 allegorical figures of Tragedy and Comedy by the noted sculptor William Rush (1756–1833) were placed in exterior niches on either side of the large central "Venetian" window above the main entrance. In 1816, the Chestnut Street became the first American theater illuminated by gas. In 1820, however, it was destroyed by fire. Latrobe's disciple William Strickland (1787–1854) designed the next Chestnut Street Theatre, again featuring niches on the façade for Rush's statues, which had been saved from the fire. That building lasted until 1855, but Rush's statues have survived and are now located in the Philadelphia Museum of Art. Meanwhile, the postcolonial period saw the addition of other Philadelphia theaters: Rickett's Amphitheater (a.k.a. Art Pantheon, 1795), the Olympic (1809), and Washington Hall (1816).

In Boston the way was paved for the city's first facility constructed specifically for use as a theater with the 1792 publication of a pamphlet titled "Effects of the Stage on the Manners of the People; and the Propriety of Encouraging and Establishing a Virtuous Theatre: By a Bostonian." The opening on February 3, 1794 of the Federal Street Theatre (a.k.a. the "Old Boston" Theatre), designed by Charles Bulfinch, did indeed mark a change in the local attitude toward theater, which was reported as "the triumph of taste and liberal feeling over bigotry and prejudice." The spacious brick structure with a covered arcade for carriages incorporated not only a stage with a thirty-one foot proscenium opening and seating for 1,060 people, but also a "noble and elegant dancing room," card and tea rooms, and kitchens. The English-born actor-manager John Bernard (1756–1828) thought it "displayed a taste and completeness worthy of London." On February 2, 1798, just four years after its opening, a fire destroyed everything but the brick shell. Although only one share of the building's seventy-thousand-dollar cost was covered by insurance, the owners promptly commissioned Bulfinch to rebuild it, which he did, with a considerably improved interior. It served Boston's playgoers until 1852.

In 1798 New York's John Street Theatre was replaced by the Park Theatre, seating two thousand. The exterior of the building was disparaged by some. Joseph Ireland, an early chronicler of the stage, for example, called it "a plain barn-like structure, devoid of any architectural pretensions." But the upper boxes were cantilevered rather than supported by sight obstructing pillars or columns—an architectural innovation for the time. The acoustics and interior decoration also were widely praised. It was regularly refurbished and renovated. After it was destroyed by fire in 1820, a second Park Theatre

*Above, Thomas Abthorpe Cooper. From Hornblow,* A History of Theatre in America, *vol. 1, 1919.*

*Left, Anne Brunton Merry and Joseph George Holman as Romeo and Juliet. Courtesy of the Harvard Theatre Collection, the Houghton Library.*

much like the first was built on the same foundations, but it also was destroyed by fire in 1848 and not rebuilt.

These were the major—but not the only—theaters built in the immediate postwar period. In 1794, for example, a second theater, the City or Church Street Theatre, was opened in Charleston by a company of French actors. Although used fairly regularly as a theater, it was remodeled as a concert hall in 1800. From 1800 to 1812, a summer theater operated at Charleston's Vaux-Hall Gardens. In 1796, Boston also had a second theater, The Haymarket, larger, but less handsome than the Federal Street Theatre. It was in operation, however, for only six years, until 1803.

In New York, fast becoming America's largest city, with a population of almost one hundred thousand by 1810, the Park Theatre was soon joined by the Anthony Street Theatre (1813–21), the Chatham Garden Theatre (1822–34), the Lafayette Theatre (1825), and the Bowery Theatre (1826), the last of which served numerous and various companies, performers, and theatergoers until 1929.

Theater building was not confined to major metropolises. By the 1820s new, permanent theaters had been erected in a number of smaller cities and towns, including Providence, Rhode Island (1795), Lexington, Kentucky (1808, the first permanent theater in the western frontier), Albany, New York (1813), Pittsburgh (1813), Baltimore (1815), Cincinnati (1820), Mobile (1824), and Salem, Massachusetts (1828). A number of theaters were built in New Orleans during the early 1800s, including the St. Philip Street Theatre (1808, the first theater to house a permanent English-speaking company in predominantly French-speaking New Orleans), and the Camp Street (a.k.a. American) Theatre (1824). In 1798 Benjamin Latrobe completed plans for a theater in Richmond, Virginia that would have been by any standards a unique, advanced design for the time, but for various reasons, the theater was never constructed.

THE AMERICAN COMPANY spent the Revolutionary War years in Jamaica where they first occupied a theater in Kingston and then later in Spanish Town on Montego Bay. In 1779, David Douglass left the company, and its management was assumed by Lewis Hallam, Jr. (1740–1808). In 1781, John Henry rejoined the company and became a copartner with Hallam. As the war ended, the partners planned their return to America.

Henry returned in 1782 to reclaim theaters in Annapolis, Philadelphia, and New York, while Hallam recruited actors in London. By the fall of 1785, the Old American Company, as it was now called, was reorganized and playing a season at the John Street Theatre in New York. For the next twenty years, despite occasional internal strife, and changes in company membership and managerial organization, the Old American Company was a major force in the development of postcolonial theater. Indeed, throughout the late 1780s and early 1790s, it monopolized theatrical activity in New York, Philadelphia, Baltimore, Annapolis, and Richmond.

In 1790 the dominance of the Old American Company was challenged, however, by its leading man Thomas Wignell (1753–1803). Angered by Henry's refusal to allow him greater managerial and artistic control, Wignell left the company, taking several actors with him. Joining with the musician Alexander Reinagle (1756–1908), Wignell formed a company which in 1794 moved into Philadelphia's new Chestnut Street Theatre. With a number of excellent actors recruited from the English stage, including James Fennell (1766–1816), Anne Brunton Merry (1769–1808), Thomas Abthorpe Cooper (1776–1849), and William Warren (1767–1832), the Chestnut Street Theatre company quickly became America's preeminent theatrical company. Indeed, with the establishment of the Chestnut Street Theatre company, the Old American Company withdrew from its regular seasonal engagements in Philadelphia and took up nearly permanent residence in New York.

By the end of the eighteenth century, several other resident companies had been established. In Charleston, for example, there were two companies whose histories through the turn of the century were often interwoven. A company headed by the French dancer, actor, and pantomimist Alexander Placide (d. 1812) and his wife Charlotte Wrighten Placide (d. 1823) performed a varied repertoire of English and French drama and pantomime at the City Theatre, while Thomas Wade West headed a company at the Charleston Theatre. The Placide company eventually took over the Charleston Theatre and West's company moved north to Virginia to develop a circuit of theaters in Richmond, Norfolk, Petersburg, Fredericksburg, and Alexandria, where it operated until the early 1800s. In addition to contributing to the development of theater in Charleston, the Placides also established one of the first American theatrical dynasties. Five of their children had distinguished theatrical careers, including Henry (1799–1870), one of the finest character actors of his time; Caroline (1798–1881), who—first as Mrs. Leigh Waring and then as Mrs. William Rufus Blake—was a leading lady in stock companies for over forty years; and Jane (1804–35), who became known as the "Queen of Drama in New Orleans," especially admired for her Lady Macbeth and Cordelia.

Although Boston lagged behind other major cities in establishing resident companies, by the late 1790s various theater companies at the Haymarket and the Federal Street Theatres competed against one another. When in 1803 the company at the Haymarket failed, however, and the theater was subsequently demolished, the Boston Theatre company held a virtual monopoly on theatrical activities in Boston for over twenty-five years.

Each of these major metropolitan theatrical companies also developed touring circuits to the smaller cities and towns in their immediate regions where they played brief engagements. For example, the Park Theatre company toured to Hartford, while the Boston Theatre company traveled to Providence, Portsmouth, and Newport. The Philadelphia company played engagements in Baltimore, Annapolis, Alexandria, and Washington. Companies out of Charleston played brief seasons in Augusta, Savannah, Richmond, Petersburg, Norfolk, and other southern towns.

Several companies not associated with the major metropolitan theater also toured the small towns and cities of the new states and developing territories. As noted above, Thomas Wade West, after leaving Charleston in 1796, headed a fairly large company which toured a regular circuit of cities in northern Virginia. In his *Memoirs* John Durang documents his theatrical tours of small towns in western Maryland and Pennsylvania (see also the section on Canada below, pp. 106–7).

From the late 1770s, the region west of the Alleghenies, particularly those lands along the major waterways of the Ohio and Mississippi River Valleys, was increasingly settled. By 1787, Lexington, Kentucky, calling itself the "Athens of the West," was an important western community, home to a university and a regionally distributed newspaper. In 1792, Kentucky was admitted to the Union. By 1808, Lexington had an amateur thespian society performing in a permanent theater managed by Noble Luke Usher, a leader of early theatricals in Kentucky. In 1810, a troupe of professional actors led by James Douglass (no relation to David Douglass) was recruited from Montreal to play in Kentucky. Soon after their arrival, one of the members of the Douglass company, William Turner, formed his own troupe to play in Cincinnati. In 1814, Samuel Drake (1769–1854), an English émigré actor working in John Bernard's Green Street Theatre company in Albany, New York, was persuaded by Luke Usher, either the son or nephew of Noble Usher, to take up residence in Kentucky. With his three sons and two daughters—Drake's wife had died the previous year—and several additional actors from Albany, Drake arrived in Frankfort in 1815. Within a decade the Drake company had supplanted the Douglass and Turner companies to become the dominant theatrical company in Kentucky and Cincinnati. Striking out on their own, several actors in Drake's company were responsible for spreading theater into other towns along the Cumberland and Mississippi Rivers. In 1817, for example, Noah Ludlow (1795–1886), one of Drake's actors, brought a company to Nashville, Tennessee. The following year, he took the first English theater company to New Orleans with a visit to Natchez, Mississippi en route and a stop in Huntsville, Alabama on his way back to Kentucky. In 1820, both the Drake and Ludlow companies performed in St. Louis. By the early 1820s, through the efforts of Drake, Ludlow, and other pioneering managers and barnstorming actors, professional theater was well-established in many of the emergent towns and cities of the southern and western frontiers.

Although their histories are often difficult to chronicle, these early frontier companies and touring troupes, whether large or small, were significant in the development of theater in the immediate postwar period and would continue to be so as America expanded its frontiers throughout the nineteenth century. McDermott describes a three-phase process, regardless of geographic or chronological location, in the development of American theater companies. The first phase was characterized by small teams of strolling players or variety performers, or small repertory companies usually comprised of eight or ten members mostly drawn from one or two families. First-phase companies played in found spaces—inns, warehouses, barns. Most significantly, they were peripatetic, moving from town to town, region to region, sometimes never visiting the same town twice. As towns grew larger and prospered economically, theatrical companies also changed. Second-phase companies were larger, sometimes boasting as many as twenty-four members with a core of experienced actors who had made names for themselves in minor-city theaters or in a first-phase theatrical troupe. Usually second-phase companies played in buildings constructed specifically for performance, repeatedly using them in an established, regular touring circuit. Finally, when a town developed into a city, some theatrical companies were then able to take up more or less permanent residence for nine or ten months of the year, playing in elaborate theaters and no longer touring extensively. This pattern of development was not mutually exclusive, nor did every company develop through all three stages. Some companies, for example, remained second-phase operations throughout their existence. In any period of the nineteenth century, however, first-, second-, and third-phase theater companies coexisted simultaneously. The pattern would be somewhat affected by the decline of resident stock companies and the rise of combination companies after the Civil War, but overall it remained remarkably consistent through the 1890s.

Until the 1790s, American theater companies were organized as profit-sharing enterprises. In 1792, however, Hallam and Henry reorganized the Old American Company as a salaried company. Other companies soon followed their lead. Salaries were usually paid by the week for three weekly performances. In the late 1790s weekly salaries ranged from four to forty dollars depending on the company and one's position in it. John Hodgkinson (1767–1805) and his wife, for example, recruited from London for the American Company, received forty dollars a week, reportedly the highest salary received by American actors at that time. In addition to their salaries, as in England, actors usually received the proceeds after expenses of one or more benefit performances each season. The proceeds of a benefit could range from one hundred to almost one thousand dollars, a significant percentage of an actor's annual salary. Actors' salaries compared favorably with those of other salaried workers of the time whose weekly pay ranged from six to ten dollars a week for a six-day work week. Paying actors a fixed salary rather than a share in the profits offered managers opportunitites for higher incomes and more artistic power and control, but also more financial responsibility and risk. Actors were sometimes disgruntled with the power of managers. As already noted, Wignell, for example, because of a dispute with managers Hallam and Henry, left the Old American Company to form his own company. In 1813, aiming to free themselves from "managerial despots," several actors, mostly from the Park and Charleston Theatres, formed an old-style profit sharing company called the Theatrical Commonwealth. Although initially successful, the company fell victim to internal squabbles and inadequate physical facilities—without permanent theaters at their disposal, they rented circus buildings in New York and Philadelphia, for example—and finally they dissolved in 1814. Though actors would continue to grumble about despotic managers, salaried companies led by managers became the standard organization of American companies throughout most of the nineteenth century.

Managing was not an easy profession. Although they often had assistants, managers were ultimately responsible for all the myriad financial and artistic operations of the theater, including leasing the theater, casting, supervising rehearsals, arranging for scenery, costumes, lighting, stage machinery, music, and musicians, and, of course paying all the bills, salaries, taxes, fees, and so forth. Early nineteenth-century managers were frequently in debt, even bankrupt, but the potential financial rewards were such that theatrical management continued to attract ambitious men and even a few women.

Among the more notable managers of the period was Stephen Price (1783–1840) who managed the Park Theatre from 1808 until his death and for a short time—1826–30—London's Drury Lane. Unlike many other managers of the time, Price was neither an actor nor a playwright, but a shrewd, sometimes unscrupulous businessman. Washington Irving mockingly called him "King Stephen" as much for his imperious, manipulative managerial methods, as for his influence in the theater of his time. After Wignell's death in 1803, his widow Anne Brunton Merry ran the Chestnut Street Theatre for a few years, but generally there was a prejudice against women as managers. When in 1806 she married William Warren, the elder, he and his partner William B. Wood (1779–1861) assumed management of the Chestnut Street Theatre, which they successfully operated, along with theaters in Washington and Baltimore, for a quarter century. Charles Gilfert (1787–1829) ran the Charleston Company of Comedians from 1817 to 1825 and developed a touring circuit to Savannah, Richmond, and other southern cities. James H. Caldwell (1793–1863) had emigrated from England to America in 1816 to perform as leading man with the Company of Comedians, but he soon quit to manage on his own. In 1819, he organized the American Company in New Orleans, sharing the eighteenth-century St. Philip Street Theatre with a French company. Over the next twenty years, Caldwell gained a near monopoly over theatrical activities in New Orleans.

IMMEDIATELY AFTER THE war American theatrical companies were organized as self-contained, resident stock companies performing two or three times a week. But in the late 1790s and early 1800s, companies began to shift toward a system by which the resident company increasingly played in support of a traveling star, usually an English actor or actress imported from London specifically for this purpose by an enterprising manager. The first such traveling or visiting star may well have been James Fennell, a

*Above, George Frederick Cooke. From Hornblow,* A History of Theatre in America *(1919).*

*Right, George Frederick Cooke as Richard III. Courtesy Lawrence and Lee Theatre Research Institute, Ohio State University.*

handsome, tall London-born actor brought to Philadelphia by Thomas Wignell in 1792. Playing in Philadelphia, Baltimore, New York, and other cities, he was admired for his Othello, Lear, Iago, Hamlet, and Jaffier in *Venice Preserv'd*. In 1796, Fennell was followed by Thomas Abthorpe Cooper and by Anne Brunton Merry. For an engagement in New York in 1801, Merry was paid one hundred dollars a week, significantly more than any leading stock actors of the day. Stephen Price, perhaps more than any other manager of the time, was responsible for promoting visiting stars. As Hewitt noted, Price "was the first to perceive the attraction of star actors from England, and he exploited that attraction with such enterprise that he altered the pattern of theatre operation in this country."

Among the stars that Price secured early in his management of the Park Theatre was George Frederick Cooke (1756–1812). Dublin-born Cooke was a traveling actor in the English provinces from the early 1770s. In 1800 he made a successful starring debut at Covent Garden where he created a sensation with his interpretations of Richard III, Shylock, Iago, Macbeth, Sir Giles Overreach, and Macklin's Sir Pertinax Mac Sycophant. Cooke made his first New York appearance on November 11, 1810, at the Park Theatre. He subsequently played engagements in Boston, Philadelphia, Providence, and Baltimore, interspersed with return engagements in New York. Hewitt calculates that under the terms of his contract with Price and Price's partner at the time, Thomas Abthorpe Cooper, Cooke made over thirty-seven hundred dollars for the sixteen nights of his first New York engagement, while Price and Cooper profited over twelve thousand dollars. As his agents in America, Price and Cooper also took a percentage of Cooke's earnings outside of New York. For example, for twenty nights in Philadelphia, William Warren paid Price and Cooper over eighty-eight hundred dollars while Cooke made over thirty-six hundred dollars. Clearly Cooke was very profitable to Price and Cooper. Unfortunately this forceful tragic actor was also a hopeless alcoholic. He died of cirrhosis of the liver in New York in September 1812 before he was able to return to England and benefit from his American-earned riches. But Cooke had demonstrated to Price and Cooper how lucrative visiting stars could be. In fact, in 1815, Cooper sold his share of the Park Theatre management to Price to return full time to starring engagements.

After Cooke, Price brought a number of English stars to America, including James W. Wallack, the elder (1795?–1864), Joseph George Holman (1764– 1817) and his daughter Agnes (fl. 1810–30), and the popular singing actor Charles Incledon (1791–1865), but none of these had the reputation or the power of Cooke. In 1820, however, Price secured the great Edmund Kean (1789–1833) for an American tour. Kean opened in *Richard III* on November 29, to a packed house at the Anthony Street Theatre. (The Park Theatre had been destroyed in a fire in May). For sixteen nights of performing, Kean received about forty-three hundred dollars, but Price and his new partner, Edmund Stimson, made about seven thousand dollars. Kean then played in Philadelphia, Baltimore, and Boston, with a return engagement in New York. Over the next fifteen years, Price brought numerous stars to

*Left, Mary Ann Dyke Duff as Ophelia after a portrait by John Neagle. Courtesy Lawrence and Lee Theatre Research Institute, Ohio State University.*

*Right, Fanny Kemble after a painting by Sir Thomas Lawrence. Courtesy Lawrence and Lee Theatre Research Institute, Ohio State University.*

America. Several would take up permanent residence in the United States, while others would continue to shuttle back and forth across the Atlantic for their entire careers. Among the more notable of Price's stars were the gifted comedian and quick-change artist Charles Mathews (1776–1835), who toured America twice, first in 1822–23 and again in 1834; Tyrone Power (1795–1841), a specialist in Irish characters toured regularly in the 1830s; the comedy actress-singer Clara Fisher (1811–98) came in 1833. Between 1832 and 1834, under Price's aegis, the ingenue Fanny Kemble (1809–93) and her father, the distinguished actor Charles Kemble (1775–1854), brother of the famous tragedian John Phillip Kemble (1757–1823), made several highly successful starring tours.

Price and his associates were not the only managers to appreciate the popularity and profitability of stars. Snelling Powell (1758–1821), for example, manager or comanager of the Boston Theatre from 1801 to 1821, was responsible for promoting the career of Mary Ann Dyke Duff (1794–1857), whom he brought to America in 1810. Although initially unnoticed, Mrs. Duff by the 1820s was widely regarded as one of the greatest tragic actresses of her time, and was even called "the American Sarah Siddons," after the great English tragedienne. By the 1820s James Caldwell also had turned to visiting stars. In his 1821–22 season at the Orleans Theatre, for example, he featured Thomas Abthorpe Cooper, who received over thirty-three hundred dollars for sixteen nights. Cooper subsequently returned to New Orleans for eight additional engagements between 1822 and 1836. He was only the first of numerous American and visiting English stars whom Caldwell engaged over the course of his career in New Orleans.

Not all English stars were imported by managers. Junius Brutus Booth (1796–1852) came to America on his own and arrived unheralded. He made his New York debut in 1821, just a few months after Kean. Like Kean, Booth was also a practitioner of the new romantic style of acting and in 1817 he had attempted to rival Kean on the London stage. Kean played only in the major

*Junius Brutus Booth as Richard III. Courtesy of the Lawrence and Lee Theatre Research Institute, Ohio State University.*

cities of the East during his two American starring tours. Booth became a permanent American resident and for over three decades plied his art not only in the major eastern and southern cities, but also in the emerging towns and cities along the Ohio and Mississippi Rivers. Volatile, passionate, subject to occasional fits of manic-depressive behavior, Booth was also an intelligent and diligent performer. Shattuck called him "America's romantic actor *par éminence*" and credited him rather than Kean with sustaining the "natural" style of acting in America to the middle of the century. He sired the most eminent tragedian of the succeeding generation, Edwin (1833–93), and the most infamous, John Wilkes (1839–65); his eldest son, Junius Brutus Jr. (1821–83), also became a respected actor and theatrical manager.

By the mid-1820s the star system was well established with dozens of traveling stars both English and American—and in the case of opera, French and Italian—touring to an increasing number of American theaters. Although the attractiveness of the resident stock company was eroded by the star system,

*Left, Royall Tyler (1758–1826) was a successful lawyer who anonymously wrote plays and poetry. Although several of his plays were published, only* The Contrast *has survived. From Arthur Hornblow,* A History of the Theatre in North America, *vol. 1, 1919.*

*Right, Royall Tyler's* The Contrast *(1787) is the first professionally produced comedy written by an American on an American subject. It points up contrasts between true-blue patriotic Americans and those who still look to the mother country for standards in fashion and manners. From Arthur Hornblow,* A History of the Theatre in North America, *vol. 1, 1919.*

it still remained the organizational backbone of American theater. Traveling stars were supported by resident companies. Indeed, without such companies there could not have been a star system. There were, furthermore, no schools for acting. The resident company provided the only training ground for performers. Would-be actors began essentially as apprentices playing "general utility" or "walking gentleman or lady" in a stock company. If they had talent and were diligent, they gradually learned their craft, advancing over the seasons to more significant lines of business and—if lucky—even to stardom.

IF ONE EXAMINES the repertory of American theater companies in the postwar period, one finds that eighteenth- and nineteenth-century English plays or translations of continental plays were the standard fare. The plays of Shakespeare, the comedies of Sheridan and Goldsmith, the farces of John O'Keefe, George Colman, and Thomas Morton were among the more popular offerings. In this respect, the repertory of American theater companies was identical to the repertory of English provincial and metropolitan theaters. This situation continued well into the nineteenth century, even after a number of American dramatists had established national reputations in the theater. In the postwar period four playwrights emerged who contributed to the development of a nascent American drama: Royall Tyler, William Dunlap, Susanna Rowson, and John Daly Burk.

Royall Tyler (1757–1826) is credited with being the first American to write a play on a native subject which was also produced by a professional company. By profession a lawyer and eventually a justice of Vermont's Supreme Court, Tyler was a prolific writer: the author of ten plays, fifty poems, a novel, and numerous essays. His theatrical fame, however, rests on his play *The Contrast,* which was first presented by the Old American Company at the John Street Theatre on April 18, 1787. *The Contrast* is essentially a romantic comedy with a strong satiric vein along the lines of Sheridan's *The School for Scandal* or *The Rivals.* The action provides a contrast between English and American character types and attitudes. Tyler used the character of Jonathan, a wily but naive rustic, servant to the hero Colonel Manly and one of the first in a long line of similar types known collectively as "Yankee" characters, to satirize contemporary theater, fashion, and social behaviors. *The Contrast* had only five performances in New York in 1787, but between its opening and 1804, the Old American Company performed it a total of thirty-eight times in Philadelphia and Baltimore. Other companies also presented it in Boston, Charleston, Norfolk, and other Virginia towns. Several of Tyler's subsequent plays were professionally produced, but none had the success of *The Contrast.*

William Dunlap (1766–1839) is often called the first professional playwright in America, and the "Father of American Drama." He was the versatile author of some sixty plays, including adaptations of plays by contemporary foreign playwrights. Among his more notable original plays are *The Father; or, American Shandyism* (1789), the second comedy by an American author to be performed on the professional stage, *The Fatal Deception; or, The Progress of*

*Guilt* (1790, revised and published in 1806 as *Leicester*), a romantic, historical tragedy centering on an episode in the life of the Elizabethian courtier Robert Dudley, first earl of Leicester (1532–88).

Dunlap's *André* (1798), a verse tragedy in typical eighteenth-century style, is about the trial and execution of the British officer Major John André, who was captured after his meeting with Benedict Arnold. Although the characterizations are weak, the versification artificial and strained, and the tone overly sentimental, the dramatic arguments at the heart of *André* are provocative, resonating with a new nation's ideological ambivalences and its efforts to articulate appropriate social goals and values. But despite the relevancy of its theme and situation, *André* closed after only three performances. Dunlap himself thought it was "a most unfortunate subject for the stage." As Richardson notes "playgoers were not ready to accept . . . a play which sought to examine in any meaningful way the unresolved conflicts between aristocratic personal values and the demands of democratic idealism which resided just below the surface of Federalist America." Bowing to popular taste, Dunlap rewrote *André*, turning it into a patriotic spectacle by incorporating scenic effects, songs, and comic episodes and retitling it *The Glory of Columbia — Her Yeomanry* (1803). The dramatic integrity of *André* was virtually destroyed, but *The Glory of Columbia* was successful with audiences. Future critics and historians, however, would judge *André* Dunlap's best play.

With *André*, Dunlap demonstrated an interest in writing plays with a significant American content and point-of-view; but as manager of the Park Theatre from 1789–1805 and again from 1806–11, he was a practical man of the theater. Early in his career as a manager, he discovered that adaptations of popular English, German, and French melodramas were successful at the box office. In the precarious profession of management, these adaptations frequently kept the wolf of bankruptcy at bay. Increasingly Dunlap's energies focused on translation and adaptation. In 1798, for example, he scored a success with *The Stranger,* an adaptation of August von Kotzebue's *Menschenhass und Reue* (Misanthropy and repentance, 1789). He subsequently may have adapted as many as sixteen of Kotzebue's plays, including in 1800 the very popular *The Spanish in Peru; or, The Death of Rolla,* usually called *Pizarro* (1794). Although Dunlap had his greatest successes with the plays of Kotzebue, he also adapted French plays, including *The Voice of Nature* (1803), based on L. C. Caigniez's *Le Jugement de Solomon,* and *The Wife of Two Husbands* (1804) from Guilbert de Pixérécourt's *La Femme à deux maris*. With his adaptations, Dunlap, for better or worse, helped establish an American taste for melodrama which was to prevail throughout most of the nineteenth century. Indeed in America, as in England, *The Stranger* and *Pizarro* remained in the repertoire of leading tragedians until midcentury.

In addition to his contributions as a playwright and manager, Dunlap wrote *A History of the American Theatre* (1832) which, despite its factual errors, is a significant historical document. He also wrote biographies of George Frederick Cooke (1813) and the novelist Charles Brockden Brown

(1815) and historical studies of New York and the arts in America. In his various plays and nondramatic writings, Dunlap laid the foundation for and promoted a national theater.

Susanna Haswell Rowson (1762–1824) was at various times in her life a novelist, actress, essayist, musician, and teacher. In 1794 she wrote her first play *Slaves in Algiers; or, A Struggle for Freedom, A Play Interspersed with Songs,* in which she also acted in Philadelphia, Baltimore, and New York. This, her only extant play, centers on the melodramatic escape of a party of Americans from captivity in Algeria. The subject had considerable relevancy at a time when Barbary Coast pirates were with impunity enslaving American travelers and plundering American merchantmen. Rowson wrote at least three other plays, all on patriotic themes: *The Female Patriot* (1795); *The Volunteers* (1795), which dramatized support for the Whiskey Rebellion of 1794; and *The Columbian Daughter; or, Americans in England.* Regrettably these plays have been lost, but they were widely admired at the time.

Although John Daly Burk (1776–1808) is credited with seven plays, he is remembered principally for *Bunker-Hill; or, The Death of General Warren,* which had its premiere at Boston's Haymarket Theatre on February 17, 1797. *Bunker-Hill* combined a romantic plot, speeches filled with patriotic sentiment, and lavish spectacle. Act 5, for example, reenacted the historical battle, using dozens of extras and special effects—smoke, flame, cannonades, and musket fire. It proved exceptionally popular, playing for ten performances in 1797 and earning Burk two thousand dollars, an enormous, unprecedented amount paid to a playwright at the time. It was also frequently revived in later years, especially on July 4. Early critics, however, deplored the play. Dunlap, for example, called it "vile trash," although he produced it with one of his own plays as an afterpiece. William W. Clapp thought it "execrable." But perhaps these were jealous reactions by rival managers.

Tyler and Dunlap, and to a lesser extent Rowson and Burk, were the best, but not the only playwrights working in America in the immediate postwar period. Merserve names a dozen or so individuals who, in the period from 1783 to 1800, had their plays presented in theaters in New York, Boston, Philadelphia, and Charleston. Many of these were amateurs whose careers were limited to one or two plays. A number of actors and actresses also contributed pieces, often adaptations of English or French originals, to the companies in which they worked. Hodgkinson, Henry, Fennell, and Mrs. Merry, for example, all wrote plays. Many of these plays, whether spectacle, farce, romantic tragedy, or melodrama—had distinctly American content. English plays—or English adaptations of continental plays—however, remained more popular with managers, actors, and, one must assume, audiences. American plays comprised only a very small portion of the repertoire. America may have won her political independence from England, but in the theater, English culture continued to dominate.

Undaunted by the tendencies of the repertoire, if not by an outright bias against American plays, numerous playwrights continued to test their mettle with American playgoers. Increasingly with the turn of the century and especially after the War of 1812, various writers and critics argued for the merit and promotion of American art and literature, including drama, and for an American culture in general, separate and distinct from English and European culture. Among the more prominent and successful playwrights to emerge in this new nationalistic period were James Nelson Barker (1784–1858), Mordecai Noah (1785–1851), and John Howard Payne (1791–1852).

Among James Nelson Barker's better plays were *Tears and Smiles* (written 1806, performed 1807), a drawing room comedy with satirical overtones set in contemporary Philadelphia, and *The Indian Princess* (1809), the first American play with an Indian subject matter and Indian characters to actually be performed. *Marmion; or, The Battle of Flodden Field* (1812), an historical verse drama inspired by Sir Walter Scott's 1808 poem, proved Barker's most successful play, however. Set in sixteenth-century Scotland and England, *Marmion* drew parallels between historical events and America in 1812. As Richardson points out, Barker's interest was "ideological rather than aesthetic. . . . Scotland becomes America's precursor state and America's conflicts with Britain are metaphorically presented in the guise of the Scottish–British conflict in the sixteenth century." In a preface to the published edition, Barker maintained that these coincidences were "perceived and felt" by American audiences. Playgoers, however, must also have been attracted by the play's medieval pageantry and melodramatic battle scenes. First performed in New York in 1812, and in Philadelphia the following year, it was frequently revived over the next decade. Barker's last play *Superstition; or, The Fanatic Father* (1824) was set in seventeenth-century New England, with a plot centering on a revengeful, fanatic Puritan clergyman, suggestive of a type that Hawthorne would so effectively sketch a few years later. Unlike *Marmion*, *Superstition*'s content was distinctly American which, although historical, argued that Americans may have escaped English tyranny but had to remain ever alert to threats to their democratic ideals. But despite its American content and superiority to *Marmion*, *Superstition* was underappreciated by Barker's contemporaries.

Mordecai Noah authored a number of very popular plays after the War of 1812. His first success was *The Wandering Boys; or, The Castle of Olival* (1812), loosely adapted from Pixérécourt's *Le Pélerin blanc; ou, les Orphelins du hameau* (1801). First produced in Charleston, it was subsequently performed in New York and even had a fairly successful run of eight performances at Covent Garden in 1814. After the war, Noah served as Consul to Tunis for six years. This experience undoubtedly provided the material for *The Siege of Tripoli* (1820) which, capitalizing on national sentiment and the romance of the Barbary Coast, also proved to be a popular success. Among Noah's other plays were *She Would Be a Soldier; or, The Plains of Chippewa* (1819) loosely based on the 1814 Battle of Chippewa; *Marion; or, The Hero of Lake George* (1821) set during the Revolution; and *The Grecian Captive; or, The Fall of Athens* (1822) adapted from a French melodrama and set during the Greek War of Independence, a conflict which resonated with many Americans at the time.

Following his debut as Young Norval in John Home's *Douglas* at the Park Theatre in 1809, John Howard Payne established a reputation as a youthful starring actor playing such roles as Romeo, Hamlet, Rolla in *Pizarro,* and Edgar in *King Lear.* After several seasons in America, he appeared at Drury Lane and then toured the provinces and Ireland. In 1815, he visited Paris where he met the famous actor Talma, who encouraged him to translate French melodramas. Over the next five years he would continue to occasionally perform, and for one season he managed London's Sadler's Wells Theatre, but Payne, less successful as an actor and manager than he had hoped, increasingly devoted his energies to playwriting. He is generally credited with sixty plays, some original, others adaptations of French melodramas. Payne's first success was *The Tragedy of Brutus; or, The Fall of Tarquin* (1818). With its popular romantic theme of patriotic rebellion, and highly charged emotional scenes, it proved a very effective vehicle for leading actors throughout the nineteenth century, from Edmund Kean, who first played it, to Edwin Booth, who made it a mainstay of his repertoire. Among Payne's other popular successes were *Thérèse; or, The Orphan of Geneva* (1821), *Charles the Second; or, The Merry Monarch* (1824), and *Clari; or, The Maid of Milan* (1823), perhaps remembered mainly for the lyrics of the incidental song "Home, Sweet Home," which he also composed.

Although he was a prolific and popular playwright, inadequate copyright laws denied Payne appropriate financial compensation for his efforts. In 1835, following a benefit performance in New Orleans, he vented his bitterness at his situation and at American managers who neglected American dramatists in favor of the latest English comedy or melodrama. An upwelling of nationalism and Jacksonian democratic ideals even then was sweeping across America. The playwrights following Tyler, Dunlap, Barker, and Payne were more numerous and skillful, their output more extensive and diverse, but the frustrations that Payne experienced would to a large extent continue to dog them for most of the century.

## MEXICO

Censorship prevented the theater in New Spain from becoming a genuine forum for examination of the Enlightenment ideas that gained currency in political clubs and literary societies after the success of the American and French revolutions. Yet the theater did play an important role in the long war for independence (1810–21). "Nationalistic sentiment," according to González Peña, "began in the theater." For the most part, the stage of the Coliseo Nuevo was filled with *costumbrismo,* plays depicting local customs, atmosphere, and modes of speech, all of which reinforced a sense of Mexican identity distinct from that of the mother country. Generations of intermarriage between *criollos* and natives had produced a population with great numbers of *mestizos,* while certain aspects of the indigenous culture—vocabulary, cuisine, folk customs—permeated all levels of the colonial social hierarchy, except perhaps the ruling *peninsulares* (born in Spain). Such factors prepared the way for the break with the mother country.

The seeds of revolution in New Spain might be traced back to 1767 when the Spanish crown asserted the state's supremacy over religious interests by decreeing the expulsion of the Jesuits from all dominions of Spain. The resulting setback to education and intellectual life in New Spain provoked a number of local uprisings, the quick, cruel suppression of which further inflamed anti-Spanish sentiment among the *criollos*. The initiating event in the independence movement occurred on September 16, 1810, when Miguel Hidalgo y Costilla, the beloved village priest of Dolores, rang the church bells and incited his mostly Indian and *mestizo* parishioners to march against tyranny. Captured and executed nine months later, Hidalgo is remembered by Mexicans as the father of his country. Hidalgo might be tenuously linked to the theater in that his translation of Molière's *Tartuffe* had been performed in San Felipe Torresmochas. Leadership of the independence movement passed to various others during the eleven-year struggle, a period in which theater remained at a low ebb. The repertoire at the Coliseo consisted of plays so often performed and so familiar to its largely *criollo* audiences that discussions in the auditorium tended to attract more attention than did the action on stage. The topical one-liners that occasionally could be woven into a performance usually alluded to the Napoleonic occupation of Spain rather than to events in provincial areas of New Spain. The hit of the 1809–10 season, *Los Patriotas de Aragón,* scathingly mocked Napoleon's army. In 1810 the stage even accommodated a monkey uniformed like Bonaparte.

*Above, Joaquín Fernández de Lizardi (c. 1774–1827), known as "El Pensador mexicano," was a journalist who wrote popular plays. From Luís González Obregón,* México viejo: epoca colonial, *1900.*

*Right, although the Coliseo Nuevo in México was dirty and foul-smelling, theatergoers who could afford to sit in the boxes came well-dressed, like the couple shown here. From Brantz Mayer,* Mexico: Aztec, Spanish, and Republican, *1852.*

Not until 1812 was any recognition of the independence movement manifested in the capital's theater, and that was a celebration of the royalist General Calleja's victory over the insurgents. The Coliseo, hung with silk banners and garlands of flowers, honored the general with festivities so lavish that the jealous viceroy refused to attend. Calleja soon attained the appointment as viceroy and won the favors of the company's leading singer, Inés García. The public's adulation of charming, black-eyed "La Inesilla" reached a peak of frenzy at her benefit night in 1813. She cleverly announced that there would be no fixed price of admission, but that she would rely instead upon the generosity of her supporters. On Calleja's orders, his aides threw more than a hundred Spanish doubloons onto the stage. Even Calleja's wife threw a valuable set of jewelry to the feet of her husband's mistress. Others threw jewels, coins, rosaries set with precious stones, and flowers, while additional donations were left on silver platters at the entrance. The Coliseo thrived during Calleja's three years as viceroy, but by 1817 the actors were once again barely subsisting.

Won over to the cause of independence by the "three guarantees" (*trigarantes*: independence, religion, equality) negotiated by General Agustín de Iturbide, the conservative *criollo* audiences celebrated at the Coliseo on three consecutive evenings (September 27–29, 1821) for the benefit of the Trigarante army. The program for the third night characterizes the festivities:

> Theatre. Saturday 29 September 1821. The first of our coveted freedom. Third program of commemoration and benefit for the Trigarante Army. A performance of the *comedia* in three acts THE FOUR SULTANAS. Embellished with all the effects required by its action, and with a toast to be sung by Don Andrés del Castillo, with lyrics corresponding to actual circumstances. During the first intermission a PATRIOTIC MARCH will be sung by the Opera Company; and during the second the quintet from DIDO ABANDONED will be danced by the principal actors of this line of business. The price of admission will be doubled, under the same terms as the two preceding programs.

Another gala evening marked the date of the actual proclamation of independence on October 27, 1821. That occasion saw the premiere of a patriotic allegorical melodrama, *Free Mexico* (*México libre*), by Mexican poet Francisco Luís Ortega. In that work, Liberty triumphs with the aid of the classical deities Athena and Mars (Wisdom and War), overcoming Despotism, Discord, Fanaticism, and Ignorance, who all confess their misdeeds, recognize their guilt, and disappear.

The national spirit began to be evident in Mexican letters and was encouraged by playwriting contests that the earliest newspapers sponsored, beginning in 1805. Although most of the winning texts are lost, the titles point to either *costumbrismo* or local history. An 1808 competition, for example, called for a "national tragedy" drawing upon "the antiquities of this hemisphere, a field unknown to Europeans," and was won by a play titled *Xóchitl*. The literary leader of the period, José Joaquin Fernández de

Lizardi (1776–1827)—although better known as Mexico's first novelist and as a journalist who used the pseudonym "El Pensador Mexicano" (the Mexican Thinker)—wrote several plays on national subjects, including *The Miraculous Apparition of Our Lady* (*Auto Mariano para recordar la milagrosa aparición de Nuestra Madre y Señora*) about the famous appearance of the Virgin of Guadalupe in 1531 to Juan Diego, a Christianized Indian; a *pastorela* titled *The Happiest Night; or, The Reward of Innocence;* the second part of a popular melodrama, *The Sensitive Negro* (*El negro sensible*, 1825); and *El unipersonal de don Agustín de Iturbide* (1823), a verse monologue in which the military hero (who made himself emperor in 1822 and abdicated in 1823) reflects upon his mistakes. The poet José Agustín de Castro (1730–1814) also wrote plays. His religious *loas* and three *autos* (published in 1809) are interesting mainly for their local references, but his two *sainetes* (1797) make lively use of popular figures of speech and rustic manners. *The Glitzy Horseman* (*El charro*) takes place at the entrance to a convent in Puebla. *The Cobblers* (*Los remendones*) portrays two married couples in a satirical look at Mexican peasant life. Anastasio María de Ochoa y Acuña (1783–1833), best known for his light amusing poetry on Mexican themes, wrote two comedies, *Love for the Empowered* (*El amor por apoderado*) and *The Orphan of Tlalnepantla* (*La huérfana de Tlalnepantla*). His tragedy *Don Alfonso* had a successful production at the Coliseo in 1811. Two plays by an unknown Mexican author premiered at the Coliseo in 1823: *The Liberal in Chains* (*El liberal entre cadenas*), a *loa* in five short acts, praised those who had won Mexico's independence, and *Despotism Vanquished* (*El despotismo abatido*) castigated the former emperor Iturbide. The latter failed, according to Reyes de la Maza, because the Mexican people have never countenanced mockery of a fallen leader.

Independence brought economic difficulties to Mexico, and these were felt in the theater of the 1820s, as frequent attendance was no longer affordable to many. Yet the practice of subsidizing the (formerly Royal) Hospital of the Indians from the Coliseo's income continued. In 1823, a proposal to cut the actors' salaries in half in order to lower admission prices was rejected by the actors. The city council then dissolved the company, closed the Coliseo, and searched for a theater manager willing to assume the risk. Victorio Rocamora, an actor–singer, accepted the challenge. He succeeded by expanding the musical variety numbers on each bill, broadening the repertoire (even including Shakespeare), and placing new emphasis on opera.

With the opening of the Teatro del Palenque de los Gallos (Cockpit Theatre) on September 9, 1823, the capital city boasted two theaters for the first time in almost two centuries. Several Coliseo artists, including Rocamora and the star singer Cecilia Ortiz, were lured over at least temporarily to the small company run by Luciano Cortés. Because this theater was open to the sky, Cortés spent a portion of his income offering masses for clement weather. Over the years until it was destroyed by fire in 1884, this theater was known by various names: Teatro Nuevo, Moderno, de las Moras, and—most often—Provisional.

At the Coliseo, another phase in its development began with the arrival in July 1824 of the moderately renowned Spanish actor Diego María Garay. Having lost his baggage, he could offer only his "slight talents" (as he wrote in a public announcement) in a "drama illustrative of our time," *The Knights Templar* (*Los Templarios*). He thanked the city council for subsidizing improved lighting and a new curtain, and acknowledged their recognition of "the advantages people gain from a cultivated theater, which is also the barometer by which the culture of nations is moderated." He further proclaimed his desire to work with the theater administration to advance artistic and political reforms. Garay's talent and dedication quickly earned the Mexican public's approval, but his inclinations proved too liberal for the church. The announced production of a dramatic exposé titled *The Inquisition Seen from Within* (*La Inquisición por dentro*) was not permitted to open. The hard-won principle of freedom of expression met its match in the power of the clergy. Garay continued to propose thought-provoking plays while welding the Coliseo actors into a disciplined repertory company. A gala program on October 15, 1824, honoring Guadalupe Victoria, the recently elected first president of the Republic, included several offerings on patriotic themes. Garay and the returned prodigal Cecilia Ortiz reigned as popular favorites at the Coliseo, although Garay's liberal views met obstacles. For example, an Italian magician named Castelli, booked into the Coliseo in August 1824, barely escaped with his life when the public denounced his sleight-of-hand tricks as witchcraft and attempted to take on the functions of the defunct Inquisition. "El Pensador Mexicano," writing about the incident in *El Sol,* deplored the fanaticism and ignorance of his fellow *ciudadanos* (citizens).

A number of documents attest to terrible conditions in the Coliseo in the 1820s. Among the commentaries culled from periodicals of the day by Reyes de la Maza, a piece published in *El Sol* (February 13, 1825) indicts boorish theatergoers as well as a callously profit-minded theater administration. The lengthy catalogue of grievances asks, for example,

> Is it enlightenment that in a free country, rich with natural resources, the Coliseo and its actors are left in such a state that foreigners look at us with scorn? . . . Is is enlightenment that they talk so vociferously in the boxes across from the proscenium that the echo mixes in with the actors' voices? . . . Is it enlightenment . . . that the prompter screeches, that the women dress with no sense of propriety, that we are given scenery full of patches and stains, and that we are inhaling the fumes given off by the poor quality of oil burned in the lamps?

The piece is signed "An unenlightened subscriber," but—despite the snide references to a couple of minor company members—it seems to represent the point of view of the theater artist more than the theatergoer. The final paragraph may be fruitfully compared with Diego María Garay's signed letters to *El Sol,* which leads one to conjecture that he may have used this means of venting his feelings anonymously:

> And is it enlightenment, finally, that this season the theater has fallen into mercenary hands that reach for nothing beyond personal gain, and that the governor's

office has cut adrift this barometer of a people's culture, depriving them furthermore of the plays which contribute so much toward combatting fanaticism and which underscore the public image and glory of a newborn Republic?

The *Semanario Político y Literario* noted the theater's poor lighting, confusion during scene changes, old scenery used interchangeably for all kinds of plays, careless play selection, too many musical numbers during intermission to the detriment of the main play, and the ridiculous practice of actors bowing or curtseying to the audience upon their first entrance. In addition to the unpleasant smell of the oil lamps which dripped and spotted the clothing of theatergoers in the orchestra, a foul odor emanating from the sanitary facilities forced spectators to cover their noses with perfumed handkerchiefs. Nor had conditions improved by 1839, when Fanny Calderón de la Barca (née Frances Erskine Inglis, 1804–82), the Scottish-born wife of Spain's ambassador to Mexico, recorded her impressions (published as *Life in Mexico*):

> In the evening we went to the theater with the Cortinas, to their box. Anything so disgusting I never saw. Such actors! Such a theater! Dark, dirty, redolent of bad odours; the passages leading to the boxes so dirty, so ill-lighted, that one is afraid in the dark to pick one's steps through them. Such darkness—horrible odours—dirtiness—are probably unequalled in theatrical annals. . . . The prompter spoke so loudly that as 'Coming events cast their shadows before,' every word was made known to the audience in confidence, before it came out upon the stage officially.

Another American eyewitness of the 1840s, Brantz Mayer, similarly reported that

> the whole performance becomes rather a sort of mere *repetition* than *acting,* as the 'comicos' invariably follow the words, uttered in quite a loud tone by a prompter, who sits in front beneath the stage with his head only partially concealed by a wooden hood. A constant reliance on this person greatly impairs the dramatic effect, and makes the whole little better than bad reading.

Fanny Calderón's observations extended to the audience:

> The whole pit smoked, the galleries smoked, the boxes smoked, the prompter smoked—a long stream of curling smoke ascending from his box, giving something oracular and Delphic to his prophecies. And more than all, the ladies smoked—so that sociability could go no further. *Il ne manquait* but that the actors should smoke—which they did, men and women in the side-scenes most devoutly. . . . The theater is certainly unworthy of this fine city.

## CANADA

Although French hegemony over the northernmost part of the continent ended with the Treaty of Paris in 1763, Canada's colonial status continued under Great Britain until July 1, 1867, when the British North America Act confederated the various regions and created the Dominion of Canada. From the beginning, the British government worked for good relations with the

French-speaking population of its new possession by accommodating the *Canadiens'* religious institutions and assuring their civil rights, a policy that was guaranteed by passage of the Quebec Act in 1774. High birth rates among the French–Canadians steadily increased their numbers, and the English-speaking population jumped dramatically after the American Revolution with the influx of up to fifty thousand refugees who remained loyal to the British crown. In the theater, the period from 1763 to 1825 saw continuing clerical suppression of francophone theater apart from school plays. There may well have been unrecorded amateur theatricals by well-born or well-educated French immigrants, almost all of whom were Freemasons and thus not easily cowed by bishops. Meanwhile, anglophone theater remained largely in the hands of amateurs and military men.

Garrison theatricals may be traced back to Marc Lescarbot's *Théâtre de Neptune* in 1606, but it was among British soldiers that such efforts became widespread and commonplace as a means of promoting good relations with the local community, raising money for charitable causes, keeping up morale despite the tedium of fortress duty, and perhaps even asserting the primacy of British culture. Because the garrison officers were socially superior to the local élite, the military men were expected to set the standard for civilized behavior, and their theater could function as a school of manners. It appears that plays were performed in virtually every British garrison at some point during the century before Confederation. Contemporary comedies from London provided the bulk of the repertoire, with occasional productions of Molière plays in English translation. In Montreal from 1774 to 1776, Edward William, commander of the Royal Artillery, rented a hall for performances and presented at least two comedies by Molière. Not only did the officers under the Scottish Commander William play the female roles, but it is believed that they paid their respects to the local culture by performing those pieces in French. (André Bourassa notes that many Scots were bilingual, having been granted dual French and Scottish citizenship from the time of Mary Queen of Scots' marriage into the French royal family.) They also expanded the usual English repertoire, even presenting some Shakespeare, and their popularity was such that Governor Haldimand granted General McLean's request in 1780 to convert a Jesuit church vestibule into a play-house. Nine years later, when the church was turned over to Anglicans, its vestibule was no longer available for performances.

In Halifax, Nova Scotia, "Gentlemen of the Army and Navy" performed *The Suspicious Husband* by Benjamin Hoadley in 1773. A 1774 production there of an anonymous three-act antislavery comedy *Acadius; or, Love in a Calm* may well mark the first English-language play written in Canada (though the text is lost). In 1788 the officers presented *The School for Scandal,* a garrison–community cooperative effort in that two boys from Halifax played the roles of the women characters. In 1789 the garrison opened the five-hundred-seat Grand Theatre in Halifax with a production of *The Merchant of Venice*. That year also brought the first known production in Saint John, New Brunswick, in a tavern owned by Thomas Mallard, a former lieutenant in the militia. Mallard's Long Room had been "converted into a pretty theater" with a stage and numbered seating for the inaugural production: *The Busy Body* by Susannah Centlivre and *Who's the Dupe?* by Hannah Cowley on a single bill, with the proceeds going to charity. Various local assemblies used the room at Mallard's over the next few years, but it is known to have served as a theater again for five productions in 1795. Saint John's first real playhouse, the Drury Lane, was opened in 1809 as a joint endeavor by officers and local amateurs who performed a number of plays there before the regiment was transferred. In Kingston, Ontario, officers and townspeople cooperated on about thirty productions in 1816–17. In St. John's, Newfoundland, around 1818 the navy built a local theater and paid for it with the proceeds from performances. Even in the Arctic, the officers and crews of British Navy ships put on plays as early as 1819 and continued the practice until 1876. Performances of the so-called Royal Arctic Theatre sometimes took place on the decks of icebound ships and sometimes in "theaters" built of ice and snow on shore. The earliest known English performance in British Columbia, in Esquimault Harbour in 1853, also took place on a naval vessel.

While the military maintained a steady stream of theater in English, the sporadic theatrical activities of French-speaking Catholics met continuing opposition from the clergy, in spite of Pope Clement's 1735 decree that actors should no longer be denied the sacraments. In the New World—where the Church functioned as the main bulwark for preserving a non-English cultural identity—the local priest could exercise pervasive influence over the lives and attitudes of the faithful. By the 1790s, in fact, Quebec's clergymen were able to shift their antitheatrical battleground from the pulpit to the confessional; that is, instead of public condemnation of performers, they deterred potential audience members by warning of the pernicious effects of theatergoing on one's spiritual health. Besides the church, other obstacles to francophone theater were the rural pattern of French settlement outside of Quebec and Montreal, and the lack of emphasis on literature in the *collèges* (secondary schools). Nevertheless, there were a few francophone theatrical initiatives during this period that merit attention.

Two French-speaking amateur groups are known to have presented plays in 1765. In April the Troupe Comédienne organized by Pierre Chartrier dit Lavictoire performed a bowdlerized or pantomimic version of Molière's *Dom Juan; ou, le Festin de pierre,* followed by some acrobatic feats, at Jean Roi's tavern in Quebec. Upper floors of taverns often functioned as performance spaces in the years before playhouses were built, because this provided a ready source of intermission refreshment for the male theatergoers. In October a group of village women came to Quebec to present *Les Fêtes villageoises* (Village festivities), a short piece undoubtedly extracted from a Paris opera, but purportedly written by one Lanoux, "celebrated poet of Canada," with a cantata and a duet by the "great musician" Zeliot. These two events were countenanced, according to Laflamme and Tourangeau, probably because both were occasional presentations in honor of Governor Murray (not to mention the fact that the appointed bishop of Quebec, Monseigneur Briand, was away in London).

*Left, the painter Louis Dulongpré left us this portrait of his friend and theatrical collaborator Joseph Quesnel (1746–1809). Inventaire des Oeuvres d'Art-Québec.*

*Right, the English actor John Bernard (1756–1828) wrote in his memoirs of his brief visits to Montreal and Quebec. He is shown here in the role of Jack Meggot in* Suspicious Husband. *From John Bernard,* Retrospections of America, 1797–1811, *1887.*

*Montreal's first theater opened in 1804 on the second story of this stone building. Franklin Graham,* Histrionic Montreal, *1902.*

Similarly, French Catholic school theatricals often honored a dignitary. These performances tended to occur at end-of-year awards ceremonies, as exemplified by the dramatized moral lessons given at the Seminary of Quebec between 1775 and 1780. In 1775 the seminary's students of logic presented *Le Monde démasqué* (Society unmasked) and students of rhetoric presented *Le Concert ridicule* (Ridiculous concert). Some schools prohibited comedies but allowed serious plays. In no instance did boys and girls perform side by side in a play, and sometimes the text of a play would be altered to do away with female characters altogether. In 1778 when the Collège de Saint Raphaël presented *Le Sacrifice d'Abraham* before Governor Haldimand (who then donated a hundred guineas to the school), a second performance was given for an audience of girls, since they had been excluded from the one for boys.

Joseph Quesnel (1746–1809) is the most important name in francophone theater of this period. The well-educated French-born businessman, adventurer, and poet had voyaged widely before his ship was captured in 1774 during a gun-running expedition for the American revolutionaries. He settled in Montreal, married, became a Canadian citizen, and went into the fur trade. In 1789, Quesnel and another recent immigrant, painter and dancing-master Louis Dulongpré, recruited five amateur actors and formed a company, sometimes referred to as the Théâtre de Société. (*Théâtres de société* or private theatricals had been fashionable among the French aristocracy.) It is likely, as some historians maintain, that these were the same Jeunes Messieurs Canadiens who later appeared in Quebec. According to a contract signed on November 11, 1789, a stage and seating for spectators would be set up in Dulongpré's house, which would be available for at least four performances. From his sixty-pound allocation, Dulongpré would also take charge of payments for scenery (three complete settings painted on canvas: a room, a forest, and a street), lighting, music, wigs, tickets, newspaper announcements, and doorkeepers. The first program, announced for November 24—Regnard's *Le Retour imprévu* (Unforeseen return) and Florian's *Deux billets* (Two tickets)—set the pattern for subsequent bills: a full-length comedy and a musical afterpiece. The endeavor generated the controversy that led the Church to revise its strategy and exploit the confessional as a means of attacking theater, and it stirred up a three-month polemic in the *Gazette de Montréal*. On December 29, Quesnel's troupe presented Regnard's cynical comedy *Le Légataire universel* (The residuary legatee) and a one-act comic opera. In response to various attacks, including one parish priest's threatening to refuse absolution to any who attended, the *Gazette* published a statement by a member of the company: "The plays we perform, decent ones, are not those you may have seen staged in France: we choose carefully, and to convince yourself that these are in no way *filled with vice-ridden intrigues,* you should take a look at the class of prominent citizens who honor us with their presence and their applause." An Englishman also wrote in defense of the francophone players: "It has always been wisely observed that French comedy is a school of good manners, which is all to the glory of France, while our own theater has too often been a school of debauchery." Quesnel himself responded by writing an innocuous work, *Colas et Colinette; ou, le Bailli dupé* (Colas and colinette; or, The bailiff confounded), Canada's first "operetta" and first original French-language play to be produced and published. Performed in 1790 on a bill with Molière's *Le Médecin malgré lui,* Quesnel's inoffensively charming pastoral comedy with songs won a warm reception in Montreal as well as in revivals in Quebec in 1805 and 1807. For the 1805 revival by Les Jeunes Messieurs Canadiens, the jovial Quesnel (who had retired to Boucherville in 1793) wrote an "Address to the Young Actors" in verse, which was published by the *Gazette de Québec* (February 7, 1805). Quesnel also wrote two additional surviving plays—a one-act political satire, *Les Républicains français* (The French republicans, 1801), and a verse comedy set in Canada, *L'Anglomanie; ou Dîner à l'anglaise* (Anglomania; or, Dining English-style, 1803)—neither of which seems to have been performed in his lifetime.

The 1790 production of *Colas and Colinette* marked the end of live theater in Montreal for five years, perhaps because the new democratically elected Parliament in Quebec drew members of Quesnel's company there. By 1791 Les Jeunes Messieurs Canadiens rented a room above John Franks's tavern and presented two Molière plays in 1791. Although their *Malade imaginaire (The Imaginary Invalid)* and *L'Avare (The Miser)* aroused the concern of Abbé Joseph-Octave Plessis, a staunch opponent of the theater who would later become bishop of Quebec (1806–25), the troupe persevered for several years, presenting ten bills of plays, mostly by Molière but also including the earliest known Canadian performance of Beaumarchais's *Le Barbier de Séville (The Barber of Seville),* which they twice revived. Indeed, their 1791 performance of it so delighted the audience that an entire act had to be encored. Nevertheless, Les Jeunes Messieurs Canadiens seem to have ceased their activities after April 1793, probably due to the unrelenting clerical opposition, which made it difficult to recruit actors. A Société de Jeunes Messieurs Canadiens (which may have comprised performers from the earlier group) staged plays in Quebec in 1814 and in Montreal in 1815, perhaps avoiding clerical censure by not settling in either place. The various performance venues used during this period are as difficult to pinpoint as is the possible continuity of the amateur troupes. Other amateur groups appeared sporadically and briefly, but there were long dry spells in both towns—notably from 1797 to 1804 and from 1809 to 1814—when there is no record of any francophone theater at all.

The earliest known amateur production in English was *The West Indian* by Richard Cumberland, performed in Halifax in 1787. Halifax enjoyed quite a bit of theater in the 1790s, much of it presented by the Gentlemen Amateurs who were particularly stimulated by the 1794 visit of His Royal Highness Prince Edward. In Saint John a group of gentlemen actors performed in the City Hall from 1795. Toronto (then York) society enjoyed play readings in private homes before its recorded theater history began in 1809 with *The School for Scandal* performed in a ballroom.

Amateur theater was gradually overtaken by visiting foreign players. An American troupe led by Giffard and Mills played Halifax in 1768. A number of American companies toured to Canada during the Revolutionary period, 1775–83, when theater was prohibited in the rebellious colonies. Several American troupes later added Halifax, Montreal, and Quebec to their New England circuit. One such was the company of Edward Allen and William Moore, which played Montreal and Quebec for many seasons beginning in 1786, setting a new standard of professionalism in both towns. An Italian family of variety performers, La Compagnie du Sieur Donegani, led by Jean Donegani and Thomas Delvecchio, played Montreal in 1788 and 1792, between American engagements. Their talents included tumbling, wire dancing, glassblowing, and athletic feats.

The American dancer–pantomimist John Durang traveled from Philadelphia to Canada in 1797 with members of Ricketts's Equestrian and Comedy Company. After rigorous treks through backwoods areas, they built a circus in Montreal and played a season there, followed by two months in Quebec in 1798. The success of Ricketts's open-air "summer" circus led to their construction of a roofed facility which incorporated a pit and a row of elevated boxes facing an equestrian ring and stage, as well as a coffee room, dressing rooms, a dome with skylights in the roof, a gallery for the orchestra above the door where the horses entered, and stables. Durang's memoirs provide a lively account of his performances in Montreal:

> I rode the foxhunter, leaping over the bar with the mounting and dismounting while in full speed, taking a flying leap on horseback through a paper sun, in character of a drunken man on horseback, tied in a sack standing on two horses while I changed to woman's clothes; rode at full speed standing on two horses, Mr. Ricketts at the same time standing on my shoulders, with master Hutchins at the same time standing in the attitude of Mercury on Mr. Ricketts' shoulders forming a pyramid. I performed the drunken soldier on horseback, still vaulted, I danced on the stage, I was the Harlequin in the pantomimes, occasionally I sang a comic song. I tumbled on the slack rope and performed on the slack wire. I introduced mechanical exhibitions in machinery and transparencies. I produced exhibitions of fireworks. In short, I was performer, machinist, painter, designer, music compiler, the bill maker, and treasurer.

Durang and Ricketts returned to Philadelphia after that season, but the circus stood for many years.

Mr. Ormsby, a Scottish actor (his first name unknown) who had managed a theater in Albany, New York, and was now traveling alone, arrived in Montreal in 1803 and rallied support for opening the town's first theater, located on the second story of a stone warehouse; he inaugurated it in 1804 with the five-act comedy *The Busy Body* and a farcical afterpiece. 1807 saw the opening of the Montreal New Theatre (capacity six hundred; the population of Montreal was then 9,568) by Mr. Prigmore, an English actor who had performed low comedy roles in New York and Philadelphia. His one-season management brought productions of Shakespeare's *The Tempest* and *Othello* as well as performances by the pioneer Kentuckian actor–manager Noble Luke Usher; Usher's wife, the actress Harriet L'Estrange; and John

Bernard. The circumstances of Bernard's Montreal engagement are entertainingly related in his memoir, *Retrospections of America, 1797–1811:*

> I found a company playing at Montreal on a sharing scheme, but as deficient in talent as in numbers. . . . I addressed a note to the theatre, expressing my wish to perform for a few nights, but received no answer. In consequence of this neglect, . . . I gave out my bills for an evening's entertainment, and, the news of my arrival soon spreading, was waited on a few hours later by several gentlemen of the town to know why I did not perform. I referred them to the management, to whom, therefore, a note was immediately forwarded, acquainting them that there would be no attendance at the theatre unless I was engaged. A low fellow, a scene painter, was accordingly sent to me to treat for terms, who actually offered me the whole concern for £300; but, not inclined to talk of this, I told them that I would engage with them on my usual terms, viz., to perform six nights for a clear benefit, which was agreed to. As, from their slight pretensions to support, the company had hitherto met with little success, they resolved to take benefits during my six nights, as their only remaining chance of indemnification. The houses proved all good, and my own an overflow, an assurance to me what Montreal could do for a manager when any proper inducement was offered to it.

Bernard then traveled to Quebec, where he gave six performances, toyed with the idea of opening a theater there, then returned to Boston.

In 1809 an English scene-painter named Allport (probably the "low fellow" who negotiated with Bernard), succeeded to the management of the Montreal Theatre and hired, among others, a Scotsman, John Duplessis Turnbull, who had acted in London and Boston. Turnbull lent his varied talents to presenting a spectacular romantic musical melodrama *The Wood Demon; or, The Clock Has Struck*. Three days before its April 20, 1809, opening, the *Montreal Gazette* published a summary of the action in French, one of many such indications of the interculturalism of the few entertainment options during that period. Turnbull is sometimes erroneously credited as the author of *The Wood Demon*, which had premiered at London's Drury Lane in 1807, the work of M. G. Lewis. Turnbull oversaw the opening of a new seven-hundred-seat playhouse in 1818 and presented melodramas there until it burned down in 1820. Various performance spaces came into use over the next few seasons, as foreign troupes appeared with increasing frequency. The need for a commodious permanent playhouse became apparent, a need to be fulfilled in 1825 by Montreal's landmark Theatre Royal.

# 4 *Romantic Enactments: 1825–70*

## THE UNITED STATES

During the first half of the nineteenth century, there was a significant expansion of territory in America. Following the Mexican War of 1846–48, additional territories were acquired in the West and Southwest. The number of states almost tripled. With the admission of California in 1850, there were now thirty-one united states. The relationship between North and South, free and slave states, proponents of states' rights and federalism increasingly strained the Union and would eventually erupt in the tragic, bloody Civil War of 1861–65.

Population also grew rapidly, and cities and towns expanded in number. New York, for example, exploded to a city of almost half a million people by 1850. With this increase in population, New York soon replaced Philadelphia as America's new urban center of commerce and culture. Both urban and western expansion were assisted by improved transportation systems—railroads, waterways, and roads. In 1825, for example, the opening of the Erie Canal contributed to the growth of western New York and to the developing Great Lakes states. Agricultural businesses and industry expanded. Despite periodic setbacks, the era was generally marked by economic prosperity for many Americans, although in the South this prosperity was wrested from the labor of black slaves.

A spirit of nationalism, already evident earlier in the century, became even more widespread and fervent with the election of Andrew Jackson in 1828. At its best, nationalism expressed itself in a spirit of progressive patriotism, expansiveness, and idealism; at its worst, it encouraged an aggressive chauvinism. Paradoxically, even while America was asserting its unique sense of mission and political independence from foreign influence in manifestos like the Monroe Doctrine and concepts like "Manifest Destiny," it could not escape the influence of European culture. In the antebellum period, for example, many American writers and artists embraced Romanticism, the dominant European aesthetic mode. But American Romanticism, for the most part, tended to be more optimistic and constructive, less radical and iconoclastic than its European counterpart. It tended also in a more democratic, populist direction; low and high culture, elitism and egalitarianism, realism and idealism often commingled in artistic works, including theatrical performances.

*Interior of new Chestnut Street Theatre, Philadelphia, c. 1820s. Courtesy Free Library of Philadelphia.*

*Interior of Niblo's Garden Theatre c. 1855. From* Ballou's Pictorial Drawing-Room Companion *(February 24, 1855).*

WITH THE INCREASE in urban populations, new and larger theaters were built in most eastern cities. In Boston, for example, the City Theatre was built in 1823 to supplement and compete with the Federal Street Theatre. It was followed by the Tremont Theatre (1827), the Boston Museum (1841), and the Howard Athenaeum (1845). In 1854 the Boston Theatre was erected after the Federal Street and Tremont theaters were closed. With a seating capacity of over three thousand, the Boston Theatre was one of the larger theaters in America at the time. In Philadelphia, the Chestnut Street Theatre, destroyed by fire in 1820, was rebuilt. In the same year a new Philadelphia theater opened, the Walnut Street Theatre, converted from the circus amphitheater called the Olympic. It survives today as the oldest functioning playhouse in America. Philadelphia's Arch Street Theatre opened in 1828. In the 1850s, Philadelphia also became an important center for minstrel shows; in 1855 the Eleventh Street Opera House was opened as Philadelphia's first all-minstrel theater.

Among the numerous theaters built in New York to meet the entertainment demands of its rapidly growing population were the Olympic (1837), modeled after Madame Vestris's Olympic Theatre in London, and the Broadway Theatre (1847). With seating for forty-five hundred, the Broadway was the largest theater in America. In 1839 Niblo's Garden, since 1828 a home to variety entertainment, expanded its offerings to include standard theatrical fare. In 1848 William E. Burton (1804–60), an English-born comedian and the manager of theaters in Philadelphia, Washington, D.C., and Baltimore, leased Palmo's Opera House (opened in 1844). As Burton's Chambers Street Theatre, it was a popular venue for farces, burlettas, and light comedy until 1850.

Since 1816 William Henry Brown, an African–American entrepreneur, had operated a rough-hewn pleasure garden, the African Grove, for the black population of lower Manhattan; blacks were excluded from the whites-only Chatham Gardens. In 1821 Brown built the African Grove Theatre (or African Theatre), the first African–American theater in the United States, where he mounted presentations of Shakespeare's tragedies, musical recitals, and his own play, the first by an African American, *The Drama of King Shotaway* (1823), about the 1795 Carib insurrection on the island of St. Vincent. Brown's presentations attracted a sizable, principally African–American audience which, as Hay points out, posed a threat to Stephen Price at the Park Theatre. The Park had a fairly large, segregated gallery for African Americans and Brown was attracting this audience to his theater. The African Theatre also raised the hackles of the pro-slavery, racist New York City sheriff and playwright Mordecai Noah, who also was Price's friend. For two years Noah, as drama critic and editor of the *National Advocate*, ridiculed the African Theatre and using his authority as sheriff repeatedly shut down performances because they ostensibly disturbed the peace of the neighborhood. Under these pressures, Brown finally was forced to disband his company. One of his leading actors, however, James Hewlett (fl. 1821–31) continued to present solo recitals for audiences in New York and Philadelphia. Another of Brown's actors, Ira Aldridge (1807–67) would have a distinguished career, but in Europe rather than America (see below). Not until after the Civil War would other black theater companies emerge. (Black theatergoers would remain segregated in white theaters in many parts of the country until after World War II.)

In South Carolina, the Charleston Theatre had served theatergoers for two decades, but after the resignation of Charles Gilfert, who had successfully managed the theater since 1817, the theater went through a succession of managers and generally poor seasons. In 1833 the theater was sold to the Medical College of the State of South Carolina and its interior converted to classrooms, offices, and laboratories. As Hoole reports, the touring Irish star Tyrone Power quipped that the theater had been "changed into a school of anatomy; so *cutting up* is still the order of the day; only this practice is no longer confined to the poets, but extends to subjects generally." Two new theaters were almost immediately built in Charleston: the Queen Street Theatre in 1833 and Seyle's New Theatre in 1837. Neither of these theaters was as handsome or comfortable as the "New" Charleston Theatre completed in 1837. With a strong stock company and regular engagements by numerous visiting stars, it became the major Charleston theater and an important theater on the southern touring circuit until the onset of the Civil War.

In New Orleans James H. Caldwell continued to solidify his theatrical management. Through the 1820s he operated out of the Camp Street Theatre. In 1835, however, he built a new theater, the St. Charles, one of the handsomest and at a cost of about $352,000, probably the most expensive theater built in America to that date. It was destroyed by fire in 1842, but replaced by another, although lesser building. In the late 1820s and early 1830s, Caldwell also operated theaters in St. Louis, Mobile, Cincinnati, and Nashville. By the late 1830s, however, Caldwell found himself in competition in New Orleans and in other southern cities and towns with the managerial partnership of Noah Ludlow and Sol Smith (1801–69).

Ludlow and Smith are principally responsible for developing theater along the Mississippi in the late 1830s and 1840s. Ludlow's early career is sketched in chapter 3. In the 1820s Ludlow operated a theater in Mobile and toured through Alabama, Tennessee, and Kentucky. In the 1830s he worked for Caldwell, managing theaters in Mobile, St. Louis, and Nashville. Smith began his theatrical career in the early 1800s as a strolling player and sometime prompter and theater manager along the midwestern frontier. In the late 1820s and early 1830s, Smith was at various times a member of the Drake company and Caldwell's Camp Street Theatre company, but mostly he toured at the head of his own company across the South, playing dozens of towns in Kentucky, Tennessee, Alabama, Georgia, and the Carolinas. In 1835 Ludlow and Smith teamed up to found the American Theatrical Commonwealth Company and to open their first St. Louis theater. They also operated a theater in Mobile. In 1838 they opened a new theater in New Orleans, calling it the New American since the locals often referred to the Camp Street Theatre as the American to distinguish it from the French-language theaters of the city. The New American was destroyed by fire in 1842, four months after the St. Charles's destruction, but it also was quickly rebuilt. After Caldwell retired from management in 1843, Ludlow and Smith managed both the New American and the St. Charles theaters through the early 1850s.

The New American and St. Charles were not the only theaters in New Orleans. In 1849 Thomas Placide (1808–77) organized the Varieties Theatre Stock Company for the presentation of opera, comedy, vaudeville, farce, and ballet. Under several managers, including the Anglo–Irish playwright and actor, Dion Boucicault (1820–90), who managed it for one season (1855–56), the Varieties operated successfully until the Civil War. Opera, mostly French, had a long tradition in New Orleans dating back to the 1790s and flourished at the Orleans Theatre throughout the antebellum era. Ludlow and Smith continued to operate their theater in St. Louis and another theater in Mobile. When they dissolved their partnership in 1853, Benedict DeBar (1812–77), an Irish-born actor, succeeded them not only in New Orleans, but also in St. Louis where he successfully built and managed several theaters until 1873.

Typically, as cities grew, theatrical entertainment was divided among several theaters, specializing in either drama, variety entertainment, or opera, although repertories often overlapped to a certain extent. By the 1860s, for example, St. Louis had seven theaters: a variety house, two German-language theaters, two theaters for amateur productions, and two theaters for legitimate drama, including occasional presentations of opera and ballet. St. Louis was not unique in having theaters for its increasing German émigré population. Large-scale emigrations from Germany in the 1830s and 1840s led to the development of numerous German-language theaters throughout the country. New Orleans also continued to have a vital professional French-language theater, which served as a center of Creole social life through the 1860s. With a rapid growth of immigrant populations after the Civil War, there would be an increasing number and variety of active, professional foreign-language theaters in America.

In the 1830s, the remarkable Chapman family troupe were touring the towns along the Ohio and Mississippi Rivers with their "Floating Theatre." Little more than a rectangular shed on a barge that was poled downriver, the Floating Theatre became the precursor to even more elaborate "showboats" that would ply America's major waterways later in the century. After the death of the family patriarch William Chapman Sr. (1764–1839), his widow carried on the family business into the mid 1840s; but gradually members of the family left showboating to play in the established stock companies of the East and South. In the early 1850s, several members of the Chapman family, including George (c. 1832–96), his wife Mary (d. 1894), William Jr., "Uncle Billy" (1799–1857), and his daughter Caroline (1818–76), made their way to California, becoming stars on the early San Francisco stage (see below).

By the 1850s many of the larger towns and cities of the Mid-South and Middle West had permanent theaters and resident stock companies. The Adelphi Theatre Company, for example, was organized in Nashville in 1850, while Memphis had a permanent theater, the Gaiety, by 1857. In Chicago, the Illinois Theatre Company performed for several seasons (1837–39) in a theater of sorts converted from an auction house. In 1847, actor and theater manager John B. Rice (1809–74) built the first permanent theater in Chicago. Although that theater was destroyed by fire in 1850, Rice almost immediately built another theater. By the 1850s, Chicago's population had grown to about twenty thousand, but this was still insufficient to sustain two theaters. Faced by stiff competition from actor James H. McVicker (1822–96), who in 1857 erected a splendid theater bearing his own name, Rice retired from theatrical involvement in 1861 and converted his theater to a business property. (Rice subsequently served as mayor of Chicago from 1865 to 1869 and as an Illinois congressman from 1872 until his death). After the Civil War, McVicker's Theatre became one of America's leading stock companies.

Other Great Lakes cities soon followed Chicago in building theaters and organizing companies. In Cleveland, for example, a stock company was organized in 1853 by John A. Ellsler (1822–1903), who for the next thirty years dominated theatrical activities not only there, but in several other Ohio cities and towns. Milwaukee had at least two theaters—the Temple of Thalia and Young's Hall—by the early 1850s. In the same period, an entrepreneur in Toledo built two "entertainment halls"—Union Hall and Duell Hall—where companies regularly touring the upper Middle West presented a range of dramatic entertainment, including minstrel shows and performances of *Uncle Tom's Cabin.*

By the eve of the Civil War, permanent theaters and regular theatrical touring circuits were well established throughout most of the eastern half of the United States. The landmass west of the Missouri River was still a largely undeveloped frontier—called variously "Indian Territory" or "Unorganized Territory"—but in the 1850s, California began to develop as the new theatrical El Dorado. That story is covered later in this chapter.

EXPANSIONIST THEATRICAL TENDENCIES required an ever-increasing number of actors—in fact, theatrical personnel of all specialties. In the colonial and immediate postcolonial era, theaters, in large part, depended on English émigré or visiting performers. In the mid-1820s, however, this situation gradually changed as more and more native-born actors entered the profession.

American theatrical companies continued to be organized as resident stock companies supplemented by traveling stars. Typical salaries for stock actors remained modest. In the mid-1850s, for example, a salary list for Baltimore's Holliday Street Theatre discloses that the highest salary was thirty dollars a week for the "Old Man" in the company; the "Leading Man" and "Leading Lady" were each paid twenty-five dollars a week; the "Juvenile" was paid fifteen dollars; and the "utility" performers were paid either eight or five dollars, depending on their experience. A star might make several hundred dollars or more a week. As the populations of cities and towns grew, the number of urban theaters increased correspondingly. Competition for audiences remained keen, and successful managers knew that stars drew at the box office.

English stars continued to be an attraction, especially in major metropolitan theaters. Fanny Kemble's passionate but refined acting style, especially her portrayals of Julia in Sheridan Knowles's romantic drama *The Hunchback* and Shakespeare's Juliet, won the appreciation of a growing number of sophisticated American playgoers. The great tragedian William Charles Macready (1793–1873) successfully toured in 1826–27, 1843–44, and 1849, earning widespread acclaim. Nationalistic attitudes, however, made major English stars less welcome in the Jacksonian and antebellum period than in the past. English actors would continue to cross the Atlantic, but most of them would come as émigrés, rather than as touring stars.

With stars in demand, numerous ambitious, talented American actors—even many who were not particularly talented—aimed for star billing as quickly as possible. Generally stars followed the English classical tradition. They performed in Shakespeare's plays and other standard English plays of the eighteenth and nineteenth centuries, although they might also include in their repertoires roles in contemporary plays, sometimes written expressly for them. Tragedians acted principally in serious plays—tragedies and historical, romantic dramas or melodramas—but their repertoires might include a few comic roles, usually in such standard pieces as *The School for Scandal*. Versatility was one of the hallmarks of the traditional nineteenth-century tragedian. Increasingly, however, driven by a combination of audience expectations and special or limited talents, some stars began to specialize in a single type of role—romantic heroines, for example, or Irish comic characters—sometimes even in one or two specific roles. More so than in the past, in the nineteenth-century American theater, the term "star" encompassed a fairly wide range of actors, roles, and styles of acting. Among American-born actors, Edwin Forrest (1806–72) and Charlotte Cushman (1816–76) were the first to achieve major star status.

Forrest made his professional debut at the Walnut Street Theatre in 1820. For several years, he served his theatrical apprenticeship playing the towns and cities on the Ohio Valley circuit. For one season (1824–25), he was a member of Caldwell's American Theatre company in New Orleans. A turning point in his career occurred the next season when he was engaged to play second leads to Edmund Kean's performances in Albany: Iago to Kean's Othello, Richmond to his Richard III, and Titus to his Brutus (Payne's *Brutus; or, The Fall of Tarquin*). Kean recognized Forrest's talent, privately encouraged him, and publicly praised his gifts; Forrest, in turn, incorporated elements of Kean's romantic style into his own acting. In the summer of 1826, Forrest made his first New York appearance as Othello at the Park Theatre; and on the strength of this performance, he was engaged in the fall as the leading man at the Bowery Theatre. He soon struck out on his own as a traveling star playing engagements at the major theaters in the East, South, and Middle West. Over the next forty years, until his stardom was eclipsed by advancing age and by younger performers like Edwin Booth, Forrest was the most recognized and popular tragedian on the American stage. He played all the great roles in the traditional tragedian's repertoire of the time, including Richard III, Coriolanus, Hamlet, Macbeth, William Tell in an adaptation of Schiller's play, Rolla in Sheridan's adaptation of A. F. F. von Kotzebue's *Pizarro*, and Cardinal Richelieu in *Richelieu; or, The Conspiracy* by Edward Bulwer-Lytton.

*Left, Edwin Forrest as Richard III. Courtesy Lawrence and Lee Theatre Research Institute, Ohio State University.*

*Right, Edwin Forrest as Metamora. Courtesy Lawrence and Lee Theatre Research Institute, Ohio State University.*

Handsome, with a penetrating voice and a powerful physique developed through a regimen of strenuous calisthenic workouts with dumbbells, Forrest was at his best and most comfortable playing strong, uncomplicated, heroic rebels. There were not many such roles in the standard repertoire, however. In 1829, he promoted the cause of American drama and his own career and interests by offering "a prize for the best tragedy, in five acts, of which the hero . . . shall be an aboriginal of this country." The winner was John Augustus Stone's *Metamora; or, The Last of the Wampanoags*. The title character, combining traits of heroic nobility with savagery, became a popular mainstay in Forrest's repertoire throughout his career. It also stimulated a series of plays centered on Native Americans. Over the next few years, Forrest awarded thousands of dollars in prizes for original plays by American playwrights, although only a few of these remained in his permanent repertoire. Robert Montgomery Bird's (1806–54) *The Gladiator* (1831), about Spartacus, the slave and gladiator who led a slave rebellion in 71–73 B.C.E. routing several Roman armies before he was finally captured and executed, was one of Forrest's most successful roles. Robert T. Conrad's (1810–58) *Jack Cade* (1835), about the fifteenth-century rebel who, like Spartacus, led

*Edwin Forrest as Spartacus. From* The Stage and Its Stars Past and Present. *Howard Paul and George Gebbie, eds. (1890). Courtesy Curtis Theatre Collection, University of Pittsburgh Library.*

an insurrection of Kentishmen against the oppressive government of Henry VI, was also a popular Forrest impersonation. These heroic rebels and the theme of individual freedom opposed to tyranny struck a sympathetic chord with Jacksonian playgoers. They were also ideal vehicles for Forrest's muscular, emotionally passionate style of acting.

In 1836 and again in 1845, Forrest successfully starred in London and then made a starring tour of several English cities. During his second tour, Forrest was, in contrast to his first tour, cooly, even hostilely received by certain critics. On one occasion, his performance was disrupted by a claque who hissed and laughed inappropriately. Forrest suspected that the English actor William Charles Macready had influenced and arranged this reception. In fact, as his *Diaries* reveal, Macready was privately resentful and contemptuous of Forrest, but he publicly denied any responsibility for Forrest's treatment. Although in the past the two had a professionally collegial relationship, they now became bitter opponents, each nursing a grudge against the other. One night in Edinburgh, Forrest attended a Macready performance and at one point loudly hissed the eminent English tragedian. It was a scandalous breach of theatrical etiquette. Reporters on both sides of the Atlantic jumped on the incident and fanned the antagonism between the two actors. Many of Forrest's American supporters, for example, viewed his gesture as fully justified, considering the ill treatment their hero had received from Macready and the London critics.

When in 1849 Macready embarked on his third starring tour of America, numerous playgoers and some critics viewed him as the enemy of their idol Forrest. Undoubtedly this view was fueled by a widespread general resentment of foreign influence, principally among the urban working class, many of whom were rabid Forrest loyalists. The situation finally came to a head on May 7, 1849, at the Astor Place Opera House in New York during Macready's scheduled performance as Macbeth. When Macready made his first entrance, he was assaulted, mainly by the gallery audience, by hisses and catcalls. Cheers, applause, and waving handkerchiefs from the boxes were not a counterdeterrent. The attack was intensified with rotten eggs, vegetables, and asafoetida raining down on the actors, but they courageously carried on through two acts. When the gallery hooligans began throwing chairs, however, the manager rang down the curtain. Macready determined to leave for England the next day, but he was persuaded by a delegation of prominent New Yorkers, including the writers Washington Irving and Herman Melville, to attempt another performance on May 10. On this occasion, opposition to Macready and the forces to protect him were even more organized than at the earlier aborted performance. Various nativist groups such as the Native Sons of America and the Order of United Americans were organized to disrupt the performance; over three hundred policemen were positioned in the theater, and outside the theater a company of soldiers was placed at the ready, all to maintain order. Thousands crowded into Astor Place before the theater opened. When Macready entered, the audience exploded with hisses, boos, and catcalls. The police arrested three troublemakers. When the crowd outside was informed of this action, they stormed the theater hurling bricks, boards, and paving stones. The police attempted to quell the mob, but they were significantly outnumbered. The soldiers were then called in. Macready stubbornly struggled through the performance, even while a mob rioted in Astor Place. Failing to disperse the crowd by their mere appearance and then attacked themselves, the soldiers were given the order to fire. Perhaps as many as 31 rioters were killed and 150 wounded.

Throughout both incidents, Forrest had kept his distance, performing at the Broadway Theatre about a mile from Astor Place. He maintained that he had no part in organizing or even encouraging opposition to Macready. But he did nothing to prevent it and afterwards he received a number of congratulatory letters for having routed Macready. He would always be associated with the Astor Place Riot and, as Charles Shattuck notes, this would "lower his credit with cultivated and genteel folk, who . . . had never been quite at ease" with his robust, romantic acting style. Forrest's reputation, at least with certain playgoers, was damaged further in 1851, when he attempted to divorce his wife Catherine Sinclair (1817–91) on the grounds of adultery, only to be countersued on the same grounds. At a time when such proceedings were rare, the divorce trial as reported by the press caused a scandal. Forrest lost his suit, was publicly branded an adulterer, and ordered to pay alimony of three thousand dollars a year. Enraged and humiliated, Forrest contested the alimony order; the legal haggling continued for over fifteen years.

Catherine Sinclair, almost immediately after the trial, embarked on a fairly successful theatrical career in California. Forrest, protesting his innocence, was embittered by the outcome of the divorce trial. He identified even more strongly with King Lear as—"a man more sinned against than sinning." In the late 1850s, his histrionic power was diminished by gout, rheumatism, and sciatica, but he remained a popular box office attraction.

Forrest's success spawned numerous imitators and disciples. While some presented only crude caricatures of the "heroic school" of American acting, others gave Forrest genuine competition. Augustus A. Addams (d. 1851), for example, was felt by many critics to excel Forrest in many heroic roles, but premature death cut short his promising career. John R. Scott (1809–56) was also considered a rival to Forrest, but he abandoned tragedy for less demanding roles in sensational, popular melodramas. Joseph Proctor (1816–97) had a long, generally successful career on the American stage. While he acted many of the great tragic roles, he became mainly identified with the leading role in the popular frontier melodrama *Nick of the Woods,* adapted from Robert Montgomery Bird's novel by Louisa Medina (c. 1813–38), one of the era's more successful woman dramatists. As the theatrical memorialist Walter Moore Leman noted, if Proctor played "the Jibbenainosay [one of the names for the main character in *Nick of the Woods*] more frequently than Shakespeare, it is not that he loved the immortal bard less, but that the multitude loved the Jibbenainosay the more." Proctor's experience was typical of many American actors in an era when melodrama was increasingly more popular and prevalent than tragic drama.

Charlotte Cushman was widely regarded as the greatest American actress of her generation, lauded not only in her own country, but abroad as well. She originally trained as an opera singer. Her first professional engagement was in a company led by the English-born and trained actress/singer Clara Fisher at the St. Charles Theatre in New Orleans in 1835–36. Although blessed with a vocal range of almost two full registers, Cushman was a natural contralto. But since Clara Fisher was a contralto, Cushman was forced into soprano roles. The strain of almost nightly performances eventually proved too much; her voice was so badly damaged that an operatic career seemed unlikely. When she reported her anxieties to James Caldwell, he advised her instead to consider straight acting and placed her under the tutelage of James Barton (d. 1848), an old-line, experienced tragedian in the St. Charles stock company. Barton rehearsed her for Lady Macbeth and together they teamed in a very successful performance of the "Scottish play" on April 23, 1836. Lady Macbeth subsequently became one of Cushman's most popular roles.

Cushman's success in New Orleans, did not immediately catapult her to stardom. She made a successful New York debut as Lady Macbeth at the Bowery Theatre on September 12, 1836, and followed this with well-received performances in such plays as *The Stranger, Rob Roy,* and *Jane Shore.* Two weeks later, however, her career suffered a setback when the Bowery was destroyed in a fire. There followed an engagement at the Pearl Street Theatre

*Left, Charlotte Cushman as Lady Macbeth. From Hornblow,* A History of American Theatre, *vol. 1, 1919.*

*Right, Charlotte Cushman c. 1870s. From Appelbaum,* Great Actors and Actresses of the American Stage in Historic Photographs. *Courtesy Dover Publications, Inc.*

in Albany where she opened again as Lady Macbeth opposite Junius Brutus Booth. Tall for a woman of her day, large boned, and square jawed with a powerful, husky voice, she was especially popular with Albany audiences in "breeches" parts. She closed her engagement, for example, with a performance as Romeo which proved so successful that it became one of her standard roles.

Leaving Albany, Cushman continued her professional apprenticeship as a "walking lady" at the Park Theatre. Here for three seasons, she played a wide variety of roles, including two which she would claim as her own: the weird, gypsy hag Meg Merriles in an adaptation of Sir Walter Scott's *Guy Mannering* and the pathetic Nancy Sikes in an adaptation of Charles Dickens's *Oliver Twist.* At the Park, Cushman also played in support of some of the finest actors on the American stage at this time, including the transplanted English tragedian James W. Wallack, the elder, and the great Forrest.

In 1840 she was hired as the leading lady at William Burton's new National Theatre in Philadelphia. When Macready came to America in 1843, he asked that Cushman support him in several of his roles. He urged her to go to England. Although Cushman had reservations about such a venture, she realized that only through a successful engagement in London might she become a full-fledged star, a distaff equal to Forrest and Macready. After several frustrating months of attempting to arrange a London engagement, she finally opened as Bianca in *Fazio,* on February 13, 1845 at the Princess's Theatre. A romantic, melodramatic tale of betrayal, seduction, madness, and tragic death, it was an excellent vehicle for Cushman's formidable powers. London critics and audiences praised the performance. She remained in England for two years, starring at the Haymarket and Princess's Theatre—at the latter with Macready—and touring the major Provincial theaters. She reaped accolades not only for her Lady Macbeth, Nancy Sikes, and Meg Merriles, but also for her Rosalind, Emilia, Queen Katherine, and Romeo.

When Cushman came home in 1849, she, like Mary Ann Duff, was also hailed as "the Siddons of America." The next twenty-five years of her career were spent in lucrative starring engagements and tours in both America and England. Between engagements, she retired to an apartment she had leased in Rome and there she entertained visiting American and British intellectuals and artists, including Nathaniel Hawthorne, Harriet Beecher Stowe, poets Robert and Elizabeth Browning, Anthony Trollope, sculptor William Wetmore Storey, and many others.

A diagnosis of breast cancer and a series of subsequent operations, including a mastectomy in 1869, sharply curtailed Cushman's professional life. She spent her remaining years as a platform reader, delivering monologues from her celebrated performances and reciting light poetry. In November 1874, after a final performance as Lady Macbeth at Booth's Theatre, New Yorkers fêted her with an extravagant farewell celebration, unique in the annals of the American stage. Speeches, poetry readings, the presentation of a laurel crown, and a torchlight parade complete with a military band to escort her from the theater to her hotel, celebrated "our Charlotte."

Cushman had few competitors as a tragedienne in the antebellum era. Josephine Clifton (1813?–47) might have equaled Cushman had her career lasted as long. Nearly six feet tall, Clifton created a similar striking, formidable physical presence on stage, and reputably was rather more feminine and attractive than Cushman. She was, furthermore, the first American-born actress to star in England, making her London debut as Belvidera in Otway's *Venice Preserved* at Covent Garden in 1834, a decade before Cushman. She remained in England for two seasons polishing her art by playing in the companies at both Covent Garden and Drury Lane and touring the Provincial theaters. When she returned to America, "the magnificent Josephine," as she was styled, successfully toured as a star throughout the eastern seaboard, southern, and mid-western circuits, including a season touring with Forrest. (Clifton was the accused "other woman" in the Forrest–Sinclair divorce case.) She was celebrated for her Lady Macbeth, Jane Shore, and Bianca Visconti, a role created especially for her by the playwright–essayist Nathaniel Parker Willis (1806–67) in 1837. In 1846, she married Robert Place, manager at the time of the American Theatre in New Orleans, but then unexpectedly died the following year.

As an American actor, Ira Aldridge had a unique career. A year after the closing of the African Theatre, Aldridge departed the United States for England. There for the next twenty-five years, he played the provincial circuit, honing his talent and skills, and attracting a popular and critical following. In 1833, Aldridge took over as Othello for the critically ill Edmund

Kean at Covent Garden. For the first time an American actor had starred at one of the English-speaking world's major theaters. That the role was Othello and Aldridge was a black American made the achievement even more noteworthy. But critical reaction to his performance was mixed, and instead of becoming a London star Aldridge returned to the provincial circuit. In 1852 he left England for a series of starring tours on the continent, where he received popular and critical acclaim and numerous official accolades and honors. A starring engagement at Covent Garden in 1858 finally won him the approval of London's critics and audiences. For the next seven years, he played in England and Europe. In 1863 he became a British citizen. In 1865 he left England for an extended European tour, but died during an engagement at Lódz, Poland. Over the course of his career, Aldridge played over forty roles, including not only Shakespeare's Othello, but also King Lear, Macbeth, Shylock, Richard III, and Aaron in *Titus Andronicus*. A versatile actor, he included in his repertoire a range of characters, both black and white, in comic, melodramatic, and tragic roles in  both classical and contemporary dramas. His acting style was most often compared to William Charles Macready's and he was frequently praised for his naturalism and emotional restraint. That Aldridge was forced to ply his considerable talents abroad was a significant loss to the American stage .

While Forrest was the model of a uniquely American heroic style, other American tragedians of the time adhered to the time-worn classical tradition.

*Ira Aldridge. Courtesy of the Harvard Theatre Collection, the Houghton Library.*

Edward Loomis Davenport (1815–77) and James E. Murdoch (1811–93) were the exemplars of this style.

Born in Boston, Davenport made his theatrical debut in Providence playing a small role in *A New Way to Pay Old Debts* in support of Junius Brutus Booth's Sir Giles Overreach. There followed a decade of playing small roles in stock companies in Boston, Philadelphia, and New York. By the mid-1840s, he was playing leading roles at the Bowery Theatre. In 1846 Anna Cora Mowatt (1819–70)—who was best known as the author of the social comedy *Fashion* (1845), but had also started a professional starring career—hired Davenport to be her leading man for a national tour. She even wrote *Armand, the Child of the People* (1847), a romantic play in blank verse, to suit her talents and those of Davenport. In the fall of 1847, Davenport and Mowatt embarked to England for a starring tour of London and the English provinces which proved very successful. Davenport would remain in England for the next seven years, playing in support of such English stars as Gustavus Vaughan Brooke (1818–66) and Macready, and touring the provinces on his own as an American tragedian. He gradually won the admiration of the English critics for his performances as Shakespeare's Brutus, Laertes, Macduff, Iago, Othello, and Shylock, as well as William the Sailor in Douglas Jerrold's popular melodrama *Black-Eyed Susan* (1829). While in England, Davenport married Fanny Vining (1829–91), an actress and the daughter of the London comedian and theater manager Frederick Vining. Several of their children, most notably Fanny (1850–98), would also be active in the theater.

In 1854 Davenport returned to America, where for over twenty years he established a successful career as a star, playing in all the major theaters of the East and Mid-West. In the late 1850s and early 1860s, Davenport also managed several theaters, most notably Boston's Howard Athenaeum, and with James W. Wallack Jr. (1818–73) he co-managed a successful touring combination company. Davenport's repertoire ranged over dozens of characters—clowns, melodramatic villains, and tragic heroes. Until it was eclipsed by Edwin Booth, Davenport's Hamlet was considered the finest of its day. His Sir Giles Overreach was judged equal to the stirring impersonations of the elder Booth and Kean.

Davenport was capable of projecting emotional energy and intensity, but he was not known, as was Forrest, for his physical power. He was relatively tall and had a strong, melodious voice, but he was, as Charles Shattuck writes, "a master of historic technique and a precisionist rather than an overwhelmer in performance." A contemporary, Henry Dickinson Stone, observed that in Davenport's interpretations "calm judgment ruled over impulse." He was sometimes even criticized for being overly intellectual. Ultimately his versatility may have worked to his disadvantage. Playing with equal success such diverse characters as Hamlet, Dickens's Bill Sikes, and Sheridan's Lucius O'Trigger, it was his unwillingness or inability to specialize in a narrow line of business that prevented him from winning widespread popular recognition as a star. Furthermore, he had none of the offstage attitudes and behaviors that are sometimes associated with major stars. He was not reckless, eccentric, or volatile, but noted for his gentlemanliness, geniality, and patience.

James E. Murdoch was expected to enter his father's Philadelphia book-binding business, but as a teenager he joined a local amateur dramatic group and studied elocution under two of the cities noted Philadelphia elocutionists, Lemuel G. White (b. 1792) and Dr. James Rush (1786–1869). In 1829 he made his professional debut at the Arch Street Theatre in Philadelphia as Frederick in Kotzebue's *Lover's Vows*. For the next decade, he played in various stock companies in New York, Boston, Philadelphia, Pittsburgh, Mobile, New Orleans, and Augusta, Georgia, where he came to the attention of Edwin Forrest who touted young Murdoch's talent. Two years later, however, Murdoch, suffering from an attack of indigestion, mistakenly took a preparation containing arsenic. Although he recovered, his health was permanently affected. The course of his subsequent career was occasionally interrupted by periods when he temporarily left the stage to recuperate and pursue his elocution studies. In the early 1840s, Murdoch quit acting to teach and lecture on elocution, Shakespearean characters, and "The Uses and Abuses of the Stage." But in 1845, he was back in harness, appearing with distinction at the Park Theatre as Hamlet. For the next fifteen years, Murdoch, like Davenport, established a reputation as a versatile and popular traveling star. He was noted for his interpretations of Hamlet, Macbeth, Othello, Charles de Moor in Schiller's *The Robbers*, Claude Melnotte in *The Lady of Lyons,* but also for light comic roles like Charles Surface in *The School for Scandal* and Rover in *Wild Oats*. In 1853–54, he was one of the first American stars to tour California where he was very well received, but ill health again forced him to return East. In 1856, he starred in London at the Haymarket Theatre for 110 consecutive nights. During the Civil War, he again retired from the professional stage, to tour Union war camps and hospitals reciting patriotic poems. After the war, he devoted most of his time to teaching, lecturing, and writing.

Although they were not stars in the same bravura mold as Cushman and Clifton, Anna Cora Mowatt, Matilda Heron (1830–77), and Laura Keene (1826?–73) nonetheless were actresses who left their mark on the era.

Before she decided to become an actress, Mowatt was successful as an author and platform reader. Indeed, as noted above, she was best known for *Fashion,* her sprightly, very popular comedy of American manners. When her husband suffered some financial setbacks shortly after the premiere of *Fashion,* Mowatt, with no real training or acting experience, and after only three weeks of rehearsal, launched herself as a star, making her debut as Pauline in *The Lady of Lyons* at the Park Theatre in June 1845. Limiting herself to romantic heroines such as Julia in *The Hunchback* and Shakespeare's Juliet, or high comedy roles such as Katherina in *The Taming of the Shrew* or Lady Teazle, Mowatt was widely praised for the naturalness of her acting style. She proved a popular performer not only in America but also in England during two starring tours in 1847 and 1851. But in 1854 at the peak of her popularity, failing health forced her abrupt retirement.

Irish-born Matilda Heron made her debut in 1851, playing standard romantic heroines such as Shakespeare's Juliet and Bianca in Bulwer's *Fazio; or, The Bride of Mantua*. In 1854, however, during a holiday in Paris, she saw

Mme. Doche's rendition of Marguerite Gautier in Dumas's *The Lady of the Camellias* by Alexandre Dumas *fils.* She was inspired to adapt her own version, entitled *Camille,* appearing in it for the first time in New Orleans in 1855. Although she continued to play other roles, she became identified almost solely with *Camille.* Like Mowatt, Heron also was praised for her naturalistic effects. In Camille's death scene, the effects were so detailed, for example, that many spectators found the moment mordantly fascinating. Theatergoers flocked to her performances for twenty years. The noted critic William Winter commended her "elemental power," "startling personality," and "wildness of emotion." Indeed, Heron was the model for a school of so-called emotionalistic or sensation acting which peaked in popularity during the Gilded Age.

English-born Laura Keene initially appeared with Madame Vestris's noted Olympic Theatre Company in London. In 1852, however, James W. Wallack the elder hired her as leading lady for his New York theater company. Here she achieved success in such standard comic roles as Lady Teazle, Lady Gay Spanker in *London Assurance,* and Beatrice in *Much Ado about Nothing,* often playing opposite James's son Lester (1820–88) who was particularly adept in English gentlemen roles. After a season with Wallack, Keene struck off on her own as a touring star and theater manager. After managing theaters in Baltimore and San Francisco, she returned to New York in 1855 to manage and star at her own theater. Although in the course of her career, Keene played a wide range of roles, her strengths as an actress lay in high comedy and intensely passionate melodramas. She also was one of the most successful managers of the time, known for the attention and expense she lavished on her productions and for the excellence of her companies, which often included many of the best players of the day. After she retired from management, she returned to touring until her premature death.

Although many tragedians also included a few comic roles in their repertoires, comic acting was generally a specialty field. Among the leading antebellum comic actors were Henry Placide (1799–1870), William E. Burton, John Gilbert (1810–89), and William Warren (1812–88).

After a decade as a child actor, Placide, son of the actor–manager Alexander Placide, made his adult debut in 1823 at New York's Park Theatre as Zekiel Homespun, a character in George Colman's popular farce *The Heir-at-Law.* He remained at the Park for twenty years playing over five hundred mainly comic roles, ranging from middle-aged English gentleman to country bumpkins. Edwin Forrest considered him "the best general actor on the American boards."

Burton emigrated from England to America in 1834. By the early 1840s he was managing and starring at theaters in Philadelphia, Baltimore, and Washington, D.C. In 1848, as noted above, he opened his own theater in New York: Burton's Chambers Street Theatre. Burton's Theatre boasted a talented company and his scenically lavish mountings of *The Merry Wives of Windsor, The Winter's Tale,* and *A Midsummer Night's Dream* were among the finest Shakespearean productions in America to that time. But audiences

*James Henry Hackett as Falstaff. From Hornblow, A History of Theatre in America, vol. 1, 1919.*

*Left, The comedian William Warren. Theatre Cabinet Photographs Collection, Special Collections Library, University of Michigan.*

*Right, John Gilbert as Sir Anthony Absolute in Sheridan's The Rivals. Theatre Cabinet Photographs Collection, Special Collections Library, University of Michigan.*

came mainly to see Burton perform such roles as Tony Lumpkin, Bob Acres, Falstaff, and Bottom, and especially Timothy Toodles in his own play *The Toodles,* of which theatergoers seemingly never tired. Laurence Hutton (1843–1904), a theatrical historian and biographer, called Burton "the funniest man who ever lived," one who could convulse audiences with a facial expression, a posture, or a gesture without ever speaking a line.

John Gilbert played over one thousand roles during his long career, mainly at Wallack's Theatre, where he was a member of the company for over twenty-six years; but he was best known for his portrayal of old men in classic English comedies. Indeed, as Sir Anthony Absolute and Sir Peter Teazle he was considered peerless.

William Warren, called "the younger" to distinguish him from his actor father, disliked touring. For virtually his entire fifty-year career, he was a member of the Boston Museum company where he reportedly gave over thirteen thousand performances in 577 characters. He had great versatility and was capable of playing virtually any comic role, especially eccentric types such as Dogberry, Polonius, Sir Andrew Aguecheek, and Micawber in an adaptation of Dickens's *Great Expectations.*

Placide, Burton, Gilbert, and Warren were noted for their comic versatility; other comedians of the era built careers around a single type of character or even a single role. In the antebellum period, for example, a number of actors specialized in playing enormously popular Yankee roles, a type first introduced in Tyler's *The Contrast* in the character of Jonathan—a simple, but shrewd, patriotic New England rustic, skeptical of urban values and personalities, and given to an idiomatic, slangy, uniquely American brand of English. The Yankee character was first explored, ironically, by the English comedian Charles Mathews in two of his own plays—*Trip to America* and *Jonathan in England*—which he devised to display his versatility and quick change artistry during tours of America in 1822–23 and 1834.

Inspired by Mathews's success, a number of American actors began to specialize in such Yankee characters as Solon Shingle in *The People's Lawyer* (1839), Lot Sap Sago in *Yankee Land* (1834) and *The Wag of Maine* (1842), and Deuteronomy Dutiful in *The Vermont Wool Dealer* (1838). Dozens of comedians played Yankee roles, but the leaders in the field were James Henry Hackett (1800–1871), George Handel "Yankee" Hill (1809–49), often called the "most authentic" Yankee actor, and Danforth Marble (1810–49). While Hill and Marble were exclusively Yankee actors, Hackett did win acclaim playing Falstaff, and Dromio of Ephesus in Shakespeare's *The Comedy of Errors,* and the frontiersman Nimrod Wildfire in *The Lion of the West* (1831).

Other specialty roles proved almost as popular as the Yankee character. Frank S. Chanfrau (1824–84), for example, gained stardom playing Mose the Fireman in *A Glance at New York* (1848), a vehicle created expressly for him by playwright and theater manager Benjamin A. Baker (1818–90). Dressed in the red shirt, plug hat, and rolled-up trousers of the New York fireman, Mose was a recognizable urban type—brash but sentimental, always ready to volunteer to fight a fire or just to fight. So successful was *A Glance at New York,* that

Baker developed a series of plays featuring Chanfrau as Mose, including *New York As It Is* (1848), *Mose in California* (1849) and *Mose in China* (1850).

The disastrous Potato Famine forced thousands of Irish to America in the late 1840s and early 1850s. This influx of Irish promoted the popularity of the stage Irishman (and woman). The husband/wife starring teams of Billy Florence (1831–91) and his wife Malvina Pray (1831–1906) and Barney Williams (1823–76) and his wife Maria Pray Mestayer (1828–1917), sister of Malvina, were especially popular and successful in both England and America, playing Irish characters in sentimental melodramas and comedies, although both couples also played a range of traditional comedy roles and Yankee types.

Dion Boucicault and his second wife, Scottish actress Agnes Robertson (1833-1916), were also successful in Irish roles, usually in plays written by Boucicault himself—among the best of the genre—including *The Colleen Bawn* (1860), *Arrah-na-Pogue* (1865), *The O'Dowd* (1872), and *The Shaughraun* (1874).

*Billy Florence probably as Sir Lucius O'Trigger in Sheridan's* The Rivals. *Theatre Cabinet Photographs Collection, Special Collections Library, University of Michigan.*

*Left, Malvina Pray Florence as Mrs. Gilflory in the political farce* The Mighty Dollar *(1875). Theatre Cabinet Photographs Collection, Special Collections Library, University of Michigan.*

*Right, Lotta Crabtree as Little Nell. From Appelbaum,* Great Actors and Actresses of the American Stage in Historic Photographs. *Courtesy Dover Publications, Inc.*

The appeal of some stars depended not so much on a particular role or even a dramatic vehicle as on their personal magnetism and talent. Such was the case of Lotta Crabtree (1847–1924). Lotta began her career at the age of six, dancing, singing, and playing the banjo in California mining camp halls. Lola Montez (1818–61), an Irish-born *danseuse* and actress, renowned for her provocative dancing, was living in California at the time. She volunteered to tutor Lotta, honing her nascent talents. After winning the affection of San Franciscans, Lotta went east. In New York, she appeared in an adaptation of Dickens's *The Old Curiosity Shop* called *Little Nell and the Marchioness,* in which she played both eponymous roles. But these and other vehicles were mere excuses for Lotta to display her talents at mimicry, clog dancing, singing, and banjo-picking. Her career lasted until the turn-of-the-century when she retired as one of the wealthiest performers in America.

Petite—indeed, elfin—Lotta projected a winsome, appealing innocence and a girlish charm even in her mature years. Ada Isaacs Menken's (1835?–68) attraction, like that of Lola Montez, was explicitly erotic. The first few years of her career—playing romantic heroines—were undistinguished. In the early 1860s, however, she exploited the scandalous dissolution of her bigamous marriage to a noted pugilist by assuming the role of the Cossack Prince Mazeppa in the popular equestrian melodrama *Mazeppa; or, The Wild Horse of Tartary,* adapted from a heroic poem by Lord Byron. The

*Lotta Crabtree c. 1880s. Theatre Cabinet Photographs Collection, Special Collections Library, University of Michigan.*

play had often been presented, but never with a woman in the title role. The dramatic high point of the play occurs when Mazeppa is lashed naked to a real horse which then gallops across the stage. For the scene, Menken wore only a form-hugging, flesh-colored body suit that made her appear virtually nude. It was a sensational effect. For almost a decade Menken toured in *Mazeppa* and a few other melodramas which exhibited her physical and personal allure. She was especially popular in male-dominated San Francisco where she played almost continuously for a season before touring the booming silver-mining camps of western Nevada. Her West Coast sojourn earned her over fifty thousand dollars, an enormous sum for the time. Offstage Menken wrote poetry, sculpted, and reportedly spoke five languages. Her life style was often deliberately unconventional. In San Francisco, for example, she dressed in men's clothes, smoked cigars, and visited various saloons and variety halls in the company of journalist–humorist Artemus Ward. Among her friends and admirers were Mark Twain, Walt Whitman, George Sand, Alexander Dumas *père*, and Charles Dickens. After her premature death (from peritonitis), many other actresses would play Mazeppa, but none would achieve the fame of "La Menken."

THERE IS SOME evidence that Spanish language plays were being performed as early as 1789 in Monterey and there may have been a professional Spanish troupe touring the California settlements at the turn-of-the-century. By the late 1840s, there were Spanish-language performances by professional actors in both Monterey and Los Angeles. Annual productions of *pastorelas*, reenactments of the nativity story, were regularly performed by casts of Native Americans and clerics under the auspices of the Spanish missions. (*Pastorelas* continue to be presented today in many western and southwestern towns and cities.) These various early Spanish performances, whether amateur or professional, are not particularly well documented, however. Not until the latter part of the nineteenth-century was professional Spanish-language theater fairly well established in California.

The origins of English-language theater in California can be traced to March 1847, when soldiers of the Seventh Regiment of New York Volunteers arrived in San Francisco to occupy California at the end of the Mexican War. On their long voyage around Cape Horn, the soldiers had amused themselves with amateur theatricals and they continued their activities after landing with performances of melodramas and farces. As the soldiers were dispersed to other outposts at Sonoma, Monterey, Santa Barbara, and Los Angeles, they carried their theatrical enthusiasms with them.

Although San Francisco was the central *pueblo* of upper California, it was little more than a frontier village in 1847 with probably no more than two hundred inhabitants. The discovery of gold on the American River near Sacramento in January 1848, however, rapidly swelled the population of both San Francisco and Sacramento. By July 1849 the population of San Francisco jumped to five thousand, and by September—as more and more fortune seekers from the United States, South America, Europe, the British Isles, China and the Antipodes poured into the city—it climbed to over twenty thousand. Sacramento's population swelled to ten thousand. By 1853, the resident population of San Francisco was probably about thirty-five thousand, but tens of thousands passed through the city on their way to the mining camps. Many came hoping to make their fortune mining gold; others to prosper by providing various services and entertainment to the gold seekers.

Theaters developed alongside saloons, bordellos, banks, hotels, and other business establishments. By 1850 both San Francisco and Sacramento could boast the presence of a half-dozen small theaters, or "bijoux" as they were called. Though often little more than a rough platform stage inside a large canvas tent with an adjacent saloon, they were the sites of lively and various professional theatrical entertainment. Between 1849 and 1861, dozens of theatrical buildings were constructed in San Francisco and Sacramento, but many of these were washed away by regular floods or disastrous fires that destroyed dozens of flimsy, rapidly constructed buildings. Theaters continued to be built or rebuilt, however, each replacement more solid and substantial than the one before.

Between 1849 and 1869, San Francisco would become California's theatrical capital, offering a wide range of entertainments. In the decade 1850–59 alone, there were 1,105 theater productions in San Francisco: 907 plays, 48 operas (in five different languages), 84 extravaganzas, ballets or pantomimes, and 66 minstrel shows. Outside of New York, San Francisco was probably the most active theatrical center in America. Audiences, moreover, were heterogeneous, enthusiastic, and catholic in their tastes. They enjoyed Shakespeare, farce, opera, burlesque, minstrelsy, circus—whatever was available for their amusement. To meet the demand, pioneering managers changed bills frequently, promoting freshness, variety, and novelty. Unlike in the East, where managers tended to specialize in either drama or variety entertainment, California managers mixed high tragedy with burlesque, circus with Shakespeare, often on the same bill.

Popular entertainers were among the first theatrical pioneers to arrive in San Francisco. One of these was Stephen C. Massett (d. 1898), an itinerant theatrical jack-of-all-trades, who in 1849 offered a one-man medley of songs, dramatic recitations, and comic imitations, including, according to one program "imitations of seven different persons who had assembled for the purpose of suppressing the press." An inveterate wanderer, Massett did not remain long in San Francisco. He took his one-man show to Sacramento and the mining camps, then he went abroad to Australia, Europe, and the Indies. He returned to California for short stays in the 1850s, but finally ended up in Japan where he lived for almost forty years. Joseph Andrew Rowe (d. 1887), an equestrian and manager of circus companies touring the West Indies and Central and South America, arrived shortly after Massett. In the fall of 1849, he opened Rowe's Olympic Circus in a makeshift amphitheater on Kearney Street. In 1850 he built a more permanent amphitheater also called the Olympic Circus and when that burned down he erected another called the New Olympic Amphitheater. Later in his career, he built the Pioneer Circus. Rowe may also have been the first impresario to mount professional dramatic productions in  San Francisco, combining circus entertainment with performances of *Othello, Richard III,* and *The Lady of Lyons.* These productions were undistinguished, featuring obscure, second-rate American or English actors, but they proved popular with entertainment-hungry Forty-Niners. D. G. "Doc" or "Yankee" Robinson, a druggist who did "Yankee" impersonations on the side, was another early theatrical pioneer. In 1850 he and his partner James Evrard opened the 280-seat Dramatic Museum where they presented melodramas, burlesques, and comic skits often written by and featuring "Doc" himself. Throughout the 1850s, Robinson was a popular theater manager and performer, often regaling San Franciscans with his topical burlesques. When the Dramatic Museum burned down, he built the American Theatre. With a seating capacity of two thousand, it was one of the first real theaters in San Francisco.

Tom Maguire (1816–96) was the dominant and most successful of California's pioneer theatrical managers. Maguire, a prosperous but reportedly illiterate New York saloonkeeper, migrated in 1849 to San Francisco, where he became the operator of the Parker House, a hotel and gambling saloon. In the fall of 1850, Maguire opened a theater on the second floor of his hotel, naming it the Jenny Lind after the famous Swedish soprano whom he admired, although she had never visited California, nor had she ever had any association with Maguire. The first Jenny Lind was destroyed in a fire in the spring of 1851; a second was built only to burn down nine days after its opening. Undaunted, Maguire built a third Jenny Lind. A substantial three-storied building, the largest in the city to that date, it was constructed of brick with a front façade finished in straw colored sandstone imported from Australia. The handsome interior, reportedly painted in shades of light pink accented with gilding, was configured in a standard arrangement of orchestra stalls, dress circle, balcony, and galleries and had a seating capacity of about two thousand.

After only a year of operation, to meet the demands of his creditors, Maguire was forced to sell the Jenny Lind to the city of San Francisco for two hundred thousand dollars and it was converted into a city hall. Maguire, however, quickly built another theater, the San Francisco Hall or Theatre, renamed Maguire's Opera House in 1853. Over the course of the next two decades, Maguire established himself as an important theatrical entrepreneur, "the Napoleon of managers," as he was called, controlling numerous theaters not only in San Francisco, but in Sacramento and other developing towns in northern California and western Nevada.

In 1853, a third major theater, the Metropolitan, opened. It was distinguished by its three tiers of boxes and its unusually large stage and lobby area. The Metropolitan was also the first San Francisco stage to be lit by gas. The theater was placed under the management of Catherine Sinclair, who the year before had won her bitterly contested, widely publicized divorce from the tragedian Edwin Forrest. Sinclair, an actress of some talent, proved a diligent, if not always successful manager. Like so many other San Francisco theaters, the Metropolitan was completely destroyed by fire in 1857. A new Metropolitan was built on the same site in 1861 and leased by Maguire. In 1864 Maguire built the Academy of Music, which, despite its name, was a house mainly for theatrical performances.

Several other minor theaters were built during the 1860s, such as Maguire's Eureka and the Lyceum, but these were venues for variety and minstrels. Indeed, from the mid-1850s through the 1860s, minstrelsy and variety eclipsed drama and opera in popularity in San Francisco. The soon to be internationally famous San Francisco Minstrels, a company created by combining the long-established Edwin P. Christy (1815–62) and Charley Backus (1831–83) minstrel troupes, began to offer, to the delight of their audiences, "Ethiopian" burlesques of well-known plays and operas, sending up San Francisco's growing intellectual and elitist play- and opera-goers. (For the development of the minstrel show, see pages 139–41, below.) The mid-1850s also saw the rise of a score of distinctly San Franciscan variety halls known as "melodeons" after the portable reed organ which supplied much of the musical accompaniment for the variety acts. With names like What Cheer, the Apollo, the Bella Union, and the New Idea, melodeons, like eastern "concert saloons," combined a saloon with gambling and entertainment that included acts with off-color jokes and songs, satirical skits, and dance routines or tableaux featuring women in various states of undress. Admissions were nominal—one to two "bits" (twelve and a half to twenty-five cents)—or, in the case of the Bella Union, admission was free. Income was derived principally from liquor sales. Like London's East End music halls and

Montmartre's cabarets, the melodeon environment and program were mainly oriented toward men, but some of the larger melodeons offered occasional, cleaned-up family versions of the variety program. Melodeons remained popular through the turn-of-the-century until the sale of liquor in San Francisco's theaters was outlawed.

While San Francisco remained California's theatrical center, by the 1850s, Sacramento also boasted two major theaters: the Sacramento Theatre opened in 1853 and the Forrest Theatre in 1855. During the gold rush era, various northern California mining towns, including Stockton, Marysville, Downieville, and Grass Valley, built substantial theaters to accommodate troupes touring out of San Francisco and Sacramento.

In the late 1850s, the discovery of silver in northwestern Nevada, the famous Comstock Lode, led to the development of new towns along the Nevada–California boundary. By the mid-1860s, there were theaters in Frankton, Genoa, Nevada City, Carson City, Silver City, and Aurora, and itinerant performers were making regular visits. Gold also drew settlers to Oregon and by the late 1850s, there was a permanent theater in Portland, the Willamette or Stewart's Theatre, and troupers were touring from there to smaller settlements in Salem and Oregon City. Within a decade, acting troupes were venturing into Washington and Idaho.

Numerous actors, both distinguished and workaday, were drawn to the Gold Coast. Getting there was not easy. Whether one took the long voyage around Cape Horn, or a combination of two sea voyages and an overland passage across the Panamanian isthmus, or came overland, the trip was arduous and risky. But the promise of earnings which might be two or three times what could be earned in Boston or New York made the trip worthwhile. One of the first to arrive was Canadian-born James Stark (1818–75), reportedly a former pupil of Macready. He teamed with Sarah Kirby (?–1898), later to become Mrs. Stark, to manage the first Jenny Lind Theatre, where they presented a season of poetic drama, including Shakespeare's tragedies, and numerous standards such as Payne's *Brutus,* Massinger's *A New Way to Pay Old Debts,* and Knowles's *Virginius.* In 1851, Stark, at the request of several prominent San Franciscans, appeared in the title role of a well-received production of *King Lear.* Indeed, as MacMinn documents, San Franciscans liked Shakespeare, especially the tragedies. This was Stark's first effort at Lear, but the role soon became one of his most popular interpretations. Several other veteran husband–wife teams or family troupes traveled to Gold Rush California, including Charles Robert Thorne Sr. (1815–93) and his wife Anna Maria Mestayer (1815–81), the Chapmans (George, Mary, William B., and Caroline), and Lewis Baker (1823–73) and his wife Alexina Fisher Baker (1822–87). In 1851, Junius Brutus Booth Jr. came to San Francisco to manage Maguire's third Jenny Lind Theatre. In July 1852, at Junius's invitation, the elder Booth, undoubtedly the most distinguished tragedian to appear in San Francisco up to that time, began a two-week engagement at the Jenny Lind. Booth moved on to Sacramento for two weeks and then back to San Francisco for a week of performances at the Adelphi Theatre. Returning East after his California tour,

*Advertising woodcuts for* Mazeppa; or, The Wild Horse of Tartary, *adapted by Henry M. Milner from Lord Byron's poem. (London, 1831; New York, 1833). From Appelbaum,* Scenes from the 19th-Century Stage in Advertising Woodcuts. Courtesy Dover Publications, Inc.

*Ada Isaacs Menken probably c. 1860. From Hornblow,* A History of American Theatre, *vol. 1, 1919.*

Boothe died unexpectedly en route, but his sons Junius and Edwin remained in San Francisco, Junius building a solid reputation as an astute actor–manager and Edwin serving his professional apprenticeship.

In the 1850s and 1860s, many established veteran performers came to California as visiting stars, remaining for a few weeks or even a few years, but eventually returning to the established cities and theaters of the East. Golden Era San Francisco was visited among others by F. S. Chanfrau, James E. Murdoch, James William Wallack, and Mr. and Mrs. Barney Williams. Mr. and Mrs. Charles Kean, the noted English husband–wife team, played for several months in 1864–65. Edwin Forrest, at the low ebb of his histrionic power but still celebrated, was engaged for six weeks in 1866 at Maguire's Opera House which was enlarged and renovated specifically for this event. International opera stars, ballerinas, pantomimists, and vaudevillians also passed through San Francisco.

San Francisco played an even more important role in helping to develop and promote the careers of many emerging performers. The pool of talented performers was small; actors easily moved from theater to theater. In such an environment, an ambitious young actor could quickly gain a wealth of experience and lay the foundation for a career. Between 1852 and 1856, young Edwin Booth, for example, played a wide range of characters in San Francisco and Sacramento theaters, including roles in farces, historical melodramas, spectacle entertainments, and supporting and leading parts in such standards as *The Hunchback, London Assurance, The Iron Chest, Hamlet, Othello, Much Ado about Nothing,* and *The Taming of the Shrew.* No other theatrical venue in America offered such opportunities and they paved the way for Booth's meteoric rise to stardom in the next decade.

Perhaps because of the heavily male population, young attractive actresses were in particular demand. Matilda Heron, Agnes Booth (1846–1910), Laura Keene, Jean Margaret Davenport Lander (1829–1903), Julia Dean (1830–68), among others—all later to become East Coast stars—honed their developing talents in the theaters of San Francisco and Sacramento. Lola Montez and Ada Isaacs Menken, in particular, were enthusiastically embraced by the mostly male playgoers of California. During her highly publicized engagement at the American Theatre in San Francisco in 1853, Lola appeared in several dramatic roles, including Lady Teazle in *The School for Scandal,* but it was her exotic *tarantella*-inspired Spider Dance that spectators really came to see, paying as much as sixty-five dollars a seat for the opportunity. Capitalizing on Lola's appearance, "Doc" Robinson mounted his own full-length burlesque, *Who's Got the Countess?; or, The Rival Houses* at the San Francisco Theatre. It featured Caroline Chapman as Mlle. Mula, Countess of Bohemia, and her father William as Lewis Buggins, a parody of the manager of the American Theatre, Lewis Baker. The burlesque proved as popular as Lola herself.

A decade after Lola was both idolized and satirized, Ada Isaacs Menken's appeared in *Mazeppa* at Maguire's Opera House. San Francisco theatergoers were bedazzled by "La Menken." At the end of her first two-week run in

August 1863, an estimated thirty thousand people (about half the population of the city) had witnessed her performances. Menken extended her West Coast visit to the following April playing two more sold-out engagements at the Opera House and touring the silver mining towns on the California–Nevada border. The San Franciscan appetite for *Mazeppa* was not easily whetted. After Menken left, other actresses mounted "the wild house of Tartary" on various San Francisco stages for another decade.

From the arrival of the first Forty-Niners, San Francisco was an international multicultural city. Although theatrical entertainment was dominated by an Anglo–American, English-language culture, Mexican companies, French vaudevillians, and Italian opera companies performed successfully in San Francisco. The Adelphi Theatre, in particular, was associated with foreign theatricals. But the development of a Chinese theater was perhaps unique to San Francisco.

The Chinese were among the earliest émigrés to Gold Rush California. By the early 1850s, there were over twenty-five thousand Chinese statewide. Like the majority of the Forty-Niners, most were young single men, mainly from Canton province, hoping to make it rich in the gold fields. Many, however, settled in San Francisco to establish businesses of various sorts or to work as launderers, shop keepers, and restaurateurs. Like African Americans, they were excluded from white places of entertainment, so they developed their own Chinatown brothels, gambling dens, and saloons. In October 1852 a company of Chinese jugglers from Hong Kong played to capacity crowds for two nights at the American Theatre. Several days later the Tung Hook Tong Chinese Opera Troupe, 123-members strong, presented a sampling of Chinese opera with musical accompaniment on traditional instruments. Although after a few months the Tung Hook Tong Company moved on to New York, other Chinese companies would regularly visit San Francisco throughout the 1850s and 1860s. By the late 1850s two Chinese troupes were in residence in San Francisco: one at the Adelphi Theatre, the other at the Union Theatre. A decade later, the Hing Chuen Yuen Theatre was built on Jackson Street in the heart of Chinatown at a cost of forty thousand dollars. Known to non-Asians as the "Royal Chinese Theatre," it continued to present traditional Chinese opera to San Francisco's growing Asian population through the turn-of-the-century.

With the completion of the transcontinental railroad in 1869, California was joined to the rest of the country. San Francisco moved quickly toward a more metropolitan sophistication, losing much of its distinctive frontier, boomtown flavor. Indeed, the California Theatre built in 1869 was one of the most spacious and ornate theaters in the United States. San Francisco's theatrical ambience, while remaining dynamic, became generally reflective of theater across Gilded Age America. The expanding railroad network stimulated the founding of numerous towns and cities across the Great Plains and the Southwest. By the 1880s, there was a growing western circuit of theaters and stock companies. The city by the bay would remain, however, an important West Coast theater center to the present day.

ENGLISH DRAMA AND adaptations of foreign drama, especially melodrama, continued to dominate the repertoires of American theaters; but an increasing number of American playwrights—with little encouragement from audiences, critics, actors, or managers—struggled to establish a foothold for plays that drew on national themes, issues, and character types or sought, by imitating standard romantic fare, to gain a reputation comparable to their European counterparts. Few plays, however, would be produced of lasting merit. Among the more successful of the antebellum playwrights who aspired to write plays of literary substance were Robert Montgomery Bird and George Henry Boker (1823–90).

As already noted, Bird's *The Gladiator* became permanent in Forrest's repertoire. In 1834 Bird submitted another play to Forrest, *The Broker of Bogota,* a romantic melodrama, similar in style to *The Gladiator.* The central character Baptista Fero is a wealthy eighteenth-century broker in New Grenada (Colombia) and a loving but authoritarian father whose rash actions lead to his son's tragic suicide. With echoes of *King Lear* and English playwright Sheridan Knowles's popular *Virginius, The Broker of Bogota* became an excellent vehicle for Forrest's emotional range and acting style and he made thousands of dollars performing both it and *The Gladiator.* For these plays, Forrest paid Bird a paltry flat fee of one thousand dollars each. Bird believed Forrest had agreed to additional remunerations, but Forrest refused further payments. Disenchanted with Forrest, Bird abandoned playwriting, turning instead to writing novels.

George Henry Boker aspired to be a major American poet, and his lyric and narrative poems published as *Poems of the War* in 1864 are among the best of the era. Boker also achieved some commercial success and critical acclaim as a playwright both before and after the Civil War. He wrote ten plays in all, seven of which were produced. Although several of his plays were comedies, he was recognized mainly for his romantic verse tragedies set in the Renaissance period, and principally for *Francesca da Rimini* which he completed in 1853. Drawing on an episode in Dante's *Inferno,* Boker effectively dramatized the story of Francesca and Paolo, traditional star-crossed lovers who become innocent victims of their warring families, fateful circumstances, and the machinations of a malicious, vengeful villain. But in contrast to many such plays of the period, Boker's tragic situations are often relieved by irony and diverse comic and lyrical touches. The four main characters are also deftly defined and offer excellent acting roles. In 1855 E. L. Davenport produced the play and played Lanciotto, the sensitive hunchbacked brother of Paolo to whom Francesca unknowingly had been betrothed. The play was presented for eight performances in New York and four more performances in Philadelphia, a creditable run for the time; but Davenport's approach to Lanciotto was viewed by some critics as too heavyhanded and *Francesca da Rimini* was virtually forgotten for over twenty-five years. Boker essentially withdrew from writing for the stage. He continued to write poetry and after the Civil War served as an ambassador first to Turkey and then to Russia.

In 1879 the tragedian Laurence Barrett (1838–91), then approaching the peak of his popularity, rediscovered *Francesca da Rimini*. With the assistance of his friend the prominent critic William Winter (1836–1917), and over Boker's mild protests, Barrett cut and rearranged the text making it even more stageworthy. Splendidly produced, and with Barrett as Lanciotto, *Francesca da Rimini* was enthusiastically received when revived in 1882. It remained in Barrett's repertoire throughout the 1880s, proving to be one of his most successful productions. At the turn of the century, Otis Skinner (1858–1942), who had played Paolo in Barrett's production, once again revived *Francesca da Rimini* assuming the role of Lanciotto. It ran for a very respectable fifty-six performances on Broadway and then Skinner successfully toured it for a season. Other American playwrights of the antebellum era tried their hand at romantic verse tragedy, but none of their efforts rose to the level of Boker's *Francesca da Rimini*.

Imbued by the spirit of nationalism pervading the country in the 1830s and 1840s, many playwrights found success by focusing on contemporary national character types, attitudes, and issues. The "Yankee" character in various guises—peddler, ploughboy, lawyer, or merchant—continued to be a popular focus for numerous star vehicles featuring James Henry Hackett, George Handel Hill, Dan Marble, and other Yankee specialists. A variation on the character was the frontiersman or backwoodsman popularized in dramatizations of James Fenimore Cooper's novels, and in such plays as James Kirk Paulding's *The Lion of the West* (1831), Louisa Medina's aforementioned *Nick of the Woods* (1838), Mordecai Noah's *The Frontier Maid* (1840), and W. R. Derr's *Kit Carson, the Hero of the Prairie* (1850).

The success of Forrest in *Metamora* spawned a variety of plays centered on Indian characters, among the more noteworthy of which was George Washington Parke Curtis's (1781–1857) *Pocahontas; or, The Settlers of Virginia* (1830). Another Pocahontas play was *The Forest Princess; or, Two Centuries Ago* (1844) by Charlotte Mary Sanford Barnes. So popular were Indian plays and their exaggerated interpretation of the "noble red man" (or woman) that they became the subject of even more popular burlesques. In 1847, John Brougham (1810–80), an actor–playwright, successfully lampooned *Metamora* in *Met-a-mora; or, The Last of the Pollywogs*. Almost a decade later, he followed *Met-a-mora* with *Po-Ca-Hon-Tas; or, The Gentle Savage* (1855), an "Original, Aboriginal, Erratic, Operatic, Semi-Civilized, and Semi-Savage Extravaganza." Such burlesques, and a changing attitude that viewed Native Americans as more "savage" than "noble" as frontiers expanded westward and white settlers competed for Indian lands, combined to end the taste for Indian plays by the late 1850s.

Approaches toward depicting African Americans in plays remained conflicted during the Jacksonian era. In the 1820s and 1830s African Americans, for the most part, were portrayed as they had been in earlier decades as doltish but happy slaves or servants and always by white actors in blackface. The rise of the minstrel show in the early 1840s offered, at least for about a decade, a more diverse view of black life and character types, including, according to Robert C. Toll, "hunters and fishermen thrilling to the joys of the catch; young lovers flirting and courting; black frontiersmen and river boatsmen embodying American strength and independence; husbands and wives living happily together; heartbroken lovers pining for their sweethearts. . . ." Still African Americans were depicted as racially, physically, and culturally inferior and different—grotesquely bug-eyed, woolly haired and thick-lipped, given to eating "possum" and "coon," and compulsively musical. Minstrel shows also expressed a fundamental ambivalence about slavery; on the one hand portraying happy blacks dancing and singing on the plantation; on the other hand, accommodating jokes, songs, and sketches that commented, if indirectly and in the guise of humor, on the injustice and cruelty of the institution.

The origins of the minstrel show can be traced to T. D. "Daddy" Rice (1806–60). By the early 1830s Rice, in blackface makeup, was performing a comic Negro song and dance routine called "Jim Crow" after its original model, an elderly Negro stableman. By the late 1830s and 1840s, Rice had developed full-length entertainments called "Ethiopian operas" which featured his solo performance. In 1843, fiddler Dan Emmett (1815–1904) formed the Virginia Minstrels, a musical quartet playing popular tunes on fiddle, banjo, tambourine, and bones and wearing blackface makeup. Emmett also opened the first minstrel hall in Chicago in 1855. By the early 1850s, minstrelsy had rapidly become America's favorite form of popular theatrical entertainment. Dozens of minstrel troupes found permanent homes in the cities of the Northeast, some in their own theaters, commonly known as "Ethiopian Opera Houses." Many other companies toured the cities of the Midwest and South. The minstrel show was popular because it offered folksy entertainment at reasonable prices. But it also provided white Americans with a nonthreatening vehicle to cope with their racism and the "otherness" of blacks and with the problematic nature of slavery in a country that professed to be democratic and egalitarian. Minstrels rationalized white superiority and romanticized plantation life. "Blacking up" allowed whites to psychologically "black out" the realities of black life and the pressing need for social and political change.

As the abolitionist cause became in the 1850s and 1860s ever more central to the political conflict that would erupt in the Civil War, and white interests and values were challenged, the minstrel show became increasingly cartoonish in its depiction of "Negro folk life" and "characters." In the 1850s, Edwin P. Christy's Christy Minstrels standardized the minstrel show structure into three acts or parts with a focus almost exclusively on sheer entertainment; antislavery sentiments disappeared. The first part began with a "walkround" until the whitefaced master of ceremonies, Mr. Interlocuter announced "Gentlemen, be seated." Sitting in a semicircle, company members would sing songs interspersed with jokes from the "endmen," Mr. Tambo and Mr. Bones who played respectively tambourine and bones. Other members played banjo, fiddle, as well as tambourines and bones—since the Virginia Minstrels the traditional core of the minstrel band. The first part also usually featured a tenor singing romantic, sentimental love ballads. The second part consisted of a variety show or "olio" of specialty acts—for example, a song-and-dance routine, acrobats, or musical numbers. Its distinctive feature, however, was the "stump speech." Usually given by one of the endmen, its content could range from utter nonsense—an excuse for "Negro dialect" malapropisms, puns, and jokes—to comic orations on education, temperance, or women's rights. Following the olio was a one-act sketch which before 1850 was invariably set on a southern plantation replete with dancing, singing, banjo-twanging "darkies." By the mid-1850s, such plantation scenes were often replaced with blackface burlesques of Shakespeare's plays or popular melodramas. The performance concluded with a group song and dance number.

As early as 1855 many talented blacks found that minstrelsy offered performance opportunities not otherwise available to them. The number of black minstrels would remain small until after the Civil War. The earliest known all-black minstrel troupe, composed of fifteen ex-slaves, was organized in 1865 as the Georgia Slave Troupe minstrels. However, it was a later Georgia Minstrels company—under the leadership of the black entrepreneur Charles B. Hicks—that enjoyed world renown in the 1870s. Indeed, the great Sam Lucas (1840–1916), known as "King of All Colored Comedians," frequently toured with the Georgia Minstrels. Black minstrel troupes did serve to modify the image of African Americans presented in minstrels, even though they continued to work within the traditional format and audience expectations of the genre. But they also succeeded in attracting large numbers of black people to American popular entertainment and provided an outlet for talented black musicians and performers.

While minstrelsy caricatured African Americans and romanticized plantation life, slavery, and black culture, a few antebellum plays offered a more realistic view. As early as 1845, Zeke, the black servant in Anna Cora Mowatt's *Fashion,* while still essentially a comic character, speaking in Negro dialect, possessed a human dimension beyond the minstrel caricature. Few plays, however, featured African Americans as major characters, nor, considering its significance in American life, were plays about slavery particularly numerous. Perhaps the enormous popularity of the dramatization of Harriet Beecher Stowe's novel *Uncle Tom's Cabin* (1852) discouraged competition.

George L. Aiken's 1852 six-act version of *Uncle Tom's Cabin* became the standard antebellum dramatization. By the late 1850s companies called "Tommers" crisscrossed the country; by the 1870s there were fifty such companies; by the 1890s perhaps five hundred. The play was also a standard fixture on the London stage and versions were presented in Paris and Berlin. Undoubtedly the most popular American play of the nineteenth century, it continued to be revived and adapted, including several film versions, well into the twentieth century.

Essentially a sentimental melodrama, Aiken's dramatization nevertheless sharply focused on the pervasive inhumanity of slavery. Perhaps for the first time in an American play, black slaves were portrayed as fully humanized figures, rather than as minstrel caricatures. Uncle Tom is an example of heroic Christian suffering and martyrdom, while the mulatto

George Harris effectively functions as a symbol of heroic rebellion, not dissimilar from Forrest's Spartacus or Metamora. Eliza, George's wife, is equally heroic and the rascally Topsy is audacious and irreverent. The white characters range from Wilson, a businessman, and Phineas Fletcher, a frontiersman, both of whom help George and Eliza escape, to the kindly, but weak plantation owner St. Clair, to the villainous slave master Simon Legree. The white characters at best, according to Richardson, "tacitly accept slavery, ameliorating its nature through personal intervention" or at worst "they epitomize the brutal realities" of the slave system. Adhering to the melodramatic format, lavish scenic spectacle, including a scene in which Eliza flees across the ice-swollen Ohio River, often pursued by real bloodhounds, also gave *Uncle Tom's Cabin* audience appeal. Whatever its shortcomings as a drama, *Uncle Tom's Cabin* contributed to the abolitionist cause and a more human representation of black Americans.

After *Uncle Tom's Cabin,* the most popular and provocative play exploring slavery and racism was Dion Boucicault's *The Octoroon; or, Life in Louisiana* (1859). The plot centers on Zoe, "one-eighth" African American—sufficient by the miscegenation statutes of the time to be classified "colored"—the illegitimate daughter of the late Judge Peyton, a plantation owner. Peyton had freed Zoe, but died before he could legalize the action. George, Peyton's nephew, has inherited the plantation and is in love with Zoe. But the villainous M'Closky wants Zoe. He calls in his lien on the plantation and kills a messenger bringing news to George that a Liverpool firm is advancing monies for him to save the plantation and Zoe. Zoe, still legal chattel, is auctioned as a slave and bought by M'Closky. M'Closky is eventually exposed, foiled, and murdered by the "noble savage" Wahnotee, but Zoe is unaware of these developments. Rather than be owned by M'Closky, she poisons herself. Although structured as a melodrama with its particular emotional appeals and qualities—augmented by scenic spectacle—*The Octoroon,* more than other plays of the era, did critically reflect on, albeit ambiguously, questions of law, justice, and prevailing racial attitudes.

Boucicault had an established reputation as a playwright and actor in England, before he came to America in 1853. Although never a citizen, he contributed significantly to developments in the American theater throughout his career. With plays like *The Octoroon* and *The Poor of New York* (1857), he helped establish the prewar vogue for sensational melodrama. He managed theaters in New Orleans, Washington, and New York and in 1856 he expedited the enactment of a U.S. copyright law that gave playwrights "along with the right to present and publish the composition, the sole right to act, perform or represent the same." He is credited with over two hundred plays, many of which were first presented in the United States, but, after *The Octoroon,* he is probably best known for his aforementioned melodramas of Irish rural life.

The antebellum era was marked by a number of cultural tensions: between European culture, valued by a segment of American society, and mounting nationalistic sentiments which rejected all things foreign; between a growing urbanism and urbanity and a more established agrarianism; and between elitist and egalitarian values and attitudes. This cultural turbulence created a milieu rich in opportunities for social comedy.

The most successful social comedy of the period was Anna Cora Mowatt's *Fashion; or Life in New York* which satirized the social pretensions of the emerging *nouveau riche* in the vein of *The School for Scandal*. Following its opening performance at New York's Park Theatre, it ran for three continuous weeks—a long run for the time. It also was staged in other metropolitan theaters and frequently revived throughout the century. The success of *Fashion* led to a spate of social comedies in the 1850s, including *Self* (1856), by Sidney Bateman (1823–81), mother of the child-prodigy actresses Kate (1843–1917) and Ellen (1844–1936), and *Young New York* (1856) by Edward G. P. Wilkins (1829–61), the drama critic of the New York *Herald*. These plays never rose to the level of *Fashion*—much less the sparkling comedies of Sheridan or Goldsmith on which they were modeled. They did, however, contribute to a growing tradition of social comedy in American theater which had begun with Tyler's *The Contrast* and would continue to the present day.

In addition to plays centered on distinctly American ambiences, character types, or ethnic groups, a number of antebellum American plays treated a range of topical subjects and social issues. There were plays, for example, on Gold Rush California, the Mexican War of 1848–49, women's

*Dion Boucicault as Conn with Sadie Martinot (1861–1923) as Moyo in* The Shaughraun. *Theatre Cabinet Photographs Collection, Special Collections Library, University of Michigan.*

rights, and the burgeoning temperance movement. Two temperance plays in particular, William H. Smith's *The Drunkard; or, The Fallen Saved* (1844; preserved fairly faithfully on film in W. C. Fields's *The Old-Fashioned Way,* 1934) and William W. Pratt's *Ten Nights in a Bar Room* (1858), had initial long runs in New York and were frequently revived in theaters across the country throughout the century.

Plays, no matter their literary quality or genre—farce, romantic tragedy, sensational melodrama—were sometimes referred to as "legitimate drama" to distinguish them from types of performance—minstrel shows, variety acts, burlesque skits, circus, sometimes musical comedy—that modern theater historians collectively classify as "popular entertainment."

The term *legitimate* originates with England's major theaters—principally Drury Lane and Covent Garden—which were granted exclusive licenses or patents dating back to the Restoration to present traditional dramatic fare. Legally prevented from mounting productions of such plays, unlicensed English theaters emerging in the late eighteenth century carved out a market niche by developing a range of alternative theatrical entertainments which usually incorporated fair amounts of music. Such entertainments were usually thought of as lesser, "low," or bastardized forms of theater.

These two theatrical divisions to a certain extent split along class lines: popular entertainment forms for the lower or working class; legitimate drama for the educated, affluent middle and upper classes. Egalitarian America, however, never had the equivalent of England's patent theaters; and, at least in the first part of the century, as noted earlier, "legitimate drama" and "popular entertainment" overlapped or intermingled. A classical play might be followed by a comic ballet as an afterpiece, or an equestrian show might include a Shakespearean play. American theater managers tended to present whatever they thought would attract the largest possible audience. By midcentury, however, many theaters gradually began to specialize in presenting either legitimate drama or a form of popular entertainment. As in England, such specialization also tended to reinforce class divisions and to somewhat strengthen distinctions between "high" and "low" theatrical art. But audiences still frequently overlapped, if not commingled: workers went to performances of Shakespeare and Italian opera; President Lincoln attended minstrel shows.

In the antebellum era, after minstrel shows, variety was probably the next most popular form of theatrical entertainment. Variety usually consisted of solo or small group exhibitions of singing, dancing, mimicry, acrobatics, recitation, clowning, or the playing of popular, as opposed to classical music. Lotta Crabtree, for example, was essentially a variety *artiste*. As entr'actes or afterpieces, such performances had been included in the standard theatrical bill of fare throughout the eighteenth and early nineteenth centuries. But gradually variety acts found separate venues in "concert saloons," mostly all-male establishments offering liquor and attractive waitresses (and sometimes prostitutes) as well as variety entertainment. There were hundreds of such concert saloons in New York by midcentury; and, as noted earlier in this chapter, San Francisco developed its own distinctive melodeons in the Gold Rush era. Variety acts were also presented in certain legitimate theaters such as New York's Niblo's Garden and the Chatham Garden Theatre. In New York in 1841, the master showman P. T. Barnum (1810–91) opened his grandiose Barnum's American Museum and Garden and Gallery of Fine Arts. Undoubtedly, the museum's principal draw was Barnum's exhibition of unusual animals—some real, some bogus—and human oddities, such as midgets Tom Thumb (Charles Stratton; 1832–88) and Lavinia Warren (1841–1919). But in the museum's "Moral Lecture Hall," essentially a theater, Barnum presented a range of theatrical entertainment, from variety acts to productions of "moral" drama, a classification that included Shakespeare's plays along with *The Drunkard* and *Uncle Tom's Cabin*. Variety entertainment was also a mainstay of the many showboats which plied America's waterways in the 1840s and 1850s. Later in the century, variety would develop into what became known as vaudeville.

THEATRICAL CRITICISM WAS not well established in the early nineteenth-century American theater. Using the pen name Jonathan Oldstyle, Washington Irving (1783–1859), best known for his tales "The Legend of Sleepy Hollow" and "Rip Van Winkle," published a series of letters in the New York *Morning Chronicle* in 1802–3 which commented satirically on the state of the contemporary stage. Later Irving also wrote reviews for such magazines as *The Salmagundi* and the *Analectic Magazine*. He is regarded as the first American theatrical critic of any importance, but his position was unique. Few newspapers published reviews in the early decades of the nineteenth century and even fewer of these were signed. Most theatrical criticism appeared in short-lived theatrically oriented magazines such as the *Theatrical Censor* (1806), *Rambler's Magazine* and the *New York Theatrical Register* (1809) or in sporting weeklies such as the *Spirit of the Times* (1831). As the number of newspapers increased with the growth of urban populations—most of whom were not only literate, but avid readers—theatrical reviewing also became more commonplace. Reviewers, however, continued to remain anonymous for the most part. Reviews generally were not very detailed, and often amounted to little more than a few cursory observations or judgments. Among the exceptions to this tendency were the reviews of the poet and short story writer Edgar Allan Poe (1809–49), who reviewed theater for a number of journals, including the *Broadway Journal* in the mid-forties. The poet Walt Whitman (1819–92) also reviewed theatrical productions for a number of newspapers in the 1840s, including the *Brooklyn Eagle*. Both Poe and Whitman complained about the generally low level of theatrical reviewing. Poe, for example, labeled reviewers "illiterate montebanks," while Whitman railed against the common practice of paying a journalist to tout or "puff," as it was called, a particular performer or production, in the guise of a review. (Whitman himself, however, was not above "puffing" his own *Leaves of Grass* in various journals and newspapers.) In the late 1850s, Henry Clapp Jr. (1814–75) championed a higher level of the theatrical reviewing through his own reviews published in his weekly the *Saturday Press*. Indeed, Clapp would influence a number of theater reviewers emerging after the Civil War who in turn would change the entire direction of theatrical reviewing in America.

BY THE LATE 1850s the American stage, reflecting the development of the nation as a whole, had in many respects come of age. It could boast a corps of talented, skilled, experienced theater professionals who could hold their own against their European counterparts, an extensive infrastructure of numerous theaters, stock companies, and touring circuits, and a distinct national and even international identity. Continuing development, however, would be delayed by the Civil War which ripped apart the economic, social, and political fabric of the country.

## MEXICO

Mexico was ripe for the Romantic movement which swept Europe from the 1820s to the 1840s, coinciding with a period of political problems in the unstable young republic. The Romantic artist—whether poet, painter, playwright, or performer—indulged the emotions, making a virtue of extremes of passion, and drew upon the folk life, local color, national history and literature that constituted his cultural patrimony. Romanticism formed an appropriate backdrop to the strong national sentiment that permeated all levels of Mexican life. Although the Mexican theater continued to rely heavily upon both plays and performing artists from Spain (with an increasing influence from France), Mexican nationalism found various means of expression both on the stage and in the audience.

At the beginning of this period, the Coliseo Nuevo—about which Fanny Calderón de la Barca would later write so disparagingly—was still the leading theater of the capital. In January 1826 its name was changed to Teatro Principal, the name it retained until the end of its existence in 1931, long after it had ceased to be the city's principal theater. In 1826 the new name was merely cosmetic for a theater beset by problems. With no viceroy to set an example and make theatergoing socially *de rigueur*, the upper classes abandoned their boxes. Acrimonious political differences between liberals and conservatives carried over from the street to the theater auditorium where fisticuffs often broke out. The poor quality of plays in the repertoire encouraged the actors to take outrageous liberties. Furthermore, the theater administration's attempt to reinvigorate the company by hiring new artists from Spain offended the resident artists.

Andrés Prieto, the most celebrated of the imported actors, encountered some hostility from critics and theatergoers who preferred not to admit that anything worthwhile could come from Spain, but his talent finally won their respect and applause. Indeed, the huzzas at his curtain calls sometimes included the amusingly commingled plaudit and insult, "*Bravo por el gachupín!*" (Mexicans had long used *gachupín* as a derogatory term for "Spaniard.") Reviewing the season's opening production for *El Iris* (April 8,

*The principal theater of almost every town in Mexico was called Teatro Principal. In the capital, the Coliseo Nuevo was so renamed in 1826. That playhouse continued in use until it burned down in 1931.*

*Left, Miguel Valleto was a Spanish actor who braved nationalistic Mexican sentiment in his engagements at the Teatro Principal. From* El Apuntador, *1841.*

*Right, the lovely actress–dancer Soledad Cordero (1816–47) came from Spain to perform at the Teatro Principal, where she maintained a following in the 1830s.*

1826), Cuban poet José María Heredia praised Prieto: "How great was the expression of his physiognomy, how noble his attitudes, and how masterful the infections of his voice!" In May and June, however, Heredia and Prieto were exchanging heated letters in *El Iris* over Heredia's criticism of a play translation Prieto had done. Finally reconciled, both won approbation in January 1827 when Prieto chose Heredia's play *El Tiberio* as a vehicle for his histrionic gifts.

Despite the acknowledged superiority of Prieto's acting, anti-Spanish sentiment caused a drastic decline in attendance at the Principal. In an effort to rescue the theater, Colonel Luis Castrejón, a stage-struck man of means, got himself appointed to its administration. Surprisingly, his strategy was to bring in another Spanish star, the world-renowned tenor Manuel García along with his opera company and scenery. Although Castrejón poured his own money into renovating the Principal, the city council fixed admission prices that would prevent him from recovering his investment. Castrejón then decided to continue presenting the dramatic company headed by Prieto and another outstanding Spanish actor, Miguel Valleto, at the Principal, and to book the opera into the Teatro Provisional (formerly Teatro de los Gallos). Despite the Spanish-sounding title of the opera, *The Barber of Seville,* the Provisional was packed to capacity for García's opening. Before the end of the first act, however, angry murmurs were heard as spectators began walking out, shocked that García would be so brazen as to sing in Italian an opera set in Spain. While García continued to present his repertoire of operas in the languages in which they were written, attendance plummeted. Colonel Castrejón lost both theaters as well as his personal fortune. Manuel García attempted to break even by giving a series of concerts in a ballroom, but in December 1827 the chamber of deputies passed a decree expelling Spaniards from Mexico. En route to embark at Veracruz, García's coach was attacked by brigands who robbed him of everything. It is not clear to historians why Andrés Prieto and the earlier arrival from Spain, Diego María Garay, were not affected by the expulsion decree. Miguel Valleto did have to leave, but later returned.

The theaters reopened in 1829, but the only noteworthy performance that season occurred in the auditorium. Vicente Guerrero, second president of the Republic, sitting in his box at the Principal on September 20, received word of a great victory won by General Santa Anna over the Spanish (who had not yet accepted Mexico's 1821 declaration of independence). Guerrero interrupted the play to make the announcement and the audience erupted in demonstrations of jubilation, jumping onto their seats and cheering, then following the president back to the palace.

In 1830 the task of forming a theater company "worthy of the enlightenment of the capital" devolved upon Colonel Manuel de la Barrera. He followed the usual procedure: hiring actors from Spain. Having solicited advice from the Mexican-born dramatist Manuel Eduardo de Gorostiza, who was then residing in Europe, Barrera assembled an excellent company, including leading actor Bernardo Avecilla (d. 1841) and actress–dancer Soledad Cordero (1816–47). He also hired Andrés Pautret as choreographer. Barrera's

*Left, Antonio Castro (1816–63) made his acting debut at the Teatro Principal in 1834 and long remained a popular favorite.*

*Right, the American balloon ascensionist Eugene Robertson won acclaim as "the first to voyage through the Mexican air" on February 12, 1835. The engraving is by Montes de Oca.*

*Promenades in the Alameda supplemented the many entertainment options available in mid-nineteenth-century México. From Christian Sartorius,* Mexico: Landscapes and Popular Sketches, *1859.*

one questionable decision, an irrational refusal to rehire Diego María Garay, led to public demonstrations (perhaps orchestrated by Garay) and letters to the newspapers; nevertheless, not until Barrera resigned from the theater management in 1832 did Garay return to the stage of the Principal. Appointed co-artistic director of the company, Garay opened the repertoire to the newest plays from Europe, that is, melodramas with stirring action and moral lessons—plays that might be seen as the popular side of literary Romantic drama. Garay's modern preferences were balanced by his codirector Avecilla's inclination for the classics. Another boost for the Principal occurred in 1834 with the debut of the Mexican-born actor Antonio Castro (1816–63), who had studied under Avecilla and quickly rose to become the company's most popular actor.

After leaving the Principal, Barrera became manager of the Plaza de Toros (bull ring), which he packed to capacity in 1833 for a well-publicized hot-air-balloon ascension by a French aeronaut. Reyes de la Maza recounts how the nervous balloonist, whose contract gave him an out in case of bad weather, managed to delay until he saw a distant cloud, which he claimed as a deterrent. Authorities jailed him as a charlatan, but Barrera refused to refund admissions. Two years later Barrera booked an authentic balloonist, the American Eugene Robertson, who charged ten thousand pesos per ascension. Again the Plaza de Toros was sold out. The balloon rose and soon became a speck in the blue sky, causing holiday excitement throughout the city—followed by a night of distress when there was no sign of its return. Having landed over sixty miles away, Robertson made his way back overland to a triumphal welcome. His second attempted ascension failed when the balloon would not inflate properly, and the fickle public mocked him in the newspapers. Robertson reclaimed his reputation six months later (September 13, 1835) with a new balloon he had ordered from the United States. First he sent up a small balloon on which appeared a huge portrait of General Santa Anna. Then Robertson ascended in an enormous balloon, waving a Mexican flag and throwing out leaflets of patriotic poetry. For his third triumph, a month later, he carried a passenger aloft; that beautiful but nervous young woman thus became the first Mexican ever to travel by air. The first Mexican aeronaut, Benito Acosta, capped the evening after his triumphal 1842 balloon flight over the capital by attending a program in his honor at the Teatro Principal at which the leading Mexican dramatist, Fernando Calderón, recited a poem he had composed for the occasion.

Entertainment options continued to expand during the 1830s. Masked balls were held in the theaters during the pre-Lenten carnival season. The Galli opera company arrived in 1831 and began performing twice a week at the Principal, leaving the rest of the week for the dramatic company. In 1834 having maintained their popularity for three seasons, the Galli singers threatened to leave the country unless they were paid the several months salary owed to them. The government gave in, and the Galli company stayed until 1838. The first elephant arrived in Mexico in 1832 and attracted throngs of admission-paying curiosity-seekers in the three months before it died; then the bones were cleaned and tickets sold to view the skeleton. The renowned marionette company of Los Hermanos Rosete Aranda, founded in 1835 in Huamantla, Tlaxcala, moved to the capital in 1880, began its worldwide touring in 1888 and remained active until 1941. Not only did the Rosete Aranda company boast three thousand marionettes, but it toured with its own orchestra and singers as well as puppeteers and technical crew.

Born in Guadalajara, Fernando Calderón (1809–45) earned a law degree at the university there. His first play, *Reinaldo y Elina,* was produced in Guadalajara in 1827, while he was still a student. That play and seven others known only by their titles are no longer extant, although several were produced in the theaters of Guadalajara and Zacatecas. The Romantic influence of Sir Walter Scott, Victor Hugo, and others is evident in Calderón's surviving three dramas, two of them with chivalric subjects and one on English history: *The Tournament (El torneo,* 1839), *Herman; or, The Return from the Crusade (Hermán, o la vuelta del cruzado,* 1842), and *Anne Boleyn (Ana Bolena,* 1839). His one comedy, *None of the Three* (A *ninguna de las tres,* ca. 1839), gently mocks the excesses of romantic sentimentality while incorporating Mexican local color and commenting obliquely on inadequate educational opportunities for women. Although all but one of his plays premiered in provincial theaters, they found great favor when later presented in the capital. Calderón's skillful dramaturgy, poetic language, and tasteful approach to Romanticism have sustained his reputation as one of Mexico's most important dramatists.

Others also wrote plays in the Romantic vein. Strongly influenced by the French Romantics, Ignacio Rodríguez Galván (1816–42) tended toward greater excesses of passion and poetic embellishment than Calderón. *The Chapel (La capilla,* 1837) and *Muñoz, Inspector of Mexico (Muñoz, visitador de México,* 1838) both dramatize violent episodes in sixteenth-century Mexican history. The latter premiered with considerable success at the Teatro Principal when the author was only twenty-two. Rodriguez Galván's unrequited love for actress Soledad Cordero drove him to seek a foreign diplomatic post, but he died of fever in Havana. Manuel Eduardo de Gorostiza (1789–1851) counts as a Mexican writer because he was born in Veracruz (of Spanish parents) and entered into Mexico's diplomatic service in 1824. However, his plays were written and premiered abroad. In the 1830s his plays began to be produced in Mexico City, including *Pardon for All (Indulgencia para todos,* 1818), *Customs of Yesteryear (Las costumbres de antaño,* 1819), and *Bread and Onions with You (Contigo pan y cebolla,* 1833). Isabel Prieto de Landázuri (1833–76) wrote about fifteen verse plays in various genres, at least four of which were staged in Guadalajara, one in Mexico City. Two of her plays have survived: *The Two Flowers (Las dos flores,* 1861), a romantic drama; and *The Two Are Worse (Los dos son peor,* 1862), a *costumbrismo* comedy that satirizes Romantic excess. Among many lesser Romantic dramatists, Pantaleón Tovar (1828–76) must be signalled for his frequent use of Mexican subjects, including, for example, *A Sublime Dishonor (Una deshonra sublime,* 1853), a "drama of Mexican customs in five acts and in verse."

*Left, when it opened in 1844, this magnificent theater was named after President Santa Anna, but it was El Gran Teatro Nacional during most of its seventy-six-year existence. From the Secretaria de Educación Pública.*

*Right, this 1852 city map shows the location of the capital's two leading theaters in relation to the Cathedral and the Palace, which form two sides of the zócalo. The Teatro Principal was located on the Calle del Coliseo. The Gran Teatro Nacional was further up the same street, then called Calle de Vergara.*

*The eighteen-hundred-seat, gaslit Teatro Iturbide opened in 1856. Today that structure houses Mexico's Chamber of Deputies. Courtesy of Biblioteca de las Artes, Centro Nacional de las Artes, México D.F.*

The 1840s saw several new theaters opened in the capital, beginning with the Teatro de Nuevo México (also known as Teatro de Belchite), which was inaugurated on May 30, 1841 with an all-Spanish company in Fernando Calderón's *The Tournament*. The fresh white and gold interior with portraits of authors and performers on the railings of the boxes offered a glaring contrast to the deficiencies of the Teatro Principal, which were pointed out yet again in the press: low doorways, poor sightlines, stuffy boxes, inadequate wing space, disagreeable smells. But the Principal's acting company was signalled as superior. The Principal's competition intensified that year when the Teatro Provisional was roofed over, and the following year when the Teatro Nuevo México presented *Goat's Foot* (*La pata de cabra*), a fairy extravaganza that had broken box-office records in France and Spain. In 1843 one could also choose among the popular fare at the Teatro de la Unión (also known as Teatro del Puente Quebrado), nine different illuminated scenes at the Diorama, and a performing chimpanzee (the first in Mexico) that could play the violin and fold his master's clothes. Brantz Mayer, an American in Mexico at the time, characterized the three theaters "which were almost constantly in operation": the Principal drew the old aristocracy, while those who craved novelty preferred the Nuevo México, and the Puente Quebrado offered coarse jokes and broad acting designed to appeal to a popular audience. Although Mayer frequently attended the Principal, it was at the Nuevo México that he kept a box with several young friends. Boxes could be rented by the month or year. Mayer noted that some families filled them "in full dress every evening" and used them as receiving rooms for friends. "The theater is a Mexican necessary of life," he wrote. "It is the legitimate conclusion of a day, and all go to it—the old, because they have been accustomed to do so from their infancy; the middle aged, because they find it difficult to spend their time otherwise; and the young for a thousand reasons which the young will most readily understand."

The theater that some called the finest in the world opened in Mexico City on February 10, 1844, one of a number of self-glorifying initiatives of Antonio López de Santa Anna, the military leader who also served various terms as president or dictator of Mexico. Originally named El Gran Teatro de Santa Anna, the theater was also known under different governments as El Gran Teatro Nacional and El Gran Teatro Imperial. The magnificent structure featured four Corinthian columns on the façade, an enormous vestibule, and an interior portico. There were twenty rows of orchestra seats, three tiers of boxes (a total of seventy-five boxes), and seating in the balconies and galleries. Although reserved seating was limited to 2,248, the theater's total capacity with its ten standing areas was estimated at over seven thousand. The building also included ample backstage facilities. Perhaps the most glittering event of its inaugural season was the grand ball held in the theater on June 13, 1844 to celebrate Santa Anna's forty-seventh birthday. The orchestra seats were removed to make a dance floor, and the interior was lavishly appointed with flowers, candles, and a statue of the honoree. At one o'clock in the morning, the stage curtain was drawn to reveal a banquet table for two hundred. The dancing continued until 7:00 A.M. The major theatrical production of that season was the Mexican premiere of José Zorrilla's *Don Juan Tenorio,* which had opened in Madrid only eight months earlier. Hired away from the Principal, Antonio Castro played Don Luís de Mejía. The production was also noteworthy for the ghostly effects created by machinist Alerci.

A major renovation early in 1845 transformed the shabby Teatro Principal, its notoriously dim lighting helped by an abundance of new gilt decorations. Two weeks after its reopening, an earthquake closed it along with the capital's other theaters until they could be inspected for safety. The Principal closed again during the United States Army's occupation of Mexico City (September 1847–June 1848). Because the social élite would not attend the theater in time of war, some theater managers turned to spectacle and variety entertainment—rope dancers, French gymnasts, a strong man—to draw attendance from the lower end of the social spectrum. The tactic backfired in the long run, as exemplified by an incident at the Nacional in November 1848: theatergoers in the cheap gallery seats expressed their boredom with a talky play by Eugène Scribe by whistling and stomping. The protests spread to the better seats and so drowned out the actors that the curtain was rung down in midscene. Many left the theater, but the rowdy ones in the balconies shouted for some musical numbers. The theater manager refused and ordered the house lights extinguished. In response, cushions were thrown into the orchestra and at the central chandelier, which was quickly raised up to the ceiling. When the rioters ran out of cushions, they threw their chairs, causing considerable damage, until the arrival of the police ended the protest. The occasional eruption of similar incidents over the next few years gave rise to a special appellation, *cócoras,* for the agitators. One artist who did succeed with the new audiences at the Nacional was Matilde Diez, "the Pearl of the Spanish Theater," who arrived with her own company in 1855, presented a repertoire of Romantic drama from France, Spain, and Cuba, and sustained the box office for a five-month run.

As contractor for the Gran Teatro de Santa Anna (Nacional), Francisco Arbeu had sunk his entire fortune into the building. Nevertheless, as soon as he could amass the funds, he began building another theater designed by the same architect, Lorenzo Hidalga. The cornerstone for the Teatro de Iturbide was laid in 1851, and it opened in 1856 with a masquerade ball. For its first theatrical production, Arbeu appropriately chose a Mexican work, Pantaleón Tovar's *And for What? (¿Para qué?).* It was at the Iturbide in 1864 that originated a tradition still practiced throughout the Spanish-speaking world: the annual presentation of Zorrilla's *Don Juan Tenorio* for the *día de los muertos*—All Soul's Day, the first of November. Less grand than the Nacional, the Iturbide held only eighteen hundred reservable seats, but it marked a major advance with its gas lighting.

And still more theaters opened in the capital: the Teatro de Oriente and the Teatro del Relox in 1855, the Teatro de la Esmeralda (later called Teatro de la Fama, and still later the Hidalgo) and the Teatro Aéreo in 1858. The capital's larger theaters usually served as venues for the lucrative costume balls at carnival time. During the theater season, they participated in considerable interchange of companies and individual artists. In 1860, Antonio Castro, for example, performed at the Principal on weekdays and at the Nacional on Sundays. Beyond Mexico City, a number of provincial towns had or soon would have theaters. Among these were Puebla, Mérida, Querétaro, San Luis Potosí, Guanajuato, Veracruz, and Guadalajara.

Theater attendance again declined during the Wars of Reform (1858–61) and the War of French Intervention (1861–63). However, the theaters frequently presented special fundraising programs to benefit Mexican soldiers. For example, one such evening at the Nacional, on May 20, 1862, honored General Ignacio Zaragoza with a play titled *Liberty in Chains* (*La libertad en cadena*), followed by a one-act satire, *The Domestic Tyrant* (*El tirano doméstico*) by a popular playwriting team, Juan A. Mateos and Vicente Riva Palacio. The intermission entertainment included prominent poets reciting poems they had composed for the occasion. Zaragoza's death a few months later occasioned additional patriotic evenings in his memory, one of which included an appearance by twelve soldiers who had been wounded on *el cinco de Mayo* (May 5, 1862); everyone present alternated cheers and tears as poems were thrown to the men on stage. The death of the beloved actor Antonio Castro in 1863 also occasioned a lavish memorial evening at the Nacional, where a bust of him was placed in a niche.

Mexico's Second Empire (1864–66)—the two-year reign of the Hapsburgs, Maximiliano and Carlota—brought new prosperity to the theaters, as the

*Concha Méndez made her debut as actress and singer in 1862, and was soon named Imperial Court singer. After the fall of Maximilian and Carlota, she continued performing in various theaters, notably the Nacional and the Principal. Courtesy of Biblioteca de las Artes, Centro Nacional de las Artes, México D.F.*

imperial couple devoted themselves to patronage of the arts. Several theaters were awarded lavish subsidies, including twelve hundred pesos a month for the company of the Teatro Principal. In addition, a Teatro de Corte was created in one of the palace ballrooms. For the court theater's inauguration on Carlota's birthday, November 4, 1865, the Principal company gave a command performance of *Don Juan Tenorio,* at which the author himself, José Zorrilla, read a poem he had composed for the occasion. Maximiliano honored these and other outstanding performers in the capital by naming them *actores de cámera* (actors of the imperial chamber). After Maximiliano's execution on June 19, 1867 (the empress already having returned to Europe, where she was diagnosed as psychotic), the *cócoras* again found their raucous voices. When the beloved Mexican singer–actress Concha Méndez appeared on stage, the audience normally called for her signature song "La Paloma," but after a performance of *The Death of Lincoln* (*La muerte de Lincoln* by Juan A. Mateos) at the Nacional on July 21, 1867, the rowdy element demanded "Adiós, mamá Carlota," a ditty satirizing the former empress. Méndez nobly refused to mock the foreign woman who had always treated her kindly, but the *cócoras* could not respect such sensibilities. Their whistles drowned out her attempt to sing "La Paloma," and Méndez left the stage in tears. The image of the Mexican star's conflicting emotions—patriotism versus personal loyalty—provides an appropriate metaphoric closure to the Romantic era.

## THE CARIBBEAN

While Cuba chafed under its continuing status as a colony of Spain, Romantic drama with its characteristic idealization of individuality and nationalism found receptive audiences there. The way was prepared with works like *America and Apollo* (*América y Apolo*), a heroic musical drama in one act, with libretto by Manuel de Zequeira y Arango, which premiered at the Principal and was also published in Havana in 1807. Because of censorship, dramatists often set their action in historical periods and distant lands, leaving it to their audiences to see analogies with Cuba. Thus the 1820s brought a number of melodramas about colonial Mexican and United States history. The newspapers provide us with titles of now lost and uncredited playtexts like *Great Washington, Genius of the United States* (*El gran Washington, genio de los Estados Unidos,* 1820).

Author of many short populist plays with a distinctly Cuban flavor, the actor Francisco Covarrubias (1775–1850) earned posterity's accolade as the father of Cuban theater. Born in Havana, Covarrubias demonstrated a gift for comedy from childhood. He acceded to his family's wish that he study medicine, but soon joined an amateur acting group that presented plays in the open air in the afternoons. By 1800 he had attracted the attention of Eustaquio de la Fuente, manager of the humble Teatro del Campo de Marte, who arranged Covarrubias's professional debut as a low comedian at the Teatro del Circo. Interrupted only by a long illness in 1823, Covarrubias acted continuously at all the major theaters of Havana from 1801 until his retirement in 1847 at the age of seventy-two. From about 1810 he wrote one or two plays a year: light pieces—mostly *sainetes* based upon Cuban customs, speech, and topical events—interspersed with music and his widely quoted humorous verses. Because they featured rough types like wagoners, hunters, and farmhands, the unrestrained depictions of Cuban life offended some *criollo* sensibilities, yet they served as an important springboard of nationalist sentiment. Unfortunately, only the titles of his plays and some verses have survived.

At fifteen José María Heredia (1803–39) wrote three plays and acted in a performance of one of them in Matanzas. The titles are indicative of their pre-Romantic tendencies: *Edward IV; or, The Merciful Usurper* (*Eduardo IV o el Usurpador clemente*, 1819) and *Montezuma; or, The Mexicans*, both verse dramas, and a *sainete* probably influenced by Covarrubias, *The Terror-stricken Peasant* (*El campesino espantado*). After translating a number of French plays, Heredia became involved in a conspiracy against the Spanish governor and had to go into exile. He continued writing plays, most of which premiered in Mexico, where he lived from 1825. At least one of his plays, however, reached Havana audiences when it was presented anonymously at the Diorama in 1833. Another Romantic, José Jacinto Milanés (1814–63), born in Matanzas, idealized Cuban womanhood in verse dramas like *Count Alarcos* (*El conde Alarcos*, 1838) and *The Poet at Court* (*El poeta en la corte*, 1840), which even found favor in Spain. Gertrudis Gómez de Avellaneda (1814–73) was Cuban, though she spent much of her life in Spain. Author of twenty Romantic dramas in the 1840s and 1850s, Gómez de Avellaneda achieved psychological depth of character within historical settings like the twelfth-century Spain of *Munio Alfonso* (1844) or the Biblical *Belshazzar* (*Baltasar*, 1858). Despite her success in Spanish theaters, Cuban censors either banned her plays or insisted on changes that reduced their effectiveness.

Other Romantic dramatists of Cuba include Joaquín Lorenzo Luaces (1826–67), José Agustín Millán, and Bartolomé José Crespo y Borbón (1811–71). The latter took the African pseudonym Creto Gangá for his *sainetes* using Afro-Cuban dialect to attack slavery. Francisco Javier Foxá (1816–65), from Santo Domingo, wrote his plays in Cuban exile. His *Don Pedro de Castillo*, wildly applauded at the Gran Teatro Tacón in 1838, may have been the first full-fledged Romantic drama written in the Americas. On Santo Domingo, Felix María del Monte (1819–99) was outstanding among a number of dramatists who took a Romantic approach to the dramatization of native historical subjects like his *Ozema; or, The Indian Virgin* (*Ozema, o la virgen indiana*, 1870).

Several Puerto Rican dramatists used local or historical color to express their nationalism, most notably Alejandro Tapia y Rivera (1826–82). Among the historical settings of his Romantic dramas were Elizabethan England in *Roberto D'Evreux* (1856), the St. Bartholomew's Day massacre in *Bernardo de Palissy* (1857), and Spaniards in the New World, *Vasco Nuñez de Balboa* (1872). Other playwrights included Salvador Brau (1842–1912), Ramón Méndez Quiñones (1847–89), and two women: Carmen Hernández de

*The first permanent playhouse in San Juan, capital of Puerto Rico, was built in 1832 and later named after Puerto Rico's great playwright Alejandro Tapia y Rivera. Fotógrafo El Mundo.*

Araújo (1832–77) and María Bibiana Benítez (1785–1873). A number of theaters were built on the island during this period, beginning in 1820 with one in Caguas and a "provisional" or temporary theater in Ponce. The capital's first permanent playhouse, the Teatro Municipal de San Juan (later named after Tapia y Rivera), was completed in 1832.

## CANADA

Apart from a growing fondness for melodrama and, in native drama, the sporadic appearance of themes relating to national politics and identity, Romanticism is not a concept that applies to the Canadian theater of 1825 to 1867. The unrest that resulted in the abortive uprisings of 1837 contributed to the use of dramatic form for airing of issues of the day, but most such works were published rather than performed. Subsequent decades saw the appearance of two important authors of Canadian historical dramas, Antoine Gérin-Lajoie and Louis-Honoré Fréchette. On the whole, however, it was already-familiar works from England that dominated the repertoire. Garrison theater continued to be presented right up until the departure of the British troops in 1871, while amateur theatricals spread to many smaller towns. The most significant development in this period was the construction of permanent playhouses as a means of attracting professional companies and individual performers from the United States and Europe, for which there was increasing demand. The trend was spurred also by the opening of the Erie Canal in 1825 and the completion of railway connections linking many towns

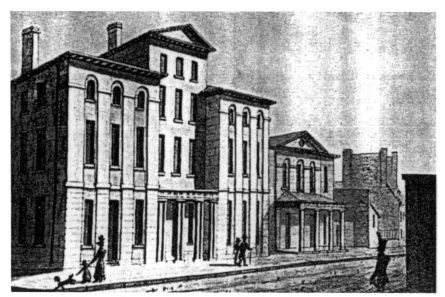

*In this 1826 drawing by John Drake, Montreal's first Theatre Royal (1825–47) is the two-story building with the portico on the far side of the Masonic Hall. Archives du Séminaire de Québec.*

*This illustration of the first Theatre Royal of Montreal shows manager Fredrick Brown and Miss Riddle on stage in* Virginius. *Franklin Graham,* Histrionic Montreal, *1902.*

in the 1850s. While rising professionalism characterized anglophone theater in this period, francophone theater remained the province of amateurs.

Eighteen different locations in Montreal are known to have been used for theatrical performances, both anglophone and francophone, between 1774 and the opening of Montreal's first permanent theater. Most venues were second-floor halls with probable capacities of no more than two hundred. The Theatre Royal (capacity one thousand) opened on November 21, 1825. The construction cost six thousand pounds, which was financed by English citizens under the leadership of principal shareholder John Molson. Considered spacious in its day, the two-story stone building, 60 by 110 feet, included a basement with two dressing rooms and a green room. The main entrance under the Doric portico led into a salon with access to the two tiers of boxes. An open gallery above the boxes and a pit with benches provided additional seating. A low partition separated the orchestra from the rest of the pit. Architect Gordon Forbes followed earlier English practice by incorporating doors in the proscenium.

The manager of the Theatre Royal's inaugural season, Frederick Brown (ca. 1794–1838), was born in England and had been acting with modest success in Boston and other American cities since 1816, but found his greatest popularity as a Shakespearean tragedian on his several appearances in Montreal. As the Theatre Royal's first lessee, Brown spared no expense. He employed a large company, including several women, mixing professionals from Boston with local amateurs. Early in 1826 he brought in an outstanding young American actor, Thomas Hamblin, and soon topped that with his engagement of Edmund Kean. Kean starred in several plays, including four of Shakespeare, supported by Brown and others of the Theatre Royal company, and was generously fêted by Montreal society. (During a subsequent Quebec engagement, Kean was initiated into the Huron tribe, made a chief, and given tribal garb, which he often wore—even as he used visiting cards with his Huron name, Alanienouidet, printed on the reverse—after his return to London.) Brown's lavish productions won praise, but his lax bookkeeping led to the loss of his lease in October 1826. From then until the razing of the theater in 1844, there were frequent changes of management and great variety in bookings, both amateur and professional. On the whole, the Theatre Royal achieved its purpose in attracting star performers from outside Canada. Among these were James Henry Hackett, Charles Kean, and Edwin Forrest in 1831, Charles Kemble and his daughter Fanny in 1833, Tyrone Power in 1835, and Charles Dickens in 1842. The penultimate season was managed by John Nickinson, who later would be closely identified with the Royal Lyceum Theatre of Toronto. A July 1844 visit by the English star William Charles Macready highlighted the Theatre Royal's final season, at the end of which the historic playhouse was razed to make space for the Bonsecours Market.

Montreal's second Theatre Royal, built in 1847, was also called Hays' House after Moses Hays, the businessman who owned that block in the city's fashionable quarter. With a capacity of twenty-four hundred and a 110-by-76-foot stage, the four-story facility proved best suited to opera and dance extravaganzas, despite the success of the first season's Shakespeare productions booked by manager George Skerrett (1810–55). After it burned down in 1852, a third Theatre Royal opened that year, with a smaller capacity (fifteen hundred), many safety features, and a removable floor for extending the stage level to the boxes so that the theater could be used for balls and meetings. Its first manager, John Wellington Buckland (1815–72), ran this Theatre Royal until 1868 and returned briefly in the 1870s. Most theatrical luminaries of their day made guest appearances with the Theatre Royal Stock Company during its summer seasons. Even the infamous John Wilkes Booth played there in 1865 shortly before he assassinated President Abraham Lincoln. Amateur groups usually rented the theater during the winter months. For a quarter of a century, this remained the fashionable theater of Montreal, but it declined after 1900 and was razed in 1913.

Although the majority of productions at the Theatre Royal were in English, francophones frequently attended, drawn especially to the musical extravaganzas. Conversely, when Montreal got its first visit by professionals from France—Scévola Victor's troupe, which had just played New York—the reception was only lukewarm. From February to May 1827, Victor's company played alternately at Montreal's Theatre Royal and Royal Circus (which had opened in 1824), followed by a short visit to Quebec. Leonard Doucette attributes Victor's lack of success not only to clerical opposition but to the French troupe's misreading of *Canadien* tastes. The Victor company's characteristic fare is evident in the list of pieces on the program for their final performance in Montreal: a one-act comedy titled *Les Mariages par circonstances* (Marriages of convenience); "a drama composed by M. Alvic, who performs it, and in which he imitates Talma," *Le Délire; ou, Les Folies de l'amour* (Ecstasy; or, Love's excesses); singing in French of the patriotic song "God Save the King;" a spectacular three-act melodrama with fighting and fireworks, *La Forêt périlleuse; ou, Les brigands de la Calabre* (The dangerous woods; or, The Calabrian brigands); a comedy–vaudeville with songs and dances, *Les Deux précepteurs* (The two mentors). Scévola Victor himself disappeared along with the company's funds, leaving the actors stranded. The salutary result was a series of benefit performances staged by amateurs. Later that year, in order to raise money and pay off the outstanding debts, Laurent Alvic created a show, *Le Comédien sans argent; ou, Le retour d'Alvic en Canada* (The penniless player; or, Alvic's return to Canada), a comedy "giving details of the flight of Mr. Victor," in which Alvic played five different roles.

Setting a better example for the francophone theater, Firmin Prud'homme, a French actor who had trained under Talma, arrived in Montreal in 1831, presented a series of dramatic recitals of French neoclassical scenes, and offered lessons in declamation. Soon he was working with Les Amateurs Canadiens. Their first program under his guidance consisted of Ducis's French adaptation of *Hamlet*, Molière's *Georges Dandin*, and Prud'homme's own historic scenes titled *Napoléon à Ste-Hélène* (Napoleon on St. Helena). Prud'hommme also performed in Quebec, where critics found his style "affected" in contrast to the praise he earned in Montreal. Residing in

Montreal until 1839, Prud'homme may be credited with raising francophone performance standards and including elements of Romanticism within the expanded repertoire he introduced. Another influential Frenchman, Hyacinthe-Poirier Leblanc de Marconnay (1794–1864) arrived in Montreal in 1834 and stayed six years. While working as a journalist, he wrote two plays for the Société Dramatique des Amateurs de Montreal. The group rented the Theatre Royal in 1836 and presented, among other pieces, his *Valentine; ou, La Nina canadienne* and *Le Soldat*, which they also published.

Another immigrant journalist, Aimé-Nicolas "Napoléon" Aubin (b. 1812) arrived in 1835 and settled in Quebec. A newspaper he founded there so riled authorities that he served two months in prison in 1839. Not long after his release, he founded a theater company called Les Amateurs Typographes, which rather contentiously presented a tragedy by the anticlerical Voltaire at Quebec's Theatre Royal. A second performance of the play—along with two entertainments by Aubin, *Le Soldat français* (The French soldier) and *Le Chant des ouvriers* (Song of the laborers), that were also perceived as seditious—elicted so much cheering and applause at "every allusion to resistance" that the audience did not disperse until 2:00 A.M. This provoked

*Left, John Nickinson (1801–64), actor–manager of the Royal Lyceum from 1853–58, is shown in the role of Havresack in the anonymous one-act* The Old Guard. *Metropolitan Toronto Reference Library.*

*Right, Toronto's first permanent theatre, the Royal Lyceum Theatre was located on King Street West, between Bay and York Streets. This woodcut appeared in* The Boy's Times *(July 21, 1858). Metropolitan Toronto Reference Library.*

the city fathers to rule that performances end by 11:00 P.M. When the Theatre Royal's management refused to rent it again to Aubin's amateurs, Aubin noisily launched a subscription drive to construct a rival playhouse. The management quickly relented.

Quebec's Theatre Royal was originally opened in 1824 as the Royal Circus by the partnership of West and Blanchard, who also opened the Royal Circus in Montreal that year. The facility's parterre had been used for equestrian spectacles created by West. Blanchard specialized in hot-air-balloon ascensions, which reportedly carried three people from the parterre to the level of the upper gallery. On the stage a pantomime or play was usually presented as a finale to the circus acts. Often the facility would be used as a circus by day and for legitimate theater in the evening. Chief Justice Henry Sewell bought the building, remodeled it, and reopened it as the Theatre Royal in 1832. The remodeling included elaborate interior decoration: the ceiling painted as a blue sky with clouds, a gilded star above the proscenium, and a sculpture of Shakespeare at the back of the stage. The theater remained in use until torn down in 1846. The Salle de Musique (Music Hall), designed by Charles Baillargé, that soon graced Quebec was built in 1852–53 as a concert hall (capacity fifteen hundred), but its well equipped stage made it suitable for legitimate drama, variety shows, public balls, and other events. Renamed Olimpic Theatre, and later Academy of Music, the building featured Quebec's finest entertainments until it burned down in 1900.

Frank's Hotel served as York's earliest theatrical venue. There, between about 1820 and 1830, theatergoers ascended an outside stair to the hotel ballroom where boxes and a pit seated about one hundred. Various other locations came into use in the 1830s and 1840s. The town (now called Toronto) got its first permanent playhouse in 1848 with the opening of the 750-seat, gaslit Royal Lyceum Theatre. Like other theaters of the day, it presented a mix of professional, amateur, and multicultural entertainments, including the Toronto Colored Young Men's Amateur Theatrical Society, which rented the Royal Lyceum for three nights in 1849. Outstanding among the theater's dozen or so managers during its quarter-century were John Nickinson from 1853 to 1859 and George Holman from 1867 to 1872. Nickinson (1808–64) had come to Canada with his British Army regiment. Stationed in Montreal, he enjoyed such success in garrison theater that he bought his discharge and embarked on a professional stage career. He honed his skills as a dialect comic and character actor over several seasons in the northeastern United States, including New York City, then toured with a troupe to Montreal, Quebec, and Toronto. In 1853 he took the lease on Toronto's Royal Lyceum. His four daughters acted with the company, as did actor–playwright Graves Simcoe Lee (1828–1912). Lee's very well received *Fiddle, Faddle, and Foozle* (1853), in which the author played Foozle, was the first play by a native-born Canadian to be staged in Toronto. Nickinson also presented Lee's farce *Saucy Kate* (1853), but his success with the Royal Lyceum rested largely on guest appearances by a number of distinguished actors. Nickinson instituted an annual Christmas spectacle and an annual tour to Hamilton, Ontario, where he also ran the Metropolitan Theatre. By 1858, however, an economic downturn led to his giving up the Royal Lyceum lease and returning to the United States. Nickinson's daughter Charlotte Morrison later managed the theater, which burned down in 1874. George W. Holman, Jr. (1821–88) ran the Royal Lyceum during the period when the Holman English Opera Troupe was in residence there. The company, composed largely of members of the Holman family, presented a variety of musical genres as well as legitimate drama, maintaining high artistic standards. One of Toronto's most beloved comedians, especially in Irish roles, the red-haired Henry Denman Thompson (1833–1911) performed at the Royal Lyceum under both Nickinson and Holman. His greatest success, however, came after 1875 when he toured as a Yankee character named Joshua Whitcomb in his own play, eventually titled *The Old Homestead*.

While theater as entertainment steadily gathered steam, drama as a vehicle for ideas erupted at crucial junctures in Canada's political life. Francophone Quebec produced a body of "paradramatic literature," journalistic or propagandistic material presented in a dialogue format. Doucette speculates that with a literacy rate of only 3 percent among the francophone population of Quebec province, this format encouraged those who were literate to read the articles aloud to the others, thus ensuring the widest possible dissemination. During the years of unrest leading to the Patriote Rebellion of 1837, those who rallied behind Louis-Joseph Papineau and put forward to the British government a list of grievances (the Ninety-Two Resolutions) met opposition from "Friends of the Status Quo." Doucette signals five dialogue pieces or *comédies du statu quo* (status quo comedies)—in two of which the Bureaucrates mock the Patriotes, followed by three from the Patriote point of view—published in the Quebec press in 1834. Although anonymous, these might well represent the earliest published plays by Canadian-born francophones.

The earliest *Canadien* author known to us by name is Pierre Petitclair (1813–60), the educated son of illiterate provincial Quebec farmers. Molière's influence pervades his three published plays. In *Griphon; ou, La Vengeance d'un valet* (Griphon; or, A valet's revenge, 1837), a valet dresses as a woman to dupe his eighty-year-old, womanizing master. The melodramatic *La Donation* (1842) not only bears the distinction of having been performed by Napoleon Aubin's Amateurs Typographes, but includes a number of local references as well as servants who speak the Quebec patois. Petitclair's third surviving play, *Une partie de campagne* (A country outing, 1856), humorously employs several varieties of diction and shows the folly of a French–Canadian's attempt to "anglicize" himself. Produced in Quebec in 1857 by Les Amateurs Canadiens–Français, the comedy kept the audience in fits of laughter. Although Petitclair's plays fell into long neglect, their very existence belies the infamous Report on the Affairs of British North America (1839) that Lord Durham submitted, based upon his five-month visit to Canada: "There can hardly be conceived a nationality more destitute of all that can invigorate and elevate a people, than that which is exhibited by the descendents of the French in Lower

Canada, owing to their retaining their peculiar language and manners. They are a people with no history, and no literature." Indeed, Durham's report smugly misrepresented conditions on a number of points.

The next important play by a native-born French-Canadian appeared only five years after Durham's report. Antoine Gérin–Lajoie (1824–82) excelled in his studies at the Collège de Nicolet, especially in rhetoric. At seventeen, he delivered a moving oration on Canadian history; at eighteen, he composed a long-popular patriotic song; and at nineteen, he wrote *Le Jeune Latour* (Young Latour, 1844), a three-act tragedy romanticizing an incident that had occurred in 1629. Gérin–Lajoie himself played the title role in the premiere performance at the Collège de Nicolet. One critic hailed him as "another Racine." Although there is no woman among the seven characters, two Iroquois join Latour on the side of France. Another graduate of the Collège de Nicolet, Louis-Honoré Fréchette (1839–1908) also wrote a historical drama while he was a student. First staged by an amateur group at the Salle de Musique de Québec, *Félix Poutré* (1862) went on to become the most frequently performed Canadian play of the nineteenth century. This comic melodrama about an alleged hero of the 1837 rebellion represents a dramaturgically significant advance over the work of Petitclair and Gérin–Lajoie. Fréchette wrote several additional plays, notably *Papineau* (1880), and was recognized as Canada's preeminent poet of his day. A one-act comic operetta by Elzéar Labelle (1843–75), *La Conversion d'un pêcheur de la Nouvelle-Ecosse* (The conversion of a Nova Scotia fisherman, 1869), comments on the effects of Confederation: the Acadian fisherman has fallen on hard times while the Quebec farmer, closer to sources of government handouts, has prospered.

The English-language theater too began to see plays on Canadian subjects. Although not produced, the pseudonymous *Female Consistory of Brockville* (1856) survives because it was privately published. Signed by "Caroli Candidus, Esq., a Citizen of Canada," the work seems to have been written by Mr. Whyte, the Presbyterian minister who actually had been forced from his position by some women of the congregation who found him insensitive to their needs. The play satirizes the women while suggesting that they resorted to slander to achieve their ends. Another pseudonymous dramatist, Sam Scribble, had three plays staged in 1865 at the Theatre Royal in Montreal: the satirical *The King of the Beavers* and *Dolorsolatio,* and the one-act farce *Not Dead Yet; or, The Skating Carnival.* The action of the allegorical *Dolorsolatio* occurs in Grandpapa Canada's house, where his family and guests gather. His two sons, Master East and Master West, are described respectively as "a gentleman of French education" and "an overgrown boy." Six characters represent Canadian towns: "fast" Quebec; "slow" Kingston; "blighted" London; "fashionable" Montreal; Toronto as "a young lady with a very good opinion of herself"; and Ottawa as "a young lady" just making her social debut. After witnessing from the backyard a shameful fight between the neighbors, Mr. North and Mr. South, the Canadians realize the importance of unity among themselves, thus presaging Canada's 1867 Confederation.

# 5  *Tradition and Transformation: 1870-1900*

## THE UNITED STATES

The nation was torn apart by the Civil War, but theater was surprisingly little affected. A few theaters closed for a short period at the beginning of the conflict, but most had reopened by 1862, even many in the South. Military movements and precautions disrupted civilian travel, so engagements by touring stars in the South were sharply curtailed. The quality of performance in southern theaters may have suffered as better actors moved North out of harm's way. But the Memphis Theatre company, for example, thrived during the war under the management of an occupying Union officer. The Richmond Theatre burned in 1862, but activities were moved to a temporary hall and the theater was rebuilt by 1863. New Orleans's Varieties Theatre remained in operation during the war. A few leading actors volunteered for service. Lawrence Barrett, a rising young tragedian at the beginning of the war, served with a Massachusetts regiment for a year. James E. Murdock, as noted in the preceding chapter, toured hospitals and encampments, giving public recitals of patriotic poems. Most actors, however, continued to pursue their profession and were, in fact, in demand as theatrical activity increased in the major cities of the East, especially in New York. In the turbulent years of the war, people may have needed theatrical inspiration and entertainment more than ever. After the Civil War, despite a few economic downturns, particularly in 1873, prosperity steadily mounted as industry, transportation, and financial services expanded. The completion of the transcontinental railroad in 1869, for example, was a singular achievement in a rapidly spreading, nationwide network of railways. By the mid-1880s, there were over one hundred thirty thousand miles of track, a four-fold increase since 1860. Railroads opened up the trans-Mississippi territory for uncontrolled settlement and the exploitation of natural resources, increasing tensions with the indigenous peoples of the West. Stimulated by easy access to eastern markets, giant cattle kingdoms sprawled across thousands of acres of the Great Plains. Railroads also facilitated the transportation of raw materials, especially iron ore and coal. Midwestern towns like Cleveland, Detroit, and Chicago mushroomed into

*Left, Civil War soldier audience. From Olive Logan's* Before the Footlights and Behind the Scenes, *1870.*

*Right, Steele MacKaye's double elevator stage at the Madison Square Theatre, formerly Daly's Fifth Avenue Theatre, New York, 1884. From* Scientific American, *1884.*

*Booth's Theatre, 1869. From* Harper's Weekly, *January 9, 1869.*

industrial and commercial metropolises. Energetic entrepreneurs organized business empires and amassed fortunes—for example, Andrew Carnegie in steel, John D. Rockefeller in oil, J. P. Morgan in banking, and Edward Henry Harriman in railroads. Astounding inventions—including the electric light, telephone, phonograph, radio, motion picture, automobile, and airplane—enhanced communications and the quality of life. Hundreds of new machines increased industrial productivity.

Population climbed from about thirty-nine million at the end of the war to seventy-six million at the turn of the century. New York grew from one-and-a-half million to three-and-a-half million—one-twelfth the population of the entire country. Thousands of former slaves migrated from the South. Rural communities declined as farm workers migrated to cities attracted by higher paying jobs in business, the professions, and manufacturing. Even the South, overwhelmingly agrarian before the war, gradually became more and more citified and industrial. Increased immigration also contributed to the population explosion. Wages and income generally accelerated in tandem with urbanization and industrialization. Flexing its industrial and technological muscle, the United States asserted itself as an imperialistic international power, following its quick victory in the Spanish–American War (April–October, 1898).

Affected by these powerful social and economic forces, there was an unparalleled, wholesale growth of theater—at least in the North. In the economically troubled South, a number of first-class theaters in Charleston, Mobile, and New Orleans never recovered their former standing. Growing urban populations with more disposable income and leisure time than the antebellum generation fueled a demand for recreational activities, including theatrical entertainment. The organization of the theatrical enterprise also shifted toward greater centralization and the model of commercial corporations and monopolies. At the outset of the era, theater like all the arts, was held in the sway of a conventional late-Romantic idealism, but certain modernist ideas gathered force as the century waned. The Gilded Age was a transitional, or transformational era between the Victorian world and the Modern Age, simultaneously moving forward while also sometimes nostalgically looking back. Overall, for the American stage, as for the society it reflected, it was a complex, generally progressive, dynamic time, but not without significant organizational and artistic turmoil.

BETWEEN THE END of the war and the turn of the century, thousands of theaters were built across the United States as part of the vigorous building boom that accompanied urbanization. In New York, twenty-five new theaters were built during the period, most located along or adjacent to Broadway in a commercial and residential district spreading northward roughly between Fourteenth and Forty-Second Streets. The area around Union Square at the south end of this corridor was home to various businesses servicing the burgeoning theatrical industry—dramatic agencies, costume shops, theatrical suppliers, photography studios, the offices of trade newspapers, and boarding houses, hotels, and restaurants that catered to the theater trade.

The new theaters, for the most part, followed the eclectic architectural fashion of the day with exteriors that suggested Renaissance, Second Empire, or even exotic Moorish-inspired buildings. Interiors were ornately decorated with conventional horseshoe-shaped auditoriums and picture-frame, wing-and-drop stages. Depending on whether the theater was designed for dramatic performance or more popular musical or variety entertainment, seating capacities ranged from about one thousand to twenty-five hundred.

There were few American architects of the time who specialized exclusively in theater building. The firm of J. B. McElfatrick (1829–1906) and Sons, however, built or remodeled about three hundred theaters in the United States and Canada between 1870 and 1920, including forty in New York, among which were the the Broadway (1888), the Empire (1893), Olympia (1895), the Victoria (1899), the Belasco (1900), and the Hudson (1903), all fairly conventional in design.

Several theaters built during the Gilded Age, however, were noted for their innovations both in architectural design and stage technology. Booth's Theatre, built for Edwin Booth in 1869 by the distinguished architect James Renwick Jr. (1818–95), among whose buildings were St. Patrick's Cathedral in New York and the Smithsonian Institution in Washington, D.C., was one of the finest of the era. The ornate Second Empire style of the exterior, and the lavishly decorated and appointed interior were impressive and handsome but conventional, although its orchestra seating and sweeping tiers of balconies broke with the earlier box, pit, and gallery configuration. The narrow apron and sunken orchestra pit, furthermore, anticipated features of Wagner's celebrated Bayreuth *Festspielhaus* which would open in 1876. Backstage, Booth's Theatre contained a number of mechanical innovations. Scenery was changed using huge, hydraulic lifts positioned below the stage to vertically raise a series of moving bridges and platforms. This mechanism allowed Booth's scenic artists to abandon the old-fashioned wing-and-drop system in favor of realistically detailed, architectural, three-dimensional scenic units. The theater also included a forced-air heating and cooling system, a sprinkler system for fire protection, and an electrical spark ignition device that for the first time in the United States permitted both the auditorium and stage lights to be extinguished during performance. In 1879, Steele MacKaye, a virtual Gilded Age "Renaissance man" of the theater, variously successful as an actor, manager, playwright, and inventor, redesigned the interior of the Madison Square Theatre, formerly Daly's Fifth Avenue, to include a double elevator stage on two levels. While one scene was being played at stage level, another scene could be arranged on a parallel stage located immediately below stage level. When the act drop was lowered, a scenic change was effected by raising the entire basement level setting to stage level, while the stage-level setting rose simultaneously into the area above the proscenium arch where stage hands could set up a new scene if necessary. At the next curtain, this setting could then be lowered to stage level while the stage-level setting sank to the basement. Scenes could be changed within two minutes using the system and the cycle could be repeated as often as necessary. He

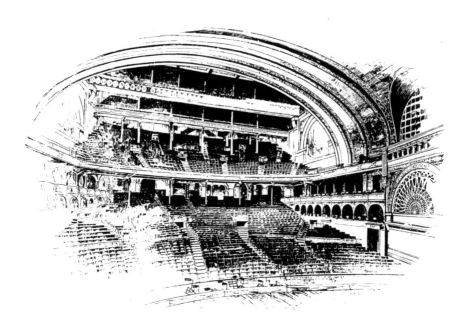

*Interior of Auditorium Theatre, Chicago. From a contemporaneous sketch. Courtesy Auditorium Theatre Council.*

*Interior of Auditorium Theatre, Chicago, 1889. Courtesy Auditorium Theatre Council.*

*Interior of Auditorium Theatre, Chicago, 1965. Courtesy of the Auditorium Theatre Council.*

also eliminated the apron, relocated the orchestra to a box directly above the proscenium opening, and reduced the seating capacity to seven hundred making it a much more intimate theater appropriate for realistic, modern drama. MacKaye continued his efforts to modernize theater architecture in the Lyceum Theatre (1885), which among its several mechanical innovations included an orchestra pit on an elevator.

In the Midwest, Chicago architect Dankmar Adler (1844–1900) built and remodeled numerous theaters in Chicago and other midwestern towns and cities. Adler was particularly innovative in designing auditoriums in which seating was arranged in a curvilinear fashion with a steep rise away from the stage, a design that promoted effective sightlines and especially acoustics. In 1885, for example, Adler and his partner Louis Sullivan (1856–1924) modified the auditorium of McVicker's Theatre, so that it followed his so-called isacoustic principle. He also installed a new heating and electrical lighting system.

Undoubtedly, Adler and Sullivan's finest achievement was the Chicago Auditorium Theatre. It was the first theater in the United States in which the fan-shaped, curvilinear auditorium departed completely from the traditional prevailing horseshoe shaped designs and in which most of the seats on several levels faced the stage. The Auditorium was designed to seat over forty-two hundred for operatic, choral, or orchestra performances. A special hinged ceiling could be lowered to close off the upper galleries, while a hanging curtain could be drawn across the rear of the auditorium, reducing capacity to about twenty-five hundred for dramatic presentations. The theater also had an innovative air cooling system. The stage was equipped with hydraulic lifts and a flexible stage floor, similar to that at Booth's Theatre, for changing scenery and a cyclorama for creating realistic sky effects. The handsome auditorium decor, combining bare electric light bulbs with gilded geometrical design and tasteful allegorical murals, was also completely fire resistant. Opened in 1889, the Auditorium Theatre was used mainly for opera and ballet performances until 1942 when it was abandoned. (Its hinged ceiling never worked properly or safely and despite excellent acoustics, it simply proved too large for a dramatic theater.) In the late 1960s, it was restored and reopened and continues to be used today for large-scale musicals, and dance and popular music concerts.

The New Theatre built in 1909 also deserves mention for its design inovations. Designed by the noted Beaux-Arts architects John Merven Carrère (1858–1911) and Thomas Hastings (1860–1929), it had sweeping flying balconies similar to the Auditorium Theatre and its state-of-the-art stage equipment boasted an electrically powered revolving stage, the first in America. But unlike the Auditorium Theatre, the acoustics were dreadful and with a seating capacity of over two thousand it was also too large to be a viable dramatic theater. Renamed the Century Theatre in 1911, it was converted to a house used mainly for lavishly staged musicals and operettas until 1930, after which it was demolished.

Despite the design innovations of the Auditorium Theatre and the New Theatre, American theater architects would not make a complete break with the conventions of the past until after World War II.

SPURRED BY AUDIENCE expectations and prosperity, visually elaborate and artistic productions became the norm during the Gilded Age. Scenic artists and costumers generally adhered to the established conventions of scenic realism with its demand for historical accuracy and authentic detail. Charles W. Witham (1842–1926) was one of the more prolific scenic artists of the era. Edwin Booth hired Witham first for his Winter Garden Theatre and then his Booth's Theatre scenic staff. Witham created the settings for all of Booth's scenically spectacular Shakespearean revivals at both theaters, including *Merchant of Venice* (1867), *Romeo and Juliet* (1869), *Hamlet* (1864–70), and *Julius Caesar* (1871). When Booth gave up management, Witham designed scenery for Augustin Daly's revivals of a series of Shakespearean comedies in the late 1870s and 1880s. Showing his versatility, in the 1880s Witham also designed scenery re-creating actual New York locales for actor–playwright Edward Harrigan's *Mulligan Guard* comedies. As a freelance scenic artist at the turn of the century, Witham worked for a number of producers and touring stars, including Fanny Davenport and Sarah Bernhardt. Among other leading scenic artists of the period were Ernest Gros, David Belasco's designer; Richard Marston (1842?–1917), an English scene painter, who designed numerous Broadway productions; and Edward G. Unitt, who worked for the Frohman brothers.

Only major producers had the resources to maintain resident scenic artists. Other theaters relied on a number of scenic studios to supply settings. A few leading scenic artists complained that the studios offered second-rate scenery, and that they prevented the development of scenic art. But several scenic studios prospered for decades and the quality of their products did improve. The Armbruster Studio, founded by German émigré scene painter Matias Armbruster in 1875, supplied stock scenery to local theaters and touring companies until the late 1950s. The Lee Lash Studio, founded in 1891, continued to operate until the mid-1940s. Some first-class designers opened their own scenery companies. In partnership with Joseph Wickes, Unitt, for example, organized his own studio at the turn of the century.

The invention of the carbon filament light bulb by Thomas Edison in 1879 also contributed to advances in scenic realism and in safety and comfort. By the turn of the century, most theaters had made the change from gas to electricity. Stage lighting consisted of lamps arranged in strips as borderlights, footlights, or winglights, and individual instruments—spotlights, and floodlights. Increasingly sophisticated switchboards and dimmer boards, lenses, and filaments were developed to control lights, their brightness and efficiency.

For the first half of the nineteenth century, actors and actresses generally supplied their own costumes. The pressures of historical accuracy gradually led some stars to commission designers for special costumes. Andrew Jackson Allen (1776–1853), for example, designed costumes for Edwin Forrest. Edwin Booth hired Thomas Joyce (1821–73) to design historically based costumes and manage an extensive costume department at Booth's Theatre. Critics of the time rarely commented on costumes, but Joyce's tasteful and authoritative designs were occasionally singled out for praise. H. A. Ogden (1856–1922) designed costumes for E. H. Sothern and Viola Allen, while E. Hamilton Bell, an English costume designer, created gowns for Ada Rehan and Julia Marlowe. Sometimes stars or producers commissioned gowns from European *couturiers* like Charles Frederick Worth (1825–95). Costume houses such as Dazian founded in 1842, Van Horne founded in 1852, Eaves founded in 1867, and Brooks founded in 1906, were important suppliers as theatrical production expanded. Indeed, the latter three lasted until the 1980s when they finally were merged as the Eaves Costume Company. By the turn of the century, the costume designer was an increasingly recognized theatrical artisan.

IN THE DECADE after the Civil War, the resident stock company, supplemented by the visiting star, remained the organizational backbone of the American theater. Most cities had at least one resident stock company; major metropolises might have two or three. For the most part, these companies continued to mount seasons which mixed standard favorites with new plays. Productions were rotated on a fairly regular basis, but long runs of a hundred or more continuous performances were not unusual before the war and would become commonplace in the 1870s and 1880s. The stock company was usually led by an actor–manager who generally adhered to time-honored practices—

traditional lines of business, repertory, and the use of stars. It functioned as a theatrical training school; for the talented and ambitious actor, it also provided a base to launch a career as a touring star. The resident stock company had its shortcomings and critics, but it provided a certain stability and financial security for the common player, handsome incomes for most stars, and respectable profits for managers. There were few pressures for change.

In the North several of the best antebellum companies continued to flourish after the war. At the Arch Street Theatre in Philadelphia, for example, Louisa Lane Drew (1820–97) managed a distinguished traditional stock company. Not only was Mrs. Drew a respected and gifted comedienne, she had a reputation as a skillful stage director and acting coach, with a sharp eye for spotting promising talents. Numerous rising Gilded Age stars would benefit from her tutelage, including her son John Drew Jr. (1853–1927), and daughter Georgiana Drew (1856–93), wife of the gifted émigré English actor Maurice Barrymore (1847–1905). Boston had two first-class companies: the Boston Museum Company, managed by Richard Montgomery Field from 1864 to 1893, and the Boston Theatre Company, managed most successfully by Junius Brutus Booth Jr. from 1866 to 1873 and then by Eugene Thompkins (1850–1909) from 1878 to 1885. Until his death in 1877, Benedict DeBar operated the stock company he had founded in St. Louis in 1855. In Chicago, James H. McVicker managed what was widely regarded as the best stock company in the best theater in the Midwest for over forty years.

The most prestigious companies were in New York, America's established theatrical capital. In the immediate postwar period, Wallack's Theatre was America's leading stock company. It was founded by English-born

*Left, Georgiana Drew Barrymore (left) with her mother Louisa Lane Drew c. 1880s. Theatre Cabinet Photographs Collection, Special Collections Library, University of Michigan.*

*Right, the New Wallack's Theatre, Broadway at Thirteenth Street (1861). From Lester Wallack's* Memories of Fifty Years, *1889.*

*Wallack's Theatre (1882) on Broadway at Thirtieth Street. From Lester Wallack's* Memories of Fifty Years, *1889.*

James William Wallack. After the elder Wallack's death in 1864, his son Lester assumed management of the theater. Lester, born in America, but sent by his father to England to be educated, was regarded as the handsomest man on the American stage and without peer in English gentleman roles or as a swashbuckling hero—Rob Roy, for example. Unusual for the period, Wallack's operated without stars, although both father and son were regarded as stars by the fashionable audience that patronized their theater. Under Lester's management, Wallack's solidified an enviable reputation for forceful ensemble acting, especially in classic English comedy and romantic melodrama, the company's stock-in-trade. Wallack's also had exclusive United States rights to the plays of several popular English dramatists of the day, including Tom Taylor, T. W. Robertson, H. J. Byron, and Watts Phillips. Many of the most talented and popular actors of the era were at various times associated with Wallack's. Some remained with the company for years or even decades. John Gilbert (1810–89), known for his portrayal of classic old men roles was with the company for twenty-six years; George Holland (1791–1870), a gifted low comedian, was a Wallack's member for fourteen years; Rose Coghlan (1851?–1932), unsurpassed in her day as a light comedienne, was connected with Wallack's off and on for over thirteen years; Elizabeth Ponisi (1818–99), who played old women's roles, was at Wallack's for seventeen years. Experience playing together over numerous seasons undoubtedly contributed to the quality of the Wallack's ensemble. In 1882, Lester built a new theater on Broadway and Thirtieth Street, which he managed until his retirement in 1887.

In 1869, the premier position of Wallack's Theatre was challenged when Augustin Daly (1838–99) organized his own company at the Fifth Avenue Theatre. Unlike most managers of the time, Daly was not an actor. His pre-

*Lester Wallack as Benedick in* Much Ado about Nothing. *From Hornblow,* A History of Theatre in America, *vol.1, 1919.*

vious theatrical experience had been as a drama critic and successful playwright and play adaptor. Actor–managers had always exercised a certain authority over theatrical production, but Daly quickly established himself as a stage autocrat, exercising total control over every aspect of production—play selection, casting, rehearsing, and preparation of the *mise-en-scène*. In this respect, he was one of American stage's first producer–directors or *régisseurs*. Daly produced a wide range of plays—Restoration comedies, Shakespeare, his own original melodramas and adaptations of new French and German plays and novels, and new American social comedies by Bronson Howard (1842–1908) and Olive Logan (1839–1909). Like Wallack, Daly also generally eschewed stars, although he occasionally presented major stars—Edwin Booth, for example—for limited runs. Daly also eliminated traditional lines of business: actors played as cast by Daly. Daly generally preferred to hire promising young performers over veterans, especially actresses—"Daly Debutantes" they were called. He would then mold their talents and public appeal by casting them in vehicles tailored to their abilities and personalities. Daly was an astute judge of talent and a skillful teacher and director, but some actors chafed under his autocratic methods. After a few seasons with "The Governor," as he was known, they would transfer to a rival company or strike out as independent stars. Dozens of Gilded Age stars owed their careers to Daly, including such luminaries as Clara Morris (1846–1925) and Fanny Davenport (1850–98). Other Daly actors were intensely loyal to him and remained with his company for decades, including

*Left, Lester Wallack as Young Marlowe in Oliver Goldsmith's* She Stoops to Conquer. *Theatre Cabinet Photographs Collection, Special Collections Library, University of Michigan.*

*Right, Augustin Daly c. 1880s. From Joseph Francis Daly's* The Life of Augustin Daly,

*Augustin Daly c. 1870s. From Joseph Francis Daly's* The Life of Augustin Daly, *1917.*

Otis Skinner (1858–1942) and Bijou Heron (1863–1937), daughter of Matilda Heron (1830–77) and later the wife of actor-producer Henry Miller (1859–1929). Ada Rehan (1860–1916), Daly's principal leading lady, John Drew, his principal leading man, Mrs. Gilbert (1822–1904), a specialist in old women roles, James Lewis (1840–96), one of the era's most versatile and talented comedians, and Charles Fisher (1816–1911), noted for his skill in classic English comic roles—all were members of Daly's company for virtually their entire careers.

In 1879, Daly moved his company to a renovated theater on Broadway and Thirty-Ninth Street, which he renamed Daly's Theatre. For the next twenty years, he solidified his reputation as a *régisseur*. Indeed, he became the prototype for the producer–directors who would increasingly dominate the turn-of-the-century stage. In 1884, Daly expanded his sphere by touring his company during the summer months, including an engagement in London. Daly's was the first American stock company to perform in London. In 1886, the Daly company followed their second London tour with engagements in Hamburg, Berlin, Paris, and the English Provinces. In 1892, Daly built his own London theater where his company performed annually in the summer months throughout the 1890s. A highlight of these years were Daly's scenically splendid revivals of ten of Shakespeare's comedies, featuring his "Big Four"—Rehan, Drew, Gilbert, and Lewis—supported by a rigorously rehearsed company of younger performers.

Wallack and Daly remained the leading managers in the 1880s, but they faced increasing competition from rival managers. In 1872, for example, A. M. Palmer (1838–1905), a lawyer attracted by the theater, but with virtually no theatrical experience, took over the management of the Union Square Theatre, a variety house. Palmer reoriented the theater toward legitimate drama with lavish stagings of new French, English, and American plays. Over the next ten years, he developed one of the largest and best companies in New York, often enticing actors away from Wallack's and Daly's with significantly higher salaries and a management style that was businesslike, but amiable and supportive. Like Daly, Palmer also broke with the traditional lines of business and actors were cast in various roles, both large and small; but unlike Daly and Wallack, Palmer did feature or star company actors, and he regularly used visiting stars as well. Unlike Daly, Palmer preferred experienced, even seasoned, actors rather than neophytes, but he did foster the careers of Agnes Booth (1846–1910), William H. Crane (1845–1928), Richard Mansfield (1854–1907), James O'Neill (1847–1920), and William Gillette (1853–1937). In 1883, Palmer left the Union Square theater for the Madison Square Theatre where he continued his now established managerial practices. In 1888, following Lester Wallack's death, he took over Wallack's Theatre, renamed it Palmer's and in 1891 he moved his company to this theater. At all of his theaters, Palmer fostered the production of high-class plays of contemporary life, often commissioning new plays, translations, and adaptations. He promoted American drama, producing Bronson Howard's *The Banker's Daughter* (1878), Bartley Campbell's *My Partner* (1879), Clyde Fitch's *Beau Brummel* (1890), James A. Hern's *Margaret*

*Fleming* (1891), and Augustus Thomas's *Alabama* (1891). He also produced the plays of contemporary British playwrights Oscar Wilde, Henry Arthur Jones, and W. S. Gilbert. A dramatization of George du Maurier's sensational novel *Trilby* (1895) proved one of his most successful productions.

In the late 1880s, the Frohman brothers, Daniel (1851–1940) and Charles (1860–1915), joined Daly and Palmer as important New York theatrical managers. Before becoming managers, the Frohmans had worked on the business side of theater, but never in any artistic capacity. Daniel managed the Lyceum Theatre from 1887 to 1908 where he developed a fine acting company, which at various times included such notables as E. H. Sothern (1859–1933), Georgia Cayvan (1858–1906), and Minnie Maddern Fiske (1864–1932). After several lucrative successes as an independent producer, Charles Frohman formed his own company in 1893 at the new Empire Theatre, which he had built on Broadway and Fortieth Street. The Frohmans were essentially theatrical entrepreneurs. They were not without artistic interests, but their principal orientation was commercial. To a greater extent than most of their contemporaries, they exploited the commercial possibilities of the long run and stars. Success was measured largely by the box-office draw; and both Frohmans, but especially Charles, had a keen, almost unerring, sense of what would appeal to the playgoers of their day. Charles's notable productions included many new American and British plays, among them David Belasco's and Franklin Fyles's western melodrama *The Girl I Left Behind Me* (1893)—later made into an epic film by director John Ford—Clyde Fitch's *Barbara Frietchie* (1899) and *Captain Jinks of the Horse Marines* (1901), James M. Barrie's *The Little Minister* (1897) and *Peter Pan* (1899), and Oscar Wilde's *The Importance of Being Ernest* (1895). Many of these productions also operated as star vehicles for featured members of Frohman's Empire Theatre company. Charles Frohman acquired an estimable

*Minnie Maddern Fiske c. 1880s. Theatrical Cabinet Photographs Collection, Special Collections Library, University of Michigan.*

*Minnie Maddern Fiske c. 1880s. Theatrical Cabinet Photographs Collection, Special Collections Library, University of Michigan.*

reputation as a "starmaker." Among the many stars who benefited from his patronage were William H. Crane, Maude Adams (1872–1953), Julia Marlowe (1866–1950), Viola Allen (1869–1948), Arnold Daly (1875–1927), Ethel Barrymore (1879–1959), and Margaret Anglin (1876–1958). At the turn of the century, the Frohmans were the most successful producers in America. The Empire Theatre company was widely regarded as Broadway's glittering jewel. To star or have one's play produced at the Empire was the goal of every ambitious actor and playwright.

Building on his Empire Theatre successes, Charles Frohman acquired five more theaters in New York, several theaters in other cities, and the Duke of York's Theatre in London. In the last decade of his management, he was producing as many as twelve productions annually and had thousands of employees, including several hundred actors. Frohman was killed in 1915 as a passenger aboard the torpedoed *Lusitania,* but his managerial style continued to influence theatrical tastes and practices long after his death.

After 1900, Charles Frohman's chief managerial rival was David Belasco (1853–1931). Unlike other major New York managers of his generation, Belasco had a theatrical background. He began his career as an actor in San Francisco, his hometown, then worked as a stage manager, producer, and playwright. In the early 1880s, after coproducing a successful revival of *The Octoroon* at Baldwin's Theatre with another Frohman brother, Gustave (1854–1930), Belasco was hired as the stage manager and resident dramatist at the Madison Square Theatre. When A. M. Palmer took over the Madison Square, Belasco moved to Daniel Frohman's Lyceum Theatre. In the mid-1890s, he left Frohman to become an independent producer and playwright, achieving notable successes with his own plays *Madame Butterfly* (1900), the basis for Puccini's famous opera, and *Du Barry* (1901).

*A scene from David Belasco's* The Girl of the Golden West. *Belasco Theatre, 1905. Scenery: Ernest Gros; costumes, E. S. Freisinger. Frank Keenan, left. Blanche Bates with outstretched arm as Minnie. Robert Hilliard (1857–1927), leaning on bar as Dick Johnson. Courtesy of the Museum of the City of New York. The Byron Collection.*

Belasco's most productive period began in 1902 when he began to operate his own theater, becoming an influential producer and *régisseur*. He extended his ideal of scenic naturalism which he had been promoting since his apprentice years in California. "Everything must be real" was his aesthetic dictum. Belasco's productions pushed nineteenth-century stage realism to new extremes with solid, three-dimensional scenic units, actual objects, elaborate, historically accurate costuming, and "natural" lighting effects. Like Daly, Belasco controlled every aspect of production and he also tended to hire relatively inexperienced performers whom he then cast in vehicles—usually written by himself—tailored to their particular talents and personalities. He rehearsed his productions for an unheard of ten weeks (four was normal, although Palmer usually rehearsed six weeks) and he was a demanding, but effective acting coach and director. Although his own plays were romantic, sentimental, and melodramatic, Belasco championed an acting style that emphasized the personality of the performer, but that was also natural, spontaneous, and emotionally truthful. Under his tutelage a number of actors rose to stardom, including Blanche Bates (1873–1941), the original Cho-Cho-San in *Madame Butterfly* and Minnie in *The Girl of the Golden West* (1905), which was also operatized by Puccini; Mrs. Leslie Carter (1862–1937) who would become one of the leading emotionalistic actresses of the time; and David Warfield (1866–1951), whom Belasco changed from a vaudevillian comic to a preeminent character actor, often praised for his unaffected, natural style.

Belasco was the last of the nineteenth-century *régisseurs*. In the final decade of his career, his plays and production methods were considered old-fashioned, although they were being absorbed and successfully exploited by the movie industry; Belasco-trained actors continued to perform throughout the 1920s and 1930s.

As early as the mid-1870s, the rise of the combination company threatened the centrality of the resident company in the organization of the American stage. A combination was a theatrical company organized to tour a single play, or perhaps a small repertoire of two or three plays, featuring a prominent star, or occasionally, stars. Combination companies traveled with their own stock of scenery, properties, and costumes and a cadre of at least essential support personnel—for example, a company manager, a bookkeeper, and a dresser or two.

How the combination company arose is not altogether clear. Traveling companies were common in the early development of the American theater, but they usually toured a repertoire of plays, not a single play. Nor did they travel with scenery as elaborate as that of the late-nineteenth-century combination companies. They were, to a large extent, traveling stock companies and they were virtually phased out with the rise of the stock and star system in the 1830s and 1840s. Joseph Jefferson III (1828–1905) claims that he and the English actor–manager Charles Wyndham (1837–1919), who lived in the United States from 1862–72, simultaneously, but independently, established the combination system in 1868 when they toured their own productions, respectively, of *Rip Van Winkle* and *The Lancers*. Laura Keene, however, toured a combination company as early as 1862–63. Certainly the growth of railroads stimulated the organization of the combination company. In 1860, there were about thirty thousand miles of track. After the Civil War, with the laying of the transcontinental system, railways expanded rapidly. By the mid-1880s, there were over one hundred thirty thousand miles of track. The combination system was firmly established by 1875 with nearly a hundred companies on the road. In the early 1880s, the number increased to almost 140. By the early 1890s, there were over 230 companies; in the peak season, 1904, there were 420 companies touring. Charles Frohman was particularly successful utilizing the "star and combination" system. Members of his Empire Theatre company would be promoted as "stars" as quickly as possible and then sent, with a supporting cast, on national tours in their latest New York hit. For example, in 1897 he presented Maude Adams as Lady Babbie in James M. Barrie's *The Little Minister*. It ran for three hundred consecutive performances in New York, after which it toured for a year.

Resident companies declined in number with the increase in combinations. In the early 1870s, for example, there were about fifty permanent companies nationwide. By the end of the decade, there were fewer than ten companies in operation. The famous New York companies continued to prosper in the late 1880s and 1890s in large part by embracing the long run followed by a combination tour. David Belasco maintained a company until he retired in 1930. By the turn of the century, however, the resident company had virtually ceased to exist, their theaters becoming combination, or "road," houses.

By 1905, *Julius Cahn's Official Theatrical Guide*, the "bible" for the theatrical producer, listed over seventeen hundred theaters nationwide available to touring combinations, and there may have been another thousand unlisted theaters. Theater in America became virtually synonymous with touring. Even major stars eventually succumbed to the combination company. Between 1886 and 1891, Edwin Booth, for example, completed five nationwide, combination tours organized by his close friend and fellow tragedian, Lawrence Barrett, including three "joint starring" tours with Barrett and a tour featuring the Polish émigré tragedienne Helena Modjeska (1840–1909).

The Booth–Barrett tours represented the acme of high theatrical art in the Gilded Age, and they were also unique in that they toured a repertoire of plays. Most combinations, for example, offered only a single play—a classical tragedy, a standard comedy, or a popular melodrama. Combination touring productions of *Uncle Tom's Cabin*—"Tom shows," they were called— were especially prolific. Stars often found themselves locked into one popular role which they then had to relentlessly tour season after season. Although Joseph Jefferson played a few other roles, he was almost exclusively identified as Rip Van Winkle in the play of that title which he toured season after season, first as a traveling star and then with combination companies for his entire career. Jefferson seemed never to tire of Rip, a role which the charismatic actor invested with warmth and humor. In contrast, James O'Neill (1846–1920), father of the playwright Eugene O'Neill (1888–1953), believed he had squandered his talent playing one role season after season for over twenty-five years: that of Edmund Dantès in a dramatization of Alexandre Dumas's *The Count of Monte Cristo*. O'Neill would occasionally appear in other roles, but they were never as popular as Dantès. In the popular mind, O'Neill was exclusively "The Count of Monte Cristo." It was the same story for many other Gilded Age stars. Frank Mayo (1839–96), for example, had achieved some success as a leading stock actor, then as a traveling star in a range of standard and new roles. In 1872, he acted Davy Crockett in a play by Frank Murdoch (1843–72), a role which proved so popular that he played it continuously for the next twenty years.

The problems arising from the sheer number of theatrical attractions on the road each season led to the formation of new theatrical associations and businesses to more effectively coordinate and organize touring attractions. One way of organizing touring was through a theatrical circuit. Theater managers or owners within the same geographical area or along a principle railroad route banded together as a collective or circuit to book touring combinations as a block. Usually collective booking was less expensive than single booking. Combinations were also less likely to cancel an agreement with a circuit than with a single manager or owner. There was, for example, an eastern circuit for cities between New York and Halifax, a Kansas–Missouri circuit, a Saginaw Valley circuit for towns in Michigan, the Lone Star circuit in Texas, to name just a few of the dozen or so circuits in operation. Touring also led to the rise of the booking office which negotiated contracts between circuit managers and touring productions. Dramatic agencies also arose to negotiate contracts for leading actors. Stock companies were self-contained units producing their scenery, costumes, properties, and so forth "in house." With the breakdown of this system, new theatrical service industries developed, ranging from costume houses to professionally oriented journals. Theater gradually became more and more a business enterprise or commercial industry, following the model of other industries then developing in the United States. Theatrical production passed from the control of actor-managers to that of entrepreneurial, business-oriented producers.

In 1896 a partnership, known as the Theatrical Trust or Syndicate, was formed among Charles Frohman; Alf Hayman (1866–1921), who controlled most of the theaters in a western circuit between San Francisco and Omaha; Marc Klaw (1858–1936) and Abraham Erlanger (1860–1930), who together operated one of the largest booking agencies; and Fred Nixon (né Nirdlinger; 1877?–1931) and Fred Zimmerman (1841?–1925), who together operated theaters in Philadelphia and other mid-Atlantic cities. The original partners were soon joined by the Boston managers and producers William Harris Sr. (1844–1916) and Isaac Rich (1827–1908). By the early 1900s, the Syndicate owned, leased, or, by striking deals with circuit managers, operated most of the first-class theaters across America—perhaps as many as seven hundred theaters.

The Syndicate was essentially a monopolistic booking agency, organized, like most monopolies of the era, to reduce competition and maximize profits. Their contract with theater managers demanded exclusivity: they were to be the sole agency supplying touring productions. They dictated which productions would be booked to tour, in which theaters they would play and when, and on what terms. So large was its network that theater owners, producers, and star actors not associated with the Syndicate—"independents," they were called—soon discovered that it was difficult, if not impossible, to tour without a Syndicate agreement.

On the positive side, the Syndicate brought stability and efficiency to the complex, sometimes chaotic touring circuit. They renovated old theaters and built new ones; they increased access to first-class productions; and they made money for their partnership and its constituent members. Some popular stars, however, long accustomed to negotiating bookings and terms directly with managers, balked at losing their autonomy. Most eventually succumbed to Syndicate pressure and came into the fold. For those who did, the financial rewards could be substantial. Those who doggedly tried to maintain their independence usually found themselves blacklisted or boycotted from Syndicate productions and theaters. When, for example, Minnie Maddern Fiske tried to book a national tour in her usual way, she soon found that she was completely shut out of Syndicate theaters and forced to play in second-rate houses or in alternative spaces—skating rinks, convention halls, hotel ballrooms, or circus-style tents. In 1904, David Belasco, one of the independent producers, had planned to tour his popular, romantic melodrama, *The Darling of the Gods,* set in "old" Japan, to St. Louis for the World's Fair crowd. The Syndicate had reserved St. Louis's only first-class theater, the

Olympic, for their own attractions. Belasco, undeterred, booked an independent, but second-class house, whereon the Syndicate revoked their previous agreements with him for bookings in other cities. Moreover, the Syndicate spitefully scheduled their own "Japanese" production, *The Japanese Nightingale,* against Belasco to "steal his thunder" and reduce his profits. In fact, this became a typical Syndicate ploy to undermine a rival production or star. The Syndicate also selected plays to produce in accordance with their own conventional taste and, especially, estimations of profitability. Stars managed by the Syndicate, who might have preferred a higher caliber drama, were often forced to tour in shallow, but profitable, romantic claptrap. Serious "modern" plays, whether European or American, had little chance of being produced.

Recent studies suggest that many of the charges brought against the Syndicate were not wholly justified; but at the time, the organization was regularly castigated by theater critics and independent producers and stars. In their view, theater had become unduly commercial under Syndicate control. After the Sherman Anti-Trust Act became law in 1905, several suits were brought against the Syndicate for illegal business practices—unfair competition, restraint of trade, discrimination—but the actions were either dismissed or decided in favor of the Syndicate.

An effort to break the Syndicate's stranglehold on touring was initiated in 1902 by a group of actors and managers led by the Fiskes. Calling themselves the Independent Booking Agency, they claimed to control over four hundred theaters, including a circuit of popular priced theaters in Michigan and Ohio managed by John H. Havlin (1847–1924) and Edward D. Stair (1859–1951)—indeed, Stair and Havlin were a sort of minor Syndicate. None of these theaters were first-class houses, however. After two seasons, the Independent Agency was crushed when the Syndicate struck a deal with Stair and Havlin.

Eventually the Syndicate's monopoly was broken not by outraged critics, actors, and producers, but by rival monopolists. The brothers Shubert—Lee (1875?–1953), Sam S. (1877?–1905), and Jacob J. (1879–1963)—arrived in New York around 1900 from Syracuse where they managed a circuit of upstate theaters. They leased the Herald Square Theatre and established themselves as producers with several outstanding presentations, including a Richard Mansfield starring engagement. Gradually they began leasing, purchasing, or building additional theaters in New York and other cities. Initially the Shuberts worked with the Syndicate, but the Syndicate soon realized the competitive potential of the Shuberts and tried to restrain their expansion. The Shuberts were not cowed. They formed an alliance with Belasco and the Fiskes, and then with backing from various financiers, they bought or built more theaters. For a decade, the Syndicate and the Shuberts battled for supremacy; but by the early 1920s, what was now the Shubert Theatre Corporation reigned as the most powerful theatrical management and producing company in America. They controlled as many as a thousand theaters, produced up to fifty new attractions each season, and employed hundreds of actors, singers, dancers, and other theatrical workers. The Shuberts promoted numerous performers, especially musical comedy stars, and they produced some especially notable operettas, musicals, and revues, but whether they contributed more than the Syndicate to elevating theatrical standards or to the art of the theater is debatable. The struggle between art and commercialism would continue to be an ongoing theme in the American theater.

THE ACTING PROFESSION went through a number of changes in the post-Civil War era. The growth of theater, especially the touring phenomenon, brought unparalleled opportunities for Gilded Age actors. In 1888, for example, *The New York Dramatic Mirror* estimated that there were over twenty-four hundred legitimate actors working in the United States. By the turn of the century, the number of actors had grown to probably over fifteen thousand. If one includes professional showwomen and showmen—i.e., dancers, circus performers, and variety artists—there were perhaps as many as thirty to forty thousand employed in some form of theater or popular entertainment.

These numbers undoubtedly apply mainly, perhaps solely, to white actors. For black actors the situation was rather different. Errol Hill reports that in the decades after the Civil War a score or more of black dramatic companies—mostly amateur or semiprofessional groups—were organized in cities across America. During the 1880s, New York's Astor Place Company

*Left, Frank Mayo as Davy Crockett. Theatre Cabinet Photographs Collection, Special Collections Library, University of Michigan.*

*Right, Steele MacKaye c. 1880s. Theatrical Cabinet Photograph Collection, Special Collections Library, University of Michigan.*

of Colored Tragedians (founded in 1878) was a leading black professional theater company. Under the leadership of J. A. Arneaux (1855–?), the Astor Place Company mounted productions of Shakespeare and other standard tragedies at various venues around the city. The company also toured to Philadelphia and Providence. Arneaux's career as a tragedian was brief, roughly three years between 1884 and 1887, but during this time he earned a reputation for his interpretations of Iago, Macbeth, Romeo, and especially Richard III which were favorably compared to the performances of the leading tragedians of the time, including Edwin Booth. Within the black community, a number of African Americans would earn distinction as classical actors during the Gilded Age. For over thirty years, Henrietta Vinton Davis (1860–1941) won acclaim for her solo recitals and performances with other black actors of scenes from Shakespeare's plays. Davis also produced and starred in touring productions of original plays by African–American dramatists. But Davis was a notable exception. Excluded from white companies and with a paucity of professional black theater companies, apart from minstrel troupes, the opportunities for black actors whose talents and interests lay in the legitimate theater sphere were very limited. Not until the turn of the century would there be a genuine flowering of African–American actors and companies committed to the performance of legitimate drama.

Dozens of star actors and actresses achieved prominence on the late-nineteenth-century stage, many of whom earned princely incomes of one hundred thousand dollars or more each season, principally from touring. Below the stars were numerous leading actors, comedians, character, and utility actors whose salaries ranged from as much as two hundred fifty dollars a week for a leading man or lady to eighteen dollars a week for a general utility player. There was no uniform salary scale; actors, or their agents, negotiated their own terms and there could be a significant range of pay even for comparable roles, depending on where you worked, whether on Broadway or in a touring company. Actors were hired on a seasonal basis, but company members could reasonably expect to be rehired from season to season. As noted above, some actors remained with a single company for their entire careers. As a general rule though, most stayed with a company only for a season or two and then they moved on for better roles or higher pay. But actors who worked steadily enjoyed annual incomes which compared favorably with other middle-class occupations of the time. Many actors, however, experienced periods of regular unemployment. There were always more actors than jobs; competition remained keen. McArthur notes that in 1900, with more companies touring than ever before, nearly 30 percent of the actors and 40 percent of the actresses reported they were unemployed.

Despite increased opportunity, entrance into the profession was not easy. Many late-nineteenth-century actors were born into theatrical families—the Booths, the Davenports, the Drew-Barrymores, and the Jeffersons, for example. Typically, the children of actors followed in their parents' footsteps, often making their first stage appearances as children or teenagers. Aspiring actors without such connections petitioned managers for an audition. If the audition was successful, then a young professional started out on the lowest rung in the company as a general utility player. Gradually one might advance to larger roles as a walking lady or gentleman, then to juvenile or ingenue, and finally to principal character actor or leading man or lady. An occasional young actress endowed with special beauty, talent, and a magnetic personality might begin her career as a leading lady or star, but this was the exception rather than the rule. Once in the company, actors could improve their skills by taking private classes in elocution, singing, dancing, or fencing, but there was no systematic approach to actor training. One learned one's craft principally through experience. This generally worked as long as there were stock companies. With the rise of the long run and touring, a new approach to actor training was demanded.

Steele MacKaye was an early advocate and organizer of acting schools. In 1869–70 he studied in Paris with the noted French acting teacher and theorist François Delsarte (1811–71) who had invented a system to promote natural acting. Returning to America, MacKaye called for the establishment of an acting school based on the Delsarte method. MacKaye's first acting schools were, for various reasons, relatively short-lived; but in 1884, in association with Franklin H. Sargent (1856–1923), a teacher of elocution and stage director, MacKaye organized the Lyceum Theatre School. MacKaye left the Lyceum after a year, but under Sargent's leadership, the renamed (in 1892) American Academy of Dramatic Arts, became America's premier acting school. Over the course of four years students took classes in diction, pantomime, dancing, stage business and rehearsal, fencing, and makeup. They were also given opportunities to act in professional companies associated with the school or in productions mounted by the school itself.

Other American acting schools founded around the turn of the century include Boston's Emerson College of Oratory, Samuel Silas Curry's Boston School of Expression, the Leland Powers School of the Spoken Word, the Stanhope– Wheatcroft School which was connected with Charles Frohman's Empire Theatre, and F. F. MacKay's National Dramatic Conservatory. While many of these schools closed in the early decades of the new century as their founders retired or died, the American Academy of Dramatic Arts remained a leading professional acting school down to the present day. Gradually the acting school became an accepted avenue into the profession. Between 1886 and 1925, for example, nearly two thousand students graduated from the American Academy of Dramatic Arts, many of whom became active on the stage and in the nascent film industry. As McTeague notes, furthermore, these American acting schools were teaching and exploring techniques of realistic acting before Constantin Stanislavsky's ideas impacted American actor training in the 1920s and 1930s.

In the latter part of the century, as their numbers increased, actors also began to assert a new sense of professional identity by professional organizations and societies. In 1882, for example, the Actors' Fund of America was initiated to assist actors who might find themselves in financial need. With such prominent actors and managers as Edwin Booth, Joseph Jefferson, A. M.

*Left, Edwin Booth as Othello. From* Edwin Booth in Twelve Dramatic Characters, *1871. Drawings by W. J. Hennessy, wood engraving by W. J. Linton. Courtesy of the Hampden–Booth Theatre Library at The Players.*

*Right, Edwin Booth as Iago. Courtesy of the Hampden–Booth Theatre Library at The Players.*

Palmer, and P. T. Barnum serving as trustees, the fund raised thousands of dollars through a series of benefit performances. In 1902, the fund also established the Actors' Fund Home on Staten Island to offer a final refuge to aged players. The Actors' Fund was not the first American theatrical charity. It was preceded by, among others, the General Theatrical Fund (1829) and the American Dramatic Fund Association (1848). But the Actors' Fund was the most successful and it continues to operate to the present day. In 1894 the Actors' Society of America (ASA) was founded to promote a professional image for actors and to address their employment problems—e.g., the lack of standardized contracts and wages. ASA published a list of disreputable managers, and worked to improve working conditions, enhance communication within the profession, and raise performance standards. ASA's actual accomplishments were modest; but it did succeed in raising professional consciousness and it was the parent organization of the powerful Actors' Equity Association (AEA or Equity) founded in 1916.

Professional life was also enhanced with the founding of theatrical clubs in the nineteenth century. Although its primary purpose was charitable, the Actors' Order of Friendship, founded in 1849, is generally considered the first theatrical club in America, since the organization maintained club houses in both New York and Philadelphia where actors could socialize. The Benevolent and Protective Order of Elks was founded in 1868 by a group of

variety entertainers. Actors dominated the membership of the Elks throughout the 1880s, but as the society increasingly attracted members from business and the professions, its distinctively theatrical character and membership
gradually disappeared. Several exclusive gentlemen's clubs existed in New
York City, including the Union, the Knickerbocker, and the Century, but,
reflecting a longstanding prejudice against the profession, actors were, for the
most part, excluded from these clubs. Founded in 1875, the Lambs Club was
the first important New York club for actors. After occupying leased rooms
for a decade, in 1905 the Lambs Club moved to a handsome clubhouse,
designed by the noted Beaux-Arts architect Stanford White. In 1888, Edwin
Booth founded The Players. With his own funds, he purchased a four-story
residence on Gramercy Park, an exclusive neighborhood in New York, and
had Stanford White remodel it for a clubhouse. Booth also donated his own
extensive collection of theatrical books for the members' library. The clubhouse rooms were decorated with various theatrical portraits and memora-
bilia, creating an atmosphere that was partly dignified gentlemen's club, and
partly theatrical museum, much like London's Garrick Club (founded in
1831). In addition to theatrical professionals, members of The Players included other artists and prominent businessmen interested in the theater.
Theatrical critics were pointedly excluded from membership. In 1904, a third
theatrical club, the Friars Club was founded mainly as a social organization
for dramatic agents and managers, but actors were soon invited to join. The
Lambs Club, The Players, and the Friars Club continue to operate to the present day. Since these theatrical men's clubs excluded women members,
actresses founded two clubs of their own in the 1890s: The Twelfth Night
Club in 1891 and the Professional Women's League in 1892. The latter had
a social function, but it also offered a range of services to actresses, including
legal advice, and classes on sewing, music, French, and stage dancing.

The rise of mass market illustrated magazines, which often ran feature
stories about actors, contributed to their increasing public recognition.
Inexpensive individual *carte de visite* or "cabinet" photographs and illustrated programs were sold in theaters and bookstores. Regular theatergoers
could collect photographs of their favorite stars, much like sports enthusiasts
might collect baseball or football cards today. Celebrity was a mixed bless-
ing. It resulted in a loss of privacy, for example, but it could also bring a certain social and political influence. With the notorious exception of John
Wilkes Booth, American actors were generally not active in political or social
causes. In the latter part of the century, however, a number of actors used
their public prominence to lobby for social changes. Olive Logan, Julia
Marlowe, and Minnie Maddern Fiske, for example, were among several well-
known actresses who fought for suffrage and women's rights. Actor and playwright James A. Herne (1839–1901) campaigned for tax reform. By the turn
of the century, actors had achieved a more widespread and much higher level
of public respectability in America than ever before.

In the Gilded Age Edwin Booth was the widely acknowledged leader of
the profession. He made his debut in 1849 in a small role in support of his

father's Richard III. From 1852 to 1856, he played dozens of roles in theaters in San Francisco and Sacramento. In 1854, in partnership with Laura Keene he made a brief starring tour to Australia. Then in 1856, he returned east, steadily building a reputation as a promising star. Engagements in London, Manchester, and Liverpool in 1861–62 enhanced his professional standing and deepened his theatrical technique and knowledge. Beginning in the early 1860s, Booth also took on the management of several theaters, including the Winter Garden (1864–67) and his own Booth's Theatre (1869–74).

At the Winter Garden, Booth set out to mount an innovative series of "historically accurate" productions of Shakespeare and other serious drama. His production of *Hamlet* (1864–65) was enthusiastically received and played continuously for one hundred performances, an unprecedented run at the time for a Shakespearean play. Booth's triumph was short-lived. Three weeks after the close of *Hamlet*, Booth's brother John Wilkes assassinated President Abraham Lincoln. Booth was exonerated from any involvement in the conspiracy, but he felt compelled to announce his retirement. His career seemed over; but after almost a year, his supporters finally persuaded him to return to the stage. When the curtain went up on his performance as Hamlet on January 3, 1866, the audience greeted him with thunderous applause, cheers, and waving handkerchiefs for a full five minutes.

Encouraged by this reception, Booth continued his postponed series of Winter Garden revivals. But a year later, disaster struck again when the Winter Garden itself and Booth's entire stock of scenery, costumes, and properties were destroyed by fire. With uncommon resiliency, Booth rebounded from this setback. He set about building his own theater—Booth's Theatre. Over the course of four years, beginning in 1869, he mounted and played the leading roles in eight scenically spectacular productions, including *Romeo and Juliet, Othello, Hamlet* (even more splendid than his "Hundred Nights" Winter Garden production), *Julius Caesar, Macbeth,* and *Richelieu.* But the revivals were expensive and Booth soon found himself financially overextended. Poor business management and the financial panic of 1873 plunged Booth into bankruptcy and the resultant loss of his theater.

Booth never again attempted management; rather he spent the next twenty years of his career as a touring star. He made starring tours to England in 1881–82 and in 1883. On the first tour, he alternated the roles of Othello and Iago with Henry Irving, the reigning English player king. In 1883, he also made a highly successful tour of Germany and Austria, playing, of course, in English supported by German-speaking companies. As noted above, from 1886 until his retirement, he made several acclaimed nationwide tours in association with Lawrence Barrett. A generous starring actor, over the course of his career Booth willingly shared the stage with visiting foreign stars, including the German star Bogumil Dawison, the Italian tragedian Tommaso Salvini, and the émigré Polish actress Helena Modjeska. By the mid-1880s Booth was widely regarded as America's foremost classical tragedian and one of the truly great actors of the time.

His mature repertoire consisted of fifteen roles which he played repeatedly, polishing them to diamondlike brilliance. He was at his best in the portrayal

*Left, John McCullough as Othello. Theatre Cabinet Photographs Collection, Special Collections Library, University of Michigan.*

*Right, Otis Skinner as Count de Grammont, his first starring role, in Clyde Fitch's romantic melodrama* His Grace de Grammont (1894). *Theatrical Cabinet Photograph Collection, Special Collections Library, University of Michigan.*

of brooding, melancholy characters like Hamlet—his greatest creation—or Brutus, or in capturing darkly sinister characters like Iago, or Richard III. But he was a versatile actor equally successful with light comic characters like Benedick and Petruchio or as the wily, histrionic Cardinal Richelieu.

Although Booth was blessed with physical beauty and a clear, musical voice, the hallmark of his acting style was its air of restraint or "quietude." It was the chief quality that distinguished his acting from the emotional excesses of the earlier Romantic school to which his father had belonged. He aimed for a certain natural, "conversational" quality. He delivered Shakespeare's dialogue, for example, as if it were "conversation," breaking up the regular, formal meter, to create a new rhythm which emphasized meaning. His gestures and physical business appeared spontaneous and dynamic, although they were often carefully planned. Booth was also exceptionally attentive to his costuming and makeup. On balance, the outward details of his acting and his expression of feeling seemed to audiences of the day natural and real; still the overall effect impressed viewers, in their own words, as "poetic," or "spiritual"—that is, ideal. This interplay between the real and the ideal echoed the prevailing aesthetic values and tastes of his era. It was a style widely admired by many Gilded Age actors and critics and a precursor to the style of psychological realism that would increasingly dominate acting in America

During the 1880s Booth suffered a number of personal setbacks, including the death of an infant son, a generally unhappy second marriage, a nearly fatal carriage accident, an attempt on his own life, and the long illness, insanity, and death of his second wife Mary McVicker, daughter of Chicago manager, James H. McVicker. These shocks enriched and deepened his interpretations. The parallels between his personal life and his characterizations did not escape his notice. Late in his career he wrote his friend the critic William Winter that in the "mimic world" of the theater, "I almost nightly find the actual sufferings of my real life rehearsed."

Lawrence Barrett's reputation was second only to Booth's. He began his career in the 1850s playing various roles in stock companies in New York and Boston. After a year of war service Barrett toured as a visiting star and managed the California Theatre in San Francisco. Returning to New York in 1870, he won plaudits for his explosive Cassius in a revival of *Julius Caesar*. He then played second leads to Booth for a season at Booth's Theatre, but also starred on his own as James Harebell in English playwright W. G. Wills's romantic tragedy *The Man O'Airlee* (one of his most acclaimed characterizations) and as Leontes in *The Winter's Tale*. An unfortunate rift with Booth forced Barrett to leave New York. For over a decade, he toured relentlessly—hundreds of performances in scores of cities, including a stint in London in 1884. Gradually he built an estimable reputation as a tragedian. Eventually Booth and Barrett reconciled their differences and became close friends and professional partners.

With deep-set, glowing eyes, and a high broad forehead which evoked intellectual strength, Barrett was most effective in portraying characters close to his own disciplined, but sometimes impetuous personality. Cassius, for example, fitted Barrett's temperament like a glove and his interpretation was regarded as definitive at the time. His Hamlet also impressed, but it was largely inspired and overshadowed by Booth's interpretation. Toward the end of his career, he was often praised for his eloquent portrayal of Lear. But his major achievements were in a wide range of non-Shakespearean roles, usually in contemporary, romantic tragedies. His interpretation of Lanciotto, the morose, physically deformed antihero of George Henry Boker's *Francesca da Rimini*, was considered among his acting masterpieces.

Barrett also earned distinction as a theatrical producer. His productions were especially noted for the quality of their ensemble effects and their handsome scenery and costumes. He commissioned new plays, adaptations, and translations, and revived several older American and European romantic dramas. His highly successful management of Booth's five national tours, in three of which he also starred, was his crowning achievement as both an actor and producer.

Although Edwin Forrest continued to act after the Civil War, he was well beyond the peak of his powers. In the early 1860s, Forrest had hired a promising young actor to play second leads in his support. Irish-born John McCullough (1837–85) had arrived in America at age fifteen, reportedly illiterate and destitute. A cousin in Philadelphia offered him a job in his factory. McCullough began to teach himself to read and write. Introduced to

*Left, Fanny Janauschek. Theatre Cabinet Photographs, Special Collections Library, University of Michigan.*

*Right, Helena Modjeska probably as Camille. Theatre Cabinet Photographs Collection, Special Collections Library, University of Michigan.*

Shakespeare by a fellow worker, he became interested in acting. Amateur performances, a chance opportunity to perform utility roles at Philadelphia's Arch Street Theatre, lessons from the famous elocutionist Lemuel White, who had also taught Forrest, and McCullough soon found himself on the road to a career.

Tall, well-built, and classically handsome with a strong voice and a diligent approach to his work, McCullough complemented Forrest's heroic mold and acting style. He toured with Forrest for six years, playing Macduff to the star's Macbeth, Laertes to his Hamlet, Iago to his Othello, Richmond to his Richard, and so on. Inevitably McCullough's acting style was influenced by Forrest. In 1866, McCullough accompanied Forrest to San Francisco for an engagement at Maguire's Opera House. Forrest urged his protégé to remain in California and develop his own style and following. Except for periodic starring tours, McCullough remained in California for a decade as the leading actor and manager of the California Theatre. When Forrest died in 1872, McCullough assumed several of his former mentor's roles, including Spartacus, Virginius, and Jack Cade. In 1874, when he played his first starring engagement in New York, comparisons with Forrest were inevitable.

Some older critics branded him a second-rate Forrest, but others recognized a control and subtlety often absent from Forrest's performances.

Always eager to learn and improve, McCullough took acting lessons from Steele MacKaye. Gradually critics and audiences warmed to McCullough's increasingly more refined heroic style and to his engaging off-stage personality. Indeed, his colleagues affectionately called him "Genial John." He made those roles formerly associated with Forrest distinctively his own. In Shakespearean roles, although he fell short of Booth and Barrett, McCullough's commanding, but sensitive portrayals of Lear and, especially, Othello won widespread admiration, and his Coriolanus was considered a definitive representation. At the peak of his career, Genial John succumbed to the ravages of advanced syphilis. Institutionalized for a short time, he then died at his home in Philadelphia. Hundreds attended his funeral and mourned his loss to the American stage.

With McCullough's death, the classic heroic style fell out of fashion. Some of its features, however, were absorbed by a new generation of actors specializing in playing the dashing heroes of romantic historical melodramas, an

*Left, Helena Modjeska as Camille. Theatre Cabinet Photographs Collection, Special Collections Library, University of Michigan.*

*Right, Mary Anderson as Juliet. Theatrical Cabinet Photograph Collection, Special Collections Library, University of Michigan.*

increasingly popular genre at the turn of the century. As noted earlier, James O'Neill became famous and wealthy playing the eponymous hero of Dumas's *The Count of Monte Cristo*. Romantic heroes also formed a large part of the early repertoire of Otis Skinner (1858–1942), although over the course of his long career, this remarkably versatile actor proved equally adept in classic, light comedy, and character roles. Other notable actors who specialized in Romantic heroes include William Faversham (1868–1940) and James K. Hackett (1869–1926), son of the actor–manager James Henry Hackett.

When Charlotte Cushman retired in 1875, her place was taken principally by two émigrée tragediennes. Fanny Janauschek (1830–1904), born in Prague, was a recognized star in the German theater when she came to America in 1867. Indeed, for several years she acted in German in America. At the urging of Augustin Daly, however, she learned English, and in 1873–74, she made her debut as an English-speaking star. Her accent remained noticeably pronounced, but she had a powerful presence and fierce intensity that was especially effective in roles like Lady Macbeth, Brunhilde (in a stage adaptation of the Nibelungen saga written especially for her), Queen Katherine in Shakespeare's *Henry VIII*, Mary Stuart, and Medea. Although her style of acting was to a large extent "old school," she retained a following down to the turn of the century.

*Left, Richard Mansfield as Baron von Wiener Schnitzel in an English language adaptation of Jacques Offenbach's operetta* La Vie Parisienne. *New York, 1884. Theatre Cabinet Photographs Collection, Special Collections Library, University of Michigan.*

*Right, Richard Mansfield in the title role of Clyde Fitch's* Beau Brummell *(1890). It was his most popular characterization, remaining in his repertoire until his death. Theatrical Cabinet Photographs Collection, Special Collections Library, University of Michigan.*

Like Janauschek, Helena Modjeska (1840–1909) was an established star in her native Poland before she emigrated to America in 1876. After intensive English-language study, she made her American debut in an adaptation of Scribe's *Adrienne Lecouvreur*. For the next several years she toured, playing mainly in English-language adaptations of French melodramas such as Dumas's *Camille*, Henri Meilhac and Ludovic Halévy's *Frou-Frou*, and Eugène Scribe's *Adrienne Lecouvreur*—plays in which her accent would not seem out of place. Slender, with a sensitive beauty and silvery voice, she seemed ideally suited to such heroines and quickly won critical and public approval.

In her early career, Modjeska had played a number of Shakespeare's heroines in Polish. In the 1880s, she gradually added to her English language repertoire the roles of Rosalind, Viola, Beatrice, Imogen, and Isabella in *Measure for Measure*, the latter a play only rarely seen on the American stage of the time. With her reputation established in America, she regularly returned to the continent for starring engagements in the 1880s and 1890s. In 1889, she toured in consort with Edwin Booth, playing Ophelia, Portia, and Lady Macbeth. Indeed, her Lady Macbeth became a mainstay of her later repertoire. Finally, in the last decade of her career, she would add Queen Katherine, Queen Constance in *King John*, and at the age of fifty-eight, Cleopatra. Widely recognized as a Shakespearean interpreter, she also continued to play in contemporary dramas by Dumas, Hermann Sudermann, and Victorien Sardou.

Among native-born actresses of the era, Mary Anderson (1859–1940) was the leading exemplar of classical acting. Almost entirely self-taught, patterning her style after that of Edwin Booth, she made her debut as Shakespeare's Juliet in 1875. For the next several years, she toured extensively, playing romantic heroines like Julia in *The Hunchback*, Pauline in *The Lady of Lyons*, Bianca in *Fazio*, and Parthenia in *Ingomar*. In 1877, she made her first New York appearance, winning public acclaim. Unusually tall for a woman of her day, with classical features, arresting grey eyes, a mass of wavy brown hair, and a deep, expressive voice, she won over theatergoers with her physical loveliness and the warmth of her personality. Critics conceded her beauty and talent, but noted lapses in acting technique. By the early 1880s, however, Anderson had succeeded in gaining greater artistic control and confidence. In 1883–84, she played a season at the Lyceum Theatre where audiences flocked to see her as Galatea in W. S. Gilbert's *Pygmalion and Galatea*. While in England, Anderson showed an estimable flair as a producer. In 1884, for example, she mounted an historically accurate, scenically lavish production of *Romeo and Juliet*. The production and Anderson's Juliet were outstanding critical and popular successes. The next year, her production of *As You Like It*, in which she played Rosalind, was presented at Stratford-upon-Avon as a benefit for the Shakespeare Memorial Theatre. It subsequently toured the provincial circuit and then the United States. In 1887–88, she revived *The Winter's Tale* at the Lyceum Theatre, boldly undertaking the roles of both Hermoine and Perdita. The following season, she brought this production to

America where it and her tour-de-force dual performances were hailed her finest achievements. But then at the height of her career, she abruptly retired from the stage, married an English solicitor, and moved to a village near Stratford-upon-Avon.

Richard Mansfield (1857–1907) was widely regarded as the leader of the profession after Booth's retirement. Trained by his mother, a noted opera singer, Mansfield's earliest roles were in W. S. Gilbert and Arthur Sullivan's operettas. His vocal strength and flexibility would remain one of his strengths. In 1882, he made his mark as Baron Chevrial, a wealthy, aging roué, in an adaptation of Octave Feuillet's melodramatic *A Parisian Romance*. Mansfield's performance, an exquisite portrait of physical and moral depravity, riveted spestators. By 1886, he was a recognized star, usually touring at the head of his own company, and steadily adding to his repertoire of roles.

In several respects, Mansfield's acting reflected a traditional, classical approach, but on balance, he was more a character actor than a traditional tragedian like Booth or Barrett. He mounted splendid productions of *Richard III*, *The Merchant of Venice*, *Henry V*, and *Julius Caesar*, but his Shakespearean performances, with the exception of *Henry V*, were limited successes. He never even attempted Hamlet, the touchstone of the classical tragedian. He was at his

*Richard Mansfield as Richard III. Courtesy Lawrence and Lee Theatre Research Institute, Ohio State University.*

*Left, Clara Morris c. 1870s. Courtesy Lawrence and Lee Theatre Research Institute, Ohio State University.*

*Right, Fanny Davenport in Augustin Daly's* The Princess Royal *(1877). Courtesy the Lawrence and Lee Theatre Research Institute, Ohio State University.*

best in vivid, strongly theatrical or eccentric roles whether comic or melodramatic. Conversant in several languages, Mansfield reveled in dialect parts. Among his notable portrayals, for example, were his electrifying performance as both Dr. Jekyll and Mr. Hyde in an adaption of Robert Louis Stevenson's famous tale, as well as roles like Ivan the Terrible, Don Juan, and Beau Brummel, the last one of his most popular creations.

Throughout his career, Mansfield flirted with what was called the "new"—that is, "modern"—drama. In the 1890s, for example, he introduced George Bernard Shaw to America, playing Bluntschli in *Arms and the Man* and Dick Dudgeon in *The Devil's Disciple,* but he was not prepared for Shaw's even more political plays. He rejected *Candida,* for example, and *Man of Destiny,* which was written expressly for him, because Shaw's Napoleon was unheroic. Instead, he chose to act Napoleon in an old-fashioned historical melodrama. He produced Henrik Ibsen's *A Doll's House* in order that his actress–wife Beatrice Cameron (1863–1940) could play Nora, but he was decidedly not an Ibsenite. He remained a mainstream Victorian and a romantic. In 1898–99, he achieved tremendous public and critical success in Rostand's *Cyrano de Bergerac.* It was just the colorful, grand heroic role that ideally suited Mansfield's interests and temperament. In the first decade of the twentieth century, he added to his reputation with performances as Molière's Alceste, Schiller's Don Carlos, and Ibsen's Peer Gynt.

Despite waning public interest in classical drama, several older performers tried to carry on the tradition. One of the more successful was Robert
Bruce Mantell (1854–1928). Born in Scotland, but raised in Ireland, Mantell
spent his journeyman years on England's provincial circuit. In the late 1870s,
he tried on several occasions to establish himself in America, but the roles he
obtained were small and the tours brief, so he retreated back to England. In
the 1880s, he finally succeeded in America as a touring star, mainly playing
leads in popular romantic melodramas, but also winning some acclaim as
Romeo, Othello, and Hamlet. But Mantell's private life suddenly stalled a
propitious professional start. Like Edwin Forrest, he became enmeshed in a
scandalous divorce. When he failed to keep up alimony payments, the State
of New York indicted him for contempt and threatened arrest. For a decade,
Mantell toured from coast to coast, everywhere but New York, allowing his
alimony debt to increase by tens of thousands of dollars. Isolated from the
theatrical center where his reputation could have advanced, he almost sank
into stage oblivion. At the turn of the century, Mantell negotiated a settlement with his ex-wife and the contempt citation was withdrawn. In 1904,
Mantell played in New York City as Richard III, but in a second-class theater
in a shoddy production. His powerful interpretation, however, won favorable

*Fanny Davenport as Cleo-
patra. Courtesy of Lawrence
and Lee Theatre Research
Institute, Ohio State University.*

critical notice. Well-received performances as Othello, Richelieu, Hamlet, Macbeth, and Lear revived his flagging career. For the next twenty-five years, Mantell would play a repertoire almost exclusively Shakespearean, appearing in all the major cities (nine times in New York between 1904 and 1919) and numerous towns across America and winning a considerable following.

In the last decades of the century, however, domestic melodrama and light comedy became the stock-in-trade for most American performers, especially for star actresses. After Matilda Heron's death, Clara Morris (1847–1925) emerged as the greatest emotionalistic actress of the era. In the 1860s, she played a range of roles in John Ellsler's Cleveland stock company. Then after a season as the leading lady at Woods Theatre in Cincinnati, she won an engagement with Augustin Daly. In the next three years, she established a reputation for playing the heroines in a series of domestic melodramas, several adapted from French originals, plays that revolved around women trapped in destructive, usually illicit love affairs and driven, as a consequence, to madness and death. Morris was unrivaled in her ability to capture realistically the struggles of such characters. Her face was described as "girlish" or "innocent," but capable of projecting seductive allure. She was able apparently to weep profusely on cue. Her tearful voice, quivering lip, and heaving breasts became trademarks. Regularly criticized for physical awkwardness and mannerisms, and faulty elocution, these flaws were forgotten in the magnetism of her performances.

Fanny Davenport (1850–98), the daughter of midcentury tragedian E. L. Davenport, began her career playing classic, light comedy roles—for example, Lady Gay Spanker in Dion Boucicault's *London Assurance* or Rosalind in *As You Like It*. Tallish, youthfully radiant, with a charming onstage personality, she was well suited to such parts. In the early 1870s, as she matured, she was increasingly cast in dramatic roles, and achieved a notable success as Mabel Renfrew, the central character in Daly's domestic melodrama *Pique*. As Mabel, Davenport exhibited various emotional reactions, particularly in the climactic scenes in which she rescues her son from thuggish kidnappers. *Pique* was enormously popular; running for 238 performances in New York, it elevated Davenport to star status. For several seasons, she continued to act in Daly's company, playing a range of roles, including Imogen, Beatrice, Lady Macbeth, Lady Teazle, and Nancy Sykes. In the early 1880s, however, she struck out as a touring star and began to specialize in playing the volatile heroines of Sardou's *Fedora, Tosca, Cleopatra,* and *Gismonda*, roles originally created for Sarah Bernhardt. Davenport, in fact, was the first actress to play these roles in English in America. Her voluptuous figure, statuesque, commanding prescence, and ability to project various stages of jealousy, hate, rage, and ardor worked to good advantage in such parts and she reached a level of celebrity almost equal to that of Morris.

Mrs. Leslie Carter (1862–1937), *née* Caroline Louise Dudley, owed her stage career to an early failed marriage. At the age of eighteen she married a prominent and wealthy Chicagoan, but the marriage ended nine years later in a highly publicized divorce. Left without any means of support, but strikingly beautiful, she capitalized on her public notoriety by trying the stage. Two Broadway appearances in 1890–91 were essentially failures, but David Belasco saw her potential and took her on as a student. In 1895, he starred her in his play *The Heart of Maryland* as Maryland Calvert, a role which Belasco specifically tailored to suit Carter's talent and abilities. Her "virago-like intensity," as one critic described it, and her almost uncontrolled emotional outbursts, seeming to verge on hysteria, created a sensation. Belasco wrote other sensational melodramas for Mrs. Carter, including *Zaza* (1899), *Du Barry* (1901), and *Adrea* (1904). In all of these, she had opportunities to weep vociferously, rant to the point of hoarseness, and writhe passionately about the floor. Such over-the-top acting was disdained by many critics, but audiences were thrilled. Carter eventually broke with Belasco and starred on her own in *Zaza* and *Du Barry* as well as in *Camille* and *Tosca*. As popular taste turned away from sensational melodramas and toward a more restrained realism, Carter modified her style, achieving success most notably as Lady Catherine in Somerset Maughan's social drama *The Circle* (1921).

Standing at the opposite extreme of their emotionalistic sisters were a group of Gilded Age actresses who made their mark not in sensational melodramas, but in light comedy or in sentimental dramas. These plays provided vehicles for an actress to play characters that were invariably beautiful, charming and refined, and sexy, but in an entirely wholesome way. Indeed, often the actress's own personality was so close to the character portrayed that personality and character, or person and persona, were virtually indistinguishable. Personality actresses, as they were called, were frequently accused of playing themselves no matter the role. But unlike many emotionalistic actresses, they usually had served a standard theatrical apprenticeship before becoming stars and they relied less on intuition and spontaneity than on studied stage technique. More than any other actresses of the era, furthermore, personality actresses established the prototype of the female star for succeeding generations up to the present day.

In the immediate postwar period, Maggie Mitchell (1832–1918) was perhaps the pioneer example of a personality actress. Petite, with a tomboyish energy, she was cast initially in boys' roles, breeches parts, or as the soubrette in popular sentimental comedies—Dot in an adaptation of Dickens's *The Cricket on the Hearth,* for example. In 1860 at the St. Charles Theatre in New Orleans, she played the title role in *Fanchon, the Cricket,* an adaptation of George Sand's *La Petite Fadette.* Fanchon, a simple country girl, simultaneously arch and delicate, childlike and womanly, ideally suited Mitchell's personality and made her famous. Over the course of her career, she added other child or childlike, morally good heroines to her repertoire—for example, Jane Eyre in an adaptation of Charlotte Bronte's famous novel—and was regularly praised for her naturalness and seeming absence of art. Fanchon, however, was Mitchell's *chef d'oeuvre.* Advancing age apparently had little effect on Mitchell's appeal as Fanchon; she was still playing the role in her late fifties.

Mitchell was virtually a one-role performer. Other leading personality actresses exhibited more range, although light comedies and sentimental

*Left, Ada Rehan c. 1900. Theatrical Cabinet Photograph Collection, Special Collections Library, University of Michigan.*

*Right, Julia Marlowe as Prince Hal in* 1. Henry IV, *1895–96. Theatrical Cabinet Photograph Collection, Special Collections Library, University of Michigan.*

*Julia Marlowe as Imogen in* Cymbeline. *Theatrical Cabinet Photograph Collection, Special Collections Library, University of Michigan.*

dramas were the mainstays of their repertoires. Ada Rehan, Viola Allen, and Maude Adams were singular models of the school.

Born in Ireland, Rehan came to America with her family at age five. She served her apprenticeship in the mid-1870s in Louisa Lane Drew's Arch Street Theatre company and in stock companies in Louisville and Albany. In 1879 she joined Augustin Daly's company, quickly becoming his leading lady, a position she held for the next twenty years. With an attractive, generously proportioned figure, masses of reddish hair and grey-blue eyes, and a voice that was most often described as "caressing" or "melodious" with perfect articulation or diction, Rehan captivated with her loveliness, charm, and warmth. Over the course of her career, she played over two hundred roles—mostly a string of farces and melodramas adapted from German originals by Daly. In the 1880s, however, Daly showcased her talents in a series of scenically splendid revivals of Shakespeare's comedies. In both New York and London, where Daly took his company almost annually from 1888 to 1899, Rehan played Kate in *The Taming of the Shrew,* Helena in *A Midsummer Night's Dream,* Mistress Ford in *The Merry Wives of Windsor,* Rosalind, Viola, Portia and Beatrice. Critics found her irresistible, although they recognized her limitations: no matter the role, she was always Ada Rehan. After Daly's death, without his inspiration and coaching, Rehan's acting was seen as increasingly mannered and artificial. She toured on her own for a few seasons, but could never recapture her glory days with Daly; she retired at the early age of forty-five.

Viola Allen spent the first part of her career mainly playing in support of John McCullough, Lawrence Barrett, and the Italian tragedian Tommaso Salvini on his tour of America in the 1880s. She also played Lydia Languish in a famous all-star tour of Sheridan's *The Rivals,* headed by Joseph Jefferson as Bob Acres. In the early 1890s, she joined Charles Frohman's Empire Theatre company as a leading lady. She won national prominence in two morally uplifting melodramas, *The Christian* (1898) and *The Eternal City* (1902) which Hall Caine (1853–1931) adapted from his own popular novels. In the early years of the new century, Allen was acclaimed for revivals of Shakespeare's *As You Like It, Cymbeline,* and *The Winter's Tale,* in which she starred as her namesake Viola, Imogen, and, following in Mary Anderson's footsteps, as both Hermoine and Perdita. Some critics complained that she lacked variety in these characterizations; and, indeed, in photographs of Allen in these and other characters in her repertoire, her demeanor—a pensive "look"—is invariably the same. Other critics commended her sensitive, sympathetic, intelligent interpretations. After 1909, she returned to starring in sentimental melodramas like *The White Sister* (1909) in which she played a nun caught in an ethical romantic dilemma. But in 1916, to celebrate Shakespeare's tercentenary, she and James K. Hackett mounted a production of *Macbeth.* Allen's approach to Lady Macbeth was innovative, neither bullying, like Cushman's or Janauschek's interpretations, nor a sexy *femme fatale* as Ellen Terry had played the role; rather she mothered Macbeth, wheedling and patronizing him like a spoiled child. It failed to win critical appreciation, however. Her career on the wane, Allen retired in 1918.

*Maude Adams as Peter Pan. Courtesy Lawrence and Lee Theatre Research Institute, Ohio State University.*

Maude Adams began her career at the age of seven as a child performer working with her mother Annie Adams, a stock actress traveling the western circuit. In 1888, she made her New York debut in *The Paymaster,* an undistinguished melodrama, and then quickly established a reputation as a gifted ingenue, appearing with distinction in a number of contemporary sentimental dramas and comedies. For several seasons, she played second leads to John Drew, invariably garnering praise for her performances. Her breakthrough role came in 1897 as Barbie in James M. Barrie's *The Little Minister* which reportedly the Scots writer, impressed by an Adams performance that he had witnessed, adapted from his novel expressly for her. In a double role as a mysterious, beautiful Gypsy girl who is then revealed to be in actuality a well-born lady, Adams displayed her range: spirited and beguiling as the Gypsy girl, compassionate and sincere as Lady Barbara. *The Little Minister* ran for three hundred performances and propelled Adams into stardom. With a figure more girlish than womanly, large blue eyes, and wavy brown hair, perhaps more pretty than beautiful, Adams was particularly adept in roles that were delicate or winsome and that evoked tender sympathies. The distinctive quality of her voice, especially her laugh, was frequently singled out. Capitalizing on these qualities, Barrie wrote one starring vehicle after another for her, including *Quality Street* (1901), *What Every Woman Knows* (1908), and *A Kiss for Cinderella* (1916). Undoubtedly, her greatest role, and the one for which she is best remembered, was as Barrie's Peter Pan (1905). So successfully did she capture the charm and spirit of "the boy who wouldn't grow up" that for an entire generation Maude Adams simply *was* Peter Pan. Adams did succeed in other roles, most notably in Edmond Rostand's whimsical *Chantecler* (1911) as the rooster who believes his crowing makes the sun rise. She did attempt to play a few classical roles—Juliet, Viola, and Rosalind, for example—but these generally were not well received. Grievously stricken by influenza during the pandemic of 1918, Adams, although at the height of her popularity, decided to retire from the stage. The death of Charles Frohman, Adams's producer and friend, may also have affected her decision. With a long-standing interest in stage lighting, in the 1920s Adams worked as a lighting consultant for General Electric. In 1931, she briefly toured with Otis Skinner in *The Merchant of Venice*. Finally at the age of sixty-five, she began a distinguished teaching career as the founder of the drama department at Stephens College in Missouri where she remained until 1953.

Julia Marlowe (1866–1950) had a versatility and range beyond that of the typical personality actress, although in the early part of her career she was sometimes placed in this school. She began her career in the early 1880s as a teenager playing small roles in various second-class touring companies. Although she was making steady progress, in 1884 she left the stage to study with Ada Dow (1847–1926), a retired actress and producer. After three years of old-fashioned stage training, Marlowe appeared in New York in 1887 as Juliet, Viola, and Parthenia in the romantic melodrama *Ingomar*. Critics thought she was promising, but overall their judgment was lukewarm. For a decade, however, Marlowe continued to tour in a classical repertoire. Although she developed an enthusiastic following on the road, her success in New York was stymied by William Winter's negative reviews and by Augustin Daly who, not wanting her competition, countered Marlowe's productions of *Twelfth Night* and *As You Like It* with his own spectacular revivals featuring Ada Rehan. Discouraged in her efforts to succeed as a classical actress, Marlowe contracted to tour the Syndicate circuit in a series of historical romances, including *For Bonnie Prince Charlie* (1897), Clyde Fitch's Civil War drama *Barbara Frietchie* (1901), and *When Knighthood Was in Flower* (1902), in which as Mary Tudor she scored her greatest popular successes. Marlowe became one of the Syndicate's top box-office attractions, but she felt confined by a repertoire of romantic melodramas. A turning point came in 1904 when producer Daniel Frohman teamed her with Edward H. Sothern (1859–1933) to tour in a series of Shakespeare revivals.

E. H. Sothern, son of the English comedian Edward Askew Sothern (1826–81), was Daniel Frohman's leading man at the Lyceum Theatre where for a decade he had specialized in gentlemanly light comedy roles and dashing romantic heroes like Prince Rudolf in *The Prisoner of Zenda* (1895) and D'Artagnan in *The King's Musketeers*. Although highly successful in such roles, Sothern, like Marlowe, wanted recognition as a classical actor. In 1900 he played Hamlet in New York, garnering judicious critical praise and generating good audiences. For the next four years, he regularly offered performances as Hamlet; but, while he was undoubtedly interested, he did not attempt other Shakespeare roles—until he partnered Julia Marlowe.

*Left, E. H. Sothern as Ernanton de Launay in Robert N. Stephens's* An Enemy to the People, *a romantic melodrama set in seventeenth-century France. The Sanders Theatre Collection, Special Collections Library, University of Michigan.*

*Right, William H. Crane as Falstaff. Theatre Cabinet Photographs Collection, Special Collections Library, University of Michigan.*

Season after season, Sothern and Marlowe toured the country, playing mainly a Shakespeare repertoire, including *Hamlet, Romeo and Juliet, Much Ado about Nothing, The Taming of the Shrew, Twelfth Night* and *The Merchant of Venice.* In 1909, they played *Antony and Cleopatra* and in 1910 *Macbeth.* Critical consensus judged them at their best in comedy. As Rosalind and Viola, for example, Marlowe's feminine charm, beauty, intelligence, and thrilling, rich contralto voice were seen to their best advantage. But her Ophelia, especially the mad scene, was considered innovative in the simplicity of her approach and genuinely touching in its effect. In a like vein, her Lady Macbeth was also found deeply moving in the banquet and sleepwalking scenes. Sothern invested Petruchio and Benedick with a swashbuckling charm and energy carried over from his romantic hero roles. He was particularly adept at signaling to the audience with a playful smile, a wink, or a blown kiss that however gruff or cruel he might seem, he was head-over-heels for Katherine or Beatrice. Sothern's Malvolio, "a fantastic, tragically comic thing," one critic called it, may have been the definitive interpretation of the era. Critics were divided about the tragic stature of Sothern's Hamlet, Shylock, and Macbeth, although his careful, thoughtful study, inventiveness, physical energy, and skillful execution were regularly commended. Gifted producer–directors, Marlowe and Sothern staged all of their own productions which were admired as models of the idealized, historically accurate tradition. In 1911, they became offstage partners. During the war years, Sothern (joined occasionally by Marlowe) entertained the troops with recitations and solo scenes from Shakespeare. In 1919, they again reformed their company and toured continuously until 1924, winning universal recognition as America's most distinguished acting couple and Shakespearean producers.

Comic acting in the Gilded Age continued in the directions and traditions established earlier in the century. Standard comedies such as Sheridan's *The Rivals* or Colman's *The Heir-at-Law,* featuring star performers, remained as popular as ever. An adaptation of Mark Twain's *The Gilded Age* (1873), which named the era, offered comedian John T. Raymond (1836–87) the role of Colonel Mullberry Sellers, a very successful Yankee character type. William H. Crane and Stuart Robson (1836–1903), after independent careers as comic stock actors, became a very popular starring team in the 1870s and 1880s appearing as the two Dromios in *The Comedy of Errors,* as Sir Andrew (Robson) and Sir Toby (Crane) in *Twelfth Night,* as Falstaff (Crane) and Slender (Robson) in *The Merry Wives of Windsor,* and in Bronson Howard's *The Henrietta* which was written especially for them. In the 1890s, they once again pursued independent careers. Crane achieved a major success touring as Senator Hannibal Rivers in *The Senator,* a "Yankee" role created for him. Robson was less successful without his former partner, but he continued to be an attraction in a number of farce comedies for the next decade.

Ethnic comic character types remained popular as thousands of new immigrants poured into America's cities, especially into New York. Beginning in the late 1870s, Edward Harrigan (1844–1911) wrote a series of farces about an Irish pseudomilitary company called the "Mulligan Guard" and their conflicts and relationships with their rivals: the German Lochmuller family and other Italian and Negro neighbors and friends. Harrigan himself

*Joseph Jefferson as Rip Van Winkle. From Hornblow,* A History of American Theatre, *vol. 1, 1919.*

played Dan Mulligan, the leader of the guards, while his partner Tony Hart (1855–91) played various characters, including in a dress, wig, and blackface makeup, a character called Rebecca Alleys. Mixing low comedy gags, songs, dancing, and knockabout action with realistic portrayals of character types and interactions on New York's Lower East Side, the Mulligan Guard plays—some forty in all—proved enormously popular, with many running for over one hundred consecutive performances. William Dean Howells, one of Harrigan and Hart's staunchest fans, so admired Harrigan's skills as a comic playwright that he called him the "American Goldoni."

Although never quite as popular as vehicles for the stage Irishman, plays or variety sketches featuring the "Dutchman"—an American corruption of the German *Deutsch*—proved an American comedy staple through the turn of the century. Inspired in part by Harrigan and Hart, Joseph Weber (1867–1942) and Lew Fields (1867–1941) developed a series of hilarious knockabout routines involving two "Dutch" characters—Mike (Weber) and Meyer (Fields). By the 1880s Weber and Fields were stars. In the 1880s and 1900s, they expanded their interests into theater management and also became important producers of musical burlesques and comedies in which they were often featured. Their "Dutch comic" routine in various disguises remained popular on the vaudeville circuit, on radio, and in movies through the 1930s.

The most famous and popular comic actor of the period was Joseph Jefferson III (1829–1905). Jefferson, scion of an Anglo-American acting family that can be traced back to the age of Garrick, was on stage from age four. For three decades, he was a strolling player, initially acting within the family troupe, then with various stock companies from New Orleans to New York.

*Lew Fields and Joe Weber c. 1890s. From Appelbaum and Camner,* Stars of the American Musical Theatre in Historic Photographs. *Courtesy Dover Publications, Inc.*

With Laura Keene's company in the late 1850s, he scored successes as Dr. Pangloss in the farce *The Heir-at-Law* and as Asa Trenchard in *Our American Cousin*. Following the death of his wife in 1861, Jefferson spent four years touring California and Australia, winding up in London where in 1865 he first appeared as Rip Van Winkle, the role with which he was most identified for the next forty years. His portrayal was noted for its naturalness, pathos, and whimsical humor. As Jefferson matured, Rip matured with him until the characterization was a polished masterpiece. So popular was Jefferson as Rip that he became virtually a one-role actor. He continued to play Bob Acres, Dr. Pangloss, and Caleb Plummer in *The Cricket on the Hearth*, but for some critics these were not distinctive characterizations, merely Rip in different guises. Jefferson's projected warmth and charm, both on- and offstage, made him one of the most beloved actors of his era.

Numerous foreign stars visited America during the Gilded Age as faster and safer ships reduced the hazards of transoceanic travel. Furthermore, the well-developed and organized touring circuit offered foreign stars, like their American counterparts, opportunities for enormous earnings. American theatrical impresarios promoted these visitors and theatergoers generally flocked to their performances.

Among the English stars who traveled to America were Charles Albert Fechter (1824–79); Adelaide Neilson (1846?–80), who visited four times in the 1870s; Lillie Langtry (1853–1929) who visited four times in the 1880s; Johnston Forbes-Robertson (1853–1937) who first came in 1885 to play in support of Mary Anderson, then returned as a star in his own right to tour America seven times between 1891 and 1916; Mrs. Patrick Campbell (1865–1940) who toured on numerous occasions between 1902 and 1916; and Herbert Beerbohm Tree (1853–1917) who visited in 1895, 1896, and 1916. Henry Irving (1838–1905) with his costar Ellen Terry (1848–1928) and his entire Lyceum Theatre company came on eight occasions between 1883 and 1905.

Italian, French, and German singers had graced America's opera houses for decades. In 1855, the French actress Rachel (1820–58) toured America, but at best her reception was a *succès d'estime*. In the Gilded Age, however, numerous continental stars achieved critical and popular success in America. With a few exceptions, these stars performed in their native language. Despite the waves of new émigrés, particularly from Italy, Germany, and Eastern Europe, it is likely that only a minority of spectators who attended these foreign-language performances actually understood the dialogue. But the stars often played roles familiar to the audience. Moreover, their frequently emotionally charged performance styles, rich in expressive gesture and movement, generally transcended the language barrier.

The Italian actress Adelaide Ristori (1822–1906) was one of the first continental stars to tour the United States after the Civil War. In 1866–67, she performed the title roles in *Elizabeth the Queen, Mary Stuart,* and *Marie Antoinette* in over a dozen cities from New York to Chicago to New Orleans. Knepler reports that Ristori's net profit was $270,000. She played America three more times in 1867–68, in 1875, and finally in 1885. During her last tour, she played in English, including performances of Lady Macbeth to the

Macbeth of Edwin Booth. Ristori's compatriot, Tommaso Salvini (1829–1915), toured America five times—in 1873, 1881, 1882–83, 1885–86, and 1889–90. He was especially lionized for his powerful, passionate Othello which in 1886, he acted (in Italian) to Edwin Booth's celebrated Iago. In 1881–82, Ernesto Rossi (1827–96) tried to follow in Salvini's footsteps but failed to capture critical enthusiasm.

Eleonora Duse (1859–1924) made four tours in 1893, 1896, 1902, and 1923. On each occasion, American reviewers marvelled at the "naturalness" of her style, her complete absorption into the character, and her seeming absence of "technique." Although her first and third tours were financially disappointing, her choice of repertoire, rather than her artistry, was the chief culprit. In 1893, for example, she played in such standards as *Camille, Fedora,* and *Divorçons,* roles long familiar to American audiences from performances by other actresses, including Sarah Bernhardt, Helena Modjeska, Clara Morris, and Fanny Davenport. In 1902, she erred in the opposite way by offering a completely unfamiliar repertoire of Gabriele D'Annunzio's plays. By 1923, her fame was such that repertoire was not a factor in attracting audiences. For one performance at the Metropolitan Opera House in Ibsen's *Lady from the Sea,* hardly a box-office draw at that time (or any other), Duse brought in more than thirty thousand dollars, a record for the era.

Americans never seemed to tire of Sarah Bernhardt. She made nine national tours between 1880 and 1918, playing a wide range of fallen women, *femme fatales,* historical figures, even a Frenchified and feminized Hamlet in 1900. Among other French actors touring America in the Gilded Age were the great comedian Constant-Benôit Coquelin (1841–1909), who on his third tour in 1900 introduced Americans to his famous interpretation of Cyrano de Bergerac. The distinguished tragedian, Jean Mounet–Sully (1841–1916), however, utterly failed in 1894 with a classic repertoire ranging from Corneille through Hugo. Gabriele Réjane (1856–1920), a gifted comedienne, had somewhat more success in 1895 touring with her own company from Paris's Vaudeville Theatre, enough to motivate a return in 1904.

Among the distinguished stars of the German and Austrian stage playing in America in the last quarter of the century were Ludwig Barnay (1842–1924), Ernst Possart (1841–1921), Adolphe von Sonnenthal (1834–1909), and Josef Kainz (1858–1910). Invariably, they performed only in the large, well-organized German-language stock companies in New York, Chicago, Cincinnati, Milwaukee, St. Louis, and New Orleans. Bogumil Dawison (1818–72), Polish-born, but a star of the German stage, did "cross over" from German-language theater to predominantly mainstream theaters when he performed Othello to Edwin Booth's Iago in the 1860s. It was, however, another bilingual affair: Booth and the ensemble in English, Dawison in German, and the Desdemona, German–American actress Maria Methua-Schiller, alternating between German and English.

How influential these foreign performers—whatever their language—were on American stage culture is difficult to ascertain. Sarah Bernhardt and certain English actresses undoubtedly reinforced a taste for the emotionalis-

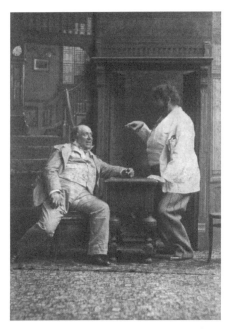

*Scenes from David Belasco's* May Blossom, *a melodrama with a Civil War background presented at the Madison Square Theatre for 169 performances in 1884. As the eponymous May Blossom, Georgia Cayvan (1858–1906) was launched as a popular star. Left: W. J. Le Moyne (1831–1905) and De Wolf Hopper (1862–1935). Right: Georgia Cayvan and W. J. Le Moyne. Theatre Cabinet Photograph Collection, Special Collections Library, University of Michigan.*

*Scene from David Belasco's* May Blossom. *Georgia Cayvan and Joseph Wheelock (1871–1910). Theatre Cabinet Photograph Collection, Special Collections Library, University of Michigan.*

tic and personality schools. Irving probably inspired high standards in production and ensemble playing. Duse almost certainly contributed to a growing appreciation of psychological realism. Although to a lesser extent than in the Gilded Age, foreign performers would continue to enrich the American stage into the twentieth century.

MANY OF THE dramatic tendencies established before the Civil War continued throughout the nineteenth century. Melodrama, for example, remained a dominant form; with an ever wider range of subjects—historical, romantic, frontier, and crime. With continuing waves of immigration, ethnic comedy also remained popular. Dramatic standards of the antebellum period, contemporary English drama, and adaptations of French sensation drama and German melodrama continued to weigh importantly in the bill of fare, but original American plays represented an increasingly significant share of the theatrical repertoire. Responding to various social and artistic forces, from the horrors and disillusionment of the war, to the growing materialism that gave the Gilded Age its name, to the rise of realism in literature and the visual arts, American drama became more realistic and socially conscious.

Augustin Daly was one of the first new playwrights to emerge in the postwar period. He began by adapting French and German melodramas and considering the dramatic preferences of the time and his own proclivities, his first original plays were also sensational melodramas, including *Under the Gaslight* (1867) and *A Flash of Lightning* (1868). The former was celebrated especially for a suspenseful scene in which the heroine discovers that her protector, a one-armed Civil War veteran, has been tied across the railroad tracks by the villain. With the train approaching, she manages to untie him just in the nick of time. Although Daly never completely abandoned such melodramatic effects, he did gradually temper them with realistically drawn characters and locales and elements of social commentary and satire. *Horizon* (1871), a frontier melodrama, for example, has numerous melodramatic situations and incidents, but it was one of the first plays to bring the issue of western expansion into the theater and its caricature of a corrupt politician did provide social satire. Similarly *Divorce* (1871) and *Pique* (1875), while essentially constructed as romantic melodramas, also examined Gilded Age marital relationships and values. Prolific, with over ninety plays to his credit, many in collaboration with his brother Joseph (1840–1916), a distinguished jurist, Daly set the stage for the next generation of American playwrights.

The career of Bronson Howard (1842–1908) began when Augustin Daly produced his *Saratoga* (1870), a comedy about fashionable society in an upstate New York spa. Over the next thirty years, Howard would write a score of plays, mostly social comedies that skillfully integrated elements of realism, melodrama, romance, and satire. It was a combination that made him one of the most commercially successful playwrights of the time—the first truly professional American playwright to earn a decent, even handsome income solely from his plays. In an era of industrial robber-barons and wheeling-and-dealing tycoons, Howard took as his special theme the world of

American business. He explored the subjects in several plays, including *The Banker's Daughter* (1873), but his most successful business play was *The Henrietta* (1887). With a plot that centers on internecine family conflict against a background of stock exchange machinations, and featuring the comedy team of Stuart Robson and William H. Crane, *The Henrietta* ran for over a year, grossing almost a half-million dollars. It continued to be revived and toured to the turn of the century. Although a departure from the bulk of his work, after *The Henrietta,* Howard's most successful play was *Shenandoah* (1888), a sweeping Civil War melodrama which chronicles the tribulations of two romantically entwined couples—one Southern and one Northern—as they are caught up in the events of the war from the firing on Fort Sumter to the surrender at Appomatox. *Shenandoah* failed to address the political issues that gave rise to the war or its social consequences, but its romantic plot and sprawling epic structure proved very popular.

*Shenandoah* was not the first Civil War play. Numerous plays about Civil War battles and major figures such as General Grant were staged during and immediately after the war, but their merits as drama are not high. A. Daly's *Norwood* (1867) includes an act played out against the Battle of Gettysburg. In 1874, Dion Boucicault offered his Civil War melodrama *Belle Lamar,* but it was a comparative failure. The first really successful Civil War play was *Held by the Enemy* (1886), a spy melodrama, authored and starring the actor–dramatist William Gillette. Gillette's *The Secret Service* (1895), also a spy drama, was an ever greater success perhaps as much for its suspenseful action and Gillette's realistic portrayal of the central hero as for its Civil War setting. David Belasco's *The Heart of Maryland* (1895) combined elements of romance with espionage, but the dramatic situations are much more contrived than *Shenandoah* or Gillette's spy plays.

Although melodrama in one form or another dominated the Gilded Age, there was a steady drift away from its conventions, contrivances, and escapism and toward a new, more realistic drama. The novelist William Dean Howells (1837–1920) was a pioneering champion of realist drama. For over five decades, in the pages of *Atlantic Monthly* and *Harper's,* Howells outlined the aims and principles of realist drama, praised realist plays and playwrights, and castigated the artificialties of melodrama. Howells was also a skillful playwright. *A Counterfeit Presentment* (1877) is essentially a contemporary romantic comedy, but its realistic style and tone and, especially, its examination of gender roles and ethical values mark it as an advance over other similar plays of the time. Lawrence Barrett produced and starred in it on tour for a season, but he never brought it to New York and Howells's monetary rewards were paltry. Ironically, Howells, the arch-realist, scored a financial success with his adaptation of *Yorick's Love* (1878), a florid, romantic Spanish verse drama which Barrett also produced and in which he starred. Thereafter, except for an occasional adaptation, Howells kept his playwriting efforts offstage. He wrote a score of one-act plays which he published in *Atlantic Monthly* and *Harper's.* Howells himself called them "farces," but they are sharply observed, realistic comedies of middle-class society and social issues, comparable in several respects to the one-act farces of Chekhov and Shaw. They were widely read as models of realist style, but never professionally produced in America. (*The Garroters* [1886] and *The Mouse Trap* [1889] were given special matinee performances in London at the turn of the century.)

Several playwrights in the late 1870s and 1880s contributed to the progress toward realism in American drama. Steele MacKaye's *Hazel Kirke* (1880), set in the Lancashire countryside, is a romantic melodrama, but unlike traditional melodramas it is absent a conventional villain, the action is relatively restrained, and the principal characters are more complex and sharply etched than usual. It ran for almost two years in New York and then toured for several seasons. MacKaye's *Paul Kauvar; or, Anarchy* (1887), set during the French Reign of Terror, is a more traditionally structured historical melodrama, but it resonates American class conflict of the sort which led to the Chicago Haymarket Riot of 1876 and its aftermath.

James A. Herne began his career as an actor and stage manager. In the late 1870s, he collaborated with David Belasco in authoring a number of romantic melodramas in which Herne and his actress wife, Katherine Corcoran (1857–1943), were often featured. In 1888, Herne's play *Drifting Apart*, a drama set among the fishing and seafaring folk of Gloucester, gained the attention of Howells and the realist, "local color" novelist Hamlin Garland (1860–1940), both of whom encouraged Herne's growing interest in developing realistic drama about the lives of real people—a drama of character and content, rather than events and situations. Herne's next play, *Margaret Fleming* (1890), is considered to be the first American realistic play. The plot of *Margaret Fleming* revolves around marital infidelity. Philip, Margaret's husband, is discovered to have fathered a child by a worker in his mill. The millworker dies shortly after the birth. Margaret goes blind, her acute glaucoma presumably aggravated by her husband's betrayal. Guilt-stricken, Philip temporarily runs away from his responsibility, but Margaret adopts the child. When Philip returns home, expecting the worst, Margaret compassionately forgives him, but indicates that she demands from Philip a new level of responsibility and a new marital relationship. Herne skillfully undercuts much of the melodramatic potential of this plot with restrained, conversational dialogue rather than emotional reaction, and carefully drawn, believable characters. Furthermore, he does not attempt to simplify the issues, but invites thoughtful consideration of its complexities. It was the closest American drama came to Ibsen until the emergence of O'Neill. *Margaret Fleming* was admired by supporters of realism, but many critics and playgoers found the subject matter and Herne's approach distasteful. Herne persisted and two of his later plays—*Shore Acres* (1892) and *Sag Harbor* (1899)—equally realistic in style, but comedic rather than tragic and less provocative in subject matter, were critical and popular successes. But on balance, audiences, for the most part, were still not ready for either Ibsen or for an American-style Ibsenism, although by the 1890s other playwrights were moving in this direction.

PARALLELING THE GROWTH of legitimate theater, popular entertainment also expanded after the Civil War. Showboating, for example, which had virtually disappeared during the Civil War made a dramatic come-back during the Gilded Age. Augustus Byron French (1832–1902) operated five different boats—all named the *New Sensation*—between the late 1870s and the turn of the century. Other successful showboat operators include Edwin Price (1846–1931), the husband–wife team of E. E. Eisenbarth and Susan Henderson, William R. Markle (1856–1930), and Ralph Emerson, who had started his showboat career as Price's advance man, essentially an advertising agent who traveled ahead of the showboat to promote its arrival.

Typically showboats presented variety bills, although some operators, such as Eisenbarth and Henderson, presented dramatic productions ranging from Shakespeare to popular sentimental melodrama. A special feature of showboats was their steam-powered calliopes. A calliope "concert" heralded the showboat's arrival and entertained potential customers.

Showboats gradually grew larger and more luxurious in their appointments. William Markle's *Queen,* built in 1901, seated almost a thousand spectators. In the early decades of the twentieth century, there were over twenty boats active on the major waterways. The rise of the vaudeville circuit and then movies significantly affected the popularity of showboats and the Great Depression brought a virtual end to this unique form of American theater. The showboat *Majestic,* however, has been in almost continuous operation along the Ohio River and its tributaries since 1923. It is currently operated by the Cincinnati Recreation Commission principally as a summer theater venue for musical comedies and variety shows.

Minstrel shows remained popular into the 1880s. In 1878, Colonel Jack H. Haverly (1837–1901) consolidated four troupes into one enormous company which he called the United Mastadon Minstrels. In the same year, Haverly also took control of Callender's Colored Minstrels, an African–American troupe. Until the mid-1880s, he successfully managed these enormously popular companies, touring them season after season usually to engagements in his own theaters in New York, Chicago, Philadelphia, and San Francisco. Generally, the format of the minstrel show did not change during the Gilded Age, although costumes and settings became much more lavish than in the antebellum era. Succeeding Haverly, Lew Dockstader (1856–1925) with his partner George Primrose (1852–1919) managed the most successful minstrel troupe at the turn of the century. Unlike Haverly, Dockstader was a minstrel performer as well as a manager. The musical comedy star Al Jolson (1886–1950) received his early training as a Dockstader minstrel. In the 1910s and 1920s Jolson continued to perform in blackface in a series of Broadway musicals which were little more than vehicles for his singing and infectiously exuberant personality.

Although minstrelsy perpetuated a degrading, caricaturish image of African Americans and of black life, it did provide opportunities for numerous black entertainers and performers, many of whom—like Billy Kersands (c. 1842–1915) and Sam Lucas (1848–1916)—became well-known, popular

*The showboat* Majestic, *with its tow, c. 1950s. Courtesy Theatre Museum of Repertoire Americana and the Society for the Preservation of Tent, Folk, and Repertoire Theatre, Mt. Pleasant, Iowa.*

*The showboat* Majestic *in 1997. Courtesy Cincinnati Recreation Commission/ Showboat Majestic.*

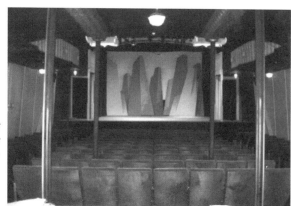

*Interior of the showboat* Majestic *in 1997. Courtesy Cincinnati Recreation Commission/Showboat Majestic.*

stars. A break with the black minstrel format occurred as early as the mid-1870s when Anna Madah (1855–1920?) and Emma Louise (1857–1901?) Hyers organized their own combination to tour full-scale productions of original black musical comedies. Indeed, both Kersands and Lucas were featured in several of the Hyers Sisters (as they were known) productions. Still most black performers were engaged as minstrels. The 1890 census tallied 1,490 black Americans in the acting profession, and according to Allen Woll, almost all of them toured in minstrel companies. But the Hyers Sisters had pointed black performers in a different direction. *The Creole Show,* produced by the white Chicago burlesque theater owner Sam T. Jack (1853–99), eased the transition by keeping the minstrel interlocutor for the first act, but casting a woman in the role. With that innovation as well as an all-female chorus, Jack could boast "a show to glorify the colored girl." Sam Lucas had apparently conceived the idea of a black burlesque company, and his presence as star of *The Creole Show* helped to attract other top black performers, including songwriter–singer Irving Jones. Lavish costuming and an urban setting (as opposed to the plantation lowlife parameters of the minstrel show) contributed to the runaway success of this first all-black burlesque. (For more on the rise of burlesque, see below.) Soon other all-black productions were featuring women in major roles and furthering the evolution toward the full-fledged musical. Among these were two shows—*The Octoroons* (1895) and *Oriental America* (1896)—put together by John W. Isham (1866–1902), an African American who had managed *The Creole Show. Oriental America* opened on Broadway, then toured for a season. *Black Patti's Troubadours* (1896) starred Sissieretta Jones (1869–1933), an operatic soprano who had sung at the White House in 1892.

Also helping to prepare the way for the first great wave of black musicals (1897–1909) was the fad for so-called coon songs. These syncopated ditties in "Negro dialect" became a staple of the variety stage beginning with "All Coons Look Alike to Me" (1890)—in which the female vocalist debates her choice between two handsome blacks—written by composer–comedian Ernest "the Unbleached American" Hogan (1859?–1909). The blue-eyed, blond May Irwin (1862–1938), the struggling young comedienne Fanny Brice (1891–1951), and numerous other white performers took up "coon shouting," sometimes in blackface, sometimes not. Hogan went on to tour with *Black Patti's Troubadours* and to star in *Clorindy; or, The Origin of the Cakewalk* (1898), a musical afterpiece by Will Marion Cook (1869–1944) and Paul Laurence Dunbar (1872–1906). Produced at New York's Casino Roof Garden in July 1898, *Clorindy* was the first African–American musical to play to mostly white audiences. It exploited a nationwide craze for cakewalk dances that had been initiated by two rising young black vaudeville performers, Bert Williams (1874–1922) and George Walker (1873–1911). The distinction of being the first full-length musical comedy written, produced, directed, and performed by blacks belongs to Bob Cole (1869–1911) and Billy Johnson's (1858–1916) *A Trip to Coontown,* which opened on Broadway in April 1898. Cole's efforts to work with white producers had repeatedly led to disappointment, so he decided to produce his own work with performers from other black shows to which he had contributed material, including *Black Patti's Troubadours*. The *New York Times* review (April 16, 1898) called *A Trip to Coontown* "one of the most artistic farce comedy shows that New York has seen in a long time. . . . There is many a white comedian who could sit at the feet of these Negro actors and learn a thing or two."

Bob Cole's best work was in partnership with the classically trained composer J. Rosamond Johnson (1873–1954). Cole also worked with Rosamond's brother, the poet and playwright James Weldon Johnson (1871–1938). The songwriting partnership of Cole and Rosamond Johnson succeeded in selling songs to many of Broadway's leading producers and performers, a success that enabled them to set their own standards and refuse to supply the "coon songs" that pandered to stereotyped notions. Their greatest hit, "Under the Bamboo Tree," sung by Marie Cahill (1870–1933) in *Sally in Our Alley* (1902), sold over four hundred thousand copies of sheet music in its first year. Bob Cole and Rosamond Johnson also performed successfully together as a vaudeville team, and wrote two additional musicals before Cole's death: *The Shoo-fly Regiment* (1907), about patriotic black soldiers in the Spanish– American War, and *The Red Moon* (1909), which combined the folklore and music of African–American and Native American cultures.

When Bert Williams and George Walker billed themselves as "Two Real Coons" and made a hit with their cakewalk at Koster and Bial's vaudeville house in New York City in 1897, they also sang a Cole and Johnson song, "The Black 400's Ball." Williams and Walker then toured for years with various companies, refining their stage personae, discovering that they worked best if the tall intellectual Williams darkened his light complexion and played the slow, shuffling "Jonah man" (a human magnet for hard luck), while the nimble Walker functioned as the fast-talking dandy or "urban sport." Although these roles reflected minstrel stereotypes, Williams and Walker gradually added complexities to enrich them. Their hit musical shows include *The Policy Players* (1899), *Sons of Ham* (1902), *In Dahomey* (1903), *Abyssinia* (1906), and *Bandanna Land* (1908). *In Dahomey* was the first all-black musical to play in a major New York legitimate theater. Their two subsequent shows also reached Broadway with great success and featured Walker's wife, Ada Overton Walker (1880–1914). After Walker retired in 1909, Bert Williams became a solo performer, regularly appearing in annual editions of the Ziegfeld *Follies* from 1910 to 1919. (See chapter 6 for more on the Ziegfeld *Follies.*) He is perhaps best remembered for his signature song "Nobody."

Vaudeville arose out of the post-Civil War concert saloon boom. In the 1870s in New York alone, for example, there were seventy-five to eighty concert saloons offering a range of variety entertainment, along with an assortment of alcoholic beverages. As noted in chapter 4, concert saloons were usually all-male establishments and the atmosphere could be rowdy. The origin of

*Left, vaudevillian Eddie Foy. Theatre Cabinet Photographs Collection, Special Collections Library, University of Michigan.*

*Right, the Dolly Sisters. From Appelbaum and Camner,* Stars of the American Musical Theatre in Historic Photographs. *Courtesy Dover Publications, Inc.*

the term "vaudeville" is not altogether clear, but by the early nineteenth century it defined a genre of French farce which included songs comprised of topical, satirical lyrics set to popular tunes. Since American vaudeville had no similarities to French vaudeville, it has been suggested that the term was borrowed simply to give a respectable air to variety acts long associated with the concert saloon milieu. Tony Pastor (1837–1908), a variety performer and theater manager, is usually credited with creating American vaudeville by moving variety out of the saloons and into a regular theater and promoting it as "family entertainment." Pastor, however, continued to use the term variety, not vaudeville. Several attempts to achieve his goal in the 1860s and early 1870s were unsuccessful. But in 1881, he moved into a theater near Union Square. Here he established the vaudeville format of a succession of short variety acts, principally comic sketches and song-and-dance routines. Pastor prohibited salacious "blue" or "off-color" material in these acts—common in the concert saloons—and banned drinking and smoking from his theater to attract respectable, middle-class families in large numbers. In the 1880s and 1890s, Pastor's was America's leading variety theater. Numerous turn-of-the-century vaudeville and musical comedy stars got their start at Pastor's, including Edward Harrigan and Tony Hart, Joe Weber and Lew Fields, the eccentric comedian and impersonator Nat Goodwin (1857–1919), the Canadian-born singer–comedienne May Irwin (1862–1938), and Lillian Russell (1861–1922), a singing actress as much celebrated for her full-figured beauty as her talent, and whose career eventually cut across operetta, musical comedy, burlesque, and comic drama.

In the 1880s, Boston theatrical entrepreneurs B. F. Keith (1846–1914) and Edward F. Albee (1857–1930) formed a partnership to produce vaudeville. Gradually they added to their circuit by building or leasing theaters in New York, and other cities. Keith is often credited with introducing the term "vaudeville" to distinguish respectable variety from saloon entertainment, although it had been used by a few other variety producers as early as the 1840s. By the early 1900s, Keith and Albee, through their United Booking Office founded in 1906, exercised a monopolistic control—comparable to the Shuberts or the Syndicate in the legitimate field—over the first-class vaudeville touring circuit in America. Maintaining a policy of "clean" entertainment, Keith–Albee made vaudeville the most popular form of theatrical entertainment in the early decades of the twentieth century, operating over twenty theaters in New York alone. Initially Keith–Albee had competitors, among them F. F. Proctor (1851–1929), who controlled a circuit of a dozen theaters in the East, and Martin Beck (1867–1940), who booked a circuit of over two hundred theaters in the West. Proctor, however, eventually joined Keith–Albee's United Booking Office. Then in 1928, Beck and Albee merged to form the Keith–Albee Orpheum Corporation, controlling a circuit of seven hundred theaters in the United States and Canada, including New York's Palace Theatre, the mecca of vaudeville performers.

Early in the new century, vaudeville had settled into a standard pattern of nine or so ten-to-twenty-minute acts, or "numbers" or "turns" as they were called, with an intermission after the fifth act. Position in the sequence was important. The major star or "headliner," as he or she (or sometimes a duo) was called, usually was the penultimate act. In first-class metropolitan theaters, there were usually two performances a day; in second-class small town, suburban, or neighborhood theaters, performances might be continuous between 10:00 A.M. and 10:00 P.M. In addition to comics and song-and-dance artists, or "hoofers," as they were called, vaudeville included jugglers, animal acts, acrobats, mimes, ventriloquists, magicians, and male and female impersonators. Many of vaudeville's early performers were drawn from America's teeming working-class ethnic populations, especially the Irish, Jewish, and African–American communities. Vaudeville had dozens of leading stars during its heyday in the late 1910s and 1920s. A short list of a few of the most notable vaudevillians would include singer–comedian Eddie Foy (1856–1928); W. C. Fields (1880–1946), who in the role of the bibulous, wisecracking tramp regaled audiences with his comic juggling and trick pool-playing act; Will Rogers (1879–1935), who did rope tricks while delivering folksy, wry social commentary; singer–comedienne Elsie Janis (1889–1956), one of vaudeville's greatest stars; singer Sophie Tucker (1884–1966), who was billed as "The Last of the Red Hot Mamas" both for her robust figure and jazz-inspired song style; dancers Fred (1899–1987) and Adele (1898–1981) Astaire, whose grace elevated ballroom dancing to an art form; the dancing, singing Dolly Sisters, Jenny

*Left, George L. Fox as Humpty Dumpty. Theatre Cabinet Photographs Collection, Special Collections Library, University of Michigan.*

*Right, Chorus members from* The Black Crook. *Merriman Scrapbooks, Curtis Theatre Collection, University of Pittsburgh Library.*

*Left, Lydia Thompson as Robinson Crusoe in an 1877 burlesque version of Dafoe's famous novel. Theatre Cabinet Photograph Collection, Special Collections Library, University of Michigan.*

*Right, The Esquire Theatre, Toledo, Ohio, a typical burlesque theatre of the 1950s. Courtesy John and Jennifer Rockwood.*

(1893–1941) and Rosie (1893–1970); the Marx Brothers, Gummo (1897–1977), Groucho (1895–1977), Chico (1891–1961), Harpo (1893–1964) and Zeppo (1901–79), famous for their inimitable zany, madcap comic sketches; and Julian Eltinge (1883–1941), a renowned female impersonator–quick change artist. Like most American theater, vaudeville was segregated. In the 1910s and 1920s, black vaudevillians worked a separate circuit of segregated theaters, located mainly in the South and organized under the umbrella of the Theatre Owners' Booking Association (TOBA). Although the pay scale was poor—black entertainers caustically read TOBA as an acronym for "tough on black actors"—the "Chitlin circuit," as it was also called, offered employment and entertainment to many African Americans.

In the late 1920s, vaudeville's popularity was eroded by the rise of musical comedy and revues, radio, and especially the motion picture. A movie showing, in fact, was often the final "act" of many vaudeville performances by the mid-1920s. Entrepreneur Marcus Loew (1870–1927) built a large circuit of cheap-priced vaudeville theaters in which live entertainment was presented between film showings. In 1930, the Keith–Albee Orpheum circuit was combined with the Radio Corporation of America (RCA) to create the Radio–Keith–Orpheum (RKO) corporation, a major radio, movie, and later television company. Loew organized the Metro–Goldwyn–Mayer (MGM) movie company and his vaudeville theaters were quickly converted to movie palaces. Indeed, vaudeville theaters became movie houses in the late 1920s and early 1930s, including the famous Palace Theatre in 1932. Vaudevillians, in turn, were absorbed into musical comedy and revue, radio, movies, and (after World War II) television.

Burlesque, a musicalized travesty centering on provocatively costumed female performers, was second only to vaudeville as popular entertainment at the turn of the century. Originally the term referred to travesties of serious plays, personalities, or events, a form of dramatic entertainment that had been popular in England and America since the 1840s. As noted in chapter 4, in the antebellum period, actor–playwright John Brougham, in such plays as *Metamora; or, The Last of the Pollywogs,* lampooned the popularity of romantic melodramas centering on Native American heroes. Lola Montez's dancing and personal life and careers also inspired numerous burlesques. In the early 1870s, the brilliant comedian and mime George L. Fox's (1825–77) burlesque versions of Edwin Booth's Hamlet and Richelieu were enormously successful. Fox's pantomime *Humpty-Dumpty,* first presented in 1867 and regularly revised and revived thereafter until the mid-1870s, also contained burlesque elements.

The female component of burlesque is usually traced to the popularity of *The Black Crook* (1866), a scenically spectacular musical extravaganza, loosely based on a melodramatic treatment of the Faust story, which featured a chorus of female dancers attired in tights and short dresses. Despite outcries from some quarters that *The Black Crook* degraded theatrical art and women, "legs" and scenic spectacle won out. *The Black Crook* ran for over a year in New York, grossed a million dollars, and spawned numerous imitations, including *Evangeline; or, The Belle of Arcadia* (1874), a spoof of Longfellow's famous poem. The spectacle of women in tights—"leg shows," they were called—was bolstered by the tours in the late 1860s of the British Blondes, a troupe of women—all blondes—led by English burlesque star Lydia Thompson (1836–1908). The Blondes presented lampoons of classical myths and well-known exotic stories such as "Ali Baba and the Forty Thieves" and "Sinbad the Sailor." In the spirit of classical burlesque, these dramatized stories served mainly as a skeletal structure on which to hang parodic songs, topical jokes, risqué dances, and displays of skimpily costumed, attractive women. For a complex of aesthetic, moral, and social reasons, Thompson's Blondes provoked a storm of antiburlesque protest, although, in fact, little in their performances was original to the American stage. Adah Isaacs Menken as Mazeppa, for example, had performed in revealing tights; the scenic extravaganza and burlesque component had been preceded by *The Black Crook* and its offshoots. But Thompsonian burlesque with its emphasis on female display, male impersonation, saucy humor, and indecorous dancing challenged conventional Victorian notions of gender roles, female sexuality, and the representation of women on stage. Despite criticism from women's rights advocates, clergymen, and drama critics, burlesque troupes multiplied in the 1880s and 1890s. Thompson herself toured the United States regularly through 1891.

Theatrical impresario Michael B. Leavitt (1843–1935) is usually credited with organizing the first American burlesque company. In the late 1870s, he merged a female minstrel company which he managed—Mme. Rentz's Female Minstrels—with elements of vaudeville and musical travesty into a production format which he called burlesque. With singer–dancer Mabel Santley as the star, Leavitt's Rentz–Santley Novelty and Burlesque Company established the model for burlesque companies in the 1880s and 1890s. Following the format of minstrel performance, burlesque shows were also divided into three parts: the first part combined song-and-dance numbers with low comedy sketches by male comics; the second part featured a series of specialty variety acts; the third part, a sort of grand finale, was a musical travesty. Under pressure of competition, costumes became increasingly alluring and the humor more sexually suggestive.

Sam T. Jack, the Chicago burlesque producer and theater owner, after seeing the exotic dancer Little Egypt perform at the 1893 Chicago World's Fair, introduced a form of Middle-Eastern "belly dancing," called "hootchycootchy" or "cootch" dancing, into burlesque performance. Increasingly physically revealing and sexually explicit, the cootch dance quickly became an integral part of burlesque performance.

By the turn of the century, there were over fifty burlesque companies touring the United States, most catering to a white working-class and lower-middle-class male audience. Like their counterparts in legitimate theater and vaudeville, burlesque theater owners and producers organized themselves into the Travelling Vaudeville and Burlesque Manager's Association of America in 1900. The organization was not as effective or as unified as the Syndicate or the Vaudeville Managers' Association and burlesque companies soon split into two rival theater circuits or "wheels": the Western or Empire Circuit and the Eastern or Columbia Circuit. The Empire became known for its "hot" or "dirty" shows, while the Columbia circuit maintained a policy of respectable or "clean" shows. Competition continued to factionalize the circuits in the early decades of the twentieth century.

In the early 1910s, the Minsky brothers—Abe (1882–1949), Billy (1887–1932), Herbert K. (1891–1959), and Morton (1902–87)—carved out a niche as independent burlesque producers. They are credited with introducing an illuminated runway into the theater auditorium so that patrons might ogle the dancers more closely. Some burlesque dancers were disrobing at least down to flesh-colored tights by the turn of the century. By the early 1920s, the "striptease," a cootch dance in which the performer disrobed down to virtual nudity had become a dominant feature of burlesque. The Minskys became famous for a format that was limited to cootch dancers, stripteasers, and low comedy routines filled with suggestive, double-entendre humor. In the late 1920s and early 1930s, the Minskys operated several burlesque (former legitimate theaters) off Broadway on Forty-Second Street and had become virtually synonymous with burlesque. Although some burlesque acts retained a certain sly wit and rambunctious humor, most burlesque was reduced to increasingly coarse and artless striptease dancing by the 1930s. Attacked by various civic and religious leaders and organizations, the

*Gypsy Rose Lee c. 1940s. From Appelbaum and Camner, Stars of the American Musical Theatre in Historic Photographs. Courtesy Dover Publications, Inc.*

Minsky's were driven out of business and then burlesque was legally prohibited in New York in 1937. Striptease moved into tawdry nightclubs and raunchy "topless" bars.

A few burlesque queens—perhaps most notably Gypsy Rose Lee (1914?–70)—and the better comics—Phil Silvers (1911–85), Bud Abbott (1895–1974) and Lou Costello (1906–59), Jackie Gleason (1916–87), Red Buttons (b. 1918), and Red Skelton (1910–97)—moved into musical revue, vaudeville, radio, movies, and then television, all becoming celebrated performers. In the 1960s striptease dancer Ann Corio revived the golden age of burlesque in a production called *This Was Burlesque* which had a successful long run on Broadway and on tour. In the late 1970s, the musical revue *Sugar Babies* based on the "respectable" burlesque format and featuring movie stars Mickey Rooney (b. 1920) and Ann Miller (b. 1919), also enjoyed success in New York and on tour. Both productions succeeded in providing a glimpse at an almost extinct form of entertainment.

As THE NINETEENTH century waned, the American stage still clung to some of the conventions and practices of the past. But in many areas the grip was tenuous. The Gilded Age had witnessed significant changes in the organizational size and structure of the theatrical enterprise and also, although to a lesser extent, in artistic approaches, styles, and genres. As the new century dawned, however, the American theater was on the cusp of an even more remarkable, dynamic era of change, expansion, and influence.

## MEXICO

With the fall of Emperor Maximilian, Benito Juárez made a triumphal return to the capital from the northern provinces where he had led a resistance movement and a Republican government in exile. When Mexico City's theaters reopened in June 1867 after the turmoil of the transition period, virtually all of them held gala evenings to celebrate the restoration of the Republic. (Juárez, a Zapotec Indian who had risen from orphanhood to the governorship of Oaxaca to the presidency, was reelected president of the Republic that year and served until his death in 1872.) The Gran Teatro Nacional honored Juárez with a sumptuous event on July 18, and the Teatro Principal presented a series of festive programs: July 5 for General Porfirio Díaz, July 7 for General Vicente Riva Palacio (who also wrote plays in collaboration with Juan A. Mateos), July 25 for President Juárez. The latter occasion included a historical drama by Mexican actor Felipe Suárez, *The Triumph of Liberty* (*El Triunfo de la libertad*). Six days later Juárez attended a second performance of Suárez's play, which was again presented on a multiple bill.

Outstanding among the patriotic spectacles of the period, *Fatherland!* (*La patria!*, 1868) by Mexican poet C. Joaquín Villalobos premiered on *el cinco de mayo* (commemorating an important Mexican victory over French invaders on May 5, 1862) at the Teatro de Iturbide, where a company headed by actor Eduardo González (d. 1871) was then engaged. The Spanish-born

*This partial view of México's Zócalo shows the side fronted by the National Palace. In the nineteenth century the large open square became a mecca for entertainment booths called* jacalones. *From Juan N. del Valle,* El Viajero en México, 1859.

*With the fad for short light entertainment pieces called tandas, the Teatro Principal gained a reputation as the "cathedral of tanda." Here a fashionable audience gathers outside the theater before the show.*

*The fanciful costumes of* Las Tandas del Tinglado *lit up the stage of México's vener-able Teatro Principal. Courtesy of Biblioteca de las Artes, Centro Nacional de las Artes.*

González had already made his mark in the capital by working out a scheme to keep the theater running during Lent without offending the devout. He announced that one-fifth of the Lenten-period profits would go to the poor— thus giving theatergoers a charitable pretext to enjoy themselves. *La patria!* featured new scenery: moonlit woods with a painted vista of the volcanos Popocatépetal and Ixtaccíhuatl. A noble Indian woman personifying Mexico comes upon statues of Hidalgo (the father of Mexican independence, played by González) and Minerva (Goddess of Wisdom) in the deep woods and anx-iously tells them of an invading army's threat to her. They give her the nation-al flag (faith) and a sword (force), and Mexico goes off to defend her honor. In part 2, four years later, the two statues wonder what has become of the Indian woman. Just then a sweet melody introduces the Zephyrs, nine dancers who throw flowers and report a new era. Mexico enters as the orchestra plays "Zaragoza's March." She returns the flag and the sword, pre-sents the flags of the conquered nations in tribute, and in redemptive verses urges her countrymen to offer the vanquished a generous pardon and Christian reconciliation. The popularity of this three-character patriotic alle-gory led to its revival on *el cinco de mayo* for many years to come.

Two trends dominate Mexican theater during the last decades of the nineteenth century: the unabating demand for light musical entertainment and the sudden appearance of a great number of Mexican dramatists. One kind of light theatrical fare originated in the tiny theaters (*jacalones*) or pup-pet booths that operated on and near the Zócalo, the main square opposite the National Palace in Mexico City. Traditionally tied to the November fairs held there, the little shows attracted ever-larger audiences. Beginning in the 1850s, the puppets of Don Soledad "Chole" Aycardo delighted spectators ranging from the social élite to the poor who saw themselves in his most famous puppet creation, the happy-go-lucky character called El Negrito Poeta (Little Black Poet). Aycardo's other long-lived characters included Juan Panadero (Johnny Breadbaker) and La Muerte Torera (Death-as-Bullfighter). From 1857 Aycardo made the Teatro de Reloj his center of operations. There, his offerings ranged from dramatic performances by live actors to circus acts in which he played the leading clown role himself. Beloved even by the *cócoras* for his easygoing manner, Don Chole also earned his following with the verses he wrote to compliment his audience, criticize vices like drinking and gambling, and serve as prologues to his shows.

Other enterprises—including the Teatro de América and the Salón Gótico, both of which opened in 1867—based their appeal on low ticket prices and musical selections. The available entertainment further extended to operatic numbers, pantomime, rope-dancing, magic shows, dissolving views, and other variety acts. Soon the idea of presenting several short musical playlets in one evening evolved into the wildly popular *tandas* ("hour pieces") at the Principal and other major theaters. Indeed, the *tandas del Principal* became an annual event during the November fiesta season and continued from 1869 until the theater itself burned down in 1931. At the Principal, four of these colorful, cleverly topical, short musical revues would be presented in an evening, and the bill was changed weekly. In 1874 the Zócalo area boasted eight *jacalones*, including the Teatro de la Exposición where *tandas* were presented continuously from four o'clock in the afternoon, culminating in the infamous *tanda de confianza* (intimate show) at 11:00 P.M.

Surprisingly, though the French occupation of Mexico had ended only a few years earlier, a fashion for all things French swept the capital beginning with the 1869 opening of a *café-cantante*, modeled after the Parisian

*The "cancanomania" that swept México in the 1870s was one of the many light entertainment forms that so delighted audiences in the capital's theaters. Courtesy of Biblioteca de las Artes, Centro Nacional de las Artes.*

*cafés-concerts* of the period. Then came the cancan. According to Reyes de la Maza, performers and public alike were transformed from one day to the next as the joyously infectious music of Jacques Offenbach captivated their spirits and overcame their sense of decorum. It all began on June 22, 1869, when the *zarzuela* company of Joaquín Gaztambide presented *Los dioses del Olimpo* (The Olympian gods), a Spanish adaptation of Offenbach and Halévy's *Orpheus in the Underworld*, at the Gran Teatro Nacional. A reviewer hailed Offenbach and the famous Parisian cancan dancer Rigolboche as "the two missionaries of progress and merriment" (*El Renacimiento*, July 3, 1869). At the Nacional, Amalia Gómez executed the titillating high kicks à la Rigolboche; a few families were scandalized enough to leave at intermission. But most stayed to cheer, demanding ten curtain calls. "Cancanomania," though decried by upholders of public morals, penetrated the *zarzuelas* at other theaters, giving rise to a category of musicals called *zarzuelas can-canescas*. Even dramatic companies, struggling for audiences during the craze, either capped their bills with a cancan number or came up with plays on the subject. A benefit evening at the Principal, for example, included an *apropósito* (occasional piece) called *A Family Council; or, The Effects of the Can-Can* (*Un concilio de familia o los efectos del can-can*, 1869), in which a censorious village priest ends up participating in the dance.

The following year brought the first *revista* (musical revue) in Mexico. The company of Eduardo González presented *La revista del año 1869* at the Nacional on January 30, 1870. Enrique de Olavarría (who later wrote the seminal history of Mexican theater) penned the light verse satire of politics and customs. Whether it was due to Olavarría's discretion as a foreigner by birth or the public's general satisfaction with its lot, this revue did not jab as sharply as would those of more unstable times, especially from 1910 to 1930.

It was *zarzuelas* (Spanish-style musical comedies) above all that filled the theaters of the last decades of the nineteenth century. Numerous *zarzuela* companies came and went from one theater to another, interspersed by the occasional Italian opera company on tour. (The leading opera singers who toured to Mexico with their companies included soprano Angela Peralta, "the Mexican nightingale," who had made her career in Europe and returned to the land of her birth in 1871 with tenor Enrico Tamberlick, and in 1877, and Adelina Patti in 1886.) Among the more successful *zarzuela* companies were those of José Joaquín Cleofas Moreno and Manuel Estrada y Cordero. There was even a *zarzuela* company composed entirely of child performers, the Compañía Infantil de Zarzuela, booked at the Principal in 1874. In 1890, with *zarzuelas* running concurrently in so many theaters, one critic commented that the capital had been *enzarzuelizada* (zarzuela-ized).

The flavor of both the musical and dramatic theater in Mexico is conveyed to us by a wealth of reportage in various periodicals. (Many of those theater reviews, commentaries, and even reader-response letters have been collected in an invaluable series of books edited by Luis Reyes de la Maza.) Among such writing published from 1867 to 1890, one writer's name stands

*Ignacio Manuel Altamirano (1834–93), a diplomat and prolific man of letters, endeavored with his theatre criticism to raise artistic standards and uphold Mexican national identity. Courtesy of Biblioteca de las Artes, Centro Nacional de las Artes.*

out ahead of the others. Still acknowledged as the *maestro* of Mexican critics, Ignacio Manuel Altamirano (1834–93), a full-blooded Indian, strove to define the national culture and raise its standards through his contributions in various genres including poetry, the novel, biography, literary criticism, and political analysis. According to José Luis Martínez, Altamirano revered literature as "the faithful expression of our nationality and an active element of cultural integration." While there was "no publication of liberal ideas that didn't count on his collaboration," his theater commentaries most often appeared in *El Renacimiento*, which he founded in 1869. Altamirano in turn expressed profound respect for the critical acumen of Manuel Peredo, a poet–playwright–translator who often reviewed theater for *El Renacimiento* as well as for *El Semanario Ilustrado*. Another important theater critic, Enrique Chávarri, used the pen-name "Juvenal" for his columns in *El Monitor Republicano*. Manuel Guttiérrez Nájara (1859–1915) wrote on theater for various publications, using various pseudonyms, including El Cronista, Rabagás, Nemo, Pomponnet, and Mr. Can-Can. The Baron (Alfredo G.) Gostkowski published his strong opinions on the cultural scene in *El Domingo*. In addition to providing the permanent descriptive record of theater in their time, these critics actively contributed to cultural advancement through their encouragement of—and sometimes personal participation in—the arts.

When the great Spanish actor José Valero performed at the Nacional in May 1868, Altamirano analyzed the sixty-year-old's physical qualities and performance style, and cited his approach as a welcome alternative to the exaggerated histrionics of the Romantic school: ". . . from the time I began reviewing, I've been suggesting to our artists and audiences this kind of simplicity combined with the extraordinary but apparently shocking idea of introducing naturalness into dramatic interpretation." Altamirano further praised Valero for his repertoire of classic plays that had never before been produced in Mexico. During Valero's engagement at the Nacional, the company at the Principal found itself playing to nearly empty houses, so the latter theater went dark. Valero then generously performed a benefit at the Nacional for the Principal's actors. Because Valero headed the Dramatic Conservatory in Madrid, his presence served as impetus for a project Altamirano had long advocated: the founding of a dramatic training school in Mexico City. A four-month extension of Valero's run enabled him to participate in planning for the school, which was organized as a branch of the Sociedad Filarmónica. The subjects taught were dramatic literature, elocution, speech, music, fencing, and dance.

In May 1873 Valero returned to Mexico only to discover both major theaters fully booked. Thus the star of Spain's legitimate stage was obliged to open at the lowly Teatro Hidalgo. Besides offering well-mounted productions of good plays, Valero gave charitable benefits and even found employment in his company for the displaced actors who normally performed at the Hidalgo on Thursdays and Sundays. Attracting audiences away from the better playhouses by such tactics, it took Valero only two weeks to oust the *zarzuela* company from the Nacional and transfer his company there. For his farewell performance on July 26, 1873, Valero revived a Mexican play that had premiered at the Principal the year before. *The Past* (*El pasado*, 1872), by an impoverished young medical student, Manuel Acuña (1850–73), had triumphed on its opening night and with a second performance a month later at which the twenty-three-year-old poet had been honored. Since then, Acuña had been barely subsisting. At the Nacional, Valero's wife Salvadora Cairón gave an inspired performance in the leading role, drawing tears and audible sobs from the audience. Called onstage with her at the end, Acuña was visibly moved by the ovations. He shared the plight of many Mexican dramatists of the epoch: a night of glory, but little financial reward. Less than five months later Acuña committed suicide.

Conditions began to seem more hopeful for Mexican dramatists during the presidency of Sebastián Lerdo de Tejada (1872–76). Although Lerdo's leadership did not satisfy everyone, he was the first Mexican president to authorize subsidization of a theater company. Enrique Guasp de Péris, a Spanish-born actor of long residency in the capital, took the initiative of proposing government support for a project to promote Mexican drama as a means by which Lerdo de Tejada could gain the approval of intellectuals. Awarded three hundred pesos a month, Guasp began in November 1875 at the Teatro Principal to present plays by Mexican writers. Over the next thirteen months—continuing even after the fall of Lerdo de Tejada and thus the end of the subsidy—he produced twenty-eight new Mexican plays. Also in 1876, the peak year for Mexican drama until well into the twentieth century, other Mexican plays premiered at the Nacional, Nuevo México, and Hidalgo theaters, bringing the total to forty-three Mexican plays in one year.

José Peón Contreras (1843–1907), by far the most important and prolific of the playwrights launched by Guasp, practiced medicine before turning seriously to poetry and drama. Three of the Yucatán-born author's early (now lost) plays had productions in 1861–62 at the Teatro de San Carlos in

Mérida, his home town. Beginning in 1871, he published several collections of ballads (*romances*), some on subjects from Mexican history, such as "Moctezuma" and "Xocoyotzin." After submitting a playscript to José Valero who rejected it without a glance, Peón Contreras would have given up writing for the theater if Guasp had not announced his project. In 1876, from January 11 to December 7, ten of the Mexican plays premiered by Guasp's company were by Peón Contreras. *The King's Daughter* (*La hija del rey*, 1876), written for actress Concepción Padilla and still considered the best of his historical dramas in verse, had a wildly successful premiere at the Principal. A subsequent performance at the Nacional culminated in a ceremony honoring the author, who received a gold pen, a gold filigree crown, and a laurel wreath. José Peón Contreras wrote over forty plays.

When Peón Contreras arrived on the scene, the grand old man of Mexican drama was Juan A. Mateos (1831–1913), a lawyer, journalist, and prolific playwright. He and General Vicente Riva Palacio (1832–96) had initiated a "theatrical assault" with the very successful production of their first collaboration, *Hereditary Hate* (*Odio hereditario*), at the Teatro de Iturbide in January 1861. Together for three seasons they had over a doezen plays

*Left, Concepción Padilla made her debut as a dramatic actress at the Gran Teatro Nacional on January 1, 1871. This photograph is inscribed "a memento of friendship and affection to my friend and companion Felipe Montoya, Guanajuato, February 1883." Courtesy of Biblioteca de las Artes, Centro Nacional de las Artes.*

*Right, Juan A. Mateos (1831–1913) drew upon his experience as a lawyer to write many successful comedies in the 1870s.*

*Left, a popular favorite at the Circo Orrin was the clown Ricardo Bell.*

*Right, completely rebuilt in its old shell after the earthquake of 1894, the Teatro Principal reopened with electric lighting. This period illustration shows the audience on opening night in 1895.*

produced, many later published in a collection, *Las Liras hermanas* (1871). On his own from 1863, Mateos made a point of depicting national customs and problems at all social levels in a great variety of comedies (some dealing with judicial corruption), melodramas, and historical dramas. Among his major audience-pleasers were *The Millstone of Justice* (*La muela de juicio*, 1864); *The Kidnapping* (*El plagio*, 1872); *The Gods Depart* (*Los dioses se van*, 1878), which Chávarri called "his best work;" and *The Man Who Laughs* (*El hombre que ríe*, 1878), based upon Victor Hugo's *Le Roi s'amuse*.

Two plays by the lyric poet José Rosas Moreno (1838–83) premiered in 1876 under Guasp's project: *Daily Bread* (*El pan de cada día*), a moralizing verse comedy on the subject of gossip, and *Sor Juana Inés de la Cruz*, about the pre-convent days of the brilliant seventeenth-century nun. Rosas Moreno is also noteworthy as the first in Mexico to write children's plays. José Martí, who would later win recognition as the hero of the Cuban struggle for independence, first came to the attention of the Mexican public when Guasp presented his *Love Repaid with Love* (*Amor con amor se paga*). Alberto G. Bianchi saw two of his plays staged during that *annus mirabilis*, one by Guasp's company, the other at the Teatro de Nuevo México. The latter, *Martyrs of the People* (*Los martirios de un pueblo*), brought its working class audience to a fever pitch of emotion with its political satire. Afterward, carrying Bianchi through the streets on their shoulders, they called for an end to

*The Circo Orrin (1891–1910) offered variety entertainment and was nostalgically remembered by residents of the capital long after its disappearance.*

*Aquatic spectacles like the one depicted in this woodcut were featured at the Circo Orrin.*

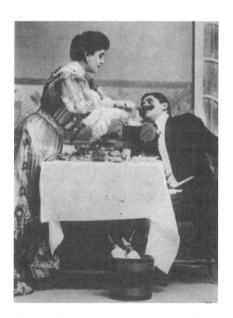

*The internationally renowned actress Virginia Fábregas (1870–1950) began her career in the 1880s. Here she played opposite Francisco Cardona in Victorien Sardou's* Let's Get a Divorce! *(Divorcie-monos). Courtesy of Biblioteca de las Artes, Centro Nacional de las Artes, México D.F.*

the Lerdo government. The result was a one-year prison sentence for Bianchi. After Lerdo's fall seven months later, Bianchi was released and *Martyrs of the People* performed at the Nacional.

Other dramatists came to the fore without Guasp's aid. Alfredo Chavero (1841–1906) held important government posts and wrote numerous plays as a sideline. Drawn especially to historical subjects, he displayed a romantic nationalism in dramas like *Xóchitl* (Flower, 1877), about an Indian mistress of Hernán Cortés, and *Quetzalcóatl* (1878). The well-known poet Manuel José Othón (1858–1906) composed several verse plays for the theater in his home town, San Luis Potosí, which he rarely left. His dramatic work achieved sudden prominence when Mexico's leading actress, María de Jesús Servín, brought his *After Death* (*Después de la muerte*, 1885) to the stage of the Teatro Principal in the capital. Servín, who also managed a theater company for a time, saw her own work staged when her adaptation of a French play, *My Husband Allows It* (*Mi marido me lo permite*), premiered at the Principal in 1876.

The capital got an elegant new theater in 1875 when Porfirio Macedo opened the Teatro Arbeu, one of the last theaters with an old-fashioned horseshoe-shaped auditorium and the first to feature the convenience of fold-up orchestra seats. José Joaquín Cleofas Moreno, who became the Arbeu's colorful manager, presented a mixture of *zarzuelas* and French operettas. For *el cinco de mayo*, he put together a major show and personally invited President Lerdo de Tejada, who promised to attend. At nine o'clock curtain time, a full house awaited the expected occupant of the presidential box. Around 10:30 P.M., according to Chávarria (*El Monitor Republicano*, May 9, 1875), some gave up and went home. Finally, at 11:00 P.M. the military band in the portico announced Lerdo's arrival, and the performance could begin. The press chastised the soon-to-be ex-president for his lack of courtesy.

In a season at the Gran Teatro Nacional in 1886, the *zarzuela* company of Arcaraz and Palou presented one of the landmark shows of the late nineteenth century. *The Fair at Santa Anita* (*Una fiesta en Santa Anita*), a musical *aproposito*, united the talents of librettist Juan de Dios Peza and composer Luis Arcaraz with Mexican popular melodies and colorful folk elements. The applause began when the curtain rose on a view of a Mexican village with floating gardens (*chinampas*) and canoes gliding in canals. Myriad visual and aural details gave the scene its distinctively Mexican flavor and established the frequently revived *Fair at Santa Anita* as the forerunner of the Mexican (not Spanish-style) *zarzuela*.

Among other noteworthy events near the end of the century was the debut in 1888 of seventeen-year-old Virginia Fábregas (1870–1950), who would go on to a fifty-year career and international recognition as Mexico's greatest actress. In 1889 residents of the capital heard that a panther was prowling the city; the scare inspired an *aproposito* called *The Panther of San Cosme* and a folk saying used by parents to frighten their children into good behavior. Beginning in a tent theater in 1881, the Orrin brothers presented circus entertainment in the capital. The opening of their Circo Orrin in 1891 provided a permanent and extremely popular venue for aquatic pantomimes, performing animals, and such beloved stars of variety entertainment as the great clown Ricardo Bell, the dwarf Pirrimplín, and the amazing quick-change artist Leopoldo Frégoli who played all five characters in a one-act comedy he had written. Fond memories of the Circo Orrin lingered among residents of the capital long after the razing of the building in 1910.

At the Teatro Principal—where the old façade had been demolished and replaced in 1880, and electric lighting had been installed in 1893—an earthquake in 1894 brought down some walls and the roof over the stage. The theater reopened nearly a year later, completely reconstructed within the original framework, with much improved stage equipment, lighting, and ventilation. Graced by the presence of the phenomenally popular Rosario Soler, the Principal reigned in the late 1890s as the "supreme temple" of *tandas* and other musical entertainment. More theaters were needed, however, to meet the demand for *zarzuelas*. The Teatro Mignon opened in 1899, followed in 1900 by the Teatro del Renacimiento (later Teatro Mexicano; after 1932, Teatro Virginia Fábregas). By the turn of the century, only the Hidalgo was still regularly providing legitimate drama in the capital.

## THE CARIBBEAN

From 1868 to 1901, Cuba's almost constant involvement in wars for independence retarded its artistic development. Romantic drama continued to be produced alongside realistic social problems plays from France and Spain. As in Mexico, however, it was light musical entertainment that dominated. In the mid-1860s a distinctly Cuban form of popular theater appeared, called *bufos habaneros*. Usually featuring a Negro character, these musical

*A Cuban theater is used as a public ballroom in this sketch. Here as elsewhere in the nineteenth century, the box office for a ball often exceeded that for performance of a play. From Samuel Hazard,* Cuba with Pen and Pencil, *1871.*

comedy sketches used situations from working-class Cuban life to mock the showier Spanish *zarzuelas. Bufos habaneros* quickly attracted a following, and soon there were at least nine amateur groups presenting them in the capital. When the War for Independence broke out and the *bufos habaneros* were banned, some groups toured to Mexico while others simply gave them a new designation, *bufos de Salas,* and continued performing them in Havana. In the 1880s Raimundo Cabrera (1852–1923) combined the musical satire form of the *bufos* with his more sophisticated writing; his *From the Park to the Moon (Del parque a la luna),* for example, ran 106 performances at the Teatro Cervantes. Federico Villoch (1866–1954) emerged in the 1890s as a successful writer of *bufos* and was still making a political impact well into the twentieth century.

José Martí (1853–95)—the Cuban revolutionary leader, poet, playwright, and journalist—wrote most of his plays in exile. At sixteen he published his first play, *Abdala* (1869), a patriotic drama in verse, in the only issue of *La Patria Libre* (January 23, 1869). For that and other revolutionary activities, he served a year of forced labor, after which he lived abroad (Spain, United States, Venezuela, Mexico), devoting himself to the cause of Cuban independence through his writing and organization of labor groups. He wrote his prose drama *Adultress (Adúltera,* 1874) in Spain. His two-character one-act comedy in verse *Love Repaid by Love (Amor con amor se paga,* 1875) premiered to extraordinary acclaim at the Teatro Principal in Mexico City. In Guatemala he wrote *Fatherland and Liberty (Patria y libertad,* 1895), a patriotic allegory in verse, in which two native women, Coana and Indiana, symbolically achieve independence for the two Americas. Martí's other

*Fanciful headdresses and costumes are worn by revellers dancing in the streets at carnival time in mid-nineteenth century Cuba. From Samuel Hazard,* Cuba with Pen and Pencil, *1871.*

dramatic writing survives only in fragments and play titles, but he also published numerous essays about dramatic literature and the theater.

On Puerto Rico, Eugenio Astol (1843–1904), a remarkable actor and engaging personality, excelled in roles ranging from Romantic heroes to comic characters. He ran various companies, built at least one theater in San Juan, and traveled widely in Latin America. Astol's talent gave considerable impetus to Alejandro Tapia y Riveras and other Puerto Rican playwrights of that generation and after. Without entirely abandoning his Romanticism, Tapia y Rivera explored some social problems in his later work. The antiracist sentiment in his *The Quadroon* (*La cuaterona*, 1867) delayed its premiere in Puerto Rico until five years after the 1873 abolition of slavery there. The *jíbaro* (peasant) figure, which had appeared in Puerto Rican literature as early as 1820, became a staple of late nineteenth-century Puerto Rican drama beginning with *Wagering on Cocks; or, The African Fresh off the Boat* (*La juega de gallos o El negro bozal*, 1851), a *costumbrista* play by Ramón C. F. Caballero. Ramón Méndez Quiñones (1847–99) earned recognition as a folklorist and a following among rural audiences by employing the *jíbaro* in a series of plays in the 1870s and 1880s. His 1878 play, *A Jíbaro Like Few Others* (*Un jíbaro como hay pocos*), premiered in Aguadilla with Astol in the title role.

On Santo Domingo this period marked the appearance of many amateur and academic theater groups that used simple staging.

## CANADA

Trends that had begun before the 1867 Confederation intensified during the last three decades of the nineteenth century: more playhouses constructed, more foreign stars and companies touring to Canada, continuing westward expansion of theatrical activity, increasing numbers of plays by Canadian writers though the foreign repertoire maintained its hegemony. Most importantly, some permanent professional Canadian companies established themselves.

On the negative side, this period brought an end to the informal accommodation that had existed between church and theater. Although Monseigneur de Saint-Vallier's 1694 ordinance against theater was still technically in effect, it could be overlooked as long as francophone theater maintained a low profile by its infrequency, presented only the most scrupulously moral texts, and did not involve women. By the 1850s, however, French–Canadian urban young people were bilingual and finding their way in droves to the English-language comedies and melodramas at the Theatre Royal, which featured actresses and which the francophone press condemned as displaying "immoral tendencies." Visits by professional French troupes presenting the latest Paris successes fueled the flame, and the francophone theater began to experience its harshest attacks since the days of Saint-Vallier.

In 1859 the extremely conservative bishop of Montreal, Monseigneur Ignace Bourget, circulated a pastoral letter instructing his clergy to warn their parishioners "against Opera, Theatre, Circus, and other secular entertainments that are today, throughout our towns and rural areas, a genuine subject of scandal." He went on to suggest that "these disorders are all the more regrettable in that they could bring down on us the terrible punishment of a poor harvest," and he called for "rightfully angry indignation against those faithless foreigners who come thus to expose us to the wrath of Heaven, poisoning our land with their dangerous shows! Alas!" Thus, the following year, when a francophone troupe began performing three times a week in Montreal's Salle Bonaventure, the company managers Vilbon and Trottier prudently announced in advance their moral intentions:

> One will see on the French stage of Montreal only plays of incontestable moral cachet, and for that purpose we have engaged the services of a censor who, after reading, rereading and revising the texts on the basis of the strictest standards of appropriate behavior and decent language, will himself then submit them to a committee of respectable people of our city whose final approbation alone will accord these dramatic works the privilege of citizenship on the French stage of Montreal.

In the process of periodically reiterating such sentiments, spokesmen for the enterprise moved from a defensive to an offensive position, promoting the theater as a moral alternative to the taverns and brothels that might otherwise attract young men, and as a school of virtue, where young ladies could learn lessons in modesty and decorum. By 1863 the troupe was in a position to undertake a subscription drive toward hiring some actors from France and assuring themselves a permanent place in Montreal's cultural scene. However, less high-minded groups undermined those efforts.

A French company presenting operettas by Offenbach in 1868 once again provoked the bishop of Montreal; Monseigneur Bourget condemned such fare for its "revolting immorality." He suggested that the churches

Toronto's 1,323-seat Grand Opera House opened in 1874. It burned in 1879, but was reconstructed in about two months and reopened, with increased seating capacity, on February 9, 1880. This illustration appeared in the Canadian Illustrated News (August 29, 1874). Metropolitan Toronto Reference Library.

Rideau Hall, a fully equipped proscenium stage in the ballroom of the governor general's residence in Ottawa, opened in 1873, because Lord Dufferin enjoyed private theatricals with his family. From Canadian Illustrated News. Metropolitan Toronto Reference Library.

schedule novenas "around seven o'clock in the evening, a time convenient to good souls, about the same time that some go to the theater, so that sacred songs and fervent prayers will substitute for the risqué songs and dissolute words that attract socialites to the shows." The bishop could scarcely object, however, when patriotic plays trumpeted the glory of France and other noble sentiments. Thus the announcement of a play titled *Les Prussians en Lorraine* shortly after the Franco–Prussian War of 1870–71 was well calculated to draw francophone crowds to the Theatre Royal. The manager of the French company, Alfred Maugard arrived in Montreal in 1871 by way of the Antilles. His Compagnie Lyrique et Dramatique specialized in operettas, by which they won an especially enthusiastic following at Quebec's Salle de Musique. In Quebec, Maugard met Félix-Gabriel Marchand (1832–1900), a respected journalist and public servant (later prime minister of Quebec province) who also wrote poetry and plays. On December 4, 1872, Maugard presented a gala evening of two plays by French–Canadian authors: Rodolphe Tanguay's dramatization of Joseph Marmette's 1872 novel *L'Intendant Bigot* and Marchand's own two-act *vaudeville* (light comedy with songs using familiar tunes) *Erreur n'est pas compte; ou Les Inconvénients d'une ressemblance* (Mistakes don't count; or, The inconvenience of looking alike, 1872). The ecstatic critical response led Maugard and his wife to settle their company permanently in Quebec. Little by little, however, the power of the box office led them to liberalize the repertoire. After several "charitable" warnings, the bishop of Quebec, Monseigneur Taschereau, circulated a letter (November 7, 1873) to be read in all of the city's churches: Catholics were henceforth forbidden to attend the theater. Maugard's company was forced to disband.

In Montreal in the spring of 1874, Monseigneur Bourget again took the offensive, provoked by the arrival of Achille Fay-Génot's Société Dramatique Française:

> Already the columns of certain newspapers are carrying announcements to the public of the arrival of a group of French actors coming to spread throughout our city and its surrrounding area the contamination of the most abominable vice. Already the mindless theater-lovers have been alerted to plays that are notorious for their excessive immorality, some of them arising from the most noxious sewer of all the revoltingly immodest filth produced by the French theater.

Other attacks were occasioned by the Algerian-born operetta singer Marie-Aimé (1852–87) with her New French Opera Bouffe Company at Montreal's Theatre Royal in October 1874, by the Genuine New-York *Black Crook* Company in Quebec (although *Black Crook* companies had previously toured Canada), by Montreal's Théâtre des Nouveautés in 1906, and by the several visits of Sarah Bernhardt.

The legendary Sarah Bernhardt's first visit to Montreal in 1880 sparked such anticipation that over five thousand cheering people (in a city of one hundred forty-one thousand) awaited her at the train station despite the temperature of minus-seven degrees Fahrenheit. There Louis-Honoré Fréchette declaimed a poem he had written in her honor. The florid, fleshy Fréchette later accompanied the star on a tour to the Iroquois village of Caughnawaga, an outing that occasioned her remark to the press: "Amazing country! The savages are civilized, and the poets are well-fed." Bernhardt performed at Montreal's lavishly appointed Academy of Music (capacity two thousand), which had opened in 1875. She initiated her four-performance run with Scribe and Legouvé's *Adrienne Lecouvreur,* a choice that had provoked Monseigneur Edouard Fabre, bishop of Montreal, to publish a denunciatory letter in the newspapers (December 21, 1880). Still the performance sold out, as did *Frou-frou* the following evening. However, *The Lady of the Camelias* (matinee) and *Hernani* were hampered by being scheduled on Christmas Day. The perfor-mance of *Adrienne Lecouvreur* on December 23, opened with the singing of "La Marseillaise" by a two hundred-voice choir, at the first notes of which everyone—including Governor General Lorne, married to Princess Louise, fourth daughter of Queen Victoria—jumped to their feet. Afterward, an emotional outpouring of applause continued for a few moments until the gov-ernor general respectfully signaled the orchestra to play "God Save the Queen." At the curtain call, white doves were released and a French flag-draped laurel wreath presented. Even the conservative newspaper *La Minerve* reported that *Adrienne Lecouvreur* "does not deserve the severe judgment it was given in these columns," though it was regrettable that Bernhardt did not apply her tal-ent to "plays more in accord with our ideas of beauty and greatness."

Sarah Bernhardt returned to Canada in 1891 (April and December), 1896, 1905, 1910, and 1916. Her 1905 tour brought particularly vehement condemnations from the archbishops of both Montreal and Quebec, Monseigneurs Bruchési and Bégin, who objected to the apparent anticleric-al-ism in Sardou's *The Sorceress* (*La Sorcière*). Although the play drew packed houses in both cities, Bernhardt incautiously expressed her views in an inter-view published in Quebec's *L'Evènement* (December 5, 1905): "I don't under-stand your people at all. You have English–Canadians, Irish–Canadians, French–Canadians, Iroquois–Canadians. But how dare you call yourselves French–Canadians? You have nothing French about you! . . . You have no painters, no authors, no sculptors, no poets." She also blamed the Catholic clergy for leading cultural development backwards, away from the artistic achievements of France and toward something more primitive. Her remarks so inflamed Quebec's French–Canadian students that a street demonstration verged on violence when her company departed. Indeed, an actress in the company wrote in a letter that "they threw stones at our carriages. . . . When we arrived at the station we had to get our bags off and pay the coachman in a hail of sticks and stones." Despite the problems, Bernhardt did arouse nationalistic French pride among the *Canadiens,* thus encouraging a long line of French professional theater companies and individual performers to try their luck in Canada. Among the French stars who came were Coquelin, Mounet–Sully, and Réjane.

The English-language stage also attracted stars, many from the American theater. The Americans included Benedict DeBar (who worked for a time with Buckland at Montreal's Theatre Royal), William H. Crane, Lawrence Barrett, Blind Tom (a Georgia slave-born pianist of international renown), Frank Mayo, Genevieve Ward, Steele Mackaye, James O'Neill,

*A fashionable audience filled Rideau Hall for a private performance. From* Canadian Illustrated News *(March 29, 1973). Metropolitan Toronto Reference Library.*

General and Mrs. Tom Thumb, George L. Fox, Marie Wainwright, Nat C. Goodwin Jr., Rose Eytinge, Richard Mansfield, Maurice Barrymore, Mary Anderson, Joseph Jefferson III. Touring stars from continental Europe and England included Charles Fechter, Daniel E. Bandmann, Fanny Janauschek, Helena Modjeska, Adelaide Nielson, Tommaso Salvini, Ernesto Rossi, Adelaide Ristori, Ellen Terry, Sir Henry Irving, Fanny Davenport, E. A. Sothern, Robert Bruce Mantell, and Lily Langtry. Beginning in the 1880s, their tours often extended beyond Montreal and Quebec, as theaters opened in other towns. Grand Opera Houses proliferated: Ottawa (1875; capacity 1,400), Kingston (1879), London (1880; capacity 1,228), Hamilton (1880; capacity 1,120); Chatham (1880s; capacity 1,336), Barrie (1890s; capacity 1,000). Other towns had opera houses named after their manager, as was Bradburn's Opera House (capacity 1,000) in Peterborough. Others, like the Princess Theatre in Winnipeg (1883), were named for royalty. Some towns supported more than one opera house: Toronto's Grand Opera House (1880; capacity 1,751) was rivaled by the Toronto Opera House (1880s; capacity 1,900) and the Princess Theatre (1896; capacity 1,815); the city's Royal Opera House and the Queen's Theatre both burned in 1883. Ottawa's Russell Theatre (1897) surpassed its Grand Opera in capacity. In addition, Ottawa's social élite enjoyed private theatricals in a ballroom theater in the official residence of the governor general. This facility, known as Rideau Hall, opened in 1873 with a fully equipped proscenium stage for the use of Lord Dufferin and his family. Subsequent governors general continued the tradition of family theatricals and/or *théâtre de société* until the end of the century. Numerous smaller towns constructed town halls with auditorium facilities. Meanwhile, Montreal was also adding performance venues: the Crystal Palace (1884; capacity 1,500), the Victoria Theatre (1884), the Queen's Theatre (1891), Empire Theatre (1893, later called Théâtre Français), Le Monument National (1894), Her Majesty's Theatre (1898), and the Théâtre National (1900).

Canada began producing its own outstanding actors during this period, but most sought validation on the New York stage, and many became expatriates, as did the Montreal-born William Burke Wood (1779–1861), who acted under Thomas Wignell in Philadelphia and later shared the management of several American theaters with William Warren. William Rufus Blake (1802–63) made his professional debut in Halifax in 1817, but it was with an American company; most of his career was in American theater, although he played an 1831 starring engagement in Montreal and Quebec, and briefly managed a theater in Halifax. The popular blackface minstrel performer Cool Burgess (b. 1840) worked in partnership with the American J. H. Haverly from 1862 to 1866, after which Burgess formed his own minstrel company and included Ontario on almost every season's tour. Julia Arthur (1869–1950) toured with Daniel Bandmann's company, beginning in her hometown, Hamilton, Ontario; her international career included engagements with Henry Irving's Lyceum Theatre, with Arthur Hopkins's 1921 *Macbeth* in New York as Lady Macbeth opposite Lionel Barrymore, and with the Theatre Guild in the title role of Shaw's *Saint Joan* (1924), yet she often returned to tour Canada. Margaret Anglin (1876–1958), born in Ottawa and trained in New York, achieved renown in touring and resident companies in both the United States and Canada. Toronto's beloved John Nickinson had launched his professional acting career in Albany and ended it in Cincinnati. Even francophone actors seeking to make the leap from amateurism to a professional career used the American stage as a rite of passage, as exemplified by Alphonse-Victor Brazeau (1839–98), who may have been the first professional French–Canadian actor. Brazeau made his amateur debut at eighteen with the Société des Amateurs Canadiens at Montreal's Theatre Royal, playing ingenues so charmingly that deluded gentlemen inundated him with flowers. Later, his "beauty" marred by smallpox, Brazeau turned to comic character roles. He joined a professional francophone company in New Orleans, the Troupe Saint-Louis, which toured to Montreal in 1878 with Brazeau at its head. Other Canadians, francophone and anglophone, who made late-nineteenth-century stage careers on both sides of the border include Graves Simcoe Lee, Arthur McKee Rankin, Fanny Reeves, Clara Morris, Mae Edwards, Julien Daoust, and May Irwin.

The rise of professional companies enabled some Canadian performers to make careers largely in Canada. Until the 1870s it was mainly the foreign stars who toured, playing with the resident stock company in each town they visited. From around 1880 whole troupes began to tour by rail. Indeed, according to Mary M. Brown, towns as small as London, Ontario, would see over a hundred professional touring companies during the August to May theatrical season. The playhouses themselves were locally owned and operated, but their managers often made use of booking agencies that informally placed them in a "circuit." These Canadian circuits were never as fixed as the ones in the United States, and thus theater managers more successfully resisted the kind of syndication that put control of the American stage into the hands of a few men around 1896.

One of Canada's prominent theater managers, Charlotte Morrison (1832–1910), balanced her own resident stock company with booked-in touring companies. Morrison had been Toronto's most beloved actress from the management days of her father, John Nickinson, at the Royal Lyceum, and she had toured the provinces of Quebec and Ontario as a star performer. After management stints at the Royal Lyceum and at the Toronto Opera House, she became the first manager of Toronto's Grand Opera House (1874–78), where she played leading roles in performances by her company on the evenings when there was no touring star or troupe. It was Morrison's stock company

*Left, Ontario-born actress Julia Arthur (1869–1950) is shown here in the role of Imogen in Shakespeare's* Cymbeline. *Metropolitan Toronto Reference Library.*

*Right, Toronto's Grand Opera House reached its zenith under the management of Charlotte Morrison from 1874 to 1878. This playbill shows the fare on her benefit night, December 18, 1876: the five-act French comedy* A Scrap of Paper *(a translation of Victorien Sardou's* Les Pattes de mouche, *1860), followed by a comic afterpiece,* Bonnie Fish Wife. *Metropolitan Toronto Reference Library.*

that nurtured the talents of Ida Van Cortland (1854–1924), who moved from walk-ons to speaking roles in the 1877–78 season there. Van Cortland later recalled: "In that one season I worked under twenty different stars, and played at least forty different parts." The regular stock season was thirty weeks with a weekly change of bill; ten of those weeks would be devoted to the eight Shakespeare plays in the repertoire. If a touring star came to perform with the resident company, there would usually be a nightly change of bill. Van Cortland also reminisced, as reported by Murray D. Edwards:

> As I watched in the wings, and listened, in those old days, it seems to me the actors were never weary of discussing readings, expressions, emphasis and action. The Couldrock reading of a line was contrasted with a Booth interpretation; and the phrase was discussed pro and con, the meaning analyzed word by word, and the methods of inflection necessary to bring that meaning out.

In 1879 Van Cortland joined a touring company run by William Nannary (b.1839), who made his headquarters in Halifax. In 1881 she married comic actor Albert Tavernier (1854–1929), who had also joined Nannary's company, having previously acted with Eugene A. McDowell (1845–93), a very successful actor–manager of both touring and stock companies in Canada. Tavernier and Van Cortland toured with various other itinerant troupes, including that of the wide-ranging Harry Lindley (1839–1913). Then they formed their own Tavernier Dramatic Company, playing Canada and the United States from 1882 to 1896.

One of the most remarkable and far-reaching Canadian theatrical enterprises was that of the seven Marks Brothers, who came from a farm near Christie Lake, Ontario. Murray D. Edwards has pieced together the saga of how they took quality entertainment to small Ontario communities that were not on the more profitable circuits. The eldest brother, Robert William Marks (1853–1937), entered show business as a result of a chance encounter with an itinerant magician. Marks formed a partnership with "King Kennedy, the Mysterious Hindu from the Bay of Bengal" and learned the tricks of the trade. In 1879 Bob Marks began touring with his brother Thomas, reaching as far west as Winnipeg, where they were hailed as among the earliest professional entertainers to visit there in those days before the Manitoba town had a rail connection. Then Bob Marks brought his other brothers and their wives into the business, which eventually split into three separate companies, each called Marks Brothers Dramatic Company and each comprising about twelve people. Bob, Ernie, and Tom Marks headed the three companies. During the summer they would return to the family farm to plan the following forty-two week season. Standard melodramas filled the bill, all geared to the family audience. What distinguished the Marks Brothers besides their respect for the conservative tastes of the small-town public was the lavishness of their production values by comparison with most touring companies of the period. Rather than relying on stock scenes, they created a new, specific setting for each locale in the play. Bob Marks would sometimes even employ a scene-painter to create new scenery when he played an extended run in one town.

Canadian actress Ida Van Cortland (1854–1924) is shown here in the role of Billie Piper in a dramatization of Joaquin Miller's The Danites. *Metropolitan Toronto Reference Library.*

*The shows of the Ontario-based Marks Brothers Dramatic Company were transported great distances by horse-drawn wagon. All seven Marks Brothers appear in this photograph. Metropolitan Toronto Reference Library.*

*All seven Marks Brothers appear on this 1905 poster. Robert Marks, at center, was the eldest; he started the family touring-theater business in 1879. Metropolitan Toronto Reference Library.*

As trappers, miners, and settlers moved into the plains and far western lands, theater followed closely behind, albeit crude in form and circumstances. Women were few in those early outposts, and the men entertained themselves by storytelling, fiddling, and dancing. Settlers in the Red River valley saw a magician, Magnus McGregor, as early as 1833, according to E. Ross Stuart, and in the 1840s, a Mr. Desjarlais performed for locals who paid one buffalo sinew apiece to crowd into a farm kitchen and see his sleight of hand. As towns were established, community concerts often included dramatic readings. Winnipeg's first performance venue for such events was an upstairs room called Red River Hall; the audience was asked not to applaud, for fear of causing the shaky building to collapse. After its 1866 inauguration, however, Red River Hall, with its beams propped up by poles, withstood two years of frequent use. A Theatre Royal with a capacity of two hundred (serving Winnipeg's tiny population of 215) opened in 1870. Winnipeg's lively amateur theater scene (with women performing by 1874) was centered in a different space every couple of years. The City Hall Theatre, a five- hundred-seat upstairs auditorium used from 1876 to 1883, was the site of the first professional performance in Winnipeg, by the minstrel Cool Burguess in 1877 and 1878. McDowell's company played four weeks there in 1879, presenting sixteen different plays. When City Hall closed because its walls were buckling, the Princess Theatre replaced it. Victoria Hall, which opened in 1882, shook when the drop curtain was lowered after each act, but an 1891 renovation allowed it to continue in use as the Bijou. Perhaps the two most influential figures in early Winnipeg theater history were critic Charles W. Handscomb (1867–1906) and manager–entrepreneur Corliss Power Walker (1853–1942). Handscomb had written *The Big Boom* (1886), a satire on Winnipeg land speculation, that was produced by McDowell's troupe, and he had toured with Haverly's Minstrels. He settled in Winnipeg as music and drama critic for the *Manitoba Free Press*, then founded his own weekly *Town Topics* in 1898. To review theater, he hired Harriet Walker, wife of his close friend, the theater manager C. P. Walker. Writing under the sobriquet "The Matinee Girl," Mrs. Walker proved to be an independent thinker, while Handscomb unhesitatingly used his forum to promote what he saw as "morally healthy" fare. C. P. Walker had moved to Winnipeg after brief theater management experience at the Fargo Opera House. He leased the Winnipeg Theatre, gradually acquired a chain of theaters along the railroad between the two cities, worked with the American Theatrical Syndicate to monopolize Winnipeg theater, and crowned his career with the construction in 1907 of the magnificent, fireproof Walker Theatre, which operated year round and hosted an impressive roster of stars.

The prairie lands that would become Saskatchewan and Alberta in 1905 were settled more slowly than Manitoba (which became a province in 1870) and, even farther west, British Columbia (admitted to dominion in 1871). Thus in those areas the theater remained much longer in the hands of amateurs, including the Royal Canadian Mounted Police who enjoyed putting on

*The Marks Brothers productions were renowned for attractive décor, as evidenced in this scene from act 3 of* At the Point of the Sword. *Metropolitan Toronto Reference Library.*

*The American-born actor-manager Eugene A. McDowell (1845–1943) spent most of his career touring Canada, often in the western territories. He is shown here as Conn in Dion Boucicault's* The Shaughraun. *Metropolitan Toronto Reference Library.*

minstrel shows in the 1880s. Regina's first town hall theater opened above the jail in 1886, Saskatoon's at about the same time, while Edmonton and Calgary long used a variety of venues: schoolhouse, skating rink, barn, or meeting room in a hotel, church, or community hall. Not until 1892 was Edmonton reached by rail, and that year brought its first professional performers. In Calgary the earliest primitive facilities were replaced in 1893 by the seven-hundred-seat, two-story, gas-lit Hull's Opera House.

Shipboard and garrison theatricals served the entertainment needs of early colonials in British Columbia and on Vancouver Island. The Fraser River gold rush of 1858 lured thousands of former California forty-niners into the area, and numerous small mining camps sprang up in the remote Cariboo district in the 1860s. Most miners spent the winters in Victoria, where George Chapman's Pioneer Dramatic Company, featuring his own family, was the first professional troupe. In 1860 Chapman opened the 360-seat Colonial Theatre, which boasted segregated seating: parquet seats for one dollar were "suitable for ladies; Indians and such ilk will have a corner by themselves;" that is, for fifty cents, miners could sit in the pit and Native Americans in the gallery. For the few hundred miners who wintered in the camps, saloons offered variety entertainment: boxing, magic acts, singing. A Cariboo Amateur Dramatic Association was formed in 1865 and sponsored amateur theatricals at a saloon in Barkerville. That group bought the Parlor Saloon in 1868 and reopened it as the Theatre Royal (capacity 250 in a permanent settlement of two thousand). After the whole town burned down that year, the upper floor of the Williams Creek Fire Brigade Hall served as the new Theatre Royal, which survived until 1937. Meanwhile, Victoria boasted a new eight-hundred-seat facility, the Victoria Theatre (1885), and The Nanaimo Opera opened in 1889. With railway linkages completed in 1887,

*From 1861 to 1882, the major theatre in Victoria, British Columbia, was the wooden structure shown here and called the Theatre Royal. Courtesy of the B.C. Archives (photo no. HP008720).*

*Western music halls combined the attractions of the saloon and the stage show to draw miners who lived in town during the winter. Victoria's St. Charles Music Hall, shown here around 1880, was typical. Courtesy of the B.C. Archives (photo no. HP057179).*

*Sarah Anne Curzon (1833–98) grew up in England, but lived in Canada when she wrote her plays. From* Literary Garland *(May 1846).*

Vancouver began to surpass Victoria in population and playhouses; among these were Herring's Opera House (1887), the Imperial Opera House (1889), and the 1,211-seat Vancouver Opera House (1891). In the Yukon, Dawson City had a log Opera House by 1898, followed by various other facilities, and finally the seven-hundred-seat Palace Grand Theatre (1899).

The repertoires of most troupes were limited to popular fare like melodramas, farces, and operettas. Among the few companies specializing in Shakespeare and the classics were the German-born Daniel E. Bandmann's Shakespeare Repertory Company, which toured Canada in the 1880s, and Margaret Anglin's company, which toured Canada in 1898. But there was no perceptible demand for material beyond the tried and true. Nevertheless, a number of new Canadian plays were published, even if not produced, during the last decades of the nineteenth century. Poetic drama had begun to appear during the pre-Confederation period with *Saul* (1857), a lengthy religious drama in verse by English-born Charles Heavysege (1816–76). It garnered excessive praise for its literary qualities and was given a public reading in Montreal by the author, but did not get produced. Eliza Lanesford Cushing (1794–1886) also wrote verse plays either on Biblical subjects, like *Esther* (1838), or geared to women's interests; her ten plays were published in periodicals. Wilfred Campbell drew on myth and legend for his verse plays like *Mordred* (1895). Thomas Bush wrote blank verse for most of the characters in his melodrama, *Santiago* (1866), though some of the ethnic stereotypes speak their heavy dialect in prose. John Hunter–Duvar (1821–99) wrote historical verse tragedies, *The Enamorado* (1879) and *De Roberval* (1888). Sarah Anne Curzon (1833–98) composed a verse drama, *Laura Secord, the Heroine of 1812* (1887), about the popular figure in Canadian folk history. Her women's rights play, *The Sweet Girl Graduate* (1882), was also published but not produced.

*Dawson City in the Yukon opened its seven-hundred-seat Palace Grand Theatre in 1899. This Larss and Duclos photograph of the exterior was taken that year. Thomas Gibson Album, photo 59-804-6N from the Archives and Manuscripts Collections, Alaska and Polar Regions Department, Elmer E. Rasmuson Library, University of Alaska Fairbanks.*

*Dawson City's Palace Grand could also be used for community festivities as well as theater. Here the main floor of the auditorium serves as a ballroom on St. Andrew's Night, 1899. From the McLennan Collection (YA 6485), courtesy of the Yukon Archives, Whitehorse.*

*A one-act operetta,* The Maire of St. Brieux *by Frederick Augustus Dixon (1843–1919), is shown on stage at Rideau Hall, where a number of Dixon's plays were staged. From* Canadian Illustrated News *(April 24, 1875). Metropolitan Toronto Reference Library.*

Historical subjects served polemicists as well as poets and melodramatists. Charles Mair (1838–1927) cofounded an anti-American, antifrancophone nationalist movement called Canada First in 1874; his blank verse tragedy *Tecumseh* (1886), about the legendary Shawnee leader, served as a vehicle for the heavyhanded expression of those sentiments. Conservative politician Nicholas Flood Davin (1843–1901) wrote "a farce" satirizing political opportunism: *The Fair Grit; or, The Advantages of Coalition* (1876). William Henry Fuller's *The Unspecific Scandal* (1874) and *H.M.S. Parliament; or, The Lady who Loved a Government Clerk* (1880) attacked the corrupt government of prime minister John A. Macdonald. The latter work, a comic opera incorporating tunes from Gilbert and Sullivan's *H.M.S. Pinafore* (which had been presented in hundreds of Canadian and American theaters in 1878–79), actually got staged, opening at Montreal's Academy of Music on February 16, 1880 to critical and popular acclaim. Having produced it lavishly, Eugene A. McDowell then took it on the road for a season, playing at least twenty-seven towns and cities, including Ottawa (there is no evidence that Macdonald attended), from the Maritime provinces to Manitoba. Another comic opera, this one mocking Canadians taken in by the economic lure of the United States, had three performances in Hamilton, Ontario, where its composer John Edmond Paul Aldous headed the music school. Jean Newton McIlwraith wrote the text of *Ptarmigan; or, A Canadian Carnival* (1895), in which the heroine, named Maple Leaf, is described as "an athletic *Canadienne*, in love with her country," and the hero Ptarmigan— who has seen that American girls dominate their husbands—ends up with a "new woman." Catharine Nina Merritt (1859–1926) celebrated Canada's ties to Britain in *When George III Was King* (1897).

Writing prolifically in various dramatic genres, Frederick Augustus Dixon saw many of his works produced. As tutor for Lord Dufferin's sons, he wrote children's plays that were presented in Rideau Hall in the 1870s, most notably *Fifine, the Fisher-Maid; or, The Magic Shrimps* (1877). His one-act operetta *The Maire of St. Brieux* (1875), composed by Frederick W. Mills, so delighted audiences at Rideau Hall that it was revived in 1876 at Ottawa's Grand Opera House. Also at the Grand Opera House, his *Masque Entitled 'Canada's Welcome'* (1879), composed by Arthur A. Clappé, greeted the arrival of the new governor general. William A. Tremayne (1864–1939) moved from film acting to screen and stage writing, then to directing in Montreal, where he exercised considerable influence over early twentiety-century theater. Among his melodramas that won great popular success are *The Secret Warrant* (1897) and *The Black Feather* (1916). Actor McKee Rankin (1841–1914) sometimes wrote his own material, and enjoyed partic-ular success with *The Danites* (based upon a work by Joaquin Miller, 1877), *The Canuck* (1890), and *Abraham Lincoln* (1891).

Several French–Canadian dramatists from this period must also be sig-naled. Félix-Gabriel Marchand's interest in theater has already been men-tioned in connection with Alfred Maugard's attempt to establish a company in Quebec. Produced plays by Marchand, who later became premier of

*W. H. Fuller's* H.M.S. Parliament, *one of many late-nineteenth-century political satires on the Canadian stage, borrowed plot elements and tunes from the well-known Gilbert and Sullivan operetta* H.M.S. Pinafore. *Scenes and characters from the show are shown on the cover of the* Canadian Illustrated News *(February 28, 1880). Metropolitan Toronto Refer-ence Library.*

Quebec province, include: *Fatenville* (1869), *Erreur n'est pas comte* (1872), *Un Bonheur en attire un autre* (Luck brings luck, 1883) as well as the posthumously performed *Les Faux brilliants* (All that glitters) and *Le Lauréat* (The laureate). Marchand's daughter, Joséphine Dandurand, also wrote plays, including *Rancune* (1888). Elzéar Paquin (1850–1947) is known for one play, an epic historical tragedy, *Riel* (1886), about the instigator of the 1885 Métis rebellion and his execution.

Thus the nineteenth century closed with continuing expressions of national heritage and identity—whether British–Canadian or French–Canadian or simply Canadian—published as dramatic literature and occasionally even finding their way to the stage.

# 6 Entertainment and Art: 1900–1945

## THE UNITED STATES

From the turn of the century to the onset of the Great Depression was one of the most dynamic eras in American history. Mounting industrial and commercial expansion fueled the flight from the farm to the city. In one of the greatest mass migrations in world history, millions of immigrants poured into the United States between 1900 and 1930—almost nine million in the decade 1900–1910. The populations of many American cities doubled or even tripled within a single generation. Inventive engineers attacked urban growth by building incredible water projects, bridges, subways, and elevated trains. Steel-skeleton technology led to higher and higher commercial buildings—skyscrapers, as they were called. The Empire State Building completed in 1931 was the tallest manmade structure to date, soaring over one hundred stories to 1,250 feet. Cities expanded upward and outward into residential suburbs, becoming great commercial and cultural megalopolises. But overcrowding strained city services and intensified the problems of the urban poor.

Progressive political leaders, muckraking journalists, social philosophers, and activists exposed problems in government, business, and industry, and lobbied for legislative regulations and sweeping humanitarian reform. Women gradually wrested some improvements in their legal and social status, culminating in the Nineteenth Amendment granting them voting rights.

The long wave of economic prosperity that began in the Gilded Age brought most Americans a higher standard of living and more discretionary income. A plethora of consumer products—washing machines, electric stoves, an array of manufactured food products—made daily life easier and increased the time available for leisure activities. The automobile, initially a luxury, was increasingly a necessity. A mushrooming system of intra- and interurban roadways gave many Americans unprecedented mobility. By 1900, the Great Plains were settled and the frontier was closed. The United States—forty-eight by 1912—was a borderless country from the Atlantic to the Pacific and from Canada to Mexico. The territorial status of Puerto Rico (later upgraded to a Commonwealth) and of Alaska and Hawaii (subsequently admitted as the forty-ninth and fiftieth states, respectively) extended the American sphere into the Caribbean, the Far North, and the Pacific.

In the 1920s, one could drive, if so moved, for thousands of miles in any direction within the "lower forty eight." Intercity passenger railway service—streamliners—and an increasing number of commercial airlines whisked travelers to their destinations with relative rapidity and in comparative luxury. Nationwide radio broadcasts enhanced American homogeneity and solidarity. Movies also produced a sense of a shared, common culture. Daily family gatherings around a radio or a weekly trip to the local movie theater became rituals for many Americans.

In the late 1910s and 1920s, a new generation of American writers, artists, composers, scientists, and philosophers achieved international renown, bolstering American cultural pride and confidence. In 1930, novelist Sinclair Lewis, for example, became the first American to win the Nobel Prize for Literature. American artists of all sorts were also prime contributors to the new, modernist aesthetic emerging after World War I.

It was generally a progressive, exuberant time, but not entirely a "golden age." Prosperity nurtured a shallow consumerism; mobility, paradoxically, fostered rootlessness. Protected by ocean barriers, Americans could be narrow, smug, even xenophobic. The nation entered World War I with a naive self-confidence and jingoistic idealism. The reality of the war, however, left many Americans feeling alienated and disillusioned. But America could no longer retreat into insularity. After World War I, America was politically, economically, and culturally connected to the world, and conversely, the world was connected to America. The 1920s was a strange, schizophrenic decade, another transitional period fraught with competing values and interests: isolationist and international, traditional and modern, engaged and detached, confident and anxious, richly creative and wildly self-destructive, liberating for some, but oppressive for others. Then with the stock market crash in October 1929, the "Roaring Twenties" collapsed. The Great Depression was a collective psychological, as well as economic crisis.

As always, the stage mirrored the times. Reflecting the building boom, hundreds of new theaters were built. The number of productions presented annually in New York tripled from the turn of the century to the end of the 1920s. In large part, this theatrical expansion was generated by economic prosperity and a burgeoning, middle-class population. Demand for theatrical entertainment of all sorts, from provocative dramas to farce to musical comedies and variety performance, sparked competition and an openness to novelty and experimentation. Late Victorian theatrical conventions were challenged by modernist notions of theater art. Alternative organizational models and forward-thinking producers vied with older entrepreneurs. A fresh crop of stars, endowed with magnetic stage personalities and the techniques of natural acting, brightened the stage. Innovative scenic designers, often working with inventive stage directors, radically altered the look of theater. Talented playwrights emerged to create works of genuine dramatic distinction and win international recognition, while a new generation of critics voiced their impatience with outworn approaches and styles. Indeed, dissatisfaction with the increasingly commercial orientation of the American theater mounted from various quarters. Lastly, that new marvel—the motion picture—would profoundly impact the theatrical industry as a whole.

IN 1912, THE redoubtable critic and theatrical chronicler William Winter estimated that there were not fewer than eight thousand theaters in America, a several thousand increase since the 1880s. New York City was the leader *sans pareil* in new theater construction. Stimulated not only by population explosion, but also by new and more efficient intraurban transportation systems, and a booming real estate market, over eighty new theaters were built in New York between 1900 and 1930. Most of these theaters were clustered on the side streets off of Times Square at the confluence of Broadway and Seventh Avenue. By the 1920s, Times Square, in fact, had replaced Union Square as the new center of New York's theatrical industry. The new theaters were conventionally designed with traditional proscenium stages and compact, intimate auditoriums, seating between eight hundred and one thousand spectators. The leading theater architect of the period, Herbert J. Krapp (1887–1973), designed over twenty New York theaters built during the 1920s, many of which are still in use today, including the Ethel Barrymore Theatre, the Broadhurst Theatre, the Neil Simon (Alvin) Theatre, and the John Golden (Theatre Masque) Theatre. Krapp also designed numerous theaters outside of New York, many for the Shubert theatrical empire.

In the 1910s and 1920s virtually all first-class professional theater in America was centralized on "Broadway," as this theater district came to be called. Broadway, in turn, was controlled by commercially oriented producers and production companies. Like his Gilded Age predecessor, the new Broadway producer selected the play he wanted to present, cast it, and either staged it himself or hired a director to do it. Furthermore, he often owned his own theater or theaters. A. L. Erlanger (the sole remaining member of the Syndicate) and the Shuberts were the leading producers, but their success fostered competitors. Theatrical producing was a risky business; nearly seventy percent of the productions mounted each season failed. But the potential profits from a successful long run show, followed by a national tour, could be enormous. In the 1920s, the Shuberts, Bernheim reports, sometimes had annual net profits of one million dollars or more; while Erlanger had a net worth of five million dollars in 1926. Poggi reports that *Lightnin'*, a rural comedy–melodrama, was produced for about six thousand dollars in 1918; after a three-year run in New York, it had grossed over one million dollars and it continued to tour season after season until 1925. Anne Nichols's (1891?–1966) *Abie's Irish Rose* (1922), a sentimental, romantic comedy, pitting young lovers—a Jewish boy and an Irish Catholic girl—against their hidebound parents, ran for over five years and earned perhaps five times more than *Lightnin'*. A flourishing economy provided capital for almost any enterprise, no matter how speculative. The number of productions on Broadway steadily increased from an average of one hundred in the seasons 1900 to 1904, to 192 in 1920–21, to a peak of 297 in 1926–27. Leiter reports that in the decade of the 1920s nearly twenty-five hundred productions were presented on Broadway, or an average of 250 a season. Theater

*Producer John Golden. Courtesy of the Flora Ward Hineline Papers, the Ward M. Canaday Center for Special Collections, University of Toledo Libraries.*

in America had become a big, multimillion dollar industry employing thousands of workers from seamstresses to actors.

Among the leading producers of the 1910s and 1920s were: Sam Harris (1872–1941), who teamed with the playwright and musical comedy star George M. Cohan (1878–1942) to produce over fifty plays from the early 1900s through the 1920s; Archibald (1877?–1959) and Edgar Selwyn (1875–1944), who, in addition to being producers, joined in 1914 with Elisabeth Marbury (1856–1933), the first dramatist's agent in America, to form the American Play Company, a worldwide play brokerage agency; John Golden (1874–1955), the producer of *Lightnin'* and 150 other plays, many of which were long-run successes; A. H. Woods (1870–1951), a producer of popular low-budget melodramas; Theodore Liebler (1852–1941) and George C. Tyler (1867–1946), who founded Liebler and Company in 1897, a partnership that would eventually produce some three hundred plays; and Florenz Ziegfeld (1869–1932), who, in addition to presenting annual editions of his famous *Follies* musical revue, produced numerous musical comedies and operettas. Other notable producers are discussed throughout this chapter.

MANY PRODUCERS—LIKE businessmen of any era—were mainly interested in minimizing their costs and increasing their profits. Elevating theatrical tastes and standards and fostering fair and equitable working conditions were a secondary consideration. In an enterprise where one's entire investment could be lost overnight—and often was—there was a marked potential for labor abuses. Following the example of American industrial workers, who had been organizing since after the Civil War, theater workers also began to organize themselves into craft guilds and unions. In 1885, for example, scene-painters formed the Protective Alliance of Scene Painters. In 1886, stagehands organized the Theatrical Protective Union of New York to force managers to hire them to change scenery, rather than actors; stagehands in other cities followed suit. In 1893, representatives from these local groups met and founded the National Alliance of Theatrical Stage Employees. In 1898, the National Alliance affiliated with Canadian stagehands and became the International Alliance of Theatrical Stage Employees (IATSE), a powerful union representing several different theatrical crafts. Actors working in New York's numerous Yiddish-language theaters organized the Hebrew Actors Union and achieved collective bargaining rights after a short strike against producers in 1899. In 1900, vaudevillians formed a union called the White Rats which in 1910 won a charter from the increasingly powerful American Federation of Labor (AFL) formed in 1886. The White Rats attempted to wrest some agreements from vaudeville producers, but the union was crushed in a lock-out of performers in 1916. A new organization, the National Vaudeville Artists, was formed, but not until the American Guild of Variety Artists (AGVA) was organized in 1939 did variety performers have strong union representation.

The organization of the acting profession was especially contentious. Actors regularly charged Broadway producers with abusive labor practices. Actors, for example, were expected to rehearse without pay, usually from six to ten weeks. There is on record the case of an actor who rehearsed for twenty-two weeks without pay, then received only four days pay when the production was abruptly closed. Actors could be laid off without notice; their salaries cut without warning; and their number of weekly performances increased without additional compensation. These and numerous other abuses, as noted in chapter 5, led to the formation of the Actors' Society of America (ASA) in 1894. The ASA's efforts to lobby on behalf of the profession were ignored by producers. As early as 1897, in an effort to gain additional clout, the ASA moved to affiliate with the American Federation of Labor (AFL). But many actors thought of themselves as artists not workers and they thwarted ASA's efforts. By 1912, the ASA was effectively dissolved and a new organization, the Actors' Equity Association (AEA or Equity) was founded. Led by its first president, comedian and singer Francis Wilson (1854–1935), Equity struggled for the next six years to negotiate a standard minimum contract for all classes of productions with the organizations that represented theater managers and producers—first the United Managers' Protective Association (UMPA), then in 1918 its successor organization, the Producing Managers' Association (PMA). But the producers steadfastly refused to make any concessions. Equity gradually overcame persistent unionization fears among many of its members and gained AFL membership in 1919, assuming the charter once held by the White Rats.

With producers still refusing to negotiate a standard contract, Equity called a strike. It quickly spread to eight cities, closed thirty-seven plays and prevented sixteen others from opening. The strike divided the profession with actors on both sides of the issue. George M. Cohan, who was both a performer and a producer, was particularly vehement in his opposition to Equity and unionism. He went so far as to organize a rival association of actors who supported the producers, the Actors' Fidelity League or "Fidos," as they were called. In a show of solidarity, other unionized workers—stagehands, musicians, teamsters, and theatrical bill posters—joined with Equity in their cause. The strike also had widespread public support. After thirty days and the loss of millions of dollars, the producers capitulated. A standard contract was agreed to and Equity became the sole representative of legitimate professional actors. Over the next decade, Equity negotiated additional agreements, including minimum wage and minimum rehearsal pay provisions, and an important closed-shop clause, forcing producers to hire only Equity members.

In the next two decades, other theatrical or entertainment unions were organized, including United Scenic Artists (1918) for scenic and costume designers, the Dramatists and Screen Writers Guilds (1920); and the Association of Theatrical Press Agents and Managers (1928). In 1933, actors in movies organized the Screen Actors' Guild. Producers also organized various associations through the 1920s, in large part to deal with an increasing number of theatrical trade unions, which ultimately led to the League of New York Theatres and Producers in 1930. (In 1985, in recognition of its national constituency, it changed its name to the League of American Theatres and Producers [LATP]). By the end of the 1930s virtually every group of workers associated directly or indirectly with theatrical productions had been organized into a union. Producers remained a significant force in the American theater, but unionization effectively circumscribed their powers—some would argue to the detriment of advancements in American theatrical art.

TOURING, WHICH IN large measure was responsible for the Syndicate and Shubert theatrical empires, and for the rise of Broadway, began to decline precipitously in the second decade of the new century. From a peak of over four hundred productions touring in 1904, by 1920 the average was about seventy productions a season. Poggi attributes the decline to a score of reasons. Undoubtedly rising production costs—a total increase of as much as 300 percent between 1900 and 1925—adversely affected the profitability of touring. Higher ticket prices to cover these costs, growing competition from family-oriented and more cheaply priced vaudeville entertainment, even cheaper movies, and free radio, were also factors affecting the decline.

Ironically, the decline of the road sparked a revival of stock companies. Most of these were organized as popular-priced houses, with tickets usually scaled at ten, twenty, and thirty cents—giving rise to the expression "ten-twent'-thirt' houses"—and rarely exceeding seventy-five cents. They often employed young or second-rate actors, and normally presented old-fashioned, sentimental comedies and melodramas, with occasional forays into Shakespeare or classic English comedy. Such companies had actually existed since the late 1890s, offering an alternative to higher priced touring productions. When the number of touring combinations declined, and also began to

bypass smaller communities, local stock companies once again became principal venues for dramatic entertainment, although they also faced stiff competition from touring vaudeville companies and emerging motion-picture
halls, or nickelodeons, as they were called. A number of companies located
in resort or vacation areas operated only during the summer months. These
summer stock companies were generally superior to winter stock since they
could attract a higher caliber actor during the "off" season. By the 1920s,
there were perhaps as many as two hundred popular-priced companies in
operation, but significantly fewer than in the heyday of the first-class metropolitan stock company. Some popular-priced companies were well-regarded,
such as Boston's Castle Square Theatre company, but generally stock had a
reputation, even if unmerited, for artistic inferiority. Actors who could play
on Broadway, did not act in stock. For all theater artists, a long run on
Broadway, followed by a tour, if possible, was the ultimate goal.

Another alternative to the decline of the road—and the centralization of
commercial theater in New York—was the tent show. Tent shows were itinerant repertory companies presenting popular-priced melodrama or variety
entertainment, mainly to rural towns and villages, during the summer. Poorly
ventilated local theaters usually closed in the summer, so the companies
played in tents. These companies were particularly prevalent in the central
states after World War I where, traveling by motor car and truck, they usually played a regular circuit of rural communities. Rural or folk comedies
centering on a red-haired, freckle-faced rustic named "Toby" were especially
popular. By the late 1920s, the Tent and Repertoire Managers' Protective
Association advertised that there were four hundred tent—or Toby—shows
touring rural America.

"Little theaters" also provided an alternative to commercial theater.
This term was used to describe collectively a number of mostly amateur theatrical groups that sprang up in America in the second decade of the twentieth century. The founders of these theaters were usually dissatisfied with
the commercial theatrical fare offered by tours or stock companies. They
modeled their aspirations after such European art theaters as André
Antoine's Théâtre-Libre, Otto Brahm's Freie Bühne, J. T. Grein's
Independent Theatre, the Moscow Art Theatre, and Dublin's Abbey Theatre.
Like their models, little theater organizers shared an enthusiasm for the
modern European drama of Henrik Ibsen, August Strindberg, Anton
Chekhov, John Galsworthy, and Bernard Shaw, for new serious American
drama, and for dramatic classics, plays which were ordinarily not presented
by typical commercial producers. By the late 1920s, there were hundreds of
little theaters across America. Among the more important seminal groups
were: Chicago's Little Theatre (1912)—which gave the movement its name—
New York's Neighborhood Playhouse (1915) and Washington Square
Players (1915), the Cleveland Playhouse (1915), the Provincetown Players
(1914), and the Pasadena Playhouse (1917). Some retained an amateur community theater status, while others eventually evolved into semi- or fully
professional theaters, like Chicago's Goodman Theatre, founded in 1925.

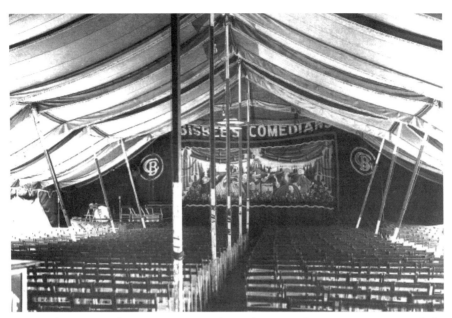

*The Bisbee's Comedians tent touring the midwest in the 1920s. Courtesy of the Theatre Museum of Repertoire Americana and the Society for the Preservation of Tent, Folk, and Repertoire Theatre, Mt. Pleasant, Iowa.*

*Walter Hampden as Cyrano de Bergerac. Courtesy of The Hampden–Booth Library at The Players.*

Although commercial interests dominated the American theater for the first third of the new century, a few entrepreneurs and producers worked to promote high-quality dramatic art. In 1909, for example, a consortium of wealthy businessmen, led by millionaire arts patron Otto Kahn (1867–1934), established what they hoped would be an American equivalent of Europe's great national theaters—the Théâtre Français or Vienna Burgtheater. Not only did they build the architecturally splendid New Theatre, but they endowed or subsidized its operation, presumably freeing its management from commercial concerns. They installed Winthrop Ames (1871–1937), a young producer-director at Boston's Castle Square Theatre, as artistic director. Ames, Harvard-educated, and with a private income, had first-hand experience with contemporary European theater practice. In 1907, he had spent several months seeing productions in London, Paris, Berlin, Munich, and Vienna. Ames assembled a company of old and new actors and planned a repertory season mixing revivals of classics with new modern plays. The New Theatre opened with a scenically sumptuous production of *Antony and Cleopatra,* the redoubtable Sothern and Marlowe in the title roles. But the New Theatre was large and its acoustics so poor that actors could not always be heard, and there were interminable "waits" while the settings were changed. Sothern and Marlowe were considered miscast as tragic lovers. The production as a whole was judged an embarrassing failure, but Ames, sticking to his plan, repeated it twice a week for the next three months in rotation with several modern plays, including John Galsworthy's *Strife* and American playwright Edward Sheldon's provocative *The Nigger.* Sothern and Marlowe had been slated for a revival of *Twelfth Night,* but stung by critical reaction to their *Antony and Cleopatra,* they resigned from the New Theatre's company. It was a serious blow to the enterprise, but Ames pressed on for another season, presenting some classics, but mainly new European plays, including Arthur Wing Pinero's *The Thunderbolt,* and Maurice Maeterlinck's *Mary Magdalen* and *The Blue Bird.* The productions were generally distinguished, but insufficiently popular to break even in the cavernous New Theatre. Ames's financial backers finally conceded failure; the debt was larger than they were willing to sustain. The theater, as noted in chapter 5, was sold to the Shuberts, who renamed it the Century, and used it as a house for musicals and operettas. (Ironically, Sothern and Marlowe would return to the Century in the autumn of 1921 for a fairly successful six-week run of their popular Shakespeare repertoire.) Ames clung to his vision of a commercial art theater, but he had learned one important lesson. He built two small theaters—the Little Theatre (1912, five hundred seats) and the Booth Theatre (1913, eight hundred seats)—where for the next two decades he successfully mounted productions of plays by Galsworthy, Arthur Schnitzler, Bernard Shaw, Maeterlinck, and other modern dramatists.

In the 1910s and 1920s, Ames was joined by other producers who occasionally aimed beyond mere financial success. In 1911, veteran producer William A. Brady (1863–1950) built the one-thousand-seat Playhouse Theatre where he starred his wife, Grace George (1879–1961) in a number of modern plays, including Shaw's *Major Barbara* (1915) and *Captain Brassbound's Conversion* (1916). Producer–director John D. Williams (1886?–1941) staged a number of provocative plays including Galsworthy's *Justice* (1916), Augustus Thomas's *The Copperhead* (1918), Somerset Maugham's *Our Betters* (1917) and *Rain* (1922) and Eugene O'Neill's *Beyond the Horizon* (1920). George C. Tyler was responsible for all-star revivals of *The School for Scandal* (1925) and Pinero's *Trelawney of the Wells* (1927), the latter featuring John Drew as Sir William Grover in his last performance. Tyler produced Booth Tarkington's *Clarence* (1919) and George S. Kaufman and Marc Connelly's first successful farce, *Dulcy* (1921). Although these comedies seem old-fashioned by current standards, they were considered among the finest light comedies of their day, a cut above the usual Broadway fare. Tyler also presented Eugene O'Neill's *Chris Christopherson* (1919), an early version of *Anna Christie,* and *The Straw* (1921), although neither play proved successful. Arthur Hopkins (1878–1950) was perhaps the most influential independent producer–director of the 1920s. Early in his career, he scored notable successes with Tolstoy's *Redemption* (*The Living Corpse* 1918), starring John Barrymore, and Edward Sheldon's *The Jest* (1919, an adaptation of Italian playwright Sam Benelli's florid, historical melodrama *La cena delle beffe),* starring both John and Lionel Barrymore. Subsequently, Hopkins starred John Barrymore in outstanding revivals of *Richard III* (1920) and *Hamlet* (1922) and Lionel in a revival of *Macbeth* (1921). In 1918, Hopkins starred the Russian émigré actress Alla Nazimova (1879–1945) in revivals (in English) of Ibsen's *The Wild Duck, Hedda Gabler,* and *A Doll's House.* Among the many new modern plays which Hopkins produced were O'Neill's *Anna Christie* (1921) and *The Hairy Ape* (1922) and Philip Barry's (1869–1949) *Paris Bound* (1927) and *Holiday* (1928).

As noted in chapter 5, several essentially nineteenth-century-style actor–managers remained active well into the 1920s, preserving the classical tradition. Robert Mantell and the team of Julia Marlowe and E. H. Sothern, for example, continued to offer high quality productions of Shakespeare, while Minnie Maddern Fiske, in association with her husband Harrison Grey Fiske (1861–1942), promoted the production of serious realist drama, especially the plays of Ibsen. Walter Hampden (1879–1955) and Eva LeGallienne (1899–1991) aimed to follow in the footsteps of this older generation of classical actor– managers. Hampden was born in New York, but received his early theatrical experience in England where, as a member of Frank R. Benson's (1858–1939) repertory company, he played dozens of roles in London and the provinces in the early years of the century. In 1907, he returned to America, playing second leads to Alla Nazimova and Viola Allen. In 1908, he shot to prominence playing the Christlike butler, Manson, in Charles Rann Kennedy's (1871–1950) allegorical drama *The Servant in the House* (1908) which had a long run on Broadway and then a successful tour. Hampden subsequently appeared in other contemporary plays, including Clyde Fitch's *The City* (1909), but Hampden's physical assets, training, and temperament were better suited to a classical repertoire. And, in fact, he was more interested in Shakespeare and poetic plays, than in modern drama. In 1916, he played Caliban in a Shakespeare tercentenary production of *The Tempest* at the New (Century) Theatre, receiving good notices for the power of his performance. Two years later, with assistance from several wealthy patrons, he formed his own company and starred as Hamlet, Macbeth, and as Marc Antony. After a New York run, Hampden toured this repertoire for several months. The tour was so successful that Hampden continued to alternate limited New York runs with touring for the next four years, offering a range of Shakespeare's tragedies and comedies. Generally critics compared Hampden's Hamlet favorably with the performances of E. H. Sothern and Johnston Forbes–Robertson. There was widespread agreement that Romeo was his finest interpretation, with Macbeth and Othello displaying his vocal strength and flexibility, but flawed in their overall design and execution. But his range as a Shakespearean actor and his talents as a producer–director were universally admired.

In 1923, Hampden's company took up residence in New York, first at the National Theatre, then at the Colonial Theatre which he renamed Hampden's Theatre. For the next seven years, Hampden continued to stage new romantic historical plays, often reflecting his personal interest in theosophy, and revivals of Shakespeare and modern classics. Among his more notable productions were *Cyrano de Bergerac* (1923), revivals of *Othello*, *Hamlet* , and *The Merchant of Venice* in 1925, *Caponsacchi* (1926), adapted from Robert Browning's "The Ring and the Book," Ibsen's *An Enemy of the People* (1927), *Henry V* (1928), and Bulwer–Lytton's *Richelieu* (1929). In the tradition of nineteenth-century actor–managers, Hampden's productions were usually carefully and lavishly staged. *The Light of Asia* (1928), for example, about Prince Siddhartha's transformation into Buddha, had spectacular scenery and costumes and exotic choreography by modern dance pioneer Ruth St. Denis (1877–1968). Although he wanted to establish a reputation as a Shakespearean actor, Hampden's Cyrano was always his most popular and esteemed role. Many critics thought it better than the interpretations by Richard Mansfield or Constant Coquelin. He reportedly played it over one thousand times, twice as many performances as Coquelin. The Depression forced him to disband his company in 1930. Hampden continued to perform in various productions in the 1930s and 1940s, earning a reputation as a thoughtful and consistent performer, widely respected in the profession. His last role on Broadway was as Danforth in Arthur Miller's *The Crucible* (1953).

In 1926, actress Eva Le Gallienne tried to combine a European art theater ideal with an American popular-priced stock-company model. Born in London and educated there and in Paris, Le Gallienne came to America in 1915. After several years playing minor roles, she had a notable success as Julie in Ferenc Molnár's *Liliom*, which played for a year on Broadway and then toured for another season. (Later Oscar Hammerstein II and Richard Rodgers adapted *Liliom* for their famous musical *Carousel,* 1945.) In the mid-1920s, Le Gallienne also achieved success in Molnár's *The Swan*, Schnitzler's *The Call of Life,* and Ibsen's *The Master Builder* and *John*

*Gabriel Borkman.* She was initially inspired by Sarah Bernhardt whom she saw numerous times as a teenager growing up in Paris. But after witnessing Eleonora Duse in London in the early 1920s, and then on several occasions during Duse's last American tour, Le Gallienne worked to develop a style of playing that was, like Duse's, psychologically real, emotionally restrained, and seemingly absent "technique." It served her well in the modern roles that best suited her and which she preferred. She disdained the Broadway commercial theater, however. In 1926, she founded the Civic Repertory Theatre, located in an old theater on Fourteenth Street, forty blocks south of the Broadway theater district. It was a turning point in her career. For almost a decade, Le Gallienne produced, directed, and starred in a series of notable productions of classics and new American and foreign plays. Plays were presented in repertory fashion and at popular prices. Generous patrons sustained the Civic through financial shortfalls, but generally Le Gallienne demonstrated that a classic repertory theater could be relatively successful. Over seven seasons, the Civic mounted over thirty productions, including notable productions of Chekhov's *Three Sisters* and *The Cherry Orchard,* Ibsen's *Hedda Gabler,* and *Peter Pan.*

The Great Depression and a serious injury to her arm and hand conspired to force Le Gallienne to close the Civic Repertory Theatre in 1933. She

*Eva LeGallienne as the Duc de Reichstadt in Edmond Rostand's* l'Aiglon *(The eaglet) a role originally created for Sarah Bernhardt. Courtesy of The Hampden–Booth Library at The Players.*

remained a forceful presence in the American theater, however, as an actress, producer, and director for another fifty years. She continued to promote modern drama, especially the plays of Ibsen and Chekhov, several of which she translated for her own productions, and to espouse the repertory ideal. Her American Repertory Theatre, founded in 1946, failed after a single season; but the National Repertory Theatre, which she founded in 1959, successfully toured until 1965. In 1976 she played Fanny Cavendish in a highly successful revival of *The Royal Family*, one of her last stage roles. In addition to her stage work, beginning in the late 1950s, she appeared in several distinguished television productions. For her role in the film *Resurrection* (1980), she was nominated for an Academy Award. In the last decade of her career, she was celebrated for her lifelong commitment to the highest standards of theater art, receiving the National Medal of Arts in 1986.

Two New York little theaters would also impact Broadway's commercial establishments. The Provincetown Players began informally in the summer of 1915 when a score of fledgling performers and playwrights, including Eugene O'Neill, staged a series of one-act plays in a makeshift theater on an old wharf in Provincetown, Massachusetts. They repeated the experiment the following summer; and then flush with enthusiasm, they relocated to a small theater in Greenwich Village, New York's bohemian neighborhood, becoming one of the first of what would later be called Off-Broadway theaters. Under the leadership of director and playwright, George Cram Cook (1873–1924) the Provincetown Players continued to mount plays that aspired to high dramatic standards. Over the course of its first six seasons, the Provincetown Players mounted over ninety new plays, mostly one-acts, by emerging talents, including all of O'Neill's early plays, and plays by Susan Glaspell (1876–1948), poet Edna St. Vincent Millay (1892–1950), and novelist Edna Ferber (1885–1968). For these writers, the Provincetown Players offered a first opportunity to see and hear their plays performed, and as such the company contributed significantly to nurturing their talent and honing their skills. It also gave a start to the careers of a number of actors, directors, and designers. Although after a few seasons, some of its members were paid, the Provincetown Players remained largely amateur and resolutely experimental. But it established a growing reputation for inventive stagings of compelling dramas. Internal squabbles and the premature death of Cook complicated the original organizational structure of the group. With O'Neill, designer Robert Edmund Jones (1887–1954), and theater critic Kenneth McGowan (1888–1963) in leadership, the Provincetown Players became more professionally oriented in the mid-1920s. They remained committed to quality drama, however, presenting a number of notable productions throughout the 1920s, including O'Neill's *All God's Chillun Got Wings* (1923), and *Desire under the Elms* (1924), and Paul Green's Pulitzer Prize-winning drama *In Abraham's Bosom* (1926), a moving folk tragedy about a black idealist's struggles to improve the lot of his rural community. The Provincetown Players regularly transferred their more successful productions to Broadway for relatively long commercial runs. Despite their successes, the organization was in constant financial straits; shortly after the stock market crash of 1929, the company dissolved.

The Washington Square Players was founded in 1914 to present realist and symbolist plays, preferably by American authors. During four seasons, they presented over sixty productions, predominantly one-act plays, most by American writers, but including plays by Chekhov, Maeterlinck, Shaw, and Oscar Wilde. They remained an amateur, volunteer organization—although some actors and business and technical personnel did receive token salaries. The Washington Square Players steadily built a critical and popular following, but when key members were conscripted for service in World War I, the organization was disbanded in 1918. A year later, members of the Washington Square Players reorganized as the Theatre Guild.

Like its parent organization, the Theatre Guild was mainly interested in modernist plays by American and foreign dramatists. The Guild intended to be self-supporting; it never sought subsidies. But it did emphasize artistic merit over commercial concerns. To capitalize their enterprise and to organize interested playgoers, the Guild offered tickets by subscription to a series of their productions. Subscription tickets were significantly discounted from the per-production, single-ticket box-office price even though Guild prices were cheaper than tickets to commercial productions. Subscribers became Guild "members." While subscriptions were common for concert and operatic series, it was unusual for theater companies, although Augustin Daly had offered subscriptions to his seasons as early as 1888. Theatergoers were slow to embrace the system, but by 1925, the Guild had twenty-five thousand member subscribers. Eventually the subscription list swelled to seventy-five thousand members. Their success inspired other resident companies and little theaters to offer subscriptions. The Guild mounted the American premieres of numerous foreign plays, including works by Shaw, Molnár, Leonid Andreyev, Luigi Pirandello, and new American plays by Elmer Rice (1892–1967), S. N. Behrman (1893–1973), Maxwell Anderson (1888–1959), O'Neill, and many others. Under the leadership of Lawrence Langner (1890–1962) and Theresa Helburn (1887–1959), the Guild founded an acting school, maintained an acting company, and, beginning in 1926, initiated a variation on the repertory system, rotating two plays on a weekly, rather than nightly basis. In the late 1920s, the Guild began to tour with a repertoire of four plays, which in the larger cities were also offered by subscription. Although the Guild featured the play and its company rather than particular actors, it nurtured an entire generation of stars. Combining high theatrical standards with often innovative business savvy, the Guild successfully—and uniquely— synthesized the conflicting demands of art and commercialism and became the American theater's leading standard bearer until World War II.

SINCE THE GILDED Age, American acting had moved steadily toward an increasingly more natural style. Several interlocking factors account for the trend, including, perhaps foremost, a contemporary realistic drama, both native and foreign, that focused on ordinary people and, in particular, their inner, psychological lives. Indeed, realism of this sort was increasingly perva-sive in American literature and art. The development of modern psychology with its interest in the complexities of consciousness was a significant influ-ence. Acting schools, acting teachers, and a number of forceful actors also made contributions.

Minnie Maddern Fiske was an early champion of realistic drama and an exemplar of the more subdued, subtler acting style appropriate to its repre-sentation. In 1894, for a single benefit performance, she acted Nora in *A Doll's House*. (She was not the first to play the role in America. Helena Modjeska presented her adaptation as early as 1882, and, as noted earlier in chapter 5, Beatrice Cameron, wife of Richard Mansfield, acted the role in 1890.) Mrs. Fiske then regularly included it in her repertoire and subse-quently added *Hedda Gabler* (1903), *Rosmersholm* (1907), *The Pillars of Society* (1910) and *Ghosts* (1927), the last daringly staged in contemporary 1920s dress. Mrs. Fiske also enjoyed notable successes as Tess in an adapta-tion of Thomas Hardy's *Tess of the D'Urbervilles* (1897), as the eponymous *Becky Sharp* (1899), adapted from William Thackeray's *Vanity Fair*, and in several new American plays, including Langdon Mitchell's *The New York Idea* (1906), two realistic plays by Edward Sheldon, *Salvation Nell* (1908) and *The High Road* (1912), and Harry James Smith's (1880–1918) *Mrs. Bumpstead–Leigh* (1911), a comedy of contemporary manners.

In whatever play she performed, whether somber realistic drama or social comedy, Mrs. Fiske was invariably praised for her naturalness, realis-tically detailed, telling gestures, and seemingly complete identification with the character. Like that of Duse, her technique was suggestive, emotionally contained, and wholly untheatrical. As the manager of her own company, the Manhattan Theatre company, from 1904 to 1914, Mrs. Fiske inspired and trained numerous young actors, urging them toward an honest projection of emotion and demanding clarity in execution. On Broadway and on tour, she won thousands of converts to her artistry, and was widely regarded by the late 1920s as one of the finest actors of her generation.

Unlike Mrs. Fiske, William H. Gillette advanced a reputation for realistic acting not in modern social dramas, but principally in his own well-crafted melodramas. After a decade playing various comic and romantic roles, Gillette found his true *métier* as the cool-headed man of action, first as the Union spy Captain Thorne in his own Civil War melodrama, *The Secret Service* (1895), and then even more successfully as the famous sleuth *Sherlock Holmes* (1899) in his own dramatization of Arthur Conan Doyle's stories. Tall, slim, with chis-eled features and a manner that projected a detached, collected personality, Gillette was ideal for such roles. He cultivated a complementary style of acting principally characterized by sincerity, skillful underplaying, and a repressed emotional intensity. He also had a crisp, staccato way of delivering dialogue that seemed entirely natural and appropriate to the characters he played. But often it was not what he said, but what he did that was most telling. Critics commented on his economical but evocative gestures—for example, a twitch-ing finger, a compression of the lips, a tightening of the face muscles. Gillette applied his approach to a range of roles in farces, light comedies, and melodramas. His notable successes included starring roles in James M. Barrie's romantic fantasies, *The Admirable Crichton* (1903) and *Dear Brutus* (1918), for which he garnered critical praise for his naturalness and credibility. Sherlock Holmes was his mainstay; he played it over thirteen hundred times. In 1928, when he came out of an eight-year retirement to play Holmes one more time, he was still able to move audiences with his compellingly realistic approach.

The visits of two foreign companies also had an effect on the rise of realistic acting. Dublin's Abbey Theatre company, touring America in 1911 and 1915, impressed many with their natural, unaffected style. The Moscow Art Theatre (MAT) company, which toured on several occasions between 1923 and 1925, had an even more widespread and lasting influence. Although they played in Russian, which probably only a few playgoers and critics understood, they were heralded for their realistic, ensemble acting. During the course of the MAT's American visits, the company's leader Constantin Stanislavski published an English-language version of his autobiography *My Life in Art* (1924). Later scholarship has demonstated that this English-language version is in significant instances misleadingly, ambiguously translated, but at the time it was read as an authoritative introduction or "preface" to Stanislavski's renowned system of actor training. The 1936 American, English-language publication of Stanislavski's *An Actor Prepares* was even more influential, although it was filled with inaccurate translations as well and contained but a fragment of the Russian version published two years later.

The Stanislavski system would also be promoted in America by several of Stanislavski's disciples. In 1923, for example, the MAT was greeted in New York by Richard Boleslavski (1887–1937), a former MAT company member who had fled Moscow in the wake of the Revolution and had eventually arrived in America in 1922. Shortly after the MAT opened its New York engagement, Boleslavski presented a series of lectures outlining Stanislavski's system. Six months later, with the assistance of Maria Ouspenskaya (1881–1949), a MAT member who had decided to remain in America, Boleslavski set up the American Laboratory Theatre (ALT). Until it was disbanded in 1933 at the height of the Depression, the ALT was the principal school teaching the Stanislavski system in America.

In 1931, three theater artists—Lee Strasberg (1901–82), one of Boleslavski's students, Harold Clurman (1901–80), who would subsequently become an important director and critic, and Cheryl Crawford (1902–86), who had been working as a production assistant with the Theatre Guild—founded the Group Theatre. Dedicated to developing a systemized approach to actor training based on the Stanislavski model—what Strasberg would later refer to as "the Method"—and to the production of new realistic plays, the Group Theatre became an important theater organization until it disbanded in 1941. It mounted a number of notable productions, most significantly seven plays by Clifford Odets (1906–63). Dozens of actors were associated with the Group including Stella Adler (1903–92), also a Boleslavski student, and her brother Luther (1903–84), Morris Carnovsky (1897–1992), and Lee J. Cobb (1911–76). As inspiring acting teachers, several members of the Group would continue to have a profound effect on the course of actor training in America to the present day.

Stella Adler, for example, actually studied with Stanislavski in Paris in 1934. At her own studio, the Stella Adler Conservatory founded in 1949, and at the Yale School of Drama, she dedicated herself for over forty years to training aspiring actors emphasizing Stanislavski's techniques of "given circumstances" and the "magic if." Beginning in 1935, Sanford Meisner (1905–97) taught acting at the Neighborhood Playhouse School of Theatre for over fifty years, becoming one of the most respected acting teachers in America. In 1947, Group Theatre members Cheryl Crawford, director Elia Kazan (b. 1909) and actor–director Robert Lewis (b. 1909) founded the Actors Studio. In 1950, Lee Strasberg joined the Studio and from 1951 until his death served as its forceful artistic director. The Studio was intended as a workshop for professional actors where they could continue to develop their skills and explore their craft free from the pressures and criticism of the commercial theater. Under Strasberg, the Studio tended to concentrate on exploring the actor's own emotional resources—Stanislavski's "emotional memory" techniques—to the exclusion of other elements of the Stanislavksi system and physical and vocal training. In the 1950s, the Actor's Studio became a signal force in shaping a distinctive style of American acting. Critics of the Studio, however, believed that the Method with its emphasis on subjective emotional responses, on temperament rather than analytical character development, produced a style of acting that was self-indulgent and limiting. Method-trained actors, for example, are often thought effective only in contemporary, naturalistic plays and films and are unable to act in classic drama. But the Method did result in acting that was remarkably natural and emotionally compelling. Among the graduates of the Studio are many of the finest actors in the American theater and film, including Marlon Brando (b. 1924), Geraldine Page (1924–87), Shelley Winters (b. 1922), Dustin Hoffman (b. 1937), Al Pacino (b. 1940), and Robert De Niro (b. 1943).

THE BARRYMORES—LIONEL (1878–1954), Ethel (1879–1959), and John (1882–1942)—were among the brightest stars of the new twentieth-century stage. Children of actors Maurice Barrymore and Georgiana Drew, their first theatrical experiences were at Philadelphia's Arch Street Theatre managed by their celebrated grandmother Mrs. John Drew. Their uncle John Drew Jr. was also an early model and mentor. Uniquely gifted, physically attractive, with charismatic personalities and solid stage experience and technique, they each had become by the early 1920s not only significant actors but also well-known social celebrities.

Lionel Barrymore, the elder sibling, made his debut in 1893 in his grandmother's road tour of *The Rivals*. There followed a range of experiences in stock, touring, and in the emerging film industry, where he appeared in dozens of one-reel silent "flickers," as they were called. In 1918, Lionel played the simple Illinois farmer Milton Shanks in Augustus Thomas's Civil

*John Barrymore as Hamlet. Courtesy of the Lawrence and Lee Theatre Research Institute, Ohio State University.*

War drama *The Copperhead.* Lionel's remarkable physical transformation as he aged forty years between acts 1 and 2 was judged an acting triumph. He successfully costarred with his brother John in *The Jest* (1919). Then in 1921, he acted Macbeth in a production directed by Arthur Hopkins and designed by Robert Edmond Jones. Lionel's unconventional, psychological interpretation was imaginative but unappreciated by the critics. Jones's abstract, modernist scenery and lighting may also have negatively affected Lionel's reception. But later in the season, he won critical acclaim in a French social drama called *The Claw* (1921). In 1923, he triumphed again as Tito Beppi, a Pagliacci-like figure in a melodrama adapted from the Italian called *Laugh, Clown, Laugh* (1923). Lionel continued to act on Broadway for two more seasons in a series of turgid melodramas. His notices were often mixed and the plays were flops. Frustrated with Broadway and the direction of his career, he left for Hollywood. Between 1925 and 1953, he appeared in almost two hundred movies, among which were roles in such classics as *You Can't Take It with You* (1938), *It's a Wonderful Life* (1946), *Duel in the Sun* (1947), and *Key Largo* (1948). He never returned to the stage.

John Barrymore played supporting roles in a number of contemporary dramas and comedies in the early 1900s. In 1904–5, for example, he had a small role in a comic adventure drama called *The Dictator.* He rose to stardom in *The Fortune Hunter* (1909), an above-average romantic comedy about a young man's pursuit of a country heiress. There followed other roles principally in comedies, most of them forgettable. Blessed with elegant good looks—a striking profile, in particular—and a warm, musical voice, John seemed destined to a career as a light comedian. But in 1916 with his performance as the check-forging clerk William Falder in John Galsworthy's social drama *Justice,* he gained a reputation as a serious actor. There followed notable successes in Edward Sheldon's adaptation of English writer George du Maurier's popular novel *Peter Ibbetson* (1917; Lionel costarred as Colonel Ibbetson), in Leo Tolstoy's *Redemption,* and as noted, *The Jest.* In all three plays, John was commended for his depth of feeling and the subtle ways in which he nuanced his characterizations. His standing in the profession was elevated with a forceful performance as Richard III (1920) and then even more so two years later as Hamlet.

For many playgoers, Barrymore's Hamlet—quietly cerebral, reserved, utterly simple and natural—was the finest Hamlet since Edwin Booth's; and as if to underscore this estimation *Hamlet* was repeated for 101 consecutive performances, breaking Booth's record of one hundred nights. A cross-country tour in 1923–24 was followed by a London engagement in 1925. London's critics were judicious, but generally appreciative. English actors John Gielgud, twenty at the time, and Laurence Olivier, then aged seventeen, both later to be celebrated for their own Hamlets, witnessed Barrymore's Hamlet and were sufficiently impressed to remember it long after the fact. Then at the peak of his career, Barrymore abandoned the stage for Hollywood. He appeared in over forty films, giving distinguished performances in many of them, including *Grand Hotel* (1923), *Reunion in Vienna* (1933), and *Twentieth Century* (1934), but chronic alcoholism, and a cavalier attitude toward his career, ate away at his talent. He returned to the stage only once, in 1939–40, in a comedy vehicle called *My Dear Children.* His unique stage magnetism still shone through, but, on balance, he seemed a

*Ethel Barrymore c. 1950 as Kate in a revival of James M. Barrie's* The Twelve Pound Look, *one of her signature roles. Courtesy the Flora Ward Hineline Papers, The Ward M. Canaday Center for Special Collections, University of Toledo Libraries.*

mere parody of the actor he once was. Had he continued after his performance as Hamlet to pursue ever more challenging roles, he might have become a great actor, the legitimate heir of Edwin Booth.

At the age of fourteen, Ethel Barrymore was touring as Julia in her grandmother's production of *The Rivals*. At eighteen, she was playing in London with Henry Irving and Ellen Terry. In 1901, her career skyrocketed as Madame Trentoni in Charles Frohman's production of Clyde Fitch's society comedy *Captain Jinks of the Horse Marines*. Tall, willowy, with huge blue eyes, wavy ash-blond hair, and a distinctive throaty voice, Ethel captivated as much with her beauty as with her talent and effortless acting style. Frohman capitalized on his new star's looks and personality, casting her in a series of light sentimental comedies including James Barrie's *Alice-Sit-by-the-Fire* (1905) and *The Twelve Pound Look* (1911), in which Ethel rivaled Maude Adams.

As she matured, Ethel opted for more serious roles in Edna Ferber's *Our Mrs. McChesney* (1915), Zoë Akins's *Déclassée* (1919), Gerhart Hauptmann's *Rose Bernd* (1922), Pinero's *The Second Mrs. Tanqueray* (1925), and Somerset Maugham's *The Constant Wife* (1926). In 1925, she also played Ophelia and Portia to Walter Hampden's Hamlet and Shylock. Her Portia in particular received admiring notices. Throughout the 1930s, Ethel added to her reputation on Broadway and on tour, including notable successes in an adaptation of Canadian novelist Mazo de La Roche's popular family epic *The Whiteoaks of Jalna* (1938), in which she played a 102-year-old matriarch, and in Welsh actor and writer Emlyn Williams's autobiographical *The Corn Is*

*Alfred Lunt and Lynn Fontanne as Trigorin and Arkadina in Chekhov's* The Seagull. *Courtesy of Lawrence and Lee Theatre Research Institute, Ohio State University.*

*Lynn Fontanne as Madame Arkadina in Anton Chekhov's* The Seagull. *Courtesy of the Hampden–Booth Library at the Players.*

*Green* (1940). As the dedicated teacher Mrs. Moffat in the latter, she was universally praised for her forceful, sensitive performance. Unlike Lionel and John, she did not desert the stage for the movies, although she starred with them in the film *Rasputin and the Empress* in 1923. In the mid-1940s, however, Ethel, now in her sixties, succumbed to Hollywood, appearing with distinction in over twenty-five films, including *None But the Lonely Heart* (1944) with Cary Grant, for which she won an Oscar as best supporting actress.

After the Barrymores, the husband–wife team of Alfred Lunt (1892–1977) and Lynn Fontanne (1887–1983) were among the more celebrated and successful stage stars of the 1920s and 1930s. Lunt's theatrical apprenticeship was served in Boston's Castle Square Theatre stock company where, between 1912 and 1915, he played a range of roles in dozens of melodramas and farces and an occasional classic. Leaving Boston, he played in support of several touring stars, including Margaret Anglin, Laura Hope Crews (1879–1942), a well-known actress of her day, and the aging British star Lillie Langtry in her last American visits. In 1919, he joined producer George C. Tyler's Washington, D.C., National Theatre company whose members included a young English actress, Lynn Fontanne.

As a teenager, Fontanne had the good fortune to be given acting lessons by Ellen Terry, who also arranged her professional debut in a pantomime. There followed minor roles in various touring productions and finally a series of London engagements. A turning point in her nascent career came in 1915 when the young American star Laurette Taylor (1884–1946) recruited Fontanne for her American company. In the United States, Fontanne played in Taylor's support in several plays, then she was cast in a leading role in

George S. Kaufman's first play, *Someone in the House* (1918), produced by George C. Tyler. Fontanne received rave reviews, but the great influenza epidemic, which caused playgoers to stay at home and theaters to close prematurely, ended the run. Tyler persuaded his new star to join his Washington, D.C., company until he could develop her next vehicle.

George C. Tyler, perhaps intuiting their compatibility, regularly featured Lunt and Fontanne in the same plays. In turn, they discovered an immediate physical attraction offstage and a remarkable performance chemistry onstage, but it would be several more years before they became "The Lunts." They rose to major stardom in separate vehicles—Lunt in Booth Tarkington's *Clarence* (1919) and Fontanne in George S. Kaufman and Marc Connelly's farce *Dulcy* (1921). In 1922 they married, but continued to pursue independent careers. They were brought together by the Theatre Guild's 1924 production of Ferenc Molnár's high comedy, *The Guardsman*. As the Actor/Guardsman and the Actress, Lunt and Fontanne were a resounding success.

For the next thirty-five years, the Lunts acted almost exclusively together. They were particularly admired for their delicate approach to sophisticated comedy, their meticulous attention to the details of characterization—from costumes to stage business—and, when the play called for it, their witty sexual byplay. In their years of playing together, they developed a unique technique of overlapping their dialogue which heightened the naturalism and sometimes the comic effect of their acting. Urbane comedy was their special strength. Among plays written for them were S. N. Behrman's *The Second Man* (1927) and *Amphitryon 38* (1937; adapted from Jean Giraudoux's play), Robert Sherwood's *Reunion in Vienna* (1931) and *Idiot's Delight* (1936), Noël Coward's *Design for Living* (1933), and Howard Lindsay and Russel Crouse's *The Great Sebastians* (1956). The Lunts were also acclaimed for their performances in *The Taming of the Shrew* (1935)—a performance that years later inspired the Cole Porter musical *Kiss Me, Kate* (1948)—and as Madame Arkadina and Trigorin in *The Seagull* (1938). They made their last stage appearance in Friedrich Duerrenmatt's ironic modern drama *The Visit* (1958), staged by the noted British director Peter Brook, which proved to be one of their greatest successes.

In the mid-1930s, as coproducers with the Theatre Guild, the Lunts exercised complete artistic control over productions in which they appeared. After a Broadway run, they would invariably tour the country playing small towns and large cities, in regular theaters and high-school auditoriums. They also regularly brought their productions to London, even in the middle of World War II. They had many offers, but unlike the Barrymores after filming *The Guardsman* in 1931, they refused to make movies. Television enticed them in the 1960s, and they appeared in several video-plays, notably in *The Magnificent Yankee* (1965), about jurist Oliver Wendell Holmes and his wife Fanny; but the Lunts remained quintessential stars of the stage.

Apart from Walter Hampden and Alfred Lunt, few actors achieved lasting distinction on the American stage between the wars. In addition to Eva

Le Gallienne, Ethel Barrymore, and Lynn Fontanne, however, a number of actresses stood out—two in particular.

Katharine Cornell (1893–1974) served her theatrical apprenticeship with the Washington Square Players. In 1911, Jesse Bonstelle (1871?–1932), a leading stock actress and manager of theaters in Buffalo and Detroit—she later founded the Detroit Civic Theatre (1928)—produced a stage version of Louisa May Alcott's popular novel *Little Women* which successfully toured for several years. In 1919, for the London production of *Little Women*, Bonstelle cast Cornell in the pivotal role of Jo March. Cornell's Jo received glowing reviews from London's pundits. Returning to New York, she received good notices for roles in a number of contemporary sentimental dramas, including Clemence Dane's *A Bill of Divorcement* (1921), her first leading role, Arthur Wing Pinero's *The Enchanted Cottage* (1923) and Sidney Howard's *Casanova* (1923), but the title role in Bernard Shaw's *Candida* (1924) established her as a star of the first magnitude. Statuesque and athletically slender, with a dark, exotic beauty, and velvety, but resonant voice, Cornell was especially adept at playing vulnerable, sensitive heroines, such as Leslie Crosbie in Somerset Maugham's *The Letter* (1927), Countess Olenska in an adaptation of Edith Wharton's *The Age of Innocence* (1928), or the poetess Elizabeth Barrett in *The Barretts of Wimpole Street* (1931).

*Left, Katharine Cornell as St. Joan (1936–37). Courtesy the Hampden–Booth Library at The Players.*

*Right, Helen Hayes in* Victoria Regina. *From Appelbaum,* Great Actors and Actresses of the American Stage in Historic Photographs. *Courtesy Dover Publications, Inc.*

*Helen Hayes in* Victoria Regina. *Courtesy the Flora Ward Hineline Papers, the Ward M. Canaday Center for Special Collections, University of Toledo Libraries.*

In 1921, Cornell married Guthrie McClintic (1893–1961), a young actor turned director, whom she had met in Detroit. In the early 1930s, they organized their own production company with Cornell as star and McClintic as director. Like the Lunts, Cornell and McClintic would be highly successful partners for almost thirty-five years. Season after season, they mounted a series of distinguished productions of contemporary plays and classics—twenty-nine, in all—including *Romeo and Juliet* (1933–34), Shaw's *Saint Joan* (1936) and *The Doctor's Dilemma* (1941), Maxwell Anderson's *The Wingless Victory* (1936–37), *The Three Sisters* (1942), *Antony and Cleopatra* (1947), and Christopher Fry's *The Dark Is Light Enough* (1955). Cornell–McClintic usually toured their productions after a New York run. (The Lunts and Cornell–McClintic were good friends and to avoid duplicating or overlapping each other, they shared their plans and touring schedules.) Their first tour covered over seventeen thousand miles in which they gave 225 performances in over seventy towns and cities. Cornell's last tour—Jerome Kilty's *Dear Liar* (1959), a play based on the letters of turn-of-the-century British star Mrs. Patrick Campbell (Cornell) and Bernard Shaw (played by British actor Brian Aherne)—went to sixty-seven towns and cities over twenty-seven weeks. By the onset of World War II, she was widely held to be the most distinguished actress in the American theater—the leading lady of her time. Like the Lunts, Cornell also refused movie offers, but late in her career, she did appear on television, notably in a production of *The Barretts of Wimpole Street* in 1955. When McClintic died, Cornell retired from the stage.

Helen Hayes (1900–1993) was on stage from the age of five, appearing in musicals as a child actress. As a petite and perky teenager she progressed to ingénue roles, playing the sweetheart, the "girl next door," or the carefree 1920s flapper in light romantic comedies like Booth Tarkington's *Clarence*

(1919). In the mid-1920s, Hayes succeeded in redirecting her career toward a more varied repertoire with roles such as Constance Neville in *She Stoops to Conquer* (1924), Cleopatra in the Theatre Guild's staging of Shaw's *Caesar and Cleopatra* (1925), Maggie Shane in a revival of Barrie's *What Every Woman Knows* (1926), and Norma Besant in George Abbott and Ann Preston Bridgers's tragic social drama *Coquette* (1927), in which Hayes's emotional range ran from the coquettish to the suicidal. *Coquette* ran for almost a year on Broadway and then toured for two seasons. But it was Hayes's tour de force performances as *Mary of Scotland* (1933) and *Victoria Regina* (1935), in which she portrayed Queen Victoria from a young newly-wed to an aged empress, that brought her special distinction.

For the next forty years, Helen Hayes proved to be a remarkably flexible leading actress, appearing in plays as wide ranging as the historical drama *Harriet* (1943), about Harriet Beecher Stowe, to the comedy *Mrs. McThing* (1952), in which she played a society lady turned charwoman, to Eugene O'Neill's tragic *A Touch of the Poet* (1958) in which she played Con Melody's long-suffering wife Nora. In the 1960s, under the aegis of the Department of State, she starred in several international tours, playing a repertoire of American plays such as *The Skin of Our Teeth* and *The Glass Menagerie*. As she aged, she made a graceful transition from "leading lady" to character roles, playing the mother in a revival of George Kelly's *The Show-Off* (1967) and the tragic, drug-addicted Mary Tyrone in O'Neill's *Long Day's Journey into Night* (1971), her last stage role.

Unlike other stage stars of her era, Hayes moved easily between Broadway and Hollywood. As a child, she had appeared in several silent films and was always attracted to movies. In 1932 she won her first Academy Award for *The Sin of Madelon Claudet* written by her husband, playwright Charles MacArthur (1895–1956). Almost forty years later, in 1970, she won a second Oscar for playing a sweet, little old lady stowaway in *Airport*. In between there were distinguished performances in *A Farewell to Arms* (1932), *My Son, John* (1951), and *Anastasia* (1956). In the 1940s, she had her own radio program, "The Helen Hayes Theatre," and in the 1950s she also made numerous television appearances. Her many awards and honors include the first George S. Kaufman Award for Lifetime Achievement in the Theatre (1987) and the National Medal of Arts (1988).

Ethel Barrymore, Lynn Fontanne, Katharine Cornell, and Helen Hayes were preeminent as "First Ladies of the American Theatre," but there were other leading actresses of the pre-World War II period who merit acknowledgment. Judith Anderson (1898–1992), Australian by birth, came to America in 1918. After several seasons in stock, she rose to stardom as the sinister seductress Elsie Van Zile in the melodrama *Cobra* (1924). There followed more significant roles, replacing Fontanne as Nina Leeds in O'Neill's *Strange Interlude* (1929), playing Lavinia in *Mourning Becomes Electra* (1932), and Delia in Zoë Akins's Pulitzer Prize-winning *The Old Maid* (1935). In the late 1930s, she established a reputation as a classical actress, playing Gertrude to John Gielgud's *Hamlet* (1936), Lady Macbeth, first

*Left, Ina Claire in* Grounds for Divorce *(1924) by Guy Bolton. From Appelbaum,* Great Actors and Actresses of the American Stage in Historic Photographs. *Courtesy Dover Publications, Inc.*

*Right, Judith Anderson as Delia in Zoë Akins's* The Old Maid. *Courtesy of the Flora Ward Hineline Papers, the Ward M. Canaday Center for Special Collections, University of Toledo Libraries.*

opposite Laurence Olivier in London (1937), then opposite Maurice Evans (1941) in the United States, and Olga in Katharine Cornell's celebrated revival of Chekhov's *The Three Sisters* (1942). One of her greatest roles was as Medea (1947) in Robinson Jeffers's adaptation of Euripides' tragedy. She also appeared in numerous films, usually as characters that are malevolent or manipulative—e.g., Mrs. Danvers in *Rebecca* (1940) or Big Mama in the film version of Tennessee Williams's *Cat on a Hot Tin Roof* (1958).

Ina Claire (1892?–1985) began her career in vaudeville, and in musical comedies and revues where her skills as a mimic and singer brought her early prominence. In the 1920s and 1930s, she became one of Broadway's most popular stars, usually playing a witty cosmopolitan in a string of sophisticat- ed light comedies. Elegantly attractive and graceful with impeccable timing, Claire's gifts as a comedienne were unsurpassed. She was especially success- ful in roles in three S. N. Behrman comedies: as Marion Froude in *Biography* (1932), Leonie Frothingham in *End of Summer* (1936), and Enid Fuller in *The Talley Method* (1941). Her talent also graced a number of movie come- dies in the 1930s and 1940s including the film version of George S. Kaufman and Edna Ferber's play about a family of eminent actors *The Royal Family* (1930) in which she portrayed Fanny Cavendish, delightfully mimicking

Ethel Barrymore on whom the character was based. Her last stage performance was in T. S. Eliot's comedy of ideas *The Confidential Clerk* (1954). In
another era, Claire might have played a range of roles in classic English
comedies from Shakespeare to Shaw, but she confined herself to contemporary plays. By the end of her career, audience taste for such vehicles and
Claire's brand of comedy had waned.

REALISM WAS THE prevailing style in scenery in the first decades of the new
century. By the late teens, realism was increasingly challenged, however, by
more modernist European scenic practices. Inspired principally by the visionary designs and theoretical writings of English designer Edward Gordon
Craig (1872–1966) and Swiss designer Adolphe Appia (1862–1928) and by
the inventive, eclectic directorial approach of Austrian *régisseur* Max
Reinhardt, the "new stagecraft," as it was called, rejected Belasco-style pho-
tographic realism and historical accuracy in favor of abstraction, suggestion,
selective and simplified realism, and visual symbolism and metaphor.

The Viennese émigré designer Joseph Urban (1871–1933) was one of the
first to introduce the new stagecraft to the United States. In 1911, after
almost a decade of designing at Vienna's Burgtheater and for various
European operatic productions, Urban was commissioned to design for the
Boston Opera. He remained in the United States, designing for Florenz
Ziegfield's *Follies* and for the Metropolitan Opera. Urban's designs were
noted for their simplicity of line, lush color, and impressionistic suggestive-
ness, the latter often achieved by applying certain pointillist techniques to
scene painting. In association with architect Thomas A. Lamb, Urban also
designed the Ziegfeld Theatre in 1927. With a carefully coordinated art deco
exterior and interior and with the latest in stage equipment, the Ziegfeld was
one of the most elegant and modern theaters of the era. A highpoint of
Urban's career was his designs for the celebrated musical *Showboat* which
was staged at the Ziegfeld Theatre in 1927.

The American designer, Livingston Platt (1885–1968) was also an early
pioneer of the new stagecraft. In 1911 after a sojourn in Europe, he began to
design settings for both Boston's Toy Theatre, an alternative "little" theater,
and the Castle Square Theatre. His designs, based on a few architectural elements—walls, towers, platforms—and atmospheric lighting to suggest a
locale, clearly mirror the influence of Craig and Appia. Actress and director
Margaret Anglin was sufficiently impressed to commission Platt to design her
notable revivals of ancient Greek tragedies and touring Shakespearean productions. Throughout the 1920s and early 1930s, Platt designed numerous
Broadway productions, including such hits as Vicki Baum's *Grand Hotel*
(1930) and George S. Kaufman and Edna Ferber's *Dinner at Eight* (1933).

Max Reinhardt himself promoted the new stagecraft movement when he
brought his exotic Arabian Nights–style pantomime *Sumurum* to New York
in 1912. Three years later English director–playwright Harley Granville–
Barker (1877–1946), demonstrated his own variation on new stagecraft style
with his New York presentations of *A Midsummer Night's Dream*, Shaw's

*Androcles and the Lion* and Anatole France's *The Man Who Married a Dumb Wife,* a farcical curtain-raiser set in the Middle Ages.

American designer Robert Edmond Jones's scenery and costumes for *The Man Who Married a Dumb Wife* , which wittily and economically suggested medievalism without resorting to heavy-handed historical accuracy, signaled his allegiance to the new stagecraft. In the next twenty years, Jones established a reputation as one of America's leading designers. His imaginative, often strikingly minimalistic and abstract scenery for numerous productions, including Arthur Hopkins's revivals of *Macbeth* (1921) and *Hamlet* (1922), and Eugene O'Neill's *Anna Christie* (1921), *The Hairy Ape* (1922), *Desire under the Elms* (1924), and *Mourning Becomes Electra* (1931), contributed significantly to elevating the art of American scene design.

Comparable to Jones in both talent and influence, Lee Simonson (1888–1967) helped found the Theatre Guild and became its principal designer for the next twenty years. Simonson's designs, notable for their simplified realism and architectural strength, contributed to the success of many outstanding Guild productions, including Shaw's *Heartbreak House* (1920) and *Back to Methuselah* (1922), Elmer Rice's *The Adding Machine* (1923), O'Neill's *Marco Millions* (1928), and Behrman's adaptation of Giraudoux's *Amphytrion 38* (1938).

Other young designers joined with Jones and Simonson to advance American scenic art, usually adapting new stagecraft techniques to a range of different modernist dramatic styles whether naturalism, expressionism, or symbolism. Rollo Peters (1892–1967) designed settings for the Washington Square Players and then the Theatre Guild; Cleon Throckmorton (1897–1965) designed several of O'Neill's early plays, including *The Emperor Jones* (1920) and *S. S. Glencairn* (1924); Aline Bernstein (1880–1955) designed many of the productions at Eva LeGallienne's Civic Repertory Theatre; Norman Bel Geddes (1893–1958) worked in various styles, but was best known for his detailed, realistic setting for Max Reinhardt's *The Miracle* (1924), which transformed the interior of the Century (New) Theatre into a remarkable semblance of a Gothic cathedral nave, and for the authentic-looking New York street he created for Sidney Kingsley's *Dead End* (1935); Mordecai Gorelik (1899–1990), the chief designer for the Group Theatre in the 1930s, was especially noted for his strongly expressionistic designs for Sidney Kingsley's *Men in White* (1933) and Robert Ardrey's *Thunder Rock* (1939); and Boris Aronson (1898–1980), a Russian émigré designer, began his long career on the American stage working for the Yiddish Art Theatre, the Group Theatre, and the Theatre Guild designing such productions as Clifford Odets's *Awake and Sing* (1935) and William Saroyan's *The Time of Your Life* (1939). By the mid-1920s, in fact, although conventional realistic stage design remained popular, the new stagecraft was an established and admired alternative.

In the late 1920s, new design talents emerged. Jo Mielziner (1901–75) and Donald Oenslager (1902–75) developed a more painterly, impressionistic scenic style known as poetic or lyrical realism. Jones, Simonson, Mielziner, and Oenslager dominated American scenic design from the late 1920s to the early 1960s, designing the sets for most of the major productions during this period. Mielziner's outstanding settings in the early part of his career include O'Neill's *Strange Interlude* (1928), Elmer Rice's *Street Scene* (1929), and Maxwell Anderson's *Winterset* (1935). Oenslager, after assisting Jones in the early 1920s, struck out on his own, designing numerous productions in the 1930s, including the Cole Porter musical *Anything Goes* (1934), George S. Kaufman and Moss Hart's *You Can't Take It with You* (1936), and John Steinbeck's *Of Mice and Men* (1937). Oenslager also exercised considerable influence over American scenic design as a professor of design at Yale University from 1925 to 1971. Many of his students would go on to successful careers in the American theater. By the early 1940s dozens of professional designers were active on Broadway.

As a separate specialty, costume design lagged behind scenic design. Many scenic designers of the 1920s and 1930s also designed costumes for their productions. Lee Simonson, for example, both designed and collected historical costumes and clothing. His collection became the foundation for New York's Metropolitan Museum of Art's renowned Costume Institute. Irene Sharaff (b.1912) was one of the first designers to specialize in costumes. Sharaff initially designed costumes for the Civic Repertory Theatre in the 1920s, then for numerous Broadway plays and musicals and for films through the 1960s. Helene Pons (?–1990), who designed costumes for Theatre Guild Productions, Lucinda Ballard (b. 1908), Raoul Pène DuBois (1914–85), and Alvin Colt (b. 1915) were also important costume designers whose careers began in the late 1920s and early 1930s. Ballard received the first Antoinette Perry ("Tony") Award for costume design in 1947. The art of costume design was bolstered when United Scenic Artists recognized the specialty in 1936. By the 1940s, costume designers were regularly credited in New York playbills.

New lighting inventions spurred the art of theatrical lighting. David Belasco with his electrician Louis Hartmann (1878–1941) pioneered many innovations in stage lighting, including use of small spotlights and the elimination of the traditional footlights. In the 1920s, the development of more refined lenses gave spotlights both great intensity and flexibility. Several new stagecraft designers, the actress Maude Adams, and the producer– director Winthrop Ames are also credited with early use of spotlights to complement scenic design and to create visual focus and interest. Stanley McCandless (1897–1967) was a pioneer in the development of theatrical lighting systems, including pre-set lighting control boards. His book *A Method of Lighting the Stage* (1932) became the foundation for a systematic approach to lighting design. Abe Feder (1909–97) was one of the first professional lighting designers on the American stage. In the early 1930s, he began designing for Broadway shows and Group Theatre productions. He remained an important lighting designer and consultant for over fifty years. Jean Rosenthal (1912–69), one of McCandless's students, and initially Feder's assistant, was lighting productions on her own by the late 1930s. For over thirty years, she designed lighting for Martha Graham's (1894–1991) dance company, for the New York City Ballet, and for hundreds of Broadway productions, becoming America's leading lighting designer. There would continue to be technological advances in lighting instruments and control boards, and dozens of talented lighting designers would join Feder and Rosenthal in illuminating stage, film, and television productions. By the 1940s, the profession of lighting designer was well established and in 1962 United Scenic Artists recognized lighting as a separate design specialty.

VARIOUS FORMS OF musical theater, from burlesque extravaganza to grand opera, were an integral part of the nineteenth-century American stage. At the turn of the century, however, operetta, revue, and musical comedy emerged as dominant forms of musical theater. The operettas of W. S. Gilbert and Arthur Sullivan, especially their *H.M.S. Pinafore,* which had its American premiere in 1879, were enormously popular in America, as they were in England, in the 1880s. Although overwhelmed by the Gilbert and Sullivan vogue, Viennese operettas by such composers as Franz von Suppé (1819–95), Karl Millöcker (1842–99) and especially Johann Strauss the younger (1829–99) were also popular. Inspired by Gilbert and Sullivan and the Viennese school, composer Reginald De Koven (1859–1920) and lyricist Harry B. Smith (1860–1936) created in *Robin Hood* (1891) the first genuinely successful American operetta of the era. But it was Victor Herbert (1859–1924) who created an American operetta comparable to the Viennese. Born in Ireland and educated in Germany, Herbert came to the United States at the age of twenty-seven. A talented cellist and conductor—in 1900 he became permanent conductor of the Pittsburgh Symphony Orchestra—Herbert turned to composing operettas in the mid-1890s. *The Wizard of the Nile* (1895) enjoyed a long run in New York and on tour and was the first American operetta to be mounted in both Vienna and Prague. Among Herbert's numerous successes were *Babes in Toyland* (1903), *The Red Mill* (1906), and especially *Naughty Marietta* (1910), which set a new standard for American operetta.

Undoubtedly, American operetta was also promoted by a new generation of Viennese operettas. The 1907 New York production of Franz Lehar's (1870–1948) *The Merry Widow,* for example, created a vogue equal to the *Pinafore* craze of the 1880s. World War I put a damper on Germanic music and theater in America, but in the 1920s operetta roared back into popularity mainly because of two émigré composers. Prague-born Rudolf Friml (1879–1972) came to the United States in 1903. Beginning with his first operetta, *The Firefly* (1912), he composed dozens of popular operettas, including *Rose Marie* (1924) and *The Vagabond King* (1925). Hungarian Sigmund Romberg's (1887–1951) numerous hits include *Maytime* (1917), *Blossom Time* (1921), based on the life and music of Franz Shubert, *The Student Prince* (1924), *The Desert Song* (1926), and *New Moon* (1928). By the late 1920s, the popularity of operetta waned as tastes turned toward musical comedy, although the operettas of Herbert,

Friml, and Romberg would have a second life as movie adaptations in the late 1930s and early 1940s.

Combining topical comedy sketches, songs, dance, lavish spectacle, and a chorus of beautiful young women, the musical revue can trace its origins to aspects of the minstrel show, burlesque, and vaudeville. *The Passing Show* (1894) produced by George W. Lederer (1861–1938) is usually considered to be the first American musical revue. Throughout the Gay Nineties and the turn of the century, revues with such titles as *In Gay New York* (1897), *The Whirl of the Town* (1898), and *About Town* (1906) abounded, but producer Florenz Ziegfeld is generally credited with popularizing the form. Beginning with *The Follies of 1907,* Ziegfeld mounted an annual series of revues until his death in 1932. Ziegfeld's *Follies* were noted especially for their choruses of willowy, erotically costumed young women—as many as seventy-five or eighty chorines by the 1920s. Ziegfeld, however, also attracted to his *Follies* the most talented vaudeville singers, dancers, and comics of the era, including Eddie Cantor (1892–1964), Will Rogers, Marilyn Miller (1898–1936), and Fanny Brice (1891–1951). Music and songs were written by leading musical theater composers and by Tin Pan Alley songsmiths, including Irving Berlin (1888–1989), Victor Herbert, and Rudolf Friml. After 1915, the *Follies* had spectacular decor designed by Joseph Urban. The success of the *Follies* spawned numerous competitors in the 1910s and 1920s. The Shuberts, for example, mounted *The Passing Show* from 1912 to 1924, and then between 1923 and 1943, six editions of *Artists and Models* which featured a virtually nude chorus. In 1919, George White (1890–1968), a former vaudeville and *Follies* dancer, weighed in with the *George White Scandals* which often featured the inspired music of George (1898–1937) and Ira (1896–1983) Gershwin. Earl Carroll's (1892–1948) *Vanities* and Irving Berlin's *Music Box Revues* were also among the more popular and successful revue series. (The rise of black musical revues is discussed in a separate section later in this chapter.)

Affected by the Depression and the rise of movie musicals, the Ziegfeld-style revue faded from the theater in the 1930s, although the flexibility of the revue form continued to be used for various musical entertainments. *Pins and Needles* (1937), for example, was a revue that in song and dance spoofed Depression-era labor issues and leftist political organizations, and ran for over a thousand performances on Broadway. Berlin's *This Is the Army* (1942), a successor to his World War I army show *Yip, Yip Yaphank* (1918)—Yaphank was the Long Island army camp where Berlin was stationed—celebrated army life with a chorus of soldiers rather than showgirls. African-American dancer and choreographer Katherine Dunham's (b. 1912) *A Tropical Revue* (1943) showcased the talents of black dancers and choreographers and had a long run on Broadway and then on tour. Showman Billy Rose (1899–1966), whose interests ranged from nightclubs to legitimate theatrical productions, attempted to revive the lavish Ziegfeld-style revue with *The Seven Lively Arts* (1944) which featured music by Cole Porter and Igor Stravinsky, lavish settings by Norman Bel Geddes, comic sketches by prominent playwrights Moss Hart (1904–61) and George S. Kaufman, and the

*Left,* Ziegfeld Follies *poster. The poster model was Billie Burke (1885–1970), a notable stage and screen star and Ziegfeld's second wife. Courtesy of the Museum of the City of New York.*

*Right, George M. Cohan c. 1937, striking a typical President Roosevelt pose for his role in* I'd Rather Be Right. *Courtesy the Flora Ward Hineline Papers, the Ward M. Canaday Center for Special Collections, University of Toledo Libraries.*

talents of comic actor Bert Lahr (1897–1967) and jazz clarinetist Benny Goodman, among others. The material was not up to the usual standards of the talented writers and composers; critics thought the show too sophisticated and too lavish for wartime; and it was closed after a relatively short twenty-week run. Revues which featured topical humor, or reviewed the work of musical theater composers—including Porter, Berlin, Richard Rodgers and Oscar Hammerstein II—continued to be mounted to the present day (see chapter 7). In the 1950s, influenced as much by the Parisian Folies Bergères as by memories of Ziegfeld, spectacular revues featuring scantily clad show girls became a mainstay of several Las Vegas casino shows.

The roots of what became known as the American musical can be traced to burlesque extravaganza, to the musical farces of Edward Harrigan and Tony Hart, and to the influence of foreign comic operas, operettas, and turn-of-the-century English musical comedies such as *A Gaiety Girl* (1893)—credited as the first to carry the designation "musical comedy"— and *Florodora* (1899), both of which enjoyed long New York runs after their London premieres. As it evolved in the first decades of the twentieth century, the American musical took on certain characteristics. Unlike the revue, for example, the musical was built around a dramatic plot, libretto, or "book," as it is called. The books for early musicals, however, were flimsy affairs, little more than skeletal frameworks for a loosely connected string of romantic ballads, satirical tunes, and lively "coon songs." The music, furthermore, was usually less sophisticated and melodic than European-influenced operettas.

At the turn of the century, George M. Cohan (1878–1942) stamped the developing musical comedy form with his own distinctive style. For over a decade, Cohan performed in vaudeville as a singer and dancer in an act that initially included his mother, father, and younger sister, and then later his wife. Beginning with *The Governor's Son* (1901), for which he was composer, lyricist, librettist, and star, Cohan moved from vaudeville to the legitimate musical stage. Through the late 1920s, there was rarely a season that did not include at least one, and often several, Cohan musical comedies, including such notable hits as *Little Johnny Jones* (1904), *Forty-Five Minutes from Broadway* (1906), *The Man Who Owns Broadway* (1909), *The Little Millionaire* (1911), *Mary* (1920), and *The Merry Malones* (1927). Cohan's plots, combining romantic complications with political and social commentary, were a cut above the average of his era; his colloquial, slangy lyrics were like Cohan himself—cocky, funny, patriotic, and sentimental; his tunes were simple, but appealing—anyone could sing a Cohan song. Many of his songs—for example, "Over There," "Give My Regards to Broadway," "Grand Old Flag," "Yankee Doodle Boy," "Mary's a Grand Old Name"—remained popular for decades after their Broadway premieres. Cohan invariably performed only in his own musicals and comedies, but late in his career he won acclaim as the father Nat Miller in O'Neill's gentle domestic drama *Ah, Wilderness!* (1933) and for his impersonation of President Franklin Roosevelt in Rodgers and Hart's *I'd Rather Be Right* (1937), a musical satirizing Depression-era politics. As producer, playwright, and performer, he became "Mr. Broadway" and his life-sized bronze statue still overlooks the square at the confluence of Broadway and Seventh Avenue.

Like Cohan, other musical entertainers used the musical theater format mainly as a vehicle to display their performing talents. After almost a decade in vaudeville and minstrel shows, Al Jolson, for example, made his musical comedy debut in *La Belle Paree* (1911) where he sang, in blackface, a song entitled "Paris Is a Paradise for Coons." His vitality and jazz-oriented, inimitable singing style created a sensation. In 1912 Jolson was featured in *Whirl of Society* in which he played Gus, a wisecracking blackfaced servant character drawn from the minstrel tradition. As Gus, Jolson starred in several other musicals, including *Robinson Crusoe, Jr.* (1916), *Sinbad* (1918), and *Bombo* (1921). The plots were as silly as the character, but audiences came mainly to hear Jolson sing. After his debut in the movie *The Jazz Singer* (1927), the first "talkie," Jolson moved to Hollywood, appearing in several films, but his subsequent Broadway appearances were limited. He also was featured on numerous radio broadcasts in the 1940s. One of the most beloved performers of the era, many of Jolson's hit songs became pop music standards, including "Swanee," "April Showers," "California, Here I Come," "Mammy," and "Sonny Boy."

Cohan's contributions notwithstanding, Jerome Kern (1885–1945) is generally considered the father of the modern American musical. Born in New York City, he studied at the New York College of Music and then in Germany in the early years of the new century. He initially intended to be a serious composer, but abandoned this goal when he realized he had neither the talent nor the technique. For several years he wrote popular songs for musical revues. Then beginning in 1915, in collaboration with librettist and playwright Guy Bolton (1883–1979), he created a series of musical comedies for producer F. Ray Comstock's (1880–1949) intimate three-hundred-seat Princess Theatre. With small casts and no stars, charming, romantic stories, a simplified approach to staging, and a tone that was colloquial but sophisticated, the Princess Theatre musicals—as they became known—stood in opposition to lavishly staged, star-studded revues and operettas and to Cohan's brassy style. *Very Good Eddie* (1915), which ran for over three hundred performances, established both Kern's reputation as a leading musical comedy composer and the commercial viability of small-scale musical comedies. *Very Good Eddie* was followed by a number of Kern–Bolton successes in the teens, including *Oh Boy!* (1917), *Leave It to Jane* (1917), and *Oh, Lady! Lady!* (1918), all with exceptionally clever lyrics by English humorist P. G. Wodehouse (1881–1975), later celebrated for his satirical stories about upper-class English life. In the 1920s, Kern moved into larger-scale musicals, scoring notable successes with *Sally* (1920) and *Sunny* (1925), both starring Marilyn Miller. Kern's *Show Boat* (1927) marked a turning point in the development of the American musical. Based on Edna Ferber's (1887–1968) popular novel, a sprawling saga covering four decades in the lives of a showboat family, *Show Boat,* with inventive lyrics by young Oscar Hammerstein II, was the first American musical drama—partly musical comedy and partly operetta. Its music and songs ranged over several different styles including ballads, Negro spirituals, and ragtime. It effectively, although not fully, integrated musical sequences with the dramatic plot, and its overall tone and characterizations were authentic and realistic. Furthermore, *Show Boat* gave Broadway its first integrated cast of African–American and white actors. Produced by Florenz Ziegfield, it ran on Broadway for almost two years, then toured for another year, had a long run in London, and successful New York revivals in 1932, 1946, and 1995. Three different movie versions were made: 1929, 1936, and 1951. Kern created several noteworthy musicals in the later 1920s and 1930s, several of which experimented with unorthodox musical and dramatic techniques, but none proved as successful as *Show Boat.*

By the early 1920s, Kern had been joined by other composers in refining the American musical form. In 1924, George and Ira Gershwin wrote the hit musical *Lady, Be Good,* which starred dancer–singers Fred and Adele Astaire. George's jazz-inspired rhythms and graceful ballads and Ira's witty rhymes and phrasing significantly elevated the standards of musical comedy. Among their subsequent successes were *Oh, Kay!* (1926), *Funny Face* (1927), *Strike Up the Band* (1930) and *Of Thee I Sing* (1931). The latter, a sharp political satire with a book by George S. Kaufman and Morrie Ryskind

*From left to right: Rose McClendon (1884–1936) as Serena, Frank Wilson (1886–1956) as Porgy and Evelyn Ellis (1894–1958) as Bess in* Porgy *(1927). From Appelbaum, Great Actors and Actresses of the American Stage in Historic Photographs. Courtesy of Dover Publications, Inc.*

*Black chorus members of* Show Boat *(1927). Courtesy of The Museum of the City of New York.*

*Cab Calloway (1908–94) as Sportin' Life in the 1952–53 tour of* Porgy *and* Bess. *Lawrence and Lee Theatre Research Institute, Ohio State University.*

(1895–1985), was the first musical to win the Pulitzer Prize for drama and the first American musical to be published in script form. The culmination of the Gershwins' talents was *Porgy and Bess* (1935) based on Dorothy and DuBose Heyward's *Porgy* (1927), a drama about the black denizens of a poor neighborhood in Charleston, South Carolina. More opera than musical, *Porgy and Bess* was not initially successful, running for only 124 performances; but a revival in 1942 ran for thirty-five weeks on Broadway and then toured. An international tour mounted in the mid-1950s established *Porgy and Bess* as a classic of the American musical theater. *Porgy and Bess* has been criticized for its sympathetic, but nonetheless stereotypical, treatment of black life and characterizations. It also has been suggested that its success discouraged the further development of black musical theater, which had seemed so promising in the 1920s and early 1930s. *Porgy and Bess,* however, provided opportunities for numerous black singers and it has been frequently revived in the United States and abroad, including productions by the Houston Grand Opera in 1976 and the Metropolitan Opera in 1985.

Despite the economic restraints of the Depression and the turbulence of World War II, the 1930s and 1940s were a Golden Age for the American musical theater. Cole Porter (1891–1964) brought to the form sophisticated, saucy lyrics and distinctive melodies, ranging from romantic ballads, to comic ditties, to Latin-inspired tangos, rhumbas, and bequines. His successful musical comedies, include *Girl Crazy* (1930), in which musical star Ethel Merman (1909–84) made her debut, *Anything Goes* (1934), and *Du Barry Was a Lady* (1939), which featured both Merman and Bert Lahr. *Kiss Me Kate* (1948), inspired by Shakespeare's *Taming of the Shrew* and featuring Alfred Drake (1914–92), a leading musical theater star, ran for over a thousand performances, won a Tony Award for best musical, and is widely

*Act 1 of Cole Porter's* Du Barry Was a Lady *with Bert Lahr at center as Louis Blore. Scenery and costumes by Raoul Pene Du Bois. 46th Street Theatre, 1939. Courtesy of the Museum of the City of New York.*

*Ethel Merman c. 1930s. From Appelbaum and Camner,* Stars of the American Musical Theatre in Historic Photographs. *Courtesy Dover Publications, Inc.*

*A scene from the London production of* Oklahoma! *Settings by Lemuel Ayers; costumes by Miles White; direction by Rouben Mamoulian. From the Isabel Bigley Barnett Collection at the Lawrence and Lee Theatre Research Institute, Ohio State University.*

considered Porter's masterpiece. In the early 1950s Porter capped his career with *Can-Can* (1953) and *Silk Stockings* (1955), both Broadway successes.

Composer Richard Rodgers (1902–79) and lyricist Lorenz Hart (1895–1943) had collaborated on songs for revues in the 1910s. From the mid-1920s to 1940, they created some of the most popular and successful musical comedies of the era, including *On Your Toes* (1935), *Babes in Arms* (1937), and *The Boys from Syracuse* (1938), the last based on Shakespeare's *Comedy of Errors. Pal Joey* (1940), a musical drama based on a series of short stories by author John O'Hara (1905–70) about an antiheroic, womanizing nightclub entertainer marked a departure for Rodgers and Hart and for the direction of the musical theater. Following Hart's premature death, Rodgers teamed with Oscar Hammerstein II in what became one of the most fruitful partnerships in the annals of the American musical stage. Before he joined Rodgers, Hammerstein had contributed either lyrics or libretto (or both) to several important musicals and operettas in the 1920s and 1930s, including Friml's *Rose Marie*, Sigmund Romberg's *Desert Song* and *New Moon,* and Jerome Kern's *Sunny* and *Show Boat.* Rodgers and Hammerstein's first collaboration produced *Oklahoma!* (1943), which artfully integrated music with the dramatic plot. It featured inspired choreography by Agnes de Mille (1909–93)—including a sophisticated "Dream Ballet" sequence—refreshing lyrics, a melodic, sweeping score, and winning performances by a cast of new talents including Alfred Drake and Celeste Holm (b.1919), both of whom would have distinguished careers on stage and screen. *Oklahoma!* was the most successful musical since *Show Boat*. It ran for over five years on Broadway. A second touring production opened in the fall 1943 and was on the road continuously for over ten years. Productions were also mounted in London, Berlin, Paris, and other foreign capitals. *Oklahoma!* was followed by a string of Rodgers and Hammerstein musicals, including *Carousel* (1945), *South Pacific* (1949), *The King and I* (1951), *Flower Drum Song* (1958) and *The Sound of Music* (1958)—notable not only for their lush scores and often trenchant lyrics, but also for their treatment of such themes as gender conflicts, totalitarianism, and racial and ethnic prejudice. Rodgers and Hammerstein moved the musical away from frothy comedic entertainment and toward drama. *South Pacific* won the Pulitzer Prize for drama, only the second musical to be so honored.

Throughout the 1920s and 1930s, Irving Berlin was known principally as a composer for revues. He did collaborate, however, with George S. Kaufman to create *The Cocoanuts* (1925), a zany musical comedy vehicle for the Marx Brothers, and with Moss Hart for *Face the Music* (1932), a political satire. In the early 1940s, with the popularity of the revue waning, Berlin turned to musical comedy. His notable hits included *Annie Get Your Gun* (1946), based on the life of trick-shot artist Annie Oakley (1860–1926), and *Call Me Madame* (1950), inspired by socialite Perle Mesta's experiences as ambassador to Liechtenstein. Both musicals starred the irrepressible Ethel Merman.

*Portrait photograph of Laurette Taylor in the 1920s. From Appelbaum,* Great Actors and Actresses of the American Stage in Historic Photographs. *Courtesy Dover Publications, Inc.*

*A scene from Jack Kirkland's dramatization of Erskine Caldwell's novel* Tobacco Road. *Courtesy of The Museum of the City of New York. Gift of Miss Ann Dene, 39.441.5.*

Emigrating from Germany to New York in 1935, Kurt Weill (1900–1950) had an established reputation for his modernist concert music and as the composer for Bertolt Brecht's *The Threepenny Opera* (1928) and *The Rise and Fall of the City of Mahagonny* (1930). Weill, in partnership with playwrights Paul Green, Maxwell Anderson, and Elmer Rice, and poets Ogden Nash (1902–71) and Langston Hughes (1902–67), created a half-dozen musicals notable for their originality and treatment of serious social issues. These included *Johnny Johnson* (1936), a moving antiwar play; *Lady in the Dark* (1941), which spoofed the vogue for psychoanalysis; *Knickerbocker Holiday* (1938), which satirized the tendency toward "big government"; and the tragic *Lost in the Stars* (1949), an exploration of racism in South Africa based on novelist Alan Paton's *Cry, the Beloved Country*. Weill's early death cut short a career still full of promise, but he had a lasting influence on American theater music and several of his musicals have become often-revived classics.

Because of the contributions principally of Kern, Porter, Berlin, Rodgers and Hammerstein, and Weill, the American musical was firmly entrenched as an important and sometimes dominant genre of American theater art by the end of World War II.

IN THE 1910s and 1920s, popular entertainment rather than serious drama ruled on Broadway. Typically a Broadway season offered a range of melodramas, farces, light sentimental comedies, and lavishly staged musical comedies, revues and operettas. Before World War I, the longest running Broadway play was J. Hartley Manners's *Peg o' My Heart* which ran for over six hundred performances in New York in 1912, played in London for a season, then had eight different companies touring it for several seasons more for a total of six thousand performances by 1918. Laurette Taylor, the star of *Peg o' My Heart* (and Manners's wife), became so identified with the title role that she was able to succeed in little else for years. The previously mentioned *Lightnin'* (1918) surpassed *Peg o' My Heart* with 1,291 performances on Broadway and a seven-year tour. *Abie's Irish Rose* (1922), however, with over twenty-five hundred performances, was the greatest hit of the 1920s, until the sensational, rural melodrama, *Tobacco Road* (1933), chalked-up over three thousand continuous performances. Running not far behind these hits were such plays as *The Gold Diggers* (1919, 720 performances), a farce about chorus girls searching for wealthy husbands, and *The Bat* (1920, 867 performances), a mystery "whodunit."

While such fare held sway, a few plays of dramatic merit continued to be mounted on Broadway with varying degrees of critical and commercial success. Indeed, the 1920s and 1930s gave rise to an American drama comparable to the best modern European drama. A number of interlocking factors set the stage for this flowering. The burgeoning demand for theatrical entertainment, for example, made it easier, as Leiter notes, for playwrights to get their plays produced. But there were also producers—including organizations like the Provincetown Players and the Theatre Guild—interested in mounting serious plays, inventive directors and designers to stage them, and actors with the training and inclination to perform them. A new breed of critics could explain and champion the work. Interest in modern drama was also stimulated by such organizations as the Drama League of America founded in 1909 to stimulate interest in modern drama and the role of theater as a cultural force. The Drama League sponsored playreading circles and circulated playscripts and information about meritorious productions. Its quarterly journal, *The Drama,* published new playscripts and articles by well-known critics. By 1920, the Drama League had tens of thousands of members and one hundred centers nationwide. *Theatre Arts,* a theatrical journal founded in 1916 by critic and theater historian Sheldon Cheney (1886–1980), also introduced its readership to modernist ideas and practices in European and American drama and theater. The success of the Drama League, *Theatre Arts,* and theater groups like the Theatre Guild, the Civic Repertory Theatre, and the Provincetown Players suggests that there was a growing audience for modern drama.

As noted in chapter 5, a movement toward a modern realist drama had begun in the 1890s, most notably in the plays of the "American Ibsen," James A. Herne. These efforts continued in the work of several playwrights succeeding Herne. Clyde Fitch (1865–1909), for example, was the prolific author of over fifty plays, many adaptations of popular novels and foreign plays. At his best, as in *The Girl with Green Eyes* (1902), *The Climbers* (1901), or *The Truth* (1906), he wrote incisive satires of upper-class

*Left, Mrs. Fiske as Salvation Nell. Courtesy of the Museum of the City of New York. Gift of Harold Friedlande, 68.80.269.*

*Right, Clyde Fitch's* The City *with Walter Hampden on left and Tully Marshall (1864–1943). Courtesy of the Museum of the City of New York.*

*Scene from Eugene Walter's* The Easiest Way. *From the left: Frances Starr (1886–1973), Robert Kelly (1875–1949), and Joseph Kilgour (1863–1933). Courtesy of the Museum of the City of New York. Gift of the New York Public Library, 37.339.229.*

hypocrisy and materialism. Fitch's last play, *The City* (1909), focused on broader social issues in the style of Herne, but this promising direction was cut short by his premature death. In *The New York Idea* (1906), Langdon Mitchell (1862–1935), like Fitch, also used the genre of comedy for a trenchant analysis of modern marriage and divorce. Marriage, and especially gender roles, were also scrutinized by Eugene Walter (1874–1941) in *The Easiest Way* (1908) and *Paid in Full* (1908) and in a dozen or more plays by Rachel Crothers (1878–1958). Crothers's *The Three of Us* (1906), her first Broadway success, was admired by critics for its realistic characterization and dialogue and ran for the entire season. Writing a play a year over the next two decades, and usually directing them as well, Crothers would earn a reputation as a skillful and thoughtful playwright. *He and She* (1920), one of her best plays, was a probing examination of double standards. In a trio of plays—*Salvation Nell* (1908), *The Nigger* (1910), and *The Boss* (1911)— Edward Sheldon (1886–1946) attempted a realistic portrayal of American working-class life and of racial and labor issues. In *The Great Divide* (1906), William Vaughn Moody (1869–1910) explored the turn-of-the-century conflict between the opportunities and freedom offered by the Western frontier and the hidebound traditions and limitations of the eastern establishment. Starring Henry Miller and Margaret Anglin, *The Great Divide* ran for more than two hundred performances on Broadway, then toured for almost a season. It would subsequently come to be regarded as the finest play of the era. Although he worked within the conventions of realistic melodrama and farce, many of the sixty-odd plays of Augustus Thomas (1857–1934) were both commercial successes and critically well-regarded pieces in their time.

American drama in the 1920s was dominated by Eugene O'Neill (1888–1953). In 1914–15 at Harvard University, O'Neill attended Professor George Pierce Baker's (1866–1935) famous Workshop 47, a laboratory for the production of student plays, many written in Baker's playwriting course. Baker was a pioneer in the academic study of practical theater, and a number of prominent playwrights of the 1920s and 1930s benefited from his tutelage, including Edward Sheldon, Philip Barry, and Sidney Howard. After his stint with Baker, O'Neill's career was launched when the Provincetown Players produced several of his one-act "sea plays," including *Bound East for Cardiff* (1916) and *Moon of the Caribbees* (1919). In 1920, O'Neill's first Broadway production, *Beyond the Horizon,* a naturalistic rural tragedy, ran for the entire season, garnering critical acclaim and winning a Pulitzer Prize. It established O'Neill as the most promising playwright of his generation. Between 1920 and 1934, twenty-one new O'Neill plays premiered in New York, ranging from the expressionistic *The Emperor Jones* (1920) and *The Hairy Ape* (1921), to historical costume dramas about explorers Ponce de Leon *(The Fountain,* 1921) and Marco Polo *(Marco Millions,* 1927), to the epic thirteen-act trilogy *Mourning Becomes Electra* (1932), a retelling of Aeschylus's *Oresteia* set against the American Civil War. O'Neill's plays also explored emotionally powerful, provocative subjects—materialism, adultery, interracial marriage, incest, and modern alienation. Despite—or perhaps because of—their somber

*Eugene O'Neill c. 1940. The Yale Collection of American Literature, Beinecke Rare Book and Manuscript Library, Yale University.*

*Act 7 of Eugene O'Neill's Strange Interlude. Directed by Philip Moeller; designed by Jo Mielziner. Lynn Fontanne as Nina Leeds, Charles Walters as Gordon Evans (as a boy), and Glen Anders as Edmund Darrell. Guild Theatre, 1928. Courtesy of the Museum of the City of New York.*

tone, experimental structure, and subject matter, most of O'Neill's plays were commercial successes, running for one hundred or more performances. Several ran for over two hundred. *Strange Interlude* (1928), a mysterious, psychological thriller in nine acts about erotic power and desire, ran for over four hundred performances. The critic Burns Mantle selected seven of O'Neill's plays as Best Plays of their respective seasons, and *Anna Christe* (1922) and *Strange Interlude* won him two more Pulitzer Prizes. It was a singular record unmatched by any other modernist American dramatist of the 1920s.

When O'Neill was awarded the Nobel Prize for Literature in 1936, the second American to receive this prestigious award, it signaled international recognition of his artistry, as well as the coming of age of American drama. At the time of the award, however, buffeted by illness, family crisis and professional disappointment with the reception of *Days without End* (1934), O'Neill had retreated from the hurley-burley of Broadway. Throughout the late 1930s and the war years, he worked on several plays, including a multi-play cycle to be called "A Tale of Possessors Self-Dispossessed," a historical epic tracing the growth of materialism in American life. In 1946, O'Neill's *The Iceman Cometh* , written in 1939, opened on Broadway. A powerful, but long and grim realistic drama set in a seedy New York saloon, it was judged a relative failure, although it ran for a respectable 136 performances. Ironically, after O'Neill's death, a revival of *The Iceman Cometh* in 1956, followed by acclaimed productions of the searing, autobiographical *Long Day's Journey into Night* (1956; but written in 1939–41; it won O'Neill his fourth and final Pulitzer Prize), and *A Touch of the Poet* (1958, the only completed play from the "A Tale of Possessors Self-Dispossessed" cycle) elevated O'Neill once again to a premiere position among American dramatists.

O'Neill was the foremost dramatist of the era, but playwriting talent abounded from the 1920s to the 1940s; it was, in fact, a "Golden Age" of American drama. Elmer Rice (1892–1967) succeeded on Broadway with his powerful courtroom drama *On Trial* (1914) and then added to his reputation with the daring, expressionistic *The Adding Machine* (1923), and the Pulitzer Prize–winning naturalistic drama *Street Scene* (1929). Beginning with *They Knew What They Wanted* (1924, another Pulitzer winner), Sidney Howard (1891–1939) crafted a dozen social dramas that were both compelling and entertaining. Robert Sherwood (1896–1955) author of the deftly written *The Petrified Forest* (1935), an exciting melodrama overlaid with social arguments, won Pulitzers for *Idiot's Delight* (1936) an absorbing antiwar drama; *Abe Lincoln in Illinois* (1938), a stirring reminder of the American past in the depths of the Depression; and *There Shall Be No Night* (1940) a provocative condemnation of the Russian invasion of Finland. S. N. Behrman (1893–1973), Philip Barry (1896–1949) and George Kelly (1887–1974) created a distinctly American social comedy, witty, smart and penetrating in its depiction of upper-class values and behavior.

Among Barry's most successful comedies were *Paris Bound* (1927), *Holiday* (1928), and *The Philadelphia Story* (1939), the last of which starred Katharine Hepburn as Tracy Lord, a charming but spoiled heiress caught in a romantic dilemma. Bolstered by Hepburn's buoyant performance, *The Philadelphia Story* played for over four hundred performances on Broadway then embarked on a national tour. The movie version (1940) starring Hepburn, Cary Grant, and James Stewart proved equally popular. From the late 1920s through the 1930s, Behrman was one of Broadway's most prolific and dependable playwrights. His best plays include *The Second Man* (1927), *Biography* (1932), and *No Time for Comedy* (1939). Often produced by the Theatre Guild and featuring such brilliant comic actors as the Lunts, Ina Claire, Jane Cowl (1884–1950), and Katharine Cornell, Behrman's urbane, sophisticated comedies usually enjoyed fairly long runs and critical acclaim. George Kelly's *The Show Off* (1924), a farce comedy centering on a ridiculous braggart, was considered one of the best American comedies of the time. In 1925 Kelly won the Pulitzer Prize for *Craig's Wife,* a lacerating, satirical exposé of a manipulative control-freak more concerned with the perfection of her home than her husband.

Maxwell Anderson's (1888–1959) talent is often favorably compared to O'Neill's. He achieved early success in 1924 with a popular, realistic antiwar drama, *What Price Glory?*, written in collaboration with Laurence Stallings (1894–1968), but he did not come into his own until the 1930s. Anderson's over thirty plays range, like O'Neill's, across several different styles. Anderson was particularly interested in verse drama and in several plays he welded poetic dialogue to historical subjects in an attempt to create a modern equivalent of classical tragedy. *Elizabeth the Queen* (1930) and its companion *Mary of Scotland* (1923) were his most popular dramas in this genre. In *Winterset* (1935) Anderson attempted to integrate poetic dialogue with a contemporary tragic story. It was a commercial failure, but *Winterset* won the Drama Critics Circle Award and is widely considered his finest play. In 1933, Anderson won his only Pulitzer Prize, for *Both Your Houses* (1933), a cleverly written, bitterly cynical political satire. *High Tor* (1936) and *The Star Wagon* (1937) were imaginative fantasy comedies; the former won the Critics Circle Award, while the latter proved one of Anderson's more commercially successful plays, running for over two hundred performances. *Key Largo* (1939) and *The Eve of St. Mark* (1942) are powerful realistic dramas addressing the issues and conflicts of World War II. Anderson's output slowed after the war, but *Joan of Lorraine* (1947), about Joan of Arc with the Swedish film star Ingrid Bergman (1915–82) in the title role, and the gripping melodrama *The Bad Seed* (1954), about an unnaturally malicious child, were long-run successes.

Dozens of women were active in the professional theater as important playwrights and lyricists in the period from 1900–1945. Susan Glaspell (1876–1948), a cofounder of the Provincetown Players, in plays such as *Trifles* (1916) and the experimentally structured *The Verge* (1921), challenged conventional notions of women's roles. In 1931, she won a Pulitzer Prize for *Alison's House,* based on the life of Emily Dickenson. Zoë Akins's (1886–1958) *Déclassée* (1919), although marred by melodramatic plotting, was one of the first serious attempts to address sexual double standards and class snobbery. In a dozen social comedies and melodramas, Akins continued

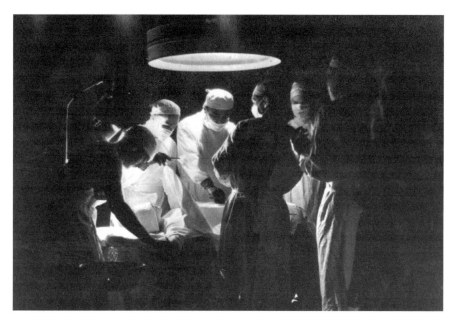

*Sidney Kingsley's* Men in White, *produced by the Group Theatre; directed by Lee Strasberg; scenery by Mordecai Gorelik. Courtesy of the Museum of the City of New York. Gift of Harold Friedlander, 68.80.6589.*

*Lillian Hellman's* The Children's Hour. *Produced and directed by Herman Shumlin. Maxine Elliott Theatre, 1934. Courtesy of the Museum of the City of New York. Gift of Mary Martin, 62.97.103.*

*Clifton Webb (c. 1889-1966) a popular stage and screen actor for over fifty years as Sheridan Whiteside in the touring production of* The Man Who Came to Dinner. *Courtesy of the Flora Ward Hineline Papers, the Ward M. Canaday Center for Special Collections, University of Toledo Libraries.*

to comment on gender issues. In 1935, Akins won a Pulitzer Prize for her adaptation of Edith Wharton's novel *The Old Maid*. Rachel Crothers never won a Pulitzer Prize, but her plays continued to be popular and widely respected. *Susan and God*, a sharply etched social drama, played for almost three hundred performances on Broadway in 1937. Rida Johnson Young (1875–1926), Dorothy Donnelly (1880–1928), and Dorothy Fields (1905–74) were leading librettists–lyricists

Lillian Hellman (1906–84) was one of the best playwrights—man or woman—of the 1930s and 1940s. In well-crafted realistic plays with distinctive characters and strong plots, such as *The Children's Hour* (1934),*The Little Foxes* (1939), and its prequel *Another Part of the Forest* (1946), she explored human tendencies toward cruelty and greed. *Watch on the Rhine* (1941) warned of the dangers of fascism, while *The Searching Wind* (1944) lambasted American foreign policy. In the late 1930s and 1940s, Hellman was also a successful screenwriter. In 1951 her long-time companion, famous mystery writer Dashiell Hammett (1894–1961), was jailed for contempt when he refused to respond to questioning by the infamous House Committee on Un-American Activities. When a year later Hellman herself was subpoenaed, she also refused to cooperate. Her reputation and gender saved her from jail, but she was subsequently blacklisted from working in Hollywood. Hellman continued to work in the theater, however. *The Autumn Garden* (1951) and *Toys in the Attic* (1960), both dramas about personal responsibility and moral choice, enjoyed long runs on Broadway. Indeed, all but four of her twelve plays were commercial successes and *The Little Foxes, Watch on the Rhine*, and *Toys in the Attic* won Drama Critics Circle Awards.

The social and political turbulence of the Great Depression and World War II gave rise to several new dramatic voices. Clifford Odets provided the Group Theatre with some of their most powerful vehicles, including *Waiting for Lefty* (1935), a galvanic agitprop play centering on a strike-call by taxi drivers, and *Awake and Sing!* (1935) and *Paradise Lost* (1935), two forceful, realistic dramas about lower middle-class Jewish families struggling with Depression-era pressures. Odets continued to write throughout the mid-1950s. His later work lacked the energy and focus of his Group Theatre plays, but *The Country Girl* (1950), a psychological drama about a has-been actor trying to make a comeback, enjoyed a long run on Broadway, was successful in a screen adaptation, and has been regularly revived. With *Men in White* (1933), a riveting hospital drama, Sidney Kingsley (b. 1906) provided the Group Theatre with one of their most successful productions and won a Pulitzer Prize. Kingsley's *Dead End* (1935) and *Detective Story* (1949) are compelling naturalistic plays about the brutalizing effects of urban life. In contrast to Odets's and Kingsley's downcast views of American society, the works of Thornton Wilder (1897–1975) and William Saroyan (1908–81) were more upbeat and philosophical. Wilder's *Our Town* (1938), a chronicle of family life in turn-of-the-century rural New Hampshire, and *The Skin of Our Teeth* (1942), an inventive survey of human history from the Ice Age to the Atomic Age, assert a positive, progressive attitude about America. Both plays won Pulitzer Prizes, had long runs on Broadway, and have become— especially *Our Town*—classics of American drama. Similarly Saroyan's *The Time of Your Life* (1939), which won both a Pulitzer Prize and a Drama Critics Circle Award, and *My Heart's in the Highlands* (1939) reaffirm the value of love, beauty, and dreams, even when life seems at its darkest.

Counteracting Depression gloom, the period between the wars also produced a score of sparkling light comedies and farces, several destined to become classics of the genre. George S. Kaufman, although he invariably worked in collaboration with other playwrights, was still considered the leading comic dramatist of the time, the coauthor of some forty plays. Kaufman had his earliest successes in consort with Marc Connelly. Their *Beggar on Horseback* (1924), for example, was a hilarious, expressionistic satire about American corporate culture. Kaufman and Moss Hart (1904–61) collaborated on six comedies, including *Once in a Lifetime* (1930), a farce about the early days of talking pictures, the Pulitzer Prize–winning *You Can't Take It with You* (1936), a zany comedy centered on an eccentric family dedicated to the "pursuit of happiness," and *The Man Who Came to Dinner* (1939), a rollicking put-down of celebrity. Kaufman also wrote several plays with the novelist Edna Ferber, most successfully *The Royal Family* (1927), a comedy loosely based on the lives of the Barrymores, and *Dinner at Eight* (1932), a biting satire about the American wealthy class.

Other comedies of the period which merit mention are Ben Hecht (1894–1964) and Charles MacArthur's (1895–1956) *The Front Page* (1928), a rowdy farce about the newspaper business; Bella (1899–1990) and Samuel (1899–1971) Spewack's *Boy Meets Girl* (1935), another comedy about

*Left, Frank Fay (1897–1961) as Elwood P. Dowd in* Harvey. *From Appelbaum,* Great
Actors and Actresses of the American Stage in Historic Photographs. *Courtesy Dover
Publications, Inc.*

*Right, Orson Welles c. 1940s. Courtesy the Flora Ward Hineline Papers, The Ward
M. Canaday Center for Special Collections, University of Toledo Libraries.*

Hollywood; Clare Boothe's (1905–87) *The Women* (1936), a savage satire
about socialites with an entirely female cast; Howard Lindsay and Russell
Crouse's *Life with Father* (1939), a charming comedy about a turn of the century New York family; Mary Chase's (1907–81) Pulitzer Prize-winning
*Harvey* (1944), a fantasy with an invisible six-foot white rabbit as its unlikely title character; and *Arsenic and Old Lace* (1941) by Joseph Kesselring, a
wacky farce about two charming, but murderous old maids. All these comedies enjoyed exceptionally long runs on Broadway. *Life with Father* ran for
eight seasons for a total of over thirty-two hundred performances, the
longest-running drama in the history of Broadway. These plays were also
adapted into popular movies and continue to be revived to the present day.

AT THE TURN of the century, stage direction generally was not held to be a separate, district theatrical craft. Ben Teal (1855–1917) is usually credited with
being the first American to exclusively pursue a career as a stage director.
Beginning in the 1880s, Teal staged over eighty productions, ranging from
spectacular melodramas like *Ben Hur* (1899) to popular musical comedies.
William Seymour (1855–1933), who started his career as a prompter and stage
manager, was also a pioneering specialist in direction who staged dozens of
plays and operas from the late 1870s to the 1920s. But Teal and Seymour were

exceptions. Usually plays were staged by an actor–manager, by the producer, or sometimes by the playwright. As long as plays and their productions adhered to the conventions of nineteenth-century realism, this approach sufficed. Unconventional plays, however, and the scenic approaches of the new stagecraft required special directorial talent to unify the sometimes competing demands of script, *mise-en-scène*, and acting ensemble. Throughout the 1920s and 1930s, the stage director was gradually accepted as a key figure in the process of play production. Directors were increasingly given credit in programs and cited in critical reviews. But most directors continued to wear several hats as producers, playwrights, actors, or designers. Several producers and actor–managers established reputations as skillful, imaginative directors, including David Belasco, Arthur Hopkins, Winthrop Ames, Mrs. Fiske, Eva Le Gallienne, and Walter Hampden. Designer Robert Edmond Jones and playwrights Clyde Fitch, George Abbott (1887–1996), Howard Lindsay, and George S. Kaufman also were recognized for their directorial prowess. By the mid-1920s, a few individuals were establishing reputations primarily, if not solely, as directors. James Light (1894–1964), for example, who began his career as an actor and designer with the Provincetown Players, gradually moved almost exclusively into directing, staging with notable success the premieres of several Eugene O'Neill plays, including *All God's Chillun Got Wings* (1924). Philip Moeller (1880–1958) was a founder of the Theatre Guild and its principal director throughout the 1920s and early 1930s. Rouben Mamoulian (1897–1987), Russian-born and trained at the famed Evgeny Vakhtangov Studio in Moscow, emigrated to the United States in the early 1920s. He made his Broadway debut as the director of *Porgy* (1927) for the Theatre Guild. His staging of O'Neill's sprawling *Marco Millions* (1928) established his special ability to integrate music, drama, and dance into an artistically unified production and he was much sought after to direct musicals. Among his notable directorial credits are the musicals *Porgy and Bess* (1935), *Oklahoma!* (1943), *Carousel* (1945), and *Lost in the Stars* (1949). He also directed a number of outstanding films from the 1930s through the 1950s. Other important American directors of the 1930s and 1940s include Orson Welles (1915–85) whose so-called voodoo *Macbeth* (1935), set in Haiti with an all-black cast, and *Julius Caesar* (1937), set in Mussolini's Italy, were considered daring and provocative; Guthrie McClintic, who, in addition to directing over twenty-five productions starring his wife Katharine Cornell, staged some sixty other productions including Maxwell Anderson's *Winterset* (1935), *High Tor* (1937), and *Key Largo* (1939); S. N. Behrman's *No Time for Comedy* (1939); and Howard Lindsay and Russell Crouse's *Life with Mother* (1948). Margaret Webster (1905–72), although English, spent most of her career in the United States, mainly directing a series of notable Shakespeare revivals, including *Richard II* (1937), *Hamlet* (1938), and *Macbeth* (1941), all featuring émigré English actor Maurice Evans (1901–89). Between 1948 and 1950, she formed a touring company that took Shakespeare's plays to hundreds of cities and towns across America and Canada. In 1950, she became the first woman to direct at the Metropolitan Opera.

Dance was an integral part of American theatrical entertainment since the colonial period, but it was the rise of musical theater in the early decades of the twentieth century that gave rise to the professional choreographer. Ziegfeld directors Julian Mitchell (1854?–1926) and Ned Wayburn (1874–1942), established reputations in the 1910s and 1920s for their dance routines for the choruses in musical revues and comedies. Early musical theater dance drew on period social dances and traditional theatrical dance conventions. Classically trained dancer Albertina Rasch (1869–1962) brought a new sophistication to musical theater dance by incorporating ballet techniques and conventions. Among her notable choreographic credits were the urbane, witty dances for *Lady in the Dark* (1943). Sammy Lee (1890?–1968) and Robert Anton (1902–57) are credited with integrating various dance styles from tap-dancing and jazz dance to modern dance into musical theater dance numbers from the late-1920s to the 1940s. Lee, for example, staged the energetic dance numbers in *Show Boat* (1927), while Alton was responsible for the dances in *Pal Joey* (1940), an eclectic mix of various dance styles from tap to ballroom. Generally, however, dances in musical comedies and dramas were viewed as *divertissements*, separate from the musical plot or characterization. This changed as pioneering modern dance choreographers entered the field of musical theater. Agnes de Mille's choreography for *Oklahoma!* (1943) is usually credited as the first to fully integrate dance with the music, book, and characterization. Other modern dancer/choreographers who contributed to the development of music theater dance include the Russian émigré George Balanchine (1904–83), the founding artistic director of the New York City Ballet, Charles Weidman (1900?–1975), Helen Tamiris (1905–66), Jack Cole (1913–74), and Hanya Holm (c. 1898–1992). Holm's dances for *Kiss Me Kate* were the first musical theater dances to be copyrighted. By the 1940s, choreographers were regularly being credited in programs and were considered to be creative partners along with the director in music theater productions. In 1959, directors and choreographers organized the Society of Stage Directors and Choreographers (SSDC) to represent their interests for contract negotiations with producers.

THEATRICAL CRITICISM IN America at the turn of the century was dominated by an older generation of New York critics who generally represented a traditional and conservative point of view. Chief among these critics were William Winter, critic of the *New York Tribune* from 1865 to 1909, English-born John Ranken Towse (1845–1933), who came to America in 1869 and served as critic of the *New York Evening Post* from 1874 to 1927, Edward Dithmar (1854–1917), critic of the *New York Times* from 1884 to 1901 and English-born Alan Dale (1861–1928) who reviewed for several papers from 1887 until his death. James G. Huneker (1857–1921) also belonged to this generation, but he was more liberal and receptive to new tendencies in theater and drama. Writing for several different papers in the late 1890s and early 1900s, including the *New York Sun* from 1905 to 1917, Huneker was especially active in promoting modern European drama. His *Iconoclasts: A Book of Dramatists* (1905) was a seminal study of Ibsen, Strindberg, Shaw, and other major European dramatists. Huneker's critical style and views encouraged a new generation of critics emerging in the early 1900s. George Jean Nathan (1882–1958) was among the leaders of the younger, progressive critics. Between 1909 and 1923 as drama critic of *Smart Set,* a rising, intellectually oriented periodical, Nathan specialized in ridiculing outmoded theatrical traditions and conventions. In 1918, Alexander Woollcott (1887–1943) was appointed drama critic at the *New York Times.* A founder of the famous Algonquin Round Table, a group of writers who met weekly at the Algonquin Hotel to discuss their work and the course of American culture, Woollcott was a witty and enthusiastic champion of modernism. In the 1920s, Woollcott left the *Times,* but he continued to write theatrical criticism for several leading New York dailies, including the *Sun,* the *Herald,* and the *World.* Burns Mantle (1873–1948) became critic for the *New York Evening Mail* in 1911, moving to the *Daily News* in 1922. An erstwhile advocate of new American drama, Mantle initiated the annual *Best Plays of the Year* series in 1919. At the end of each season, he selected ten plays which he considered the "best," then he published what he called "descriptive synopses" of them. His anthologies also included a comprehensive record of every play produced during the New York season. Mantle compiled and edited this respected series until 1947. (In the 1930s, he published two supplementary volumes, covering 1899–1909 and 1909–19. Under various editors, the *Best Play* series has continued to be published until the present day.) Percy Hammond (1873–1936) was for the last fifteen years of his life the urbane critic of the *New York Tribune.* Stark Young (1881–1963), who reviewed for the influential journal *New Republic* from 1922 to 1947, while simultaneously serving as a contributing editor for *Theatre Arts,* was one of the more intellectual critics of the era. A proponent of the new stagecraft and a friend of both Eugene O'Neill and Robert Edmund Jones, Young also worked in the theater occasionally as a director. In 1926, Brooks Atkinson (1894–1984) became the chief critic of the powerful *New York Times.* He held the post until 1960 and gained a reputation as one of the theater's most literate and humane critics. Joseph Wood Krutch (1893–1970), critic for *The Nation* from 1924 to 1952, was especially esteemed for his thoughtfulness and erudition. By the mid-1920s, there were dozens of full-time professional critics working across America, a result in part of the growing number of daily papers—fifteen in New York, for example—as well as weekly and monthly journals, many of which were distributed nationally. Although producers, playwrights, and actors often complained about critics, they were generally accepted as an important and established part of the American theater and many were widely respected.

THE FIRST SURGE of black musicals—led by Cole and Johnson, and Walker and Williams—had hit Broadway around the turn of the century. By contrast, in the teens, Broadway seemed barren of African–American-created shows, the notable exception being *His Honor the Barber* (1911), directed by S. H. Dudley (1872–1940), with specialty numbers by Ada Overton Walker.

*Left, Bill Robinson. From Appelbaum and Camner,* Stars of the American Musical Theatre in Historic Photographs. *Courtesy Dover Publications, Inc.*

*Right, Paul Robeson as Othello in 1930 London production. Van Volkenberg-Browne Collection, Special Collections Library, University of Michigan.*

Perhaps, as Allen Woll maintains, the black theater was not so much dormant as it was finding its own identity by seeking African–American audiences rather than catering to the white audiences' preconceptions about black entertainment. In 1906, for example, Robert Motts (1861–1912) founded the Pekin Stock Company in Chicago. His success led to the formation of other Pekin Companies in Cincinnati and Savannah. In 1915, actress Anita Bush (1883?–1974) organized a stock company for black actors at Harlem's Lafayette Theatre. The Lafayette Players remained active in New York until 1928 when they moved to Los Angeles where they operated until the Depression forced the company to disband. Members of the Lafayette Theatre who came to prominence included Charles Sidney Gilpin (1878–1930), Dooley Wilson (1886–1953), Abbie Mitchell (1884–1960), and Evelyn Preer (1896–1932). Such efforts heralded expanding enterprises by black artists and entrepreneurs in other cities. Between 1910 and 1930, according to Elizabeth Brown–Guillory, African Americans owned and oper-ated 157 theaters nationwide.

In the 1920s black theater—indeed, black arts and culture in general—achieved renewed visibility in American life. Although the phenomenon became known as the Harlem Renaissance, it spread far beyond New York. A combination of factors might account for this remarkable flowering of talent: blacks who had fought in World War I were eager to prove themselves in other arenas too; many blacks were migrating from the South and forming large urban communities in northern cities; W. E. B. DuBois (1868–1963) was a persuasive advocate of the black arts movement; the black jazz clubs of Harlem (the Cotton Club, Connie's Inn, and others) attracted white patrons, who thus mingled with African Americans in settings without the proscenium arch to serve as artificial barrier. The 1921 Broadway opening of the smash hit all-Negro jazz and blues musical *Shuffle Along* also provided renewed impetus to black theater production even as it initiated the process of integrating the legitimate theater audience. Before *Shuffle Along* black theatergoers had been restricted to the balcony in New York theaters, but—as *Variety* reported—"colored patrons were noticed as far front as the fifth row" at the Sixty-Third Street Theatre. By the end of the decade, racial seating restrictions had largely ceased to exist on Broadway, although they continued in other parts of the country.

*Shuffle Along*, with music by Eubie Blake (1883–1983), lyrics by Noble Sissle (1889–1975), and book by Flournoy Miller (1886–1971) and Aubrey Lyles (1884–1932), ran a remarkable 504 performances. The flimsy plot served as a mere framework for the exhilarating dances and for Blake's memorable score which included "I'm Just Wild about Harry" and "Love Will Find a Way." A number of performers launched their careers with *Shuffle Along*: the beloved Florence Mills (1895–1927), Josephine Baker (1906–75), whose expressive eyes and comic antics set her apart from the rest of the chorus line, Adelaide Hall (b. 1910), and Paul Robeson (1898–1976).

Numerous other black musicals followed in the wake of *Shuffle Along*; these include *Put and Take* (1921), *Strut Miss Lizzie* (1922), *Runnin' Wild* (the show that popularized "the Charleston," 1923), Blake and Sissle's *The Chocolate Dandies* (1924) and *Africana* (1927), in which the wonderful actress–singer Ethel Waters (1900–1977) made her Broadway debut. Of particular note, *Plantation Revue* (1922) marked the producing debut of Lew Leslie (1886–1963), a white producer who mounted a number of revues with all-black casts. The music was often by white composers and the sketches suggested minstrel and burlesque routines, but Leslie's revues offered opportunities for numerous black performers. Leslie's *Blackbirds of 1928* triumphed with Bill "Bojangles" Robinson (1878–1949) singing and dancing "Doin' the New Low-Down," and Adelaide Hall's show-stopping "Diga Diga Doo." It ran for over five hundred performances, one of the longest-running Broadway musicals of the 1920s. Leslie's subsequent editions of *Blackbirds* (1930, 1933, 1939) were less successful.

Most black performers who made it to Broadway and other highly visible venues had worked their way up on the road. After his 1911 fling at Broadway, S. H. Dudley had begun to create his own East Coast chain of theaters offering black entertainment to black audiences. In 1920 Dudley's circuit was absorbed into the white-managed Theatre Owners' Booking Association (TOBA), which, as noted in chapter 5, expanded booking opportunities for black performers, but offered notoriously low salaries and poor working conditions. In 1924 Dudley formed the Colored Actors Union to lobby for reforms. Also instrumental in effecting improvements in black show business was James Albert Jackson (1878–1960), a former minstrel performer who became an influential journalist. From 1920 to 1925, Jackson edited a column (much of which he wrote himself) in *Billboard* on black performance of all varieties. Anthony D. Hill has analyzed the far-reaching effects of "J. A. Jackson's Page."

In 1920, one of the Lafayette's leading players, Charles Sidney Gilpin, won the title role in O'Neill's *The Emperor Jones,* which was produced by the Theatre Guild. Initially presented at the small Provincetown Playhouse in Greenwich Village, *The Emperor Jones* quickly transferred to a Broadway theater where it ran for over two hundred performances. Its success was credited not only to the innovative, expressionistic structure of the play, but also to Gilpin's riveting performance as Brutus Jones, the ex-Pullman porter become dictator. Like many black performers of the day, Gilpin had moved from black minstrelsy to vaudeville to a range of roles in the Pekin Stock Company of Chicago, and then to the Lafayette Players. Between acting engagements, he took various jobs as a printer, barber, and Pullman porter. In 1919, he landed his first Broadway role as the slave Custis in English playwright John Drinkwater's *Abraham Lincoln. The Emperor Jones* was one of the first Broadway productions by a white playwright to feature a black performer. It was not the first; in 1917, three short plays about Negro life by white poet Ridgely Torrence (1874–1950) were presented on Broadway with an entirely black cast. But Gilpin was the first black actor to achieve prominence on Broadway. In 1926, *The Emperor Jones*, again with Gilpin in the title role, was revived for a successful short-run. Talented and experienced, but bedeviled by alcoholism and hampered by limited opportunities, Gilpin never again appeared on Broadway.

The Harlem Renaissance also brought a wealth of legitimate drama. The trailblazer was Angelina Weld Grimké (1880–1958), whose *Rachel* (1916), produced by the NAACP, is the earliest surviving full-length play by a black woman. It influenced other women to write plays, and to use the stage as a forum for attacking racial injustices. An entire category of "antilynching plays" flowed from the pens of women responding to the horrifying lynchings of black men—approximately 1,886 men between 1901 and 1931—in the South. Noteworthy among the black women who wrote plays in the 1910s and 1920s were Georgia Douglas Johnson (1880–1966), Mary P. Burrill (1884—1946), Zora Neale Hurston (1891–1960), Eulalie Spence (1894–1981), Marita Bonner (1899–1971), May Miller (b. 1899), and Myrtle Smith Livingston (b. 1901). The Negro little theatre movement meant that many of their works could get productions by groups like the Howard Players (Washington, D.C., 1921), the Gilpin Players (later called Karamu; Cleveland, 1921), the Ethiopian Art Theatre (Chicago, 1922), and the Krigwa Players (founded by W. E. B. DuBois, 1926). Willis Richardson (1889–1977) also took inspiration from Grimké's *Rachel* and became a prolific writer of one-acts, most of them produced at Howard University. His one-act folk piece *The Chip Woman's Fortune* (1923) was premiered in Chicago by the Ethiopian Art Players, who then took the production to Broadway for a short two-week run

In 1925 *Appearances* by Garland Anderson (1887–1939) became the first full-length serious drama by a black author to be produced on Broadway. Although Anderson had only a fourth-grade education, he believed in hard work and positive thinking. While working as a San Francisco hotel bellhop, he was given a theater ticket; seeing a play inspired him to write one himself. The plot centers upon an honest black bellhop who is falsely accused of rape by a white woman, and this leads to a stirring trial scene. Anderson sent his script to Al Jolson, who helped him get it to a producer. With three black actors in the cast of fourteen, *Appearances*—in the wake of Eugene O'Neill's integrated productions—contributed to the demise of the old Broadway practice of having black characters played by whites in blackface. *Appearances* toured for two years, was revived in new York in 1929, and went on to a London engagement. In contrast to the optimism of *Appearances,* the gritty side of black life was portrayed in *Harlem* (1929) by Wallace Thurman (1902–34). Langston Hughes's *Mulatto* (1935), an intense drama about race relations in the South, enjoyed a 373-performance run on Broadway, followed by a national tour.

The success of Charles Gilpin pried open the Broadway door for other black actors. Rose McClendon (1884–1936), trained at the American Academy of Dramatic Art, had leading roles in Paul Green's *In Abraham's Bosom* (1926) and in Dorothy and DuBose Heyward's all-black cast *Porgy* (1927). *Porgy*, produced by the Theatre Guild, ran for nearly four hundred performances. McClendon appeared on Broadway in numerous plays throughout the 1930s, most notably in the Group Theatre's production of Paul Green's *The House of Connelly* (1931), in Langston Hughes's *Mulatto*, and in Archibald MacLeish's (1892–1982) *Panic* (1935). Richard B. Harrison (1864–1935) achieved widespread fame on Broadway, and later on tour, as De Lawd in Marc Connelly's biblical folk drama *The Green Pastures* (1930). Canada Lee (1907–52) appeared notably in Paul Peters and George Sklar's left-wing antilynching drama *Stevedore* (1934), as Banquo in Orson Welles's celebrated "voodoo" *Macbeth* (1936), as Bigger Thomas in Richard Wright's dramatization of his novel *Native Son* (1941), and as Caliban in Margaret Webster's revival of *The Tempest* (1945).

Paul Robeson was the most prominent black star of the era. A graduate of Columbia University's law school, Robeson's outstanding basso voice and natural acting abilities led him instead to a career as a concert singer and actor. He played Brutus Jones in revivals of *The Emperor Jones* in 1924 and 1925 and the lawyer Jim Harris in O'Neill's controversial *All God's Chillun Got Wings* (1924). In the late 1920s, Robeson went to England where he played in the London productions of *The Emperor Jones* and Jerome Kern's *Show Boat*, in which he triumphed as Joe with his moving interpretation of "Ol' Man River." In 1930 Robeson was cast in a London production of *Othello*, the first African American to play the role there since Ira Aldridge's appearances in 1865. Robeson had no previous experience acting Shakespeare. Critical notices ranged from "magnificent" to "disappointing." But with an excellent supporting cast that included Peggy Ashcroft (Desdemona), Ralph Richardson (Roderigo), and Sybil Thorndyke (Emilia), the production had a respectable six-week run and then briefly toured the Provincial circuit. Returning to New York, Robeson reprised Joe in Florenz Ziegfeld's revised and updated revival of *Show Boat* (1932). In the 1930s, Robeson also achieved international renown as a concert singer. He also showed his range and "star quality" as a featured actor in a number of English and American films, including black film pioneer Oscar Micheaux's *Body and Soul* (1924), film versions of *The Emporor Jones* (1933) and *Show Boat* (1936), and *Song of Freedom* (1936). In 1943, he returned to Broadway as Othello in a very successful production directed by Margaret Webster with Uta Hagen (b. 1919) as Desdemona and Puerto Rican–American actor José Ferrer (1912– 92) as Iago. Robeson was the first African American to play Othello in America with a white supporting cast. Some critics complained about his technical shortcomings as a Shakespearean actor, but overall Robeson and the production were judged a resounding success. With this performance Robeson claimed Othello for future generations of African–American actors and furthered progress toward racial equality and recognition of black acting talent.

Offstage, Robeson was an articulate activist for human rights. He was also asssociated with several leftist political organizations. As he was an outspoken black man in the racist and virulent anti-Communist 1950s, it was inevitable that he would run afoul of numerous reactionary groups, government agencies, and congressional committees. Like many other left-leaning artists of the time, he was eventually blacklisted from working either on Broadway or in Hollywood. When the Department of State revoked his passport, international travel was also impossible. He continued to give concerts, however, often as benefits for social and political causes.

In the late 1950s, Robeson's passport was finally returned and in 1959 he reprised his Othello in a new production in Stratford-upon-Avon. The supporting cast included British actors Mary Ure (Desdemona), Albert Finney (Cassio), and the expatriate American actor Sam Wanamaker (Iago)—another victim of 1950s blacklisting. Once again, Robeson garnered high praise from critics and numerous friends and admirers for his powerful, stately interpretation. Had social conditions been different, Robeson might have become a major stage and screen star. But his achievements as a singer, actor, and political activist were significant and they laid the ground work for the successes of the next generation of African–American actors.

MILLIONS OF IMMIGRANTS, principally from Eastern, Central, and Southern Europe poured into the United States between 1880 and 1930—almost nine million, for example, in the decade 1900–1910. A range of theaters oriented toward these new immigrant communities—Armenian, Hungarian, Polish, and Slovak—flourished in the early part of the twentieth century. Many of

*Left, Rudolph Schildkraut as Shylock. Courtesy of The Museum of the City of New York. Gift of Mrs. Joseph Schildkraut, 65.4.1.*

*Right, Paul Muni in* Counsellor at Law *(1931) by Elmer Rice. From Appelbaum,* Great Actors and Actresses of the American Stage in Historic Photographs. *Courtesy Dover Publications, Inc.*

these theaters were amateur operations, but there were vital professional Italian theaters in New York and San Francisco, and a professional Swedish company toured the Scandinavian communities of the upper Midwest.

The Mexican Revolution (1910–20) and periods of political unrest in Cuba and Puerto Rico from the late nineteenth century on drove numerous Latinos to the United States, swelling the established Spanish-speaking populations of many American cities. In the 1920s, Los Angeles and San Antonio were active centers of Mexican/Hispanic theatrical activity with dozens of permanent theaters, and locally acclaimed performers and playwrights. The large Hispanic population of New York, which included many émigré and expatriate Cubans and Puerto Ricans, was also served by a number of professional theaters from the early 1920s through the 1930s. In addition, Spanish and Mexican companies toured Hispanic communities across the nation, especially in California, Texas and the Southwest, New York, and Tampa, Florida. Hispanic audiences could experience a range of dramas and theatrical entertainments: classical Spanish plays, contemporary Hispanic dramas, *zarzuelas,* musical revues *(revistas),* and variety acts *(variedades). Carpas teatros* (tent theaters) toured rural towns in the southwest with satirical, topical musical farces, a precursor to the Chicano *teatros* of the 1960s.

As a result of the Depression, World War II, and the rise of movies, Hispanic–American theater declined in the late 1930s and 1940s, but after the war it would experience an even greater flowering.

Yiddish theater was one of the largest and more influential of America's ethnic theaters. After the Civil War there were about two hundred thousand Jews in America, most in New York City. Russian persecution, however, forced millions of Eastern European Jews to emigrate between the 1880s and World War I. Yiddish, a Germanic language with elements of Russian, Polish, and Hebrew, had long been the *lingua franca* of Northern and Eastern European Jewry. Jewish immigration coincided with the development of a modern Yiddish culture; indeed, the "father of Yiddish theater," playwright Avrom Goldfaden (1840–1908), was among the first of the new Jewish arrivals, landing in New York in 1887. In dozens of musical folk comedies and dramas, Goldfaden created many of the conventional stock characters and situations that would become Yiddish theater traditions. The first Yiddish theater production in New York preceded Goldfaden's arrival by five years. By the 1890s, led by playwright–producers Joseph Lateiner (1853–1937) and, especially, Jacob Gordin (1853–1909), Yiddish theater was well established in New York. Yiddish theaters sprang up wherever there was a concentration of Jewish émigrés, in Baltimore, Boston, Chicago, and Detroit. New York, however, was the flourishing capital of Yiddish theater, and, as events in Europe took their toll, world Jewish culture. By the 1920s, there were more than a dozen Yiddish theater companies in New York, many located on the Lower East Side, the heart of the émigré Jewish community.

Influenced principally by Goldfaden, early Jewish theater was dominated by slapstick farce, sentimental melodrama, musical comedy, and variety performance. A new generation of Yiddish playwrights, among whom were Gordin, Sholom Asch (1880–1957), Peretz Hirshbein (1880–1948), H. Leivick (Leivick Halper, 1888–1962—whose *The Golem* became a world drama classic), and David Pinski (1872–1959), elevated Yiddish drama to a high literary level. Yiddish low comedy and vaudeville remained popular, but a growing Jewish intelligensia disparaged it as *shund* (trash) theater. In the 1910s and 1920s several Yiddish art theaters emerged, including the Yiddish Art Theatre, founded in 1915 by Maurice Schwartz (1890–1960); the short-lived Jewish Art Theatre (1919–21) founded by actor Jacob Ben-Ami (1890–1977); and ARTEF (Arbeiter Teater Farband or Workers' Theatre Association) organized in 1925. The Yiddish Art Theatre produced a variety of plays from the Yiddish repertoire and Yiddish translations of world classics from Schiller to Shaw. ARTEF was particularly noted for its stylized expressionistic and agitprop productions of modern Yiddish, Russian, and American plays. The Yiddish Art Theatre and ARTEF remained active through the 1930s.

Actors had a place of special prominence in Yiddish theater. Major stars included Jacob Adler (1855–1926) and Boris Thomashevsky (1868–1939), both of whom were regarded as serious artists despite their old-fashioned grandiloquent acting style. Adler in particular, was widely admired beyond the Yiddish-speaking world, and uptown audiences, critics, and actors frequently went downtown to see his performances. Adler's moving rendition of Shylock in a Yiddish adaptation of *The Merchant of Venice* became sufficiently famous that in 1903 he presented it on Broadway in Yiddish with an English-speaking supporting cast. Reportedly John Barrymore studied Adler in Tolstoy's *Redemption* in preparation for his own acclaimed performance. Adler was also famous for the eponymous role in Gordin's *The Jewish King Lear* (1892). But Adler's most important legacy to the American stage were his children, especially Stella whose teaching influenced hundreds of actors for over forty years.

Adler, Thomashevsky, and other actors of their generation worked exclusively in the Yiddish theater, but many Jewish actors of the succeeding generation also achieved prominence on the mainstream Broadway stage. Jacob Ben-Ami, for example, was a member of Theatre Guild and Eva Le Gallienne's Civic Repertory Theatre in the 1920s and 1930s and was a featured player in numerous Broadway productions through 1972. Joseph Schildkraut (1896–1964), son of actor Rudolph Schildkraut (1862–1930), began his career acting with his father on the Yiddish stage, but from the 1920s on he was an often acclaimed Broadway and Hollywood star. Other famous actors who began their careers in the Yiddish theater, but achieved later mainstream prominence, include, in addition to Luther and Stella Adler, Molly Picon (1898–1992), Joseph Buloff (1899–1985), and Paul Muni (1897?–1967), who moved from Broadway to Hollywood, becoming a major film star in the 1930s and 1940s.

Immigration restrictions after World War I, increasing assimilation, and migration to the suburbs contributed to a decline of Yiddish theater. World War II and its aftermath had a devastating effect on the Eastern European wellsprings of Yiddish culture and thus on American Yiddish theater. Yiddish theater was preserved by the Folksbeine (People's Stage), an amateur New York theater company founded in 1915, that continued to present at least one production a year to the present day. Beginning in the 1970s, there was a resurgence of interest in Yiddish theater. Theaters oriented toward Jewish culture mounted traditional Yiddish-language plays and revues, sometimes with simultaneous English translation, or in English-language, or bilingual adaptations. *Kuni-Leml* (Clownish louts, 1984), an adaptation of a Goldfaden musical farce, enjoyed a long Off-Broadway run. Alan Knee's contemporary comedies such as *Second Avenue Rag* (1980) and *Schmulnik's Waltz* (1985) also recapture the spirit of Yiddish theater. The legacy of the Yiddish theater also marks numerous Jewish–American plays from Clifford Odets's *Awake and Sing* (1935) to Paddy Chayefsky's (1923–81) *The Tenth Man* (1959) to William Finn (b. 1952) and James Lapine's (b. 1949) *Falsettoland* (1989) and Herb Gardner's (b. 1934) *Conversations with My Father* (1994).

In the 1920s and 1930s, most of the ethnic theaters that had developed from the 1890s on gradually disappeared as new laws restricted immigration and as immigrant communities became increasingly "Americanized" and assimilated into mainstream English-language culture. World War I put a damper on German cultural expression and even the several long established German-language theaters of New York and Milwaukee ceased to flourish. After World War II, however, new groups of immigrants and new ethnic theaters would enrich the American stage.

BEGINNING IN THE early 1900s, movies became increasingly popular. Estimates vary, but Bernheim, for example, noted that in 1909 there were seven thousand movie theaters nationwide, increasing by the late 1920s to over twenty thousand. He also calculated that in 1925 weekly movie attendance was one hundred thirty million compared to a legitimate theater weekly attendance of 2.3 million. With the arrival of "talkies" in 1927, the appetite for movies grew substantially, first surpassing and then replacing vaudeville and popular-priced stock as the leading form of popular entertainment. By the end of the 1930s, Hollywood was producing over four hundred feature films a year, four times the number of theatrical productions of all kinds available in New York.

As a class, actors were disdainful of the dramatically vapid, technically crude "flickers," and—at least initially—movie salaries, roughly comparable to stock salaries of the time, offered little incentive to compromise one's talent. Still most early silent film stars were stage trained. Douglas Fairbanks (1883–1939) and cowboy star William S. Hart (1872–1946), for example, each had decades of stage experience in stock companies, touring, and on Broadway before they became screen idols. When the nascent film industry was centered near New York, actors might easily divide their time between film shooting and stage performance—and many did. The industry's relocation to Hollywood in the early 1910s, however, made such a schedule difficult. Many actors either moved to Hollywood permanently or forswore the movies, although a rare few would succeed as both stage and screen stars.

As the quality of films and especially their financial rewards increased, few actors could resist a Hollywood offer. In the late 1920s, a few top legitimate stars could command a thousand to fifteen hundred dollars a week (musical and vaudeville stars even more); leading supporting players might make as much as five hundred dollars; common players, one hunded dollars. After his triumph as *Hamlet* in London in 1925, Peters reports that John Barrymore was offered over seventy-six thousand dollars per film. Furthermore, if the shooting schedule went beyond the usual three weeks, he was paid an extra $7,625 per week of additional shooting. By the early 1930s, Barrymore was earning a half-million dollars a year. Even Lionel Barrymore, a lesser star, was earning one hundred thousand dollars a year. Hollywood also held out the lure of national celebrity and a glamorous, sybaritic lifestyle, formerly available only to the wealthy social élite and never to mere players. Numerous promising and experienced actors were gobbled up by Hollywood producers, insatiable for new stars to feature in the hundreds of films they were producing annually.

The Broadway stage, weakened by Hollywood's inroads was further crippled by the 1929–40 Depression. Some companies floundered—the Civic Repertory Theatre and Walter Hampden's company, for example—while others, such as the Theatre Guild, managed to survive. New organizations, such as the Group Theatre, emerged. A few established stars and commercial producers flourished. But overall, the 1930s, with a few exceptions, was a debilitating decade for the American theater.

As Leiter records, the number of new productions dwindled from a high of 280 in 1927–28 to a low of 69 in 1940–41. In 1930–31 in New York, there were 239 productions of all types, including revivals, revues, and puppet plays; in 1939–40, there were 109. At one point, the production failure rate, a relatively high 70 percent in the 1920s, rose to over 80 percent in the early 1930s. Theaters stood empty; some were converted into movie palaces, or along Forty-Second Street, the brightly lit center of the Broadway theater district, into tawdry burlesque houses. With monies for capitalization limited, theatrical producers cut costs, eliminated stars, reduced cast sizes, and skimped on scenery, costumes, or music. Despite new economic realities theatrical unions were reluctant to compromise on hard-won agreements, exacerbating the difficulties of mounting Broadway productions. Touring companies which once numbered in the hundreds each season, shrank to an annual average of twenty during the 1930s. Stock companies dropped from a high of 257 companies in 1926–27, to 200 companies in 1929, to a paltry 5 in 1939. Many of Broadway's established and promising stars opted for the relative financial security of Hollywood, largely immune to the country's economic woes. The quality of many Broadway productions generally spiraled downward, further affecting attendance which in turn led to more failures and even fewer productions.

The extent to which the Depression directly affected the theatrical professions is difficult to determine. Actors as a rule were perennially unemployed. In the late 1920s, there were about ten thousand members of Equity. Data collected by Bernheim during the peak 1927–28 season on six thousand New York performers revealed that very few averaged more than fourteen weeks work in the theater. By 1934, Equity reported that in New York there were five thousand unemployed actors, roughly half its membership. In Hollywood in 1932, according to Flanagan, twenty-two thousand actors registered with casting bureaus, but most were probably inexperienced laymen looking for work as extras in one of the few industries with jobs. One might assume, however, that with the drop in productions, employment opportunities for theatrical artists and workers were even more limited than usual.

The Federal Theatre Project (FTP) was established in 1935 as an arm of the Federal government's Works Progress Administration (WPA), an ambitious program designed to put people to work by creating numerous public works projects. Hallie Flanagan (1890–1969), the director of Vassar College's Experimental Theatre, was appointed national director of the FTP, whose primary goal was to create jobs for thousands of unemployed theater workers, from actors to stage hands. But Flanagan also believed that the FTP could be an instrument to bolster the communal, social value of theater. In contrast to the Broadway model, the FTP was organized as a noncommercial, egalitarian, community-oriented enterprise. Performances were offered to the public at very low cost—tickets ranged from ten cents to one dollar—or for free. Flanagan was particularly interested in fostering new plays and initiatives that encouraged experimentation; but to attract the broadest possible audience, the FTP supported an array of theatrical activities including revivals of classics, historical dramas, children's theater, ethnic drama, vaudeville shows, and circus.

The administration of FTP was divided into a number of semi-autonomous geographical regions. Each region was coordinated by its own director from a producing center located in a regional capitol—Chicago for the Midwest, Los Angeles for the West, and so on. At its height, the FTP had activities in about forty states, employed about thirteen thousand people, and was presenting hundreds of different programs to a total audience of several hundred thousand spectators. It was an extremely complex bureaucracy, but its accomplishments over a relatively short period of time were remarkable. In New York City, for example, which was so large that it was a "region" unto itself, the FTP ran a half-dozen major producing programs, including a Gilbert and Sullivan operetta company, a Yiddish theater company, and a circus.

New York's special Negro Theatre unit housed at Harlem's Lafayette Theatre provided unprecedented opportunities for African–American actors, directors, designers, playwrights and technicians. One of the FTP's first hits was the Negro Theatre company's "voodoo" *Macbeth* (1936). The production featured an all-black cast headed by veteran actors Jack Carter (d. 1963) as the Thane, Canada Lee as Banquo, and Edna Thomas (1886–1974) as Lady Macbeth. Orson Welles, the young, white, and virtually unknown director of *Macbeth*, imaginatively transposed Shakespeare's play from ancient Scotland to nineteenth-century Haiti. *Macbeth* ran for sixty-four sold-out performances at the Lafayette Theatre then moved downtown to Broadway for another eleven performances, after which it was toured to Cleveland, Detroit, Chicago, and other cities. Other outstanding Negro Theatre productions included *Haiti* (1938), about the nineteenth-century Haitian revolutionary Henri Chistophe, powerfully played by Rex Ingram (1896–1969), an actor previously known for his portrayal of De Lawd in the movie version of *Green Pastures* (1936). *Haiti* ran for over 160 performances. Black theater companies were also organized in other cities. By 1939, there were over twenty black companies in operation. One of the notable hits of the Chicago company was Theodore Ward's (1902–83) provocative *Big White Fog* (1938) which examined African–American responses to the political options of the day from Marcus Garvey's nationalistic "Back to Africa" movement to communism.

In 1936, the FTP offered Orson Welles and John Houseman (1902–88)—who was, in partnership with Rose McClendon, the Negro Theatre company's coproducer—their own company to mount productions of classics. Among Welles and Houseman's notable productions were an adaptation of the nineteenth-century farce *The Italian Straw Hat* by Eugene Labiche, which they retitled *Horse Eats Hat* (1936), and Christopher Marlowe's *Tragical History of Dr. Faustus* (1937). Their controversial production of Marc Blitzstein's (1905–64) musical *The Cradle Will Rock* (1937), about ongoing efforts to unionize workers in the steel industry, ran into a series of bureaucratic hurdles resulting in the cancellation of its opening. Balking at what they regarded as artistic censorship, Welles and Houseman opened the production in a scaled-down version and then resigned their FTP positions.

After leaving the FTP, Welles and Houseman founded the Mercury Theatre and produced a number of distinguished revivals of classics, including the aforementioned *Julius Caesar* (1937), set in Fascist Italy, Thomas Dekker's *The Shoemaker's Holiday* (1938), and Shaw's *Heartbreak House* (1938). Houseman would subsequently hold several key positions in the American theater, including artistic director of the American Shakespeare Festival (1956–59), Head of the Drama Division of the Juilliard School of the Performing Arts (1968–76), and founder in 1972 of the Acting Company, a leading American touring company to the present day. In 1939, Welles moved to Hollywood where he established a distinguished reputation as a film actor and director, especially for his work in the remarkable film *Citizen Kane* (1940). But he continued to work off and on in the theater as an actor and director—sometimes brilliantly so—through the 1950s.

New York's Living Newspaper unit was one of the FTP's more original and prominent, but also controversial programs. Living Newspapers were a style of docu-drama inspired in part by postrevolutionary Russian agitprop plays which were designed to promote Soviet cultural and political goals. In 1926, with the support of a John Simon/Guggenheim Memorial Fellowship, Hallie Flanagan, the first woman to win this prestigious fellowship, had studied Soviet theater, and the organization of European theater. In a series of dramatized scenes, supplemented by projected newspaper headlines, charts, graphs, and other documents, radio announcements, film clips, lighting and sound effects, and music, Living Newspapers examined current social problems and issues. Arthur Arent (1904–72) was the most successful Living Newspaper dramatist. His *Triple-A Plowed Under* (1936) traced the history of farm problems from World War I through the 1930s. The title referred to the Agricultural Adjustment Administration (AAA), a program established in 1933 to raise crop prices and farm income. In 1936, however, the Supreme Court declared the AAA unconstitutional, to the consternation of the Roosevelt administration and farmer organizations. The play suggested, in fact, that the AAA for all its good intentions may have inadvertently benefited large farmers, food processors, and commodity speculators more than small farmers and the American consumer. In one scene, farmers and workers are seen trying to organize a new political party to represent their interests. Arent's *Power* (1937) questioned the power of huge utilities companies, including the rural electrification program sponsored by the Tennessee Valley Authority (TVA). *One-Third of a Nation* (1938) attacked New York City's long-standing working-class housing problem. Adapted to local housing conditions, *One-Third of a Nation* was also presented in ten other cities, including New Orleans, Detroit, and Philadelphia. Living Newspapers were enormously popular and effective in educating the public and calling attention to legislative shortcomings.

Although Living Newspapers and provocative productions like *The Cradle Will Rock* represented only a small percentage of the FTP's total theatrical output, they fanned the flames of anti-FTP sentiment. The FTP had its staunch supporters, but from the outset it was sniped at by Equity and commercial producers for "amateurism" and unfair competition. A powerful conservative anti-New Deal element of Congress feared FTP as a hotbed of radical ideas and in June 1939, they succeeded in abolishing the Federal Theatre Project. It is estimated that over the course of its four years, the FTP presented over sixty-three thousand performances of over one thousand productions to a total audience of over thirty million. As the economy slowly improved in 1938–39, thousands of FTP "graduates" were returned to jobs in Hollywood, on Broadway, and in community theaters, many of which were fostered by the FTP. The FTP experiment was short-lived, but its legacy would live on well into the post-World War II era.

The onset of World War II stimulated industrial growth, created jobs, and ultimately broke the back of the great Depression. It would take decades, however, for theater in America to recapture the palmy days of the 1920s.

## MEXICO

While some historians claim that the twentieth century began for Mexico with the revolution in 1910, a number of significant changes did occur at the actual turn of the century. In the capital, the year 1900 saw the wooden sidewalks replaced by cement, the mule-drawn trams replaced by electric ones, the completion of a drainage project to prevent flooding during heavy rains, and the razing of the Gran Teatro Nacional, which held its final performance on October 3, 1900. Demolition of the 1844 building allowed the continuation of the street of El Cinco de Mayo as far as the Alameda. This creation of a long avenue was one of many public works initiatives intended to "Europeanize" the city under the "constitutional dictatorship" of Porfirio Díaz, who served as Mexico's President (with only a brief hiatus) from 1876 to 1911. The government consoled opera lovers for the loss of the city's only theater large enough to present Italian grand opera companies by promising a magnificent replacement theater near the Alameda.

Construction of a new Teatro Nacional began in 1905, but the revolution halted progress until 1919. During the thirty years it took to complete the building, some design modifications occurred, so that the exterior of the three-story Carrara marble edifice is the work of the original Italian architect and sculptors, whereas the interior was completed according to the 1932 plans of Mexican architect Federico Mariscal. A New York firm did the major construction work, and a German company installed the elaborate stage machinery. The rigid, incombustible stage curtain of Tiffany crystal—a mosaic depicting the two volcanoes of the Valley of Mexico—was in place as early as 1910. The inauguration of the long-awaited Teatro Nacional on September 29, 1934 occasioned the formation of a new acting company by María Tereza Montoya and Alfredo Gómez de la Vega to present Juan Ruíz de Alarcón's seventeenth-century masterpiece, *La verdad sospecha*. Soon renamed the Palacio de Bellas Artes (Palace of Fine Arts), the magnificent building incorporates offices, library and art exhibition areas, as well as the centerpiece Teatro de Bellas Artes. Shifting patterns of subsidy resulted in the operation of the theater largely as a rental facility over the next four decades rather than as the permanent home of a resident national company. Moreover, the classics continued to dominate the repertoire as long as the Palacio and its theater were run by the government's old department of fine arts. The 1946 creation of the Instituto Nacional de Bellas Artes (INBA) constituted a complete reorganization of the government's patronage of the arts, resulting in greater innovation as well as encouragement for Mexican artists. Salvador Novo (1904–74) was appointed to head the theater section of INBA. Not until 1972 did the Teatro de Bellas Artes house a permanent Compañía Nacional de Teatro.

The closing of the old Teatro Nacional in 1900 was partially mitigated by the opening of the Teatro del Renacimiento on September 17, 1900. Though relatively small in size, the new theater boasted the first orchestra seating area with a raked floor, a much appreciated amenity in those days of fashionably large ladies' hats. That summer also saw several improvements undertaken at the capital's Teatro Principal: wooden flashings over the entrances, new lighting under the portico, a portion of the lobby converted into a waiting room, and water outlets installed as a fire precaution near the proscenium arch. Other theaters opened in the capital in the early years of the century: the Teatro Lírico (1907), Teatro Colón (1909), Teatro-Circo Xicoténcatl (1912, renamed Teatro Esperanza Iris in 1918). The latter featured a good electric lighting system and fixed seating—that is, seats bolted to the floor—which was still fairly unusual. Located close to the Chamber of Deputies (which was housed in the remodeled former Teatro Iturbide), the Teatro-Circo Xicoténcatl operated under the threat of revocation of its license if any noise should ever disturb the work of the deputies.

To a number of cities elsewhere in Mexico, "porfirismo" brought construction of large flashy theaters, including San Luis Potosí's Teatro de la Paz, Guadalajara's Teatro Degollado, Guanajuato's Juárez, Jerez's Hinojosa, Tlaxcala's Xicoténcatl (with a removable orchestra floor, so that the playhouse could also serve as a cockpit or circus), and Oaxaca's Macedonio Alcalá. Mérida's second Teatro José Peón Contreras—replacing an earlier theater named after the city's eminent poet–playwright (who flourished in the 1870s and died in 1907) and inaugurated in December 1908—boasted an Italian Renaissance-style façade and, according to Henry A. Case, a stage area of over six thousand square feet. Unfortunately, the miscalculated distribution of its two thousand seats meant that companies often played to only half-full houses while many interested ticketbuyers had to be turned away. The problem was the availability of only twelve hundred seats on a per-show basis at popular prices. The remaining eight hundred seats in the eighty boxes were rented by the season to wealthy families who did not attend every performance. Another entertainment facility in Mérida was the Circo Teatro,

*The columned façade of México's Gran Teatro Nacional is seen at the end of the street not long before the building's demolition in 1900, which allowed the continuation of the Calle de Cinco de Mayo.*

*The Palacio de Bellas Artes, across from the Alameda in Mexico D.F., was almost thirty years in construction. Inaugurated in 1934, the imposing structure serves as a center for many arts events. The weight of the three-story Carrara marble exterior is causing the building to sink slightly. Photograph by Felicia Londré.*

*Among the many new theaters constructed during the Porfirio Díaz presidency was the two-thousand-seat Italian Renaissance-style Teatro Peón Contreras in Mérida, a city of sixty thousand in northern Yucatán. It was named after the city's famous nineteenth-century playwright. From Henry A. Case,* Views on and of Yucatán, *1911.*

which could be adapted to various uses. Case reports that bullfights held there on Sunday afternoons in the dry season might be attended by three thousand or so, and that same evening the ring would be filled with chairs for up to eight hundred who would pay considerably lower prices to see a drama or opera there.

The *género chico* (short pieces of lightweight entertainment) continued to dominate Mexican theater. By 1902 five theaters in the capital regularly offered that genre (the Principal, Riva Palacio, María Guerrero—popularly known as "el Tepache"—Apolo, and Guillermo Prieto), while opera found a home at the Teatro Arbeu. Two sisters, "las Moriones," both former singers and both widows of leading theatrical entrepreneurs (José Joaquín Cleofas Moreno and Pedro Arcaraz) exercised tyrannical control over much of the musical entertainment in the capital. In 1902, however, Romualda and Genara Moriones found themselves embroiled in a media-created controversy. For fifty years it had been a tradition to celebrate the one-hundred-performance milestone of any show with a special presentation of it at which the entire cast reversed the gender of their roles. The focus of the brouhaha was the hundredth performance of a *zarzuela* produced by the Moriones, *Free Education* (*Enseñanza libre*), by a very popular and prolific team of *zarzuela* creators, Guillermo Perrín and José de Palacios. Not long before that, police had raided a homosexual dance show, arrested the forty-one people they found there, and consigned them to forced labor in the Yucatán. In response to what was perceived as a fashion for homosexuality, the press then denounced the "disgusting" commemorative performance of *Free Education* and even accused the sisters of audaciously rehearsing a new *zarzuela* titled *The Forty-One.* The Moriones vociferously defended the crossdressed one-hundredth-performance tradition, but apparently scrapped any plans they may have had for a topical *zarzuela*.

A number of legendary performers are associated with the musical theater of this era. Chole Alvarez earned her nickname "La Morronga" when she appeared in *Free Education* and sang a tango called "Morrongo" (slang for "cat"). She triumphed also in the title roles in Aurelio González Carrasco's *The Woman Sergeant* (*La sargenta,* 1903) and Perrín and

*Left, the popular singer–actress Esperanza Iris (1888–1962) and the comic actor Alfonso Castillo are shown in the operetta* Eivalzertraum *(El encanto de un vals) by Oscar Strauss, produced by Esperanza Iris's own operetta company in a season at the Teatro Arbeu in 1911. Courtesy of Biblioteca de las Artes, Centro Nacional de las Artes, México D.F.*

*Right, the petite singer–actress Maria Conesa (1892–1978) enjoyed a sixty-five-year career as a popular favorite. Courtesy of Biblioteca de las Artes, Centro Nacional de las Artes, México D.F.*

*Left, the trio of widows in* Pharaoh's Court *(1910) sing their big number,* "Consejos de las viudas." *From a period illustration.*

*Right, Paco Gavilanes (1860-1924) starred in the title role of* Pharaoh's Court *(1910). From a period illustration.*

Palacios's *Chestnut-Hair* (*La morenita*, 1903). The charming singer Esperanza Iris (1888–1962) began winning acclaim at the Principal in 1901, inaugurated the Teatro Ideal in 1914, and remained a favorite of Mexican theatergoers during her long career. She starred in what was undoubtedly the most popular *zarzuela* of the twentieth century, *Chin-Chun-Chan* (1904). Written by José F. Elizondo and Rafael Medina, and composed by Luis Jordá, *Chin-Chun-Chan* was the first Mexican theater piece to achieve one thousand performances. Audiences demanded reprises of virtually every song, including Iris's comic number with fractured English phrases. The opening lines declared:

| | |
|---|---|
| Because the Yankee is invading, | *Como el yanqui nos invade,* |
| our English had better get good, | *el inglés hay que aprender,* |
| so when we greet our cousins | *para que con nuestros primos* |
| we'll be understood. | *nos podamos entender.* |

In another big number, Esperanza Iris joined several other singers, all equipped with bells, receivers, and antennae, representing *telefonistas* (telephone operators). Manuel Noriega played a harried husband who attempts to escape his wife by making himself up to look Chinese. Thus he is mistaken for the Mandarin millionaire Chin-Chun-Chan. The mistaken identities plot also afforded some excellent material for the comic monologuist Paco Gavilanes. Anastasio "Tacho" Otero (1883–1924) played the *payaso* (bumpkin), which became his signature character type in subsequent shows. *Chin-Chun-Chan* ended with a cakewalk that always brought ovations.

Paco Gavilanes (1860–1924) enjoyed further acclaim for his comic song "Pom-Pom!" in a 1904 *zarzuela*, *Poor Valbuena* (*El pobre Valbuena*). In 1910 he played the title role in Perrín and Palacios's *Pharaoh's Court* (*La corte de Faraón*), from which came "Babylonian Song" ("*Una canción babilónica*"), a tune that soon everyone in the city was whistling. Another popular number (with lyrics which today sound impossibly sexist) was a trio sung by three widows giving advice to brides. From 1907 the beloved singer-actress María Conesa (1892–1978), familiarly known as *la gatita* (little cat), made the Principal her artistic home. For sixty-five years (she was still performing at the age of eighty) that tiny but radiant figure charmed audiences with the carefree manner of her singing and dancing. Similarly, Prudencia Grifell (1880–1960) enjoyed a six-decade career, first starring in *zarzuelas* and later running her own legitimate theater company.

While light musical entertainment remained the staple of Mexican theater throughout the revolutionary period (1910–20), current events got some airing in the theater as performers followed the old practice of interjecting topical asides to the audience. The turbulent decade began auspiciously with a frenzy of theatrical activity to commemorate the centenary of Mexican Independence. On September 16, 1910, every theater offered a Mexican *zarzuela*, patriotic allegory, or singing of the national anthem by a star performer. Less than a month later Francisco Madero's Plan of San Luís Potosí became the rallying manifesto for revolution.

Two dramatists particularly reflected the spirit of the times in plays that applied a naturalistic approach to nationalistic themes. Federico Gamboa (1864–1939) won his greatest renown as a novelist, especially for *Santa* (1903), his widely popular, Emile Zola–influenced story of a prostitute. His 1904 play *Serf's Revenge* (*La venganza de la gleba*) focuses on *mestizos* in a rural atmosphere and prefigures the revolution; it has been signaled as the Mexican theater's first serious denunciation of the sufferings of the peon. Gamboa wrote another rural drama, *Part Payment* (*A buena cuenta*, 1914) and a contemporary tragedy, *Among Brothers* (*Entre hermanos*, 1928). Marcelino Dávalos (1871–1923), a lawyer, was appreciated for his faithful adherence to Mexican subjects along with his social criticism. His plays include *Guadalupe* (1903), *Thus They Pass . . .* (*Así pasan . . .* , 1908), *Marciano's Crime* (*El crímen de Marciano*, 1909), *Tragic Gardens* (*Jardines trágicos*, 1909), *The Old* (*Lo viejo*, 1911), *Eagles and Stars* (*Aguilas y estrellas*, 1916). Virginia Fábregas (1870–1950) starred in several of those plays by Dávalos.

Folkloric elements held a tenuous place in the theater, as exemplified by the work of Rafael M. Saavedra, Luis Quintanilla, and others. Saavedra founded his short-lived Teatro Regional Mexicano in 1921, giving impetus to the construction of an open-air theater in San Juan Teotihuacán for the reenactment of preconquest rituals and dances by natives of the region. A 1922 performance there with the pre-Colombian pyramids as scenic background was attended by the secretary of public education as well as members of the cultural commission, but the government's attempt to administer the project brought its demise. Saavedra turned in 1923 to another initiative, the Teatro Sintético, founded for the purpose of synthesizing a variety of popular performance styles and folk customs. Luis Quintanilla took inspiration from the colorful and internationally renowned Russian cabaret theater, Nikita Baliev's *Chauve-souris* (The bat), and founded his own "Bat" Theatre, the Teatro Mexicano del Murciélago (1924), noting that the *murciélago* was sacred to the indigenous peoples of the Oaxaca region. With the goal of offering "a shop full of toys for the soul," Quintanilla integrated native, rural, and popular elements in a dance-based presentation for the commercial stage. For a 1926 revival, the Teatro del Murciélago joined with La Casa del Estudiante Indígena for a fuller presentation of native musicality.

Regional vernacular theater flourished notably in the Yucatán. The survival there of ancient forms of evangelical drama, including elements of Maya performance traditions, provided a fertile climate for playlets featuring indigenous or *mestizo* heroes and performed in a mixture of languages, often interspersed with song and dance. Because they were largely improvised, only a few of the hundreds of *yucateco* pieces that toured the region from the early nineteenth century have survived. They peaked in popularity in the 1920s. In succeeding years, various government initiatives (notably the Misiones Culturales) promoted theater as an educational tool in rural areas, through the presentation of didactic dramas about proper sanitary habits, crop rotation, and the significance of the Revolution.

The nationalist impulse that grew out of the revolutionary decade also manifested itself in a fashion for Mexican character types. Actor Leopoldo

*Left, Leopoldo Beristáin, shown here with his wife Carolina Aguilar, played Mexican character types and earned the nickname "el Cuatezón." Courtesy of Biblioteca de las Artes, Centro Nacional de las Artes, México D.F.*

*Right, comedian Roberto "Panzón" Soto (1886–1960) may have hampered his stage career by his political outspokenness.*

*Left, comedienne Lupe Rivas Cacho often played opposite Leopoldo "Cuatezón" Beristáin. Courtesy of Biblioteca de las Artes, Centro Nacional de las Artes, México D.F.*

*Right, the baggy-pants comedian Cantinflas (Mario Moreno, 1911–93), "the Mexican Charlie Chaplin," got his start in a carpa and went on to international renown on stage and screen. Courtesy of Biblioteca de las Artes, Centro Nacional de las Artes,*

Beristáin (1875–1948), nicknamed "Cuatezón" (Buddy), led the way with his creation of *el payo* (the rustic lout). Miguel Covarrubias describes this stage character as an "uncouth but naive ranchman always in conflict with new-fangled ideas." Under pressure from the police, Beristáin softened the porno-graphic tone of his early work at the Teatro Apolo, moved to the Teatro María Guerrero and teamed up with Lupe Rivas Cacho, whose *borrachita* (drunk woman) character complemented *el payo* with great verve. The port-ly comedian Roberto Soto (1886?–1960) then developed his *ranchero gritón* (the loud-mouthed rancher). "Panzón" (Big-Belly) Soto long enjoyed a pop-ular following not only for his spontaneous—and often off-color—humor, but for the courage of his biting political commentary from the stage, espe-cially as manifested in his satirical impersonations of the corrupt labor union boss Luis Morones. Joaquín Padavé and Delia Magaña brought their own quick wits to play off of the versatile Soto's range of characterizations. Other beloved performers of the 1920s and 1930s included Amelia Wilhelmy, who specialized in aggressive lower-class women, and the short but agile comic dancer Don Catarino.

Another popular figure was the roguish urban *pícaro* created by Mario Moreno (1911–93), using the stage name "Cantinflas." Son of a postal employee, Moreno preferred dancing and clowning in the streets to attending school. At sixteen he left his agricultural school to join a traveling *carpa* troupe. These tent shows became widespread during the postrevolutionary period. Housing a small stage and some rows of benches for their lively pop-ulist audiences, these canvas tents could be set up quickly on a street corner, vacant lot, or town square. For a few pesos, the diversion-seeker could enjoy a couple of *tandas* or other variety entertainment accompanied by a three- or four-piece "orchestra." Hired as a dancer, Moreno found his stock character by accident when he was asked on a moment's notice to fill in for the compa-ny's announcer. Overcome by stage fright, he garbled his words so badly that someone in the laughter-convulsed audience called out the nonsense word "cantinflas," which he adopted along with the verbal style. Indeed, due to his widespread popularity, the language acquired a new verb, *cantinflear*, mean-ing to talk incessantly but meaninglessly. According to Covarrubias, the genius of Cantinflas lay in his "relentless dribble that never achieves a phrase with sense, . . . a mad, rascally humor of the most surrealist variety." He often played opposite "the devastatingly placid Manuel Medel who hides a true Brighella personality under baggy clothes, shaggy wigs and messy make-up." By 1937 Cantinflas had risen to the status of headliner at the Folies Bergères in the capital. That year he married Valentina Subarev, a *carpa* dancer of Russian parentage. Sometimes called "the Mexican Charlie Chaplin," Cantinflas made forty-nine feature films, beginning in 1940. As a millionaire, he contributed generously to social programs and led many successful fundraising drives to build housing and hospitals for the poor of Mexico City.

After the revolution, a decade of political instability along with the growing popularity of movies took a toll. By 1920 the stages had been removed from at least five theaters in the capital to convert them into movie houses. By 1930 the venerable Teatro Principal opened for business only on Sundays and holidays. Roberto Soto's Compañía Mexicana de Revistas was booked at the Principal on the night it burned down. The Sunday March 1, 1931 performance of the revue *Saturday Calamity* (*El fracaso del sábado*) was just drawing to a close at 12:35 A.M. when the black backcloth went up in flames. Joaquín Pardavé tried to calm the public and was the last performer to stand upon the historic stage. Panic caused many to be wounded in addition to performers and audience members who were killed. The 178-year history of the Coliseo Nuevo–Teatro Principal de México came to an end.

The vitality of Mexican popular entertainment could not mask the relative paucity and mediocrity of legitimate theater in the early part of the century. Actors affected Castilian pronunciation along with an outmoded acting style derived from imitating performers on tour from Spain. Given such falseness, coupled with continuing reliance on the very audible prompter and a repertoire that relied heavily on European melodrama, it was difficult to arouse the general public's interest in serious drama. Even comedy won its biggest audiences with a genre imported from Spain: the slapstick *astrakán*, broad comedy that builds to a mere gag, a genre popularized by Spanish playwrights Pedro Muñoz Seca and Carlos Arniches. Headquarters for that fare was the Teatro Ideal, which in 1913 began operating as La Casa de la Risa

On March 1, 1931, the capital's venerable Teatro Principal was destroyed in a tragic fire that killed a number of theatre personnel as well as audience members. Today the site where a theatre had stood for 178 years is marked only by a small plaque on a wall in Calle Bolivar. Courtesy of Biblioteca de las Artes, Centro Nacional de las Artes, México D.F.

*María Tereza Montoya (1898–1974) shares a scene with Ricardo Mondragón in a 1935 production of* Canadá *by Cesare Griobo Viola, produced by the Gran Compañía de Drama y Alta Comedia María Tereza Montoya at the Teatro María Tereza Montoya. Courtesy of Biblioteca de las Artes, Centro Nacional de las Artes, México D.F.*

*Open-air theater in rural communities like these performances in Tabasco was an educational tool of government-sponsored groups like the Misiones Culturales in the 1920s. Courtesy of Biblioteca de las Artes, Centro Nacional de las Artes, México D.F.*

(House of Laughter), under the successful management of two sisters, Anita and Isabelita Blanch. Meanwhile, the increasingly fossilized audiences for operetta found nostalgic pleasure in the same works that had held the stage since their youth; the six o'clock Sunday "vermouth performances" provided them at least with a weekly social occasion. Most people recognized that the theater was in a deplorable state, especially after a 1921 Mexican tour by Argentine actress Camila Quiroga demonstrated the possibilities of colloquial pronunciation and a higher standard of production. Fortunately, several initiatives in 1922–23 prepared the way for a revitalization of Mexican theater.

The appointment of José Vasconcelos (1881–1959) to the Secretaría de Educación Pública (SEP)—making him, in effect, minister of education and culture from 1921 to 1924—brought a man of letters into an important government position. Vasconcelos created the department of fine arts in 1921; he oversaw the introduction of the Spanish language in remote areas; he promoted literacy by opening hundreds of schools and libraries, providing government subsidy for publication and distribution of classic literature, and creating respect for the teaching profession. Indeed, it was this philosopher–lawyer's enthusiasm for classical Greek drama with its sense of community expressed in large-scale architecture that led to the Misiones Culturales and the construction of some open-air theaters in provincial areas. Recognizing that theatrical performance constituted the only viable means of reaching and communicating with Mexico's huge rural population, the Misiones Culturales involved sending teachers into small communities during the summer to work with the locals on social concerns through dramatic activities. Despite the dubious success of the educational function (aesthetics were never a consideration), the Misiones Culturales prepared the way for a much larger undertaking (see CREFAL in chapter 7) in the 1950s.

In 1923 the outstanding actress María Tereza Montoya (1898–1974) organized a municipally subsidized series of four Mexican plays. From the age of two, Montoya had played speaking roles in melodramas alongside her actor father at the Teatro Hidalgo. Throughout childhood and adolescence she had performed with various companies, and at seventeen formed her own company, which toured the country. After the favorable reception of her company's first season in the capital in 1922, she was emboldened to pursue her dream of presenting Mexican dramatists. She claimed in her memoirs, *El teatro en mi vida*, that she brought to the fore almost all of the Mexican playwrights of that era. The obstacles facing such a venture are evident in her listing of the 513 plays in which she performed between 1900 and 1956, of which—according to Guillermo Schmidhuber's tally—only 83 are Mexican, and most of them came after 1938.

Another step forward in 1923 occurred with the formation of the Unión de Autores Dramáticos (UDAD). That year also saw the emergence of the Grupo de Siete, a group of seven dramatists whose nationalistic ideals prompted them to turn to the European avant-garde as a source of inspiration for renewing Mexican drama; thus the seven were dubbed "los Pirandellos," and some critics waggishly referred to them as "seven authors in search of an audience." José Joaquín Gamboa (1878–1931) had seen a number of his plays produced between 1899 and 1908, then left theater and journalism for a diplomatic career. His association with the Group of Seven marked a second phase in his playwriting, a realistic period during which his best works were *The Devil Is Cold* (*El diablo tiene frío,* 1923), *The Revillagigedo Family* (*Los Revillagigedo,* 1925), and *The Same Case* (*El mismo caso,* 1929). A third phase comprised such abstract and symbolic dramas as *She* (*Alucinación; o Ella,* 1930) and his masterpiece *The Gentleman, Death, and the Devil* (*El caballero, la muerte y el diablo,* 1931). Víctor Manuel Díez Barroso (1890–1930) betrayed a Pirandellian influence in *Control Yourself* (*Véncete a ti mismo,* 1925). His highly original work, often dealing with the subconscious in a melodramatic or farcical vein, culminated in *He and His Body* (*El y su cuerpo,* 1930). The distinguished scholar Francisco Monterde (1894–1985) wrote over twenty plays, including *Proteus* (*Proteo,* 1931). Carlos Noriega Hope (1896–1934) is remembered for the wit and irony of plays like *Miss Goodwill* (*La señorita voluntad,* 1925) and *A Flapper* (*Una flapper,* 1925). Ricardo Parada León (1902–72) focused on manual laborers in plays of considerable power, beginning with *Agony* (*La agonía,* 1923) and *The Slave* (*La esclava,* 1923). The Lozano García brothers, Lázaro (1899–1973) and Carlos (b. 1902), wrote six plays in collaboration, all strongly nationalistic, beginning with *Woman at Last* (*Al fin mujer,* 1925).

It is possible, as Guillermo Schmidhuber believes, that the plays of the Group of Seven might never have reached the stage had it not been for a collaboration with la Comedia Mexicana. The origin of this seminal producing group is unclear, though playwright Amalia González Caballero de Castillo Ledón (1898–1986) is credited as founder. The year 1929 marked the Comedia Mexicana's first theater season that was publicized under that name; however, the rubric was in place as early as 1922 when the organization presented a two-month season of five Mexican plays at the Teatro Lírico. Similar seasons occurred at various playhouses in the capital in 1923 (Montoya's contribution), 1925 (a season presented under the name Pro Arte Nacional), 1926, 1929, 1931, 1936, 1937, and 1938. During those nine seasons (which might be grouped into two series, 1922–26 and 1929–38), the Comedia Mexicana produced works by other dramatists besides the Group of Seven, and they included a number of women: Teresa Farías de Isassi (1878–1930), Catalina D'Erzell (1897–1950), Concepción Sada (1899–1981), and María Luisa Ocampo (1908–74). The latter, five of whose plays were presented by the organization, funded part of the 1926 season with her lottery winnings. Another outstanding author, Carlos Díaz Dufoo (1861–1941) added dramatic writing to his literary endeavors when the Comedia Mexicana produced his first play *Father Merchant* (*Padre mercader*) in 1929, and it became the first Mexican work to run one hundred consecutive performances.

Several experimental theater groups emerged after 1928, beginning with the Teatro de Ulises, organized by heiress and playwright Antonieta Rivas Mercado (1900–1931). Having traveled in Europe, she was eager to promote

*Left, Julio Bracho founded several small theater groups in the 1930s. He was inter-ested in producing the classics. Courtesy of Biblioteca de las Artes, Centro Nacional de las Artes, México D.F.*

*Right, Salvador Novo (1904–74) was a poet, playwright, actor, journalist, art critic, and scholar. He was a founder of Teatro Ulises as well as of the School of Dramatic Art of the National Institute for Fine Artes (INBA), where he taught and, from 1946 to 1952, directed the theater section. Courtesy of Biblioteca de las Artes, Centro Nacional de las Artes, México D.F.*

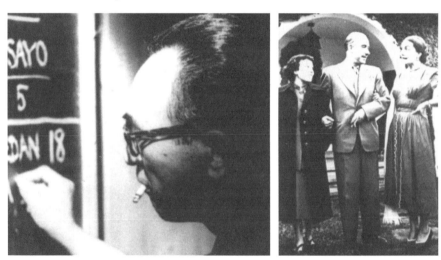

*Left, the Japanese-born director Seki Sano (1905–66) gained theater experience in the Soviet Union in the 1930s, then came to Mexico, where he influenced a generation or more of theater practicioners. Courtesy of Biblioteca de las Artes, Centro Nacional de las Artes, México D.F.*

*Right, Rodolfo Usigli (1905–79) is a seminal figure in the modern Mexican theater. He is shown here with actress Argentina Casas. Courtesy of Biblioteca de las Artes, Centro Nacional de las Artes, México D.F.*

the kind of theatrical experimentation she had seen abroad. She returned to Mexico to work with Xavier Villaurrutia (1903–50) and Salvador Novo (1904–74), who were publishing *Ulises*, a small journal of avant-garde arts. They then founded a theater of the same name. This group emphasized a conceptual approach to theater as opposed to the Group of Seven's nationalistic agenda. During its short existence (until the suicide of Rivas Mercado in Notre Dame Cathedral in Paris), the Teatro de Ulises presented six plays, four of them French, as well as the first Eugene O'Neill play performed in Mexico. The writers affiliated with Ulises, many of them poets and translators, also acted and directed nonprofessionally. Many theater historians now signal Ulises as the key endeavor of the 1920s leading to the revitalization of Mexican theater. According to Frank Dauster, Ulises was "exotic, cosmopolitan, an opening to world theatre."

Following the trail blazed by Ulises, Julio Bracho founded in 1931 el Grupo Escolares de Teatro in order to explore directorial approaches. With a small government subsidy, the Escolares staged J. M. Synge's *Riders to the Sea*, Strindberg's *The Stronger*, and one Mexican play, Francisco Monterde's *Proteus*. Bracho later founded another experimental theater company, Trabajadores de Teatro. By 1936, with his Teatro Universitario, Bracho was producing Greek tragedy and putting the focus on the actor. Yet another of Bracho's projects was la Compañía Dramática Andrea Palma, which has been signaled as the first experimental theater group from the capital to tour the provinces.

Building upon the work of both the Teatro de Ulises and the Escolares, the Teatro de Orientación announced its discontent with the "inertia, vulgarity, and decadence of commercial shows." Under the leadership of playwright Celestino Gorostiza (1904–67), the group obtained substantial funding from the office of public education and the Institute of Fine Arts. (As Schmidhuber notes, one facet of the lasting impact of the Orientación was the tradition of government subsidization for noncommercial theater). During its first two seasons, July to December 1932 and spring 1933, the Orientación presented only foreign plays in translation (including O'Neill, Jean Cocteau, Molière, Chekhov, Shakespeare, Synge), but the third season, autumn 1933, included two Mexican plays: *Appearance of a Lie* (*Parece mentira*) by Xavier Villaurrutia (1903–50) and *School of Love* (*La escuela del amor*) by Gorostiza. The last two seasons, 1938 and 1939, were presented under the direct sponsorship of the department of fine arts. The complete production record of this extremely influential company comprised twenty-six plays, seven of which were by Mexican authors. In 1943 Gorostiza and Villaurrutia together founded the state-subsidized Teatro de México, which lasted three seasons, producing mostly Mexican plays. Xavier Vallaurrutia's own plays, especially his early ones of the 1920s and 1930s, are among the most experimental of the period.

Less known and shorter-lived but more experimental than the Teatro de Orientación, the Ciclo Post-Romántico presented eleven plays in 1932–33, notably three German expressionist works by Georg Kaiser and Ernst Toller.

The Teatro de Ahora, founded in 1932 by two lawyers, Mauricio Magdaleno (1906–86) and Juan Bustillo Oro (1904–89), attempted to infuse dramatic explorations of Mexican social reality with revolutionary fervor. Four plays comprised Ahora's only season (February–March 1932), including Magdaleno's dramatizations of aspects of the revolution, *Emiliano Zapata* and *Pánuco 137*, and Bustillo Oro's portrayal of Mexican immigrants in the United States (according to Schmidhuber, the first Mexican play on a *chicano* theme), *Those Who Return (Los que vuelven)*. Widely perceived as crudely didactic, the plays failed to attract audiences, and the disillusioned authors abandoned the theater.

The international recognition accorded Mexican painters José Clemente Orozco (1883–1949), Diego Rivera (1886–1957), and David Siqueiros (1896–1974) seemed to provide an impetus for scene designers. Indeed, Orozco and Rivera both painted drops for ballets based on Mexican history. Other important scenic artists of the period include Manuel Rodriguez Lozano, Rufino Tamayo, Carlos Gonzalez, Julio Castellanos, and Gabriel Fernandez Ledesma. Agustín Lazo studied in Paris and brought a French influence to his costume designs for the Mexican stage.

One amateur group contributed to the theatrical ferment of those years. In 1938 the electrical workers' union, SME (Sindicato Mexicano de Electristas), began producing plays in a private theater. Its first season of five plays included one by Villaurrutia. In 1939 the SME began a joint venture with the Japanese-born director Seki Sano (1905–66), who had arrived in Mexico that year. As head of his own theater company in Tokyo, Seki Sano had been the youngest director in Japan. During the 1930s he traveled and studied in various countries, including the United States and Russia. In Moscow he trained under Stanislavski and worked for five years as an

*In 1964 Wilberto Cantón revived Rodolfo Usigli's* El gesticulador *at the Teatro Fábregas. This moment from the second act features actors Manuel Zozaya and Enrique Aguilar. Courtesy of Biblioteca de las Artes, Centro Nacional de las Artes, México D.F.*

*The original production of Rodolfo Usigli's* The Imposter *(El gesticulador) at the Palacio de Bellas Artes in 1947 was directed by Wilberto Cantón. Courtesy of Biblioteca de las Artes, Centro Nacional de las Artes, México D.F. Courtesy of Biblioteca de las Artes, Centro Nacional de las Artes, México D.F.*

assistant to the great Russian director Vsevolod Meyerhold. With the SME in Mexico City in 1939, he founded the Teatro de las Artes, dedicated to a populist ideal: "theater of the people for the people." Seki Sano continued working with the SME until 1941, by which time he had many other projects. With painter Gabriel Fernández Ledesma and choreographer Waldeen Falkestain, he mounted the theatrical ballet *La coronela* by Silvestre Revueltas in 1940. That year he also founded a studio of dramatic arts. During his years as a teacher of acting at the Palacio de Bellas Artes, he worked with over sixty-five hundred students of various nationalities. While he clearly had a lasting impact on the theater of Mexico, he also made enemies by his outspoken criticism of its problems.

Seki Sano's work with SME inspired a number of other groups, including Proa, which also enjoyed SME support. Directed by José de J. Aceves, Proa lasted from 1942 to 1947, producing a mixture of Mexican and contemporary foreign plays. La Linterna Mágica, another experimental company aided by SME, began in 1946, under the direction of Ignacio Retes, to seek its own resident dramatist. After three seasons of producing classic, foreign, and Mexican plays, it allied itself with playwright José Revueltas. Jebert Darién, a disciple of Seki Sano, teamed with actress Lola Bravo in 1947 to found the Teatro de Arte Moderno.

Rodolfo Usigli (1905–79) has been hailed as the redeemer of Mexican theater, the one who made it his mission to lead into the modern period a theater that had not been perceptibly touched by the revolution. Although many did contribute to the theater's long-overdue revitalization, the standard wisdom—as indicated by Peter Beardsell—is that Usigli's "contribution was both unique and—in a crucial period—paramount." As a journalist, Usigli began publishing his commentaries on theater in 1931. His sharp criticism—coupled with enthusiasm for what the theater could be—inspired and influenced the postrevolutionary generation, especially with the publication of his books: *Mexico in the Theatre* (*México en el teatro*, 1932), *Development of Mexican Theatre* (*Caminos del teatro en México*, 1933), and *Itinerary of a Dramatist* (*Itinerario del autor dramático*, 1941).

It was as a dramatist that Usigli made his greatest impact. He had already written several plays when, in 1935, he and Xavier Villarrutia were awarded scholarships to study under George Pierce Baker at Yale University. One of Usigli's plays that grew out of that opportunity, *The Imposter* (*El gesticulador*, 1937) stands as the single most significant work in twentieth-century Mexican theater. Subtitled "a play for demagogues, with epilogue on the hypocrisy of the Mexican, twelve notes, and an essay on the present state of dramatic poetry," the provocative piece finally reached the stage, at the Palacio de Bellas Artes in May 1947, fully ten years after it was written. Despite the popular success of the production, *El gesticulador* succumbed to pressure from authorities and closed after a two-week run. It was published in 1948. The play's title character is a mediocre history professor who takes advantage of the fact that his name, César Rubio, is the same as that of a presumed-dead revolutionary hero. Rubio's assumption of an identity he has not earned leads to a series of deceptions within his family and in the larger society, and ultimately costs him his life. The play operates on various levels—realistic, allegorical, metatheatrical—to probe human and national weaknesses.

During the 1930s Usigli also taught history at the Universidad Nacional Autónoma de México, and he translated and directed plays for the Teatro de Orientación. In 1940 he founded the Teatro de Medianoche (named for its midnight curtain time) with the intention of developing a theater audience for high-quality productions of Mexican and international plays. He also declared his refusal of government subsidy, planning to operate entirely on box-office proceeds. The experiment lasted one three-month season. From 1944 to 1946 he served as Mexican cultural attaché in Paris. Among his early plays in addition to *El gesticulador* are *The Apostle* (*El apóstel*, 1931), *Middle Class* (*Medio tono*, 1937), *Women Don't Work Miracles* (*La mujer no hace milagros*, 1939), *The Family Dines at Home* (*La familia cena en casa*, 1942), and *Another Springtime* (*Otro primavera*, 1945). Usigli's commitment to present Mexican reality on stage informed all thirty-nine of his plays, the best-known of which—apart from *El gesticulador*—were written after 1945.

## THE CARIBBEAN

Although Cuba finally achieved its independence from Spain in 1898 and was proclaimed a republic in 1902, a series of corrupt leaders retarded its cultural development. The public demanded nothing more than light, escapist entertainment. Havana's Teatro Alhambra (1900–1934) presented a steady stream of colorful, somewhat risqué musical revues and came to symbolize popular culture for male audiences in those decades. The Alhambra's impresario, Federico Villoch (1868–1954), wrote close to four hundred works, often satirical and featuring character types descended from the *bufos habaneros*. The *bufo* settled into a formula, according to Willis Knapp Jones, by which "the quick-witted and unscrupulous Negro, frequently aided by his mulatto girlfriend, got the better of a stupid and parsimonious Galician immigrant, usually the owner of a grocery store." Other characters might include a Galician woman, La Gallega, and a backwoods farmer named Liborio. Cuban *zarzuelas*—notably those composed by Ernesto Lecuona (1896–1963)—peaked in the early 1930s.

A society to promote serious theater, the Sociedad del Fomento del Teatro, founded in 1910 and headed by the outstanding actress Luisa Martínez Casado (1860–1926), commemorated that year's eighth anniversary of the Cuban republic with productions of plays by nineteenth-century Cuban dramatists Gertrudis Gómez de Avellaneda and José Martí at the old Teatro Tacón. Although the Sociedad soon failed, one of its members, José Antonio Ramos (1885–1946), emerged as the leading Cuban playwright during a career of nearly four decades, 1906–44. Interested in new dramatic forms and social themes, Ramos absorbed elements of Ibsen and Pirandello, but took his subjects from Cuban life and politics. His major work, *Tremor* (*Tembladera*, 1917), focuses on a rural family while examining issues like foreign land-ownership and exploitation of the poor. It won the prize for literature that year and is considered to be one of the best Cuban plays of all time. Ramos continued to question received wisdom in later plays like *In the Hands of God* (*En las manos de Diós*, 1935). Other theatrical initiatives included the Teatro la Cueva, founded in 1936 by playwright Luis A. Baralt (1892–1969), the Teatro Cubano de Selección (1938), the Patronato del Teatro (1942), the politically oriented Teatro Popular (1943) for audiences of workers, and the influential though short-lived Academía de Artes Dramáticas (ADAD, 1945).

Puerto Rico, ceded to the United States by Spain under the terms of the Treaty of Paris (1902) after the Spanish–American War, saw various theatrical currents in the early decades of the century: political theater, especially dealing with the problems of the working class; poetic drama; drama incorporating folkloric elements along the lines of Spanish *costumbrismo*; and realistic plays influenced by Ibsen and Shaw. Puerto Rican theater began to find its identity in 1938 as a result of a playwriting competition sponsored by the Ateneo Puertorriqueño, which then produced the three winning plays. Emilio Belaval (1909–72), president of that cultural association, soon founded his own theater company, Areyto (1940–41), which premiered four Puerto Rican plays. Belaval's own plays incorporate departures from realism while pointing up the failures of modern life. Early plays by Manuel Méndez Ballester (b. 1909) came to the fore in both of Belaval's projects: *The Cry of the Furrows* (*El clamor de los surcos*) at the Ateneo, and *The Dead Season* (*Tiempo muerto*, 1940) at Areyto. Méndez Ballester continued to figure prominently in Puerto Rican theater through the 1960s.

## CANADA

Ever since the 1825 opening of the first Theatre Royal, Montreal had been an important center for English-language professional theater, while French-language theater remained in the hands of amateurs. The 1890s brought an unprecedented explosion of theatrical activity in the city, including a burgeoning professional francophone theater, to the extent that the period from 1890 to 1914 has been called "the golden age of Montreal theater." According to Jean-Marc Larrue, Montreal had never had more than three permanent playhouses at any given time before 1890, but by the end of the decade there were ten, all devoted to professional theater. Similarly, there had never been more than one local professional company at a time, but between 1892 and 1899 there were eight such troupes, five of them francophone. During the 1890s the number of performances (11,321) as well as the number of different titles presented (1,899) nearly doubled the corresponding figures for the 1880s.

The Empire Theatre, a much-remodeled and renamed facility owned and managed by anglophones, can be signaled as the first permanent Montreal theater to present an exclusively francophone repertoire, beginning in 1893. Although troupes of both languages had been booked into an earlier incarnation of the building (when it was called Lyceum Opera House), the particular success of the Compagnie Franco-Canadienne, bolstered by its star performer Blanche de la Sablonnière, provided the incentive for the French programming. An imported French opera company played there for three seasons (1893–96), but the third season saw a drastic decline in receipts, due to a downturn in the local economy as well as to another wave of clerical opposition. On February 11, 1896 the French performers refused to perform, explaining to the waiting audience that they were striking because none of them had been paid for forty days. A citizens' committee soon formed to help out the artists and pay their passage back to France. The grateful troupe gave two farewell performances in Sohmer Park, a popular site for band concerts and variety entertainers. In 1896, the Empire was renamed Théâtre Français, but, ironically, it now housed an anglophone resident company. With Beryl Hope as its popular featured actress, the Théâtre Français troupe continued to attract good audiences until the building burned down in 1900.

Le Monument National, constructed as a headquarters for the Montreal branch of the Société Saint-Jean-Baptiste, opened in 1894. Its second-floor theater (capacity 1,496) was used for a variety of attractions from popular lectures to opera. Indeed, the anglophone troupe from the Théâtre Français performed there on the evening after the fire destroyed their playhouse. Of all the amateur groups that used the Monument National, perhaps the most significant for the development of French–Canadian theater was a project called "Les Soirées de famille" (Family Evenings), initiated in November 1898 by Elzéar Roy, a professor at the Collège Saint-Laurent. Building upon the elocution courses offered for young people at the Monument National, Roy won the clergy to his view that the tasteful performance of carefully chosen, high quality Canadian and French plays would delight, instruct, and edify both the young performers and their family audiences. "Les Soirées de famille" presented eighty-five programs—standard, Church-approved comedies and melodramas—during its three-year existence. However, increasing competition from touring professional companies that presented the same repertoire with greater expertise brought the demise of the "Soirées de famille" in May 1901. A number of those who had participated in the performances went on to outstanding careers in public life. And at least one professional theater career was launched: Juliette Béliveau (1890–1975) made her stage debut there at age ten and was dubbed "la petite Sarah" by Louis-Honoré Fréchette. The petite francophone actress maintained a strong following throughout her many featured engagements in operetta, legitimate drama, music hall, film, radio, and television.

Recognizing the need for a resident professional francophone company in Montreal, two Frenchmen who taught elocution and worked with "Les Soirées de famille" founded the Théâtre des Variétés. Antoine Bailly (who took the stage name Antoine Godeau, as it was not seemly for a professor to be identified as an actor) and Léon Petitjean recruited local talent, among whom was a young man who had just completed his law degree but readily succumbed to the lure of the stage: Joseph Archambault (1871–1950). Using the stage name Palmieri (taken from a character he played in a melodrama), Archambault enjoyed a long successful career in francophone theater. Godeau too would become a leading actor–manager. Opening in 1898, about a week after the first "Soirée," the Variétés quickly earned a reputation for artistic quality despite the company's cramped facilities in a small second-floor room. The Théâtre des Variétés lasted only until August 1900, but in its first twelve months it had presented 289 performances of forty-two different plays. Its end came when the Théâtre National opened on August 12, 1900 and absorbed the leading artists from the Variétés.

Julien Daoust (1866–1943) was the driving force behind the opening of the Théâtre National, the first Montreal playhouse purpose-built for French-language theater. Located at the corner of Sainte-Catherine and Baudry Streets, the building designed by architect Albert Sincennes functioned as the center of francophone cultural life until World War I curtailed the visits of French troupes even as local actors answered the call to arms. Daoust had already established himself as an actor, having toured and performed for several seasons in the United States, and he had directed an amateur production of *Cyrano de Bergerac* at the Monument National. At the Théâtre National, Daoust continued to act and direct as well as to write a number of successful melodramas on religious subjects, but he quickly turned over the management to Georges Gauvreau. In September 1900 Gauvreau appointed Paul Cazeneuve (1871–1925) as artistic director. Born in France and raised in the

*French–Canadian theatergoers long depended upon school productions of classic plays like this 1875 production of* Antigone *at the Petit Séminaire de Montréal. Courtesy of André Bourassa.*

*Montreal's Academy of Music, opened in 1875, served as a center for francophone performances early in the twentieth century. From Franklin Graham,* Histrionic Montreal, *1902.*

*Joseph Archambault (1871–1950) took the stage name Palmieri and was one of the leading francophone actors of the twentieth century. From Palmieri,* Mes Souvenirs de théâtre.

United States, Cazeneuve had toured with stars like Edwin Booth and Helena Modjeska; thus during a Montreal engagement he had come to Gauvreau's attention. Cazeneuve's success at the Théâtre National rested partly on his canny choice of repertoire to please his clientele. His translations–adaptations of American stage hits even succeeded in drawing audiences from the anglophone theaters. His gradual introduction of French psychological dramas may have helped to refine his audience's tastes, but the public's love of action melodrama scarcely diminished. Indeed, the company's stage villains— Palmieri, Elzéar Hamel, and Frédéric Lombard—were popularly dubbed "Les Trois Poignards" (The Three Daggers). Besides Palmieri, Godeau, Daoust, Hamel, Lombard, and Cazeneuve himself, outstanding resident actors during the golden years of the Théâtre National included Blanche de la Sablonnière and Jean-Paul Filion. Their grueling schedule involved matinee and evening performances, weekly changes of bill, and only one week of preparation time to rehearse and stage each new four- or five-act play. In Filion's nostalgic recollection:

> Ah! how we worked in those days! There was rehearsal every morning except Monday and Thursday, and often at night after the performance. We performed every afternoon and every evening, except Friday afternoon. Thus, on Tuesday there was rehearsal from 9:30 to 12:30, matinee and evening performances, then night rehearsal; on Wednesday, blocking; Thursday morning off; Friday morning, rehearsal with prompter; Saturday morning, rehearsal; then Sunday evening, dress preview. Opening night was every Monday.

When Cazeneuve left the Théâtre National in 1910, it had offered over four thousand performances of three hundred different titles in 405 weeks.

While the Théâtre National pleased the general public, others hoped to set a higher tone at the Théâtre des Nouveautés, which opened in February 1902. Its organizers, the Société Anonyme des Théâtres, explained their purpose: "Until now most Montreal theaters have devoted themselves to melodrama and vaudeville. These genres, melodrama particularly, accommodate the tastes and inclinations of the masses but cannot completely fulfill the needs of the cultivated audience. We have therefore decided to tackle the great works." One of the directors, Gonzalve Désaulniers, even voyaged to Paris to engage some players. An orchestra provided musical underscoring for the mainpiece, accompanied the one-act operetta offered as an afterpiece, and played intermission music. Although the bill might change a couple of times a week, the only matinee was on Saturday. Plot synopses printed in English in the programs are evidence of a multicultural audience. Thirteen-year-old Juliette Béliveau joined the troupe, which was regularly replenished with French artists.

The closure of the Nouveautés in May 1908 resulted from a showdown with Monseigneur Bruchési, archbishop of Montreal, after a series of provocations on both sides. The problems might be traced back to 1906 when puritan groups in the Maritimes and Ontario formed a Lords' Day Alliance to agitate for a federal law prohibiting business dealings and entertainment events that charged admission on the Sabbath. Monseigneur Bruchési demonstrated his support by issuing to the clergy of his diocese (February 6, 1906) a formal interdiction of Sunday theater and concerts "even for charity." However, the proposed law was considerably softened as a result of protests from the people of Quebec who balked at giving up their Sunday pleasures and from merchants who argued for the salutary ripple effect that the theater had on the entire economy. Two developments provoked Monseigneur Bruchési to stronger action on the issue. One was a journalistic comment, cited by Laflamme and Tourangeau, that "this law won't have much effect in the province of Quebec." The other was Ernest Ouimet's opening of his Ouimétoscope, Montreal's first cinema. The idea of a fully darkened auditorium was likened to "a night school run by the devil." On November 25, 1907, the archbishop renewed and reinforced his earlier edict, with added injunctions against the cinema:

> These presentations and various attractions must be discontinued on Sundays: we issue this express order to all under our jurisdiction. On other days, we expect that morality will be scrupulously respected, and that only scenes beyond reproach will be played before our theatregoers. . . . Everything we have said about the theaters must apply equally to this new mode of performance [cinema]. Those in charge must remember their duty and their responsibility. It is also crucial that their auditoriums never be plunged into total darkness and that serious vigilance prevent all disorderliness and all danger.

Of even greater consequence for the theaters than the question of Sunday performances was the perennial issue of censorship of the repertoire and of newspaper advertising of theater. Company managers understood the need for caution in the selection of plays: only one in ten met the standards deemed appropriate for the *Canadien* public. Even then, it was common practice to cut and rewrite words, phrases, and whole passages, to the point that one newspaper editorialized: "We must object to the pruning of play texts, to this or that person reworking a masterpiece." In September 1906, the Théâtre des Nouveautés made the mistake of presenting *Le Bercail* (The fold, 1904) by Henry Bernstein, a prolific and successful dramatist of Paris boulevard theater. This was a naturalist drama in which adultery figures as a plot element. Monseigneur Bruchési met privately with the theater managers and elicited their promise never again to present an immoral play. The following spring, however, the visit of Rose Syma, a rising star in the Paris theater, occasioned the staging of another naturalist drama by Bernstein: *La Rafale* (The squall, 1905). Reacting to "a play that is merely a display case of base sensuality and a defense of suicide" as well as to the effrontery of presenting it during Holy Week, the archbishop issued an edict (March 30, 1907) explicitly forbidding "all Catholics in our diocese to attend performances at the Théâtre des Nouveautés." Although the managers agreed to submit to a censorship committee in return for the lifting of the interdiction, the damage had been done; the faithful abandoned the theater. The Théâtre des Nouveautés eked out another year, but finally succumbed to financial losses and closed.

Two additional Montreal theaters exhausted Monseigneur Bruchési's patience. The Theatre Royal drew attention to itself by some suggestive advertising: "The path to pleasure," "Theatre lovers will see the other side of Paris at the Theatre Royal," "Pretty and charming women abound in this troupe." In a missive dated May 10, 1909, the archbishop likened himself to a father who sees his children's virtue exposed to certain danger, and thus he forbade the Catholics of his diocese to attend any performance at the Theatre Royal. Not long after that, actor–director Paul Marcel began putting together a company of francophone actors, which he installed in Montreal's Academy of Music. Marcel met with the archbishop and promised that his choice of plays would be irreproachable. On that basis, Marcel was able to win subscribers. Opening September 6, 1909, the "Comédie-Française de Montréal" garnered critical praise for the talents of its actors. For two weeks that month they performed only one-acts, leaving the rest of the bill for a starring engagement by exotic dancer Loïe Fuller. As they moved into the season, however, family theatergoers began to register complaints over plays like Victorien Sardou's *Divorçons!* (Let's get a divorce!, 1880) and Alexandre Dumas fils's social thesis tragedy *Denise* (1885). Even some of the play titles sounded pretentious: *L'Amour veille* (Watchful love), *La Rivale* (The other woman), *Les Femmes qui pleurent* (Women who weep), and *Les Francs-Maçons* (Freemasons). Monseigneur Bruchési dutifully read the plays and declared them "indecent and dangerous." Anyone exposed to them would gain "fatal familiarity with wickedness. . . . All the worst instincts of human nature are revealed in them. Whether one wishes it or not, at no matter what age one begins to attend the theater, one is at the school for sin." Nor would cuts and alterations make a difference: "The plays are in themselves corrupt." Although the archbishop stopped short of explicitly forbidding theatergoing at the Academy of Music, the company's closing performance came only four months later; the building was demolished the next day.

Given the restrictions, it is not surprising that few francophones were drawn to write for the stage. Julien Daoust, however, wrote close to thirty dramatic works that were produced but not published. In addition to religious melodramas like *Le Triomphe de la croix* (Triumph of the cross, 1903), the frequently-revived *Le Chemin des larmes* (Road of tears, 1915), and *La Conscience d'un prêtre* (Conscience of a priest, 1920), he contributed to the 1910s vogue for musical revues, notably with *La Belle Montréalaise* (The Montreal beauty, 1913). Probably a revision of Daoust's 1912 revue *Mademoiselle Canada*, *La Belle Montréalaise* continued its stage life in the 1920s as *Allo Québécoise*. The work brims with songs and dances (including a chorus of dancing firemen), metatheatrical parody mingling comedy and melodrama, and allegorical characters like Mademoiselle Canada, Electricity, and Time.

The long popularity of melodrama might be said to have peaked with *Aurore l'enfant martyr* (Aurora, the martyred child), which premiered in 1921 at Montreal's Théâtre Alcazar and continued to be performed about two hundred times a year for the next thirty years throughout francophone Canada and even in New England parish halls. Authors Léon Petitjean and Henri Rollin based the melodrama on the true story of a wicked stepmother in the village of Sainte-Eulalie whose torture of her ten-year-old stepdaughter—burning her hands on a red-hot stove, forcing her to eat bars of soap—resulted in the child's death. Hampered by the outcome of the notorious trial (the convicted woman was pregnant and, thus spared hanging, was sent to a prison for the mentally ill in Kingston), the Rollin–Nohcor troupe originally took a *grand guignol* approach to the material, treating it as theater of horrors interspersed with comic bits and songs. A later version of the much-doctored script incorporated a trial sequence culminating in a (historically untrue) sentencing of Aurora's stepmother to the gallows. Finally, purged of comic elements, a five-act melodrama version enjoyed a new surge of success in 1929. The copyright passed through many hands, and a script was not published until 1982.

Other dramatists may be accorded passing mention. Paris-born Henry Deyglun (1903–71) came to Montreal in 1921, having worked under Jacques Copeau; he combined an acting career with writing for the stage and, later, radio. Among his seventeen plays one might signal *Coeur de maman* (Mama's heart, 1936) and *Notre maître l'amour* (Our master love, 1937). Léopold Houlé (1883–1953) could boast two hundred performances of his moralizing *Le Presbytère en fleurs* (Blossoming presbytery, 1929). Father Gustave Lamarche (1895–1987) combined poetic use of language, symbolist tendencies, religious subjects, and a panoramic theatricality. His thirty-four plays, many presented pageant-style in outdoor settings, include *Jonathas* (1934), *La Défaite de l'enfer* (Hell's undoing, 1938), and *Notre-Dame-de-la-couronne* (Our Lady of the crown, 1947). The most polished dramatist of the

1930s, Yvette Mercier–Gouin (1895–1984), portrayed Montreal's contemporary upper-class society in plays like *Cocktail* (1935) and *Le Jeune dieu* (The young god, 1936).

In 1907, the French actor Eugène Lassalle, who had been hired by the Nouveautés shortly before its demise, founded the Conservatoire d'Art Dramatique Canadien, a francophone theater training school that also presented the classics. Lassalle saw it as the base upon which to build a national French–Canadian theater and he even succeeded in getting subsidization from the provincial government for a time. Although Lassalle gave up hope of a professional theater after his best pupils formed their own troupe in 1910, the Conservatoire Lassalle continued. Beginning in 1909 it was the theaters that subsidized the government's good works with the institution of an entertainment tax. By 1925 the tax was fixed at ten percent of the ticket price, and in 1941 it rose to a 12.5 percent surtax. Along with the escalating costs of production and touring star engagements, a proliferation of cinemas—Cinématographe, Supériograph parisien, Vitascope, Nationoscope, Mont-Royaloscope, and others—took a toll on theater attendance. Indeed, some theater facilities were converted to moviehouses with just enough stage space for vaudeville acts between screenings. World War I administered the *coup de grace* to live theater. Little of consequence in French–Canadian theater occurred during the two decades after the war.

Meanwhile, English-language theater continued its long struggle to resist American influence. The founding of the Theatrical Syndicate in 1896 exacerbated existing circumstances by which touring companies from New York dominated the Canadian theatrical landscape. In 1911, protesting that "Canada is the only nation in the world whose stage is entirely controlled by aliens," critic B. K. Sandwell urged as a countermeasure the importation of British theater companies. A British–Canadian Theatrical Organization (BCTO), organized in 1912, facilitated tours by British stars like John Martin–Harvey. While the 1910s and early 1920s did indeed see increased British presence and influence, other factors actually served to "de-annex" the Canadian theater from the United States and to boost discovery of its own identity. As early as 1902 to 1910, for example, Harold Nelson Shaw (1865?–1937) was touting his troupe as "all-Canadian." The Harold Nelson company took an ambitious repertoire, in which Shakespeare's plays figured prominently, to small-town opera houses throughout western Canada. By the 1930s neither American nor British touring companies could hold their own economically against the growing competition from movies and radio, and they abandoned the theatrical arena to Canadians.

Ironically, one of the most effective Canadian theater ventures involved association with an American company to achieve a bookings monopoly modeled after the American syndicate. Ambrose J. Small (1866–?) worked with Detroit's C. J. Whitney, who controlled a theater circuit in the Great Lakes region. After Whitney's death in 1903, Small continued his theatrical booking operation while building a chain of thirty-four theaters, half of them in Ontario. The A. J. Small Circuit, advertised as "the most carefully

booked territory in the world," brought an unprecedented range of professional theater—Shakespeare, modern classics, star vehicles, minstrel
shows—to towns like Hamilton, Stratford, Brockville, Sarnia for nearly two
decades. Small's contribution was to uphold an artistic standard for audiences long accustomed to less. However, the gradual decline of the road led
Small in 1919 to sell his holdings to Trans-Canada Theatre Society (TCTS).
Scarcely had Ambrose Small deposited the one-million-dollar down payment in his bank account when he disappeared, his fate never to be known.
Soon TCTS gained control of C. P. Walker's chain of theaters in the Red
River Valley. The resulting monopoly allowed TCTS to foist poorer-quality
British productions on the public, a tactic which failed and led to the demise
of TCTS by 1922. C.P. Walker then resumed the management of his flagship
facility, the Walker Theatre (1907) in Winnipeg, and ran it successfully for
a decade with a varied repertoire.

Radio had also been subject to American influence in its early days; however, with the rise of radio drama beginning in 1925, Canadian radio not only
found its own voice but also provided a proving ground for a generation of
Canadian dramatists. By the 1980s Howard Fink could claim that "for six
decades radio drama has been inextricably interwoven with the history of
Canadian theater." Canada boasted the first commercial radio network in North
America—CN Radio, launched by Canadian National Railways in 1924—with
eight affiliate stations across the nation from Halifax to Vancouver by 1925. In
1927 Jack Gillmore created the CNRV Players, which broadcast weekly radio
dramas (ranging from adaptations of Shakespeare to new Canadian pieces)
from the Vancouver station. The first such series comprising all-Canadian
material came in 1931 when Merrill Denison wrote fourteen historical dramas that were directed by Tyrone Guthrie and broadcast from CNRM
(Montreal) as "The Romance of Canada." Their popularity led to a second
season, under the direction of Rupert Caplan. Private stations too produced
radio drama, notably Alberta's CKUA (Edmunton) with a series lasting from
1928 to 1941, and including work by writers like Gwen Pharis Ringwood and
Elsie Park Gowan, who would later emerge as prominent regional dramatists
for the stage. The nationalization of the CNR network in 1932, a protectionist measure against American broadcasting, brought government subsidies
and a national listening audience of millions for radio drama. From 1944,
under the leadership of Andrew Allan (1907–74), the Canadian Broadcasting
Corporation's Drama Department broadcast a Sunday night live "Stage"
drama series that lasted twelve seasons and showcased numerous Canadian
writers. A Wednesday night series begun in 1947 presented the classics and a
foreign repertoire. Approximately thirty-five hundred original Canadian
plays were broadcast during the golden age of Canadian radio drama, from
1939 through the 1950s. CBC radio not only fostered a sense of national
community and identity during the war years (with separate networks for
French and English), but served as a creative font and a springboard for thousands of Canadian actors, dramatists, and directors whose work has defined
the contemporary Canadian stage.

Perhaps the development of a distinctly Canadian theater owes the most to the little theater movement. As professional touring gradually died out, hundreds of amateur community theater groups sprang up to fill the void. In Toronto, productions by the Arts and Letters Club provided a crucial impetus. Founded in 1908, the luncheon club for artists and critics enjoyed post-prandial entertainments in the restaurants where they met. Roy Mitchell (1884–1944) served as *Prankmeister* for the occasional programs, which expanded into full productions beginning in 1910 with the rental of a performance space in the former York County Courthouse. Mitchell and other club members placed 150 crates at one end of the room to create a platform stage, and they improvised lighting equipment with tin wash basins as reflectors. The April 1911 production of Maurice Maeterlinck's symbolist play *Interior* heralded Mitchell's nonrealistic approach, informed by his theosophical beliefs. The Arts and Letters Club has continued to this day its long tradition of amateur theater, but Mitchell left in 1916 to learn through practical experience by working in New York theater for two seasons. In 1919 Mitchell was appointed the first director of the five-hundred-seat Hart House Theatre financed by arts philanthropist Vincent Massey (1887–1967) at the University of Toronto. Vincent and his brother Raymond Massey (1896–1983) both performed as amateurs there. The presentation of at least one new Canadian play each season placed Hart House Theatre at the forefront of Canada's little theater movement. During his two seasons at Hart House, Mitchell explored many of the ideas that he later put forth in his important book *The Creative Theatre* (1920): stylization through simplicity of means in order to free the imagination, emphasis on scenic beauty with striking lighting effects, flexible use of performance space, awareness of the communal role of the audience in the flow of creative energy.

Notable among theater artists inspired by Roy Mitchell, Merrill Denison (1893–1975) brought his training as an architect to work as art director and sometime set designer under Mitchell at Hart House Theatre. It was Mitchell who prompted Denison, an ardent conservationist and supporter of woman suffrage, to draw upon his knowledge of the backwoods people living on or near Denison's vast landholdings in Ontario and to write plays about them. Denison's first play, the one-act farce *Brothers in Arms* (1921), premiered at Hart House and went on to over fifteen hundred performances during the next fifty years. Other comedic one-acts and the full-length naturalistic *Marsh Hay* (1923)—published in a collection titled *The Unheroic North* (1923)—established Denison as Canada's first anglophone dramatist to focus specifically on Canadian life and character. After the great success of his full-length *Contract* (1929), directed by Carroll Aikins at Hart House, Denison turned to writing for radio.

Aikins (1888–1967) was another director whose amateur theater endeavors must be signaled for their part in creating a climate for Canadian drama. His play about indigenous people, *The God of Gods* (1919), had premiered in Birmingham, England, and it opened the hundred-seat Home Theatre on his fruit ranch near Naramata, British Columbia. For two seasons

(1920–22), students came there to train under Aikins and perform (in addition to picking fruit). Aikins served as director of Hart House Theatre from 1927 to 1929. Also in British Columbia, the English actor Llewelyn Bullock–Webster (1879–1970) founded the Prince Rupert Amateur Dramatic Society in 1911 and the British Columbia Dramatic School in 1921. He taught acting at the school until its closure in 1932, all the while involved in myriad other educational and artistic activities in the province.

In Alberta, the Medicine Hat Amateur Dramatic Society, founded in 1914, eventually gave rise to the Medicine Hat Little Theatre. Theater in Alberta—indeed, throughout all of western Canada—gained its greatest impetus from the work of Elizabeth Sterling Haynes (1897–1957). She had acted under Roy Mitchell at Hart House Theatre before moving to Edmonton in 1922. There Haynes directed productions for the University of Alberta Theatre Society, helped to found the Alberta Drama League in 1929, and served as first artistic director of the Edmonton Little Theatre, which she cofounded in 1929. In 1933 she cofounded (with Edward A. Corbett), the Banff School of Drama (later called Banff Centre School of Fine Arts). As secretary and registrar at the school in the 1930s, Gwen Pharis Ringwood (1910–84) took inspiration from Haynes as well as from the summer playwriting courses of visiting professor Frederick Koch of the Carolina Playmakers. Koch enouraged Ringwood to write plays that drew upon the people and life of the Canadian plains. Ringwood's one-act tragedy *Still Stands the House* (1938), set in an isolated farmhouse during a blizzard, remains one of Canada's most often published and produced plays. Her twenty-five *Collected Plays* (1982) include other prairie dramas, folk dramas, comedies, historical musicals, and a trilogy based upon indigenous culture. Also encouraged by Elizabeth Sterling Haynes, Elsie Park Gowan (b. 1905) wrote a number of successful plays in the 1930s for Edmondton Little Theatre.

Manitoba's anglophone amateur theater is best represented by the Community Players of Winnipeg (1921), which became the Winnipeg Little Theatre under John Craig in 1930. By then sixteen Winnipeg groups and ninety from elsewhere in the province comprised the Manitoba Drama League. Sasketchewan's little theaters included the Christ Church Dramatic Society (1921–29) and the Saskatoon Little Theatre (1922–49) in Saskatoon, and the Regina Little Theatre from 1931. That same year saw the start of two important amateur theaters in the Maritimes. The Theatre Arts Guild in Halifax, Nova Scotia, achieved a long, distinguished record of productions, many directed by H. Leslie Pigot; and the Saint John Theatre Guild, New Brunswick, lasted until 1954. The latter group nurtured the work of Jane Sweet, who wrote the prize-winning political drama *Small Potatoes* (1938).

Another long-lived group, Montreal Repertory Theatre, retained its amateur status from its 1930 inception until 1956, and served as a springboard for many leading lights of Canadian professional theater, including Yvette Brind'amour, Fred Barry, Christopher Plummer, and others. Its energetic founder Martha Allan (1895–1942) had studied theater in Paris and had acted at Pasadena Playhouse before creating the bilingual company (she acted and directed in both French and English). Rehearsals were held in the coach house of her family's estate, and performances were given in rented facilities. An experimental wing called the MRT Workshop began in 1932 to premiere plays by Canadian authors, both anglophone and francophone. Allan's 1932 coproduction of *Hamlet* with Ottawa Little Theatre aroused controversy not because of its sponsorship by the governor general, whose son played the title role, but because of Allan's decision to use the First Quarto text. In 1938 an affiliate organization was created with the same initials as Montreal Repertory Theatre—Mont-Royal Théâtre Français—to take over French-language production, though the two entities shared production staff. Allan maintained a high standard of production, won recognition for her play *All on a Summer's Day* (1936), and might well have ascended to the leadership of the Dominion Drama Festival—which she ardently supported—if not for her untimely death at forty-seven.

Various other initiatives contributed to the development of anglophone Canadian playwrights before World War II. In 1932, for example, a group of women led by Leonora McNeilly founded the Playwrights Studio Group, which presented plays at Hart House until 1940. Among the group's most successful writers, Lois Reynolds Kerr (b. 1908) drew upon her experience as a Depression-era reporter to write what she called her "society-newspaper plays" about social-climbing women: *Among Those Present* (1933), *Nellie McNabb* (1934), and *Guest of Honour* (1936). Another group, the Play Workshop, formed in 1934 in Toronto by the noted playwright–director Herman Voaden (1903–91), led the way in production of experimental plays. Voaden had acted at Hart House in 1926 and founded the Drama Club of Sarnia in 1927, then became interested in the European avant-garde. His own major plays, in a vein he called "symphonic expressionism," include *Rocks* (1932), *Earth Song* (1932), *Hill-Land* (1934), *Murder Pattern* (1936), and *Ascend as the Sun* (1942). In *Murder Pattern*, for example, the harshly beautiful land speaks for itself in counterpoint to the human story. As an early promoter of Canadian cultural nationalism, Voaden compared Canada of the 1930s to Walt Whitman's America, "awakening to a sense of unlimited power and wealth, proud in her youth, and needing only her confidence to succeed. . . . This Greater Canada must have a place in our literature and art—its spirit must inform and give breadth to what we create." Voaden's Play Workshop produced works by many other Canadian authors, including two expressionist one-acts by Bertram Booker (1888–1955), *Within* (1935) and *The Dragon* (1936).

Dora Mavor Moore (1888–1979) had acted professionally in Ottawa, New York, Chicago, and London, then devoted herself to Canadian theater. She founded three amateur groups: the University of Toronto Extension Players (1930), the Hart House Touring Players (1931), and the Village Players (1938). The latter company launched the professional New Play Society in 1946. Moore rented Toronto's Royal Ontario Museum Theatre (capactiy 450) and there, in the 1940s and 1950s, the nonprofit NPS set an unprecedented record of premiering original Canadian plays, to be discussed in chapter 7.

The 1930s also saw a Workers' Theatre movement with its own journal, *Masses*. Theatres in several Canadian cities, each supported by a local Progressive Arts Club, espoused a militant leftist political agenda. Prominent among such ventures were the Theatre of Action and the Workers' Experimental Theatre, both of Toronto. The latter produced the movement's best-known production, *Eight Men Speak* (1933), a collectively written work performed once only by thirty-five unemployed workers for an audience of about fifteen hundred. Police prevented a planned second performance in Toronto as well as a performance scheduled for Winnipeg. The episodic political satire employed standard agitprop techniques, including choral chant, documentary material, presentational acting, and mime. Such efforts represent an avant-garde of marginalized or "alternative" theater that has posed a healthy challenge to the more conservative aesthetics of mainstream fare. The full-blown movement after World War II would have an ardent leftist as its forerunner: George Luscomb (b. 1926), founder and artistic director of Toronto Workshop Productions from 1959 to 1986.

Although it remained a showcase for amateur theater and came to stand for aesthetic and social conservatism, the Dominion Drama Festival (DDF) can undeniably be credited with nourishing professional theater in Canada as well as bringing into the same arena the sometimes anatagonistic francophone and anglophone theaters. The original impetus for the creation of the DDF was to facilitate communications and foster interaction among the many amateur theater groups all across Canada. To that end, a group of theater artists—including Martha Allan, Vincent Massey, Herman Voaden, and others—met in Rideau Hall in Ottawa on October 29, 1932, with the governor general to plan an organization. Sworn in as Canada's governor general in August 1931, Vere Brabazzon Ponsonby, the ninth earl of Bessborough, had quickly demonstrated his proclivity for theatergoing. He became patron of the DDF, which was organized both as a competition and as a showcase for amateur theater. There was a precedent for such an undertaking in that Canada's ninth governor general, Lord Grey, had inititated an annual musical and dramatic competition that lasted from 1907 to 1911. That project, however, had remained in the hands of a social élite, whereas the DDF involved regional playoffs and independent adjudicators of some standing in the professional theater. Each entry, whether a one-act or an excerpt from a longer work, could run no longer than forty minutes. About ninety English-language and twenty French presentations were entered in the first round of the first DDF. The finals, held in Ottawa, on April 24–29, 1933, brought entries from eight provinces and included six French entries, with the Bessborough Trophy going to the Masquers Club of Winnipeg. For seven years the event took place in Ottawa (though Bessborough's appointment as governor general ended in fall 1935); Winnipeg hosted the DDF in 1938; London, Ontario, in 1939. World War II brought a hiatus in the festival, but it reappeared in 1947. The postwar years brought a number of challenges and changes. Beginning in 1950, full-length plays were allowed. With the renaissance of professional theater in the 1960s, amateur theater no longer played a crucial role as a national cultural standard-bearer. In 1970 the Dominion Drama Festival received a new name, Theatre Canada, and an altered mandate: the emphasis would devolve from competition to showcasing. Adjudicators gave way to *animateurs*, who commented on the work and facilitated discussions involving artists and audiences. Theatre Canada ended in 1978, but its long-range effects may be summed up in the words of Robertson Davies, who observed in his foreword to Betty Lee's *Love and Whisky: The Story of the Dominion Drama Festival* that it was

> an astounding achievement, and undoubtedly the most astonishing thing about it was that it was an artistic venture dedicated to destroying itself in the cause of art: whatever passions may have raged in the breasts of its patrons and competitors from time to time, it never lost sight of its desire to keep the art of the theater alive in a country where it was greatly threatened, and in the end to bring about a better theater, in the hands of professional artists, in which the amateurs would either have to relinquish their amateur status, or go back to seats among the audience. This is what it achieved. The foundation of our modern professional theater rests on many stones, but the largest and the strongest is the achievement of the Dominion Drama Festival.

It also succeeded in maintaining until the end Lord Bessborough's ideal of a fraternal bilingualiism and biculturalism.

The French–Canadian theater had largely stagnated throughout the 1920s. None of the episodic Canadian history plays written during this or the subsequent decade made a lasting impact. Touring companies from France appeared regularly, but local efforts remained at the amateur level. The rebirth—some would say the actual birth—of French–Canadian theater came in 1937, with the founding of Les Compagnons de Saint-Laurent. As early as 1930, however, the opening of Montreal's Stella Theatre augured better things to come. The Stella (formerly the Chantecler Theatre, capacity 443) had been used during the 1920s by various groups, including a professional troupe led by two excellent actors, Fred Barry (1887–1964) and Albert Duquesne (1890–1956). Outstanding among the struggling theater groups of the interwar period, the Barry–Duquesne company had begun in 1918 as the Barry–Duquesne–Deyglun company (with dramatist Henry Deyglun). For the Stella, they engaged Antoine Godeau as director and gathered the finest Quebec actors of the period: Godeau's daughter Marthe Thiéry (who married Duquesne), Antoinette Giroux, Bella Ouellette, Jeanne Deslauriers, Mimi d'Estée, Jeanne Demons, Gaston Dauriac, Pierre Durand, and Henry Deyglun. The Stella opened in August 1930 with *La Lettre*, a French version of Somerset Maugham's *The Letter*. The high quality of performance by a *Canadien* company attracted a strong following, but the adoption of the old tradition of a weekly change of bill proved exhausting. Critics complained of a prompter who drowned out the actors' voices. Henri Letondal became artistic director for the Stella's third season, which showed a marked decline, especially in terms of a repertoire centered more and more upon lightweight revues. The remainder of the decade saw various permutations: Letondal with a new company, the Académie Canadienne d'Art Dramatique, at the Stella in 1933–34; Antoinette Giroux's Union Artistique Canadienne at the Stella in 1934–35; the Barry–Duquesne company at the Monument National in 1937. The theater facility itself became a cinema until 1960, when Le Théâtre du Rideau Vert would restore it to artistic prominence.

While the interwar years were described by the respected critic Jean Béraud (1899–1965) as an "unhealthy climate" for Montreal's francophone theater, that same period has been called the "golden age" of francophone theater in Manitoba. The way had been prepared by school productions at the Collège de Saint-Boniface as early as 1870. Those school productions achieved particular success under the leadership of the theater and choral director Father Martial Caron, S.J., from 1933 to 1950. His lavish 1945 staging of L'Ame huronne (The Huron soul) by Father Jean Laramée, for example, capped its four academic performances with—by popular demand—a public performance that drew twelve hundred spectators. Putting on plays became a means of self-assertion by the minority francophone community in Winnipeg and other Manitoba towns, where community theater groups proliferated. One amateur group distinguished itself beyond all others and remained in the 1990s Canada's longest-existing francophone amateur company; Le Cercle Molière was founded in Saint-Boniface in 1925 by André Castelain de la Lande, Louis-Philippe Gagnon, and Raymond Bernier. Under the artistic directorship of Arthur Boutal from 1928 to 1941, Le Cercle Molière presented classical and contemporary plays from France, and earned a wide reputation for excellence, beginning with a best play award at the 1933 Dominion Drama Festival.

The year 1937 stands as a watershed in French–Canadian theater history. Not only does it mark the radio début of the character Fridolin (who would soon begin his long stage life), but that year also saw the formation of the Union des Artistes, a professional organization for francophone theater personnel. Perhaps what most affected the legitimate theater was the remarkable work of Les Compagnons de Saint-Laurent, which began that year and continued until 1952. Father Emile Legault, C.S.C. (Holy Cross), had been directing school plays for several years at the Collège de Saint-Laurent in a Montreal suburb, and since 1935 he had been in charge of Action Catholique Etudiante. With those fervent young people, Legault staged a religious pageant, Celle qui la porte fit s'ouvrir by Louis Barjon, S.J., on Saint-Laurent's cathedral square. The production attracted considerable attention and was presented again on Notre Dame cathedral square in Montreal. That was the impetus for the founding of what Legault conceived as "a parish troupe dedicated to a religious repertoire" and "an avant garde gathering of young men and women who espouse the ideal of serving their faith through the theatre." Influenced by the work of Jacques Copeau in Paris, Legault aimed for a poetry of the theater, observing that "the best theatre is not a canned version of real life, but a transposition, an interpretation of the human." Theatre must entertain above all, he acknowledged, but it could also serve as an instrument of moral elevation. The inaugural production in November 1937, La Bergère au pays des *loups* (Shepherdess in wolf territory), was the first of twelve plays by Henri Ghéon that Les Compagnons would produce in their fifteen-year existence. Ghéon's *Le Noël sur la place* (Christmas on the square), first presented in December 1937, would be revived hundreds of times. In June 1938 Legualt traveled to Quebec City to stage Ghéon's *Le Mystère de la messe* (Mystery of the mass) for the National Eucharistic Congress. The French dramatist was in attendance, along with one hundred twenty thousand others, for the performance by a cast of two thousand on a huge platform on the Plains of Abraham. Ghéon then went on to direct the Compagnons in a play written especially for them: *Le Jeu de Saint Laurent du fleuve* (The play of Saint Lawrence of the river, 1938). On his return from six months of theatergoing in France, Legault expanded the repertoire beyond religious theater. With the fall 1939 production of Molière's *The Misanthrope*, Les Compagnons de Saint-Laurent crystallized in the view of critics the "house style" that emphasized the youthfulness of the purposely anonymous cast: energy, movement, grace, lightness, acrobatics, mime, dynamism, enthusiasm, truthfulness, the physical exaltation of intellectual content. Until 1942, the Compagnons de Saint Laurent performed at the Collège de Saint Laurent. From 1942 to 1945 they used the Ermitage Theatre in Montreal, then the Gesù Theatre until 1948, when Les Compagnons became a professional company and acquired their own theater. Various factors led to the disbanding of Les Compagnons de Saint Laurent in 1952, but a number of its alumni became prominent in Canadian theater, notably Jean Gascon (1921–88), who would later become artistic director of the Stratford Festival.

A seminal figure in modern Québécois theater, Gratien Gélinas (b. 1909) distinguished himself as actor, playwright, director, and spokesman for Canadian film and French–Canadian theater. Facing the 1930s depression with a degree in classical studies from the Collège de Montréal, Gélinas worked eight years for an insurance company while, on the side, he rallied fellow alumni to form a theater group called La Troupe des Anciens du Collège de Montréal, and he also acted in both French and English with Martha Allan's Montreal Repertory Theatre. Two years of regular appearances in a radio serial (1934–36) and some one-man sketches in a 1936 stage revue led to the opportunity to write and perform his own half-hour weekly comedy for a Montreal radio station, beginning in 1937. Thus he created his cocky, wry, streetwise yet charming Fridolin, a character who spoke colloquial Quebec French and who came to represent the irrepressible French–Canadian everyman. Fridolin transferred so easily to the stage that by 1941 Gélinas abandoned the radio show. From 1938 to 1946 Gélinas presented each year a new edition of his stage revue, *Fridolinons*, maintaining a vast popular following in both Montreal and Quebec City. Through Fridolin's antics—without flinching from politics, economics, and even religion—Gélinas enabled French–Canadians to laugh at their problems.

Gélinas's first play, *Tit-Coq* (Little rooster, 1948) premiered at the Monument National under the direction of Gélinas and Fred Barry, and ran for over three hundred performances. Gélinas played the Fridolin-like title role of the illegitimate, lonely soldier whose fiancée betrays him. The character seemed to sum up the frustrations of French–Canadians who had fought in the war and still saw themselves as marginalized and who struggled with the church's restrictive power over their personal lives. Although it no longer seems as relevant as it did in 1948, *Tit-Coq* stands as a landmark play in modern French–Canadian drama. Gélinas wrote three more plays: the tragicomic *Bousille et les justes* (Bousille and the just, 1959), *Hier, les enfants dansaient* (Yesterday the children were dancing, 1966), and *La Passion de Narcisse Mondoux* (1986).

Pierre Dagenais (1924–90) was another extraordinary theatrical presence. His career peaked in the 1940s with L'Equipe (1943–47), the company he founded when he was nineteen. His 1943 staging of *Altitude 3200* by Julian Luchaire at the Monument National brought him recognition as a director, which he subsequently confirmed with his stagings of Shakespeare and various contemporary works from the English and French repertoires. He also acted in French and English, earning the epithet "the Orson Welles of Canada." Dagenais wrote plays, worked in radio theater, and became a theater critic. His efforts along with those of Père Emile Legault and Gratien Gélinas prepared the way for a great blossoming of French–Canadian theater after World War II.

# 7 *Renewal and Experimentation: 1945 to the Present*

## THE UNITED STATES

America's wartime economy boomed with military and war-related industrial expansion. With virtually full employment, Americans on the home front once again had disposable income and looked to a variety of recreational activities to provide a respite from the turmoil of war. As a major port of embarkation and with dozens of training camps surrounding the city, military personnel by the thousands joined New York's already teeming civilian population. The Times Square entertainment hub bustled with activity. "The Fabulous Invalid," as Broadway was called after the 1938 Moss Hart and George S. Kaufman play of that title, rose from its Depression-era sick bed. Leiter reports that the number of new productions increased from sixty-nine in 1940–41, to a high of ninety-seven in 1943–44, then stabilized between seventy-six and seventy-nine in the next few years. The ratio of "flops" to "hits" also decreased. This was an improvement over Depression doldrums, but only marginally so. And after the war, Broadway theatrical activity rapidly dwindled to a half-century low of only fifty-seven new productions in 1949–50.

A combination of economic factors contributed to Broadway's decline, but the swift rise of television was also a major culprit. By 1949, for example, there were about two million television sets in operation in the United States, receiving hundreds of hours of free news, drama, and variety entertainment. A decade later, 85 percent of the population had access to a television. As television programming expanded and advanced in sophistication, the audience for theater contracted. Even the movie industry, which had been growing impressively since the advent of "talkies," was affected by television. From the late 1940s to the late 1950s, movie attendance plummeted. Gradually the novelty of television faded, but its supremacy as America's principal source of information and entertainment would remain undiminished. By the 1990s, almost 99 percent of American households owned more than one television set (1.87 sets on average); over 70 percent owned a VCR, and 60 percent subscribed to a cable television system through which one could receive a dazzling array of programs.

Beginning in the 1950s, however, theater regained a precarious foothold and then over the next thirty years steadily climbed back to a moderately secure ledge on America's cultural heights. In large part, the upward progress of theater was supported by the growth of alternatives to Broadway. In New York, the first of these ventures was labeled Off-Broadway which was followed within a decade by a second development called Off-Off-Broadway. Far beyond New York, a grassroots movement led to a network of professional resident theaters located in dozens of cities and towns across the nation. New York would remain the largest, and, in many respects, the most important, but not the only theater center. New York's long-standing stranglehold on theatrical activity was broken and the American stage was once again decentralized.

Ironically, by the 1980s, theater had joined with the media industry—television, movies, recordings, videotapes—in numerous mutually supportive, symbiotic relationships. Remarkable advances in electronic technology enhanced both theatrical production and the business of theater. Indeed, complex "multimedia" or "mediated" theatrical presentations, integrating live performance with film, video, and sound and lighting effects became fairly common.

In the immediate postwar years, a mood of optimism pervaded American society, but it gradually dissipated as Americans came to grips with a number of troubling social and political realities. The 1950s seemed tranquil, but tensions simmered beneath the decade's seemingly staid surface. Despite general prosperity, there were worrisome economic ups and downs. Relationships with the Soviet Union and China were strained almost to the breaking point during the Korean War. An intricate web of "Cold War" alliances, with the world divided between the democratic West and the communist East, produced an uneasy peace. American fear of the "Red Menace" reached paranoid levels. Congressional committees hounded prominent Americans who stood to the political left—especially celebrity writers and film producers, directors, and actors. Hollywood in particular was considered a hotbed of subversive communist activity and influence. The threat of nuclear holocaust exacerbated personal and social anxiety. It was poet W. H. Auden who called the era "The Age of Anxiety," fraught with disillusion, cynicism, and a sense of defeatism and powerlessness.

The postwar generation of Americans responded to the spirit of the times in several ways. A new popular music style called "rock 'n' roll" (or simply "rock"), a synthesis of various folk and popular music genres, gave expression to a pervasive adolescent rebelliousness, sometimes simply frisky, prankish, and high-spirited, and at other times sullen and self-destructive. One generally youthful faction, collectively referred to as "hippies," rejected establishment values and institutions in favor of an anarchistic lifestyle that embraced communal living, free love, Eastern or Native American religious beliefs and practices, and the use of mind-altering drugs like marijuana, peyote, and LSD (lysergic acid diethylamide). Hippie guru Timothy Leary, a former Harvard professor of psychology, exhorted Americans to, "turn on" (to drugs), "tune in" (to another level of reality), and "drop out" (of society). Hippies expressed their antiestablishment free-spiritedness with long, flowing hair styles and brightly colored, Eastern-inspired clothing and jewelry. California, especially San Francisco, became the center of America's hippie counterculture. Paradoxically, the movement exercised considerable influence over mainstream culture, particularly in the visual arts, fashion, and popular music.

Several factions, unlike the hippies, rallied to particular social and political causes demanding changes in government, education, business and industry, and the established religions. A young Southern Baptist minister, Dr. Martin Luther King Jr., galvanized African Americans to fight oppressive segregationist laws and practices. Seeking an end to long-standing social and political discrimination, other disenfranchised groups—Native Americans, Latino farm workers, women, gays and lesbians—allied themselves with the African–American civil rights struggle. College students organized to challenge hidebound academic policies and procedures. The civil rights movement was overlapped by America's escalating involvement in the Vietnam War. By the late 1960s, the war had become one of the most divisive issues in American history. Commingled civil rights and antiwar demonstrations became commonplace. Students burned their draft cards in public rituals. Riots wreaked havoc in several major cities. The assassinations of President John F. Kennedy (1963), black leader Malcolm X (1965), Presidential candidate Robert Kennedy and Martin Luther King Jr.—both in 1968—intensified a widespread sense of outrage. In addition to the war and human rights, other issues, including environmental concerns, poverty, labor inequities, and governmental corruption, were brought to the foreground. "Power to the People" was the motto of radical protest as America was divided between the "haves" and "have-nots," war-mongering "hawks" and peacenik "doves," conservatives and liberals, despoilers of natural resources and conservationists, whites and people of color, men and women, straight and gay, young and old.

In the midst of social tumult, American theater experienced a remarkable renewal. New theater artists and companies blossomed to challenge the theatrical status quo in playwriting, acting, styles of theatrical production, and sociopolitical consciousness. Mainstream theater, whose artistic tendencies have been historically conservative and conventional, was energized and enlivened by the influence of the times and the theatrical avant-garde. Ironically, establishment institutions such as the National Endowment for the Arts (NEA), founded in 1965, and various private philanthropic foundations, the legacy of multimillionaires like Henry Ford and John D. Rockfeller, were principal financial contributors to America's alternative theater organizations. Laws allowing theaters, like private museums, libraries, and schools, to incorporate as not-for-profit cultural and educational institutions also helped the growth and development of the noncommercial, alternative theater movement. Foreign treaties and alliances and the East–West stand-off sparked the development of international theater organizations, such as the International Theatre Institute (ITI; founded in 1947), and international theater exchanges, tours, and festivals. Government agencies sponsored these international theatrical activities principally to promote national political goals, but the activities also contributed significantly to international cultural understanding and artistic cross-pollination.

America's withdrawal from Vietnam beginning in 1972, the accomplishments of the civil rights struggle and of the women's and gay liberation movements, and political détente with the Soviet Union and China deflated social and political activism. Reform seemed less urgent, although knotty national and international problems persisted, including poverty, drug trafficking, hate crimes, international terrorism, urban decay, nationalistic and religious wars, environmental pollution, AIDS, and human rights. But bolstered by a steadily expanding economy and relative political stability, America in the 1980s swung in a more conservative direction. Hippies were displaced by a post-1960s generation of materialistic, narcissistic "yuppies"—an acronym for "young, urban professionals." The American theater, always a bellwether of the national mood, seemed less daring, vibrant, and provocative than it was in the volatile 1960s and 1970s, although hundreds of outstanding productions, well-crafted plays, and compelling performances continued to arrest the attention of theatergoers. At the half-century mark, theater in America was at a low ebb. But, on balance, the forty years between 1950 and 1990 was marked by a steady increase in theaters built, theater companies founded, and theater attendance, and in the range and diversity of theatrical activity. Threatening clouds dotted the horizon, but in the waning years of the millennium, the American stage had once again reached a high-water mark.

IN THE 1960s, Broadway continued to decline; the average number of productions sank to about sixty-five a season, of which only half were nonmusical, new plays. By the late 1980s, the number of productions shrank to fewer than thirty a season. Touring companies also declined. In 1988–89, for example, there were a mere seven companies on the road. The number of theaters available for productions also decreased from almost eighty in the 1920s to about thirty-five by the mid-1960s. Furthermore, many of these theaters were often vacant at any one time during the course of a season. With so few productions and so many theaters dark, the Broadway theater district slipped into a tawdry and even dangerous condition by the late 1960s. West Forty-Second Street became a string of sleazy, pornographic film houses, massage parlors, "adult" bookstores, and cheap cafés; prostitutes and pimps, drug dealers and users, and vagrants of various sorts peopled the area; muggings of playgoers and actors on their way to or from theaters became fairly regular occurrences. Times Square, storied for its glitzy festive atmosphere, became known as "Slime Square."

In the early 1970s, however, the League of New York Theatres and Producers working in consort with municipal authorities initiated a series of programs to improve Broadway's environment and bolster the fading theatrical industry. New hotels and commercial buildings were erected and developers and businesses were offered incentives to locate in the area. Three new Broadway theaters were built, the Minskoff (1973), the Uris (1972, later renamed the Gershwin), and Circle in the Square (1972, in the same building as the Gershwin). In the 1980s, three additional new theaters were built: the Marquis Theatre inside the elephantine Marriott Marquis hotel, and two theaters in the new Criterion Center building. The Marquis Theatre, however, was built at the cost of demolishing three older theaters—the Bijou (1917), the Helen Hayes (1911), and the Morosco (1917). Several older theaters which had fallen into disuse as legitimate houses were also reclaimed for service in the 1990s, including several on benighted Forty-Second Street—e.g., the Republic (a.k.a Victory) Theatre built in 1900 and the New Amsterdam Theatre built in 1903, the latter renovated by the Walt Disney Company. The Canadian entertainment company Livent, Inc., reclaimed the Apollo and Lyric Theatres, combining them into a complex called the Ford Center for the Performing Arts (1998). Other older theaters were protected from eventual demolition by having them declared "historical landmarks."

By the mid-1990s, the environment of Broadway was regaining much of its former pizzazz. The paucity of productions was still worrisome, however. At various times during the 1990s there were hopeful signs of a genuine Broadway resurgence. In the latter part of the 1996–97 season, for example, thirty-four theaters were active with a bumper crop of new productions and revivals. The historical trend, however, remained in a downward direction.

The causes for Broadway's decline can be traced to several overlapping social and economic factors, but principally to rising production and running costs. A comedy or drama that would have cost under a hundred thousand dollars to produce in the late 1940s, cost almost three hundred thousand dollars to produce by the late 1970s. By the mid-1980s, the same production, as a result of inflation, cost seven hundred thousand dollars; and one million dollars or more by the mid-1990s. Neil Simon's *Laughter on the 23rd Floor* (1993), for example, cost 1.6 million. The costs of producing an extravagant musical in the mid 1950s, like *My Fair Lady,* was about five hundred thousand dollars; by the 1990s a comparable musical—*Sunset Boulevard* (1995), for example—could cost twelve million dollars or more. Running costs for a straight play could be as high as two hundred thousand dollars a week; as much as five hundred thousand dollars a week for a musical. To amortize its costs, a production generally had to play to capacity houses for a year or more. A genuine hit ran for years. Ticket prices spiraled upward to meet increased costs. In the 1960s, for example, top tickets were priced at about seven dollars for a straight play and ten dollars for a musical; by 1980, prices had risen to twenty dollars and twenty-seven dollars; by the mid-1990s, straight plays were as high as fifty dollars and musicals seventy-five dollars. The range of ticket prices also diminished. In 1960, a second balcony ticket could be had for as little as $2.50. In 1980 tickets might range from ten dollars to twenty-five dollars; in the 1990s, the range narrowed to sixty dollars to seventy dollars.

Despite high prices, people still went to Broadway in rising numbers throughout the late 1970s and 1980s. Producers made it easier to buy tickets by accepting credit cards and phone orders in the early 1970s. Computer technology also made ticket marketing and distribution more efficient and effective.

Subsidized by private and public sources, the Theatre Development Fund (TDF) was organized in 1967 principally to market unsold tickets at half-price on performance days. In 1973, TDF opened several discount ticket booths—called TKTS—on Broadway and at other key locations. TKTS proved a popular and successful operation. By 1980–81 with an average ticket price of almost twenty dollars, over ten million attended Broadway shows, while box office receipts were almost two hundred million dollars. Broadway attendance slacked off in the 1980s, declining by almost three million, but box office receipts climbed as ticket prices continued to be jacked up. In 1990, for example, with an average ticket price of thirty-six dollars and attendance of slightly over eight million, the box office receipts were over $280 million. In 1996–97, attendance increased to over ten million, one of the best seasons in over fifteen years, while the box office took in a record $480 million. (Broadway and national touring shows combined grossed $1.3 billion.) These large grosses, however, were generally produced by just a few musical mega-hits.

Who were these theatergoers? Beginning in the mid-1960s, a series of statistical surveys initiated by various foundations and government agencies revealed that mainstream American theatergoers were invariably college educated, affluent, middle-aged, and white. Historically, slightly more women went to the theater than men. Over three decades, with one notable exception, there were slight changes in the pattern, but no major shifts. A 1992 National Endowment for the Arts survey indicated that while whites still comprised over 80 percent of the theater audience, African–American and Hispanic theater attendance increased significantly over a 1982 survey. African–American attendance, in fact, doubled. These statistics were drawn from surveys of theatergoers nationwide. A survey solely of the Broadway theater audience taken by the League of American Theatres and Producers in 1996 confirmed in part the historical pattern. Two-thirds of the Broadway audience was over thirty-five years of age; three-quarters had annual incomes of over fifty thousand dollars and 22 percent had incomes over one hundred fifty thousand dollars. Surprisingly, while the majority of Broadway theatergoers were from New York—over 60 percent—about 26 percent came from elsewhere in the United States and nearly 13 percent came from abroad. Broadway continued to hold a position as a theater mecca.

Various surveys have indicated that Americans value theater, and the arts in general. A 1992 NEA report, however, indicated that only 13.5 percent of the adult population attended at least one theatrical performance in the course of a year, although attendance did increase by over 1.5 percentage points since 1982. The report also suggests that many Americans would attend more frequently, but are prohibited by various factors from the availability of leisure time to costs. But to date, American theatergoers across the nation seemed a solidly middle-class elite.

Considering the costs, commercial Broadway production was an increasingly risky enterprise. Enormous profits could be made, but a staggering loss was not uncommon. The 1964 revival of the musical *Fiddler on the Roof*, for example, made a net profit of over eight million on a $375,000 investment.

By 1989, the musical *Cats* (1982) which cost almost four million dollars to produce had already made a twenty-three-million-dollar profit and was still running almost a decade later. But productions regularly lost thousands, even millions of dollars. *Jerome Robbins' Broadway* (1989), a potpourri of this noted director–choreographer's most successful musical theater dance numbers, seemed a sure-fire hit, but lost four million dollars.

In the postwar era, fewer independent producers entered the Broadway arena than in its heyday in the 1920s. Among the notable Broadway producers in the period from the 1950s through the 1980s were: Leland Hayward (1902–71), producer of such successes as *Mister Roberts* (1948), *South Pacific* (1949) and *The Sound of Music* (1959); David Merrick (1912–96), the producer of over seventy plays, including the hit musical *Hello, Dolly!* (1964) and English playwright John Osborne's *Luther* (1963); Arnold Saint-Subber (1918–94), who mounted most of Neil Simon's comic hits in the 1960s; Morton Gottlieb (b. 1933), a savvy producer of well-crafted romantic comedies and stylish thrillers; Alexander H. Cohen (b. 1920) whose productions ranged from noteworthy European imports to Arthur Miller's *The Price* to a revival of *Anna Christie* (1977) to the zany musical revue *A Day in Hollywood, a Night in the Ukraine* (1980); Roger L. Stevens (b. 1910), who over a long career was associated with a series of outstanding commercial productions and several leading institutional theaters; and partners Elizabeth McCann (b. 1931) and Nelle Nugent (b. 1939), who were perhaps the most successful Broadway producers from the mid-1970s to the mid-1980s, responsible for such hits as Bernard Pomerance's *The Elephant Man* (1979) and Beth Henley's *Crimes of the Heart* (1982).

A few independent, entrepreneurial producers continued to be active in the 1990s, but Broadway was dominated by three large production companies: the Shubert Organization, operated by Gerald Schoenfeld (b. 1924) and Bernard B. Jacobs (1916–97); Nederlander Enterprises, headed by James Nederlander (b. 1922); and the Jujamcyn Theatres, headed by Rocco Landesman (b. 1947). Not coincidentally, these three companies also owned virtually all of Broadway's commercial theaters, as well as legitimate theaters in many other major cities. In the late 1990s, several entertainment or media conglomerates entered the Broadway arena, financing the production of lavish musicals, mounting them in their own renovated or new theaters, and then taking them on lucrative tours. The Walt Disney Company, for example, produced live, theatrical versions of their popular animated films *Beauty and the Beast* (1995) and *The Lion King* (1997), while the Canadian firm Livent, Inc., headed by entrepreneur Garth Drabinsky (b. 1949), mounted several productions on Broadway, including a highly successful revival of *Show Boat* (1994) and *Ragtime* (1997), a musical adaptation of E. L. Doctorow's acclaimed novel. (See the Canada section of this chapter.) To compete with these new companies, whose financial clout generally exceeded that of Broadway's traditional theatrical producers or production companies, several producers formed producing partnerships. In 1997, for example, Jujamcyn Theatres and the Pace Theatrical Group formed a partnership, mainly to produce large-scale musicals.

• • •

IN THE POSTWAR years, Broadway continued to be gripped by a fairly narrow, generally conservative range of fare, mostly musicals and comedies. A decreasing number of productions and rising production costs also limited opportunities for aspiring playwrights, actors, directors, and producers. In the late 1940s and early 1950s, Off-Broadway arose as an alternative to Broadway. The term was used by critic Burns Mantle as early as the mid-1930s to define some semiprofessional or amateur productions mounted in various locales in Manhattan. But "Off-Broadway" did not become significant until a decade later when productions at several theaters, located mainly in Greenwich Village, began to take on a more professional character and to attract critical attention. In 1949, five of these theater groups formed the Off-Broadway Theatre League and negotiated a special contract with Actors' Equity with provisions that would allow Equity members to work at greatly reduced salaries. Working with small budgets in under two-hundred-seat theaters, Off-Broadway producers and companies mounted a range of plays generally not available on Broadway—revivals of historical and modern classics and artistically meritorious contemporary European and American works. Their goal was not commercial, but they did hope to at least break even on their production costs—often under three thousand dollars—and perhaps generate a modest profit. Like the Provincetown Players or the Group Theatre, Off-Broadway theaters became a training ground for numerous new playwrights and young performers and directors.

Three companies, in particular, are usually considered seminal in the establishment of Off-Broadway: Circle in the Square, the Phoenix Theatre, and the Living Theatre. Located in a small theater-in-the-round off Sheridan Square—hence its name—Circle in the Square, founded in 1951, was one of the first Off-Broadway companies to win widespread critical attention with outstanding revivals of Tennessee Williams's *Summer and Smoke* (1952) and Eugene O'Neill's *The Iceman Cometh* (1956). Led by its principal cofounders, director José Quintero (b. 1924) and producer–director Theodore Mann (b. 1924), Circle in the Square would continue to mount distinguished new plays and revivals, ranging from Euripides' *Medea* to Shaw's *Arms and the Man*. When their original theater was demolished in 1960, Circle in the Square relocated to a theater on Bleecker Street. In 1972, Circle in the Square opened a second uptown theater, on Broadway at West Fiftieth Street, and remains the oldest continually operating theater company in New York.

The Phoenix Theatre, cofounded in 1953 by Norris Houghton (b. 1909) and T. Edward Hambleton (b. 1911) mounted an eclectic mixture of productions—French absurdist plays, the plays of Bertolt Brecht and Shakespeare, classic English comedies, and new American plays, including Arthur Kopit's (b. 1937) *Oh Dad, Poor Dad, Momma's Hung You in the Closet and I'm Feeling So Sad* (1962), one of the first American absurdist comedies. After opening Off-Broadway, *Oh Dad . . .* was transferred to Broadway. In 1964, the Phoenix Theatre joined forces with the Association of Producing Artists (APA), a company of talented young actors founded by Ellis Rabb (1930–97) in 1960. APA did not have a permanent home, but rather had spent much of its four-year history up to 1964 as a resident professional theater company first at Princeton University and then at the University of Michigan. For five seasons, the APA–Phoenix presented a program of historical and modern classics, including an inventive adaptation of Tolstoy's *War and Peace* (1965), Shaw's *Man and Superman* (1964) and revivals of George S. Kaufman and Moss Hart's *You Can't Take It with You* (1965) and George Kelly's *The Show Off* (1967). The APA–Phoenix program, however, was ambitious and costly by Off-Broadway standards. In an attempt to increase revenues, the company moved to Broadway's larger Lyceum Theatre. Yet despite critical acclaim, a large subscription audience, support from individual patrons, and a substantial grant from the Ford Foundation, deficits continued to mount. In 1970, about five hundred thousand dollars in debt, the APA–Phoenix was dissolved. Several members of the APA would subsequently have distinguished careers, including most notably Rabb himself, his British-born wife Rosemary Harris (b. 1930), and Nancy Marchand (b. 1928). Houghton would become a well-known educator and theater writer, while Hamilton remained an independent producer.

The Living Theatre was founded in 1947 by the husband–wife team of Julian Beck (1925–85) and Judith Malina (b. 1926). In the late 1940s and 1950s, mingling an anarchistic political idealism with a penchant for avant-garde theater, Beck and Malina mounted a series of antirealistic plays, from esoteric, poetic pieces like Gertrude Stein's *Doctor Faustus Lights the Lights* (1938), William Carlos Williams's *Many Loves* (1942), and Alfred Jarry's *Ubu the King* (1896), to conventional modern works like Luigi Pirandello's *Tonight We Improvise* (1930) and Brecht's *Man Is Man* (1931). These productions were the most experimental of the time, but they attracted limited attention. In 1958, the Living Theatre mounted a hyper-realistic production of Jack Gelber's *The Connection,* a slice-of-life drama about a group of hero-in-addicted jazz musicians waiting for their next fix. It ran for over 775 performances and won several awards. The Living Theatre also won acclaim when they appeared at the Théâtre des Nations festival in Paris in 1961. With their production of Kenneth Brown's *The Brig* (1963), a ritualized recreation of a day in a Marine Corps prison, the Living Theatre solidified its growing reputation as an important avant-garde theater company. Beck and Malina, however, continually courted difficulties by their antibourgeois and antibureaucratic stances. In 1964, they were convicted of tax evasion charges and served brief prison terms, after which they left the United States for Europe to regroup. But Beck and Malina had already inspired a number of experimental theater groups emerging in the 1960s. In 1968, an even more radicalized Living Theatre company would return from exile to join with other activist, avant-garde theater groups to protest the social and aesthetic status quo (see below).

After Circle in the Square, the New York Shakespeare Festival (NYSF) was the most successful of the early Off-Broadway companies. It was founded in 1954 by Joseph Papp (1921–91) principally to mount free productions of Shakespeare's plays each summer. The NYSF played in a variety of locales and spaces for several years, but finally settled in Central Park. In 1961 with a grant from publisher George T. Delacorte, a permanent, outdoor, neo-Elizabethan style theater with seating for twenty-three hundred was specially built for the company. Papp expanded his operations in 1964 with a second ensemble which toured New York's five boroughs playing in its own portable sixteen-hundred-seat outdoor theater. Productions remained free, subsidized by the municipal government of New York, principally through the parks department, and increasingly by corporate and private support. In 1965, Papp initiated his third and most ambitious expansion by persuading the city of New York to remodel the old Astor Library building in Greenwich Village, empty for a number of years, into a complex of five theaters. Christened the Public Theatre, it became the NYSF's home for a diverse range of new American plays, American premieres of contemporary foreign plays, and revivals of classics. Unlike the summer Shakespeare productions, Papp charged for tickets at the Public Theatre, although the amount, at least initially, was a nominal $2.50. Established as a not-for-profit cultural institution, the NYSF/Public Theatre—as the organization was now called—relied heavily on governmental, corporate, and private support. Papp, in fact, was a staunch believer in public funding for the arts.

Papp, however, was also a practical entrepreneur. In 1967, for example, he had a surprise hit with *Hair,* a musical celebration of the emerging "hippie" counterculture. A re-staged production of *Hair* was moved to Broadway for a long run. Papp then used the profits from *Hair* to subsidize works that were more experimental or had less mass-market appeal. Over the years, he continued this strategy. Other notable NYSF/Public Theatre productions—some seventeen in all—which enjoyed successful Broadway runs include a musical version of *The Two Gentlemen of Verona* (1971); David Rabe's *Sticks and Bones* (1971), a provocative drama about the impact of the Vietnam War on the American homefront; Jason Miller's *That Championship Season* (1972), a critically acclaimed exploration of American values set against the reunion of a champion high school basketball team; and the musical drama *A Chorus Line,* which opened in 1975 and ran continuously for fifteen years for a total of 6,137 performances, a Broadway record.

Joseph Papp also championed the work of emerging Asian–American, African–American, and Latino playwrights, nurtured the careers of actors, directors, and designers, including many minority theater artists, and hosted a score of experimental and foreign companies and productions. In the early 1980s, the NYSF/Public Theatre initiated the Festival Latino de Nueva York. In 1986, Festival Latino presented over thirty productions by a dozen or so companies from across the United States and from Latin America. By the early 1990s NYSF/Public Theatre had a budget of fifteen million dollars and was widely considered a signal producing organization, while Papp himself was regarded as a major figure in the development of postwar American theater.

The Lincoln Center Repertory Theatre was also founded as an alternative to Broadway, although in terms of its pay scale, house size, and ticket pricing, it was a Broadway not an Off-Broadway operation. It was organized as the

*Exterior of the Vivian Beaumont Theatre (designed by Eero Saarinen and Jo Mielziner). Courtesy New York Power Authority.*

legitimate theater company for the Lincoln Center for the Performing Arts. Construction of Lincoln Center was begun in 1959. Over the course of the next decade, the center, located twenty blocks north of the Broadway theater district, gradually took shape as its several planned performing spaces were completed, including in 1965 the one thousand-seat Vivian Beaumont and the smaller, 299-seat, Off-Broadway-sized Forum Theatre (later renamed the Mitzi E. Newhouse), both state-of-the-art facilities for legitimate theater. Two years before these theaters were completed, Broadway veterans director Elia Kazan (b. 1909) and producer Robert Whitehead (b. 1916) were appointed by Lincoln Center's governing board to organize a flagship theater company. The Lincoln Center Repertory Theatre was another effort, like the ill-fated turn-of-the-century New Theatre company or the postwar American Repertory Theatre, to create an American equivalent of the Comédie Française. In a temporary facility erected for them in Greenwich Village, Kazan and Whitehead mounted an ambitious season of new American plays and revivals, including Arthur Miller's *After the Fall* and *Incident at Vichy,* poet Archibald MacLeish's *J.B.* (a contemporary version of the Book of Job) Eugene O'Neill's *Marco Millions,* Molière's *Tartuffe,* and the Jacobean tragedy *The Changling.* But despite a talented company of experienced actors and skillful direction, the season proved artistically disappointing and more costly than anticipated. The Lincoln Center governing board fired Whitehead; Kazan resigned in protest. The subsequent history of Lincoln Center would continue to be a troubled one for the next two decades. From 1965 to 1967, Herbert Blau (b. 1926) and Jules Irving (1924–79), cofounders in 1955 of the celebrated San Francisco Actor's Theatre, one of the first professional theaters outside of New York, were co-artistic directors of the Lincoln Center Repertory Theatre. They mounted a series of challenging European classics and modernist plays like Georg Büchner's *Danton's Death,* Brecht's *The Caucasian Chalk Circle,* Jean

Paul Sartre's *The Condemned of Altona,* Federico García Lorca's *Yerma,* Shaw's *St. Joan,* and Ben Jonson's *The Alchemist.* Like Kazan and Whitehead, Blau and Irving also assembled an excellent company. But the plays themselves, in what many critics judged as uninspiring productions, did not excite enthusiasm. Blau resigned in 1967. Irving carried on alone, but his management on balance proved critically and financially lackluster. In 1973 Joseph Papp took over. His reign was marked by several critical and popular successes, including *A Doll's House* (1975) with the distinguished Norwegian actress Liv Ullman (b. 1939) as Nora, *The Threepenny Opera* (1976) staged by avant-garde director Richard Foreman and featuring Puerto Rican actor Raul Julia (1940–94) as Mack the Knife, and *The Cherry Orchard* (1977), imaginatively staged by Romanian émigré director Andrei Serban (b. 1943). But the operation continued to run at a substantial deficit, and Papp, citing various artistic and financial reasons, resigned his directorship in 1977.

Lincoln Center seemed cursed as a home for a theater company. After a four-year hiatus, during which the Vivian Beaumont and Mitzi E. Newman theaters were virtually dark, a new company was organized under the artistic directorship of Gregory Mosher (b. 1949), who had been the successful artistic director of the Goodman Theatre since 1978, and producer Bernard Gersten (b. 1923), who had been Joseph Papp's long-time associate until he was fired in 1978. Together Mosher and Gersten reversed Lincoln Center's fortunes with a mostly American repertoire mixing new plays with revivals. André Bishop (b. 1948), Mosher's successor since 1991, has followed the same policy with equal success.

Notwithstanding the importance of producing companies like Circle in the Square, APA–Phoenix, the NYSF/Public Theatre, and the Lincoln Center Repertory Theatre, most Off-Broadway productions in the 1950s and 1960s were presented by independent producers such as Lucille Lortel (b. 1902) who mounted numerous productions of contemporary American and foreign plays at the Theatre de Lys. (Lortel also owned the White Barn Theatre in Westport, Connecticut, an important summer theater; in 1981 the Theatre de Lys was renamed the Lucille Lortel Theatre.) Richard Barr (1917–89) was another successful Off-Broadway producer, responsible for producing the early works of numerous American playwrights, including Edward Albee (b. 1928), Lanford Wilson (b. 1937), A. R. Gurney (b. 1930), John Guare (b. 1938), and many others.

Throughout the 1950s, the number of Off-Broadway theaters and productions gradually increased. By the early 1960s there were as many as thirty Off-Broadway theaters in operation; in the 1960–61 season the number of productions jumped to over one hundred, far surpassing Broadway in the number of productions mounted annually. Another sign of Off-Broadway's growing importance was the establishment in 1956 of the Off-Broadway Theatre Awards (Obies) by New York's leading alternative, antiestablishment newspaper, the *Village Voice,* founded in 1955. Obies were soon as highly prized as the Drama Critics' Circle Award. Success brought new economic challenges, however. Costs of producing Off-Broadway steadily mounted through the 1950s. A production that might have cost three thousand dollars in the early 1950s cost by the late 1950s ten thousand dollars and, then twenty thousand dollars by the mid-1960s. Operating costs also increased with a rise in wages, both artistic and managerial, advertising budgets, and an elevation in production standards. There was a corresponding increase in ticket prices. Although Off-Broadway costs remained lower than Broadway's, the increase was sufficiently significant to deter would-be producers. The number of Off-Broadway productions dropped precipitously in the 1960s to an average of about fifty productions a season.

By the late 1960s, Off-Broadway was split between commercially oriented productions, and including the APA–Phoenix, the NYSF/Public Theatre and the Lincoln Center Repertory Theatre, a dozen or so subsidized not-for-profit producing companies, each tending to specialize in a particular repertoire. The Negro Ensemble Company (NEC) founded in 1967 with a grant from the Ford Foundation by actor–director–playwright Douglas Turner Ward (b. 1930), and actor Robert Hooks (b. 1937), quickly became America's leading African–American theater company. Over the course of the next thirty years, NEC rose to a position of renown, fostering new African–American drama, premiering Afro–Caribbean and African plays, and promoting the careers of numerous black actors, directors, and designers. The American Place Theatre (APT) was cofounded in 1961 by director and acting teacher Wynn Handman (b. 1922), who became APT's artistic director; minister Sidney Lanier (b. 1923); and actor Michael Tolin (b. 1925). Its purpose was to develop and produce new American plays. In 1978, The Women's Project, under the leadership of Julia Miles (b. 1930), was organized as an arm of APT for women playwrights. (It was renamed Women's Project and Productions and established as an independent company in 1987.) Since their founding APT and Women's Project have nurtured hundreds of playwrights and directors. Other important Off-Broadway nonprofit companies include the Chelsea Theatre Center, founded by Robert Kalfin (b. 1933) in 1965, which, until its demise in 1983, presented premieres of many important American and foreign plays; the Circle Repertory Company, which was cofounded by director Marshall Mason (b. 1940), playwright Lanford Wilson, and others in 1969, and has tended to produce new American plays; the Roundabout Theatre Company, founded in 1965 by producer–director Gene Feist (b. 1930), which became noted for its revivals of modern classics by Chekhov, Shaw, Ibsen and others; and the Manhattan Theatre Club founded in 1970, which, under the artistic direction of Lynne Meadow (b. 1946) since 1972, has championed well-crafted American and foreign plays.

With increasing costs, Off-Broadway in the 1960s was becoming more limited as a venue for the new and different. Albert Poland and Bruce Mailman, in fact, suggest, with some justification, that most early Off-Broadway companies and producers were from the outset, with a few notable exceptions, more interested in mounting revivals of classics and the plays of European avant-gardists like Samuel Beckett, Brecht, Jean Genet, and Eugene

Ionesco, than aesthetically challenging American plays or experimental pieces. Beginning in the late 1950s, an alternative to Off-Broadway itself began to emerge. Small, informal, producing groups organized to challenge established notions of theater and drama. They performed in small, usually under-one-hundred-seat makeshift theaters in church basements, coffee houses, bars, and storefronts. In such facilities, the production approach tended to be low-budget and spare. Actors, directors, playwrights, and technicians usually worked for free or for token salaries or honoraria. By the early 1960s, theater critics were using the term "Off-Off-Broadway" (OOB) to designate this loose collection of theater companies and performances.

The Caffe Cino, a Greenwich Village coffee house where owner Joe Cino (1931–67) began to present plays in 1959, is credited as the first Off-Off-Broadway theater. A range of plays was mounted at the Caffe Cino, from classics to the European avant-garde, but the Cino was especially important for championing new American plays. Ten of Lanford Wilson's plays, for example, were presented at the Cino between 1963 and 1967. The Caffe Cino was joined by other OOB groups in the early 1960s. The Judson Poets' Theatre, founded in 1961 at the Judson Memorial Methodist Church by its young assistant minister Al Carmines (b. 1936), earned a reputation for productions of distinctive musicals with stylish scores by Carmines, and sharply satirical librettos by various young playwrights. *Promenade* (1965), for example, with a book by Cuban émigré playwright Marie Irene Fornés (b. 1930) eventually moved to an Off-Broadway theater for a long commercial run. At her Cafe La Mama, founded in 1962, Ellen Stewart (b. 1920?) supported dozens of young playwriting and directing talents. In 1966, the Cafe La Mama was one of the first OOB organizations to receive a substantial grant from the Rockefeller Foundation. Renamed the La Mama ETC (Experimental Theatre Club) in 1969 and housed in a lower Manhattan complex of two nearby theaters (the larger of which was once a large warehouse), it became the premiere home base for performances by numerous American and foreign avant-garde companies.

By the late 1960s, there were a score of OOB theaters in operation. In the mid-1960s, Equity waived its rules allowing members to work in OOB productions. To promote recognition of OOB, and to help its members achieve their artistic goals, the Off-Off-Broadway Alliance was organized with support from various government agencies and foundations. By the mid-1970s, there were as many as seventy-eight major OOB producing companies, and more than a hundred secondary groups—a mixture of theaters showcasing new playwrights, culturally specific theaters—as they came to be called—and avant-garde companies exploring new methods and styles of theatrical performance. (A number of avant-garde theater artists and companies are sufficiently important to be addressed in a separate section below.)

Among the important OOB producing groups dedicated to new plays were The Ensemble Studio Theatre (founded 1971); Interart Theatre (founded 1970); the New Dramatists company (founded 1949), Playwrights Horizons (founded in 1971); and Theatre for the New City (founded 1971).

*Scene from* Heart of the Earth: A Popol Vuh Story *(1995). Book by Cherrie Moraga. Music by Glen Vélez. Puppets, Masks, and Direction by Ralph Lee. Produced by INTAR Hispanic American Arts Center. Max Ferrá, Artistic Director. Courtesy of INTAR. Photo: Jim Moore. ©1994.*

Companies like the Classic Stage Company (founded 1967) and the Jean Cocteau Repertory Company (founded 1971) mounted a range of historical and modern classics.

A number of OOB theater companies were organized to foster the work of ethnic minorities, women, and gays and lesbians. The National Black Theatre (founded 1968), the New Federal Theatre (founded 1970), the New Lafayette Theatre (1967–72) and the Urban Arts Corps (founded 1968) joined with the Negro Ensemble Company to develop new African–American drama. New York's growing Latino community was served by INTAR (International Arts Relations/Hispanic American Arts Center, founded 1966), the Puerto Rican Traveling Theatre Company (founded 1967), Repertorio Español (founded 1968), and the Thalia Spanish Theatre, which presents a range of Spanish and Latin American plays, but specializes in productions of Spanish *zarzuela*. The Pan Asian Repertory Theatre (founded 1977) was one of the first Asian–American theater companies. The Irish Rebel Theatre at the Irish Arts Center (founded 1972) presented modern and contemporary Irish drama, while the American Jewish Theatre and the Jewish Repertory Theatre (both founded in 1974) focused on old and new plays and musicals by Jewish writers. The AMAS ("You Love") Musical Theatre was a multiracial, multicultural company specializing in new, small-scale musicals and revues. The Play-House of the Ridiculous (1967–72) and its more successful offshoot the Ridiculous Theatrical Company (1967) were among the first theaters oriented to the gay community. At the Ridiculous Theatre Company, founder actor–playwright Charles Ludlam (1943–87) staged his own high-camp parodies of classic plays and operas, including *Bluebeard* (1970), *Camille* (1973), *Der Ring Gott Farblonjet* (*The Ring of the Nibelungen;* literally in Yiddish "The Ring God Mixed-Up," 1977), and *The Mystery of Irma Vep* (1984). Bizarre and zany in their mixture of high and low art, female impersonation, scatological jokes, and lavish visual effects, "ridiculous theater" was a unique phenomenon and attracted a large following, which was far from exclusively gay. TOSOS (The Other Side of Silence, 1972–77) and the Glines (1976–82) were other theaters serving the gay community. Spider Woman Theatre, named after the Hopi goddess of creation, was founded in 1975 by Lisa Mayo and Gloria and Muriel Miguel to focus on both Native American and feminist concerns. Split Britches, an important feminist and lesbian troupe, was founded as an offshoot of Spider Woman Theatre by Lois Weaver (b. 1950), Peggy Shaw (b. 1944), and Deborah Margolin. Both groups create collective theater pieces marked by an improvisatory, nonlinear, often comedic approach to issues of gender. The WOW (Women's One World) Café was organized by Weaver, Shaw, and Margolin in 1982 as a venue for a range of women's performances.

In 1978, OOB theater (and the Broadway theater district) was bolstered with the opening of Theatre Row on Forty-Second Street between Ninth and Tenth Avenues. For decades this block had been an eyesore. To clean it up, the city of New York bought properties along the street and turned them over to OOB companies for conversion into theaters, offices, and rehearsal studios. This reclamation led to a widespread revitalization of the area with new upscale restaurants, shops, the Manhattan Plaza, a subsidized apartment complex for performing artists, and new theaters. A number of OOB companies, as they became more stable and established, upgraded to Off-Broadway status. For example, the Circle Repertory Theatre, the Manhattan Theatre Club, and Playwrights Horizons, which had begun as OOB theaters became important Off-Broadway companies. By the mid-1970s, the Theatre Development Fund had expanded its ticket discount program to include both Off- and Off-Off-Broadway productions. The number of OOB companies and productions declined in the 1980s, but in the mid-1990s there were still over 120 groups of various sizes and types in operation. There was, furthermore, from the 1970s onward increasing cross-influence among Off-Broadway, Off-Off-Broadway, and Broadway as theater artists moved between the various venues, as companies upgraded their status, and as productions transferred from OOB to Off-Broadway and from Off-Broadway to Broadway. The distinctions among the various venues were more a matter of production size, ticket prices, Equity contract, and tax-paying or tax-free status, than overall artistic quality and style. By the early 1990s, mainly because of the development of Off- and Off-Off-Broadway, the New York theatrical scene was far richer and more diverse than it had been at mid-century.

AFTER WORLD WAR II, opportunities to experience high-quality professional theater outside of New York City were limited. Some cities had well-managed and financed amateur community theaters—for example, the Cleveland Playhouse or the Omaha Community Playhouse. Major metropolises were still visited by touring productions of major Broadway hits, or, as noted in chapter 6, by the Lunts, Katharine Cornell, and Margaret Webster's company. Several professional summer stock companies located in vacation areas also continued to operate. But with the availability of theater at an all-time low, many people had virtually lost the practice of playgoing. This situation began to change in the late 1940s and 1950s with the rise of resident professional theaters in a number of American cities.

Margo Jones (1913–55) founded the prototype resident theater. A successful Broadway director and producer, in 1947 Jones returned to her native Texas and opened Theatre '47 in Dallas. (The name of the theater changed yearly—Theatre '48, '49, etc.—until, following her death, it became the Margo Jones Theatre.) Jones's book *Theatre-in-the-Round* (1951) chronicled her experience and vision for a national network of resident theaters. At her theater Jones mounted fully professional productions of meritorious new American plays alongside international classics. Her notable premieres of American plays include Tennessee Williams's *Summer and Smoke* (1947), William Inge's *Dark at the Top of the Stairs* (1947), and Jerome Lawrence and Robert E. Lee's *Inherit the Wind* (1950).

In the late 1940s and early 1950s, the number of resident theaters multiplied. Inspired in part by Jones's example, Nina Vance (1915–80) founded the Alley Theatre in Houston in 1947. Movie stars Gregory Peck (b. 1916), Dorothy McGuire (b. 1919), and Mel Ferrer (b. 1917) organized the La Jolla Playhouse in 1947. Zelda Fichandler (b. 1924) with others cofounded the Arena Stage in Washington, D.C., in 1950. And in 1952 Herbert Blau and Jules Irving founded the San Francisco Actor's Workshop. Although these theaters were initially amateur, they moved rapidly in the direction of full professionalism. Other resident theaters founded in the 1950s include the Milwaukee Repertory Theatre (1954), Chicago's Court Theatre (1954), and the Dallas Theatre Center (1959).

The resident theater movement was given a major boost in 1959 when the Ford Foundation contributed grants totaling almost five hundred thousand dollars to the Alley Theatre, Arena Stage, and the Actor's Workshop, as well as to a competitively selected group of directors and playwrights. In 1962, the Ford Foundation's support to resident theaters had risen to nine million dollars; by the mid-1980s, their cumulative contribution amounted to sixty million dollars. (In addition to its support of resident theaters, the Ford Foundation also contributed handsomely to the development of the other arts.) In 1961 a Ford Foundation grant led to the organization of the Theatre Communications Group (TCG). TCG offered a range of services to resident theaters, from sponsoring combined auditions and exchange visits among directors, to maintaining theater personnel files, to the publication of playscripts, a job-placement newsletter, a monthly magazine (*American Theatre* began publication in 1980), and various reports on resident theater organization, financing, and audience development. Other private foundations soon joined with the Ford Foundation to support nonprofit resident theater companies across the country, including, as noted above, many of New York's Off- and Off-Off-Broadway companies. Professional noncommercial theaters also benefited significantly from the founding of the National Endowment for the Arts in 1965 and the consequent development of numerous state and municipal arts agencies, which, for the first time since the Depression-era New Deal programs, provided for substantial government subsidies for the arts. The League of Resident Theatres (LORT) was founded in 1965 to represent resident theaters and to negotiate a series of special contracts with Equity.

Another breakthrough for the development of resident theaters came in 1963 when the celebrated English director Tyrone Guthrie (1900–1971), who had been instrumental in founding Canada's Stratford Festival in 1954, lent his considerable prestige and expertise to the founding of the Minneapolis Theatre (later renamed the Tyrone Guthrie Theatre). With a company of experienced, well-known actors, such as Jessica Tandy (1909–94) and her husband Hume Cronyn (b. 1911) and George Grizzard (b. 1928), and housed in a new, innovative multimillion dollar facility, the Guthrie Theatre attracted national attention to the resident theater movement.

In the 1960s and 1970s the number of resident theaters founded increased from about a dozen companies to well over a hundred companies at the beginning of the 1980s. Not all resident theaters were successful. But over two decades, many more theaters opened than folded. Economic restraints and a cycle of recession and inflation slowed the number of resident theaters founded in the 1980s and 1990s; nevertheless, by the mid-1990s, TCG represented almost three hundred professional theaters, most of which were located outside New York City, spread across dozens of towns and cities nationwide. According to TCG's annual fiscal survey, *Theatre Facts 1995*, these theaters played to a total attendance of almost twenty million in the 1994–95 season, presenting almost sixty thousand performances of about twenty-six hundred productions. Furthermore, resident theaters employed a total of more than 32,500 actors, directors, designers, playwrights, and technical and managerial personnel. Taken as a whole, by the late 1990s nonprofit resident theaters comprised the largest sector of the American theater.

Resident theaters vary significantly in operating budgets, staffing, and physical plants. The largest—e.g., Actors Theatre of Louisville (founded in 1964), the Missouri Repertory Theatre (founded 1964), Atlanta's Alliance Theatre, (founded 1968), Houston's Alley Theatre, Washington, D.C.'s Arena Stage, Baltimore's Center Stage (founded in 1963), the Guthrie Theatre, the Hartford Stage Company (founded in 1964), the La Jolla Playhouse, and Chicago's Steppenwolf Theatre (founded in 1976)—are well-established, corporate-style organizations with multimillion dollar budgets, handsome physical plants housing two or more theaters, and large artistic, technical, and administrative staffs. They may present a dozen or more productions each season—a mixture of classics and contemporary American and foreign plays—to a total audience of several hundred thousand, a substantial number

*Left, a scene from the Omaha Magic Theatre's production of* Sound Fields: Are We Hear, *by Megan Terry, JoAnn Schmidman, and Sora Kimberlain. From left Jon Lindley, Hollie McClay, JoAnn Schmidman, and Sora Kimberlain. Courtesy Omaha Magic Theatre. Photo by Megan Terry c. 1992.*

*Right, from left Liza Lapira as Peony, Mimosa as Sara, and Eileen Rivera as Hyacinth in the Pan Asian Repertory Theatre's production of* Shanghai Lil's *a musical about a Chinatown restaurant transformed into a cabaret/nightclub during World War II. Book and lyrics by Lilah Kan, music by Louis Steward, direction and choreography by Tisa Chang. Courtesy Pan Asian Repertory Theatre. Photo: Carol Rosegg.*

*A scene from* Talking Bones *by Shay Youngblood as produced by the Penumbra Theatre Company in 1993–94. Directed by Robbie McCauley with, from left, Laurie Carlos and Lou Bellamy. Courtesy Penumbra Theatre.*

of whom are regular season subscribers. Initially a number of resident theaters attempted to produce plays in repertory fashion, but eventually, mainly
for economic reasons, the repertory system was abandoned. Instead, plays
are presented sequentially, generally for a limited, predetermined number of
performances. As part of their general cultural and educational missions—the
rationale for their nonprofit status—the larger resident theaters often mount
various community oriented "outreach" programs, as they are called—e.g.,
theater performances and workshops for school-aged children, tours of productions to other towns and cities in their immediate region, and in-service
professional theater training programs. In contrast, the smallest theaters may
have budgets of five hundred thousand dollars or less, operate in small two-
hundred-seat theaters, sometimes converted from business or industrial
spaces, and operate with a staff of ten or so.

Many resident theaters—large, mid-sized, or small—often have established programs, a repertory focus, or production style that give them a special distinction. In 1977, for example, the Actors Theatre of Louisville (ATL)
initiated the annual Humana Festival of New American Plays, named after
the principal corporate sponsors of the festival, Humana, Inc., one of the
largest health care companies in the world with corporate headquarters in
Louisville. Under the long-time leadership of artistic director Jon Jory (b.
1938), ATL's Humana Festival, over the course of two decades, has mounted
hundreds of productions of new plays and fostered the careers of dozens of
playwrights. Through its annual Classics in Context program begun in 1986,
ATL also has brought new attention to world drama classics. The American
Repertory Theatre (ART), founded in Cambridge, Massachusetts, in 1980 by
the influential critic and director Robert Brustein (b. 1927), has won acclaim
for its innovative staging of classics and provocative experimental works, but
ART has also mounted premieres of mainstream-oriented plays, including
*Big River* (1985), a popular, award-winning musical adaptation of Mark
Twain's *Adventures of Huckleberry Finn*. The Yale Repertory Theatre was
also founded by Robert Brustein, in 1966; under Lloyd Richards (b. 1923),
artistic director from 1979–91, it became especially noted for its productions
of South African Athol Fugard's plays and the premieres of all of August
Wilson's (b. 1945) acclaimed interpretations of the African–American experience. Philadelphia's small Wilma Theatre (founded in 1973), under the co-
artistic directorship of two Czech émigrés, Jiri and Blanka Ziska, has earned
distinction for its imaginative productions of modernist European and
American plays. Los Angeles's Odyssey Theatre (founded in 1969) has maintained a special interest in contemporary American and British plays.

Parallel with developments Off- and Off-Off-Broadway, a number of resident theaters were founded to promote the work of women and ethnic minorities. For example, Minneapolis's At the Foot of the Mountain Theatre (founded
in 1974) has concentrated on collaborative pieces on feminist themes. The
Omaha Magic Theatre (OMT), founded in 1968 by JoAnn Schmidman
(b. 1945), is woman-artist managed and since 1974 home to playwright-in-
residence Megan Terry (b. 1932), one of the more original voices in contemporary

American drama. Working collaboratively, Schmidman and Terry have created over sixty inventive pieces which address a wide range of social issues from spousal abuse to illiteracy to artistic censorship. Los Angeles's East West Players, founded by the actor Mako (b. 1932) in 1965 as the first Asian–American theater company, has championed the work of numerous talented Asian–American playwrights, actors, and directors. Other pioneering Asian–American theaters include Hawaii's Kumu Kahua Theatre (1971) and the San Francisco's Asian American Theatre Company (1973). African–American theater companies like Jomandi Productions in Atlanta (1976), the St. Louis Black Repertory Company (1976), Crossroads Theatre Company in New Brunswick, New Jersey (1978), the Penumbra Theatre Company in St. Paul, Minnesota (1978), and the Detroit Repertory Theatre (1957) have been important in promoting African–American playwrights and in casting African Americans in a range of contemporary world drama. (The Detroit Repertory Theatre has long followed a policy of nontraditional, racially mixed casting.) Beginning in the mid-1960s, Hispanic theaters were organized wherever there were concentrations of Latinos, but principally in New York and California. California's important El Teatro Campesino and its offshoots warrant separate discussion below.

By the late 1980s and early 1990s, resident theaters had become the principal venues and producers of high quality theater in America. Other cities—Chicago, Minneapolis–St. Paul, Seattle, San Francisco, and Washington, D.C.—joined with New York as important theater centers. Chicago's rise to a major theater center is often traced to a number of small, amateur improvisational comedy companies active in the 1950s and 1960s. Viola Spolin (1906–94), a gifted teacher and the creator of hundreds of inventive improvisatory theater games designed to promote creativity, was the guiding spirit behind Chicago improvisation. In the 1950s, Spolin conducted theater games workshops first at the Compass Theatre and then at the Second City theater company, both cofounded by her son Paul Sills (b. 1927). These workshops were the foundation for the improvised comic sketches and routines for which the Second City became famous not only in Chicago but nationwide. Graduates of Chicago's Second City company, and its offshoots in other American and Canadian cities, comprise a veritable Who's Who of stand-up comedians and comic actors in American theater, film, and television, including Alan Arkin (b. 1934), Dan Aykroyd (b. 1954), Linda Lavin (b. 1937), Elaine May (b. 1932), Bill Murray (b. 1950), and Mike Nichols (b. 1931). Through her book *Improvisation for the Theatre* (1963), as well as her lectures and workshops, Spolin's methods became well known and were adopted to a wide range of activities in education, psychotherapy, stage direction, and actor training. In the 1960s and 1970s, other Chicago theaters were founded, including the Body Politic Theatre (1966–95)—also cofounded by Paul Sills—the Organic Theatre (1969), the Victory Gardens Theatre (1974), the Northlight Theatre (1974), the Wisdom Bridge Company (1974), and the Steppenwolf Theatre (1976). By the mid-1990s, Chicago was the second largest theater center in the United States with some 150 theaters—a rich mélange of commercial venues, nonprofit companies, a range of culturally specific theaters, college and university theaters, improvisational comedy theaters, and suburban dinner theaters.

The Guthrie Theatre and the Children's Theatre Company, founded in 1961, stimulated an increased interest in theater among Minneapolis–St. Paul's burgeoning affluent, well-educated population. Beginning in the 1970s, a dozen or so small theater companies opened in the Twin Cities, many of which continued to operate in the mid-1990s, including the Cricket Theatre (founded 1971), the multiracial Mixed Blood Theatre (founded 1976), and the unique and critically acclaimed Franco–American Théâtre de la Jeune Lune (founded 1979) which splits its season between Minneapolis and Paris. Seattle is home to a dozen resident theaters, including the Seattle Repertory Theatre (founded 1963), A Contemporary Theatre, Inc. (founded 1965), the Northwest Asian American Theatre (founded 1972), the Intiman Theatre Company (founded 1974), and New City/Theatre Zero (founded 1982), Seattle's principal avant-garde theater company. In the early 1990s Theatre Bay Area, a theatrical service organization, listed over a hundred theater groups in the populous San Francisco Bay region, including San Francisco's flagship company the American Conservatory Theatre (founded 1966 in Pittsburgh, but relocated to San Francisco in 1968); the Magic Theatre (founded 1965), which has premiered the work of numerous important American playwrights, including Sam Shepard; Theatre Rhinoceros (founded 1977), one of the oldest resident companies focusing on gay and lesbian material; and the Berkeley Repertory Theatre (founded 1968). Washington, D.C., is the home not only for Arena Stage, but also the Shakespeare Theatre (founded 1969), the Source Theatre Company (founded 1977), and the Woolly Mammoth Theatre Company (founded 1980). Los Angeles, long dominated by the film industry, nevertheless is home to a score of theater groups—large professional resident theaters and small showcase operations—mounting a total of more than twelve hundred productions a year. Like New York, other urban theater centers have organized their own service associations and created equivalents to the Tony and Obie awards. The Chicago theater awards, for example, are called "Jeffs" after the nineteenth-century actor Joseph Jefferson.

The summer Shakespeare festival is a specialized and important sector among American resident theaters. Its origins can be traced to the early decades of the twentieth century when several North American theater producers began to embrace Shakespeare as an organizing principle for a summer festival. In 1929, for example, actor Fritz Leiber (1883–1949) created the Chicago Civic Shakespeare Society, to present several Shakespeare productions at the Chicago Civic Theatre each summer. Although the productions served primarily as a vehicle for Leiber and his actress–wife, Virginia Bronson (fl. 1900–1930s), they were an annual event for a number of years. In 1934, Thomas Wood Stevens (1880–1942), founder of the theater department at Carnegie–Mellon University (then Carnegie Institute of Technology), collaborated with émigré English director Ben Iden Payne (1881–1976) to reconstruct a conjectural version of the Elizabethan Globe Theatre at the

Chicago World's Fair where abbreviated versions of Shakespeare's plays were presented. This theater was rebuilt the following year at the Pacific International Exposition in Balboa Park in San Diego for the same purpose, ultimately giving rise to an annual festival at what became known as the Old Globe Theatre.

The modern idea of a festival of Shakespeare plays in the United States, however, began with Angus L. Bowmer (1904–79), a professor at Southern Oregon College in Ashland, who founded the Oregon Shakespeare Festival (OSF) in 1935. The OSF remains the oldest surviving Shakespeare festival and one of the largest resident theaters in the United States. The Old Globe Theatre, although it too can trace its origins to 1935, did not actually offer a summer festival of plays until 1949. In the 1950s several other important festivals were founded, including not only the New York Shakespeare Festival, but also the American Shakespeare Theatre (AST, founded 1955) located in Stratford, Connecticut. Until its demise in the late 1970s, the AST was the nation's premiere Shakespeare company, mounting a total of over seventy-five productions. Among the numerous prominent actors of the day appearing in AST productions were Morris Carnovsky, Alfred Drake, Katherine Hepburn (b. 1907), the African–American star James Earl Jones (b. 1931), and the noted Canadian actor Christopher Plummer (b. 1929).

In the early 1960s, stimulated undoubtedly by the 1964 quadricentennial of Shakespeare's birth and the growing resident theater movement, dozens of summer Shakespeare festivals were founded. The older festivals, furthermore, gradually extended their seasons and expanded their operations. The Oregon Shakespeare Festival, for example, which had been gradually moving toward becoming a fully professional company, went from a two-month summer season to virtually a year-round operation. OSF's principal theater, the outdoor Elizabethan Theatre, was rebuilt on two occasions. In 1959, an entirely new, third Elizabethan Theatre was built, modeled after reconstructions of Shakespeare's Globe Theatre. In 1970, the OSF added a modern, indoor theater—the Angus L. Bowmer Theatre—to its complex. In 1977, the OSF opened a small "studio" theater named the Black Swan. Finally in 1995, the interior of the Elizabethan Theatre was significantly remodeled for better acoustics and audience comfort. In the late 1960s and 1970s, the San Diego's Old Globe also expanded into additional theaters and a longer season. In 1984, the Alabama Shakespeare Festival (founded 1972) moved into a new two-theater, multimillion-dollar facility in Montgomery. With such expansion, these major festival theaters also stretched their repertoires well beyond Shakespeare's plays. A typical season at a Shakespeare festival theater now includes not only two or three Shakespearean plays, but also revivals of international classics and productions of contemporary comedies, dramas, and musicals.

By the early 1990s there were over eighty Shakespeare festival theaters operating in the U.S. Among the principal ones, in addition to those noted above, are the California Shakespeare Festival in Orinda; Shakespeare at Santa Cruz (California); the Utah Shakespeare Festival; Shakespeare and Company at Lenox Massachusetts; the Shakespeare Festival of Dallas; the

*The Old Globe Theatre, San Diego. Photo: Ken Howard. Courtesy of the Old Globe Theatre.*

Colorado Shakespeare Festival; the North Carolina Shakespeare Festival; and the Shakespeare Repertory Theatre of Chicago. The quality of presentation can vary widely from company to company and season to season, but the various Shakespeare companies and festivals do offer thousands of theatergoers the opportunity to experience performances of Shakespeare's plays. The OSF, for example, boasts an annual attendance of over three hundred fifty thousand people drawn from across the nation. Many of the large outdoor summer festivals—a number of which, following the example of the New York Shakespeare Festival, offer free performances—attract thousands of spectators per performance. After their regular season, Washington, D.C.'s Shakespeare Theatre, for example, offers a free production every summer in the outdoor Carter Barron Amphitheater in Rock Creek Park. Attendance is regularly about four thousand people per performance.

By the mid-1990s, resident theaters remained a vital part of the American theater, but the vigorous growth that had marked the period from 1960 to 1990 had significantly waned. Resident, nonprofit theaters nationwide were heavily dependent on contributions to balance their budgets; earned income often accounted for 50 percent or less of the total expenses. But the rate of contributions declined precipitously from 1990 to 1995, forcing many theaters to employ new strategies to close the inevitable gap between earned income and expenses, including cutting expenses, reducing the number of plays presented and the scope of production, and increasing ticket prices. Small and mid-sized resident theaters, with fewer resources for fund-raising and lacking the endowments which many large companies were able to establish, are especially vulnerable to these fiscal changes.

Especially worrisome to resident theaters is the significant decline in the budget of the National Endowment for the Arts (NEA). After years of significant growth, congressional appropriations slowed in the 1980s. After reaching a high of almost $176 million in 1992, the budget declined to $162 million in 1995. The NEA allocation to its theatre program division was about $8 million, down from a high of almost $11 million in 1981. In terms of real dollars, these decreases are even more substantial. In 1997, congressional conservatives, long-standing opponents of federal arts funding, failed in their efforts to eliminate the NEA altogether, but they did succeed in preventing any increase in its budget. Major foundations also reduced their support to the arts in the early 1990s. With nonprofit resident theaters more dependent than ever on earned income and private contributions, concerns arose that the nonprofit sector would become increasingly market driven, that the distinction between commercial and noncommercial theater would continue to blur, and that the important role resident theaters had as conservators of the classics and promoters of innovation and experimentation would be compromised. Ironically, since the nonprofit sector is one of the principal engines driving Broadway, its loss would significantly affect the vitality and diversity of American commercial theater.

OFF- AND OFF-OFF Broadway and the counterculture movement of the 1960s gave rise to a number of radical or alternative theaters bound together by a common interest in challenging the status quo. These theaters tended in two major, sometimes overlapping, directions. Several companies, for example, embraced forms of agitprop theater to press for social and political awareness and reform, while other groups were oriented more toward avant-garde, aesthetic experimentation with a point of view that was less socio-political than broadly humanistic. Whether social activist or aesthetic, alternative theaters explored approaches to theater that emphasized performance over script, the visual over the verbal, and nonlinear and nonnarrative structures. Collaboration also tended to be valued over individual effort and improvisation became the principal *modus operandi.*

The San Francisco Mime Troupe is one of America's first and oldest activist theaters. Founded by R. G. Davis (b. 1933) in the late 1950s, the Mime Troupe initially adapted *commedia dell'arte*–inspired plays to contemporary sociopolitical issues. In 1967, for example, the Mime Troupe adapted Goldoni's *L'amante militaire* (1755; The soldierly lover) as an anti-Vietnam War play. Like the historical *commedia* troupes, the Mime Troupe toured to various neighborhoods in San Francisco performing out-of-doors on portable platform stages. They also adopted the conventions of *commedia* performance—masks, stereotypical characterization, and broad exaggerated gestures and movements. In the early 1970s, the Mime Troupe moved away from the *commedia* style and toward several popular entertainment genres—nineteenth-century melodrama, silent film, cartoons and comic books, and circus. Music, songs, and dance were also featured elements of their performances. With scripts by Joan Holden (b. 1935), each production tended to focus on a particular social, political, or economic problem. *The Independent Female; or, A Man Has His Pride* (1970) was about women's liberation; *Frijoles or Beans* (1975) examined food distribution; *Hotel Universe* (1977) concerned urban renewal. Through the 1970s, the San

Francisco Mime Troupe aligned itself even more closely with working class views and issues and became increasingly a multiracial, multicultural company. *I Ain't Your Uncle* (1990), a deconstruction in their inimitable style of *Uncle Tom's Cabin*, is one of their more recent examinations of racism and race relations. San Francisco remained their home base, but tours across the United States and to Europe and Central America gave the Mime Troupe a national and international following.

The Free Southern Theatre was founded in 1963 by Gilbert Moses (1942–95) and John O'Neal (b. 1940) to support the civil rights struggle by touring free theatrical performances to cities and rural towns across the American South. One of their first productions was social historian Martin B. Duberman's *In White America* (1963), a moving docudrama based on authentic letters, speeches, and memoirs about the black struggle against racism. The Free Southern Theatre was one of the first integrated companies to play to mostly black audiences in the rural South. Before it disbanded in 1980, the Free Southern Theatre presented a range of new African–American and classic and modernist drama including *Waiting for Godot* (1953), African–American actor–playwright Ossie Davis's *Purlie Victorious* (1961), and Molière's *George Dandin* (1668), all intended to promote black pride and historical and social awareness among its audiences.

In 1965, the National Farm Workers Association, a union principally of Mexican–American—or Chicano, as they prefer to be identified—migrant laborers, organized a historic strike against the grape growers of California's San Joaquin Valley. Luis Valdéz (b. 1940) founded El Teatro Campesino (ETC, The Farmworkers' Theatre) to support the strikers and agitate for their cause. Inspired by the San Francisco Mime Troupe, Valdéz's short agitprop skits *(actos)* also adapted the comic conventions and style of *commedia dell'arte* and silent films, but with a distinct Latino flavor like the traditional *carpas teatros*. ETC's plays, for example, always used a mixture of Spanish and English—the patois of their audiences. The characters also were drawn from recognizable Anglo and Chicano types. Initially ETC focused solely on the strike, but by the late 1960s, its concerns broadened to other issues in Mexican–American life. *Los vendidos* (The sellouts, 1967), for example, addressed stereotyping and tokenism in government hiring; *No saco nada de la escuela* (I don't get anything out of school, 1969) was concerned with the experience of Chicano children in schools dominated by Anglo teachers and culture; *Vietnam campesino* (1970) examined the threats posed to farm workers and to disenfranchised minorities in general by the military and agribusiness establishment.

In 1971, Valdéz relocated ETC to San Juan Bautista, a small rural town one hundred miles south of San Francisco, where he organized El Centro Campesino Cultural as a research center and theater laboratory. Usually after premiering at El Centro, ETC productions toured to other locations in California. Over the next decade, Valdéz's plays became longer and more complex, incorporating aspects of Amerindian mythology and Chicano folklore. Less overtly political and militant, they were concerned with the struggles of the Mexican–American people as a whole and with the historical and prevailing Anglo-Hispanic relationship. *Zoot Suit* (1978), for example, was a drama with music based on an actual 1940s trial in which members of a Chicano gang in Los Angeles were wrongfully convicted of murder. Structured like a Depression era Living Newspaper, *Zoot Suit* enjoyed a long run in Los Angeles and was the first Hispanic–American play to be presented on Broadway. Other mainstream successes followed *Zoot Suit,* including *Corridos!* (1983), based on traditional Chicano folk ballads; *I Don't Have to Show You No Stinking Badges* (1986), after a character in and a line from the classic film *The Treasure of Sierra Madre* (1948); and *Bandido!* (1994), about the California bandit hero Tiburcio Vasquez. The ETC became a model for a score of Chicano *teatros* founded in the 1960s and 1970s, including the important and influential El Teatro de la Esperanza (Theatre of Hope) in San Francisco, Su Teatro (Your Theatre) in Denver, and Teatro Libertad (Free Theatre) in Tucson. In 1971 an umbrella organization, TENAZ (El Teatro Nacional de Atzlan), was founded to facilitate communication among Chicano *teatros*. By the mid-1970s, there were perhaps a hundred such groups nationwide. The *teatros* movement fostered opportunities for numerous Latino playwrights, directors, and performers, many of whom achieved prominence both within the Latino theater community, as well as in mainstream theater, film, and television.

The San Francisco Mime troupe and El Teatro Campesino were among the more prominent, but not the only theaters addressing workers' issues. Other important theaters oriented to a working-class audience which merit mention include the New York Street Theatre Caravan (1968), the Iron Clad Agreement (1976), the Modern Times Theatre (1977), and the Dakota Theatre Caravan (1977).

The Bread and Puppet Theatre, founded in 1961 in New York by German émigré Peter Schumann (b. 1934), is a particularly distinctive activist theater company. At the beginning of a Bread and Puppet Theatre performance, actors pass through the audience handing out loaves of bread, inviting spectators to tear off a piece and then pass the loaf to their neighbor. For Schumann, puppet shows, like bread, are essential to life. As writer, puppet designer, and director, Schumann is the controlling spirit behind Bread and Puppet Theatre productions. The puppets vary from hand-puppets to giant-sized, fifteen-feet tall rod puppets and actors wearing oversized full-head masks becoming essentially body puppets. The plays themselves are allegorical fables drawn from Biblical stories, folktales, and myths. While the puppets mime the action, an actor narrates the story, or it is told by a series of pictographs uncranked gradually from a large turning roll of paper. Scenery consists of a plain red cloth attached to a pole on either side. Drums, cymbals, a trumpet, toy musical instruments—a kazoo, for example—accent the action. Its productions are easily adapted to any indoor or outdoor space, but the Bread and Puppet Theatre tends to outdoor performance. Infused with a Christian idealism, the plays are more humanistic than political. *The King's Story* (1963), *A Man Says Goodbye to His*

*Mother* (1968), and *The Cry of the People for Meat* (1968), presented during the Vietnam War era, protested not only that conflict, but the institution of war and the various dehumanizing forces that lead to it: imperialism, greed, and a penchant for violence. In 1970, the nucleus of the company left New York eventually settling as a commune on a farm in northeast Vermont. Here each summer since 1974, they have mounted *The Domestic Resurrection Circus*, a weekend-long, quasi-sacred celebration of humankind's best qualities and a gentle protest against those tendencies that would despoil them. The performance usually attracts hundreds of spectators who are also invited to participate in the event by helping to build puppets, carrying banners in the parades that are part of the festivities, or playing some of the musical instruments. Since the mid-1970s the Bread and Puppet Theatre has occasionally toured a production. In 1975, it created a special piece for the University of California at Davis. *A Monument to Ishi* was conceived as an "antibicentennial pageant" memorializing the last surviving member of a northern California Indian tribe—Ishi, he was named—and decrying the tragic historical consequences of colonization and western expansion. The Bread and Puppet Theatre is a unique institution, but Schumann's expressive use of puppetry has inspired other theater artists, including most notably Julie Taymor (b. 1952). Taymor is best known for her vividly theatrical stagings in which she combines her imaginatively designed puppets with live actors. She has been especially acclaimed for *Juan Darien, a Carnival Mass* (1988), a South American folkloric tale of revenge and resurrection, and for her inventive mounting of the stage version of the Disney animated film *The Lion King* (1998).

American avant-garde companies in the 1960s were influenced by several foreign theater artists, including the Polish director and theoretician Jerzy

*Left, a scene from the Bread and Puppet Theatre's production of* The World *(1983). Photo: D. J. Watermeier.*

*Right, scene from the Open Theatre's production of Jean Claude van Itallie's* The Serpent. *Courtesy Department of Special Collections and Archives, Kent State University Libraries. Photo: Freddy Tornberg.*

Grotowski (b. 1933), the Italian director and theoretician Eugenio Barba (b. 1936), and the English director Peter Brook (b. 1925). Grotowski, especially, exercised a signal influence through his visits to New York in the late 1960s, and many American avant-garde companies adopted his "poor theater" approach. In the 1960s, the writings of Antonin Artaud and Bertolt Brecht, translated into English and published in inexpensive paperbacks or in theater journals, had a significant impact. *The Tulane Drama Review* (later renamed *TDR, The Drama Review),* founded in 1957, published numerous essays, reviews, and interviews about European and American avant-garde theater. As new avant-garde companies were founded, moreover, they tended to influence one another. A growing number of international festivals, organized to showcase the work of avant-garde theater companies, also increased the opportunities for cross-pollination.

A phenomenon called the *happening* was a major influence on developing avant-garde theaters. The form was pioneered in the late 1950s by Allan Kaprow (b. 1927), a painter and art historian. Derived from dadaist festivals, happenings were quasitheatrical affairs in which spectators were involved in a series of multimedia experiences. For example, in *18 Happenings in 6 Parts* (1959), one of Kaprow's early happenings, an art gallery was compartmentalized into several small rooms. Visitors to the gallery moved from room to room in each of which, over a short span of time, they listened to taped music or sounds, viewed slides of paintings, familiar objects, and collages, while simultaneously a live ensemble entertained them with a series of often mundane and seemingly unrelated activities: bouncing a ball; rolling and unrolling pants legs; squeezing the juice from oranges and then drinking it; painting on a roll of canvas, and so on. Sometimes attendees at a happening were expected to engage or participate in certain prescribed activities, but happenings, like the experiencing of the visual arts in general, mainly involved passive observation. Happenings and a range of similar performance events, most

*Arthur Miller's* All My Sons *with (from left) Loris Wheeler as Ann Deever, Arthur Kennedy as Chris Keller, Ed Begley as Joe Keller, and Beth Merrill as Kate Keller. Culver Pictures.*

organized by avant-garde painters, sculptors, and musicians, had a considerable vogue in the early 1960s. As a mode of artistic expression, however, happenings became increasingly self-indulgent, trivialized, and amateurish. Nevertheless, with their emphasis on spatial arrangements, activities rather than plots, simultaneity and multiple focus, the use of several media, and varying degrees of audience interaction, happenings contributed to the work of several emerging avant-garde theater companies and artists.

In 1968, after four years in Europe, the Living Theatre returned to the United States with a repertoire of four avant-garde performance pieces: an adaptation of *Antigone* by Judith Malina "after Sophocles, after Hölderlin, after Brecht" as their advertising broadsheet described it; *Frankenstein,* based on Mary Shelley's gothic novel; a mysterious, ritualistic exercise called *Mysteries and Smaller Pieces;* and *Paradise Now,* an inflammatory, dramatic diatribe. Partially scripted around collectively developed scenarios, these works consisted mainly of physical activity: yoga exercises, pseudomilitary close-order drills, erotic writhings and gropings, ritualized processions, and free, individualized improvisation; frenetic explosive movement alternated with inaction and frozen tableaux; Hindi incantations and pop songs mingled with screams, shouts, groans, and moments of silence. Eschewing scenery, costumes, and theatrical lighting, performances relied entirely on the human— sometimes naked—body. The influence of Antonin Artaud's visionary "theater of cruelty" and Jerzy Grotowski's "poor theater" concept was unmistakable. Many of the visual and kinetic effects were stirring, but the performance style was frequently inept and the overall message was exasperatingly enigmatic. For a year, the Living Theatre toured the United States inciting both enthusiasm and outrage. They were pilloried by establishment critics, but their commitment and methods were embraced by the counterculture and several avant-garde theater artists. The pressures of the tour, however, coupled with the political upheavals of 1968–69, took their toll; the company returned to performing in Europe, but broke up the following year. Beck and Malina attracted new disciples, and continued their theatrical explorations and touring activities both in the United States and abroad. But their stars gradually faded. By the mid-1970s, they were mostly forgotten, although a Living Theatre company under Malina's direction continues to operate to the present day.

During the Living Theatre's absence, the Open Theatre emerged as the most critically acclaimed and influential avant-garde company of the 1960s. It was founded in 1963 by Joseph Chaikin (b. 1935), a former member of the Living Theatre, as an actors' collective exploring alternatives to psychological realism. Using various improvisational games and exercises, many drawn from the work of Viola Spolin, the Open Theatre Company developed a distinctive, physically expressive, theatricalist acting style. In the mid-1960s, usually working with a writer to give their improvised material a shape and focus, the Open Theatre mounted several striking theater pieces. *Viet Rock* (1966) by Megan Terry (b. 1932), for example, was one of the first plays to protest the Vietnam War. *The Serpent* (1968) had a text by Jean Claude van Itallie (b. 1936) which integrated episodes from the Book of Genesis with the assassinations of John F. Kennedy and Martin Luther King Jr. Typically, however, Open Theatre plays were apolitical. *Terminal* (1969), for example, with a text by Susan Yankowitz (b. 1941), focused on human reactions to death and dying, while *The Mutation Show* (1970), scripted by Joseph Chaikin and Roberta Sklar (b. 1940), explored rituals of conformity and alienation. The Open Theatre's extensive tours in the United States and abroad significantly impacted actor training techniques and antirealistic approaches to theater, an influence which continued long after the group disbanded in 1973. Chaikin suffered a stroke in 1984 from which he has never fully recovered. But in the 1990s, he returned to the theater. Incorporating his disability into both his technique and the dramatic subject matter, he has acted in several plays which he has coauthored with Sam Shepard and Jean Claude van Itallie. He is also in demand as a director and teacher.

In 1967, Richard Schechner (b. 1934), a professor of theater at New York University and the founder of the *Tulane Drama Review,* organized the Performance Group. Drawing eclectically on a number of sources, including happenings, Grotowski, the Living Theatre, Brecht, and Artaud, Schechner created an experimental approach he called "environmental theater." For each of his productions, Schechner created a different actor–audience arrangement, an environment that would force a closer than usual integration of performer and spectator. Schechner usually used a conventional text as a starting point—for example, Euripides' *The Bacchae* for *Dionysus in 69* (1968), *Makbeth* (1969), or Brecht's *Mother Courage and Her Children* (1974)—but then he substantially altered it in the rehearsal/production process by adding contemporary references, exercises drawn from the dramatic rituals of aboriginal peoples, and the use of the created environment. *Commune* (1970), however, was a collective creation. Cobbled together from a variety of literary and historical accounts, *Commune* was a complex play-within-a-play in which actors, representing members of the infamous real-life Charles Manson "commune," reenact moments in American history from the *Mayflower* voyage to the Vietnamese War My Lai massacre as a prologue to Manson's vicious murder of actress Sharon Tate. In its time, Schechner's environmental approach was widely admired and copied. In the late 1970s, however, he dissolved his company and turned increasingly to the scholarly study of primitive dramatic ritual and performance theory.

Founded by actor–director Andre Gregory (b. 1937), the Manhattan Project was another important avant-garde, enviromental theater company of the 1970s. Using a small ensemble of actors, adapting the script to the performance space, and utilizing a stylized, highly physical, and frequently comedic approach to the dramatic material, Gregory won acclaim for his staging of an adaption of *Alice in Wonderland* (1970), Samuel Beckett's *Endgame* (1973), and Anton Chekhov's *The Seagull* (1975), the latter at the NYSF/Public Theatre. In the 1980s and 1990s, Gregory appeared as a supporting actor in mainstream productions in New York and at several regional theaters, and in a number of Hollywood films.

Robert Wilson (b. 1941) has earned a position as one of the more admired and enduring avant-garde theater artists. Trained as a painter and architect in the early 1960s, Wilson also worked as a therapist with physically and emotionally handicapped people. As a child Wilson himself had suffered from a speech impediment which he eventually overcame with the help of a gifted dance teacher named Byrd (or Bird) Hoffmann. Indeed, as a memorial to his teacher, Wilson named the school and producing organization he formed in the late 1960s the Byrd Hoffmann School of Byrds and the Byrd Hoffmann Foundation. Undoubtedly, Wilson's therapeutic experiences account for many of the characteristics of his work—e.g., their emphasis on visual and aural imagery, their detached, dreamy tone, and their snaillike pace: a simple gesture or stage-cross can take a half hour or more. Wilson's most famous pieces are, in fact, notable for their length. *Deafman Glance* (1970), for example, incorporated two earlier works—*The King of Spain* (1969) and *The Life and Times of Sigmund Freud* (1970)—and was eight hours long. In fact, Wilson as a rule tends to include all or portions of earlier work in each succeeding work which accounts in large part for their monumental length. *The Life and Times of Josef Stalin* (1973) incorporated parts of all his previous work to that point and was twelve hours in length. *KA MOUNTAIN AND GUARDenia TERRACE* (1972) created for Iran's Shiraz Festival, lasted a week.

Rejecting conventional narrative structure, Wilson's plays unfold as nonlinear collage-like accretions and progressions of images. Wilson derives his images from a panoply of sources: the lives of historical figures (Stalin, Freud, Einstein, Edison, Queen Victoria), natural phenomena (icebergs, volcanoes, dinosaurs, animals of various sorts, fire, flowers, planets), a variety of machines, (automobiles, spaceships, trains, computers, clocks), paintings, literary works, and undoubtedly his own dreams and experiences—a complex, rich mixture of symbolic, fantastical, and familiar material. Live action and theatrical effects are often integrated with film, video, and slide projections. Similarly, conventional music instruments are frequently commingled with electronically synthesized sounds to create complicated incidental music. Long periods of silence are also a major feature of Wilson's work. Wilson's "texts" are ambiguous, cryptic, and esoteric. What they are about is open to wide-ranging interpretation, but the images are frequently haunting and the accumulative experience can be both meditative and cathartic.

As Wilson's works grew increasingly complex, few American companies could afford to mount them. Since the 1980s his work has been supported by heavily subsidized European theaters—Berlin's Schaubühne and Munich's Kammerspiele, for example. Few of his major pieces have been seen in their entirety in the United States. Portions of *the CIVIL warS: a tree is best measured when it is down* (1984) have been presented by the American Repertory Theatre in Cambridge and at the Brooklyn Academy of Music (BAM). *Einstein on the Beach* (1976) was revived at BAM in 1992. Wilson's other major works include *Death and Destruction in Detroit II* (1987) and *The Black Rider: The casting of magic bullets* (1990).

Although best known for his epic scale, Robert Wilson has always simultaneously worked in a shorter, chamber theater form, focusing on one to four performers. With the great American soprano Jessye Norman, for example, he created *Great Day in the Morning* (1983), based on Negro spirituals. Beginning in the mid-1980s, while continuing to develop his own original works, both short and long, Wilson applied his unique vision and approach as a director and designer of operas and plays drawn form the classical and modern repertoire. He has, for example, staged Euripides's *Alcestis* (1986) and Ibsen's *When We Dead Awaken* (1991) for the American Repertory Theatre, Richard Strauss's *Salome* for the La Scala Opera in 1987, Mozart's *The Magic Flute* for the Paris Opera in 1991, Georg Büchner's *Danton's Death* for Houston's Alley Theatre in 1992, and Wagner's *Lohengrin* for the Metropolitan Opera in 1998. Although some critics have accused Wilson of artistic charlatanism and anti-intellectualism, the originality and inventiveness of his work has won international renown.

Richard Foreman (b. 1937) is perhaps second only to Wilson in stature as an American postmodernist theater artist. Foreman began his career writing conventional plays, but influenced by experimental filmmakers in the 1960s, his work shifted toward a more avant-garde approach. In 1968, Foreman founded the Ontological–Hysteric Theatre (OHT) as an organization for staging his plays. The name of the company signals, although not altogether clearly, Foreman's preoccupation and goals: "Ontology," an interest in the state of existence or being and "Hysteric," a reference perhaps to his goal of trying to jolt spectators out of their usual logical mode and into an altered state of psychological awareness. Foreman seems preoccupied with the process of thought, especially with the "web of disruptions," as he calls it, that continually interrupt the stream of consciousness with one thought being displaced by another often unrelated thought, and then by still another thought, *ad infinitum*. Invariably, Foreman has shaped his theatrical pieces around his own shifting states of consciousness which he meticulously records in notebooks and then dramatizes.

To date, Richard Foreman has presented over thirty works with titles ranging from the straightforward, such as *Total Recall* (1970), *Egyptology* (1985), *The Mind King* (1992), and *Benita Canova* (1998), to the cryptic, such as *Rhoda in Potato Land (Her Fall-Starts)* (1975), *Pandering to the Masses: A Misrepresentation* (1974), and *Penguin Touquet* (1981). Unlike Wilson, Foreman tends to work in a setting that, with minor variations, remains fairly constant: an unlocalized, curtainless endstage, the back wall of which might be painted in bold stripes and contain several doorways; a series of thin ropes that crisscross the space, dividing it into sectors and visually fragmenting the action; sliding screens or panels that reshape the space and create odd, distorted perspectives; and a use of colorless, nondirectional lighting that illuminates but is distinctly antitheatrical. Into this space, Foreman drops an assortment of familiar and bizarre props—couches, chairs, tables, a giant, crudely constructed penguin in *Penguin Touquet*. Sometimes props fly in and fly out. Words or verbal commentary are written or projected on elements of the set. Foreman's actors, usually costumed in everyday clothing, or frequently in various states of undress, interact with the set, props and each other in a series of robotic movements, gestures, and carefully arranged *tableaux vivants*. They intone the dialogue, frequently stare blankly or point directly at the audience, and are generally, like robots, emotionally expressionless. Unlike the pace of Wilson's works, OHT pieces move with frenetic rapidity and usually run for about one and one-half hours. The action is punctuated by the sounds of buzzers, bells, drumming, sometimes music. Foreman's own recorded voice often comments on the action; furthermore, he is a visible presence in the performance, frequently directing the action, working the light board and creating the sound, or shifting scenery and props. In recent years, however, Foreman has abandoned this practice, appearing, if at all, on videotape or film. As in Wilson's work, Foreman's pieces are enigmatic, dense, extremely difficult to puzzle out, especially in a single viewing; but the surrealistic juxtaposition of bizarre props and dreamlike activity are thought-provoking, if not consciousness altering.

Beginning in the late 1970s Foreman, like Wilson, also began directing a number of standard plays for Off-Broadway and regional theaters, including Brecht's *Threepenny Opera* (1976), H. Leivick's Yiddish theater classic *The Golem* for the New York Shakespeare Festival (1984), Molière's *Don Juan* at the Guthrie Theatre (1981), and Büchner's *Woyzeck* at the Hartford Stage Company (1990). Usually Foreman's directorial approach to these plays incorporates many of the techniques he employs in his original OHT productions. Although these productions have often sparked controversy, they have also stimulated new interest and insights into these time-worn classics.

In 1975 Elizabeth Le Compte (b. 1944) and Spalding Gray (b. 1941) founded the Wooster Group (WG) as a separate unit within Richard Schechner's Performance Group. (It was named after the Wooster Street location of the theater.) After Schechner dissolved the Performance Group, the Wooster Group organized itself as an independent company. Working improvisationally, they developed several pieces in the late 1970s based on Gray's life. *Sakonnet Point* (1977), for example, drew on Gray's boyhood summers spent at this location in Rhode Island; *Rumstick Road* (1977) is the street address where Gray grew up and focuses on his response to his mother's suicide in 1967; *Nyatt School* (1978) integrated Gray's biography with scenes from T. S. Eliot's play *The Cocktail Party* (1949); while *Point Judith* (1980) intersected Gray's recollections with O'Neill's *Long Day's Journey into Night* and other seemingly extraneous material.

These pieces established a foundation for an evolving WG style, a complex collage of evocative dancelike movement, surreal, visual images, docudrama, and the deconstruction of established texts. *Rumstick Road,* for example, used letters written by Gray's mother and father, photographs of Gray's family and home, and taped recordings of Gray eliciting responses about his mother's suicide from his father, two grandmothers, and even his mother's psychiatrist. Group improvisations were developed from this material, although in performance the connection between the documentary source and the improvised activity is not always clear. In several instances, the documents were simply read or recited as part of the performance. In one scene, Gray and the actor representing his father, called The Man, sit on stage and lip-sync to recordings which Gray had made of the actual interview. The juxtaposition of past and present in prerecorded and live performance, in this instance tended to create an ironic, unsettling effect, and this technique, extended to include filmed and videotaped material, became a WG trademark.

After Spalding Gray left the company to pursue a career as an independent monologist, the WG developed several provocative pieces based on deconstructions of classic American plays, *Route 1 & 9 (The Last Act)* (1981) juxtaposed parts of Thornton Wilder's *Our Town* with a bawdy sketch by Dewey "Pigmeat" Markham (1904–81), one of the headliners of the pre-World War II black burlesque "Chitlin' Circuit." The white WG company members performed this material in grotesque minstrel blackface, using exaggerated, stereotypical "Negro" accents and gestures. The action also incorporated at one point a film clip showing sexually explicit activities during an automobile trip on highways 1 and 9 (hence the title) which run through the heart of heavily industrialized, polluted, ugly eastern New Jersey. Although intended as a grim, ironic commentary on Wilder's idyllic representation and the reality of America, the piece provoked a storm of controversy. In *L.S.D.: Just the Highpoints* (1984), scenes from Arthur Miller's *The Crucible* were contrasted with episodes from the life of the hippie-era guru and drug advocate Timothy Leary. This piece was also intended as a dialectical commentary on American reactionary politics from the 1950s through the "Reaganite" 1980s. Miller, despite his long-standing liberal stance, took exception to this use of his play and forced the removal of *The Crucible* material from *L.S.D.* Other WG productions include *Frank Dell's The Temptation of Saint Antony* (1987), a complex collage inspired by Gustave Flaubert's *The Temptation of Saint Antony,* Ingmar Bergman's film *The Magician,* episodes from the life of the stand-up comic Lenny Bruce (who sometimes used the name "Frank Dell"), and a 1932 book about the afterlife; a deconstruction of Chekhov's *The Three Sisters* called *Brace Up!* (1991); and a treatment of O'Neill's *The Emperor Jones* (1993; revived in 1998). In 1996, WG applied its techniques to another O'Neill play—*The Hairy Ape.* Willem Dafoe (b. 1955), who since his first appearances with the Wooster Group in the 1970s had established a parallel career as a mainstream film star, played Yank. After opening at the Wooster Street Theatre, *The Hairy Ape* transferred to Broadway for a limited, but fairly successful commercial run.

Mabou Mines, named for no particular reason after a Nova Scotia mining town, was organized as a collaborative, avant-garde company in 1970. Among the founding members were Lee Breuer (b. 1937), Jo Anne Akalaitis (b. 1935), Ruth Maleczech (b. 1939), David Warrilow (b. 1934), and the composer Philip Glass (b. 1937). Mabou Mines integrates a variety of typical postmodernist theatrical techniques or strategies—video, sound effects, recorded voices, props, puppets of various sorts, bizarre props and settings, textual deconstruction—with an exploration of narrative modes and a psychologically motivated, essentially naturalistic acting style. By the mid-1980s, Mabou

Mines had mounted over thirty productions. Although several members of the company took on directorial responsibilities, Breuer and Akalaitis emerged as the principal directors and became the *de facto* leaders of the group.

Lee Breuer achieved recognition in the 1970s with a series of "animations" as he called them: *The Red House Animation* (1970), *The B. Beaver Animation* (1975) and *The Shaggy Dog Animation* (1978). In each of these pieces, metaphoric animals were used as central characters in a complex visual, aural, and verbal collage to comment on aspects of the human condition, particularly on creativity, male–female power relationships, and issues of identity. Breuer also has directed critically acclaimed productions of Samuel Beckett's *Play* and *Come and Go*—both in 1971—and *The Lost Ones* in 1974. But to date, Breuer's most successful production has been *The Gospel at Colonus* (1983), an adaptation of Sophocles's *Oedipus at Colonus* imaginatively conceptualized as a contemporary black gospel music concert. After its première at the Brooklyn Academy of Music's New Wave Festival, it was transferred to Broadway and then played limited engagements in several major regional theaters, including a staging at Houston's Grand Opera. A prolific, restless writer–director, Breuer has staged both original works and iconoclastic interpretations of historical and modernist classics. In 1990, for example, he mounted a *King Lear* transposing the action to small-town Georgia in the conservative 1950s, reversing all the gender roles, casting Ruth Maleczeck as Lear and, in fact, furthermore, making the Fool a transvestite and Edgar African American. For over a decade, he has been working on a large-scale project called *The Warrior Ant; or, The Insectiad* about the life of a metaphorical ant as it searches for life's meaning. This epic twelve-part work, only four parts of which have been mounted to date, incorporates a variety of puppets, an original score by composer Bob Telson inspired by Afro-Caribbean music, and the Mabou Mines company supplemented by a score of performers, puppeteers, and dancers. In 1991, Breuer also mounted a "work-in-progress" called *Peter Pan and Wendy*, a postmodern interpretation of James M. Barrie's famous play.

Like Breuer, Jo Anne Akalaitis has worked both with the Mabou Mines company and as an independent director alternating between creating original theater pieces and staging the work of other authors, including historical and modernist classics. *Dead End Kids: A History of Nuclear Power* (1980) explored the benefits and threats of nuclear power, using a collage technique that combined various materials from government reports, photographs, and films to excerpts from Goethe's *Faust*. Akalaitis has also achieved acclaim for her staging of a number of contemporary German playwright Franz Xaver Kroetz's neorealistic dramas, including *Through the Leaves* in 1984. Her controversial production of Beckett's *Endgame* for the American Repertory Theatre in 1984 moved the setting to a Boston subway tunnel, cast African-American actors as Hamm, Nell, and Nagg, and used percussive, dissonant postmodernist music composed by Philip Glass. Beckett sued the producer claiming artistic violation of his play, and ultimately succeeded in having his name removed from the program and advertisements.

Akalaitis continued to spark both controversy and admiration for her bold interpretations of Jean Genet's *The Screens* (1989) and Büchner's

*Leonce and Lena* for the Guthrie Theatre, John Ford's *'Tis Pity She's a Whore* (1992) for the Goodman Theatre, and Shakespeare's *Cymbeline* (1989) and *Henry IV, 1 and 2* (1991) for the New York Shakespeare Festival, the latter mixing an Elizabethan look with contemporary props—beer cans, a TV, a *Playboy* magazine—and vaudevillesque business. In 1991, Akalaitis succeeded Joseph Papp as artistic director of the New York Shakespeare Festival, but her controversial productions, including a *Woyzeck* in 1992, and her managerial style, which some viewed as abrasive, led to her dismissal in March 1993. By the mid-1990s, Mabou Mines continued as a company, and Breuer and Akalaitis remained key members, but several original members had left the company and the organization as a whole had lost much of its creative verve and focus.

Other important postmodern theater artists, include Ping Chong (b. 1946), Martha Clarke (b. 1944), Meredith Monk (b. 1942), and Laurie Anderson (b. 1947). Chong, like many postmodern writer–directors––designers, works collaboratively with a team of designers, composers, choreographers, and performers, but he is responsible for the production concept, and its overall structure, and execution. Since the early 1970s, Chong has created over two dozen highly original, imaginative pieces. He describes his approach as *bricolage,* or the assembling of diverse materials into a unified whole. His works tend in the direction of multimedia experiences combining film, video, music, sound effects, and recorded voices, the projection of slide sequences, scenic and lighting effects, a variety of puppets, choreographed movement, and dramatized scenes or narrated speeches. Chong draws on a diverse range of materials, including well-known authors, films, or historical figures. *Fear and Loathing in Gotham* (1975), for example, is Chong's version of pioneer German filmmaker Fritz Lang's *M; A.M./A.M.—The Articulated Man* (1982) is derived from "The Golem" a poem by the great Argentinean writer Jorge Luis Borges which in turn is based on sixteenth-century Yiddish legend about a manmade monster; *Noiresque: The Fallen Angel* (1989) is an ironic interpretation of Louis Carroll's classic *Alice in Wonderland;* and *Deshima* (1990) is about Vincent Van Gogh. Although a first-generation Chinese–American raised in New York's Chinatown, Chong mainitains an international and multicultural perspective. He often eclectically weaves into his pieces elements from Asian, European, and American culture, including mixing English dialogue with passages from several foreign languages. Chong's nonlinear imagistic works may seem disconnected, but they can be understood as meditations around a particular theme—for example, spiritual longing, alienation, the cyclical nature of destruction and rebirth, or historical and cultural relationships—and his craftsmanship and vision are arresting and widely admired.

Martha Clarke began her career as a modern dancer and was one of the cofounders of the innovative Pilobolus dance company. In 1978, she founded the Crowsnest Company to pursue her own collaboratively developed, conceptual dance–theater pieces. In the late 1970s and early 1980s, she staged a number of short plays, including María Irene Fornés's (b. 1930) *Dr.*

*Kheal* (1968), featuring the diminutive (4' 9", 80 lb.) actress Linda Hunt (b. 1945). In 1982, Clarke's own *A Metamorphosis in Miniature,* an adaptation of Kafka's "The Metamorphosis," won critical praise and an Obie award for Hunt. Clarke's breakthrough piece, however, was *The Garden of Earthly Delights* (1984), a wordless, but richly imagistic, dance–theater piece inspired by Hieronymous Bosch's visionary painting about earth, heaven, and hell. *Vienna Lusthaus* (1986), with a short text by Charles L. Mee Jr., music by Richard Peaslee, and costumes and set by Robert Israel, was a dense, hour-long piece evoking fin-de-siècle Vienna in a series of overlapping images and dancelike activities. Other Clarke works include *Miracolo d' Amore* (1988) based on Italo Calvino's renditions of Italian folk tales, but mixing in selections from Petrarch and Dante, *commedia dell'arte* characters and slapstick, and arresting moments depicting the abuse of women; *Endangered Species* (1990), an extravagant circus-influenced piece, set against a Civil War background, in which actors and dancers interacted with a number of animals, including an elephant; and *An Uncertain Hour* (1995) about AIDS, the war in Bosnia, and the loss of innocence, all set to Alban Berg's music. *Vienna Lusthaus,* however, remains her most well-received work. In the early 1990s, Clarke also began a career directing operas and plays, including Mozart's *The Magic Flute* at the Glimmerglass Opera in upstate New York.

The work of Meredith Monk is difficult to compartmentalize. A multi-talented dancer, choreographer, composer, director, and filmmaker, beginning in the 1960s Monk has created a steady stream of striking dance–theater works that combine ritualistic dancelike movements, a variety of nonverbal vocalizations—shouts, ululations, animal sounds—and minimalistic, but inventive, visual effects. The meaning or content of Monk's piece is not always clear, but they are nonetheless often hauntingly expressive, and invariably

*Left, Arthur Miller's* Death of a Salesman *with (from left) Mildred Dunnock as Linda and Lee J. Cobb as Willy. Graphic House.*

*Right, director Elia Kazan (right) describes Jo Mielziner's* Death of a Salesman *set to Mildred Dunnock, Lee J. Cobb, and Arthur Kennedy. Culver Pictures.*

they invoke a range of ideas and emotional responses. Among her better known works are *Juice* (1969), a "theater cantata" with a cast of eighty-five performers staged in three different locales, including the cochlea-shaped exhibition corridors of New York's Guggenheim Museum of Art; *Education of the Girlchild* (1973), a reflection on developmental experiences of women; *Quarry* (1976), an exploration of the Holocaust; and *Facing North* (1991), a two-character meditation on arctic ecology. A tireless experimenter, Monk continues to be a widely admired and influential avant-gardist.

Although she is sometimes classified as a performance artist or a pop-rock musician and composer, several of Laurie Anderson's concerts, as they are usually called, particularly *United States* (1978–83), *Empty Places* (1988–90), and *The Nerve Bible* (1994–95)—high-tech, multi-media, musical pieces—have more in common with postmodern experimental theater than performance art or rock concerts. Unlike most postmodern practitioners, Anderson, however, does have a mass following and her performances, usually staged in large concert halls or outdoor amphitheaters are invariably sold out. Some of her material, furthermore, has been recorded and videotaped for international distribution. Indeed, it should be noted that many of the techniques and approaches pioneered by postmodern writer–directors have gradually been absorbed into mainstream theatrical productions, pop-rock music concerts, and into the short film and video pieces—usually called "rock videos"—that are used to promote the recordings of rock musicians.

The emergence of a new style of one-person performance was also part of the avant-garde theater trend of the late 1980s and 1990s. Performance artists, as they were called, divided into two camps. One group tended to perform original sketches in which they played a series of characters. The tenor of these performances was usually comic, but their intent was to dissect various social types and problems. Eric Bogosian (b. 1953) in pieces like *Drinking in America* (1986), *Sex, Drugs & Rock and Roll* (1987), and *Pounding the Nails in the Floor with My Hands* (1994) savaged American maleness and contemporary urban life. Bogosian has also written full-length, multi-character satirical plays not intended for solo performance, among which are *sub Urbia* (1994) and *Griller* (1998). John Leguizamo's (b. 1965) *Mambo Mouth* (1991), *Spic-O-Rama* (1992), and *Freak* (1997), were satirical critiques of Latino culture. In *The Search for Signs of Intelligent Life in the Universe* (1985), Lily Tomlin (b. 1939) took on a dozen or so different characters and issues. Anna Devere Smith (b. 1951) has created unique performance pieces inspired by tragic social events. *Fires in the Mirror: Crown Heights, Brooklyn, and Other Identities* (1992), was about a conflict between orthodox Jews and African Americans in the neighborhood they share, while *Twilight: Los Angeles 1992* (1993) was concerned with the devastating Los Angeles riot of that year. Smith interviewed various people involved in these incidents. Then using this material, she re-created twenty or more individuals in a remarkable tour-de-force series of monologues which tended to point to racial and class divisiveness as the underlying cause of the conflicts.

Another even larger group of performance artists, like Spalding Gray, have used autobiography to construct monologues that recall personal experiences while simultaneously commenting on social issues or problems. Holly Hughes (b. 1951), for example, has lyrically evoked various experiences as a woman and lesbian. Rachel Rosenthal (b. 1926) has created surrealistic, visionary performances by integrating autobiographical monologues, ecological commentary, songs, and exotic costumes. Karen Finley's (b. 1956) scatological, transgressive pieces are designed to shock audiences into an awareness of the violence, rage, and erotic obsessiveness that undergirds certain social attitudes and behavior. In *Men on the Verge of His-panic Breakdown* (1994), Guillermo Reyes has addressed the problems of being gay and Hispanic.

Related to performance art are a diverse group of performers called "new vaudevillians" who put to use such activities as mime, clowning, juggling, and acrobatics to construct a playfully postmodern vision of contemporary life and art. Bill Irwin (b. 1950), one of the most accomplished new vaudevillians, has created a number of award winning pieces including *The Regard of Flight* (1982), *Largely New York* (1989) and *Fool Moon* (1993) which imaginatively twit, among other topics, postmodern theater itself and the pervasive influence of television. Irwin has also put his remarkable talents to use in conventional roles like Trinculo in *The Tempest* and Molière's Scapin. A trio calling themselves *The Reduced Shakespeare Company* have deflated the Bard by

*Left, Linda Loman (played by Jane Houdyshell) comforts her husband Willy Loman (Howard Witt) in a 1993 Missouri Repertory Theatre production of Arthur Miller's* Death of a Salesman *directed by George Keathley. Baker S. Smith designed the costumes. Courtesy Missouri Repertory Theatre.*

*Right, Big Daddy (played by Ken Albers) and Big Mama (Jane Houdyshell) have a confrontation on Big Daddy's birthday in Tennessee Williams's* Cat on a Hot Tin Roof *at Missouri Repertory Theatre. Courtesy Missouri Repertory Theatre.*

*Marco Barricelli played Brick to Kathleen Warfel's Maggie in* Cat on a Hot Tin Roof *by Tennessee Williams at Missouri Repertory Theatre in 1996. George Keathley directed. Courtesy Missouri Repertory Theatre.*

hilariously enacting abbreviated parodies of the entire canon—including four versions of *Hamlet*—in two hours. Other new vaudevillians include the juggling quartet The Flying Karamazov Brothers, acrobat Avner ("The Eccentric") Eisenberg, and juggler Michael Moschen (b. 1955).

MANY OF THE playwrights—Anderson, Hellman, Odets, Wilder—who had established estimable reputations in the 1930s and 1940s, continued to write well into the 1950s, but generally, with a few notable exceptions—O'Neill's posthumously produced *Long Day's Journey into Night,* for example—their later efforts were unequal to their earlier successes. In the late 1940s, two playwrights emerged whose dramatic craft and seriousness of purpose would match and in some cases surpass the work of the leading prewar dramatists.

Arthur Miller's (b. 1915) first Broadway play *The Man Who Had All the Luck* (1944) closed after four performances, but three years later *All My Sons* (1947), a wrenching drama about war profiteering and moral responsibility, won the Drama Critics' Circle Award and ran for 325 performances. With *Death of a Salesman* (1949), a portrayal of near-tragic proportions, presenting a quintessential American salesman as has-been, struggling to understand and justify his failure to himself and his family, Miller solidified his reputation as one of the leading playwrights of his generation. *Death of a Salesman* struck a responsive chord for many Americans whose immediate postwar euphoria had given way to a growing sense of disillusionment in the face of cold war political tensions and economic recession. It ran for 742 performances on Broadway and garnered the Pulitzer Prize, the Drama Critics' Circle Award, and a Tony Award as the best play of the season. Frequently revived, anthologized, and produced in translation in numerous foreign countries, including a notable production in Beijing in 1983, *Death of a Salesman* has achieved the status of an American classic.

Miller followed *Death of a Salesman* with *The Crucible* (1953), a compelling drama set against the seventeenth-century Salem witch trials but resonating with an infamous Congressional investigation of American political leftists. Miller himself was subpoenaed by the House Un-American Activities Committee, but he courageously defended his rights and refused to answer questions about his leftist associations. *A View from the Bridge* (1955) was a powerful, primal study of illicit desire and betrayal set in Brooklyn's tough dockside district. Neither *The Crucible* nor *A View from the Bridge,* however, was as successful as *Death of a Salesman.* In 1955, Miller married the celebrated film idol Marilyn Monroe (1926–62); perhaps disappointed with the reception of his last plays and embittered by the direction of American politics, Miller retreated with his famous wife to Hollywood. The marriage was a troubled one, and Monroe and Miller were eventually divorced in 1961. After Monroe's untimely death, Miller returned to Broadway with *After the Fall* (1964), a semiautobiographical play about his life with Monroe. *Incident at Vichy* (1964), about Nazi persecution of Jews, and *The Price* (1968), a wrenching drama of conflict between two brothers following the death of their father, were all absorbing dramas centering on questions of guilt, evil, and the influence of the past. Only *The Price,* running for 429 performances, was a commercial success.

From the 1970s through the 1990s, Miller authored numerous plays, including *Creation of the World and Other Business* (1972), *The Archbishop's Ceiling* (1977), *The American Clock* (1980), *The Ride down Mount Morgan* (1991) and *The Last Yankee* (1991). With varying success, most were produced Off-Broadway, in regional theaters, or in London where many of Miller's earlier plays have also enjoyed revivals. In the 1980s, he was more highly regarded abroad—especially in China with the mid-1980s production of *Death of a Salesman*—than in the United States. In 1994, however, Miller returned to Broadway with *Broken Glass* which enjoyed a relatively long run. The London production of *Broken Glass* in 1995 won a coveted Olivier award as best play of the season. By the early 1990s, octogenarian Miller was regarded as America's "greatest living playwright."

Tennessee Williams (1911–83) achieved his first success with *The Glass Menagerie* (1945), a lyrical "memory" play that drew on Williams's own relationship with his mother and sister. *The Glass Menagerie* ran for 560 performances and won the Drama Critics' Circle Award. In *A Streetcar Named Desire* (1947), Williams explored the psychological arena of sexual desire, gender conflict, alienation, and human frailty—themes that would animate a score of his plays produced in the 1950s and 1960s. While Miller generally worked within the traditions of social realism, Williams enriched realism with poetic dialogue, original dramatic structures, and an evocative use of scenery, lighting, sound effects, and music. His many notable plays include *Summer and Smoke* (1948), *The Rose Tattoo* (1951), *Camino Real* (1953), *Sweet Bird of Youth* (1959), and *Cat on a Hot Tin Roof* (1955); the latter won both the Pulitzer Prize and the Drama Critics' Circle Award and ran for almost seven hundred performances. *The Night of the Iguana* (1961), a compassionate

*Left, Arthur Hill, Uta Hagen, and Edward Albee during rehearsals of* Who's Afraid of Virginia Woolf? *Dominic.*

*Right, Arthur Hill as George and Uta Hagen as Martha in a scene from* Who's Afraid of Virginia Woolf? *Dominic.*

Born Yesterday *(1946) by Garson Kanin (b. 1912) is a classic American comedy that verges on political satire. Robert Elliott played tycoon Harry Brock in the 1990 Missouri Repertory Theatre production. Also shown are Forrest Compton and Stratton Walling. The luxury hotel setting is by James Leonard Joy, with lighting by Jeff Davis and costumes by Virgil Johnson. George Keathley directed. Courtesy Missouri Repertory Theatre.*

*Carla Noack tries to mollify the cranky, ailing, ninety-two-year-old socialite played by Patricia Fraser in Edward Albee's* Three Tall Women *at Missouri Repertory Theatre in 1997, as directed by George Keathley. Courtesy Missouri Repertory Theatre.*

drama of displacement and resolution set in Mexico, ran for a creditable 316 performances and garnered critical praise, but it was Williams's last Broadway success. Buffeted by depression, dependency on drugs and alcohol, anxieties about his creative energy, Williams continued to write but his later plays—over twenty in total—have not yet been granted the recognition due them. His major plays, however, are continually revived and anthologized; and among American playwrights, he is perhaps Eugene O'Neill's equal.

In the 1950s, William Inge (1913–73) was often ranked with Miller and Williams. His conventionally structured dramas are sympathetic studies of life in postwar middle America. His first play, *Come Back, Little Sheba* (1950), is set in a run-down neighborhood in a midwestern city and explores the tensions within an arid marriage. Both Shirley Booth (1907–92) and Sidney Blackmer (1895–1973) won Tony Awards for their stirring, naturalistic portrayals of Lola and Doc, the middle-aged, quietly desperate central characters. Two years later, in a film version of the play, Booth now playing opposite movie star Burt Lancaster as Doc, won an Oscar for her performance of Lola. Despite Booth and Blackmer's contributions, *Come Back, Little Sheba* was a critical and popular disappointment, barely eking out a run of 190 performances. *Picnic* (1953), however, about a handsome, young vagabond's impact on the lives of four women in a backwater Kansas community, won the Pulitzer Prize and ran for a respectable 477 performances. Inge had two more successes with the serio-comic *Bus Stop* (1955) and the domestic drama *The Dark at the Top of the Stairs* (1957). But in the 1960s, depression and alcoholism destroyed his potential; his last plays, uneven in quality, failed in production.

*David Mamet's* Glengarry Glen Ross *as produced by the Virginia Stage Company (1985–86). From left Geoff Pierson, Roger Serbagi, T. A. Taylor, Carl Don, Bill Geisslinger, Mitchell Thomas. Photo: Mark Atkinson. Courtesy Virginia Stage Company.*

*David Mamet's* Glengarry Glen Ross *as produced by the Virginia Stage Company (1985-86). From left: Geoff Pierson and Roger Serbagi. Photo: Mark Atkinson. Courtesy Virginia Stage Company.*

Miller, Williams, and to a lesser extent Inge were the only playwrights to sustain a body of important work during the 1950s. A number of critically and commercially successful plays merit mention, however, including Jerome Lawrence and Robert E. Lee's *Inherit the Wind* about the famous 1925 trial in Tennessee which debated whether Darwin's theory of evolution should be taught in American schools; Thornton Wilder's comedy *The Matchmaker* (set in turn-of-the-century New York and the source for the later hit musical *Hello Dolly);* Michael Gazzo's torturous study of drug addiction *A Hatful of Rain;* Ketti Frings's *Look Homeward, Angel* (1957), a moving dramatization of Thomas Wolfe's epic novel, which won both the Pulitzer Prize and the Drama Critics' Circle Award; and *J.B.* (1959), poet Archibald McLeish's (1892–1982) contemporized account of the Book of Job which won the Pulitzer Prize and Tony Award. In addition to *The Matchmaker,* other outstanding light comedies of the decade include John Patrick's (1905–96) *The Teahouse of the August Moon* (1953), a charming sentimental (but now potentially offensive) comedy about American soldiers in occupied postwar Okinawa, which ran for over a thousand performances and won the Pulitzer Prize, Drama Critics' Circle, and Tony Awards; Lawrence and Lee's *Auntie Mame,* which later became the hit musical *Mame* (1966); and Gore Vidal's (b. 1925) witty antiwar satire *Visit to a Small Planet* (1957).

In the 1960s only two playwrights achieved steady success on Broadway, Edward Albee and Neil Simon. Albee (b. 1928) began his career with several short, absurdist plays, including *The Zoo Story* (1958), *The Sandbox* (1959), and *The American Dream* (1960). In 1962 Albee's first full-length play, *Who's Afraid of Virginia Woolf?,* an emotionally charged, Strindbergian battle of the sexes, which many critics compared to O'Neill's *Long Day's Journey into Night,* ran for over 650 performances and won the Drama Critics' Circle Award. Albee won his first Pulitzer Prize for *A Delicate Balance* (1966) and a second for *Seascape* (1975), both challenging but entertaining explorations of metaphysical problems and knotty human relationships. Although Albee's reputation suffered in the 1980s from several failed productions and a dwindling output, he rebounded in 1994 with *Three Tall Women* which won him a third Pulitzer Prize, as well as a Drama Critics' Circle Award. A revival of *A Delicate Balance* in 1996 received a Tony Award for the best revival of the season.

Neil Simon (b. 1927) served his apprenticeship writing comic sketches for popular television shows and Broadway revues in the 1950s. His first Broadway play *Come Blow Your Horn* (1961), a delightful light comedy centering on the relationships among two brothers and their father, began an almost unbroken string of Broadway successes through 1972—nine comedies and the books for three musicals. Simon's theatrical record was less successful in the 1970s, although *California Suite* (1976) and *Chapter Two* (1977), a semiautobiographical drama, proved popular. Simon's facility in writing comic dialogue and his enormous commercial success led to a certain critical dismissal. However, his bittersweet autobiographical trilogy *Brighton Beach Memoirs* (1983), *Biloxi Blues* (1984), and *Broadway Bound* (1986), in which

*Beth Henley's* Crimes of the Heart *as produced by the Virginia Stage Company (1984–85). From left: Alex Bond, Debra Dean, and Cynthia Mace. Courtesy Virginia Stage Company.*

*Beth Henley's* Crimes of the Heart *as produced by the Virginia Stage Company. From left: Daniel Ahearn and Cynthia Mace. Courtesy Virginia Stage Company.*

character and situation take precedence over verbal and visual jokes, forced critical reassessment. *Brighton Beach Memoirs* won Simon his first Drama Critics' Circle Award; and *Biloxi Blues* won a Tony Award. In 1991, Simon won his first Pulitzer Prize and a second Tony Award for *Lost in Yonkers,* a comedy which also draws on his childhood experiences. In 1983, in recognition of his contribution to Broadway, the Nederlander company renamed their Alvin Theatre the Neil Simon Theatre. Simon's most recent plays are *Laughter on the 23rd Floor* (1993), a musical version of his film *The Goodbye Girl* (1993), *London Suite* (1994), and *Proposals* (1997). All had only limited success on Broadway, however. *London Suite* premiered at the Seattle Repertory Theatre and then played Off-Broadway—a sign of Broadway's continued decline. *Proposals* closed after a mere seventy-six performances.

Since the 1970s, Broadway's economic structure generally has discouraged commercial productions of untested, new plays, especially plays that deviated from the realistic mode. But Off- and Off-Off Broadway and resident theater companies promoted and sustained dozens of fresh dramatic voices, representing diverse points of view. Lanford Wilson's (b. 1937) numerous successes include *The Hot'l Baltimore* (1973), which ran for over a thousand performances Off-Broadway, a record for a nonmusical play, and *Talley's Folly* (1980) which won both the Pulitzer Prize and Drama Critics' Circle Award. Wilson's *Burn This* (1987), after limited runs at the Mark Taper Forum in Los Angeles, the Steppenwolf Theatre in Chicago, and the Circle Repertory Theatre, enjoyed critical acclaim and a long run on Broadway. Sam Shepard (b. 1943) established his career Off-Off-Broadway as the author of a dozen or so short, provocative, experimental plays. In 1979, however, he won the Pulitzer prize for *Buried Child* (1978), produced Off-Broadway. *Buried Child* was followed with Off-Broadway productions

*The teacher–student relationship takes a turn for the worse in David Mamet's* Oleanna. *The roles were played by Gary Neal Johnson and Carrie Vujcec in the 1997 Missouri Repertory Theatre production directed by Fontaine Syer. Linda K. Meyers designed the costumes, Victor En Yu Tan the lighting, and Harry Feiner the set. Courtesy Missouri Repertory Theatre.*

*Tina Howe's* Painting Churches *as produced by the Virginia Stage Company (1985–86). From left: Jordan R. Baker, Avril Gentles, and Wyman Pendleton. Photo: Ellen Forsyth. Courtesy Virginia Stage Company.*

*Tina Howe's* Painting Churches *as produced by the Virginia Stage Company (1985–86). From left: Avril Gentles, Wyman Pendleton, and Jordan R. Baker. Photo: Ellen Forsyth. Courtesy Virginia Stage Company.*

of *Fool for Love* (1979), *True West* (1980), *A Lie of the Mind* (1985), *States of Shock* (1991), and *Eyes for Consuela* (1998), powerful deconstructions of American social values and ideals. In 1996, the Steppenwolf Theatre mounted a critically acclaimed revival of *Buried Child* which was then transferred to New York as Shepard's first Broadway production. Although his plays are often criticized for their obscurity, and confusing mixture of realism and surrealism, Shepard is acknowledged as a significant contemporary dramatist. Beginning in the late 1970s, Shepard coupled playwriting with a career as a film actor. His notable film credits include the role of celebrated test-pilot Colonel Chuck Yeager in *The Right Stuff* (1983), an historical film about the development of America's space program.

*Marceline Hugot, Nicole Givens, Cherry Jones (seated) as Mabel Tidings Bigelow, Jeffrey Hayenga, William Anton, and Robert Knepper in the Old Globe Theatre's world premiere production of Tina Howe's* Pride's Crossing, *directed by Jack O'Brien in the Old Globe Theatre, January–March 1997. Photo: Ken Howard. Courtesy of the Old Globe Theatre.*

David Mamet's (b. 1947) early plays were produced in a number of Chicago theaters, principally at the St. Nicholas Theatre which he cofounded, and at the Goodman Theatre, where he was an associate director from 1974 to 1984. In 1977, *American Buffalo,* which had premiered at the Goodman in 1975, became Mamet's first Broadway production. It received a Drama Critics' Circle Award, but ran for only 135 performances; a revival in the early 1980s, however, featuring the noted stage and film actor Al Pacino (b. 1940), was more successful. Mamet's *Glengarry Glen Ross,* a production that transferred from the Goodman Theatre to Broadway in 1983 ran for 375 performances and won both a Pulitzer Prize and a Drama Critics' Circle Award. Mamet's other notable plays include *A Life in the Theatre* (1977), *Speed-the-Plow* (1987), *Oleanna* (1993), *The Cryptogram* (1995), and *Old Neighbors* (1997). Mamet's plays usually explore American materialism or gender and family conflicts in a naturalistic style marked by a distinctive approach to dialogue. Halting, repetitive, often filled with obscenities, Mamet's dialogue captures a kind of urban American speech, but it also reflects the dissolution of American urban culture.

Roused by the women's liberation movement and with the opportunities presented by Off- and Off-Off-Broadway and resident theaters, a number of women playwrights entered the theatrical mainstream in the 1980s. Among the more prominent were Beth Henley (b. 1952), Marsha Norman (b. 1947), Tina Howe (b. 1937), and Wendy Wasserstein (b. 1950). In 1981, Henley's *Crimes of the Heart* (1977), about the relationship of three sisters in a small southern town, won the Pulitzer Prize, making her the first woman to win since Frances Goodrich and Albert Hackett shared the Pulitzer for *The Diary of Anne Frank* (1956), and only the sixth woman in the history of this prestigious award. Two years later Norman won the Pulitzer for *'night Mother,* a lacerating drama in which a woman planning suicide confronts her mother. In 1989, Wendy Wasserstein's *The Heidi Chronicles,* which traces the central character's development from the turbulent mid-1960s to the late 1980s, won numerous honors, including a Tony Award and the Pulitzer Prize. With the Broadway productions of *The Sisters Rosensweig* (1992) and *An American Daughter* (1997), Wasserstein became one of the most prominent and commercially successful playwrights of her generation. Tina Howe's best known plays, *Painting Churches* (1983), *Coastal Disturbances* (1986), and *Approaching Zanzibar* (1989), explore complex familial relationships in original forms combining realism and fantasy, overlapping dialogue, and evocative visual effects. *Prides Crossing* (1997) centers on the life of Mabel Tidings Bigelow, the first woman to swim the English Channel. Rather than following a standard chronological design, Howe moves freely over events in Bigelow's life from age ten to ninety. Perhaps too distinctive for mainstream Broadway, her plays nevertheless have enjoyed long runs Off-Broadway and at numerous regional theaters. Among other leading women playwrights, with a representative sampling of their plays, are: Constance Congdon (b. 1944), *Tales of the Lost Formicans* (1988) and *Casanova* (1991); Mary Gallagher (b. 1947), *¿De Dónde?* (1989); Emily Mann (b. 1952), *Still Life* (1979) and *Execution of Justice* (1984); Jane Martin (thought by some to be a *nom de plume* for a male playwright), *Keely and Du* (1993) and *Jack and Jill* (1996); Paula Vogel (b. 1951), *The Baltimore Waltz* (1992) and the Pulitzer Prize winning *How I Learned to Drive* (1998); and Naomi Wallace, *In the Heart of America* (1994) and *One Flea Spare* (1996). In 1978, the Susan Smith Blackburn Prize was established to recognize excellent plays by women. Created as a memorial to the prize's namesake, a journalist with an avid interest in the theater, there have been hundreds of finalists for the award over the past thirty years.

Beginning in the 1950s, a number of important plays by African–American dramatists were produced on and Off-Broadway. Louis Peterson's *Take a Giant Step* (1953) was one of the first black plays to receive a Broadway production after the war. Alice Childress (1920–94), who had acted for a decade with the American Negro Theatre, turned to playwriting in the early 1950s. Her *Trouble in Mind* (1955), a powerful backstage drama exploring race relations in the 1950s, won an Obie for best new Off-Broadway play of the season; and her *Wedding Band* (1966) and *Wine in the Wilderness* (1969), which focus on strong black women characters, have been frequently produced in regional and university theaters. Loften Mitchell's (b. 1919) *A Land Beyond the River* (1957), about civil rights

August Wilson's cycle of plays exploring the African–American condition in the twentieth century focuses on the great recording artist Ma Rainey for his play set in the 1920s. Barbara D. Mills played the title role in Ma Rainey's Black Bottom in the 1993 Missouri Repertory Theatre production directed by Claude Purdy with costumes by Paul Tazewell and lighting by Phil Monat. Courtesy Missouri Repertory Theatre.

Scenes from August Wilson's The Piano Lesson as produced by Penumbra Theatre in 1992–93. Directed by Marion McClinton; setting by W. J. E. Hammer. From left: William Wilkins as Boy Willie; Lester Purry as Lymon; Rebecca Rice as Berniece; Lou Bellamy as Doaker. Courtesy Penumbra Theatre.

leader Joseph De Laine's efforts to end discrimination in public schools, was produced Off-Broadway. Mitchell's other plays include *Star of the Morning* (1971), about the black vaudevillian Bert Williams, and the successful Broadway revue *Bubbling Brown Sugar* (1976). An educator and author of several books on African–American drama and theater, including *Black Drama* (1967), Mitchell has been an influential champion of black theater. In 1959 Lorraine Hansberry's *Raisin in the Sun,* about a struggling working-class black family in Chicago, was the first play by an African American to win a Drama Critics' Circle Award, and ran for 530 performances. It also marked the Broadway acting debut of Sidney Poitier (b. 1924), who would become a major film star and the first African American to win a Best Actor Oscar, and the directorial debut of African–American director and educator Lloyd Richards (b. 1923), who in 1968 became artistic director of the National Playwrights' Conference at the Eugene O'Neill Theatre Center, dean of the Yale School of Drama, and artistic director of the Yale Repertory Theatre. *A Raisin in the Sun* was made into a successful movie in 1961, starring Poitier and featuring several members of the original Broadway cast, including veteran African–American actresses Claudia McNeil and Ruby Dee (b. 1923). Hansberry completed only one other play,

*Don Marshall played Paul Robeson in Phillip Hayes Dean's (b. 1939) one-man play* Paul Robeson *at Missouri Repertory Theatre in 1995. Courtesy Missouri Repertory Theatre.*

*Scene from R. A. Shiomi's* Yellow Fever *(1994). Ernest Abuba as Sam Shikaze and Carol Honda as Rosie. Directed by Andrew Tsao; produced by Pan Asian Repertory Theatre, Tisa Chang Artistic/Producing Director. Photo: Corky Lee. Courtesy Pan Asian Repertory Theatre.*

*A scene from Milcha Sanchez–Scott's* The Cuban Swimmer. *Presented at INTAR Hispanic American Arts Center in 1983–84. Directed by Max Merrá with sets by Ming Cho Lee. The Swimmer, Jeanette Mirabal; on boat from left, Graciela Lecube as the Grandmother; Manuela Rivera as the Brother; Lillian Hurst as the Mother; Carlos Cestero as the Father. Courtesy INTAR. Photo: Carol Halebian.*

*The Sign in Sidney Brustein's Window* (1964), before her early death from cancer. Actor Ossie Davis's (b. 1917) *Purlie Victorious* (1961), a hilarious spoof about racial stereotyping, which starred both Davis and his wife Ruby Dee, ran for seven months on Broadway. It was later the source for the musical *Purlie* which ran for almost seven hundred performances in 1970–71.

As the civil rights struggle intensified in the mid-1960s, several African–American playwrights used drama as a weapon to confront white racism, while simultaneously promoting black pride. Amiri Baraka (b. 1934) was one of the most prominent radical African–American playwrights of the 1960s. In a dozen plays, including *The Slave* (1964), *Dutchman* (1964), and *Slave Ship* (1967), the last a forceful mainly pantomimic history of the black experience from the horrors of the "middle passage" to a visionary destruction of white America, Baraka fiercely attacked racist attitudes and institutions. Ed Bullins (b. 1935) authored numerous plays, ranging from the eerie agitprop drama *The Electronic Nigger* (1968), to the realistic dramatization of a brutal rape in *The Taking of Miss Jamie* (1975), a Drama Critics' Circle Award winner, and a series of acute, troubling examinations of black anger and alienation that include *In the Wine Time* (1968), *The Duplex* (1970), and *Home Boy* (1976). Charles Gordone's (b. 1912) *No Place to Be Somebody* (1970), a taut gangster thriller, seething with repressed indignation and acerbic social commentary, was the first African–American play to win a Pulitzer Prize.

Adrienne Kennedy's (b. 1931) *Funnyhouse of a Negro,* a surreal drama examining racial and gender identity, won an Obie in 1964. Kennedy's subsequent plays, including *A Rat's Mass* (1966) and *A Movie Star Has to Star in Black and White* (1976), are structurally original and compelling and have generated critical attention, if not widespread popular interest. In 1993 Cleveland's Great Lakes Theater Festival honored Kennedy, who grew up in Cleveland, with an Adrienne Kennedy Festival staging several of her plays, including *Ohio State Murders* (1992).

August Wilson (b. 1945) is the most important and commercially successful African–American playwright to emerge in the 1980s. *Ma Rainey's Black Bottom* (1982) was the first in a series of a half-dozen plays chronicling the black experience in the twentieth century. All were first staged by Lloyd Richards at the Yale Repertory Theatre and then enjoyed long runs on Broadway. Wilson has captured numerous honors, including Pulitzer Prizes for *Fences* (1987) and *The Piano Lesson* (1990) and Drama Critics' Circle Awards for *Ma Rainey's Black Bottom, Fences, Joe Turner's Come and Gone* (1988), *The Piano Lesson, Two Trains Running* (1992), and *Seven Guitars* (1996)—more than any other playwright in the history of that award.

Wilson's plays are inventive in their use of striking visual metaphors and incidental music—blues, jazz, and spirituals predominately—but generally they follow the conventions of realism. Several other acclaimed contemporary African–American playwrights have adopted more experimental approaches to deconstruct the complexities of the black experience. Ntozake Shange (b. 1948), in her plays *for colored girls who have considered suicide when the rainbow is enuf* (1976), *spell #7* (1978), and *Betsey Brown* (1991), combines poetry, music, and dance in a unique and evocative dramatic style. George C. Wolfe's *The Colored Museum* (1986) is an astringent satirization of black stereotypes using the format of the 1920s-style musical revue. In *Jelly's Last Jam* (1991), Wolfe deconstructs the life of jazz composer and pianist "Jelly Roll" Morton. Among Suzan-Lori Parks's (b. 1963) critically acclaimed plays are *Imperceptible Mutabilities in the Third Kingdom* (1989), *The Death of the Last Black Man in the Whole Entire World* (1990), *The American Play* (1994), and *Venus* (1996). Mixing surrealism with historical events and figures, Parks's dramas are among the more inventive in the contemporary American theater.

Other African–American plays that merit mention are Joseph Walker's (b. 1935) *The River Niger* (1975), the first African–American play to win a Tony Best Play award; Charles Fuller's (b. 1939) *Soldier's Play,* which won a Pulitzer Prize in 1981; Samm-Art Williams's *Home* (1979); Lonnie Elder III's (b. 1931) critically acclaimed *Ceremonies in Dark Old Men* (1969) and *Splendid Mummer* (1988), about the black tragedian Ira Aldridge; Ron Milner's (b. 1938) *Roads to the Mountain Top* (1986) about civil rights leader Dr. Martin Luther King Jr.; director–playwright Vinnette Carroll's (b. 1922) *Don't Bother Me, I Can't Cope* (1972) and *Your Arm's Too Short to Box with God* (1977), both stirring musical plays about black issues and experiences; Carlyle Brown's *The African Company Presents Richard III*

A French diplomat stationed in China falls for a Beijing Opera performer in David Henry Hwang's M. Butterfly. Gary Neal Johnson played Gallimard and B. K. Bernal played Song Liliang in the 1993 Missouri Repertory Theatre production. Courtesy Missouri Repertory Theatre.

Terrence McNally's A Perfect Ganesh (1993) as produced by the Virginia Stage Company (1994–95). From left: Jane Moore, Sam Guncler, David McCann (Ganesh), and Deborah Mayo. Photo: Mark Atkinson. Courtesy Virginia Stage Company.

(1987); and OyamO's (b. 1943) *I Am a Man* (1993), about the volatile 1968 Memphis garbage collector's strike. By the early 1990s, dozens of black dramatists had won a distinctive place in the panorama of American theater.

Luis Valdéz and El Teatro Campesino and other *teatros* provided opportunities for dozens of Chicano playwrights, including Carlos Morton (b. 1947), among whose plays are two postmodern, neohistorical critiques of California's past and present: *Los Dorados* (1978) and *Rancho Hollywood* (1979); Josefina Lopez (b. 1969), author of *Simply Maria* (1986) and *Real Women Have Curves* (1990), both sharp comic treatments of Chicana life; Estela Portillo Trambley (b. 1936), best known for her *Sor Juana,* a compelling portrait of the seventeenth century Mexican nun poet–playwright; and Milcha Sanchez-Scott (b. 1955), whose *Roosters* (1987) is a moving, lyrical exploration of Chicano issues.

Cuban-born María Irene Fornés is probably the best known contemporary Latina playwright. Her plays, including *Fefu and Her Friends* (1977) and *The Conduct of Life* (1985), have received numerous productions in leading Off-Broadway and resident theaters. Fornés is also a director and has mentored numerous young Latino playwrights. *The Floating Island Plays* (1984–91), a tetralogy tracing the history of a Cuban family from the pre-Castro era through exile and then assimilation into the United States, by Cuban–American Eduardo Machado (b. 1953), has been critically acclaimed and widely produced.

A rich body of postwar New York Puerto Rican, or as it began to be called in the late 1960s, "Nuyorican" drama emerged after the war. René Marqués's (1917–79) *The Oxcart (La Carreta,* 1953) is considered the seminal drama exploring the central Nuyorican conflict between their Latino island culture and that of mainland, hegemonic Anglo-America. A list of notable Nuyorican playwrights would include Roberto Rodríguez Suárez, usually considered the "father" of Puerto Rican drama in the United States; Oscar Colón; Miguel Piñero (1947–88), whose prison drama *Short Eyes* won a Drama Critics' Circle Award and an Obie in 1974; and José Rivera (b. 1955) whose many plays, including *The House of Ramon Iglesias* (1983) and *Marisol* (1992), have been produced by leading Off-Broadway and regional theaters. With dialogue that is often bilingual, a social context that is bicultural, and a mixed range of styles from naturalism to surrealism, Nuyorican drama is a vital contribution to contemporary American drama.

Promoted by the several Asian–American theaters founded in the late 1960s and 1970s, a substantial body of Asian–American drama had developed by the 1980s. Among the more prominent contemporary Asian–American dramatists, with a few of their plays, are: Frank Chin (b. 1940), *Chickencoop Chinaman* (1972), *Year of the Dragon* (1977); Philip Kan Gotanda (b. 1950), *The Wash* (1987), *Yankee Dawg You Die* (1987), *Song for Nisei Fisherman* (1980), *Ballad of Yachiyo* (1995); Laurence Yep (b. 1948), *Pay the Chinaman* (1977); and Wakako Yamauchi (b. 1924), *And the Soul Shall Dance* (1977). David Henry Hwang (b. 1957) has been the most successful Asian–American playwright in mainstream theaters. A number of his plays, including *The*

*Dance and The Railroad* (1981) and *Family Devotions* (1981), have been produced Off-Broadway and at leading regional theaters. In 1988, Hwang's *M.
Butterfly*, a complex drama examining political, cultural, and gender conflict,
ran for almost eight hundred performances on Broadway and won a Tony
Award. Following Off-Broadway and regional theater productions, Hwang's
*The Golden Child* opened on Broadway to widespread critical acclaim in
1998. Increasingly in the late 1980s and 1990s, mainstream resident theaters
have mounted plays by Asian–American playwrights.

Homosexual characters—both men and women—had been presented
rarely in American plays since the 1920s, though a few noted playwrights,
such as Lillian Hellman in *The Children's Hour* (1934) and Robert Anderson
in *Tea and Sympathy* (1953), did present such portrayals. But most of these
depictions were stereotypical or caricaturish portraits of neurasthenic, effeminate men or neurotic, predatory women. Homosexual playwrights such as
Tennessee Williams, William Inge, and Edward Albee, like Oscar Wilde and
Noël Coward before them, still wrote in an era when to address the subject
directly was not deemed possible and tended to avoid homosexual material
or to veil it in double entendre and ambiguity. But the militant gay rights or
liberation movement of the 1960s led to the writing and production of
numerous plays which, for the first time in the history of the American theater, presented homosexual characters and issues in a realistic fashion.

Mart Crowley's *The Boys in the Band* (1968), centering on an ensemble of
gay characters at a birthday party, was a turning point in the representation of
homosexuals in mainstream American drama. It ran for over a thousand performances Off-Broadway, and received numerous productions in regional theaters. In the 1970s, gay playwrights such as Lanford Wilson, Robert Patrick,
Terrence McNally (b. 1939), and Albert Innaurato (b. 1948) included realistically portrayed homosexuals among the dramatis personae in several of their
respective plays. Harvey Fierstein's (b. 1954) *Torch Song Trilogy* (1983), with
a drag queen as its central character, was a humorous, sympathetic insider's
view of a strain of homosexual culture. It ran for over twelve hundred performances on Broadway and won the Tony Award as best play of the season.
Fierstein also furnished the book for the popular musical comedy *La Cage aux
Folles* (1983) about two aging gay men who operate a drag club. With the onset
of AIDS in the 1980s and 1990s, numerous poignant realist plays interpreted
the various stages of this epidemic to both gay and mainstream theatergoers,
including Larry Kramer's (b. 1939) *The Normal Heart,* William Hoffman's *As
Is* (1985), Paula Vogel's *The Baltimore Waltz* (1991), and Terrence McNally's
*Love! Valor! Compassion!* (1995). Tony Kushner's (b. 1956) *Angels in
America: A Gay Fantasia on National Themes*—an epic, seven-hour drama in
two parts, *Millennium Approaches* (1991) and *Perestroika* (1993)—explored a
number of complex social and political issues against the background of AIDS
in America. Part 1 won the Pulitzer Prize and Drama Critics' Circle Award in
1993, and both parts 1 and 2 won Tony Awards.

A number of lesbian theater groups were founded in the 1970s and 1980s,
including the Lavender Cellar in Minneapolis (1973), the Rites of Women

*Left, Marlon Brando as Stanley Kowalski in* A Streetcar Named Desire. *From Appelbaum* Great Actors and Actresses of the American Stage in Historic Photographs. *Courtesy Dover Publications, Inc.*

*Right, Katharine Hepburn c. 1939–40, as Tracy Lord in Philip Barry's* The Philadelphia Story *(1939), a role written expressly for her. Courtesy the Flora Ward Hineline papers, the Ward M. Canaday Center for Special Collections, University of Toledo Libraries.*

Lesbian Feminist Theater in Philadelphia , and the Red Dyke Theatre in Atlanta (1974). Generally lesbian theater groups have tended toward company-developed pieces and solo performance. Perhaps for this reason, the body of more conventional texts addressing lesbian issues or experience is small in comparison to gay drama. Jane Chambers's (1937–83) *Last Summer at Blue Fish Cove* (1980) was produced by a number of resident theaters. Rosalyn Drexler's (b. 1926) *Delicate Feelings* (1984), about two lesbian wrestlers, was produced Off-Off-Broadway. Karen Malpede's (b. 1945) *Sappho and Aphrodite* (1983), about the ancient poetess, was produced in London and New York. Several of Joan Schenkar's (b. 1948) provocative comedic fantasies, including *Signs of Life,* about Henry James, his sister Alice, her female lover, and P. T. Barnum and one of his female circus freaks, have been produced in regional and university theaters. Cherríe Moraga's (b. 1952) lyrical, inventive pieces have also been widely produced in leading regional theaters.

Many traditional Native American dramatic rituals have survived into the twentieth century, but the emergence of a modern Native American drama is usually traced to the Native American Theatre Ensemble founded in 1973 by Hanay Geiogamah (b. 1945?). Geiogamah himself was the author of a number of critically regarded plays, including *Body Indian* (1972) and *49* (1982). Native American sculptor, poet, and performance artist Jimmie Durham's (b. 1940) deconstruction of white America's relationship with its indigenous peoples, *Thanksgiving* (1982), *Manhattan Giveaway* (1985) and *Savagism and You* (1991), have garnered considerable critical attention. A number of Diane Glanoy's (b. 1941) plays, including *Weebjob* (1987) have been produced and published. The acclaimed American Indian Dance Theatre, codirected by Geiogamah and Barbara Schwei, has introduced a mass audience to a broad range of authentic and theatricalized Native American dances. Spiderwoman Theatre is a leading force in Native American theater and drama. But to date, despite a growing body of literature by Native American writers, there are relatively few Native American plays.

The 1980s and 1990s were especially rich in talented playwrights. Terrance McNally. for example, has authored over a dozen graceful, witty, critically acclaimed plays covering a range of contemporary concerns including, in addition to those previously cited, *Lips Together, Teeth Apart* (1991) and *The Master Class* (1995). Among the many important dramatists not previously mentioned earlier in this chapter are Christopher Durang (b. 1949) whose sharply satiric pieces include *Beyond Therapy* (1981) and *The Marriage of Bette and Boo* (1973, revised 1985); John Guare (b. 1938), author of a dozen well-received dramas including *The House of Blue Leaves* (1970) and *Six Degrees of Separation* (1990); A. R. Gurney Jr. (b. 1930), the contemporary stage's arch chronicler of the strengths and failings of America's WASPs—White, Anglo-Saxon, Protestants—in such plays as *The Dining Room* (1981), *The Cocktail Hour* (1990), and *Later Life* (1993); Arthur Kopit (b. 1937), author of a number of inventive, thought-provoking dramas, including *Indians* (1968), *Wings* (1978), *The End of the World* (1984) and *The Road to Nirvana* (1990); Romulus Linney (b. 1930), a prolific playwright whose works range from folk drama like *Holy Ghosts* (1976) to a provocative study of Nazi leader Hermann Göring, *2: Göring at Nuremberg* (1992); Richard Nelson (b. 1950) whose dissections of American contemporary life include *American Abroad* (1989) and *New England* (1994); and David Rabe (b. 1940), whose plays include *Sticks and Bones* (1971) and *Streamers* (1976), about the effects of the Vietnam War as well as other explorations of the failed American dream.

HOLLYWOOD CONTINUED TO be a mecca for American actors, in the immediate postwar decades. No sooner would an actor achieve some notability on the stage than he or she would be offered a lucrative film contract. A noted case in point is Marlon Brando (b. 1924) who achieved prominence as Stanley Kowalski in Tennessee Williams's *A Streetcar Named Desire* in 1947. His reprise of this role in the 1951 film version of Williams's drama catapulted Brando into screen stardom. Although widely considered one of the most compelling and influential actors of his generation, Brando built this reputation working exclusively in movies. Brando was but one of dozens of actors who made stage debuts in the 1930s and 1940s, then moved to Hollywood to become screen stars, and never or only rarely thereafter returned to the stage. Indeed, many of America's leading movie stars during Hollywood's "golden age" began their careers in the theater.

Even as younger actors in the 1940s and 1950s looked toward Hollywood for careers, a number of established film stars began to drift back to their theatrical roots. Fredric March (1897–1975), for example, was a leading actor with the Theatre Guild in the 1920s. For much of the 1930s he starred in the movies, winning an Oscar in 1935 for his double role in the film *Dr. Jekyll and Mr. Hyde*. In 1942, however, he returned to Broadway as Mr. Antrobus in Thornton Wilder's *The Skin of Our Teeth*. For the next two decades, March and his wife, actress Florence Eldridge (1901–88), divided their careers between movies and the stage. Among their many distinguished stage performances were the roles of James and Mary Tyrone in the premiere of Eugene O'Neill's *Long Day's Journey into Night* (1956). Henry Fonda (1905–82), long established as a film star, won acclaim for his Tony award-winning performance in the title role of *Mister Roberts* (1948). Thereafter for the next twenty-five years, Fonda successfully alternated between the stage and screen, appearing in a number of Broadway plays, including William Gibson's *Two for the See Saw* (1958), Robert Anderson's *Silent Night, Lonely Night* (1959), and as *Clarence Darrow* (1974) in a tour-de-force, one-person performance. Katharine Hepburn (b. 1907) also returned to the stage in the 1950s, playing with distinction a number of Shakespeare's heroines, including Rosalind, Portia, Beatrice, Viola, and Cleopatra, at the American Shakespeare Theatre. In 1969–71, first on Broadway and then on tour, Hepburn played the famous French fashion designer Coco Chanel in the

*Jessica Tandy and Hume Cronyn in 1944. From Appelbaum* Great Actors and Actresses of the American Stage in Historic Photographs. *Courtesy of Dover Publications, Inc.*

musical *Coco*. Lauren Bacall (b. 1924), after a long career in Hollywood, returned to Broadway in the late 1950s, winning critical acclaim in the comedy *Cactus Flower* (1965) and in the musicals *Applause* (1970) and *Woman of the Year* (1981), the latter based on a Hepburn–Spencer Tracy film vehicle. Even two pioneering stars of the silent screen—Dorothy (1898–1968) and Lillian (1893–1993) Gish—shuttled between Hollywood and Broadway in the 1940s and 1950s. Indeed, Lillian's long and distinguished stage career extended well into the 1980s and included acclaimed stage performances in John Patrick's *The Curious Savage* (1950), Horton Foote's *The Trip to Bountiful* (1953), and Robert Anderson's *I Never Sang for My Father* (1968).

The rise of Off-Broadway and resident theaters, coupled with an expansion of both film and television in the 1960s and 1970s, opened new opportunities for actors. Numerous actors found it possible to successfully maintain dual stage and movie careers. George C. Scott's (b. 1927), wide ranging stage work includes performances as Richard III, Shylock, and Marc Antony for the New York Shakespeare Festival; the role of the pampered actor Gary Essendine in Noël Coward's stylish comedy *Present Laughter* for Circle in the Square (1982); and the lead in the Broadway production of Larry Gelbart's *Sly Fox* (1976), an adaptation of Ben Jonson's *Volpone*. His numerous starring and supporting film roles include the title role in *Patton* (1970), about controversial General George S. Patton, for which Scott won an Academy Award as best actor, although he refused to accept it.

Others who gained prominence on stage and screen in the 1960s and 1970s include Jason Robards (b. 1922), perhaps our best interpreter of Eugene O'Neill's antiheroic characters; Eli Wallach (b. 1915), whose career has embraced innumerable comedic and dramatic character roles; Hal Holbrook (b. 1925), who came to notice in the mid-1950s with his one-person performance *Mark Twain Tonight!* and subsequently appeared on Broadway, in resident theaters, and in featured roles on television and in major films; Rip Torn (b. 1931), who essayed both leading and character roles on Broadway, Off-Broadway, in various resident theaters, and in films; and Geraldine Page (1924–87), who was considered one of the finest stage actresses of her time, while her film work garnered eight Oscar nominations and the award for Best Actress in the film version of Horton Foote's *The Trip to Bountiful* (1986). The partnership of Canadian-born Hume Cronyn and British-born Jessica Tandy was often compared to the Lunts. Both together and independently, in careers that stretched over half a century, they appeared in a range of classical and contemporary plays from *Hamlet* to *Death of a Salesman*, on Broadway and at leading resident theaters. They also appeared in dozens of films and television dramas. In 1990, Tandy won an Academy Award as best actress for her performance in the film adaptation of Alfred Uhry's play *Driving Miss Daisy*. Both Cronyn and Tandy were also honored with the National Medal for Arts—Tandy in 1986 and Cronyn in 1990.

By the mid-1970s, the new post-1960s generation of American actors generally expected to have careers on stage and in film and television. A number of actors, probably best known in the public mind as film or television stars, have also achieved acclaim for outstanding stage performances. Among the more prominent are Kathy Bates (b. 1948), Stockard Channing (b. 1944), Glenn Close (b. 1947), Dustin Hoffman (b. 1937), Stacy Keach (b. 1941), Kevin Kline (b. 1947), John Malkovich (b. 1953), Al Pacino (b. 1940), Meryl Streep (b. 1949), Dianne Wiest (b. 1948), and Cherry Jones (b. 1956). The African–American actor James Earl Jones (b. 1931) deserves special mention for his performances as Othello, King Lear, and Macbeth; as Troy Maxson in August Wilson's *Fences* (1987); and in many other roles.

Although film and television performance has been the route for celebrity and name recognition, a number of contemporary actors have achieved renown working mainly on stage. Philip Bosco (b. 1930), for example, has appeared in character roles in movies and television dramas, but his stage performances in Shakespeare, Shaw, and dozens of contemporary plays, have made him one of the most respected actors in the profession. Canadian-born Colleen Dewhurst (1926–91), who rarely appeared in either movies or on TV, was widely acclaimed as the premier interpreter of O'Neill's heroines. Other notable actors whose allegiance has been principally to the stage include Australian-born Zoë Caldwell (b. 1934), Olympia Dukakis (b. 1931), Alvin Epstein (b. 1925), George Grizzard (b. 1928), Uta Hagen (b. 1919), English-born Rosemary Harris (b. 1930), Julie Harris (b. 1925), Robert Prosky (b. 1930), Frances Sternhagen (b. 1930), and Irene Worth (b. 1916). A member of the Theatre Guild in the 1920s and the Group Theatre in the 1930s, Morris Carnovsky (1897–1992) won renown in the 1950s and 1960s for his interpretations of King Lear, Falstaff, Prospero, and Shylock. Indeed, Carnovsky's Lear, which he played in three different productions, was considered one of the finest of the time.

Opportunities for minority performers expanded from the 1960s onward and the American stage was enriched by many fine African–American, Asian–American, and Latino actors. Ruby Dee (b. 1923) and her husband Ossie Davis (b. 1917) are among the more celebrated African– American performers in the contemporary theater. Although James Earl Jones has received more acclaim, Earle Hyman (b. 1926) is undoubtedly the leading African–American interpreter of Shakespeare. He has played Othello, for example, in six different productions, including productions in Norway and Sweden. Hyman has also won renown for his performance in numerous modern and contemporary plays, including O'Neill's *The Emperor Jones* and Uhry's *Driving Miss Daisy*. Other notable African–American stage actors include Gloria Foster (b. 1936), Moses Gunn (1929–93), Robert Hooks (b. 1937), Charles Dutton (b. 1951), whose contributions to the success of August Wilson's *Ma Rainey's Black Bottom* and *The Piano Lesson* were significant, and Andre Braugher (b. 1962). Korean–American Randall Duk Kim (b. 1943), co-founder of the American Players Theatre, a principally Shakespearean summer theater located in Wisconsin, achieved widespread recognition in the 1980s for his interpretations of Shakespeare's Hamlet, Lear, Shylock; Sophocles' Oedipus; Chekov's Ivanov; and other classical roles. He also appeared with distinction Off-Broadway in the premieres of Frank Chin's

*Chickencoop Chinaman, Year of the Dragon,* and in David Henry Hwang's *The Golden Child* on Broadway. For his brilliant performance as the transvestite spy, Song Liling, in David Henry Hwang's *M. Butterfly,* B. D. Wong (b. 1962) was the first Asian American to win a Tony Award. In 1992, Wong won acclaim for his Peter Pan in a production at the Starlight Theatre in Kansas City; he is one of the few men and the first nonwhite actor to play this traditionally female role. Wong has also appeared in minor suporting roles in a number of commercially successful films. Other successful Asian American stage actors include Ernest Abuba (b. 1947), Tisa Chang (b. 1941), Nobu McCarthy (b. 1934), and Sab Shimono (b. 1942). Edward James Olmos (b. 1947) starred in Luis Valdéz's *Zoot Suit;* his successful career as a film and television actor and director has made him one of the more recognized Latino actors. Other Latino actors who have achieved mainstream recognition on stage and screen include José Ferrer (1912–92), who was the first actor to receive the National Medal of the Arts; Raul Julia (1940–94) who played a wide range of roles from Shakespeare's tragic heroes to farcical characters; Miriam Colón (b. 1935), founder of the Puerto Rican Traveling Theatre (1966); Rita Moreno (b. 1931), whose distinguished career has included numerous film, television, and stage awards; and Chita Rivera (b. 1933), whose impressive talents have been featured in numerous musicals from *Guys and Dolls* (1950) to *Kiss of the Spider Woman* (1993). The practice of nontraditional casting was increasingly acceptable in the American theater of the 1980s and 1990s, so that American minority actors frequently had opportunities to play characters outside of their own respective ethnic types.

Mainstream American actor training and acting style continued to be dominated by the school of psychological realism and Stanislavski and the Actor's Studio Method remained a significant influence. The physical and improvisatory techniques of Viola Spolin and Joseph Chaikin and their followers made substantial inroads on actor training from the mid-1970s onward. The work of foreign theorists and practitioners, notably Jerzy Grotowski, Eugenio Barba, and, in the 1980s, Suzuki Tadashi (b. 1939), also influenced American approaches to performance. After the war, the established training schools, like the Actor's Studio and the Neighborhood Playhouse School of Theatre, were joined by a score of schools located mostly in New York and Los Angeles. Among the most prestigious and respected are the HB Studio founded in 1946 by Herbert Berghof (1909–90) with his wife Uta Hagen, and the Stella Adler Conservatory of Acting founded by Stella Adler (1903–92) in 1949. A number of nonprofit resident theaters organized training programs, including Circle in the Square and the American Conservatory Theatre. In the late 1960s and 1970s university theater departments also moved in the direction of offering professional actor training under the auspices of bachelor of fine arts or master of fine arts degree programs. (The development of university theater is treated in a separate section below.)

Even after completion of an academic or professional training program, entry into the profession or membership in Equity or its sister guilds, the

Screen Actors' Guild (SAG) and the American Federation of Television and Radio Artists (AFTRA), was not automatic. Many young aspiring actors spend years auditioning for productions and theaters, and working in low-paying, non-Equity or Equity-waiver theaters, before gaining a foothold in the profession. Undoubtedly with the developments in movies, television, and a range of theatrical venues, there were in the 1990s more opportunities for actors than at any other time in the history of the American stage. But with thirty-five thousand members of Equity and about ninety thousand members of SAG, competition remains keen. For many work-a-day actors, earning a living solely through acting is a challenging proposition.

THE MUSICAL THEATER format established by Cole Porter, Irving Berlin, Kurt Weill, and especially Rodgers and Hammerstein, continued to flourish from the 1950s to the mid-1960s. Indeed, as noted in chapter 6, Rodgers and Hammerstein remained at the top of their form through the 1950s with *The King and I* (1951) set in exotic nineteenth-century Siam; *Flower Drum Song* (1958), about generational conflicts in San Francisco's Chinatown, and mostly cast with Asian-American performers; and *The Sound of Music* (1959), based on the experiences of the famous Trapp Family Singers of Austria. All three enjoyed critical acclaim and commercially successful long runs. As the King in *The King and I* the relatively unknown Yul Brynner (1920?–85) became an overnight star and remained closely associated with this role for the rest of his notable film and stage career. The role of Maria von Trapp in *The Sound of Music* capped the career of Mary Martin (1913–90), who had achieved major stardom as the nurse Nellie Forbush in *South Pacific* (1949). Rodgers continued to compose musicals after the death of Hammerstein in 1960, but none was successful. Cole Porter also had a major success with *Can-Can* (1953) set in turn-of-the-century Paris. *Can-Can* also launched the career of Gwen Verdon (b. 1926) who would become a star on the musical stage. *Silk Stockings* (1955), a witty, stylish send-up of cold war politics, was Porter's last musical.

Musical theater in the 1950s and 1960s was mainly marked by the ascent of a new generation of musical composers and lyricists. Leonard Bernstein (1918–90) was one of the most talented. A classically trained composer, Bernstein's first foray into musical theater was *On the Town* (1944), a romantic comedy about three sailors on shore leave in New York. With a book and sprightly lyrics by the team of Betty Comden (b. 1915) and Adolph Green (b. 1915), *On the Town* ran for almost five hundred performances. Collaborating again with Comden and Green, Bernstein's *Wonderful Town* (1950), based on the popular comedy *My Sister Eileen* (1940), by Jerome Chodorov and Joseph Fields, was even more successful. Bernstein's score for *Candide* (1956), a "comic operetta" based on Voltaire's satirical novel, was critically acclaimed, but the subject matter and production style precluded a commercial success: it closed after seventy-three performances. (A 1974 revival, however, with new lyrics by the young lyricist–composer Stephen Sondheim and direction by Harold Prince premiered

*Mary Martin c. 1940s. From Appelbaum and Camner,* Stars of the American Musical Theatre in Historic Photographs. *Courtesy Dover Publications, Inc.*

at the Chelsea Theatre Center, then transferred to Broadway where it ran for almost eight hundred performances.) *West Side Story* (1957) imaginatively relocated *Romeo and Juliet* to a rough Manhattan neighborhood of the 1950s with the Montagues and Capulets becoming rival Puerto Rican and white street gangs. Bernstein's inventive score, a mixture of operatic, jazz, and Latin music, Stephen Sondheim's alternately tough and moving lyrics, and Jerome Robbins's (b. 1918) dynamic, exciting choreography and direction marked *West Side Story* as a landmark American musical, equal to George Gershwin's *Porgy and Bess.* After this success, Bernstein abandoned musical theater to focus on his career as the principal conductor of the New York Philharmonic and to compose concert music. But his impact on other musical theater composers was significant.

After Rodgers and Hammerstein, the Viennese-born composer Frederick Loewe (1904–88) and lyricist Alan Jay Lerner (1918–86) were the most successful musical theater partnership of the late 1940s and 1950s. Their first hit was *Brigadoon* (1947), a romantic fantasy with a Scottish setting, which with its lilting score and charming lyrics enjoyed long runs in both New York and London. *Paint Your Wagon* (1951), set in California's gold rush days, was colorful, but less successful than *Brigadoon. My Fair Lady* (1956), however, adapted from Bernard Shaw's *Pygmalion,* was a runaway hit. With period settings by Oliver Smith (1918–94) and lavish costumes by Cecil Beaton (1904–80), compelling performances by English actors Rex Harrison (1908–90) as Henry Higgins and Julie Andrews (b. 1935) as Eliza Doolittle, polished choreography by Hanya Holm, and stylish direction by playwright–director Moss Hart, *My Fair Lady* ran for 2,717 performances, the longest running musical of the time. The London production had a comparable run and the national tour continued for almost seven years. *Camelot* (1960), a retelling of the legend of King Arthur, was mounted by the same artistic team, with renowned British actor Richard Burton (1925–84) as Arthur and Julie Andrews as Queen Guinevere. It was critically acclaimed, but a New York newspaper strike affected its commercial run. Subsequent revivals, however, elevated it into the pantheon of American musical classics. After *Camelot,* Loewe retired from the theater, although he did collaborate with Lerner on the score for the film *Gigi* (1959).

A plethora of musicals graced Broadway in the 1950s and 1960s. A short list of the more notable hits would include Richard Adler (b. 1923) and Jerry Ross's (1926–55) *The Pajama Game* (1954), about a labor strike in a pajama factory with echoes of *Pins and Needles,* and *Damn Yankees* (1955), an entertaining comedy mixing baseball with the Faust legend; Jerry Bock (b. 1924) and Sheldon Harnick's (b. 1925) *Fiorello* (1959), about New York mayor Fiorello LaGuardia, and *Fiddler on the Roof* (1964), based on the stories of the noted Yiddish author Sholem Aleichem; Frank Loesser (1910–69) and Abe Burrows's (1910–85) *Guys and Dolls* (1950), based on Damon Runyon's comic tales of New York sporting life, and *How to Succeed in Business without Really Trying* (1961), a sparkling lampoon of American corporate culture; Loesser's *The Most Happy Fella* (1956), based on Sidney Howard's *They Knew What They Wanted;* Meredith Wilson's *Music Man* (1957), a sentimental romance set in the turn of the century; Stephen Sondheim's *A Funny Thing Happened on the Way to the Forum* (1962), a riotous musical farce, adapted from several comedies by the ancient Roman playwrights Plautus; and Mitch Leigh (b. 1928) and Joe Darion's (b. 1917) *Man of La Mancha* (1965), based on the Don Quixote story. Jerry Herman's (b. 1932) *Hello, Dolly!* (1964), adapted from Thornton Wilder's *The Matchmaker,* was one of the most popular musicals of its time, running for over twenty-eight hundred performances. As Dolly Levi, Carol Channing (b. 1921) entered the ranks of musical comedy stardom. Over its more than fifteen-year run, numerous prominent performers played Dolly, including Mary Martin, Ethel Merman, film stars Ginger Rogers and Betty Grable, and in 1967 pop/jazz singer Pearl Bailey at the head of an all-black cast.

Although Off-Broadway was generally not a major musical theater venue, Harvey Schmidt and Tom Jones's *The Fantasticks* (1960) deserves special mention. A whimsical romance based on Edmond Rostand's *Les Romanesques, The Fantasticks,* with a cast of six, simple staging, and a four-piece combo rather than an orchestra, was the antithesis of the Broadway musical. It was still running in mid-1997 after more than sixteen thousand performances.

As the 1960s waned, two musicals, in particular, signaled a shift in the style of the American musical. John Kander (b. 1927) and Fred Ebb's (b. 1932) *Cabaret* (1966), set in prewar Berlin, is often touted as the first "concept" musical with a book that is more theme- than plot-centered. Owing more to Brechtian influences and the Kurt Weill of *Threepenny Opera* than to the traditional musical comedy formula, its sardonic tone reflected a rising cynicism and divisiveness within American society. *Hair* (1967), the

"American Tribal Love-Rock Musical," as it was subtitled, introduced rock music to the musical comedy. Furthermore its libretto which commented on various issues, including the Vietnam War, environmental pollution, racial stereotyping, drug use, and sexual freedom and experimentation, was a radical departure from traditional musical material.

On balance, *Hair* was frequently acerbic, but also lively, and generally good humored, even optimistic, but some critics berated it as vulgar, salacious, and offensive. Authorities in Boston (1970) and Chattanooga, Tennessee (1973) banned performances in their cities, but in two separate decisions, the United States Supreme Court ruled that the production of *Hair* was protected under First Amendment rights to freedom of expression. *Hair*'s rock score and spirit of youthful rebelliousness proved a winning combination, especially to younger playgoers. Ultimately it ran for 1,750 performances on Broadway and toured worldwide into the 1970s. *Hair* influenced the development of other pop/rock musicals, including the Christian-oriented *Godspell* (1971) and *Jesus Christ Superstar* (1971). But the pop/rock musical trend was short-lived and few matched *Hair*'s verve and immediacy. Ironically, during *Hair*'s run, the musical *1776* (1969) a celebratory, retelling of the events that led up to the Declaration of Independence was almost as successful as *Hair,* winning several Tonys and other establishment theater awards and running for over twelve hundred performances.

The musical revue *Oh! Calcutta!* (1969) consisted of a series of risqué comic sketches, songs, and dances that were blatantly sexual and featured both male and female nudity. Material was provided by several notable writers and composers including Sam Shepard, Samuel Beckett, and John Lennon. As it was intended to do, *Oh! Calcutta!* raised a storm of controversy about theatrical censorship. Opening Off-Broadway, it ran for over seven hundred performances then transferred to Broadway for an additional six hundred performances. In 1976, it was revived, running for almost six thousand performances before it finally closed in 1989.

In the 1970s the nonbook or concept musical gained in popularity. This tendency is often attributed to a paucity of composers and especially librettists after the dissolution of such successful partnerships as Rodgers and Hammerstein and Lerner and Loewe and the concomitant rise of forceful, imaginative directors and director–choreographers. Composer–lyricist Stephen Sondheim (b. 1930) and producer–director Harold Prince (b. 1928) were the leading popularizers of the concept musical. Among their most successful collaborations were *Company* (1970), which in an almost Brechtian fashion explored contemporary romantaic relationships; *Follies* (1971), set against the Ziegfeld Follies; *A Little Night Music* (1973), based on Ingmar Bergman's film *Smiles of a Summer Night; Pacific Overtures* (1976), about the opening of Japan to the West, which used an all-Asian cast and drew on the conventions of traditional Japanese theater to confront historical prejudice on both sides of the Pacific; and *Sweeney Todd, the Demon Barber of Fleet Street* (1979), which combined Victorian melodrama with *grand guignol* effects. Although critically acclaimed for their innovative, visually lavish stagings and musical sophistication, the Sondheim–Prince musicals had modest runs by the standards of the day—averaging roughly about five hundred to six hundred performances each—and several lost a significant amount of money. Nevertheless, by the end of the decade Sondheim and Prince had achieved a level of eminence in the world of musical theater.

Among other noteworthy large-scale concept musicals of the 1970s are John Kander and Ebb's *Chicago* (1975) which, set in the mid-1920s and structured around a set of vaudeville acts, gave director–choreographer Bob Fosse (1927–87) the opportunity to stage elaborate and exciting dance numbers. *A Chorus Line* (1975), about the anxieties and ambitions of musical theater dancers and based on interviews with two-dozen actual dancers, was the most successful concept musical of the era. Skillfully developed, choreographed, and directed by Michael Bennett (1943–87), *A Chorus Line* ran continuously for the next fifteen years, closing in April 1990 after over six thousand performances.

A scarcity of original musicals spurred a nostalgic tendency for revivals and musicals based on popular movies. *No, No, Nanette,* originally produced in 1925, initiated the trend in 1971. Other successful revivals include *Irene* (1973, originally produced in 1919); an all-black cast *Guys and Dolls* (1976), produced by the Houston Grand Opera; and *The King and I* (1977), with Yul Brynner reprising his original performance as the King of Siam. Nostalgia for the older musical theater format undoubtedly also fueled the success of such old-fashioned, sentimental book musicals as *Shenandoah* (1975) about a Virginia farm family drawn into the Civil War; *Annie* (1977) based on the comic strip character "Little Orphan Annie"; and, especially, *Grease* (1972), a light-hearted, rock 'n' roll, romantic comedy set in the 1950s. *Grease* originated at a small Chicago theater and premiered in New York Off-Broadway, but it was quickly transferred to Broadway where it ran for a total of almost thirty-four hundred performances. Among the more successful musicals based on movies were *Applause* (1970), based on the movie *All About Eve* (1950); *Gigi* (1973), which Lerner and Loewe adapted from their own motion picture; *Sugar* (1972), based on the Billy Wilder film farce *Some Like It Hot* (1959); and *On the Twentieth Century* (1978) taken from the John Barrymore–Carol Lombard screwball comedy *Twentieth Century* (1934). A search for new material and audiences also led to novel country–western musicals—for example, *The Best Little Whorehouse in Texas* (1978).

The 1970s and 1980s also saw a striking advance in the number of musicals on Broadway aimed at black audiences, among them the 1975 premiere of ragtime composer Scott Joplin's *Treemonisha* written in 1915; *Purlie* (1970) adapted from Ossie Davis's *Purlie Victorious* (1961); *Raisin* (1973), a musical version of Lorraine Hansberry's *Raisin in the Sun* (1959); and *The Wiz* (1975), a funky, satirical African–American version of *The Wizard of Oz*. A number of notable black musical revues or cavalcades were also produced, including *Bubbling Brown Sugar* (1976); *Ain't Misbehavin'* (1978), about black songwriter Fats Waller; *Eubie!* (1978), about black musical theater composer Eubie Blake (1883–1983); *One Mo' Time* (1979), a re-creation of black vaudeville entertainment of the 1920s, and *Sophisticated*

*Ladies* (1981), featuring the music of Duke Ellington. *Dreamgirls* (1981), a concept musical developed by Michael Bennett, was based on the story of the Supremes, a black vocal trio who rose to stardom in the 1960s. It ran for over fifteen hundred performances on Broadway. It should be noted that all of these shows attracted black audiences to Broadway in record numbers, but they were also equally appealing to many white theatergoers.

Since the 1920s, successful American musicals were regularly exported for production in London and other European capitals. Indeed, American musicals dominated the genre. British musical theater, however, once again began to make inroads on Broadway with English composer–lyricist Lionel Bart's *Oliver!*, a musical version of Dickens's *Oliver Twist*. After premiering in London in 1960, *Oliver!* moved to New York in 1963 for a successful long run on Broadway, followed by a national tour. At the beginning of the 1970s, the English team of composer Andrew Lloyd Webber (b. 1948) and lyricist Tim Rice established a forceful presence on Broadway with *Jesus Christ Superstar* (1970), a controversial rock-opera retelling of Jesus's last days, which, imaginatively staged by Tom O'Horgan, ran for over seven hundred performances. Lloyd Webber's star remained on the ascent for the next two decades.

The major musical trends of the 1970s continued unabated through the 1990s—e.g., lavishly produced concept and book musicals, foreign imports, revivals, and musicals based on movies. In the 1980s, Stephen Sondheim, however, moved in the direction of small-scale and increasingly refined musical material. *Sunday in the Park with George* (1984), for example, centers on French artist George Seurat (1859–91) and his painting "Sunday Afternoon on the Island of the Grand Jatte"; *Into the Woods* (1987) was inspired by psychologist Bruno Bettelheim's Freudian interpretation of classic fairy tales; *Assassins* (1991) deals with the various assassins of American presidents; and *Passion* (1994), is a strange love story set in nineteenth-century Italy. Developed in collaboration with Off-Broadway's Playwrights Horizons, Sondheim's later musicals were critically acclaimed for their musical daring, as well as for their clever, minimalistic stagings, usually by James Lapine (b. 1940), but they did not attract a mass audience. Andrew Lloyd Webber and Tim Rice, in contrast, enjoyed a string of unprecedented commercial successes, including *Evita* (1980), about the controversial Argentinean political idol Eva Perón; *Cats* (1981), a concept musical based on T. S. Eliot's collection *Old Possum's Book of Practical Cats*; *Phantom of the Opera* (1988), adapted from the novel by French author Gaston Leroux (1868–1927); and *Sunset Boulevard* (1994), based on the movie of the same title. Competing with Lloyd Webber and Rice were *Les Misérables* (1987), based on Victor Hugo's famous epic, and *Miss Saigon* (1991), a modernized version of Puccini's *Madama Butterfly* set against the US–Vietnam war. Both were the work of the French team of composer Claude Michel Schönberg and lyricist Alain Boublil, in consort with British producer Cameron Mackintosh and director Trevor Nunn, formerly artistic director of the Royal Shakespeare Company. As of mid-1997, *Cats, Phantom of the Opera, Les Misérables,* and *Miss Saigon* were still playing on Broadway. *Cats,* indeed, had become the longest running

Broadway musical with over sixty-two hundred performances. Furthermore, road companies of all four productions crisscrossed the nation, making them among the best known musicals in the history of the American stage.

Through the late 1980s and 1990s, fewer and fewer musicals were mounted on Broadway. In 1988–89, for example, only six new musicals and one revival opened. After foreign imports, the most commercially successful musical productions of the 1990s were revivals of earlier successes, including *Guys and Dolls* (1992); *Carousel* (1994); *Show Boat* (1994); *The King and I* (1996); and *A Funny Thing Happened on the Way to the Forum* (1996). It is telling, furthermore, that *Carousel* was a production mounted by England's National Theatre and premiered in London, while *Show Boat,* perhaps the most successful revival, was mounted by a Canadian production company and premiered in Toronto. Indeed, only *Rent* (1996), an exciting reworking of Puccini's *La Bohème* set in present-day New York's bohemian East Village neighborhood struck both critics and theatergoers as fresh and original. With a romantic but accessible story line, numerous references to such issues as racism, sexual orientation, and AIDS, a contemporized pop/rock score, and a vibrant, but minimalistic staging, it won numerous awards, including the prestigious Pulitzer Prize, and settled in for a long run. But *Rent* was the only bright light in an otherwise humdrum, dismal musical theater landscape. And tragically, its young composer–lyricist Jonathan Larson (1960–96) died before opening night. As early as the 1970s, a number of organizations were founded to nurture American musical theater, including the National Alliance of Musical Theatre Producers and the National Music Theatre Network. The Music Theatre Group founded in 1971 has fostered the development of a number of original experimental musical theater pieces such as Martha Clarke's *Vienna Lusthaus* and several works by the inventive Elizabeth Swados (b. 1951). As the 1990s wane, however, the future of the American musical, one of the cornerstones of the modern Broadway theater, looks bleak.

SCENIC DESIGN IN the postwar era followed several major trends. In the immediate postwar period, the painterly poetic or lyrical realism of Jo Mielziner, Donald Oenslager, Oliver Smith, and other veteran designers continued to dominate scenic design. The painterly style remained popular for realistic American dramas and traditional musicals with younger designers like John Lee Beatty (b. 1948) and Marjorie Bradley Kellogg (b. 1946), considered the new masters. Beginning in the mid-1960s, however, the painterly style gave way to a new design aesthetic. Influenced by postwar European scenic design, by trends in painting and sculpture, and by the availability of various new polymer, composite, and lightweight metal materials, the new style tended to be more sculptural than painterly, and more abstract and constructivistic than impressionistic. It was characterized by exposed metal scaffolding, a juxtaposition of different textures and materials creating a three-dimensional collage effect, and the use of metaphorical scenic pieces. Increasingly, sophisticated projected scenery also became a widely used technique. The veteran designer Boris Aronson was one of the pioneers of this approach and a major influence on the next generation of designers. A list of the leading designers working in this sculptural, constructivistic mode would include Shanghai-born Ming Cho Lee (b. 1930), Eugene Lee (b. 1939), Robin Wagner (b. 1933), and John Conklin (b. 1937). Responding to the nature of contemporary theater, the work of several designers—notably Santo Loquasto (b. 1944), Douglas Schmidt (b. 1942) and David Mitchell (b. 1932)—eclectically ranged between sculptural abstract minimalism and a more old-fashioned, multiscened, realistic approach.

Beginning in the 1980s, the tendencies of postmodern art—heterogeneity, self-reflexivity and irony, and an eclectic mix of styles and media—also marked the work of a number of American scenic designers. Influenced by such avant-garde practitioners as Robert Wilson and Richard Foreman, and by environmentalist theater practices, postmodern scenic design is characterized by either a refined, strongly imagistic, neoexpressionistic or surrealistic approach, or by a self-conscious, antiart, raw ugliness. Sometimes both approaches are combined in ironic dialectical opposition. Although postmodernism has not invaded Broadway scenic design to any great extent—the production of *Rent* being a notable exception—by the 1990s it was a commonplace approach in many regional theater productions. American scenic designers working primarily in a postmodernist style include James Clayburgh (b. 1949), Robert Israel (b. 1939), Adrianne Lobel (b. 1955), Russian-born George Tsypin (b. 1954), and Michael Yeargany (b. 1946).

Costume design and designers continued to gain recognition in the postwar American theater. Among the numerous acclaimed contemporary costume designers are Theoni Aldredge (b. 1932) whose credits include productions for the New York Shakespeare Festival, and costumes for such Broadway hits as *A Chorus Line, Dreamgirls* (1981), and *La Cage aux Folles* (1983); Patricia Zipprodt (b. 1925), the designer of costumes for a number of notable musicals, including *Fiddler on the Roof, Cabaret, Pippin* (1972), and *Sunday in the Park with George;* Florence Klotz (b. 1920?), noted for her designs for *Follies, A Little Night Music, Kiss of the Spider Woman* (1993), and the 1995 revival of *Show Boat;* Korean-born Willa Kim (b. 1930?) who has designed costumes for such lavish musicals as *The Will Rogers Follies* (1991) and *Victor/Victoria* (1995) as well as the 1986 revival of *The Front Page;* and English-born Jane Greenwood (b. 1934) who is often called on for revivals of period pieces such as *Long Day's Journey into Night* (1986), *Our Town* (1988), and *The Heiress* (1995).

Lighting design after World War II was marked by a series of technological advances in lighting control systems, instruments, and lamps. Theatrical engineer and consultant George Izenour (b. 1912), developed an improved lighting console that increased the number of stored lighting changes or combinations (known as *presets*) from three—the prewar standard—to ten. A major breakthrough came with the development of electronic control boards which utilized advances in computer technology, electronic miniaturization, and data storage. By the mid-1980s, using relatively small computerized systems a designer could store hundreds of different lighting effects and combinations. The number of lighting instruments used for large-scale theatrical productions jumped from the previous limit of several hundred to a thousand or more. The development of Vari-Lites (computer-controlled, automated lighting instruments) was another breakthrough. Armed with the potential and flexibility of the new lighting technology, lighting designers became true "artists of light," creating spectacular tonal and atmospheric effects. Among the more celebrated contemporary lighting designers are Pat Collins (b. 1932), Jennifer Tipton (b. 1937), Tharon Musser (b. 1925), Jules Fisher (b. 1937), Martin Aronstein (b. 1936), and Ken Billington (b. 1946), each of whom is responsible for hundreds of productions from the 1960s to the present.

THE IMPORTANCE OF directors mounted in the postwar American theater. The success (but rarely the failure) of a production was increasingly attributed to the director's imagination, interpretive skills, ability to coach outstanding performances from actors, and to lead a team of designers to realize a special, unified artistic vision. Directors who were able to stamp a production with a personal "signature" of sorts—a reflection of their personality or a distinctive approach to staging—were especially admired. Such directors were often regarded as the "authors" or *auteurs*—to borrow a term from French film theory—of the theatrical production, equal in importance to the author of the script.

Although a few directors worked across several different genres—musicals, comedies, dramas, classics—most tended to specialize in a particular type of drama or theater. In the immediate postwar period, for example, José Quintero (b. 1924) established a reputation as the foremost director of O'Neill's late plays. Elia Kazan (b. 1909) began his career as an actor and director with the Group Theatre. After the war, he was celebrated for his naturalistic, emotionally intense approach to staging the works of Tennessee Williams and Arthur Miller, including notable productions of Williams's *A Streetcar Named Desire* (1947) and *Cat On A Hot Tin Roof* (1955) and Miller's *Death of a Salesman* (1949). Harold Clurman's (1901–80) directorial career, like that of Kazan, started with the Group Theatre for whom he staged five of Clifford Odets's plays, including *Awake and Sing* (1935) and *Golden Boy* (1937). In the 1950s and 1960s, he was noted for his sensitive direction of Carson McCullers's *The Member of the Wedding* (1950), Lillian Hellman's *The Autumn Garden* (1951), Jean Anouilh's *The Waltz of the Toreadors* (1957), and Arthur Miller's *Incident at Vichy* (1964). Alan Schneider (1917–84) was widely admired for his special way with the plays of Samuel Beckett, Harold Pinter, and Edward Albee. Mike Nichols (b. 1931), after a highly successful career in the 1950s as a comedy act with partner Elaine May (b. 1932), achieved distinction as an adept director of contemporary comedy and drama. His credits include four Neil Simon hits, including *The Odd Couple* (1965) and *Plaza Suite* (1968), English playwright Tom Stoppard's witty comedy *The Real Thing* (1984), and two of David Rabe's controversial dramas, *Streamers* (1976) and *Hurlyburly* (1984).

A number of directors achieved distinction working principally in the field of musical theater. Gower Champion (1921–80), after a career in Hollywood in the 1950s, returned to Broadway to direct and choreograph such hits as *Bye Bye Birdie* (1960), *Hello, Dolly!* (1964), and *42nd Street* (1980); Jerome Robbins (b. 1918), one of the musical theater's leading choreographers, not only directed *West Side Story* (1957), but also *Gypsy* (1959) and *Fiddler on the Roof* (1964); Bob Fosse was one of the most successful director-choreographers of the 1960s and 1970s; Tommy Tune (b. 1939) established a record as an inventive director–choreographer with *The Best Little Whorehouse in Texas* (1978), *Nine* (1980), *Grand Hotel* (1990), and *The Will Rogers Follies* (1991). Undoubtedly the major director of musicals in the postwar theater has been Harold Prince (b. 1928), the unprecedented winner of eight Tony Awards for direction. In addition to his credits already cited, he was the award-winning director of *Phantom of the Opera* (1988) and the 1994 revival of *Show Boat*.

The rise of Off- and Off-Off-Broadway and resident theaters opened opportunities for numerous directors working in a range of styles and approaches. At the Off-Broadway Circle Repertory Company which he helped found, Marshall Mason (b. 1940), captured attention for his direction of Lanford Wilson's poetic realist plays, including *The Hot'l Baltimore* (1973) and *Burn This* (1987). Lynne Meadow (b. 1946) at the Manhattan Theatre Club is noted for her crisp stagings of a number of contemporary English and American plays. At the Off-Off-Broadway CSC Repertory Theatre, founder Christopher Martin (b. 1942) and his successor Carey Perloff (b. 1959) built reputations for inventive interpretations of classics and modern and contemporary European plays. Among resident theater directors, Adrian Hall (b. 1927) at Providence's Trinity Repertory Company, and Mark Lamos (b. 1946) at the Hartford Stage Company have been acclaimed for their daring, innovative productions of classics and provocative new plays. Hall's productions, mainly for Providence's Trinity Repertory Company, have been noted for his actor-centered approach and his minimalist environmental settings created in consort with designer Eugene Lee. Lamos's has become particularly adept at transposing classics to a twentieth-century time frame, usually in a visually inventive and telling style. *Twelfth Night* (1985), for example, was set at a 1930s party with Cole Porter and George Gershwin tunes as incidental music. Liviu Ciulei (b. 1923) and Andrei Serban, two Rumanian émigré directors, contributed significantly to American theatrical staging in the 1970s and 1980s. As artistic director of the Guthrie Theatre from 1980 to 1986, Ciulei brought a new anti-illusionist, politicized theatricalism to staging such classics as *The Tempest* (1981) and *A Midsummer Night's Dream* (1985). Serban has also worked in an essentially antirealistic style, but his eclecticism and range is not easily pigeon-holed. His *Cherry Orchard* (1977) for the Lincoln Center Repertory Company, for example, was played as a farce against a pared-down setting consisting of a few chairs on a bare stage with a frieze of cherry trees at the rear. For both the Guthrie Theatre and Circle in the Square, Serban staged *The Marriage of Figaro* in a theatricalized highly physical style. To connect the present with the past, the costuming juxtaposed white contemporary clothes in the first half against black eighteenth-century dress in the second half. Actors performed on roller skates, bicycles, skateboards, wheelchairs, and a swing. The overriding concept behind this approach was not altogether clear, but it was fresh and entertaining.

Peter Sellars (b. 1957) and Anne Bogart (b. 1951) are America's leading postmodernist stage directors. Sellars earned a reputation as the *enfant terrible* of the American stage for his controversial contemporized, deconstructionist interpretations of classic plays and operas. Sellars, for example, relocated Mozart's *The Marriage of Figaro* (1988) to a lavishly appointed penthouse apartment in one of New York's towering skyscrapers where the characters cavorted like contemporary affluent "yuppies." Productions of Aeschylus's *Ajax* (1986) and *The Persians* (1993) were staged as sharply critical commentaries on contemporary American militarism. Sellars's *The Merchant of Venice* (1994) for Chicago's Goodman Theatre was set against our own high-tech, market-driven, morally ambiguous time. While Sellars has been criticized for self-indulgent, aesthetic foolishness, his interpretations are invariably inventive and thought-provoking. Like Sellars, Bogart also tends to relocate classics to our time to deconstruct their thematic content. She set *South Pacific* (1984), for example, in the rehabilitation unit of a veteran's hospital to foreground its concerns with patriotism, racism, and power. But Bogart is noted as well for her own original, postmodernist creations. *Woman and Men: A Big Dance* (1982), for example, uses a high school dance as a metaphor for American social and sexual roles, while *History, an American Dream* (1983) is a complex mainly visual and kinetic exploration of the connections between war and gender relationships. In 1992, Bogart and the noted Japanese director Suzuki Tadashi cofounded the Saratoga International Theatre Institute (SITI). Her recent works, influenced by Suzuki's physically expressive, theatricalist approach, have been *Small Lives/Big Dreams* (1994), based on Chekhov's plays, and a reworking of Elmer Rice's *The Adding Machine* (1995).

In addition to those already noted in this chapter, directors who merit mention are William Ball (1931–91), founder of the American Conservatory Theatre where he directed a score of notable productions; Arvin Brown (b. 1940), artistic director of the Long Wharf Theatre since 1967; Gordon Davidson (b. 1933), artistic director of the Center Theatre Group at Los Angeles's Mark Taper Forum since 1966; Gene Saks (b. 1921), one of Broadway's outstanding directors of contemporary comedies; Ulu Grosbard (b. 1929), a skillful director of realistic American plays, including David Mamet's *American Buffalo* (1977); Des McAnuff (b. 1952), artistic director of the La Jolla Playhouse; Gerald Gutierrez (b. 1952), who has been particularly adept at staging American revivals; Garland Wright (b. 1946), artistic director of the Guthrie Theatre (1986–95); Stephen Porter, who has directed dozens of plays for major resident theaters and is noted for his sparkling productions of Molière and Shaw; Gregory Mosher (b. 1949), who championed new American works at the Goodman Theatre (1978–85); and Jack O'Brien (b. 1939), artistic director of the Old Globe Theatre since 1969, whose credits range from Shakespeare, to musicals, contemporary comedies and dramas; Frank Galati (b. 1943), a Chicago director known especially for his stage adaptations of such novels as John Steinbeck's *The Grapes of Wrath* and *East of Eden.* Gerald Freedman (b. 1927), artistic director of the Great Lakes Theater Festival (1985–97), Michael Kahn (b. 1937), artistic director of the American Shakespeare Theatre (1969–74) and Washington, D.C.'s Shakespeare Theatre since 1986, and Jerry Turner (b. 1927), artistic director of the Oregon Shakespeare Festival (1971–91), should be singled out for their contributions to American Shakespeare direction.

Dance and the role of the choreographer in American musical theater mounted in importance from the 1950s. Dances were increasingly integrated into the staging and book to such an extent that distinctions between direction and choreography, libretto and dancing, often disappeared. Musical theater dance generally continued to draw on various dance styles from classical ballet to modern dance, but a distinctive form of theater dance derived from jazz dance emerged in the 1950s. Bob Fosse and Jerome Robbins were the principal creators of this dance idiom which was strikingly visible in *The Pajama Game* (1955) and *Damn Yankees* (1956), both choreographed by Fosse, and *West Side Story* (1958), choreographed by Robbins. The numerous new social dances that developed with the rock 'n' roll phenomenon were introduced into musical theater in *Hair* (1968) and *Grease* (1972). Contemporary musical theater dance ranges from jazz and rock dance styles to the recreation of period dances for new musicals like *Hello, Dolly!* (1961), set at the turn of the century, or for revivals like *No, No, Nanette* (1971). The prominence of dance in contemporary musical theater was celebrated in such musicals as *A Chorus Line,* Bob Fosse's *Dancin'* (1978), and in the all-dance revue, *Jerome Robbins' Broadway* (1989). Although theatrical dance is associated mainly with mainstream musical theater, from the 1980s on dance became an increasingly important part of nonmusical theater, as well.

From the late 1940s to the early 1990s a half-dozen director–choreographers —Bob Fosse, Jerome Robbins, Gower Champion, Michael Kidd (b. 1917), Michael Bennett, and Tommy Tune—choreographed most of Broadway's award-winning musicals. Other choreographers who merit mention are Joe Layton (1931–94), whose credits include *Wonderful Town* (1953), *The Sound of Music* (1959) and *George M!* (1968); Patricia Birch (b. 1930?), who choreographed *Grease* and created the innovative subtle dances in *A Little Night Music;* Susan Stroman (b. 194?), who won Tony Awards for her choreography for *Crazy for You* and the revival of *Show Boat* (1995); and Graciela Daniele (b. 1940?), who invented the period inspired dances for the hit revival of Gilbert and Sullivan's *The Pirates of Penzance* (1980), *The Mystery of Edwin Drood* (1985), and *Ragtime* (1997).

IN THE SECOND half of the century, college and university theater was a mounting presence across the spectrum of American theatrical training and activity. Extracurricular, amateur theater performances had been a feature of academic life from the earliest days of the country. In the nineteenth century, especially, such performances flourished and clubs like Brown University's Thalian Dramatic Association and Harvard's Hasty Pudding Club became well known for their theatrical presentations. The actual beginnings of formalized academic study of theater is unclear, but, as noted in chapter 6, Professor George Pierce Baker initiated one of the first practical theater courses at Harvard in 1905. With the title "English 47: Techniques of Drama," it was essentially a course in playwriting. In 1912, Baker added "47 Workshop" as a laboratory theater for producing the plays written in English 47. In 1925, frustrated with Harvard's reluctance to expand his program, Baker moved to Yale University where he founded the drama department that eventually became the Yale School of Drama.

Predating Baker's efforts at Yale, the first department of theater in the United States was established by Thomas Wood Stevens in 1914 at Pittsburgh's Carnegie–Mellon Institute of Technology. Other pioneers of academic theater include Frederick H. Koch at the University of North Carolina, Thomas H. Dickenson at the University of Wisconsin, Alexander Drummond at Cornell University, and E. C. Mabie at Iowa University. Gradually, the number of college theater programs multiplied. In 1936, the American Educational Theatre Association (AETA) was founded with eighty members pledged "to encourage the highest possible standards of teaching, production, and research in the educational theater field." (AETA subsequently became the American Theatre Association [ATA] and then in 1986 the Association for Theatre in Higher Education [ATHE]).

Many of the first programs of theater study were housed in departments of English or departments of Speech, but by the early 1960s there was a growing trend toward autonomous departments of theater. By the mid-1960s, roughly half of the U.S.'s over fifteen hundred accredited colleges offered a degree in theater, while over 75 percent offered courses in theater. In 1967 there were about eighteen thousand undergraduate theater majors and about three thousand bachelors degrees, two thousand masters degrees, and nine hundred doctoral degrees were awarded with an emphasis in theater. Furthermore, there were about ten thousand productions of plays in college and university theaters for an audience of about five million. A decade later, the number of presentations and the total audience had roughly doubled.

Beginning in the early 1960s, university theater programs also expanded in other directions. As part of a nationwide boom in the construction of theater and cultural complexes, many universities built new theaters or performing arts centers to house their theater and fine arts departments. A 1963 AETA survey indicated that almost three hundred academic institutions were building or planning to build new theatrical facilities. In 1969 the University of Illinois, for example, opened the Krannert Center for the Performing Arts. With four state-of-the art theaters and various auxiliary spaces—classrooms, shops, rehearsal rooms, offices—the Krannert Center was one of the finest theatrical complexes in America.

In consort with these new physical plants, a number of university theater programs moved to combine traditional liberal arts education with training for careers in the professional theater. To achieve this goal, some universities began to hire professional actors, designers, and directors as adjunct or full-time professors. Special courses of study in acting, directing, scenery, costume, lighting design, theatrical technology, and theater management, at both the undergraduate and graduate level, proliferated. Several university theater departments also aligned themselves with a resident theater company to strengthen the relationship between university programs of study and the professional theater. The University of Minnesota, for example, formed an alliance with the Guthrie Theatre. Close ties were also built between the University of Missouri–Kansas City and the Missouri Repertory Theatre, the Yale School of Drama and the Yale Repertory Theatre, and the University of San Diego and the Old Globe Theatre—to name but a few partnerships. In 1967, the University/Resident Theatre Association (URTA) was founded to coordinate these joint university theater programs. By the early 1980s, professionally oriented university theater programs were commonplace. Although building programs and university theater enrollments slowed in the late 1980s and 1990s, university departments of theater remained important training schools for careers in the professional theater.

BEGINNING IN THE early 1960s, there was a surge in new theater building across America. Many of these new theaters broke with the traditional multi-tiered auditorium and proscenium stage configuration, adopting instead various arena, thrust, or end-stage arrangements. The noted American architect Frank Lloyd Wright, for example, designed an innovative theater for the Dallas Theatre Center (1959) which, inspired by ancient Greek and Elizabethan theaters, had a broad fan-shaped auditorium sweeping around a curved, modified thrust stage. In 1961, Washington, D.C.'s Arena Stage moved into a new theater facility which, as the company's name dictated, was an arena configuration seating about eight hundred spectators. A decade later, Arena Stage opened a second five hundred-seat theater, the Kreeger Theatre, which, instead of an arena, had a modified proscenium arrangement. For the Guthrie Theatre (1963) in Minneapolis, Tyrone Guthrie and stage designer Tanya Moiseiwitsch, working with architect Ralph Rapson, created an asymmetrical auditorium and thrust stage suggested by, but not replicating, their earlier Festival Theatre (1953–57) in Stratford, Ontario. The thrust configuration was also adapted for Theatre Atlanta (1965), the Mark-Taper Forum (1967) at the Music Center of Los Angeles County, Dallas's Alley Theatre (1968), and dozens of other theaters built in the 1960s and 1970s.

Another tendency in theater architecture was toward a multiple-use space for which a single auditorium and stage could be mechanically reconfigured for different performance uses or staging arrangements. Noted architect Eero Saarinen and scenic designer Jo Mielziner designed the Vivian Beaumont Theatre (1965) at the Lincoln Center for Performing Arts in New York City so that it could be used in either a proscenium or thrust arrangement. George Izenour was responsible for a score of multi-use theaters and

*The Krannert Center for the Performing Arts at the University of Illinois-Urbana-Champaign. Courtesy University of Illinois.*

*Lincoln Center for the Performing Arts. At left, the New York State Theatre (1964); center, the Metropolitan Opera (1966); right, Avery Fisher Hall (1962).Courtesy New York Power Authority.*

auditoriums in the United States, including Fort Wayne Indiana's Theatre of Performing Arts (1973), Uihlein Hall (1969) in Milwaukee, the Jesse Jones Hall for the Performing Arts in Houston (1966), and the Edwin Thomas Hall Performing Arts Hall at the University of Akron (1973).

A number of new theaters were built as part of performing arts or cultural complexes. One of the first and largest of these was the Lincoln Center for the Performing Arts located on New York City's Upper West Side. Lincoln Center was the model for other major performing arts centers built in the 1960s and 1970s including the Music Center of Los Angeles County (1964–68), the Atlanta Memorial Arts Center (1968), Washington, D.C.'s John F. Kennedy Center for the Performing Arts (1971), and the Denver Center for the Performing Arts (1979). Usually these complexes contain several theaters for music, dance, opera, and drama performances.

Some communities, instead of building new theaters or performing arts centers restored older theaters which had fallen into disuse as theater declined in the 1930s. In some instances, theaters originally designed as movie houses were converted into legitimate theaters. In 1980, for example, Cleveland renovated three contiguous theaters in its downtown area—the State, the Palace, and the Ohio, all built in the 1920s—to legitimate theater use. St. Louis's Fox Theatre was one of the nation's largest and most lavishly appointed movie palaces in the 1930s, but by the 1950s, it had fallen into a dilapidated state. In 1982 a completely restored Fox was reopened as a theater for Broadway touring musicals and various popular entertainments. Dozens of older theaters and movie palaces were reclaimed for legitimate use in the 1970s and 1980s. In addition, numerous nontheatrical spaces—churches, schools, libraries, commercial buildings—were converted into theaters. The Actors Theatre of Louisville, for example, is housed in a former bank building. The theater building boom reached its apex in the early 1980s, leaving the United States with probably the most diverse assortment of theaters in the world.

As RADIO, AND then to an even greater degree television, absorbed the news reporting industry, the number of newspapers nationwide, but especially in New York, declined significantly. In New York, for example, the number of daily newspapers shrank from a high of about twenty in the 1920s to seven in 1950, to a mere three in 1970—two tabloids the *New York Post* and the *Daily News,* and the venerable *New York Times;* in 1985, a fourth tabloid *New York Newsday* briefly entered the market but retreated again to serving just suburban Long Island in the mid-1990s, and there have been no further additions to the present day. A succession of *Times* reviewers wielded an unprecedented influence over the success or failure of theatrical productions in New York. The list of powerful *Times* critics includes Walter Kerr (1913–97), perhaps one of the most perceptive and humane theater critics of the 1960s and 1970s; Frank Rich (b. 1949), chief critic from 1980 to 1993; and David Richards (b. 1942) who was first Sunday, then daily critic from 1990–94. With the decline of daily newspapers, critics for magazines and special interest newspapers gained in importance, particularly for

*Left, exterior of the restored Fox Theatre, St. Louis. Courtesy of Fox Theatre/Fox Associates.*

*Right, lobby staircase of the restored Fox Theatre, St. Louis. Courtesy of Fox Theatre/Fox Associates.*

*Auditorium of the restored Fox Theatre, St. Louis. Courtesy of Fox Theatre/Fox Associates.*

a national readership. Among the new critics emerging in the late 1960s and 1970s, many of whom would remain influential into the 1980s and 1990s, were T. E. Kalem (1919–85) and William A. Henry III (1950–94) of *Time*; Jack Kroll of *Newsweek*; Henry Hewes (b. 1917) of *Saturday Review*; Edith Oliver (1913–98) of the *New Yorker*; John Simon (b. 1925) of *New York Magazine*, one of the most acerbic of theater critics; and Edwin Wilson (b. 1927) of the *Wall Street Journal*. The *Village Voice*, founded in 1955, became an important voice on Off- and Off-Off-Broadway theater through critics such as Julius Novik (b. 1939) and Michael Feingold (b. 1945). Robert Brustein (b. 1927), writing mainly for *The New Republic* since 1959, has been one of the most astute of American theater critics.

As resident theaters developed in the 1960s, a number of theater critics for metropolitan daily newspapers outside of New York gained a recognition beyond their local readership. Over his long tenure at the *Washington Post* (1946–79), Richard Coe (1916–95), for example, earned a national reputation as a keen, but generally supportive critic. Similarly, Claudia Cassidy (1905–96), critic for the *Chicago Tribune* from 1942 to 1965, was widely admired for her fairness and high standards. Other critics who deserve mention are Daniel Sullivan (b. 1935) and Sylvie Drake (b. 1930), critics of the *Los Angeles Times* from the 1970s to the early 1990s, and Bernard Weiner (b. 1941), chief drama critic of the influential *San Francisco Chronicle* from 1971 to 1991. In 1974, the American Theatre Critics' Association was formed to facilitate communication among its 250 members.

With the growth of the academic study of theater, there was a corresponding increase in the number of scholarly journals and monographs concerned with the history and criticism of American theater. Journals such as *The Drama Review, Performing Arts Journal,* and *Theatre Magazine* were especially important for their articles about American avant-garde theater and contemporary American playwrights, directors, musical theater, acting theory, and numerous other theatrical subjects.

Producers in particular continued to rail against critics. On a few occasions, producers became so outraged by a critic that they refused the usual complimentary tickets to review their productions. Yet producers and other theater artists regularly vied for the numerous annual awards established by critics both in New York and other cities, including the Drama Critics' Circle Award (established in 1936), the Outer Critics' Circle Award (established in 1950 by critics of suburban New York newspapers), and the Drama Desk Awards (established 1968).

## MEXICO

The years following World War II brought remarkable growth in the Mexican economy, while industrialization led to rapid urbanization. The Mexican film industry won international recognition in the late 1940s, the Pan-American Highway was completed in 1951, and women gained voting and elective office-holding rights in 1953. Advances in public education

*Left, directed by Seki Sano, Tennessee Williams's* A Streetcar Named Desire *opened in México D. F. in 1948. Humberto Zurita and Jacqueline Andere are shown as Stanley and Blanche at the Teatro Manolo Fábregas. Courtesy of Biblioteca de las Artes, Centro Nacional de las Artes, México D.F.*

*Right, Rodolfo Usigli's* Corona de fuego *(Crown of fire, 1960) is a historical drama set in the time of the Spanish Conquistadores and Cuahutémoc, the Aztec successor to Moctezuma II. Courtesy of Biblioteca de las Artes, Centro Nacional de las Artes, México D.F.*

*Virginia Fábregas (1870–1950) was one of Mexico's most internationally renowned actresses. Courtesy of Biblioteca de las Artes, Centro Nacional de las Artes, México D.F.*

*In 1951 Seki Sano directed Rodolfo Usigli's* Corona de sombra *(Crown of shadows, 1947), a play about the ill-fated Maximiliano and Carlota (played by Carlos Bribiesca and Lilian Opperheim), at the Palacio de Bellas Artes. Julio Prieto designed the sets. Courtesy of Biblioteca de las Artes, Centro Nacional de las Artes, México D.F.*

included the 1953 opening of a beautiful new campus for the four-hundred-year-old Universidad Nacional Autónoma de México (UNAM), which became an important center for the arts. The 1949 opening of the 140-seat Teatro del Caracol set an example for other small, commercial theater ventures. The Caracol's founders, Antonio Arce and José de Jesús Aceves, had the good fortune to present Rodolfo Usigli's *The Boy and the Cloud* (*El niño y la niebla*), which achieved a seven-month run. The capital's theater scene then saw an explosion of activity with the opening of dozens of *teatros de bolsillo* (pocket theaters) ranging in capacity from 93 (Teatro de la Capilla, 1953) to 1,141 (Teatro de los Insurgentes, 1953), most of them seating around 200. A new Teatro Virginia Fábregas (1954, capacity 960) was built on the site of the old one. In 1955 alone, eight new playhouses opened in Mexico City, followed by four more in 1956, four in 1957, and three in 1958. In addition to those independent theaters, a government-subsidized National Auditorium, constructed in Chapultepec Park, seated eighteen hundred. By 1985 Mexico City boasted over fifty theaters. With this proliferation of theaters came new audiences from the expanding middle class, new directors (including a number of Europeans who had arrived during the war), and a new generation of dramatists.

New dramatists and directors both were galvanized by the first production of a Tennessee Williams play in Mexico. *A Streetcar Named Desire* (*Un tranvía llamado deseo*) opened in December 1948 and brought critical

*Emilio Carballido's (b. 1925)* I Too Speak of the Rose *(Yo también hablo de la rosa) deals with the problems of two teenagers who derail a train and their subsequent confrontations with authority figures. Courtesy of Biblioteca de las Artes, Centro Nacional de las Artes, México D.F.*

acclaim for Seki Sano as best director of the 1948–49 season. It marked the first time in Mexico that a production had been rehearsed as long as three months. In a 1979 interview cited by Fernando de Ita, playwright Luisa Josefina Hernández recalled its impact:

> The theatre in Mexico had been sentimental and ridden with cliché. Then *A Streetcar Named Desire* broke away from all that and gave us honest portraits of people who are quite frank or openly cruel and unsympathetic. It had a tremendous influence in that it opened up new possibilities for our dramatists: to see realism for real. . . . I began writing plays about a month after seeing Seki Sano's production.

The playwrights known as the "generation of the 1950s" almost all considered themselves disciples of Rodolfo Usigli (1905–78), whose early work has been covered in chapter 6. In the course of his diplomatic service for the Mexican government, Usigli lived abroad for a total thirty-four years, and yet he wrote over thirty plays, always taking Mexico as his subject. According to Fernando de Ita, Usigli's evocation of the Mexican ethos in the theater could be considered the equivalent of the work of the great Mexican muralists Diego Rivera, José Clemente Orozco, and David Siqueiros. Usigli himself considered his most important dramatic work to be not his galvanizing *El gesticulador* (The imposter, 1937), but a trilogy on the subject of nationalism, devoted to what he called "the three fundamental Mexican myths." *Crown of Fire (Corona de fuego*, 1960) deals with territorial sovereignty as seen in the tragedy of the last Aztec ruler, Cuahutémoc, who was defeated by Cortés. *Crown of Light (Corona de luz*, 1963) examines spiritual sovereignty through the legend of the Virgin of Guadalupe's 1531 appearance to the

*Carballido, one of Mexico's finest and most prolific playwrights, has also worked to promoted quality theater for children and to encourage young playwrights. He is shown here addressing young people in the lobby of the Palacio de Bellas Artes. Courtesy of Biblioteca de las Artes, Centro Nacional de las Artes, México D.F.*

native Juan Diego. *Crown of Shadows* (*Corona de sombra*, 1947) treats political sovereignty through the fall of Maximilian and Carlotta. The three *Crowns*, according to Frank Dauster, do not so much look at the past in the light of the present, as interpret the present through the past. For many years Usigli taught theater history and dramatic composition at UNAM, where his students included Emilio Carballido, Luisa Josefina Hernández, Sergio Magaña, Luis G. Basurto, Jorge Ibargüengoitia, and Héctor Azár, all of whom were to become important playwrights.

Two plays produced in 1950 heralded the generation of brilliant young dramatists whose works, according to Carlos Solórzano, "even in the 1990s still comprise the basis of the national dramaturgy." *The Quadrant of Loneliness* (*El cuadrante de la soledad*) by José Revueltas (1914–76), directed by Ignacio Retes (b. 1918) and designed by Diego Rivera, dramatized urban overcrowding. The production would have continued its triumphant run, but the author acceded to political pressure from the Populist Party and withdrew his play after one hundred performances. The major revelation of 1950 was the talent of Emilio Carballido (b. 1925), whose *Rosalba and the Llavero Family* (*Rosalba y los Llaveros*) premiered to great acclaim under Salvador Novo's direction at the Palacio de Bellas Artes. Rosalba is an independent-minded city girl whose visit to her provincial relatives exposes their social and racial hypocrisies. Touching upon national issues and concerns within the framework of light comedy, that play is noteworthy as the initial success of Mexico's most prolific and internationally known dramatist of the twentieth century. Carballido's most characteristic plays employ a blend of realism and fantasy to probe philosophical or metaphysical concepts, as in *The Clockmaker from Córdoba* (*El relojero de Córdoba*, 1960). His extraordinary one-act *I Too Speak of the Rose* (*Yo también hablo de la rosa*, 1966) juxtaposes several realities in a work of poetic and theatrical metaphor as well as social concern.

Luisa Josefina Hernández (b. 1928) came to prominence in 1954 when she won *El Nacional*'s first prize in drama for *Model Boutique* (*Botica modelo*). Outstanding among her early plays of psychological realism are *Fallen Fruit* (*Los frutos caídos*, 1957), which Seki Sano directed, and *The Royal Guests* (*Los huéspedes reales*, 1958). Her later plays reveal a Brechtian influence in both form (departures from realism) and content (broad social concerns), as in *The Mulatto's Orgy* (*La fiesta del mulato*, 1979). She has also turned to pre-Columbian history in plays like *Quetzalcóatl* (1968) and *Popol Vuh* (1974). Similarly, Sergio Magaña (1924–90) found his early success in realism—with *The Signs of the Zodiac* (*Los signos del zodíaco*, 1951)—and later turned to pre-Columbian themes with *Moctezuma II* (1953) and a retelling of the *Rabinal Achí* titled *Enemies* (*Los enemigos*, 1970). Sometimes labeled an existentialist, sometimes an expressionist, Carlos Solórzano (b. 1922), has certainly taken an allegorial approach in his major works, which include *The Hands of God* (*Las manos de Diós*, 1956) and *The Puppets* (*Los fantoches*, 1958). Also notable in the generation of the 1950s are Elena Garro (b. 1920), Rafael Solana (1915–92), and Wilberto Cantón (1923–79). Even the venerable Celestino Gorostiza (1904–67) contributed a major work in this decade; *The Color of Our Skin* (*El color de nuestra piel*, 1952) attacked unconscious racism of the middle class. His last play, *Malinche* (*La malinche*, 1958) reexamined the conquest through the relationship between Cortés and his native mistress Malinche. Working in a more commercial vein were Luis G. Basurto (1920–91) and Jorge Ibargüengoitia (b. 1928).

Four playwrights of particular interest began their careers in the period between the generation of the 1950s and the so called new dramatists of the 1970s. Maruxa Vilalta (b. 1932) evolved from her didactic expressionism of the 1960s to a more complex dramaturgy influenced by Brecht. Hugo Argüelles (b. 1932) writes plays of "magic realism" with a streak of black humor and cruelty. Felipe Santander (b. 1934) found early success with his light comedies, but left the theater to become an agronomic engineer. That experience impelled him to write a play in a more didactic vein: *The Extension Agent* (*El extensionista*, 1978). With over sixty thousand performances, it became one of the most successful works in Mexican theater history. Santander made it part of a rural trilogy by following it with *The Brothers* (*Los hermanos*) and *The Miracle* (*El milagro*).

Originally known as a novelist, Vicente Leñero (b. 1933) built a substantial and complex body of work for the theater, for which many consider him alongside Usigli and Carballido as one of the leading dramatists of the century. As early as 1968, with his *People Rejected* (*Pueblo rechazado*, 1968), Leñero was exploring a documentary approach (combined with some Brechtian techniques) to historical drama and contemporary social issues. Despite problems with censorship occasioned by its strong language, *The Bricklayers* (*Los albañiles*, 1973), a drama set among the urban poor, won the major prizes for play-writing and direction, and was seen by seventy thousand people in its first season. According to Fernando de Ita, the 1980 production of Leñero's *The Move* (*La mudanza*) marked the birth of a "new dramatic realism." Working closely with director Luis de Tavira, Leñero presented reality as if captured in a photograph that merely records data from daily life without attempting to interpret it or get under the surface of it. The technique, which Leñero carried to greater extremes in *Visit of the Angel* (*La visita del angel*, 1981) and has been labeled *hyperrealism*, was subsequently employed by playwrights Victor Hugo Rascón Banda (b. 1948), Jesús González Dávila (b. 1942), and others.

If the 1950s belonged to the dramatist, it was the director who came to the fore in the 1960s. The way had been paved by foreign directors like Seki Sano, Charles Rooner, and Fernando Wagner, who introduced the ideas of

El Extensionista *(The extension agent, 1978) by Felipe Santander has been widely performed in rural communities. Courtesy of Biblioteca de las Artes, Centro Nacional de las Artes, México D.F.*

*Rodolfo Usigli and Hugo Agüelles are two of Mexico's outstanding twentieth-century dramatists. Courtesy of Biblioteca de las Artes, Centro Nacional de las Artes, México D.F.*

*Poesía en Voz Alta (Poetry Out Loud) was an influential group that promoted the work of new playwrights from 1956 to 1963. Courtesy of Biblioteca de las Artes, Centro Nacional de las Artes, México D.F.*

Stanislavsky, Meyerhold, and Copeau (Artaud and Brecht would be added later). With the 1954 opening of the Teatro del Granero, Mexico's first arena theater, Xavier Rojas set the standard for staging in the round. Héctor Mendoza (b. 1932), undoubtedly the most influential director since Seki Sano, first won renown as a playwright with his powerful realistic drama *Drowned* (*Ahogados*, 1952) and his tender adolescent comedy *Simple Things* (*Las cosas simples*, 1953). In 1956, Mendoza had just begun his career as a professional director when he joined with actor Juan José Arreola, poet Octavio Paz, painters Juan Soriano and Leonora Carrington, and others in an experimental venture called Poesía en Voz Alta (Poetry Out Loud). Arreola had conceived the project as a series of university-sponsored poetry recitals, but Paz pushed for the staging of plays that used language imaginatively. Carlos Fuentes described the mission of Poesía en Voz Alta in the playbill for the second production (which included Paz's only play, *La hija de Rappacini*, an unfettered dramatization of Hawthorne's story "Rappacini's Daughter"): "These programs . . . place us at the starting point—the archetypal freshness—of all great theatre, rooted in the word. . . . They restore and proclaim the essence of artistic creation: reality is not something given; it needs to be discovered and created anew in the imagination." Mendoza proved to be the right director, unleashing the imaginative powers of the actors, exercising a theatricality not tied to scenic elements or literal renditions of the text. Although Juan Soriano was the only one of the founders to stay with Poesía en Voz Alta through all eight of its programs, 1956–63, Mendoza left his stamp on the venture whose short existence belies its lasting impact. Indeed, several of those who began their careers under Mendoza have earned recognition as leading contemporary directors: Juan José Gurrola, José Luis Ibáñez, and Nancy Cárdenas. In his subsequent directorial work, Mendoza continued to prefer neglected classics and poetic works.

Like Mendoza, Juan José Gurrola (b. 1935) emphasizes the poetic and the theatrical, but is more inclined to spring surprises on his audience and even

*Héctor Azar is one of Mexico's leading directors and dramatists. Courtesy of Biblioteca de las Artes, Centro Nacional de las Artes, México D.F.*

scandalize them by his irreverent treatment of the classics. The Chilean-born Alejandro Jodorowsky directed in Mexico for the first time in 1966, bringing the influence of the European avant-garde: Beckett, Ionesco, Fernando Arrabal. Subsequent directors like Julio Castillo (1944–88), Luis de Tavira (b. 1949), Enrique Pineda, and Jesusa Rodríguez (b. 1955) often seem to flout the text, preferring to create in scenic metaphors. Castillo was particularly prone to visual richness and strong lighting effects. Tavira brings a mystical or ritualistic quality to his staging. Rodríguez, who is also an actress and set and lighting designer, may be the most innovative of her generation of directors. With her own company, Divas A.C., she audaciously mingled sex and religion in *Donna Giovanna* (1985), a controversial adaptation, featuring a woman in the title role, of Mozart's opera. Her work continues to provoke as she displays a fascination for pre-Columbian aesthetics (including nudity) and satirizes three favorite targets—religion, government, and the mass media (especially television)—in productions like *The Council of Love* (*El Concilio de amor*, 1988) and *Coatlicue's Mammary Tour* (*La gira mamal de la Coatlicue*, 1990). In 1991 Rodríguez and actress Liliana Felipe restored the Teatro de la Capilla, an independent theater in Coyoacán (a suburb of Mexico City) and there opened an eighty-seat cabaret, El Habito. Other leading directors since the 1950s include Héctor Azar (b. 1930), Marta Luna (b. 1944), Lola Bravo (b. 1918), Ludwik Margules (b. 1933), and Miguel Sabido (b. 1938).

The 1970s saw the emergence of so many promising playwrights at Universidad Nacional Autónoma de México (UNAM) that professor Guillermo Serret dubbed them collectively Los Nuevos Dramaturgos or La Nueva Dramaturgia Mexicana (the new dramatists or new Mexican dramaturgy). In a series of modest productions and lectures, Serret introduced thirty-seven new dramatists. Others whose work premiered during that decade have been placed under the same banner, which signals a generation rather than any cohesive artistic credo. Among the most important of the new dramatists are Sabina Berman (b. 1953), Jesús González Dávila (b. 1941), Alejandro Licona (b. 1953), Oscar Liera (b. 1946), Willebaldo López (b. 1944), Victor Hugo Rascón Banda (b. 1950), Guillermo Schmidhuber de la Mora (b. 1943), Juan Tovar (b. 1941), Tomás Urtusástegui (b. 1933), and Oscar Villegas (b. 1943). Berman, Liera, Tovar, and Villegas do share one trait: their plays provide latitude for the director and scenic designer to function, in effect, as co-authors. Indeed, that characteristic has been credited with the emergence of some successful directors of the 1980s and 1990s, like Jesusa Rodríguez.

Education-related initiatives played a part in the revitalization of Mexican theater. The School of Theatre (Escuela de Teatro) of the Faculty of Philosophy and Letters at the UNAM had been founded by Fernando Wagner (1905–71), a German immigrant teaching there from 1934 as well as directing professionally. UNAM's Taller de Investigación Teatral was founded in 1970. At the Instituto Nacional de Bellas Artes (INBA), Salvador Novo founded the School of Theatre Art (Escuela de Arte Teatral) in 1947. In 1963 INBA created Mascarones as a touring wing to take theater to the provinces. Within a generation, most of the outstanding actors of the Mexican stage had been trained either at UNAM or INBA. By the 1990s, strong theater programs existed at other universities, including those of Veracruz, Nueva León, Guanajuato, Guadalajara, in addition to a number of fine private theater schools.

The Teatro Estudiantil Autónomo (Independent Student Theatre), which—despite its name—had no educational affiliation, took inspiration from Federico García Lorca's La Barraca, which had toured Golden Age classics to rural Spain. Xavier Rojas rallied some students and other young people to create TEA around 1950. That group presented a mixture of foreign and Mexican plays in provincial villages. Also fostering the development of new talent through old plays was the UNAM-sponsored Teatro en Coapa. Héctor Azar (b. 1930), a literature professor, initiated the project, which combined outdoor performance with the revival of classic works of the sixteenth and seventeenth centuries. Azar went on to form the Centro Universitario de Teatro in 1962. In 1964 his Teatro Universitario traveled to Nancy, France, to compete with twenty-nine other student companies in the Festival of University Theatres and won first prize. The group repeated its triumph in 1965 with Azar's own play *Olímpica*.

The student protest movement that began in Paris in May 1968 spread to Mexico City that summer and, like its European prototype, gave rise to street performances and various popular art forms adapted to political ends. The worst of the clashes between student demonstrators and police occurred on October 2, on the Tlatelolco plaza, a site of Aztec sacrifices. There the students were fired upon, leaving over three hundred dead, five hundred wounded, and two thousand arrested. A number of theater groups grew out of the manifestations and many of them later came together under the umbrella group known as CLETA (Centro Libre de Experimentación Teatral y Artística), founded in 1973 by UNAM theater students who occupied the university-owned Foro Isabelino, a theater in downtown Mexico City, and the Foro Abierto de la Casa del Lago, an outdoor theater in Chapultepec Park. CLETA evolved into a cultural organization promoting class consciousness through popular theater for workers as well as students. Within a decade or so, CLETA counted affiliate groups in fifteen different provincial cities. In the capital, CLETA gave performances in schools, factories, streets, metro stations, and markets as well as in the UNAM spaces. Some theater groups founded under CLETA's aegis later separated from it to function independently while others simply started up as independent initiatives, benefitting from the favorable climate that CLETA had created for such ventures. Enrique Cisneros (b. 1948), a founder of CLETA, headed the circus-oriented Equipo de los Chidos, but alienated many by his insistence on the primacy of revolutionary politics over artistry. His brother Luís Cisneros (b. 1950) founded the Teatro Taller Tecolete (TTT) and settled into the Foro Isabelino; he—like other spin-offs of CLETA—preferred to uphold artistic standards. The Grupo Zopilote and the Grupo Zumbón both specialized in collective creation, the latter drawing upon the *Popol Vuh* for its production of *Why the Toad Cannot Run* (*Por qué el sapo no puede correr*). The Grupo Cultural Zero, based in Cuernavaca, mingled various popular performance styles in its touring productions. Given the climate of unrest in Chiapas and Enrique Cisneros's declared sympathy for the zapatistas, CLETA's continuing residence at the Foro Abierto (located only a stone's throw from the presidential palace) became problematic; the government closed the outdoor theater in January 1996.

Other popular theater initiatives since the 1940s have been government-subsidized, usually through INBA. Some, like the UNESCO-sponsored Centro Regional para la Educación Fondamental de América Latina (CREFAL, 1950–64), have been educational in nature and aimed specifially at rural areas, not unlike the Misiones Culturales of the 1920s. Beginning in 1978, INBA organized an annual festival of provincial theater (Muestra Nacional de Teatro de Provincia), held each year in a different city. From 1972 to 1976, el Teatro CONASUPO (Companía Nacional de Subsistencias Populares) de Orientación Campesino pursued similar goals. Directed by Rodolfo Valencia, CONASUPO employed professional actors who had trained either at UNAM or at INBA's Escuela de Arte Teatral. With the sudden devaluation of the peso in 1976, CONASUPO and a number of other cultural projects were terminated. However, those who had been taking theater to the villages and seeing the results rallied to present a plan to the Secretaria de Educación Pública. This resulted in the formation of el Taller de Arte Escénico Popular (AEP, 1977–82) and thus little break in the continuity of professionally presented theater for rural audiences. This project even managed to offer some work in local indigenous languages. In the state of Tabasco, the Laboratorio de Teatro Campesino e Indígena (LTCI), founded in 1983, distinguished itself by its lack of didactic purpose. Its purely aesthetic goals included the training of theater performers, designers, and technicians who would in turn teach the craft to others of their ethnic community, providing a forum for sharing a cultural heritage, and achieving visibility at national and international festivals. Under the artistic leadership and anthropological sensitivity of María Alicia Martínez Medrano (b. 1937), LTCI achieved its goals within five years. Perhaps the most important heir to CONASUPO is the Asociacion Nacional "Teatro-Comunidad, A.C." (TECOM), founded in 1987 and still active in providing a forum for Mexico's many ethnicities to express through theater their particular sense of community. Under the leadership of a national coordinator (Domingo Adame was the first; Susana Jones holds the post in the late 1990s), TECOM has sponsored an annual festival of community theater that brings together as many as 150 performance groups.

In 1990 indigenous peoples comprised about 8 percent of Mexico's population; that is, more than six million people belong to fifty-six surviving ethnic groups, some on the verge of extinction. Donald Frischmann points out that many of these groups have become conscious of themselves as belonging to a culture other than the dominant one and that their growing sense of need to perpetuate their own culture has resulted in a blossoming of performance actitivities. Two native theater companies in particular have won recognition well beyond their own regions and have even begun to spawn other such groups. The Sac Nicté (White Flower), a Yucatán Maya theater group founded in 1978 by Carlos Armando Dzul Ek, is dedicated to preserving through performance the Maya conception of the supernatural however overlaid with Christianity, as well as recovering and reviewing events of indigenous import from the historical past. A staple of their repertoire is *Little Armadillo* (*Chan Wech*), a song–story–guessing game that makes fun of the Spanish. *The Inquisition; or, The Collision of Two Cultures* (*El auto de fe, o choque de dos culturas*, 1988–91) reinterprets the horrifying torture of the natives conducted by Fray Diego de Landa at Maní, Yucatán, in 1562. Because Sac Nicté's audiences are largely bilingual, such plays are performed with Maya characters speaking Yucatec Mayan and Spanish characters speaking Spanish. Dzul Ek, who also directs the Dorothy Arango Bilingual School in Maní, works improvisationally with the Sac Nicté performers; they have created over fifteen productions since 1978. In the neighboring state of Chiapas, in San Cristóbal de las Casas, the Sna Jtz'ibajom (the Writers' House) project is a collaborative effort of two ethnic Maya groups, the Tzotziles and the Tzeltales. Their plays and puppet shows have presented native legends and folklore on tours to remote highland villages, where they usually perform in Tzotzil Mayan. Although much of Sna Jtz'ibajom's work draws upon oral tradition, a 1992 production, *Dynasty of Jaguars* (*Dinastía de jaguares*), synthesizes several sources in a historically based cautionary tale about the need for cooperation among various indigenous groups before they can achieve an acceptable peace with the colonizers.

## THE CARIBBEAN

With Fidel Castro's ascension to power in Cuba in 1959 came a socialist government with Soviet-style subsidy and control of the arts. A National Council for Culture (Consejo Nacional de Cultura) was created in 1961 to oversee the burgeoning theatrical scene: the refurbishment of old theaters, new employment opportunities for professional actors and directors, many new Cuban plays entering the repertoire, productions or tours reaching all parts of the island, a lively amateur theater scene, and the hosting of a number of festivals of Latin American theater in Havana. The National School of Art (Escuela Nacional de Arte) opened in 1962. In 1963 Havana counted fourteen theaters in operation, eight of them government-subsidized, five independent, and one at the university.

Prominent among provincial theater companies, Teatro Escambray was founded in 1968 under the leadership of Sergio Corrieri (b. 1938). This community-oriented collective—with the overt political aim of promoting the goals of the revolution—settled in the undeveloped Escambray region and developed productions related to local concerns, with discussions following every performance. *The Showcase* (*La vitrina*, 1970) by Albio Paz (b. 1937) focused on the Castro government's plan to introduce collective-dairy farming in the area; it remained in the company's repertoire (occasionally revised according to immediate circumstances) until 1978. Corrieri's mother Gilda Hernández (1913–89) figured prominently in the company, both as actress and as author of another frequently-presented play, *The Trial* (*El juicio*, 1973). The productions always incorporated music, but the work of the 1980s and after tended to focus more strongly on musical and visual elements. The example of Teatro Escambray led to a number of similar ventures, including Teatro Político Bertolt Brecht (1973), Teatro de Participación Popular (1973), Cabildo Teatral de Santiago (1973), and Cubano de Acero (1977).

Among the leading Cuban dramatists, Virgilio Piñera (1912–79) was well established before the revolution, beginning with *Electra Garrigó* (1948), which used classical mythology to comment on Cuban violence. Piñera's *Cold Air* (*Aire frío*, 1959) realistically portrays the life of the pre-revolutionary Cuban middle class. José Triana (b. 1931) also drew upon classical Greek myth for *Medea in the Mirror* (*Medea en el espejo*, 1960). He won international acclaim for his harrowing but highly theatrical *Night of the Assassins* (*La noche de los asesinos*, 1965). Mythology similarly informs the work of Eugenio Hernández Espinosa (b. 1936), but in his case the origin is Nigeria. The Yoruba legends of his Afro-Cuban heritage resonate in plays like *María Antonia* (1964), *La Simona* (1977), and *Odebí the Hunter* (*Odebí el cazador*, 1980).

Cuba's leading stage director Vicente Revuelta (b. 1929) began as an actor in the 1940s, worked with several great directors in Paris, returned to Cuba in 1954, and founded the Teatro Estudio in 1958. The company won international renown for its productions of Brecht as well as contemporary Latin American plays. Revuelta won the 1982 best director award for his staging of Shakespeare's *Twelfth Night*. Other important Cuban directors include Berta Martínez (b. 1931), Roberto Blanco (b. 1936), and Armando Suárez del Villar (b. 1936).

A major impetus to the development of Puerto Rican theater has been— beginning in 1958, under the sponsorship of the Puerto Rican Cultural Institute—the annual festival of plays by commonwealth dramatists. Francisco

Arriví (b. 1915), a longtime director of the institute's theater section, had founded an influential theater company, Tinglado Puertorriqueño, in 1945. Among
his own best-known plays, which often explore racial prejudice, is the trilogy
*Máscara puertorriqueño*, which includes *Masquerade* (*Vejigantes*, 1958). Puerto
Rico has produced a number of other outstanding dramatists and directors,
notably René Marqués (1919–79), who first earned international recognition
with the naturalistic *The Oxcart* (*La carreta*, 1953). *The Fanlights* (*Los soles
truncos*, 1958) and *A Blue Boy for That Shadow* (*Un niño para esa sombra*,
1960) have also been widely produced. The range of his fifteen or so plays
includes poetic realism, existentialism, plays of social concern, and biblical dramas. Puerto Rican directors of particular distinction are Gilda Navarra (b.
1921), who creates mime dramas with her Taller de Histriones; Myrna Casas
(b. 1934), who is also a playwright; and Victoria Espinosa (b. 1922).

## CANADA

The search for Canadian cultural identity intensified in the decades after
World War II. Canada's crucial contribution to the Allied war effort unleashed
new energy and national self-awareness in the arts as in other aspects of life.
The groundwork for a professional theater independent of British, French,
and American influence had been laid by the prewar advancements in radio
drama and little theater. Postwar prosperity made possible the widespread
proliferation of professional theater companies in the 1950s and 1960s, followed by the opening of new facilities to house them. While those theaters that
depended upon mainstream audiences to fill their seats had little incentive to
produce new works by Canadian authors, a number of smaller, "alternative"
theaters rose to the challenge and began to produce native dramatists; the late
1960s brought several landmark productions. The 1970s saw a remarkable
blossoming of alternative theaters, collective creation, documentary drama,
regional drama, and plays of Canadian history. Many of the playwrights who
came to prominence in that decade have achieved international recognition as
well as canonical status in Canada. Thus their work began to be staged in the
"establishment" theaters, and this led to some blurring of boundaries in the
1980s between producers of classic and commercial plays and those who
experimented with other forms. Although the 1990s brought cuts in funding
to the arts, Canadian theater and drama had achieved a firm foundation that
seems to assure their continuing ascendancy on the world scene.

In the 1940s, the vast majority of Canadian citizens had no hope of ever
attending a live concert or theater, while those few who had seen professional
theater knew only dreary second-rate touring companies from Europe and
the United States. Art treasures shared space with dinosaur bones in the inadequate National Museum; symphonies played in sports arenas; professionally performed plays on Canadian subjects existed only on the radio. To
returning servicemen who had been exposed to the wealth of European culture and to the wave of educated postwar European immigrants, the arts in
Canada needed a jolt. Lobbying for government support of the arts began

even as the war was drawing to a close. A so-called March on Ottawa on June 21, 1944, brought artists representing sixteen cultural organizations to testify before the House of Commons Special Committee on Reconstruction and Reestablishment. Despite the persuasiveness of the case for the arts, it was not until 1949 that the government appointed a Royal Commission on National Development in the Arts, Letters, and Sciences, headed by Vincent Massey, to investigate—according to its mandate—how to encourage endeavors "which express national feeling, promote common understanding and add to the variety and richness of Canadian life." In 1951, the Massey Commission submitted its report, and most of its recommendations were implemented by the end of the decade. Most significantly, the report called for the creation of an independent body to oversee the distribution of state aid to the arts. The resulting Canada Council, endowed in 1957, had an epoch-making effect on the arts. Materially, its funding provided opportunities for numerous individual artists, which in turn promoted the rise of Canadian professional theater. It also stimulated increasing numbers of nonprofit institutions. Less tangibly, but ultimately of equal importance, the Canada Council gave the arts respectability in the eyes of the public, raised artistic standards, and engendered a spirit of cultural nationalism.

Even before the availability of government subsidy, some new professional theater companies appeared, precursors to the regional theaters of the 1960s. The earliest, Vancouver's Everyman Theatre Company was founded in 1946 by Sydney Risk (1908–85) to carry on the kind of innovative production in repertory that he had admired in England. Risk began with a company of fourteen, but did not find a permanent performance space until 1950. Meanwhile, his work earned recognition through touring in the prairie provinces. Although his repertoire was largely European, Risk did stage a play by Alberta's Elsie Park Gowan. After Joy Coghill joined the company as codirector in 1951, Everyman won a following for children's plays as well. A 1953 production of *Tobacco Road* opened to a favorable reception, but the text's explicitness led to police intervention—the arrest of the five actors on stage in mid-performance—during the second week. Facing litigation that the financially precarious company could not afford, Risk closed Everyman. Vancouver's second professional theater company, Totem Theatre, founded by Thor Arngrim and Stuart Baker, opened in 1951 in a rented hall. After two ambitious seasons, the company moved to a playhouse in Victoria, where it survived until 1954. The amateur Theatre under the Stars, which presented musicals in Vancouver's Stanley Park from 1940, must be signaled for one original work amid the usual Broadway fare: *Timber!!* (1952) may well be the earliest all-Canadian musical.

While Everyman Theatre was gearing up in Vancouver, Dora Mavor Moore (1888–1979) in Toronto was preparing to transform her amateur Village Players into a professional company. Aiming "to establish a living theatre in Canada on a professional but non-profit basis," she pooled her savings and war bonds to incorporate the New Play Society. The company made its debut on October 11, 1946 with J. M. Synge's *The Playboy of the Western*

*World*, performing in the 450-seat Royal Ontario Museum, a nonunion basement facility that she rented for one hundred dollars per night. The first six NPS productions—each performed twice (Friday and Saturday)—opened at two-week intervals, culminating in a Christmas program of medieval nativity plays presented with the St. Mary Magdalen Church choir. The second series of six plays, in the spring of 1947, included a Canadian drama, *The Man in the Blue Moon* by Lister Sinclair (b. 1921), as well as a guest appearance by Montreal's Les Compagnons de Saint Laurent, performing Molière in French. Shakespeare's *Macbeth* emerged as the favorite of the fall 1947 series; the demand for tickets led NPS to tour it to Ontario schools. Despite critical praise for the artistic excellence of NPS productions, its audience comprised largely intellectuals and European-immigrants—until the 1948 breakthrough to a popular audience with *Spring Thaw*, a topical musical revue which the company hastily created to substitute for an unfinished adaptation. Taking their cue from Gratien Gélinas's humorous look at Quebec life in his annual *Fridolinons* (discussed in chapter 6), the New Play Society used jokes, skits, and songs to satirize anglophone Canada. An annual event from 1948 to 1971 and from 1980 to 1986, *Spring Thaw* launched the careers of many Canadian comedians and singers.

In January 1949 the New Play Society presented its second Canadian play: *To Tell the Truth* by Morley Callaghan. At the invitation of theater manager Ernest Rawley, the production transferred to Toronto's Royal Alexandra Theatre for a week-long run in February. Thus *To Tell the Truth* became the first play written and produced by Canadians to appear at the venerable 1907 Toronto landmark "Royal Alex." The NPS peaked in 1949–50 with a season that included five new Canadian plays, among them the acclaimed *Riel* by John Coulter (1888–1980). The Irish-born Coulter had seen his plays produced in Belfast, Dublin, and London, but it was his Canadian-history epic about the nineteenth-century Métis leader Louis Riel for which he is remembered. Giving the controversial Riel heroic stature, Coulter explored issues that continued to resonate in Canadian thought. Anton Wagner signals Coulter as "the first major 20th century English–Canadian playwright with a strongly articulated political consciousness." In 1966 the Canada Council commissioned Coulter to write a small-cast version of the play suitable for amateur production; this was *The Crime of Louis Riel*. In 1967 Coulter wrote a third version, the documentary drama *The Trial of Louis Riel* for Canada's centennial.

The New Play Society presented its fiftieth production in 1952. When the Museum Theatre became a union house in 1950, the New Play Society ended its subscription-series format, but continued mounting occasional productions there until 1954, after which the repertoire took a commercial turn. A contributing factor in the change of emphasis may have been the siphoning away to the Stratford Festival (which opened in 1953) talent that had been developed at NPS. Ironically, Dora Mavor Moore's generous assistance had been instrumental in the creation of the festival, and her son Mavor Moore (b. 1919), a prodigiously accomplished actor and director as well as author of over one hundred produced plays, served on the Stratford Festival's board of governors from 1953 to 1974. During the 1950s, too, the New Play Society's professional training school became Dora Mavor Moore's major focus. She dissolved the company in 1971 (she was eighty-three), having worked closely with many of Canada's leading actors and writers of stage and radio: her son Mavor Moore, Jane Mallett (1899–1984), Donald Harron (b. 1924), William Needles (b. 1919), Robert Christie (b. 1913), Peter Mews, Lloyd Bochner, Tommy Tweed (1908–71), Donald Davis (b. 1928), John Drainie, Andrew Allan (1907–74), and Toby Robins (1931–86). Dora Mavor Moore's contributions were recognized with many honors during her lifetime, and since 1981 Toronto's annual theater awards have borne her name.

The Stratford Festival began in the mind of Tom Patterson, a journalist from Stratford, Ontario, concerned about the hardships that the 1930s Depression had wreaked upon the small town's limited economy. Serving in Europe during the war, Patterson took further inspiration from the theater he saw there. By 1951 he was ready to act upon his idea of capitalizing on the town's name and its association with Shakespeare to create an open-air festival of Shakespeare plays. Patterson turned to Dora Mavor Moore for advice on how to proceed, and she put him in touch with the great British director Tyrone Guthrie. Guthrie accepted the invitation to direct the project in part because he had his own dream: he wanted to direct Shakespeare in a format that would approximate the Elizabethan thrust stage. He got Tanya Moiseiwitsch to design an innovative open platform stage for an enclosed space. Because of budgetary and time constraints, the original enclosure (used for four seasons) was a huge tent. Two years of planning and fundraising led to the Stratford Festival's inaugural performance on July 3, 1953: *Richard III* with Alec Guinness in the title role. *All's Well That Ends Well* opened the following evening, starring Guiness and Irene Worth. Both productions, directed by Guthrie and designed by Moisewitsch, ran in rotating repertory, with a one-week extended run, until late August. That first season's attendance reached sixty-eight thousand.

*Exterior of the Stratford Festival's Festival Theatre, c. 1997, after renovations and additions to the theater. Photo: Terry Manzo. Courtesy Stratford Festival.*

*Interior of the Stratford Festival's Festival Theatre with open stage designed by Tanya Moiseiwitsch. Photo: Terry Manzo. Courtesy Stratford Festival.*

Michael Langham succeeded Guthrie as artistic director in 1956, having directed *Julius Caesar* for the festival the preceding summer. The young English director demonstrated his sensitivity to Canadian concerns by staging *Henry V* with francophone actors playing the French characters (including Gratien Gélinas as King Charles). Christopher Plummer, a bilingual actor from Montreal, played the title role to great acclaim and often performed at the Stratford Festival for more than a decade thereafter. The festival tent was replaced by the permanent Festival Theatre, constructed in 1956–57 and inaugurated with *Hamlet* (played by Plummer) on July 1, 1957. The new facility achieved an impression of intimacy with its seating for 2,262 spectators arranged in a 220-degree arc around the thrust stage. The success of its design exerted a strong influence over international theater architecture, notably the Guthrie Theatre (1963) of Minneapolis. Within its first two seasons, the Stratford Festival was employing auxiliary facilities for small-scale productions and concerts. These spaces were eventually acquired by the festival, remodeled, and remain in use today as the Avon Theatre (proscenium stage; capacity 1,107) and the Tom Patterson Theatre (flexible/thrust stage; capacity 494).

Michael Langham proved to be a superb leader for the Stratford Festival, his tenure lasting until 1967. The climate for the arts had changed considerably in Canada when Jean Gascon was appointed artistic director with John Hirsch as his associate. Hirsch resigned in 1969, but returned in 1981 for a five-year stint as artistic director, during which he plunged the festival deeply into debt. However, the festival faced its greatest controversy with the appointment of Robin Phillips as Gascon's successor in 1974. Many vigorously protested the selection of yet another Englishman to run the Canadian festival (Phillips's years at the helm, 1974–81, were scrutinized in the Spring 1981 issue of *Canadian Theatre Review*), yet he did strengthen the festival in many ways, particularly in the quality of production. Subsequent artistic directors were John Neville, 1986–89; David William, 1989–94; and since 1994, Richard Monette. The example of the Stratford Festival figured prominently in the creation of other summer theater festivals: the Shaw Festival (1962) in Niagara-on-the-Lake, Ontario; The Charlottetown Festival (1965) in Charlottetown, Prince Edward Island; and the Blyth Festival of new Canadian plays (1975) in Blyth, Ontario. In terms of its artistic prestige and continuing power to attract theatergoers from around the world to a small town in Ontario, the Stratford Festival must be counted one of the foremost classical repertory theaters in the world. As such, however, it has often become a lightning rod for controversy, a standard against which other Canadian theaters have either measured themselves or rebelled.

Besides the Stratford Festival several other anglophone companies begun in the 1950s contributed to the growing professionalism of Canada's theater. In Ottawa the Canadian Repertory Theatre arose from an earlier amateur society. Its first production, Esther McCracken's *Quiet Weekend*, opened in October 1949 with a cast that included nineteen-year-old Christopher Plummer. Surviving its 1949–50 season of thirty-five plays in thirty-five weeks in a school auditorium, the Canadian Repertory Theatre reorganized in 1950

*A scene from the Stratford Festival's production of* World of Wonders *adapted from Robertson Davies's novel by Elliott Hayes. Directed by Richard Rose; settings by Stephen Osler; costumes by Molly Harris Campbell. From left: Michelle Risk as Zingara, the Fortune Teller; William Vickers as Charlie, the Barker; Diego Matamoros as Andro, the Hermaphrodite/Gus; Patrick Finnigan as Paul Dempster; Brian McKay as Frank Molza, the Fire Eater. Courtesy Stratford Festival.*

under the leadership of Amelia Hall (1916–84). During her four years with the company, Hall directed about forty productions and acted in close to one hundred fifty. (As Lady Anne at Stratford in 1953, this outstanding actress was the first woman to speak from the festival stage.) The demise of the Canadian Repertory Theatre in 1956 deprived Ottawa of professional theater until 1967. Newfoundland's first resident professional company, The London Theatre Company, created in 1951 in St John's, produced about one hundred plays from a British-oriented repertoire during its six-year existence.

Somewhat more assiduous at including Canadian plays amidst the standard fare were two Toronto ventures: the Jupiter Theatre (1951–54) and the Crest Theatre (1953–66). The latter was founded by brothers Murray Davis (b. 1924) and Donald Davis (b. 1928), who had gained professional experience through their own successful summer stock company, the Straw Hat Players, from 1948 to 1955. Donald Davis had been acting since childhood and had performed regularly at Hart House Theatre under Robert Gill, whom he regarded as his mentor. Indeed, as Jill Tomasson Goodwin notes, Davis spent his early life in "preparations for a profession that did not exist within Canada." Thus, the founding of the Crest Theatre—with the help of the Davis brothers' sister, actress Barbara Chilcott (b. 1923)—contributed significantly to creating professional theater opportunities for directors and actors as well as dramatists. It operated in a converted cinema (capacity 822), the rental of which necessitated a grueling year-round schedule with the brothers sharing the administrative duties that left them fewer opportunities to perform than they would have liked. Although it became a nonprofit organization in 1957 and received funding from the Canada Council, the Crest faced continuing financial difficulties that led to its closure in 1966. During its thirteen seasons and approximately 140 productions, the Crest premiered many Canadian works, including Bernard Slade's (b. 1930) first comedy *Simon Says Get Married* (1961). A particularly fruitful association for both the Straw Hat Players and the Crest was with playwright–novelist Robertson Davies (1913–95). Among his plays staged by those theaters were *Fortune My Foe* in 1950, *At My Heart's Core* in 1951, *Overlaid* in 1952, *A Jig for the Gypsy* in 1954, and *Hunting Stuart* in 1955. Davies's work for the stage includes five one-act and nine full-length plays, often treating Canadian philistinism (or cultural deprivation) and spiritual values. If his plays have endured less well than his novels, it is probably due to their quasi-Shavian literary quality.

The 1958 founding of Manitoba Theatre Centre (MTC) marks the beginning of Canada's regional professional nonprofit theater movement. The MTC was created through a merger of the amateur Winnipeg Little Theatre (1921–37, 1948–58) and the semiprofessional Theatre 77. The latter, located in a studio space exactly 77 steps from Winnipeg's main downtown intersection, was a fairly new company begun by Tom Hendry (b. 1929) and John Hirsch (1930–89). Hendry, an accountant turned producer–playwright–dramaturg, and Hirsch, who had been running the Muddiwater Puppet Company, shared a vision of "a decentralized national theatre network in Canada." They understood the need to educate audiences by interspersing light fare with the classics and by reaching out to young audiences with touring school programs. Although Hendry and Hirsch moved on to other projects in the 1960s, their creation remained the prototype of regional cultural anchor that the Canada Council encouraged. For twelve years the MTC operated out of Winnipeg's eight-hundred-seat Dominion Theatre. Finally, in 1970, MTC moved into a complex—incorporating both a proscenium theater and a flexible theater—specifically constructed according to the needs of a resident company serving a regional constituency.

Theatre New Brunswick, another important regional theater, had a reverse genesis; that is, first, the construction of the playhouse, and then the creation of a company to use it. The edifice was the one-thousand-seat Playhouse that opened in Fredericton in September 1964. Given to the people of New Brunswick by Lord and Lady Beaverbrook through their Foundations, The Playhouse was at that time the province's only theater adequately equipped to serve professional touring companies. For four seasons it functioned largely as a rental house for road companies, supplemented by a local amateur group's offerings. A turning point came in 1968 with the appointment of Walter Learning (b. 1938) as artistic director of the Playhouse. He earned the confidence of the Board by producing a summer season that paid for itself at the box office. Then he founded Theatre New Brunswick (TNB), making it truly regional in that the mainstage productions toured to other New Brunswick towns on a 650-mile circuit. Learning himself traveled about the province and recognized "an obligation to the school curriculum." Soon the popular repertoire was supplemented by the classics. He added a Canadian component with the quite successful plays he wrote in collaboration with poet Alden Nowlan (1933–83). A 1972 remodeling of the Playhouse moved the stage forward and reduced the capacity to 763. In 1974 Learning founded the TNB Young Company. He left TNB in 1978 to head the Canada Council's Theatre Section, where he exercised considerable influence with his encouragement of "three C" programming: a mix of contemporary, classic, and Canadian. Learning went on to serve as artistic director of Vancouver Playhouse from 1982 to 1986 and of the Charlottetown Festival, from 1987. TNB has continued in the forefront of Canadian regional theaters under subsequent artistic directors: Malcolm Black, 1978–84, Janet Amos, 1984–88, and Sharon Pollock. By 1984, thirteen theaters fit the Canada Council's profile for regional theaters: Alberta's Citadel Theatre (Edmonton) and Theatre Calgary; British Columbia's Bastion Theatre (Victoria) and Vancouver Playhouse; Manitoba's MTC; New Brunswick's TNB; Nova Scotia's Neptune Theatre (Halifax); Ontario's Grand Theatre (London) and CentreStage (Toronto); Quebec's Centaur Theatre and Théâtre du Nouveau Monde (Montreal) and Théâtre du Trident (Quebec City); Saskatchewan's Globe Theatre (Regina).

With increasing numbers of regional and other new theater companies and the opportunities they brought for actors, directors, and dramatists, there was an acute need for theater facilities all across the nation. Most of the surviving nineteenth-century playhouses had been converted to cinemas. The first wave of postwar construction followed the somewhat misguided notion that the same stagehouses and auditoriums could be used for everything from grand opera to psychological drama. Among the multipurpose facilities of the 1950s were Alberta's twin Jubilee Auditoriums in Calgary and Edmonton (1957), the Queen Elizabeth Theatre in Vancouver (1959), and the O'Keefe Centre in Toronto (1960). The 1960s and 1970s brought a boom in both renovation of existing buildings and new construction to create playhouses particularly suited to legitimate drama. A few examples are indicative of the trend: The Vancouver Playhouse complex (1962) was built to encompass the existing Queen Elizabeth Theatre. A former church was converted into the Vancouver East Cultural Centre (1973). The Arts Club, a Vancouver theater group founded in 1958, supplemented its 125-seat hall by converting warehouses into larger performance spaces in 1979 and 1983. In Victoria, the McPherson Playhouse (1965) opened in a remodeled vaudeville theater to house the Bastion Theatre Company. Edmonton's Citadel Theatre began its existence in a renovated Salvation Army hall (1965), and in 1976 moved into its new three-theater complex. Regina's former City Hall (1909) was remodeled in 1981 to provide a home for the Globe Theatre, which Ken and Sue Kramer had founded in 1966. Theatre Calgary, founded in 1968, opened its 750-seat Max Bell Theatre in the Calgary Centre for Performing Arts in 1985. Toronto's Young People's Theatre, founded in 1966, acquired permanent quarters in 1977 by renovating a historic 1881 building (the stable for Toronto Street Railway Company) that had stood empty since 1909. Montreal's Place des Arts opened in 1963, and the Saidye Bronfman Centre in 1967. On Prince Edward Island, the huge Confederation Centre of the Arts was opened by Queen Elizabeth II in 1964. Canada's centennial in 1967 spurred planning for complexes like Toronto's St Lawrence Centre for the Performing Arts (1970). In Ottawa the forty-six-million-dollar National Arts Centre, completed in 1969, incorporates four performance spaces. The preservation and refurbishing of historic theaters, often backed by commercial interests, has added to the cultural wealth. For example, Ed Mirvish purchased Toronto's Royal Alexandra in 1963 for very successful use as a roadhouse for major touring shows. Also in Toronto, the magnificent Thomas W. Lamb-designed Elgin and Winter Garden Theatres, opened one above the other in 1913–14 as vaudeville houses, had been used as cinemas and then allowed to stand dormant; the 1980s restoration of these theaters put them back into service as venues for long-running spectacles.

For francophone Canada, the 1950s brought a proliferation of theater companies, both amateur and professional, surpassing anglophone Canada. Rapid urbanization in the immediate postwar period, especially in Quebec, undoubtedly contributed to the demand for more entertainment options. Facing that reality, the Catholic church adopted a new stance toward the theater, as evidenced by a pastoral letter (February 14, 1950) on "The Issue of Labor and the Social Doctrine of the Church." The document acknowledged the validity of entertainment as a healthy respite as long as it would promote the "development of intellectual faculties and moral virtues." A test case came in 1948 when the semiprofessional Compagnons de Saint-Laurent

(1937–52, discussed in chapter 6), headed by Father Emile Legault, announced André Obey's poetic drama *Le Viol de Lucrèce* (The rape of Lucrece), which they presented under the title *Lucrèce*. In this instance it was not the Church that raised objections to a production, but a Montreal journalist, René-O. Boivin. Countering Boivin's virulent attacks on "sensation-seeking," journalist Louis Morrisset came out in defense of Les Compagnons as a leading exemplar of French–Canadian theater art. The ensuing polemic escalated to the point that at least one report suggested that the Church was up to its old habits of censorship. The truth was that Monseigneur Alexandre Vachon, archbishop of Ottawa, did decide against bringing the production to Ottawa on tour, but specified that this decision in no way constituted a condemnation of the production of *Lucrèce* as immoral. He further insisted upon the high esteem in which he held the troupe, its leader, and its exceptional cultural accomplishments. In Montreal, the eight performances (March 6, 9, 11–13, 18–20, 1948, all but the first at the Jesuit-run Gesù Hall), proceeded without incident, and Father Legault used the occasion to reiterate the troupe's mission: "to create in a climate of Christianity a theater of beauty."

In artistic quality and numbers of francophone theater companies, Montreal continued to hold the lead among cities with large French-speaking populations. One of the city's earliest postwar companies, Le Théâtre du Rideau Vert was founded in 1948 by actress Yvette Brind'amour (1918–92). She struggled to keep it afloat with challenging plays from Broadway and Paris until 1952, when financial difficulties necessitated a hiatus. Le Théâtre du Rideau Vert resumed operations in 1955, having found a light comedy style that worked for the company and attracted a following. A few French–Canadian dramatists saw their work produced there in the 1950s, notably Félix Leclerc (1914–88), who had acted with Les Compagnons de Saint-Laurent and became an internationally-known singer-guitarist. Among his light comedies of Quebec life, the theater staged *Sonnez les matines* (Ring the morning bells, 1954) and *Le P'tit Bonheur* (A touch of luck, 1956). But it was in the 1960s, after the troupe's move to the former Théâtre Stella, that it achieved a remarkable streak of important productions by French–Canadian dramatists.

Françoise Loranger (b. 1913) was well established as a writer and director for radio and television when Le Théâtre du Rideau Vert premiered her first play for the stage, *Une Maison . . . un jour* (A house . . . one day) in 1965. It typified Loranger's early work, which focused on the disintegration of the bourgeois family, as threats to that long stable milieu raised questions of identity and conscience. This production toured not only to Quebec City, but also to Moscow, Leningrad, and Paris. The Rideau Vert then produced *Encore cinq minutes* (Five minutes more, 1967), which—with its strong matriarchal role—remains Loranger's most successful play. In her later plays, premiered at various other theaters, Loranger moved from the bourgeois milieu to works of heightened theatricality and nationalistic content; prominent in this latter group are *Double jeu* (Double game, 1969) and *Médium saignant* (Medium rare, 1970).

Les Belles-soeurs *by Michel Tremblay premiered at the Théâtre du Rideau Vert in Montreal from August 28 to October 13, 1968 under the direction of André Brassard. René Ouellette designed the set, and François Barbeau the costumes. Photograph by Guy Dubois, courtesy of Théâtre du Rideau Vert.*

Two of the most momentous premieres in the history of the Théâtre du Rideau Vert came in 1968: *L'Exécution* by Marie-Claire Blais and *Les Belles-soeurs* (The sisters-in-law) by Michel Tremblay. Yvette Brind'amour directed *L'Exécution* (The execution), a disturbing drama set in a Catholic boys' boarding school where a charismatic student instigates the murder of an innocent younger student. The complicity of the other boys brings a gross miscarriage of justice. Blais (b. 1939) wrote several other stage plays, but remains best known as a novelist. Even more important was Tremblay's *Les Belles-soeurs*, now a classic of both anglophone and francophone Canadian theater, though it encountered rejection by producing groups for three years after Tremblay completed it in 1965, and it engendered considerable controversy when the Rideau Vert premiered it in 1968. This and many subsequent plays by Michel Tremblay (b. 1942) reflect the working-class East Montreal milieu into which he was born. (Tremblay has claimed that he was twelve before he became aware of the existence of English-speaking people—at which time he also learned of the extreme difference between his marginalized world and their world of opportunity.) He wrote *Les Belles-soeurs*, his first produced play, under the encouragement of his friend André Brassard (b. 1946) after the two attended a French–Canadian movie and noted the falseness of the characters speaking European French. What most bothered the critics of *Les Belles-soeurs* was the unprecedented use of *joual*, a French–Canadian slang considered too crude for the stage. The play rankled French–Canadian audiences by its exposure of a poverty that was as much intellectual and emotional as it was material. Also disconcerting to many was the play's bold mingling of realism and theatricalism, misery and farce. Brassard directed the production, working closely with Tremblay and bringing to bear his own experience in the avant-garde theater. The fifteen characters in the play are all working-class French–Canadian women ranging in age from twenty to ninety-three, all hemmed in by social and religious restrictions symbolized by the unseen husbands and priests who dominate their lives. Neighbors and relatives have gathered to help the middle-aged Germaine lick the million trading stamps she has won, to fill the stamp booklets that she will redeem for consumer goods. The women's envy, greed, and pettiness culminate in a free-for-all with the booklets, followed by a rain of gold stamps to the strains of "O Canada!" The anthem seems to comment ironically on the unliklihood that either the nation or providence will effect any change in the squalid existence of those who live on rue Fabre.

The Rideau Vert's production of *Les Belles-soeurs* was undoubtedly a watershed event in French–Canadian theater, even as it helped to effect the transition to the more politicized notion of Québécois theater. Indeed, according to Jane Moss, Tremblay's work was the spark that ignited the theatrical revolution of the 1970s in Quebec, that transformed French–Canadian identity (with its colonialist overtones) into Québécois, an independent identity based in a distinctive reality; this was achieved through "the fusion of avant-garde dramaturgy with popular language and Québécois subject matter." Tremblay wrote other "rue Fabre" plays, including *En pièces détachées* (Like death warmed over, 1970), *A toi, pour toujours, ta Marie-Lou* (Forever yours, Mary Lou, 1973), and *Bonjour là, bonjour* (1974). Another cycle of plays by Tremblay centers on the Main, a tawdry Montreal nightlife district frequented by colorful characters like the eponymous *La Duchesse de Langeais* (1970) and the transvestite *Hosanna* (1973). Although in the 1980s he turned increasingly to writing novels, Tremblay maintained his characteristic raw vitality in later plays like the masterful *Albertine en cinq temps* (Albertine in five periods, 1984), *Le Vrai Monde?* (The real world, 1987), and *La Maison suspendue* (Timeless house, 1992), as well as in his musical theater (including the bilingual opera *Nelligan*, 1990, composed by André Gagnon, directed by Brassard) and screenplays.

Le Théâtre du Rideau Vert's 1973 production of *La Sagouine* initiated its long, fruitful association with New Brunswick playwright Antonine Maillet (b. 1923). What Michel Tremblay did for Québécois identity and culture with his use of *joual*, Maillet did for Acadia (the French-populated area of today's Maritime provinces) with its own archaic dialect. The title character of the one-woman drama *La Sagouine* is a seventy-two-year-old menial laborer who scrubs floors and recalls in sixteen separate monologues the travails she has known, including the harsh existence of the coastal fisherman's family and her

*Viola Léger played the title role in* La Sagouine *by Antonine Maillet. The play premiered at Montreal's Théâtre du Rideau Vert in the 1972-73 season. Photograph by Guy Dubois, courtesy of Théâtre du Rideau Vert.*

own recourse to prostitution to support her surviving children. Naive and yet intelligent, devout and yet cognizant of the Church's hypocrisy, La Sagouine is, in the words of Maillet, "a revolutionary without bitterness." The role has been closely identified with its creator, Viola Léger, who toured it for several years and performed it in Paris, and who has continued to play the strong central roles in Maillet's plays. The character of La Sagouine had appeared as a woman in her forties in Maillet's earlier play *Les Crasseux* (The scum, 1968). Among Antonine Maillet's later plays—all premiered at the Rideau Vert—are *Maria-agélas* (1974), *Evangéline Deusse* (a modern riposte to Henry Wadsworth Longfellow's romantic treatment of the Evangeline legend, 1976), *La Veuve enragée* (Enraged widow, 1977), *Emmanuel à Joseph à Dâvit* (1979), *Garrochés en Paradis* (Stoned in paradise, 1986), and many others.

In the decade or so following the opening of Le Théâtre du Rideau Vert, dozens of professional francophone companies came into being in Montreal. One of the longest running and most important for developing new acting and directing talent was the Théâtre du Nouveau Monde (TNM), founded in 1951. This professional company had its origin in an earlier venture, Le Théâtre d'Essai de Montréal, begun in 1949 by Jean-Louis Roux (b. 1923) to produce his own play *Rose Latulippe* as well as *Un Fils à tuer* (A son to kill), which was to become the best known play of Eloi de Grandmont (1921–70). Roux and Grandmont then joined with three others who had acted with Les Compagnons de Saint-Laurent—Jean Gascon (1921–88), Guy Hoffman (1916–86), and Georges Groulx—to found TNM. As artistic director, Gascon remained with the company fifteen years. When Gascon moved to the artistic directorship of the Stratford Festival, Roux succeeded him as

TNM's artistic director from 1966 to 1982. With only two artistic directors during its first thirty years, TNM enjoyed great continuity of leadership and gradually reached its goals: paying actors a living wage, obtaining a permanent theater facility (which it did in 1971), and expanding the repertoire beyond the Molière and Feydeau plays that dominated the early seasons. The company's European tours in the 1950s—during which they had the chutzpah to take a Molière production to Paris—earned it an international reputation. Notable among the Canadian plays premiered by TNM were *Klondyke* (music by Gabriel Charpentier, 1965) by Jacques Languirand (b. 1931); *Le Temps sauvage* (Savage period, 1966) by Anne Hébert (b. 1916); *Les Grands Soleils* (Full sun, 1968) by Jacques Ferron (1921–85); *Bilan* (1968) and *Les Beaux dimanches* (1968) by Marcel Dubé (b. 1930); *La Guerre, Yes Sir!* (1971) and *Floralie, où es tu?* (1974), both dramatized from his own novels by Roch Carrier (b. 1937); *Les Oranges sont vertes* (Oranges are green, 1972) by Claude Gauvreau (1925–71); and Denise Boucher's *Les Fées ont soif* (The fairies are thirsty, 1978), a feminist play in which the depiction of the Virgin Mary was seen as blasphemous by some and which generated unsuccessful attempts to have the work banned.

Paul Buissonneau founded the Théâtre de Quat'Sous in 1955 to present daring new work that challenged aesthetic norms; he continued as artistic director until 1984. The company played in various Montreal facilities, finally acquiring its own 160-seat theater in 1965; some of its offerings were coproduced with other theaters. Apart from *Les Belles-soeurs*, all of Michel Tremblay's "rue Fabre" plays premiered at the Théâtre de Quat'Sous. Indeed,

*Montreal's Théâtre du Nouveau Monde (TNM), founded in 1951, continues to thrive, presenting an eclectic repertoire under strong artistic leadership, in a fine facility across the street from the Place des Arts. Photo by Felicia Londré.*

*Montreal's Place des Arts is a large centrally located complex incorporating facilities for theatre, symphony, and dance, as well as art exhibitions. Photo by Felicia Londré.*

by 1972, journalist Michel Bélair (*Le Devoir*) could signal the Théâtre de Quat'Sous as "a launching pad for young Québécois dramatists" and even as the "official stage" for Québécois theater.

Montreal's Le Théâtre Club, opened in 1953 by Jacques Létourneau (b. 1929) and Monique Lepage (b. 1930), emphasized polished production of the classics, modern European and Canadian plays, and children's plays. Lepage, a veteran of Les Compagnons de Saint-Laurent, managed the company until 1965 as well as acting and directing in French and English. In 1956 dramatist Jacques Languirand founded Le Théâtre de Dix Heures, which produced French absurdist drama as well as his own plays, the most important of which is *Les Grands départs* (Great departures, 1958). Gratien Gélinas also founded a theater, the Comédie-Canadienne (1958–70), which presented many new Quebec plays, including Marcel Dubé's important drama *Un Simple Soldat* (1958). Janine Beaubien opened the 150-seat Théâtre de la Poudrière in 1958 and fifteen years later could look back on a record of productions in French, English, and German. 1959 brought Le Théâtre de l'Egrégore, which announced itself as "the first professional avant garde theater."

Spurring such abundance of professional theater was the opening in Montreal of the Conservatoire d'Art Dramatique du Québec in 1954, followed by a Quebec City branch in 1958. In addition, the long-anticipated, bilingual National Theatre School of Canada opened in Montreal in 1960. The Centre d'Essai des Auteurs Dramatiques (CEAD), founded in 1965 in Montreal, promoted the work of francophone Canadian dramatists by its sponsorship of readings and workshops. CEAD, today known simply as the Association Québécoise des Auteurs Dramatiques (AQAD), maintains a Centre de Documentation housing over two thousand Québécois plays and other archives that are available to theater professionals and scholars, and it works closely with the Association Québécoise des Auteurs Dramatiques. Amateur theater also had its support organization, L'Association Canadienne du Théâtre d'Amateurs (ACTA), founded in 1958; it sponsored an annual festival perhaps inspired by the mostly anglophone Dominion Drama Festival. ACTA's founder, Guy Beaulne (b. 1921) directed it until 1963. The Québécois militancy of the late 1960s and the concommitant growth of collective creation brought about the substitution of the word "nonprofessional" for "amateur" and, in 1972, ACTA's name change to L'Association Québécoise du Jeune Théâtre (AQJT); the organization lasted until 1985.

Although it remained resolutely amateur during its twelve-season existence (1955–67), Les Apprentis-Sorciers must be mentioned not only for the professional quality of its productions of absurdists like Ionesco and socially committed writers like Brecht, but also because it spawned two other significant Montreal companies. Les Saltimbanques, an amateur group formed in 1962 by members of Les Apprentis-Sorciers who wanted to focus on more avant-garde work, earned notoriety in 1967 with Pierre Moretti's *Equation pour un homme actuel* (Equation for a man of today), which was banned for indecency, but received funding for a tour to Europe. In 1969 Les Saltimbanques, Les Apprentis-Sorciers, and André Brassard's company, Le Mouvement Contemporain, combined to form a company that would produce Québécois plays exclusively: Le Théâtre d'Aujourd'hui. Under the artistic directorship of Jean-Claude Germain (b. 1939) from its founding until 1982, the Théâtre d'Aujourd'hui took a pronounced political bent. Also in 1969 Germain founded the Théâtre du Même Nom (TMN)—its acronym reversing that of le Théâtre du Nouveau Monde, at which TMN poked fun for not producing enough Quebec plays—and wrote a steady stream of plays for it. Exuberantly skewing Canadian sacred cows, mindsets, and institutions, for example, are Germain's *Diguidi, diguidi, ha! ha! ha!* (1970) and *A Canadian Play/ Une Plaie Canadienne* (/A Canadian wound, 1980).

Montreal's proliferation of professional companies continued during the turbulent 1960s and in the 1970s. La Nouvelle Compagnie Théâtrale began in 1964 with an emphasis on European classics, but by the end of that decade—in which the "quiet revolution" (1960–66) brought a changed outlook in Quebec province, liberating its people from the influence of the Catholic Church and of English-speaking institutions—Québécois dramatists formed an important segment of the repertoire. Le Théâtre de la Marmaille, founded in 1973, expanded the range of children's theater under the leadership of Monique Rioux and playwright Marie-Francine Hébert. Other francophone children's theaters followed. Actor Jean Duceppe (b. 1924) brought vast experience in Quebec theater to founding his own company in 1973. Highlighting his inaugural season was *Charbonneau & le Chef* (1968) by John Thomas McDonough (b. 1924), a Dominican priest whose play, based upon a 1949 workers' strike, targets the collusion of church and state in a miscarriage of social justice. Duceppe played le Chef (Premier Maurice Duplessis) in several francophone productions of this very popular work. The Compagnie Jean Duceppe has necessarily presented largely popular fare to fill seats in the Théâtre Port Royal (capacity nine hundred), where it is the resident company. The Port Royal is one of three theaters in Montreal's Place des Arts complex completed in 1967.

Quebec City depended on touring companies from Montreal for its professional theater throughout the 1950s. There were a number of amateur companies in the city, but they were somewhat slow to stage Canadian plays. The best record was achieved by the Théâtre de l'Estoc, begun by students in 1957 and slipping the occasional play by writers like Jacques Languirand or Marie-Claire Blais into the line-up of modern European plays. L'Estoc became a professional company in 1963 and, with a continuing emphasis on contemporary drama, lasted until 1967. Playwright Jean Barbeau (b. 1945) founded the Théâtre Quotidien du Québec in 1969 as a forum for Québécois plays, including his own, the most important of which was *Joualez-moi d'amour* (Slang me some love, 1971). Théâtre Euh!, also founded in 1969, took a populist and militantly political approach to theater. Other initiatives were based outside the city; for example, the Théâtre de Marjolaine performed in a barn in Eastman, Quebec from 1960. Le Théâtre Populaire du Québec (TPQ), founded in 1963 by Jean Valcourt, was based in Montreal, but regularly toured to Quebec City as well as to the Maritimes and Ontario. Albert Millaire, artistic director from 1969 to 1972, reoriented the TPQ from the classics to works by Québécois dramatists, and Jean-Guy Sabourin, artistic director 1972–76, continued that policy.

Mainstream theater in Quebec City truly came into its own with the opening of Le Grand Théâtre de Québec, a cultural center located near the government buildings and housing two theater auditoriums, rehearsal rooms, an art gallery, and Quebec's conservatory of music. Intended to commemorate the 1967 centenary of confederation, the facility was finally inaugurated on January 16, 1971. As director general of the Grand Théâtre de Québec from 1970 to 1976, Guy Beaulne functioned both as administrator and artist; he envisioned the center as a locus for popular and regional creative expression. The larger of the two theaters, the Salle Louis-Fréchette (capacity eighteen hundred), is well equipped for opera and ballet. The smaller Salle Octave-Crémazie is a flexible space that can accommodate between 300 and 650 spectators, depending upon the configuration used for a given production. It houses Le Théâtre du Trident, a professional theater producing group formed in 1970 by the amalgamation of three preexisting troupes specializing in three different kinds of theater (hence the name Trident, evoking Neptune's three-pronged sceptre): Le Théâtre du Vieux-Québec (traditional theater), L'Estoc (cutting-edge theater), and Le Théâtre pour Enfants (children's plays). The Trident's inaugural production, Jean Barbeau's *O–71* (1971) spoofed the current fad for bingo games. The Trident's artistic director Paul Hébert noted that because the organization did not function as a permanent troupe with a regular corps of actors and a subscription series, each production was to be sold to the public on its own merits as an individual event. While all of the Trident productions did well at the box office, the big hit of that season was John Thomas McDonough's *Charbonneau & le Chef*, which the company premiered. Its eighty-nine performances (including an extended run) boasted a total attendance of 53,236, thus playing to better than 100 percent capacity. The Trident's success contributed significantly to attendance figures for the Grand Théâtre de Québec. In 1973, on the second anniversary of the Grand

Théâtre's opening, Guy Beaulne announced that six hundred fifty thousand spectators had attended the 780 performances in the complex.

Besides Françoise Loranger, Michel Tremblay, and Antonine Maillet, a few other postwar francophone dramatists merit special mention. Attracted to theater from childhood, Marcel Dubé (b. 1930) sensed the importance of Gratien Gélinas's *Tit-Coq* in 1948 and saw it five times. Dubé soon founded his own amateur theater group, La Jeune Scène (1949–56), which produced his earliest plays, including *Zone* (the grand prize-winner for best play at the 1953 Dominion Drama Festival) and *Chambres à louer* (Rooms to rent), which won in 1955. *Zone*, a portrait of French–Canadian youth betrayed by a society that exploits them and cuts them adrift, became one of the most produced plays of the 1950s. Other major plays by this prolific dramatist include *Un Simple Soldat* (1958), *Le Temps des lilas* (Lilac time, 1958), *Florence* (1960), *Les Beaux Dimanches* (1968), *Au Retour des oies blanches* (The white geese, 1966), and *Le Réformiste* (1977). Whether he focuses on middle-class life or Quebec politics, Dubé's plays tend to take a fatalistic view of French–Canadian life.

Robert Gurik (b. 1932) uses farce and parable to expose social problems in plays like *Le Pendu* (The hanged man, 1970). Also widely produced were his allegorical treatment of Quebec politics *Hamlet, prince du Québec* (1968), and his trial drama *Le Procès de Jean-Baptiste M.* (1972). Jacques Ferron (1921–85) focused on Quebec politics, yet could not conceal the influence of French literature; his plays include *Les Grands soleils* (written 1958, premiered 1968), *La Tête du roi* (The king's head, 1963), and *Le Don Juan chrétien* (The Christian Don Juan, 1968). Marie Laberge (b. 1950) brings her experience as an actress and director as well as a feminist perspective to her playwriting. Her prize-winning *C'était avant la guerre à l'Anse-à-Gilles* (It was before the war at Anse-à-Gilles, 1981), in which the woman protagonist apparently breaks free of restrictive gender roles, has had many productions. Despite their difficult pasts, Laberge's women reveal remarkable capacity for love, as in *Aurélie, ma soeur* (Aurelia, my sister, 1988).

After the "quiet revolution" propelled Québécois drama to the fore, ironically, francophone theatrical production seemed to develop in ways parallel to what was going on in anglophone theater. If French Canada had begun in the 1960s to assert its own identity as distinct from English-speaking Canada, the latter also showed signs of asserting itself apart from British and American influence. The 1965 adoption of the red and white maple leaf flag was one outward manifestation of a process that was to culminate in 1982 with Queen Elizabeth II's official return of Canada's constitution, which had been held in the British parliament. Thus, in the two Canadian cultures, a postcolonial mentality gave rise to the cultural nationalism of the 1970s. That cultural nationalism found expression in a number of ways, all so closely interrelated that it is difficult to discuss them as separate phenomena: alternate theater, collective creation, documentary theater, political theater, Canadian history plays, and regionalist or community-centered work.

Alternate theater—known in Quebec as *le jeune théâtre*—might be described as theater that consciously defines itself as an alternative to "establishment" theater. If mainstream theater privileges the dramatic text and the director, then alternate theater would give place to the actor and audience. If institutional theater is oriented to selling a well-packaged cultural product, then alternate theater would focus on the process of experimenting with new forms and nontraditional subject matter. The movement grew partly out of the activism (including the American counterculture) of the 1960s combined with the growing sense of nationalism in Canada, and thus there has often been a strong political component in alternate theater. A decade or more of government support for the arts had produced a generation of artist–intellectuals who were open to aesthetic innovation. Appropriately, it was at a Festival of Underground Theatre (FUT) in Toronto in 1970 that the term "alternate theater" first came into use. FUT was organized by a loose group of young directors (including Ken Gass and Jim Garrard) who saw an opportunity to showcase their work by cooperating with the newly inaugurated St Lawrence Center for the Performing Arts. The directors were taken seriously, granted major funding, and produced an event that brought in such renowned groups as Peter Schumann's Bread and Puppet and Jérôme Savary's Paris company later known as the Grand Magic Circus. Given such visibility, the alternate theater movement rapidly bore fruit. According to Alan Filewood, "in 1965 there were fewer than a dozen professional theaters in English Canada; ten years later there were well over a hundred (and as many again in Quebec)." Although some of the most prominent alternate theaters are based in Toronto, the movement was truly nationwide.

Toronto Workshop Productions (TWP) is often signaled as anglophone Canada's first alternate theater—or at least the company that prepared the way for alternate theater. Founded by George Luscomb in 1959, it is also the oldest continuously operating company in Toronto. During his three years in England as a member of Joan Littlewood's Theatre Workshop, Luscomb had learned improvisation as a technique for the formation of a creative ensemble. He applied the technique with his own company, first to existing texts and then to company-created work beginning with *Hey, Rube!* (1961), a spectacularly successful show about circus people. TWP's most successful production, *Ten Lost Years* (1974), about the 1930s Depression in Canada, enjoyed a long run in Toronto and a nationwide tour. Despite setbacks including a serious theater fire, Luscomb stayed with the company twenty-seven years, forging a strong ensemble and maintaining strong leftist political slant in most of the work.

Celebrating its thirtieth anniversary in 1997–98, Theatre Passe Muraille (TPM) could boast of having produced over three hundred new Canadian plays. It also achieved one of Canadian theater's most successful records of collective creation (twenty-two shows in its first decade) and it exercised leadership in the creation of community-based production as well as in the encouragement of plays of Canadian history. Jim Garrard (b. 1939) founded TPM in 1968, naming the company to reflect Antonin Artaud's dictum that "theatre is event, not architecture." Not only did the Toronto-based company not have a permanent facility until 1975, but its production approach figuratively demolished any invisible wall between performers and audience. The most important production during Garrard's tenure as artistic director was *Futz* (1965) by American playwright Rochelle Owens. Everyone connected with the production was charged with indecency at each performance during the three-week run at the Central Library Theatre, and TPM benefited by the sensationalizing media coverage. Garrard and his producers were brought to trial, but eventually acquitted.

Under Paul Thompson's artistic directorship, 1972–82, TPM enjoyed its golden age of collective creation. The process of collective creation, just as the term implies, involves all company members in research on a given topic and improvisations based upon that research to lead to dramatic expression of the group's shared ideas; eventually this work coalesces into a production, often involving mime, monologue, collage sequences, song, and dance. TPM's first, highly acclaimed, and extremely influential collective creation, *The Farm Show* (1972), was developed under the directorial eye of Paul Thompson; however, the work itself was the product of the entire company's residence of several weeks in Clinton, Ontario. After immersing themselves in the life of the farm community, they premiered the show in a local barn, revived it in Toronto that fall, toured it across Canada and to England, and revived it in 1985 in Clinton. The collective worked collaboratively with writer Rick Salutin (b. 1942) to create *1837: The Farmers' Revolt*, which is perhaps TPM's greatest success; it was revived in 1997. Salutin's "diary" of the creative process (published in *Modern Canadian Plays I*, edited by Jerry Wasserman) chronicles the dramatic shaping of the historical material about the grassroots democracy movement in Upper Canada. Other notable TPM collective creations are *Doukhobors* (1971), *Under the Greywacke* (1973), *I Love You, Baby Blue* (1973), and *Shakespeare for Fun and Profit* (1977). Another important work resulted from Thompson's collaboration as a director with Linda Griffiths, who wrote the one-person play *Maggie and Pierre* (1979) and performed both of the eponymous roles.

The Factory Theatre Lab (FTL), founded in 1970 by playwright Ken Gass (b. 1945), weathered a number of setbacks, including moves to various less-than-adequate performance spaces in Toronto, and yet it distinguished itself for its policy of producing only Canadian plays. Among FTL's important premieres were *Creeps* (1971) by David Freeman (b. 1947) about the marginalization of the disabled; *Esker Mike and His Wife, Agiluk* (written 1969, produced 1971) by Herschel Hardin; *Strawberry Fields* (1973) by Michael Hollingsworth (b. 1950); *The Stonehenge Trilogy* (1975) by Larry Fineberg (b. 1945); *Underground* (1975) and *This Side of the Rockies* (1977) by Bryan Wade (b. 1950). FTL's most important contribution may be the discovery and nurturing of playwright George F. Walker (b. 1947). Walker had attended only one play in his life and was working as a taxi-driver when he saw FTL's script-solicitation flyer on a lamppost. Gass not only produced Walker's one-act submission, *The Prince of Naples* (1971), but he made Walker playwright-in-residence. Over the years most of Walker's plays have premiered at FTL, although his most produced work, *Zastrozzi* (1977), premiered at Toronto

Free Theatre (TFT). Founded in 1971, TFT maintained a free admission policy until 1973 (and since the 1982 founding of its subsidiary outdoor summer festival, the Dream in High Park, has annually presented free Shakespeare). TFT gained a certain notoriety in 1973 with the production of Michael Hollingsworth's *Clear Light*, a work almost universally regarded as depraved and revolting, to the extent that several company members refused to act in it. In 1988 TFT merged with CentreStage Company to become the Canadian Stage Company (CSC). In 1997, with twenty thousand subscribers to the mainstage season at the Bluma Appel Theatre in the St Lawrence Center, CSC continued to feature Canadian plays in its programming.

Toronto's Tarragon Theatre also boasts a strong record of presenting Canadian work including Québécois drama in translation. Bill Glassco (b. 1935), artistic director until 1982, founded the company with his wife Jane in 1971. Bill Glassco and John Van Burek together translated into English six of Michel Tremblay's plays, which the Tarragon then produced. The 1972 production of *Leaving Home* by David French initiated a long and rewarding director–dramatist collaboration that yielded "the Mercer plays," a very well received series of realistic dramas about a Catholic working-class family in Newfoundland. The Tarragon also premiered the next two Mercer plays, *Of the Fields, Lately* (1973) and *Salt-Water Moon* (1984), as well as French's popular backstage comedy *Jitters* (1979). Glassco directed the fourth Mercer play, *1949* (1988) at Canadian Stage Company, where he was then sharing the artistic directorship with Guy Sprung. Canadian plays staged at the Tarragon

*In 1986, Toronto's Tarragon Theatre produced the English-language premiere of Michel Tremblay's* Albertine, in Five Times *(Albertine en cinq temps). Shown left to right are Patricia Hamilton, Susan Coyne, Clare Coulter, Doris Petrie, Joy Coghill. Courtesy of Tarragon Theatre.*

have tended to employ a traditional dramaturgy and this, coupled with the company's continuing success, has prompted some to regard it as more mainstream than alternate. However, this is a criticism that might apply to virtually any alternate theater of the 1970s that survived into the 1980s and 1990s.

A late-comer to the Toronto alternate theater scene, the NDWT (1975–82) is best remembered for the director–dramatist collaboration of the company's founder Keith Turnbull (b. 1944) with James Reaney (b. 1926), who was already an established playwright. Reaney's *Colours in the Dark* (1967), for example, had premiered at the Stratford Festival and been produced at Vancouver Playhouse. Reaney and Turnbull worked together eight years to develop Reaney's important historical trilogy known as "The Donnellys": *Sticks and Stones* (1973), *The St. Nicholas Hotel—Wm. Donnelly, Prop.* (1974), and *Handcuffs* (1975). Although the three plays had premiered at the Tarragon, NDWT toured them across Canada and presented all three in a long-remembered one-day marathon, December 14, 1975, in Toronto. Because NDWT emphasized touring, its initials—supposedly connoting Ne'er-Do-Well Thespians—have also been taken to stand for No Drama Without Travel. Toronto, with its relatively small francophone population base, has also supported a French-language theater. Founded in 1967 by John Van Burek as an amateur group, Le Théâtre du P'tit Bonheur became professional in 1973 and changed its name to Le Théâtre Français de Toronto in 1987; it survived on a mixed repertoire of European classics and Québécois plays.

English-language alternate theaters outside Toronto include Vancouver's Tamahnous Theatre (the name means "magic" in the Chilcotin Indian language), founded in 1971 by John Gray. Other Vancouver troupes devoted to Canadian drama include the New Play Centre, founded in 1970 by Douglas Bankson and Sheila Neville, and Northern Light Theatre, founded in 1975. One might also signal as alternate theater the various projects undertaken in Vancouver and other western cities by John Juliani under the rubric Savage God. In Alberta, there have been a number of "alternatives" to Theatre Calgary and Citadel Theatre; these include Workshop West, Chinook Theatre, Catalyst Theatre, Theatre Three, Theatre Network, and Teatro La Quindicina in Edmonton; and Alberta Theatre Projects and Loose Moose in Calgary. In addition, since 1982 Edmonton has hosted an annual Fringe Festival that showcases professional, amateur, and academic theater. The 25th Street House, founded in 1971 in Saskatoon, Saskatchewan, presented a number of collective creations, garnering nationwide attention with *Paper Wheat* (1977), about the hard lives of those who settled on the prairies. Founded in 1972 as an alternative to Winnipeg's Manitoba Theatre Centre, Manitoba Theatre Workshop later became the Prairie Theatre Exchange.

On the Atlantic side, collective creation worked well for three touring companies: Newfoundland's Mummers Troupe and CODCO, and Nova Scotia's Mulgrave Road Co-op Theatre. The Mummers Troupe began as 1960s-style street theater, constituted itself as a troupe in 1972, and under the leadership of Chris Brookes, using the mummers' hobbyhorse as emblem, developed a distinctive community-oriented populist style; it disbanded in

1982. CODCO got its name (for Cod Company) in 1974, but the six actors who founded the troupe had first formed a collective in Toronto in 1973 when Paul Thompson, artistic director of Theatre Passe Muraille, provided an incentive for the Newfoundlanders to create their own material. The result, *Cod on a Stick*, presented at a TPM venue, won such acclaim that the group took it back to Newfoundland, first to St. John's and then on an eight-week tour to twenty-three towns and villages. Between 1973 and 1976 CODCO collectively created five works of Newfoundland life, after which the original performers gradually dispersed, although the company iteslf continued to create works for stage and television. The Mulgrave Road Co-op Theatre, founded in 1977 and based in the small town of Guysborough, Nova Scotia, developed numerous scripts dealing with the concerns of its rural coastal audiences.

Francophone theaters also embraced collective creation during the 1970s. The Grand Cirque Ordinaire (1969–78) was founded after the seven students of the graduating class at the National Theatre School presented the administration with a radical manifesto demanding changes in the curriculum. When that was turned down, the students withdrew from the school and, led by Raymond Cloutier, became the *comédiens–créateurs* (actor-creators) of their own largely nonverbal, improvisation-based, "sociopoetic" material. Their first and best-known production was the collectively created *T'es pas tannée, Jeanne d'Arc?* (Aren't you fed up, Joan of Arc?, 1969). Les Enfants du Paradis, founded in Montreal in 1975 and later changing its name to Carbone 14, stressed mime and improvisation. Le Théâtre Experimental de Montréal (1975–78) split into two companies, Le Nouveau Théâtre Experimental de Montréal and Le Théâtre Experimental des Femmes. Another women's troupe, Le Théâtre des Cuisines (1973–81), also became known for its collective creations. Others include Le Théâtre de Carton (1972–94), Théâtre Parminou, and Gens d'en Bas.

Mainstream theater did not lie dormant during the heyday of alternate theater. Some established theaters presented important new Canadian plays and playwrights, while some new companies offered traditional mixes of classics and foreign plays. George Ryga (1932–87), for example, had worked in radio and television until Vancouver Playhouse premiered his break-through play *The Ecstasy of Rita Joe* (1967) about a Native American woman trapped between her own indigenous cultural heritage and the uncomprehending expectations of urban white society. Vancouver Playhouse also premiered Ryga's next play, *Grass and Wild Strawberries* (1969) and commissioned a third. The latter work, however, *Captives of the Faceless Drummer* (1970), dealt disturbingly with recent political events and was canceled by the Playhouse board; it premiered in the Vancouver Art Gallery. Manitoba Theatre Centre's 1967 (centennial year) premiere of a Canadian play was *Lulu Street* by Ann Henry (b. 1914); the play is a family drama set during a 1919 labor strike in Winnipeg. Saskatoon's leading professional company, Persephone Theatre (founded 1974) and Theatre Newfoundland and Labrador (founded 1979 in Stephenville, Newfoundland) followed the

*The spirited Canadian World War I flying ace Billy Bishop recalls his exploits in this moment from John Gray's 1978 play, as presented at Missouri Repertory Theatre in 1991. Benjamin Evett played the title role in* Billy Bishop Goes to War.

*Michael Deep at the piano and Benjamin Evett performed John Gray's* Billy Bishop Goes to War *at Missouri Repertory Theatre in 1991. Dennis Rosa directed.*

lead of the regional theaters in offering the "three Cs": classical, contemporary international, and Canadian.

Among the regional theaters, the Centaur Theatre has upheld an impressive record of presenting and premiering Canadian plays since its founding in 1969 by artistic director Maurice Podbrey (b. 1934). By 1974 the nonprofit corporation was able to purchase and renovate the Old Stock Exchange, where it had been leasing a small auditorium; the complex now incorporates two theaters, Centaur 1 (capacity 255) and Centaur 2 (capacity 440). While recognized as Montreal's leading English-language theater, the Centaur often employs francophone theater professionals like the distinguished Quebec actress Denise Pelletier (1929–76), who played the title role in Jacques Beyderwellen's *La Divine Sarah* at the Centaur in 1976. Preeminent among the dramatists developed at the Centaur, David Fennario (b. 1947) saw three of his plays premiered there in four seasons, 1974–78, followed by what may have been Canada's first bilingual play, *Balconville* (1979), which remains Fennario's most popular work. About his controversial political play *The Death of René Lévesque* (1991), which Paul Thompson directed at the Centaur, Podbrey commented: "David has taken on a subject which Anglophones in Quebec have difficulty in addressing. The nationalist movement in Quebec affects their lives profoundly but there are few avenues or opportunities for them to address and evaluate the subject constructively. The use of six Francophone actors working in English gives the occasion an edge that is also exciting." Apart from Fennario's plays, one of the Centaur's most important premieres also dealt with political ramifications of Quebec's situation in Canada. The theater commissioned Rick Salutin to write a play about the Montreal Canadiens. Working with hockey goalie Ken Dryden, Salutin wrote a quasidocumentary play with historical overtones, using ice-hockey as a metaphor. Directed by Guy Sprung, *Les Canadiens* premiered at the Centaur in 1977 and won the Chalmers best play award. Productions at Toronto Workshop Productions and at Vancouver's Arts Club Theatre quickly followed.

The remarkable outpouring of Canadian drama of all kinds since the 1970s makes it impossible even to catalogue all the important names and play titles. A few examples beyond those already mentioned must serve to hint at the riches. John Herbert's (b. 1926) *Fortune and Men's Eyes*, an unflinching, funny, and moving drama dealing with homosexuality and prison hierarchy, premiered in New York in 1967, having been refused full production at the Stratford Festival, where its workshop version had been deemed inappropriate. Widely produced internationally, the play finally had its first full production in Canada at Toronto's Phoenix Theatre in 1975. One of Canadian theater's many works based upon the nation's history, the one-man musical *Billy Bishop Goes to War* (1978) by John Gray (b. 1946), with Eric Peterson, who created the title role, explores the nature of heroism through the persona of the World War I flying ace who shot down seventy-two German planes. Sharon Pollock (b. 1936) also employed historical subjects in plays like *Walsh* (1973) about Sitting Bull's futile attempt to find refuge for his people in Canada, and *Blood Relations* (1980) about Lizzie

Borden. John Murrell's (b. 1945) most often produced plays are *Waiting for the Parade* (1977) about five Calgary women during World War II, and *Memoir* (1978) about Sarah Bernhardt. Joanna Glass (b. 1936) draws upon her own experience for plays like *Artichoke* (1975) and *If We Are Women* (1993). Anne Chislett (b. 1942), who in 1975 cofounded the Blyth Summer Festival for new Canadian plays, writes intelligent plays of subtle power: *The Tomorrow Box* (1980), *Quiet in the Land* (1981), and *Another Season's Promise* (1986). Judith Thompson's (b. 1954) *The Crackwalker* (1980) and *Lion in the Streets* (1990) epitomize the hypnotic rawness of speech and action. Dan Needles has won a popular following with his hilarious "Wingfield plays" feauring Walt Wingfield and a motley assortment of characters in Persephone Township.

While theater companies and dramatists have taken focus in this necessarily cursory survey of modern Canadian theater, the work of a few other significant artists must be signaled at least in passing. Robert Prévost (1927–82) designed sets and costumes for virtually every major Canadian theater, ballet, and opera company, beginning with Les Compagnons de Saint-Laurent. Other important set designers are Jacques Pelletier (1909–74), Jean-Claude Rinfret (b. 1929), Cameron Porteous (b. 1937), Michael Eagan (b. 1942), Mark

*Left,* If We Are Women *by Joanna Glass examines three generations of women. John Dillon directed the 1994 Missouri Repertory Theatre production with Heather Ayres (seated) and her two grandmothers played by Marjorie Kellogg and Nora Denney.*

*Right, Judith Thompson's* Lion in the Streets *premiered at the Tarragon Theatre in Toronto in 1990. Pictured are Andrew Gillies, Tracy Wright, Maggie Huculak, and Jane Spidell. Photograph by Michael Cooper, courtesy of Tarragon Theatre.*

Negin (b. 1942), Paul Bussières (b. 1943), Astrid Janson (b. 1947), Mary Kerr (b. 1950), and Claude Goyette (b. 1954). Laure Cabana (b. 1910), François Barbeau (b. 1945), and Julia Tribe (b. 1958) are leading costume designers. Allan Watts, Susan Benson (b. 1942), Sue LePage (b. 1951), and Debra Hanson (b. 1951) design both sets and costumes. Although born in England, set and costume designer Desmond Heeley (b. 1930), like Tanya Moiseiwitsch, remains closely idenified with the theater of Canada. Major lighting designers include Jeffrey Dallas (1945–89), Michael J. Whitfield (b. 1944), Nick Cernovich, and Claude Accolas. Among directors, Albert Millaire (b. 1935) has worked successfully for both anglophone and francophone theaters. Janet Amos (b. 1945) has held aristic directorships of the Blyth Festival, 1980–84, and Theatre New Brunswick, 1984–88. Certain critics have also made very positive contributions to theatrical development, above all Herbert Whittaker (b. 1910), who began by designing sets and served as a vividly constructive critic for the *Toronto Globe and Mail* from 1949 until his retirement in 1975. Others are Nathan Cohen (1923–71) and his successor Urjo Kareda for the *Toronto Star*, and Zelda Heller for the *Montreal Star*.

One of the most significant developments of the 1980s and 1990s has been the sudden visibility of Native American performance. This has taken two forms: first, recuperated ceremonial traditions that were once condemned, even criminalized, by the colonizing society, but are now regarded with respect and awe by non-Natives who are privileged to witness them; second, Native dramatists and theater companies that employ the English language and elements of non-Native dramaturgy to give widely accessible cultural expression to the experience of a particular Native nation. Even in the first category, some compromising of authenticity is inevitable when the event is viewed and reported by non-Natives, and yet the very existence of such performances is to be celebrated. There are, for example, the pow-wow dancing of the Lyons Dance Troupe of Ontario, the masked Xwe-Xwe ritual of the Coast Salish, the southern Kwakiutl mystery play, the Inuit spirit play, the Kaviatchaq dance of the Inupiat Eskimo, and thousands more. There are contemporary arrangements of old forms like the 1972 production of 'Ksan, a two-hour collage of dances and spirit plays reconstructed by the Tshimshian people of British Columbia; 'Ksan toured to the National Arts Centre in Ottawa.

The second type of Native theater is enjoying a great surge of activity and interest. Leading that surge, Tomson Highway, a full-blooded Cree, employs Native elements—like the trickster figure (Nanabush)—in a form influenced by his studies of western drama under James Reaney at the University of Western Ontario. His first full-length play, *The Rez Sisters* (1986), premiered by Native Earth Performing Arts Company in Toronto, toured Canada, was performed at the Edinburgh Festival, got a new production at the Centaur Theatre in 1989, and has scarcely been absent from the stage—or the university classroom—since then. Highway's other most produced play, *Dry Lips Oughta Move to Kapuskasing*, generated feminist criticism when it premiered at the Theatre Passe Muraille in 1989, but the production was revived in 1991 at the large commerical Royal Alexandra

*Tomson Highway's* The Rez Sisters *won the Dora Mavor Moore Award for Best New Play and the Chalmers Award for Outstanding Canadian Play when it was produced by Native Earth Performing Arts in 1986. Pictured from left to right are Anne Anglin, Sally Singal, Margaret Cozry, Muriel Miguel, Monique Mojica, and—as Nanabush— René Highway. Courtesy of Tomson Highway and Native Earth Performing Arts.*

Theatre. Ojibway dramatist Drew Hayden Taylor, who succeeded Highway as artistic director of Native Earth Performing Arts, writes comedies in conscious opposition to the tendency to emphasize the dark side of Native experience; among his works are *Toronto at Dreamer's Rock* (1989), *The Bootlegger Blues* (1990), and *Dead White Writer on the Floor* (1996). Maria Campbell's 1973 autobiography *Halfbreed* served as a starting point for her work with non-Native actress–playwright Linda Griffiths in an exploration of cross-cultural portrayals; this resulted in the play *The Book of Jessica: A Theatrical Transformation*. Other Native works of note include *Princess Pocahontas and the Blue Spots* (1991) by Monique Mojica (Métis), *Moonlodge* (1989) by Margo Kane (Saulteaux), and *Coyote City* (1988) by Daniel David Moses (Delaware).

Its Toronto location and its association with playwright–directors Tomson Highway and Drew Hayden Taylor make Native Earth Performing Arts the best known of theater organizations devoted to indigenous work. Founded in 1982, Native Earth has since 1989 presented an annual festival of new Native plays under the patronage of Weesageechak (an incarnation of the trickster). Other companies devoted to Native plays include the Red

Roots Theatre Company and Awasikan Theatre in Winnipeg, Saskatchewan's Upisasik Theatre, De-ba-jeh-mu-jig Theatre Group of Manitoulin Island in northern Ontario, Alberta's Four Winds Theatre and Takwakin Theatre, and Vancouver's Spirit Song.

While Canadian theater continues to gather strength from many different ethnic initiatives—black, Jewish, Asian, and others—in addition to those of its various Native nations, some commercial interests are becoming major players in an increasingly global market. Toronto businessman Edwin Mirvish (b. 1914), for example, not only spent lavishly to renovate the Royal Alexandra, but also moved into Broadway and West End production, and purchased London's Old Vic. The most remarkable success story is that of Garth Drabinsky (b. 1950), whose Toronto-based Livent (Live Entertainment of Canada) company is changing the way the commercial theater business operates, not only in Canada but in the United States as well. John Lahr described Livent as "a nineties theatre-production company structured like a thirties film studio." Indeed, the earlier phase of Drabinsky's career was movie-oriented: he produced six movies and built up a chain (Cineplex Odeon) of over eighteen hundred movie houses in North America and Great Britain. When the company became financially overextended, Drabinsky and his partner Martin Gottlieb were bought out, but they retained the live-theater division, which consisted of one Toronto theater and one musical production, *The Phantom of the Opera*. On that basis, in 1989 Livent was founded. In eight years it grew to ownership of six important theaters, including New York's Times Square–revitalizing Ford Center for the Performing Arts, created out of the former Apollo and Lyric theaters on West Forty-Third Street, which opened in early 1998.

Livent is more than real estate. It is also the first publicly traded company in the history of the live theater; it creates and markets the product it houses. Because Drabinsky closely monitors the development of his productions, actively recruiting the very best talent available, pushing his artists to outdo themselves and paying them handsomely, Livent boasts a track record of artistic excellence and commercial success in New York as well as in Toronto, Los Angeles, Chicago, Vancouver: *Kiss of the Spider Woman* (1993, seven Tony Awards, including best musical), *Show Boat* (1994, Tony Award for best musical), *Barrymore* (1997, Tony Award for best actor Christopher Plummer). Drabinsky finances new projects on the profits from his numerous long-running road shows. This represents a drastic change from the old Broadway practice of hustling investors for each new, high-risk production. The musical version of *Ragtime*, three years in development and scheduled to open the Ford Center on Times Square, exemplifies Drabinsky's belief that musicals are the supreme medium for making a powerful statement: "*Ragtime, Show Boat,* and *Parade* are all strong indictments of racism and anti-Semitism." Despite the apparent extravagance of expenditures on preproduction development and putting as much as 12 percent of the gross of any show into advertising, Drabinsky runs a tight business, keeping watch over daily balance sheets and having all his productions built in Canada, where costs are about 35 percent lower than in the United States.

At the end of the 1990s, Canada's most internationally renowned creators of theater may well be two forms of "imagistic" entertainment: the Montreal-based Cirque du Soleil (founded 1984) and Quebec City's performer–*animateur* Robert Lepage (b. 1957). Le Cirque du Soleil originated in street performances—stilt-walking, juggling, acrobatics—by a group of young people contributing to Quebec's celebration of the 450th anniversary of Jacques Cartier's discovery of Canada. That early version of circus arts (without animals) in a storytelling format under a yellow-and-blue tent (capacity eight hundred) toured to ten Quebec towns in 1984. The following year the troupe toured Canada all the way to Vancouver, and in 1987 the company brought a show called *Cirque Réinventé* (Reinvented circus) to the Los Angeles Festival. Over the years the tent grew to seat twenty-five hundred, the company expanded to over seventy performers, and the tours had reached eighteen countries by 1996. The 1994 production, *Mystère*, settled for a time in Las Vegas. *Quidam* (1996), directed by Franco Dragone, continued to elicit superlatives from audiences and critics dazzled by the startling visual images, graceful stunts, and what Richard Corliss called "wordless drama" that "transforms motion into emotion."

After theater studies at the Conservatoire d'Art Dramatique de Québec and in Paris, Robert Lepage founded Théâtre Hummm . . . with Richard Fréchette. The company staged several works, both classic texts and collective creations. In 1982 Lepage and Fréchette joined Quebec City's Théâtre Repère (founded in 1980 by Jacques Lessard), and soon Lepage attracted attention by his directing. Among his important productions are *Vinci* (1986), *La Trilogie des dragons* (Dragon trilogy, 1985–87), *Le Polygraphe* (1987), *Plaques tectoniques* (Tectonic plates, 1988–90), *Les Aiguilles et l'opium* (Needles and opium, 1991), *A Midsummer Night's Dream*, 1992), and a number of Shakespeare variations. As the productions toured worldwide, Lepage constantly revised them. Like many postmodern theater artists, Lepage creates works so structurally complex that it is difficult to describe them. They tend to employ multiple narratives that are not always advanced in a linear fashion, but are complicated by a dense mosaic of stage imagery. Lepage is particularly adept at combining scenic elements, lighting effects, costume pieces, objects both unusual and commonplace, snippets of film, and ritualized actions and dancelike movement to evoke a compelling, mysterious atmosphere.

Lepage's works are subject to a range of interpretations, but most often they seem to be meditations on the interconnections between history, geography, and culture. *Dragon Trilogy*, for example, is an epic saga which, over the course of six hours, traces the lives of two cousins—Jeanne and Françoise—from the 1930s through the 1980s. The action moves from Quebec City to Toronto to Vancouver and back to Quebec City. The Chinatowns in each of these cities, as well as the cities of Hong Kong and Hiroshima, and an assortment of Chinese, Japanese, British and Anglo– and French–Canadian characters are interwoven into the stories of Jeanne and Françoise. Personal history is thus foregrounded against both Canadian and world history. By turns lyrical, surrealistic, and naturalistic,

*Dragon Trilogy* is a compelling treatment of existential and cultural perplexities. In *Needles and Opium*, a remarkable solo performance, Lepage explores the nature of creativity through the intertwined lives of French poet–filmmaker Jean Cocteau, the jazz musician Miles Davis, and Robert (Lepage's alter ego), a young Québecois visiting Paris. *Alanienouidet* (1992) focuses on the English tragedian Edmund Kean's 1826 tour to Montreal and Québec. For Kean, a high point of his tour was a meeting with a Huron Indian delegation which attended his performance of *Richard III* and then made him an honorary chief with the name Alanienouidet (meaning "strong wind on drifting snow"). The incident provides a framework for a consideration of a range of Native and European issues.

In 1994 Lepage founded the multidisciplinary Ex Machina company, of which he is artistic director. Its major productions are *Les Sept branches de la rivière Ota* (The seven streams of the River Ota, 1995), a seven-hour work inspired by Lepage's visit to Hiroshima, and *Elseneur* (1995), a one-man version of *Hamlet* performed by Lepage. His work has been hailed as brilliantly innovative, but criticized as increasingly shallow as a result of his heavy reliance on technological effects. According to Margaret Croyden, "Perhaps Lepage's work is too expressive, too complicated, too varied to warrant a label. To attribute his aesthetic to any one technique, any one style, any one idea, would be difficult. He is a man whose imagination and talent are fluid, who is forever searching and forever changing. One thing is certain, Lepage's creativity will always produce theater that is astonishing and magical."

A bright vision of the totality of Canadian culture as it is and will be is compellingly expressed by Cree dramatist Tomson Highway. In an interview with Ann Wilson, he said:

> I think that every society is constantly in a state of change, of transformation, of metamorphosis. I think it is very important that it continue to be so to prevent the stagnation of our imaginations, our spirits, our soul. It is bad enough that our bodies and our physical environment are in danger of stagnating. I think the very fact that British and French and Czechoslovakian, Yugoslavian and Polish, are now living on this continent means that we need a different experience, one that changes any identification, even if by the very nature of the fact that all are called Canadians, Ontarians, Torontonians. Right there, you have Indian names. There is an additional psychic magic that happens there, just as a result of that name. So I think that white culture in Canada is very much changing and transforming as a result of living with native culture; likewise Cree culture, native culture. It is impossible for me to live in a tent for the rest of my life, even though I was born in one. . . . What I really find fascinating about the future of my life, the life of my people, the life of my fellow Canadians is the searching for this new voice, this new identity, this new tradition, this magical transformation that potentially is quite magnificent. It is the combination of the best of both worlds, . . . combining them and coming up with something new—I think that's the most exciting thing.

# Bibliography

GENERAL WORKS

Applebaum, Stanley, ed. *Great Actors and Actresses of the American Stage in Historic Photographs: 1850–1950*. New York: Dover, 1983.
————. *The New York Stage: Famous Productions in Photographs: 1883–1939*. New York: Dover, 1976.
———— and James Camner, eds. *Stars of the American Musical Theater in Historic Photographs: 1860s to 1950*. New York: Dover, 1981.
Archer, Stephen M. *American Actors and Actresses: A Guide to Information Sources*. Detroit: Gale Research Press, 1983.
Arrom, José Juan. *Historia de la literatura dramática Cubana*. New Haven, Conn.: Yale University Press, 1944.
Ball, John and Richard Plant, eds. *Bibliography of Theatre History in Canada: The Beginnings Through 1984*. Oakville, Ontario: ECW Press, 1993.
Banham, Martin, Errol Hill, and George Woodyard, eds. *The Cambridge Guide to African and Caribbean Theatre*. Cambridge: Cambridge University Press, 1994.
Beauchamp, Hélène, John Hare, and Paul Wyczynski, eds. *Archives des lettres canadiennes*. Vol. 5, *Le Théâtre canadien–français*. Montreal: Fides, 1976.
Benson, Eugene and L. W. Conolly. *English–Canadian Theatre*. Toronto: Oxford University Press, 1987.
————, eds. *The Oxford Companion to Canadian Theatre*. Don Mills, Ontario: Oxford University Press, 1989.
Béraud, Jean. *350 Ans de théâtre au Canada français*. Ottawa: Le Cercle du Livre de France, 1958.
Bernheim, Alfred L. *The Business of the American Theatre: An Economic History of the American Theatre, 1750–1932*. New York: Benjamin Blom, 1964 (originally published, 1932).
*Best Plays of [various volumes]*. Ed. Burns Mantle; John Chapman; Louis Kronenberger; Henry Hewes; Otis L. Grunsey Jr. (since 1963). New York: Dodd, Mead, 1921–1994; Applause Books, 1995– .
Bigsby, C. W. E. *A Critical Introduction to Twentieth-Century American Drama*. Vol. 1, *1900–1940*; vol. 2, *Williams/Miller/Albee*; vol. 3, *Beyond Broadway*. Cambridge: Cambridge University Press, 1982–85.
Bogard, Travis, Richard Moody, and Walter J. Meserve. *The Revels History of Drama in English*. Vol. 8, *American Drama*. London: Methuen, 1977.

Bordman, Gerald. *American Musical Comedy: From "Adonis" to "Dream-girls."* New York: Oxford University Press, 1982.

———. *American Musical Revue: From "The Passing Show" to "Sugar Babies."* New York: Oxford University Press, 1985.

———. *American Musical Theatre: A Chronicle.* 2d ed. New York: Oxford University Press, 1992.

———. *American Operetta: From "H. M. S. Pinafore" to "Sweeney Todd."* New York: Oxford University Press, 1981.

Brask, Per and William Morgan, eds. *Aboriginal Voices: Amerinidan, Inuit, and Sami Theater.* Baltimore: Johns Hopkins University Press, 1992.

Brown, T. Allston. *History of the American Stage.* New York: Burt Franklin (originally published 1870), 1969.

Bryan, George B. *Stage Deaths: A Biographical Guide to International Theatrical Obituaries.* Westport, Conn.: Greenwood Press, 1991.

———. *Stage Lives: A Bibliography and Index to Theatrical Biographies in English.* Westport, Conn.: Greenwood Press, 1985.

Burge, James C. *Lines of Business: Casting Practice and Policy in the American Theatre, 1752–1899.* New York: Peter Lang, 1986.

Camara Zavala, Gonzalo. *Historia del teatro Peón Contreras.* Mexico: Talleres Gráficos Laguna, 1946.

Ceballos, Edgar. *Diccionario enciclopédico básico de teatro Mexicano.* México D.F.: Escenología, 1996.

Chavrán, Richard and Rafael Chabrán, eds. *The Latino Encyclopedia.* 6 vols. New York: Marshall Cavendish, 1996.

Clapp, William W., Jr. *A Record of the Boston Stage.* New York: Greenwood Press (originally published in 1853 by James Monroe), 1969.

Coad, Oral Sumner and Edwin Mims Jr. *The American Stage.* New Haven, Conn.: Yale University Press, 1929.

Dizikes, John. *Opera in America: A Cultural History.* New Haven, Conn.: Yale University Press, 1993.

Doucette, Leonard E. *Theatre in French Canada: Laying the Foundations 1606–1867.* Toronto: University of Toronto Press, 1984.

Dudden, Faye E. *Women in the American Theatre: Actresses & Audiences 1790–1870.* New Haven, Conn.: Yale University Press, 1994.

Duerr, Edwin. *The Length and Depth of Acting.* New York: Holt, Reinhart, & Winston, 1962.

Durham, Weldon B., ed. *American Theatre Companies, 1749–1887.* New York: Greenwood Press, 1986.

———. *American Theatre Companies, 1888–1930.* New York: Greenwood Press, 1985.

———. *American Theatre Companies, 1931–86.* New York: Greenwood Press, 1989.

Edwards, Murray D. *A Stage in Our Past: English-Language Theatre in Eastern Canada from the 1790s to 1914.* Toronto: University of Toronto Press, 1968.

*Escenarios de dos mundos: Inventario teatral de Iberoamérica.* Vol. 2 , *Cuba*; vol. 3, *México*; vol. 4, *Puerto Rico, República Dominicana.* Madrid: Centro de Documentación Teatral (Moisés Pérez Coterillo, director), 1988.

Frick, John W. and Stephen M. Vallillo. *Theatrical Directors: A Biographical Dictionary.* Westport, Conn.: Greenwood Press, 1994.

Glazer, Irvin R. *Philadelphia Theatres, A–Z: A Comprehensive, Descriptive Record of 813 Theatres Constructed since 1724.* Westport, Conn.: Greenwood Press, 1986.

González Obregón, Luis. *México viejo: época colonial; noticias históricas, tradiciones, leyendas y costumbres.* México: C. Bouret, 1900.

González Peña, Carlos. *History of Mexican Literature.* Trans. Gusta Barfield Nance and Florene Johnson Dunstan. Dallas: Southern Methodist University Press, 1969.

Graham, Franklin. *Histrionic Montreal: Annals of the Montreal Stage with Biographical and Critical Notices of the Plays and Players of a Century.* New York: Benjamin Blom (originally published 1902), 1969.

Green, Stanley. *Encyclopedia of the Musical Theatre.* New York: Dodd, Mead, 1976. (Reprint, DaCapo Press, 1979.)

———. *Broadway Musicals: Show by Show.* 5th ed. Milwaukee, Wisc.: Hal Leonard Corporation, 1996.

Hare, John E. "Panorama des spectacles à Québec: de la Conquête au XXe siècle." In *Le Théâtre canadien français.* Ed. Hélène Beauchamp, Bernard Julien, and Paul Wyczynski, 60–107. Vol. 5 of *Archives des Lettres Canadiennes.* Montréal: Fides, 1976.

Hay, Samuel A. *African–American Theatre: A Historical and Critical Analysis.* New York: Cambridge University Press, 1994.

Henderson, Mary C. *The City and the Theatre: New York Playhouses from Bowling Green to Times Square.* Clifton, N.J.: James T. White, 1973.

———. *Theatre in America: 200 Years of Plays, Players, and Productons.* 2d ed. New York: Harry Abrams, 1996.

Hill, Errol. *Shakespeare in Sable: A History of Black Shakespearean Actors.* Amherst: University of Massachusetts Press, 1984.

———. *The Theatre of Black Americans.* Vol. 1, *Roots & Rituals/The Image Makers*; vol. 2, *The Presenters/The Participators.* Englewood Cliffs, N.J.: Prentice–Hall, 1980.

Hornblow, Arthur. *A History of the Theatre in America: From Its Beginnings to the Present Time.* 2 vols. Philadelphia: J. B. Lippincott Company, 1919. (Reprint, New York: Benjamin Blom, 1965.)

Ireland, Joseph N. *Records of the New York Stage: From 1750 to 1860,* 2 vols. New York: Burt Franklin (originally published 1866–67), 1968.

Jackson, Kenneth T. *The Encyclopedia of New York City.* New Haven, Conn.: Yale University Press, 1995.

Jones, Willis Knapp. *Behind Spanish American Footlights.* Austin: University of Texas Press, 1966.

Laflamme, Jean and Rémi Tourangeau. *L'Eglise et le théâtre au Québec.* Montréal: Fides, 1979.

Lamb, Ruth S. *Mexican Theatre of the Twentieth Century: Bibliography and Study.* Claremont: Ocelot Press, 1975.

Lamb, W. Kaye. *The History of Canada: From Discovery to Present Day.* New York: American Heritage Press, 1971.

Larson, Orville K. *Scene Design in the American Theatre From 1915 to 1960.* Fayetteville: University of Arkansas Press, 1989.

Londré, Felicia Hardison. *The History of World Theater: From the English Restoration to the Present.* New York: Continuum, 1991.

Magaña Esquivel, Antonio and Ruth S. Lamb. *Breve historia del teatro mexicano.* México: Ediciones de Andrea, 1958.

Mañon, Manuel. *Historia del Teatro Principal de México.* México: Editorial Cultura, 1932.

McConachie, Bruce A. and Daniel Friedman. *Theatre for Working-Class Audiences in the United States, 1830–1980.* Westport, Conn.: Greenwood Press, 1985.

Mendoza López, Margarita. *Teatro mexicano del siglo XX,* 6 vols. México D.F.: Instituto Mexicano del Seguro Social, 1989–94.

Meserve, Walter J. *An Outline History of American Drama.* 2d rev ed. New York: Feedback Theatrebooks & Propero Press, 1994.

Miller, Robert Ryal. *Mexico: A History.* Norman: University of Oklahoma Press, 1985.

Monterde, Francisco. *Bibliografía del teatro mexicano.* New York: Burt Franklin, 1970 (originally published 1933).

Morton, Desmond. *A Short History of Canada,* 2d ed. Toronto: McClelland & Stewart, 1994.

Moses, Montrose J. *Famous Actor-Families in America.* New York: Thomas Crowell, 1906. (Reprint, Greenwood Press, 1968.)

Mullin, Donald. *Victorian Actors and Actresses in Review: A Dictionary of Contemporary Views of Representative British and American Actors and Actresses, 1837–1901.* Westport, Conn.: Greenwood Press, 1983.

———. *The Development of the Playhouse: A Survey of Theatre Architecture from the Renaissance to the Present.* Berkeley and Los Angeles: University of California Press, 1970.

New, William H., ed. *Dramatists in Canada: Selected Essays.* Vancouver: University of British Columbia Press, 1972.

Olavarría y Ferrari, Enrique de. *Reseña historica del teatro en México 1539–1911.* 5 vols. México: Editorial Porrua, 1961.

Owen, Bobbi. *Costume Design on Broadway: Designers and Their Credits, 1915–85.* New York: Greenwood Press, 1987.

———. *Lighting Design on Broadway. Designers and Their Credits, 1915–90.* New York: Greenwood Press, 1991.

———. *Scenic Design on Broadway: Designers and Their Credits, 1915–90.* New York: Greenwood Press, 1991.

Pasarell, Emilio J. *Origenes y desarrollo de la afición teatral en Puerto Rico.* Vol. 1, San Juan: Universidad de Puerto Rico, 1951; vol. 2, Río Piedras: Universidad de Puerto Rico, 1967.

Poggi, Jack. *Theatre in America: The Impact of Economic Forces, 1870–1967.* Ithaca, N.Y.: Cornell University Press, 1968.

Quinn, Arthur Hobson. *A History of the American Drama From the Beginning to the Civil War.* 2d ed. New York: Appleton-Century-Crofts, 1943.

Reyes de la Maza, Luis. *Cien años de teatro en México (1810–1910).* México: Sep/Setentas, 1972.

Richardson, Gary A. *American Drama From the Colonial Period Through World War I: A Critical History.* New York: Twayne Publishers, 1993.

Robinson, Alice M., Vera Mowry Roberts, and Milly S. Barranger, eds. *Notable Women in the American Theatre: A Biographical Dictionary.* New York: Greenwood Press, 1989.

Rubin, Don, ed. *The World Encyclopedia of Contemporary Theatre.* Vol. 2, *Americas.* London: Routledge, 1996.

Saddlemyer, Ann, ed. *Early Stages: Theatre in Ontario 1800–1914.* Toronto: University of Toronto Press, 1990.

Schlarman, J. H. *Mexico: A Land of Volcanoes: From Cortés to Alemán.* Milwaukee: Bruce Publishing, 1950.

Seller, Maxine Schwartz, ed. *Ethnic Theatre in the United States.* Westport, Conn.: Greenwood Press, 1983.

Shattuck, Charles H. *Shakespeare on the American Stage: From the Hallams to Edwin Booth.* Washington, D.C.: The Folger Shakespeare Library, 1976.

Smith, Bradley. *Mexico: A History in Art.* Garden City: Doubleday, 1968.

Smith, Cecil and Glenn Linton. *Musical Comedy in America.* New York: Theatre Arts Books, 1981.

Southern, Eileen. *The Music of Black Americans: A History.* 3d ed. New York: W. W. Norton, 1997.

Spritz, Kenneth. *Theatrical Evolution: 1776–1976.* Yonkers, N.Y.: Hudson River Museum, 1976.

Teurbe Tolón, Edwin and Jorge Antonio González. *Historia del teatro en La Habana.* Vol. 1. Santa Clara, Cuba: Universidad Central de las Villas, 1961.

*Theatre World.* Ed. Daniel Blum (1944–64); John Willis (1965–present). New York: Crown Publishers, 1944–91; Applause Books, 1992–present.

Usigli, Rodolfo. *Mexico in the Theater.* Trans. Wilder P. Scott. University, Miss.: Romance Monographs, 1976.

Versényi, Adam. *Theatre in Latin America: Religion, Politics, and Culture from Cortés to the 1980s.* Cambridge: Cambridge University Press, 1993.

Wagner, Anton, ed. *Canada's Lost Plays.* Vol. 4, *Colonial Quebec: French–Canadian Drama, 1606–1966.* Toronto: Canadian Theatre Review Publications, 1982.

Wagner, Anton and Richard Plant, eds. *Canada's Lost Plays.* Vol. 1, *The Nineteenth Century.* Toronto: Canadian Theatre Review Publications, 1978.

Weiss, Jonathan M. *French Canadian Theater.* Boston: Twayne Publishers, 1986.

Wilmeth, Don B., ed. (with Tice L. Miller). *Cambridge Guide to American Theatre.* (updated version) New York: Cambridge University Press, 1996.

Wilson, Garff. *A History of American Acting.* Bloomington: Indiana University Press, 1966. (Reprint, Greenwood Press, 1980.)

Witham, Barry B., ed. *Theatre in the United States: A Documentary History.* Vol. 1, *1750–1915: Theatre in the Colonies and United States.* New York: Cambridge University Press, 1996.

Woll, Allen. *Black Musical Theatre: From "Coontown" to "Dreamgirls."* Baton Rouge: Louisiana State University Press, 1989.

Young, William C. *Documents of American Theatre History.* Vol. 1, *Famous American Playhouses, 1716–1899*; vol. 2, *Famous American Playhouses, 1900–1971.* Chicago: American Library Association, 1973.

———. *Famous Actors and Actresses on the American Stage: Documents of American Theatre History.* 2 vols. New York: R. R. Bowker, 1975.

## 1: PRE-COLUMBIAN PERFORMANCE

Acuña, René. *Farsas y representaciones escénicas de los mayas antiguos.* Mexico: Universidad Nacional Autónoma de México, 1978.

———. *Introducción al estudio del Rabinal Achí.* Mexico: UNAM, Instituto de Investigaciones Filológicas, 1975.

Arrom, José Juan. "Drama of the Ancients." *Américas* 4 (March 1952), 16–19.

Austin, Mary. "American Indian Dance Drama." *The Yale Review* 19:4 (June 1930), 732–45.

———. "Primitive Stage Setting." *Theatre Arts Monthly* 12 (January 1928), 49–59.

Azor, Ileana. *Orígen y presencia del teatro en nuestra América.* La Habana, Cuba: Editorial Las Letras Cubanas, 1988.

Bailey, Forence Merriam. "Some Plays and Dances of the Taos Indians." *Natural History* 24 (1924), 85–95.

Balmori, Clemente H. "Teatro aborígen americano." *Estudios americanos* 9:45 (1955), 577–601.

Blanchard, David. "Entertainment, Dance, and Northern Mohawk Showmanship." *American Indian Quarterly* 7:1 (1983), 2–26.

Blish, Helen. "The Drama of the Sioux Sun Dance." *Theatre Arts Monthly* (August 1933), 629–34.

Brenner, Anita. *Idols Behind Altars.* New York: Biblo & Tannen, 1967.

Breslin, Patrick. "Coping with Change: The Maya Discover the Play's the Thing." *Smithsonian* 23:5 (August 1992), 78–87.

Carrasco, David and Eduardo Matos Moctezuma. *Moctezuma's Mexico: Visions of the Aztec World.* Niwot: University Press of Colorado, 1992.

Cid Perez, Jose and Dolores Marti de Cid. *Teatro indio precolombino: El Güegüense o macho ratón, El varón de Rabinal, Ollantay.* Avila, Spain: Aguilar, 1964.

Clendinnen, Inga. *Aztecs: An Interpretation.* New York: Cambridge University Press, 1993.

Coe, Michael, Dean Snow, and Elizabeth Benson. *Atlas of Ancient America.* New York: Facts on File, 1990.

Craven, Roy C. *Ceremonial Centers of the Maya.* With an introduction by William R. Bullard Jr. Gainesville: University Presses of Florida, 1974.

Díaz, Gisele and Alan Rodgers. *The Codex Borgia: A Full-Color Restoration of the Ancient Mexican Manuscript.* With a new introduction and commentary by Bruce E. Byland. New York: Dover, 1993.

Drucker, Philip. *Cultures of the North Pacific Coast.* San Francisco: Chandler Publishing, 1965.

———. "Kwakiutl Dancing Societies." *Anthropological Records* 2:6 (1940), 201–30.

Durán, Fray Diego. *The Aztecs: The History of the Indies of New Spain.* Trans., with notes, Doris Heyden and Fernando Horcasitas. New York: Orion Press, 1964.

———. *Book of the Gods and Rites and the Ancient Calendar.* Trans. and ed. Fernando Horcasitas and Doris Heyden. Norman: University of Oklahoma Press, 1971.

———. *Historia de las Indias de Nueva España y Islas de Tierra Firme.* Mexico: Editiones de Ramírez, 1880.

Erdman, Harley. "Náhuatl Performance: Feasts and Farces of Pre-Columbian Mexico." *Theatre Topics* 2:2 (September 1992), 149–59.

Ernst, Alice Henson. "Masks of the Northwest Coast." *Theatre Arts Monthly* (August 1933), 646–56.

Freidel, David, Linda Schele, and Joy Parker. *Maya Cosmos: Three Thousand Years on the Shaman's Path.* New York: William Morrow, 1993.

Frisbie, Charlotte, ed. *Southwestern Indian Ritual Drama.* Albuquerque: University of New Mexico Press, 1980.

Gilmore, Frances. *The King Danced in the Marketplace.* Salt Lake City: University of Utah Press, 1977.

Girard, Rafael. "Una obra maestra del teatro maya." *Cuadernos americanos* 36 (Nov.–Dec. 1947), 157–88.

Harvey, Byron, III. *Ritual in Pueblo Art: Hopi Life in Hopi Painting.* Vol. 24 of Contributions from the Museum of the American Indian. New York: Heye Foundation, 1970.

Hayes, H. R. *Children of the Raven: The Seven Indian Nations of the Northwest Coast.* New York: McGraw–Hill, 1975.

Heth, Charlotte, ed. *Native American Dance: Ceremonies and Social Traditions.* Washington, D.C.: National Museum of the American Indian, Smithsonian Institution with Starwood Publishing, 1993.

Highwater, Jamake. *Arts of the Indian Americas: Leaves from the Sacred Tree.* New York: Harper & Row, 1983.

Hoffman, James. "Towards an Early British Columbia Theatre: The Hamatsa Ceremony as Drama." *Canadian Drama/ L'Art dramatique canadien* 11:1 (1985), 231–44.

Huntsman, Jeffrey F. "Native American Theatre." In *Ethnic Theatre in the United States*. Ed. Maxine Schwartz Seller, 355–85. Westport, Conn.: Greenwood Press, 1983.

Iglesia, Ramón. *Columbus, Cortés, and Other Essays*. Trans. and ed. Lesley Byrd Simpson. Berkeley and Los Angeles: University of California Press, 1969.

International Institute for Comparative Music Studies. *Inuit Games and Songs/Chants et Jeux des Inuit, Canada*. Berlin/Venice: UNESCO Collection "Musical Sources."

Isaacs, Edith J. R., ed. *Theatre Arts Monthly* 17:8 (August 1933). Special issue: "The Dramatic Arts of the American Indian."

Jennings, Francis. *The Founders of America: From the Earliest Migrations to the Present*. New York: W. W. Norton, 1993.

Josephy, Alvin M., Jr. *500 Nations: An Illustrated History of North American Indians*. New York: Alfred A. Knopf, 1994.

Kelly, Isabel T. "Southern Paiute Shamanism." *Anthropological Records* 2:4 (1939), 151–67.

Landa, Diego de. *Landa's Relación de las cosas de Yucatán: A Translation*. Ed., with notes, by Alfred M. Tozzer. Vol. 18 of Papers of the Peabody Museum of American Archaeology and Ethnology. Cambridge, Mass.: Harvard University Press, 1941. (Reprint, Kraus Reprint Corporation, 1966.)

Lantis, Margaret. *Alaskan Eskimo Ceremonialism*. Seattle: University of Washington Press, 1947. (Reprint, 1966.)

Laski, Vera P. "The Raingod Ceremony of the Tewa: A Religious Drama." In *The Masterkey for Indian Lore and History*, 76–84. Los Angeles: Southwest Museum, 1957.

———. *Seeking Life*. Philadelphia: American Folklore Society, 1958.

Leon–Portilla, Miguel. *Literatura de Mexico antiguo: los textos en lengua nahuatl*. Caracas: Biblioteca Ayacucho, 1978.

———. *Literaturas indígenas de México*. México: Editorial Mapfre: Fondo de Cultura Económica, 1995.

———. "Teatro nahuatl prehispanico." *La Palabra y el hombre* 9 (Feb.–Mar. 1959), 13–36.

Lothrop, S. K. "A Note on Indian Ceremonies in Guatemala." *Indian Notes* 4 (1927), 68–81.

Mace, Carroll E. "New Information about Dance–Dramas of Rabinal and the *Rabinal-Achí*." *Xavier University Studies* 1 (1967), 1–20.

Maxwell, James A., ed. *America's Fascinating Indian Heritage*. Pleasantville, N.Y.: Reader's Digest Association, 1978.

Monterde, Francisco. *Bibliografía del teatro en Mexico*. New York: Burt Franklin, 1970. (Reprint of 1933 edition.)

———. "Prólogo." *Teatro Indígena prehispánico (Rabinal Achí)*. Mexico: Ediciones de la Universidad Nacional Autonoma, 1955.

Mooney, James. *The Ghost-Dance Religion and the Sioux Outbreak of 1890*. Annual report 14, part 2. Washington, D.C.: Bureau of American Ethnology, 1896.

Ortiz, Alfonso, ed. *New Perspectives on the Pueblos*. Albuquerque: University of New Mexico Press, 1972.

Radin, Paul. *The Road of Life and Death: A Ritual Drama of the American Indians*. Bollingen Series 5. Princeton: Princeton University Press, 1991.

Ravicz, Marillyn Ekdahl. *Early Colonial Religious Drama in Mexico: From Tzompantli to Golgotha*. Washington, D.C.: Catholic University of America Press, 1970.

Ray, Dorothy Jean. *Eskimo Masks: Art and Ceremony*. Seattle: University of Washington Press, 1967.

Raynaud, Georges. *Teatro indígena prehispánica (Rabinal Achí)*. Mexico: Ediciones de la Universidad Autonoma, 1955.

Rodriguez Rouanet, Francisco. "Notas sobre una representación actual del Rabinal Achí o Baile del Tun." *Guatemala indígena* 2:1 (1962), 45–56.

Roediger, Virginia More. *Ceremonial Costumes of the Pueblo Indians: Their Evolution, Fabrication, and Significance in the Prayer Drama*. With new introduction by Fred Eggan. Berkeley and Los Angeles: University of California Press, 1991.

Royaards, Rense. *Mexican Drama*. Trans. Christine Bloom. Amsterdam: International Theatre Bookshop, 1992.

Sahagún, Fray Bernardino de. *Historia general de las cosas de Nueva España*, 4 vols. Mexico: Ed. Porrúa, 1956.

———. *Florentine Codex: General History of the Things of New Spain*. Book 2, *The Ceremonies*. Trans. from the Aztec into English, with notes and illustrations, by Arthur J. O. Anderson and Charles E. Dibble. Monographs of the School of American Research, no. 14, part 3. Santa Fe: 1951.

Salmoral, Manuel Lucena. *America 1492: Portrait of a Continent Five Hundred Years Ago*. New York: Facts on File, 1990.

Schele, Linda and Mary Ellen Miller. *The Blood of Kings: Dynasty and Ritual in Maya Art*. New York: George Braziller, 1986.

Séjourné, Laurette. *Teotihuacan, métropole de l'amérique*. Paris: François Maspero, 1969.

Shank, Theodore. "A Return to Mayan and Aztec Roots." *The Drama Review* 18:4 (Dec. 1974), 56–70.

Soustelle, Jacques. *The Olmecs: The Oldest Civilization in Mexico*. Trans. Helen R. Lane. Garden City, N.Y.: Doubleday, 1984.

Sten, María. *Vida y muerte del teatro náhuatl*. México D.F.: Secretaria de Educación Pública, 1974.

Stuart, Gene S. and George E. Stuart. *Lost Kingdoms of the Maya*. Washington, D.C.: National Geographic Society, 1993.

Symington, Fraser. *The Canadian Indian: The Illustrated History of the Great Tribes of Canada*. Toronto: McClelland & Stewart, 1969.

Tedlock, Barbara "Zuñi Sacred Theatre." *American Indian Quarterly* 7:3 (Summer 1983), 93–110.

Thomas, David Hurst, Jay Miller, Richard White, Peter Nabokov, and Philip J. Deloria. *The Native Americans: An Illustrated History*. Atlanta: Turner Publishing, 1993.

Toriz, Martha. *La fiesta prehispánica: un espectáculo teatral*. México D.F.: Instituto Nacional de Bellas Artes, 1993.

Townsend, Richard Fraser. *The Aztecs*. London: Thames & Hudson, 1992.

———. *State and Cosmos in the Art of Tenochtitlan*. Vol. 20 of Studies in Pre-Columbian Art and Archaeology. Washington, D.C.: Trustees for Harvard University, 1979.

Walker, James R. *Lakota Belief and Ritual*. Ed. Raymond J. DeMallie and Elaine A. Jahner. Lincoln: University of Nebraska Press, 1980.

## 2: THEATRE IN NEW SPAIN, THE AMERICAN COLONIES, AND NEW FRANCE

### New Spain and the Caribbean

Aguirre, Yolanda. *Apuntes en torno al Teatro Colonial en Cuba (1790–1833)*. La Habana: Impresora Universitaria "Andre Voisin," 1969.

Alonso, Amado. "Biografía de Fernán González de Eslava." *Revista de Filología Hispánica* 2:3 (1940), 213–321.

Arrom, José Juan. "Criollo: definición y mátices de un concepto." *Hispania* 34:2 (May 1951), 172–76.

———. *Historia del teatro hispanoamericano (epoca colonial)*. Mexico: Ediciones de Andrea, 1967.

Arróniz, Othón. *Teatro de evangelización en nueva españa*. Mexico: Universidad Nacional Autónoma de México, 1979.

Barker, George C., ed. and trans. *The Shepherds' Play of the Prodigal Son (Coloquio de pastores del hijo pródigo)* Berkeley and Los Angeles: University of California Press, 1953.

Burkhart, Louise M. *Holy Wednesday: A Nahua Drama from Early Colonial Mexico*. Philadelphia: University of Pennsylvania Press, 1996.

Castañeda, C. E. "The First American Play." *The Catholic World* 134:802 (January 1932), 429–37.

Cortés, Hernan. *Letters from Mexico*. Trans. and ed. Anthony Pagden. With an introduction by J. H. Elliott. New Haven, Conn.: Yale University Press, 1986.

de la Cruz, Sor Juana Inés. *A Sor Juana Anthology*. Trans. Alan S. Trueblood. With a foreword by Octavio Paz. Cambridge: Harvard University Press, 1988.

———. *Obras completas*. Prologue by Francisco Monterde. México: Editorial Porrúa, 1992.

Díaz del Castillo, Bernal. *The Discovery and Conquest of Mexico*. Trans. with an introduction and notes by A. P. Maudslay, and a new introduction by Hugh Thomas. New York: Da Capo Press, 1996.

Frischman, Donald H. "Active Ethnicity: Nativism, Otherness, and Indian Theatre in Mexico." *Gestos* 6:11 (April 1991), 113–26.

Flynn, Gerard. *Sor Juana Inés de la Cruz*. New York: Twayne Publishers, 1971.

García Icazbalceta, D. J. *Obras*. Vol. 2, Opúscolos varios. Mexico: V. Agüeros, 1896.

Garibay, Angel María. *Historia de la literatura nahuatl.* Vol. 2. Mexico: Editorial Porrua, 1954.

Gillmore, Frances. "The Dance Dramas of Mexican Villages." *University of Arizona Bulletin* (Humanities Bulletin 5) 14:2 (April 1, 1943), 5–28.

———. "Spanish Texts of Three Dance Dramas from Mexican Villages." *University of Arizona Bulletin* (Humanities Bulletin 4) 13:4 (October 1, 1942), 3–83.

González de Eslava, Fernán. *Coloquios espirituales y sacramentales.* 2 vols. Mexico: Porrua, 1958.

Gorham, Sarah. "The Celibate Matriarch." *Et Ultra* (Winter–Spring 1991), 10–12.

Hill, Errol. *The Jamaican Stage 1655–1900: Profile of a Colonial Theatre.* Amherst: University of Massachusetts Press, 1992.

Horcasitas, Fernando. *El teatro náhuatl: epocas novohispana y moderna.* Mexico: Universidad Nacional Autonóma de Mexico, 1974.

Icaza, Francisco A. de. "Orígenes del teatro en México." *Boletín de la real academia española* 2 (1915), 57–76. (Includes text of *Desposorio espiritual* [1574] by Juan Perez Ramirez.)

Iglesia, Ramón. *Columbus, Cortés, and Other Essays.* Trans. and ed. Lesley Byrd Simpson. Berkeley and Los Angeles: University of California Press, 1969.

Johnson, Harvey L. "El primer dramaturgo americano—Fernán González de Eslava." *Hispania* 24:2 (May 1941), 161–70.

———. "The Staging of González de Eslava's *Coloquios.*" *Hispanic Review* 8:4 (October 1940), 343–46.

Le Clézio, J. M. G. *The Mexican Dream; or, The Interrupted Thought of Amerindian Civilizations.* Trans. Teresa Lavender Fagan. Chicago: University of Chicago Press, 1993.

Leonard, Irving A. "The 1790 Theater Season of the Mexico City Coliseo." *Hispanic Review* 19:2 (April 1951), 104–20.

Lockhart, James. *The Nahuas After the Conquest: A Social and Cultural History of the Indians of Central Mexico, Sixteenth through Eighteenth Centuries.* Stanford: Stanford University Press, 1992.

———, Frances Berdan, Arthur J. O. Anderson. *The Tlaxcalan Actas: A Compendium of the Records of the Cabildo of Tlaxcala (1545–1627).* Salt Lake City: University of Utah Press, 1986.

Magnus, Jaime Chabaud. "Directoras de escena novohispanas del siglo XVII." *Latin American Theatre Review* 23:1 (Fall 1989), 111–17.

Mañon, Manuel. *Historia del teatro principal de México.* México: Editorial Cultura, 1932.

María y Campos, Armando de. *Guía de representaciones teatrales en la Nueva España (siglos XVI al XVIII).* Ed. B. Costa-Amic. México D.F.: Colleción La Máscara, 1959.

McKendrick, Melveena. *Theatre in Spain 1490–1700.* Cambridge: Cambridge University Press, 1989.

Motolinía, Fray Toribio de Benavente. *Historia de los indios de la nueva España.* Mexico: Editorial Salvador Chavez Hayhoe, 1941.

Paz, Octavio. *Sor Juana; or, The Traps of Faith.* Trans. Margaret Sayers Peden. Cambridge, Mass.: Belknap Press of Harvard University Press, 1988.

Pazos, P. Manuel R. "El teatro franciscano en Méjico, durante el siglo XVI." *Archivo Ibero–Americano* 11:42 (April–June 1951), 129–89.

Rael, Juan B. *The Sources and Diffusion of the Mexican Shepherds' Plays.* Guadalajara: Libreria La Joyita, 1965.

Ramos Smith, Maya. *El Actor en México: Entre el Coliseo y el Principal (1753–1821).* México: Grupo Editorial Gaceta, 1994.

Ravicz, Marilyn Ekdahl. *Early Colonial Religious Drama in Mexico: From Tzompantli to Golgotha.* Washington, D.C.: Catholic University of America Press, 1970. (This study includes English translations of *The Last Judgment*, *The Destruction of Jerusalem*, and other early religious dramas.)

Recchia, Giovanna. *Espacio Teatral en la ciudad de méxico siglos XVI–XVIII.* México D.F.: INBA/CITRU, 1993.

Robe, Stanley L., ed. *Coloquios de pastores from Jalisco, Mexico.* Berkeley and Los Angeles: University of California Press, 1954.

Rojas Garcidueñas, José. *El teatro de Nueva España en le siglo XVI.* Mexico: Luís Alvarez, 1935.

Schilling, Hildburg. *Teatro profano en la Nueva España.* Mexico: Imprenta Universitaria, 1958.

Spell, J.R. "The Theatre in New Spain in the Early Eighteenth Century." *Hispanic Review* 15 (1947), 137–64.

Tolón, Edwin Teurbe and Jorge Antonio González. *Historia del teatro en La Habana.* Santa Clara: Universidad Central de las Villas, 1961.

Torres Rioseco, A. *Ensayos sobre literatura latinoamericana.* Mexico: Tezontle, 1953.

Trenti Rocamora, J. Luis. *El Teatro en la America colonial.* Buenos Aires: Editorial Huarpes

Tyre, Carl Allen, ed. *Religious Plays of 1590.* Vol. 8 of University of Iowa Studies in Spanish Language and Literature. Iowa City: University of Iowa, 1938.

Usigli, Rodolfo. *Mexico in the Theatre.* Trans. with an introduction by Wilder P. Scott. University, Miss.: Romance Monographs, 1976.

Versényi, Adeam. "Getting under the Aztec Skin: Evangelical Theatre in the New World." *New Theatre Quarterly* 5 (August 1989), 217–26.

Viveros, Germán. *Teatro dieciochesco de Nueva España.* México: Universidad Nacional Autónoma de México, 1990.

Weiss, Judith A. *Latin American Popular Theatre: The First Five Centuries.* Albuquerque: University of New Mexico Press, 1993.

Xirau, Ramón. *Genio y figura de Sor Juana Inés de la Cruz.* Buenos Aires: Editorial Universitaria, 1967.

### The American Colonies

Brown, Jared. *The Theatre in America during the Revolution.* New York: Cambridge University Press, 1995.

Dunlap, William. *History of the American Theatre.* New York: Burt Franklin, 1963.

Gutierrez, Ramón A. "El drama de la conquista de Nuevo México." *Gestos* 4:8 (Nov. 1989), 73–86.

Hawke, David Freeman. *Everyday Life in Early America.* Perennial Library. New York: Harper & Row, 1989.

Holifield, E. Brooks. *Era of Persuasion: American Thought and Culture 1521–1680.* Boston: Twayne, 1989.

Kahan, Gerald. *George Alexander Stevens and The Lecture on Heads.* Athens: University of Georgia Press, 1984.

Kritzer, Amelia Howe, ed. *Plays by Early American Women, 1775–1850.* Ann Arbor: University of Michigan Press, 1995.

Rankin, Hugh F. *The Theater in Colonial America.* Chapel Hill: University of North Carolina Press, 1965.

Ritchey, David, ed. *A Guide to the Baltimore Stage in the Eighteenth Century: A History and Day Book Calendar.* Westport, Conn.: Greenwood Press, 1982.

Willis, Eola. *The Charleston Stage in the XVIII Century.* New York: Benjamin Blom, 1968. (Originally published 1933.)

### New France

Arbour, Roméo. "*Le Théâtre de Neptune* de Marc Lescarbot." In *Archives des lettres canadiennes.* Vol. 5, *Le Théâtre canadien–français,* 21–31. Montreal: Fides, 1976.

Bond, F. Fraser. "America's Premier 'First Night'—1606." *Dalhousie Review* 36 (Winter 1957), 392–98.

Burger, Baudouin. "Les Spectacles dramatiques en Nouvelle-France (1606–1760)." In *Archives des lettres canadiennes.* Vol. 5, *Le Théâtre canadien–français,* 33–57. Montreal: Fides, 1976.

Hicks, R.K. "Le Théâtre de Neptune." *Queen's Quarterly* 34 (October 1926), 215–23.

Lescarbot, Marc. *The Theatre of Neptune in New France.* Trans. Eugene Benson and Renate Benson. In *Canada's Lost Plays,* Vol. 4. Ed. Anton Wagner. Toronto: Canadian Theatre Review Publications, 1982.

Macdougall, Angus J., S.J. "An Historical Sidelight—Quebec 1658." *Culture* 11 (January 1950), 15–28.

Marion, Séraphin. "Le Tartuffe et Mgr de Saint-Vallier." Chap. 1 in *Les Lettres canadiennes d'autrefois.* Vol. 8, *Littérateurs et Moralistes du Canada français d'autrefois,* 15–37. Ottawa: Editions de l'Université, 1954.

Roquebrune, Robert de. "Le Théâtre au Canada en 1694: L'affaire du Tartuffe." *Revue de l'histoire des colonies françaises* 19 (March–April 1931), 181–94.

Waldo, Lewis P. *The French Drama in America in the Eighteenth Century and its Influence on the American Drama of that Period, 1701–1800.* Baltimore: Johns Hopkins Press, 1942.

**3: THE POSTCOLONIAL STRUGGLE FOR NATIONAL IDENTITY**

### United States

Archer, Stephen M. *Junius Brutus Booth; Theatrical Prometheus.* Carbondale: Southern Illinois University Press, 1992.

Clapp, William W. Jr. *A Record of the Boston Stage.* New York: Greenwood Press, 1969. (Reprint of 1853 edition published by James Monroe and Co.)

Dunlap, William. *History of the American Theatre.* 2 vols., 1832. (Reprint, New York: Burt Franklin, 1963.)

Glazer, Irvin R. *Philadelphia Theatre: A Pictorial Architectural History.* New York: Atheneum of Philadelphia and Dover Publications, 1994.

Hill, West T. *The Theatre in Early Kentucky: 1790–1820.* Lexington: University Press of Kentucky, 1971.

Hewitt, Bernard. "King Stephen' of the Park and Drury Lane" in *The Theatrical Manager in England and America.* Ed. Joseph W. Donohue Jr. Princeton, N.J.: Princeton University Press, 1971.

Hoole, W. Stanley. *The Ante-Bellum Charleston Theatre.* Tuscaloosa: University of Alabama Press, 1946.

Kendall, John S. *The Golden Age of the New Orleans Theatre.* New York: Greenwood Press, 1968.

McDermott, Douglas. "The Development of Theatre on the American Frontier, 1750–1890." *Theatre Survey* 19:1 (May 1978), 63–78.

McNamara, Brooks. *The American Playhouse in the Eighteenth Century.* Cambridge, Mass.: Harvard University Press, 1969.

Meserve, Walter J. *An Emerging Entertainment: The Drama of the American People to 1828.* Bloomington and London: Indiana University Press, 1977.

Péladeau, Marius B., ed. *The Verse of Royall Tyler.* Charlottesville: University Press of Virginia, 1968.

Porter, Susan L. *With an Air Debonnair: Musical Theatre in America, 1785–1815.* Washington and London: Smithsonian Institution Press, 1991.

Shockley, Martin Staples. *The Richmond Stage: 1784–1812.* Charlottesville: University Press of Virginia, 1977.

Shattuck, Charles. "The Romantic Acting of Junius Brutus Booth." *Nineteenth Century Theatre Research* 5 (Spring 1977), 1–26.

Smith, Geddeth. *Thomas Abthorpe Cooper: America's Premier Tragedian.* Madison, N.J.: Fairleigh Dickinson Press, 1996.

### Mexico

Calderón de la Barca, Fanny. *Life in Mexico.* Ed., and annotated by Howard T. Fisher and Marion Hall Fisher. New York: Doubleday, 1966.

Reyes de la Maza, Luis. *El teatro en México durante la independencia (1810–39).* México: Universidad Nacional Autónoma de México, 1969.

### Canada

Bernard, John. *Retrospections of America 1797–1811.* New York: Harper & Bros., 1887.

Bourassa, André. "The Rebirth of French Theatre in the Province of Quebec, 1765–1825." *Theatre Symposium* 2 (Spring 1994), 82–96.

———. "Renaissance de la culture française au Québec après la cession de la colonie aux Britanniques: rôle des gens de théâtre venus du sud-est américain." *Canadian Review of American Studies* 24:3 (Fall 1994), 53–101.

Burger, Baudouin. *L'Activité théâtrale au Québec (1765–1825).* Montreal: Les Editions Parti Pris, 1974.

Hayne, David M. "Le Théâtre de Joseph Quesnel" in *Le Théâtre canadien français* 5 (1976), 109–17.


## 4: ROMANTIC ENACTMENTS, 1825–70

### United States

Bank, Rosemarie K. *Theatre Culture in America, 1825–60.* New York: Cambridge University Press, 1997.

Barnes, Eric Wollencott. *The Lady of Fashion: The Life and the Theatre of Anna Cora Mowatt.* New York: Charles Scribner's Sons, 1954.

Berson, Misha. *The San Francisco Stage,* part 1, *From the Gold Rush to Golden Spike, 1849–69. San Francisco Performing Arts Library & Museum Journal* 2 (1989).

Carson, G. B. William. *Managers in Distress: The St. Louis Stage, 1840–44.* St. Louis: St. Louis Historical Documents Foundation, 1949.

———. *The Theatre on the Frontier: The Early Years of the St. Louis Stage.* Chicago: University of Chicago, 1932. (2d ed. Benjamin Blom, 1965.)

Dempsey, David with Raymond P. Baldwin. *The Triumphs and Trials of Lotta Crabtree.* New York: William Morrow, 1968.

Ernst, Alice Henson. *Trouping in the Oregon Country: A History of Frontier Theatre.* Portland: Oregon Historical Society, 1961. (Reprint, Greenwood Press, 1974.)

Gagey, Edmond. *The San Francisco Stage: A History.* New York: Columbia University Press, 1950. (Reprint, Greenwood Press, 1970.)

Grimsted, David. *Melodrama Unveiled: American Theatre and Culture, 1800–1850.* Chicago: University of Chicago Press, 1968.

Hodge, Francis. *Yankee Theatre: The Image of America on the Stage, 1825–50.* Austin: University of Texas Press, 1964.

Hutton, Lawrence. *Plays and Players.* New York: Hurd & Houghton, 1875.

Koon, Helene Wickham. *How Shakespeare Won the West: Players and Performances in America's Gold Rush, 1849–65.* Jefferson, N.C.: McFarland, 1989.

Leach, Joseph. *Bright, Particular Star.* New Haven: Yale University Press, 1970.

MacMinn, George R. *The Theatre of the Golden Era in California.* Caldwell, Idaho: Caxton Printers, 1941.

Mankowitz, Wolf. *Mazeppa.* London: Blond & Briggs, 1982.

Marshall, Dorothy. *Fanny Kemble.* New York: St. Martin's Press, 1977.

Martin, George. *Verdi at the Golden Gate: Opera and San Francisco in the Gold Rush Years.* Berkeley and Los Angeles: University of California Press, 1993.

Mason, Jeffrey D. *Melodrama and the Myth of America.* Bloomington: Indiana University Press, 1993.

Meserve, Walter J. *Heralds of Promise: The Drama of the American People during the Age of Jackson, 1829–49.* New York: Greenwood Press, 1986.

Moody, Richard. *Edwin Forrest: First Star of the American Stage.* New York: Alfred A. Knopf, 1960.

Murdoch, James E. *The Stage; or Recollections of Actors and Acting from an Experience of Fifty Years, 1880.* (Reprint, Benjamin Blom, 1969.)

Overmyer, Grace. *America's First Hamlet* [John Howard Payne]. New York: New York University Press, 1957.

Riddle, Ronald. *Flying Dragons, Flowing Streams: Music in the Life of San Francisco's Chinese.* Westport, Conn.: Greenwood Press, 1983.

Saxon, A. H. *P. T. Barnum: The Legend and the Man.* New York: Columbia University Press, 1989.

Southern, Eileen. "The Georgia Minstrels: The Early Years." *Inside the Minstrel Mask: Readings in Nineteenth-Century Blackface Minstrelsy.* Ed. Annemarie Bean, James V. Hatch, and Brooks McNamara, 163–75. Hanover: Wesleyan University Press, 1996.

Toll, Robert C. *Blacking Up: The Minstrel Show in Nineteenth-Century America.* New York: OUP, 1974.

Watson, Margaret G. *Silver Theatre: Amusements of the Mining Frontier in Early Nevada, 1850–64.* Glendale, Calif.: Arthur H. Clarke, 1964.

Wickham Koon, Helene. *How Shakespeare Won the West: Players and Performances in America's Gold Rush, 1849–65.* Jefferson, N.C.: McFarland, 1989.

### Mexico

Carilla, Emilio. *El teatro romántico en Hispanoamérica.* Bogotá: Instituto Caro y Cuervo, 1959.

Mayer, Brantz. *Mexico, As It Was and As It Is,* 3d ed. Philadelphia: G. B. Zieber, 1847.

Monterde, Francisco. "Una evasión romántica de Fernando Calderón." *Revista Iberoamericana* 17:33 (February 1951), 81–89.

Reyes de la Maza, Luis. *El teatro en 1857 y sus antecedentes (1855–56).* With an introduction by José Rojas de Garciolueñas. México: Instituto de Investigaciones Estéticas, 1956.

———. *El teatro en México durante el segundo imperio (1862–67).* México: Imprenta Universitaria, 1959.

———. *El teatro en México durante la independencia (1810–39).* México: Universidad Nacional Autónoma de México, 1969.

———. *El teatro en México entre la reforma y el imperio (1858–61).* México: Imprenta Universitaria, 1958.

Tolón, Edwin Teurbe and Jorge Antonio González. *Historia del teatro en La Habana.* Santa Clara: Universidad Central de las Villas, 1961.

Urbina, Alberto Trueba. *El Teatro de la República: Biografía de un gran coliseo* [Teatro Iturbide in Querétaro]. México: Ediciones Botas, 1954.

## Canada

Playfair, Giles. *The Flash of Lightning: A Portrait of Edmund Kean*. London: William Kimber, 1983.

Scribble, Sam. "Dolorsolatio." In *Canada's Lost Plays*. Vol. 1, *The Nineteenth Century*. Ed. Anton Wagner and Richard Plant. Toronto: CTR Publications, 1978.


## 5: TRADITION AND TRANSFORMATION: 1870–1900

### United States

Auster, Albert. *Actresses and Suffragists: Women in the American Theatre, 1890–1920*. New York: Praeger, 1984.

Bryan, Vernanne. *Laura Keene: A British Actress on the American Stage, 1826–73*. Jefferson, N.C.: McFarland, 1997.

Carlson, Marvin. *The Italian Shakespearians: Performances by Ristori, Salvini, and Rossi in England and America*. Washington, D.C.: Folger Shakespeare Library, 1985.

Clapp, John B. and Edwin F. Edgett, *Players of the Present*. Series 2, vols. 9, 11, 12. New York: The Dunlap Society, 1899–1901. (Reprint, Benjamin Blom, 1969.)

Coleman, Marion Moore. *Fair Rosalind: The American Career of Helena Modjeska*. 1969.

Curry, Jane Kathleen. *Nineteenth-Century American Women Theatre Managers*. Westport, Conn.: Greenwood Press, 1994.

Daly, Joseph Francis. *The Life of Augustin Daly*. New York: Macmillan, 1917.

Gregersen, Charles E. *Dankmar Adler, His Theatres and Auditoriums*. Athens: Ohio University Press, 1990.

Henneke, Ben Graf. *Laura Keene: Actress, Innovator, and Impresario*. Tulsa, Okla.: Council Oak Books, 1990.

Hornblow, Arthur. *Training for the Stage: Some Hints for Those About to Choose the Player's Career*. Philadelphia: J. B. Lippincott, 1916.

Hutton, Laurence. *Plays and Players*. New York: Hurd & Houghton, 1875.

Johnson, Claudia D. *American Actress: Perspective on the Nineteenth Century*. Chicago: Nelson–Hall, 1984.

Kimmel, Stanley. *The Mad Booths of Maryland*. Revised edition. New York: Dover, 1969.

Knepler, Henry. *The Gilded Stage: The Years of the Great International Actresses*. New York: William Morrow, 1968.

Kotsilibas–Davis, James. *Great Times, Good Times: The Odyssey of Maurice Barrymore*. Garden City, N.Y.: Doubleday, 1977.

Lewis, Philip C. *Trouping: How the Show Came to Town*. New York: Harper & Row, 1973.

Londré, Felicia Hardison. "Eleonora Duse: An Italian Actress on the American Stage," *Studies in Popular Culture* 8:2 (1985), 60–70.

Magnuson, Landis K. *Circle Stock Theatre: Touring American Small Towns, 1900–1960.* Jefferson, N.C.: McFarland, 1995.

McArthur, Benjamin. *Actors and American Culture, 1880–1920.* Philadelphia: Temple University Press, 1984.

McKay, Frederic Edward and Charles E. L. Wingate, eds. *Famous American Actors of Today.* 2 vols. New York: Thomas Y. Crowell, 1896.

McTeague, James H. *Before Stanislavsky: American Professional Acting Schools and Acting Theory, 1875–1925.* Metuchen, N.J.: Scarecrow Press, 1993.

Patterson, Ada. *Maude Adams, a Biography.* New York: Meyer Bros., 1908.

Robbins, Phyllis. *Maude Adams, an Intimate Biography.* New York: Putnam, 1956.

Sampson, Henry T. *The Ghost Walks: A Chronological History of Blacks in Show Business, 1865–1910.* Metuchen, N.J.: Scarecrow Press, 1988.

Seller, Maxine Schwartz, ed. *Ethnic Theatre in the United States.* Westport, Conn.: Greenwood Press, 1983.

Shattuck, Charles H. *The Hamlet of Edwin Booth.* Champaign: University of Illinois Press, 1969.

———. *Shakespeare on the American Stage: From Booth and Barrett to Sothern and Marlowe,* vol. 2. Washington, D.C.: Folger Shakespeare Library, 1987.

Skinner, Otis. *Footlights and Spotlights: Recollections of My Life on the Stage.* Indianapolis, Ind.: Bobbs–Merrill, 1923.

Sothern, Edward H. *The Melancholy Tale of "Me": My Remembrances.* New York: Charles Scribner's Sons, 1916.

Strang, Lewis C. *Famous Actors of the Day.* 1st Series. Boston: L. C. Page, 1899.

———. *Famous Actresses of the Day.* 1st Series. Boston: L. C. Page, 1899.

Stoddard, Richard. "Thomas Joyce, Edwin Booth's Costumer." *Educational Theatre Journal* 22 (March 1970), 71–77.

Toll, Robert C. *On with the Show: The First Century of Show Business in America.* New York: Oxford University Press, 1976.

Turner, Mary M. *Forgotten Leading Ladies of the American Theatre.* Jefferson, N.C.: McFarland, 1990.

Wallack, Lester. *Memories of Fifty Years.* New York: Charles Scribner's Sons, 1889.

Warde, Frederick. *Fifty Years of Make Believe.* New York: International Press Syndicate, 1920.

Watermeier, Daniel J., ed. *Edwin Booth's Performances: The Mary Isabella Stone Commentaries.* Ann Arbor, Mich.: UMI Research Press, 1990.

Wilson, Francis. *Francis Wilson's Life of Himself.* Boston: Houghton Mifflin, 1924.

Wilson, Garff B. *A History of American Acting.* Bloomington: Indiana University Press, 1966. (Reprint, Greenwood Press, 1980.)

Wilstach, Paul. *Richard Mansfield: The Man and the Actor.* New York: Charles Scribner's Sons, 1909.

Winter, William. *Ada Rehan: A Study.* New York: 1891. (Rev. ed., 1898.)

———. *Brief Chronicles.* New York: Dunlap Society, 1889. (Reprint, Burt Franklin, 1970.)

———. *Life and Art of Edwin Booth.* New York: Macmillan, 1893.

———. *Life and Art of Joseph Jefferson.* New York: Macmillan, 1984.

———. *Life and Art of Richard Mansfield.* 2 vols. New York: Moffat, Yard, 1913.

———. *Life of Tyrone Power.* New York: Moffat, Yard, 1913.

———. *Other Days: Being Chronicles and Memories of the Stage.* New York: Moffat, Yard, 1908.

———. *Shadows of the Stage.* New York: Macmillan, 1892.

———. *Shakespeare on the Stage.* 3 vols. New York: Macmillan, 1911–16.

———. *The Wallet of Time.* 2 vols. 1913. (Reprint, Benjamin Blom, 1969.)

## Mexico

Altamirano, Ignacio M. *La Literatura nacional: revistas, ensayos, biografías y prólogos.* 3 vols. Ed. with an introduction by José Luis Martinez. México: Editorial Porrua, 1949.

Guttiérrez Nájaro, Manuel. *Obras III: Crónicas y artículos sobre teatro, I (1876–80)* México: UNAM, 1974.

María y Campos, Armando de. *Los payasos, poetas del pueblo.* México: Ediciones Botas, 1939.

Martí, José. *Teatro.* Introduction by Rine Leal. La Habana: Editorial Letras Cubanas, 1981.

Olavarría y Ferrari, Enrique de. *Reseña historica del teatro en México, 1538–1911.* Vol. 2 and 3. México: Editorial Porrua, 1961.

Reyes de la Maza, Luis. *El teatro en México con Lerdo y Díaz (1873–79).* México: Imprenta Universitaria, 1963.

———. *El teatro en México en la época de Juárez (1868–72).* México: Imprenta Universitaria, 1961.

Rivera de Alvarez, Josefina. "Orígenes del teatro puertorriqueño: 'La juega de gallos o El negro bozal' de Ramón C. F. Caballero." *Revista del Instituto de Cultura Puertorriqueña* 3 (April–June 1959), 20–25.

## Canada

Beasley, David. "McKee Rankin: The Actor as Playwright." *Theatre History in Canada* 10:2 (Fall 1989), 115–31.

Booth, Michael R. "Gold Rush Theatres of the Klondike." *The Beaver,* no. 292 (Winnipeg, 1962), 32–37.

Brown, Mary M. "Entertainers of the Road." in *Early Stages: Theatre in Ontario 1800–1914.* Ed. Ann Saddlemyer, 123–65. Toronto: University of Toronto Press, 1990.

Craig, Irene. "Grease Paint on the Prairies." *Papers Read Before the Historical and Scientific Society of Manitoba* 3 (1947), 38–55.

Edwards, Murray D. *A Stage in Our Past: English-Language Theatre in Eastern Canada from the 1790s to 1914.* Toronto: University of Toronto Press, 1968.

Evans, Chad. *Frontier Theatre: A History of Nineteenth-Century Theatrical Entertainment in the Canadian Far West and Alaska.* Victoria, British Columbia: Sono Nis Press, 1983.

Filewood, Alan. "National Battles: Canadian Monumental Drama and the Investiture of History." *Modern Drama* 38 (1995), 71–85.

Gold, Arthur and Robert Fizdale. *The Divine Sarah: A Life of Sarah Bernhardt.* New York: Alfred A. Knopf, 1991.

Lawrence, Robert G. "Dramatic History: H. M. S. Parliament." *Canadian Theatre Review* 19 (Summer 1978), 38–45.

Marion, Séraphin. "Dramaturges français et moralistes canadiens." In *Les Lettres canadiennes d'autrefois.* Vol. 8, *Littérateurs et moralistes du Canada français d'autrefois.* Ottawa: Editions de l'Université, 1954.

Massicotte, E. Z. "A. V. Brazeau, auteur et comédien." *Bulletin des recherches historiques* 23:2 (1917), 62–63.

———. "Eglise, théâtre, manufacture." *Bulletin des recherches historiques* 45:10 (1949), 316–19.

Shrive, Norman. "Poets and Patriotism: Charles Mair and *Tecumseh.*" In *Dramatists in Canada: Selected Essays.* Ed. William H. New, 27–38. Vancouver: University of British Columbia Press, 1972.

Stuart, E. Ross. *The History of Prairie Theatre: The Development of Theatre in Alberta, Manitoba, and Saskatchewan 1833–1982* (Canadian Theatre History No. 2). Toronto: Simon & Pierre, 1984.

## 6: ENTERTAINMENT AND ART: 1900–1945

### United States

Allen, Robert C. *Horrible Prettiness: Burlesque and American Culture.* Chapel Hill: University of North Carolina Press, 1991.

Barrow, Kenneth. *Helen Hayes, First Lady of the American Theatre.* Garden City, N.Y.: Doubleday, 1985.

Binns, Archie. *Mrs. Fiske and the American Theatre.* New York: Crown Publisher, 1955.

Bordman, Gerald. *American Theatre: A Chronicle of Comedy and Drama, 1914–30.* New York: Oxford University Press, 1995.

———. *American Theatre: A Chronicle of Comedy and Drama, 1930–45.* New York: Oxford University Press, 1996.

Brown–Guillory, Elizabeth. *Their Place on the Stage: Black Women Playwrights in America.* Westport, Conn.: Greenwood Press, 1988.

Brown, Jared. *The Fabulous Lunts.* New York: Atheneum, 1986.

Callow, Simon. *Orson Welles: The Road to Xanadu.* New York: Viking, 1995.

Corio, Ann. *This Was Burlesque.* New York: Grosset & Dunlap, 1968.

Duberman, Martin Bauml. *Paul Robeson.* New York: Alfred A. Knopf, 1988.

Edwards, Christine. *The Stanislavsky Heritage: Its Contribution to the Russian and American Theatre.* New York: New York University Press, 1965.

Eustis, Morton. *Broadway, Inc.: The Theatre as a Business.* New York: Dodd, Mead, 1934.

Flanagan, Hallie. *Arena.* New York: Duell, Sloan & Pearce, 1940.

Fox, Ted. *Showtime at the Apollo.* New York: Holt, Rinehart, & Winston, 1983.

France, Richard, ed. *Orson Welles on Shakespeare: The W. P. A. and Mercury Theatre Playscripts.* New York: Greenwood Press, 1990.

Gill, Glenda E. *White Grease Paint on Black Performers: A Study of the Federal Theatre, 1935–39.* New York: Peter Lang, 1988.

Green, Abel and Joe Laurie, Jr. *Show Biz: From Vaudeville to Video.* New York: Henry Holt, 1951.

Hatch, James V. and Leo Hamalian, eds. *Lost Plays of the Harlem Renaissance, 1920–40.* Detroit: Wayne State University Press, 1996.

Hatch, James V. and Ted Shine, eds. *Black Theatre USA: Plays by African Americans: The Early Period, 1847–1938.* New York: Free Press, 1996.

Henderson, Amy and Dwight Blocker Bowers. *Red, Hot, & Blue: A Smithsonian Salute to the American Musical.* Washington, D.C.: Smithsonian Institute Press, 1996.

Hill, Anthony D. *Pages from the Harlem Renaissance: A Chronicle of Performance.* New York: Peter Lang, 1996.

Hirsch, Foster. *A Method to Their Madness: The History of the Actor's Studio.* New York: W. W. Norton, 1984.

Houseman, John. *Run-through: A Memoir.* New York: Simon and Schuster, 1972.

Kanellos, Nicholás. *A History of Hispanic Theatre in the United States, Origins to 1940.* Austin: University of Texas Press, 1990.

Leiter, Samuel L. *The Encyclopedia of the New York Stage, 1920–30.* New York: Greenwood Press, 1985.

———. *The Encyclopedia of the New York Stage, 1930–40.* New York: Greenwood Press, 1989.

———. *The Encyclopedia of the New York Stage, 1940–50.* New York: Greenwood Press, 1992.

Matthews, Jane De Hart. *The Federal Theatre: Plays, Relief, and Politics.* Princeton, N.J.: Princeton University Press, 1967.

Miller, Jordan Y. and Winifred L. Frazer. *American Drama Between the Wars: A Critical History.* Boston: Twayne Publishers, 1991.

Mosel, Tad (with Gertrude Macy). *Leading Lady: The World and Theatre of Katharine Cornell.* Boston: Little, Brown, 1978.

Perkins, Kathy A. *Black Female Playwrights.* Bloomington: Indiana University Press, 1989.

Peters, Margot. *The House of Barrymore.* New York: Alfred A. Knopf, 1991.

Roberts, J. W. *Richard Boleslavsky: His Life and Work in the Theatre.* Ann Arbor, Mich.: UMI Research Press, 1981.

Senelick, Laurence, ed. *Wandering Stars: Russian Emigré Theatre, 1905–40.* Iowa City: University of Iowa Press, 1992.

Shanke, Robert. *Shattered Applause: The Lives of Eva LeGallienne.* Carbondale: Southern Illinois University Press, 1992.

Sheehy, Helen. *Eva LeGallienne.* New York: Alfred E. Knopf, 1997.

Smith, Bill. *The Vaudevillians.* New York: Macmillan, 1976.

Smith, Wendy. *Real Life Drama: The Group Theatre and America, 1931–40.* New York: Alfred A. Knopf, 1990.

Snyder, Robert W. "Immigrants, Ethnicity, and Mass Culture: The Vaudeville Stage in New York City: 1880–1930." In *Budapest and New York: Studies in Metropolitan Transformation: 1870–1930.* Thomas E. Bender and Carl E. Schorske, eds. New York: Russell Sage Foundation, 1994.

Sobel, Bernard. *Burleycue: An Underground History of Burlesque Days.* New York: Farrar & Rinehart, 1931.

Stein, Charles W., ed. *American Vaudeville As Seen by Its Contemporaries.* New York: Alfred A. Knopf, 1984.

Waldau, Roy S. *Vintage Years of the Theatre Guild: 1928–39.* Cleavland: Case Western Reserve University Press, 1972

Woll, Allen. *Dictionary of the Black Theatre: Broadway, Off-Broadway, and Selected Harlem Theatres.* Westport, Conn.: Greenwood Press, 1983.

Ziegfeld, Richard and Paulette. *The Ziegfeld Touch: The Life and Times of Florenz Ziegfeld, Jr.* New York: Harry N. Abrams, 1993.

## Mexico

Argudin, Yolanda. *Historia del teatro en México.* Mexico D.F.: Panorama Editorial, 1985.

Beardsell, Peter. *A Theatre for Cannibals: Rodolfo Usigli and the Mexican Stage.* Rutherford: Fairleigh Dickinson Press, 1992.

Bonfil, Carlos. *Cantinflas: Aguila o sol.* México D.F.: Consejuo Nacional para la Cultura y las Artes, 1993.

Case, Henry A. *Views on and of Yucatán.* Mérida de Yucatán: Henry A. Case, 1911.

Covarrubias, Miguel. "Slapstick and Venom: Politics, Tent Shows and Comedians." *Theatre Arts Monthly* 22:8 (August 1938), 587–96.

Cucuel, Madeleine. "Les recherches théâtrales au Mexique (1923–47)." *Cahiers du C.R.I.A.R.* (Centre de Recherches d'Etudes Ibériques et Ibéro–Américaines) 7 (1987), 7–54.

Dauster, Frank. "The Contemporary Mexican Theater." *Hispania* 38 (March 1955), 31–34.

———. " La generación de 1924: el dilema del realismo." *Latin American Theatre Review* 18:2 (Spring 1985), 13–27.

Everaert Dubernard, Luis. *México 1900.* México: Salvat, 1994.

Gonzalez Freire, Natividad. *Teatro cubano (1927–61).* La Habana: Ministerio de Relaciones Exteriores, 1961.

Jiménez, Victor and Alejandrina Escudero. *El Palacio de Bellas Artes: Construcción e historia.* México: INBA, 1994.

Konijn, Elly A. "Seki Sano and His Actor Training Program: Sano in Comparison to Stanislavski and Meyerhold." Unpublished paper presented at IFTR/FIRT congress, Universidad de las Américas–Puebla, June 26, 1997.

Leñero, Estela, ed. *Seki Sano, 1905–66.* Book 10 in the series, *Una vida en el teatro.* México: INBA, 1996.

María y Campos, Armando de. *Cronicas de teatro de "hoy"*. México: Ediciones Botas, 1941.

———. *Memoria de Teatro: Cronicas (1943–45)*. Mexico: Compañía de Ediciones Populares, 1946.

———. *El Teatro de género chico en la revolución mexicana*. México D.F.: Cien de México, 1996 (originally published 1956).

Meade de Angulo, Mercedes. "La empresa nacional de autómatas de los Hermanos Rosete Aranda." *Coloquio de teatro de Tlaxcala*, ed. Emiliano Pérez Cruz, 23–28. Tlaxcala: Patronato Estatal de Promotores Voluntarios en Tlaxcala, 1996.

Mendoza López, Margarita. "Teatro de las Bellas Artes de la Ciudad de México." *Latin American Theatre Review* 18:2 (Spring 1985), 7–11.

Merlin, Socorro. *Vida y milagros de las carpas: La carpa en México 1930–50*. México D.F.: INBA, 1995.

Monterde, Francisco, prólogo y nótas. *Teatro mexicano del siglo XX*. Mexico: Fondo de Cultura Económica, 1956.

Montoya, María Tereza. *El Teatro en mi vida*. Mexico: Ediciones Botas, 1956.

Nomland, John B. *Teatro mexicano contemporáneo, 1900–1950*, trans. Paloma Gorostiza de Zozaya and Luis Reyes de la Maza. Mexico: Instituto Nacional de Bellas Artes, 1967.

Novo, Salvador. "Spellbound Stages." *Theatre Arts Monthly* 32 (August 1938), 569–78.

Prida Santacilla, Pablo. *Y se levanta el telón*. México: Impresora Juan Pablos, 1960.

Rutherford, John. *Mexican Society during the Revolution*. Oxford: Clarendon Press, 1971.

Schmidhuber, Guillermo. *El Teatro Mexicano en Cierne, 1922–38*. New York: Peter Lang, 1992.

Tanaka, Michiko. "Seki Sano's Search for a New Theatre for the People in Latin America." Unpublished paper presented at IFTR/FIRT congress, Universidad de las Américas–Puebla, June 26, 1996.

Usigli, Rodolfo. *Mexico in the Theater*. Trans. with an introduction by Wilder P. Scott. University, Miss.: Romance Monographs, 1976.

———. *Two Plays by Rodolfo Usigli: Crown of Light and One of These Days*. Trans. Thomas Bledsoe with an introduction by Willis Knapp Jones. Carbondale: Southern Illinois University Press, 1971.

Villaurrutia, Xavier. "Hope and Curiosity: Experimental Theatre." *Theatre Arts Monthly* 22:8 (August 1938), 607–9.

———. "Mexican Painters and the Theatre." *World Theatre* 1:3 (1951), 36–40.

Villatoro, Gustavo. *El problema de nuestro Teatro Nacional*. La Habana: Ucar, García y Cía., 1933–34.

### Canada

Brown, Mary. "Ambrose Small: A Ghost in Spite of Himself." In *Theatrical Touring and Founding in North America*. Ed. L. W. Conolly. Westport, Conn.: Greenwood Press, 1982.

Caron, Anne. *Le père Emile Legault et le théâtre au Québec.* Montréal: Fides, 1978.

Corriveau, Jeanne. "Le Théâtre collégial au Québec: L'apport de Gustave Lamarche." In *Archives des lettres canadiennes.* Vol. 5, *Le Théâtre canadien–français,* 169–201. Montreal: Fides, 1976.

Cotnam, Jacques. *Le Théâtre québecois instrument de contestation sociale et politique.* Montreal: Fides, 1976.

Fink, Howard. *Canadian National Theatre on the Air, 1925–61: CBC–CRBC–CNR Radio Drama in English: A Descriptive Bibliography and Union List.* Toronto: University of Toronto Press, 1983.

———. "A National Radio Drama in English." In *Contemporary Canadian Theatre: New World Visions.* Ed. Anton Wagner, 176–85. Toronto: Simon & Pierre, 1985.

———. "Radio Drama in English." In *The Oxford Companion to Canadian Theatre.* Ed. Eugene Benson and L. W. Conolly, 452–56. Toronto: Oxford University Press, 1989

Godin, Jean-Cléo. "Une 'Belle Montréalaise' en 1913." *Revue d'histoire littéraire du Québec et du Canada français* 5 (1983), 55–62.

Hare, John E. "Le Théâtre professionel à Montréal de 1898 à 1937." In *Archives des lettres canadiennes.* Vol. 5, *Le Théâtre canadien–français,* 239–47. Montreal: Fides, 1976.

Hoffman, James. "L. Bullock–Webster and the B. C. Dramatic School." *Histoire du théâtre au Canada/Theatre History in Canada* 8 (Fall 1987), 204–20.

Larrue, Jean-Marc. *Le Théâtre à Montréal à la fin du XIXe siècle.* Montreal: Fides, 1981.

Leblanc, Alonzo. "La Tradition théâtrale à Québc (1790–1973)." In *Archives des lettres canadiennes.* Vol. 5, *Le Théâtre canadien–français.* Montreal: Fides, 1976.

Lee, Betty. *Love and Whiskey: The Story of the Dominion Drama Festival.* Toronto: McClelland & Stewart, 1973.

Legault, Emile. "Quelques notes sur les Compagnons de Saint-Laurent (1937–52)." In *Archives des lettres canadiennes.* Vol. 5, *Le Théâtre canadien–français,* 249–66. Montreal: Fides, 1976.

Marks, Kitty, with Frank Croft. "My Life with the Original Marks Brothers." *Maclean's* (June 21, 1958), 16–17, 58–62.

Martinson, Denyse. *Juliette Béliveau.* Montréal: Les Editions de l'Homme, 1970.

Palmieri. *Mes Souvenirs de Théâtre.* Montréal: Les Editions de l'Etoile, 1944.

Saint-Pierre, Annette. *Le Rideau se lève au Manitoba.* Saint-Boniface, Manitobe: Les Editions des Plaines, 1980.

Usmiani, Renate. "Roy Mitchell: Prophet in Our Past." *Histoire du théâtre au Canada/ Theatre History in Canada* 8 (Fall 1987), 147–68.

Voaden, Herman. "A View from the Thirties." *Canadian Theatre Review* 28 (Fall 1980), 10–17.

Wagner, Anton, ed. *Canada's Lost Plays.* Vol. 3, *The Developing Mosaic: English–Canadian Drama to Mid-Century.* Toronto: Canadian Theatre Review Publications, 1980.

7: RENEWAL AND EXPERIMENTATION: 1945 TO THE PRESENT

*United States*

Adler, Thomas P. *American Drama, 1940–60: A Critical History.* New York: Twayne, 1994.

*American Participation in Theatre.* National Endowment for the Arts Research Division Report #35. Santa Ana, Calif.: Seven Locks Press, 1996.

Behr, Edward. *The Complete Book of "Les Misérables."* New York: Arcade, 1989.

Berson, Misha. *Between Worlds: Contemporary Asian–American Plays.* New York: Theatre Communications Group, 1990.

Blumenthal, Eileen and Julie Taymor. *Julie Taymor, Playing with Fire.* New York: Harry N. Abrams, 1995.

Brockett, Oscar G. and Robert Findlay. *Century of Innovation: A History of European and American Theatre and Drama Since the Late Nineteenth Century.* 2d ed. Boston: Allyn & Bacon, 1991.

Breuer, Lee. *Animations: A Trilogy for Mabou Mines.* New York: Performing Arts Journal Publications, 1979.

Case, Sue-Ellen. *Split Britches: Lesbian Practice/Feminist Performance.* New York: Routledge, 1996.

Champagne, Lenora. *Out from Under: Texts by Women Performance Artists.* New York: Theatre Communications Group, 1990.

Clum, John, ed. *Staging Gay Lives: An Anthology of Contemporary Gay Theatre.* Boulder, Colo.: Westview Press, Inc., 1996.

Coleman, Janet. *The Compass.* New York: Alfred A. Knopf, 1990.

Croyden, Margaret. *Lunatics, Lovers, and Poets: The Contemporary Experimental Theatre.* New York: Dell Publishing, 1974.

Curtin, Kaier. *"We Can Always Call Them Bulgarians": The Emergence of Lesbians and Gay Men on the American Stage.* Boston: Alyson Publications, 1987.

Davy, Kate. *Richard Foreman and the Ontological-Hysteric Theatre.* Ann Arbor, Mich.: UMI Research Press, 1981.

Delgado, Maria M. and Paul Heritage, eds. *In Contact with the Gods? Directors Talk Theatre.* New York: Manchester University Press, 1996.

Dixon, Michael Bigelow and Liz Engelman. *Humana Festival '96: The Complete Plays, Including a Chronological History of the Festival.* Lyme, N.H.: Smith & Kraus, 1996.

Engle, Ron, Felicia Hardinson Londré and Daniel J. Watermeier. *Shakespeare Companies and Festivals: An International Guide.* Westport, Conn.: Greenwood Press, 1995.

Epstein, Helen. *Joe Papp: An American Life.* Boston: Little, Brown, 1994.

Feyder, Linda, ed. *Shattering the Myth: Plays by Hispanic Women* (selected by Denise Chávez). Houston, Tex.: Arté Publico Press, 1992.

Foreman, Richard. *Plays and Manifestos.* New York: New York University Press, 1976.

———. *Reverberation Machines: The Later Plays and Essays.* Barrytown, N.Y.: Station Hill Press, 1985.

Gard, Robert E., Marston Balch and Pauline B. Temkin. *Theatre in America: Appraisal and Challenge.* New York: Theatre Arts Books, 1968.

Goldman, William. *The Season: A Candid Look at Broadway.* New York: Harcourt, Brace & World, 1969.

Horn, Barbara Lee. *The Age of "Hair": Evolution and Impact of Broadway's First Rock Musical.* New York: Greenwood Press, 1991.

Huerta, Jorge, ed. *Necessary Theatre: Six Plays About the Chicano Experience.* Houston, Tex.: Arté Publico Press, 1989.

Ilson, Carol. *Harold Prince From "Pajama Game" to "Phantom of the Opera."* Ann Arbor, Mich.: UMI Research Press, 1989.

Izenour, George C. *Theatre Design.* New York: McGraw–Hill, 1977.

Kanellos, Nicholás and Jorge Huerta, eds. *Nuevo Pasos: Chicano and Puerto Rican Drama.* Houston, Tex.: Arté Publico Press, 1989.

Kilgore, Emilie S., ed. *Contemporary Plays by Women: Outstanding Winners and Runner-Up for the Susan Smith Blackburn Prize (1978–90).* New York: Prentice Hall, 1991.

King, Bruce. *Contemporary American Theatre.* New York: St. Martin's Press, 1991.

Langley, Stephen, ed. *Producers on Producing.* New York: Drama Book Specialists, 1976.

Laufe, Abe. *Broadway's Greatest Musicals.* (Rev. ed.) New York: Funk & Wagnalls, 1977.

Lee, Josephine. *Performing Asian America.* Philadelphia: Temple University Press, 1997.

Leiter, Samuel L. *The Great Stage Directors: 100 Distinguished Careers of the Theatre.* New York: Facts on File, 1994.

———. *Ten Seasons: New York Theatre in the Seventies.*

Little, Stuart W. *After the Fact: Conflict and Consensus, A Report on the First American Congress of Theatre.* New York: Arno, 1975.

———. *Off-Broadway: The Prophetic Theatre.* New York: Coward, McCann & Geoghegan, 1972.

Malpede, Karen. *Three Works by the Open Theatre.* New York: Drama Book Specialists, 1974.

Mann, Mary A. *The Los Angeles Theatre Book.* North Hollywood, Calif.: privately published, 1984.

Martin, Carol. *A Source Book of Feminist Theatre and Performance: On and beyond the Stage.* New York: Routledge, 1996.

Maufort, Marc, ed. *Staging Difference: Cultural Pluralism in American Theatre and Drama.* New York: Peter Lang, 1995.

Moy, James S. *Marginal Sights: Staging the Chinese in America.* Iowa City: University of Iowa Press, 1993.

Napoleon, Davi. *Chelsea on the Edge: The Adventures of an American Theatre.* Ames: Iowa State University Press, 1991.

Neff, Renfreu. *The Living Theatre: USA.* New York: Bobbs–Merrill, 1970.

Pasolli, Robert. *A Book on the Open Theatre.* New York: Bobbs–Merrill, 1970.

Perkins, Kathy A. and Roberta Uno, eds. *Contemporary Plays by Women of Color.* New York: Routledge, 1996.

Poland, Albert and Bruce Mailman. *The Off Off Broadway Book: The Plays, People, Theatre.* New York: Bobbs–Merrill, 1972.

Pottlitzer, Joanne. *Hispanic Theatre in the United States and Puerto Rico: A Report to the Ford Foundation.* New York: Ford Foundation, 1988.

Price, Julia S. *The Off-Broadway Theatre.* New York: Scarecrow Press, Inc., 1962.

Roudané, Matthew C. *American Drama since 1960: A Critical History.* New York: Twayne, 1996.

Ryzuk, Mary S. *The Circle Repertory Company: The First Fifteen Years.* Ames: Iowa State University Press, 1989.

Savran, David. *The Wooster Group, 1975–85: Breaking the Rules.* Ann Arbor, Mich.: UMI Research Press, 1986.

*Theatre Profiles: The Illustrated Reference Guide to America's Nonprofit Theatre.* Published annually, 1973–96, vols. 1–12. New York: Theatre Communications Group.

Shank, Theodore. *American Alternative Theatre.* New York: St. Martin's Press, 1982.

Vogel, Harold L. *Entertainment Industry Economics: A Guide for Financial Analysis.* 3d ed. New York: Cambridge University Press, 1994.

### Mexico

Angel Quemain, Miguel. "El Laboratorio de Teatro Campesino e Indigena." *Escenarios de dos mundos* 3 (1988), 153–54.

Brun, Josefina. "El teatro universitario de la UNAM." *Escenarios de dos mundos* 3 (1988), 159–62.

Burgess, Ronald D. *The New Dramatists of Mexico, 1967–85.* Lexington: University Press of Kentucky, 1991.

Cajiao Salas, Teresa and Margarita Vargas, eds. *Women Writing Women: An Anthology of Spanish–American Theater of the 1980s.* Albany: State University of New York Press, 1997.

Carballido, Emilio. *The Golden Thread and Other Plays.* Trans. Margaret Sayers Peden. Austin: University of Texas Press, 1970.

Chabaud Magnus, Jaime. "El teatro rural en México." *Escenarios de dos mundos* 3 (1988), 149–52.

Dauster, Frank. "La generación de 1924: el dilema del realismo." *Latin American Theatre Review* 18:2 (Spring 1985), 13–27.

———, ed. *Perspectives on Contemporary Spanish American Theatre.* Lewisburg: Bucknell University Press, 1996.

Enríquez, José Ramón, ed. *Teatro para la escena.* México D.F.: Ediciones El Milagro, 1996.

Foster, David William. *Estudios sobre teatro mexicano contemporáneo.* New York: Peter Lang, 1984.

Franco, Jean. "A Touch of Evil: Jesusa Rodríguez's Subversive Church." In *Negotiating Performance: Gender, Sexuality, & Theatricality in Latin America.* Ed. Diana Taylor and Juan Villegas. Durham, N.C. and London: Duke University Press, 1994.

Frischmann, Donald H. "Active Ethnicity: Nativism, Otherness, and Indian Theatre in Mexico." *Gestos* 6:11 (April 1991), 113–26.

———. "The Age-Old Tradition of Mexico's Popular Theatre." *Theatre Research International* 14 (Summer 1989), 111–22.

———. "Contemporary Mayan Theatre and Ethnic Conflict: The Recovery and (Re)Interpretation of History." In *Imperialism and Theatre: Essays on World Theatre, Drama, and Performance.* Ed. J. Ellen Gainor, 71–84. New York: Routledge, 1995.

———. "El nuevo teatro popular en México: posturas ideológicas y estéticas." *Latin American Theatre Review* 18:2 (Spring 1985), 29–37.

Ita, Fernando de. "La danza de la pirámide: Historia, exaltación y crítica de las nuevas tendencias del teatro en México." *Latin American Theatre Review* 23:1 (Fall 1989), 9–17.

———. "De Seki Sano a Luis de Tavira: Itinerario de la puesta en escena." *Escenarios de dos mundos* 3 (1988), 139–42.

———, ed. and intro. *Teatro Mexicano Contemporáneo: Antología.* Madrid: Centro de Documentación Teatral, 1991.

Leñero, Vicente, ed. *La Nueva Dramaturgia Mexicana.* México D.F.: Ediciones El Milagro, 1996.

María y Campos, Armando de. *El teatro esta siempre en crisis (Cronicas de 1946 a 1950).* México: Arriba el Telón, 1954.

Mendoza López, Margarita. *Teatro Méxicano del siglo XX, 1900–1986: Catálogo de obras teatrales.* México D.F.: Instituto Mexicano de Seguro Social, 1987.

Meyran, Daniel. *Tres Ensayos sobre Teatro Mexicano.* Roma: Bulzoni, 1996.

Nigro, Kirsten F. "Luisa Josefina Hernández." *Contemporary World Writers,* 2d ed. Ed. Tracy Chevalier, 250–52. Detroit: St. James Press, 1993.

Partida Tayzan, Armando. "1950–87: De la posguerra a nuestros días" and "La nueva dramaturgia." *Escenarios de dos mundos* 3 (1988), 101–11, 124–26.

Peden, Margaret Sayers. *Emilio Carballido.* Boston: Twayne, 1980.

Peralta, Braulio. "Héctor Mendoza: Todo un estilo." *Escenarios de dos mundos* 3 (1988), 134–38.

Pérez Quitt, Ricardo, ed. *Dramaturgos de Puebla en un acto.* México: Comisión Puebla V Centenario, 1991.

*Qué pasa con el teatro en México?* México: Organización Editorial Novaro, 1967.

Rabell, Malkah. "La generación de los cincuenta." *Escenarios de dos mundos* 3 (1988), 117–20.

Solórzano, Carlos. "México." Trans. Joanne Rotermundt-De la Parra. *The World Encyclopedia of Contemporary Theatre.* Vol 2, *Americas.* Ed. Don Rubin, 310–30. London: Routledge, 1996.

———. *Testimonios teatrales de México.* Universidad Nacional Autónoma de México, 1973.

Swansey, Bruce. "Cinco directores de vanguardia." *Escenarios de dos mundos* 3 (1988), 143–48.

Tavira, Luis de. "Vicente Leñero: o teatro o silencio." In *La Noche de Hernán Cortés* by Vicente Leñero, 9–16. Madrid: Centro de Documentación Teatral, 1992,

Unger, Roni. *Poesía en Voz Alta in the Theater of Mexico.* Columbia: University of Missouri Press, 1981.

Usigli, Rodolfo. *Two Plays*, Trans. Thomas Bledsoe, with an introduction by Willis Knapp Jones. Carbondale: Southern Illinois University Press, 1971.

Weiss, Judith A. "Traditional Popular Culture and the Cuban 'New Theatre': Teatro Escambray and the Cabildo de Santiago." *Theatre Research International* 14 (Summer 1989), 142–52.

## Canada

Adilman, Sid. "Robert Lepage's Vision." *Toronto Star* (November 4, 1995), H1, H7.

Anthony, Geraldine, ed. *Stage Voices: Twelve Canadian Playwrights Talk about Their Lives and Work.* Toronto: Doubleday Canada, 1978.

Beauchamp–Rank, Hélène. "La Vie théâtrale à Montréal de 1950 à 1970: théâtres, troupes, saisons, répertoires." In *Archives des lettres canadiennes.* Vol. 5, *Le Théâtre canadien–français,* 267–90. Montreal: Fides, 1976.

Brask, Per, ed. *Contemporary Issues in Canadian Drama.* Winnipeg: Blizzard Publishing, 1995.

Charest, Rémy. *Robert Lepage: Quelques zones de liberté.* Québec: L'Instant même, 1995.

Collet, Paulette. "La Sagouine: un regard perçant et lucide, source d'espoir." *Canadian Drama/ L'Art dramatique canadien* 13 (1987), 43–49.

Conolly, L. W., ed. *Canadian Drama and the Critics.* Vancouver: Talonbooks, 1987.

Corliss, Richard. "Forgive the Mimes: Cirque du Soleil's *Quidam.*" *Time* (October 14, 1996).

Courtney, Richard. "Indigenous Theatre: Indian and Eskimo Ritual Drama" In *Contemporary Canadian Theatre.* Ed. Anton Wagner, 206–15. Toronto: Simon & Pierre, 1985.

Croyden, Margaret. "Lepage Makes a Splash in *The River Ota.*" *TheaterWeek* (December 2–8, 1996), 44–47.

Filewood, Alan. *Collective Encounters: Documentary Theatre in English Canada.* Toronto: University of Toronto Press, 1987.

———. "The Political Dramaturgy of the Mummers Troupe." *Canadian Drama/ L'Art dramatique canadien* 13:1 (1987), 60–71.

———. "Receiving Aboriginality: Tomson Highway and the Crisis of Cultural Authenticity." *Theatre Journal* 46 (October 1994), 363–73.

Frazer, Robin. "Indian Culture." *Performing Arts in Canada* 9 (Summer 1972), 7–13.

Germain, Jean-Claude. "Théâtre Québécois or Théâtre Protestant?" *Canadian Theatre Review* 11 (Summer 1976), 8–21.

Goodwin, Jill Tomasson. "A Career in Review: Donald Davis, Canadian Actor, Producer, Director." *Theatre History in Canada/Histoire du Théâtre au Canada* 10 (Fall 1989), 132–51.

Grant, Agnes. "Native Drama: A Celebration of Native Culture." In *Contemporary Issues in Canadian Drama*. Ed. Per Brask, 102–13. Winnipeg: Blizzard Publishing, 1995.

Hamblet, Edwin C. *Marcel Dubé and French–Canadian Drama*. New York: Exposition Press, 1970.

Highway, Tomson. "The First and Founding Nations Respond." An interview by Ann Wilson. In *Other Solitudes: Canadian Multicultural Fictions*. Ed. Linda Hutcheon and Marion Richmon, 350–55. Toronto: Oxford University Press, 1990.

Johnston, Denis W. "Drama in British Columbia: A Special Place" In *Contemporary Issues in Canadian Drama*. Ed. Per Brask. Winnipeg: Blizzard Publishing, 1995.

———. *Up the Mainstream: The Rise of Toronto's Alternative Theatres, 1968–75*. Toronto: University of Toronto Press, 1991.

Lahr, John. "Profile: The High Roller," [Garth Drabinsky]. *The New Yorker* (June 2, 1997), 70–77.

Leblanc, Alonzo. "La Tradition théâtrale à Québec (1790–1973)." In *Archives des lettres canadiens*, Vol. 5, *Le Théâtre canadien–français*, 203–38. Montreal: Fides, 1976.

Leitch, Adelaide. *Floodtides of Fortune: The Story of Stratford and the Progress of the City through Two Centuries*. Stratford, Ontario: Corporation of the City of Stratford, 1980.

Lévesque, Robert. "Trucs pour jouer *Hamlet* seul: *Elseneur*." *Le Devoir* (November 13, 1995), B8.

Mead, Rebecca. "Party On, Garth." *New York* (June 2, 1997), 22–29.

Moss, Jane. "Québécois Theatre: Michel Tremblay and Marie Laberge." *Theatre Research International* 21 (Autumn 1996), 196–207.

Munday, Jenny. "Mulgrave Road Co-Op Theatre: The View from Inside the Electrolux." *Canadian Theatre Review* 71 (Summer 1992), 88–91.

Nardocchio, Elaine F. "1958–68: Ten Formative Years in Quebec's Theatre History." *Canadian Theatre Review* 12 (1986), 33–35.

Nothof, Anne. "Accommodating Voices in Canadian Native Drama: Who Speaks? Who Listens?" Unpublished paper presented at Association for Theatre in Higher Education, San Francisco, August 1995.

———. "Collective Creativity—Working *Odd Jobs*." *Canadian Drama/ L'Art dramatique canadien* 13:1 (1987), 34–42.

———. "Cultural Collision and Magical Transformation: The Plays of Tomson Highway." *Studies in Canadian Literature/Etudes en Littérature Canadienne* 20:2 (1995), 34–43.

Peters, Helen. *The Plays of CODCO*. New York: Peter Lang, 1992.

Poteet, Susan. "Mind Your Own Language." [On Michel Tremblay's *Nelligan*.] *Theatrum* 20 (Sept.–Oct. 1990), 16–19.

Rabillard, Sheila. "Absorption, Elimination, and the Hybrid: Some Impure Questions of Gender and Culture in the Trickster Drama of Tomson Highway." *Essays in Theatre/ Etudes Théâtrales* 12 (November 1993), 3–27.

Rewa, Natalie. "Clichés of Ethnicity Subverted: Robert Lepage's *La Trilogie des dragons.*" *Theatre History in Canada/ Histoire du Théâtre au Canada* 11 (Fall 1990), 148–61.

Sabbath, Lawrence. "Denise Pelletier." *Canadian Theatre Review* 11 (Summer 1976), 119–21.

Salter, Denis, "Six Characters in Search of a Hero: David Fennario's *The Death of René Lévesque.*" *Canadian Theatre Review* 69 (Winter 1991), 87–91.

Salutin, Rick. *Les Canadiens.* Vancouver: Talonbooks, 1977.

Somerset, J. Alan B. *The Stratford Festival Story: A Catalogue–Index to the Stratford, Ontario Festival 1953–90.* Westport, Conn.: Greenwood Press, 1991.

Sweets, Ellen. "Cirque du Soleil Takes Your Breath Away." *The Kansas City Star* (March 3, 1996), I-1, I-8.

Tepper, Bill. "The Forties and Beyond: The New Play Society." *Canadian Theatre Review* 28 (Fall 1980), 18–33.

Usmiani, Renaate. *Second Stage: The Alternative Theatre Movement in Canada.* Vancouver: University of British Columbia Press, 1983.

Wagner, Anton, ed. *Contemporary Canadian Theatre: New World Visions.* Toronto: Simon & Pierre, 1985.

———. "John Coulter: Death of a Griot." *Canadian Theatre Review* 30 (Spring 1981), 117–21.

Wallace, Robert. *Producing Marginality: Theatre and Criticism in Canada.* Saskatoon: Fifth House Publishers, 1990.

Wasserman, Jerry, ed. *Modern Canadian Plays.* Vols. 1 and 2. Vancouver: Talonbooks, 1993.

Watermeier, Daniel J. "Stratford Festival of Canada." In *Shakespeare Companies and Festivals: An International Guide.* Ed. Ron Engle, Felicia Hardison Londré, and Daniel J. Watermeier. Westport, Conn.: Greenwood Press, 1995.

Whittaker, Herbert. "Whittaker's Montreal: A Theatrical Autobiography 1910–49." Ed. and with an introduction by Rota Herzberg Lister. *Canadian Drama/ L'Art dramatique canadien* 12:2, 233–341.

———. *Whittaker's Theatre: A Critic Looks at Stages in Canada and Thereabouts 1944–75.* Ed. Ronald Bryden with Boyd Neil. Greenbank. Ontario: Whittaker Project, 1985.

Zoglin, Richard. "The Drabinsky Rag." *Time* (June 30, 1997).

# Index of Names

# Subject Index